Library of Congress Cataloging in Publication Data
Main entry under title:

The Official Scrabble® players dictionary.

1. Scrabble® (Game) — Glossaries, vocabularies, etc.
GV1507.S3036   793.7′3   78-3681
ISBN 0-87779-020-5

Made in the United States of America

6RRD8079

TheOf
SCRAB
Playe
Dictio

G. & C. MERRIAM COMPA

SPRINGFIELD, MASSAC

OUR TRADEMARK ● **SCRABBLE**® Selchow & Righter Company takes pride in offering this dictionary to owners of its SCRABBLE® Brand line of word games and to participants in tournaments and contests sponsored by its subsidiary, SCRABBLE® Crossword Game Players, Inc. The SCRABBLE® trademark, registered in the United States Patent and Trademark Office, is one of our most valued assets as it represents our seal and reputation for excellence and quality.

As a trademark, it must be capitalized, and when describing products be followed by a generic name of the game such as SCRABBLE® crossword game, SCRABBLE® crossword cubes, SCRABBLE® sentence cubes, and the like. The SCRABBLE® trademark means "Made by" or "Sponsored by" Selchow & Righter Company or its subsidiary.

Your cooperation in the continued proper use of our trademark is appreciated and we hope that this dictionary will enhance enjoyment of our products.

SELCHOW & RIGHTER COMPANY

REFACE ● This word book has been long awaited by lovers of the SCRABBLE® Brand crossword games, and Scrabble® Crossword Game Players, Inc., a subsidiary of Selchow & Righter Co., is very pleased to present it to them. All who have looked for a guide to settle challenges that arise in the course of play now have one of authority. This is the dictionary of first reference for all official SCRABBLE® Players crossword game tournaments.

It is important to remember that The Official Scrabble® Players Dictionary was edited solely with this limited purpose in mind. It is not intended to serve as a general dictionary of English; thus, such important features of general dictionaries as definitions of multiple senses, pronunciation respellings, etymologies, and usage labels are omitted.

The plan of the dictionary and the policies that governed its editing were developed under the direction of Scrabble® Crossword Game Players, Inc. The finished manuscript was prepared for the typesetter and the dictionary was seen into print by members of the Editorial Department of G. & C. Merriam Company under the supervision of James G. Lowe, Associate Editor.

The detailed organization and special features of the dictionary are explained in the Introduction which immediately follows. It should be read with care by all who use the dictionary. Now that this work is available, we are confident that it will afford satisfaction and enjoyment to SCRABBLE® crossword game players everywhere.

Scrabble® Crossword Game Players, Inc.

NTRODUCTION ● **MAIN ENTRIES** ● Main entries are
listed in boldface type and are set flush with the left-hand margin of
each column. Except for an occasional cross-reference (such as
GUNFOUGHT past tense of gunfight), main entries contain from two to
eight letters since words within this range are considered to be most
useful to SCRABBLE® crossword game players. Only words that are
permissible in SCRABBLE® crossword games are included in this
dictionary. Thus, proper names, words requiring hyphens or
apostrophes, words considered foreign, and abbreviations have been
omitted. Because dictionaries have different standards for selecting
entries, several current desk dictionaries were consulted in preparing
the list of main entries for this book in order to insure a wider range of
entries than any single dictionary of that kind offers. Words that
exceed eight letters in length and are not inflected forms of words
entered in this dictionary should be looked up in a desk dictionary
such as Webster's New Collegiate Dictionary. No attempt was made to
omit obsolete, archaic, slang, or nonstandard words since they are
permitted by the rules of the game. All variant forms of a main entry
are shown at their own alphabetical places and defined in terms of the
principal form.

RUN-ON ENTRIES ● A main entry may be followed by one or
more derivatives in boldface type with a different part-of-speech label.
These are run-on entries. Run-on entries are not defined since their
meanings are readily derivable from the meaning of the root word.

JOYOUS	*adj* joyful **JOYOUSLY** *adv*
KNOW	*v* KNEW, KNOWN, KNOWING, KNOWS to have a true understanding of **KNOWABLE** *adj*

No entry has been run on at another if it would fall alphabetically
more than two places from the entry. **When you do not find a word at
its own place, it is always wise to check several entries above and
below to see if it is run on.**

CROSS-REFERENCES ● A cross-reference is a main entry that
is an inflected form (such as the plural form of a noun, the past tense
form of a verb, or the comparative form of an adjective) of another
word. An inflected form is entered as a main entry only if it undergoes
a spelling change in addition to or instead of suffixation *and* if it falls
alphabetically three or more places away from the root word.

For example, in the entries reproduced below **GAGGED** is a main
entry because it involves a spelling change (the final -*g* of *gag* is
doubled) besides the addition of the -*ed* ending and because it falls

alphabetically three or more places away from the entry **GAG**. On the other hand, *gags* is not a main entry because it involves no spelling change beyond the addition of the ending -*s*. Equally, while **GAGING** is a main entry, *gaged* is not, because, even though it involves a spelling change (the final -*e* of *gage* is dropped) beyond the addition of the -*ed* ending, it would not fall three or more places from **GAGE**.

GAG	*v* GAGGED, GAGGING, GAGS to stop up the mouth
GAGA	*adj* crazy
GAGE	*v* GAGED, GAGING, GAGES to pledge as security
GAGER	*n* pl. -S gauger
GAGGED	past tense of gag
GAGGER	*n* pl. -S one that gags
GAGGING	present participle of gag
GAGGLE	*v* -GLED, -GLING, -GLES to cackle
GAGING	present participle of gage

This policy is intended to make the word desired as easy to find as possible without wasting space. Nevertheless, many inflected forms will appear only at the main entry.

Users of the book should always look at several entries above and below the expected place if they do not find the desired word as a main entry.

Cross-reference entries for present tense third person singular forms of verbs use the abbreviation "sing."

PARTS OF SPEECH ● An italic label indicating a part of speech follows each main entry except cross-references (such as **JOLLIED**, **JOLLIER, JOLLIES, JOLLIEST**), for which the label is given at the root word. The eight traditional parts of speech are indicated as follows:

n	noun	*pron*	pronoun
v	verb	*prep*	preposition
adj	adjective	*conj*	conjunction
adv	adverb	*interj*	interjection

The label *n/pl* is given to two kinds of nouns. One is the plural noun that has no singular form.

VIBES	*n/pl* a percussion instrument

The other is the plural noun of which the singular is not entered in this dictionary. Singular forms are omitted if they contain more than eight letters.

ROSTELLA *n/pl* small, beaklike structures

Rostellum, the singular form, has nine letters and is not entered.

When a word can be used as more than one part of speech, each part of speech is entered separately if the inflected forms are not spelled alike. For example, both the adjective *lazy* and the verb *lazy* are entered because the inflected forms vary.

LAZY *adj* LAZIER, LAZIEST disinclined
to work or exertion

LAZY *v* LAZIED, LAZYING, LAZIES to
move or lie lazily

On the other hand, the verb *suit* is entered while the noun *suit* is not because the inflected form *suits* at the verb is spelled the same as the plural form of the noun. In a dictionary for SCRABBLE® crossword game players, entry of the noun is therefore redundant. Homographs (words spelled alike) which may be used as the same part of speech are treated in the same way. For example, *lepton* is entered as a noun twice because the plurals are spelled differently.

LEPTON *n* pl. -TA a monetary unit of
Greece

LEPTON *n* pl. -S an atomic
particle . . .

If both plurals were spelled alike, only one *lepton* would be entered in this dictionary. In this way the dictionary includes as many different spellings as possible yet avoids wasting space with repeated entry of words spelled in the same way. The SCRABBLE® crossword game player, after all, needs only one entry to justify his play.

INFLECTED FORMS ● Inflected forms include the past tense,
past participle, present participle, and present tense third person singular of verbs, the plural of nouns, and the comparative and superlative of adjectives and adverbs. They are shown in capital letters immediately following the part-of-speech label. Irregular inflected forms are listed as main entries when they fall three or more alphabetical places away from the root word (see **Cross-References** above). All inflected forms are allowable as entries in SCRABBLE® crossword games.

The principal parts of the majority of verbs are shown as -ED, -ING, -S (or -ES when applicable). This indicates that the past tense and past participle are formed simply by adding -*ed* to the entry word, that the present participle is formed simply by adding -*ing* to the entry word, and that the present third person singular is formed simply by adding -*s* (or -*es*) to the entry word.

TALK *v* -ED, -ING, -S to communicate
by speaking

When inflection of an entry word involves any spelling change in addition to the suffixal ending (such as the dropping of a final -*e,* the doubling of a final consonant, or the changing of a final -*y* to -*i*-) or when the inflection is irregular, the inflected forms given indicate such changes.

WASTE   *v* WASTED, WASTING, WASTES
to use thoughtlessly

DIM   *v* DIMMED, DIMMING, DIMS to
make dim

TRY   *v* TRIED, TRYING, TRIES to
attempt

RISE   *v* ROSE, RISEN, RISING, RISES
to move upward

For verbs of more than one syllable either the last syllable or the last two syllables are shown.

ABDICATE   *v* -CATED, -CATING, -CATES to
give up formally

BEGIN   *v* -GAN, -GUN, -GINNING, -GINS
to start

The plurals of nouns are preceded by the abbreviation "pl." Most plurals are shown as -S (or -ES when applicable) to indicate that the plural is formed simply by adding the given suffix to the entry word.

VINTNER   *n* pl. -S a wine merchant

When pluralizing a noun involves any spelling change in addition to the suffixal ending (such as the changing of a final -*y* to -*i*- or a final -*f* to -*v*-) or when the plural is irregular, the plural form shown indicates such change.

BEVY   *n* pl. BEVIES a group

LEAF   *n* pl. LEAVES a usually green,
flattened organ of vascular
plants

CHILD   *n* pl. CHILDREN a young person

In such cases involving polysyllabic nouns at least the last syllable is shown.

SUDATORY   *n* pl. -RIES a hot-air bath for
inducing sweating

For the sake of clarity, two groups of nouns that are confusing to many, those ending in -*o* and those ending in -*y,* are always indicated in this dictionary by showing at least the last syllable, even though no spelling change is involved.

RONDO   *n* pl. -DOS a type of musical
composition

SAWNEY   *n* pl. -NEYS a foolish person

Variant plurals are shown wherever they add another word permissible in SCRABBLE® crossword games.

GLOSSA   *n* pl. -SAE or -SAS the tongue

Plurals which have the same form as the singular are shown only when they are the only plural for that entry. This is done to show that for the entry in question it is not permissible to add -*s* (or -*es*) to the singular to create a plural.

HAIKU   *n* pl. HAIKU a Japanese poem
CALENDS   *n* pl. CALENDS the first day of
the Roman month

Otherwise, they are omitted and only the plural with the inflection is shown.

DEER   *n* pl. -S a ruminant mammal

The comparative and superlative forms of adjectives and adverbs are shown, when applicable, immediately following the part-of-speech label. Any spelling changes are indicated in the forms shown.

WEAK   *adj* WEAKER, WEAKEST lacking
strength
OFTEN   *adv* -ENER, -ENEST frequently
BALKY   *adj* BALKIER, BALKIEST
stubborn . . .

Not all adjectives or adverbs can be inflected, and only those inflected forms shown are acceptable. None of the adjectives and adverbs listed as run-on entries in this dictionary have inflected forms.

DEFINITIONS ● In most cases, only one very brief definition is given for each main entry since definitions do not play a significant role in the SCRABBLE® crossword game. This definition serves only to orient the player in a general way to a single meaning of the word. It is not intended to have all the precision and detail of a definition in a good general dictionary.

When a word consisting of eight letters or less appears in a definition but is not an entry in this dictionary, it is glossed in parentheses. For example, at the entry for the verb *bomb*, the noun "bombs" is used in the definition and is glossed because the noun *bomb* is not a separate entry.

BOMB   *v* -ED, -ING, -S to attack with
bombs (explosive projectiles)

A main entry that is a variant form of another entry is defined in terms of the most common form, which is entered and defined at its own alphabetical place.

AMPOULE   *n* pl. -S ampule
AMPUL   *n* pl. -S ampule
AMPULE   *n* pl. -S a small glass vial

SCRABBLE® crossword game players in Canada will be pleased to learn that variant forms such as *honour, centre,* and *cheque,* which are often omitted from general dictionaries, have also been included in this book.

LISTS OF UNDEFINED WORDS   ●   Lists of undefined words appear after the entries of the prefixes **RE-** and **UN-**. These words are not defined because they are self-explanatory: their meanings are simply the sum of a meaning of the prefix combined with a meaning of the root word. All of their inflected forms are given, however.

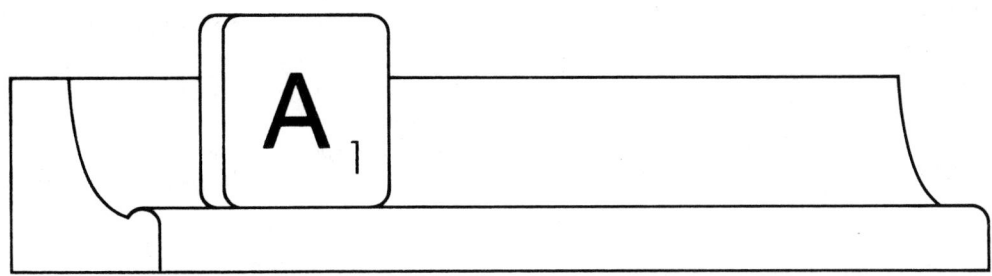

AA	*n* pl. -S rough, cindery lava
AAH	*v* -ED, -ING, -S to exclaim in amazement, joy, or surprise
AAL	*n* pl. -S an East Indian shrub
AALII	*n* pl. -S a tropical tree
AARDVARK	*n* pl. -S an African mammal
AARDWOLF	*n* pl. -WOLVES an African mammal
AASVOGEL	*n* pl. -S a vulture
ABA	*n* pl. -S a sleeveless garment worn by Arabs
ABACA	*n* pl. -S a Philippine plant
ABACK	*adv* toward the back
ABACUS	*n* pl. -CI or -CUSES a calculating device
ABAFT	*adv* toward the stern
ABAKA	*n* pl. -S abaca
ABALONE	*n* pl. -S an edible shellfish
ABAMP	*n* pl. -S abampere
ABAMPERE	*n* pl. -S a unit of electric current
ABANDON	*v* -ED, -ING, -S to leave or give up completely
ABASE	*v* ABASED, ABASING, ABASES to lower in rank, prestige, or esteem **ABASEDLY** *adv*
ABASER	*n* pl. -S one that abases
ABASH	*v* -ED, -ING, -ES to make ashamed or embarrassed
ABASING	present participle of abase
ABATE	*v* ABATED, ABATING, ABATES to reduce in degree or intensity **ABATABLE** *adj*
ABATER	*n* pl. -S one that abates
ABATIS	*n* pl. -TISES a barrier made of felled trees
ABATOR	*n* pl. -S one that unlawfully seizes an inheritance
ABATTIS	*n* pl. -TISES abatis
ABATTOIR	*n* pl. -S a slaughterhouse
ABAXIAL	*adj* situated away from the axis
ABAXILE	*adj* abaxial
ABBACY	*n* pl. -CIES the office of an abbot
ABBATIAL	*adj* pertaining to an abbot
ABBE	*n* pl. -S an abbot
ABBESS	*n* pl. -ES the female superior of a convent of nuns
ABBEY	*n* pl. -BEYS a monastery or convent
ABBOT	*n* pl. -S the superior of a monastery
ABBOTCY	*n* pl. -CIES abbacy
ABDICATE	*v* -CATED, -CATING, -CATES to give up formally
ABDOMEN	*n* pl. -MENS or -MINA the body cavity containing the viscera
ABDUCE	*v* -DUCED, -DUCING, -DUCES to abduct
ABDUCENS	*n* pl. -CENTES a cranial nerve
ABDUCENT	*adj* serving to abduct
ABDUCING	present participle of abduce
ABDUCT	*v* -ED, -ING, -S to draw away from the original position
ABDUCTOR	*n* pl. -ES or -S an abducent muscle
ABEAM	*adv* at right angles to the keel of a ship
ABED	*adv* in bed
ABELE	*n* pl. -S a Eurasian tree
ABELMOSK	*n* pl. -S a tropical herb

ABERRANT	*n* pl. -S a deviant
ABET	*v* ABETTED, ABETTING, ABETS to encourage and support
ABETMENT	*n* pl. -S the act of abetting
ABETTAL	*n* pl. -S abetment
ABETTED	past tense of abet
ABETTER	*n* pl. -S abettor
ABETTING	present participle of abet
ABETTOR	*n* pl. -S one that abets
ABEYANCE	*n* pl. -S temporary inactivity
ABEYANCY	*n* pl. -CIES abeyance
ABEYANT	*adj* marked by abeyance
ABFARAD	*n* pl. -S a unit of capacitance
ABHENRY	*n* pl. -RIES or -RYS a unit of inductance
ABHOR	*v* -HORRED, -HORRING, -HORS to loathe
ABHORRER	*n* pl. -S one that abhors
ABIDANCE	*n* pl. -S the act of abiding
ABIDE	*v* ABODE or ABIDED, ABIDING, ABIDES to accept without objection
ABIDER	*n* pl. -S one that abides
ABIGAIL	*n* pl. -S a lady's maid
ABILITY	*n* pl. -TIES the quality of being able to do something
ABIOSIS	*n* pl. -OSES absence of life **ABIOTIC** *adj*
ABJECT	*adj* sunk to a low condition **ABJECTLY** *adv*
ABJURE	*v* -JURED, -JURING, -JURES to renounce under oath
ABJURER	*n* pl. -S one that abjures
ABLATE	*v* -LATED, -LATING, -LATES to remove by cutting
ABLATION	*n* pl. -S surgical removal of a bodily part
ABLATIVE	*n* pl. -S a grammatical case
ABLAUT	*n* pl. -S a patterned change in root vowels of verb forms
ABLAZE	*adj* being on fire
ABLE	*adj* ABLER, ABLEST having sufficient power, skill, or resources
ABLE	*n* pl. -S a communications code word for the letter A
ABLEGATE	*n* pl. -S a papal envoy
ABLER	comparative of able
ABLEST	superlative of able
ABLINGS	*adv* ablins
ABLINS	*adv* perhaps
ABLOOM	*adj* blooming
ABLUENT	*n* pl. -S a cleansing agent
ABLUSH	*adj* blushing
ABLUTED	*adj* washed clean
ABLUTION	*n* pl. -S a washing
ABLY	*adv* in an able manner
ABMHO	*n* pl. -MHOS a unit of electrical conductance
ABNEGATE	*v* -GATED, -GATING, -GATES to deny to oneself
ABNORMAL	*n* pl. -S a mentally deficient person
ABO	*n* pl. ABOS an aborigine (an original inhabitant)
ABOARD	*adv* into, in, or on a ship, train, or airplane
ABODE	*v* ABODED, ABODING, ABODES to forebode
ABOHM	*n* pl. -S a unit of electrical resistance
ABOIDEAU	*n* pl. -DEAUS or -DEAUX a type of dike
ABOIL	*adj* boiling
ABOITEAU	*n* pl. -TEAUS or -TEAUX aboideau
ABOLISH	*v* -ED, -ING, -ES to do away with
ABOLLA	*n* pl. -LAE a cloak worn in ancient Rome
ABOMA	*n* pl. -S a South American snake
ABOMASAL	*adj* pertaining to the abomasum
ABOMASUM	*n* pl. -SA the fourth stomach of a ruminant
ABOMASUS	*n* pl. -MASI abomasum
ABOON	*adv* above
ABORAL	*adj* situated away from the mouth **ABORALLY** *adv*
ABORNING	*adv* while being born
ABORT	*v* -ED, -ING, -S to bring forth a fetus prematurely
ABORTER	*n* pl. -S one that aborts
ABORTION	*n* pl. -S induced expulsion of a nonviable fetus
ABORTIVE	*adj* failing to succeed
ABOUGHT	past tense of aby and abye
ABOULIA	*n* pl. -S abulia **ABOULIC** *adj*

ABOUND   *v* -ED, -ING, -S to have a large number or amount

ABOUT   *adv* approximately

ABOVE   *n* pl. -S something that is above (in a higher place)

ABRADANT   *n* pl. -S an abrasive

ABRADE   *v* ABRADED, ABRADING, ABRADES to wear away by friction

ABRADER   *n* pl. -S a tool for abrading

ABRASION   *n* pl. -S the act of abrading

ABRASIVE   *n* pl. -S an abrading substance

ABREACT   *v* -ED, -ING, -S to release repressed emotions by reliving the original traumatic experience

ABREAST   *adv* side by side

ABRI   *n* pl. -S a bomb shelter

ABRIDGE   *v* ABRIDGED, ABRIDGING, ABRIDGES to reduce the length of

ABRIDGER   *n* pl. -S one that abridges

ABROACH   *adj* astir

ABROAD   *adv* out of one's own country

ABROGATE   *v* -GATED, -GATING, -GATES to abolish by authoritative action

ABRUPT   *adj* -RUPTER, -RUPTEST rudely brief **ABRUPTLY** *adv*

ABSCESS   *v* -ED, -ING, -ES to form an abscess (a localized collection of pus surrounded by inflamed tissue)

ABSCISE   *v* -SCISED, -SCISING, -SCISES to cut off

ABSCISIN   *n* pl. -S a regulatory substance found in plants

ABSCISSA   *n* pl. -SAS or -SAE a particular geometric coordinate

ABSCOND   *v* -ED, -ING, -S to depart suddenly and secretly

ABSENCE   *n* pl. -S the state of being away

ABSENT   *v* -ED, -ING, -S to take or keep away

ABSENTEE   *n* pl. -S one that is not present

ABSENTER   *n* pl. -S one that absents himself

ABSENTLY   *adv* in an inattentive manner

ABSINTH   *n* pl. -S absinthe

ABSINTHE   *n* pl. -S a bitter liqueur

ABSOLUTE   *adj* -LUTER, -LUTEST free from restriction

ABSOLUTE   *n* pl. -S something that is absolute

ABSOLVE   *v* -SOLVED, -SOLVING, -SOLVES to free from the consequences of an action

ABSOLVER   *n* pl. -S one that absolves

ABSONANT   *adj* unreasonable

ABSORB   *v* -ED, -ING, -S to take up or in

ABSORBER   *n* pl. -S one that absorbs

ABSTAIN   *v* -ED, -ING, -S to refrain voluntarily

ABSTERGE   *v* -STERGED, -STERGING, -STERGES to cleanse by wiping

ABSTRACT   *adj* -STRACTER, -STRACTEST difficult to understand

ABSTRACT   *v* -ED, -ING, -S to take away

ABSTRICT   *v* -ED, -ING, -S to form by cutting off

ABSTRUSE   *adj* -STRUSER, -STRUSEST difficult to understand

ABSURD   *adj* -SURDER, -SURDEST ridiculously incongruous or unreasonable **ABSURDLY** *adv*

ABSURD   *n* pl. -S the condition in which man exists in an irrational and meaningless universe

ABUBBLE   *adj* bubbling

ABULIA   *n* pl. -S loss of will power **ABULIC** *adj*

ABUNDANT   *adj* present in great quantity

ABUSE   *v* ABUSED, ABUSING, ABUSES to use wrongly or improperly **ABUSABLE** *adj*

ABUSER   *n* pl. -S one that abuses

ABUSIVE   *adj* characterized by wrong or improper use

ABUT   *v* ABUTTED, ABUTTING, ABUTS to touch along a border

ABUTILON   *n* pl. -S a flowering plant

ABUTMENT   *n* pl. -S something that abuts

ABUTTAL   *n* pl. -S an abutment

ABUTTED   past tense of abut

ABUTTER   *n* pl. -S one that abuts

ABUTTING   present participle of abut

ABUZZ   *adj* buzzing

ABVOLT   *n* pl. -S a unit of electromotive force

ABWATT   *n* pl. -S a unit of power

ABY   *v* ABOUGHT, ABYING, ABYS to pay the penalty for

ABYE   v ABOUGHT, ABYING, ABYES to aby

ABYSM   n pl. -S an abyss

ABYSMAL   adj immeasurably deep

ABYSS   n pl. -ES a bottomless chasm
ABYSSAL adj

ACACIA   n pl. -S a flowering tree or shrub

ACADEME   n pl. -S a place of instruction

ACADEMIA   n pl. -S scholastic life or environment

ACADEMIC   n pl. -S a college student or teacher

ACADEMY   n pl. -MIES a secondary school

ACAJOU   n pl. -S a tropical tree

ACALEPH   n pl. -LEPHAE or -LEPHS a jellyfish

ACALEPHE   n pl. -S acaleph

ACANTHUS   n pl. -THI or -THUSES a prickly herb

ACARI   pl. of acarus

ACARID   n pl. -S any of an order of arachnids

ACARIDAN   n pl. -S acarid

ACARINE   n pl. -S acarid

ACAROID   adj resembling an acarid

ACARPOUS   adj not producing fruit

ACARUS   n pl. -RI a mite

ACAUDAL   adj having no tail

ACAUDATE   adj acaudal

ACAULINE   adj having no stem

ACAULOSE   adj acauline

ACAULOUS   adj acauline

ACCEDE   v -CEDED, -CEDING, -CEDES to consent

ACCEDER   n pl. -S one that accedes

ACCENT   v -ED, -ING, -S to pronounce with prominence

ACCENTOR   n pl. -S a songbird

ACCEPT   v -ED, -ING, -S to receive willingly

ACCEPTEE   n pl. -S one that is accepted

ACCEPTER   n pl. -S one that accepts

ACCEPTOR   n pl. -S accepter

ACCESS   v -ED, -ING, -ES to get at

ACCIDENT   n pl. -S an unexpected or unintentional occurrence

ACCIDIE   n pl. -S acedia

ACCLAIM   v -ED, -ING, -S to shout approval of

ACCOLADE   n pl. -S an expression of praise

ACCORD   v -ED, -ING, -S to bring into agreement

ACCORDER   n pl. -S one that accords

ACCOST   v -ED, -ING, -S to approach and speak to first

ACCOUNT   v -ED, -ING, -S to give an explanation

ACCOUTER   v -ED, -ING, -S to equip

ACCOUTRE   v -TRED, -TRING, -TRES to accouter

ACCREDIT   v -ED, -ING, -S to give official authorization to

ACCRETE   v -CRETED, -CRETING, -CRETES to grow together

ACCRUAL   n pl. -S the act of accruing

ACCRUE   v -CRUED, -CRUING, -CRUES to come as an increase or addition

ACCURACY   n pl. -CIES the quality of being accurate

ACCURATE   adj free from error

ACCURSED   adj damnable

ACCURST   adj accursed

ACCUSAL   n pl. -S the act of accusing

ACCUSANT   n pl. -S an accuser

ACCUSE   v -CUSED, -CUSING, -CUSES to make an assertion against

ACCUSER   n pl. -S one that accuses

ACCUSTOM   v -ED, -ING, -S to make familiar

ACE   v ACED, ACING, ACES to score a point against in a single stroke

ACEDIA   n pl. -S apathy

ACELDAMA   n pl. -S a place of bloodshed

ACENTRIC   adj having no center

ACEQUIA   n pl. -S an irrigation ditch or canal

ACERATE   adj acerose

ACERATED   adj acerose

ACERB   adj ACERBER, ACERBEST sour

ACERBATE   v -BATED, -BATING, -BATES to make sour

ACERBIC   adj acerb

ACERBITY   n pl. -TIES sourness

ACEROLA   n pl. -S a West Indian shrub

ACEROSE   adj needle-shaped

ACEROUS   adj acerose

ACERVATE   *adj* growing in compact clusters

ACERVULI   *n/pl* spore-producing organs of certain fungi

ACESCENT   *n* pl. -S something that is slightly sour

ACETA   pl. of acetum

ACETAL   *n* pl. -S a flammable liquid

ACETAMID   *n* pl. -S an amide of acetic acid

ACETATE   *n* pl. -S a salt of acetic acid **ACETATED** *adj*

ACETIC   *adj* pertaining to vinegar

ACETIFY   *v* -FIED, -FYING, -FIES to convert into vinegar

ACETONE   *n* pl. -S a flammable liquid **ACETONIC** *adj*

ACETOSE   *adj* acetous

ACETOUS   *adj* tasting like vinegar

ACETOXYL   *n* pl. -S a univalent radical

ACETUM   *n* pl. -TA vinegar

ACETYL   *n* pl. -S a univalent radical **ACETYLIC** *adj*

ACHE   *v* ACHED, ACHING, ACHES to suffer a dull, continuous pain

ACHENE   *n* pl. -S a type of fruit **ACHENIAL** *adj*

ACHIER   comparative of achy

ACHIEST   superlative of achy

ACHIEVE   *v* ACHIEVED, ACHIEVING, ACHIEVES to carry out successfully

ACHIEVER   *n* pl. -S one that achieves

ACHINESS   *n* pl. -ES the state of being achy

ACHING   present participle of ache

ACHINGLY   *adv* in an aching manner

ACHIOTE   *n* pl. -S a yellowish red dye

ACHOO   *interj* ahchoo

ACHROMAT   *n* pl. -S a type of lens

ACHROMIC   *adj* having no color

ACHY   *adj* ACHIER, ACHIEST aching

ACICULA   *n* pl. -LAE or -LAS a needlelike part or process **ACICULAR** *adj*

ACID   *n* pl. -S a type of chemical compound

ACIDHEAD   *n* pl. -S one who uses LSD

ACIDIC   *adj* sour

ACIDIFY   *v* -FIED, -FYING, -FIES to convert into an acid

ACIDITY   *n* pl. -TIES sourness

ACIDLY   *adv* sourly

ACIDNESS   *n* pl. -ES acidity

ACIDOSIS   *n* pl. -DOSES an abnormal condition of the blood **ACIDOTIC** *adj*

ACIDY   *adj* sour

ACIERATE   *v* -ATED, -ATING, -ATES to turn into steel

ACIFORM   *adj* needle-shaped

ACING   present participle of ace

ACINUS   *n* pl. -NI a small, saclike division of a gland **ACINAR, ACINIC, ACINOSE, ACINOUS** *adj*

ACLINIC   *adj* having no inclination

ACME   *n* pl. -S the highest point **ACMATIC, ACMIC** *adj*

ACNE   *n* pl. -S a skin disease **ACNED** *adj*

ACNODE   *n* pl. -S an element of a mathematical set that is isolated from the other elements

ACOCK   *adj* cocked

ACOLD   *adj* cold

ACOLYTE   *n* pl. -S an assistant

ACONITE   *n* pl. -S a poisonous herb **ACONITIC** *adj*

ACONITUM   *n* pl. -S aconite

ACORN   *n* pl. -S the fruit of the oak tree

ACOUSTIC   *n* pl. -S a hearing aid

ACQUAINT   *v* -ED, -ING, -S to cause to know

ACQUEST   *n* pl. -S something acquired

ACQUIRE   *v* -QUIRED, -QUIRING, -QUIRES to come into possession of

ACQUIRER   *n* pl. -S one that acquires

ACQUIT   *v* -QUITTED, -QUITTING, -QUITS to free or clear from a charge of fault or crime

ACRASIN   *n* pl. -S a substance secreted by the cells of a slime mold

ACRE   *n* pl. -S a unit of area

ACREAGE   *n* pl. -S area in acres

ACRED   *adj* owning many acres

ACRID   *adj* -RIDER, -RIDEST sharp and harsh to the taste or smell

ACRIDINE   *n* pl. -S a chemical compound

ACRIDITY   *n* pl. -TIES the state of being acrid

ACRIDLY   *adv* in an acrid manner

ACRIMONY *n* pl. -NIES sharpness or bitterness of speech or temper

ACROBAT *n* pl. -S one skilled in feats of agility and balance

ACRODONT *n* pl. -S an animal having rootless teeth

ACROGEN *n* pl. -S a plant growing at the apex only

ACROLEIN *n* pl. -S a flammable liquid

ACROLITH *n* pl. -S a type of statue

ACROMION *n* pl. -MIA the outward end of the shoulder blade **ACROMIAL** *adj*

ACRONIC *adj* occurring at sunset

ACRONYM *n* pl. -S a word formed from the initials of a compound term or series of words

ACROSS *prep* from one side of to the other

ACROSTIC *n* pl. -S a poem in which certain letters taken in order form a word or phrase

ACROTISM *n* pl. -S weakness of the pulse **ACROTIC** *adj*

ACRYLATE *n* pl. -S an acrylic

ACRYLIC *n* pl. -S a type of resin

ACT *v* -ED, -ING, -S to do something

ACTA *n/pl* recorded proceedings

ACTABLE *adj* suitable for performance on the stage

ACTIN *n* pl. -S a protein in muscle tissue

ACTINAL *adj* having tentacles

ACTING *n* pl. -S the occupation of an actor

ACTINIA *n* pl. -IAE or -IAS a marine animal

ACTINIAN *n* pl. -S actinia

ACTINIC *adj* pertaining to actinism

ACTINIDE *n* pl. -S any of a series of radioactive elements

ACTINISM *n* pl. -S the property of radiant energy that effects chemical changes

ACTINIUM *n* pl. -S a radioactive element

ACTINOID *n* pl. -S an actinide

ACTINON *n* pl. -S an isotope of radon

ACTION *n* pl. -S the process of acting

ACTIVATE *v* -VATED, -VATING, -VATES to set in motion

ACTIVE *n* pl. -S a participating member of an organization

ACTIVELY *adv* with activity

ACTIVISM *n* pl. -S a doctrine that emphasizes direct and decisive action

ACTIVIST *n* pl. -S an advocate of activism

ACTIVITY *n* pl. -TIES brisk action or movement

ACTOR *n* pl. -S a theatrical performer **ACTORISH** *adj*

ACTRESS *n* pl. -ES a female actor

ACTUAL *adj* existing in fact **ACTUALLY** *adv*

ACTUARY *n* pl. -ARIES a statistician who computes insurance risks and premiums

ACTUATE *v* -ATED, -ATING, -ATES to set into action or motion

ACTUATOR *n* pl. -S one that actuates

ACUATE *adj* sharp

ACUITY *n* pl. -ITIES sharpness

ACULEATE *adj* having a sting

ACUMEN *n* pl. -S mental keenness

ACUTANCE *n* pl. -S a measure of photographic clarity

ACUTE *adj* ACUTER, ACUTEST marked by sharpness or severity **ACUTELY** *adv*

ACUTE *n* pl. -S a type of accent mark

ACYCLIC *adj* not cyclic

ACYL *n* pl. -S a univalent radical

ACYLATE *v* -ATED, -ATING, -ATES to introduce acyl into

AD *n* pl. -S an advertisement

ADAGE *n* pl. -S a traditional saying expressing a common observation **ADAGIAL** *adj*

ADAGIO *n* pl. -GIOS a musical composition or movement played in a slow tempo

ADAMANCE *n* pl. -S adamancy

ADAMANCY *n* pl. -CIES unyielding hardness

ADAMANT *n* pl. -S an extremely hard substance

ADAMSITE *n* pl. -S a lung-irritating gas

ADAPT *v* -ED, -ING, -S to make suitable

ADAPTER *n* pl. -S one that adapts

ADAPTION *n* pl. -S the act of adapting **ADAPTIVE** *adj*

ADAPTOR   *n* pl. -S adapter

ADAXIAL   *adj* situated on the same side as

ADD   *v* -ED, -ING, -S to combine or join so as to bring about an increase **ADDABLE** *adj*

ADDAX   *n* pl. -ES a large antelope

ADDEDLY   *adv* additionally

ADDEND   *n* pl. -S a number to be added to another

ADDENDUM   *n* pl. -DA something added or to be added

ADDER   *n* pl. -S a venomous snake

ADDIBLE   *adj* capable of being added

ADDICT   *v* -ED, -ING, -S to devote or surrender to something habitually or compulsively

ADDITION   *n* pl. -S something added

ADDITIVE   *n* pl. -S a substance added to another to impart desirable qualities

ADDLE   *v* -DLED, -DLING, -DLES to confuse

ADDRESS   *v* -DRESSED or -DREST, -DRESSING, -DRESSES to speak to

ADDUCE   *v* -DUCED, -DUCING, -DUCES to bring forward as evidence

ADDUCENT   *adj* serving to adduct

ADDUCER   *n* pl. -S one that adduces

ADDUCING   present participle of adduce

ADDUCT   *v* -ED, -ING, -S to draw toward the main axis

ADDUCTOR   *n* pl. -S an adducent muscle

ADEEM   *v* -ED, -ING, -S to take away

ADENINE   *n* pl. -S an alkaloid

ADENITIS   *n* pl. -TISES inflammation of a lymph node

ADENOID   *n* pl. -S an enlarged lymphoid growth behind the pharynx

ADENOMA   *n* pl. -MAS or -MATA a tumor of glandular origin

ADENYL   *n* pl. -S a univalent radical

ADEPT   *adj* ADEPTER, ADEPTEST highly skilled **ADEPTLY** *adv*

ADEPT   *n* pl. -S an adept person

ADEQUACY   *n* pl. -CIES the state of being adequate

ADEQUATE   *adj* sufficient for a specific requirement

ADHERE   *v* -HERED, -HERING, -HERES to become or remain attached or close to something

ADHEREND   *n* pl. -S the surface to which an adhesive adheres

ADHERENT   *n* pl. -S a supporter

ADHERER   *n* pl. -S one that adheres

ADHERING   present participle of adhere

ADHESION   *n* pl. -S the act of adhering

ADHESIVE   *n* pl. -S a substance that causes adhesion

ADHIBIT   *v* -ED, -ING, -S to take or let in

ADIEU   *n* pl. ADIEUS or ADIEUX a farewell

ADIOS   *interj* — used to express farewell

ADIPOSE   *n* pl. -S animal fat **ADIPIC** *adj*

ADIPOSIS   *n* pl. -POSES obesity

ADIPOUS   *adj* pertaining to adipose

ADIT   *n* pl. -S an entrance

ADJACENT   *adj* next to

ADJOIN   *v* -ED, -ING, -S to lie next to

ADJOINT   *n* pl. -S a type of mathematical matrix

ADJOURN   *v* -ED, -ING, -S to suspend until a later time

ADJUDGE   *v* -JUDGED, -JUDGING, -JUDGES to determine judicially

ADJUNCT   *n* pl. -S something attached in a subordinate position

ADJURE   *v* -JURED, -JURING, -JURES to command solemnly

ADJURER   *n* pl. -S one that adjures

ADJUROR   *n* pl. -S adjurer

ADJUST   *v* -ED, -ING, -S to bring to a more satisfactory state

ADJUSTER   *n* pl. -S one that adjusts

ADJUSTOR   *n* pl. -S adjuster

ADJUTANT   *n* pl. -S an assistant

ADJUVANT   *n* pl. -S an assistant

ADMAN   *n* pl. -MEN a man employed in the advertising business

ADMASS   *adj* pertaining to a society strongly influenced by advertising

ADMIRAL   *n* pl. -S a high-ranking naval officer

ADMIRE   *v* -MIRED, -MIRING, -MIRES to regard with wonder, pleasure, and approval

ADMIRER   *n* pl. -S one that admires

ADMIT   *v* -MITTED, -MITTING, -MITS to allow to enter

ADMITTER   *n* pl. -S one that admits

ADMIX   *n* -MIXED or -MIXT, -MIXING, -MIXES to mix

ADMONISH   *n* -ED, -ING, -ES to reprove mildly or kindly

ADNATE   *adj* joined to another part or organ

ADNATION   *n* pl. -S the state of being adnate

ADNEXA   *n/pl* conjoined anatomical parts **ADNEXAL** *adj*

ADNOUN   *n* pl. -S an adjective when used as a noun

ADO   *n* pl. ADOS bustling excitement

ADOBE   *n* pl. -S an unburnt, sun-dried brick

ADOPT   *v* -ED, -ING, -S to take into one's family by legal means

ADOPTEE   *n* pl. -S one that is adopted

ADOPTER   *n* pl. -S one that adopts

ADOPTION   *n* pl. -S the act of adopting **ADOPTIVE** *adj*

ADORABLE   *adj* worthy of being adored **ADORABLY** *adv*

ADORE   *v* ADORED, ADORING, ADORES to love deeply

ADORER   *n* pl. -S one that adores

ADORN   *v* -ED, -ING, -S to add something to for the purpose of making more attractive

ADORNER   *n* pl. -S one that adorns

ADOWN   *adv* downward

ADOZE   *adj* dozing

ADRENAL   *n* pl. -S an endocrine gland

ADRIFT   *adj* drifting

ADROIT   *adj* ADROITER, ADROITEST skillful **ADROITLY** *adv*

ADSCRIPT   *n* pl. -S a distinguishing symbol written after another character

ADSORB   *v* -ED, -ING, -S to gather on a surface in a condensed layer

ADULARIA   *n* pl. -S a mineral

ADULATE   *v* -LATED, -LATING, -LATES to praise excessively

ADULATOR   *n* pl. -S one that adulates

ADULT   *n* pl. -S a fully developed individual

ADULTERY   *n* pl. -TERIES voluntary sexual intercourse between a married person and someone other than his or her spouse

ADULTLY   *adv* in a manner typical of an adult

ADUMBRAL   *adj* shadowy

ADUNC   *adj* bent inward

ADUNCATE   *adj* adunc

ADUNCOUS   *adj* adunc

ADUST   *adj* scorched

ADVANCE   *v* -VANCED, -VANCING, -VANCES to move or cause to move ahead

ADVANCER   *n* pl. -S one that advances

ADVENT   *n* pl. -S arrival

ADVERB   *n* pl. -S a word used to modify the meaning of a verb, adjective, or other adverb

ADVERSE   *adj* acting in opposition

ADVERT   *v* -ED, -ING, -S to call attention

ADVICE   *n* pl. -S recommendation regarding a decision or course of conduct

ADVISE   *v* -VISED, -VISING, -VISES to give advice to

ADVISEE   *n* pl. -S one that is advised

ADVISER   *n* pl. -S one that advises

ADVISING   present participle of advise

ADVISOR   *n* pl. -S adviser

ADVISORY   *n* pl. -RIES a report giving information

ADVOCACY   *n* pl. -CIES the act of advocating

ADVOCATE   *v* -CATED, -CATING, -CATES to speak in favor of

ADVOWSON   *n* pl. -S the right of presenting a nominee to a vacant church office

ADYNAMIA   *n* pl. -S lack of physical strength **ADYNAMIC** *adj*

ADYTUM   *n* pl. -TA an inner sanctuary in an ancient temple

ADZ   *n* pl.-ES a cutting tool

ADZE   *n* pl. -S adz

AE   *adj* one

AECIA   pl. of aecium

AECIAL   *adj* pertaining to an aecium

AECIDIUM   *n* pl. -IA an aecium

AECIUM   *n* pl. -IA a spore-producing organ of certain fungi

AEDES   *n* pl. AEDES any of a genus of mosquitoes

AEDILE   *n* pl. -S a magistrate of ancient Rome

AEDINE   *adj* pertaining to an aedes

AEGIS   *n* pl. -GISES protection

AENEOUS   *adj* having a greenish gold color

AENEUS   *adj* aeneous

AEOLIAN   *adj* eolian

AEON   *n* pl. -S eon

AEONIAN   *adj* eonian

AEONIC   *adj* eonian

AERATE   *v* -ATED, -ATING, -ATES to supply with air

AERATION   *n* pl. -S the act of aerating

AERATOR   *n* pl. -S one that aerates

AERIAL   *n* pl. -S a metallic apparatus for sending and receiving electromagnetic waves

AERIALLY   *adv* in a manner pertaining to the air

AERIE   *n* pl. -S a bird's nest built high on a mountain or cliff **AERIED** *adj*

AERIER   comparative of aery

AERIES   pl. of aery

AERIEST   superlative of aery

AERIFORM   *adj* having the form of air

AERIFY   *v* -FIED, -FYING, -FIES to aerate

AERILY   *adv* in an aery manner

AERO   *adj* pertaining to aircraft

AEROBE   *n* pl. -S an organism that requires oxygen to live **AEROBIC** *adj*

AEROBIUM   *n* pl. -BIA aerobe

AERODUCT   *n* pl. -S a type of jet engine

AERODYNE   *n* pl. -S an aircraft that is heavier than air

AEROFOIL   *n* pl. -S airfoil

AEROGEL   *n* pl. -S a highly porous solid

AEROGRAM   *n* pl. -S an airmail letter

AEROLITE   *n* pl. -S a meteorite containing more stone than iron

AEROLITH   *n* pl. -S aerolite

AEROLOGY   *n* pl. -GIES the study of the atmosphere

AERONAUT   *n* pl. -S one who operates an airship

AERONOMY   *n* pl. -MIES the study of the upper atmosphere

AEROSOL   *n* pl. -S a gaseous suspension of fine solid or liquid particles

AEROSTAT   *n* pl. -S an aircraft that is lighter than air

AERUGO   *n* pl. -GOS a green film that forms on copper

AERY   *adj* AERIER, AERIEST airy

AERY   *n* pl. AERIES aerie

AESTHETE   *n* pl. -S esthete

AESTIVAL   *adj* estival

AETHER   *n* pl. -S the upper region of the atmosphere **AETHERIC** *adj*

AFAR   *n* pl. -S a great distance

AFEARD   *adj* afraid

AFEARED   *adj* afeard

AFF   *adv* off

AFFABLE   *adj* easy to talk to **AFFABLY** *adv*

AFFAIR   *n* pl. -S anything done or to be done

AFFAIRE   *n* pl. -S a brief amorous relationship

AFFECT   *v* -ED, -ING, -S to give a false appearance of

AFFECTER   *n* pl. -S one that affects

AFFERENT   *adj* conducting toward an organ or part

AFFIANCE   *v* -ANCED, -ANCING, -ANCES to betroth

AFFIANT   *n* pl. -S one who makes a written declaration under oath

AFFICHE   *n* pl. -S a poster

AFFINE   *n* pl. -S a relative by marriage

AFFINED   *adj* closely related

AFFINELY   *adv* in the manner of a type of mathematical mapping

AFFINITY   *n* pl. -TIES a natural attraction or inclination

AFFIRM   *v* -ED, -ING, -S to state positively

AFFIRMER   *n* pl. -S one that affirms

AFFIX   *v* -ED, -ING, -ES to attach

AFFIXAL   *adj* pertaining to a prefix or suffix

AFFIXER   *n* pl. -S one that affixes

AFFIXIAL   *adj* affixal

AFFLATUS *n* pl. -ES a creative inspiration

AFFLICT *v* -ED, -ING, -S to distress with mental or physical pain

AFFLUENT *n* pl. -S a stream that flows into another

AFFLUX *n* pl. -ES a flowing toward a point

AFFORD *v* -ED, -ING, -S to have sufficient means for

AFFOREST *v* -ED, -ING, -S to convert into forest

AFFRAY *v* -ED, -ING, -S to frighten

AFFRAYER *n* pl. -S one that affrays

AFFRIGHT *v* -ED, -ING, -S to frighten

AFFRONT *v* -ED, -ING, -S to insult openly

AFFUSION *n* pl. -S an act of pouring a liquid on

AFGHAN *n* pl. -S a woolen blanket or shawl

AFGHANI *n* pl. -S a monetary unit of Afghanistan

AFIELD *adv* in the field

AFIRE *adj* being on fire

AFLAME *adj* flaming

AFLOAT *adj* floating

AFLUTTER *adj* nervously excited

AFOOT *adv* on foot

AFORE *adv* before

AFOUL *adj* entangled

AFRAID *adj* filled with apprehension

AFREET *n* pl. -S an evil spirit in Arabic mythology

AFRESH *adv* anew

AFRIT *n* pl. -S afreet

AFT *adv* toward the stern

AFTER *prep* behind in place or order

AFTERS *n/pl* dessert

AFTERTAX *adj* remaining after payment of taxes

AFTMOST *adj* nearest the stern

AFTOSA *n* pl. -S a disease of hoofed mammals

AGA *n* pl. -S a high-ranking Turkish military officer

AGAIN *adv* once more

AGAINST *prep* in opposition to

AGALLOCH *n* pl. -S the fragrant wood of a tropical tree

AGALWOOD *n* pl. -S agalloch

AGAMA *n* pl. -S a tropical lizard

AGAMETE *n* pl. -S an asexual reproductive cell

AGAMIC *adj* asexual

AGAMOUS *adj* agamic

AGAPE *n* pl. -PAE or -PAI the love of God for mankind **AGAPEIC** *adj*

AGAR *n* pl. -S a viscous substance obtained from certain seaweeds

AGARIC *n* pl. -S any of a family of fungi

AGATE *n* pl. -S a variety of quartz **AGATOID** *adj*

AGATIZE *v* -IZED, -IZING, -IZES to cause to resemble agate

AGAVE *n* pl. -S a tropical plant

AGAZE *adj* gazing

AGE *v* AGED, AGING or AGEING, AGES to grow old

AGEDLY *adv* oldly

AGEDNESS *n* pl. -ES oldness

AGEE *adv* to one side

AGEING *n* pl. -S aging

AGELESS *adj* never growing old

AGELONG *adj* lasting for a long time

AGENCY *n* pl. -CIES an organization that does business for others

AGENDA *n* pl. -S a list of things to be done

AGENDUM *n* pl. -S an item on an agenda

AGENE *n* pl. -S a chemical compound used in bleaching flour

AGENESIA *n* pl. -S agenesis

AGENESIS *n* pl. AGENESES absence or imperfect development of a bodily part **AGENETIC** *adj*

AGENIZE *v* -NIZED, -NIZING, -NIZES to treat with agene

AGENT *n* pl. -S one who is authorized to act for another **AGENTIAL** *adj*

AGENTRY *n* pl. -RIES the office or duties of an agent

AGER *n* pl. -S one that ages

AGERATUM *n* pl. -S a flowering plant

AGGER *n* pl. -S a mound of earth used as a fortification

AGGIE *n* pl. -S a type of playing marble

AGGRADE *v* -GRADED, -GRADING, -GRADES to fill with detrital material

AGGRESS *v* -ED, -ING, -ES to commit the first act of hostility

AGGRIEVE *v* -GRIEVED, -GRIEVING, -GRIEVES to distress

AGHA *n* pl. -S aga

AGHAST *adj* shocked by something horrible

AGILE *adj* able to move quickly and easily **AGILELY** *adv*

AGILITY *n* pl. -TIES the quality of being agile

AGIN *prep* against

AGING *n* pl. -S the process of growing old

AGINNER *n* pl. -S one that is against change

AGIO *n* pl. AGIOS a premium paid for the exchange of one currency for another

AGIOTAGE *n* pl. -S the business of a broker

AGIST *v* -ED, -ING, -S to feed and take care of for a fee, as livestock

AGITATE *v* -TATED, -TATING, -TATES to move with a violent, irregular action **AGITABLE** *adj*

AGITATO *adj* fast and stirring — used as a musical direction

AGITATOR *n* pl. -S one that agitates

AGITPROP *n* pl. -S pro-Communist propaganda

AGLARE *adj* glaring

AGLEAM *adj* gleaming

AGLEE *adv* agley

AGLET *n* pl. -S a metal sheath at the end of a lace

AGLEY *adv* awry

AGLIMMER *adj* glimmering

AGLITTER *adj* glittering

AGLOW *adj* glowing

AGLY *adv* agley

AGLYCON *n* pl. -S a type of chemical compound

AGLYCONE *n* pl. -S aglycon

AGMA *n* pl. -S eng

AGMINATE *adj* clustered together

AGNAIL *n* pl. -S a piece of loose skin at the base of a fingernail

AGNATE *n* pl. -S a relative on the father's side **AGNATIC** *adj*

AGNATION *n* pl. -S the relationship of agnates

AGNIZE *n* -NIZED, -NIZING, -NIZES to acknowledge

AGNOMEN *n* pl. -MINA or -MENS an additional name given to an ancient Roman

AGNOSTIC *n* pl. -S one who disclaims any knowledge of God

AGO *adv* in the past

AGOG *adv* in a state of eager curiosity

AGON *n* pl. -S or -ES the dramatic conflict between the main characters in a Greek play

AGONAL *adj* pertaining to agony

AGONE *adv* ago

AGONES a pl. of agon

AGONIC *adj* not forming an angle

AGONIES pl. of agony

AGONISE *v* -NISED, -NISING, -NISES to agonize

AGONIST *n* pl. -S one that is engaged in a struggle

AGONIZE *v* -NIZED, -NIZING, -NIZES to suffer extreme pain

AGONY *n* pl. -NIES extreme pain

AGORA *n* pl. -RAS or -RAE a marketplace in ancient Greece

AGORA *n* pl. AGOROT or AGOROTH a monetary unit of Israel

AGOUTI *n* pl. -S or -ES a burrowing rodent

AGOUTY *n* pl.- TIES agouti

AGRAFE *n* pl. -S agraffe

AGRAFFE *n* pl. -S an ornamental clasp

AGRAPHA *n/pl* the sayings of Jesus not found in the Bible

AGRAPHIA *n* pl. -S a mental disorder marked by inability to write **AGRAPHIC** *adj*

AGRARIAN *n* pl. -S one who favors equal distribution of land

AGREE *v* AGREED, AGREEING, AGREES to have the same opinion

AGRESTAL *adj* growing wild

AGRESTIC *adj* rural

AGRIMONY *n* pl. -NIES a perennial herb

AGROLOGY *n* pl. -GIES the science of soils in relation to crops

AGRONOMY *n* pl. -MIES the application of scientific principles to the cultivation of land

AGROUND *adv* on the ground

AGUE *n* pl. -S a malarial fever **AGUELIKE, AGUISH** *adj* **AGUISHLY** *adv*

AGUEWEED *n* pl. -S a flowering plant

AH *interj* — used to express delight, relief, or contempt

AHA *interj* — used to express surprise, triumph, or derision

AHCHOO *interj* — used to represent the sound of a sneeze

AHEAD *adv* at or to the front

AHEM *interj* — used to attract attention

AHIMSA *n* pl. -S the Hindu principle of nonviolence

AHOLD *n* pl. -S a hold or grasp of something

AHORSE *adv* on a horse

AHOY *interj* — used in hailing a ship or person

AHULL *adj* abandoned and flooded, as a ship

AI *n* pl. -S a three-toed sloth

AIBLINS *adv* ablins

AID *v* -ED, -ING, -S to help

AIDE *n* pl. -S an assistant

AIDER *n* pl. -S one that aids

AIDFUL *adj* helpful

AIDLESS *adj* helpless

AIDMAN *n* pl. -MEN a corpsman

AIGLET *n* pl. -S aglet

AIGRET *n* pl. -S aigrette

AIGRETTE *n* pl. -S a tuft of feathers worn as a head ornament

AIGUILLE *n* pl. -S a sharp, pointed mountain peak

AIKIDO *n* pl. -DOS a Japanese art of self-defense

AIL *v* -ED, -ING, -S to cause pain or discomfort to

AILERON *n* pl. -S a movable control surface on an airplane wing

AILMENT *n* pl. -S a physical or mental disorder

AIM *v* -ED, -ING, -S to direct toward a specified object or goal

AIMER *n* pl. -S one that aims

AIMFUL *adj* full of purpose **AIMFULLY** *adv*

AIMLESS *adj* lacking direction or purpose

AIN *n* pl. -S ayin

AINE *adj* elder or eldest

AINEE *adj* aine

AINSELL *n* pl. -S own self

AIR *v* -ED, -ING, -S to expose to the air (the mixture of gases that surrounds the earth)

AIR *adv* AIRER, AIREST early

AIRBOAT *n* pl. -S a boat used in swampy areas

AIRBORNE *adj* flying

AIRBOUND *adj* stopped up by air

AIRBRUSH *v* -ED, -ING, -ES to apply in a fine spray by compressed air, as paint

AIRBURST *n* pl. -S an explosion in the air

AIRBUS *n* pl. -BUSES or -BUSSES a passenger airplane

AIRCOACH *n* pl. -ES the cheaper class of accommodations in commercial aircraft

AIRCRAFT *n* pl. AIRCRAFT any machine or device capable of flying

AIRCREW *n* pl. -S the crew of an aircraft

AIRDROME *n* pl. -S an airport

AIRDROP *v* -DROPPED, -DROPPING, -DROPS to drop from an aircraft

AIRFIELD *n* pl. -S an airport

AIRFLOW *n* pl. -S a flow of air

AIRFOIL *n* pl. -S a part of an aircraft designed to provide lift or control

AIRFRAME *n* pl. -S the framework and external covering of an airplane

AIRGLOW *n* pl. -S a glow in the upper atmosphere

AIRHEAD *n* pl. -S an area in hostile territory secured by paratroops

AIRIER comparative of airy

AIRIEST superlative of airy

AIRILY *adv* in an airy manner

AIRINESS *n* pl. -ES the state of being airy

AIRING *n* pl. -S an exposure to the air

AIRLESS *adj* having no air

AIRLIFT *v* -ED, -ING, -S to transport by airplane

AIRLIKE	*adj* resembling air
AIRLINE	*n* pl. -S an air transportation system
AIRLINER	*n* pl. -S a large passenger aircraft
AIRMAIL	*v* -ED, -ING, -S to send mail by airplane
AIRMAN	*n* pl. -MEN an aviator
AIRN	*n* pl. -S iron
AIRPARK	*n* pl. -S a small airport
AIRPLANE	*n* pl. -S a winged aircraft propelled by jet engines or propellers
AIRPORT	*n* pl. -S a tract of land maintained for the landing and takeoff of aircraft
AIRPOST	*n* pl. -S a system of conveying mail by airplane
AIRPROOF	*v* -ED, -ING, -S to make impermeable to air
AIRSCREW	*n* pl. -S an airplane propeller
AIRSHIP	*n* pl. -S a lighter-than-air aircraft having propulsion and steering systems
AIRSICK	*adj* nauseated from flying in an airplane
AIRSPACE	*n* pl. -S the portion of the atmosphere above a particular land area
AIRSPEED	*n* pl. -S the speed of an aircraft with relation to the air
AIRSTRIP	*n* pl. -S a runway
AIRT	*v* -ED, -ING, -S to guide
AIRTH	*v* -ED, -ING, -S to airt
AIRTIGHT	*adj* not allowing air to escape or enter
AIRWARD	*adv* toward the sky
AIRWAVE	*n* pl. -S the medium of radio and television transmission
AIRWAY	*n* pl. -WAYS a passageway in which air circulates
AIRWISE	*adj* skillful in aviation
AIRWOMAN	*n* pl. -WOMEN a female aviator
AIRY	*adj* AIRIER, AIRIEST having the nature of air
AISLE	*n* pl. -S a passageway between sections of seats **AISLED** *adj*
AIT	*n* pl. -S a small island
AITCH	*n* pl. -ES the letter H
AIVER	*n* pl. -S a draft horse
AJAR	*adj* partly open
AJEE	*adv* agee
AJIVA	*n* pl. -S inanimate matter
AJOWAN	*n* pl. -S the fruit of an Egyptian plant
AKEE	*n* pl. -S a tropical tree
AKELA	*n* pl. -S a leader of a cub scout pack
AKENE	*n* pl. -S achene
AKIMBO	*adj* having hands on hips and elbows bent outward
AKIN	*adj* related by blood
AKVAVIT	*n* pl. -S aquavit
ALA	*n* pl. ALAE a wing or winglike part
ALACK	*interj* — used to express sorrow or regret
ALACRITY	*n* pl. -TIES cheerful promptness
ALAE	pl. of ala
ALAMEDA	*n* pl. -S a shaded walkway
ALAMO	*n* pl. -MOS a softwood tree
ALAMODE	*n* pl. -S a silk fabric
ALAN	*n* pl. -S a large hunting dog
ALAND	*n* pl. -S alan
ALANE	*adj* alone
ALANG	*adv* along
ALANIN	*n* pl. -S alanine
ALANINE	*n* pl. -S an amino acid
ALANT	*n* pl. -S alan
ALANYL	*n* pl. -S a univalent radical
ALAR	*adj* pertaining to wings
ALARM	*v* -ED, -ING, -S to frighten by a sudden revelation of danger
ALARMISM	*n* pl. -S the practice of alarming others needlessly
ALARMIST	*n* pl. -S one who alarms others needlessly
ALARUM	*v* -ED, -ING, -S to alarm
ALARY	*adj* alar
ALAS	*interj* — used to express sorrow or regret
ALASKA	*n* pl. -S a heavy fabric
ALASTOR	*n* pl. -S an avenging deity in Greek tragedy
ALATE	*adj* having wings
ALATED	*adj* alate
ALATION	*n* pl. -S the state of having wings
ALB	*n* pl. -S a long-sleeved vestment

ALBA *n* pl. -S the white substance of the brain

ALBACORE *n* pl. -S a marine food fish

ALBATA *n* pl. -S an alloy of copper, nickel, and zinc

ALBEDO *n* pl. -DOS the ratio of the light reflected by a planet to that received by it

ALBEIT *conj* although

ALBICORE *n* pl. -S albacore

ALBINAL *adj* albinic

ALBINIC *adj* pertaining to albinism

ALBINISM *n* pl. -S the condition of being an albino

ALBINO *n* pl. -NOS an organism lacking normal pigmentation

ALBITE *n* pl. -S a mineral **ALBITIC** *adj*

ALBUM *n* pl. -S a book for preserving photographs or stamps

ALBUMEN *n* pl. -S the white of an egg

ALBUMIN *n* pl. -S a simple protein

ALBUMOSE *n* pl. -S a proteose

ALBURNUM *n* pl. -S sapwood

ALCADE *n* pl. -S alcalde

ALCAHEST *n* pl. -S alkahest

ALCAIC *n* pl. -S a type of verse form

ALCAIDE *n* pl. -S the commander of a Spanish fortress

ALCALDE *n* pl. -S the mayor of a Spanish town

ALCAYDE *n* pl. -S alcaide

ALCAZAR *n* pl. -S a Spanish fortress or palace

ALCHEMY *n* pl. -MIES a medieval form of chemistry **ALCHEMIC** *adj*

ALCHYMY *n* pl. -MIES alchemy

ALCIDINE *adj* pertaining to a family of seabirds

ALCOHOL *n* pl. -S a flammable liquid

ALCOVE *n* pl. -S a recessed section of a room **ALCOVED** *adj*

ALDEHYDE *n* pl. -S a type of chemical compound

ALDER *n* pl. -S a shrub or small tree

ALDERMAN *n* pl. -MEN a member of a municipal legislative body

ALDOL *n* pl. -S a chemical compound

ALDOLASE *n* pl. -S an enzyme

ALDOSE *n* pl. -S a type of sugar

ALDRIN *n* pl. -S an insecticide

ALE *n* pl. -S an alcoholic beverage

ALEATORY *adj* pertaining to luck

ALEC *n* pl. -S a herring

ALEE *adv* toward the side of a vessel sheltered from the wind

ALEF *n* pl. -S aleph

ALEGAR *n* pl. -S sour ale

ALEHOUSE *n* pl. -S a tavern where ale is sold

ALEMBIC *n* pl. -S an apparatus formerly used in distilling

ALEPH *n* pl. -S a Hebrew letter

ALERT *adj* ALERTER, ALERTEST ready for sudden action **ALERTLY** *adv*

ALERT *v* -ED, -ING, -S to warn

ALEURON *n* pl. -S aleurone

ALEURONE *n* pl. -S protein matter found in the seeds of certain plants

ALEVIN *n* pl. -S a young fish

ALEWIFE *n* pl. -WIVES a marine fish

ALEXIA *n* pl. -S a cerebral disorder marked by the loss of the ability to read

ALEXIN *n* pl. -S a substance in the blood that aids in the destruction of bacteria

ALEXINE *n* pl. -S alexin

ALFA *n* pl. -S a communications code word for the letter A

ALFAKI *n* pl. -S alfaqui

ALFALFA *n* pl. -S a plant cultivated for use as hay and forage

ALFAQUI *n* pl. -S a teacher of Muslim law

ALFAQUIN *n* pl. -S alfaqui

ALFORJA *n* pl. -S a leather bag

ALFRESCO *adv* outdoors

ALGA *n* pl. -GAE or -GAS any of a group of primitive aquatic plants **ALGAL** *adj*

ALGAROBA *n* pl. -S the mesquite

ALGEBRA *n* pl. -S a branch of mathematics

ALGERINE *n* pl. -S a woolen fabric

ALGICIDE *n* pl. -S a substance used to kill algae

ALGID *adj* cold

ALGIDITY *n* pl. -TIES coldness

ALGIN   *n* pl. -S a viscous substance obtained from certain algae

ALGINATE   *n* pl. -S a chemical salt

ALGOID   *adj* resembling algae

ALGOLOGY   *n* pl. -GIES the study of algae

ALGOR   *n* pl. -S coldness

ALGORISM   *n* pl. -S the Arabic system of arithmetic notation

ALGUM   *n* pl. -S almug

ALIAS   *n* pl. -ES an assumed name

ALIBI   *v* -BIED, -BIING, -BIES or -BIS to make excuses for oneself

ALIBLE   *adj* nourishing

ALIDAD   *n* pl. -S alidade

ALIDADE   *n* pl. -S a device used in angular measurement

ALIEN   *v* -ED, -ING, -S to transfer to another, as property

ALIENAGE   *n* pl. -S the state of being foreign

ALIENATE   *v* -ATED, -ATING, -ATES to make indifferent or unfriendly

ALIENEE   *n* pl. -S one to whom property is transferred

ALIENER   *n* pl. -S alienor

ALIENISM   *n* pl. -S alienage

ALIENIST   *n* pl. -S a physician who treats mental disorders

ALIENLY   *adv* in a foreign manner

ALIENOR   *n* pl. -S one that transfers property

ALIF   *n* pl. -S an Arabic letter

ALIFORM   *adj* shaped like a wing

ALIGHT   *v* ALIGHTED or ALIT, ALIGHTING, ALIGHTS to come down from something

ALIGN   *v* -ED, -ING, -S to arrange in a straight line

ALIGNER   *n* pl. -S one that aligns

ALIKE   *adj* having close resemblance

ALIMENT   *v* -ED, -ING, -S to nourish

ALIMONY   *n* pl. -NIES an allowance paid to a woman by her divorced husband

ALINE   *v* ALINED, ALINING, ALINES to align

ALINER   *n* pl. -S aligner

ALIPED   *n* pl. -S an animal having a membrane connecting the toes

ALIQUANT   *adj* not dividing evenly into another number

ALIQUOT   *n* pl. -S a number that divides evenly into another

ALIST   *adj* leaning to one side

ALIT   a past tense of alight

ALIUNDE   *adv* from a source extrinsic to the matter at hand

ALIVE   *adj* having life

ALIYAH   *n* pl. -S the immigration of Jews to Israel

ALIZARIN   *n* pl. -S a red dye

ALKAHEST   *n* pl. -S the hypothetical universal solvent sought by alchemists

ALKALI   *n* pl. -LIES or -LIS a type of chemical compound **ALKALIC** *adj*

ALKALIFY   *v* -FIED, -FYING, -FIES to alkalize

ALKALIN   *adj* alkaline

ALKALINE   *adj* containing an alkali

ALKALISE   *v* -LISED, -LISING, -LISES to alkalize

ALKALIZE   *v* -LIZED, -LIZING, -LIZES to convert into an alkali

ALKALOID   *n* pl. -S a type of chemical compound

ALKANE   *n* pl. -S a type of chemical compound

ALKANET   *n* pl. -S a European plant

ALKENE   *n* pl. -S a type of chemical compound

ALKINE   *n* pl. -S alkyne

ALKOXY   *adj* containing a univalent radical composed of alkyl united with oxygen

ALKYD   *n* pl. -S a synthetic resin

ALKYL   *n* pl. -S a univalent radical **ALKYLIC** *adj*

ALKYLATE   *v* -ATED, -ATING, -ATES to combine with alkyl

ALKYNE   *n* pl. -S a type of chemical compound

ALL   *n* pl. -S everything that one has

ALLANITE   *n* pl. -S a mineral

ALLAY   *v* -ED, -ING, -S to reduce in intensity or severity

ALLAYER   *n* pl. -S one that allays

ALLEGE   *v* -LEGED, -LEGING, -LEGES to assert without proof or before proving

ALLEGER *n* pl. -S one that alleges

ALLEGORY *n* pl. -RIES a story presenting a moral principle

ALLEGRO *n* pl. -GROS a musical passage played in rapid tempo

ALLELE *n* pl. -S any of several forms of a gene **ALLELIC** *adj*

ALLELISM *n* pl. -S the state of possessing alleles

ALLELUIA *n* pl. -S a song of praise to God

ALLERGEN *n* pl. -S a substance capable of inducing an allergy

ALLERGIC *adj* pertaining to allergy

ALLERGIN *n* pl. -S allergen

ALLERGY *n* pl. -GIES a state of hypersensitive reaction to certain things

ALLEY *n* pl. -LEYS a narrow passageway

ALLEYWAY *n* pl. -WAYS an alley

ALLHEAL *n* pl. -S a medicinal herb

ALLIABLE *adj* capable of being allied

ALLIANCE *n* pl. -S an association formed to further the common interests of its members

ALLIED past tense of ally

ALLIES present 3d person sing. of ally

ALLIUM *n* pl. -S a bulbous herb

ALLOBAR *n* pl. -S a change in barometric pressure

ALLOCATE *v* -CATED, -CATING, -CATES to set apart for a particular purpose

ALLOD *n* pl. -S allodium

ALLODIUM *n* pl. -DIA land held in absolute ownership **ALLODIAL** *adj*

ALLOGAMY *n* pl. -MIES fertilization of a flower by pollen from another

ALLONGE *n* pl. -S an addition to a document

ALLONYM *n* pl. -S the name of one person assumed by another

ALLOPATH *n* pl. -S one who treats diseases by producing effects incompatible with those of the disease

ALLOT *v* -LOTTED, -LOTTING, -LOTS to give as a share or portion

ALLOTTEE *n* pl. -S one to whom something is allotted

ALLOTTER *n* pl. -S one that allots

ALLOTTING present participle of allot

ALLOTYPE *n* pl. -S a type of antibody

ALLOTYPY *n* pl. -TYPIES the condition of being an allotype

ALLOVER *n* pl. -S a fabric having a pattern extending over the entire surface

ALLOW *v* -ED, -ING, -S to put no obstacle in the way of

ALLOXAN *n* pl. -S a chemical compound

ALLOY *v* -ED, -ING, -S to combine to form an alloy (a homogenous mixture of metals)

ALLSEED *n* pl. -S a plant having many seeds

ALLSPICE *n* pl. -S a tropical tree

ALLUDE *v* -LUDED, -LUDING, -LUDES to make an indirect reference

ALLURE *v* -LURED, -LURING, -LURES to attract with something desirable

ALLURER *n* pl. -S one that allures

ALLUSION *n* pl. -S the act of alluding **ALLUSIVE** *adj*

ALLUVIA a pl. of alluvium

ALLUVIAL *n* pl. -S soil composed of alluvium

ALLUVION *n* pl. -S alluvium

ALLUVIUM *n* pl. -VIA or -VIUMS detrital material deposited by running water

ALLY *v* -LIED, -LYING, -LIES to unite in a formal relationship

ALLYL *n* pl. -S a univalent radical **ALLYLIC** *adj*

ALMA *n* pl. -S almah

ALMAGEST *n* pl. -S a medieval treatise on astrology or alchemy

ALMAH *n* pl. -S an Egyptian girl who sings and dances professionally

ALMANAC *n* pl. -S an annual publication containing general information

ALME *n* pl. -S almah

ALMEH *n* pl. -S almah

ALMEMAR *n* pl. -S a bema

ALMIGHTY *adj* having absolute power over all

ALMNER *n* pl. -S almoner

ALMOND *n* pl. -S the edible nut of a small tree

ALMONER *n* pl. -S one that distributes alms

ALMONRY   *n* pl. -RIES a place where alms are distributed

ALMOST   *adv* very nearly

ALMS   *n* pl. ALMS money or goods given to the poor

ALMSMAN   *n* pl. -MEN one who receives alms

ALMUCE   *n* pl. -S a hooded cape

ALMUD   *n* pl. -S a Spanish unit of capacity

ALMUDE   *n* pl. -S almud

ALMUG   *n* pl. -S a precious wood mentioned in the Bible

ALNICO   *n* pl. -COES a magnetic alloy

ALODIUM   *n* pl. -DIA allodium **ALODIAL** *adj*

ALOE   *n* pl. -S an African plant **ALOETIC** *adj*

ALOFT   *adv* in or into the air

ALOGICAL   *adj* being outside the bounds of that to which logic can apply

ALOHA   *n* pl. -S love — used as a greeting or farewell

ALOIN   *n* pl. -S a laxative

ALONE   *adj* apart from others

ALONG   *adv* onward

ALOOF   *adj* distant in interest or feeling **ALOOFLY** *adv*

ALOPECIA   *n* pl. -S baldness **ALOPECIC** *adj*

ALOUD   *adv* audibly

ALOW   *adv* in or to a lower position

ALP   *n* pl. -S a high mountain

ALPACA   *n* pl. -S a ruminant mammal

ALPHA   *n* pl. -S a Greek letter

ALPHABET   *v* -ED, -ING, -S to arrange in the customary order of the letters of a language

ALPHORN   *n* pl. -S a wooden horn used by Swiss herdsmen

ALPHOSIS   *n* pl. -SISES lack of skin pigmentation

ALPHYL   *n* pl. -S a univalent radical

ALPINE   *n* pl. -S a plant native to high mountain regions

ALPINELY   *adv* in a lofty manner

ALPINISM   *n* pl. -S mountain climbing

ALPINIST   *n* pl. -S a mountain climber

ALREADY   *adv* by this time

ALRIGHT   *adj* satisfactory

ALSIKE   *n* pl. -S a European clover

ALSO   *adv* in addition

ALT   *n* pl. -S a high-pitched musical note

ALTAR   *n* pl. -S a raised structure used in worship

ALTER   *v* -ED, -ING, -S to make different

ALTERANT   *n* pl. -S something that alters

ALTERER   *n* pl. -S one that alters

ALTHAEA   *n* pl. -S althea

ALTHEA   *n* pl. -S a flowering plant

ALTHO   *conj* although

ALTHORN   *n* pl. -S a brass wind instrument

ALTHOUGH   *conj* despite the fact that

ALTITUDE   *n* pl. -S the vertical elevation of an object above a given level

ALTO   *n* pl. -TOS a low female singing voice

ALTRUISM   *n* pl. -S selfless devotion to the welfare of others

ALTRUIST   *n* pl. -S one that practices altruism

ALUDEL   *n* pl. -S a pear-shaped vessel

ALULA   *n* pl. -LAE a tuft of feathers on the first digit of a bird's wing **ALULAR** *adj*

ALUM   *n* pl. -S a chemical compound

ALUMIN   *n* pl. -S alumina

ALUMINA   *n* pl. -S an oxide of aluminum

ALUMINE   *n* pl. -S alumina

ALUMINUM   *n* pl. -S a metallic element **ALUMINIC** *adj*

ALUMNA   *n* pl. -NAE a female graduate

ALUMNUS   *n* pl. -NI a male graduate

ALUMROOT   *n* pl. -S a flowering plant

ALUNITE   *n* pl. -S a mineral

ALVEOLAR   *n* pl. -S a sound produced with the tongue touching a place just behind the front teeth

ALVEOLUS   *n* pl. -LI a small anatomical cavity

ALVINE   *adj* pertaining to the abdomen and lower intestines

ALWAY   *adv* always

ALWAYS   *adv* at all times

ALYSSUM   *n* pl. -S a flowering plant

AM   present 1st person sing. of be

AMA   *n* pl. -S amah

AMADAVAT   *n* pl. -S an Asian songbird

AMADOU *n* pl. -S a substance prepared from fungi for use as tinder

AMAH *n* pl. -S an Oriental nurse

AMAIN *adv* with full strength

AMALGAM *n* pl. -S an alloy of mercury with another metal

AMANDINE *adj* prepared with almonds

AMANITA *n* pl. -S any of a genus of poisonous fungi

AMARANTH *n* pl. -S a flowering plant

AMARELLE *n* pl. -S a variety of sour cherry

AMARNA *adj* pertaining to a certain historical period of ancient Egypt

AMASS *v* -ED, -ING, -ES to gather

AMASSER *n* pl. -S one that amasses

AMATEUR *n* pl. -S one that engages in an activity for pleasure

AMATIVE *adj* amorous

AMATOL *n* pl. -S a powerful explosive

AMATORY *adj* pertaining to sexual love

AMAZE *v* AMAZED, AMAZING, AMAZES to overwhelm with surprise or wonder **AMAZEDLY** *adv*

AMAZON *n* pl. -S a tall, powerful woman

AMBAGE *n* pl. -S a winding path

AMBARI *n* pl. -S ambary

AMBARY *n* pl. -RIES an East Indian plant

AMBEER *n* pl. -S tobacco juice

AMBER *n* pl. -S a fossil resin

AMBEROID *n* pl. -S ambroid

AMBERY *n* pl. -BERIES ambry

AMBIANCE *n* pl. -S ambience

AMBIENCE *n* pl. -S the character, mood, or atmosphere of a place or situation

AMBIENT *n* pl. -S ambience

AMBIT *n* pl. -S the external boundary of something

AMBITION *v* -ED, -ING, -S to seek with eagerness

AMBIVERT *n* pl. -S a person whose personality type is intermediate between introvert and extravert

AMBLE *v* -BLED, -BLING, -BLES to saunter

AMBLER *n* pl. -S one that ambles

AMBO *n* pl. AMBOS or AMBONES a pulpit in an early Christian church

AMBOINA *n* pl. -S amboyna

AMBOYNA *n* pl. -S the mottled wood of an Indonesian tree

AMBRIES pl. of ambry

AMBROID *n* pl. -S a synthetic amber

AMBROSIA *n* pl. -S the food of the Greek and Roman gods

AMBRY *n* pl. -BRIES a recess in a church wall for sacred vessels

AMBSACE *n* pl. -S bad luck

AMBULANT *adj* ambulating

AMBULATE *v* -LATED, -LATING, -LATES to move or walk about

AMBUSH *v* -ED, -ING, -ES to attack from a concealed place

AMBUSHER *n* pl. -S one that ambushes

AMEBA *n* pl. -BAS or -BAE amoeba **AMEBAN, AMEBIC, AMEBOID** *adj*

AMEBEAN *adj* alternately responding

AMEER *n* pl. -S amir

AMEERATE *n* pl. -S amirate

AMELCORN *n* pl. -S a variety of wheat

AMEN *n* pl. -S a word used at the end of a prayer to express agreement

AMENABLE *adj* capable of being persuaded **AMENABLY** *adv*

AMEND *v* -ED, -ING, -S to improve

AMENDER *n* pl. -S one that amends

AMENITY *n* pl. -TIES the quality of being pleasant or agreeable

AMENT *n* pl. -S a mentally deficient person

AMENTIA *n* pl. -S mental deficiency

AMERCE *v* AMERCED, AMERCING, AMERCES to punish by imposing an arbitrary fine

AMERCER *n* pl. -S one that amerces

AMESACE *n* pl. -S ambsace

AMETHYST *n* pl. -S a variety of quartz

AMI *n* pl. -S a friend

AMIA *n* pl. -S a freshwater fish

AMIABLE *adj* having a pleasant disposition **AMIABLY** *adv*

AMIANTUS *n* pl. -ES a variety of asbestos

AMICABLE *adj* friendly **AMICABLY** *adv*

AMICE *n* pl. -S a vestment worn about the neck and shoulders

AMID	*n* pl. -S amide
AMIDASE	*n* pl. -S an enzyme
AMIDE	*n* pl. -S a type of chemical compound **AMIDIC** *adj*
AMIDIN	*n* pl. -S the soluble matter of starch
AMIDO	*adj* containing an amide united with an acid radical
AMIDOGEN	*n* pl. -S a univalent chemical radical
AMIDOL	*n* pl. -S a chemical compound
AMIDSHIP	*adv* toward the middle of a ship
AMIDST	*prep* in the midst of
AMIE	*n* pl. -S a female friend
AMIGA	*n* pl. -S a female friend
AMIGO	*n* pl. -GOS a friend
AMIN	*n* pl. -S amine
AMINE	*n* pl. -S a type of chemical compound **AMINIC** *adj*
AMINITY	*n* pl. -TIES the state of being an amine
AMINO	*adj* containing an amine united with a nonacid radical
AMIR	*n* pl. -S a Muslim prince or governor
AMIRATE	*n* pl. -S the rank of an amir
AMISS	*adj* being out of proper order
AMITOSIS	*n* pl. -TOSES a type of cell division **AMITOTIC** *adj*
AMITROLE	*n* pl. -S an herbicide
AMITY	*n* pl. -TIES friendship
AMMETER	*n* pl. -S an instrument for measuring amperage
AMMINE	*n* pl. -S a type of chemical compound
AMMINO	*adj* pertaining to an ammine
AMMO	*n* pl. -MOS ammunition
AMMOCETE	*n* pl. -S the larva of a lamprey
AMMONAL	*n* pl. -S a powerful explosive
AMMONIA	*n* pl. -S a pungent gas
AMMONIAC	*n* pl. -S a gum resin
AMMONIC	*adj* pertaining to ammonia
AMMONIFY	*v* -FIED, FYING, -FIES to treat with ammonia
AMMONITE	*n* pl. -S the coiled shell of an extinct mollusk
AMMONIUM	*n* pl. -S a univalent chemical radical
AMMONOID	*n* pl. -S ammonite
AMNESIA	*n* pl. -S loss of memory
AMNESIAC	*n* pl. -S one suffering from amnesia
AMNESIC	*n* pl. -S amnesiac
AMNESTIC	*adj* pertaining to amnesia
AMNESTY	*v* -TIED, -TYING, -TIES to pardon
AMNION	*n* pl. -NIONS or -NIA a membranous sac enclosing an embryo **AMNIC, AMNIONIC, AMNIOTIC** *adj*
AMNIOTE	*n* pl. -S a vertebrate that develops an amnion during the embryonic stage
AMOEBA	*n* pl. -BAS or -BAE a unicellular microscopic organism **AMOEBAN, AMOEBIC, AMOEBOID** *adj*
AMOEBEAN	*adj* amebean
AMOK	*n* pl. -S a murderous frenzy
AMOLE	*n* pl. -S a plant root used as a substitute for soap
AMONG	*prep* in the midst of
AMONGST	*prep* among
AMORAL	*adj* lacking a sense of right and wrong **AMORALLY** *adv*
AMORETTO	*n* pl. -TI or -TOS a cupid
AMORINO	*n* pl. -NI an amoretto
AMORIST	*n* pl. -S a lover
AMOROSO	*adv* tenderly — used as a musical direction
AMOROUS	*adj* pertaining to love
AMORT	*adj* being without life
AMORTISE	*v* -TISED, TISING, TISES to amortize
AMORTIZE	*v* -TIZED, -TIZING, -TIZES to liquidate gradually, as a debt
AMOTION	*n* pl. -S the removal of a corporate officer from his office
AMOUNT	*v* -ED, -ING, -S to combine to yield a sum
AMOUR	*n* pl. -S a love affair
AMP	*n* pl. -S ampere
AMPERAGE	*n* pl. -S the strength of an electric current expressed in amperes
AMPERE	*n* pl. -S a unit of electric current strength
AMPHIBIA	*n/pl* organisms adapted for life both on land and in water
AMPHIOXI	*n/pl* lancelets
AMPHIPOD	*n* pl. -S a small crustacean

AMPHORA *n* pl. -RAE or -RAS a narrow-necked jar used in ancient Greece **AMPHORAL** *adj*

AMPLE *adj* -PLER, -PLEST abundant **AMPLY** *adv*

AMPLIFY *v* -FIED, FYING, FIES to make larger or more powerful

AMPOULE *n* pl. -S ampule

AMPUL *n* pl. -S ampule

AMPULE *n* pl. -S a small glass vial

AMPULLA *n* pl. -LAE a globular bottle used in ancient Rome **AMPULLAR** *adj*

AMPUTATE *v* -TATED, -TATING, -TATES to cut off by surgical means

AMPUTEE *n* pl. -S one that has had a limb amputated

AMREETA *n* pl. -S amrita

AMRITA *n* pl. -S a beverage that bestows immortality in Hindu mythology

AMTRAC *n* pl. -S a military vehicle equipped to move on land and water

AMTRACK *n* pl. -S amtrac

AMU *n* pl. -S a unit of mass

AMUCK *n* pl. -S amok

AMULET *n* pl. -S an object worn to protect against evil or injury

AMUSE *v* AMUSED, AMUSING, AMUSES to occupy pleasingly **AMUSABLE** *adj* **AMUSEDLY** *adv*

AMUSER *n* pl. -S one that amuses

AMUSIVE *adj* amusing

AMYGDALA *n* pl. -LAE an almond-shaped anatomical part

AMYGDALE *n* pl. -S amygdule

AMYGDULE *n* pl. -S a small gas bubble in lava

AMYL *n* pl. -S a univalent radical

AMYLASE *n* pl. -S an enzyme

AMYLENE *n* pl. -S a flammable liquid

AMYLIC *adj* pertaining to amyl

AMYLOID *n* pl. -S a hard protein deposit resulting from degeneration of tissue

AMYLOSE *n* pl. -S the relatively soluble component of starch

AMYLUM *n* pl. -S starch

AN *indefinite article* — used before words beginning with a vowel sound

ANA *n* pl. -S a collection of miscellaneous information about a particular subject

ANABAENA *n* pl. -S a freshwater alga

ANABAS *n* pl. -ES a freshwater fish

ANABASIS *n* pl. -ASES a military advance

ANABATIC *adj* pertaining to rising wind currents

ANABLEPS *n* pl. -ES a freshwater fish

ANABOLIC *adj* pertaining to a process by which food is built up into protoplasm

ANACONDA *n* pl. -S a large snake

ANADEM *n* pl. -S a wreath for the head

ANAEMIA *n* pl. -S anemia **ANAEMIC** *adj*

ANAEROBE *n* pl. -S an organism that does not require oxygen to live

ANAGLYPH *n* pl. -S a type of carved ornament

ANAGOGE *n* pl. -S a spiritual interpretation of words **ANAGOGIC** *adj*

ANAGOGY *n* pl. -GIES anagoge

ANAGRAM *v* -GRAMMED, -GRAMMING, -GRAMS to transpose the letters of a word or phrase to form a new one

ANAL *adj* pertaining to the anus

ANALCIME *n* pl. -S analcite

ANALCITE *n* pl. -S a mineral

ANALECTA *n/pl* analects

ANALECTS *n/pl* selections from a literary work or group of works

ANALEMMA *n* pl. -MAS or -MATA a type of graduated scale

ANALGIA *n* pl. -S inability to feel pain

ANALITY *n* pl. -TIES a type of psychological state

ANALLY *adv* at or through the anus

ANALOG *n* pl. -S analogue

ANALOGIC *adj* pertaining to an analogy

ANALOGUE *n* pl. -S something that bears an analogy to something else

ANALOGY *n* pl. -GIES resemblance in some respects between things otherwise unlike

ANALYSE *v* -LYSED, -LYSING, -LYSES to analyze

ANALYSER *n* pl. -S analyzer

ANALYSIS *n* pl. -YSES the separation of a whole into its parts

ANALYST	*n* pl. -S one that analyzes	**ANDESITE**	*n* pl. -S a volcanic rock
ANALYTIC	*adj* pertaining to analysis	**ANDESYTE**	*n* pl. -S andesite
ANALYZE	*v* -LYZED, LYZING, -LYZES to subject to analysis	**ANDIRON**	*n* pl. -S a metal support for holding wood in a fireplace
ANALYZER	*n* pl. -S one that analyzes	**ANDROGEN**	*n* pl. -S a male sex hormone
ANANKE	*n* pl. -S a compelling necessity in ancient Greek religion	**ANDROID**	*n* pl. -S a synthetic man
		ANE	*n* pl. -S one
ANAPAEST	*n* pl. -S anapest	**ANEAR**	*v* -ED, -ING, -S to approach
ANAPEST	*n* pl. -S a type of metrical foot	**ANECDOTE**	*n* pl. -DOTES or -DOTA a brief story
ANAPHASE	*n* pl. -S a stage of mitosis		
ANAPHORA	*n* pl. -S the repetition of a word or phrase at the beginning of several successive verses or sentences	**ANECHOIC**	*adj* neither having nor producing echoes
		ANELE	*v* ANELED, ANELING, ANELES to anoint
ANARCH	*n* pl. -S an advocate of anarchy	**ANEMIA**	*n* pl. -S a disorder of the blood **ANEMIC** *adj*
ANARCHY	*n* pl. -CHIES absence of government **ANARCHIC** *adj*		
		ANEMONE	*n* pl. -S a flowering plant
ANASARCA	*n* pl. -S a form of dropsy	**ANENST**	*prep* anent
ANATASE	*n* pl. -S a mineral	**ANENT**	*prep* in regard to
ANATHEMA	*n* pl. -MAS or -MATA a formal ecclesiastical ban or curse	**ANERGIA**	*n* pl. -S anergy
ANATOMY	*n* pl. -MIES the structure of an organism **ANATOMIC** *adj*	**ANERGY**	*n* pl. -GIES lack of energy **ANERGIC** *adj*
ANATOXIN	*n* pl. -S a toxoid	**ANEROID**	*n* pl. -S a type of barometer
ANATTO	*n* pl. -TOS annatto	**ANESTRUS**	*n* pl. -TRI a period of sexual dormancy
ANCESTOR	*n* pl. -S a person from whom one is descended		
		ANETHOL	*n* pl. -S anethole
ANCESTRY	*n* pl. -TRIES a line or body of ancestors	**ANETHOLE**	*n* pl. -S a chemical compound
		ANEURISM	*n* pl. -S aneurysm
ANCHOR	*v* -ED, -ING, -S to secure by means of an anchor (a device for holding a floating vessel in place)	**ANEURYSM**	*n* pl. -S an abnormal blood-filled dilation of a blood vessel
		ANEW	*adv* once more
		ANGA	*n* pl. -S any of the eight practices of yoga
ANCHORET	*n* pl. -S a recluse		
ANCHOVY	*n* pl. -VIES a small food fish	**ANGARIA**	*n* pl. -S angary
ANCHUSA	*n* pl. -S a hairy-stemmed plant	**ANGARY**	*n* pl. -RIES the right of a warring state to seize neutral property
ANCHUSIN	*n* pl. -S a red dye		
ANCIENT	*adj* -CIENTER, -CIENTEST of or pertaining to time long past	**ANGEL**	*n* pl. -S a winged celestial being **ANGELIC** *adj*
		ANGELICA	*n* pl. -S an aromatic herb
ANCIENT	*n* pl. -S one who lived in ancient times	**ANGELUS**	*n* pl. -ES a Roman Catholic prayer
ANCILLA	*n* pl. -LAE or -LAS a helper		
ANCON	*n* pl. -ES the elbow **ANCONAL, ANCONEAL, ANCONOID** *adj*	**ANGER**	*v* -ED, -ING, -S to make angry
		ANGERLY	*adv* in an angry manner
ANCONE	*n* pl. -S ancon	**ANGINA**	*n* pl. -S a disease marked by spasmodic attacks of intense pain **ANGINAL, ANGINOSE, ANGINOUS** *adj*
ANCRESS	*n* pl. -ES a female recluse		
AND	*n* pl. -S an added condition or stipulation		
ANDANTE	*n* pl. -S a moderately slow musical passage	**ANGIOMA**	*n* pl. -MAS or -MATA a tumor composed of blood or lymph vessels

ANGLE	v -GLED, -GLING, -GLES to fish with a hook and line	**ANION**	n pl. -S a negatively charged ion **ANIONIC** adj
ANGLEPOD	n pl. -S a flowering plant	**ANISE**	n pl. -S a North African plant
ANGLER	n pl. -S one that angles	**ANISEED**	n pl. -S the seed of the anise used as a flavoring
ANGLICE	adv in readily understood English	**ANISETTE**	n pl. -S a liqueur flavored with aniseed
ANGLING	n pl. -S the sport of fishing		
ANGORA	n pl. -S the long, silky hair of a domestic goat	**ANISIC**	adj pertaining to an anise
		ANISOLE	n pl. -S a chemical compound
ANGRY	adj -GRIER, -GRIEST feeling strong displeasure or hostility **ANGRILY** adv	**ANKERITE**	n pl. -S a mineral
		ANKH	n pl. -S an Egyptian symbol of enduring life
ANGST	n pl. -S a feeling of anxiety or dread	**ANKLE**	n pl. -S the joint connecting the foot and the leg
ANGSTROM	n pl. -S a unit of length	**ANKLET**	n pl. -S an ornament for the ankle
ANGUINE	adj resembling a snake		
ANGUISH	v -ED, -ING, -ES to suffer extreme pain	**ANKUS**	n pl. -ES an elephant goad
		ANKUSH	n pl. -ES ankus
ANGULAR	adj having sharp corners	**ANKYLOSE**	v -LOSED, -LOSING, -LOSES to unite or grow together, as the bones of a joint
ANGULATE	v -LATED, -LATING, -LATES to make angular		
ANGULOSE	adj angular	**ANLACE**	n pl. -S a medieval dagger
ANGULOUS	adj angular	**ANLAGE**	n pl. -GEN or -GES the initial cell structure from which an embryonic organ develops
ANHINGA	n pl. -S an aquatic bird		
ANI	n pl. -S a tropical American bird	**ANLAS**	n pl. -ES anlace
ANIL	n pl. -S a West Indian shrub	**ANNA**	n pl. -S a former coin of India and Pakistan
ANILE	adj resembling an old woman		
ANILIN	n pl. -S aniline	**ANNAL**	n pl. -S a record of a single year
ANILINE	n pl. -S a chemical compound		
ANILITY	n pl. -TIES the state of being anile	**ANNALIST**	n pl. -S a historian
		ANNATES	n/pl the first year's revenue of a bishop paid to the pope
ANIMA	n pl. -S the soul		
ANIMAL	n pl. -S a living organism typically capable of voluntary motion and sensation	**ANNATTO**	n pl. -TOS a yellowish-red dye
		ANNEAL	v -ED, -ING, -S to toughen
		ANNEALER	n pl. -S one that anneals
ANIMALLY	adv physically	**ANNELID**	n pl. -S any of a phylum of segmented worms
ANIMATE	v -MATED, -MATING, -MATES to give life to		
ANIMATER	n pl. -S animator	**ANNEX**	v -ED, -ING, -ES to add or attach
ANIMATO	adv in a lively manner — used as a musical direction	**ANNEXE**	n pl. -S something added or attached
ANIMATOR	n pl. -S one that animates	**ANNOTATE**	v -TATED, -TATING, -TATES to furnish with critical or explanatory notes
ANIME	n pl. -S a resin obtained from a tropical tree		
ANIMI	n pl. -S anime	**ANNOUNCE**	v -NOUNCED, -NOUNCING, -NOUNCES to make known publicly
ANIMISM	n pl. -S the belief that souls may exist apart from bodies		
		ANNOY	v -ED, -ING, -S to be troublesome to
ANIMIST	n pl. -S an adherent of animism		
ANIMUS	n pl. -ES a feeling of hostility	**ANNOYER**	n pl. -S one that annoys

ANNUAL *n* pl. -S a publication issued once a year

ANNUALLY *adv* once a year

ANNUITY *n* pl. -TIES an allowance or income paid at regular intervals

ANNUL *v* -NULLED, -NULLING, -NULS to make or declare void or invalid

ANNULAR *adj* shaped like a ring

ANNULATE *adj* composed of or furnished with rings

ANNULET *n* pl. -S a small ring

ANNULI a pl. of annulus

ANNULLED past tense of annul

ANNULLING present participle of annul

ANNULUS *n* pl. -LI or -LUSES a ring or ringlike part **ANNULOSE** *adj*

ANOA *n* pl. -S a wild ox

ANODE *n* pl. -S a positively charged electrode **ANODAL, ANODIC** *adj* **ANODALLY** *adv*

ANODIZE *v* -IZED, -IZING, -IZES to coat with a protective film by chemical means

ANODYNE *n* pl. -S a medicine that relieves pain **ANODYNIC** *adj*

ANOINT *v* -ED, -ING, -S to apply oil to as a sacred rite

ANOINTER *n* pl. -S one that anoints

ANOLE *n* pl. -S a tropical lizard

ANOLYTE *n* pl. -S the part of an electricity-conducting solution nearest the anode

ANOMALY *n* pl. -LIES a deviation from the common rule, type, or form

ANOMIE *n* pl. -S a collapse of the social structures governing a given society **ANOMIC** *adj*

ANOMY *n* pl. -MIES anomie

ANON *adv* at another time

ANONYM *n* pl. -S a false or assumed name

ANOOPSIA *n* pl. -S a visual defect

ANOPIA *n* pl. -S anoopsia

ANOPSIA *n* pl. -S anoopsia

ANORAK *n* pl. -S a parka

ANORETIC *adj* lacking appetite

ANOREXIA *n* pl. -S loss of appetite

ANOREXY *n* pl. -OREXIES anorexia

ANORTHIC *adj* denoting a certain type of crystal system

ANOSMIA *n* pl. -S loss of the sense of smell **ANOSMIC** *adj*

ANOTHER *adj* one more

ANOXEMIA *n* pl. -S a disorder of the blood **ANOXEMIC** *adj*

ANOXIA *n* pl. -S absence of oxygen **ANOXIC** *adj*

ANSA *n* pl. -SAE the projecting part of Saturn's rings

ANSATE *adj* having a handle

ANSATED *adj* ansate

ANSERINE *n* pl. -S a chemical compound

ANSEROUS *adj* silly

ANSWER *v* -ED, -ING, -S to say, write, or act in return

ANSWERER *n* pl. -S one that answers

ANT *n* pl. -S a small insect

ANTA *n* pl. -TAE or -TAS a pilaster formed at the termination of a wall

ANTACID *n* pl. -S a substance that neutralizes acid

ANTALGIC *n* pl. -S an anodyne

ANTE *v* ANTED or ANTEED, ANTEING, ANTES to put a fixed stake into the pot before the cards are dealt in poker

ANTEATER *n* pl. -S any of several mammals that feed on ants

ANTECEDE *v* -CEDED, -CEDING, -CEDES to precede

ANTED a past tense of ante

ANTEDATE *v* -DATED, -DATING, -DATES to be of an earlier date than

ANTEFIX *n* pl. -FIXES or -FIXA an upright ornament at the eaves of a tiled roof

ANTELOPE *n* pl. -S a ruminant mammal

ANTENNA *n* pl. -NAE or -NAS a sensory appendage on the head of an insect, myriapod, or crustacean **ANTENNAL** *adj*

ANTEPAST *n* pl. -S an appetizer

ANTERIOR *adj* situated in or toward the front

ANTEROOM *n* pl. -S a waiting room

ANTETYPE *n* pl. -S an earlier form

ANTEVERT *v* -ED, -ING, -S to displace by tipping forward

ANTHELIA *n/pl* halolike areas seen in the sky opposite the sun

ANTHELIX *n* pl. -LICES the inner curved ridge on the cartilage of the external ear

ANTHEM *v* -ED, -ING, -S to praise in a song

ANTHEMIA *n/pl* decorative floral patterns used in Greek art

ANTHER *n* pl. -S the pollen-bearing part of a stamen **ANTHERAL** *adj*

ANTHERID *n* pl. -S a male reproductive organ of certain plants

ANTHESIS *n* pl. -THESES the full bloom of a flower

ANTHILL *n* pl. -S a mound formed by ants in building their nest

ANTHODIA *n/pl* flower heads of certain plants

ANTHOID *adj* resembling a flower

ANTHRAX *n* pl. -THRACES an infectious disease

ANTI *n* pl. -S one that is opposed

ANTIAR *n* pl. -S an arrow poison

ANTIARIN *n* pl. -S antiar

ANTIBODY *n* pl. -BODIES a body protein that produces immunity against certain microorganisms or toxins

ANTIC *v* -TICKED, -TICKING, -TICS to act in a clownish manner

ANTICK *v* -ED, -ING, -S to antic

ANTICLY *adv* in a clownish manner

ANTIDOTE *n* pl. -S a remedy to counteract the effects of a poison

ANTIFAT *adj* preventing the formation of fat

ANTIGEN *n* pl. -S a substance that stimulates the production of antibodies

ANTIGENE *n* pl. -S antigen

ANTIHERO *n* pl. -ROES a protagonist who is notably lacking in heroic qualities

ANTIKING *n* pl. -S a usurping king

ANTILOG *n* pl. -S the number corresponding to a given logarithm

ANTILOGY *n* pl. -GIES a contradiction in terms or ideas

ANTIMASK *n* pl. -S a comic performance between the acts of a masque

ANTIMERE *n* pl. -S a part of an organism symmetrical with a part on the opposite side of the main axis

ANTIMONY *n* pl. -NIES a metallic element

ANTING *n* pl. -S the deliberate placing, by certain birds, of living ants among the feathers

ANTINODE *n* pl. -S a region between adjacent nodes

ANTINOMY *n* pl. -MIES a contradiction between two seemingly valid principles

ANTIPHON *n* pl. -S a psalm or hymn sung responsively

ANTIPODE *n* pl. -S an exact opposite

ANTIPOLE *n* pl. -S the opposite pole

ANTIPOPE *n* pl. -S one claiming to be pope in opposition to the one chosen by church law

ANTIPYIC *n* pl. -S a medicine that prevents the formation of pus

ANTIQUE *v* -TIQUED, TIQUING, TIQUES to give an appearance of age to

ANTIQUER *n* pl. -S one that antiques

ANTIRUST *n* pl. -S something that prevents rust

ANTISERA *n/pl* serums that contain antibodies

ANTISKID *adj* designed to prevent skidding

ANTISMOG *adj* designed to reduce pollutants that cause smog

ANTITANK *adj* designed to combat tanks

ANTITAX *adj* opposing taxes

ANTITYPE *n* pl. -S an opposite type

ANTIWAR *adj* opposing war

ANTLER *n* pl. -S the horn of an animal of the deer family **ANTLERED** *adj*

ANTLIKE *adj* resembling an ant

ANTLION *n* pl. -S a predatory insect

ANTONYM *n* pl. -S a word opposite in meaning to another

ANTONYMY *n* pl. -MIES the state of being an antonym

ANTRA pl. of antrum

ANTRAL *adj* pertaining to an antrum

ANTRE *n* pl. -S a cave

ANTRORSE *adj* directed forward or upward

ANTRUM *n* pl. -TRA a cavity in a bone

ANURAN *n* pl. -S a frog or toad

ANURESIS *n* pl. -RESES inability to urinate **ANURETIC** *adj*

ANURIA *n* pl. -S absence of urine **ANURIC** *adj*

ANUROUS *adj* having no tail

ANUS *n* pl. -ES the excretory opening at the end of the alimentary canal

ANVIL *v* -VILED, -VILING, -VILS or -VILLED, -VILLING, -VILS to shape on an anvil (a heavy iron block)

ANVILTOP *n* pl. -S an anvil-shaped cloud mass

ANXIETY *n* pl. -ETIES painful or apprehensive uneasiness of mind

ANXIOUS *adj* full of anxiety

ANY *adj* one, no matter which

ANYBODY *n* pl. -BODIES a person of some importance

ANYHOW *adv* in any way

ANYMORE *adv* at the present time

ANYONE *pron* any person

ANYPLACE *adv* in any place

ANYTHING *n* pl. -S a thing of any kind

ANYTIME *adv* at any time

ANYWAY *adv* in any way

ANYWAYS *adv* anyway

ANYWHERE *n* pl. -S any place

ANYWISE *adv* in any way

AORIST *n* pl. -S a verb tense **AORISTIC** *adj*

AORTA *n* pl. -TAS or -TAE a main artery **AORTAL, AORTIC** *adj*

AOUDAD *n* pl. -S a wild sheep

APACE *adv* swiftly

APACHE *n* pl. -S a Parisian gangster

APAGOGE *n* pl. -S establishment of a thesis by showing its contrary to be absurd **APAGOGIC** *adj*

APANAGE *n* pl. -S appanage

APAREJO *n* pl. -JOS a type of saddle

APART *adv* not together

APATETIC *adj* having coloration serving as natural camouflage

APATHY *n* pl. -THIES lack of emotion

APATITE *n* pl. -S a mineral

APE *v* APED, APING, APES to mimic

APEAK *adv* in a vertical position

APEEK *adv* apeak

APELIKE *adj* resembling an ape (a large, tailless primate)

APER *n* pl. -S one that apes

APERCU *n* pl. -S a brief summary

APERIENT *n* pl. -S a mild laxative

APERITIF *n* pl. -S an alcoholic drink taken before a meal

APERTURE *n* pl. -S an opening

APERY *n* pl. -ERIES the act of aping

APETALY *n* pl. -ALIES the state of having no petals

APEX *n* pl. APEXES or APICES the highest point

APHAGIA *n* pl. -S inability to swallow

APHANITE *n* pl. -S an igneous rock

APHASIA *n* pl. -S loss of the ability to use words

APHASIAC *n* pl. -S one suffering from aphasia

APHASIC *n* pl. -S aphasiac.

APHELION *n* pl. -ELIA the point in a planetary orbit farthest from the sun **APHELIAN** *adj*

APHESIS *n* pl. -ESES the loss of an unstressed vowel from the beginning of a word **APHETIC** *adj*

APHID *n* pl. -S any of a family of small, soft-bodied insects

APHIDIAN *n* pl. -S an aphid

APHIS *n* pl. APHIDES an aphid

APHOLATE *n* pl. -S a chemical used to control houseflies

APHONIA *n* pl. -S loss of voice

APHONIC *n* pl. -S one affected with aphonia

APHORISE *v* -RISED, -RISING, -RISES to aphorize

APHORISM *n* pl. -S a brief statement of a truth or principle

APHORIST *n* pl. -S one that aphorizes

APHORIZE *v* -RIZED, -RIZING, -RIZES to write or speak in aphorisms

APHOTIC *adj* lacking light

APHTHA *n* pl. -THAE a small blister in the mouth or stomach **APHTHOUS** *adj*

APHYLLY *n* pl. -LIES the state of being leafless

APIAN *adj* pertaining to bees

APIARIAN *n* pl. -S an apiarist

APIARIST   *n* pl. -S a person who raises bees

APIARY   *n* pl. -ARIES a place where bees are kept

APICAL   *adj* situated at the apex **APICALLY** *adv*

APICES   a pl. of apex

APICULUS   *n* pl. -LI a sharp point at the end of a leaf

APIECE   *adv* for each one

APIMANIA   *n* pl. -S an excessive interest in bees

APING   present participle of ape

APIOLOGY   *n* pl. -GIES the study of bees

APISH   *adj* slavishly or foolishly imitative **APISHLY** *adv*

APLASIA   *n* pl. -S defective development of an organ or part

APLASTIC   *adj* not plastic

APLENTY   *adj* being in sufficient quantity

APLITE   *n* pl. -S a fine-grained rock **APLITIC** *adj*

APLOMB   *n* pl. -S self-confidence

APNEA   *n* pl. -S temporary cessation of respiration **APNEAL, APNEIC** *adj*

APNOEA   *n* pl. -S apnea **APNOEAL, APNOEIC** *adj*

APOCARP   *n* pl. -S a fruit having separated carpels

APOCARPY   *n* pl. -PIES the state of being an apocarp

APOCOPE   *n* pl. -S an omission of the last sound of a word **APOCOPIC** *adj*

APOCRINE   *adj* pertaining to a type of gland

APODAL   *adj* having no feet or footlike appendages

APODOSIS   *n* pl. -OSES the main clause of a conditional sentence

APODOUS   *adj* apodal

APOGAMY   *n* pl. -MIES a form of plant reproduction **APOGAMIC** *adj*

APOGEE   *n* pl. -S the point in the orbit of a celestial body which is farthest from the earth **APOGEAL, APOGEAN, APOGEIC** *adj*

APOLLO   *n* pl. -LOS a handsome young man

APOLOG   *n* pl. -S apologue

APOLOGAL   *adj* pertaining to an apologue

APOLOGIA   *n* pl. -GIAS or -GIAE a formal justification or defense

APOLOGUE   *n* pl. -S an allegory

APOLOGY   *n* pl. -GIES an expression of regret for some error or offense

APOLUNE   *n* pl. -S the point in the orbit of a celestial body which is farthest from the moon

APOMICT   *n* pl. -S an organism produced by apomixis

APOMIXIS   *n* pl. -MIXES a type of reproductive process

APOPHYGE   *n* pl. -S a concave curve in a column

APOPLEXY   *n* pl. -PLEXIES a sudden loss of sensation and muscular control

APORT   *adv* on or toward the left side of a ship

APOSTACY   *n* pl. -CIES apostasy

APOSTASY   *n* pl. -SIES an abandonment of one's faith or principles

APOSTATE   *n* pl. -S one who commits apostasy

APOSTIL   *n* pl. -S a marginal note

APOSTLE   *n* pl. -S a disciple sent forth by Christ to preach the gospel

APOTHECE   *n* pl. -S a spore-producing organ of certain fungi

APOTHEGM   *n* pl. -S a maxim

APOTHEM   *n* pl. -S the perpendicular from the center to any side of a regular polygon

APPAL   *v* -PALLED, -PALLING, -PALS to appall

APPALL   *v* -ED, -ING, -S to fill with horror or dismay

APPANAGE   *n* pl. -S land or revenue granted to a member of a royal family

APPARAT   *n* pl. -S a political organization

APPAREL   *v* -ELED, -ELING, -ELS or -ELLED, -ELLING, -ELS to provide with outer garments

APPARENT   *adj* easily seen

APPEAL   *v* -ED, -ING, -S to make an earnest request

APPEALER   *n* pl. -S one that appeals

APPEAR   *v* -ED, -ING, -S to come into view

APPEASE   *v* -PEASED, -PEASING, -PEASES to bring to a state of peace or contentment

APPEASER   *n* pl. -S one that appeases

APPEL   *n* pl. -S a feint in fencing

APPELLEE   *n* pl. -S the defendant in a type of judicial proceeding

APPELLOR   *n* pl. -S a confessed criminal who accuses an accomplice

APPEND   *v* -ED, -ING, -S to add as a supplement

APPENDIX   *n* pl. -DIXES or -DICES a collection of supplementary material at the end of a book

APPESTAT   *n* pl. -S the mechanism in the central nervous system that regulates appetite

APPETENT   *adj* marked by strong desire

APPETITE   *n* pl. -S a desire for food or drink

APPLAUD   *v* -ED, -ING, -S to express approval by clapping the hands

APPLAUSE   *n* pl. -S the sound made by persons applauding

APPLE   *n* pl. -S an edible fruit

APPLIER   *n* pl. -S one that applies

APPLIQUE   *v* -QUED, -QUEING, -QUES to apply as a decoration to a larger surface

APPLY   *v* -PLIED, -PLYING, -PLIES to bring into contact with something

APPOINT   *v* -ED, -ING, -S to name or assign to a position or office

APPOSE   *v* -POSED, -POSING, -POSES to place side by side

APPOSER   *n* pl. -S one that apposes

APPOSITE   *adj* relevant

APPRAISE   *v* -PRAISED, -PRAISING, -PRAISES to set a value on

APPRISE   *v* -PRISED, -PRISING, -PRISES to notify

APPRISER   *n* pl. -S one that apprises

APPRIZE   *v* -PRIZED, -PRIZING, -PRIZES to appraise

APPRIZER   *n* pl. -S one that apprizes

APPROACH   *v* -ED, -ING, -ES to come near or nearer to

APPROVAL   *n* pl. -S the act of approving

APPROVE   *v* -PROVED, -PROVING, -PROVES to regard favorably

APPROVER   *n* pl. -S one that approves

APPULSE   *n* pl. -S the approach of one moving body toward another

APRAXIA   *n* pl. -S loss of the ability to perform coordinated movements **APRACTIC, APRAXIC** *adj*

APRICOT   *n* pl. -S an edible fruit

APRON   *v* -ED, -ING, -S to provide with an apron (a garment worn to protect one's clothing)

APROPOS   *adj* relevant

APSE   *n* pl. -S a domed, semicircular projection of a building **APSIDAL** *adj*

APSIS   *n* pl. -SIDES an apse

APT   *adj* APTER, APTEST suitable

APTERAL   *adj* apterous

APTEROUS   *adj* having no wings

APTERYX   *n* pl. -ES the kiwi

APTITUDE   *n* pl. -S an ability

APTLY   *adv* in an apt manner

APTNESS   *n* pl. -ES the quality of being apt

APYRASE   *n* pl. -S an enzyme

APYRETIC   *adj* having no fever

AQUA   *n* pl. AQUAE or AQUAS water

AQUACADE   *n* pl. -S a swimming and diving exhibition

AQUANAUT   *n* pl. -S a scuba diver trained to live in underwater installations

AQUARIA   a pl. of aquarium

AQUARIAL   *adj* pertaining to an aquarium

AQUARIAN   *n* pl. -S a member of the old sects that used water rather than wine in religious ceremonies

AQUARIST   *n* pl. -S one who keeps an aquarium

AQUARIUM   *n* pl. -IUMS or -IA a water-filled enclosure in which aquatic animals are kept

AQUATIC   *n* pl. -S an organism living or growing in or near water

AQUATINT   *v* -ED, -ING, -S to etch, using a certain process

AQUATONE   *n* pl. -S a type of printing process

AQUAVIT   *n* pl. -S a Scandinavian liquor

AQUEDUCT   *n* pl. -S a water conduit

AQUEOUS   *adj* pertaining to water

AQUIFER   *n* pl. -S a water-bearing rock formation

AQUILINE   *adj* curving like an eagle's beak

AQUIVER	*adj* quivering
AR	*n* pl. -S the letter R
ARABESK	*n* pl. -S a design of intertwined floral figures
ARABIZE	*v* -IZED, -IZING, -IZES to cause to acquire Arabic customs
ARABLE	*n* pl. -S land suitable for cultivation
ARACEOUS	*adj* belonging to the arum family of plants
ARACHNID	*n* pl. -S any of a class of segmented invertebrate animals
ARAK	*n* pl. -S arrack
ARANEID	*n* pl. -S a spider
ARAPAIMA	*n* pl. -S a large food fish
ARAROBA	*n* pl. -S a Brazilian tree
ARBALEST	*n* pl. -S a type of crossbow
ARBALIST	*n* pl. -S arbalest
ARBITER	*n* pl. -S one chosen or appointed to judge a disputed issue **ARBITRAL** *adj*
ARBOR	*n* pl. -S a shady garden shelter
ARBOR	*n* pl. -ES a tree
ARBOREAL	*adj* living in trees
ARBORED	*adj* having trees
ARBORETA	*n/pl* places for the study and exhibition of trees
ARBORIST	*n* pl. -S a tree specialist
ARBORIZE	*v* -IZED, -IZING, -IZES to form many branches
ARBOROUS	*adj* pertaining to trees
ARBOUR	*n* pl. -S a shady garden shelter **ARBOURED** *adj*
ARBUSCLE	*n* pl. -S a dwarf tree
ARBUTE	*n* pl. -S an evergreen tree **ARBUTEAN** *adj*
ARBUTUS	*n* pl. -ES an evergreen tree
ARC	*v* ARCED, ARCING, ARCS or ARCKED, ARCKING, ARCS to move in a curved course
ARCADE	*v* -CADED, -CADING, -CADES to provide with an arcade (a series of arches)
ARCADIA	*n* pl. -S a region of simple pleasure and quiet
ARCADIAN	*n* pl. -S one who lives in an arcadia
ARCADING	*n* pl. -S an arcade
ARCANE	*adj* mysterious
ARCANUM	*n* pl. -NA a mystery
ARCATURE	*n* pl. -S a small arcade
ARCH	*v* -ED, -ING, -ES to bend like an arch (a curved structure spanning an opening)
ARCHAIC	*adj* pertaining to an earlier time
ARCHAISE	*v* -ISED, -ISING, -ISES to archaize
ARCHAISM	*n* pl. -S an archaic word, idiom, or expression
ARCHAIST	*n* pl. -S one that archaizes
ARCHAIZE	*v* -IZED, -IZING, -IZES to use archaisms
ARCHDUKE	*n* pl. -S an Austrian prince
ARCHER	*n* pl. -S one that shoots with a bow and arrow
ARCHERY	*n* pl. -CHERIES the sport of shooting with a bow and arrow
ARCHIL	*n* pl. -S orchil
ARCHINE	*n* pl. -S a Russian unit of linear measure
ARCHING	*n* pl. -S a series of arches
ARCHIVE	*v* -CHIVED, -CHIVING, -CHIVES to file in an archive (a place where records are kept) **ARCHIVAL** *adj*
ARCHLY	*adv* slyly
ARCHNESS	*n* pl. -ES slyness
ARCHON	*n* pl. -S a magistrate of ancient Athens
ARCHWAY	*n* pl. -WAYS a passageway under an arch
ARCIFORM	*adj* having the form of an arch
ARCKED	a past tense of arc
ARCKING	a present participle of arc
ARCO	*adv* with the bow — used as a direction to players of stringed instruments
ARCTIC	*n* pl. -S a warm, waterproof overshoe
ARCUATE	*adj* curved like a bow
ARCUATED	*adj* arcuate
ARCUS	*n* pl. -ES an arch-shaped cloud
ARDEB	*n* pl. -S an Egyptian unit of capacity
ARDENCY	*n* pl. -CIES ardor
ARDENT	*adj* characterized by intense emotion **ARDENTLY** *adv*
ARDOR	*n* pl. -S intensity of emotion
ARDOUR	*n* pl. -S ardor

ARDUOUS   *adj* involving great labor or hardship

ARE   *n* pl. -S a unit of surface measure

AREA   *n* pl. AREAE a section of the cerebral cortex having a specific function

AREA   *n* pl. -S a particular extent of space or surface **AREAL** *adj* **AREALLY** *adv*

AREAWAY   *n* pl. -WAYS a sunken area leading to a basement entrance

ARECA   *n* pl. -S a tropical tree

AREIC   *adj* pertaining to a region of the earth contributing little surface drainage

ARENA   *n* pl. -S an enclosed area for contests

ARENOSE   *adj* sandy

ARENOUS   *adj* arenose

AREOLA   *n* pl. -LAE or -LAS a small space in a network of leaf veins **AREOLAR, AREOLATE** *adj*

AREOLE   *n* pl. -S areola

AREOLOGY   *n* pl. -GIES the study of the planet Mars

ARETE   *n* pl. -S a sharp mountain ridge

ARETHUSA   *n* pl. -S a flowering plant

ARF   *interj* — used to express the bark of a dog

ARGAL   *n* pl. -S argol

ARGALI   *n* pl. -S a wild sheep

ARGENT   *n* pl. -S silver **ARGENTAL, ARGENTIC** *adj*

ARGENTUM   *n* pl. -S silver

ARGIL   *n* pl. -S a white clay

ARGINASE   *n* pl. -S an enzyme

ARGININE   *n* pl. -S an amino acid

ARGLE   *v* -GLED, -GLING, -GLES to argue

ARGOL   *n* pl. -S a crust deposited in wine casks during aging

ARGON   *n* pl. -S a gaseous element

ARGONAUT   *n* pl. -S a marine mollusk

ARGOSY   *n* pl. -SIES a large merchant ship

ARGOT   *n* pl. -S a specialized vocabulary **ARGOTIC** *adj*

ARGUABLE   *adj* capable of being argued about **ARGUABLY** *adv*

ARGUE   *v* -GUED, -GUING, -GUES to present reasons for or against

ARGUER   *n* pl. -S one that argues

ARGUFIER   *n* pl. -S one that argufies

ARGUFY   *v* -FIED, -FYING, -FIES to argue stubbornly

ARGUING   present participle of argue

ARGUMENT   *n* pl. -S a discussion involving differing points of view

ARGUS   *n* pl. -ES an East Indian pheasant

ARGYLE   *n* pl. -S a knitting pattern

ARGYLL   *n* pl. -S argyle

ARHAT   *n* pl. -S a Buddhist who has attained nirvana

ARIA   *n* pl. -S an elaborate melody for a single voice

ARID   *adj* -IDER, -IDEST extremely dry **ARIDLY** *adv*

ARIDITY   *n* pl. -TIES the state of being arid

ARIDNESS   *n* pl. -ES aridity

ARIEL   *n* pl. -S an African gazelle

ARIETTA   *n* pl. -S a short aria

ARIETTE   *n* pl. -S arietta

ARIGHT   *adv* rightly; correctly

ARIL   *n* pl. -S an outer covering of certain seeds **ARILED, ARILLATE, ARILLOID** *adj*

ARILLODE   *n* pl. -S a type of aril

ARIOSE   *adj* characterized by melody

ARIOSO   *n* pl. -SOS or -SI a musical passage resembling an aria

ARISE   *v* AROSE, ARISEN, ARISING, ARISES to get up

ARISTA   *n* pl. -TAE or -TAS a bristlelike structure or appendage **ARISTATE** *adj*

ARK   *n* pl. -S a large boat

ARLES   *n/pl* money paid to bind a bargain

ARM   *v* -ED, -ING, -S to supply with weapons

ARMADA   *n* pl. -S a fleet of warships

ARMAMENT   *n* pl. -S a military force equipped for war

ARMATURE   *v* -TURED, -TURING, -TURES to furnish with armor

ARMBAND   *n* pl. -S a band worn around an arm (an upper appendage of the human body)

ARMCHAIR *n* pl. -S a chair with armrests

ARMER *n* pl. -S one that arms

ARMET *n* pl. -S a medieval helmet

ARMFUL *n* pl. ARMFULS or ARMSFUL as much as the arm can hold

ARMHOLE *n* pl. -S an opening for the arm in a garment

ARMIES pl. of army

ARMIGER *n* pl. -S one who carries the armor of a knight

ARMIGERO *n* pl. -GEROS armiger

ARMILLA *n* pl. -LAE or -LAS a thin membrane around the stem of certain fungi

ARMING *n* pl. -S the act of one that arms

ARMLESS *adj* having no arms

ARMLET *n* pl. -S an armband

ARMLIKE *adj* resembling an arm

ARMLOAD *n* pl. -S an armful

ARMOIRE *n* pl. -S a large, ornate cabinet

ARMONICA *n* pl. -S a type of musical instrument

ARMOR *v* -ED, -ING, -S to furnish with armor (a defensive covering for the body)

ARMORER *n* pl. -S one that makes or repairs armor

ARMORIAL *n* pl. -S a treatise on heraldry

ARMORY *n* pl. -MORIES a place where weapons are stored

ARMOUR *v* -ED, -ING, -S to armor

ARMOURER *n* pl. -S armorer

ARMOURY *n* pl. -MOURIES armory

ARMPIT *n* pl. -S the hollow under the arm at the shoulder

ARMREST *n* pl. -S a support for the arm

ARMSFUL a pl. of armful

ARMURE *n* pl. -S a woven fabric

ARMY *n* pl. -MIES a large body of men trained and armed for war

ARMYWORM *n* pl. -S a destructive moth larva

ARNATTO *n* pl. -TOS annatto

ARNICA *n* pl. -S a perennial herb

ARNOTTO *n* pl. -TOS a tropical tree

AROID *n* pl. -S a flowering plant

AROINT *v* -ED, -ING, -S to drive away

AROMA *n* pl. -S a pleasant odor

AROMATIC *n* pl. -S a fragrant plant or substance

AROSE past tense of arise

AROUND *prep* on all sides of

AROUSAL *n* pl. -S the act of arousing

AROUSE *v* AROUSED, AROUSING, AROUSES to stimulate

AROUSER *n* pl. -S one that arouses

AROYNT *v* -ED, -ING, -S to aroint

ARPEGGIO *n* pl. -GIOS a technique of playing a musical chord

ARPEN *n* pl. -S arpent

ARPENT *n* pl. -S an old French unit of area

ARQUEBUS *n* pl. -ES an early portable firearm

ARRACK *n* pl. -S an Oriental liquor

ARRAIGN *v* -ED, -ING, -S to call before a court of law to answer an indictment

ARRANGE *v* -RANGED, -RANGING, -RANGES to put in definite or proper order

ARRANGER *n* pl. -S one that arranges

ARRANT *adj* outright **ARRANTLY** *adv*

ARRAS *n* pl. ARRAS a tapestry **ARRASED** *adj*

ARRAY *v* -ED, -ING, -S to place in proper or desired order

ARRAYAL *n* pl. -S the act of arraying

ARRAYER *n* pl. -S one that arrays

ARREAR *n* pl. -S an unpaid and overdue debt

ARREST *v* -ED, -ING, -S to seize and hold by legal authority

ARRESTEE *n* pl. -S one that is arrested

ARRESTER *n* pl. -S one that arrests

ARRESTOR *n* pl. -S arrester

ARRHIZAL *adj* rootless

ARRIS *n* pl. -RISES a ridge formed by the meeting of two surfaces

ARRIVAL *n* pl. -S the act of arriving

ARRIVE *v* -RIVED, -RIVING, -RIVES to reach a destination

ARRIVER *n* pl. -S one that arrives

ARROBA *n* pl. -S a Spanish unit of weight

ARROGANT *adj* overly convinced of one's own worth or importance

ARROGATE *v* -GATED, -GATING, -GATES to claim or take without right

ARROW   v -ED, -ING, -S to indicate the proper position of by means of a linear figure with a wedge-shaped end

ARROWY   adj moving swiftly

ARROYO   n pl. -ROYOS a brook or creek

ARSE   n pl. -S the buttocks — usually considered vulgar

ARSENAL   n pl. -S a collection or supply of weapons

ARSENATE   n pl. -S a chemical salt

ARSENIC   n pl. -S a metallic element

ARSENIDE   n pl. -S an arsenic compound

ARSENITE   n pl. -S a chemical salt

ARSENO   adj containing a certain bivalent chemical radical

ARSENOUS   adj pertaining to arsenic

ARSHIN   n pl. -S archine

ARSINE   n pl. -S a poisonous gas

ARSINO   adj containing a certain univalent chemical radical

ARSIS   n pl. ARSES the unaccented part of a musical measure

ARSON   n pl. -S the malicious or fraudulent burning of property **ARSONOUS** adj

ARSONIST   n pl. -S one that commits arson

ART   n pl. -S an esthetically pleasing and meaningful arrangement of elements

ARTAL   a pl. of rotl

ARTEFACT   n pl. -S artifact

ARTEL   n pl. -S a collective farm in Russia

ARTERIAL   n pl. -S a type of highway

ARTERY   n pl. -TERIES a vessel that carries blood away from the heart

ARTFUL   adj crafty **ARTFULLY** adv

ARTICLE   v -CLED, -CLING, -CLES to charge with specific offenses

ARTIER   comparative of arty

ARTIEST   superlative of arty

ARTIFACT   n pl. -S an object made by man

ARTIFICE   n pl. -S a clever stratagem

ARTILY   adv in an arty manner

ARTINESS   n pl. -ES the quality of being arty

ARTISAN   n pl. -S a trained or skilled workman

ARTIST   n pl. -S one who practices one of the fine arts

ARTISTE   n pl. -S a skilled public performer

ARTISTIC   adj characteristic of art

ARTISTRY   n pl. -RIES artistic quality or workmanship

ARTLESS   adj lacking cunning or guile

ARTWORK   n pl. -S illustrative or decorative work in printed matter

ARTY   adj ARTIER, ARTIEST showily or pretentiously artistic

ARUM   n pl. -S a flowering plant

ARUSPEX   n pl. -PICES haruspex

ARVAL   adj pertaining to plowed land

ARVO   n pl. -VOS afternoon

ARYL   n pl. -S a univalent radical

ARYTHMIA   n pl. -S an irregularity in the rhythm of the heartbeat **ARYTHMIC** adj

AS   adv to the same degree

ASARUM   n pl. -S a perennial herb

ASBESTOS   n pl. -ES a mineral **ASBESTIC** adj

ASBESTUS   n pl. -ES asbestos

ASCARID   n pl. -S a parasitic worm

ASCARIS   n pl. -RIDES ascarid

ASCEND   v -ED, -ING, -S to go or move upward

ASCENDER   n pl. -S one that ascends

ASCENT   n pl. -S the act of ascending

ASCESIS   n pl. -CESES the conduct of an ascetic

ASCETIC   n pl. -S one who practices extreme self-denial for religious reasons

ASCI   pl. of ascus

ASCIDIAN   n pl. -S a small marine animal

ASCIDIUM   n pl. -DIA a flask-shaped plant appendage

ASCITES   n pl. ASCITES accumulation of serous fluid in the abdomen **ASCITIC** adj

ASCOCARP   n pl. -S a spore-producing organ of certain fungi

ASCORBIC   adj relieving scurvy

ASCOT   n pl. -S a broad neck scarf

ASCRIBE   v -CRIBED, -CRIBING, -CRIBES to attribute to a specified cause, source, or origin

ASCUS	*n* pl. ASCI a spore sac in certain fungi
ASDIC	*n* pl. -S sonar
ASEA	*adv* at sea
ASEPSIS	*n* pl. -SEPSES the condition of being aseptic
ASEPTIC	*adj* free from germs
ASEXUAL	*adj* occurring or performed without sexual action
ASH	*v* -ED, -ING, -ES to convert into ash (the residue of a substance that has been burned)
ASHAMED	*adj* feeling shame, guilt, or disgrace
ASHCAN	*n* pl. -S a metal receptacle for garbage
ASHEN	*adj* consisting of ashes
ASHIER	comparative of ashy
ASHIEST	superlative of ashy
ASHLAR	*v* -ED, -ING, -S to build with squared stones
ASHLER	*v* -ED, -ING, -S to ashlar
ASHLESS	*adj* having no ashes
ASHMAN	*n* pl. -MEN one who collects and removes ashes
ASHORE	*adv* toward or on the shore
ASHPLANT	*n* pl. -S a walking stick
ASHRAM	*n* pl. -S a secluded dwelling of a Hindu sage
ASHTRAY	*n* pl. -TRAYS a receptacle for tobacco ashes
ASHY	*adj* ASHIER, ASHIEST covered with ashes
ASIDE	*n* pl. -S a comment by an actor intended to be heard by the audience but not the other actors
ASININE	*adj* obstinately stupid or silly
ASK	*v* -ED, -ING, -S to put a question to
ASKANCE	*adv* with a side glance
ASKANT	*adv* askance
ASKER	*n* pl. -S one that asks
ASKESIS	*n* pl. ASKESES ascesis
ASKEW	*adv* to one side
ASKING	*n* pl. -S the act of one who asks
ASLANT	*adj* slanting
ASLEEP	*adj* sleeping
ASLOPE	*adj* sloping
ASOCIAL	*adj* avoiding the company of others
ASP	*n* pl. -S a venomous snake
ASPECT	*n* pl. -S appearance of something to the eye or mind
ASPEN	*n* pl. -S any of several poplars
ASPER	*n* pl. -S a Turkish money of account
ASPERATE	*v* -ATED, ATING, -ATES to make uneven
ASPERGES	*n* pl. ASPERGES a Roman Catholic rite
ASPERITY	*n* pl. -TIES acrimony
ASPERSE	*v* -PERSED, -PERSING, -PERSES to spread false charges against
ASPERSER	*n* pl. -S one that asperses
ASPERSOR	*n* pl. -S asperser
ASPHALT	*v* -ED, -ING, -S to coat with asphalt (a substance used for paving and roofing)
ASPHERIC	*adj* varying slightly from an exactly spherical shape
ASPHODEL	*n* pl. -S a flowering plant
ASPHYXIA	*n* pl. -S unconsciousness caused by lack of oxygen
ASPHYXY	*n* pl. -PHYXIES asphyxia
ASPIC	*n* pl. -S the asp
ASPIRANT	*n* pl. -S one that aspires
ASPIRATA	*n* pl. -TAE a type of plosive
ASPIRATE	*v* -RATED, -RATING, -RATES to pronounce with an initial release of breath
ASPIRE	*v* -PIRED, -PIRING, PIRES to have an earnest desire or ambition
ASPIRER	*n* pl. -S an aspirant
ASPIRIN	*n* pl. -S a pain reliever
ASPIRING	present participle of aspire
ASPIS	*n* pl. -PISES aspic
ASPISH	*adj* resembling an asp
ASQUINT	*adv* with a sidelong glance
ASRAMA	*n* pl. -S ashram
ASS	*n* pl. -ES a hoofed mammal
ASSAGAI	*v* -GAIED, -GAIING, -GAIS to pierce with a light spear
ASSAI	*n* pl. -S a tropical tree
ASSAIL	*v* -ED, -ING, -S to attack
ASSAILER	*n* pl. -S one that assails

ASSASSIN	*n* pl. -S a murderer
ASSAULT	*v* -ED, -ING, -S to attack
ASSAY	*v* -ED, -ING, -S to attempt
ASSAYER	*n* pl. -S one that assays
ASSEGAI	*v* -GAIED, -GAIING, -GAIS to assagai
ASSEMBLE	*v* -BLED, -BLING, -BLES to come or bring together
ASSEMBLY	*n* pl. -BLIES the act of assembling
ASSENT	*v* -ED, -ING, -S to express agreement
ASSENTER	*n* pl. -S one that assents
ASSENTOR	*n* pl. -S assenter
ASSERT	*v* -ED, -ING, -S to state positively
ASSERTER	*n* pl. -S one that asserts
ASSERTOR	*n* pl. -S asserter
ASSESS	*v* -ED, -ING, -ES to estimate the value of for taxation
ASSESSOR	*n* pl. -S one that assesses
ASSET	*n* pl. -S a useful quality or thing
ASSIGN	*v* -ED, -ING, -S to set apart for a particular purpose
ASSIGNAT	*n* pl. -S one of the notes issued as currency by the French revolutionary government
ASSIGNEE	*n* pl. -S one to whom property or right is legally transferred
ASSIGNER	*n* pl. -S one that assigns
ASSIGNOR	*n* pl. -S one who legally transfers property or right
ASSIST	*v* -ED, -ING, -S to give aid or support to
ASSISTER	*n* pl. -S one that assists
ASSISTOR	*n* pl. -S assister
ASSIZE	*n* pl. -S a session of a legislative or judicial body
ASSLIKE	*adj* resembling an ass
ASSOIL	*v* -ED, -ING, -S to pardon
ASSONANT	*n* pl. -S a word or syllable that resembles another in sound
ASSORT	*v* -ED, -ING, -S to distribute into groups according to kind or class
ASSORTER	*n* pl. -S one that assorts
ASSUAGE	*v* -SUAGED, -SUAGING, -SUAGES to make less severe
ASSUME	*v* -SUMED, -SUMING, SUMES to take on
ASSUMER	*n* pl. -S one that assumes
ASSURE	*v* -SURED, -SURING, -SURES to insure
ASSURED	*n* pl. -S an insured person
ASSURER	*n* pl. -S one that assures
ASSURING	present participle of assure
ASSUROR	*n* pl. -S assurer
ASSWAGE	*v* -SWAGED, -SWAGING, -SWAGES to assuage
ASTASIA	*n* pl. -S inability to stand resulting from muscular incoordination
ASTATIC	*adj* unstable
ASTATINE	*n* pl. -S a radioactive element
ASTER	*n* pl. -S a flowering plant
ASTERIA	*n* pl. -S a gemstone cut to exhibit asterism
ASTERISK	*v* -ED, -ING, -S to mark with an asterisk (a star-shaped printing mark)
ASTERISM	*n* pl. -S a property of certain minerals of showing a starlike luminous figure
ASTERN	*adv* at or toward the rear of a ship
ASTERNAL	*adj* not connected to the sternum
ASTEROID	*n* pl. -S a type of celestial body
ASTHENIA	*n* pl. -S lack of strength
ASTHENIC	*n* pl. -S a slender, lightly muscled person
ASTHENY	*n* pl. -NIES asthenia
ASTHMA	*n* pl. -S a respiratory disease
ASTIR	*adj* moving about
ASTOMOUS	*adj* having no stomata
ASTONISH	*v* -ED, -ING, -ES to fill with sudden wonder or surprise
ASTONY	*v* -TONIED, -TONYING, -TONIES to astonish
ASTOUND	*v* -ED, -ING, -S to amaze
ASTRAGAL	*n* pl. -S a convex molding
ASTRAL	*n* pl. -S a type of oil lamp
ASTRALLY	*adv* in a stellar manner
ASTRAY	*adv* off the right course
ASTRICT	*v* -ED, -ING, -S to restrict
ASTRIDE	*adv* with one leg on each side
ASTRINGE	*v* -TRINGED, -TRINGING, -TRINGES to bind or draw together

ASTUTE	*adj* shrewd **ASTUTELY** *adv*
ASTYLAR	*adj* having no columns
ASUNDER	*adv* into pieces
ASWARM	*adj* swarming
ASWIRL	*adj* swirling
ASWOON	*adj* swooning
ASYLUM	*n* pl. -LUMS or -LA an institution for the care of the mentally ill or aged
ASYNDETA	*n/pl* omissions of certain conjunctions
AT	*prep* in the position of
ATABAL	*n* pl. -S a type of drum
ATAGHAN	*n* pl. -S yataghan
ATALAYA	*n* pl. -S a watchtower
ATAMAN	*n* pl. -S a hetman
ATAMASCO	*n* pl. -COS a flowering plant
ATARAXIA	*n* pl. -S peace of mind
ATARAXIC	*n* pl. -S a drug that relieves nervous tension
ATARAXY	*n* pl. -RAXIES ataraxia
ATAVIC	*adj* pertaining to a remote ancestor
ATAVISM	*n* pl. -S the reappearance of a genetic characteristic after several generations of absence
ATAVIST	*n* pl. -S an individual displaying atavism
ATAXIA	*n* pl. -S loss of muscular coordination
ATAXIC	*n* pl. -S one suffering from ataxia
ATAXY	*n* pl. ATAXIES ataxia
ATE	*n* pl. -S blind impulse or reckless ambition that drives one to ruin
ATECHNIC	*adj* lacking technical knowledge
ATELIC	*adj* pertaining to a type of verb form
ATELIER	*n* pl. -S a workshop or studio
ATHANASY	*n* pl. -SIES immortality
ATHEISM	*n* pl. -S the belief that there is no God
ATHEIST	*n* pl. -S a believer in atheism
ATHELING	*n* pl. -S an Anglo-Saxon prince or nobleman
ATHENEUM	*n* pl. -S a literary institution
ATHEROMA	*n* pl. -MAS or -MATA a disease of the arteries

ATHIRST	*adj* having a strong desire
ATHLETE	*n* pl. -S one skilled in feats of physical strength and agility **ATHLETIC** *adj*
ATHODYD	*n* pl. -S a type of jet engine
ATHWART	*adv* from side to side
ATILT	*adj* being in a tilted position
ATINGLE	*adj* tingling
ATLAS	*n* pl. ATLANTES or ATLASES a male figure used as a supporting column
ATLATL	*n* pl. -S a device for throwing a spear or dart
ATMA	*n* pl. -S atman
ATMAN	*n* pl. -S the individual soul in Hinduism
ATOLL	*n* pl. -S a ring-shaped coral island
ATOM	*n* pl. -S the smallest unit of an element **ATOMIC, ATOMICAL** *adj*
ATOMICS	*n/pl* the science dealing with atoms
ATOMISE	*v* -ISED, -ISING, -ISES to atomize
ATOMISM	*n* pl. -S the theory that the universe is composed of simple, indivisible, minute particles
ATOMIST	*n* pl. -S an adherent of atomism
ATOMIZE	*v* -IZED, -IZING, -IZES to reduce to a fine spray
ATOMIZER	*n* pl. -S a device for atomizing liquids
ATOMY	*n* pl. -MIES a tiny particle
ATONAL	*adj* lacking tonality **ATONALLY** *adv*
ATONE	*v* ATONED, ATONING, ATONES to make amends or reparation **ATONABLE** *adj*
ATONER	*n* pl. -S one that atones
ATONIC	*n* pl. -S an unaccented syllable or word
ATONING	present participle of atone
ATONY	*n* pl. -NIES muscular weakness
ATOP	*adj* being on or at the top
ATOPY	*n* pl. -PIES a type of allergy **ATOPIC** *adj*
ATRAZINE	*n* pl. -S an herbicide
ATREMBLE	*adj* trembling
ATRESIA	*n* pl. -S absence or closure of a natural bodily passage
ATRIA	a pl. of atrium

ATRIAL	*adj* pertaining to an atrium	**ATTORNEY**	*n* pl. -NEYS a lawyer
ATRIP	*adj* aweigh	**ATTRACT**	*v* -ED, -ING, -S to cause to approach or adhere
ATRIUM	*n* pl. ATRIA or ATRIUMS the main room of an ancient Roman house	**ATTRITE**	*adj* attrited
		ATTRITED	*adj* worn down by rubbing
ATROCITY	*n* pl. -TIES a heinous act	**ATTUNE**	*v* -TUNED, -TUNING, -TUNES to bring into harmony
ATROPHIA	*n* pl. -S a wasting away of the body or any of its parts **ATROPHIC** *adj*	**ATWAIN**	*adv* in two
		ATWEEN	*prep* between
ATROPHY	*v* -PHIED, -PHYING, -PHIES to waste away	**ATWITTER**	*adj* twittering
ATROPIN	*n* pl. -S atropine	**ATYPIC**	*adj* atypical
ATROPINE	*n* pl. -S a poisonous alkaloid	**ATYPICAL**	*adj* not typical
ATROPISM	*n* pl. -S atropine poisoning	**AUBADE**	*n* pl. -S a morning song
ATTACH	*v* -ED, -ING, -ES to connect as an associated part	**AUBERGE**	*n* pl. -S an inn
		AUBURN	*n* pl. -S a reddish brown color
ATTACHE	*n* pl. -S a diplomatic official	**AUCTION**	*v* -ED, -ING, -S to sell publicly to the highest bidder
ATTACHER	*n* pl. -S one that attaches		
ATTACK	*v* -ED, -ING, -S to set upon violently	**AUDACITY**	*n* pl. -TIES boldness
		AUDAD	*n* pl. -S aoudad
ATTACKER	*n* pl. -S one that attacks	**AUDIBLE**	*n* pl. -S a type of play in football
ATTAIN	*v* -ED, -ING, -S to gain or achieve by mental or physical effort	**AUDIBLY**	*adv* in a way so as to be heard
		AUDIENCE	*n* pl. -S a group of listeners or spectators
ATTAINER	*n* pl. -S one that attains		
ATTAINT	*v* -ED, -ING, -S to disgrace	**AUDIENT**	*n* pl. -S one that hears
ATTAR	*n* pl. -S a fragrant oil	**AUDILE**	*n* pl. -S one whose mental imagery is chiefly auditory
ATTEMPER	*v* -ED, -ING, -S to modify the temperature of	**AUDING**	*n* pl. -S the process of hearing, recognizing, and interpreting a spoken language
ATTEMPT	*v* -ED, -ING, -S to make an effort to do or accomplish		
		AUDIO	*n* pl. -DIOS sound reception or transmission
ATTEND	*v* -ED, -ING, -S to be present at		
ATTENDEE	*n* pl. -S an attender	**AUDIT**	*v* -ED, -ING, -S to examine with intent to verify
ATTENDER	*n* pl. -S one that attends		
ATTENT	*adj* heedful	**AUDITION**	*v* -ED, -ING, -S to give a trial performance
ATTEST	*v* -ED, -ING, -S to affirm to be true or genuine		
		AUDITIVE	*n* pl. -S an auditory
ATTESTER	*n* pl. -S one that attests	**AUDITOR**	*n* pl. -S one that audits
ATTESTOR	*n* pl. -S attester	**AUDITORY**	*n* pl. -RIES a group of listeners
ATTIC	*n* pl. -S a story or room directly below the roof of a house	**AUGEND**	*n* pl. -S a number to which another is to be added
ATTICISM	*n* pl. -S a concise and elegant expression		
		AUGER	*n* pl. -S a tool for boring
ATTICIST	*n* pl. -S one who uses atticisms	**AUGHT**	*n* pl. -S a zero
ATTIRE	*v* -TIRED, -TIRING, -TIRES to clothe	**AUGITE**	*n* pl. -S a mineral **AUGITIC** *adj*
		AUGMENT	*v* -ED, -ING, -S to increase
ATTITUDE	*n* pl. -S a state of mind with regard to some matter	**AUGUR**	*v* -ED, -ING, -S to foretell from omens
ATTORN	*v* -ED, -ING, -S to acknowledge a new owner as one's landlord	**AUGURAL**	*adj* pertaining to augury
		AUGURER	*n* pl. -S one that augurs

AUGURY   *n* pl. -RIES the practice of auguring

AUGUST   *adj* -GUSTER, -GUSTEST inspiring reverence or admiration **AUGUSTLY** *adv*

AUK   *n* pl. -S a diving seabird

AUKLET   *n* pl. -S a small auk

AULD   *adj* AULDER, AULDEST old

AULIC   *adj* pertaining to a royal court

AUNT   *n* pl. -S the sister of one's father or mother

AUNTHOOD   *n* pl. -S the state of being an aunt

AUNTIE   *n* pl. -S aunt

AUNTLIKE   *adj* resembling an aunt

AUNTLY   *adj* -LIER, -LIEST of or suggesting an aunt

AUNTY   *n* pl. AUNTIES aunt

AURA   *n* pl. -RAS or -RAE an invisible emanation

AURAL   *adj* pertaining to the ear **AURALLY** *adv*

AURAR   pl. of eyrir

AURATE   *adj* having ears

AURATED   *adj* aurate

AUREATE   *adj* golden

AUREI   pl. of aureus

AUREOLA   *n* pl. -LAS or -LAE a halo

AUREOLE   *v* -OLED, -OLING, -OLES to surround with a halo

AURES   pl. of auris

AUREUS   *n* pl. -REI a gold coin of ancient Rome

AURIC   *adj* pertaining to gold

AURICLE   *n* pl. -S an ear or ear-shaped part **AURICLED** *adj*

AURICULA   *n* pl. -LAS or -LAE an auricle

AURIFORM   *adj* ear-shaped

AURIS   *n* pl. AURES the ear

AURIST   *n* pl. -S a specialist in diseases of the ear

AUROCHS   *n* pl. -ES an extinct European ox

AURORA   *n* pl. -RAS or -RAE the rising light of the morning **AURORAL, AUROREAN** *adj*

AUROUS   *adj* pertaining to gold

AURUM   *n* pl. -S gold

AUSPEX   *n* pl. -PICES a soothsayer of ancient Rome

AUSPICE   *n* pl. -S a favorable omen

AUSTERE   *adj* -TERER, -TEREST grave in disposition or appearance

AUSTRAL   *adj* pertaining to the south

AUTACOID   *n* pl. -S a hormone

AUTARCHY   *n* pl. -CHIES absolute rule or power

AUTARKY   *n* pl. -KIES national economic self-sufficiency **AUTARKIC, AUTARKIK** *adj*

AUTECISM   *n* pl. -S the development of the entire life cycle of a parasitic fungus on a single host

AUTHOR   *v* -ED, -ING, -S to write

AUTISM   *n* pl. -S extreme withdrawal into fantasy **AUTISTIC** *adj*

AUTO   *v* -ED, -ING, -S to ride in an automobile

AUTOBAHN   *n* pl. -BAHNS or -BAHNEN a German superhighway

AUTOBUS   *n* pl. -BUSES or -BUSSES a bus

AUTOCADE   *n* pl. -S a procession of automobiles

AUTOCOID   *n* pl. -S autacoid

AUTOCRAT   *n* pl. -S an absolute ruler

AUTODYNE   *n* pl. -S a type of electrical circuit

AUTOGAMY   *n* pl. -MIES fertilization of a flower by its own pollen

AUTOGENY   *n* pl. -NIES the production of living organisms from inanimate matter

AUTOGIRO   *n* pl. -ROS a type of airplane

AUTOGYRO   *n* pl. -ROS autogiro

AUTOLYZE   *v* -LYZED, -LYZING, -LYZES to break down tissue by the action of self-contained enzymes

AUTOMATA   *n/pl* robots

AUTOMATE   *v* -MATED, -MATING, -MATES to convert to a system of automatic control

AUTONOMY   *n* pl. -MIES the state of being self-governing

AUTOPSIC   *adj* pertaining to an autopsy

AUTOPSY   *v* -SIED, -SYING, -SIES to examine a dead body to determine the cause of death

AUTOSOME   *n* pl. -S a type of chromosome

AUTOTOMY   *n* pl. -MIES the shedding of a damaged body part

AUTOTYPE　*n* pl. -S a type of photographic process

AUTOTYPY　*n* pl. -TYPIES autotype

AUTUMN　*n* pl. -S a season of the year **AUTUMNAL** *adj*

AUTUNITE　*n* pl. -S a mineral

AUXESIS　*n* pl. AUXESES an increase in cell size without cell division

AUXETIC　*n* pl. -S a substance that promotes auxesis

AUXIN　*n* pl. -S a substance used to regulate plant growth **AUXINIC** *adj*

AVA　*adv* at all

AVAIL　*v* -ED, -ING, -S to be of use or advantage to

AVARICE　*n* pl. -S greed

AVAST　*interj* — used as a command to stop

AVATAR　*n* pl. -S the incarnation of a Hindu deity

AVAUNT　*interj* — used as an order of dismissal

AVE　*n* pl. -S an expression of greeting or farewell

AVELLAN　*adj* having the four arms shaped like filberts — used of a heraldic cross

AVELLANE　*adj* avellan

AVENGE　*v* AVENGED, AVENGING, AVENGES to exact retribution for

AVENGER　*n* pl. -S one that avenges

AVENS　*n* pl. -ES a perennial herb

AVENTAIL　*n* pl. -S ventail

AVENUE　*n* pl. -S a wide street

AVER　*v* AVERRED, AVERRING, AVERS to declare positively

AVERAGE　*v* -AGED, -AGING, -AGES to calculate the arithmetic mean of

AVERMENT　*n* pl. -S the act of averring

AVERRED　past tense of aver

AVERRING　present participle of aver

AVERSE　*adj* opposed; reluctant **AVERSELY** *adv*

AVERSION　*n* pl. -S a feeling of repugnance **AVERSIVE** *adj*

AVERT　*v* -ED, -ING, -S to turn away

AVGAS　*n* pl. -GASES or -GASSES gasoline for airplanes

AVIAN　*n* pl. -S a bird

AVIANIZE　*v* -IZED, -IZING, -IZES to make less severe by repeated culture in a chick embryo, as a virus

AVIARIST　*n* pl. -S the keeper of an aviary

AVIARY　*n* pl. -ARIES a large enclosure for live birds

AVIATE　*v* -ATED, -ATING, -ATES to fly an aircraft

AVIATION　*n* pl. -S the act of aviating

AVIATOR　*n* pl. -S one that aviates

AVIATRIX　*n* pl. -TRICES or -TRIXES a female aviator

AVICULAR　*adj* pertaining to birds

AVID　*adj* eager

AVIDIN　*n* pl. -S a protein found in egg white

AVIDITY　*n* pl. -TIES the state of being avid

AVIDLY　*adv* in an avid manner

AVIDNESS　*n* pl. -ES avidity

AVIFAUNA　*n* pl. -NAS or -NAE the bird life of a particular region

AVIGATOR　*n* pl. -S one that navigates aircraft

AVION　*n* pl. -S an airplane

AVIONICS　*n/pl* the science of electronics applied to aviation **AVIONIC** *adj*

AVISO　*n* pl. -SOS advice

AVO　*n* pl. AVOS a monetary unit of Macao

AVOCADO　*n* pl. -DOS or -DOES the edible fruit of a tropical tree

AVOCET　*n* pl. -S a shore bird

AVODIRE　*n* pl. -S an African tree

AVOID　*v* -ED, -ING, -S to keep away from

AVOIDER　*n* pl. -S one that avoids

AVOSET　*n* pl. -S avocet

AVOUCH　*v* -ED, -ING, -ES to affirm

AVOUCHER　*n* pl. -S one that avouches

AVOW　*v* -ED, -ING, -S to declare openly **AVOWABLE** *adj* **AVOWABLY, AVOWEDLY** *adv*

AVOWAL　*n* pl. -S an open declaration

AVOWER　*n* pl. -S one that avows

AVULSE　*v* AVULSED, AVULSING, AVULSES to tear off forcibly

AVULSION　*n* pl. -S the act of avulsing

AW　*interj* — used to express protest, disgust, or disbelief

AWA	*adv* away	**AWOKE**	a past tense of awake
AWAIT	*v* -ED, -ING, -S to wait for	**AWOKEN**	a past participle of awake
AWAITER	*n* pl. -S one that awaits	**AWOL**	*n* pl. -S one who is absent without leave
AWAKE	*v* AWAKED or AWOKE, AWOKEN, AWAKING, AWAKES to wake up	**AWRY**	*adv* with a turn or twist to one side
AWAKEN	*v* -ED, -ING, -S to awake	**AX**	*v* -ED, -ING, -ES to work on with an ax (a type of cutting tool)
AWAKENER	*n* pl. -S one that awakens		
AWAKING	present participle of awake	**AXAL**	*adj* axial
AWARD	*v* -ED, -ING, -S to grant as due or merited	**AXE**	*v* AXED, AXING, AXES to ax
		AXEL	*n* pl. -S a jump in figure skating
AWARDEE	*n* pl. -S one that is awarded something	**AXEMAN**	*n* pl. -MEN axman
AWARDER	*n* pl. -S one that awards	**AXENIC**	*adj* free from germs
AWARE	*adj* having perception or knowledge	**AXES**	pl. of axis
		AXIAL	*adj* pertaining to or forming an axis **AXIALLY** *adv*
AWASH	*adj* covered with water		
AWAY	*adv* from a certain place	**AXIALITY**	*n* pl. -TIES the state of being axial
AWAYNESS	*n* pl. -ES the state of being distant	**AXIL**	*n* pl. -S the angle between the upper side of a leaf and its supporting stem
AWE	*v* AWED, AWING or AWEING, AWES to inspire with awe (reverential fear)		
		AXILE	*adj* axial
AWEARY	*adj* weary	**AXILLA**	*n* pl. -LAE or -LAS the armpit
AWEATHER	*adv* toward the windward side of a vessel	**AXILLAR**	*n* pl. -S a feather on the undersurface of a bird's wing
AWED	past tense of awe	**AXILLARY**	*n* pl. -LARIES an axillar
AWEE	*adv* awhile	**AXING**	present participle of axe
AWEIGH	*adj* hanging just clear of the bottom — used of an anchor	**AXIOLOGY**	*n* pl. -GIES the study of values and value judgments
AWELESS	*adj* lacking awe	**AXIOM**	*n* pl. -S a self-evident truth
AWESOME	*adj* inspiring awe	**AXIS**	*n* pl. AXES a straight line about which a body rotates **AXISED** *adj*
AWFUL	*adj* -FULLER, -FULLEST extremely bad or unpleasant **AWFULLY** *adv*		
		AXIS	*n* pl. AXISES an Asian deer
AWHILE	*adv* for a short time	**AXITE**	*n* pl. -S a fiber of an axon
AWHIRL	*adj* whirling	**AXLE**	*n* pl. -S a shaft upon which a wheel revolves **AXLED** *adj*
AWING	a present participle of awe		
AWKWARD	*adj* -WARDER, -WARDEST lacking skill, dexterity, or grace	**AXLETREE**	*n* pl. -S a type of axle
		AXLIKE	*adj* resembling an ax
AWL	*n* pl. -S a pointed tool for making small holes	**AXMAN**	*n* pl. -MEN one who wields an ax
AWLESS	*adj* aweless	**AXOLOTL**	*n* pl. -S a salamander of Mexico and western United States
AWLWORT	*n* pl -S an aquatic plant		
AWMOUS	*n* pl. AWMOUS alms	**AXON**	*n* pl. -S the central process of a neuron **AXONAL, AXONIC** *adj*
AWN	*n* pl. -S a bristlelike appendage of certain grasses **AWNED, AWNLESS, AWNY** *adj*		
		AXONE	*n* pl. -S axon
		AXOPLASM	*n* pl. -S the protoplasm of an axon
AWNING	*n* pl. -S a rooflike canvas cover **AWNINGED** *adj*		
		AXSEED	*n* pl. -S a European herb

AY   *n* pl. AYS aye

AYAH   *n* pl. -S a native maid or nurse in India

AYE   *n* pl. -S an affirmative vote

AYIN   *n* pl. -S a Hebrew letter

AZALEA   *n* pl. -S a flowering shrub

AZAN   *n* pl. -S a Muslim call to prayer

AZIDE   *n* pl. -S a type of chemical compound **AZIDO** *adj*

AZIMUTH   *n* pl. -S an angle of horizontal deviation

AZINE   *n* pl. -S a type of chemical compound

AZO   *adj* containing nitrogen

AZOIC   *adj* pertaining to geologic periods that precede the appearance of life

AZOLE   *n* pl. -S a type of chemical compound

AZON   *n* pl. -S a radio-controlled aerial bomb

AZONAL   *adj* pertaining to a type of a soil group

AZONIC   *adj* not restricted to any particular zone

AZOTE   *n* pl. -S nitrogen **AZOTED** *adj*

AZOTEMIA   *n* pl. -S an excess of nitrogenous substances in the blood **AZOTEMIC** *adj*

AZOTH   *n* pl. -S mercury

AZOTIC   *adj* pertaining to azote

AZOTISE   *v* -TISED, -TISING, -TISES to azotize

AZOTIZE   *v* -TIZED, -TIZING, -TIZES to treat with nitrogen

AZOTURIA   *n* pl. -S an excess of nitrogenous substances in the urine

AZURE   *n* pl. -S a blue color

AZURITE   *n* pl. -S a mineral

AZYGOS   *n* pl. -ES an azygous anatomical part

AZYGOUS   *adj* not being one of a pair

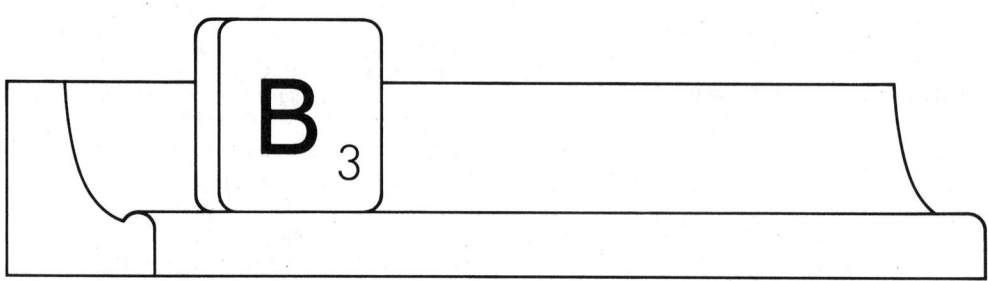

BA   *n* pl. -S the eternal soul, in Egyptian mythology

BAA   *v* -ED, -ING, -S to bleat

BAAL   *n* pl. -S or -IM a false god

BAALISM   *n* pl. -S the worship of a baal

BABA   *n* pl. -S a rum cake

BABASSU   *n* pl. -S a palm tree

BABBITT   *v* -ED, -ING, -S to line with a type of metal

BABBLE   *v* -BLED, -BLING, -BLES to talk idly or excessively

BABBLER   *n* pl. -S one that babbles

BABBLING   *n* pl. -S idle talk

BABBOOL   *n* pl. -S babul

BABE   *n* pl. -S a baby

BABEL   *n* pl. -S confusion

BABESIA   *n* pl. -S a parasitic protozoan

BABICHE   *n* pl. -S rawhide thongs

BABIED   past tense of baby

BABIES   present 3d person sing. of baby

BABIRUSA   *n* pl. -S a wild pig

BABKA   *n* pl. -S a coffee cake

BABOO   *n* pl. -BOOS a Hindu gentleman

BABOOL   *n* pl. -S babul

BABOON   *n* pl. -S a large ape

BABU   *n* pl. -S baboo

BABUL   *n* pl. -S a North African tree

BABUSHKA   *n* pl. -S a woman's scarf

BABY   *v* -BIED, -BYING, -BIES to coddle

BABYHOOD   *n* pl. -S the state of being a baby (an infant)

BABYISH   *adj* resembling a baby

BACCA   *n* pl. -CAE a berry

BACCARA   *n* pl. -S baccarat

BACCARAT   *n* pl. -S a card game

BACCATE   *adj* pulpy like a berry

BACCATED   *adj* baccate

BACCHANT   *n* pl. -S or -ES a carouser

BACCHIC   *adj* riotous

BACCHIUS   *n* pl. -CHII a type of metrical foot

BACH   *v* -ED, -ING, -ES to live as a bachelor

BACHELOR   *n* pl. -S an unmarried man

BACILLAR   *adj* rod-shaped

BACILLUS   *n* pl. -LI any of a class of rod-shaped bacteria

BACK   *v* -ED, -ING, -S to support

BACKACHE   *n* pl. -S a pain in the back

BACKBEND   *n* pl. -S an acrobatic feat

BACKBITE   *v* -BIT, -BITTEN, -BITING, -BITES to slander

BACKBONE   *n* pl. -S the spine

BACKDOOR   *adj* secretive

BACKDROP   *n* pl. -S a stage setting

BACKER   *n* pl. -S a supporter

BACKFILL   *v* -ED, -ING, -S to refill

BACKFIRE   *v* -FIRED, -FIRING, -FIRES to result in undesirable consequences

BACKHAND   *v* -ED, -ING, -S to strike with the back of the hand

BACKHOE   *n* pl. -S an excavating machine

BACKING   *n* pl. -S support

BACKLASH	*v* -ED, -ING, -ES to cause a reaction	**BADGERLY**	*adj* bothersome
BACKLESS	*adj* having no back	**BADGING**	present participle of badge
BACKLIST	*n* pl. -S a publisher's list of older book titles	**BADINAGE**	*v* -NAGED, -NAGING, -NAGES to banter
BACKLIT	*adj* illuminated from behind	**BADLAND**	*n* pl. -S a barren, hilly area
BACKLOG	*v* -LOGGED, -LOGGING, -LOGS to accumulate	**BADLY**	*adv* in a bad manner
BACKMOST	*adj* hindmost	**BADMAN**	*n* pl. -MEN an outlaw
BACKOUT	*n* pl. -S a reversal of launching procedures	**BADMOUTH**	*v* -ED, -ING, -S to criticize
		BADNESS	*n* pl. -ES the state of being bad
BACKPACK	*v* -ED, -ING, -S to hike with a pack on one's back	**BAFF**	*v* -ED, -ING, -S to strike under a golf ball
BACKREST	*n* pl. -S a back support	**BAFFIES**	pl. of baffy
BACKSAW	*n* pl. -S a type of saw	**BAFFLE**	*v* -FLED, -FLING, -FLES to confuse
BACKSEAT	*n* pl. -S a rear seat		
BACKSET	*n* pl. -S a setback	**BAFFLER**	*n* pl. -S one that baffles
BACKSIDE	*n* pl. -S the hind part	**BAFFY**	*n* pl. -FIES a wooden golf club
BACKSLAP	*v* -SLAPPED, -SLAPPING, -SLAPS to show much approval	**BAG**	*v* BAGGED, BAGGING, BAGS to put into a bag (a flexible container)
BACKSLID	past tense of backslide (to revert to sin)	**BAGASS**	*n* pl. -ES bagasse
		BAGASSE	*n* pl. -S crushed sugarcane
BACKSPIN	*n* pl. -S a backward rotation	**BAGEL**	*n* pl. -S a ring-shaped roll
BACKSTAY	*n* pl. -STAYS a support for a mast	**BAGFUL**	*n* pl. BAGFULS or BAGSFUL as much as a bag will hold
BACKSTOP	*v* -STOPPED, -STOPPING, -STOPS to bolster	**BAGGAGE**	*n* pl. -S luggage
BACKUP	*n* pl. -S a substitute	**BAGGED**	past tense of bag
BACKWARD	*adv* toward the back	**BAGGIE**	*n* pl. -S the stomach
BACKWASH	*v* -ED, -ING, -ES to spray water backward	**BAGGING**	*n* pl. -S material for making bags
BACKWOOD	*adj* uncouth	**BAGGY**	*adj* -GIER, -GIEST loose-fitting **BAGGILY** *adv*
BACKYARD	*n* pl. -S an area at the rear of a house	**BAGMAN**	*n* pl. -MEN a traveling salesman
BACON	*n* pl. -S a side of a pig cured and smoked	**BAGNIO**	*n* pl. -NIOS a brothel
BACTERIA	*n/pl* microscopic organisms	**BAGPIPE**	*n* pl. -S a wind instrument
BACTERIN	*n* pl. -S a vaccine prepared from dead bacteria	**BAGPIPER**	*n* pl. -S one that plays bagpipes
		BAGSFUL	a pl. of bagful
BACULINE	*adj* pertaining to a rod	**BAGUET**	*n* pl. -S baguette
BAD	*adj* WORSE, WORST not good in any way	**BAGUETTE**	*n* pl. -S a rectangular gem
BAD	*n* pl. -S something that is bad	**BAGWIG**	*n* pl. -S a type of wig
BADDIE	*n* pl. -S a bad person	**BAGWORM**	*n* pl. -S the larva of certain moths
BADDY	*n* pl. -DIES baddie	**BAH**	*interj* — an exclamation of disgust
BADE	past tense of bid		
BADGE	*v* BADGED, BADGING, BADGES to supply with an insignia	**BAHADUR**	*n* pl. -S a Hindu title of respect
		BAHT	*n* pl. -S a monetary unit of Thailand
BADGER	*v* -ED, -ING, -S to harass	**BAIDARKA**	*n* pl. -S bidarka

BAIL	*v* -ED, -ING, -S to transfer property temporarily **BAILABLE** *adj*
BAILEE	*n* pl. -S a person to whom property is bailed
BAILER	*n* pl. -S bailor
BAILEY	*n* pl. -LEYS an outer castle wall
BAILIE	*n* pl. -S a Scottish magistrate
BAILIFF	*n* pl. -S a court officer
BAILMENT	*n* pl. -S the act of bailing
BAILOR	*n* pl. -S a person who bails property to another
BAILOUT	*n* pl. -S the act of parachuting from an aircraft
BAILSMAN	*n* pl. -MEN one who provides security for another
BAIRN	*n* pl. -S a child **BAIRNISH** *adj*
BAIRNLY	*adj* -LIER, -LIEST childish
BAIT	*v* -ED, -ING, -S to lure
BAITER	*n* pl. -S one that baits
BAITH	*adj* both
BAIZA	*n* pl. -S a monetary unit of Oman
BAIZE	*n* pl. -S a green, woolen fabric
BAKE	*v* BAKED, BAKING, BAKES to prepare food in an oven
BAKEMEAT	*n* pl. -S a pastry
BAKER	*n* pl. -S one that bakes
BAKERY	*n* pl. -ERIES a place where baked goods are sold
BAKESHOP	*n* pl. -S a bakery
BAKING	*n* pl. -S a quantity baked
BAKLAVA	*n* pl. -S a Turkish pastry
BAKLAWA	*n* pl. -S baklava
BAKSHISH	*v* -ED, -ING, -ES to give a tip
BAL	*n* pl. -S a balmoral
BALANCE	*v* -ANCED, -ANCING, -ANCES to weigh
BALANCER	*n* pl. -S one that balances
BALAS	*n* pl. -ES a red variety of spinel
BALATA	*n* pl. -S a tropical tree
BALBOA	*n* pl. -S a monetary unit of Panama
BALCONY	*n* pl. -NIES an elevated platform
BALD	*adj* BALDER, BALDEST lacking hair
BALD	*v* -ED, -ING, -S to become bald
BALDHEAD	*n* pl. -S a bald person
BALDISH	*adj* somewhat bald
BALDLY	*adv* in a plain and blunt manner
BALDNESS	*n* pl. -ES the state of being bald
BALDPATE	*n* pl. -S a baldhead
BALDRIC	*n* pl. -S a shoulder belt
BALDRICK	*n* pl. -S baldric
BALE	*v* BALED, BALING, BALES to form into tightly compressed bundles
BALEEN	*n* pl. -S whalebone
BALEFIRE	*n* pl. -S a bonfire
BALEFUL	*adj* menacing
BALER	*n* pl. -S one that bales
BALING	present participle of bale
BALISAUR	*n* pl. -S a long-tailed badger
BALK	*v* -ED, -ING, -S to stop short and refuse to proceed
BALKER	*n* pl. -S one that balks
BALKLINE	*n* pl. -S the starting line in track events
BALKY	*adj* BALKIER, BALKIEST stubborn **BALKILY** *adv*
BALL	*v* -ED, -ING, -S to form into a ball (a spherical object)
BALLAD	*n* pl. -S a narrative poem or song **BALLADIC** *adj*
BALLADE	*n* pl. -S a type of poem
BALLADRY	*n* pl. -RIES ballad poetry
BALLAST	*v* -ED, -ING, -S to stabilize
BALLER	*n* pl. -S one that balls
BALLET	*n* pl. -S a classical dance form **BALLETIC** *adj*
BALLISTA	*n* pl. -TAE an ancient weapon
BALLON	*n* pl. -S lightness of movement
BALLONET	*n* pl. -S a small balloon
BALLONNE	*n* pl. -S a ballet jump
BALLOON	*v* -ED, -ING, -S to swell out
BALLOT	*v* -ED, -ING, -S to vote
BALLOTER	*n* pl. -S one that ballots
BALLROOM	*n* pl. -S a large room for dancing
BALLY	*adj* damned
BALLYHOO	*v* -ED, -ING, -S to promote by uproar
BALLYRAG	*v* -RAGGED, -RAGGING, -RAGS to bullyrag
BALM	*n* pl. -S a fragrant resin **BALMLIKE** *adj*

BALMORAL	*n* pl. -S a type of shoe
BALMY	*adj* BALMIER, BALMIEST mild **BALMILY** *adv*
BALNEAL	*adj* pertaining to baths
BALONEY	*n* pl. -NEYS bologna
BALSA	*n* pl. -S a tropical tree
BALSAM	*v* -ED, -ING, -S to anoint with balsam (an aromatic, resinous substance)
BALSAMIC	*adj* containing balsam
BALUSTER	*n* pl. -S a railing support
BAMBINO	*n* pl. -NOS or -NI a baby
BAMBOO	*n* pl. -BOOS a tropical grass
BAN	*v* BANNED, BANNING, BANS to prohibit
BAN	*n* pl. BANI a Rumanian coin
BANAL	*adj* ordinary **BANALLY** *adv*
BANALITY	*n* pl. -TIES something banal
BANANA	*n* pl. -S an edible fruit
BANAUSIC	*adj* practical
BANCO	*n* pl. -COS a bet in certain gambling games
BAND	*v* -ED, -ING, -S to decorate with flexible strips of material
BANDAGE	*v* -DAGED, -DAGING, -DAGES to cover a wound with a strip of cloth
BANDAGER	*n* pl. -S one that bandages
BANDANA	*n* pl. -S bandanna
BANDANNA	*n* pl. -S a large, colored handkerchief
BANDBOX	*n* pl. -ES a lightweight box
BANDEAU	*n* pl. -DEAUX or -DEAUS a headband
BANDER	*n* pl. -S one that bands
BANDEROL	*n* pl. -S a streamer
BANDIED	past tense of bandy
BANDIES	present 3d person sing. of bandy
BANDIT	*n* pl. -DITS or -DITTI a robber
BANDITRY	*n* pl. -TRIES robbery by bandits
BANDOG	*n* pl. -S a watchdog
BANDORA	*n* pl. -S bandore
BANDORE	*n* pl. -S an ancient lute
BANDSMAN	*n* pl. -MEN a member of a musical band
BANDY	*v* -DIED, -DYING, -DIES to throw to and fro
BANE	*v* BANED, BANING, BANES to kill with poison
BANEFUL	*adj* poisonous
BANG	*v* -ED, -ING, -S to hit sharply
BANGER	*n* pl. -S a sausage
BANGKOK	*n* pl. -S a straw hat
BANGLE	*n* pl. -S a bracelet
BANGTAIL	*n* pl. -S a racehorse
BANI	pl. of ban
BANIAN	*n* pl. -S a Hindu merchant
BANING	present participle of bane
BANISH	*v* -ED, -ING, -ES to expel
BANISHER	*n* pl. -S one that banishes
BANISTER	*n* pl. -S a handrail
BANJO	*n* pl. -JOS or -JOES a musical instrument
BANJOIST	*n* pl. -S one who plays the banjo
BANK	*v* -ED, -ING, -S to keep money in a bank (an institution dealing in money matters) **BANKABLE** *adj*
BANKBOOK	*n* pl. -S a depositor's book
BANKER	*n* pl. -S one who works in a bank
BANKING	*n* pl. -S the business of a bank
BANKNOTE	*n* pl. -S a promissory note
BANKROLL	*v* -ED, -ING, -S to supply the capital for
BANKRUPT	*v* -ED, -ING, -S to impoverish
BANKSIA	*n* pl. -S an Australian plant
BANKSIDE	*n* pl. -S the slope of a river bank
BANNED	past tense of ban
BANNER	*n* pl. -S a flag
BANNERET	*n* pl. -S a small banner
BANNEROL	*n* pl. -S a banderol
BANNET	*n* pl. -S a bonnet
BANNING	present participle of ban
BANNOCK	*n* pl. -S a type of cake
BANNS	*n/pl* a marriage notice
BANQUET	*v* -ED, -ING, -S to feast
BANSHEE	*n* pl. -S a female spirit
BANSHIE	*n* pl. -S banshee
BANTAM	*n* pl. -S a small fowl
BANTER	*v* -ED, -ING, -S to exchange mildly teasing remarks

BANTERER	*n* pl. -S one that banters	**BAREBACK**	*adv* without a saddle
BANTLING	*n* pl. -S a very young child	**BAREFIT**	*adj* barefoot
BANYAN	*n* pl. -S an East Indian tree	**BAREFOOT**	*adj* being without shoes
BANZAI	*n* pl. -S a Japanese battle cry	**BAREGE**	*n* pl. -S a sheer fabric
BAOBAB	*n* pl. -S a tropical tree	**BAREHEAD**	*adv* without a hat
BAPTISE	*v* -TISED, -TISING, -TISES to baptize	**BARELY**	*adv* scarcely
		BARENESS	*n* pl. -ES the state of being bare
BAPTISIA	*n* pl. -S a flowering plant	**BARER**	comparative of bare
BAPTISM	*n* pl. -S a Christian ceremony	**BARESARK**	*n* pl. -S an ancient warrior
BAPTIST	*n* pl. -S one who baptizes	**BAREST**	superlative of bare
BAPTIZE	*v* -TIZED, -TIZING, -TIZES to administer baptism to	**BARF**	*v* -ED, -ING, -S to vomit
BAPTIZER	*n* pl. -S a baptist	**BARFLY**	*n* pl. -FLIES a drinker who frequents bars
BAR	*v* BARRED, BARRING, BARS to exclude	**BARGAIN**	*v* -ED, -ING, -S to discuss terms for selling or buying
BARATHEA	*n* pl. -S a silk fabric	**BARGE**	*v* BARGED, BARGING, BARGES to move by barge (a long, large boat)
BARB	*v* -ED, -ING, -S to furnish with a barb (a sharp projection)		
BARBAL	*adj* pertaining to the beard	**BARGEE**	*n* pl. -S a bargeman
BARBARIC	*adj* uncivilized	**BARGEMAN**	*n* pl. -MEN the master or a crew member of a barge
BARBASCO	*n* pl. -COS a tropical tree	**BARGHEST**	*n* pl. -S a goblin
BARBATE	*adj* bearded	**BARGING**	present participle of barge
BARBE	*n* pl. -S a medieval cloth headdress	**BARGUEST**	*n* pl. -S barghest
BARBECUE	*v* -CUED, -CUING, -CUES to cook over live coals or an open fire	**BARHOP**	*v* -HOPPED, -HOPPING, -HOPS to visit a number of bars during an evening
BARBEL	*n* pl. -S an organ of a fish	**BARIC**	*adj* pertaining to barium
BARBELL	*n* pl. -S an exercise apparatus	**BARILLA**	*n* pl. -S a chemical compound
BARBER	*v* -ED, -ING, -S to cut hair	**BARING**	present participle of bare
BARBERRY	*n* pl. -RIES a shrub	**BARITE**	*n* pl. -S a mineral
BARBET	*n* pl. -S a tropical bird	**BARITONE**	*n* pl. -S a male singing voice
BARBETTE	*n* pl. -S a platform	**BARIUM**	*n* pl. -S a metallic element
BARBICAN	*n* pl. -S an outer fortification	**BARK**	*v* -ED, -ING, -S to cry like a dog
BARBICEL	*n* pl. -S a part of a feather	**BARKEEP**	*n* pl. -S a bartender
BARBITAL	*n* pl. -S a sedative	**BARKER**	*n* pl. -S one that barks
BARBLESS	*adj* having no barbs	**BARKLESS**	*adj* having no bark; unable to bark
BARBULE	*n* pl. -S a small barb		
BARBUT	*n* pl. -S a type of helmet	**BARKY**	*adj* BARKIER, BARKIEST covered with bark (tough outer covering of a root or stem)
BARBWIRE	*n* pl. -S barbed wire		
BARD	*v* -ED, -ING, -S to armor a horse	**BARLEDUC**	*n* pl. -S a fruit jam
BARDE	*v* BARDED, BARDING, BARDES to bard	**BARLESS**	*adj* having no restraints
		BARLEY	*n* pl. -LEYS a cereal grass
BARDIC	*adj* poetic	**BARLOW**	*n* pl. -S a jackknife
BARE	*adj* BARER, BAREST naked	**BARM**	*n* pl. -S the foam on malt liquors
BARE	*v* BARED, BARING, BARES to expose	**BARMAID**	*n* pl. -S a female bartender

BARMAN	*n* pl. -MEN a male bartender	**BARRETTE**	*n* pl. -S a hair clip
BARMIE	*adj* barmy	**BARRIER**	*n* pl. -S an obstacle
BARMY	*adj* BARMIER, BARMIEST full of barm; frothy	**BARRING**	present participle of bar and barre
BARN	*n* pl. -S a large storage building	**BARRIO**	*n* pl. -RIOS a district
BARNACLE	*n* pl. -S a shellfish	**BARROOM**	*n* pl. -S a room where liquor is sold
BARNY	*adj* BARNIER, BARNIEST resembling a barn in size, shape, or smell	**BARROW**	*n* pl. -S a type of cart
		BARSTOOL	*n* pl. -S a stool in a barroom
BARNYARD	*n* pl. -S a yard near a barn	**BARTEND**	*v* -ED, -ING, -S to tend a barroom
BAROGRAM	*n* pl. -S a barometric reading		
BARON	*n* pl. -S a lower member of nobility	**BARTER**	*v* -ED, -ING, -S to trade
		BARTERER	*n* pl. -S one that barters
BARONAGE	*n* pl. -S the rank of a baron	**BARTISAN**	*n* pl. -S bartizan
BARONESS	*n* pl. -ES the wife of a baron	**BARTIZAN**	*n* pl. -S a small turret
BARONET	*n* pl. -S the holder of a rank below that of a baron	**BARWARE**	*n* pl. -S barroom equipment
BARONG	*n* pl. -S a broad knife	**BARYE**	*n* pl. -S a unit of pressure
BARONIAL	*adj* pertaining to a baron	**BARYON**	*n* pl. -S an atomic particle **BARYONIC** *adj*
BARONNE	*n* pl. -S a baroness		
BARONY	*n* pl. -ONIES the domain of a baron	**BARYTA**	*n* pl. -S a compound of barium **BARYTIC** *adj*
BAROQUE	*n* pl. -S an ornate object	**BARYTE**	*n* pl. -S barite
BAROUCHE	*n* pl. -S a type of carriage	**BARYTONE**	*n* pl. -S baritone
BARQUE	*n* pl. -S a sailing vessel	**BASAL**	*adj* pertaining to the foundation **BASALLY** *adv*
BARRABLE	*adj* capable of being barred		
BARRACK	*v* -ED, -ING, -S to shout boisterously	**BASALT**	*n* pl. -S a volcanic rock **BASALTIC** *adj*
BARRAGE	*v* -RAGED, -RAGING, -RAGES to subject to a massive attack	**BASALTES**	*n* pl. BASALTES unglazed stoneware
		BASCULE	*n* pl. -S a type of seesaw
BARRANCA	*n* pl. -S a steep ravine	**BASE**	*adj* BASER, BASEST morally low
BARRANCO	*n* pl. -COS barranca	**BASE**	*v* BASED, BASING, BASES to found
BARRATER	*n* pl. -S barrator		
BARRATOR	*n* pl. -S one who commits barratry	**BASEBALL**	*n* pl. -S a type of ball
		BASEBORN	*adj* of low birth
BARRATRY	*n* pl. -TRIES fraud committed by a master or crew of a ship	**BASED**	past tense of base
		BASING	present participle of base
BARRE	*v* BARRED, BARRING, BARRES to play a type of guitar chord	**BASELESS**	*adj* having no foundation
		BASELINE	*n* pl. -S a line at either end of a court in certain sports
BARRED	past tense of bar		
BARREL	*v* -RELED, -RELING, -RELS or -RELLED, -RELLING, -RELS to move fast	**BASELY**	*adv* in a base manner
		BASEMAN	*n* pl. -MEN a certain player in baseball
BARREN	*adj* -RENER, -RENEST unproductive **BARRENLY** *adv*	**BASEMENT**	*n* pl. -S the part of a building below ground level
BARREN	*n* pl. -S a tract of barren land	**BASENESS**	*n* pl. -ES the state of being base
BARRET	*n* pl. -S a flat cap		
BARRETOR	*n* pl. -S barrator	**BASENJI**	*n* pl. -S a barkless dog
BARRETRY	*n* pl. -TRIES barratry		

BASER comparative of base

BASES pl. of basis

BASEST superlative of base

BASH v -ED, -ING, -ES to smash

BASHAW n pl. -S a pasha

BASHER n pl. -S one that bashes

BASHFUL adj shy; timid

BASHLYK n pl. -S a cloth hood

BASIC n pl. -S a fundamental

BASICITY n pl. -TIES the state of being alkaline

BASIDIUM n pl. -IA a structure on a fungus **BASIDIAL** adj

BASIFIER n pl. -S one that basifies

BASIFY v -FIED, -FYING, -FIES to alkalize

BASIL n pl. -S an aromatic herb

BASILAR adj basal

BASILARY adj basilar

BASILIC adj pertaining to a basilica

BASILICA n pl. -CAS or -CAE an ancient Roman building

BASILISK n pl. -S a fabled serpent

BASIN n pl. -S an enclosed body of water **BASINAL, BASINED** adj

BASINET n pl. -S a medieval helmet

BASION n pl. -S a part of the skull

BASIS n pl. BASES the foundation of something

BASK v -ED, -ING, -S to lie in a pleasant warmth

BASKET n pl. -S a wooden container

BASKETRY n pl. -RIES basket weaving

BASOPHIL n pl. -S a type of cell

BASQUE n pl. -S a bodice

BASS n pl. -ES an edible fish

BASSET v -SETED, -SETING, -SETS or -SETTED, -SETTING, -SETS to outcrop

BASSI a pl. of basso

BASSINET n pl. -S a basket used as a baby's crib

BASSIST n pl. -S a person who plays a double bass

BASSLY adv in a low-pitched manner

BASSNESS n pl. -ES the state of being low in pitch

BASSO n pl. -SOS or -SI a low-pitched singer

BASSOON n pl. -S a low-pitched instrument

BASSWOOD n pl. -S a linden tree

BASSY adj low in pitch

BAST n pl. -S a woody fiber

BASTARD n pl. -S an illegitimate child

BASTARDY n pl. -TARDIES the state of being a bastard

BASTE v BASTED, BASTING, BASTES to sew loosely together

BASTER n pl. -S one that bastes

BASTILE n pl. -S bastille

BASTILLE n pl. -S a prison

BASTING n pl. -S the thread used by a baster

BASTION n pl. -S a fortified place

BAT v BATTED, BATTING, BATS to hit a baseball

BATBOY n pl. -BOYS a boy who minds baseball equipment

BATCH v -ED, -ING, -ES to bring together

BATCHER n pl. -S one that batches

BATE v BATED, BATING, BATES to reduce the force of

BATEAU n pl. -TEAUX a flat-bottomed boat

BATFISH n pl. -ES a batlike fish

BATFOWL v -ED, -ING, -S to catch birds at night

BATH n pl. -S a washing

BATHE v BATHED, BATHING, BATHES to wash

BATHER n pl. -S one that bathes

BATHETIC adj trite

BATHING present participle of bathe

BATHLESS adj not having had a bath

BATHOS n pl. -ES triteness

BATHROBE n pl. -S a housecoat

BATHROOM n pl. -S a room in which to bathe

BATHTUB n pl. -S a tub in which to bathe

BATHYAL adj pertaining to deep water

BATIK n pl. -S a dyeing process

BATING present participle of bate

BATISTE n pl. -S a sheer fabric

BATLIKE adj resembling a bat (a flying mammal)

BATMAN	*n* pl. -MEN an orderly
BATON	*n* pl. -S a short rod
BATSMAN	*n* pl. -MEN one who bats
BATT	*n* pl. -S a sheet of cotton
BATTALIA	*n* pl. -S a military unit
BATTEAU	*n* pl. -TEAUX bateau
BATTED	past tense of bat
BATTEN	*v* -ED, -ING, -S to fasten with strips of wood
BATTENER	*n* pl. -S one that battens
BATTER	*v* -ED, -ING, -S to beat repeatedly
BATTERIE	*n* pl. -S a ballet movement
BATTERY	*n* pl. -TERIES a device for generating an electric current
BATTIER	comparative of batty
BATTIEST	superlative of batty
BATTIK	*n* pl. -S batik
BATTING	*n* pl. -S a batt
BATTLE	*v* -TLED, -TLING, -TLES to fight
BATTLER	*n* pl. -S one that battles
BATTU	*adj* pertaining to a ballet movement
BATTUE	*n* pl. -S a type of hunt
BATTY	*adj* -TIER, -TIEST crazy
BATWING	*adj* shaped like a bat's wing
BAUBEE	*n* pl. -S bawbee
BAUBLE	*n* pl. -S a cheap trinket
BAUD	*n* pl. -S a unit of data transmission speed
BAUDEKIN	*n* pl. -S a brocaded fabric
BAUDRONS	*n* pl. -ES a cat
BAULK	*v* -ED, -ING, -S to balk
BAULKY	*adj* BAULKIER, BAULKIEST balky
BAUSOND	*adj* having white marks
BAUXITE	*n* pl. -S an ore of aluminum **BAUXITIC** *adj*
BAWBEE	*n* pl. -S a Scottish coin
BAWCOCK	*n* pl. -S a fine fellow
BAWD	*n* pl. -S a madman
BAWDIER	comparative of bawdy
BAWDIES	pl. of bawdy
BAWDIEST	superlative of bawdy
BAWDILY	*adv* in a bawdy manner
BAWDRIC	*n* pl. -S baldric
BAWDRY	*n* pl. -RIES obscenity
BAWDY	*adj* BAWDIER, BAWDIEST obscene
BAWDY	*n* pl. BAWDIES obscene language
BAWL	*v* -ED, -ING, -S to cry loudly
BAWLER	*n* pl. -S one that bawls
BAWSUNT	*adj* bausond
BAWTIE	*n* pl. -S a dog
BAWTY	*n* pl. -TIES bawtie
BAY	*v* -ED, -ING, -S to howl
BAYADEER	*n* pl. -S bayadere
BAYADERE	*n* pl. -S a dancing girl
BAYAMO	*n* pl. -MOS a strong wind
BAYARD	*n* pl. -S a horse
BAYBERRY	*n* pl. -RIES a berry tree
BAYONET	*v* -NETED, -NETING, -NETS or -NETTED, -NETTING, -NETS to stab with a dagger-like weapon
BAYOU	*n* pl. -S a marshy body of water
BAYWOOD	*n* pl. -S a coarse mahogany
BAZAAR	*n* pl. -S a marketplace
BAZAR	*n* pl. -S bazaar
BAZOOKA	*n* pl. -S a small rocket launcher
BDELLIUM	*n* pl. -S a gum resin
BE	*v* present sing. 1st person AM, 2d ARE or ART, 3d IS, past sing. 1st and 3d persons WAS, 2d WERE or WAST or WERT, past participle BEEN, present participle BEING to have actuality
BEACH	*v* -ED, -ING, -ES to drive ashore
BEACHBOY	*n* pl. -BOYS a male beach attendant
BEACHY	*adj* BEACHIER, BEACHIEST sandy or pebbly
BEACON	*v* -ED, -ING, -S to warn or guide
BEAD	*v* -ED, -ING, -S to adorn with beads (round pieces of glass)
BEADIER	comparative of beady
BEADIEST	superlative of beady
BEADILY	*adv* in a beady manner
BEADING	*n* pl. -S beaded material
BEADLE	*n* pl. -S a parish official
BEADLIKE	*adj* beady
BEADMAN	*n* pl. -MEN beadsman
BEADROLL	*n* pl. -S a list of names

BEADSMAN *n* pl. -MEN one who prays for another

BEADWORK *n* pl. -S beading

BEADY *adj* BEADIER, BEADIEST resembling beads

BEAGLE *n* pl. -S a small hound

BEAK *n* pl. -S a bird's bill **BEAKED, BEAKLESS, BEAKLIKE** *adj*

BEAKER *n* pl. -S a large cup

BEAKY *adj* BEAKIER, BEAKIEST resembling a beak

BEAM *v* -ED, -ING, -S to emit in beams (rays of light)

BEAMIER comparative of beamy

BEAMIEST superlative of beamy

BEAMILY *adv* in a beamy manner

BEAMISH *adj* cheerful

BEAMLESS *adj* having no beam

BEAMLIKE *adj* resembling a beam

BEAMY *adj* BEAMIER, BEAMIEST beaming

BEAN *v* -ED, -ING, -S to hit on the head

BEANBAG *n* pl. -S a small cloth bag

BEANBALL *n* pl. -S a baseball thrown at the head

BEANERY *n* pl. -ERIES a cheap restaurant

BEANIE *n* pl. -S a small cap

BEANLIKE *adj* resembling a bean

BEANO *n* pl. BEANOS a form of bingo

BEANPOLE *n* pl. -S a thin pole

BEAR *v* BORE, BORNE or BORN, BEARING, BEARS to endure **BEARABLE** *adj* **BEARABLY** *adv*

BEARCAT *n* pl. -S a small mammal

BEARD *v* -ED, -ING, -S to oppose boldly

BEARER *n* pl. -S one that bears

BEARING *n* pl. -S demeanor

BEARISH *adj* resembling a bear (a large mammal)

BEARLIKE *adj* bearish

BEARSKIN *n* pl. -S the skin of a bear

BEAST *n* pl. -S an animal

BEASTIE *n* pl. -S a tiny animal

BEASTLY *adj* -LIER, -LIEST resembling a beast

BEAT *v* BEAT, BEATEN, BEATING, BEATS to strike repeatedly **BEATABLE** *adj*

BEATER *n* pl. -S one that beats

BEATIFIC *adj* blissful

BEATIFY *v* -FIED, -FYING, -FIES to make happy

BEATING *n* pl. -S a defeat

BEATLESS *adj* having no rhythm

BEATNIK *n* pl. -S a nonconformist

BEAU *n* pl. BEAUX or BEAUS a boyfriend **BEAUISH** *adj*

BEAUT *n* pl. -S something beautiful

BEAUTIFY *v* -FIED, -FYING, -FIES to make beautiful

BEAUTY *n* pl. -TIES one that is lovely

BEAUX a pl. of beau

BEAVER *v* -ED, -ING, -S to work hard

BEBEERU *n* pl. -S a tropical tree

BEBLOOD *v* -ED, ING, -S to cover with blood

BEBOP *n* pl. -S a type of jazz

BEBOPPER *n* pl. -S one that likes bebop

BECALM *v* -ED, -ING, -S to make calm

BECAME past tense of become

BECAP *v* -CAPPED, -CAPPING, -CAPS to put a cap on

BECARPET *v* -ED, -ING, -S to cover with a carpet

BECAUSE *conj* for the reason that

BECHALK *v* -ED, -ING, -S to cover with chalk

BECHAMEL *n* pl. -S a white sauce

BECHANCE *v* -CHANCED, -CHANCING, -CHANCES to befall

BECHARM *v* -ED, -ING, -S to hold under a spell

BECK *v* -ED, -ING, -S to beckon

BECKET *n* pl. -S a securing rope

BECKON *v* -ED, -ING, -S to signal by sign or gesture

BECKONER *n* pl. -S one that beckons

BECLAMOR *v* -ED, -ING, -S to clamor loudly

BECLASP *v* -ED, -ING, -S to embrace

BECLOAK *v* -ED, -ING, -S to place a cloak on

BECLOG *v* -CLOGGED, -CLOGGING, -CLOGS to clog thoroughly

BECLOTHE	v -CLOTHED, -CLOTHING, -CLOTHES to clothe
BECLOUD	v -ED, -ING, -S to make cloudy
BECLOWN	v -ED, -ING, -S to cause to appear ridiculous
BECOME	v -CAME, -COMING, -COMES to come to be
BECOMING	n pl. -S a process of change
BECOWARD	v -ED, -ING, -S to accuse of cowardice
BECRAWL	v -ED, -ING, -S to crawl over
BECRIME	v -CRIMED, -CRIMING, -CRIMES to make guilty of a crime
BECROWD	v -ED, -ING, -S to crowd closely
BECRUST	v -ED, -ING, -S to cover with a crust
BECUDGEL	v -GELLED, -GELLING, -GELS or -GELED, -GELING, -GELS to cudgel thoroughly
BECURSE	v -CURSED or -CURST, -CURSING, -CURSES to curse severely
BED	v BEDDED, BEDDING, BEDS to provide with a bed (a piece of furniture used for sleeping)
BEDABBLE	v -BLED, -BLING, -BLES to soil
BEDAMN	v -ED, -ING, -S to swear at
BEDARKEN	v -ED, -ING, -S to darken
BEDAUB	v -ED, -ING, -S to besmear
BEDAZZLE	v -ZLED, -ZLING, -ZLES to confuse
BEDBUG	n pl. -S a bloodsucking insect
BEDCHAIR	n pl. -S a chair near a bed
BEDCOVER	n pl. -S a cover for a bed
BEDDED	past tense of bed
BEDDER	n pl. -S one that makes up beds
BEDDING	n pl. -S material for making up a bed
BEDEAFEN	v -ED, -ING, -S to deafen
BEDECK	v -ED, -ING, -S to clothe with finery
BEDEL	n pl. -S an English university officer
BEDELL	n pl. -S bedel
BEDEMAN	n pl. -MEN beadsman
BEDESMAN	n pl. -MEN beadsmen
BEDEVIL	v -ILED, -ILING, -ILS or -ILLED, -ILLING, -ILS to harass
BEDEW	v -ED, -ING, -S to wet with dew
BEDFAST	adj confined to bed

BEDFRAME	n pl. -S the frame of a bed
BEDGOWN	n pl. -S a dressing gown
BEDIAPER	v -ED, -ING, -S to ornament with a kind of design
BEDIGHT	v -ED, -ING, -S to bedeck
BEDIM	v -DIMMED, -DIMMING, -DIMS to make dim
BEDIMPLE	v -PLED, -PLING, -PLIES to dimple
BEDIRTY	v -DIRTIED, -DIRTYING, -DIRTIES to make dirty
BEDIZEN	v -ED, -ING, -S to dress gaudily
BEDLAM	n pl. -S confusion
BEDLAMP	n pl. -S a lamp near a bed
BEDLESS	adj having no bed
BEDLIKE	adj resembling a bed
BEDMAKER	n pl. -S one that makes beds
BEDMATE	n pl. -S a bed companion
BEDOTTED	adj covered with dots
BEDOUIN	n pl. -S a nomadic Arab
BEDPAN	n pl. -S a toilet pan
BEDPLATE	n pl. -S a frame support
BEDPOST	n pl. -S a post of a bed
BEDQUILT	n pl. -S a quilt for a bed
BEDRAIL	n pl. -S a board at the side of a bed
BEDRAPE	v -DRAPED, -DRAPING, -DRAPES to drape
BEDRENCH	v -ED, -ING, -ES to drench thoroughly
BEDRID	adj bedfast
BEDRIVEL	v -ELLED, -ELLING, -ELS or -ELED, -ELING, -ELS to cover with saliva
BEDROCK	n pl. -S the rock under soil
BEDROLL	n pl. -S a portable roll of bedding
BEDROOM	n pl. -S a room for sleeping
BEDRUG	v -DRUGGED, -DRUGGING, -DRUGS to make sleepy
BEDSIDE	n pl. -S the side of a bed
BEDSONIA	n pl. -S a virus
BEDSORE	n pl. -S a type of sore
BEDSTAND	n pl. -S a table next to a bed
BEDSTEAD	n pl. -S a support for a bed
BEDSTRAW	n pl. -S a woody herb
BEDTICK	n pl. -S the cloth case of a mattress

BEDTIME	*n* pl. -S a time for going to bed
BEDUIN	*n* pl. -S bedouin
BEDUMB	*v* -ED, -ING, -S to render speechless
BEDUNCE	*v* -DUNCED, -DUNCING, -DUNCES to make a dunce of
BEDWARD	*adv* toward bed
BEDWARDS	*adv* bedward
BEDWARF	*v* -ED, -ING, -S to cause to appear small by comparison
BEE	*n* pl. -S a winged insect
BEEBEE	*n* pl. -S a pellet
BEEBREAD	*n* pl. -S a pollen mixture
BEECH	*n* pl. -ES a type of tree **BEECHEN** *adj*
BEECHNUT	*n* pl. -S the nut of a beech
BEECHY	*adj* BEECHIER, BEECHIEST abounding in beeches
BEEF	*n* pl. BEEFS or BEEVES a steer or cow fattened for food
BEEF	*v* -ED, -ING, -S to add bulk to
BEEFCAKE	*n* pl. -S pictures of male physiques
BEEFIER	comparative of beefy
BEEFIEST	superlative of beefy
BEEFILY	*adv* in a beefy manner
BEEFLESS	*adj* being without beef
BEEFWOOD	*n* pl. -S a hardwood tree
BEEFY	*adj* BEEFIER, BEEFIEST brawny
BEEHIVE	*n* pl. -S a hive for bees
BEELIKE	*adj* resembling a bee
BEELINE	*n* pl. -S a direct route
BEEN	past participle of be
BEEP	*v* -ED, -ING, -S to honk a horn
BEEPER	*n* pl. -S a signaling device
BEER	*n* pl. -S an alcoholic beverage
BEERY	*adj* BEERIER, BEERIEST affected by beer
BEESWAX	*n* pl. -ES a type of wax
BEESWING	*n* pl. -S a crust that forms on old wines
BEET	*n* pl. -S a garden plant
BEETLE	*v* -TLED, -TLING, -TLES to jut out
BEETROOT	*n* pl. -S the root of the beet
BEEVES	a pl. of beef
BEFALL	*v* -FELL, -FALLEN, -FALLING, -FALLS to happen to
BEFINGER	*v* -ED, -ING, -S to touch all over
BEFIT	*v* -FITTED, -FITTING, -FITS to be suitable to
BEFLAG	*v* -FLAGGED, -FLAGGING, -FLAGS to deck with flags
BEFLEA	*v* -ED, -ING, -S to infest with fleas
BEFLECK	*v* -ED, -ING, -S to fleck
BEFLOWER	*v* -ED, -ING, -S to cover with flowers
BEFOG	*v* -FOGGED, -FOGGING, -FOGS to envelop in fog
BEFOOL	*v* -ED, -ING, -S to deceive
BEFORE	*adv* previously
BEFOUL	*v* -ED, -ING, -S to foul
BEFOULER	*n* pl. -S one that befouls
BEFRET	*v* -FRETTED, -FRETTING, -FRETS to gnaw
BEFRIEND	*v* -ED, -ING, -S to act as a friend to
BEFRINGE	*v* -FRINGED, -FRINGING, -FRINGES to border with a fringe
BEFUDDLE	*v* -DLED, -DLING, -DLES to confuse
BEG	*v* BEGGED, BEGGING, BEGS to plead
BEGALL	*v* -ED, -ING, -S to make sore by rubbing
BEGAN	past tense of begin
BEGAZE	*v* -GAZED, -GAZING, -GAZES to gaze at
BEGET	*v* -GOT or -GAT, -GOTTEN, -GETTING, -GETS to cause to exist
BEGETTER	*n* pl. -S one that begets
BEGGAR	*v* -ED, -ING, -S to impoverish
BEGGARLY	*adj* very poor
BEGGARY	*n* pl. -GARIES extreme poverty
BEGGED	past tense of beg
BEGGING	present participle of beg
BEGIN	*v* -GAN, -GUN, -GINNING, -GINS to start
BEGINNER	*n* pl. -S one that begins
BEGIRD	*v* -GIRT or -GIRDED, -GIRDING, -GIRDS to surround
BEGIRDLE	*v* -DLED -DLING, -DLES to surround
BEGLAD	*v* -GLADDED, -GLADDING, -GLADS to gladden
BEGLOOM	*v* -ED, -ING, -S to make gloomy

BEGONE	*interj* — used as an order of dismissal	**BEING**	*n* pl. -S somthing that exists
BEGONIA	*n* pl. -S a tropical herb	**BEJEWEL**	*v* -ELED, -ELING, -ELS or -ELLED, -ELLING, -ELS to adorn with jewels
BEGORAH	*interj* begorra		
BEGORRA	*interj* — used as a mild oath	**BEJUMBLE**	*v* -BLED, -BLING, -BLES to jumble
BEGORRAH	*interj* begorra	**BEKISS**	*v* -ED, -ING, -ES to cover with kisses
BEGOT	a past tense of beget		
BEGOTTEN	past participle of beget	**BEKNIGHT**	*v* -ED, -ING, -S to raise to knighthood
BEGRIM	*v* -GRIMMED, -GRIMMING, -GRIMS to begrime	**BEKNOT**	*v* -KNOTTED, -KNOTTING, -KNOTS to tie in knots
BEGRIME	*v* -GRIMED, -GRIMING, -GRIMES to dirty	**BEL**	*n* pl. -S a unit of power
BEGROAN	*v* -ED, -ING, -S to groan at	**BELABOR**	*v* -ED, -ING, -S to discuss for an absurd amount of time
BEGRUDGE	*v* -GRUDGED, -GRUDGING, -GRUDGES to concede reluctantly	**BELABOUR**	*v* -ED, -ING, -S to belabor
		BELACED	*adj* adorned with lace
BEGUILE	*v* -GUILED, -GUILING, -GUILES to deceive	**BELADY**	*v* -DIED, -DYING, -DIES to apply the title of lady to
BEGUILER	*n* pl. -S one that beguiles	**BELATED**	*adj* late or too late
BEGUINE	*n* pl. -S a lively dance	**BELAUD**	*v* -ED, -ING, -S to praise
BEGULF	*v* -ED, -ING, -S to engulf	**BELAY**	*v* -ED, -ING, -S to fasten a rope
BEGUM	*n* pl. -S a Muslim lady of high rank	**BELCH**	*v* -ED, -ING, -ES to expel gas through the mouth
BEGUN	past participle of begin	**BELCHER**	*n* pl. -S one that belches
BEHALF	*n* pl. -HALVES interest, support, or benefit	**BELDAM**	*n* pl. -S an old woman
		BELDAME	*n* pl. -S beldam
BEHAVE	*v* -HAVED, -HAVING, -HAVES to act properly	**BELEAP**	*v* -LEAPT or -LEAPED, -LEAPING, -LEAPS to leap upon
BEHAVER	*n* pl. -S one that behaves	**BELFRY**	*n* pl. -FRIES a bell tower **BELFRIED** *adj*
BEHAVIOR	*n* pl. -S demeanor		
BEHEAD	*v* -ED, -ING, -S to cut off the head of	**BELGA**	*n* pl. -S a former Belgian monetary unit
BEHELD	past tense of behold	**BELIE**	*v* -LIED, -LYING, -LIES to misrepresent
BEHEMOTH	*n* pl. -S a large beast		
BEHEST	*n* pl. -S a command	**BELIEF**	*n* pl. -S acceptance of the truth or actuality of something
BEHIND	*n* pl. -S the buttocks		
BEHOLD	*n* -HELD, -HOLDING, -HOLDS to view	**BELIER**	*n* pl. -S one that belies
		BELIEVE	*v* -LIEVED, -LIEVING, -LIEVES to accept as true or real
BEHOLDEN	*adj* indebted		
BEHOLDER	*n* pl. -S one that beholds	**BELIEVER**	*n* pl. -S one that believes
BEHOOF	*n* pl. -HOOVES use, advantage, or benefit	**BELIKE**	*adv* perhaps
		BELIQUOR	*v* -ED, -ING, -S to soak with liquor
BEHOOVE	*v* -HOOVED, -HOOVING, -HOOVES to be proper for	**BELITTLE**	*v* -TLED, -TLING, -TLES to disparage
BEHOVE	*v* -HOVED, -HOVING, -HOVES to behoove	**BELIVE**	*adv* in due time
BEHOWL	*v* -ED, -ING, -S to howl at	**BELL**	*v* -ED, -ING, -S to provide with a bell (a ringing device)
BEIGE	*n* pl. -S a tan color		
BEIGY	*adj* of the color beige	**BELLBIRD**	*n* pl. -S a tropical bird

BELLBOY   *n* pl. -BOYS a hotel's errand boy

BELLE   *n* pl. -S an attractive woman

BELLEEK   *n* pl. -S a very thin translucent porcelain

BELLHOP   *n* pl. -S a bellboy

BELLIED   past tense of belly

BELLIES   present 3d person sing. of belly

BELLMAN   *n* pl. -MEN a town crier

BELLOW   *v* -ED, -ING, -S to shout in a deep voice

BELLOWER   *n* pl. -S one that bellows

BELLPULL   *n* pl. -S a cord pulled to ring a bell

BELLWORT   *n* pl. -S a flowering plant

BELLY   *v* -LIED, -LYING, -LIES to swell out

BELLYFUL   *n* pl. -S an excessive amount

BELONG   *v* -ED, -ING, -S to be a member of

BELOVED   *n* pl. -S one who is loved

BELOW   *n* pl. -S something that is beneath

BELT   *v* -ED, -ING, -S to fasten with a belt (a strap or band worn around the waist)

BELTLESS   *adj* having no belt

BELTING   *n* pl. -S material for belts

BELTLINE   *n* pl. -S the waistline

BELTWAY   *n* pl. -WAYS a highway around an urban area

BELUGA   *n* pl. -S a white sturgeon

BELYING   present participle of belie

BEMA   *n* pl. -MATA or -MAS a platform in a synagogue

BEMADAM   *v* -ED, -ING, -S to call by the title of madam

BEMADDEN   *v* -ED, -ING, -S to madden

BEMEAN   *v* -ED, -ING, -S to debase

BEMINGLE   *v* -GLED, -GLING, -GLES to mix together

BEMIRE   *v* -MIRED, -MIRING, -MIRES to soil with mud

BEMIST   *v* -ED, -ING, -S to envelop in a mist

BEMIX   *v* -MIXED or -MIXT, -MIXING, -MIXES to mix thoroughly

BEMOAN   *v* -ED, -ING, -S to lament

BEMOCK   *v* -ED, -ING, -S to mock

BEMUDDLE   *v* -DLED, -DLING, -DLES to confuse completely

BEMURMUR   *v* -ED, -ING, -S to murmur at

BEMUSE   *v* -MUSED, -MUSING, -MUSES to confuse

BEMUZZLE   *v* -ZLED, -ZLING, -ZLES to muzzle

BEN   *n* pl. -S an inner room

BENAME   *v* -NAMED, -NEMPT or -NEMPTED, -NAMING, -NAMES to name

BENCH   *v* -ED, -ING, -ES to take a player out of a game

BENCHER   *n* pl. -S a magistrate

BEND   *v* BENT or BENDED, BENDING, BENDS to curve **BENDABLE** *adj*

BENDAY   *v* -ED, -ING, -S to reproduce using a certain process

BENDEE   *n* pl. -S bendy

BENDER   *n* pl. -S one that bends

BENDWAYS   *adv* bendwise

BENDWISE   *adv* diagonally

BENDY   *n* pl. -DYS okra

BENE   *n* pl. -S benne

BENEATH   *prep* under

BENEDICK   *n* pl. -S benedict

BENEDICT   *n* pl. -S a newly married man

BENEFIC   *adj* kindly

BENEFICE   *v* -FICED, -FICING, -FICES to endow with land

BENEFIT   *v* -FITED, -FITING, -FITS or -FITTED, -FITTING, -FITS to be helpful or useful to

BENEMPT   a past participle of bename

BENEMPTED   a past participle of bename

BENIGN   *adj* kind **BENIGNLY** *adv*

BENISON   *n* pl. -S a blessing

BENJAMIN   *n* pl. -S benzoin

BENNE   *n* pl. -S the sesame plant

BENNET   *n* pl. -S a perennial herb

BENNI   *n* pl. -S benne

BENNY   *n* pl. -NIES an amphetamine tablet

BENT   *n* pl. -S an inclination

BENTHAL   *adj* benthic

BENTHIC   *adj* pertaining to oceanic depths

BENTHOS   *n* pl. -ES benthic sea life

BENTWOOD *n* pl. -S wood bent for use in furniture

BENUMB *v* -ED, -ING, -S to make numb

BENZAL *adj* pertaining to a certain chemical group

BENZENE *n* pl. -S a volatile liquid

BENZIDIN *n* pl. -S a hydrocarbon

BENZIN *n* pl. -S benzine

BENZINE *n* pl. -S a volatile liquid

BENZOATE *n* pl. -S a chemical salt

BENZOIN *n* pl. -S a gum resin **BENZOIC** *adj*

BENZOL *n* pl. -S a benzene

BENZOLE *n* pl. -S benzol

BENZOYL *n* pl. -S a univalent chemical radical

BENZYL *n* pl. -S a univalent chemical radical **BENZYLIC** *adj*

BEPAINT *v* -ED, -ING, -S to tinge

BEPIMPLE *v* -PLED, -PLING, -PLES to cover with pimples

BEQUEATH *v* -ED, -ING, -S to grant by testament

BEQUEST *n* pl. -S a legacy

BERASCAL *v* -ED, -ING, -S to accuse of being a rascal

BERAKE *v* -RAKED, -RAKING, -RAKES to rake all over

BERATE *v* -RATED, -RATING, -RATES to scold severely

BERBERIN *n* pl. -S a medicinal alkaloid

BERCEUSE *n* pl. -S a lullaby

BEREAVE *v* -REAVED or -REFT, -REAVING, -REAVES to deprive

BEREAVER *n* pl. -S one that bereaves

BERET *n* pl. -S a soft, flat cap

BERETTA *n* pl. -S biretta

BERG *n* pl. -S an iceberg

BERGAMOT *n* pl. -S a citrus tree

BERHYME *v* -RHYMED, -RHYMING, -RHYMES to compose in rhyme

BERIBERI *n* pl. -S a thiamine deficiency disease

BERIME *v* -RIMED, -RIMING, -RIMES to berhyme

BERINGED *adj* adorned with rings

BERLIN *n* pl. -S a type of carriage

BERLINE *n* pl. -S a limousine

BERM *n* pl. -S a ledge

BERME *n* pl. -S berm

BERNICLE *n* pl. -S a wild goose

BEROBED *adj* wearing a robe

BEROUGED *adj* obviously or thickly rouged

BERRETTA *n* pl. -S biretta

BERRY *v* -RIED, -RYING, -RIES to produce berries (fleshy fruits)

BERSEEM *n* pl. -S a clover

BERSERK *n* pl. -S a fierce warrior

BERTH *v* -ED, -ING, -S to provide with a mooring

BERTHA *n* pl. -S a wide collar

BERYL *n* pl. -S a green mineral **BERYLINE** *adj*

BESCORCH *v* -ED, -ING, -ES to scorch

BESCOUR *v* -ED, -ING, -S to scour thoroughly

BESCREEN *v* -ED, -ING, -S to screen

BESEECH *v* -SOUGHT or -SEECHED, -SEECHING, -SEECHES to implore

BESEEM *v* -ED, -ING, -S to be suitable

BESET *v* -SET, -SETTING, -SETS to assail

BESETTER *n* pl. -S one that besets

BESHADOW *v* -ED, -ING, -S to cast a shadow on

BESHAME *v* -SHAMED, -SHAMING, -SHAMES to put to shame

BESHIVER *v* -ED, -ING, -S to break into small pieces

BESHOUT *v* -ED, -ING, -S to shout at

BESHREW *v* -ED, -ING, -S to curse

BESHROUD *v* -ED, -ING, -S to cover

BESIDE *prep* next to

BESIDES *adv* in addition

BESIEGE *v* -SIEGED, -SIEGING, -SIEGES to surround

BESIEGER *n* pl. -S one that besieges

BESLAVED *adj* filled with slaves

BESLIME *v* -SLIMED, -SLIMING, -SLIMES to cover with slime

BESMEAR *v* -ED, -ING, -S to smear over

BESMILE *v* -SMILED, SMILING, -SMILES to smile on

BESMIRCH *v* -ED, -ING, -ES to dirty

BESMOKE *v* -SMOKED, -SMOKING, -SMOKES to soil with smoke

BESMOOTH *v* -ED, -ING, -S to smooth

BESMUDGE	v -SMUDGED, -SMUDGING, -SMUDGES to smudge	**BETEL**	n pl. -S a climbing plant
BESMUT	v -SMUTTED, -SMUTTING, -SMUTS to blacken with smut	**BETELNUT**	n pl. -S a seed chewed as a stimulant
BESNOW	v -ED, -ING, -S to cover with snow	**BETH**	n pl. -S a Hebrew letter
		BETHANK	v -ED, -ING, -S to thank
BESOM	n pl. -S a broom	**BETHEL**	n pl. -S a holy place
BESOOTHE	v -SOOTHED, -SOOTHING -SOOTHES to soothe	**BETHINK**	v -THOUGHT, -THINKING, -THINKS to consider
BESOT	v -SOTTED, -SOTTING, -SOTS to stupefy	**BETHORN**	v -ED, -ING, -S to fill with thorns
BESOUGHT	a past tense of beseech	**BETHUMP**	v -ED, -ING, -S to thump soundly
BESPEAK	v -SPOKE or -SPAKE, -SPOKEN, -SPEAKING, -SPEAKS to claim in advance	**BETIDE**	v -TIDED, -TIDING, -TIDES to befall
		BETIME	adv betimes
BESPOUSE	v -SPOUSED, -SPOUSING, -SPOUSES to marry	**BETIMES**	adv soon
BESPREAD	v -SPREAD, -SPREADING, -SPREADS to spread over	**BETISE**	n pl. -S stupidity
		BETOKEN	v -ED, -ING, -S to indicate
BESPRENT	adj sprinkled over	**BETON**	n pl. -S a type of concrete
BEST	v -ED, -ING, -S to outdo	**BETONY**	n pl. -NIES a European herb
BESTEAD	v -ED, -ING, -S to help	**BETOOK**	past tense of betake
BESTIAL	adj pertaining to beasts	**BETRAY**	v -ED, -ING, -S to aid an enemy of
BESTIARY	n pl. -ARIES a collection of animal fables	**BETRAYAL**	n pl. -S the act of betraying
BESTIR	v -STIRRED, -STIRRING, -STIRS to rouse	**BETRAYER**	n pl. -S one that betrays
BESTOW	v -ED, -ING, -S to present as a gift	**BETROTH**	v -ED, -ING, -S to engage to marry
BESTOWAL	n pl. -S a gift	**BETTA**	n pl. -S a freshwater fish
BESTREW	v -STREWED, -STREWN, -STREWING, -STREWS to scatter	**BETTED**	a past tense of bet
		BETTER	v -ED, -ING, -S to improve
		BETTING	present participle of bet
BESTRIDE	v -STRODE or -STRID, -STRIDDEN, -STRIDING, -STRIDES to straddle	**BETTOR**	n pl. -S one that bets
		BETWEEN	prep in the space that separates
BESTROW	v -STROWED, -STROWN, -STROWING, -STROWS to bestrew	**BETWIXT**	prep between
		BEUNCLED	adj having many uncles
		BEVATRON	n pl. -S a proton accelerator
BESTUD	v -STUDDED, -STUDDING, -STUDS to dot	**BEVEL**	v -ELED, -ELING, -ELS or -ELLED, -ELLING, -ELS to cut at an angle
BESWARM	v -ED, -ING, -S to swarm all over	**BEVELER**	n pl. -S one that bevels
BET	v BET or BETTED, BETTING, BETS to wager	**BEVELLER**	n pl. -S beveler
		BEVELLING	a present participle of bevel
BETA	n pl. -S a Greek letter	**BEVERAGE**	n pl. -S a liquid for drinking
BETAINE	n pl. -S an alkaloid	**BEVIES**	pl. of bevy
BETAKE	v -TOOK, -TAKEN, -TAKING, -TAKES to cause to go	**BEVOMIT**	v -ED, -ING, -S to vomit all over
		BEVOR	n pl. -S a piece of armor for the lower face
BETATRON	n pl. -S an electron accelerator		
BETATTER	v -ED, -ING, -S to tatter	**BEVY**	n pl. BEVIES a group
BETAXED	adj burdened with taxes		

BEWAIL	v -ED, -ING, -S to lament		**BIAS**	v -ASED, -ASING, -ASES or -ASSED, -ASSING -ASSES to prejudice **BIASEDLY** adv
BEWAILER	n pl. -S one that bewails			
BEWARE	v -WARED, -WARING, -WARES to be careful		**BIASNESS**	n pl. -ES the state of being slanted
BEWEARY	v -WEARIED, -WEARYING, -WEARIES to make weary		**BIATHLON**	n pl. -S an athletic contest
			BIAXAL	adj biaxial
BEWEEP	v -WEPT, -WEEPING, -WEEPS to lament		**BIAXIAL**	adj having two axes
BEWIG	v -WIGGED, -WIGGING, -WIGS to adorn with a wig		**BIB**	v BIBBED, BIBBING, BIBS to tipple
BEWILDER	v -ED, -ING, -S to confuse		**BIBASIC**	adj dibasic
BEWINGED	adj having wings		**BIBB**	n pl. -S a mast support
BEWITCH	v -ED, -ING, -ES to affect by witchcraft or magic		**BIBBED**	past tense of bib
			BIBBER	n pl. -S a tippler
BEWORM	v -ED, -ING, -S to infest with worms		**BIBBERY**	n pl. -BERIES the act of bibbing
			BIBBING	present participle of bib
BEWORRY	v -RIED, -RYING, -RIES to worry		**BIBCOCK**	n pl. -S a type of faucet
BEWRAP	v -WRAPPED or -WRAPT, -WRAPPING, -WRAPS to wrap completely		**BIBELOT**	n pl. -S a trinket
			BIBLE	n pl. -S an authoritative publication **BIBLICAL** adj
BEWRAY	v -ED, -ING, -S to divulge			
BEWRAYER	n pl. -S one that bewrays		**BIBLESS**	adj having no bib (a cloth covering)
BEY	n pl. BEYS a Turkish ruler		**BIBLIKE**	adj resembling a bib
BEYLIC	n pl. -S the domain of a bey		**BIBULOUS**	adj given to drinking
BEYLIK	n pl. -S beylic		**BICARB**	n pl. -S sodium bicarbonate
BEYOND	n pl. -S something that lies farther ahead		**BICE**	n pl. -S a blue or green pigment
BEZANT	n pl. -S a coin of ancient Rome		**BICEPS**	n pl. -ES an arm muscle
BEZEL	n pl. -S a slanted surface		**BICHROME**	adj two-colored
BEZIL	n pl. -S bezel		**BICKER**	v -ED, -ING, -S to argue
BEZIQUE	n pl. -S a card game		**BICKERER**	n pl. -S one that bickers
BEZOAR	n pl. -S a gastric mass		**BICOLOR**	n pl. -S something having two colors
BEZZANT	n pl. -S bezant			
BHAKTA	n pl. -S one who practices bhakti		**BICOLOUR**	n pl. -S bicolor
			BICONVEX	adj convex on both sides
BHAKTI	n pl. -S a selfless devotion to a deity in Hinduism		**BICORN**	adj having two horns
			BICORNE	n pl. -S a type of hat
BHANG	n pl. -S the hemp plant		**BICRON**	n pl. -S one billionth of a meter
BHEESTIE	n pl. -S bheesty		**BICUSPID**	n pl. -S a tooth
BHEESTY	n pl. -TIES a water carrier		**BICYCLE**	v -CLED, -CLING, -CLES to ride a bicycle (a two-wheeled vehicle)
BHISTIE	n pl. -S bheesty			
BHOOT	n pl. -S bhut		**BICYCLER**	n pl. -S one that bicycles
BHUT	n pl. -S a small whirlwind		**BICYCLIC**	adj having two cycles
BI	n pl. -S a bisexual		**BICYCLING**	present participle of bicycle
BIACETYL	n pl. -S a chemical flavor enhancer		**BID**	v BADE, BIDDEN, BIDDING, BIDS to make a bid (an offer of a price)
BIALY	n pl. -ALYS an onion roll			
BIANNUAL	adj occurring twice a year		**BIDARKA**	n pl. -S an Eskimo canoe

BIDARKEE	*n* pl. -S bidarka	**BIGGER**	comparative of big
BIDDABLE	*adj* obedient **BIDDABLY** *adv*	**BIGGEST**	superlative of big
BIDDEN	past participle of bid	**BIGGETY**	*adj* biggity
BIDDER	*n* pl. -S one that bids	**BIGGIE**	*n* pl. -S one that is big
BIDDING	*n* pl. -S a command	**BIGGIN**	*n* pl. -S a house
BIDDY	*n* pl. -DIES a hen	**BIGGING**	*n* pl. -S biggin
BIDE	*v* BIDED or BODE, BIDING, BIDES to wait	**BIGGISH**	*adj* somewhat big
		BIGGITY	*adj* conceited
BIDENTAL	*adj* having two teeth	**BIGHEAD**	*n* pl. -S a disease of animals
BIDER	*n* pl. -S one that bides	**BIGHORN**	*n* pl. -S a wild sheep
BIDET	*n* pl. -S a low basin used for washing	**BIGHT**	*v* -ED, -ING, -S to fasten with a loop of rope
BIDING	present participle of bide	**BIGLY**	*adv* in a big manner
BIELD	*v* -ED, -ING, -S to shelter	**BIGMOUTH**	*n* pl. -S a talkative person
BIENNIAL	*n* pl. -S an event that occurs every two years	**BIGNESS**	*n* pl. -ES the state of being big
BIENNIUM	*n* pl. -NIA or -NIUMS a period of two years	**BIGNONIA**	*n* pl. -S a climbing plant
		BIGOT	*n* pl. -S a prejudiced person
BIER	*n* pl. -S a coffin stand	**BIGOTED**	*adj* intolerant
BIFACIAL	*adj* having two faces	**BIGOTRY**	*n* pl. -RIES prejudice
BIFF	*v* -ED, -ING, -S to hit	**BIGWIG**	*n* pl. -S an important person
BIFFIN	*n* pl. -S a cooking apple	**BIHOURLY**	*adj* occurring every two hours
BIFFY	*n* pl. -FIES a toilet	**BIJOU**	*n* pl. -JOUX or -JOUS a jewel
BIFID	*adj* divided into two parts **BIFIDLY** *adv*	**BIJUGATE**	*adj* two-paired
		BIJUGOUS	*adj* bijugate
BIFIDITY	*n* pl. -TIES the state of being bifid	**BIKE**	*v* BIKED, BIKING, BIKES to bicycle
BIFILAR	*adj* having two threads	**BIKER**	*n* pl. -S one that bikes
BIFLEX	*adj* bent in two places	**BIKEWAY**	*n* pl. -WAYS a route for bikes
BIFOCAL	*n* pl. -S a type of lens	**BIKING**	present participle of bike
BIFOLD	*adj* twofold	**BIKINI**	*n* pl. -S a type of bathing suit **BIKINIED** *adj*
BIFORATE	*adj* having two perforations		
BIFORKED	*adj* divided into two branches	**BILABIAL**	*n* pl. -S a sound articulated with both lips
BIFORM	*adj* having two forms		
BIFORMED	*adj* biform	**BILANDER**	*n* pl. -S a small ship
BIG	*adj* BIGGER, BIGGEST of considerable size	**BILBERRY**	*n* pl. -RIES an edible berry
BIGAMIES	pl. of bigamy	**BILBO**	*n* pl. -BOS or -BOES a finely tempered sword
BIGAMIST	*n* pl. -S one who commits bigamy	**BILBOA**	*n* pl. -S bilbo
		BILE	*n* pl. -S a fluid secreted by the liver
BIGAMOUS	*adj* guilty of bigamy		
BIGAMY	*n* pl. -MIES the crime of being married to two people simultaneously	**BILGE**	*v* BILGED, BILGING, BILGES to spring a leak
		BILGY	*adj* BILGIER, BILGIEST smelling like seepage
BIGAROON	*n* pl. -S a type of cherry		
BIGEMINY	*n* pl. -NIES the state of having a double pulse	**BILIARY**	*adj* pertaining to bile
		BILINEAR	*adj* pertaining to two lines
BIGEYE	*n* pl. -S a marine fish	**BILIOUS**	*adj* pertaining to bile

BILK	*v* -ED, -ING, -S to cheat	**BINATE**	*adj* growing in pairs **BINATELY** *adv*
BILKER	*n* pl. -S one that bilks		
BILL	*v* -ED, -ING, -S to present a statement of costs to **BILLABLE** *adj*	**BINAURAL**	*adj* hearing with both ears
		BIND	*v* BOUND, BINDING, BINDS to tie or secure **BINDABLE** *adj*
BILLBUG	*n* pl. -S a weevil	**BINDER**	*n* pl. -S one that binds
BILLER	*n* pl. -S one that bills	**BINDERY**	*n* pl. -ERIES a place where books are bound
BILLET	*v* -ED, -ING, -S to lodge soldiers		
BILLETER	*n* pl. -S one that billets	**BINDING**	*n* pl. -S the cover and fastenings of a book
BILLFISH	*n* pl. -ES a fish with long, slender jaws	**BINDLE**	*n* pl. -S a bundle
BILLFOLD	*n* pl. -S a wallet	**BINDWEED**	*n* pl. -S a twining plant
BILLHEAD	*n* pl. -S a letterhead	**BINE**	*n* pl. -S a twining plant stem
BILLHOOK	*n* pl. -S a cutting tool	**BINGE**	*n* pl. -S a drunken carousal
BILLIARD	*n* pl. -S a carom shot in billiards	**BINGO**	*n* pl. -GOS a game of chance
BILLIE	*n* pl. -S a comrade	**BINIT**	*n* pl. -S a unit of computer information
BILLIES	pl. of billy	**BINNACLE**	*n* pl. -S a compass stand
BILLING	*n* pl. -S the relative position in which a performer is listed	**BINNED**	past tense of bin
BILLION	*n* pl. -S a number	**BINNING**	present participle of bin
BILLON	*n* pl. -S an alloy of silver and copper	**BINOCLE**	*n* pl. -S a binocular
		BINOMIAL	*n* pl. -S an algebraic expression
BILLOW	*v* -ED, -ING, -S to swell	**BINT**	*n* pl. -S a woman
BILLOWY	*adj* -LOWIER, -LOWIEST swelling; surging	**BIO**	*n* pl. BIOS a biography
BILLY	*n* pl. -LIES a short club	**BIOASSAY**	*v* -ED, -ING, -S to find the strength of a substance
BILLYCAN	*n* pl. -S a pot for heating water	**BIOCIDE**	*n* pl. -S a substance destructive to living organisms **BIOCIDAL** *adj*
BILOBATE	*adj* having two lobes		
BILOBED	*adj* bilobate	**BIOCLEAN**	*adj* free of harmful organisms
BILSTED	*n* pl. -S a hardwood tree	**BIOCYCLE**	*n* pl. -S a life-supporting region
BILTONG	*n* pl. -S dried and cured meat	**BIOGEN**	*n* pl. -S a hypothetical protein molecule
BIMA	*n* pl. -S bema		
BIMAH	*n* pl. -S bema	**BIOGENIC**	*adj* produced by living organisms
BIMANOUS	*adj* two-handed	**BIOGENY**	*n* pl. -NIES the development of life from preexisting life
BIMANUAL	*adj* done with two hands		
BIMENSAL	*adj* occurring every two months	**BIOHERM**	*n* pl. -S a mass of marine fossils
BIMESTER	*n* pl. -S a two-month period		
BIMETAL	*n* pl. -S something composed of two metals	**BIOLOGIC**	*n* pl. -S a drug obtained from an organic source
BIMETHYL	*n* pl. -S ethane	**BIOLOGY**	*n* pl. -GIES the science of life
BIMODAL	*adj* having two statistical modes	**BIOLYSIS**	*n* pl. -YSES death **BIOLYTIC** *adj*
BIN	*v* BINNED, BINNING, BINS to store in a large receptacle	**BIOMASS**	*n* pl. -ES an amount of living matter
BINAL	*adj* twofold	**BIOME**	*n* pl. -S an ecological community
BINARY	*n* pl. -RIES a combination of two things	**BIOMETRY**	*n* pl. -TRIES the statistical study of biological data

BIONICS *n/pl* a science joining biology and electronics **BIONIC** *adj*

BIONOMY *n* pl. -MIES ecology **BIONOMIC** *adj*

BIONT *n* pl. -S a living organism **BIONTIC** *adj*

BIOPLASM *n* pl. -S living matter

BIOPSY *n* pl. -SIES the examination of tissue **BIOPSIC, BIOPTIC** *adj*

BIOSCOPE *n* pl. -S an early movie projector

BIOSCOPY *n* pl. -PIES a type of medical examination

BIOTA *n* pl. -S the flora and fauna of a region

BIOTIC *adj* pertaining to life

BIOTICAL *adj* biotic

BIOTICS *n/pl* a life science

BIOTIN *n* pl. -S a B vitamin

BIOTITE *n* pl. -S a form of mica **BIOTITIC** *adj*

BIOTOPE *n* pl. -S a stable habitat

BIOTRON *n* pl. -S a climate control chamber

BIOTYPE *n* pl. -S a group of genetically similar organisms **BIOTYPIC** *adj*

BIOVULAR *adj* derived from two ova

BIPACK *n* pl. -S a pair of films

BIPAROUS *adj* producing offspring in pairs

BIPARTED *adj* having two parts

BIPARTY *adj* of two parties

BIPED *n* pl. -S a two-footed animal **BIPEDAL** *adj*

BIPHENYL *n* pl. -S a hydrocarbon

BIPLANE *n* pl. -S a type of airplane

BIPOD *n* pl. -S a two-legged support

BIPOLAR *adj* having two poles

BIRACIAL *adj* including members of two races

BIRADIAL *adj* having dual symmetry

BIRAMOSE *adj* biramous

BIRAMOUS *adj* divided into two branches

BIRCH *v* -ED, -ING, -ES to whip

BIRCHEN *adj* made of birch wood

BIRD *v* -ED, -ING, -S to hunt birds (winged, warm-blooded vertebrates)

BIRDBATH *n* pl. -S a bath for birds

BIRDCAGE *n* pl. -S a cage for birds

BIRDCALL *n* pl. -S the call of a bird

BIRDER *n* pl. -S a bird hunter

BIRDFARM *n* pl. -S an aircraft carrier

BIRDIE *v* BIRDIED, BIRDIEING, BIRDIES to shoot in one stroke under par in golf

BIRDLIKE *adj* resembling a bird

BIRDLIME *v* -LIMED, -LIMING, -LIMES to trap small birds

BIRDMAN *n* pl. -MEN one who keeps birds

BIRDSEED *n* pl. -S a mixture of seeds used for feeding birds

BIRDSEYE *n* pl. -S a flowering plant

BIREME *n* pl. -S an ancient galley

BIRETTA *n* pl. -S a cap worn by clergymen

BIRK *n* pl. -S a birch tree

BIRKIE *n* pl. -S a lively person

BIRL *v* -ED, -ING, -S to rotate a floating log

BIRLE *v* BIRLED, BIRLING, BIRLES to carouse

BIRLER *n* pl. -S one that birls

BIRLING *n* pl. -S a lumberjack's game

BIRR *v* -ED, -ING, -S to make a whirring noise

BIRRETTA *n* pl. -S biretta

BIRSE *n* pl. -S a bristle

BIRTH *v* -ED, -ING, -S to originate

BIRTHDAY *n* pl. -DAYS an anniversary of a birth

BIS *adv* twice

BISCUIT *n* pl. -S a small cake of shortened bread

BISE *n* pl. -S a cold wind

BISECT *v* -ED, -ING, -S to cut into two parts

BISECTOR *n* pl. -S something that bisects

BISEXUAL *n* pl. -S one who is attracted to both sexes

BISHOP *v* -ED, -ING, -S to appoint as a bishop (the head of a diocese)

BISK *n* pl. -S bisque

BISMUTH *n* pl. -S a metallic element

BISNAGA *n* pl. -S a type of cactus

BISON *n* pl. -S an ox-like animal

BISQUE *n* pl. -S a thick soup

BISTATE *adj* pertaining to two states

BISTER	n pl. -S a brown pigment **BISTERED** adj
BISTORT	n pl. -S a perennial herb
BISTOURY	n pl. -RIES a surgical knife
BISTRE	n pl. -S bister **BISTRED** adj
BISTRO	n pl. -TROS a small tavern **BISTROIC** adj
BIT	v BITTED, BITTING, BITS to restrain
BITABLE	adj capable of being bitten
BITCH	v -ED, -ING, -ES to complain
BITCHERY	n pl. -ERIES bitchy behavior
BITCHY	adj BITCHIER, BITCHIEST malicious **BITCHILY** adv
BITE	v BIT, BITTEN, BITING, BITES to seize with the teeth **BITEABLE** adj
BITER	n pl. -S one that bites
BITEWING	n pl. -S a dental X-ray film
BITING	present participle of bite
BITINGLY	adv sarcastically
BITSTOCK	n pl. -S a brace on a drill
BITSY	adj tiny
BITT	v -ED, -ING, -S to secure a cable
BITTE	interj please
BITTED	past tense of bit
BITTEN	a past participle of bite
BITTER	adj -TERER, -TEREST having a disagreeable taste **BITTERLY** adv
BITTER	v -ED, -ING, -S to make bitter
BITTERN	n pl. -S a wading bird
BITTIER	comparative of bitty
BITTIEST	superlative of bitty
BITTING	n pl. -S an indentation in a key
BITTOCK	n pl. -S a small amount
BITTY	adj -TIER, -TIEST fragmented
BITUMEN	n pl. -S an asphalt
BIVALENT	n pl. -S a pair of chromosomes
BIVALVE	n pl. -S a bivalved mollusk
BIVALVED	adj having a two-valved shell
BIVINYL	n pl. -S a flammable gas
BIVOUAC	v -OUACKED, -OUACKING, -OUACKS or -OUACS to make a camp
BIWEEKLY	n pl. -LIES a publication issued every two weeks
BIYEARLY	adj occurring every two years
BIZARRE	n pl. -S a strangely striped flower
BIZE	n pl. -S bise
BIZNAGA	n pl. -S bisnaga
BIZONE	n pl. -S two combined zones **BIZONAL** adj
BLAB	v BLABBED, BLABBING, BLABS to talk idly
BLABBER	v -ED, -ING, -S to blab
BLABBY	adj talkative
BLACK	adj BLACKER, BLACKEST being of the darkest color
BLACK	v -ED, -ING, -S to make black
BLACKBOY	n pl. -BOYS an Australian plant
BLACKCAP	n pl. -S a small European bird
BLACKEN	v -ED, -ING, -S to make black
BLACKFIN	n pl. -S a food fish
BLACKFLY	n pl. -FLIES a biting fly
BLACKGUM	n pl. -S a tupelo
BLACKING	n pl. -S black shoe polish
BLACKISH	adj somewhat black
BLACKLEG	n pl. -S a cattle disease
BLACKLY	adv in a black manner
BLACKOUT	n pl. -S a light failure
BLACKTOP	v -TOPPED, -TOPPING, -TOPS to pave with asphalt
BLADDER	n pl. -S a saclike receptacle **BLADDERY** adj
BLADE	n pl. -S a cutting edge **BLADED** adj
BLAE	adj bluish-black
BLAH	n pl. -S nonsense
BLAIN	n pl. -S a blister
BLAMABLE	adj being at fault **BLAMABLY** adv
BLAME	v BLAMED, BLAMING, BLAMES to find fault with
BLAMEFUL	adj blamable
BLAMER	n pl. -S one that blames
BLAMING	present participle of blame
BLANCH	v -ED, -ING, -ES to whiten
BLANCHER	n pl. -S a whitener
BLAND	adj BLANDER, BLANDEST soothing **BLANDLY** adv
BLANDISH	v -ED, -ING, -ES to coax by flattery

BLANK *adj* BLANKER, BLANKEST empty

BLANK *v* -ED, -ING, -S to delete

BLANKET *v* -ED, -ING, -S to cover uniformly

BLANKLY *adv* in a blank manner

BLARE *v* BLARED, BLARING, BLARES to sound loudly

BLARNEY *v* -NEYED, -NEYING, -NEYS to beguile with flattery

BLASE *adj* indifferent

BLAST *v* -ED, -ING, -S to use an explosive

BLASTEMA *n* pl. -MAS or -MATA a region of embryonic cells

BLASTER *n* pl. -S one that blasts

BLASTIE *n* pl. -S a dwarf

BLASTIER comparative of blasty

BLASTIEST superlative of blasty

BLASTING *n* pl. -S the act of one that blasts

BLASTOFF *n* pl. -S the launching of a rocket

BLASTOMA *n* pl. -MAS or -MATA a type of tumor

BLASTULA *n* pl. -LAS or -LAE an early embryo

BLASTY *adj* BLASTIER, BLASTIEST gusty

BLAT *v* BLATTED, BLATTING, BLATS to bleat

BLATANCY *n* pl. -CIES something blatant

BLATANT *adj* obvious

BLATE *adj* timid

BLATHER *v* -ED, -ING, -S to talk foolishly

BLATTED past tense of blat

BLATTER *v* -ED, -ING, -S to chatter

BLATTING present participle of blat

BLAUBOK *n* pl. -S an extinct antelope

BLAW *v* BLAWED, BLAWN, BLAWING, BLAWS to blow

BLAZE *v* BLAZED, BLAZING, BLAZES to burn brightly

BLAZER *n* pl. -S a lightweight jacket

BLAZON *v* -ED, -ING, -S to proclaim

BLAZONER *n* pl. -S one that blazons

BLAZONRY *n* pl. -RIES a great display

BLEACH *v* -ED, -ING, -ES to whiten

BLEACHER *n* pl. -S one that bleaches

BLEAK *adj* BLEAKER, BLEAKEST dreary

BLEAK *n* pl. -S a freshwater fish

BLEAKISH *adj* somewhat bleak

BLEAKLY *adv* in a bleak manner

BLEAR *v* -ED, -ING, -S to dim

BLEARY *adj* BLEARIER, BLEARIEST dimmed **BLEARILY** *adv*

BLEAT *v* -ED, -ING, -S to utter the cry of a sheep

BLEATER *n* pl. -S one that bleats

BLEB *n* pl. -S a blister **BLEBBY** *adj*

BLEED *v* BLED, BLEEDING, BLEEDS to lose blood

BLEEDER *n* pl. -S one that bleeds

BLEEDING *n* pl. -S the act of losing blood

BLELLUM *n* pl. -S a babbler

BLEMISH *v* -ED, -ING, -ES to mar

BLENCH *v* -ED, -ING, -ES to flinch

BLENCHER *n* pl. -S one that blenches

BLEND *v* BLENDED or BLENT, BLENDING, BLENDS to mix smoothly and inseparably together

BLENDE *n* pl. -S a shiny mineral

BLENDER *n* pl. -S one that blends

BLENNY *n* pl. -NIES a marine fish

BLENT a past tense of blend

BLESBOK *n* pl. -S a large antelope

BLESBUCK *n* pl. -S blesbok

BLESS *v* BLESSED or BLEST, BLESSING, BLESSES to sanctify

BLESSED *adj* -EDER, -EDEST holy

BLESSER *n* pl. -S one that blesses

BLESSING *n* pl. -S a prayer

BLEST a past tense of bless

BLET *n* pl. -S a decay of fruit

BLETHER *v* -ED, -ING, -S to blather

BLEW past tense of blow

BLIGHT *v* -ED, -ING, -S to cause decay

BLIGHTER *n* pl. -S one that blights

BLIGHTY *n* pl. BLIGHTIES a wound causing one to be sent home to England

BLIMEY *interj* — used as an expression of surprise

BLIMP *n* pl. -S a nonrigid aircraft **BLIMPISH** *adj*

BLIMY	*interj* blimey
BLIN	*n* pl. BLINI or BLINIS a blintze
BLIND	*adj* BLINDER, BLINDEST sightless
BLIND	*v* -ED, -ING, -S to make sightless
BLINDAGE	*n* pl. -S a protective screen
BLINDER	*n* pl. -S an obstruction to sight
BLINDLY	*adv* in a blind manner
BLINI	a pl. of blin
BLINIS	a pl. of blin
BLINK	*v* -ED, -ING, -S to open and shut the eyes
BLINKARD	*n* pl. -S one who habitually blinks
BLINKER	*v* -ED, -ING, -S to put blinders on
BLINTZ	*n* pl. -ES blintze
BLINTZE	*n* pl. -S a thin pancake
BLIP	*v* BLIPPED, BLIPPING, BLIPS to remove sound from a videotape
BLISS	*n* pl. -ES happiness **BLISSFUL** *adj*
BLISTER	*v* -ED, -ING, -S to cause blisters (skin swellings)
BLISTERY	*adj* having blisters
BLITE	*n* pl. -S an annual herb
BLITHE	*adj* BLITHER, BLITHEST merry **BLITHELY** *adv*
BLITHER	*v* -ED, -ING, -S to blather
BLITZ	*v* -ED, -ING, -ES to subject to a sudden attack
BLIZZARD	*n* pl. -S a heavy snowstorm
BLOAT	*v* -ED, -ING, -S to swell
BLOATER	*n* pl. -S a smoked herring
BLOB	*v* BLOBBED, BLOBBING, BLOBS to splotch
BLOC	*n* pl. -S a coalition
BLOCK	*v* -ED, -ING, -S to obstruct
BLOCKADE	*v* -ADED, -ADING, -ADES to block
BLOCKAGE	*n* pl. -S the act of blocking
BLOCKER	*n* pl. -S one that blocks
BLOCKISH	*adj* blocky
BLOCKY	*adj* BLOCKIER, BLOCKIEST short and stout
BLOKE	*n* pl. -S a fellow
BLOND	*adj* BLONDER, BLONDEST light-colored
BLOND	*n* pl. -S a blond person
BLONDE	*n* pl. -S blond
BLONDISH	*adj* somewhat blond
BLOOD	*v* -ED, -ING, -S to stain with blood (the fluid circulated by the heart)
BLOODFIN	*n* pl. -S a freshwater fish
BLOODIED	past tense of bloody
BLOODIER	comparative of bloody
BLOODIES	present 3d person sing. of bloody
BLOODIEST	superlative of bloody
BLOODILY	*adv* in a bloody manner
BLOODING	*n* pl. -S a fox hunting ceremony
BLOODRED	*adj* of the color of blood
BLOODY	*adj* BLOODIER, BLOODIEST stained with blood
BLOODY	*v* BLOODIED, BLOODYING, BLOODIES to make bloody
BLOOM	*v* -ED, -ING, -S to bear flowers
BLOOMER	*n* pl. -S a blooming plant
BLOOMERY	*n* pl. -ERIES a furnace for smelting iron
BLOOMY	*adj* BLOOMIER, BLOOMIEST covered with flowers
BLOOP	*v* -ED, -ING, -S to hit a short fly ball
BLOOPER	*n* pl. -S a public blunder
BLOSSOM	*v* -ED, -ING, -S to bloom
BLOSSOMY	*adj* having blossoms
BLOT	*v* BLOTTED, BLOTTING, BLOTS to spot or stain
BLOTCH	*v* -ED, -ING, -ES to mark with large spots
BLOTCHY	*adj* BLOTCHIER, BLOTCHIEST blotched
BLOTLESS	*adj* spotless
BLOTTED	past tense of blot
BLOTTER	*n* pl. -S a piece of ink-absorbing paper
BLOTTIER	comparative of blotty
BLOTTIEST	superlative of blotty
BLOTTING	present participle of blot
BLOTTO	*adj* drunk
BLOTTY	*adj* -TIER, -TIEST spotty
BLOUSE	*v* BLOUSED, BLOUSING, BLOUSES to hang loosely
BLOUSON	*n* pl. -S a woman's garment

BLOUSY *adj* BLOUSIER, BLOUSIEST blowsy **BLOUSILY** *adv*

BLOW *v* BLEW, BLOWN, BLOWING, BLOWS to drive or impel by a current of air

BLOWBACK *n* pl. -S an escape of gases

BLOWBY *n* pl. -BYS leakage of exhaust fumes

BLOWER *n* pl. -S one that blows

BLOWFISH *n* pl. -ES a marine fish

BLOWFLY *n* pl. -FLIES a type of fly

BLOWGUN *n* pl. -S a tube through which darts may be blown

BLOWHARD *n* pl. -S a braggart

BLOWHOLE *n* pl. -S an air or gas vent

BLOWIER comparative of blowy

BLOWIEST superlative of blowy

BLOWN past participle of blow

BLOWOFF *n* pl. -S the expelling of gas

BLOWOUT *n* pl. -S a sudden rupture

BLOWPIPE *n* pl. -S a blowgun

BLOWSED *adj* blowsy

BLOWSY *adj* -SIER, -SIEST slovenly **BLOWSILY** *adv*

BLOWTUBE *n* pl. -S a blowgun

BLOWUP *n* pl. -S an explosion

BLOWY *adj* BLOWIER, BLOWIEST windy

BLOWZED *adj* blowzy

BLOWZY *adj* -ZIER, -ZIEST blowsy **BLOWZILY** *adv*

BLUBBER *v* -ED, -ING, -S to weep noisily

BLUBBERY *adj* fat; swollen

BLUCHER *n* pl. -S a half boot

BLUDGEON *v* -ED, -ING, -S to hit with a club

BLUE *adj* BLUER, BLUEST having the color of the clear sky

BLUE *v* BLUED, BLUEING or BLUING, BLUES to make blue

BLUEBALL *n* pl. -S a medicinal herb

BLUEBELL *n* pl. -S a flowering plant

BLUEBILL *n* pl. -S the scaup duck

BLUEBIRD *n* pl. -S a songbird

BLUEBOOK *n* pl. -S an examination booklet

BLUECAP *n* pl. -S a flowering plant

BLUECOAT *n* pl. -S a policeman

BLUED past tense of blue

BLUEFIN *n* pl. -S a large tuna

BLUEFISH *n* pl. -ES a marine fish

BLUEGILL *n* pl. -S an edible sunfish

BLUEGUM *n* pl. -S a timber tree

BLUEHEAD *n* pl. -S a marine fish

BLUEING *n* pl. -S bluing

BLUEISH *adj* bluish

BLUEJACK *n* pl. -S an oak tree

BLUEJAY *n* pl. -JAYS a corvine bird

BLUELINE *n* pl. -S a line that divides a hockey rink

BLUELY *adv* in a blue manner

BLUENESS *n* pl. -ES the state of being blue

BLUENOSE *n* pl. -S a puritanical person

BLUER comparative of blue

BLUESMAN *n* pl. -MEN one who plays the blues

BLUEST superlative of blue

BLUESTEM *n* pl. -S a prairie grass

BLUESY *adj* resembling the blues (a musical form)

BLUET *n* pl. -S a meadow flower

BLUEWEED *n* pl. -S a bristly weed

BLUEWOOD *n* pl. -S a shrub

BLUEY *n* pl. BLUEYS a bag of clothing carried in travel

BLUFF *v* -ED, -ING, -S to mislead

BLUFF *adj* BLUFFER, BLUFFEST having a broad front **BLUFFLY** *adv*

BLUFFER *n* pl. -S one that bluffs

BLUING *n* pl. -S a fabric coloring

BLUISH *adj* somewhat blue

BLUME *v* BLUMED, BLUMING, BLUMES to blossom

BLUNDER *v* -ED, -ING, -S to make a mistake

BLUNGE *v* BLUNGED, BLUNGING, BLUNGES to mix clay with water

BLUNGER *n* pl. -S one that blunges

BLUNT *adj* BLUNTER, BLUNTEST not sharp or pointed **BLUNTLY** *adv*

BLUNT *v* -ED, -ING, -S to make blunt

BLUR *v* BLURRED, BLURRING, BLURS to make unclear

BLURB *n* pl. -S a note on a book jacket

BLURRY *adj* -RIER, -RIEST unclear **BLURRILY** *adv*

BLURT   *v* -ED, -ING, -S to speak abruptly

BLURTER   *n* pl. -S one that blurts

BLUSH   *v* -ED, -ING, -ES to become red

BLUSHER   *n* pl. -S one that blushes

BLUSHFUL   *adj* of a red color

BLUSTER   *v* -ED, -ING, -S to blow violently

BLUSTERY   *adj* windy

BLYPE   *n* pl. -S a shred

BO   *n* pl. BOS a pal

BOA   *n* pl. -S a large snake

BOAR   *n* pl. -S a male pig

BOARD   *v* -ED, -ING, -S to take meals for a fixed price

BOARDER   *n* pl. -S one that boards

BOARDING   *n* pl. -S a surface of wooden boards

BOARDMAN   *n* pl. -MEN a board member

BOARFISH   *n* pl. -ES a marine fish

BOARISH   *adj* swinish; coarse

BOART   *n* pl. -S bort

BOAST   *v* -ED, -ING, -S to brag

BOASTER   *n* pl. -S one that boasts

BOASTFUL   *adj* given to boasting

BOAT   *v* -ED, -ING, -S to travel by boat (watercraft) **BOATABLE** *adj*

BOATBILL   *n* pl. -S a wading bird

BOATEL   *n* pl. -S a waterside hotel

BOATER   *n* pl. -S one that boats

BOATING   *n* pl. -S the sport of traveling by boat

BOATLOAD   *n* pl. -S the amount that a boat holds

BOATMAN   *n* pl. -MEN one who works on boats

BOATSMAN   *n* pl. -MEN boatman

BOATYARD   *n* pl. -S a marina

BOB   *v* BOBBED, BOBBING, BOBS to move up and down

BOBBER   *n* pl. -S one that bobs

BOBBERY   *n* pl. -BERIES a disturbance

BOBBIES   pl. of bobby

BOBBIN   *n* pl. -S a thread holder

BOBBINET   *n* pl. -S a machine-made net

BOBBING   present participle of bob

BOBBLE   *v* -BLED, -BLING, -BLES to fumble

BOBBY   *n* pl. -BIES a policeman

BOBCAT   *n* pl. -S a lynx

BOBECHE   *n* pl. -S a glass collar on a candle holder

BOBOLINK   *n* pl. -S a songbird

BOBSLED   *v* -SLEDDED, -SLEDDING, -SLEDS to ride on a bobsled (a racing sled)

BOBSTAY   *n* pl. -STAYS a steadying rope

BOBTAIL   *v* -ED, -ING, -S to cut short

BOBWHITE   *n* pl. -S a game bird

BOCACCIO   *n* pl. -CIOS a rockfish

BOCCE   *n* pl. -S boccie

BOCCI   *n* pl. -S boccie

BOCCIA   *n* pl. -S boccie

BOCCIE   *n* pl. -S an Italian bowling game

BOCHE   *n* pl. -S a German — a derogatory term

BOCK   *n* pl. -S a dark beer

BOD   *n* pl. -S a body

BODE   *v* BODED, BODING, BODES to be an omen of

BODEGA   *n* pl. -S a grocery store

BODEMENT   *n* pl. -S an omen

BODICE   *n* pl. -S a corset

BODIED   past tense of body

BODIES   present 3d person sing. of body

BODILESS   *adj* lacking material form

BODILY   *adj* of the body

BODING   *n* pl. -S an omen

BODINGLY   *adv* ominously

BODKIN   *n* pl. -S a sharp instrument

BODY   *v* BODIED, BODYING, BODIES to give form to

BODYSURF   *v* -ED, -ING, -S to ride a wave without a surfboard

BODYWORK   *n* pl. -S a vehicle body

BOEHMITE   *n* pl. -S a mineral

BOFF   *n* pl. -S a hearty laugh

BOFFIN   *n* pl. -S a scientific expert

BOFFO   *n* pl. -FOS a boff

BOFFOLA   *n* pl. -S a boff

BOG   *v* BOGGED, BOGGING, BOGS to impede

BOGAN   *n* pl. -S a backwater or tributary

BOGBEAN   *n* pl. -S a marsh plant

BOGEY	v -GEYED, -GEYING, -GEYS to shoot in one stroke over par in golf
BOGEYMAN	n pl. -MEN a terrifying creature
BOGGED	past tense of bog
BOGGIER	comparative of boggy
BOGGIEST	superlative of boggy
BOGGING	present participle of bog
BOGGISH	adj boggy
BOGGLE	v -GLED, -GLING, -GLES to hesitate
BOGGLER	n pl. -S one that causes another to boggle
BOGGY	adj -GIER, -GIEST marshy
BOGIE	n pl. -S bogy
BOGIES	pl. of bogy
BOGLE	n pl. -S a bogy
BOGUS	adj not genuine; fake
BOGWOOD	n pl. -S preserved tree wood
BOGY	n pl. -GIES a goblin
BOGYISM	n pl. -S behavior characteristic of a bogy
BOGYMAN	n pl. -MEN bogeyman
BOHEA	n pl. -S a black tea
BOHEMIA	n pl. -S a community of bohemians
BOHEMIAN	n pl. -S an unconventional person
BOHUNK	n pl. -S an unskilled laborer
BOIL	v -ED, -ING, -S to vaporize liquid **BOILABLE** adj
BOILER	n pl. -S a vessel for boiling
BOITE	n pl. -S a nightclub
BOLA	n pl. -S a throwing weapon
BOLAR	adj pertaining to bole
BOLAS	n pl. -ES bola
BOLD	adj BOLDER, BOLDEST daring **BOLDLY** adv
BOLDFACE	v -FACED, -FACING, -FACES to print in thick type
BOLDNESS	n pl. -ES the quality of being bold
BOLE	n pl. -S a fine clay
BOLERO	n pl. -ROS a Spanish dance
BOLETE	n pl. -S boletus
BOLETUS	n pl. -TUSES or -TI a fungus
BOLIDE	n pl. -S an exploding meteor
BOLIVAR	n pl. -S or -ES a unit of Venezuelan currency
BOLIVIA	n pl. -S a soft fabric
BOLL	v -ED, -ING, -S to form pods
BOLLARD	n pl. -S a thick post on a ship or wharf
BOLLIX	v -ED, -ING, -ES to bungle
BOLLOX	v -ED, -ING, -ES to bollix
BOLLWORM	n pl. -S the larva of a certain moth
BOLO	n pl. -LOS a machete
BOLOGNA	n pl. -S a seasoned sausage
BOLONEY	n pl. -NEYS bologna
BOLSON	n pl. -S a flat arid valley
BOLSTER	v -ED, -ING, -S to support
BOLT	v -ED, -ING, -S to sift
BOLTER	n pl. -S a sifting machine
BOLTHEAD	n pl. -S a matrass
BOLTONIA	n pl. -S a perennial herb
BOLTROPE	n pl. -S a rope sewn to a sail
BOLUS	n pl. -ES a large pill
BOMB	v -ED, -ING, -S to attack with bombs (explosive projectiles)
BOMBARD	v -ED, -ING, -S to bomb
BOMBAST	n pl. -S pompous language
BOMBE	n pl. -S a frozen dessert
BOMBER	n pl. -S one that bombs
BOMBLOAD	n pl. -S the quantity of bombs being carried
BOMBYCID	n pl. -S a moth
BOMBYX	n pl. -ES a silkworm
BONACI	n pl. -S an edible fish
BONANZA	n pl. -S a rich mine
BONBON	n pl. -S a sugared candy
BOND	v -ED, -ING, -S to join together **BONDABLE** adj
BONDAGE	n pl. -S slavery
BONDER	n pl. -S one that bonds
BONDMAID	n pl. -S a female slave
BONDMAN	n pl. -MEN a male slave
BONDSMAN	n pl. -MEN bondman
BONDUC	n pl. -S a prickly seed
BONE	v BONED, BONING, BONES to debone
BONEFISH	n pl. -ES a slender marine fish
BONEHEAD	n pl. -S a stupid person

BONELESS *adj* having no bones (hard connective tissue)

BONER *n* pl. -S a blunder

BONESET *n* pl. -S a perennial herb

BONEY *adj* BONIER, BONIEST bony

BONEYARD *n* pl. -S a junkyard

BONFIRE *n* pl. -S an open fire

BONG *v* -ED, -ING, -S to make a deep, ringing sound

BONGO *n* pl. -GOS or -GOES a small drum

BONGOIST *n* pl. -S a bongo player

BONHOMIE *n* pl. -S friendliness

BONIER comparative of bony or boney

BONIEST superlative of bony or boney

BONIFACE *n* pl. -S an innkeeper

BONINESS *n* pl. -ES the state of being bony

BONING present participle of bone

BONITA *n* pl. -S bonito

BONITO *n* pl. -TOS or -TOES a marine food fish

BONKERS *adj* crazy

BONNE *n* pl. -S a housemaid

BONNET *v* -ED, -ING, -S to provide with a bonnet (a type of hat)

BONNIE *adj* bonny

BONNOCK *n* pl. -S bannock

BONNY *adj* -NIER, -NIEST pretty **BONNILY** *adv*

BONSAI *n* pl. BONSAI a potted shrub that has been dwarfed

BONSPELL *n* pl. -S bonspiel

BONSPIEL *n* pl. -S a curling match or tournament

BONTEBOK *n* pl. -S an antelope

BONUS *n* pl. -ES an additional payment

BONY *adj* BONIER, BONIEST full of bones

BONZE *n* pl. -S a Buddhist monk

BONZER *adj* very good

BOO *v* -ED, -ING, -S to cry "boo"

BOOB *n* pl. -S a dolt

BOOBOO *n* pl. -BOOS a mistake

BOOBY *n* pl. -BIES a dolt

BOODLE *v* -DLED, -DLING, -DLES to take bribes

BOODLER *n* pl. -S one that boodles

BOOGER *n* pl. -S a bogeyman

BOOGIE *n* pl. -S a jazz form

BOOGYMAN *n* pl. -MEN bogeyman

BOOHOO *v* -ED, -ING, -S to weep noisily

BOOK *v* -ED, -ING, -S to engage services

BOOKCASE *n* pl. -S a case which holds books (literary volumes)

BOOKEND *n* pl. -S a support for a row of books

BOOKER *n* pl. -S one that books

BOOKIE *n* pl. -S a bet taker

BOOKING *n* pl. -S an engagement

BOOKISH *adj* pertaining to books

BOOKLET *n* pl. -S a small book

BOOKLORE *n* pl. -S book learning

BOOKMAN *n* pl. -MEN a scholar

BOOKMARK *n* pl. -S a marker for finding a place in a book

BOOKRACK *n* pl. -S a support for an open book

BOOKREST *n* pl. -S a bookrack

BOOKSHOP *n* pl. -S a store where books are sold

BOOKWORM *n* pl. -S an avid book reader

BOOM *v* -ED, -ING, -S to make a deep, resonant sound

BOOMER *n* pl. -S one that booms

BOOMIER comparative of boomy

BOOMIEST superlative of boomy

BOOMKIN *n* pl. -S a bumkin

BOOMLET *n* pl. -S a small increase in prosperity

BOOMTOWN *n* pl. -S a prospering town

BOOMY *adj* BOOMIER, BOOMIEST prospering

BOON *n* pl. -S a timely benefit

BOONIES *n/pl* a backwoods area

BOOR *n* pl. -S a rude person

BOORISH *adj* rude

BOOST *v* -ED, -ING, -S to support

BOOSTER *n* pl. -S one that boosts

BOOT *v* -ED, -ING, -S to provide with boots (protective coverings for the feet)

BOOTEE *n* pl. -S a baby's boot

BOOTERY *n* pl. -ERIES a shoe store

BOOTH	*n* pl. -S a small enclosure
BOOTIE	*n* pl. -S bootee
BOOTIES	pl. of booty
BOOTJACK	*n* pl. -S a device for pulling off boots
BOOTLACE	*n* pl. -S a shoelace
BOOTLEG	*v* -LEGGED, -LEGGING, -LEGS to smuggle
BOOTLESS	*adj* useless
BOOTLICK	*v* -ED, -ING, -S to flatter servilely
BOOTY	*n* pl. -TIES a rich gain or prize
BOOZE	*v* BOOZED, BOOZING, BOOZES to drink liquor excessively
BOOZER	*n* pl. -S one that boozes
BOOZY	*adj* BOOZIER, BOOZIEST drunken **BOOZILY** *adv*
BOP	*v* BOPPED, BOPPING, BOPS to hit or strike
BOPPER	*n* pl. -S a bebopper
BORA	*n* pl. -S a cold wind
BORACES	a pl. of borax
BORACIC	*adj* boric
BORACITE	*n* pl. -S a mineral
BORAGE	*n* pl. -S a medicinal herb
BORANE	*n* pl. -S a chemical compound
BORATE	*n* pl. -S a salt of boric acid **BORATED** *adj*
BORAX	*n* pl. -RAXES or -RACES a white crystalline compound
BORAZON	*n* pl. -S a hard boron compound
BORDEL	*n* pl. -S a brothel
BORDELLO	*n* pl. -LOS a brothel
BORDER	*v* -ED, -ING, -S to put a border (an edge) on
BORDERER	*n* pl. -S one that borders
BORDURE	*n* pl. -S a border around a shield
BORE	*v* BORED, BORING, BORES to pierce with a rotary tool
BOREAL	*adj* pertaining to the north
BORECOLE	*n* pl. -S kale
BORED	past tense of bore
BOREDOM	*n* pl. -S tedium
BORER	*n* pl. -S one that bores
BORIC	*adj* pertaining to boron
BORIDE	*n* pl. -S a boron compound
BORING	*n* pl. -S an inner cavity
BORINGLY	*adv* tediously
BORN	*adj* having particular qualities from birth
BORNE	a past participle of bear
BORNEOL	*n* pl. -S an alcohol
BORNITE	*n* pl. -S an ore of copper
BORON	*n* pl. -S a nonmetallic element **BORONIC** *adj*
BOROUGH	*n* pl. -S an incorporated town
BORROW	*v* -ED, -ING, -S to take on loan
BORROWER	*n* pl. -S one that borrows
BORSCH	*n* pl. -ES borscht
BORSCHT	*n* pl. -S a beet soup
BORSHT	*n* pl. -S borscht
BORSTAL	*n* pl. -S a reformatory
BORT	*n* pl. -S a low-quality diamond **BORTY** *adj*
BORTZ	*n* pl. -ES bort
BORZOI	*n* pl. -S a Russian hound
BOSCAGE	*n* pl. -S a thicket
BOSCHBOK	*n* pl. -S bushbuck
BOSH	*n* pl. -ES nonsense
BOSHBOK	*n* pl. -S bushbuck
BOSHVARK	*n* pl. -S a wild hog
BOSK	*n* pl. -S a small wooded area
BOSKAGE	*n* pl. -S boscage
BOSKER	*adj* fine; very good
BOSKET	*n* pl. -S a thicket
BOSKY	*adj* BOSKIER, BOSKIEST wooded; bushy
BOSOM	*v* -ED, -ING, -S to embrace
BOSOMY	*adj* swelling outward
BOSON	*n* pl. -S an atomic particle
BOSQUE	*n* pl. -S bosk
BOSQUET	*n* pl. -S bosket
BOSS	*v* -ED, -ING, -ES to supervise
BOSSDOM	*n* pl. -S the domain of a political boss
BOSSIER	comparative of bossy
BOSSIES	pl. of bossy
BOSSISM	*n* pl. -S control by political bosses
BOSSY	*adj* BOSSIER, BOSSIEST domineering **BOSSILY** *adv*
BOSSY	*n* pl. BOSSIES a cow
BOSTON	*n* pl. -S a card game

BOSUN	*n* pl. -S a boatswain		**BOULDER**	*n* pl. -S a large rock **BOULDERY** *adj*
BOT	*n* pl. -S the larva of a botfly		**BOULE**	*n* pl. -S buhl
BOTANIC	*adj* pertaining to botany		**BOULLE**	*n* pl. -S buhl
BOTANIES	pl. of botany		**BOUNCE**	*v* BOUNCED, BOUNCING, BOUNCES to spring back
BOTANISE	*v* -NISED, -NISING, -NISES to botanize		**BOUNCER**	*n* pl. -S one that bounces
BOTANIST	*n* pl. -S one skilled in botany		**BOUNCY**	*adj* BOUNCIER, BOUNCIEST tending to bounce **BOUNCILY** *adv*
BOTANIZE	*v* -NIZED, -NIZING, -NIZES to study plants		**BOUND**	*v* -ED, -ING, -S to leap
BOTANY	*n* pl. -NIES the science of plants		**BOUNDARY**	*n* pl. -ARIES a dividing line
BOTCH	*v* -ED, -ING, -ES to bungle		**BOUNDEN**	*adj* obliged
BOTCHER	*n* pl. -S one that botches		**BOUNDER**	*n* pl. -S one that bounds
BOTCHERY	*n* pl. -ERIES something botched		**BOUNTY**	*n* pl. -TIES a reward **BOUNTIED** *adj*
BOTCHY	*adj* BOTCHIER, BOTCHIEST badly done **BOTCHILY** *adv*		**BOUQUET**	*n* pl. -S a bunch of flowers
BOTEL	*n* pl. -S boatel		**BOURBON**	*n* pl. -S a whiskey
BOTFLY	*n* pl. -FLIES a type of fly		**BOURDON**	*n* pl. -S a part of a bagpipe
BOTH	*adj* being the two		**BOURG**	*n* pl. -S a medieval town
BOTHER	*v* -ED, -ING, -S to annoy		**BOURGEON**	*v* -ED, -ING, -S to burgeon
BOTONEE	*adj* having arms ending in a trefoil — used of a heraldic cross		**BOURN**	*n* pl. -S a stream
			BOURNE	*n* pl. -S bourn
BOTONNEE	*adj* botonee		**BOURREE**	*n* pl. -S an old French dance
BOTRYOID	*adj* resembling a cluster of grapes		**BOURSE**	*n* pl. -S a stock exchange
			BOURTREE	*n* pl. -S a European tree
BOTRYOSE	*adj* botryoid		**BOUSE**	*v* BOUSED, BOUSING, BOUSES to haul by means of a tackle
BOTT	*n* pl. -S bot		
BOTTLE	*v* -TLED, -TLING, -TLES to put into a bottle (a rigid container)		**BOUSOUKI**	*n* pl. -KIA or -KIS bouzouki
BOTTLER	*n* pl. -S one that bottles		**BOUSY**	*adj* boozy
BOTTOM	*v* -ED, -ING, -S to comprehend		**BOUT**	*n* pl. -S a contest
BOTTOMER	*n* pl. -S one that bottoms		**BOUTIQUE**	*n* pl. -S a small shop
BOTTOMRY	*n* pl. -RIES a maritime contract		**BOUZOUKI**	*n* pl. -KIA or KIS a stringed musical instrument
BOTULIN	*n* pl. -S a nerve poison		
BOTULISM	*n* pl. -S botulin poisoning		**BOVID**	*n* pl. -S a bovine
BOUCLE	*n* pl. -S a knitted fabric		**BOVINE**	*n* pl. -S an ox-like animal
BOUDOIR	*n* pl. -S a woman's bedroom		**BOVINELY**	*adj* stolidly
BOUFFANT	*n* pl. -S a woman's hairdo		**BOVINITY**	*n* pl. -TIES the state of being a bovine
BOUFFE	*n* pl. -S a comic opera		
BOUGH	*n* pl. -S a tree branch **BOUGHED** *adj*		**BOW**	*v* -ED, -ING, -S to bend forward
			BOWEL	*v* -ELED, -ELING, -ELS or -ELLED, -ELLING, -ELS to disbowel
BOUGHPOT	*n* pl. -S a large vase		
BOUGHT	past tense of buy		**BOWER**	*v* -ED, -ING, -S to embower
BOUGHTEN	*adj* purchased		**BOWERY**	*n* -ERIES a colonial Dutch farm
BOUGIE	*n* pl. -S a wax candle		**BOWFIN**	*n* pl. -S a freshwater fish
BOUILLON	*n* pl. -S a clear soup		**BOWFRONT**	*adj* having a curved front

BOWHEAD *n* pl. -S an arctic whale

BOWING *n* pl. -S the technique of managing the bow of a stringed instrument

BOWINGLY *adv* in a bowing manner

BOWKNOT *n* pl. -S a type of knot

BOWL *v* -ED, -ING, -S to play at bowling

BOWLDER *n* pl. -S boulder

BOWLEG *n* pl. -S an outwardly curved leg

BOWLER *n* pl. -S one that bowls

BOWLESS *adj* being without an archery bow

BOWLFUL *n* pl. -S as much as a bowl can hold

BOWLIKE *adj* curved

BOWLINE *n* pl. -S a type of knot

BOWLING *n* pl. -S a game in which balls are rolled at objects

BOWLLIKE *adj* concave

BOWMAN *n* pl. -MEN an archer

BOWPOT *n* pl. -S boughpot

BOWSE *v* BOWSED, BOWSING, BOWSES to bouse

BOWSHOT *n* pl. -S the distance an arrow is shot

BOWSPRIT *n* pl. -S a ship's spar

BOWWOW *n* pl. -S the bark of a dog

BOWYER *n* pl. -S a maker of archery bows

BOX *v* -ED, -ING, -ES to put in a box (a rectangular container)

BOXBERRY *n* pl. -RIES an evergreen plant

BOXCAR *n* pl. -S a roofed freight car

BOXER *n* pl. -S one who packs boxes

BOXFISH *n* pl. -ES a marine fish

BOXFUL *n* pl. -S as much as a box can hold

BOXHAUL *v* -ED, -ING, -S to veer a ship around

BOXIER comparative of boxy

BOXIEST superlative of boxy

BOXINESS *n* pl. -ES the state of being boxy

BOXING *n* pl. -S a casing

BOXLIKE *adj* resembling a box

BOXTHORN *n* pl. -S a thorny shrub

BOXWOOD *n* pl. -S an evergreen shrub

BOXY *adj* BOXIER, BOXIEST resembling a box

BOY *n* pl. BOYS a male child

BOYAR *n* pl. -S a former Russian aristocrat

BOYARD *n* pl. -S boyar

BOYARISM *n* pl. -S the rule of boyars

BOYCOTT *v* -ED, -ING, -S to refuse to buy

BOYHOOD *n* pl. -S the state of being a boy

BOYISH *adj* resembling a boy **BOYISHLY** *adv*

BOYLA *n* pl. -S a witch doctor

BOYO *n* pl. BOYOS a boy

BOZO *n* pl. -ZOS a fellow

BRA *n* pl. -S a brassiere

BRABBLE *v* -BLED, -BLING, -BLES to quarrel noisily

BRABBLER *n* pl. -S one that brabbles

BRACE *v* BRACED, BRACING, BRACES to support

BRACELET *n* pl. -S a wrist ornament

BRACER *n* pl. -S one that braces

BRACERO *n* pl. -ROS a Mexican laborer

BRACH *n* pl. -ES a hound bitch

BRACHET *n* pl. -S a brach

BRACHIAL *n* pl. -S a part of the arm

BRACHIUM *n* pl. -IA the upper part of arm

BRACING *n* pl. -S a brace or reinforcement

BRACKEN *n* pl. -S a large fern

BRACKET *v* -ED, -ING, -S to classify

BRACKISH *adj* salty

BRACT *n* pl. -S a leaflike plant part **BRACTEAL, BRACTED** *adj*

BRACTLET *n* pl. -S a small bract

BRAD *v* BRADDED, BRADDING, BRADS to fasten with thin nails

BRADAWL *n* pl. -S a type of awl

BRADOON *n* pl. -S bridoon

BRAE *n* pl. -S a hillside

BRAG *adj* BRAGGER, BRAGGEST first-rate

BRAG *v* BRAGGED, BRAGGING, BRAGS to speak vainly of one's deeds

BRAGGART *n* pl. -S one who brags

BRAGGER *n* pl. -S a braggart

BRAGGEST	superlative of brag
BRAGGING	present participle of brag
BRAGGY	*adj* -GIER, -GIEST tending to brag
BRAHMA	*n* pl. -S a large domestic fowl
BRAID	*v* -ED, -ING, -S to weave together
BRAIDER	*n* pl. -S one that braids
BRAIDING	*n* pl. -S something made of braided material
BRAIL	*v* -ED, -ING, -S to haul in a sail
BRAILLE	*v* BRAILLED, BRAILLING, BRAILLES to write in braille (raised writing for the blind)
BRAIN	*v* -ED, -ING, -S to hit on the head
BRAINIER	comparative of brainy
BRAINIEST	superlative of brainy
BRAINILY	*adv* in a brainy manner
BRAINISH	*adj* impetuous
BRAINPAN	*n* pl. -S the skull
BRAINY	*adj* BRAINIER, BRAINIEST smart
BRAISE	*v* BRAISED, BRAISING, BRAISES to cook in fat
BRAIZE	*n* pl. -S a marine fish
BRAKE	*v* BRAKED, BRAKING, BRAKES to slow down or stop
BRAKEAGE	*n* pl. -S the act of braking
BRAKEMAN	*n* pl. -MEN a trainman
BRAKING	present participle of brake
BRAKY	*adj* BRAKIER, BRAKIEST abounding in shrubs or ferns
BRAMBLE	*v* -BLED, -BLING, -BLES to gather berries
BRAMBLY	*adj* -BLIER, -BLIEST prickly
BRAN	*v* BRANNED, BRANNING, BRANS to soak in water mixed with bran (the outer coat of cereals)
BRANCH	*v* -ED, -ING, -ES to form branches (offshoots)
BRANCHIA	*n* pl. -CHIAE a respiratory organ of aquatic animals
BRANCHY	*adj* BRANCHIER, BRANCHIEST having many branches
BRAND	*v* -ED, -ING, -S to mark with a hot iron
BRANDER	*n* pl. -S one that brands
BRANDISH	*v* -ED, -ING, -ES to wave menacingly
BRANDY	*v* -DIED, -DYING, -DIES to mix with brandy (a liquor)
BRANK	*n* pl. -S a device used to restrain the tongue
BRANNED	past tense of bran
BRANNER	*n* pl. -S one that brans
BRANNING	present participle of bran
BRANNY	*adj* -NIER, -NIEST containing bran
BRANT	*n* pl. -S a wild goose
BRANTAIL	*n* pl. -S a singing bird
BRASH	*adj* BRASHER, BRASHEST rash; hasty **BRASHLY** *adv*
BRASH	*n* pl. -ES a mass of fragments
BRASHY	*adj* BRASHIER, BRASHIEST brash
BRASIER	*n* pl. -S brazier
BRASIL	*n* pl. -S brazil
BRASILIN	*n* pl. -S brazilin
BRASS	*n* pl. -ES an alloy of copper and zinc
BRASSAGE	*n* pl. -S a fee for coining money
BRASSARD	*n* pl. -S an insignia
BRASSART	*n* pl. -S brassard
BRASSICA	*n* pl. -S a tall herb
BRASSIE	*n* pl. -S a golf club
BRASSISH	*adj* resembling brass
BRASSY	*adj* BRASSIER, BRASSIEST resembling brass **BRASSILY** *adv*
BRAT	*n* pl. -S a spoiled child **BRATTISH** *adj*
BRATTICE	*v* -TICED, -TICING, -TICES to partition
BRATTLE	*v* -TLED, -TLING, -TLES to clatter
BRATTY	*adj* -TIER, -TIEST resembling a brat
BRAUNITE	*n* pl. -S a mineral
BRAVA	*n* pl. -S a shout of approval
BRAVADO	*n* pl. -DOS or -DOES false bravery
BRAVE	*adj* BRAVER, BRAVEST showing courage **BRAVELY** *adv*
BRAVE	*v* BRAVED, BRAVING, BRAVES to face with courage
BRAVER	*n* pl. -S one that braves
BRAVERY	*n* pl. -ERIES courage
BRAVEST	superlative of brave
BRAVING	present participle of brave

BRAVO *n* pl. -VOS or -VOES a hired killer

BRAVO *v* -ED, -ING, -ES to applaud by shouting "bravo"

BRAVURA *n* pl. -RAS or -RE fine musical technique

BRAW *adj* BRAWER, BRAWEST splendid

BRAWL *v* -ED, -ING, -S to fight

BRAWLER *n* pl. -S a fighter

BRAWLIE *adv* splendidly

BRAWLY *adj* BRAWLIER, BRAWLIEST inclined to brawl

BRAWN *n* pl. -S muscular strength

BRAWNY *adj* BRAWNIER, BRAWNIEST muscular **BRAWNILY** *adv*

BRAWS *n/pl* fine clothes

BRAXY *n* pl. BRAXIES a fever of sheep

BRAY *v* BRAYED, BRAYING, BRAYS to utter a harsh cry

BRAYER *n* pl. -S a roller used to spread ink

BRAZA *n* pl. -S a Spanish unit of length

BRAZE *v* BRAZED, BRAZING, BRAZES to solder together

BRAZEN *v* -ED, -ING, -S to face boldly

BRAZENLY *adv* boldly

BRAZER *n* pl. -S one that brazes

BRAZIER *n* pl. -S one who works in brass

BRAZIL *n* pl. -S a dyewood

BRAZILIN *n* pl. -S a chemical compound

BRAZING present participle of braze

BREACH *v* -ED, -ING, -ES to break through

BREACHER *n* pl. -S one that breaches

BREAD *v* -ED, -ING, -S to cover with bread crumbs

BREADNUT *n* pl. -S a tropical fruit

BREADTH *n* pl. -S width

BREAK *v* BROKE, BROKEN, BREAKING, BREAKS to reduce to fragments

BREAKAGE *n* pl. -S the act of breaking

BREAKER *n* pl. -S one that breaks

BREAKING *n* pl. -S the change of a pure vowel to a diphthong

BREAKOUT *n* pl. -S an escape

BREAKUP *n* pl. -S the act of breaking up

BREAM *v* -ED, -ING, -S to clean a ship's bottom

BREAST *v* -ED, -ING, -S to confront boldly

BREATH *n* pl. -S air inhaled and exhaled

BREATHE *v* BREATHED, BREATHING, BREATHES to inhale and exhale air

BREATHER *n* pl. -S one that breathes

BREATHY *adj* BREATHIER, BREATHIEST marked by loud breathing

BRECCIA *n* pl. -S a type of rock **BRECCIAL** *adj*

BRECHAM *n* pl. -S a collar for a horse

BRECHAN *n* pl. -S brecham

BRED past tense of breed

BREDE *n* pl. -S a braid

BREE *n* pl. -S broth

BREECH *v* -ED, -ING, -ES to clothe with breeches (trousers)

BREED *v* BRED, BREEDING, BREEDS to cause to give birth

BREEDER *n* pl. -S one that breeds

BREEDING *n* pl. -S upbringing

BREEKS *n/pl* breeches

BREEZE *v* BREEZED, BREEZING, BREEZES to move swiftly

BREEZY *adj* BREEZIER, BREEZIEST windy **BREEZILY** *adv*

BREGMA *n* pl. -MATA a junction point of the skull **BREGMATE** *adj*

BRENT *n* pl. -S brant

BRETHREN a pl. of brother

BREVE *n* pl. -S a symbol used to indicate a short vowel

BREVET *v* -VETED, -VETING, -VETS or -VETTED, -VETTING, -VETS to confer an honorary rank upon

BREVETCY *n* pl. -CIES an honorary rank

BREVIARY *n* pl. -RIES a prayer book

BREVIER *n* pl. -S a size of type

BREVITY *n* pl. -TIES shortness of duration

BREW *v* -ED, -ING, -S to make beer or the like

BREWAGE *n* pl. -S a brewed beverage

BREWER *n* pl. -S one that brews

BREWERY *n* pl. -ERIES a place for brewing

BREWING *n* pl. -S a quantity brewed at one time

BREWIS *n* pl. BREWISES broth

BRIAR *n* pl. -S brier **BRIARY** *adj*

BRIARD *n* pl. -S a large dog

BRIBE *v* BRIBED, BRIBING, BRIBES to practice bribery **BRIBABLE** *adj*

BRIBER *n* pl. -S one that bribes

BRIBERY *n* pl. -ERIES an act of influencing corruptly

BRIBING present participle of bribe

BRICK *v* -ED, -ING, -S to build with bricks (blocks of clay)

BRICKBAT *n* pl. -S a piece of brick

BRICKLE *adj* brittle

BRICKY *adj* BRICKIER, BRICKIEST made of bricks

BRICOLE *n* pl. -S a cushion shot in billiards

BRIDAL *n* pl. -S a wedding

BRIDALLY *adv* in a manner befitting a bride

BRIDE *n* pl. -S a woman just married or about to be married

BRIDGE *v* BRIDGED, BRIDGING, BRIDGES to connect

BRIDGING *n* pl. -S a bracing

BRIDLE *v* -DLED, -DLING, -DLES to control with a restraint

BRIDLER *n* pl. -S one that bridles

BRIDOON *n* pl. -S a device used to control a horse

BRIE *n* pl. -S bree

BRIEF *adj* BRIEFER, BRIEFEST short

BRIEF *v* -ED, ING, -S to summarize

BRIEFER *n* pl. -S one that briefs

BRIEFING *n* pl. -S a short lecture

BRIEFLY *adv* in a brief manner

BRIER *n* pl. -S a thorny shrub **BRIERY** *adj*

BRIG *n* pl. -S a two-masted ship

BRIGADE *v* -GADED, -GADING, -GADES to group together

BRIGAND *n* pl. -S a bandit

BRIGHT *adj* BRIGHTER, BRIGHTEST emitting much light **BRIGHTLY** *adv*

BRIGHT *n* pl. -S a light-hued tobacco

BRIGHTEN *v* -ED, -ING, -S to make bright

BRILL *n* pl. -S an edible flatfish

BRIM *v* BRIMMED, BRIMMING, BRIMS to fill to the top

BRIMFUL *adj* ready to overflow

BRIMFULL *adj* brimful

BRIMLESS *adj* having no brim (an upper edge)

BRIMMED past tense of brim

BRIMMER *n* pl. -S a brimming cup or glass

BRIMMING present participle of brim

BRIN *n* pl. -S a rib of a fan

BRINDED *adj* brindled

BRINDLE *n* pl. -S a brindled color

BRINDLED *adj* streaked

BRINE *v* BRINED, BRINING, BRINES to treat with brine (salted water)

BRINER *n* pl. -S one that brines

BRING *v* BROUGHT, BRINGING, BRINGS to take with oneself to a place

BRINGER *n* pl. -S one that brings

BRINIER comparative of briny

BRINIES pl. of briny

BRINIEST superlative of briny

BRINISH *adj* resembling brine

BRINK *n* pl. -S an extreme edge

BRINY *n* pl. BRINIES the sea

BRINY *adj* BRINIER, BRINIEST salty

BRIO *n* pl. BRIOS liveliness

BRIOCHE *n* pl. -S a rich roll

BRIONY *n* pl. -NIES bryony

BRIQUET *v* -QUETTED, -QUETTING, -QUETS to mold into small bricks

BRISANCE *n* pl. -S the shattering effect of an explosive **BRISANT** *adj*

BRISK *adj* BRISKER, BRISKEST lively

BRISK *v* -ED, -ING, -S to make brisk

BRISKET *n* pl. -S the breast of an animal

BRISKLY *adv* in a brisk manner

BRISLING *n* pl. -S a small herring

BRISTLE *v* -TLED, -TLING, -TLES to rise stiffly

BRISTLY *adj* -TLIER, -TLIEST stiffly erect

BRISTOL *n* pl. -S a smooth cardboard

BRIT *n* pl. -S a young herring

BRITCHES *n/pl* breeches; trousers

BRITSKA *n* pl. -S an open carriage

BRITT *n* pl. -S brit

BRITTLE *adj* -TLER, -TLEST likely to break

BRITTLE   *v* -TLED, -TLING, -TLES to become brittle

BRITZKA   *n* pl. -S britska

BRITZSKA   *n* pl. -S britska

BROACH   *v* -ED, -ING, -ES to pierce so as to withdraw a liquid

BROACHER   *n* pl. -S one that broaches

BROAD   *adj* BROADER, BROADEST wide

BROAD   *n* pl. -S an expansion of a river

BROADAX   *n* pl. -ES a broad-edged ax

BROADAXE   *n* pl. -S broadax

BROADEN   *v* -ED, -ING, -S to make broad

BROADISH   *adj* somewhat broad

BROADLY   *adv* in a broad manner

BROCADE   *v* -CADED, -CADING, -CADES to weave with a raised design

BROCATEL   *n* pl. -S a heavy fabric

BROCCOLI   *n* pl. -S a vegetable related to the cabbage

BROCHE   *adj* brocaded

BROCHURE   *n* pl. -S a pamphlet

BROCK   *n* pl. -S a badger

BROCKAGE   *n* pl. -S an imperfectly minted coin

BROCKET   *n* pl. -S a small, red deer

BROCOLI   *n* pl. -S broccoli

BROGAN   *n* pl. -S a heavy shoe

BROGUE   *n* pl. -S an Irish accent

BROGUERY   *n* pl. -ERIES the use of an Irish accent

BROGUISH   *adj* resembling a brogue

BROIDER   *v* -ED, -ING, -S to adorn with needlework

BROIDERY   *n* pl. -DERIES the act of broidering

BROIL   *v* -ED, -ING, -S to cook by direct heat

BROILER   *n* pl. -S a device for broiling

BROKAGE   *n* pl. -S the business of a broker

BROKE   past tense of break

BROKEN   *adj* shattered **BROKENLY** *adv*

BROKER   *n* pl. -S an agent who buys and sells stocks

BROLLY   *n* pl. -LIES an umbrella

BROMAL   *n* pl. -S a medicinal liquid

BROMATE   *v* -MATED, -MATING, -MATES to combine with bromine

BROME   *n* pl. -S a tall grass

BROMELIN   *n* pl. -S an enzyme

BROMIC   *adj* containing bromine

BROMID   *n* pl. -S bromide

BROMIDE   *n* pl. -S a bromine compound

BROMIDIC   *adj* commonplace; trite

BROMIN   *n* pl. -S bromine

BROMINE   *n* pl. -S a volatile liquid element

BROMISM   *n* pl. -S a diseased condition of the skin

BROMO   *n* pl. -MOS a medicinal compound

BRONC   *n* pl. -S bronco

BRONCHI   pl. of bronchus

BRONCHIA   *n/pl* the main air passages of the lungs

BRONCHO   *n* pl. -CHOS bronco

BRONCHUS   *n* pl. -CHI a tracheal branch

BRONCO   *n* pl. -COS a wild horse

BRONZE   *v* BRONZED, BRONZING, BRONZES to make brown or tan

BRONZER   *n* pl. -S one that bronzes

BRONZING   *n* pl. -S a brownish coloring

BRONZY   *adj* BRONZIER, BRONZIEST of a brownish color

BROO   *n* pl. BROOS a bree

BROOCH   *n* pl. -ES a decorative pin

BROOD   *v* -ED, -ING, -S to ponder gloomily

BROODER   *n* pl. -S one that broods

BROODY   *adj* BROODIER, BROODIEST tending to brood

BROOK   *v* -ED, -ING, -S to tolerate

BROOKITE   *n* pl. -S a mineral

BROOKLET   *n* pl. -S a small brook or creek

BROOM   *v* -ED, -ING, -S to sweep

BROOMY   *adj* BROOMIER, BROOMIEST abounding in broom (a type of shrub)

BROSE   *n* pl. -S a porridge

BROSY   *adj* smeared with brose

BROTH   *n* pl. -S a thin clear soup

BROTHEL   *n* pl. -S a house of prostitution

BROTHER   *n* pl. -S or BRETHREN a male sibling

BROTHER   *v* -ED, -ING, -S to treat like a brother

BROTHY   *adj* resembling broth

BROUGHAM *n* pl. -S a type of carriage

BROUGHT past tense of bring

BROUHAHA *n* pl. -S an uproar

BROW *n* pl. -S the forehead

BROWBEAT *v* -BEAT, -BEATEN, -BEATING, -BEATS to intimidate

BROWLESS *adj* lacking eyebrows

BROWN *adj* BROWNER, BROWNEST of a dark color

BROWN *v* -ED, -ING, -S to make brown

BROWNIE *n* pl. -S a small sprite

BROWNIER comparative of browny

BROWNIEST superlative of browny

BROWNISH *adj* somewhat brown

BROWNOUT *n* pl. -S a power reduction

BROWNY *adj* BROWNIER, BROWNIEST somewhat brown

BROWSE *v* BROWSED, BROWSING, BROWSES to look at casually

BROWSER *n* pl. -S one that browses

BRUCELLA *n* pl. -LAE or -LAS any of a genus of harmful bacteria

BRUCIN *n* pl. -S brucine

BRUCINE *n* pl. -S a poisonous alkaloid

BRUGH *n* pl. -S a borough

BRUIN *n* pl. -S a bear

BRUISE *v* BRUISED, BRUISING, BRUISES to injure without breaking the surface of the skin

BRUISER *n* pl. -S a big, husky man

BRUIT *v* -ED, -ING, -S to spread news of

BRUITER *n* pl. -S one that bruits

BRULOT *n* pl. -S a biting fly

BRULYIE *n* pl. -S a noisy quarrel

BRULZIE *n* pl. -S brulyie

BRUMAL *adj* wintry

BRUMBY *n* pl. -BIES a wild horse

BRUME *n* pl. -S fog **BRUMOUS** *adj*

BRUNCH *v* -ED, -ING, -ES to eat a late morning meal

BRUNET *n* pl. -S a dark-haired male

BRUNETTE *n* pl. -S a dark-haired female

BRUNIZEM *n* pl. -S a prairie soil

BRUNT *n* pl. -S the main impact

BRUSH *v* -ED, -ING, -ES to touch lightly

BRUSHER *n* pl. -S one that brushes

BRUSHIER comparative of brushy

BRUSHIEST superlative of brushy

BRUSHOFF *n* pl. -S an abrupt dismissal

BRUSHUP *n* pl. -S a quick review

BRUSHY *adj* BRUSHIER, BRUSHIEST shaggy; rough

BRUSK *adj* BRUSKER, BRUSKEST brusque

BRUSQUE *adj* BRUSQUER, BRUSQUEST abrupt in manner

BRUT *adj* very dry

BRUTAL *adj* cruel; savage **BRUTALLY** *adv*

BRUTE *v* BRUTED, BRUTING, BRUTES to shape a diamond by rubbing it with another diamond

BRUTELY *adv* in a brutal manner

BRUTIFY *v* -FIED, -FYING, -FIES to make brutal

BRUTING present participle of brute

BRUTISH *adj* brutal

BRUTISM *n* pl. -S the state of being brutal

BRUXISM *n* pl. -S a nervous grinding of the teeth

BRYOLOGY *n* pl. -GIES the study of mosses

BRYONY *n* pl. -NIES a climbing plant

BRYOZOAN *n* pl. -S a type of small aquatic animal

BUB *n* pl. -S young fellow

BUBAL *n* pl. -S a large antelope

BUBALE *n* pl. -S bubal

BUBALINE *adj* pertaining to the bubal

BUBALIS *n* pl. -LISES bubal

BUBBIES pl. of bubby

BUBBLE *v* -BLED, -BLING, -BLES to form bubbles (bodies of gas contained within a liquid)

BUBBLER *n* pl. -S a drinking fountain

BUBBLY *n* pl. -BLIES champagne

BUBBLY *adj* -BLIER, -BLIEST full of bubbles

BUBBY *n* pl. -BIES a breast — often considered vulgar

BUBINGA *n* pl. -S an African tree

BUBO *n* pl. -BOES a swelling of a lymph gland **BUBOED** *adj*

BUBONIC *adj* pertaining to a bubo

BUCCAL *adj* pertaining to the cheek **BUCCALLY** *adv*

BUCK	v -ED, -ING, -S to leap forward and upward suddenly	**BUFF**	v -ED, -ING, -S to polish **BUFFABLE** adj
BUCKAROO	n pl. -ROOS a cowboy	**BUFFALO**	n pl. -LOES or -LOS an ox-like animal
BUCKAYRO	n pl. -ROS buckaroo		
BUCKBEAN	n pl. -S a marsh plant	**BUFFALO**	v -ED, -ING, -ES to intimidate
BUCKEEN	n pl. -S a poor man who acts as if wealthy	**BUFFER**	v -ED, -ING, -S to cushion
		BUFFET	v -ED, -ING, -S to hit sharply
BUCKER	n pl. -S a bucking horse	**BUFFETER**	n pl. -S one that buffets
BUCKEROO	n pl. -ROOS buckaroo	**BUFFIER**	comparative of buffy
BUCKET	v -ED, -ING, -S to hurry	**BUFFIEST**	superlative of buffy
BUCKEYE	n pl. -S a nut-bearing tree	**BUFFO**	n pl. -FI or -FOS an operatic clown
BUCKISH	adj foppish		
BUCKLE	v -LED, -LING, -LES to bend under pressure	**BUFFOON**	n pl. -S a clown
		BUFFY	adj BUFFIER, BUFFIEST of a yellowish-brown color
BUCKLER	v -ED, -ING, -S to shield		
BUCKO	n pl. BUCKOES a bully	**BUG**	v BUGGED, BUGGING, BUGS to annoy
BUCKRA	n pl. -S a white man — often used disparagingly		
		BUGABOO	n pl. -BOOS a bugbear
BUCKRAM	v -ED, -ING, -S to stiffen	**BUGBANE**	n pl. -S a perennial herb
BUCKSAW	n pl. -S a wood-cutting saw	**BUGBEAR**	n pl. -S an object or source of dread
BUCKSHEE	n pl. -S something extra obtained free		
		BUGEYE	n pl. -S a small boat
BUCKSHOT	n pl. -S a large lead shot	**BUGGED**	past tense of bug
BUCKSKIN	n pl. -S the skin of a male deer	**BUGGER**	v -ED, -ING, -S to commit sodomy with — usually considered vulgar
BUCKTAIL	n pl. -S a fishing lure		
BUCOLIC	n pl. -S a pastoral poem		
BUD	v BUDDED, BUDDING, BUDS to put forth buds (undeveloped plant parts)	**BUGGERY**	n pl. -GERIES sodomy
		BUGGING	present participle of bug
		BUGGY	n pl. -GIES a light carriage
BUDDER	n pl. -S one that buds	**BUGGY**	adj -GIER, -GIEST infested with bugs
BUDDIES	pl. of buddy		
BUDDING	adj being in an early stage of development	**BUGHOUSE**	n pl. -S an insane asylum
		BUGLE	v -GLED, -GLING, -GLES to play a bugle (a brass wind instrument)
BUDDLE	n pl. -S an apparatus on which crushed ore is washed		
BUDDLEIA	n pl. -S a tropical shrub	**BUGLER**	n pl. -S one that plays a bugle
BUDDY	n pl. -DIES a good friend	**BUGLOSS**	n pl. -ES a coarse plant
BUDGE	v BUDGED, BUDGING, BUDGES to move slightly	**BUGSEED**	n pl. -S an annual herb
		BUGSHA	n pl. -S buqsha
BUDGER	n pl. -S one that budges	**BUHL**	n pl. -S a style of furniture decoration
BUDGET	v -ED, -ING, -S to estimate expenditures		
		BUHLWORK	n pl. -S buhl
BUDGETER	n pl. -S one that budgets	**BUHR**	n pl. -S a heavy stone
BUDGIE	n pl. -S a small parrot	**BUILD**	v BUILT or BUILDED, BUILDING, BUILDS to construct
BUDGING	present participle of budge		
BUDLESS	adj being without buds	**BUILDER**	n pl. -S one that builds
BUDLIKE	adj resembling a bud	**BUILDING**	n pl. -S something that is built
		BUILDUP	n pl. -S an accumulation

BUILT	a past tense of build	**BULLOUS**	*adj* resembling bullae
BUIRDLY	*adj* burly	**BULLPEN**	*n* pl. -S an enclosure for bulls
BULB	*n* pl. -S an underground bud **BULBAR, BULBED** *adj*	**BULLPOUT**	*n* pl. -S a bullhead
		BULLRING	*n* pl. -S a bullfight arena
BULBEL	*n* pl. -S bulbil	**BULLRUSH**	*n* pl. -ES bulrush
BULBIL	*n* pl. -S a small bulb	**BULLSHIT**	*v* -SHITTED, -SHITTING, -SHITS to mislead — usually considered vulgar
BULBOUS	*adj* bulb-shaped; bulging		
BULBUL	*n* pl. -S a songbird	**BULLWEED**	*n* pl. -S knapweed
BULGE	*v* BULGED, BULGING, BULGES to swell out	**BULLWHIP**	*v* -WHIPPED, -WHIPPING, -WHIPS to strike with a long whip
BULGER	*n* pl. -S a golf club		
BULGUR	*n* pl. -S crushed wheat	**BULLY**	*v* -LIED, -LYING, -LIES to treat abusively
BULGY	*adj* BULGIER, BULGIEST bulging		
BULIMIA	*n* pl. -S insatiable appetite **BULIMIC, BULIMIAC** *adj*	**BULLY**	*adj* -LIER, -LIEST wonderful
		BULLYBOY	*n* pl. -BOYS a ruffian
BULK	*v* -ED, -ING, -S to gather into a mass	**BULLYRAG**	*v* -RAGGED, -RAGGING, -RAGS to bully
BULKAGE	*n* pl. -S a peristaltic stimulant	**BULRUSH**	*n* pl. -ES a tall marsh plant
BULKHEAD	*n* pl. -S an upright partition in a ship	**BULWARK**	*v* -ED, -ING, -S to fortify with a defensive wall
BULKY	*adj* BULKIER, BULKIEST massive **BULKILY** *adv*	**BUM**	*v* BUMMED, BUMMING, BUMS to live idly
BULL	*v* -ED, -ING, -S to push ahead	**BUMBLE**	*v* -BLED, -BLING, -BLES to bungle
BULLA	*n* pl. -LAE a large blister		
BULLACE	*n* pl. -S a purple plum	**BUMBLER**	*n* pl. -S one that bumbles
BULLATE	*adj* having a blistered appearance	**BUMBLING**	*n* pl. -S an instance of clumsiness
BULLBAT	*n* pl. -S a nocturnal bird	**BUMBOAT**	*n* pl. -S a boat used to peddle wares to larger ships
BULLDOG	*v* -DOGGED, -DOGGING, -DOGS to throw a steer		
		BUMF	*n* pl. -S paperwork
BULLDOZE	*v* -DOZED, -DOZING, -DOZES to bully	**BUMKIN**	*n* pl. -S a ship's spar
		BUMMED	past tense of bum
BULLET	*v* -ED, -ING, -S to move swiftly	**BUMMER**	*n* pl. -S one that bums
BULLETIN	*v* -ED, -ING, -S to issue a news item	**BUMMING**	present participle of bum
		BUMP	*v* -ED, -ING, -S to knock against
BULLFROG	*n* pl. -S a large frog	**BUMPER**	*v* -ED, -ING, -S to fill to the brim
BULLHEAD	*n* pl. -S a freshwater catfish	**BUMPKIN**	*n* pl. -S an unsophisticated rustic
BULLHORN	*n* pl. -S an electric megaphone		
BULLIED	past tense of bully	**BUMPY**	*adj* BUMPIER, BUMPIEST of uneven surface **BUMPILY** *adv*
BULLIER	comparative of bully		
BULLIES	present 3d person sing. of bully	**BUN**	*n* pl. -S a small bread roll
BULLIEST	superlative of bully	**BUNCH**	*v* -ED, -ING, -ES to group together
BULLION	*n* pl. -S uncoined gold or silver		
BULLISH	*adj* stubborn	**BUNCHY**	*adj* BUNCHIER, BUNCHIEST clustered **BUNCHILY** *adv*
BULLNECK	*n* pl. -S a thick neck		
BULLNOSE	*n* pl. -S a disease of swine	**BUNCO**	*v* -ED, -ING, -S to swindle
BULLOCK	*n* pl. -S a castrated bull **BULLOCKY** *adj*	**BUNCOMBE**	*n* pl. -S nonsense
		BUND	*n* pl. -S a political association

BUNDIST	*n* pl. -S a member of a bund
BUNDLE	*v* -DLED, -DLING, -DLES to fasten a group of objects together
BUNDLER	*n* pl. -S one that bundles
BUNDLING	*n* pl. -S a former courtship custom
BUNG	*v* -ED, -ING, -S to plug with a cork or stopper
BUNGALOW	*n* pl. -S a small cottage
BUNGHOLE	*n* pl. -S a hole in a keg or barrel
BUNGLE	*v* -GLED, -GLING, -GLES to work, make, or do clumsily
BUNGLER	*n* pl. -S one that bungles
BUNGLING	*n* pl. -S an instance of clumsiness
BUNION	*n* pl. -S a painful swelling of the foot
BUNK	*v* -ED, -ING, -S to go to bed
BUNKER	*v* -ED, -ING, -S to store in a large bin
BUNKMATE	*n* pl. -S a person with whom sleeping quarters are shared
BUNKO	*v* -ED, -ING, -S to bunco
BUNKUM	*n* pl. -S nonsense
BUNN	*n* pl. -S bun
BUNNY	*n* pl. -NIES a rabbit
BUNT	*v* -ED, -ING, -S to butt
BUNTER	*n* pl. -S one that bunts
BUNTING	*n* pl. -S a fabric used for flags
BUNTLINE	*n* pl. -S a rope used to haul up a sail
BUNYA	*n* pl. -S an evergreen tree
BUOY	*v* -ED, -ING, -S to mark with a buoy (a warning float)
BUOYAGE	*n* pl. -S a group of buoys
BUOYANCE	*n* pl. -S buoyancy
BUOYANCY	*n* pl. -CIES the tendency to float
BUOYANT	*adj* having buoyancy
BUQSHA	*n* pl. -S a monetary unit of Yemen
BUR	*v* BURRED, BURRING, BURS to burr
BURA	*n* pl. -S buran
BURAN	*n* pl. -S a violent windstorm
BURBLE	*v* -BLED, -BLING, -BLES to speak quickly and excitedly
BURBLER	*n* pl. -S one that burbles
BURBLY	*adj* -BLIER, -BLIEST burbling
BURBOT	*n* pl. -S a freshwater fish
BURD	*n* pl. -S a maiden
BURDEN	*v* -ED, -ING, -S to load heavily
BURDENER	*n* pl. -S one that burdens
BURDIE	*n* pl. -S burd
BURDOCK	*n* pl. -S a coarse weed
BUREAU	*n* pl. -REAUS or -REAUX a chest of drawers
BURET	*n* pl. -S burette
BURETTE	*n* pl. -S a measuring tube
BURG	*n* pl. -S a city or town
BURGAGE	*n* pl. -S a feudal tenure
BURGEE	*n* pl. -S a small flag
BURGEON	*v* -ED, -ING, -S to develop rapidly
BURGER	*n* pl. -S a hamburger
BURGESS	*n* pl. -ES a citizen of an English borough
BURGH	*n* pl. -S a Scottish borough **BURGHAL** *adj*
BURGHER	*n* pl. -S a citizen of a borough
BURGLAR	*n* pl. -S one who commits burglary
BURGLARY	*n* pl. -GLARIES a felonious theft
BURGLE	*v* -GLED, -GLING, -GLES to commit burglary
BURGONET	*n* pl. -S an open helmet
BURGOO	*n* pl. -GOOS a thick oatmeal
BURGOUT	*n* pl. -S burgoo
BURGRAVE	*n* pl. -S a German nobleman
BURGUNDY	*n* pl. -DIES a red wine
BURIAL	*n* pl. -S the act of burying
BURIED	past tense of bury
BURIER	*n* pl. -S one that buries
BURIES	present 3d person sing. of bury
BURIN	*n* pl. -S an engraving tool
BURKE	*v* BURKED, BURKING, BURKES to murder by suffocation
BURKER	*n* pl. -S one that burkes
BURKITE	*n* pl. -S a burker
BURL	*v* -ED, -ING, -S to finish cloth by removing lumps
BURLAP	*n* pl. -S a coarse fabric
BURLER	*n* pl. -S one that burls
BURLESK	*n* pl. -S a type of stage show
BURLEY	*n* pl. -LEYS a light tobacco

BURLY	*adj* -LIER, -LIEST heavy and muscular **BURLILY** *adv*
BURN	*v* BURNED or BURNT, BURNING, BURNS to destroy by fire **BURNABLE** *adj*
BURNER	*n* pl. -S one that burns
BURNET	*n* pl. -S a perennial herb
BURNIE	*n* pl. -S a brooklet
BURNING	*n* pl. -S the firing of ceramic materials
BURNISH	*v* -ED, -ING, -ES to polish
BURNOOSE	*n* pl. -S a hooded cloak
BURNOUS	*n* pl. -ES burnoose
BURNOUT	*n* pl. -S a destructive fire
BURNT	a past tense of burn
BURP	*v* -ED, -ING, -S to belch
BURR	*v* -ED, -ING, -S to remove a rough edge from
BURRED	past tense of bur
BURRER	*n* pl. -S one that burrs
BURRIER	comparative of burry
BURRIEST	superlative of burry
BURRING	present participle of bur
BURRO	*n* pl. -ROS a small donkey
BURROW	*v* -ED, -ING, -S to dig a hole or tunnel in the ground
BURROWER	*n* pl. -S one that burrows
BURRY	*adj* -RIER, -RIEST prickly
BURSA	*n* pl. -SAS or -SAE a bodily pouch **BURSAL** *adj*
BURSAR	*n* pl. -S a college treasurer
BURSARY	*n* pl. -RIES a college treasury
BURSATE	*adj* pertaining to a bursa
BURSE	*n* pl. -S a small bag or pouch
BURSEED	*n* pl. -S a coarse weed
BURSITIS	*n* pl. -TISES inflammation of a bursa
BURST	*v* BURST or BURSTED, BURSTING, BURSTS to break open suddenly or violently
BURSTER	*n* pl. -S one that bursts
BURSTONE	*n* pl. -S a heavy stone
BURTHEN	*v* -ED, -ING, -S to burden
BURTON	*n* pl. -S a hoisting tackle
BURWEED	*n* pl. -S a coarse weed
BURY	*v* BURIED, BURYING, BURIES to put in the ground and cover with earth
BUS	*v* BUSED, BUSING, BUSES or BUSSED, BUSSING, BUSSES to transport by bus (a large motor vehicle)
BUSBOY	*n* pl. -BOYS a waiter's assistant
BUSBY	*n* pl. -BIES a tall fur hat
BUSH	*v* -ED, -ING, -ES to cover with bushes (shrubs)
BUSHBUCK	*n* pl. -S a small antelope
BUSHEL	*v* -ELED, -ELING, -ELS or -ELLED, -ELLING, -ELS to mend clothing
BUSHELER	*n* pl. -S one that bushels
BUSHER	*n* pl. -S a minor league baseball player
BUSHFIRE	*n* pl. -S a fire in a wooded area
BUSHGOAT	*n* pl. -S a bushbuck
BUSHIDO	*n* pl. -DOS the code of the samurai
BUSHIER	comparative of bushy
BUSHIEST	superlative of bushy
BUSHILY	*adv* in a bushy manner
BUSHING	*n* pl. -S a lining for a hole
BUSHLAND	*n* pl. -S unsettled forest land
BUSHLESS	*adj* having no bushes
BUSHLIKE	*adj* resembling a bush
BUSHMAN	*n* pl. -MEN a woodsman
BUSHTIT	*n* pl. -S a titmouse
BUSHY	*adj* BUSHIER, BUSHIEST covered with bushes
BUSIED	past tense of busy
BUSIER	comparative of busy
BUSIES	present 3d person sing. of busy
BUSIEST	superlative of busy
BUSILY	*adv* in a busy manner
BUSINESS	*n* pl. -ES an occupation, profession, or trade
BUSING	*n* pl. -S the act of transporting by bus
BUSK	*v* -ED, -ING, -S to prepare
BUSKER	*n* pl. -S a roaming entertainer
BUSKIN	*n* pl. -S a high shoe **BUSKINED** *adj*
BUSMAN	*n* pl. -MEN a bus operator
BUSS	*v* -ED, -ING, -ES to kiss
BUSSED	a past tense of bus
BUSSES	a present 3d person sing. of bus

BUSSING	*n* pl. -S busing
BUST	*v* -ED, -ING, -S to burst
BUSTARD	*n* pl. -S a game bird
BUSTER	*n* pl. -S one that breaks up something
BUSTIC	*n* pl. -S a tropical tree
BUSTLE	*v* -TLED, -TLING, -TLES to move energetically
BUSTY	*adj* BUSTIER, BUSTIEST full-bosomed
BUSULFAN	*n* pl. -S a medicine
BUSY	*adj* BUSIER, BUSIEST occupied
BUSY	*v* BUSIED, BUSYING, BUSIES to make busy
BUSYBODY	*n* pl. -BODIES a nosy person
BUSYNESS	*n* pl. -ES the state of being busy
BUSYWORK	*n* pl. -S active but valueless work
BUT	*n* pl. -S a flatfish
BUTANE	*n* pl. -S a flammable gas
BUTANOL	*n* pl. -S a flammable alcohol
BUTANONE	*n* pl. -S a flammable ketone
BUTCH	*n* pl. -ES a lesbian with mannish traits
BUTCHER	*v* -ED, -ING, -S to slaughter
BUTCHERY	*n* pl. -ERIES wanton or cruel killing
BUTENE	*n* pl. -S butylene
BUTEO	*n* pl. -TEOS a hawk
BUTLER	*n* pl. -S a male servant
BUTLERY	*n* pl. -LERIES a storage room
BUTT	*v* -ED, -ING, -S to hit with the head
BUTTALS	*n/pl* boundary lines
BUTTE	*n* pl. -S an isolated hill
BUTTER	*v* -ED, -ING, -S to spread with butter (a milk product)
BUTTERY	*adj* -TERIER, -TERIEST containing butter
BUTTERY	*n* pl. -TERIES a wine cellar
BUTTIES	pl. of butty
BUTTOCK	*n* pl. -S either of the two rounded parts of the rump
BUTTON	*v* -ED, -ING, -S to fasten with a button (a small disk)
BUTTONER	*n* pl. -S one that buttons
BUTTONY	*adj* resembling a button
BUTTRESS	*v* -ED, -ING, -ES to prop up
BUTTY	*n* pl. -TIES a fellow workman
BUTUT	*n* pl. -S a unit of Gambian currency
BUTYL	*n* pl. -S a hydrocarbon radical
BUTYLATE	*v* -ATED, -ATING, -ATES to add a butyl to
BUTYLENE	*n* pl. -S a gaseous hydrocarbon
BUTYRAL	*n* pl. -S a chemical compound
BUTYRATE	*n* pl. -S a chemical salt
BUTYRIC	*adj* derived from butter
BUTYRIN	*n* pl. -S a chemical compound
BUTYROUS	*adj* resembling butter
BUTYRYL	*n* pl. -S a radical of butyric acid
BUXOM	*adj* -OMER, -OMEST heathily plump **BUXOMLY** *adv*
BUY	*v* BOUGHT, BUYING, BUYS to purchase **BUYABLE** *adj*
BUYER	*n* pl. -S one that buys
BUZZ	*v* -ED, -ING, -ES to make a vibrating sound
BUZZARD	*n* pl. -S a large bird of prey
BUZZER	*n* pl. -S a signaling device
BUZZWIG	*n* pl. -S a large, thick wig
BUZZWORD	*n* pl. -S a word used to impress someone
BWANA	*n* pl. -S master; boss
BY	*n* pl. BYS a pass in certain card games
BYE	*n* pl. -S a side issue
BYELAW	*n* pl. -S bylaw
BYGONE	*n* pl. -S a past occurrence
BYLAW	*n* pl. -S a secondary law
BYLINE	*v* -LINED, -LINING, -LINES to write under a byline (a line giving the author's name)
BYLINER	*n* pl. -S one that writes under a byline
BYNAME	*n* pl. -S a secondary name
BYPASS	*v* -ED, -ING, -ES to avoid by going around
BYPAST	*adj* past; gone by
BYPATH	*n* pl. -S an indirect road
BYPLAY	*n* pl. -PLAYS secondary action
BYRE	*n* pl. -S a cowshed
BYRL	*v* -ED, -ING, -S to birle
BYRNIE	*n* pl. -S an armored shirt
BYROAD	*n* pl. -S a side road

BYSSUS	*n* pl. BYSSUSES or BYSSI a fine linen
BYSTREET	*n* pl. -S a side street
BYTALK	*n* pl. -S small talk
BYTE	*n* pl. -S a group of adjacent binary digits
BYWAY	*n* pl. -WAYS a side road
BYWORD	*n* pl. -S a well-known saying
BYWORK	*n* pl. -S work done during leisure time
BYZANT	*n* pl. -S bezant

CAB	*n* pl. -S a taxicab	**CABOB**	*n* pl. -S kabob
CABAL	*v* -BALLED, -BALLING, -BALS to conspire	**CABOCHED**	*adj* full-faced — used of an animal's head in heraldry
CABALA	*n* pl. -S an occult or secret doctrine	**CABOCHON**	*n* pl. -S a precious stone
		CABOODLE	*n* pl. -S a collection
CABALISM	*n* pl. -S adherence to a cabala	**CABOOSE**	*n* pl. -S the last car of a freight train
CABALIST	*n* pl. -S one who practices cabalism		
CABALLED	past tense of cabal	**CABOSHED**	*adj* caboched
CABALLING	present participle of cabal	**CABOTAGE**	*n* pl. -S coastal trade
CABANA	*n* pl. -S a small cabin	**CABRESTA**	*n* pl. -S cabestro
CABARET	*n* pl. -S a music hall	**CABRESTO**	*n* pl. -TOS cabestro
CABBAGE	*v* -BAGED, -BAGING, -BAGES to steal	**CABRETTA**	*n* pl. -S a soft leather
		CABRILLA	*n* pl. -S a sea bass
CABBALA	*n* pl. -S cabala	**CABRIOLE**	*n* pl. -S a curved furniture leg
CABBALAH	*n* pl. -S cabala	**CABSTAND**	*n* pl. -S a place where cabs await hire
CABBIE	*n* pl. -S cabby		
CABBY	*n* pl. -BIES a driver of a cab	**CACAO**	*n* pl. -CAOS a tropical tree
CABER	*n* pl. -S a heavy pole thrown as a trial of strength	**CACHALOT**	*n* pl. -S a large whale
		CACHE	*v* CACHED, CACHING, CACHES to store in a hiding place
CABESTRO	*n* pl. -TROS a lasso		
CABEZON	*n* pl. -S a large, edible fish	**CACHEPOT**	*n* pl. -S an ornamental container for a flowerpot
CABEZONE	*n* pl. -S cabezon		
CABILDO	*n* pl. -DOS a town council	**CACHET**	*n* pl. -S an official seal
CABIN	*v* -ED, -ING, -S to live in a cabin (a roughly built house)	**CACHEXIA**	*n* pl. -S general ill health **CACHEXIC** *adj*
CABINET	*n* pl. -S a piece of furniture with shelves and drawers	**CACHEXY**	*n* pl. -CHEXIES cachexia
		CACHING	present participle of cache
CABLE	*v* -BLED, -BLING, -BLES to fasten with a cable (a heavy rope)	**CACHOU**	*n* pl. -S catechu
		CACHUCHA	*n* pl. -S a Spanish dance
		CACIQUE	*n* pl. -S a tropical oriole
CABLET	*n* pl. -S a small cable	**CACKLE**	*v* -LED, -LING, -LES to make the sound of a hen
CABLEWAY	*n* pl. -WAYS a suspended cable		
CABMAN	*n* pl. -MEN a driver of a cab	**CACKLER**	*n* pl. -S one that cackles

CACODYL *n* pl. -S a poisonous liquid

CACOMIXL *n* pl. -S a raccoon-like mammal

CACTUS *n* pl. -TI or -TUSES a plant native to arid regions **CACTOID** *adj*

CAD *n* pl. -S an ungentlemanly man

CADASTER *n* pl. -S a public record of land ownership

CADASTRE *n* pl. -S cadaster

CADAVER *n* pl. -S a corpse

CADDICE *n* pl. -S caddis

CADDIE *v* -DIED, -DYING, -DIES to serve as a golfer's assistant

CADDIS *n* pl. -DISES a coarse woolen fabric

CADDISH *adj* resembling a cad

CADDY *v* -DIED, -DYING, -DIES to caddie

CADE *n* pl. -S a European shrub

CADELLE *n* pl. -S a small, black beetle

CADENCE *v* -DENCED, -DENCING, -DENCES to make rhythmic

CADENCY *n* pl. -CIES a rhythm

CADENT *adj* having rhythm

CADENZA *n* pl. -S an elaborate musical passage

CADET *n* pl. -S a student at a military school

CADGE *v* CADGED, CADGING, CADGES to get by begging

CADGER *n* pl. -S one that cadges

CADGY *adj* cheerful

CADI *n* pl. -S a Muslim judge

CADMIUM *n* pl. -S a metallic element **CADMIC** *adj*

CADRE *n* pl. -S a nucleus of trained personnel

CADUCEUS *n* pl. -CEI a heraldic wand or staff **CADUCEAN** *adj*

CADUCITY *n* pl. -TIES senility

CADUCOUS *adj* transitory; perishable

CAECUM *n* pl. -CA cecum **CAECAL** *adj* **CAECALLY** *adv*

CAEOMA *n* pl. -S a spore-forming organ of a fungus

CAESIUM *n* pl. -S cesium

CAESTUS *n* pl. -ES cestus

CAESURA *n* pl. -RAS or -RAE a pause in a line of verse **CAESURAL**, **CAESURIC** *adj*

CAFE *n* pl. -S a restaurant

CAFFEIN *n* pl. -S caffeine

CAFFEINE *n* pl. -S a bitter alkaloid used as a stimulant

CAFTAN *n* pl. -S a full-length tunic

CAGE *v* CAGED, CAGING, CAGES to confine

CAGELING *n* pl. -S a caged bird

CAGEY *adj* CAGIER, CAGIEST shrewd and careful

CAGIER comparative of cagy

CAGIEST superlative of cagy

CAGILY *adv* in a cagey manner

CAGINESS *n* pl. -ES the quality of being cagey

CAGING present participle of cage

CAGY *adj* CAGIER, CAGIEST cagey

CAHIER *n* pl. -S a notebook

CAHOOT *n* pl. -S partnership

CAHOW *n* pl. -S a sea bird

CAID *n* pl. -S a Muslim leader

CAIMAN *n* pl. -S a tropical reptile

CAIN *n* pl. -S kain

CAIQUE *n* pl. -S a long, narrow rowboat

CAIRD *n* pl. -S a gypsy

CAIRN *n* pl. -S a mound of stones set up as a memorial **CAIRNED**, **CAIRNY** *adj*

CAISSON *n* pl. -S a watertight chamber

CAITIFF *n* pl. -S a despicable person

CAJAPUT *n* pl. -S cajeput

CAJEPUT *n* pl. -S an Australian tree

CAJOLE *v* -JOLED, -JOLING, -JOLES to persuade by flattery

CAJOLER *n* pl. -S one that cajoles

CAJOLERY *n* pl. -ERIES persuasion by flattery

CAJOLING present participle of cajole

CAJON *n* pl. -ES a steep-sided canyon

CAJUPUT *n* pl. -S cajeput

CAKE *v* CAKED, CAKING, CAKES to form into a hardened mass

CAKEWALK *v* -ED, -ING, -S to step stylishly

CALABASH *n* pl. -ES a gourd

CALADIUM *n* pl. -S a tropical plant

CALAMAR *n* pl. -S calamary

CALAMARY *n* pl. -MARIES a squid

CALAMI   pl. of calamus

CALAMINE   v -MINED, -MINING, -MINES to apply an ointment for skin ailments

CALAMINT   n pl. -S a perennial herb

CALAMITE   n pl. -S an extinct treelike plant

CALAMITY   n pl. -TIES a grievous misfortune

CALAMUS   n pl. -MI a marsh plant

CALANDO   adj gradually diminishing

CALASH   n pl. -ES a light carriage

CALATHOS   n pl. -THI a fruit basket

CALATHUS   n pl. -THI calathos

CALCANEA   n/pl calcanei

CALCANEI   n/pl bones of the heel

CALCAR   n pl. -CARIA an anatomical projection

CALCAR   n pl. -S a type of oven

CALCEATE   adj wearing shoes

CALCES   a pl. of calx

CALCIC   adj pertaining to lime or calcium

CALCIFIC   adj containing salts of calcium

CALCIFY   v -FIED, -FYING, -FIES to harden

CALCINE   v -CINED, -CINING, -CINES to reduce to a calx by heat

CALCITE   n pl. -S a mineral **CALCITIC** adj

CALCIUM   n pl. -S a metallic element

CALCSPAR   n pl. -S a calcite

CALCTUFA   n pl. -S a mineral deposit

CALCTUFF   n pl. -S calctufa

CALCULUS   n pl. -LI or -LUSES a branch of mathematics

CALDERA   n pl. -S a large crater

CALDRON   n pl. -S a large kettle or boiler

CALECHE   n pl. -S calash

CALENDAL   adj pertaining to calends

CALENDAR   v -ED, -ING, -S to schedule

CALENDER   v -ED, -ING, -S to smooth by pressing between rollers

CALENDS   n pl. CALENDS the first day of the Roman month

CALESA   n pl. -S a calash

CALF   n pl. CALVES or CALFS a young cow or bull **CALFLIKE** adj

CALFSKIN   n pl. -S the skin of a calf

CALIBER   n pl. -S the diameter of a gun barrel

CALIBRE   n pl. -S caliber **CALIBRED** adj

CALICES   pl. of calix

CALICHE   n pl. -S a mineral deposit

CALICLE   n pl. -S a cup-shaped, anatomical structure

CALICO   n pl. -COES or -COS a cotton fabric

CALIF   n pl. -S caliph

CALIFATE   n pl. -S the domain of a calif

CALIPASH   n pl. -ES an edible part of a turtle

CALIPEE   n pl. -S an edible part of a turtle

CALIPER   v -ED, -ING, -S to use a type of measuring device

CALIPH   n pl. -S a Muslim leader **CALIPHAL** adj

CALISAYA   n pl. -S the medicinal bark of the cinchona

CALIX   n pl. -LICES a cup

CALK   v -ED, -ING, -S to caulk

CALKER   n pl. -S one that calks

CALKIN   n pl. -S a gripping projection on a horseshoe

CALL   v -ED, -ING, -S to summon **CALLABLE** adj

CALLA   n pl. -S a tropical plant

CALLAN   n pl. -S callant

CALLANT   n pl. -S a lad

CALLBACK   n pl. -S a recall of a defective product

CALLBOY   n pl. -BOYS a bellboy

CALLER   n pl. -S one that calls

CALLET   n pl. -S a prostitute

CALLING   n pl. -S a vocation or profession

CALLIOPE   n pl. -S a keyboard musical instrument

CALLIPEE   n pl. -S calipee

CALLIPER   v -ED, -ING, -S to caliper

CALLOSE   n pl. -S a part of a plant cell wall

CALLOUS   v -ED, -ING, -ES to make or become hard

CALLOW   adj -LOWER, -LOWEST immature

CALLUS   v -ED, -ING, -ES to form a hard growth

CALM   adj CALMER, CALMEST free from agitation **CALMLY** adv

CALM   v -ED, -ING, -S to make calm

CALMNESS *n* pl. -ES the state of being calm

CALOMEL *n* pl. -S a chemical compound used as a purgative

CALORIC *n* pl. -S heat

CALORIE *n* pl. -S a unit of heat

CALORY *n* pl. -RIES calorie

CALOTTE *n* pl. -S a skullcap

CALOYER *n* pl. -S a monk of the Eastern Church

CALPAC *n* pl. -S a sheepskin hat

CALPACK *n* pl. -S calpac

CALQUE *v* CALQUED, CALQUING, CALQUES to model a word's meaning upon that of an analogous word in another language

CALTHROP *n* pl. -S caltrop

CALTRAP *n* pl. -S caltrop

CALTROP *n* pl. -S a spiny plant

CALUMET *n* pl. -S a ceremonial pipe

CALUMNY *n* pl. -NIES a false and malicious accusation

CALUTRON *n* pl. -S a device used for separating isotopes

CALVADOS *n* pl. -ES a dry apple brandy

CALVARIA *n* pl. -S the dome of the skull

CALVARY *n* pl. -RIES a representation of the Crucifixion

CALVE *v* CALVED, CALVING, CALVES to give birth to a calf

CALVES a pl. of calf

CALX *n* pl. -ES or CALCES a mineral residue

CALYCATE *adj* calycine

CALYCEAL *adj* calycine

CALYCES a pl. of calyx

CALYCINE *adj* pertaining to a calyx

CALYCLE *n* pl. -S an outer calyx

CALYCULI *n/pl* small, cup-shaped structures

CALYPSO *n* pl. -SOS or -SOES an improvised song

CALYPTER *n* pl. -S calyptra

CALYPTRA *n* pl. -S a hood-shaped organ of flowers

CALYX *n* pl. -LYXES or -LYCES the outer protective covering of a flower

CAM *n* pl. -S a rotating or sliding piece of machinery

CAMAIL *n* pl. -S a piece of armor for the neck **CAMAILED** *adj*

CAMAS *n* pl. -ES camass

CAMASS *n* pl. -ES a perennial herb

CAMBER *v* -ED, -ING, -S to arch slightly

CAMBIA a pl. of cambium

CAMBIAL *adj* pertaining to cambium

CAMBISM *n* pl. -S the theory and practice of exchange in commerce

CAMBIST *n* pl. -S a dealer in bills of exchange

CAMBIUM *n* pl. -BIUMS or -BIA a layer of plant tissue

CAMBOGIA *n* pl. -S a gum resin

CAMBRIC *n* pl. -S a fine linen

CAME *n* pl. -S a leaden window rod

CAMEL *n* pl. -S a large, humped mammal

CAMELEER *n* pl. -S a camel driver

CAMELIA *n* pl. -S camellia

CAMELLIA *n* pl. -S a tropical shrub

CAMEO *v* -ED, -ING, -S to portray in sharp, delicate relief

CAMERA *n* pl. -ERAS or -ERAE a judge's chamber **CAMERAL** *adj*

CAMION *n* pl. -S a military truck

CAMISA *n* pl. -S a shirt or chemise

CAMISADE *n* pl. -S camisado

CAMISADO *n* pl. -DOS or -DOES an attack made at night

CAMISE *n* pl. -S a loose shirt or gown

CAMISIA *n* pl. -S camise

CAMISOLE *n* pl. -S a brief negligee

CAMLET *n* pl. -S a durable fabric

CAMOMILE *n* pl. -S a medicinal herb

CAMORRA *n* pl. -S an unscrupulous secret society

CAMP *v* -ED, -ING, -S to live in the open

CAMPAGNA *n* pl. -PAGNE a flat, open plain

CAMPAIGN *v* -ED, -ING, -S to conduct a series of operations to reach a specific goal

CAMPER *n* pl. -S one that camps

CAMPFIRE *n* pl. -S an outdoor fire

CAMPHENE *n* pl. -S camphine

CAMPHINE	n pl. -S an explosive liquid	**CANCEL**	v -CELLED, -CELLING, -CELS or -CELED, -CELING, -CELS to annul
CAMPHOL	n pl. -S borneol		
CAMPHOR	n pl. -S a volatile compound	**CANCELER**	n pl. -S one that cancels
CAMPI	pl. of campo	**CANCER**	n pl. -S a malignant growth
CAMPIER	comparative of campy	**CANCHA**	n pl. -S a jai alai court
CAMPIEST	superlative of campy	**CANCROID**	n pl. -S a skin cancer
CAMPILY	adv in a campy manner	**CANDELA**	n pl. -S a unit of luminous intensity
CAMPING	n pl. -S the act of living outdoors		
		CANDENT	adj glowing
CAMPION	n pl. -S an herb	**CANDID**	adj -DIDER, -DIDEST frank and sincere
CAMPO	n pl. -PI an open space in a town		
		CANDID	n pl. -S an unposed photograph
CAMPO	n pl. -POS a level, grassy plain	**CANDIDA**	n pl. -S a parasitic fungus
CAMPONG	n pl. -S kampong	**CANDIDLY**	adv in a candid manner
CAMPOREE	n pl. -S a gathering of Boy Scouts	**CANDIED**	past tense of candy
		CANDIES	present 3d person sing. of candy
CAMPSITE	n pl. -S an area suitable for camping		
		CANDLE	v -DLED, -DLING, -DLES to examine eggs in front of a light
CAMPUS	n pl. -ES the grounds of a school		
		CANDLER	n pl. -S one that candles
CAMPY	adj CAMPIER, CAMPIEST comically exaggerated	**CANDOR**	n pl. -S frankness; sincerity
		CANDOUR	n pl. -S candor
CAMSHAFT	n pl. -S a shaft fitted with cams	**CANDY**	v -DIED, -DYING, -DIES to coat with sugar
CAN	v CANNED, CANNING, CANS to put in a can (a cylindrical container)		
		CANE	v CANED, CANING, CANES to beat with a rod
CAN	v present sing. 2d person CAN or CANST, past sing. 2d person COULD, COULDEST, or COULDST — used as an auxiliary to express ability	**CANELLA**	n pl. -S a medicinal tree bark
		CANER	n pl. -S one that canes
		CANEWARE	n pl. -S a yellowish stoneware
		CANFIELD	n pl. -S a card game
CANAILLE	n pl. -S the common people	**CANFUL**	n pl. CANFULS or CANSFUL as much as a can holds
CANAKIN	n pl. -S cannikin		
CANAL	v -NALLED, -NALLING, -NALS or -NALED, -NALING, -NALS to dig an artificial waterway through	**CANGUE**	n pl. -S an ancient Chinese punishing device
		CANIKIN	n pl. -S cannikin
CANALISE	v -ISED, -ISING, -ISES to canalize	**CANINE**	n pl. -S a dog
		CANING	present participle of cane
CANALIZE	v -IZED, -IZING, -IZES to canal	**CANINITY**	n pl. -TIES the state of being a canine
CANALLED	a past tense of canal		
CANALLER	n pl. -S a freight boat	**CANISTER**	n pl. -S a small, metal box
CANALLING	a present participle of canal	**CANITIES**	n pl. CANITIES the turning gray of the hair
CANAPE	n pl. -S a food served before a meal		
		CANKER	v -ED, -ING, -S to affect with ulcerous sores
CANARD	n pl. -S a false story		
CANARY	n pl. -NARIES a songbird	**CANNA**	n pl. -S a tropical plant
CANASTA	n pl. -S a card game	**CANNABIC**	adj pertaining to cannabis
CANCAN	n pl. -S a dance marked by high kicking	**CANNABIN**	n pl. -S a resin extracted from cannabis

CANNABIS *n* pl. -BISES hemp

CANNED past tense of can

CANNEL *n* pl. -S an oily, compact coal

CANNELON *n* pl. -S a stuffed roll

CANNER *n* pl. -S one that cans food

CANNERY *n* pl. -NERIES a place where food is canned

CANNIBAL *n* pl. -S one who eats his own kind

CANNIE *adj* -NIER, -NIEST canny

CANNIER comparative of canny

CANNIEST superlative of canny

CANNIKIN *n* pl. -S a small can or cup

CANNILY *adv* in a canny manner

CANNING *n* pl. -S the business of preserving food in airtight containers

CANNON *v* -ED, -ING, -S to fire a cannon (a heavy firearm)

CANNONRY *n* pl. -RIES artillery

CANNOT the negative form of can

CANNULA *n* pl. -LAS or -LAE a tube inserted into a bodily cavity **CANNULAR** *adj*

CANNY *adj* -NIER, -NIEST prudent

CANOE *v* -NOED, -NOEING, -NOES to paddle a canoe (a light, slender boat)

CANOEIST *n* pl. -S one who canoes

CANON *n* pl. -S a law decreed by a church council **CANONIC** *adj*

CANONESS *n* pl. -ES a woman who lives according to a canon

CANONISE *v* -ISED, -ISING, -ISES to canonize

CANONIST *n* pl. -S a specialist in canon law

CANONIZE *v* -IZED, -IZING, -IZES to declare to be a saint

CANONRY *n* pl. -RIES a clerical office

CANOPY *v* -PIED, -PYING, -PIES to cover from above

CANOROUS *adj* melodic

CANSFUL a pl. of canful

CANSO *n* pl. -SOS a love song

CANST a present 2d person sing. of can

CANT *v* -ED, -ING, -S to tilt or slant

CANTALA *n* pl. -S a tropical plant

CANTATA *n* pl. -S a vocal composition

CANTDOG *n* pl. -S a device used to move logs

CANTEEN *n* pl. -S a small container for carrying water

CANTER *v* -ED, -ING, -S to ride a horse at a moderate pace

CANTHUS *n* pl. -THI a corner of the eye **CANTHAL** *adj*

CANTIC *adj* slanted

CANTICLE *n* pl. -S a hymn

CANTINA *n* pl. -S a saloon

CANTLE *n* pl. -S the rear part of a saddle

CANTO *n* pl. -TOS a division of a long poem

CANTON *v* -ED, -ING, -S to divide into cantons (districts)

CANTONAL *adj* pertaining to a canton

CANTOR *n* pl. -S a religious singer

CANTRAIP *n* pl. -S cantrip

CANTRAP *n* pl. -S cantrip

CANTRIP *n* pl. -S a magic spell

CANTUS *n* pl. CANTUS a style of church music

CANTY *adj* cheerful

CANULA *n* pl. -LAS or -LAE cannula

CANULATE *v* -LATED, -LATING, -LATES to insert a canula into

CANVAS *v* -ED, -ING, -ES to canvass

CANVASER *n* pl. -S one that canvases

CANVASS *v* -ED, -ING, -ES to examine thoroughly

CANYON *n* pl. -S a deep valley with steep sides

CANZONA *n* pl. -S canzone

CANZONE *n* pl. -NI or -NES a form of lyric poetry

CANZONET *n* pl. -S a short song

CAP *v* CAPPED, CAPPING, CAPS to provide with a cap (a type of head covering)

CAPABLE *adj* -BLER, -BLEST having ability **CAPABLY** *adv*

CAPACITY *n* pl. -TIES the ability to receive or contain

CAPE *n* pl. -S a sleeveless garment **CAPED** *adj*

CAPELAN *n* pl. -S capelin

CAPELET *n* pl. -S a small cape

CAPELIN	*n* pl. -S a small, edible fish	**CAPSTONE**	*n* pl. -S the top stone of a structure
CAPER	*v* -ED, -ING, -S to frolic		
CAPERER	*n* pl. -S one that capers	**CAPSULAR**	*adj* enclosed and compact
CAPESKIN	*n* pl. -S a soft leather	**CAPSULE**	*v* -SULED, -SULING, -SULES to condense into a brief form
CAPEWORK	*n* pl. -S a bullfighting technique		
CAPFUL	*n* pl. -S as much as a cap can hold	**CAPTAIN**	*v* -ED, -ING, -S to lead or command
		CAPTAN	*n* pl. -S a fungicide
CAPH	*n* pl. -S kaph	**CAPTION**	*v* -ED, -ING, -S to provide with a title
CAPIAS	*n* pl. -ES a judicial writ		
CAPITA	pl. of caput	**CAPTIOUS**	*adj* tending to find fault
CAPITAL	*n* pl. -S the upper part of a column	**CAPTIVE**	*n* pl. -S a prisoner
		CAPTOR	*n* pl. -S one who takes or holds a captive
CAPITATE	*adj* head-shaped		
CAPITOL	*n* pl. -S a building occupied by a state legislature	**CAPTURE**	*v* -TURED, -TURING, -TURES to take by force or cunning
CAPITULA	*n/pl* flower clusters	**CAPTURER**	*n* pl. -S one that captures
CAPLESS	*adj* being without a cap	**CAPUCHE**	*n* pl. -S a hood or cowl **CAPUCHED** *adj*
CAPLIN	*n* pl. -S capelin		
CAPMAKER	*n* pl. -S one that makes caps	**CAPUCHIN**	*n* pl. -S a long-tailed monkey
CAPO	*n* pl. -POS a pitch raising device for fretted instruments	**CAPUT**	*n* pl. CAPITA a head or head-like part
CAPON	*n* pl. -S a gelded rooster	**CAPYBARA**	*n* pl. -S a large rodent
CAPONIER	*n* pl. -S a type of defense	**CAR**	*n* pl. -S an automobile
CAPONIZE	*v* -IZED, -IZING, -IZES to geld a rooster	**CARABAO**	*n* pl. -BAOS a water buffalo
		CARABID	*n* pl. -S a predatory beetle
CAPORAL	*n* pl. -S a coarse tobacco	**CARABIN**	*n* pl. -S carbine
CAPOTE	*n* pl. -S a hooded cloak or overcoat	**CARABINE**	*n* pl. -S carbine
		CARACAL	*n* pl. -S an African lynx
CAPOUCH	*n* pl. -ES capuche	**CARACARA**	*n* pl. -S a large hawk
CAPPED	past tense of cap	**CARACK**	*n* pl. -S carrack
CAPPER	*n* pl. -S a capmaker	**CARACOL**	*v* -COLLED, -COLLING, -COLS to caracole
CAPPING	*n* pl. -S a wax covering in a honeycomb		
CAPRIC	*adj* pertaining to a goat	**CARACOLE**	*v* -COLED, -COLING, -COLES to perform a half turn on a horse
CAPRICCI	*n/pl* caprices	**CARACUL**	*n* pl. -S karakul
CAPRICE	*n* pl. -S a whim	**CARAFE**	*n* pl. -S a glass bottle
CAPRIFIG	*n* pl. -S a European tree	**CARAGANA**	*n* pl. -S an Asian shrub
CAPRINE	*adj* capric	**CARAGEEN**	*n* pl. -S an edible seaweed
CAPRIOLE	*v* -OLED, -OLING, -OLES to leap	**CARAMEL**	*n* pl. -S a chewy candy
CAPSICIN	*n* pl. -S a liquid used as a flavoring	**CARANGID**	*n* pl. -S a marine fish
		CARAPACE	*n* pl. -S a hard, protective outer covering
CAPSICUM	*n* pl. -S a tropical herb		
CAPSID	*n* pl. -S the outer shell of a virus particle **CAPSIDAL** *adj*	**CARAPAX**	*n* pl. -ES carapace
		CARASSOW	*n* pl. -S curassow
CAPSIZE	*v* -SIZED, -SIZING, -SIZES to overturn	**CARAT**	*n* pl. -S a unit of weight for gems
CAPSTAN	*n* pl. -S a machine used to hoist weights	**CARATE**	*n* pl. -S a tropical skin disease

CARAVAN	*v* -VANED, -VANING, -VANS or -VANNED, -VANNING, -VANS to travel in a group
CARAVEL	*n* pl. -S a small sailing ship
CARAWAY	*n* pl. -WAYS an herb used in cooking
CARBAMIC	*adj* pertaining to a type of acid
CARBAMYL	*n* pl. -S a chemical radical
CARBARN	*n* pl. -S a garage for buses
CARBARYL	*n* pl. -S an insecticide
CARBIDE	*n* pl. -S a carbon compound
CARBINE	*n* pl. -S a light rifle
CARBINOL	*n* pl. -S an alcohol
CARBON	*n* pl. -S a nonmetallic element **CARBONIC** *adj*
CARBONYL	*n* pl. -S a chemical compound
CARBORA	*n* pl. -S a wood-boring worm
CARBOXYL	*n* pl. -S a univalent acid radical
CARBOY	*n* pl. -BOYS a bottle enclosed in a protective basket **CARBOYED** *adj*
CARBURET	*v* -RETED, -RETING, -RETS or -RETTED, -RETTING, -RETS to combine chemically with carbon
CARCAJOU	*n* pl. -S a carnivorous mammal
CARCANET	*n* pl. -S a jeweled necklace
CARCASE	*n* pl. -S carcass
CARCASS	*n* pl. -ES the body of a dead animal
CARCEL	*n* pl. -S a unit of illumination
CARD	*v* -ED, -ING, -S to provide with a card (a stiff piece of paper)
CARDAMOM	*n* pl. -S a tropical herb
CARDAMON	*n* pl. -S cardamom
CARDAMUM	*n* pl. -S cardamom
CARDCASE	*n* pl. -S a case for holding cards
CARDER	*n* pl. -S one that does carding
CARDIA	*n* pl. -DIAS or -DIAE an opening of the esophagus
CARDIAC	*n* pl. -S a person with a heart disorder
CARDIGAN	*n* pl. -S a type of sweater
CARDINAL	*n* pl. -S a high-ranking official of the Roman Catholic Church
CARDING	*n* pl. -S the process of combing and cleaning cotton fibers; cleaned and combed fibers
CARDIOID	*n* pl. -S a heart-shaped curve
CARDITIS	*n* pl. -TISES inflammation of the heart **CARDITIC** *adj*
CARDOON	*n* pl. -S a perennial plant
CARE	*v* CARED, CARING, CARES to be concerned or interested
CAREEN	*v* -ED, -ING, -S to lurch while moving
CAREENER	*n* pl. -S one that careens
CAREER	*v* -ED, -ING, -S to go at full speed
CAREERER	*n* pl. -S one that careers
CAREFREE	*adj* being without worry or anxiety
CAREFUL	*adj* -FULLER, -FULLEST cautious
CARELESS	*adj* inattentive; negligent
CARER	*n* pl. -S one that cares
CARESS	*v* -ED, -ING, -ES to touch lovingly
CARESSER	*n* pl. -S one that caresses
CARET	*n* pl. -S a proofreaders' symbol
CAREWORN	*adj* haggard
CAREX	*n* pl. CARICES a marsh plant
CARFARE	*n* pl. -S payment for a bus or car ride
CARFUL	*n* pl. -S as much as a car can hold
CARGO	*n* pl. -GOS or -GOES conveyed merchandise
CARHOP	*n* pl. -S a waitress at a drive-in restaurant
CARIBE	*n* pl. -S the piranha
CARIBOU	*n* pl. -S a large deer
CARICES	pl. of carex
CARIES	*n* pl. CARIES tooth decay **CARIED** *adj*
CARILLON	*v* -LONNED, -LONNING, -LONS to play a set of bells
CARINA	*n* pl. -NAS or -NAE a carinate anatomical part **CARINAL** *adj*
CARINATE	*adj* shaped like the keel of a ship
CARING	present participle of care
CARIOCA	*n* pl. -S a South American dance
CARIOLE	*n* pl. -S a small, open carriage
CARIOUS	*adj* decayed
CARK	*v* -ED, -ING, -S to worry
CARL	*n* pl. -S a peasant
CARLE	*n* pl. -S carl
CARLESS	*adj* being without a car

CARLIN	*n* pl. -S an old woman
CARLINE	*n* pl. -S carling
CARLING	*n* pl. -S a beam supporting a ship's deck
CARLISH	*adj* resembling a carl
CARLOAD	*n* pl. -S as much as a car can hold
CARMAKER	*n* pl. -S an automobile manufacturer
CARMAN	*n* pl. -MEN a streetcar driver
CARMINE	*n* pl. -S a vivid red color
CARN	*n* pl. -S cairn
CARNAGE	*n* pl. -S great and bloody slaughter
CARNAL	*adj* pertaining to bodily appetites **CARNALLY** *adv*
CARNAUBA	*n* pl. -S a palm tree
CARNEY	*n* pl. -NEYS carny
CARNIE	*n* pl. -S carny
CARNIES	pl. of carny
CARNIFY	*v* -FIED, -FYING, -FIES to form into flesh
CARNIVAL	*n* pl. -S a traveling amusement show
CARNY	*n* pl. -NIES a carnival
CAROACH	*n* pl. -ES caroche
CAROB	*n* pl. -S an evergreen tree
CAROCH	*n* pl. -ES caroche
CAROCHE	*n* pl. -S a stately carriage
CAROL	*v* -OLED, -OLING, -OLS or -OLLED, -OLLING, -OLS to sing joyously
CAROLER	*n* pl. -S one that carols
CAROLI	a pl. of carolus
CAROLLED	a past tense of carol
CAROLLER	*n* pl. -S caroler
CAROLLING	a present participle of carol
CAROLUS	*n* pl. -LUSES or -LI an old English coin
CAROM	*v* -ED, -ING, -S to collide with and rebound
CAROTENE	*n* pl. -S a plant pigment
CAROTID	*n* pl. -S an artery in the neck
CAROTIN	*n* pl. -S carotene
CAROUSAL	*n* pl. -S a boisterous drinking party
CAROUSE	*v* -ROUSED, -ROUSING, -ROUSES to engage in a carousal
CAROUSEL	*n* pl. -S an amusement park ride
CAROUSER	*n* pl. -S one that carouses
CAROUSING	present participle of carouse
CARP	*v* -ED, -ING, -S to find fault unreasonably
CARPAL	*n* pl. -S carpale
CARPALE	*n* pl. -LIA a bone of the wrist
CARPEL	*n* pl. -S a simple pistil
CARPER	*n* pl. -S one that carps
CARPET	*v* -ED, -ING, -S to cover a floor with a heavy fabric
CARPI	pl. of carpus
CARPING	*n* pl. -S the act of one who carps
CARPORT	*n* pl. -S a shelter for a car
CARPUS	*n* pl. -PI the wrist
CARRACK	*n* pl. -S a type of merchant ship
CARREL	*n* pl. -S a desk in a library stack for solitary study
CARRELL	*n* pl. -S carrel
CARRIAGE	*n* pl. -S a wheeled, horse-drawn vehicle
CARRIED	past tense of carry
CARRIER	*n* pl. -S one that carries
CARRIES	present 3d person sing. of carry
CARRIOLE	*n* pl. -S cariole
CARRION	*n* pl. -S dead and putrefying flesh
CARRITCH	*n* pl. -ES a religious handbook
CARROCH	*n* pl. -ES caroche
CARROM	*v* -ED, -ING, -S to carom
CARROT	*n* pl. -S an edible orange root
CARROTIN	*n* pl. -S carotene
CARROTY	*adj* -ROTIER, -ROTIEST resembling a carrot in color
CARRY	*v* -RIED, -RYING, -RIES to convey from one place to another
CARRYALL	*n* pl. -S a light covered carriage
CARRYON	*n* pl. -S a small piece of luggage
CARRYOUT	*n* pl. -S a take-out order of food
CARSE	*n* pl. -S low, fertile land along a river
CARSICK	*adj* nauseated from riding in a car

CART *v* -ED, -ING, -S to convey in a cart (a two-wheeled vehicle) **CARTABLE** *adj*

CARTAGE *n* pl. -S the act of carting

CARTE *n* pl. -S a menu

CARTEL *n* pl. -S a business organization

CARTER *n* pl. -S one that carts

CARTLOAD *n* pl. -S as much as a cart can hold

CARTON *v* -ED, -ING, -S to pack in a cardboard box

CARTOON *v* -ED, -ING, -S to sketch a humorous representation of

CARTOP *adj* able to fit on top of a car

CARTOUCH *n* pl. -ES a scroll-like tablet

CARUNCLE *n* pl. -S a fleshy outgrowth

CARVE *v* CARVED, CARVING, CARVES to form by cutting

CARVEL *n* pl. -S caravel

CARVEN *adj* carved

CARVER *n* pl. -S one that carves

CARVING *n* pl. -S a carved figure or design

CARYATID *n* pl. -S or -ES a sculptured female figure used as a column

CARYOTIN *n* pl. -S karyotin

CASA *n* pl. -S a dwelling

CASABA *n* pl. -S a variety of melon

CASAVA *n* pl. -S cassava

CASCABEL *n* pl. -S the rear part of a cannon

CASCABLE *n* pl. -S cascabel

CASCADE *v* -CADED, -CADING, -CADES to fall like a waterfall

CASCARA *n* pl. -S a medicinal tree bark

CASE *v* CASED, CASING, CASES to put in a case (a container or receptacle)

CASEASE *n* pl. -S an enzyme

CASEATE *v* -ATED, -ATING, -ATES to become cheesy

CASEBOOK *n* pl. -S a law textbook

CASED past tense of case

CASEFY *v* -FIED, -FYING, -FIES to caseate

CASEIN *n* pl. -S a milk protein **CASEIC** *adj*

CASEMATE *n* pl. -S a bombproof shelter

CASEMENT *n* pl. -S a type of window

CASEOSE *n* pl. -S a proteose

CASEOUS *adj* cheesy

CASERN *n* pl. -S a barracks for soldiers

CASERNE *n* pl. -S casern

CASETTE *n* pl. -S cassette

CASEWORK *n* pl. -S a form of social work

CASEWORM *n* pl. -S an insect larva

CASH *v* -ED, -ING, -ES to convert into cash (ready money) **CASHABLE** *adj*

CASHAW *n* pl. -S cushaw

CASHBOOK *n* pl. -S a book of monetary records

CASHBOX *n* pl. -ES a container for money

CASHEW *n* pl. -S a nut-bearing tree

CASHIER *v* -ED, -ING, -S to dismiss in disgrace

CASHLESS *adj* having no cash

CASHMERE *n* pl. -S a fine wool

CASHOO *n* pl. -SHOOS catechu

CASIMERE *n* pl. -S a woolen fabric

CASIMIRE *n* pl. -S casimere

CASING *n* pl. -S a protective outer covering

CASINO *n* pl. -NOS a gambling room

CASK *v* -ED, -ING, -S to store in a cask (a strong barrel)

CASKET *v* -ED, -ING, -S to place in a burial case

CASKY *adj* resembling a cask

CASQUE *n* pl. -S a helmet **CASQUED** *adj*

CASSABA *n* pl. -S casaba

CASSAVA *n* pl. -S a tropical plant

CASSETTE *n* pl. -S a small case containing audiotape or videotape

CASSIA *n* pl. -S a variety of cinnamon

CASSINO *n* pl. -NOS a card game

CASSIS *n* pl. -SISES a European bush

CASSOCK *n* pl. -S a long garment worn by clergymen

CAST *v* CAST, CASTING, CASTS to throw with force

CASTANET *n* pl. -S a rhythm instrument

CASTAWAY *n* pl. -WAYS an outcast

CASTE *n* pl. -S a system of distinct social classes

CASTEISM *n* pl. -S the use of a caste system

CASTER	*n* pl. -S a small, swiveling wheel
CASTING	*n* pl. -S something made in a mold
CASTLE	*v* -TLED, -TLING, -TLES to make a certain move in chess
CASTOFF	*n* pl. -S a discarded person or thing
CASTOR	*n* pl. -S caster
CASTRATE	*v* -TRATED, -TRATING, -TRATES to remove the testes of
CASTRATO	*n* pl. -TI a singer castrated in boyhood
CASUAL	*n* pl. -S one who works occasionally
CASUALLY	*adv* informally
CASUALTY	*n* pl. -TIES a victim of war or disaster
CASUIST	*n* pl. -S one who resolves ethical problems
CASUS	*n* pl. CASUS a legal occurrence or event
CAT	*v* CATTED, CATTING, CATS to hoist an anchor to the cathead
CATACOMB	*n* pl. -S an underground cemetery
CATALASE	*n* pl. -S an enzyme
CATALO	*n* pl. -LOS or -LOES a hybrid between a buffalo and a cow
CATALOG	*v* -ED, -ING, -S to classify information descriptively
CATALPA	*n* pl. -S a tree
CATALYST	*n* pl. -S a substance that accelerates a chemical reaction
CATALYZE	*v* -LYZED, -LYZING, -LYZES to act as a catalyst
CATAMITE	*n* pl. -S a boy used in sodomy
CATAPULT	*v* -ED, -ING, -S to hurl through the air
CATARACT	*n* pl. -S a tremendous waterfall
CATARRH	*n* pl. -S inflammation of a mucous membrane
CATBIRD	*n* pl. -S a songbird
CATBOAT	*n* pl. -S a small sailboat
CATBRIER	*n* pl. -S a thorny vine
CATCALL	*v* -ED, -ING, -S to deride by making shrill sounds
CATCH	*v* CAUGHT, CATCHING, CATCHES to capture after pursuit
CATCHALL	*n* pl. -S a container for odds and ends

CATCHER	*n* pl. -S one that catches
CATCHFLY	*n* pl. -FLIES an insect-catching plant
CATCHUP	*n* pl. -S ketchup
CATCHY	*adj* CATCHIER, CATCHIEST pleasing and easily remembered
CATE	*n* pl. -S a choice food
CATECHIN	*n* pl. -S a chemical used in dyeing
CATECHOL	*n* pl. -S a chemical used in photography
CATECHU	*n* pl. -S a resin used in tanning
CATEGORY	*n* pl. -RIES a division in any system of classification
CATENA	*n* pl. -NAS or -NAE a closely linked series
CATENARY	*n* pl. -NARIES a mathematical curve
CATENATE	*v* -NATED, -NATING, -NATES to link together
CATENOID	*n* pl. -S a geometric surface
CATER	*v* -ED, -ING, -S to provide food and service for
CATERAN	*n* pl. -S a brigand
CATERER	*n* pl. -S one that caters
CATERESS	*n* pl. -ES a woman who caters
CATFACE	*n* pl. -S a deformity of fruit
CATFALL	*n* pl. -S an anchor line
CATFISH	*n* pl. -ES a scaleless, large-headed fish
CATGUT	*n* pl. -S a strong cord
CATHEAD	*n* pl. -S a beam projecting from a ship's bow
CATHECT	*v* -ED, -ING, -S to invest with psychic energy
CATHEDRA	*n* pl. -DRAS or -DRAE a bishop's throne
CATHETER	*n* pl. -S a medical instrument
CATHEXIS	*n* pl. -THEXES the concentration of psychic energy on a person or idea
CATHODE	*n* pl. -S a negatively charged electrode **CATHODIC** *adj*
CATHOLIC	*adj* universal
CATHOUSE	*n* pl. -S a brothel
CATION	*n* pl. -S a positively charged ion **CATIONIC** *adj*
CATKIN	*n* pl. -S a flower cluster
CATLIKE	*adj* resembling a cat; stealthy; silent

CATLIN	*n* pl. -S catling
CATLING	*n* pl. -S a surgical knife
CATMINT	*n* pl. -S catnip
CATNAP	*v* -NAPPED, -NAPPING, -NAPS to doze
CATNAPER	*n* pl. -S one that steals cats
CATNIP	*n* pl. -S an aromatic herb
CATSPAW	*n* pl. -S a light wind
CATSUP	*n* pl. -S ketchup
CATTAIL	*n* pl. -S a marsh plant
CATTALO	*n* pl. -LOS or -LOES catalo
CATTED	past tense of cat
CATTIE	*n* pl. -S an Asian unit of weight
CATTIER	comparative of catty
CATTIEST	superlative of catty
CATTILY	*adv* in a catty manner
CATTING	present participle of cat
CATTISH	*adj* catty
CATTLE	*n/pl* domesticated bovines
CATTLEYA	*n* pl. -S a tropical orchid
CATTY	*adj* -TIER, -TIEST catlike; spiteful
CATWALK	*n* pl. -S a narrow walkway
CAUCUS	*v* -CUSED, -CUSING, -CUSES or -CUSSED, -CUSSING, -CUSSES to hold a political meeting
CAUDAD	*adv* toward the tail
CAUDAL	*adj* taillike **CAUDALLY** *adv*
CAUDATE	*adj* having a tail
CAUDATED	*adj* caudate
CAUDEX	*n* pl. -DICES or -DEXES the woody base of some plants
CAUDILLO	*n* pl. -LLOS a military dictator
CAUDLE	*n* pl. -S a warm beverage
CAUGHT	past tense of catch
CAUL	*n* pl. -S a fetal membrane
CAULD	*n* pl. -S cold
CAULDRON	*n* pl. -S caldron
CAULES	pl. of caulis
CAULICLE	*n* pl. -S a small stem
CAULINE	*adj* pertaining to a stem
CAULIS	*n* pl. -LES a plant stem
CAULK	*v* -ED, -ING, -S to make the seams of a ship watertight
CAULKER	*n* pl. -S one that caulks

CAULKING	*n* pl. -S the material used to caulk
CAUSABLE	*adj* capable of being caused
CAUSAL	*n* pl. -S a word expressing cause or reason
CAUSALLY	*adv* by way of causing
CAUSE	*v* CAUSED, CAUSING, CAUSES to bring about
CAUSER	*n* pl. -S one that causes
CAUSERIE	*n* pl. -S an informal conversation
CAUSEWAY	*v* -ED, -ING, -S to build a raised roadway over
CAUSEY	*n* pl. -SEYS a paved road
CAUSING	present participle of cause
CAUSTIC	*n* pl. -S a corrosive substance
CAUTERY	*n* pl. -TERIES something used to destroy tissue
CAUTION	*v* -ED, -ING, -S to warn
CAUTIOUS	*adj* exercising prudence to avoid danger
CAVALERO	*n* pl. -ROS a horseman
CAVALIER	*v* -ED, -ING, -S to behave haughtily
CAVALLA	*n* pl. -S a large food fish
CAVALLY	*n* pl. -LIES cavalla
CAVALRY	*n* pl. -RIES a mobile army unit
CAVATINA	*n* pl. -NAS or -NE a simple song
CAVE	*v* CAVED, CAVING, CAVES to hollow out
CAVEAT	*n* pl. -S a legal warning
CAVEATOR	*n* pl. -S one that files a caveat
CAVED	past tense of cave
CAVEFISH	*n* pl. -ES a sightless fish
CAVELIKE	*adj* resembling a cave (an underground chamber)
CAVEMAN	*n* pl. -MEN a cave dweller
CAVER	*n* pl. -S one that caves
CAVERN	*v* -ED, -ING, -S to hollow out
CAVETTO	*n* pl. -TOS or -TI a concave molding
CAVIAR	*n* pl. -S the roe of sturgeon
CAVIARE	*n* pl. -S caviar
CAVICORN	*adj* having hollow horns
CAVIE	*n* pl. -S a hencoop
CAVIES	pl. of cavy
CAVIL	*v* -ILED, -ILING, -ILS or -ILLED, -ILLING, -ILS to carp

CAVILER	n pl. -S one that cavils	**CELEB**	n pl. -S a celebrity; a famous person
CAVILLER	n pl. -S caviler	**CELERIAC**	n pl. -S a variety of celery
CAVILLING	a present participle of cavil	**CELERITY**	n pl. -TIES swiftness
CAVING	present participle of cave	**CELERY**	n pl. -ERIES a plant with edible stalks
CAVITARY	adj pertaining to the formation of cavities in tissue		
CAVITATE	v -TATED, -TATING, -TATES to form cavities	**CELESTA**	n pl. -S a keyboard instrument
		CELESTE	n pl. -S celesta
CAVITY	n pl. -TIES an unfilled space within a mass **CAVITIED** adj	**CELIAC**	adj pertaining to the abdomen
		CELIBACY	n pl. -CIES abstention from sexual intercourse
CAVORT	v -ED, -ING, -S to frolic		
CAVORTER	n pl. -S one that cavorts	**CELIBATE**	n pl. -S one who lives a life of celibacy
CAVY	n pl. -VIES a short-tailed rodent		
CAW	v -ED, -ING, -S to utter the sound of a crow	**CELL**	v -ED, -ING, -S to store in a honeycomb
		CELLA	n pl. -LAE the interior of an ancient temple
CAY	n pl. CAYS a small, low island		
CAYENNE	n pl. -S a hot seasoning **CAYENNED** adj	**CELLAR**	v -ED, ING, -S to store in an underground room
CAYMAN	n pl. -S caiman	**CELLARER**	n pl. -S the steward of a monastery
CAYUSE	n pl. -S an Indian pony		
CAZIQUE	n pl. -S cacique	**CELLARET**	n pl. -S a cabinet for wine bottles
CEASE	v CEASED, CEASING, CEASES to stop	**CELLIST**	n pl. -S one who plays the cello
CEBID	n pl. -S ceboid	**CELLO**	n pl. -LOS or -LI a stringed musical instrument
CEBOID	n pl. -S one of a family of monkeys		
		CELLULAR	adj pertaining to a cell (a basic unit of life)
CECUM	n pl. CECA a bodily cavity with one opening **CECAL** adj **CECALLY** adv	**CELLULE**	n pl. -S a small cell
		CELOM	n pl. -LOMS or -LOMATA coelom
CEDAR	n pl. -S an evergreen tree **CEDARN** adj	**CELT**	n pl. -S a primitive ax
CEDE	v CEDED, CEDING, CEDES to yield	**CEMBALO**	n pl. -LI or -LOS a harpsichord
		CEMENT	v -ED, -ING, -S to bind firmly
CEDER	n pl. -S one that cedes	**CEMENTER**	n pl. -S one that cements
CEDI	n pl. -S a monetary unit of Ghana	**CEMENTUM**	n pl. -TA the hard tissue covering the roots of the teeth
CEDILLA	n pl. -S a pronunciation mark	**CEMETERY**	n pl. -TERIES a burial ground
CEDING	present participle of cede	**CENACLE**	n pl. -S a small dining room
CEDULA	n pl. -S a Philippine tax	**CENOBITE**	n pl. -S a member of a religious order
CEE	n pl. -S the letter C		
CEIBA	n pl. -S a tropical tree	**CENOTAPH**	n pl. -S an empty tomb
CEIL	v -ED, -ING, -S to furnish with a ceiling	**CENOTE**	n pl. -S a sinkhole in limestone
		CENSE	v CENSED, CENSING, CENSES to perfume with incense
CEILER	n pl. -S one that ceils		
CEILING	n pl. -S the overhead lining of a room	**CENSER**	n pl. -S a vessel for burning incense
CEINTURE	n pl. -S a belt for the waist	**CENSOR**	v -ED, -ING, -S to delete an objectionable word or passage
CELADON	n pl. -S a pale green color		

CENSUAL	*adj* pertaining to the act of censusing
CENSURE	*v* -SURED, -SURING, -SURES to criticize severely
CENSURER	*n* pl. -S one that censures
CENSUS	*n* -ED, -ING, -ES to take an official count of
CENT	*n* pl. -S the 100th part of a dollar
CENTAL	*n* pl. -S a unit of weight
CENTARE	*n* pl. -S a measure of land area
CENTAUR	*n* pl. -S a mythological creature
CENTAURY	*n* pl. -RIES a medicinal herb
CENTAVO	*n* pl. -VOS a coin of various Spanish-American nations
CENTER	*v* -ED, -ING, -S to place at the center (the midpoint)
CENTESIS	*n* pl. -TESES a surgical puncture
CENTIARE	*n* pl. -S centare
CENTILE	*n* pl. -S a value of a statistical variable
CENTIME	*n* pl. -S the 100th part of a franc
CENTIMO	*n* pl. -MOS any of various small coins
CENTNER	*n* pl. -S a unit of weight
CENTO	*n* pl. -TONES or -TOS a literary work made up of parts from other works
CENTRA	a pl. of centrum
CENTRAL	*n* pl. -S a telephone exchange
CENTRAL	*adj* -TRALER, -TRALEST situated at, in, or near the center
CENTRE	*n* -TRED, -TRING, -TRES to center
CENTRIC	*adj* situated at the center
CENTRING	*n* pl. -S a temporary framework for an arch
CENTRISM	*n* pl. -S moderate political philosophy
CENTRIST	*n* pl. -S an advocate of centrism
CENTROID	*n* pl. -S the center of mass of an object
CENTRUM	*n* pl. -TRUMS or -TRA the body of a vertebra
CENTUM	*n* pl. -S one hundred
CENTUPLE	*v* -PLED, -PLING, -PLES to increase a hundredfold
CENTURY	*n* pl. -RIES a period of 100 years
CEORL	*n* pl. -S a freeman of low birth **CEORLISH** *adj*
CEPHALAD	*adv* toward the head
CEPHALIC	*adj* pertaining to the head
CEPHALIN	*n* pl. -S a bodily chemical
CERAMAL	*n* pl. -S a heat-resistant alloy
CERAMIC	*n* pl. -S an item made of baked clay
CERAMIST	*n* pl. -S one who makes ceramics
CERASTES	*n* pl. CERASTES a venomous snake
CERATE	*n* pl. -S a medicated ointment
CERATED	*adj* covered with wax
CERATIN	*n* pl. -S keratin
CERATOID	*adj* hornlike
CERCARIA	*n* pl. -IAE or -IAS a parasitic worm
CERCIS	*n* pl. -CISES a shrub
CERCUS	*n* pl. CERCI a sensory appendage of an insect
CERE	*v* CERED, CERING, CERES to wrap in a waxy cloth
CEREAL	*n* pl. -S a food made from grain
CEREBRAL	*n* pl. -S a kind of consonant
CEREBRUM	*n* pl. -BRUMS or -BRA a part of the brain **CEREBRIC** *adj*
CERED	past tense of cere
CEREMENT	*n* pl. -S a waxy cloth
CEREMONY	*n* pl. -NIES a formal observance
CEREUS	*n* pl. -ES a tall cactus
CERIA	*n* pl. -S a chemical compound
CERIC	*adj* containing cerium
CERING	present participle of cere
CERIPH	*n* pl. -S serif
CERISE	*n* pl. -S a red color
CERITE	*n* pl. -S a mineral
CERIUM	*n* pl. -S a metallic element
CERMET	*n* pl. -S ceramal
CERNUOUS	*adj* drooping or nodding
CERO	*n* pl. CEROS a large food fish
CEROTIC	*adj* pertaining to beeswax
CEROTYPE	*n* pl. -S a process of engraving using wax
CEROUS	*adj* pertaining to cerium

CERTAIN	adj -TAINER, -TAINEST absolutely confident	**CHAFE**	v CHAFED, CHAFING, CHAFES to warm by rubbing
CERTES	adv in truth	**CHAFER**	n pl. -S a large beetle
CERTIFY	v -FIED, -FYING, -FIES to confirm	**CHAFF**	v -ED, -ING, -S to poke fun at
		CHAFFER	v -ED, -ING, -S to bargain or haggle
CERULEAN	n pl. -S a blue color		
CERUMEN	n pl. -S a waxy secretion of the ear	**CHAFFY**	adj CHAFFIER, CHAFFIEST worthless
		CHAFING	present participle of chafe
CERUSE	n pl. -S a lead compound	**CHAGRIN**	v -GRINED, -GRINING, -GRINS or -GRINNED, -GRINNING, -GRINS to humiliate
CERUSITE	n pl. -S a lead ore		
CERVELAT	n pl. -S a smoked sausage		
CERVICAL	adj pertaining to the cervix	**CHAIN**	v -ED, -ING, -S to bind with a chain (a series of connected rings)
CERVINE	adj pertaining to deer		
CERVIX	n pl. -VICES or -VIXES the neck	**CHAINE**	n pl. -S a series of ballet turns
CESAREAN	n pl. -S a method of child delivery	**CHAINMAN**	n pl. -MEN a surveyor's assistant who uses a measuring chain
CESARIAN	n pl. -S cesarean		
CESIUM	n pl. -S a metallic element	**CHAIR**	v -ED, -ING, -S to install in office
CESS	v -ED, -ING, -ES to tax or assess		
		CHAIRMAN	n pl. -MEN the presiding officer of a meeting
CESSION	n pl. -S the act of ceding		
CESSPIT	n pl. -S a cesspool	**CHAIRMAN**	v -MANED, -MANING, -MANS or -MANNED, -MANNING, -MANS to act as chairman of
CESSPOOL	n pl. -S a covered well or pit for sewage		
		CHAISE	n pl. -S a light carriage
CESTA	n pl. -S a basket used in jai alai	**CHALAH**	n pl. -LAHS, -LOTH or -LOT challah
CESTI	pl. of cestus		
CESTODE	n pl. -S a tapeworm	**CHALAZA**	n pl. -ZAS or -ZAE a band of tissue in an egg **CHALAZAL** adj
CESTOID	n pl. -S cestode		
CESTOS	n pl. -TOI cestus	**CHALCID**	n pl. -S a tiny fly
CESTUS	n pl. -TI a belt or girdle	**CHALDRON**	n pl. -S a unit of dry measure
CESTUS	n pl. -ES a hand covering for ancient Roman boxers	**CHALEH**	n pl. -S challah
		CHALET	n pl. -S a Swiss cottage
CESURA	n pl. -RAS or -RAE caesura	**CHALICE**	n pl. -S a drinking cup **CHALICED** adj
CETACEAN	n pl. -S an aquatic mammal	**CHALK**	v -ED, -ING, -S to mark with chalk (a soft limestone)
CETANE	n pl. -S a diesel fuel		
CETE	n pl. -S a group of badgers	**CHALKY**	adj CHALKIER, CHALKIEST resembling chalk
CETOLOGY	n pl. -GIES the study of whales		
CHABOUK	n pl. -S a type of whip	**CHALLAH**	n pl. -LAHS, -LOTH, or -LOT a kind of bread
CHABUK	n pl. -S chabouk		
CHACMA	n pl. -S a large baboon	**CHALLIE**	n pl. -S challis
CHACONNE	n pl. -S an ancient dance	**CHALLIES**	pl. of chally
CHAD	n pl. -S a scrap of paper **CHADLESS** adj	**CHALLIS**	n pl. -LISES a light fabric
		CHALLOT	a pl. of challah
CHADARIM	a pl. of cheder	**CHALLOTH**	a pl. of challah
CHAETA	n pl. -TAE a bristle or seta **CHAETAL** adj	**CHALLY**	n pl. -LIES challis
		CHALONE	n pl. -S a hormone

CHALOT	a pl. of chalah
CHALOTH	a pl. of chalah
CHALUTZ	*n* pl. -LUTZIM halutz
CHAM	*n* pl. -S a khan
CHAMADE	*n* pl. -S a signal made with a drum
CHAMBER	*v* -ED, -ING, -S to put in a chamber (a room)
CHAMBRAY	*n* pl. -BRAYS a fine fabric
CHAMFER	*v* -ED, -ING, -S to groove
CHAMFRON	*n* pl. -S armor for a horse's head
CHAMISE	*n* pl. -S chamiso
CHAMISO	*n* pl. -SOS a flowering shrub
CHAMMY	*v* -MIED, -MYING, -MIES to chamois
CHAMOIS	*n* pl. -OIX a soft leather
CHAMOIS	*v* -ED, -ING, -ES to prepare leather like chamois
CHAMP	*v* -ED, -ING, -S to chew noisily
CHAMPAC	*n* pl. -S champak
CHAMPAK	*n* pl. -S an East Indian tree
CHAMPER	*n* pl. -S one that champs
CHAMPION	*v* -ED, -ING, -S to defend or support
CHAMPY	*adj* broken up by the trampling of beasts
CHANCE	*v* CHANCED, CHANCING, CHANCES to risk
CHANCEL	*n* pl. -S an area around a church altar
CHANCERY	*n* pl. -CERIES a court of public record
CHANCIER	comparative of chancy
CHANCIEST	superlative of chancy
CHANCILY	*adv* in a chancy manner
CHANCING	present participle of chance
CHANCRE	*n* pl. -S a hard-based sore
CHANCY	*adj* CHANCIER, CHANCIEST risky
CHANDLER	*n* pl. -S a dealer in provisions
CHANFRON	*n* pl. -S chamfron
CHANG	*n* pl. -S a cattie
CHANGE	*v* CHANGED, CHANGING, CHANGES to make different
CHANGER	*n* pl. -S one that changes
CHANNEL	*v* -NELED, -NELING, -NELS or -NELLED, -NELLING, -NELS to direct along some desired course
CHANSON	*n* pl. -S a song
CHANT	*v* -ED, -ING, -S to sing
CHANTAGE	*n* pl. -S blackmail
CHANTER	*n* pl. -S one that chants
CHANTEY	*n* pl. -TEYS a sailor's song
CHANTIES	pl. of chanty
CHANTOR	*n* pl. -S chanter
CHANTRY	*n* pl. -TRIES an endowment given to a church
CHANTY	*n* pl. -TIES chantey
CHAOS	*n* pl. -ES a state of total disorder; a confused mass **CHAOTIC** *adj*
CHAP	*v* CHAPPED or CHAPT, CHAPPING, CHAPS to split, crack, or redden
CHAPBOOK	*n* pl. -S a small book of popular tales
CHAPE	*n* pl. -S a part of a scabbard
CHAPEAU	*n* pl. -PEAUX or -PEAUS a hat
CHAPEL	*n* pl. -S a place of worship
CHAPERON	*v* -ED, -ING, -S to accompany
CHAPITER	*n* pl. -S the capital of a column
CHAPLAIN	*n* pl. -S a clergyman attached to a chapel
CHAPLET	*n* pl. -S a wreath for the head
CHAPMAN	*n* pl. -MEN a peddler
CHAPPED	a past tense of chap
CHAPPING	present participle of chap
CHAPT	a past tense of chap
CHAPTER	*v* -ED, -ING, -S to divide a book into main sections
CHAQUETA	*n* pl. -S a jacket worn by cowboys
CHAR	*v* CHARRED, CHARRING, CHARS to burn slightly
CHARACID	*n* pl. -S characin
CHARACIN	*n* pl. -S a tropical fish
CHARADE	*n* pl. -S a word represented by pantomime
CHARAS	*n* pl. -ES hashish
CHARCOAL	*v* -ED, -ING, -S to blacken with charcoal (a dark, porous carbon)
CHARD	*n* pl. -S a variety of beet

CHARE v CHARED, CHARING, CHARES to do small jobs

CHARGE v CHARGED, CHARGING, CHARGES to accuse formally

CHARGER n pl. -S one that charges

CHARIER comparative of chary

CHARIEST superlative of chary

CHARILY adv in a chary manner

CHARING present participle of chare

CHARIOT v -ED, -ING, -S to ride in a type of cart

CHARISM n pl. -S charisma

CHARISMA n pl. -MATA a special magnetic appeal

CHARITY n pl. -TIES something given to the needy

CHARK v -ED, -ING, -S to char

CHARKA n pl. -S charkha

CHARKHA n pl. -S a spinning wheel

CHARLADY n pl. -DIES a cleaning woman

CHARLOCK n pl. -S a troublesome weed

CHARM v -ED, -ING, -S to attract irresistibly

CHARMER n pl. -S one that charms

CHARMING adj -INGER, -INGEST pleasing

CHARNEL n pl. -S a room where corpses are placed

CHARPAI n pl. -S charpoy

CHARPOY n pl. -POYS a bed used in India

CHARQUI n pl. -S a type of meat **CHARQUID** adj

CHARR n pl. -S a small-scaled trout

CHARRED past tense of char

CHARRIER comparative of charry

CHARRIEST superlative of charry

CHARRING present participle of char

CHARRO n pl. -ROS a cowboy

CHARRY adj -RIER, -RIEST resembling charcoal

CHART v -ED, -ING, -S to map out

CHARTER v -ED, -ING, -S to lease or hire

CHARTIST n pl. -S a stock market specialist

CHARY adj CHARIER, CHARIEST cautious

CHASE v CHASED, CHASING, CHASES to pursue

CHASER n pl. -S one that chases

CHASING n pl. -S a design engraved on metal

CHASM n pl. -S a deep cleft in the earth **CHASMAL, CHASMED, CHASMIC, CHASMY** adj

CHASSE v CHASSED, CHASSEING, CHASSES to perform a dance movement

CHASSEUR n pl. -S a cavalry soldier

CHASSIS n pl. CHASSIS the frame of a car

CHASTE adj CHASTER, CHASTEST morally pure **CHASTELY** adv

CHASTEN v -ED, -ING, -S to chastise

CHASTISE v -TISED, -TISING, -TISES to discipline by punishment

CHASTITY n pl. -TIES moral purity

CHASUBLE n pl. -S a sleeveless vestment

CHAT v CHATTED, CHATTING, CHATS to converse informally

CHATEAU n pl. -TEAUX or -TEAUS a large country house

CHATTEL n pl. -S a slave

CHATTER v -ED, -ING, -S to talk rapidly and trivially **CHATTERY** adj

CHATTING present participle of chat

CHATTY adj -TIER, -TIEST talkative **CHATTILY** adv

CHAUFER n pl. -S chauffer

CHAUFFER n pl. -S a small furnace

CHAUNT v -ED, -ING, -S to chant

CHAUNTER n pl. -S one that chaunts

CHAUSSES n/pl medieval armor

CHAW v -ED, -ING, -S to chew

CHAWER n pl. -S one that chaws

CHAYOTE n pl. -S a tropical vine

CHAZAN n pl. -ZANS or -ZANIM a cantor

CHAZZEN n pl. -ZENS or -ZENIM chazan

CHEAP adj CHEAPER, CHEAPEST inexpensive

CHEAP n pl. -S a market

CHEAPEN v -ED, -ING, -S to make cheap

CHEAPIE n pl. -S one that is cheap

CHEAPISH adj somewhat cheap

CHEAPLY adv in a cheap manner

CHEAT v -ED, -ING, -S to defraud

CHEATER n pl. -S one that cheats

CHEBEC n pl. -S a small bird

CHECHAKO _n_ pl. -KOS a newcomer

CHECK _v_ -ED, -ING, -S to inspect

CHECKER _v_ -ED, -ING, -S to mark with squares

CHECKOFF _n_ pl. -S a method of collecting union dues

CHECKOUT _n_ pl. -S a test of a machine

CHECKROW _v_ -ED, -ING, -S to plant in rows which divide the land into squares

CHECKUP _n_ pl. -S an examination

CHEDDAR _n_ pl. -S a type of cheese

CHEDDITE _n_ pl. -S chedite

CHEDER _n_ pl. CHADARIM or CHEDERS heder

CHEDITE _n_ pl. -S an explosive

CHEEK _v_ -ED, -ING, -S to speak impudently to

CHEEKFUL _n_ pl. -S the amount held in one's cheek

CHEEKY _adj_ CHEEKIER, CHEEKIEST impudent **CHEEKILY** _adv_

CHEEP _v_ -ED, -ING, -S to chirp

CHEEPER _n_ pl. -S one that cheeps

CHEER _v_ -ED, -ING, -S to applaud with shouts of approval

CHEERER _n_ pl. -S one that cheers

CHEERFUL _adj_ -FULLER, -FULLEST full of spirits

CHEERIER comparative of cheery

CHEERIEST superlative of cheery

CHEERILY _adv_ in a cheery manner

CHEERIO _n_ pl. -IOS a greeting

CHEERO _n_ pl. CHEEROS cheerio

CHEERY _adj_ CHEERIER, CHEERIEST cheerful

CHEESE _v_ CHEESED, CHEESING, CHEESES to stop

CHEESY _adj_ CHEESIER, CHEESIEST resembling cheese (a food made from milk curds) **CHEESILY** _adv_

CHEETAH _n_ pl. -S a swift-running wildcat

CHEF _n_ pl. -S a chief cook

CHEFDOM _n_ pl. -S the status or function of a chef

CHEGOE _n_ pl. -S chigoe

CHELA _n_ pl. -LAE a pincerlike claw

CHELA _n_ pl. -S a pupil of a guru

CHELATE _v_ -LATED, -LATING, -LATES to subject a compound to combination with a metal ion

CHELATOR _n_ pl. -S one that chelates

CHELOID _n_ pl. -S keloid

CHEMIC _n_ pl. -S a chemist

CHEMICAL _n_ pl. -S a substance obtained by a process of chemistry (the science of the various properties and transformations of substances)

CHEMISE _n_ pl. -S a loose dress

CHEMISM _n_ pl. -S chemical attraction

CHEMIST _n_ pl. -S one versed in chemistry

CHEMURGY _n_ pl. -GIES a branch of applied chemistry

CHENILLE _n_ pl. -S a soft fabric

CHENOPOD _n_ pl. -S a flowering plant

CHEQUE _n_ pl. -S a written order directing a bank to pay money

CHEQUER _v_ -ED, -ING, -S to checker

CHERISH _v_ -ED, -ING, -ES to hold dear

CHEROOT _n_ pl. -S a square-cut cigar

CHERRY _n_ pl. -RIES a fruit

CHERT _n_ pl. -S a compact rock

CHERTY _adj_ CHERTIER, CHERTIEST resembling chert

CHERUB _n_ pl. -UBS or -UBIM an angel **CHERUBIC** _adj_

CHERVIL _n_ pl. -S an aromatic herb

CHESS _n_ pl. -ES a weed

CHESSMAN _n_ pl. -MEN one of the pieces used in chess (a board game for two players)

CHEST _n_ pl. -S a part of the body **CHESTED** _adj_

CHESTFUL _n_ pl. -S as much as a chest or box can hold

CHESTNUT _n_ pl. -S an edible nut

CHESTY _adj_ CHESTIER, CHESTIEST proud

CHETAH _n_ pl. -S cheetah

CHETH _n_ pl. -S heth

CHEVALET _n_ pl. -S a part of a stringed instrument

CHEVERON _n_ pl. -S chevron

CHEVIED past tense of chevy

CHEVIES present 3d person sing. of chevy

CHEVIOT	*n* pl. -S a coarse fabric
CHEVRON	*n* pl. -S a V-shaped pattern
CHEVY	*v* CHEVIED, CHEVYING, CHEVIES to chase about
CHEW	*v* -ED, -ING, -S to crush or grind with the teeth **CHEWABLE** *adj*
CHEWER	*n* pl. -S one that chews
CHEWINK	*n* pl. -S a common finch
CHEWY	*adj* CHEWIER, CHEWIEST not easily chewed
CHEZ	*prep* at the home of
CHI	*n* pl. -S a Greek letter
CHIA	*n* pl. -S a Mexican herb
CHIAO	*n* pl. CHIAO a monetary unit of China
CHIASM	*n* pl. -S chiasma
CHIASMA	*n* pl. -MATA or -MAS an anatomical junction **CHIASMAL, CHIASMIC** *adj*
CHIASMUS	*n* pl. -MI a reversal of word order between parallel phrases **CHIASTIC** *adj*
CHIAUS	*n* pl. -ES a Turkish messenger
CHIBOUK	*n* pl. -S a tobacco pipe
CHIC	*n* pl. -S elegance
CHICANE	*v* -CANED, -CANING, -CANES to trick
CHICANER	*n* pl. -S one that chicanes
CHICCORY	*n* pl. -RIES chicory
CHICHI	*n* pl. -S elaborate ornamentation
CHICK	*n* pl. -S a young bird
CHICKEN	*v* -ED, -ING, -S to lose one's nerve
CHICKPEA	*n* pl. -S an Asian herb
CHICLE	*n* pl. -S a tree gum
CHICLY	*adv* in an elegant manner
CHICNESS	*n* pl. -ES elegance
CHICO	*n* pl. -COS a prickly shrub
CHICORY	*n* pl. -RIES a perennial herb
CHIDE	*v* CHIDED or CHID, CHIDDEN, CHIDING, CHIDES to scold
CHIDER	*n* pl. -S one that chides
CHIEF	*adj* CHIEFER, CHIEFEST highest in authority
CHIEF	*n* pl. -S the person highest in authority
CHIEFDOM	*n* pl. -S the domain of a chief
CHIEFLY	*adv* above all
CHIEL	*n* pl. -S chield
CHIELD	*n* pl. -S a young man
CHIFFON	*n* pl. -S a sheer fabric
CHIGETAI	*n* pl. -S a wild ass
CHIGGER	*n* pl. -S a parasitic mite
CHIGNON	*n* pl. -S a woman's hairdo
CHIGOE	*n* pl. -S a tropical flea
CHILD	*n* pl. CHILDREN a young person
CHILDBED	*n* pl. -S the state of a woman giving birth
CHILDE	*n* pl. -S a youth of noble birth
CHILDING	*adj* pregnant
CHILDISH	*adj* resembling a child
CHILDLY	*adj* -LIER, -LIEST resembling a child
CHILDREN	pl. of child
CHILE	*n* pl. -S chili
CHILI	*n* pl. -ES a hot pepper
CHILIAD	*n* pl. -S a group of one thousand
CHILIASM	*n* pl. -S a religious doctrine
CHILIAST	*n* pl. -S a supporter of chiliasm
CHILL	*v* -ED, -ING, -S to make cold
CHILL	*adj* CHILLER, CHILLEST cool
CHILLER	*n* pl. -S one that chills
CHILLI	*n* pl. -ES chili
CHILLUM	*n* pl. -S a part of a water pipe
CHILLY	*adj* CHILLIER, CHILLIEST cool **CHILLILY** *adv*
CHILOPOD	*n* pl. -S a multi-legged insect
CHIMAERA	*n* pl. -S a marine fish
CHIMAR	*n* pl. -S chimere
CHIMB	*n* pl. -S the rim of a cask
CHIMBLEY	*n* pl. -BLEYS chimley
CHIMBLY	*n* pl. -BLIES chimley
CHIME	*v* CHIMED, CHIMING, CHIMES to ring harmoniously
CHIMER	*n* pl. -S one that chimes
CHIMERA	*n* pl. -S an imaginary monster
CHIMERE	*n* pl. -S a bishop's robe
CHIMERIC	*adj* imaginary; unreal
CHIMING	present participle of chime
CHIMLA	*n* pl. -S chimley
CHIMLEY	*n* pl. -LEYS a chimney
CHIMNEY	*n* pl. -NEYS a flue
CHIMP	*n* pl. -S a chimpanzee

CHIN	v CHINNED, CHINNING, CHINS to hold with the chin (the lower part of the face)	**CHIRRUP**	v -ED, -ING, -S to chirp repeatedly **CHIRRUPY** adj
CHINA	n pl. -S fine porcelain ware	**CHISEL**	v -ELED, -ELING, -ELS or -ELLED, -ELLING, -ELS to use a chisel (a cutting tool)
CHINBONE	n pl. -S the lower jaw		
CHINCH	n pl. -ES a bedbug	**CHISELER**	n pl. -S one that chisels
CHINCHY	adj CHINCHIER, CHINCHIEST stingy	**CHIT**	n pl. -S a short letter
		CHITAL	n pl. CHITAL an Asian deer
CHINE	v CHINED, CHINING, CHINES to cut through the backbone of	**CHITCHAT**	v -CHATTED, -CHATTING, -CHATS to indulge in small talk
CHINK	v -ED, -ING, -S to fill cracks or fissures in	**CHITIN**	n pl. -S the main component of insect shells
CHINKY	adj CHINKIER, CHINKIEST full of cracks	**CHITLIN**	n pl. -S chitling
		CHITLING	n pl. -S a part of the small intestine of swine
CHINLESS	adj lacking a chin	**CHITON**	n pl. -S a tunic worn in ancient Greece
CHINNED	past tense of chin		
CHINNING	present participle of chin	**CHITTER**	v -ED, -ING, -S to twitter
CHINO	n pl. -NOS a strong fabric	**CHITTY**	n pl. -TIES a chit
CHINONE	n pl. -S quinone	**CHIVALRY**	n pl. -RIES knightly behavior and skill
CHINOOK	n pl. -S a warm wind		
CHINTS	n pl. -ES chintz	**CHIVAREE**	v -REED, -REEING, -REES to perform a mock serenade
CHINTZ	n pl. -ES a cotton fabric		
CHINTZY	adj CHINTZIER, CHINTZIEST gaudy; cheap	**CHIVARI**	v -ED, -ING, -S to chivaree
		CHIVE	n pl. -S an herb used as a seasoning
CHIP	v CHIPPED, CHIPPING, CHIPS to break a small piece from		
		CHIVVY	v -VIED, -VYING, -VIES to chevy
CHIPMUCK	n pl. -S a chipmunk	**CHIVY**	v CHIVIED, CHIVYING, CHIVIES to chevy
CHIPMUNK	n pl. -S a small rodent		
CHIPPED	past tense of chip	**CHLAMYS**	n pl. -MYSES or -MYDES a garment worn in ancient Greece
CHIPPER	v -ED, -ING, -S to chirp		
CHIPPIE	n pl. -S chippy	**CHLORAL**	n pl. -S a chemical compound
CHIPPING	present participle of chip	**CHLORATE**	n pl. -S a chemical salt
CHIPPY	n pl. -PIES a prostitute	**CHLORDAN**	n pl. -S a toxic compound of chlorine
CHIRK	v -ED, -ING, -S to make a shrill noise		
		CHLORIC	adj pertaining to chlorine
CHIRK	adj CHIRKER, CHIRKEST cheerful	**CHLORID**	n pl. -S chloride
		CHLORIDE	n pl. -S a chlorine compound
CHIRM	v -ED, -ING, -S to chirp	**CHLORIN**	n pl. -S chlorine
CHIRO	n pl. -ROS a marine fish	**CHLORINE**	n pl. -S a gaseous element
CHIRP	v -ED, -ING, -S to utter a short, shrill sound	**CHLORITE**	n pl. -S a mineral group
		CHLOROUS	adj pertaining to chlorine
CHIRPER	n pl. -S one that chirps	**CHOCK**	v -ED, -ING, -S to secure with a wedge of wood or metal
CHIRPY	adj CHIRPIER, CHIRPIEST cheerful **CHIRPILY** adv		
CHIRR	v -ED, -ING, -S to make a harsh, vibrant sound	**CHOICE**	n pl. -S one that is chosen
		CHOICE	adj CHOICER, CHOICEST of fine quality **CHOICELY** adv
CHIRRE	v CHIRRED, CHIRRING, CHIRRES to chirr		
		CHOIR	v -ED, -ING, -S to sing in unison

CHOIRBOY *n* pl. -BOYS a boy who sings in a body of church singers

CHOKE *v* CHOKED, CHOKING, CHOKES to impede the breathing of

CHOKER *n* pl. -S one that chokes

CHOKEY *adj* CHOKIER, CHOKIEST choky

CHOKING present participle of choke

CHOKY *adj* CHOKIER, CHOKIEST tending to cause choking

CHOLATE *n* pl. -S a chemical salt

CHOLER *n* pl. -S anger

CHOLERA *n* pl. -S an acute disease

CHOLERIC *adj* bad-tempered

CHOLINE *n* pl. -S a B vitamin

CHOLLA *n* pl. -S a treelike cactus

CHOMP *v* -ED, -ING, -S to champ

CHON *n* pl. CHON a monetary unit of South Korea

CHOOSE *v* CHOSE, CHOSEN, CHOOSING, CHOOSES to take by preference

CHOOSER *n* pl. -S one that chooses

CHOOSEY *adj* CHOOSIER, CHOOSIEST choosy

CHOOSING present participle of choose

CHOOSY *adj* CHOOSIER, CHOOSIEST hard to please

CHOP *v* CHOPPED, CHOPPING, CHOPS to sever with a sharp tool

CHOPIN *n* pl. -S chopine

CHOPINE *n* pl. -S a type of shoe

CHOPPED past tense of chop

CHOPPER *n* pl. -S one that chops

CHOPPING present participle of chop

CHOPPY *adj* CHOPPIER, CHOPPIEST full of short, rough waves **CHOPPILY** *adv*

CHORAGUS *n* pl. -GI or -GUSES the leader of a chorus or choir **CHORAGIC** *adj*

CHORAL *n* pl. -S chorale

CHORALE *n* pl. -S a hymn that is sung in unison

CHORALLY *adv* harmoniously

CHORD *v* -ED, -ING, -S to play a chord (a combination of three or more musical tones)

CHORDAL *adj* pertaining to a chord

CHORDATE *n* pl. -S any of a large phylum of animals

CHORE *v* CHORED, CHORING, CHORES to do small jobs

CHOREA *n* pl. -S a nervous disorder **CHOREAL, CHOREIC** *adj*

CHOREGUS *n* pl. -GI or -GUSES choragus

CHOREMAN *n* pl. -MEN a menial worker

CHOREOID *adj* resembling chorea

CHORIAL *adj* pertaining to the chorion

CHORIAMB *n* pl. -S a type of metrical foot

CHORIC *adj* pertaining to a chorus

CHORINE *n* pl. -S a chorus girl

CHORING present participle of chore

CHORIOID *n* pl. -S choroid

CHORION *n* pl. -S an embryonic membrane

CHORIZO *n* pl. -ZOS a highly seasoned sausage

CHOROID *n* pl. -S a membrane of the eye

CHORTLE *v* -TLED, -TLING, -TLES to chuckle with glee

CHORTLER *n* pl. -S one that chortles

CHORUS *v* -RUSED, -RUSING, -RUSES or -RUSSED, -RUSSING, -RUSSES to sing in unison

CHOSE *n* pl. -S an item of personal property

CHOSEN past participle of choose

CHOTT *n* pl. -S a saline lake

CHOUGH *n* pl. -S a crow-like bird

CHOUSE *v* CHOUSED, CHOUSING, CHOUSES to swindle

CHOUSER *n* pl. -S one that chouses

CHOUSH *n* pl. -ES chiaus

CHOUSING present participle of chouse

CHOW *v* -ED, -ING, -S to eat

CHOWCHOW *n* pl. -S a relish of mixed pickles in mustard

CHOWDER *v* -ED, -ING, -S to make a thick soup of

CHOWSE *v* CHOWSED, CHOWSING, CHOWSES to chouse

CHOWTIME *n* pl. -S mealtime

CHRESARD *n* pl. -S the available water of the soil

CHRISM *n* pl. -S a consecrated oil **CHRISMAL** *adj*

CHRISMON *n* pl. -MA or -MONS a Christian monogram

CHRISOM *n* pl. -S chrism

CHRISTEN   v -ED, -ING, -S to baptize

CHRISTIE   n pl. -S christy

CHRISTY   n pl. -TIES a skiing turn

CHROMA   n pl. -S the purity of a color

CHROMATE   n pl. -S a chemical salt

CHROME   v CHROMED, CHROMING, CHROMES to plate with chromium

CHROMIC   adj pertaining to chromium

CHROMIDE   n pl. -S a tropical fish

CHROMING   present participle of chrome

CHROMITE   n pl. -S a chromium ore

CHROMIUM   n pl. -S a metallic element

CHROMIZE   v -MIZED, -MIZING, -MIZES to chrome

CHROMO   n pl. -MOS a type of color picture

CHROMOUS   adj pertaining to chromium

CHROMYL   adj containing chromium

CHRONAXY   n pl. -AXIES the time required to excite a nerve cell electrically

CHRONIC   n pl. -S one that suffers from a long-lasting disease

CHRONON   n pl. -S a hypothetical unit of time

CHTHONIC   adj pertaining to the gods of the underworld

CHUB   n pl. -S a freshwater fish

CHUBASCO   n pl. -COS a violent thunderstorm

CHUBBY   adj -BIER, -BIEST plump CHUBBILY adv

CHUCK   v -ED, -ING, -S to throw

CHUCKIES   pl. of chucky

CHUCKLE   v -LED, -LING, -LES to laugh quietly

CHUCKLER   n pl. -S one that chuckles

CHUCKY   n pl. CHUCKIES a little chick

CHUDDAH   n pl. -S chuddar

CHUDDAR   n pl. -S a large, square shawl

CHUDDER   n pl. -S chuddar

CHUFA   n pl. -S a European sedge

CHUFF   adj CHUFFER, CHUFFEST gruff

CHUFF   v -ED, -ING, -S to chug

CHUFFY   adj -FIER, -FIEST plump

CHUG   v CHUGGED, CHUGGING, CHUGS to move with a dull explosive sound

CHUGGER   n pl. -S one that chugs

CHUKAR   n pl. -S a game bird

CHUKKA   n pl. -S a type of boot

CHUKKAR   n pl. -S chukker

CHUKKER   n pl. -S a period of play in polo

CHUM   v CHUMMED, CHUMMING, CHUMS to be close friends with someone

CHUMMY   adj -MIER, -MIEST friendly CHUMMILY adv

CHUMP   v -ED, -ING, -S to munch

CHUMSHIP   n pl. -S friendship

CHUNK   v -ED, -ING, -S to make a dull explosive sound

CHUNKY   adj CHUNKIER, CHUNKIEST stocky CHUNKILY adv

CHUNTER   v -ED, -ING, -S to mutter

CHURCH   v -ED, -ING, -ES to bring to church (a building for Christian worship)

CHURCHLY   adj -LIER, -LIEST pertaining to a church

CHURCHY   adj CHURCHIER, CHURCHIEST churchly

CHURL   n pl. -S a rude person CHURLISH adj

CHURN   v -ED, -ING, -S to stir briskly in order to make butter

CHURNER   n pl. -S one that churns

CHURNING   n pl. -S the butter churned at one time

CHURR   v -ED, -ING, -S to make a vibrant sound

CHUTE   v CHUTED, CHUTING, CHUTES to convey by chute (a vertical passage)

CHUTIST   n pl. -S a parachutist

CHUTNEE   n pl. -S chutney

CHUTNEY   n pl. -NEYS a sweet and sour sauce

CHUTZPA   n pl. -S chutzpah

CHUTZPAH   n pl. -S supreme self-confidence

CHYLE   n pl. -S a digestive fluid CHYLOUS adj

CHYME   n pl. -S semi-digested food

CHYMIC   n pl. -S chemic

CHYMIST   n pl. -S chemist

CHYMOSIN   n pl. -S rennin

CHYMOUS   adj pertaining to chyme

CIAO *interj* — used as an expression of greeting and farewell

CIBOL *n* pl. -S a variety of onion

CIBORIUM *n* pl. -RIA a vessel for holding holy bread

CIBOULE *n* pl. -S cibol

CICADA *n* pl. -DAS or -DAE a winged insect

CICALA *n* pl. -LAS or -LE cicada

CICATRIX *n* pl. -TRICES scar tissue

CICELY *n* pl. -LIES a fragment herb

CICERO *n* pl. -ROS a unit of measure in printing

CICERONE *n* pl. -NES or -NI a tour guide

CICHLID *n* pl. -LIDS or -LIDAE a tropical fish

CICISBEO *n* pl. -BEI a lover of a married woman

CICOREE *n* pl. -S a perennial herb

CIDER *n* pl. -S the juice pressed from apples

CIGAR *n* pl. -S a roll of tobacco leaf for smoking

CIGARET *n* pl. -S a narrow roll of finely cut tobacco for smoking

CILANTRO *n* pl. -TROS an herb used in cooking

CILIA pl. of cilium

CILIARY *adj* pertaining to cilia

CILIATE *n* pl. -S one of a class of ciliated protozoans

CILIATED *adj* having cilia

CILICE *n* pl. -S a coarse cloth

CILIUM *n* pl. CILIA a short, hairlike projection

CIMEX *n* pl. -MICES a bedbug

CINCH *v* -ED, -ING, -ES to girth

CINCHONA *n* pl. -S a Peruvian tree

CINCTURE *v* -TURED, -TURING, -TURES to gird or encircle

CINDER *v* -ED, -ING, -S to reduce to cinders (ashes)

CINDERY *adj* containing cinders

CINE *n* pl. -S a motion picture

CINEAST *n* pl. -S a devotee of motion pictures

CINEASTE *n* pl. -S cineast

CINEMA *n* pl. -S a motion-picture theater

CINEOL *n* pl. -S a liquid used as an antiseptic

CINEOLE *n* pl. -S cineol

CINERARY *adj* used for cremated ashes

CINERIN *n* pl. -S a compound used in insecticides

CINGULUM *n* pl. -LA an anatomical band or girdle

CINNABAR *n* pl. -S the principal ore of mercury

CINNAMON *n* pl. -S a spice obtained from tree bark **CINNAMIC** *adj*

CINNAMYL *n* pl. -S a chemical used to make soap

CINQUAIN *n* pl. -S a stanza of five lines

CINQUE *n* pl. -S the number five

CION *n* pl. -S a cutting from a plant or tree

CIPHER *v* -ED, -ING, -S to solve problems in arithmetic

CIPHONY *n* pl. -NIES the electronic scrambling of voice transmissions

CIPOLIN *n* pl. -S a type of marble

CIRCA *prep* about; around

CIRCLE *v* -CLED, -CLING, -CLES to move or revolve around

CIRCLER *n* pl. -S one that circles

CIRCLET *n* pl. -S a small ring or ring-shaped object

CIRCLING present participle of circle

CIRCUIT *v* -ED, -ING, -S to move around

CIRCUITY *n* pl. -ITIES lack of straightforwardness

CIRCULAR *n* pl. -S a leaflet intended for wide distribution

CIRCUS *n* pl. -ES a public entertainment **CIRCUSY** *adj*

CIRQUE *n* pl. -S a deep, steep-walled basin

CIRRATE *adj* having cirri

CIRRI pl. of cirrus

CIRRIPED *n* pl. -S any of an order of crustaceans

CIRROSE *adj* cirrous

CIRROUS *adj* having cirri

CIRRUS *n* pl. -RI a tendril or similar part

CIRSOID *adj* varicose

CISCO *n* pl. -COS or -COES a freshwater fish

CISLUNAR *adj* situated between the earth and the moon

CISSOID *n* pl. -S a type of geometric curve

CIST *n* pl. -S a prehistoric stone coffin

CISTERN *n* pl. -S a water tank

CISTERNA *n* pl. -NAE a fluid-containing sac

CISTRON *n* pl. -S a segment of DNA

CITABLE *adj* citeable

CITADEL *n* pl. -S a fortress or stronghold

CITATION *n* pl. -S the act of citing **CITATORY** *adj*

CITE *v* CITED, CITING, CITES to quote as an authority or example

CITEABLE *adj* suitable for citation

CITER *n* pl. -S one that cites

CITHARA *n* pl. -S an ancient stringed instrument

CITHER *n* pl. -S cittern

CITHERN *n* pl. -S cittern

CITHREN *n* pl. -S cittern

CITIED *adj* having cities

CITIES pl. of city

CITIFY *v* -FIED, -FYING, -FIES to urbanize

CITING present participle of cite

CITIZEN *n* pl. -S a resident of a city or town

CITOLA *n* pl. -S a cittern

CITOLE *n* pl. -S citola

CITRAL *n* pl. -S a lemon flavoring

CITRATE *n* pl. -S a salt of citric acid **CITRATED** *adj*

CITREOUS *adj* having a lemonlike color

CITRIC *adj* derived from citrus fruits

CITRIN *n* pl. -S a citric vitamin

CITRINE *n* pl. -S a variety of quartz

CITRON *n* pl. -S a lemonlike fruit

CITROUS *adj* pertaining to a citrus tree

CITRUS *n* pl. -ES any of a genus of tropical, fruit-bearing trees

CITTERN *n* pl. -S a pear-shaped guitar

CITY *n* pl. CITIES a large town

CITYFIED *adj* having the customs and manners of city people

CITYWARD *adv* toward the city

CIVET *n* pl. -S a catlike mammal

CIVIC *adj* pertaining to a city

CIVICISM *n* pl. -S a system of government based upon individual rights

CIVICS *n/pl* the science of civic affairs

CIVIE *n* pl. -S civvy

CIVIL *adj* pertaining to citizens

CIVILIAN *n* pl. -S a nonmilitary person

CIVILISE *v* -LISED, -LISING, -LISES to civilize

CIVILITY *n* pl. -TIES courtesy; politeness

CIVILIZE *v* -LIZED, -LIZING, -LIZES to bring out of savagery

CIVILLY *adv* politely

CIVISM *n* pl. -S good citizenship

CIVVY *n* pl. -VIES a civilian

CLABBER *v* -ED, -ING, -S to curdle

CLACH *n* pl. -S clachan

CLACHAN *n* pl. -S a hamlet

CLACK *v* -ED, -ING, -S to make an abrupt, dry sound

CLACKER *n* pl. -S one that clacks

CLAD *v* CLAD, CLADDING, CLADS to coat one metal over another

CLADDING *n* pl. -S something that overlays

CLADODE *n* pl. -S a leaflike part of a stem

CLAG *v* CLAGGED, CLAGGING, CLAGS to clog

CLAIM *v* -ED, -ING, -S to demand as one's due

CLAIMANT *n* pl. -S one that asserts a right or title

CLAIMER *n* pl. -S one that claims

CLAM *v* CLAMMED, CLAMMING, CLAMS to dig for clams (bivalve mollusks)

CLAMANT *adj* noisy

CLAMBAKE *n* pl. -S a beach picnic

CLAMBER *v* -ED, -ING, -S to climb awkwardly

CLAMMED past tense of clam

CLAMMING present participle of clam

CLAMMY *adj* CLAMMIER, CLAMMIEST cold and damp **CLAMMILY** *adv*

CLAMOR *v* -ED, -ING, -S to make loud outcries

CLAMORER *n* pl. -S one that clamors

CLAMOUR *v* -ED, -ING, -S to clamor

CLAMP   *v* -ED, -ING, -S to fasten with a clamp (a securing device)

CLAMPER   *n* pl. -S a device worn on shoes to prevent slipping on ice

CLAMWORM   *n* pl. -S a marine worm

CLAN   *n* pl. -S a united group of families

CLANG   *v* -ED, -ING, -S to ring loudly

CLANGOR   *v* -ED, -ING, -S to clang repeatedly

CLANGOUR   *v* -ED, -ING, -S to clangor

CLANK   *v* -ED, -ING, -S to make a sharp, metallic sound

CLANNISH   *adj* characteristic of a clan

CLANSMAN   *n* pl. -MEN a member of a clan

CLAP   *v* CLAPPED or CLAPT, CLAPPING, CLAPS to strike one palm against the other

CLAPPER   *n* pl. -S one that claps

CLAPTRAP   *n* pl. -S pretentious language

CLAQUE   *n* pl. -S a group of hired applauders

CLAQUER   *n* pl. -S claqueur

CLAQUEUR   *n* pl. -S a member of a claque

CLARENCE   *n* pl. -S a closed carriage

CLARET   *n* pl. -S a dry red wine

CLARIES   pl. of clary

CLARIFY   *v* -FIED, -FYING, -FIES to make clear

CLARINET   *n* pl. -S a woodwind instrument

CLARION   *v* -ED, -ING, -S to proclaim by blowing a medieval trumpet

CLARITY   *n* pl. -TIES the state of being clear

CLARKIA   *n* pl. -S an annual herb

CLARO   *n* pl. -ROS or -ROES a mild cigar

CLARY   *n* pl. CLARIES an aromatic herb

CLASH   *v* -ED, -ING, -ES to conflict or disagree

CLASHER   *n* pl. -S one that clashes

CLASP   *v* CLASPED or CLASPT, CLASPING, CLASPS to embrace tightly

CLASPER   *n* pl. -S one that clasps

CLASS   *v* -ED, -ING, -ES to classify

CLASSER   *n* pl. -S one that classes

CLASSES   pl. of classis

CLASSIC   *n* pl. -S a work of enduring excellence

CLASSIER   comparative of classy

CLASSIEST   superlative of classy

CLASSIFY   *v* -FIED, -FYING, -FIES to arrange according to characteristics

CLASSIS   *n* pl. CLASSES a governing body in certain churches

CLASSY   *adj* CLASSIER, CLASSIEST stylish; elegant **CLASSILY** *adv*

CLAST   *n* pl. -S a fragment of rock

CLASTIC   *n* pl. -S a rock made up of other rocks

CLATTER   *v* -ED, -ING, -S to move with a rattling noise

CLATTERY   *adj* having a rattling noise

CLAUCHT   a past tense of cleek

CLAUGHT   *v* -ED, -ING, -S to clutch

CLAUSE   *n* pl. -S a distinct part of a composition **CLAUSAL** *adj*

CLAVATE   *adj* shaped like a club

CLAVE   a past tense of cleave

CLAVER   *v* -ED, -ING, -S to gossip

CLAVICLE   *n* pl. -S a bone of the shoulder

CLAVIER   *n* pl. -S a keyboard instrument

CLAW   *v* -ED, -ING, -S to scratch with claws (sharp, curved toenails)

CLAWER   *n* pl. -S one that claws

CLAWLESS   *adj* having no claws

CLAXON   *n* pl. -S klaxon

CLAY   *v* -ED, -ING, -S to treat with clay (a fine-grained, earthy material)

CLAYBANK   *n* pl. -S a yellow-brown color

CLAYEY   *adj* CLAYIER, CLAYIEST resembling clay

CLAYISH   *adj* resembling or containing clay

CLAYLIKE   *adj* resembling clay

CLAYMORE   *n* pl. -S a type of sword

CLAYPAN   *n* pl. -S a shallow natural depression

CLAYWARE   *n* pl. -S pottery

CLEAN   *adj* CLEANER, CLEANEST free from dirt or stain

CLEAN   *v* -ED, -ING, -S to rid of dirt or stain

CLEANER   *n* pl. -S one that cleans

CLEANLY *adj* -LIER, -LIEST habitually clean

CLEANSE *v* CLEANSED, CLEANSING, CLEANSES to clean

CLEANSER *n* pl. -S one that cleanses

CLEANUP *n* pl. -S an act of cleaning

CLEAR *adj* CLEARER, CLEAREST clean and pure

CLEAR *v* -ED, -ING, -S to remove obstructions

CLEARER *n* pl. -S one that clears

CLEARING *n* pl. -S an open space

CLEARLY *adv* in a clear manner

CLEAT *v* -ED, -ING, -S to strengthen with a strip of wood or iron

CLEAVAGE *n* pl. -S the act of cleaving

CLEAVE *v* CLEAVED, CLEFT, CLOVE or CLAVE, CLOVEN, CLEAVING, CLEAVES to split or divide

CLEAVER *n* pl. -S a heavy knife

CLEEK *v* CLAUCHT or CLEEKED, CLEEKING, CLEEKS to clutch

CLEF *n* pl. -S a musical symbol

CLEFT *n* pl. -S a space or opening made by cleavage

CLEMATIS *n* pl. -TISES a flowering vine

CLEMENCY *n* pl. -CIES mercy

CLEMENT *adj* merciful

CLENCH *v* -ED, -ING, -ES to grasp firmly

CLEOME *n* pl. -S a tropical plant

CLEPE *v* CLEPED or CLEPT, CLEPING, CLEPES to call by name

CLERGY *n* pl. -GIES the body of men ordained for religious service

CLERIC *n* pl. -S a member of the clergy

CLERICAL *n* pl. -S a cleric

CLERID *n* pl. -S a predatory beetle

CLERIHEW *n* pl. -S a humorous poem

CLERISY *n* pl. -SIES the well-educated class

CLERK *v* -ED, -ING, -S to serve as a clerk (an office worker)

CLERKDOM *n* pl. -S the status or function of a clerk

CLERKISH *adj* resembling or suitable to a clerk

CLERKLY *adj* -LIER, -LIEST pertaining to a clerk

CLEVEITE *n* pl. -S a radioactive mineral

CLEVER *adj* -ERER, -EREST mentally keen **CLEVERLY** *adv*

CLEVIS *n* pl. -ISES a metal fastening device

CLEW *v* -ED, -ING, -S to roll into a ball

CLICHE *n* pl. -S a trite expression **CLICHED** *adj*

CLICK *v* -ED, -ING, -S to make a short, sharp sound

CLICKER *n* pl. -S one that clicks

CLIENT *n* pl. -S a customer **CLIENTAL** *adj*

CLIFF *n* pl. -S a high, steep face of rock

CLIFFY *adj* CLIFFIER, CLIFFIEST abounding in cliffs

CLIFT *n* pl. -S cliff

CLIMATE *n* pl. -S the weather conditions characteristic of an area **CLIMATAL, CLIMATIC** *adj*

CLIMAX *v* -ED, -ING, -ES to reach a high or dramatic point

CLIMB *v* CLIMBED or CLOMB, CLIMBING, CLIMBS to ascend

CLIMBER *n* pl. -S one that climbs

CLIME *n* pl. -S climate

CLINAL *adj* pertaining to a cline

CLINALLY *adv* in a clinal manner

CLINCH *v* -ED, -ING, -ES to settle a matter decisively

CLINCHER *n* pl. -S a decisive fact or remark

CLINE *n* pl. -S a series of changes within a species

CLING *v* CLUNG, CLINGING, CLINGS to adhere closely

CLING *v* -ED, -ING, -S to make a high-pitched ringing sound

CLINGER *n* pl. -S one that clings

CLINGY *adj* CLINGIER, CLINGIEST adhesive

CLINIC *n* pl. -S a medical facility **CLINICAL** *adj*

CLINK *v* -ED, -ING, -S to make a soft, sharp, ringing sound

CLINKER *v* -ED, -ING, -S to form fused residue in burning

CLIP *v* CLIPPED, CLIPT, CLIPPING, CLIPS to trim by cutting

CLIPPER *n* pl. -S one that clips

CLIPPING   *n* pl. -S something that is clipped out or off

CLIPT   a past participle of clip

CLIQUE   *v* CLIQUED, CLIQUING, CLIQUES to form a clique (an exclusive group of persons)

CLIQUEY   *adj* CLIQUIER, CLIQUIEST inclined to form cliques

CLIQUISH   *adj* cliquey

CLIQUY   *adj* CLIQUIER, CLIQUIEST cliquey

CLITELLA   *n/pl* regions in the body walls of certain annelids

CLITORIS   *n* pl. -RISES a sex organ **CLITORAL, CLITORIC** *adj*

CLIVERS   *n* pl. CLIVERS an annual herb

CLOACA   *n* pl. -ACAE a sewer **CLOACAL** *adj*

CLOAK   *v* -ED, -ING, -S to conceal

CLOBBER   *v* -ED, -ING, -S to trounce

CLOCHE   *n* pl. -S a bell-shaped hat

CLOCK   *v* -ED, -ING, -S to time with a stopwatch

CLOCKER   *n* pl. -S one that clocks

CLOD   *n* pl. -S a dolt **CLODDISH** *adj*

CLODDY   *adj* -DIER, -DIEST lumpy

CLODPATE   *n* pl. -S a stupid person

CLODPOLE   *n* pl. -S clodpate

CLODPOLL   *n* pl. -S clodpate

CLOG   *v* CLOGGED, CLOGGING, CLOGS to block up or obstruct

CLOGGY   *adj* -GIER, -GIEST clogging or able to clog

CLOISTER   *v* -ED, -ING, -S to seclude

CLOMB   a past tense of climb

CLOMP   *v* -ED, -ING, -S to walk heavily and clumsily

CLON   *n* pl. -S a group of asexually derived organisms **CLONAL** *adj* **CLONALLY** *adv*

CLONE   *v* CLONED, CLONING, CLONES to reproduce by asexual means

CLONIC   *adj* pertaining to clonus

CLONISM   *n* pl. -S the condition of having clonus

CLONK   *v* -ED, -ING, -S to make a dull thumping sound

CLONUS   *n* pl. -ES a form of muscular spasm

CLOOT   *n* pl. -S a cloven hoof

CLOP   *v* CLOPPED, CLOPPING, CLOPS to make the sound of a hoof striking pavement

CLOSE   *adj* CLOSER, CLOSEST near **CLOSELY** *adv*

CLOSE   *v* CLOSED, CLOSING, CLOSES to block against entry or passage **CLOSABLE** *adj*

CLOSEOUT   *n* pl. -S a clearance sale

CLOSER   *n* pl. -S one that closes

CLOSEST   superlative of close

CLOSET   *v* -ED, -ING, -S to enclose in a private room

CLOSING   *n* pl. -S a concluding part

CLOSURE   *v* -SURED, -SURING, -SURES to cloture

CLOT   *v* CLOTTED, CLOTTING, CLOTS to form into a clot (a thick mass)

CLOTH   *n* pl. -S fabric

CLOTHE   *v* CLOTHED or CLAD, CLOTHING, CLOTHES to provide with clothing

CLOTHIER   *n* pl. -S one who makes or sells clothing

CLOTHING   *n* pl. -S wearing apparel

CLOTTED   past tense of clot

CLOTTING   present participle of clot

CLOTTY   *adj* tending to clot

CLOTURE   *v* -TURED, -TURING, -TURES to end a debate by calling for a vote

CLOUD   *v* -ED, -ING, -S to cover with clouds (masses of visible vapor)

CLOUDLET   *n* pl. -S a small cloud

CLOUDY   *adj* CLOUDIER, CLOUDIEST overcast with clouds **CLOUDILY** *adv*

CLOUGH   *n* pl. -S a ravine

CLOUR   *v* -ED, -ING, -S to knock or bump

CLOUT   *v* -ED, -ING, -S to hit with the hand

CLOUTER   *n* pl. -S one that clouts

CLOVE   *n* pl. -S a spice

CLOVEN   *adj* split; divided

CLOVER   *n* pl. -S a plant

CLOWDER   *n* pl. -S a group of cats

CLOWN   *v* -ED, -ING, -S to act like a clown (a humorous performer)

CLOWNERY *n* pl. -ERIES clownish behavior

CLOWNISH *adj* resembling or befitting a clown

CLOY *v* -ED, -ING, -S to gratify beyond desire

CLOZE *adj* pertaining to a type of reading comprehension test

CLUB *v* CLUBBED, CLUBBING, CLUBS to form a club (an organized group of persons)

CLUBABLE *adj* sociable

CLUBBER *n* pl. -S a member of a club

CLUBBING present participle of club

CLUBBY *adj* -BIER, -BIEST characteristic of a club

CLUBFOOT *n* pl. -FEET a deformed foot

CLUBHAND *n* pl. -S a deformed hand

CLUBHAUL *v* -ED, -ING, -S to put a vessel about

CLUBMAN *n* pl. -MEN a male member of a club

CLUBROOT *n* pl. -S a plant disease

CLUCK *v* -ED, -ING, -S to make the sound of a hen

CLUE *v* CLUED, CLUEING or CLUING, CLUES to give guiding information

CLUMBER *n* pl. -S a stocky spaniel

CLUMP *v* -ED, -ING, -S to form into a thick mass

CLUMPISH *adj* resembling a clump (a thick mass)

CLUMPY *adj* CLUMPIER, CLUMPIEST lumpy

CLUMSY *adj* -SIER, -SIEST awkward **CLUMSILY** *adv*

CLUNG past tense of cling

CLUNK *v* -ED, -ING, -S to thump

CLUNKER *n* pl. -S a jalopy

CLUPEID *n* pl. -S a fish of the herring family

CLUPEOID *n* pl. -S a clupeid

CLUSTER *v* -ED, -ING, -S to form into a cluster (a group of similar objects)

CLUSTERY *adj* pertaining to a cluster

CLUTCH *v* -ED, -ING, -ES to grasp and hold tightly

CLUTCHY *adj* tending to clutch

CLUTTER *v* -ED, -ING, -S to pile in a disorderly state

CLYPEUS *n* pl. CLYPEI a shield-like structure **CLYPEAL, CLYPEATE** *adj*

CLYSTER *n* pl. -S an enema

COACH *v* -ED, -ING, -ES to tutor or train

COACHER *n* pl. -S one that coaches

COACHMAN *n* pl. -MEN one who drives a coach or carriage

COACT *v* -ED, -ING, -S to act together

COACTIVE *adj* mutually active

COACTION *n* pl. -S joint action

COADMIRE *v* -MIRED, -MIRING, -MIRES to admire together

COADMIT *v* -MITTED, -MITTING, -MITS to admit several things equally

COAEVAL *n* pl. -S coeval

COAGENCY *n* pl. -CIES a joint agency

COAGENT *n* pl. -S a person, force, or other agent working together with another

COAGULUM *n* pl. -LA or -LUMS a clot

COAL *v* -ED, -ING, -S to supply with coal (a carbon fuel)

COALA *n* pl. -S koala

COALBIN *n* pl. -S a bin for storing coal

COALBOX *n* pl. -ES a box for storing coal

COALER *n* pl. -S one that supplies coal

COALESCE *v* -ALESCED, -ALESCING, -ALESCES to blend

COALFISH *n* pl. -ES a blackish fish

COALHOLE *n* pl. -S a compartment for storing coal

COALIFY *v* -FIED, -FYING, -FIES to convert into coal

COALLESS *adj* lacking coal

COALPIT *n* pl. -S a pit from which coal is obtained

COALSACK *n* pl. -S a dark region of the Milky Way

COALSHED *n* pl. -S a shed for storing coal

COALYARD *n* pl. -S a yard for storing coal

COAMING *n* pl. -S a raised border

COANNEX *v* -ED, -ING, -ES to annex jointly

COAPPEAR *v* -ED, -ING, -S to appear together or at the same time

COAPT *v* -ED, -ING, -S to fit together and make fast

COARSE *adj* COARSER, COARSEST rough **COARSELY** *adv*

COARSEN	v -ED, -ING, -S to make coarse
COASSIST	v -ED, -ING, -S to assist jointly
COASSUME	v -SUMED, -SUMING, -SUMES to assume together
COAST	v -ED, -ING, -S to slide down a hill
COASTAL	adj pertaining to or located near a seashore
COASTER	n pl. -S a sled
COASTING	n pl. -S coastal trade
COAT	v -ED, -ING, -S to cover with a coat (an outer garment)
COATEE	n pl. -S a small coat
COATER	n pl. -S one that coats
COATI	n pl. -S a tropical mammal
COATING	n pl. -S a covering layer
COATLESS	adj lacking a coat
COATRACK	n pl. -S a rack or stand for coats
COATROOM	n pl. -S a room for storing coats
COATTAIL	n pl. -S the back lower portion of a coat
COATTEND	v -ED, -ING, -S to attend together
COATTEST	v -ED, -ING, -S to attest jointly
COAUTHOR	v -ED, -ING, -S to write together
COAX	v -ED, -ING, -ES to cajole
COAXAL	adj coaxial
COAXER	n pl. -S one that coaxes
COAXIAL	adj having a common axis
COB	n pl. -S a corncob
COBALT	n pl. -S a metallic element **COBALTIC** adj
COBB	n pl. -S a sea gull
COBBER	n pl. -S a comrade
COBBIER	comparative of cobby
COBBIEST	superlative of cobby
COBBLE	v -BLED, -BLING, -BLES to mend
COBBLER	n pl. -S a mender of shoes
COBBY	adj -BIER, -BIEST stocky
COBIA	n pl. -S a large game fish
COBLE	n pl. -S a small fishing boat
COBNUT	n pl. -S an edible nut
COBRA	n pl. -S a venomous snake
COBWEB	v -WEBBED, -WEBBING, -WEBS to cover with cobwebs (spider webs)

COBWEBBY	adj -BIER, -BIEST covered with cobwebs
COCA	n pl. -S a South American shrub
COCAIN	n pl. -S cocaine
COCAINE	n pl. -S a narcotic alkaloid
COCCAL	adj pertaining to a coccus
COCCI	pl. of coccus
COCCIC	adj coccal
COCCID	n pl. -S an insect
COCCIDIA	n/pl parasitic protozoans
COCCOID	n pl. -S a spherical cell or body
COCCUS	n pl. COCCI a spherical bacterium **COCCOUS** adj
COCCYX	n pl. -CYGES or -CYXES a bone of the spine
COCHAIR	v -ED, -ING, -S to serve jointly as chairman of
COCHIN	n pl. -S a large domestic chicken
COCHLEA	n pl. -CHLEAE or -CHLEAS a part of the ear **COCHLEAR** adj
COCINERA	n pl. -S a cook
COCK	v -ED, -ING, -S to tilt to one side
COCKADE	n pl. -S an ornament worn on a hat **COCKADED** adj
COCKATOO	n pl. -TOOS a parrot
COCKBILL	v -ED, -ING, -S to raise the yardarm on a ship
COCKBOAT	n pl. -S a small boat
COCKCROW	n pl. -S daybreak
COCKER	v -ED, -ING, -S to pamper
COCKEREL	n pl. -S a young rooster
COCKEYE	n pl. -S a squinting eye **COCKEYED** adj
COCKIER	comparative of cocky
COCKIEST	superlative of cocky
COCKILY	adv in a cocky manner
COCKISH	adj cocky
COCKLE	v -LED, -LING, -LES to wrinkle or pucker
COCKLIKE	adj resembling a rooster
COCKLOFT	n pl. -S a small attic
COCKNEY	n pl. -NEYS a resident of the East End of London
COCKPIT	n pl. -S a pilot's compartment in certain airplanes
COCKSHUT	n pl. -S the close of day

COCKSHY	*n* pl. -SHIES a target in a throwing contest
COCKSPUR	*n* pl. -S a thorny plant
COCKSURE	*adj* certain
COCKTAIL	*v* -ED, -ING, -S to drink alcoholic beverages
COCKUP	*n* pl. -S a turned-up part of something
COCKY	*adj* COCKIER, COCKIEST arrogantly self-confident
COCO	*n* pl. -COS a tall palm tree
COCOA	*n* pl. -S chocolate
COCOANUT	*n* pl. -S coconut
COCOBOLA	*n* pl. -S cocobolo
COCOBOLO	*n* pl. -LOS a tropical tree
COCOMAT	*n* pl. -S a matting made from coir
COCONUT	*n* pl. -S the fruit of the coco
COCOON	*v* -ED, -ING, -S to wrap or envelop tightly
COCOTTE	*n* pl. -S a prostitute
COCREATE	*v* -ATED, -ATING, -ATES to create together
COD	*n* pl. -S a marine food fish
CODA	*n* pl. -S a passage at the end of a musical composition
CODABLE	*adj* capable of being coded
CODDER	*n* pl. -S a cod fisherman
CODDLE	*v* -DLED, -DLING, -DLES to pamper
CODDLER	*n* pl. -S one that coddles
CODE	*v* CODED, CODING, CODES to convert into symbols
CODEBTOR	*n* pl. -S one that shares a debt
CODEIA	*n* pl. -S codeine
CODEIN	*n* pl. -S codeine
CODEINA	*n* pl. -S codeine
CODEINE	*n* pl. -S a narcotic alkaloid
CODELESS	*adj* being without a set of laws
CODEN	*n* pl. -S a coding classification
CODER	*n* pl. -S one that codes
CODERIVE	*v* -RIVED, -RIVING, -RIVES to derive jointly
CODEX	*n* pl. -DICES an ancient manuscript
CODFISH	*n* pl. -ES the cod
CODGER	*n* pl. -S an old man
CODICES	pl. of codex

CODICIL	*n* pl. -S a supplement to a will
CODIFIER	*n* pl. -S one that codifies
CODIFY	*v* -FIED, -FYING, -FIES to arrange or systematize
CODING	present participle of code
CODLIN	*n* pl. -S codling
CODLING	*n* pl. -S an unripe apple
CODON	*n* pl. -S a triplet of nucleotides (basic components of DNA)
CODPIECE	*n* pl. -S a cover for the crotch in men's breeches
COED	*n* pl. -S a female student
COEDITOR	*n* pl. -S one who edits with another person
COEFFECT	*n* pl. -S an accompanying effect
COELIAC	*adj* celiac
COELOM	*n* pl. -LOMS or -LOMATA a body cavity in some animals **COELOMIC** *adj*
COELOME	*n* pl. -S coelom
COEMBODY	*v* -BODIED, -BODYING, -BODIES to embody jointly
COEMPLOY	*v* -ED, -ING, -S to employ together
COEMPT	*v* -ED, -ING, -S to buy up the entire supply of a product
COENACT	*v* -ED, -ING, -S to enact jointly or at the same time
COENAMOR	*v* -ED, -ING, -S to inflame with mutual love
COENDURE	*v* -DURED, -DURING, -DURES to endure together
COENURE	*n* pl. -S coenurus
COENURUS	*n* pl. -RI a tapeworm larva
COENZYME	*n* pl. -S a substance necessary for the functioning of certain enzymes
COEQUAL	*n* pl. -S one who is equal with another
COEQUATE	*v* -QUATED, -QUATING, -QUATES to equate with something else
COERCE	*v* -ERCED, -ERCING, -ERCES to compel by force or threat
COERCER	*n* pl. -S one that coerces
COERCION	*n* pl. -S the act of coercing
COERCIVE	*adj* serving to coerce
COERECT	*v* -ED, -ING, -S to erect together
COEVAL	*n* pl. -S one of the same era or period as another

COEVALLY	*adv* contemporarily	**COHERE**	*v* -HERED, -HERING, -HERES to stick together
COEXERT	*v* -ED, -ING, -S to exert jointly		
COEXIST	*v* -ED, -ING, -S to exist together	**COHERENT**	*adj* sticking together
COEXTEND	*v* -ED, -ING, -S to extend through the same space or time as another	**COHERER**	*n* pl. -S a device used to detect radio waves
		COHERING	present participle of cohere
COFACTOR	*n* pl. -S a coenzyme	**COHESION**	*n* pl. -S the act or state of cohering **COHESIVE** *adj*
COFF	*v* COFT, COFFING, COFFS to buy	**COHO**	*n* pl. -HOS a small salmon
COFFEE	*n* pl. -S an aromatic, mildly stimulating beverage	**COHOBATE**	*v* -BATED, -BATING, -BATES to distill again
COFFER	*v* -ED, -ING, -S to put in a strongbox	**COHOG**	*n* pl. -S a quahog
COFFIN	*v* -ED, -ING, -S to put in a coffin (a burial case)	**COHORT**	*n* pl. -S a companion or associate
		COHOSH	*n* pl. -ES a medicinal plant
COFFING	present participle of coff	**COHUNE**	*n* pl. -S a palm tree
COFFLE	*v* -FLED, -FLING, -FLES to chain slaves together	**COIF**	*v* -ED, -ING -S to style the hair
COFFRET	*n* pl. -S a small strongbox	**COIFFE**	*v* COIFFED, COIFFING, COIFFES to coif
COFT	past tense of coff		
COG	*v* COGGED, COGGING, COGS to cheat at dice	**COIFFEUR**	*n* pl. -S a male hairdresser
		COIFFURE	*v* -FURED, -FURING, -FURES to coif
COGENCY	*n* pl. -CIES the state of being cogent	**COIGN**	*v* -ED, -ING, -S to quoin
COGENT	*adj* convincing **COGENTLY** *adv*	**COIGNE**	*v* COIGNED, COIGNING, COIGNES to quoin
COGGED	past tense of cog		
COGGING	present participle of cog	**COIL**	*v* -ED, -ING, -S to wind in even rings
COGITATE	*v* -TATED, -TATING, -TATES to ponder	**COILER**	*n* pl. -S one that coils
COGITO	*n* pl. -TOS a philosophical principle	**COIN**	*v* -ED, -ING, -S to make coins (metal currency) **COINABLE** *adj*
COGNAC	*n* pl. -S a brandy	**COINAGE**	*n* pl. -S the act of making coins
COGNATE	*n* pl. -S one that is related to another	**COINCIDE**	*v* -CIDED, -CIDING, -CIDES to be in the same place
COGNISE	*v* -NISED, -NISING, -NISES to cognize	**COINER**	*n* pl. -S one that coins
		COINFER	*v* -FERRED, -FERRING, -FERS to infer jointly
COGNIZE	*v* -NIZED, -NIZING, -NIZES to become aware of in one's mind	**COINHERE**	*v* -HERED, -HERING, -HERES to inhere jointly
COGNIZER	*n* pl. -S one that cognizes	**COINMATE**	*n* pl. -S a fellow inmate
COGNOMEN	*n* pl. -MENS or -MINA a family name	**COINSURE**	*v* -SURED, -SURING, -SURES to insure with another
COGNOVIT	*n* pl. -S a written admission of liability	**COINTER**	*v* -TERRED, -TERRING, -TERS to bury together
COGON	*n* pl. -S a tall tropical grass	**COIR**	*n* pl. -S a fiber obtained from coconut husks
COGWAY	*n* pl. -WAYS a railway operating on steep slopes		
		COISTREL	*n* pl. -S a knave
COGWHEEL	*n* pl. -S a toothed wheel	**COISTRIL**	*n* pl. -S coistrel
COHABIT	*v* -ED, -ING, -S to live together as man and wife while unmarried	**COITION**	*n* pl. -S coitus
COHEIR	*n* pl. -S a joint heir	**COITUS**	*n* pl. -ES sexual intercourse **COITAL** *adj* **COITALLY** *adv*

COKE   v COKED, COKING, COKES to change into a carbon fuel

COL   n pl. -S a depression between two mountains

COLA   n pl. -S a carbonated beverage

COLANDER   n pl. -S a kitchen utensil for draining off liquids

COLD   adj COLDER, COLDEST having little or no warmth

COLD   n pl. -S the relative lack of heat; a chill

COLDISH   adj somewhat cold

COLDLY   adv in a cold manner

COLDNESS   n pl. -ES the state of being cold

COLE   n pl. -S a plant of the cabbage family

COLESEED   n pl. -S colza

COLESLAW   n pl. -S a salad made of shredded raw cabbage

COLESSEE   n pl. -S a joint lessee

COLESSOR   n pl. -S a joint lessor

COLEUS   n pl. -ES a tropical plant

COLEWORT   n pl. -S cole

COLIC   n pl. -S acute abdominal pain

COLICIN   n pl. -S an antibacterial substance

COLICINE   n pl. -S colicin

COLICKY   adj pertaining to or associated with colic

COLIES   pl. of coly

COLIFORM   n pl. -S a bacillus of the colon

COLIN   n pl. -S the bobwhite

COLINEAR   adj lying in the same straight line

COLISEUM   n pl. -S a large structure for public entertainment

COLISTIN   n pl. -S an antibiotic

COLITIS   n pl. -TISES inflammation of the colon **COLITIC** adj

COLLAGE   n pl. -S a kind of artistic composition

COLLAGEN   n pl. -S a protein

COLLAPSE   v -LAPSED, -LAPSING, -LAPSES to crumble suddenly

COLLAR   v -ED, -ING, -S to provide with a collar (something worn around the neck)

COLLARD   n pl. -S a variety of kale

COLLARET   n pl. -S a small collar

COLLATE   v -LATED, -LATING, -LATES to compare critically

COLLATOR   n pl. -S one that collates

COLLECT   v -ED, -ING, -S to bring together in a group

COLLEEN   n pl. -S an Irish girl

COLLEGE   n pl. -S a school of higher learning

COLLEGER   n pl. -S a student supported by funds from his college

COLLEGIA   n/pl soviet executive councils

COLLET   v -ED, -ING, -S to set a gem in a rim or ring

COLLIDE   v -LIDED, -LIDING, -LIDES to come together with violent impact

COLLIE   n pl. -S a large dog

COLLIED   past tense of colly

COLLIER   n pl. -S a coal miner

COLLIERY   n pl. -LIERIES a coal mine

COLLIES   present 3d person sing. of colly

COLLINS   n pl. -ES an alcoholic beverage

COLLOGUE   v -LOGUED, -LOGUING, -LOGUES to conspire

COLLOID   n pl. -S a type of chemical suspension

COLLOP   n pl. -S a small portion of meat

COLLOQUY   n pl. -QUIES a conversation

COLLUDE   v -LUDED, -LUDING, -LUDES to conspire

COLLUDER   n pl. -S one that colludes

COLLUVIA   n/pl rock debris

COLLY   v -LIED, -LYING, -LIES to blacken with coal dust

COLLYRIA   n/pl medicinal lotions

COLOCATE   v -CATED, -CATING, -CATES to place two or more housing units in close proximity

COLOG   n pl. -S the logarithm of the reciprocal of a number

COLOGNE   n pl. -S a scented liquid **COLOGNED** adj

COLON   n pl. -S a section of the large intestine

COLON   n pl. -ES a monetary unit of Costa Rica

COLONEL   n pl. -S a military officer

COLONI   pl. of colonus

COLONIAL   n pl. -S a citizen of a colony

COLONIC	*adj* pertaining to the colon
COLONIES	pl. of colony
COLONISE	*v* -NISED, -NISING, -NISES to colonize
COLONIST	*n* pl. -S one who settles a colony
COLONIZE	*v* -NIZED, -NIZING, -NIZES to establish a colony
COLONUS	*n* pl. -NI a freeborn serf
COLONY	*n* pl. -NIES a group of emigrants living in a new land
COLOPHON	*n* pl. -S an inscription placed at the end of a book
COLOR	*v* -ED, -ING, -S to give color (a visual attribute of objects) to
COLORADO	*adj* of medium strength and color — used of cigars
COLORANT	*n* pl. -S a pigment or dye
COLORED	*n* pl. -S a nonwhite person
COLORER	*n* pl. -S one that colors
COLORFUL	*adj* full of color
COLORING	*n* pl. -S appearance in regard to color
COLORISM	*n* pl. -S coloring
COLORIST	*n* pl. -S a person skilled in the use of color
COLOSSAL	*adj* gigantic
COLOSSUS	*n* pl. -LOSSI or -LOSSUSES a gigantic statue
COLOTOMY	*n* pl. -MIES a surgical incision of the colon
COLOUR	*v* -ED, -ING, -S to color
COLOURER	*n* pl. -S colorer
COLPITIS	*n* pl. -TISES a vaginal inflammation
COLT	*n* pl. -S a young male horse **COLTISH** *adj*
COLTER	*n* pl. -S a blade on a plow
COLUBRID	*n* pl. -S any of a large family of snakes
COLUGO	*n* pl. -GOS a small mammal
COLUMBIC	*adj* pertaining to niobium
COLUMEL	*n* pl. -S a small column-like anatomical part
COLUMN	*n* pl. -S a vertical cylindrical support **COLUMNAL, COLUM-NAR, COLUMNED** *adj*
COLURE	*n* pl. -S an astronomical circle
COLY	*n* pl. COLIES an African bird
COLZA	*n* pl. -S a plant of the cabbage family
COMA	*n* pl. -S a condition of prolonged unconsciousness
COMA	*n* pl. -MAE a tuft of silky hairs
COMAKER	*n* pl. -S one who assumes financial responsibility for another's default
COMAL	*adj* comose
COMATE	*n* pl. -S a companion
COMATIC	*adj* having blurred vision as a result of coma
COMATIK	*n* pl. -S komatik
COMATOSE	*adj* affected with coma
COMATULA	*n* pl. -LAE a marine animal
COMB	*v* -ED, -ING, -S to arrange or clean with a comb (a toothed instrument)
COMBAT	*v* -BATED, -BATING, -BATS or -BATTED, -BATTING, -BATS to fight against
COMBATER	*n* pl. -S one that combats
COMBE	*n* pl. -S a narrow valley
COMBER	*n* pl. -S one that combs
COMBINE	*v* -BINED, -BINING, -BINES to blend
COMBINER	*n* pl. -S one that combines
COMBINGS	*n/pl* hair removed by a comb
COMBINING	present participle of combine
COMBLIKE	*adj* resembling a comb
COMBO	*n* pl. -BOS a small jazz band
COMBUST	*v* -ED, -ING, -S to burn
COME	*v* CAME, COMING, COMES or COMETH to move toward something or someone
COMEBACK	*n* pl. -S a return to former prosperity
COMEDIAN	*n* pl. -S a humorous entertainer
COMEDIC	*adj* pertaining to comedy
COMEDIES	pl. of comedy
COMEDO	*n* pl. -DOS or -DONES a skin blemish
COMEDOWN	*n* pl. -S a drop in status
COMEDY	*n* pl. -DIES a humorous play, movie, or other work
COMELY	*adj* -LIER, -LIEST pleasing to look at **COMELILY** *adv*
COMER	*n* pl. -S one showing great promise

COMET   *n* pl. -S a celestial body
     COMETARY *adj*

COMETH   a present 3d person sing. of come

COMETHER   *n* pl. -S an affair or matter

COMETIC   *adj* pertaining to a comet

COMFIER   comparative of comfy

COMFIEST   superlative of comfy

COMFIT   *n* pl. -S a candy

COMFORT   *v* -ED, -ING, -S to soothe in time of grief

COMFREY   *n* pl. -FREYS a coarse herb

COMFY   *adj* -FIER, -FIEST comfortable

COMIC   *n* pl. -S a comedian

COMICAL   *adj* funny

COMING   *n* pl. -S arrival

COMITIA   *n* pl. COMITIA a public assembly in ancient Rome
     COMITIAL *adj*

COMITY   *n* pl. -TIES civility

COMMA   *n* pl. -MAS or -MATA a fragment of a few words or feet in ancient prosody

COMMAND   *v* -ED, -ING, -S to direct with authority

COMMANDO   *n* pl. -DOES or -DOS a military unit

COMMATA   a pl. of comma

COMMENCE   *v* -MENCED, -MENCING, -MENCES to begin

COMMEND   *v* -ED, -ING, -S to praise

COMMENT   *v* -ED, -ING, -S to remark

COMMERCE   *v* -MERCED, -MERCING, -MERCES to commune

COMMIE   *n* pl. -S a Communist

COMMIES   pl. of commy

COMMIT   *v* -MITTED, -MITTING, -MITS to do, perform, or perpetrate

COMMIX   *v* -MIXED or -MIXT, -MIXING, -MIXES to mix together

COMMODE   *n* pl. -S a cabinet

COMMON   *adj* -MONER, -MONEST ordinary

COMMON   *n* pl. -S a tract of publicly used land

COMMONER   *n* pl. -S one of the common people

COMMONLY   adv in a common manner

COMMOVE   *v* -MOVED, -MOVING, -MOVES to move violently

COMMUNAL   *adj* belonging to a community; public

COMMUNE   *v* -MUNED, -MUNING, -MUNES to converse intimately

COMMUTE   *v* -MUTED, -MUTING, -MUTES to exchange

COMMUTER   *n* pl. -S one that commutes

COMMY   *n* pl. -MIES commie

COMOSE   *adj* bearing a tuft of silky hairs

COMOUS   *adj* comose

COMP   *v* -ED, -ING, -S to play a jazz accompaniment

COMPACT   *adj* -PACTER, -PACTEST closely and firmly united

COMPACT   *v* -ED, -ING, -S to pack closely together

COMPADRE   *n* pl. -S a close friend

COMPANY   *v* -NIED, -NYING, -NIES to associate with

COMPARE   *v* -PARED, -PARING, -PARES to represent as similar

COMPARER   *n* pl. -S one that compares

COMPART   *v* -ED, -ING, -S to divide into parts

COMPASS   *v* -ED, -ING, -ES to go around

COMPEER   *v* -ED, -ING, -S to equal or match

COMPEL   *v* -PELLED, -PELLING, -PELS to urge forcefully

COMPEND   *n* pl. -S a brief summary

COMPERE   *v* -PERED, -PERING, -PERES to act as master of ceremonies

COMPETE   *v* -PETED, -PETING, -PETES to vie

COMPILE   *v* -PILED, -PILING, -PILES to collect into a volume

COMPILER   *n* pl. -S one that compiles

COMPLAIN   *v* -ED, -ING, -S to express discontent

COMPLEAT   *adj* highly skilled

COMPLECT   *v* -ED, -ING, -S to weave together

COMPLETE   *adj* -PLETER, -PLETEST having all necessary parts

COMPLETE   *v* -PLETED, -PLETING, -PLETES to bring to an end

COMPLEX   *adj* -PLEXER, -PLEXEST complicated

COMPLEX   *v* -ED, -ING, -ES to make complex

COMPLICE *n* pl. -S an associate

COMPLIED past tense of comply

COMPLIER *n* pl. -S one that complies

COMPLIES present 3d person sing. of comply

COMPLIN *n* pl. -S compline

COMPLINE *n* pl. -S the last liturgical prayer of the day

COMPLOT *v* -PLOTTED, -PLOTTING, -PLOTS to conspire

COMPLY *v* -PLIED, -PLYING, -PLIES to obey

COMPO *n* pl. -POS a mixed substance

COMPONE *adj* compony

COMPONY *adj* composed of squares of alternating colors

COMPORT *v* -ED, -ING -S to conduct oneself in a certain way

COMPOSE *v* -POSED, -POSING, -POSES to form the substance of

COMPOSER *n* pl. -S one that writes music

COMPOST *v* -ED, -ING, -S to fertilize

COMPOTE *n* pl. -S fruit stewed in syrup

COMPOUND *v* -ED, -ING, -S to add to

COMPRESS *v* -ED, -ING, -ES to compact

COMPRISE *v* -PRISED, -PRISING, -PRISES to include or contain

COMPRIZE *v* -PRIZED, -PRIZING, -PRIZES to comprise

COMPT *v* -ED, -ING, -S to count

COMPUTE *v* -PUTED, -PUTING, -PUTES to determine by mathematical means

COMPUTER *n* pl. -S a machine that computes automatically

COMRADE *n* pl. -S a close friend

COMTE *n* pl. -S a French nobleman

CON *v* CONNED, CONNING, CONS to study carefully

CONATION *n* pl. -S the inclination to act purposefully **CONATIVE** *adj*

CONATUS *n* pl. CONATUS an effort

CONCAVE *v* -CAVED, -CAVING, -CAVES to make concave (curving inward)

CONCEAL *v* -ED, -ING, -S to keep from sight or discovery

CONCEDE *v* -CEDED, -CEDING, -CEDES to acknowledge as true

CONCEDER *n* pl. -S one that concedes

CONCEIT *v* -ED, -ING, -S to imagine

CONCEIVE *v* -CEIVED, -CEIVING, -CEIVES to understand

CONCENT *n* pl. -S harmony

CONCEPT *n* pl. -S a general idea

CONCERN *v* -ED, -ING, -S to be of interest to

CONCERT *v* -ED, -ING, -S to plan

CONCERTO *n* pl. -TOS or -TI a musical composition

CONCH *n* pl. -S or -ES a marine mollusk

CONCHA *n* pl. -CHAE an anatomical shell-like structure **CONCHAL** *adj*

CONCHOID *n* pl. -S a type of geometric curve

CONCHY *n* pl. -CHIES a conscientious objector

CONCISE *adj* -CISER, -CISEST succinct

CONCLAVE *n* pl. -S a secret meeting

CONCLUDE *v* -CLUDED, -CLUDING, -CLUDES to finish

CONCOCT *v* -ED, -ING, -S to prepare by combining ingredients

CONCORD *n* pl. -S a state of agreement

CONCRETE *v* -CRETED, -CRETING, -CRETES to solidify

CONCUR *v* -CURRED, -CURRING, -CURS to agree

CONCUSS *v* -ED, -ING, -ES to injure the brain by a violent blow

CONDEMN *v* -ED, -ING, -S to criticize severely

CONDENSE *v* -DENSED, -DENSING, -DENSES to compress

CONDIGN *adj* deserved; appropriate

CONDOLE *v* -DOLED, -DOLING, -DOLES to mourn

CONDOLER *n* pl. -S one that condoles

CONDOM *n* pl. -S a prophylactic

CONDONE *v* -DONED, -DONING, -DONES to forgive or overlook

CONDONER *n* pl. -S one that condones

CONDOR *n* pl. -S or -ES a coin of Chile

CONDUCE *v* -DUCED, -DUCING, -DUCES to contribute to a result

CONDUCER *n* pl. -S one that conduces

CONDUCT *v* -ED, -ING, -S to lead or guide

CONDUIT *n* pl. -S a channel or pipe for conveying fluids

CONDYLE *n* pl. -S a protuberance on a bone **CONDYLAR** *adj*

CONE v CONED, CONING, CONES to shape like a cone (a geometric solid)

CONELRAD n pl. -S a system of defense in the event of air attack

CONENOSE n pl. -S a bloodsucking insect

CONEPATE n pl. -S a skunk

CONEPATL n pl. -S conepate

CONEY n pl. -NEYS cony

CONFAB v -FABBED, -FABBING, FABS to chat

CONFECT v -ED, -ING, -S to prepare from various ingredients

CONFER v -FERRED, -FERRING, -FERS to bestow

CONFEREE n pl. -S one upon whom something is conferred

CONFERVA n pl. -VAE or -VAS a freshwater alga

CONFESS v -ED, -ING, -ES to acknowledge or disclose

CONFETTO n pl. -TI a bonbon

CONFIDE v -FIDED, -FIDING, -FIDES to reveal in trust or confidence

CONFIDER n pl. -S one that confides

CONFINE v -FINED, -FINING, -FINES to shut within an enclosure

CONFINER n pl. -S one that confines

CONFIRM v -ED, -ING, -S to assure the validity of

CONFLATE v -FLATED, -FLATING, -FLATES to blend

CONFLICT v -ED, -ING, -S to come into opposition

CONFLUX n pl. -ES a flowing together of streams

CONFOCAL adj having the same focus or foci

CONFORM v -ED, -ING, -S to become the same or similar

CONFOUND v -ED, -ING, -S to confuse

CONFRERE n pl. -S a colleague

CONFRONT v -ED, -ING, -S to face defiantly

CONFUSE v -FUSED, -FUSING, -FUSES to mix up mentally

CONFUTE v -FUTED, -FUTING, -FUTES to disprove

CONFUTER n pl. -S one that confutes

CONGA v -ED, -ING, -S to perform a Latin American dance

CONGE n pl. -S permission to depart

CONGEAL v -ED, -ING, -S to change from a fluid to a solid

CONGEE v -GEED, -GEEING, -GEES to bow politely

CONGENER n pl. -S one of the same kind or class

CONGER n pl. -S a marine eel

CONGEST v -ED, -ING, -S to fill to excess

CONGIUS n pl. -GII an ancient unit of measure

CONGLOBE v -GLOBED, -GLOBING, -GLOBES to become a globule

CONGO n pl. -GOS congou

CONGO n pl. -GOES an eellike amphibian

CONGOU n pl. -S a Chinese tea

CONGRESS v -ED, -ING, -ES to assemble together

CONI pl. of conus

CONIC n pl. -S a geometric curve

CONICAL adj shaped like a cone

CONICITY n pl. -TIES the state of being conical

CONIDIUM n pl. -NIDIA a fungus spore **CONIDIAL, CONIDIAN** adj

CONIES pl. of cony

CONIFER n pl. -S an evergreen tree

CONIINE n pl. -S a poisonous alkaloid

CONIN n pl. -S coniine

CONINE n pl. -S coniine

CONING present participle of cone

CONIUM n pl. -S a poisonous herb

CONJOIN v -ED, -ING, -S to join together **CONJOINT** adj

CONJUGAL adj pertaining to marriage

CONJUNCT n pl. -S one that is joined with another

CONJURE v -JURED, -JURING, -JURES to summon a spirit

CONJURER n pl. -S a sorcerer

CONJUROR n pl. -S conjurer

CONK v -ED, -ING, -S to hit on the head

CONKER n pl. -S a chestnut used in a British game

CONKY adj full of a tree fungus

CONN v -ED, -ING, -S to direct the steering of a ship

CONNATE adj innate

CONNECT   v -ED, -ING, -S to join together

CONNED   past tense of con

CONNER   n pl. -S one that cons

CONNING   present participle of con

CONNIVE   v -NIVED, -NIVING, -NIVES to feign ignorance of wrongdoing

CONNIVER   n pl. -S one that connives

CONNOTE   v -NOTED, -NOTING, -NOTES to imply another meaning besides the literal one

CONODONT   n pl. -S a fossil

CONOID   n pl. -S a geometric solid **CONOIDAL** adj

CONQUER   v -ED, -ING, -S to overcome by force

CONQUEST   n pl. -S the act of conquering

CONQUIAN   n pl. -S a card game

CONSENT   v -ED, -ING, -S to permit or approve

CONSERVE   v -SERVED, -SERVING, -SERVES to protect from loss or depletion

CONSIDER   v -ED, -ING, -S to think about

CONSIGN   v -ED, -ING, -S to give over to another's care

CONSIST   v -ED, -ING, -S to be made up or composed

CONSOL   n pl. -S a government bond

CONSOLE   v -SOLED, -SOLING, -SOLES to comfort

CONSOLER   n pl. -S one that consoles

CONSOMME   n pl. -S a clear soup

CONSORT   v -ED, -ING, -S to keep company

CONSPIRE   v -SPIRED, -SPIRING, -SPIRES to plan secretly with another

CONSTANT   n pl. -S something that does not vary

CONSTRUE   v -STRUED, -STRUING, -STRUES to interpret

CONSUL   n pl. -S an official serving abroad **CONSULAR** adj

CONSULT   v -ED, -ING, -S to ask an opinion of

CONSUME   v -SUMED, -SUMING, -SUMES to use up

CONSUMER   n pl. -S one that consumes

CONTACT   v -ED, -ING, -S to communicate with

CONTAGIA   n/pl causative agents of infectious diseases

CONTAIN   v -ED, -ING, -S to hold within

CONTE   n pl. -S a short story

CONTEMN   v -ED, -ING, -S to scorn

CONTEMPT   n pl. -S the feeling of one who views something as mean, vile, or worthless

CONTEND   v -ED, -ING, -S to vie

CONTENT   v -ED, -ING, -S to satisfy

CONTEST   v -ED, -ING, -S to compete for

CONTEXT   n pl. -S the part of a discourse in which a particular word or phrase appears

CONTINUA   n/pl mathematical sets

CONTINUE   v -UED, -UING, -UES to go on with

CONTINUO   n pl. -UOS a type of intrumental part

CONTO   n pl. -TOS a Portuguese money of account

CONTORT   v -ED, -ING, -S to twist out of shape

CONTOUR   v -ED, -ING, -S to make the outline of

CONTRA   prep against

CONTRACT   v -ED, -ING, -S to decrease in size or volume

CONTRAIL   n pl. -S a visible trail of water vapor from an aircraft

CONTRARY   n pl. -TRARIES an opposite

CONTRAST   v -ED, -ING, -S to place in opposition to set off differences

CONTRITE   adj deeply sorry for one's sins

CONTRIVE   v -TRIVED, -TRIVING, -TRIVES to devise

CONTROL   v -TROLLED, -TROLLING, -TROLS to exercise authority over

CONTUSE   v -TUSED, -TUSING, -TUSES to bruise

CONUS   n pl. CONI an anatomical part in mammals

CONVECT   v -ED, -ING, -S to transfer heat by a process of circulation

CONVENE   v -VENED, -VENING, -VENES to assemble

CONVENER   n pl. -S one that convenes

CONVENT   v -ED, -ING, -S to convene

CONVERGE   v -VERGED, -VERGING, -VERGES to come together

CONVERSE   v -VERSED, -VERSING, -VERSES to speak together

CONVERT	*v* -ED, -ING, -S to change into another form
CONVEX	*n* pl. -ES a surface or body that is convex (curving outward)
CONVEXLY	*adv* in a convex manner
CONVEY	*v* -ED, -ING, -S to transport
CONVEYER	*n* pl. -S one that conveys
CONVEYOR	*n* pl. -S conveyer
CONVICT	*v* -ED, -ING, -S to prove guilty
CONVINCE	*v* -VINCED, -VINCING, -VINCES to cause to believe something
CONVOKE	*v* -VOKED, -VOKING, -VOKES to cause to assemble
CONVOKER	*n* pl. -S one that convokes
CONVOLVE	*v* -VOLVED, -VOLVING, -VOLVES to roll together
CONVOY	*v* -ED, -ING, -S to escort
CONVULSE	*v* -VULSED, -VULSING, -VULSES to shake violently
CONY	*n* pl. CONIES a rabbit
COO	*v* COOED, COOING, COOS to make the sound of a dove
COOCH	*n* pl. -ES a sinuous dance
COOEE	*v* COOEED, COOEEING, COOEES to cry out shrilly
COOER	*n* pl. -S one that coos
COOEY	*v* -EYED, -EYING, -EYS to cooee
COOF	*n* pl. -S a dolt
COOINGLY	*adv* in the manner of cooing doves; affectionately
COOK	*v* -ED, -ING, -S to prepare food by heating **COOKABLE** *adj*
COOKBOOK	*n* pl. -S a book of recipes
COOKER	*n* pl. -S one that cooks
COOKERY	*n* pl. -ERIES the art of cooking
COOKEY	*n* pl. -EYS cookie
COOKIE	*n* pl. -S a small, flat cake
COOKIES	pl. of cooky
COOKING	*n* pl. -S the act of one that cooks
COOKLESS	*adj* having no person that cooks
COOKOUT	*n* pl. -S a meal eaten and prepared outdoors
COOKSHOP	*n* pl. -S a shop that sells cooked food
COOKWARE	*n* pl. -S utensils used in cooking
COOKY	*n* pl. COOKIES cookie
COOL	*adj* COOLER, COOLEST moderately cold
COOL	*v* -ED, -ING, -S to make less warm
COOLANT	*n* pl. -S a fluid used to cool engines
COOLER	*n* pl. -S something that cools
COOLIE	*n* pl. -S an Oriental laborer
COOLIES	pl. of cooly
COOLISH	*adj* somewhat cool
COOLLY	*adv* in a cool manner
COOLNESS	*n* pl. -ES the state of being cool
COOLY	*n* pl. COOLIES coolie
COOMB	*n* pl. -S combe
COOMBE	*n* pl. -S combe
COON	*n* pl. -S a raccoon
COONCAN	*n* pl. -S conquian
COONSKIN	*n* pl. -S the pelt of a raccoon
COONTIE	*n* pl. -S a tropical plant
COOP	*v* -ED, -ING, -S to confine
COOPER	*v* -ED, -ING, -S to make or mend barrels
COOPERY	*n* pl. -ERIES the trade of coopering
COOPT	*v* -ED, -ING, -S to elect or appoint
COOPTION	*n* pl. -S the act of coopting
COOT	*n* pl. -S an aquatic bird
COOTIE	*n* pl. -S a body louse
COP	*v* COPPED, COPPING, COPS to steal
COPAIBA	*n* pl. -S a resin
COPAL	*n* pl. -S a resin
COPALM	*n* pl. -S a hardwood tree
COPARENT	*n* pl. -S a fellow parent
COPASTOR	*n* pl. -S one that shares the duties of a pastor
COPATRON	*n* pl. -S a fellow patron
COPE	*v* COPED, COPING, COPES to contend or strive
COPECK	*n* pl. -S kopeck
COPEMATE	*n* pl. -S an antagonist
COPEN	*n* pl. -S a blue color
COPEPOD	*n* pl. -S a minute crustacean
COPER	*n* pl. -S a horse dealer
COPIED	past tense of copy
COPIER	*n* pl. -S one that copies
COPIES	present 3d person sing. of copy

COPIHUE	*n* -pl. -S a climbing vine
COPILOT	*n* pl. -S a pilot who assists the pilot in command
COPING	*n* pl. -S the top part of a wall
COPIOUS	*adj* abundant
COPLANAR	*adj* lying in the same plane
COPLOT	*v* -PLOTTED, -PLOTTING, -PLOTS to plot together
COPPED	past tense of cop
COPPER	*v* -ED, -ING, -S to cover with copper (a metallic element)
COPPERAH	*n* pl. -S copra
COPPERAS	*n* pl. -ES a compound used in making inks
COPPERY	*adj* resembling copper
COPPICE	*n* pl. -S a thicket **COPPICED** *adj*
COPPING	present participle of cop
COPPRA	*n* pl. -S copra
COPRA	*n* pl. -S dried coconut meat
COPRAH	*n* pl. -S copra
COPREMIA	*n* pl. -S a form of blood poisoning **COPREMIC** *adj*
COPSE	*n* pl. -S a coppice
COPTER	*n* pl. -S a helicopter
COPULA	*n* pl. -LAS or -LAE something that links **COPULAR** *adj*
COPULATE	*v* -LATED, -LATING, -LATES to engage in coitus
COPY	*v* COPIED, COPYING, COPIES to imitate
COPYBOOK	*n* pl. -S a book used in teaching penmanship
COPYBOY	*n* pl. -BOYS an office boy
COPYCAT	*v* -CATTED, -CATTING, -CATS to imitate
COPYDESK	*n* pl. -S an editor's desk in a newspaper office
COPYHOLD	*n* pl. -S a type of ownership of land
COPYIST	*n* pl. -S an imitator
COQUET	*v* -QUETTED, -QUETTING, -QUETS to flirt
COQUETRY	*n* pl. -TRIES flirtatious behavior
COQUETTE	*v* -QUETTED, -QUETTING, -QUETTES to coquet
COQUILLE	*n* pl. -S a cooking utensil
COQUINA	*n* pl. -S a small marine clam
COQUITO	*n* pl. -TOS a palm tree
CORACLE	*n* pl. -S a small boat
CORACOID	*n* pl. -S a bone of the shoulder girdle
CORAL	*n* pl. -S a mass of marine animal skeletons
CORANTO	*n* pl. -TOS or -TOES courante
CORBAN	*n* pl. -S an offering to God
CORBEIL	*n* pl. -S a sculptured fruit basket
CORBEL	*v* -BELED, -BELING, -BELS or -BELLED, -BELLING, -BELS to provide a wall with a bracket
CORBIE	*n* pl. -S a raven or crow
CORBINA	*n* pl. -S a food and game fish
CORBY	*n* pl. CORBIES corbie
CORD	*v* -ED, -ING, -S to fasten with a cord (a thin rope)
CORDAGE	*n* pl. -S the amount of wood in an area
CORDATE	*adj* heart-shaped
CORDER	*n* pl. -S one that cords
CORDIAL	*n* pl. -S a liqueur
CORDITE	*n* pl. -S an explosive powder
CORDLESS	*adj* having no cord
CORDLIKE	*adj* resembling a cord
CORDOBA	*n* pl. -S a monetary unit of Nicaragua
CORDON	*v* -ED, -ING, -S to form a barrier around
CORDOVAN	*n* pl. -S a fine leather
CORDUROY	*v* -ED, -ING, -S to build a type of road
CORDWAIN	*n* pl. -S cordovan
CORDWOOD	*n* pl. -S wood used for fuel
CORE	*v* CORED, CORING, CORES to remove the core (the central part) of
COREDEEM	*v* -ED, -ING, -S to redeem jointly
COREIGN	*n* pl. -S a joint reign
CORELATE	*v* -LATED, -LATING, -LATES to place into mutual or reciprocal relation
CORELESS	*adj* having no core
COREMIUM	*n* pl. -MIA an organ of certain fungi
CORER	*n* pl. -S a utensil for coring apples
CORF	*n* pl. CORVES a wagon used in a mine
CORGI	*n* pl. -S a short-legged dog
CORING	present participle of core

CORIUM	*n* pl. -RIA a skin layer
CORK	*v* -ED, -ING, -S to stop up
CORKAGE	*n* pl. -S a charge for wine in a restaurant
CORKER	*n* pl. -S one that corks
CORKIER	comparative of corky
CORKIEST	superlative of corky
CORKLIKE	*adj* resembling cork (a porous tree bark)
CORKWOOD	*n* pl. -S a small tree
CORKY	*adj* CORKIER, CORKIEST corklike
CORM	*n* pl. -S a stem of certain plants **CORMOID, CORMOUS, CORMLIKE** *adj*
CORMEL	*n* pl. -S a small corm
CORN	*v* -ED, -ING, -S to preserve with salt
CORNBALL	*n* pl. -S a hick
CORNCAKE	*n* pl. -S a cake made of cornmeal
CORNCOB	*n* pl. -S the woody core of an ear of corn
CORNCRIB	*n* pl. -S a building in which corn is stored
CORNEA	*n* pl. -S a part of the eye **CORNEAL** *adj*
CORNEL	*n* pl. -S a hardwood tree or shrub
CORNEOUS	*adj* of a hornlike texture
CORNER	*v* -ED, -ING, -S to gain control of
CORNET	*n* pl. -S a trumpetlike instrument
CORNETCY	*n* -CIES a rank in the British cavalry
CORNFED	*adj* fed on corn
CORNHUSK	*n* pl. -S the husk covering an ear of corn
CORNICE	*v* -NICED, -NICING, -NICES to decorate with a molding
CORNICHE	*n* pl. -S a road built along a cliff
CORNICLE	*n* pl. -S a part of an aphid
CORNIER	comparative of corny
CORNIEST	superlative of corny
CORNILY	*adv* in a corny manner
CORNMEAL	*n* pl. -S meal made from corn
CORNU	*n* pl. -NUA a hornlike bone formation **CORNUAL** *adj*
CORNUS	*n* pl. -ES a cornel
CORNUTE	*adj* horn-shaped
CORNUTED	*adj* cornute
CORNUTO	*n* pl. -TOS the husband of an unfaithful wife
CORNY	*adj* CORNIER, CORNIEST trite
CORODY	*n* pl. -DIES an allowance of food or clothes
COROLLA	*n* pl. -S a protective covering of a flower
CORONA	*n* pl. -NAS or -NAE a luminous circle around a celestial body
CORONACH	*n* pl. -S a dirge
CORONAL	*n* pl. -S a wreath worn on the head
CORONARY	*n* pl. -NARIES an artery supplying blood to the heart
CORONEL	*n* pl. -S coronal
CORONER	*n* pl. -S an officer who investigates questionable deaths
CORONET	*n* pl. -S a small crown
COROTATE	*v* -TATED, -TATING, -TATES to rotate together
CORPORA	pl. of corpus
CORPORAL	*n* pl. -S a military rank
CORPS	*n* pl. CORPS a military unit
CORPSE	*n* pl. -S a dead body
CORPSMAN	*n* pl. -MEN an enlisted man trained to give minor medical treatment
CORPUS	*n* pl. -PORA a human or animal body
CORRADE	*v* -RADED, -RADING, -RADES to erode
CORRAL	*v* -RALLED, -RALLING, -RALS to place livestock in an enclosure
CORRECT	*v* -ED, -ING, -S to make free from error
CORRECT	*adj* -RECTER, -RECTEST free from error
CORRIDA	*n* pl. -S a bullfight
CORRIDOR	*n* pl. -S a narrow hallway
CORRIE	*n* pl. -S a cirque
CORRIVAL	*n* pl. -S a rival or opponent
CORRODE	*v* -RODED, -RODING, -RODES to eat away gradually
CORRODY	*n* pl. -DIES corody
CORRUPT	*adj* -RUPTER, -RUPTEST dishonest and venal
CORRUPT	*v* -ED, -ING, -S to subvert the honesty or integrity of

CORSAC	*n* pl. -S an Asian fox
CORSAGE	*n* pl. -S a small bouquet of flowers
CORSAIR	*n* pl. -S a pirate
CORSE	*n* pl. -S a corpse
CORSELET	*n* pl. -S a piece of body armor
CORSET	*v* -ED, -ING, -S to fit with a corset (a supporting undergarment)
CORSLET	*n* pl. -S corselet
CORTEGE	*n* pl. -S a retinue
CORTEX	*n* pl. -TICES or -TEXES the outer layer of an organ **CORTICAL** *adj*
CORTIN	*n* pl. -S a hormone
CORTISOL	*n* pl. -S a hormone
CORUNDUM	*n* pl. -S a hard mineral
CORVEE	*n* pl. -S an obligation to perform feudal service
CORVES	pl. of corf
CORVET	*n* pl. -S corvette
CORVETTE	*n* pl. -S a swift warship
CORVINA	*n* pl. -S corbina
CORVINE	*adj* pertaining or belonging to the crow family of birds
CORYMB	*n* pl. -S a flower cluster **CORYMBED** *adj*
CORYPHEE	*n* pl. -S a ballet dancer
CORYZA	*n* pl. -S a head cold **CORYZAL** *adj*
COS	*n* pl. -ES a variety of lettuce
COSEC	*n* pl. -S cosecant
COSECANT	*n* pl. -S a trigonometric function of an angle
COSET	*n* pl. -S a mathematical subset
COSEY	*n* pl. -SEYS a cozy
COSH	*v* -ED, -ING, -ES to bludgeon
COSHER	*v* -ED, -ING, -S to coddle
COSIE	*n* pl. -S a cozy
COSIER	comparative of cosy
COSIES	pl. of cosy
COSIEST	superlative of cosy
COSIGN	*v* -ED, -ING, -S to sign jointly
COSIGNER	*n* pl. -S one that cosigns
COSILY	*adv* in a cosy manner
COSINE	*n* pl. -S a trigonometric function of an angle
COSINESS	*n* pl. -ES coziness
COSMETIC	*n* pl. -S a beauty preparation
COSMIC	*adj* pertaining to the cosmos
COSMICAL	*adj* cosmic
COSMISM	*n* pl. -S a philosophical theory
COSMIST	*n* pl. -S a supporter of cosmism
COSMOS	*n* pl. -ES the universe regarded as an orderly system
COSS	*n* pl. COSS kos
COSSACK	*n* pl. -S a Russian cavalryman
COSSET	*v* -ED, -ING, -S to fondle
COST	*v* COST or COSTED, COSTING, COSTS to estimate a price for production of
COSTA	*n* pl. -TAE a rib **COSTAL** *adj*
COSTAR	*v* -STARRED, -STARRING, -STARS to star with another actor
COSTARD	*n* pl. -S a large cooking apple
COSTATE	*adj* having a rib or ribs
COSTER	*n* pl. -S a hawker of fruit or vegetables
COSTIVE	*adj* constipated
COSTLESS	*adj* free of charge
COSTLY	*adj* -LIER, -LIEST expensive
COSTMARY	*n* pl. -MARIES an herb used in salads
COSTREL	*n* pl. -S a flask
COSTUME	*v* -TUMED, -TUMING, -TUMES to supply with a costume (a style of dress)
COSTUMER	*n* pl. -S one that costumes
COSTUMEY	*adj* of or pertaining to a costume
COSTUMING	present participle of costume
COSY	*adj* COSIER, COSIEST cozy
COSY	*n* pl. COSIES a cozy
COT	*n* pl. -S a light, narrow bed
COTAN	*n* pl. -S a trigonometric function of an angle
COTE	*v* COTED, COTING, COTES to pass by
COTEAU	*n* pl. -TEAUX the higher ground of a region
COTENANT	*n* pl. -S one who is a tenant with another in the same place
COTERIE	*n* pl. -S a clique
COTHURN	*n* pl. -S a buskin worn by ancient Roman actors
COTHURNI	*n/pl* cothurns

COTIDAL *adj* indicating coincidence of the tides

COTILLON *n* pl. -S a ballroom dance

COTING present participle of cote

COTQUEAN *n* pl. -S a vulgar woman

COTTA *n* pl. -TAE or -TAS a short surplice

COTTAGE *n* pl. -S a small house **COTTAGEY** *adj*

COTTAGER *n* pl. -S one that lives in a cottage

COTTAR *n* pl. -S cotter

COTTER *n* pl. -S a tenant farmer

COTTIER *n* pl. -S cotter

COTTON *v* -ED, -ING, -S to take a liking

COTTONY *adj* resembling cotton (a soft, fibrous material)

COTYLOID *adj* cup-shaped

COTYPE *n* pl. -S a taxonomic type

COUCH *v* -ED, -ING, -ES to put into words

COUCHANT *adj* lying down

COUCHER *n* pl. -S one that couches

COUCHING *n* pl. -S a form of embroidery

COUDE *adj* pertaining to a type of telescope

COUGAR *n* pl. -S a mountain lion

COUGH *v* -ED, -ING, -S to expel air from the lungs noisily

COUGHER *n* pl. -S one that coughs

COULD past tense of can

COULDEST a past 2d person sing. of can

COULDST a past 2d person sing. of can

COULEE *n* pl. -S a small ravine

COULISSE *n* pl. -S a side scene of a theater stage

COULOIR *n* pl. -S a deep gorge or gully

COULOMB *n* pl. -S an electrical measure

COULTER *n* pl. -S colter

COUMARIN *n* pl. -S a chemical compound **COUMARIC** *adj*

COUMAROU *n* pl. -S the seed of a tropical tree

COUNCIL *n* pl. -S a group of persons appointed for a certain function

COUNSEL *v* -SELED, -SELING, -SELS or -SELLED, -SELLING, -SELS to advise

COUNT *v* -ED, -ING, -S to list or mention the units of one by one to ascertain the total

COUNTER *v* -ED, -ING, -S to oppose

COUNTESS *n* pl. -ES a noblewoman

COUNTIAN *n* pl. -S a resident of a county

COUNTRY *n* pl. -TRIES the territory of a nation

COUNTY *n* pl. -TIES an administrative division of a state

COUP *v* -ED, -ING, -S to overturn

COUPE *n* pl. -S an automobile with two doors

COUPLE *v* -PLED, -PLING, -PLES to unite in pairs

COUPLER *n* pl. -S one that couples

COUPLET *n* pl. -S a pair of successive lines of verse

COUPLING *n* pl. -S a joining device

COUPON *n* pl. -S a certificate entitling the holder to certain benefits

COURAGE *n* pl. -S the quality that enables one to face danger fearlessly; spirit

COURANT *n* pl. -S courante

COURANTE *n* pl. -S an old, lively dance

COURANTO *n* pl. -TOS or -TOES courante

COURIER *n* pl. -S a messenger

COURLAN *n* pl. -S a wading bird

COURSE *v* COURSED, COURSING, COURSES to cause hounds to chase game

COURSER *n* pl. -S one that courses

COURSING *n* pl. -S the pursuit of game by hounds

COURT *v* -ED, -ING, -S to woo

COURTESY *v* -SIED, -SYING, -SIES to curtsy

COURTIER *n* pl. -S one who attends a royal court

COURTLY *adj* -LIER, -LIEST stately

COUSCOUS *n* pl. -ES a North African cereal

COUSIN *n* pl. -S a child of one's aunt or uncle **COUSINLY** *adj*

COUSINRY *n* pl. -RIES cousins collectively

COUTEAU *n* pl. -TEAUX a knife

COUTER *n* pl. -S a piece of armor for the elbow

COUTH *adj* COUTHER, COUTHEST sophisticated

COUTH *n* pl. -S refinement

COUTHIE adj COUTHIER, COUTHIEST friendly

COUTURE n pl. -S the business of dressmaking

COUVADE n pl. -S a primitive birth ritual

COVALENT adj sharing electron pairs

COVE v COVED, COVING, COVES to curve over or inward

COVEN n pl. -S a group of thirteen witches

COVENANT v -ED, -ING, -S to enter into a binding agreement

COVER v -ED, -ING, -S to place something over or upon

COVERAGE n pl. -S the extent to which something is covered

COVERALL n pl. -S a one-piece work garment

COVERER n pl. -S one that covers

COVERING n pl. -S something that covers

COVERLET n pl. -S a bed covering

COVERLID n pl. -S a coverlet

COVERT n pl. -S a hiding place

COVERTLY adv secretly

COVET v -ED, -ING, -S to desire greatly

COVETER n pl. -S one that covets

COVETOUS adj excessively desirous

COVEY n pl. -EYS a flock of birds

COVING n pl. -S a concave molding

COW n pl. -S or KINE a farm animal

COW v -ED, -ING, -S to intimidate

COWAGE n pl. -S a tropical vine

COWARD n pl. -S one who lacks courage

COWARDLY adj lacking courage

COWBANE n pl. -S a poisonous plant

COWBELL n pl. -S a bell around a cow's neck

COWBERRY n pl. -RIES a pasture shrub

COWBIND n pl. -S a species of bryony

COWBIRD n pl. -S a blackbird

COWBOY n pl. -BOYS a ranch worker

COWEDLY adv in a cowed manner

COWER v -ED, -ING, -S to cringe

COWFISH n pl. -ES an aquatic mammal

COWGIRL n pl. -S a female ranch worker

COWHAGE n pl. -S cowage

COWHAND n pl. -S a cowboy

COWHERB n pl. -S an annual herb

COWHERD n pl. -S one who tends cattle

COWHIDE v -HIDED, -HIDING, -HIDES to flog with a leather whip

COWIER comparative of cowy

COWIEST superlative of cowy

COWINNER n pl. -S one of two or more winners

COWL v -ED, -ING, -S to cover with a hood

COWLICK n pl. -S a lock of unruly hair

COWLING n pl. -S a covering for an aircraft engine

COWMAN n pl. -MEN one who owns cattle

COWORKER n pl. -S a fellow worker

COWPAT n pl. -S a dropping of cow dung

COWPEA n pl. -S a black-eyed pea

COWPOKE n pl. -S a cowboy

COWPOX n pl. -ES a cattle disease

COWRIE n pl. -S cowry

COWRY n pl. -RIES a glossy seashell

COWSHED n pl. -S a shelter for cows

COWSKIN n pl. -S the hide of a cow

COWSLIP n pl. -S a flowering plant

COWY adj COWIER, COWIEST suggestive of a cow

COX v -ED, -ING, -ES to coxswain

COXA n pl. COXAE the hip or hip joint **COXAL** adj

COXALGIA n pl. -S pain in the hip **COXALGIC** adj

COXALGY n pl. -GIES coxalgia

COXCOMB n pl. -S a conceited dandy

COXSWAIN v -ED, -ING, -S to steer a racing rowboat

COY adj COYER, COYEST shy

COY v -ED, -ING, -S to caress

COYISH adj somewhat coy

COYLY adv in a coy manner

COYNESS n pl. -ES the state of being coy

COYOTE n pl. -S a small wolf

COYPOU n pl. -S coypu

COYPU n pl. -S an aquatic rodent

COZ n pl. COZES or COZZES a cousin

COZEN v -ED, -ING, -S to deceive

COZENAGE n pl. -S the practice of cozening

COZENER	*n* pl. -S one that cozens
COZEY	*n* pl. -ZEYS cozy
COZIE	*n* pl. -S cozy
COZIER	comparative of cozy
COZIES	pl. of cozy
COZINESS	*n* pl. -ES the state of being cozy
COZY	*adj* COZIER, COZIEST snug and comfortable **COZILY** *adv*
COZY	*n* pl. -ZIES a covering for a teapot
COZZES	a pl. of coz
CRAAL	*v* -ED, -ING, -S to kraal
CRAB	*v* CRABBED, CRABBING, CRABS to complain
CRABBER	*n* pl. -S one that crabs
CRABBY	*adj* -BIER, -BIEST grumpy
CRABWISE	*adv* sideways
CRACK	*v* -ED, -ING, -S to break without dividing into parts
CRACKER	*n* pl. -S a thin, crisp biscuit
CRACKING	*n* pl. -S a chemical process
CRACKLE	*v* -LED, -LING, -LES to make a succession of snapping sounds
CRACKLY	*adj* -LIER, -LIEST brittle
CRACKNEL	*n* pl. -S a hard, crisp biscuit
CRACKPOT	*n* pl. -S an eccentric person
CRACKUP	*n* pl. -S a collision
CRACKY	*interj* — used to express surprise
CRADLE	*v* -DLED, -DLING, -DLES to nurture during infancy
CRADLER	*n* pl. -S one that cradles
CRAFT	*v* -ED, -ING, -S to make by hand
CRAFTY	*adj* CRAFTIER, CRAFTIEST skillful in deceiving **CRAFTILY** *adv*
CRAG	*n* pl. -S a rough rock **CRAGGED** *adj*
CRAGGY	*adj* -GIER, -GIEST full of crags **CRAGGILY** *adv*
CRAGSMAN	*n* pl. -MEN one who climbs crags
CRAKE	*n* pl. -S a small, harsh-voiced bird
CRAM	*v* CRAMMED, CRAMMING, CRAMS to fill or pack tightly
CRAMBE	*n* pl. -S an annual herb
CRAMBO	*n* pl. -BOS or -BOES a word game
CRAMMED	past tense of cram
CRAMMER	*n* pl. -S one that crams
CRAMMING	present participle of cram
CRAMOISY	*n* pl. -SIES crimson cloth
CRAMP	*v* -ED, -ING, -S to restrain or confine
CRAMPIT	*n* pl. -S a piece of equipment used in curling
CRAMPON	*n* pl. -S a device for raising heavy objects
CRAMPOON	*n* pl. -S crampon
CRANCH	*v* -ED, -ING, -ES to craunch
CRANE	*v* CRANED, CRANING, CRANES to stretch out one's neck
CRANIA	a pl. of cranium
CRANIAL	*adj* pertaining to the skull
CRANIATE	*n* pl. -S one that has a skull
CRANING	present participle of crane
CRANIUM	*n* pl. -NIUMS or -NIA the skull
CRANK	*v* -ED, -ING, -S to start manually
CRANK	*adj* CRANKER, CRANKEST lively
CRANKIER	comparative of cranky
CRANKIEST	superlative of cranky
CRANKILY	*adv* in a cranky manner
CRANKLE	*v* -KLED, -KLING, -KLES to crinkle
CRANKLY	*adv* in a crank manner
CRANKOUS	*adj* cranky
CRANKPIN	*n* pl. -S the handle of a crank
CRANKY	*adj* CRANKIER, CRANKIEST grumpy
CRANNIED	*adj* having crannies
CRANNIES	pl. of cranny
CRANNOG	*n* pl. -S an artificial island
CRANNOGE	*n* pl. -S crannog
CRANNY	*n* pl. -NIES a crevice
CRAP	*v* CRAPPED, CRAPPING, CRAPS to defecate — usually considered vulgar
CRAPE	*v* CRAPED, CRAPING, CRAPES to crepe
CRAPPER	*n* pl. -S a toilet — usually considered vulgar
CRAPPIE	*n* pl. -S an edible fish
CRAPPING	present participle of crap
CRAPPY	*adj* -PIER, -PIEST markedly inferior in quality
CRASES	pl. of crasis

CRASH	*v* -ED, -ING,- ES to collide noisily
CRASHER	*n* pl. -S one that crashes
CRASIS	*n* pl. CRASES a vowel contraction
CRASS	*adj* CRASSER, CRASSEST grossly vulgar or stupid **CRASSLY** *adv*
CRATCH	*n* pl. -ES a manger
CRATE	*v* CRATED, CRATING, CRATES to put in a packing box
CRATER	*v* -ED, -ING, -S to form cavities in a surface
CRATON	*n* pl. -S a part of the earth's crust **CRATONIC** *adj*
CRAUNCH	*v* -ED, -ING, -ES to crunch
CRAVAT	*n* pl. -S a necktie
CRAVE	*v* CRAVED, CRAVING, CRAVES to desire greatly
CRAVEN	*v* -ED, -ING, -S to make cowardly
CRAVENLY	*adv* in a cowardly manner
CRAVER	*n* pl. -S one that craves
CRAVING	*n* pl. -S a great desire
CRAW	*n* pl. -S the stomach of certain animals
CRAWDAD	*n* pl. -S a crayfish
CRAWFISH	*v* -ED, -ING, -ES to back out or retreat
CRAWL	*v* -ED, -ING, -S to move with the body on or near the ground
CRAWLER	*n* pl. -S one that crawls
CRAWLWAY	*n* pl. -WAYS a small, low tunnel
CRAWLY	*adj* CRAWLIER, CRAWLIEST creepy
CRAYFISH	*n* pl. -ES a crustacean
CRAYON	*v* -ED, -ING, -S to use a drawing implement
CRAZE	*v* CRAZED, CRAZING, CRAZES to make insane
CRAZY	*adj* -ZIER, -ZIEST insane **CRAZILY** *adv*
CREAK	*v* -ED, -ING, -S to squeak
CREAKY	*adj* CREAKIER, CREAKIEST creaking **CREAKILY** *adv*
CREAM	*v* -ED, -ING, -S to form cream (a part of milk)
CREAMER	*n* pl. -S a cream pitcher
CREAMERY	*n* pl. -ERIES a dairy

CREAMY	*adj* CREAMIER, CREAMIEST rich in cream **CREAMILY** *adv*
CREASE	*v* CREASED, CREASING, CREASES to make a fold or wrinkle in
CREASER	*n* pl. -S one that creases
CREASY	*adj* CREASIER, CREASIEST having folds or wrinkles
CREATE	*v* -ATED, -ATING, -ATES to cause to exist
CREATIN	*n* pl. -S creatine
CREATINE	*n* pl. -S a chemical compound
CREATION	*n* pl. -S something created
CREATIVE	*adj* having the ability to create
CREATOR	*n* pl. -S one that creates
CREATURE	*n* pl. -S a living being
CRECHE	*n* pl. -S a day nursery
CREDAL	*adj* pertaining to a creed
CREDENCE	*n* pl. -S belief
CREDENDA	*n/pl* articles of faith
CREDENT	*adj* believing
CREDENZA	*n* pl. -S a piece of furniture
CREDIBLE	*adj* believable **CREDIBLY** *adv*
CREDIT	*v* -ED, -ING, -S to accept as true
CREDITOR	*n* pl. -S one to whom money is owed
CREDO	*n* pl. -DOS a creed
CREED	*n* pl. -S a statement of belief **CREEDAL** *adj*
CREEK	*n* pl. -S a watercourse smaller than a river
CREEL	*n* pl. -S a fish basket
CREEP	*v* CREPT, CREEPING, CREEPS to crawl
CREEPAGE	*n* pl. -S gradual movement
CREEPER	*n* pl. -S one that creeps
CREEPIE	*n* pl. -S a low stool
CREEPY	*adj* CREEPIER, CREEPIEST repugnant **CREEPILY** *adv*
CREESE	*n* pl. -S kris
CREESH	*v* -ED, -ING, -ES to grease
CREMAINS	*n/pl* the ashes of a cremated body
CREMATE	*v* -MATED, -MATING, -MATES to reduce to ashes by burning
CREMATOR	*n* pl. -S one that cremates
CREME	*n* pl. -S cream

CRENATE	*adj* having an edge with rounded projections
CRENATED	*adj* crenate
CRENEL	*v* -ELED, -ELING, -ELS or -ELLED, -ELLING, -ELS to provide with crenelles
CRENELLE	*n* pl. -S a rounded projection
CREODONT	*n* pl. -S an extinct carnivore
CREOLE	*n* pl. -S a type of mixed language
CREOSOL	*n* pl. -S a chemical compound
CREOSOTE	*v* -SOTED, -SOTING, -SOTES to treat with a wood preservative
CREPE	*v* CREPED, CREPING, CREPES to frizz the hair
CREPEY	*adj* CREPIER, CREPIEST crinkly
CREPT	past tense of creep
CREPY	*adj* CREPIER, CREPIEST crepey
CRESCENT	*n* pl. -S the figure of the moon in its first or last quarter
CRESIVE	*adj* increasing
CRESOL	*n* pl. -S a chemical disinfectant
CRESS	*n* pl. -ES a plant used in salads
CRESSET	*n* pl. -S a metal cup for burning oil
CREST	*v* -ED, -ING, -S to reach a crest (a peak)
CRESTAL	*adj* pertaining to a crest
CRESTING	*n* pl. -S a decorative coping
CRESYL	*n* pl. -S tolyl
CRESYLIC	*adj* pertaining to cresol
CRETIC	*n* pl. -S a type of metrical foot
CRETIN	*n* pl. -S an idiot
CRETONNE	*n* pl. -S a heavy fabric
CREVALLE	*n* pl. -S a food and game fish
CREVASSE	*v* -VASSED, -VASSING, -VASSES to fissure
CREVICE	*n* pl. -S a cleft **CREVICED** *adj*
CREW	*v* -ED, -ING, -S to serve aboard a ship
CREWEL	*n* pl. -S a woolen yarn
CREWLESS	*adj* being without any crewmen
CREWMAN	*n* pl. -MEN one who serves on a ship
CRIB	*v* CRIBBED, CRIBBING, CRIBS to confine closely
CRIBBAGE	*n* pl. -S a card game
CRIBBER	*n* pl. -S one that cribs
CRIBBING	*n* pl. -S a supporting framework
CRIBBLED	*adj* covered with dots
CRIBROUS	*adj* pierced with small holes
CRIBWORK	*n* pl. -S a framework of logs
CRICETID	*n* pl. -S a small rodent
CRICK	*v* -ED, -ING, -S to cause a spasm of the neck
CRICKET	*v* -ED, -ING, -S to play cricket (a ball game)
CRICOID	*n* pl. -S a cartilage of the larynx
CRIED	past tense of cry
CRIER	*n* pl. -S one that cries
CRIES	present 3d person sing. of cry
CRIME	*n* pl. -S a violation of the law
CRIMINAL	*n* pl. -S one who has committed a crime
CRIMMER	*n* pl. -S krimmer
CRIMP	*v* -ED, -ING, -S to pleat
CRIMPER	*n* pl. -S one that crimps
CRIMPLE	*v* -PLED, -PLING, -PLES to wrinkle
CRIMPY	*adj* CRIMPIER, CRIMPIEST wavy
CRIMSON	*v* -ED, -ING, -S to make crimson (a red color)
CRINGE	*v* CRINGED, CRINGING, CRINGES to shrink in fear
CRINGER	*n* pl. -S one that cringes
CRINGLE	*n* pl. -S a small loop of rope
CRINITE	*n* pl. -S a fossil crinoid
CRINKLE	*v* -KLED, -KLING, -KLES to wrinkle
CRINKLY	*adj* -KLIER, -KLIEST crinkled
CRINOID	*n* pl. -S a marine animal
CRINUM	*n* pl. -S a tropical herb
CRIOLLO	*n* pl. -LLOS a person of Spanish ancestry
CRIPPLE	*v* -PLED, -PLING, -PLES to disable or impair
CRIPPLER	*n* pl. -S one that cripples
CRIS	*n* pl. -ES kris
CRISIS	*n* pl. CRISES a crucial turning point **CRISIC** *adj*
CRISP	*adj* CRISPER, CRISPEST brittle
CRISP	*v* -ED, -ING, -S to make crisp
CRISPATE	*adj* curled
CRISPEN	*v* -ED, -ING, -S to make crisp
CRISPER	*n* pl. -S one that crisps

CRISPLY	*adv* in a crisp manner
CRISPY	*adj* CRISPIER, CRISPIEST crisp **CRISPILY** *adv*
CRISSUM	*n* pl. CRISSA a region of feathers on a bird **CRISSAL** *adj*
CRISTA	*n* pl. -TAE a part of a cell
CRISTATE	*adj* having a projection on the head
CRITERIA	*n/pl* standards of judgment
CRITIC	*n* pl. -S one who judges the merits of something **CRITICAL** *adj*
CRITIQUE	*v* -TIQUED, -TIQUING, -TIQUES to judge as a critic
CRITTER	*n* pl. -S a creature
CRITTUR	*n* pl. -S critter
CROAK	*v* -ED, -ING, -S to utter a low, hoarse sound
CROAKER	*n* pl. -S one that croaks
CROAKY	*adj* CROAKIER, CROAKIEST low and hoarse **CROAKILY** *adv*
CROCEIN	*n* pl. -S a red dye
CROCEINE	*n* pl. -S crocein
CROCHET	*v* -ED, -ING, -S to do a type of needlework
CROCI	a pl. of crocus
CROCINE	*adj* pertaining to the crocus
CROCK	*v* -ED, -ING, -S to stain or soil
CROCKERY	*n* pl. -ERIES pottery
CROCKET	*n* pl. -S an architectural ornament
CROCOITE	*n* pl. -S a mineral
CROCUS	*n* pl. -CUSES or -CI a flowering plant
CROFT	*n* pl. -S a small tenant farm
CROFTER	*n* pl. -S a tenant farmer
CROJIK	*n* pl. -S a triangular sail
CROMLECH	*n* pl. -S a dolmen
CRONE	*n* pl. -S a withered old woman
CRONY	*n* pl. CRONIES a close friend
CRONYISM	*n* pl. -S a kind of political favoritism
CROOK	*v* -ED, -ING, -S to bend
CROOKED	*adj* -EDER, -EDEST dishonest
CROON	*v* -ED, -ING, -S to sing softly
CROONER	*n* pl. -S one that croons
CROP	*v* CROPPED, CROPPING, CROPS to cut off short

CROPLAND	*n* pl. -S farmland
CROPLESS	*adj* being without crops (agricultural produce)
CROPPED	past tense of crop
CROPPER	*n* pl. -S one that crops
CROPPING	present participle of crop
CROQUET	*v* -ED, -ING, -S to drive a ball away in a certain game
CROQUIS	*n* pl. CROQUIS a sketch
CRORE	*n* pl. -S a monetary unit of India
CROSIER	*n* pl. -S a bishop's staff
CROSS	*v* -ED, -ING, -ES to intersect
CROSS	*adj* CROSSER, CROSSEST ill-tempered **CROSSLY** *adv*
CROSSARM	*n* pl. -S a horizontal bar
CROSSBAR	*v* -BARRED, -BARRING, -BARS to fasten with crossarms
CROSSBOW	*n* pl. -S a kind of weapon
CROSSCUT	*v* -CUT, -CUTTING, -CUTS to cut across
CROSSE	*n* pl. -S a lacrosse stick
CROSSER	*n* pl. -S one that crosses
CROSSING	*n* pl. -S an intersection
CROSSLET	*n* pl. -S a heraldic symbol
CROSSTIE	*n* pl. -S a transverse beam
CROSSWAY	*n* pl. -WAYS a road that crosses another road
CROTCH	*n* pl. -ES an angle formed by two diverging parts **CROTCHED** *adj*
CROTCHET	*n* pl. -S a small hook
CROTON	*n* pl. -S a tropical plant
CROUCH	*v* -ED, -ING, -ES to stoop
CROUP	*n* pl. -S a disease of the throat
CROUPE	*n* pl. -S the rump of certain animals
CROUPIER	*n* pl. -S an attendant in a casino
CROUPOUS	*adj* pertaining to croup
CROUPY	*adj* CROUPIER, CROUPIEST affected with croup **CROUPILY** *adv*
CROUSE	*adj* lively **CROUSELY** *adv*
CROUTON	*n* pl. -S a small cube of toasted bread
CROW	*v* -ED, -ING, -S to boast
CROWBAR	*n* pl. -S a steel bar used as a lever

CROWD	*v* -ED, -ING, -S to press into an insufficient space
CROWDER	*n* pl. -S one that crowds
CROWDIE	*n* pl. -S crowdy
CROWDY	*n* pl. -DIES porridge
CROWER	*n* pl. -S one that crows
CROWFOOT	*n* pl. -FOOTS or -FEET a flowering plant
CROWN	*v* -ED, -ING, -S to supply with a crown (a royal headpiece)
CROWNER	*n* pl. -S a coroner
CROWNET	*n* pl. -S a coronet
CROWSTEP	*n* pl. -S a step on top of a wall
CROZE	*n* pl. -S a tool used in barrel-making
CROZER	*n* pl. -S a croze
CROZIER	*n* pl. -S crosier
CRUCES	a pl. of crux
CRUCIAL	*adj* of supreme importance
CRUCIAN	*n* pl. -S a European fish
CRUCIATE	*adj* cross-shaped
CRUCIBLE	*n* pl. -S a heat-resistant vessel
CRUCIFER	*n* pl. -S one who carries a cross
CRUCIFIX	*n* pl. -ES a cross bearing an image of Christ
CRUCIFY	*v* -FIED, -FYING, -FIES to put to death on a cross
CRUD	*v* CRUDDED, CRUDDING, CRUDS to curd
CRUDDY	*adj* trashy
CRUDE	*adj* CRUDER, CRUDEST unrefined **CRUDELY** *adv*
CRUDE	*n* pl. -S unrefined petroleum
CRUDITY	*n* pl. -TIES the state of being crude
CRUEL	*adj* CRUELER, CRUELEST or CRUELLER, CRUELLEST indifferent to the pain of others **CRUELLY** *adv*
CRUELTY	*n* pl. -TIES a cruel act
CRUET	*n* pl. -S a glass bottle
CRUISE	*v* CRUISED, CRUISING, CRUISES to sail about touching at several ports
CRUISER	*n* pl. -S a boat that cruises
CRULLER	*n* pl. -S a small sweet cake
CRUMB	*v* -ED, -ING, -S to break into crumbs (small pieces)
CRUMBER	*n* pl. -S one that crumbs

CRUMBIER	comparative of crumby
CRUMBIEST	superlative of crumby
CRUMBLE	*v* -BLED, -BLING, -BLES to break into small pieces
CRUMBLY	*adj* -BLIER, -BLIEST easily crumbled
CRUMBY	*adj* CRUMBIER, CRUMBIEST full of crumbs
CRUMMIE	*n* pl. -S a cow with crooked horns
CRUMMY	*adj* -MIER, -MIEST of little or no value
CRUMP	*v* -ED, -ING, -S to crunch
CRUMPET	*n* pl. -S a small cake cooked on a griddle
CRUMPLE	*v* -PLED, -PLING, -PLES to wrinkle
CRUMPLY	*adj* full of wrinkles
CRUNCH	*v* -ED, -ING, -ES to chew with a crackling sound
CRUNCHER	*n* pl. -S one that crunches
CRUNCHY	*adj* CRUNCHIER, CRUNCHIEST crisp
CRUNODE	*n* pl. -S a point at which a curve crosses itself **CRUNODAL** *adj*
CRUOR	*n* pl. -S clotted blood
CRUPPER	*n* pl. -S the rump of a horse
CRURAL	*adj* pertaining to the thigh or leg
CRUS	*n* pl. CRURA a part of the leg
CRUSADE	*v* -SADED, -SADING, -SADES to engage in a holy war
CRUSADER	*n* pl. -S one that crusades
CRUSADO	*n* pl. -DOES or -DOS a Portuguese coin
CRUSE	*n* pl. -S a small bottle
CRUSET	*n* pl. -S a melting pot
CRUSH	*v* -ED, -ING, -ES to press or squeeze out of shape
CRUSHER	*n* pl. -S one that crushes
CRUSILY	*adj* covered with crosslets
CRUST	*v* -ED, -ING, -S to form a crust (an outer surface)
CRUSTAL	*adj* pertaining to the crust of the earth
CRUSTOSE	*adj* forming a thin, brittle crust
CRUSTY	*adj* CRUSTIER, CRUSTIEST surly **CRUSTILY** *adv*
CRUTCH	*v* -ED, -ING, -ES to prop up or support

CRUX	*n* pl. CRUXES or CRUCES a basic or decisive point
CRUZADO	*n* pl. -DOES or -DOS crusado
CRUZEIRO	*n* pl. -ROS a monetary unit of Brazil
CRWTH	*n* pl. -S an ancient stringed musical instrument
CRY	*v* CRIED, CRYING, CRIES to weep **CRYINGLY** *adv*
CRYBABY	*n* pl. -BIES a person who cries easily
CRYOGEN	*n* pl. -S a substance for producing low temperatures
CRYOGENY	*n* pl. -NIES a branch of physics
CRYOLITE	*n* pl. -S a mineral
CRYONICS	*n/pl* the practice of freezing dead bodies for future revival **CRYONIC** *adj*
CRYOSTAT	*n* pl. -S a refrigerating device
CRYOTRON	*n* pl. -S an electronic device
CRYPT	*n* pl. -S a burial vault **CRYPTAL** *adj*
CRYPTIC	*adj* mysterious
CRYPTO	*n* pl. -TOS one who belongs secretly to a group
CRYSTAL	*n* pl. -S a transparent mineral
CTENIDIA	*n/pl* comblike anatomical structures
CTENOID	*adj* comblike
CUB	*n* pl. -S the young of certain animals
CUBAGE	*n* pl. -S cubature
CUBATURE	*n* pl. -S cubical content
CUBBISH	*adj* resembling a cub
CUBBY	*n* pl. -BIES a small, enclosed space
CUBE	*v* CUBED, CUBING, CUBES to form into a cube (a regular solid)
CUBEB	*n* pl. -S a woody vine
CUBER	*n* pl. -S a device that cubes meat
CUBIC	*n* pl. -S a mathematical equation or expression
CUBICAL	*adj* shaped like a cube
CUBICITY	*n* pl. -TIES the state of being cubical
CUBICLE	*n* pl. -S a small chamber
CUBICLY	*adv* in the form of a cube
CUBICULA	*n/pl* burial chambers
CUBIFORM	*adj* shaped like a cube
CUBING	present participle of cube
CUBISM	*n* pl. -S a style of art **CUBISTIC** *adj*
CUBIST	*n* pl. -S an adherent of cubism
CUBIT	*n* pl. -S an ancient measure of length **CUBITAL** *adj*
CUBOID	*n* pl. -S a bone of the foot **CUBOIDAL** *adj*
CUCKOLD	*v* -ED, -ING, -S to make a cuckold (a cornuto) of
CUCKOO	*v* -ED, -ING, -S to repeat monotonously
CUCUMBER	*n* pl. -S a garden vegetable
CUCURBIT	*n* pl. -S a gourd
CUD	*n* pl. -S a portion of food to be chewed again
CUDBEAR	*n* pl. -S a red dye
CUDDIE	*n* pl. -S cuddy
CUDDIES	pl. of cuddy
CUDDLE	*v* -DLED, -DLING, -DLES to hug tenderly
CUDDLY	*adj* -DLIER, -DLIEST fit for cuddling
CUDDY	*n* pl. -DIES a donkey
CUDGEL	*v* -ELED, -ELING, -ELS or -ELLED, -ELLING, -ELS to beat with a heavy club
CUDGELER	*n* pl. -S one that cudgels
CUDWEED	*n* pl. -S a perennial herb
CUE	*v* CUED, CUING or CUEING, CUES to give a signal to an actor
CUESTA	*n* pl. -S a type of land elevation
CUFF	*v* -ED, -ING, -S to furnish with a cuff (a part of a sleeve)
CUFFLESS	*adj* having no cuff
CUIF	*n* pl. -S coof
CUING	a present participle of cue
CUIRASS	*v* -ED, -ING, -ES to cover with a type of armor
CUISH	*n* pl. -ES cuisse
CUISINE	*n* pl. -S a style of cooking
CUISSE	*n* pl. -S a piece of armor for the thigh
CUITTLE	*v* -TLED, -TLING, -TLES to coax
CUKE	*n* pl. -S a cucumber
CULCH	*n* pl. -ES an oyster bed

CULET   *n* pl. -S a piece of armor for the lower back

CULEX   *n* pl. CULICES a mosquito

CULICID   *n* pl. -S a culicine

CULICINE   *n* pl. -S a mosquito

CULINARY   *adj* pertaining to cookery

CULL   *v* -ED, -ING, -S to select from others

CULLAY   *n* pl. -LAYS quillai

CULLER   *n* pl. -S one that culls

CULLET   *n* pl. -S broken glass gathered for remelting

CULLIED   past tense of cully

CULLIES   present 3d person sing. of cully

CULLION   *n* pl. -S a vile fellow

CULLIS   *n* pl. -LISES a gutter in a roof

CULLY   *v* -LIED, -LYING, -LIES to trick

CULM   *v* -ED, -ING, -S to form a hollow stem

CULOTTE   *n* pl. -S a divided skirt

CULPA   *n* pl. -PAE negligence for which one is liable

CULPABLE   *adj* deserving blame or censure **CULPABLY** *adv*

CULPRIT   *n* pl. -S one that is guilty

CULT   *n* pl. -S a religious society **CULTIC** *adj*

CULTCH   *n* pl. -ES culch

CULTI   a pl. of cultus

CULTIGEN   *n* pl. -S a cultivar

CULTISM   *n* pl. -S devotion to a cult

CULTIST   *n* pl. -S a member of a cult

CULTIVAR   *n* pl. -S a variety of plant originating under cultivation

CULTRATE   *adj* sharp-edged and pointed

CULTURAL   *adj* produced by breeding

CULTURE   *v* -TURED, -TURING, -TURES to make fit for raising crops

CULTUS   *n* pl. -TUSES or -TI a cult

CULVER   *n* pl. -S a pigeon

CULVERIN   *n* pl. -S a medieval musket

CULVERT   *n* pl. -S a conduit

CUM   *prep* together with

CUMARIN   *n* pl. -S coumarin

CUMBER   *v* -ED, -ING, -S to hinder

CUMBERER   *n* pl. -S one that cumbers

CUMBROUS   *adj* unwieldy

CUMIN   *n* pl. -S a plant used in cooking

CUMMER   *n* pl. -S a godmother

CUMMIN   *n* pl. -S cumin

CUMQUAT   *n* pl. -S kumquat

CUMSHAW   *n* pl. -S a gift

CUMULATE   *v* -LATED, -LATING, -LATES to heap

CUMULUS   *n* pl. -LI a type of cloud **CUMULOUS** *adj*

CUNDUM   *n* pl. -S condom

CUNEAL   *adj* cuneate

CUNEATE   *adj* wedge-shaped; triangular

CUNEATED   *adj* cuneate

CUNEATIC   *adj* cuneate

CUNIFORM   *n* pl. -S wedge-shaped writing characters

CUNNER   *n* pl. -S a marine fish

CUNNING   *adj* -NINGER, -NINGEST crafty

CUNNING   *n* pl. -S skill in deception

CUNT   *n* pl. -S the female pudendum — usually considered obscene

CUP   *v* CUPPED, CUPPING, CUPS to place in a cup (a small, open container)

CUPBOARD   *n* pl. -S a cabinet

CUPCAKE   *n* pl. -S a small cake

CUPEL   *v* -PELED, -PELING, -PELS or -PELLED, -PELLING, -PELS to refine gold or silver in a cuplike vessel

CUPELER   *n* pl. -S cupeller

CUPELLER   *n* pl. -S one that cupels

CUPFUL   *n* pl. CUPFULS or CUPSFUL as much as a cup can hold

CUPID   *n* pl. -S a naked, winged representation of the Roman god of love

CUPIDITY   *n* pl. -TIES greed; lust

CUPLIKE   *adj* resembling a cup

CUPOLA   *v* -ED, -ING, -S to shape like a dome

CUPPA   *n* pl. -S a cup of tea

CUPPED   past tense of cup

CUPPER   *n* pl. -S one that performs cupping

CUPPING   *n* pl. -S an archaic medical process

CUPPY	*adj* -PIER, PIEST cuplike
CUPREOUS	*adj* containing copper
CUPRIC	*adj* containing copper
CUPRITE	*n* pl. -S an ore of copper
CUPROUS	*adj* containing copper
CUPRUM	*n* pl. -S copper
CUPSFUL	a pl. of cupful
CUPULA	*n* pl. -LAE a cup-shaped anatomical structure
CUPULAR	*adj* cupulate
CUPULATE	*adj* cup-shaped
CUPULE	*n* pl. -S a cup-shaped anatomical structure
CUR	*n* pl. -S a mongrel dog
CURABLE	*adj* capable of being cured **CURABLY** *adv*
CURACAO	*n* pl. -S a type of liqueur
CURACOA	*n* pl. -S curacao
CURACY	*n* pl. -CIES the office of a curate
CURAGH	*n* pl. -S currach
CURARA	*n* pl. -S curare
CURARE	*n* pl. -S an arrow poison
CURARI	*n* pl. -S curare
CURARINE	*n* pl. -S a poisonous alkaloid
CURARIZE	*v* -RIZED, -RIZING, -RIZES to poison with curare
CURASSOW	*n* pl. -S a turkey-like bird
CURATE	*n* pl. -S a clergyman in charge of a parish
CURATIVE	*n* pl. -S something that cures
CURATOR	*n* pl. -S a museum manager
CURB	*v* -ED, -ING, -S to restrain **CURBABLE** *adj*
CURBER	*n* pl. -S one that curbs
CURBING	*n* pl. -S a concrete border along a street
CURCH	*n* pl. -ES a kerchief
CURCULIO	*n* pl. -LIOS a weevil
CURCUMA	*n* pl. -S a tropical plant
CURD	*v* -ED, -ING, -S to curdle
CURDIER	comparative of curdy
CURDIEST	superlative of curdy
CURDLE	*v* -DLED, -DLING, -DLES to congeal
CURDLER	*n* pl. -S one that curdles

CURDY	*adj* CURDIER, CURDIEST curdled
CURE	*v* CURED, CURING, CURES to restore to health
CURELESS	*adj* not curable
CURER	*n* pl. -S one that cures
CURET	*n* pl. -S a surgical instrument
CURETTE	*v* -RETTED, -RETTING, -RETTES to treat with a curet
CURING	present participle of cure
CURF	*n* pl. -S an incision made by a cutting tool
CURFEW	*n* pl. -S a regulation concerning the hours which one may keep
CURIA	*n* pl. -RIAE a court of justice **CURIAL** *adj*
CURIE	*n* pl. -S a unit of radioactivity
CURIO	*n* pl. -RIOS an unusual art object
CURIOSA	*n/pl* pornographic books
CURIOUS	*adj* -OUSER, -OUSEST eager for information
CURITE	*n* pl. -S a radioactive mineral
CURIUM	*n* pl. -S a radioactive element
CURL	*v* -ED, -ING, -S to form into ringlets
CURLER	*n* pl. -S one that curls
CURLEW	*n* pl. -S a shore bird
CURLICUE	*v* -CUED, -CUING, -CUES to decorate with curlicues (fancy spiral figures)
CURLING	*n* pl. -S a game played on ice
CURLY	*adj* CURLIER, CURLIEST tending to curl **CURLILY** *adv*
CURLYCUE	*n* pl. -S curlicue
CURN	*n* pl. -S grain
CURR	*v* -ED, -ING, -S to purr
CURRACH	*n* pl. -S a coracle
CURRAGH	*n* pl. -S currach
CURRAN	*n* pl. -S curn
CURRANT	*n* pl. -S an edible berry
CURRENCY	*n* pl. -CIES money
CURRENT	*n* pl. -S a continuous flow
CURRICLE	*n* pl. -S a light carriage
CURRIE	*v* -RIED, -RYING, -RIES to prepare food a certain way
CURRIED	past tense of curry
CURRIER	*n* pl. -S one that curries leather

CURRIERY	*n* pl. -ERIES the shop of a currier
CURRISH	*adj* resembling a cur
CURRY	*v* -RIED, -RYING, -RIES to prepare leather for use or sale
CURRYING	present participle of currie
CURSE	*v* CURSED or CURST, CURSING, CURSES to wish evil upon
CURSED	*adj* CURSEDER, CURSEDEST wicked **CURSEDLY** *adv*
CURSER	*n* pl. -S one that curses
CURSING	present participle of curse
CURSIVE	*n* pl. -S a style of print
CURSORY	*adj* hasty and superficial
CURST	a past tense of curse
CURT	*adj* CURTER, CURTEST abrupt
CURTAIL	*v* -ED, -ING, -S to cut short
CURTAIN	*v* -ED, -ING, -S to provide with a hanging piece of fabric
CURTAL	*n* pl. -S an animal with a clipped tail
CURTALAX	*n* pl. -ES a cutlass
CURTATE	*adj* shortened
CURTESY	*n* pl. -SIES a type of legal tenure
CURTLY	*adv* in a curt manner
CURTNESS	*n* pl. -ES the quality of being curt
CURTSEY	*v* -ED, -ING, -S to curtsy
CURTSY	*v* -SIED, -SYING, -SIES to bow politely
CURULE	*adj* of the highest rank
CURVE	*v* CURVED, CURVING, CURVES to deviate from straightness
CURVET	*v* -VETED, -VETING, -VETS or -VETTED, -VETTING, -VETS to prance
CURVEY	*adj* CURVIER, CURVIEST curvy
CURVING	present participle of curve
CURVY	*adj* CURVIER, CURVIEST curved
CUSCUS	*n* pl. -ES an arboreal mammal
CUSEC	*n* pl. -S a volumetric unit of flow of liquids
CUSHAT	*n* pl. -S a pigeon
CUSHAW	*n* pl. -S a variety of squash
CUSHIER	comparative of cushy
CUSHIEST	superlative of cushy
CUSHILY	*adj* in a cushy manner
CUSHION	*v* -ED, -ING, -S to pad with soft material
CUSHIONY	*adj* soft
CUSHY	*adj* CUSHIER, CUSHIEST easy
CUSK	*n* pl. -S a marine food fish
CUSP	*n* pl. -S a pointed end **CUSPATE, CUSPATED, CUSPED** *adj*
CUSPID	*n* pl. -S a pointed tooth
CUSPIDAL	*adj* having a cusp
CUSPIDOR	*n* pl. -S a spittoon
CUSPIS	*n* pl. -PIDES a cusp
CUSS	*v* -ED, -ING, -ES to curse
CUSSEDLY	*adv* in a cranky manner
CUSSER	*n* pl. -S one that cusses
CUSSO	*n* pl. -SOS an Ethiopian tree
CUSSWORD	*n* pl. -S a profane or obscene word
CUSTARD	*n* pl. -S a dessert
CUSTODES	pl. of custos
CUSTODY	*n* pl. -DIES guardianship
CUSTOM	*n* pl. -S a habitual practice
CUSTOMER	*n* pl. -S one who buys something
CUSTOS	*n* pl. -TODES a guardian or keeper
CUSTUMAL	*n* pl. -S a written record of laws and customs
CUT	*v* CUT, CUTTING, CUTS to divide into parts with a sharp-edged instrument
CUTAWAY	*n* pl. -AWAYS a type of coat
CUTBACK	*n* pl. -S a reduction
CUTCH	*n* pl. -ES catechu
CUTCHERY	*n* pl. -CHERIES a judicial office in India
CUTDOWN	*n* pl. -S a reduction
CUTE	*adj* CUTER, CUTEST pleasingly attractive **CUTELY** *adv*
CUTENESS	*n* pl. -ES the quality of being cute
CUTES	a pl. of cutis
CUTEST	superlative of cute
CUTESY	*adj* -SIER, -SIEST self-consciously cute
CUTEY	*n* pl. -TEYS cutie
CUTGRASS	*n* pl. -ES a swamp grass
CUTICLE	*n* pl. -S the epidermis

CUTICULA   *n* pl. -LAE the outer hard covering of an insect

CUTIE   *n* pl. -S a cute person

CUTIN   *n* pl. -S a waxy substance found on plants

CUTINISE   *v* -ISED, -ISING, -ISES to cutinize

CUTINIZE   *v* -IZED, -IZING, -IZES to become coated with cutin

CUTIS   *n* pl. -TES or -TISES the corium

CUTLAS   *n* pl. -ES cutlass

CUTLASS   *n* pl. -ES a short sword

CUTLER   *n* pl. -S one who sells and repairs cutting tools

CUTLERY   *n* pl. -LERIES the occupation of a cutler

CUTLET   *n* pl. -S a slice of meat

CUTLINE   *n* pl. -S a caption

CUTOFF   *n* pl. -S the point at which something terminates

CUTOUT   *n* pl. -S something cut out

CUTOVER   *adj* cleared of trees

CUTPURSE   *n* pl. -S a pickpocket

CUTTABLE   *adj* capable of being cut

CUTTAGE   *n* pl. -S a means of plant propagation

CUTTER   *n* pl. -S one that cuts

CUTTING   *n* pl. -S a section cut from a plant

CUTTLE   *v* -TLED, -TLING, -TLES to fold cloth in a particular fashion

CUTTY   *n* pl. -TIES a thickset girl

CUTUP   *n* pl. -S a mischievous person

CUTWATER   *n* pl. -S the front part of a ship's prow

CUTWORK   *n* pl. -S a type of embroidery

CUTWORM   *n* pl. -S a caterpillar

CUVETTE   *n* pl. -S a small tube or vessel

CWM   *n* pl. -S a cirque

CYAN   *n* pl. -S a blue color

CYANAMID   *n* pl. -S a chemical compound

CYANATE   *n* pl. -S a chemical salt

CYANIC   *adj* blue or bluish

CYANID   *n* pl. -S a compound of cyanogen

CYANIDE   *v* -NIDED, -NIDING, -NIDES to treat an ore with cyanid

CYANIN   *n* pl. -S cyanine

CYANINE   *n* pl. -S a blue dye

CYANITE   *n* pl. -S a mineral **CYANITIC** *adj*

CYANO   *adj* pertaining to cyanogen

CYANOGEN   *n* pl. -S a reactive compound of carbon and nitrogen

CYANOSIS   *n* pl. -NOSES bluish discoloration of the skin **CYANOSED, CYANOTIC** *adj*

CYBORG   *n* pl. -S a human linked to a mechanical device for life support

CYCAD   *n* pl. -S a tropical plant

CYCAS   *n* pl. -ES a tropical plant

CYCASIN   *n* pl. -S a sugar derivative

CYCLAMEN   *n* pl. -S a flowering plant

CYCLASE   *n* pl. -S an enzyme

CYCLE   *v* -CLED, -CLING, -CLES to ride a bicycle

CYCLECAR   *n* pl. -S a type of motor vehicle

CYCLER   *n* pl. -S a cyclist

CYCLIC   *adj* moving in complete circles **CYCLICLY** *adv*

CYCLICAL   *adj* cyclic

CYCLING   *n* pl. -S the act of riding a bicycle

CYCLIST   *n* pl. -S one who rides a bicycle

CYCLITOL   *n* pl. -S a chemical compound

CYCLIZE   *v* -CLIZED, -CLIZING, -CLIZES to form one or more rings in a chemical compound

CYCLO   *n* pl. -CLOS a three-wheeled motor vehicle

CYCLOID   *n* pl. -S a geometric curve

CYCLONE   *n* pl. -S a rotating system of winds **CYCLONAL, CYCLONIC** *adj*

CYCLOPS   *n* pl. CYCLOPS a freshwater animal

CYCLOSIS   *n* pl. -CLOSES the circulation of protoplasm within a cell

CYDER   *n* pl. -S cider

CYESIS   *n* pl. CYESES pregnancy

CYGNET   *n* pl. -S a young swan

CYLINDER   *v* -ED, -ING, -S to furnish with a cylinder (a chamber in an engine)

CYLIX   *n* pl. CYLICES kylix

CYMA   *n* pl. -MAS or -MAE a curved molding

CYMAR   *n* pl. -S simar

CYMATIUM	*n* pl. -TIA a cyma	**CYST**	*n* pl. -S a sac
CYMBAL	*n* pl. -S a percussion instrument	**CYSTEIN**	*n* pl. -S cysteine
CYMBALER	*n* pl. -S one that plays the cymbals	**CYSTEINE**	*n* pl. -S an amino acid
		CYSTIC	*adj* pertaining to a cyst
CYMBLING	*n* pl. -S cymling	**CYSTINE**	*n* pl. -S an amino acid
CYME	*n* pl. -S a flower cluster	**CYSTITIS**	*n* pl. -TITIDES inflammation of the urinary bladder
CYMENE	*n* pl. -S a hydrocarbon		
CYMLIN	*n* pl. -S cymling	**CYSTOID**	*n* pl. -S a cyst-like structure
CYMLING	*n* pl. -S a variety of squash	**CYTASTER**	*n* pl. -S a structure formed in a cell during mitosis
CYMOGENE	*n* pl. -S a volatile compound		
CYMOID	*adj* resembling a cyma	**CYTIDINE**	*n* pl. -S a compound containing cytosine
CYMOL	*n* pl. -S cymene		
CYMOSE	*adj* resembling a cyme **CYMOSELY** *adv*	**CYTOGENY**	*n* pl. -NIES the formation of cells
CYMOUS	*adj* cymose	**CYTOLOGY**	*n* pl. -GIES a study of cells
CYNIC	*n* pl. -S a cynical person	**CYTON**	*n* pl. -S the body of a nerve cell
CYNICAL	*adj* distrusting the motives of others	**CYTOSINE**	*n* pl. -S a component of DNA and RNA
CYNICISM	*n* pl. -S cynical quality		
CYNOSURE	*n* pl. -S a center of attraction	**CZAR**	*n* pl. -S an emperor or king
CYPHER	*v* -ED, -ING, -S to cipher	**CZARDAS**	*n* pl. CZARDAS a Hungarian dance
CYPRES	*n* pl. -ES a legal doctrine		
CYPRESS	*n* pl. -ES a thin fabric	**CZARDOM**	*n* pl. -S the domain of a czar
CYPRIAN	*n* pl. -S a prostitute	**CZAREVNA**	*n* pl. -S the daughter of a czar
CYPRINID	*n* pl. -S a small freshwater fish	**CZARINA**	*n* pl. -S the wife of a czar
CYPRUS	*n* pl. -ES cypress	**CZARISM**	*n* pl. -S autocratic government
CYPSELA	*n* pl. -LAE an achene in certain plants	**CZARIST**	*n* pl. -S a supporter of czarism
		CZARITZA	*n* pl. -S a czarina

DA	*prep* of; from — used in names	**DAFF**	*v* -ED, -ING, -S to thrust aside
DAB	*v* DABBED, DABBING, DABS to touch lightly	**DAFFODIL**	*n* pl. -S a flowering plant
		DAFFY	*adj* -FIER, -FIEST silly
DABBER	*n* pl. -S one that dabs	**DAFT**	*adj* DAFTER, DAFTEST insane **DAFTLY** *adv*
DABBLE	*v* -BLED, -BLING, -BLES to splash		
		DAFTNESS	*n* pl. -ES the quality of being daft
DABBLER	*n* pl. -S one that dabbles		
DABBLING	*n* pl. -S a superficial interest	**DAG**	*n* pl. -S a hanging end or shred
DABCHICK	*n* pl. -S a small grebe	**DAGGER**	*v* -ED, -ING, -S to stab with a small knife
DABSTER	*n* pl. -S a bungler		
DACE	*n* pl. -S a freshwater fish	**DAGGLE**	*v* -GLED, -GLING, -GLES to drag in mud
DACHA	*n* pl. -S a Russian cottage		
DACKER	*v* -ED, -ING, -S to waver	**DAGLOCK**	*n* pl. -S a dirty or tangled lock of wool
DACOIT	*n* pl. -S a bandit in India		
DACOITY	*n* pl. -COITIES robbery by dacoits	**DAGO**	*n* pl. -GOS or -GOES an Italian or Spaniard — a derogatory term
DACTYL	*n* pl. -S a type of metrical foot	**DAGOBA**	*n* pl. -S a Buddhist shrine
DACTYLIC	*n* pl. -S a verse consisting of dactyls	**DAH**	*n* pl. -S a dash in Morse code
		DAHABEAH	*n* pl. -S a large passenger boat
DACTYLUS	*n* pl. -LI a leg joint of certain insects	**DAHABIAH**	*n* pl. -S dahabeah
		DAHABIEH	*n* pl. -S dahabeah
DAD	*n* pl. -S father	**DAHABIYA**	*n* pl. -S dahabeah
DADA	*n* pl. -S an artistic and literary movement	**DAHLIA**	*n* pl. -S a flowering plant
		DAHOON	*n* pl. -S an evergreen tree
DADAISM	*n* pl. -S the dada movement	**DAIKER**	*v* -ED, -ING, -S to dacker
DADAIST	*n* pl. -S a follower of dadaism	**DAILY**	*n* pl. -LIES a newspaper published every weekday
DADDLE	*v* -DLED, -DLING, -DLES to diddle		
		DAIMEN	*adj* occasional
DADDY	*n* pl. -DIES father	**DAIMIO**	*n* pl. -MIOS a former Japanese nobleman
DADO	*v* -ED, -ING, -ES or -S to set into a groove		
		DAIMON	*n* pl. -S or -ES an attendant spirit **DAIMONIC** *adj*
DAEDAL	*adj* skillful		
DAEMON	*n* pl. -S demon **DAEMONIC** *adj*	**DAIMYO**	*n* pl. -MYOS daimio

DAINTY	*n* pl. -TIES something delicious
DAINTY	*adj* -TIER, -TIEST delicately pretty **DAINTILY** *adv*
DAIQUIRI	*n* pl. -S a cocktail
DAIRY	*n* pl. DAIRIES an establishment dealing in milk products
DAIRYING	*n* pl. -S the business of a dairy
DAIRYMAN	*n* pl. -MEN a man who works in or owns a dairy
DAIS	*n* pl. -ISES a raised platform
DAISHIKI	*n* pl. -S dashiki
DAISY	*n* pl. -SIES a flowering plant **DAISIED** *adj*
DAK	*n* pl. -S transportation by relays of men and horses
DAKERHEN	*n* pl. -S a European bird
DAKOIT	*n* pl. -S dacoit
DAKOITY	*n* pl. -TIES dacoity
DALAPON	*n* pl. -S an herbicide used on unwanted grasses
DALASI	*n* pl. DALASI a unit of Gambian currency
DALE	*n* pl. -S a valley
DALESMAN	*n* pl. -MEN one living in a dale
DALETH	*n* pl. -S a Hebrew letter
DALLES	*n/pl* rapids
DALLIER	*n* pl. -S one that dallies
DALLY	*v* -LIED, -LYING, -LIES to waste time
DALMATIC	*n* pl. -S a wide-sleeved vestment
DALTONIC	*adj* pertaining to a form of color blindness
DAM	*v* DAMMED, DAMMING, DAMS to build a barrier to obstruct the flow of water
DAMAGE	*v* -AGED, -AGING, -AGES to injure
DAMAGER	*n* pl. -S one that damages
DAMAN	*n* pl. -S a small mammal
DAMAR	*n* pl. -S dammar
DAMASK	*v* -ED, -ING, -S to weave with elaborate design
DAME	*n* pl. -S a matron
DAMEWORT	*n* pl. -S a flowering plant
DAMMED	past tense of dam
DAMMAR	*n* pl. -S a hard resin
DAMMER	*n* pl. -S dammar
DAMMING	present participle of dam

DAMN	*v* -ED, -ING, -S to curse
DAMNABLE	*adj* detestable **DAMNABLY** *adv*
DAMNDEST	*n* pl. -S utmost
DAMNED	*adj* DAMNEDER, DAMNEDEST or DAMNDEST damnable
DAMNER	*n* pl. -S one that damns
DAMNIFY	*v* -FIED, -FYING, -FIES to cause loss or damage to
DAMOSEL	*n* pl. -S damsel
DAMOZEL	*n* pl. -S damsel
DAMP	*adj* DAMPER, DAMPEST moist
DAMP	*v* -ED, -ING, -S to moisten
DAMPEN	*v* -ED, -ING, -S to moisten
DAMPENER	*n* pl. -S one that dampens
DAMPER	*n* pl. -S one that damps
DAMPISH	*adj* somewhat damp
DAMPLY	*adv* in a damp manner
DAMPNESS	*n* pl. -ES the state of being damp
DAMSEL	*n* pl. -S a maiden
DAMSON	*n* pl. -S a small purple plum
DANCE	*v* DANCED, DANCING, DANCES to move rhythmically to music
DANCER	*n* pl. -S one that dances
DANDER	*v* -ED, -ING, -S to stroll
DANDIER	comparative of dandy
DANDIES	pl. of dandy
DANDIEST	superlative of dandy
DANDIFY	*v* -FIED, -FYING, -FIES to cause to resemble a dandy
DANDILY	*adv* in a dandy manner
DANDLE	*v* -DLED, -DLING, -DLES to fondle
DANDLER	*n* pl. -S one that dandles
DANDRIFF	*n* pl. -S dandruff
DANDRUFF	*n* pl. -S a scurf that forms on the scalp
DANDY	*adj* -DIER, -DIEST fine
DANDY	*n* pl. -DIES a man who is overly concerned about his appearance
DANDYISH	*adj* suggestive of a dandy
DANDYISM	*n* pl. -S the style or conduct of a dandy
DANEGELD	*n* pl. -S an annual tax in medieval England
DANEWEED	*n* pl. -S a danewort
DANEWORT	*n* pl. -S a flowering plant

DANG   *v* -ED, -ING, -S to damn

DANGER   *v* -ED, -ING, -S to endanger

DANGLE   *v* -GLED, -GLING, -GLES to hang loosely

DANGLER   *n* pl. -S one that dangles

DANIO   *n* pl. -NIOS an aquarium fish

DANK   *adj* DANKER, DANKEST unpleasantly damp **DANKLY** *adv*

DANKNESS   *n* pl. -ES the state of being dank

DANSEUR   *n* pl. -S a male ballet dancer

DANSEUSE   *n* pl. -S a female ballet dancer

DAP   *v* DAPPED, DAPPING, DAPS to dip lightly or quickly into water

DAPHNE   *n* pl. -S a flowering shrub

DAPHNIA   *n* pl. -S a minute freshwater crustacean

DAPPED   past tense of dap

DAPPER   *adj* -PERER, -PEREST neat and trim in appearance

DAPPING   present participle of dap

DAPPLE   *v* -PLED, -PLING, -PLES to mark with spots

DAPPERLY   *adv* in a dapper manner

DARB   *n* pl. -S something considered extraordinary

DARBIES   *n/pl* handcuffs

DARE   *v* DARED or DURST, DARING, DARES to have the necessary courage

DAREFUL   *adj* brave

DARER   *n* pl. -S one that dares

DARESAY   *v* to venture to say — DARESAY is the only form of this verb; it is not conjugated

DARIC   *n* pl. -S an ancient Persian coin

DARING   *n* pl. -S bravery

DARINGLY   *adv* in a brave manner

DARIOLE   *n* pl. -S a type of pastry

DARK   *adj* DARKER, DARKEST having little or no light

DARK   *v* -ED, -ING, -S to darken

DARKEN   *v* -ED, -ING, -S to make dark

DARKENER   *n* pl. -S one that darkens

DARKEY   *n* pl. -EYS darky

DARKIE   *n* pl. -S darky

DARKIES   pl. of darky

DARKISH   *adj* somewhat dark

DARKLE   *v* -KLED, -KLING, -KLES to become dark

DARKLY   *adv* -LIER, -LIEST in a dark manner

DARKNESS   *n* pl. -ES the state of being dark

DARKROOM   *n* pl. -S a room in which film is processed

DARKSOME   *adj* dark

DARKY   *n* pl. DARKIES a black person — a derogatory term

DARLING   *n* pl. -S a much-loved person

DARN   *v* -ED, -ING, -S to mend with interlacing stitches

DARNDEST   *n* pl. -S damndest

DARNED   *adj* DARNEDER, DARNEDEST or DARNDEST damned

DARNEL   *n* pl. -S an annual grass

DARNER   *n* pl. -S one that darns

DARNING   *n* pl. -S things darned or to be darned

DART   *v* -ED, -ING, -S to move suddenly or swiftly

DARTER   *n* pl. -S one that darts

DARTLE   *v* -TLED, -TLING, -TLES to dart repeatedly

DASH   *v* -ED, -ING, -ES to strike violently

DASHEEN   *n* pl. -S a tropical plant

DASHER   *n* pl. -S one that dashes

DASHIER   comparative of dashy

DASHIEST   superlative of dashy

DASHIKI   *n* pl. -S an African tunic

DASHPOT   *n* pl. -S a shock absorber

DASHY   *adj* DASHIER, DASHIEST stylish

DASSIE   *n* pl. -S a hyrax

DASTARD   *n* pl. -S a base coward

DASYURE   *n* pl. -S a flesh-eating mammal

DATA   a pl. of datum

DATARY   *n* pl. -RIES a cardinal in the Roman Catholic Church

DATCHA   *n* pl. -S dacha

DATE   *v* DATED, DATING, DATES to determine or record the date of **DATABLE, DATEABLE** *adj*

DATEDLY   *adv* in an old-fashioned manner

DATELESS   *adj* having no date

DATELINE   *v* -LINED, -LINING, -LINES to provide a news story with a line giving its date and place of origin

DATER   *n* pl. -S one that dates

DATING   present participle of date

DATIVE   *n* pl. -S a grammatical case **DATIVAL** *adj* **DATIVELY** *adv*

DATO   *n* pl. -TOS datto

DATTO   *n* pl. -TOS a Philippine tribal chief

DATUM   *n* pl. -TA or -TUMS something used as a basis for calculating

DATURA   *n* pl. -S a flowering plant **DATURIC** *adj*

DAUB   *v* -ED, -ING, -S to smear

DAUBE   *n* pl. -S a braised meat stew

DAUBER   *n* pl. -S one that daubs

DAUBERY   *n* pl. -ERIES a bad or inexpert painting

DAUBRY   *n* pl. -RIES daubery

DAUBY   *adj* DAUBIER, DAUBIEST smeary

DAUGHTER   *n* pl. -S a female child

DAUNDER   *v* -ED, -ING, -S to dander

DAUNT   *v* -ED, -ING, -S to intimidate

DAUNTER   *n* pl. -S one that daunts

DAUPHIN   *n* pl. -S the eldest son of a French king

DAUPHINE   *n* pl. -S the wife of a dauphin

DAUT   *v* -ED, -ING, -S to fondle

DAUTIE   *n* pl. -S a small pet

DAVEN   *v* -ED, -ING, -S to utter Jewish prayers

DAVIT   *n* pl. -S a hoisting device on a ship

DAVY   *n* pl. -VIES a safety lamp

DAW   *v* DAWED, DAWEN, DAWING, DAWS to dawn

DAWDLE   *v* -DLED, -DLING, -DLES to waste time

DAWDLER   *n* pl. -S one that dawdles

DAWEN   past participle of daw

DAWK   *n* pl. -S dak

DAWN   *v* -ED, -ING, -S to begin to grow light in the morning

DAWNLIKE   *adj* suggestive of daybreak

DAWT   *v* -ED, -ING, -S to daut

DAWTIE   *n* pl. -S dautie

DAY   *n* pl. DAYS the time between sunrise and sunset

DAYBED   *n* pl. -S a couch that can be converted into a bed

DAYBOOK   *n* pl. -S a diary

DAYBREAK   *n* pl. -S the first appearance of light in the morning

DAYDREAM   *v* -DREAMED or -DREAMT, -DREAMING, -DREAMS to fantasize

DAYFLY   *n* pl. -FLIES a mayfly

DAYGLOW   *n* pl. -S airglow seen during the day

DAYLIGHT   *v* -LIGHTED or -LIT, -LIGHTING, -LIGHTS to illuminate with the light of day

DAYLILY   *n* pl. -LILIES a flowering plant

DAYLONG   *adj* lasting all day

DAYMARE   *n* pl. -S a nightmarish fantasy experienced while awake

DAYROOM   *n* pl. -S a room for reading and recreation

DAYSIDE   *n* pl. -S the sun side of a planet or the moon

DAYSMAN   *n* pl. -MEN an arbiter

DAYSTAR   *n* pl. -S a planet visible in the east just before sunrise

DAYTIME   *n* pl. -S day

DAZE   *v* DAZED, DAZING, DAZES to stun **DAZEDLY** *adv*

DAZZLE   *v* -ZLED, -ZLING, -ZLES to blind by bright light

DAZZLER   *n* pl. -S one that dazzles

DE   *prep* of; from — used in names and phrases

DEACON   *v* -ED, -ING, -S to read a hymn aloud

DEACONRY   *n* pl. -RIES a clerical office

DEAD   *adj* DEADER, DEADEST deprived of life

DEAD   *n* pl. -S the period of greatest intensity

DEADBEAT   *n* pl. -S a loafer

DEADEN   *v* -ED, -ING, -S to diminish the sensitivity or vigor of

DEADENER   *n* pl. -S one that deadens

DEADEYE   *n* pl. -S an expert marksman

DEADFALL   *n* pl. -S a type of animal trap

DEADHEAD   *v* -ED, -ING, -S to travel without freight

DEADLIER   comparative of deadly

DEADLIEST   superlative of deadly

DEADLINE   *n* pl. -S a time limit

DEADLOCK v -ED, -ING, -S to come to a standstill

DEADLY adj -LIER, -LIEST fatal

DEADNESS n pl. -ES the state of being dead

DEADPAN v -PANNED, -PANNING, -PANS to act without emotion

DEADWOOD n pl. -S a reinforcement in a ship's keel

DEAERATE v -ATED, -ATING, -ATES to remove air or gas from

DEAF adj DEAFER, DEAFEST lacking the sense of hearing

DEAFEN v -ED, -ING, -S to make deaf

DEAFISH adj somewhat deaf

DEAFLY adv in a deaf manner

DEAFNESS n pl. -ES the state of being deaf

DEAIR v -ED, -ING, -S to remove air from

DEAL v DEALT, DEALING, DEALS to trade or do business

DEALATE n pl. -S an insect divested of its wings **DEALATED** adj

DEALER n pl. -S one that deals

DEALFISH n pl. -ES a marine fish

DEALING n pl. -S a business transaction

DEALT past tense of deal

DEAN v -ED, -ING, -S to serve as dean (the head of a faculty)

DEANERY n pl. -ERIES the office of a dean

DEANSHIP n pl. -S deanery

DEAR adj DEARER, DEAREST greatly loved

DEAR n pl. -S a loved one

DEARIE n pl. -S deary

DEARIES pl. of deary

DEARLY adv in a dear manner

DEARNESS n pl. -ES the state of being dear

DEARTH n pl. -S scarcity

DEARY n pl. DEARIES darling

DEASH v -ED, -ING, -ES to remove ash from

DEASIL adv clockwise

DEATH n pl. -S the end of life

DEATHBED n pl. -S the bed on which a person dies

DEATHCUP n pl. -S a poisonous mushroom

DEATHFUL adj fatal

DEATHLY adj fatal

DEATHY adj deathly

DEAVE v DEAVED, DEAVING, DEAVES to deafen

DEB n pl. -S a debutante

DEBACLE n pl. -S a sudden collapse

DEBAR v -BARRED, -BARRING, -BARS to exclude

DEBARK v -ED, -ING, -S to unload from a ship

DEBASE v -BASED, -BASING, -BASES to lower in character, quality, or value

DEBASER n pl. -S one that debases

DEBATE v -BATED, -BATING, -BATES to argue about

DEBATER n pl. -S one that debates

DEBAUCH v -ED, -ING, -ES to corrupt

DEBILITY n pl. -TIES weakness

DEBIT v -ED, -ING, -S to charge with a debt

DEBONAIR adj suave

DEBONE v -BONED, -BONING, -BONES to remove the bones from

DEBONER n pl. -S a bone remover

DEBOUCH v -ED, -ING, -ES to march into the open

DEBOUCHE n pl. -S an opening for the passage of troops

DEBRIEF v -ED, -ING, -S to question after a mission

DEBRIS n pl. DEBRIS fragments or scattered remains

DEBRUISE v -BRUISED, -BRUISING, -BRUISES to cross a coat of arms

DEBT n pl. -S something that is owed **DEBTLESS** adj

DEBTOR n pl. -S one who owes something to another

DEBUG v -BUGGED, -BUGGING, -BUGS to remove insects from

DEBUNK v -ED, -ING, -S to expose the sham or falseness of

DEBUNKER n pl. -S one that debunks

DEBUT v -ED, -ING, -S to make one's first public appearance

DEBUTANT n pl. -S one who is debuting

DEBYE n pl. -S a unit of measure for electric dipole moments

DECADE   *n* pl. -S a period of ten years
DECADAL *adj*

DECADENT   *n* pl. -S one in a state of mental
or moral decay

DECAGON   *n* pl. -S a ten-sided polygon

DECAGRAM   *n* pl. -S dekagram

DECAL   *n* pl. -S a picture or design
made to be transferred from
specially prepared paper

DECAMP   *v* -ED, -ING, -S to depart from a
camping ground

DECANAL   *adj* pertaining to a dean

DECANE   *n* pl. -S a hydrocarbon

DECANT   *v* -ED, -ING, -S to pour from one
container into another

DECANTER   *n* pl. -S a decorative bottle

DECAPOD   *n* pl. -S a ten-legged crustacean

DECARE   *n* pl. -S dekare

DECAY   *v* -ED, -ING, -S to decompose

DECAYER   *n* pl. -S one that decays

DECEASE   *v* -CEASED, -CEASING,
-CEASES to die

DECEDENT   *n* pl. -S a deceased person

DECEIT   *n* pl. -S the act of deceiving

DECEIVE   *v* -CEIVED, -CEIVING, -CEIVES
to mislead by falsehood

DECEIVER   *n* pl. -S one that deceives

DECEMVIR   *n* pl. -VIRS or -VIRI one of a
body of ten Roman magistrates

DECENARY   *n* pl. -RIES a tithing

DECENCY   *n* pl. -CIES the state of being
decent

DECENNIA   *n/pl* decades

DECENT   *adj* -CENTER, -CENTEST
conforming to recognized
standards of propriety
DECENTLY *adv*

DECENTER   *v* -ED, -ING, -S to put out of
center

DECENTRE   *v* -TRED, -TRING, -TRES to
decenter

DECERN   *v* -ED, -ING, -S to decree by
judicial sentence

DECIARE   *n* pl. -S a metric unit of area

DECIBEL   *n* pl. -S a unit of sound intensity

DECIDE   *v* -CIDED, -CIDING, -CIDES to
make a choice or judgment

DECIDER   *n* pl. -S one that decides

DECIDUA   *n* pl. -UAS or -UAE a mucous
membrane of the uterus
DECIDUAL *adj*

DECIGRAM   *n* pl. -S one tenth of a gram

DECILE   *n* pl. -S a statistical interval

DECIMAL   *n* pl. -S a fraction whose
denominator is some power of
ten

DECIMATE   *v* -MATED, -MATING, -MATES to
destroy a large part of

DECIPHER   *v* -ED, -ING, -S to determine the
meaning of

DECISION   *n* pl. -S the act of deciding

DECISIVE   *adj* conclusive

DECK   *v* -ED, -ING, -S to adorn

DECKEL   *n* pl. -S deckle

DECKER   *n* pl. -S something having a
specified number of levels,
floors, or layers

DECKHAND   *n* pl. -S a seaman who performs
manual duties

DECKING   *n* pl. -S material for a ship's
deck

DECKLE   *n* pl. -S a frame used in making
paper by hand

DECLAIM   *v* -ED, -ING, -S to speak
formally

DECLARE   *v* -CLARED, -CLARING,
-CLARES to make known clearly

DECLARER   *n* pl. -S one that declares

DECLASS   *v* -ED, -ING, -ES to lower in
status

DECLASSE   *adj* lowered in status

DECLINE   *v* -CLINED, -CLINING, -CLINES
to refuse

DECLINER   *n* pl. -S one that declines

DECOCT   *v* -ED, -ING, -S to extract the
flavor of by boiling

DECODE   *v* -CODED, -CODING, -CODES to
convert a coded message into
plain language

DECODER   *n* pl. -S one that decodes

DECOLOR   *v* -ED, -ING, -S to deprive of
color

DECOLOUR   *v* -ED, -ING, -S to decolor

DECOR   *n* pl. -S style or mode of
decoration

DECORATE   *v* -RATED, -RATING, -RATES to
adorn

DECOROUS   *adj* proper

DECORUM   *n* pl. -S conformity to social
conventions

DECOY   *v* -ED, -ING, -S to lure into a
trap

DECOYER	*n* pl. -S one that decoys
DECREASE	*v* -CREASED, -CREASING, -CREASES to diminish
DECREE	*v* -CREED, -CREEING, -CREES to order or establish by law or edict
DECREER	*n* pl. -S one that decrees
DECREPIT	*adj* worn out by long use
DECRETAL	*n* pl. -S a papal edict
DECRIAL	*n* pl. -S the act of decrying
DECRIED	past tense of decry
DECRIER	*n* pl. -S one that decries
DECROWN	*v* -ED, -ING, -S to deprive of a crown; depose
DECRY	*v* -CRIED, -CRYING, -CRIES to denounce
DECRYPT	*v* -ED, -ING, -S to decode
DECUMAN	*adj* extremely large
DECUPLE	*v* -PLED, -PLING, -PLES to increase tenfold
DECURION	*n* pl. -S a commander of a decury
DECURVE	*v* -CURVED, -CURVING, -CURVES to curve downward
DECURY	*n* pl. -RIES a group of ten soldiers in ancient Rome
DEDAL	*adj* daedal
DEDANS	*n* pl. DEDANS a gallery for tennis spectators
DEDICATE	*v* -CATED, -CATING, -CATES to set apart for some special use
DEDUCE	*v* -DUCED, -DUCING, -DUCES to infer
DEDUCT	*v* -ED, -ING, -S to subtract
DEE	*n* pl. -S the letter D
DEED	*v* -ED, -ING, -S to transfer by deed (a legal document)
DEEDLESS	*adj* being without deeds
DEEDY	*adj* DEEDIER, DEEDIEST industrious
DEEJAY	*n* pl. -JAYS a disc jockey
DEEM	*v* -ED, -ING, -S to hold as an opinion
DEEMSTER	*n* pl. -S a judicial officer of the Isle of Man
DEEP	*adj* DEEPER, DEEPEST extending far down from a surface
DEEP	*n* pl. -S a place or thing of great depth
DEEPEN	*v* -ED, -ING, -S to make deep
DEEPENER	*n* pl. -S one that deepens
DEEPLY	*adv* at or to a great depth
DEEPNESS	*n* pl. -ES the quality of being deep
DEER	*n* pl. -S a ruminant mammal
DEERFLY	*n* pl. -FLIES a bloodsucking fly
DEERSKIN	*n* pl. -S the skin of a deer
DEERWEED	*n* pl. -S a bushlike herb
DEERYARD	*n* pl. -S an area where deer herd in winter
DEEWAN	*n* pl. -S dewan
DEFACE	*v* -FACED, -FACING, -FACES to mar the appearance of
DEFACER	*n* pl. -S one that defaces
DEFAME	*v* -FAMED, -FAMING, -FAMES to attack the good name of
DEFAMER	*n* pl. -S one that defames
DEFAT	*v* -FATTED, -FATTING, -FATS to remove fat from
DEFAULT	*v* -ED, -ING, -S to fail to do something required
DEFEAT	*v* -ED, -ING, -S to win victory over
DEFEATER	*n* pl. -S one that defeats
DEFECATE	*v* -CATED, -CATING, -CATES to discharge feces
DEFECT	*v* -ED, -ING, -S to desert an allegiance
DEFECTOR	*n* pl. -S one that defects
DEFENCE	*n* pl. -S something that defends
DEFEND	*v* -ED, -ING, -S to protect
DEFENDER	*n* pl. -S one that defends
DEFENSE	*v* -FENSED, -FENSING, -FENSES to guard against a specific attack
DEFER	*v* -FERRED, -FERRING, -FERS to postpone
DEFERENT	*n* pl. -S an imaginary circle around the earth
DEFERRAL	*n* pl. -S the act of deferring
DEFERRED	past tense of defer
DEFERRER	*n* pl. -S one that defers
DEFERRING	present participle of defer
DEFI	*n* pl. -S a challenge
DEFIANCE	*n* pl. -S bold opposition
DEFIANT	*adj* showing defiance
DEFICIT	*n* pl. -S a shortage

DEFIED	past tense of defy
DEFIER	n pl. -S one that defies
DEFIES	present 3d person sing. of defy
DEFILADE	v -LADED, -LADING, -LADES to shield from enemy fire
DEFILE	v -FILED, -FILING, -FILES to make dirty
DEFILER	n pl. -S one that defiles
DEFINE	v -FINED, -FINING, -FINES to state the meaning of
DEFINER	n pl. -S one that defines
DEFINITE	adj known for certain
DEFLATE	v -FLATED, -FLATING, -FLATES to release the air or gas from
DEFLATOR	n pl. -S one that deflates
DEFLEA	v -ED, -ING, -S to rid of fleas
DEFLECT	v -ED, -ING, -S to turn aside
DEFLEXED	adj bent downward
DEFLOWER	v -ED, -ING, -S to deprive of flowers
DEFOAM	v -ED, -ING, -S to remove foam from
DEFOAMER	n pl. -S one that defoams
DEFOG	v -FOGGED, -FOGGING, -FOGS to remove fog from
DEFOGGER	n pl. -S one that defogs
DEFORCE	v -FORCED, -FORCING, -FORCES to withhold by force
DEFOREST	v -ED, -ING, -S to clear of forests
DEFORM	v -ED, -ING, -S to spoil the form of
DEFORMER	n pl. -S one that deforms
DEFRAUD	v -ED, -ING, -S to swindle
DEFRAY	v -ED, -ING, -S to pay
DEFRAYAL	n pl. -S the act of defraying
DEFRAYER	n pl. -S one that defrays
DEFROCK	v -ED, -ING, -S to unfrock
DEFROST	v -ED, -ING, -S to remove frost from
DEFT	adj DEFTER, DEFTEST skillful **DEFTLY** adv
DEFTNESS	n pl. -ES the quality of being deft
DEFUNCT	adj deceased
DEFUSE	v -FUSED, -FUSING, -FUSES to remove the fuse from
DEFUZE	v -FUZED, -FUZING, -FUZES to defuse
DEFY	v -FIED, -FYING, -FIES to resist openly and boldly
DEGAGE	adj free and relaxed in manner
DEGAME	n pl. -S a tropical tree
DEGAMI	n pl. -S degame
DEGAS	v -GASSED, -GASSING, -GASSES or -GASES to remove gas from
DEGASSER	n pl. -S one that degasses
DEGAUSS	v -ED, -ING, -ES to demagnetize
DEGERM	v -ED, -ING, -S to remove germs from
DEGLAZE	v -GLAZED, -GLAZING, -GLAZES to remove the glaze from
DEGRADE	v -GRADED, -GRADING, -GRADES to debase
DEGRADER	n pl. -S one that degrades
DEGREASE	v -GREASED, -GREASING, -GREASES to remove the grease from
DEGREE	n pl. -S one of a series of stages **DEGREED** adj
DEGUM	v -GUMMED, -GUMMING, -GUMS to free from gum
DEGUST	v -ED, -ING, -S to taste with pleasure
DEHISCE	v -HISCED, -HISCING, -HISCES to split open
DEHORN	v -ED, -ING, -S to deprive of horns
DEHORNER	n pl. -S one that dehorns
DEHORT	v -ED, -ING, -S to try to dissuade
DEI	prep of; from — used in names
DEICE	v -ICED, -ICING, -ICES to free from ice
DEICER	n pl. -S one that deices
DEICIDE	n pl. -S the killing of a god **DEICIDAL** adj
DEICTIC	adj proving directly
DEIFIC	adj godlike
DEIFICAL	adj deific
DEIFIED	past tense of deify
DEIFIER	n pl. -S one that deifies
DEIFORM	adj having the form of a god
DEIFY	v -FIED, -FYING, -FIES to make a god of
DEIGN	v -ED, -ING, -S to lower oneself to do something
DEIL	n pl. -S the devil

DEIONIZE *v* -IZED, -IZING, -IZES to remove ions from

DEISM *n* pl. -S a religious philosophy

DEIST *n* pl. -S an adherent of deism **DEISTIC** *adj*

DEITY *n* pl. -TIES a god or goddess

DEJECT *v* -ED, -ING, -S to depress

DEJECTA *n/pl* excrements

DEJEUNER *n* pl. -S a late breakfast

DEKAGRAM *n* pl. -S a measure equal to ten grams

DEKARE *n* pl. -S a measure equal to ten ares

DEKE *v* DEKED, DEKING, DEKES to feint in hockey

DEL *n* pl. -S an operator in differential calculus

DELAINE *n* pl. -S a wool fabric

DELATE *v* -LATED, -LATING, -LATES to accuse

DELATION *n* pl. -S the act of delating

DELATOR *n* pl. -S one that delates

DELAY *v* -ED, -ING, -S to put off to a later time

DELAYER *n* pl. -S one that delays

DELE *v* DELED, DELEING, DELES to delete

DELEAD *v* -ED, -ING, -S to remove lead from

DELEGACY *n* pl. -CIES the act of delegating

DELEGATE *v* -GATED, -GATING, -GATES to appoint as one's representative

DELETE *v* -LETED, -LETING, -LETES to remove written or printed matter

DELETION *n* pl. -S the act of deleting

DELF *n* pl. -S delft

DELFT *n* pl. -S an earthenware

DELI *n* pl. DELIS a delicatessen

DELICACY *n* pl. -CIES a choice food

DELICATE *n* pl. -S a delicacy

DELICT *n* pl. -S an offense against civil law

DELIGHT *v* -ED, -ING, -S to give great pleasure to

DELIME *v* -LIMED, -LIMING, -LIMES to free from lime

DELIMIT *v* -ED, -ING, -S to mark the boundaries of

DELIRIUM *n* pl. -IUMS or -IA wild excitement

DELIST *v* -ED, -ING, -S to remove from a list

DELIVER *v* -ED, -ING, -S to take to the intended recipient

DELIVERY *n* pl. -ERIES the act of delivering

DELL *n* pl. -S a small, wooded valley

DELLY *n* pl. DELLIES deli

DELOUSE *v* -LOUSED, -LOUSING, -LOUSES to remove lice from

DELTA *n* pl. -S an alluvial deposit at the mouth of a river **DELTAIC, DELTIC** *adj*

DELTOID *n* pl. -S a shoulder muscle

DELUDE *v* -LUDED, -LUDING, -LUDES to mislead the mind or judgment of

DELUDER *n* pl. -S one that deludes

DELUGE *v* -UGED, -UGING, -UGES to flood

DELUSION *n* pl. -S the act of deluding

DELUSIVE *adj* tending to delude

DELUSORY *adj* delusive

DELUSTER *v* -ED, -ING, -S to lessen the sheen of

DELUXE *adj* of special elegance or luxury

DELVE *v* DELVED, DELVING, DELVES to search in depth

DELVER *n* pl. -S one that delves

DEMAGOG *n* pl. -S an unethical leader

DEMAGOGY *n* pl. -GOGIES the rule of a demagog

DEMAND *v* -ED, -ING, -S to ask for with authority

DEMANDER *n* pl. -S one that demands

DEMARCHE *n* pl. -S a procedure

DEMARK *v* -ED, -ING, -S to delimit

DEMAST *v* -ED, -ING, -S to strip masts from

DEME *n* pl. -S a Greek district

DEMEAN *v* -ED, -ING, -S to conduct oneself in a particular manner

DEMEANOR *n* pl. -S the manner in which one conducts oneself

DEMENT *v* -ED, -ING, -S to make insane

DEMENTIA *n* pl. -S mental illness

DEMERIT *v* -ED, -ING, -S to lower in rank or status

DEMESNE *n* pl. -S the legal possession of land as one's own

DEMIES   pl. of demy

DEMIGOD   n pl. -S a lesser god

DEMIJOHN   n pl. -S a narrow-necked jug

DEMILUNE   n pl. -S a half-moon

DEMIREP   n pl. -S a prostitute

DEMISE   v -MISED, -MISING, -MISES to bequeath

DEMIT   v -MITTED, -MITTING, -MITS to resign

DEMIURGE   n pl. -S a magistrate of ancient Greece

DEMIVOLT   n pl. -S a half turn made by a horse

DEMO   n pl. DEMOS a demonstration

DEMOB   v -MOBBED, -MOBBING, -MOBS to discharge from military service

DEMOCRAT   n pl. -S one who believes in political and social equality

DEMODE   adj demoded

DEMODED   adj out-of-date

DEMOLISH   v -ED, -ING, -ES to destroy

DEMON   n pl. -S an evil spirit

DEMONESS   n pl. -ES a female demon

DEMONIAC   n pl. -S one regarded as possessed by a demon

DEMONIAN   adj demonic

DEMONIC   adj characteristic of a demon

DEMONISE   v -ISED, -ISING, -ISES to demonize

DEMONISM   n pl. -S belief in demons

DEMONIST   n pl. -S one who believes in demons

DEMONIZE   v -IZED, -IZING, -IZES to make a demon of

DEMOS   n pl. -ES the people of an ancient Greek state

DEMOTE   v -MOTED, -MOTING, -MOTES to lower in rank or grade

DEMOTIC   adj pertaining to a simplified form of ancient Egyptian writing

DEMOTICS   n/pl the study of people in society

DEMOTING   present participle of demote

DEMOTION   n pl. -S the act of demoting

DEMOTIST   n pl. -S a student of demotic writings

DEMOUNT   v -ED, -ING, -S to remove from a mounting

DEMPSTER   n pl. -S a deemster

DEMUR   v -MURRED, -MURRING, -MURS to object

DEMURE   adj -MURER, -MUREST shy and modest DEMURELY adv

DEMURRAL   n pl. -S the act of demurring

DEMURRED   past tense of demur

DEMURRER   n pl. -S one that demurs

DEMURRING   present participle of demur

DEMY   n pl. -MIES a size of paper

DEN   v DENNED, DENNING, DENS to live in a lair

DENARIUS   n pl. DENARII a coin of ancient Rome

DENARY   adj containing ten

DENATURE   v -TURED, -TURING, -TURES to deprive of natural qualities

DENAZIFY   v -FIED, -FYING, -FIES to rid of Nazism

DENDRITE   n pl. -S a branched part of a nerve cell

DENDROID   adj shaped like a tree

DENDRON   n pl. -S a dendrite

DENE   n pl. -S a valley

DENGUE   n pl. -S a tropical disease

DENIABLE   adj capable of being denied DENIABLY adv

DENIAL   n pl. -S the act of denying

DENIED   past tense of deny

DENIER   n pl. -S one that denies

DENIES   present 3d person sing. of deny

DENIM   n pl. -S a durable fabric

DENIZEN   v -ED, -ING, -S to make a citizen of

DENNED   past tense of den

DENNING   present participle of den

DENOTE   v -NOTED, -NOTING, -NOTES to indicate DENOTIVE adj

DENOUNCE   v -NOUNCED, -NOUNCING, -NOUNCES to condemn openly

DENSE   adj DENSER, DENSEST compact DENSELY adv

DENSIFY   v -FIED, -FYING, -FIES to make denser

DENSITY   n pl. -TIES the state of being dense

DENT   v -ED, -ING, -S to make a depression in

DENTAL   n pl. -S a dentally produced sound

DENTALIA	*n/pl* mollusks with long, tapering shells
DENTALLY	*adv* with the tip of the tongue against the upper front teeth
DENTATE	*adj* having teeth
DENTATED	*adj* dentate
DENTICLE	*n* pl. -S a small tooth
DENTIL	*n* pl. -S a small rectangular block
DENTIN	*n* pl. -S the hard substance forming the body of a tooth **DENTINAL** *adj*
DENTINE	*n* pl. -S dentin
DENTIST	*n* pl. -S one who treats the teeth
DENTOID	*adj* resembling a tooth
DENTURE	*n* pl. -S a set of teeth **DENTURAL** *adj*
DENUDATE	*v* -DATED, -DATING, -DATES to denude
DENUDE	*v* -NUDED, -NUDING, -NUDES to strip of all covering
DENUDER	*n* pl. -S one that denudes
DENY	*v* -NIED, -NYING, -NIES to declare to be untrue
DEODAND	*n* pl. -S property forfeited to the crown under a former English law
DEODAR	*n* pl. -S an East Indian cedar
DEODARA	*n* pl. -S deodar
DEPAINT	*v* -ED, -ING, -S to depict
DEPART	*v* -ED, -ING, -S to go away
DEPEND	*v* -ED, -ING, -S to rely
DEPERM	*v* -ED, -ING, -S to demagnetize
DEPICT	*v* -ED, -ING, -S to portray
DEPICTER	*n* pl. -S one that depicts
DEPICTOR	*n* pl. -S depicter
DEPILATE	*v* -LATED, -LATING, -LATES to remove hair from
DEPLANE	*v* -PLANED, -PLANING, -PLANES to get off an airplane
DEPLETE	*v* -PLETED, -PLETING, -PLETES to lessen or exhaust the supply of
DEPLORE	*v* -PLORED, -PLORING, -PLORES to regret strongly
DEPLORER	*n* pl. -S one that deplores
DEPLOY	*v* -ED, -ING, -S to position troops for battle
DEPLUME	*v* -PLUMED, -PLUMING, -PLUMES to deprive of feathers
DEPOLISH	*v* -ED, -ING, -ES to remove the gloss or polish of
DEPONE	*v* -PONED, -PONING, -PONES to testify under oath
DEPONENT	*n* pl. -S one that depones
DEPORT	*v* -ED, -ING, -S to expel from a country
DEPORTEE	*n* pl. -S one who is deported
DEPOSAL	*n* pl. -S the act of deposing
DEPOSE	*v* -POSED, -POSING, -POSES to remove from office
DEPOSER	*n* pl. -S one that deposes
DEPOSIT	*v* -ED, -ING, -S to place
DEPOT	*n* pl. -S a railroad or bus station
DEPRAVE	*v* -PRAVED, -PRAVING, -PRAVES to corrupt in morals
DEPRAVER	*n* pl. -S one that depraves
DEPRESS	*v* -ED, -ING, -ES to make sad
DEPRIVAL	*n* pl. -S the act of depriving
DEPRIVE	*v* -PRIVED, -PRIVING, -PRIVES to take something away from
DEPRIVER	*n* pl. -S one that deprives
DEPSIDE	*n* pl. -S an aromatic compound
DEPTH	*n* pl. -S deepness
DEPURATE	*v* -RATED, -RATING, -RATES to free from impurities
DEPUTE	*v* -PUTED, -PUTING, -PUTES to delegate
DEPUTIZE	*v* -TIZED, -TIZING, -TIZES to appoint as a deputy
DEPUTY	*n* pl. -TIES one appointed to act for another
DERAIGN	*v* -ED, -ING, -S to dispute a claim
DERAIL	*v* -ED, -ING, -S to run off the rails of a track
DERANGE	*v* -RANGED, -RANGING, -RANGES to disorder
DERAT	*v* -RATTED, -RATTING, -RATS to rid of rats
DERAY	*n* pl. -RAYS disorderly revelry
DERBY	*n* pl. -BIES a type of hat
DERE	*adj* dire
DERELICT	*n* pl. -S something abandoned
DERIDE	*v* -RIDED, -RIDING, -RIDES to ridicule
DERIDER	*n* pl. -S one that derides

DERINGER   *n* pl. -S a short-barreled pistol

DERISION   *n* pl. -S the act of deriding

DERISIVE   *adj* expressing derision

DERISORY   *adj* derisive

DERIVATE   *n* pl. -S something derived

DERIVE   *v* -RIVED, -RIVING, -RIVES to obtain or receive from a source

DERIVER   *n* pl. -S one that derives

DERM   *n* pl. -S derma

DERMA   *n* pl. -S a layer of the skin **DERMAL** *adj*

DERMIS   *n* pl. -MISES derma **DERMIC** *adj*

DERMOID   *adj* resembling skin

DERNIER   *adj* last

DEROGATE   *v* -GATED, -GATING, -GATES to detract

DERRICK   *n* pl. -S a hoisting apparatus

DERRIERE   *n* pl. -S the buttocks

DERRIS   *n* pl. -RISES a climbing plant

DERRY   *n* pl. -RIES a meaningless word used as part of a chorus in old songs

DERVISH   *n* pl. -ES a member of a Muslim religious order

DES   *prep* of the — used in names

DESALT   *v* -ED, -ING, -S to remove the salt from

DESALTER   *n* pl. -S one that desalts

DESAND   *v* -ED, -ING, -S to remove sand from

DESCANT   *v* -ED, -ING, -S to sing

DESCEND   *v* -ED, -ING, -S to come or go down

DESCENT   *n* pl. -S the act of descending

DESCRIBE   *v* -SCRIBED, -SCRIBING, -SCRIBES to give a verbal account of

DESCRIER   *n* pl. -S one that descries

DESCRY   *v* -SCRIED, -SCRYING, -SCRIES to discern

DESELECT   *v* -ED, -ING, -S to dismiss from a training program

DESERT   *v* -ED, -ING, -S to abandon

DESERTER   *n* pl. -S one that deserts

DESERTIC   *adj* arid and barren

DESERVE   *v* -SERVED, -SERVING, -SERVES to be entitled to or worthy of

DESERVER   *n* pl. -S one that deserves

DESEX   *v* -ED, -ING, -ES to castrate or spay

DESIGN   *v* -ED, -ING, -S to conceive and plan out

DESIGNEE   *n* pl. -S one who is designated

DESIGNER   *n* pl. -S one that designs

DESILVER   *v* -ED, -ING, -S to remove the silver from

DESINENT   *adj* terminating

DESIRE   *v* -SIRED, -SIRING, -SIRES to wish for

DESIRER   *n* pl. -S one that desires

DESIROUS   *adj* desiring

DESIST   *v* -ED, -ING, -S to cease doing something

DESK   *n* pl. -S a writing table

DESKMAN   *n* pl. -MEN one who works at a desk

DESMAN   *n* pl. -S an aquatic mammal

DESMID   *n* pl. -S a freshwater alga

DESMOID   *n* pl. -S a very hard tumor

DESOLATE   *v* -LATED, -LATING, -LATES to lay waste

DESORB   *v* -ED, -ING, -S to remove by the reverse of absorption

DESPAIR   *v* -ED, -ING, -S to lose all hope

DESPATCH   *v* -ED, -ING, -ES to dispatch

DESPISE   *v* -SPISED, -SPISING, -SPISES to loathe

DESPISER   *n* pl. -S one that despises

DESPITE   *v* -SPITED, -SPITING, -SPITES to treat with contempt

DESPOIL   *v* -ED, -ING, -S to plunder

DESPOND   *v* -ED, -ING, -S to lose spirit or hope

DESPOT   *n* pl. -S a tyrant **DESPOTIC** *adj*

DESSERT   *n* pl. -S something served as the last course of a meal

DESTAIN   *v* -ED, -ING, -S to remove stain from

DESTINE   *v* -TINED, -TINING, -TINES to determine beforehand

DESTINY   *n* pl. -NIES the fate or fortune to which one is destined

DESTRIER   *n* pl. -S a war horse

DESTROY   *v* -ED, -ING, -S to damage beyond repair or renewal

DESTRUCT   *v* -ED, -ING, -S to destroy

DESUGAR   *v* -ED, -ING, -S to remove sugar from

DESULFUR v -ED, -ING, -S to free from sulfur

DETACH v -ED, -ING, -ES to unfasten and separate

DETACHER n pl. -S one that detaches

DETAIL v -ED, -ING, -S to report with complete particulars

DETAILER n pl. -S one that details

DETAIN v -ED, -ING, -S to hold in custody

DETAINEE n pl. -S one who is detained

DETAINER n pl. -S the unlawful withholding of another's property

DETECT v -ED, -ING, -S to discover or perceive

DETECTER n pl. -S detector

DETECTOR n pl. -S one that detects

DETENT n pl. -S a mechanical device that either stops or releases a movement

DETENTE n pl. -S an easing of international tension

DETER v -TERRED, -TERRING, -TERS to stop from proceeding

DETERGE v -TERGED, -TERGING, -TERGES to cleanse

DETERGER n pl. -S one that deterges

DETERRED past tense of deter

DETERRER n pl. -S one that deters

DETERRING present participle of deter

DETEST v -ED, -ING, -S to dislike intensely

DETESTER n pl. -S one that detests

DETHRONE v -THRONED, -THRONING, -THRONES to remove from a throne

DETICK v -ED, -ING, -S to remove ticks from

DETICKER n pl. -S one that deticks

DETINUE n pl. -S an action to recover property wrongfully detained

DETONATE v -NATED, -NATING, -NATES to cause to explode

DETOUR v -ED, -ING, -S to take an indirect route

DETOXIFY v -FIED, -FYING, -FIES to remove a toxin from

DETRACT v -ED, -ING, -S to take away

DETRAIN v -ED, -ING, -S to get off a railroad train

DETRITUS n pl. DETRITUS particles of rock **DETRITAL** adj

DETRUDE v -TRUDED, -TRUDING, -TRUDES to thrust out

DEUCE v DEUCED, DEUCING, DEUCES to bring a tennis score to a tie

DEUCEDLY adv extremely

DEUTERIC adj pertaining to heavy hydrogen

DEUTERON n pl. -S an atomic particle

DEUTZIA n pl. -S an ornamental shrub

DEV n pl. -S deva

DEVA n pl. -S a Hindu god

DEVALUE v -UED, -UING, -UES to lessen the worth of

DEVEIN v -ED, -ING, -S to remove the dorsal vein from

DEVEL v -ED, -ING, -S to strike forcibly

DEVELOP v -ED, -ING, -S to bring to a more advanced or effective state

DEVELOPE v -OPED, -OPING, -OPES to develop

DEVEST v -ED, -ING, -S to divest

DEVIANCE n pl. -S the behavior of a deviant

DEVIANCY n pl. -CIES deviance

DEVIANT n pl. -S one that deviates from a norm

DEVIATE v -ATED, -ATING, -ATES to turn aside from a course or norm

DEVIATOR n pl. -S one that deviates

DEVICE n pl. -S something devised or constructed for a specific purpose

DEVIL v -ILED, -ILING, -ILS or -ILLED, -ILLING, -ILS to prepare food with pungent seasoning

DEVILISH adj fiendish

DEVILKIN n pl. -S a small demon

DEVILLED a past tense of devil

DEVILLING a present participle of devil

DEVILRY n pl. -RIES deviltry

DEVILTRY n pl. -TRIES mischief

DEVIOUS adj indirect

DEVISAL n pl. -S the act of devising

DEVISE v -VISED, -VISING, -VISES to form in the mind

DEVISEE n pl. -S one to whom a will is made

DEVISER	*n* pl. -S one that devises		**DEXIES**	*n/pl* tablets of dex
DEVISING	present participle of devise		**DEXTER**	*adj* situated on the right
DEVISOR	*n* pl. -S one who makes a will		**DEXTRAL**	*adj* pertaining to the right
DEVOICE	*v* -VOICED, -VOICING, -VOICES to unvoice		**DEXTRAN**	*n* pl. -S a substance used as a plasma substitute
DEVOID	*adj* completely lacking		**DEXTRIN**	*n* pl. -S a substance used as an adhesive
DEVOIR	*n* pl. -S an act of civility or respect		**DEXTRINE**	*n* pl. -S dextrin
DEVOLVE	*v* -VOLVED, -VOLVING, -VOLVES to transfer from one person to another		**DEXTRO**	*adj* turning to the right
			DEXTROSE	*n* pl. -S a form of glucose
			DEXTROUS	*adj* adroit
DEVON	*n* pl. -S one of a breed of small, hardy cattle		**DEY**	*n* pl. DEYS a former North African ruler
DEVOTE	*v* -VOTED, -VOTING, -VOTES to give oneself wholly to		**DEZINC**	*v* -ZINCKED, -ZINCKING, -ZINCS or -ZINCED, -ZINCING, -ZINCS to remove zinc from
DEVOTEE	*n* pl. -S an ardent follower or supporter		**DHAK**	*n* pl. -S an Asian tree
DEVOTION	*n* pl. -S the act of devoting		**DHARMA**	*n* pl. -S conformity to Hindu law **DHARMIC** *adj*
DEVOUR	*v* -ED, -ING, -S to eat up voraciously		**DHARNA**	*n* pl. -S a form of protest in India
DEVOURER	*n* pl. -S one that devours		**DHOLE**	*n* pl. -S a wild dog of India
DEVOUT	*adj* pious **DEVOUTLY** *adv*		**DHOOLY**	*n* pl. -LIES dooly
DEW	*v* -ED, -ING, -S to wet with dew (condensed moisture)		**DHOORA**	*n* pl. -S durra
DEWAN	*n* pl. -S an official in India		**DHOOTI**	*n* pl. -S dhoti
DEWATER	*v* -ED, -ING, -S to remove water from		**DHOOTIE**	*n* pl. -S dhoti
DEWAX	*v* -ED, -ING, -ES to remove wax from		**DHOTI**	*n* pl. -S a loincloth worn by Hindu men
DEWBERRY	*n* pl. -RIES an edible berry		**DHOURRA**	*n* pl. -S durra
DEWCLAW	*n* pl. -S a vestigial toe		**DHOW**	*n* pl. -S an Arabian sailing vessel
DEWDROP	*n* pl. -S a drop of dew		**DHURNA**	*n* pl. -S dharna
DEWFALL	*n* pl. -S the formation of dew		**DHUTI**	*n* pl. -S dhoti
DEWIER	comparative of dewy		**DIABASE**	*n* pl. -S an igneous rock **DIABASIC** *adj*
DEWIEST	superlative of dewy			
DEWILY	*adv* in a dewy manner		**DIABETES**	*n* pl. DIABETES a metabolic disorder
DEWINESS	*n* pl. -ES the state of being dewy		**DIABETIC**	*n* pl. -S one who has diabetes
DEWLAP	*n* pl. -S a fold of loose skin under the neck		**DIABLERY**	*n* pl. -RIES sorcery
			DIABOLIC	*adj* devilish
DEWLESS	*adj* having no dew		**DIABOLO**	*n* pl. -LOS a game requiring manual dexterity
DEWOOL	*v* -ED, -ING, -S to remove the wool from		**DIACETYL**	*n* pl. -S biacetyl
DEWORM	*v* -ED, -ING, -S to rid of worms		**DIACID**	*n* pl. -S a type of acid **DIACIDIC** *adj*
DEWY	*adj* DEWIER, DEWIEST moist with dew			
DEX	*n* pl. -ES a sulfate used as a central nervous system stimulant		**DIACONAL**	*adj* pertaining to a deacon
			DIADEM	*v* -ED, -ING, -S to adorn with a crown

DIAGNOSE   v -NOSED, -NOSING, -NOSES to recognize a disease by its signs and symptoms

DIAGONAL   n pl. -S an oblique line

DIAGRAM   v -GRAMED, -GRAMING, -GRAMS or -GRAMMED, -GRAMMING, -GRAMS to illustrate by a diagram (a graphic design)

DIAGRAPH   n pl. -S a drawing device

DIAL   v DIALED, DIALING, DIALS or DIALLED, DIALLING, DIALS to manipulate a calibrated disk

DIALECT   n pl. -S a regional variety of a language

DIALER   n pl. -S one that dials

DIALING   n pl. -S the measurement of time by sundials

DIALIST   n pl. -S a dialer

DIALLAGE   n pl. -S a mineral

DIALLED   a past tense of dial

DIALLEL   adj pertaining to a genetic crossing

DIALLER   n pl. -S dialer

DIALLING   n pl. -S dialing

DIALLIST   n pl. -S dialist

DIALOG   v -LOGGED, -LOGGING, -LOGS to dialogue

DIALOGER   n pl. -S one that dialogs

DIALOGIC   adj conversational

DIALOGUE   v -LOGUED, -LOGUING, -LOGUES to converse

DIALYSE   v -LYSED, -LYSING, -LYSES to dialyze

DIALYSER   n pl. -S dialyzer

DIALYSIS   n pl. -YSES the separation of substances in a solution by diffusion through a membrane

DIALYTIC   adj pertaining to dialysis

DIALYZE   v -LYZED, -LYZING, -LYZES to subject to dialysis

DIALYZER   n pl. -S an apparatus used for dialysis

DIAMETER   n pl. -S a straight line passing through the center of a circle and ending at the periphery

DIAMIDE   n pl. -S a chemical compound

DIAMIN   n pl. -S diamine

DIAMINE   n pl. -S a chemical compound

DIAMOND   v -ED, -ING, -S to adorn with diamonds (precious gems)

DIANTHUS   n pl. -ES an ornamental herb

DIAPASON   n pl. -S a burst of harmonious sound

DIAPAUSE   v -PAUSED, -PAUSING, -PAUSES to undergo dormancy

DIAPER   v -ED, -ING, -S to put a diaper (a baby's breechcloth) on

DIAPHONE   n pl. -S a low-pitched foghorn

DIAPHONY   n pl. -NIES organum

DIAPIR   n pl. -S a bend in a layer of rock **DIAPIRIC** adj

DIAPSID   adj pertaining to a type of reptile

DIARCHY   n pl. -CHIES a government with two rulers **DIARCHIC** adj

DIARIES   pl. of diary

DIARIST   n pl. -S one who keeps a diary

DIARRHEA   n pl. -S an intestinal disorder

DIARY   n pl. -RIES a personal journal

DIASPORA   n pl. -S migration

DIASPORE   n pl. -S a mineral

DIASTASE   n pl. -S an enzyme

DIASTEMA   n pl. -MATA a space between teeth

DIASTER   n pl. -S a stage in mitosis **DIASTRAL** adj

DIASTOLE   n pl. -S the normal rhythmical dilation of the heart

DIATOM   n pl. -S any of a class of algae

DIATOMIC   adj composed of two atoms

DIATONIC   adj pertaining to a type of musical scale

DIATRIBE   n pl. -S a bitter and abusive criticism

DIAZEPAM   n pl. -S a tranquilizer

DIAZIN   n pl. -S diazine

DIAZINE   n pl. -S a chemical compound

DIAZO   adj containing a certain chemical group

DIAZOLE   n pl. -S a chemical compound

DIB   v DIBBED, DIBBING, DIBS to fish by letting the bait bob lightly on the water

DIBASIC   adj having two replaceable hydrogen atoms

DIBBER   n pl. -S a planting implement

DIBBING   present participle of dib

DIBBLE   v -BLED, -BLING, -BLES to dib

DIBBLER   n pl. -S one that dibbles

DIBBUK   *n* pl. -BUKS or -BUKIM dybbuk

DICAST   *n* pl. -S a judge of ancient Athens **DICASTIC** *adj*

DICE   *v* DICED, DICING, DICES to cut into small cubes

DICENTRA   *n* pl. -S a perennial herb

DICER   *n* pl. -S a device that dices food

DICEY   *adj* DICIER, DICIEST dangerous

DICHASIA   *n/pl* flower clusters

DICHOTIC   *adj* affecting the two ears differently

DICHROIC   *adj* having two colors

DICIER   comparative of dicey

DICIEST   superlative of dicey

DICING   present participle of dice

DICK   *n* pl. -S a detective

DICKENS   *n* pl. -ES devil

DICKER   *v* -ED, -ING, -S to bargain

DICKEY   *n* pl. -EYS a blouse front

DICKIE   *n* pl. -S dickey

DICKY   *n* pl. DICKIES dickey

DICLINY   *n* pl. -NIES the state of having stamens and pistils in separate flowers

DICOT   *n* pl. -S a plant with two seed leaves

DICOTYL   *n* pl. -S dicot

DICROTAL   *adj* dicrotic

DICROTIC   *adj* having a double pulse beat

DICTA   a pl. of dictum

DICTATE   *v* -TATED, -TATING, -TATES to read aloud for recording

DICTATOR   *n* pl. -S one that dictates

DICTION   *n* pl. -S choice and use of words in speech or writing

DICTUM   *n* pl. -TA or -TUMS an authoritative statement

DICYCLIC   *adj* having two maxima of population each year

DICYCLY   *n* pl. -CLIES the state of being dicyclic

DID   a past tense of do

DIDACT   *n* pl. -S a didactic person

DIDACTIC   *adj* instructive

DIDACTYL   *adj* having two digits at the end of each limb

DIDAPPER   *n* pl. -S a dabchick

DIDDLE   *v* -DLED, -DLING, -DLES to swindle

DIDDLER   *n* pl. -S one that diddles

DIDIES   pl. of didy

DIDO   *n* pl. -DOS or -DOES a mischievous act

DIDST   a past tense of do

DIDY   *n* pl. -DIES a diaper

DIDYMIUM   *n* pl. -S a mixture of rare-earth elements

DIDYMOUS   *adj* occurring in pairs

DIDYNAMY   *n* pl. -MIES the state of having four stamens in pairs of unequal length

DIE   *v* DIED, DYING, DIES to cease living

DIE   *v* DIED, DIEING, DIES to cut with a die (a device for shaping material)

DIEBACK   *n* pl. -S a gradual dying of plant shoots

DIECIOUS   *adj* dioicous

DIED   past tense of die

DIEHARD   *n* pl. -S a stubborn person

DIEL   *adj* involving a full day

DIELDRIN   *n* pl. -S an insecticide

DIEMAKER   *n* pl. -S one that makes dies

DIENE   *n* pl. -S a chemical compound

DIERESIS   *n* pl. DIERESES the separation of two vowels into two syllables **DIERETIC** *adj*

DIES   present 3d person sing. of die

DIESEL   *n* pl. -S a type of engine

DIESIS   *n* pl. DIESES a reference mark in printing

DIESTER   *n* pl. -S a type of chemical compound

DIESTOCK   *n* pl. -S a frame for holding dies

DIESTRUM   *n* pl. -S diestrus

DIESTRUS   *n* pl. -ES a period of sexual inactivity

DIET   *v* -ED, -ING, -S to regulate one's daily sustenance

DIETARY   *n* pl. -ETARIES a system of dieting

DIETER   *n* pl. -S one that diets

DIETETIC   *adj* pertaining to diet

DIFFER   *v* -ED, -ING, -S to be unlike

DIFFRACT   *v* -ED, -ING, -S to separate into parts

DIFFUSE   v -FUSED, -FUSING, -FUSES to spread widely or thinly

DIFFUSER   n pl. -S one that diffuses

DIFFUSOR   n pl. -S diffuser

DIG   v DUG or DIGGED, DIGGING, DIGS to break up, turn over, or remove earth

DIGAMIST   n pl. -S one who practices digamy

DIGAMMA   n pl. -S a Greek letter

DIGAMY   n pl. -MIES a second legal marriage **DIGAMOUS** adj

DIGEST   v -ED, -ING, -S to render food usable for the body

DIGESTER   n pl. -S an apparatus in which substances are softened or decomposed

DIGESTOR   n pl. -S digester

DIGGED   a past tense of dig

DIGGER   n pl. -S one that digs

DIGGING   present participle of dig

DIGGINGS   n/pl an excavation site

DIGHT   v -ED, -ING, -S to adorn

DIGIT   n pl. -S a finger or toe

DIGITAL   n pl. -S a piano key

DIGITATE   adj having digits

DIGITIZE   v -TIZED, -TIZING, -TIZES to put data into digital notation

DIGLOT   n pl. -S a bilingual book or edition

DIGNIFY   v -FIED, -FYING, -FIES to add dignity to

DIGNITY   n pl. -TIES stateliness and nobility of manner

DIGOXIN   n pl. -S a poisonous steroid

DIGRAPH   n pl. -S a pair of letters representing a single speech sound

DIGRESS   v -ED, -ING, -ES to stray from the main topic

DIHEDRAL   n pl. -S a dihedron

DIHEDRON   n pl. -S a figure formed by two intersecting planes

DIHYBRID   n pl. -S an offspring of parents differing in two pairs of genes

DIHYDRIC   adj containing two hydroxyl radicals

DIKDIK   n pl. -S a small antelope

DIKE   v DIKED, DIKING, DIKES to furnish with an embankment

DIKER   n pl. -S one that dikes

DIKTAT   n pl. -S a harsh settlement imposed on a defeated nation

DILATANT   n pl. -S a dilator

DILATATE   adj dilated

DILATE   v -LATED, -LATING, -LATES to make wider or larger

DILATER   n pl. -S dilator

DILATION   n pl. -S the act of dilating

DILATIVE   adj tending to dilate

DILATOR   n pl. -S one that dilates

DILATORY   adj tending to delay

DILDO   n pl. -DOS an object used as a penis substitute

DILDOE   n pl. -S dildo

DILEMMA   n pl. -S a perplexing situation **DILEMMIC** adj

DILIGENT   adj persevering

DILL   n pl. -S an annual herb

DILLY   n pl. DILLIES something remarkable

DILUENT   n pl. -S a diluting substance

DILUTE   v -LUTED, -LUTING, -LUTES to thin or reduce the concentration of

DILUTER   n pl. -S one that dilutes

DILUTION   n pl. -S the act of diluting

DILUTIVE   adj tending to dilute

DILUTOR   n pl. -S diluter

DILUVIA   a pl. of diluvium

DILUVIAL   adj pertaining to a flood

DILUVIAN   adj diluvial

DILUVION   n pl. -S diluvium

DILUVIUM   n pl. -VIA or -VIUMS coarse rock material deposited by glaciers

DIM   adj DIMMER, DIMMEST obscure

DIM   v DIMMED, DIMMING, DIMS to make dim

DIME   n pl. -S a coin of the United States

DIMER   n pl. -S a molecule composed of two identical molecules

DIMERIC   adj dimerous

DIMERISM   n pl. -S the state of being dimerous

DIMERIZE   v -IZED, -IZING, -IZES to form a dimer

DIMEROUS   adj composed of two parts

DIMETER *n* pl. -S a verse of two metrical feet

DIMETHYL *n* pl. -S ethane

DIMETRIC *adj* pertaining to a type of crystal system

DIMINISH *v* -ED, -ING, -ES to lessen

DIMITY *n* pl. -TIES a cotton fabric

DIMLY *adv* in a dim manner

DIMMABLE *adj* capable of being dimmed

DIMMED past tense of dim

DIMMER *n* pl. -S a device for varying the intensity of illumination

DIMMEST superlative of dim

DIMMING present participle of dim

DIMNESS *n* pl. -ES the state of being dim

DIMORPH *n* pl. -S either of two distinct forms

DIMOUT *n* pl. -S a condition of partial darkness

DIMPLE *v* -PLED, -PLING, -PLES to mark with indentations

DIMPLY *adj* -PLIER, -PLIEST dimpled

DIMWIT *n* pl. -S a dunce

DIN *v* DINNED, DINNING, DINS to make a loud noise

DINAR *n* pl. -S an ancient gold coin of Muslim areas

DINDLE *v* -DLED, -DLING, -DLES to tingle

DINE *v* DINED, DINING, DINES to eat dinner

DINER *n* pl. -S one that dines

DINERIC *adj* pertaining to the interface between two immiscible liquids

DINERO *n* pl. -ROS a former silver coin of Peru

DINETTE *n* pl. -S a small dining room

DING *v* -ED, -ING, -S to ring

DINGBAT *n* pl. -S a typographical ornament

DINGDONG *v* -ED, -ING, -S to make a ringing sound

DINGEY *n* pl. -GEYS dinghy

DINGHY *n* pl. -GHIES a small boat

DINGIER comparative of dingy

DINGIEST superlative of dingy

DINGILY *adv* in a dingy manner

DINGLE *n* pl. -S a dell

DINGO *n* pl. -GOES a wild dog of Australia

DINGUS *n* pl. -ES a gadget or object whose name is unknown or forgotten

DINGY *n* pl. -GIES dinghy

DINGY *adj* DINGIER, DINGIEST grimy

DINING present participle of dine

DINK *v* -ED, -ING, -S to adorn

DINKEY *n* pl. -KEYS a small locomotive

DINKIER comparative of dinky

DINKIES pl. of dinky

DINKIEST superlative of dinky

DINKLY *adv* neatly

DINKUM *adj* genuine

DINKY *n* pl. -KIES dinkey

DINKY *adj* -KIER, -KIEST small

DINNED past tense of din

DINNER *n* pl. -S the main meal of the day

DINNING present participle of din

DINOSAUR *n* pl. -S one of a group of extinct reptiles

DINT *v* -ED, -ING, -S to dent

DIOBOL *n* pl. -S a coin of ancient Greece

DIOBOLON *n* pl. -S diobol

DIOCESAN *n* pl. -S a bishop

DIOCESE *n* pl. -S an ecclesiastical district

DIODE *n* pl. -S a type of electron tube

DIOECISM *n* pl. -S the state of being dioicous

DIOICOUS *adj* unisexual

DIOL *n* pl. -S a chemical compound

DIOLEFIN *n* pl. -S a hydrocarbon

DIOPSIDE *n* pl. -S a mineral

DIOPTASE *n* pl. -S a mineral

DIOPTER *n* pl. -S a measure of refractive power **DIOPTRAL** *adj*

DIOPTRE *n* pl. -S diopter

DIOPTRIC *adj* aiding the vision by refraction

DIORAMA *n* pl. -S a three-dimensional exhibit **DIORAMIC** *adj*

DIORITE *n* pl. -S an igneous rock **DIORITIC** *adj*

DIOXANE *n* pl. -S a flammable liquid

DIOXID	*n* pl. -S dioxide
DIOXIDE	*n* pl. -S a type of oxide
DIP	*v* DIPPED or DIPT, DIPPING, DIPS to immerse briefly into a liquid
DIPHASE	*adj* having two phases
DIPHASIC	*adj* diphase
DIPHENYL	*n* pl. -S biphenyl
DIPLEGIA	*n* pl. -S paralysis of the same part on both sides of the body
DIPLEX	*adj* pertaining to the simultaneous transmission or reception of two radio signals
DIPLOE	*n* pl. -S a bony tissue of the cranium **DIPLOIC** *adj*
DIPLOID	*n* pl. -S a cell having the basic chromosome number doubled
DIPLOIDY	*n* pl. -DIES the condition of being a diploid
DIPLOMA	*n* pl. -MAS or -MATA a certificate of an academic degree
DIPLOMA	*v* -ED, -ING, -S to furnish with a diploma
DIPLOMAT	*n* pl. -S a governmental official
DIPLONT	*n* pl. -S an organism having a particular chromosomal structure
DIPLOPIA	*n* pl. -S double vision **DIPLOPIC** *adj*
DIPLOPOD	*n* pl. -S a multi-legged insect
DIPLOSIS	*n* pl. -LOSES a method of chromosome formation
DIPNOAN	*n* pl. -S a lungfish
DIPODY	*n* pl. -DIES a dimeter **DIPODIC** *adj*
DIPOLE	*n* pl. -S a pair of equal and opposite electric charges **DIPOLAR** *adj*
DIPPABLE	*adj* capable of being dipped
DIPPED	a past tense of dip
DIPPER	*n* pl. -S one that dips
DIPPING	present participle of dip
DIPPY	*adj* -PIER, -PIEST foolish
DIPSAS	*n* pl. DIPSADES a fabled serpent
DIPSTICK	*n* pl. -S a measuring rod
DIPT	a past tense of dip
DIPTERA	pl. of dipteron
DIPTERAL	*adj* having two rows or columns
DIPTERAN	*n* pl. -S a two-winged fly
DIPTERON	*n* pl. -TERA dipteran
DIPTYCA	*n* pl. -S diptych
DIPTYCH	*n* pl. -S an ancient writing tablet
DIQUAT	*n* pl. -S an herbicide
DIRDUM	*n* pl. -S blame
DIRE	*adj* DIRER, DIREST disastrous
DIRECT	*v* -ED, -ING, -S to control or conduct the affairs of
DIRECT	*adj* -RECTER, -RECTEST straightforward **DIRECTLY** *adv*
DIRECTOR	*n* pl. -S one that directs
DIREFUL	*adj* dreadful
DIRELY	*adv* in a dire manner
DIRENESS	*n* pl. -ES the state of being dire
DIRER	comparative of dire
DIREST	superlative of dire
DIRGE	*n* pl. -S a funeral song **DIRGEFUL** *adj*
DIRHAM	*n* pl. -S a monetary unit of Morocco
DIRIMENT	*adj* nullifying
DIRK	*v* -ED, -ING, -S to stab with a small knife
DIRL	*v* -ED, -ING, -S to tremble
DIRNDL	*n* pl. -S a woman's dress
DIRT	*n* pl. -S earth or soil
DIRTY	*adj* DIRTIER, DIRTIEST unclean **DIRTILY** *adv*
DIRTY	*v* DIRTIED, DIRTYING, DIRTIES to make dirty
DISABLE	*v* -ABLED, -ABLING, -ABLES to render incapable or unable
DISABUSE	*v* -ABUSED, -ABUSING, -ABUSES to free from false or mistaken ideas
DISAGREE	*v* -AGREED, -AGREEING, -AGREES to differ in opinion
DISALLOW	*v* -ED, -ING, -S to refuse to allow
DISANNUL	*v* -NULLED, -NULLING, -NULS to annul
DISARM	*v* -ED, -ING, -S to deprive of weapons
DISARMER	*n* pl. -S one that disarms
DISARRAY	*v* -ED, -ING, -S to disorder
DISASTER	*n* pl. -S a calamity
DISAVOW	*v* -ED, -ING, -S to disclaim responsibility for

DISBAND   *v* -ED, -ING, -S to break up

DISBAR   *v* -BARRED, -BARRING, -BARS to expel from the legal profession

DISBOSOM   *v* -ED, -ING, -S to confess

DISBOUND   *adj* not having a binding

DISBOWEL   *v* -ELED, -ELING, -ELS or -ELLED, -ELLING, -ELS to remove the intestines of

DISBUD   *v* -BUDDED, -BUDDING, -BUDS to remove buds from

DISBURSE   *v* -BURSED, -BURSING, -BURSES to pay out

DISC   *v* -ED, -ING, -S to disk

DISCANT   *v* -ED, -ING, -S to descant

DISCARD   *v* -ED, -ING, -S to throw away

DISCASE   *v* -CASED, -CASING, -CASES to remove the case of

DISCEPT   *v* -ED, -ING, -S to debate

DISCERN   *v* -ED, -ING, -S to perceive

DISCI   a pl. of discus

DISCIPLE   *v* -PLED, -PLING, -PLES to cause to become a follower

DISCLAIM   *v* -ED, -ING, -S to renounce any claim to or connection with

DISCLIKE   *adj* disklike

DISCLOSE   *v* -CLOSED, -CLOSING, -CLOSES to reveal

DISCO   *n* pl. -COS a discotheque

DISCOID   *n* pl. -S a disk

DISCOLOR   *v* -ED, -ING, -S to alter the color of

DISCORD   *v* -ED, -ING, -S to disagree

DISCOUNT   *v* -ED, -ING, -S to reduce the price of

DISCOVER   *v* -ED, -ING, -S to gain sight or knowledge of

DISCREET   *adj* -CREETER, -CREETEST tactful

DISCRETE   *adj* separate

DISCROWN   *v* -ED, -ING, -S to deprive of a crown

DISCUS   *n* pl. -CUSES or -CI a disk hurled in athletic competition

DISCUSS   *v* -ED, -ING, -ES to talk over or write about

DISDAIN   *v* -ED, -ING, -S to scorn

DISEASE   *v* -EASED, -EASING, -EASES to make unhealthy

DISENDOW   *v* -ED, -ING, -S to deprive of endowment

DISEUSE   *n* pl. -S a female entertainer

DISFAVOR   *v* -ED, -ING, -S to regard with disapproval

DISFROCK   *v* -ED, -ING, -S to unfrock

DISGORGE   *v* -GORGED, -GORGING, -GORGES to vomit

DISGRACE   *v* -GRACED, -GRACING, -GRACES to bring shame or discredit upon

DISGUISE   *v* -GUISED, -GUISING, -GUISES to alter the appearance of

DISGUST   *v* -ED, -ING, -S to cause nausea or loathing in

DISH   *v* -ED, -ING, -ES to put into a dish (a concave vessel)

DISHELM   *v* -ED, -ING, -S to deprive of a helmet

DISHERIT   *v* -ED, -ING, -S to deprive of an inheritance

DISHEVEL   *v* -ELED, -ELING, -ELS or -ELLED, -ELLING, -ELS to make messy

DISHFUL   *n* pl. -S as much as a dish can hold

DISHIER   comparative of dishy

DISHIEST   superlative of dishy

DISHLIKE   *adj* resembling a dish

DISHONOR   *v* -ED, -ING, -S to deprive of honor

DISHPAN   *n* pl. -S a pan for washing dishes

DISHRAG   *n* pl. -S a cloth for washing dishes

DISHWARE   *n* pl. -S tableware used in serving food

DISHY   *adj* DISHIER, DISHIEST attractive

DISINTER   *v* -TERRED, -TERRING, -TERS to exhume

DISJECT   *v* -ED, -ING, -S to disperse

DISJOIN   *v* -ED, -ING, -S to separate

DISJOINT   *v* -ED, -ING, -S to put out of order

DISJUNCT   *n* pl. -S an alternative in a logical disjunction

DISK   *v* -ED, -ING, -S to break up land with a type of farm implement

DISKLIKE   *adj* resembling a disk (a flat, circular plate)

DISLIKE *v* -LIKED, -LIKING, -LIKES to regard with aversion

DISLIKER *n* pl. -S one that dislikes

DISLIMN *v* -ED, -ING, -S to make dim

DISLODGE *v* -LODGED, -LODGING, -LODGES to remove from a firm position

DISLOYAL *adj* not loyal

DISMAL *n* pl. -S a track of swampy land

DISMAL *adj* -MALER, -MALEST cheerless and depressing **DISMALLY** *adv*

DISMAST *v* -ED, -ING, -S to remove the mast of

DISMAY *v* -ED, -ING, -S to deprive of courage or resolution

DISME *n* pl. -S a former coin of the United States

DISMISS *v* -ED, -ING, -ES to permit or cause to leave

DISMOUNT *v* -ED, -ING, -S to get down from an elevated position

DISOBEY *v* -ED, -ING, -S to fail to obey

DISOMIC *adj* having a number of chromosomes duplicated

DISORDER *v* -ED, -ING, -S to put out of order

DISOWN *v* -ED, -ING, -S to deny the ownership of

DISPART *v* -ED, -ING, -S to separate

DISPATCH *v* -ED, -ING, -ES to send off with speed

DISPEL *v* -PELLED, -PELLING, -PELS to drive off in various directions

DISPEND *v* -ED, -ING, -S to squander

DISPENSE *v* -PENSED, -PENSING, -PENSES to distribute

DISPERSE *v* -PERSED, -PERSING, -PERSES to scatter

DISPIRIT *v* -ED, -ING, -S to lower in spirit

DISPLACE *v* -PLACED, -PLACING, -PLACES to remove from the usual or proper place

DISPLANT *v* -ED, -ING, -S to dislodge

DISPLAY *v* -ED, -ING, -S to make evident or obvious

DISPLODE *v* -PLODED, -PLODING, -PLODES to explode

DISPLUME *v* -PLUMED, -PLUMING, -PLUMES to deplume

DISPORT *v* -ED, -ING, -S to amuse oneself

DISPOSAL *n* pl. -S the act of disposing

DISPOSE *v* -POSED, -POSING, -POSES to put in place

DISPOSER *n* pl. -S one that disposes

DISPREAD *v* -SPREAD, -SPREADING, -SPREADS to spread out

DISPRIZE *v* -PRIZED, -PRIZING, -PRIZES to disdain

DISPROOF *n* pl. -S the act of disproving

DISPROVE *v* -PROVED, -PROVEN, -PROVING, -PROVES to refute

DISPUTE *v* -PUTED, -PUTING, -PUTES to argue about

DISPUTER *n* pl. -S one that disputes

DISQUIET *v* -ED, -ING, -S to deprive of quiet, rest, or peace

DISRATE *v* -RATED, -RATING, -RATES to lower in rating or rank

DISROBE *v* -ROBED, -ROBING, -ROBES to undress

DISROBER *n* pl. -S one that disrobes

DISROOT *v* -ED, -ING, -S to uproot

DISRUPT *v* -ED, -ING, -S to throw into confusion

DISSAVE *v* -SAVED, -SAVING, -SAVES to use savings for current expenses

DISSEAT *v* -ED, -ING, -S to unseat

DISSECT *v* -ED, -ING, -S to cut apart for scientific examination

DISSEISE *v* -SEISED, -SEISING, -SEISES to deprive

DISSEIZE *v* -SEIZED, -SEIZING, -SEIZES to disseise

DISSENT *v* -ED, -ING, -S to disagree

DISSERT *v* -ED, -ING, -S to discuss in a learned or formal manner

DISSERVE *v* -SERVED, -SERVING, -SERVES to treat badly

DISSEVER *v* -ED, -ING, -S to sever

DISSOLVE *v* -SOLVED, -SOLVING, -SOLVES to make into a solution

DISSUADE *v* -SUADED, -SUADING, -SUADES to persuade not to do something

DISTAFF *n* pl. -TAFFS or -TAVES a type of staff

DISTAIN *v* -ED, -ING, -S to stain

DISTAL *adj* located far from the point of origin **DISTALLY** *adv*

DISTANCE	v -TANCED, -TANCING, -TANCES to leave behind	**DITHEISM**	n pl. -S belief in two coequal gods
DISTANT	adj far off or apart	**DITHEIST**	n pl. -S an adherent of ditheism
DISTASTE	v -TASTED, -TASTING, -TASTES to dislike	**DITHER**	v -ED, -ING, -S to act nervously or indecisively
DISTAVES	a pl. of distaff	**DITHERY**	adj nervously excited
DISTEND	v -ED, -ING, -S to swell	**DITHIOL**	adj containing two chemical groups both of which include sulfur and hydrogen
DISTENT	adj distended		
DISTICH	n pl. -S a couplet	**DITTANY**	n pl. -NIES a perennial herb
DISTIL	v -TILLED, -TILLING, -TILS to distill	**DITTO**	v -ED, -ING, -S to repeat
		DITTY	n pl. -TIES a short, simple song
DISTILL	v -ED, -ING, -S to extract by vaporization and condensation	**DIURESIS**	n pl. DIURESES excessive discharge of urine
DISTINCT	adj -TINCTER, -TINCTEST clearly different	**DIURETIC**	n pl. -S a drug which increases urinary discharge
DISTOME	n pl. -S a parasitic flatworm	**DIURNAL**	n pl. -S a diary
DISTORT	v -ED, -ING, -S to twist or bend out of shape	**DIURON**	n pl. -S an herbicide
DISTRACT	v -ED, -ING, -S to divert the attention of	**DIVA**	n pl. -S a distinguished female operatic singer
DISTRAIN	v -ED, -ING, -S to seize and hold property as security	**DIVAGATE**	v -GATED, -GATING, -GATES to wander
DISTRAIT	adj absentminded	**DIVALENT**	adj having a valence of two
DISTRESS	v -ED, -ING, -ES to cause anxiety or suffering to	**DIVAN**	n pl. -S a sofa or couch
		DIVE	v DIVED or DOVE, DIVING, DIVES to plunge headfirst into water
DISTRICT	v -ED, -ING, -S to divide into localities		
DISTRUST	v -ED, -ING, -S to have no trust in	**DIVER**	n pl. -S one that dives
DISTURB	v -ED, -ING, -S to interrupt the quiet, rest, or peace of	**DIVERGE**	v -VERGED, -VERGING, -VERGES to move in different directions from a common point
DISULFID	n pl. -S a chemical compound	**DIVERSE**	adj different
DISUNION	n pl. -S the state of being disunited	**DIVERT**	v -ED, -ING, -S to turn aside
DISUNITE	v -UNITED, -UNITING, -UNITES to separate	**DIVERTER**	n pl. -S one that diverts
		DIVEST	v -ED, -ING, -S to strip or deprive of anything
DISUNITY	n pl. -TIES lack of unity	**DIVIDE**	v -VIDED, -VIDING, -VIDES to separate into parts, areas, or groups
DISUSE	v -USED, -USING, -USES to stop using		
DISVALUE	v -UED, -UING, -UES to treat as of little value	**DIVIDEND**	n pl. -S a quantity to be divided
		DIVIDER	n pl. -S one that divides
DISYOKE	v -YOKED, -YOKING, -YOKES to free from a yoke	**DIVIDING**	present participle of divide
		DIVIDUAL	adj capable of being divided
DIT	n pl. -S a dot in Morse code	**DIVINE**	v -VINED, -VINING, -VINES to foretell by occult means
DITA	n pl. -S a Philippine tree		
DITCH	v -ED, -ING, -ES to dig a long, narrow excavation in the ground	**DIVINE**	adj -VINER, -VINEST pertaining to or characteristic of a god **DIVINELY** adv
DITCHER	n pl. -S one that ditches	**DIVINER**	n pl. -S one that divines
DITE	n pl. -S a small amount	**DIVING**	present participle of dive

DIVINING	present participle of divine	**DOBBIN**	n pl. -S a farm horse
DIVINISE	v -NISED, -NISING, -NISES to divinize	**DOBBY**	n pl. -BIES a fool
		DOBIE	n pl. -S adobe
DIVINITY	n pl. -TIES the state of being divine	**DOBIES**	pl. of doby
DIVINIZE	v -NIZED, -NIZING, -NIZES to make divine	**DOBLA**	n pl. -S a former gold coin of Spain
DIVISION	n pl. -S the act of dividing	**DOBLON**	n pl. -S or -ES a former gold coin of Spain and Spanish America
DIVISIVE	adj causing disunity or dissension		
		DOBRA	n pl. -S a former gold coin of Portugal
DIVISOR	n pl. -S a number by which a dividend is divided	**DOBSON**	n pl. -S an aquatic insect larva
DIVORCE	v -VORCED, -VORCING, -VORCES to terminate the marriage contract between	**DOBY**	n pl. -BIES dobie
		DOC	n pl. -S doctor
DIVORCEE	n pl. -S a divorced woman	**DOCENT**	n pl. -S a college or university lecturer
DIVORCER	n pl. -S one that divorces		
DIVORCING	present participle of divorce	**DOCETIC**	adj pertaining to a religious doctrine
DIVOT	n pl. -S a piece of turf		
DIVULGE	v -VULGED, -VULGING, -VULGES to reveal	**DOCILE**	adj easily trained **DOCILELY** adv
DIVULGER	n pl. -S one that divulges	**DOCILITY**	n pl. -TIES the quality of being docile
DIVVY	v -VIED, -VYING, -VIES to divide		
DIWAN	n pl. -S dewan	**DOCK**	v -ED, -ING, -S to bring into a dock (a wharf)
DIXIT	n pl. -S a statement	**DOCKAGE**	n pl. -S a charge for the use of a dock
DIZEN	v -ED, -ING, -S to dress in fine clothes		
		DOCKER	n pl. -S a dock worker
DIZYGOUS	adj developed from two fertilized ova	**DOCKET**	v -ED, -ING, -S to supply with an identifying statement
DIZZY	adj -ZIER, -ZIEST having a sensation of whirling **DIZZILY** adv	**DOCKHAND**	n pl. -S a docker
		DOCKLAND	n pl. -S the part of a port occupied by docks
DIZZY	v -ZIED, -ZYING, -ZIES to make dizzy	**DOCKSIDE**	n pl. -S the area adjacent to a dock
DJEBEL	n pl. -S jebel	**DOCKYARD**	n pl. -S a shipyard
DJELLABA	n pl. -S a long hooded garment	**DOCTOR**	v -ED, -ING, -S to treat medically
DJIN	n pl. -S jinni		
DJINN	n pl. -S jinni	**DOCTORAL**	adj pertaining to a doctor
DJINNI	n pl. DJINN jinni	**DOCTRINE**	n pl. -S a belief or set of beliefs taught or advocated
DJINNY	n pl. DJINN jinni		
DO	v DID or DIDST, DONE, DOING, present sing. 2d person DO, DOEST or DOST, 3d person DOES, DOETH or DOTH to begin and carry through to completion	**DOCUMENT**	v -ED, -ING, -S to support by conclusive information or evidence
		DODDER	v -ED, -ING, -S to totter
		DODDERER	n pl. -S one that dodders
DO	n pl. DOS the first tone of the diatonic musical scale	**DODDERY**	adj feeble
		DODGE	v DODGED, DODGING, DODGES to evade
DOABLE	adj able to be done		
DOAT	v -ED, -ING, -S to dote	**DODGER**	n pl. -S one that dodges
DOBBER	n pl. -S a float for a fishing line	**DODGERY**	n pl. -ERIES evasion

DODGING	present participle of dodge
DODGY	*adj* DODGIER, DODGIEST evasive
DODO	*n* pl. -DOES or -DOS an extinct flightless bird
DODOISM	*n* pl. -S a stupid remark
DOE	*n* pl. -S a female deer
DOER	*n* pl. -S one that does something
DOES	a present 3d person sing. of do
DOESKIN	*n* pl. -S the skin of a doe
DOEST	a present 2d person sing. of do
DOETH	a present 3d person sing. of do
DOFF	*v* -ED, -ING, -S to take off
DOFFER	*n* pl. -S one that doffs
DOG	*v* DOGGED, DOGGING, DOGS to follow after like a dog (a domesticated, carnivorous mammal)
DOGBANE	*n* pl. -S a perennial herb
DOGBERRY	*n* pl. -RIES a wild berry
DOGCART	*n* pl. -S a one-horse carriage
DOGDOM	*n* pl. -S the world of dogs
DOGE	*n* pl. -S the chief magistrate in the former republics of Venice and Genoa
DOGEDOM	*n* pl. -S the domain of a doge
DOGESHIP	*n* pl. -S the office of a doge
DOGEY	*n* pl. -GEYS dogie
DOGFACE	*n* pl. -S a soldier in the U.S. Army
DOGFIGHT	*v* -FOUGHT, -FIGHTING, -FIGHTS to engage in an aerial battle
DOGFISH	*n* pl. -ES a small shark
DOGGED	past tense of dog
DOGGEDLY	*adv* stubbornly
DOGGER	*n* pl. -S a fishing vessel
DOGGEREL	*n* pl. -S trivial, awkwardly written verse
DOGGERY	*n* pl. -GERIES surly behavior
DOGGIE	*n* pl. -S doggy
DOGGIER	comparative of doggy
DOGGIES	pl. of doggy
DOGGIEST	superlative of doggy
DOGGING	present participle of dog
DOGGISH	*adj* doglike
DOGGO	*adv* in hiding

DOGGONE	*v* -GONED, -GONING, -GONES to damn
DOGGONE	*adj* -GONER, -GONEST damned
DOGGONED	*adj* -GONEDER, -GONEDEST damned
DOGGONING	present participle of doggone
DOGGREL	*n* pl. -S doggerel
DOGGY	*n* pl. -GIES a small dog
DOGGY	*adj* -GIER, -GIEST resembling or suggestive of a dog
DOGHOUSE	*n* pl. -S a shelter for a dog
DOGIE	*n* pl. -S a stray calf
DOGIES	pl. of dogy
DOGLEG	*v* -LEGGED, -LEGGING, -LEGS to move along a bent course
DOGLIKE	*adj* resembling a dog
DOGMA	*n* pl. -MAS or -MATA a principle or belief put forth as authoritative **DOGMATIC** *adj*
DOGNAP	*v* -NAPED, -NAPING, -NAPS or -NAPPED, -NAPPING, -NAPS to steal a dog
DOGNAPER	*n* pl. -S one that dognaps
DOGSBODY	*n* pl. -BODIES a menial worker
DOGSLED	*n* pl. -S a sled drawn by dogs
DOGTOOTH	*n* pl. -TEETH a cuspid
DOGTROT	*v* -TROTTED, -TROTTING, -TROTS to move at a steady trot
DOGVANE	*n* pl. -S a small vane
DOGWATCH	*n* pl. -ES a short period of watch duty on a ship
DOGWOOD	*n* pl. -S a tree
DOGY	*n* pl. -GIES dogie
DOILED	*adj* dazed
DOILY	*n* pl. -LIES a small napkin
DOING	*n* pl. -S an action
DOIT	*n* pl. -S a former Dutch coin
DOITED	*adj* old and feeble
DOJO	*n* pl. -JOS a school that teaches judo or karate
DOL	*n* pl. -S a unit of pain intensity
DOLCE	*n* pl. -CI a soft-toned organ stop
DOLDRUMS	*n/pl* a state of inactivity or stagnation
DOLE	*v* DOLED, DOLING, DOLES to distribute in small portions
DOLEFUL	*adj* -FULLER, -FULLEST mournful
DOLERITE	*n* pl. -S a variety of basalt

DOLESOME *adj* doleful

DOLING present participle of dole

DOLL *v* -ED, -ING, -S to dress stylishly

DOLLAR *n* pl. -S a monetary unit of the United States

DOLLIED past tense of dolly

DOLLIES present 3d person sing. of dolly

DOLLISH *adj* pretty

DOLLOP *n* pl. -S a serving

DOLLY *v* -LIED, -LYING, -LIES to move on a wheeled platform

DOLMAN *n* pl. -S a Turkish robe

DOLMEN *n* pl. -S a prehistoric monument

DOLOMITE *n* pl. -S a mineral

DOLOR *n* pl. -S grief

DOLOROSO *adj* having a mournful musical quality

DOLOROUS *adj* mournful

DOLOUR *n* pl. -S dolor

DOLPHIN *n* pl. -S a marine mammal

DOLT *n* pl. -S a stupid person **DOLTISH** *adj*

DOM *n* pl. -S a title given to certain monks

DOMAIN *n* pl. -S an area of control

DOMAL *adj* domical

DOME *v* DOMED, DOMING, DOMES to cover with a dome (a rounded roof)

DOMELIKE *adj* resembling a dome

DOMESDAY *n* pl. -DAYS doomsday

DOMESTIC *n* pl. -S a household servant

DOMIC *adj* domical

DOMICAL *adj* shaped like a dome

DOMICIL *v* -ED, -ING, -S to domicile

DOMICILE *v* -CILED, -CILING, -CILES to establish in a residence

DOMINANT *n* pl. -S a controlling genetic character

DOMINATE *v* -NATED, -NATING, -NATES to control

DOMINE *n* pl. -S master

DOMINEER *v* -ED, -ING, -S to tyrannize

DOMING present participle of dome

DOMINICK *n* pl. -S one of an American breed of chickens

DOMINIE *n* pl. -S a clergyman

DOMINION *n* pl. -S supreme authority

DOMINIUM *n* pl. -S the right of ownership and control of property

DOMINO *n* pl. -NOES or -NOS a small mask

DON *v* DONNED, DONNING, DONS to put on

DONA *n* pl. -S a Spanish lady

DONATE *v* -NATED, -NATING, -NATES to contribute

DONATION *n* pl. -S something donated

DONATIVE *n* pl. -S a donation

DONATOR *n* pl. -S a donor

DONE past participle of do

DONEE *n* pl. -S a recipient of a gift

DONENESS *n* pl. -ES the state of being cooked enough

DONG *n* pl. -S a deep sound like that of a large bell

DONGOLA *n* pl. -S a type of leather

DONJON *n* pl. -S the main tower of a castle

DONKEY *n* pl. -KEYS the domestic ass

DONNA *n* pl. DONNAS or DONNE an Italian lady

DONNED past tense of don

DONNEE *n* pl. -S the set of assumptions upon which a story proceeds

DONNERD *adj* donnered

DONNERED *adj* dazed

DONNERT *adj* donnered

DONNING present participle of don

DONNISH *adj* scholarly

DONOR *n* pl. -S one that donates

DONSIE *adj* unlucky

DONSY *adj* donsie

DONUT *n* pl. -S doughnut

DONZEL *n* pl. -S a young squire

DOODAD *n* pl. -S a dingus

DOODLE *v* -DLED, -DLING, -DLES to draw or scribble aimlessly

DOODLER *n* pl. -S one that doodles

DOOLEE *n* pl. -S a stretcher for the sick or wounded

DOOLIE *n* pl. -S doolee

DOOLY *n* pl. -LIES doolee

DOOM *v* -ED, -ING, -S to destine to an unhappy fate

DOOMFUL	*adj* ominous
DOOMSDAY	*n* pl. -DAYS judgment day
DOOMSTER	*n* pl. -S a judge
DOOR	*n* pl. -S a movable barrier for opening and closing an entranceway
DOORBELL	*n* pl. -S a bell at a door
DOORJAMB	*n* pl. -S a vertical piece at the side of a doorway
DOORKNOB	*n* pl. -S a handle for opening a door
DOORLESS	*adj* having no door
DOORMAN	*n* pl. -MEN the door attendant of a building
DOORMAT	*n* pl. -S a mat placed in front of a door
DOORNAIL	*n* pl. -S a large-headed nail
DOORPOST	*n* pl. -S a doorjamb
DOORSILL	*n* pl. -S the sill of a door
DOORSTEP	*n* pl. -S a step leading to a door
DOORSTOP	*n* pl. -S a wedge for holding a door open
DOORWAY	*n* pl. -WAYS the entranceway to a room or building
DOORYARD	*n* pl. -S a yard in front of a house
DOOZER	*n* pl. -S an extraordinary one of its kind
DOOZY	*n* pl. -ZIES doozer
DOPA	*n* pl. -S an amino acid
DOPAMINE	*n* pl. -S a form of dopa
DOPANT	*n* pl. -S an impurity added to a pure substance
DOPE	*v* DOPED, DOPING, DOPES to give a narcotic to
DOPER	*n* pl. -S one that dopes
DOPESTER	*n* pl. -S a forecaster of the outcome of sports events or other contests
DOPEY	*adj* DOPIER, DOPIEST lethargic; stupid
DOPIER	comparative of dopy
DOPIEST	superlative of dopy
DOPINESS	*n* pl. -ES the state of being dopey
DOPING	present participle of dope
DOPY	*adj* DOPIER, DOPIEST dopey
DOR	*n* pl. -S a black European beetle
DORADO	*n* pl. -DOS a marine fish

DORBUG	*n* pl. -S a dor
DORHAWK	*n* pl. -S a nocturnal bird
DORIES	pl. of dory
DORM	*n* pl. -S a dormitory
DORMANCY	*n* pl. -CIES the state of being dormant
DORMANT	*adj* lying asleep
DORMER	*n* pl. -S a type of window
DORMICE	pl. of dormouse
DORMIE	*adj* being ahead by as many holes in golf as remain to be played
DORMIENT	*adj* dormant
DORMIN	*n* pl. -S a plant hormone
DORMOUSE	*n* pl. -MICE a small rodent
DORMY	*adj* dormie
DORNECK	*n* pl. -S dornick
DORNICK	*n* pl. -S a heavy linen fabric
DORNOCK	*n* pl. -S dornick
DORP	*n* pl. -S a village
DORPER	*n* pl. -S one of a breed of mutton-producing sheep
DORR	*n* pl. -S dor
DORSA	pl. of dorsum
DORSAD	*adv* dorsally
DORSAL	*n* pl. -S a dorsally located anatomical part
DORSALLY	*adv* toward the back
DORSER	*n* pl. -S dosser
DORSUM	*n* pl. -SA the back
DORTY	*adj* sullen
DORY	*n* pl. -RIES a flat-bottomed boat
DOSAGE	*n* pl. -S the amount of medicine to be given
DOSE	*v* DOSED, DOSING, DOSES to give a specified quantity of medicine to
DOSER	*n* pl. -S one that doses
DOSS	*v* -ED, -ING, -ES to sleep in any convenient place
DOSSAL	*n* pl. -S an ornamental cloth hung behind an altar
DOSSEL	*n* pl. -S dossal
DOSSER	*n* pl. -S a basket carried on the back
DOSSERET	*n* pl. -S a block resting on the capital of a column

DOSSIER *n* pl. -S a file of papers on a single subject

DOSSIL *n* pl. -S a cloth roll for wiping ink

DOST a present 2d person sing. of do

DOT *v* DOTTED, DOTTING, DOTS to cover with dots (tiny round marks)

DOTAGE *n* pl. -S a state of senility

DOTAL *adj* pertaining to a dowry

DOTARD *n* pl. -S a senile person **DOTARDLY** *adj*

DOTATION *n* pl. -S an endowment

DOTE *v* DOTED, DOTING, DOTES to show excessive affection

DOTER *n* pl. -S one that dotes

DOTH a present 3d person sing. of do

DOTIER comparative of doty

DOTIEST superlative of doty

DOTING present participle of dote

DOTINGLY *adv* in an excessively affectionate manner

DOTTED past tense of dot

DOTTEL *n* pl. -S dottle

DOTTER *n* pl. -S one that dots

DOTTEREL *n* pl. -S a shore bird

DOTTIER comparative of dotty

DOTTIEST superlative of dotty

DOTTILY *adv* in a dotty manner

DOTTING present participle of dot

DOTTLE *n* pl. -S a mass of half-burnt pipe tobacco

DOTTREL *n* pl. -S dotterel

DOTTY *adj* -TIER, -TIEST crazy

DOTY *adj* DOTIER, DOTIEST stained by decay

DOUBLE *v* -BLED, -BLING, -BLES to make twice as great

DOUBLER *n* pl. -S one that doubles

DOUBLET *n* pl. -S a close-fitting jacket

DOUBLING present participle of double

DOUBLOON *n* pl. -S a former Spanish gold coin

DOUBLURE *n* pl. -S the lining of a book cover

DOUBLY *adv* to twice the degree

DOUBT *v* -ED, -ING, -S to be uncertain about

DOUBTER *n* pl. -S one that doubts

DOUBTFUL *adj* uncertain

DOUCE *adj* sedate **DOUCELY** *adv*

DOUCEUR *n* pl. -S a gratuity

DOUCHE *v* DOUCHED, DOUCHING, DOUCHES to cleanse with a jet of water

DOUGH *n* pl. -S a flour mixture

DOUGHBOY *n* pl. -BOYS an infantryman

DOUGHIER comparative of doughy

DOUGHIEST superlative of doughy

DOUGHNUT *n* pl. -S a ring-shaped cake

DOUGHT a past tense of dow

DOUGHTY *adj* -TIER, -TIEST courageous

DOUGHY *adj* DOUGHIER, DOUGHIEST resembling dough

DOUMA *n* pl. -S duma

DOUR *adj* DOURER, DOUREST sullen

DOURA *n* pl. -S durra

DOURAH *n* pl. -S durra

DOURINE *n* pl. -S a disease of horses

DOURLY *adv* in a dour manner

DOURNESS *n* pl. -ES the state of being dour

DOUSE *v* DOUSED, DOUSING, DOUSES to plunge into water

DOUSER *n* pl. -S one that douses

DOUZEPER *n* pl. -S one of twelve legendary knights

DOVE *n* pl. -S a bird of the pigeon family

DOVECOT *n* pl. -S dovecote

DOVECOTE *n* pl. -S a roost for domesticated pigeons

DOVEKEY *n* pl. -KEYS dovekie

DOVEKIE *n* pl. -S a seabird

DOVELIKE *adj* resembling or suggestive of a dove

DOVEN *v* -ED, -ING, -S to daven

DOVETAIL *v* -ED, -ING, -S to fit together closely

DOVISH *adj* not warlike

DOW *v* DOWED or DOUGHT, DOWING, DOWS to prosper

DOWABLE *adj* entitled to an endowment

DOWAGER *n* pl. -S a dignified elderly woman

DOWDY	*adj* DOWDIER, DOWDIEST lacking in stylishness or neatness **DOWDILY** *adv* **DOWDYISH** *adj*	**DOYEN**	*n* pl. -S the senior member of a group
DOWDY	*n* pl. DOWDIES a dowdy woman	**DOYENNE**	*n* pl. -S a female doyen
DOWEL	*v* -ELED, -ELING, -ELS or -ELLED, -ELLING, -ELS to fasten with wooden pins	**DOYLEY**	*n* pl. -LEYS doily
		DOYLY	*n* pl. -LIES doily
DOWER	*v* -ED, -ING, -S to provide with a dowry	**DOZE**	*v* DOZED, DOZING, DOZES to sleep lightly
DOWERY	*n* pl. -ERIES dowry	**DOZEN**	*v* -ED, -ING, -S to stun
DOWIE	*adj* dreary	**DOZENTH**	*n* pl. -S twelfth
DOWN	*v* -ED, -ING, -S to cause to fall	**DOZER**	*n* pl. -S one that dozes
DOWNBEAT	*n* pl. -S the first beat of a musical measure	**DOZILY**	*adv* in a dozy manner
		DOZINESS	*n* pl. -ES the state of being dozy
DOWNCAST	*n* pl. -S an overthrow or ruin	**DOZING**	present participle of doze
DOWNCOME	*n* pl. -S downfall	**DOZY**	*adj* DOZIER, DOZIEST drowsy
DOWNER	*n* pl. -S a depressant drug	**DRAB**	*adj* DRABBER, DRABBEST cheerless
DOWNFALL	*n* pl. -S a sudden fall		
DOWNHAUL	*n* pl. -S a rope for hauling down sails	**DRAB**	*v* DRABBED, DRABBING, DRABS to consort with prostitutes
DOWNHILL	*n* pl. -S a downward slope	**DRABBET**	*n* pl. -S a coarse linen fabric
DOWNIER	comparative of downy	**DRABBLE**	*v* -BLED, -BLING, -BLES to draggle
DOWNIEST	superlative of downy		
DOWNPLAY	*v* -ED, -ING, -S to de-emphasize	**DRABLY**	*adv* in a drab manner
DOWNPOUR	*n* pl. -S a heavy rain	**DRABNESS**	*n* pl. -ES the quality of being drab
DOWNTIME	*n* pl. -S the time when a machine or factory is inactive	**DRACAENA**	*n* pl. -S a tropical plant
		DRACHM	*n* pl. -S a unit of weight
DOWNTOWN	*n* pl. -S the business district of a city	**DRACHMA**	*n* pl. -MAS, -MAE or -MAI a Greek coin
DOWNTROD	*adj* oppressed	**DRACONIC**	*adj* pertaining to a dragon
DOWNTURN	*n* pl. -S a downward turn	**DRAFF**	*n* pl. -S the damp remains of malt after brewing
DOWNWARD	*adv* from a higher to a lower place		
		DRAFFISH	*adj* draffy
DOWNWIND	*adv* in the direction that the wind blows	**DRAFFY**	*adj* DRAFFIER, DRAFFIEST worthless
DOWNY	*adj* DOWNIER, DOWNIEST soft	**DRAFT**	*v* -ED, -ING, -S to conscript for military service
DOWRY	*n* pl. -RIES the money or property a wife brings to her husband at marriage		
		DRAFTEE	*n* pl. -S one that is drafted
		DRAFTER	*n* pl. -S one that drafts
DOWSABEL	*n* pl. -S a sweetheart	**DRAFTING**	*n* pl. -S mechanical drawing
DOWSE	*v* DOWSED, DOWSING, DOWSES to search for underground water with a divining rod	**DRAFTY**	*adj* DRAFTIER, DRAFTIEST having or exposed to currents of air **DRAFTILY** *adv*
DOWSER	*n* pl. -S one that dowses	**DRAG**	*v* DRAGGED, DRAGGING, DRAGS to pull along the ground
DOXIE	*n* pl. -S doxy		
DOXOLOGY	*n* pl. -GIES a hymn or verse of praise to God	**DRAGEE**	*n* pl. -S a sugarcoated candy
		DRAGGER	*n* pl. -S one that drags
DOXY	*n* pl. DOXIES a doctrine	**DRAGGIER**	comparative of draggy

DRAGGIEST superlative of draggy

DRAGGING present participle of drag

DRAGGLE v -GLED, -GLING, -GLES to make wet and dirty

DRAGGY adj -GIER, -GIEST sluggish

DRAGLINE n pl. -S a line used for dragging

DRAGNET n pl. -S a net for trawling

DRAGOMAN n pl. -MANS or -MEN an interpreter in Near Eastern countries

DRAGON n pl. -S a mythical, serpentlike monster

DRAGONET n pl. -S a marine fish

DRAGOON v -ED, -ING, -S to harass by the use of troops

DRAGROPE n pl. -S a rope used for dragging

DRAGSTER n pl. -S a vehicle used in drag racing

DRAIL n pl. -S a heavy fishhook

DRAIN v -ED, -ING, -S to draw off a liquid

DRAINAGE n pl. -S the act of draining

DRAINER n pl. -S one that drains

DRAKE n pl. -S a male duck

DRAM v DRAMMED, DRAMMING, DRAMS to tipple

DRAMA n pl. -S a composition written for theatrical performance

DRAMATIC adj pertaining to drama

DRAMMED past tense of dram

DRAMMING present participle of dram

DRAMMOCK n pl. -S raw oatmeal mixed with cold water

DRAMSHOP n pl. -S a barroom

DRANK past tense of drink

DRAPE v DRAPED, DRAPING, DRAPES to arrange in graceful folds **DRAPABLE** adj

DRAPER n pl. -S a dealer in cloth

DRAPERY n pl. -ERIES cloth arranged in graceful folds

DRAPING present participle of drape

DRASTIC adj extremely severe

DRAT v DRATTED, DRATTING, DRATS to damn

DRAUGHT v -ED, -ING, -S to draft

DRAUGHTY adj DRAUGHTIER, DRAUGHTIEST drafty

DRAVE a past tense of drive

DRAW v DREW, DRAWN, DRAWING, DRAWS to move by pulling **DRAWABLE** adj

DRAWBACK n pl. -S a hindrance

DRAWBAR n pl. -S a railroad coupler

DRAWBORE n pl. -S a hole for joining a mortise and tenon

DRAWDOWN n pl. -S a lowering of a water level

DRAWEE n pl. -S the person on whom a bill of exchange is drawn

DRAWER n pl. -S one that draws

DRAWING n pl. -S a portrayal in lines of a form or figure

DRAWL v -ED, -ING, -S to speak slowly with vowels greatly prolonged

DRAWLER n pl. -S one that drawls

DRAWLY adj DRAWLIER, DRAWLIEST marked by drawling

DRAWN past participle of draw

DRAWTUBE n pl. -S a tube that slides within another tube

DRAY v -ED, -ING, -S to transport by dray (a low, strong cart)

DRAYAGE n pl. -S transportation by dray

DRAYMAN n pl. -MEN one who drives a dray

DREAD v -ED, -ING, -S to fear greatly

DREADFUL n pl. -S a publication containing sensational material

DREAM v DREAMED or DREAMT, DREAMING, DREAMS to have a dream (a series of images occurring during sleep)

DREAMER n pl. -S one that dreams

DREAMFUL adj dreamy

DREAMT a past tense of dream

DREAMY adj DREAMIER, DREAMIEST full of dreams **DREAMILY** adv

DREAR adj dreary

DREARY adj DREARIEST, DREARIER dismal **DREARILY** adv

DREARY n pl. DREARIES a dismal person

DRECK n pl. -S rubbish

DREDGE v DREDGED, DREDGING, DREDGES to clear with a scooping device

DREDGER n pl. -S one that dredges

DREDGING n pl. -S matter that is dredged up

DREE   *v* DREED, DREEING, DREES to suffer

DREG   *n* pl. -S the sediment of liquors **DREGGISH** *adj*

DREGGY   *adj* -GIER, -GIEST full of dregs

DREICH   *adj* dreary

DREIDEL   *n* pl. -S a spinning toy

DREIDL   *n* pl. -S dreidel

DREIGH   *adj* dreich

DREK   *n* pl. -S dreck

DRENCH   *v* -ED, -ING, -ES to wet thoroughly

DRENCHER   *n* pl. -S one that drenches

DRESS   *v* DRESSED or DREST, DRESSING, DRESSES to put clothes on

DRESSAGE   *n* pl. -S the training of a horse in obedience and deportment

DRESSER   *n* pl. -S one that dresses

DRESSING   *n* pl. -S material applied to cover a wound

DRESSY   *adj* DRESSIER, DRESSIEST stylish **DRESSILY** *adv*

DREST   a past tense of dress

DREW   past tense of draw

DRIB   *v* DRIBBED, DRIBBING, DRIBS to drip

DRIBBLE   *v* -BLED, -BLING, -BLES to drivel

DRIBBLER   *n* pl. -S one that dribbles

DRIBBLET   *n* pl. -S driblet

DRIBBLING   present participle of dribble

DRIBLET   *n* pl. -S a small drop of liquid

DRIED   past tense of dry

DRIER   *n* pl. -S one that dries

DRIES   present 3d person sing. of dry

DRIEST   a superlative of dry

DRIFT   *v* -ED, -ING, -S to move along in a current

DRIFTAGE   *n* pl. -S the act of drifting

DRIFTER   *n* pl. -S one that drifts

DRIFTPIN   *n* pl. -S a metal rod for securing timbers

DRIFTY   *adj* DRIFTIER, DRIFTIEST full of drifts (masses of wind-driven snow)

DRILL   *v* -ED, -ING, -S to bore a hole in

DRILLER   *n* pl. -S one that drills

DRILLING   *n* pl. -S a heavy twilled cotton fabric

DRILY   *adv* dryly

DRINK   *v* DRANK, DRUNK, DRINKING, DRINKS to swallow liquid

DRINKER   *n* pl. -S one that drinks

DRIP   *v* DRIPPED or DRIPT, DRIPPING, DRIPS to fall in drops

DRIPLESS   *adj* designed not to drip

DRIPPER   *n* pl. -S something from which a liquid drips

DRIPPING   *n* pl. -S juice drawn from meat during cooking

DRIPPY   *adj* -PIER, -PIEST very wet

DRIPT   a past tense of drip

DRIVE   *v* DROVE or DRAVE, DRIVEN, DRIVING, DRIVES to urge or propel forward **DRIVABLE** *adj*

DRIVEL   *v* -ELED, -ELING, -ELS or -ELLED, -ELLING, -ELS to let saliva flow from the mouth

DRIVELER   *n* pl. -S one that drivels

DRIVEN   past participle of drive

DRIVER   *n* pl. -S one that drives

DRIVEWAY   *n* pl. -WAYS a private road providing access to a building

DRIVING   present participle of drive

DRIZZLE   *v* -ZLED, -ZLING, -ZLES to rain lightly

DRIZZLY   *adj* -ZLIER, -ZLIEST characterized by light rain

DROGUE   *n* pl. -S a canvas bag dragged behind a ship to reduce drifting

DROIT   *n* pl. -S a legal right

DROLL   *adj* DROLLER, DROLLEST comical

DROLL   *v* -ED, -ING, -S to jest

DROLLERY   *n* pl. -ERIES something droll

DROLLY   *adv* in a droll manner

DROMON   *n* pl. -S dromond

DROMOND   *n* pl. -S a large fast-sailing medieval galley

DRONE   *v* DRONED, DRONING, DRONES to make a continuous low sound

DRONER   *n* pl. -S one that drones

DRONGO   *n* pl. -GOS a tropical bird

DRONING   present participle of drone

DRONISH   *adj* habitually lazy

DROOL   *v* -ED, -ING, -S to drivel

DROOP   *v* -ED, -ING, -S to hang downward

DROOPY   *adj* DROOPIER, DROOPIEST drooping **DROOPILY** *adv*

DROP   *v* DROPPED or DROPT, DROPPING, DROPS to fall in drops (globules)

DROPHEAD   *n* pl. -S a convertible car

DROPKICK   *n* pl. -S a type of kick in football

DROPLET   *n* pl. -S a tiny drop

DROPOUT   *n* pl. -S one who quits school prematurely

DROPPED   past tense of drop

DROPPER   *n* pl. -S a tube for dispensing liquid in drops

DROPPING   *n* pl. -S something that has been dropped

DROPSHOT   *n* pl. -S a type of shot in tennis

DROPSY   *n* pl. -SIES an excessive accumulation of serous fluid **DROPSIED** *adj*

DROPT   a past tense of drop

DROPWORT   *n* pl. -S a perennial herb

DROSERA   *n* pl. -S a sundew

DROSHKY   *n* pl. -KIES an open carriage

DROSKY   *n* pl. -KIES droshky

DROSS   *n* pl. -ES waste matter

DROSSY   *adj* DROSSIER, DROSSIEST worthless

DROUGHT   *n* pl. -S a dry period

DROUGHTY   *adj* DROUGHTIER, DROUGHTIEST dry

DROUK   *v* -ED, -ING, -S to drench

DROUTH   *n* pl. -S drought

DROUTHY   *adj* DROUTHIER, DROUTHIEST droughty

DROVE   *v* DROVED, DROVING, DROVES to drive cattle or sheep

DROVER   *n* pl. -S a driver of cattle or sheep

DROWN   *v* -ED, -ING, -S to suffocate in water

DROWND   *v* -ED, -ING, -S to drown

DROWNER   *n* pl. -S one that drowns

DROWSE   *v* DROWSED, DROWSING, DROWSES to doze

DROWSY   *adj* DROWSIER, DROWSIEST sleepy **DROWSILY** *adv*

DRUB   *v* DRUBBED, DRUBBING, DRUBS to beat severely

DRUBBER   *n* pl. -S one that drubs

DRUBBING   *n* pl. -S a severe beating

DRUDGE   *v* DRUDGED, DRUDGING, DRUDGES to do hard, menial, or tedious work

DRUDGER   *n* pl. -S one that drudges

DRUDGERY   *n* pl. -ERIES hard, menial, or tedious work

DRUDGING   present participle of drudge

DRUG   *v* DRUGGED, DRUGGING, DRUGS to affect with a medicinal substance

DRUGGET   *n* pl. -S a coarse woolen fabric

DRUGGIST   *n* pl. -S a pharmacist

DRUID   *n* pl. -S one of an ancient Celtic order of priests **DRUIDIC** *adj*

DRUIDESS   *n* pl. -ES a female druid

DRUIDISM   *n* pl. -S the religious system of the druids

DRUM   *v* DRUMMED, DRUMMING, DRUMS to beat a drum (a percussion instrument)

DRUMBEAT   *n* pl. -S the sound of a drum

DRUMBLE   *v* -BLED, -BLING, -BLES to move slowly

DRUMFIRE   *n* pl. -S heavy, continuous gunfire

DRUMFISH   *n* pl. -ES a fish that makes a drumming sound

DRUMHEAD   *n* pl. -S the material stretched over the end of a drum

DRUMLIER   comparative of drumly

DRUMLIEST   superlative of drumly

DRUMLIKE   *adj* resembling the head of a drum

DRUMLIN   *n* pl. -S a long hill of glacial drift

DRUMLY   *adj* -LIER, -LIEST dark and gloomy

DRUMMED   past tense of drum

DRUMMER   *n* pl. -S one that drums

DRUMMING   present participle of drum

DRUMROLL   *n* pl. -S a roll played on a drum

DRUNK   *adj* DRUNKER, DRUNKEST intoxicated

DRUNK   *n* pl. -S a drunken person

DRUNKARD   *n* pl. -S one who is habitually drunk

DRUNKEN   *adj* drunk

DRUPE   *n* pl. -S a fleshy fruit

DRUPELET   *n* pl. -S a small drupe

DRUSE	*n* pl. -S a crust of small crystals lining a rock cavity
DRUTHERS	*n/pl* one's preference
DRY	*adj* DRIER, DRIEST or DRYER, DRYEST having no moisture
DRY	*v* DRIED, DRYING, DRIES to make dry **DRYABLE** *adj*
DRY	*n* pl. DRYS a prohibitionist
DRYAD	*n* pl. -S or -ES a nymph of the woods **DRYADIC** *adj*
DRYER	*n* pl. -S drier
DRYLOT	*n* pl. -S an enclosure for livestock
DRYLY	*adv* in a dry manner
DRYNESS	*n* pl. -ES the state of being dry
DRYPOINT	*n* pl. -S a method of engraving
DUAD	*n* pl. -S a pair
DUAL	*n* pl. -S a linguistic form
DUALISM	*n* pl. -S a philosophical theory
DUALIST	*n* pl. -S an adherent of dualism
DUALITY	*n* pl. -TIES the state of being twofold
DUALIZE	*v* -IZED, -IZING, -IZES to make twofold
DUALLY	*adv* in two ways
DUB	*v* DUBBED, DUBBING, DUBS to confer knighthood on
DUBBER	*n* pl. -S one that dubs
DUBBIN	*n* pl. -S material for softening and waterproofing leather
DUBBING	*n* pl. -S dubbin
DUBIETY	*n* pl. -ETIES the state of being dubious
DUBIOUS	*adj* doubtful
DUBONNET	*n* pl. -S a red color
DUC	*n* pl. -S a duke
DUCAL	*adj* pertaining to a duke **DUCALLY** *adv*
DUCAT	*n* pl. -S any of several gold coins formerly used in Europe
DUCE	*n* pl. DUCES or DUCI a leader
DUCHESS	*n* pl. -ES the wife or widow of a duke
DUCHY	*n* pl. DUCHIES the domain of a duke
DUCI	a pl. of duce
DUCK	*v* -ED, -ING, -S to lower quickly
DUCKBILL	*n* pl. -S a platypus
DUCKER	*n* pl. -S one that ducks

DUCKIE	*adj* ducky
DUCKIER	comparative of ducky
DUCKIES	pl. of ducky
DUCKIEST	superlative of ducky
DUCKLING	*n* pl. -S a young duck
DUCKPIN	*n* pl. -S a type of bowling pin
DUCKTAIL	*n* pl. -S a style of haircut
DUCKWEED	*n* pl. -S an aquatic plant
DUCKY	*adj* DUCKIER, DUCKIEST excellent
DUCKY	*n* pl. DUCKIES a darling
DUCT	*v* -ED, -ING, -S to convey through a duct (a tubular passage)
DUCTILE	*adj* easily molded or shaped
DUCTING	*n* pl. -S a system of ducts
DUCTLESS	*adj* being without a duct
DUCTULE	*n* pl. -S a small duct
DUD	*n* pl. -S a bomb that fails to explode
DUDDIE	*adj* ragged
DUDDY	*adj* duddie
DUDE	*n* pl. -S a dandy
DUDEEN	*n* pl. -S a short tobacco pipe
DUDGEON	*n* pl. -S a feeling of resentment
DUDISH	*adj* resembling a dude
DUDISHLY	*adv* in the manner of a dude
DUE	*n* pl. -S something that is owed
DUECENTO	*n* pl. -TOS the thirteenth century
DUEL	*v* DUELED, DUELING, DUELS or DUELLED, DUELLING, DUELS to fight formally
DUELER	*n* pl. -S one that duels
DUELIST	*n* pl. -S a dueler
DUELLED	a past tense of duel
DUELLER	*n* pl. -S dueler
DUELLI	a pl. of duello
DUELLING	a present participle of duel
DUELLIST	*n* pl. -S duelist
DUELLO	*n* pl. -LOS or -LI the art of dueling; a duel
DUENDE	*n* pl. -S charisma
DUENESS	*n* pl. -ES the state of being owed
DUENNA	*n* pl. -S a governess

DUET	*v* DUETTED, DUETTING, DUETS to perform a duet (a musical composition for two)
DUETTIST	*n* pl. -S a participant in a duet
DUFF	*n* pl. -S a thick pudding
DUFFEL	*n* pl. -S a coarse woolen fabric
DUFFER	*n* pl. -S a clumsy person
DUFFLE	*n* pl. -S duffel
DUG	*n* pl. -S the teat or udder of a female mammal
DUGONG	*n* pl. -S an aquatic mammal
DUGOUT	*n* pl. -S a canoe made by hollowing out a log
DUI	a pl. of duo
DUIKER	*n* pl. -S a small antelope
DUIT	*n* pl. -S doit
DUKE	*n* pl. -S a high-ranking nobleman
DUKEDOM	*n* pl. -S duchy
DULCET	*n* pl. -S a soft-toned organ stop
DULCETLY	*adv* melodiously
DULCIANA	*n* pl. -S a soft-toned organ stop
DULCIFY	*v* -FIED, -FYING, -FIES to sweeten
DULCIMER	*n* pl. -S a stringed musical instrument
DULCINEA	*n* pl. -S a sweetheart
DULIA	*n* pl. -S veneration given to saints
DULL	*adj* DULLER, DULLEST mentally slow **DULLY** *adv*
DULL	*v* -ED, -ING, -S to make less sharp
DULLARD	*n* pl. -S a dolt
DULLISH	*adj* somewhat dull
DULLNESS	*n* pl. -ES the state of being dull
DULNESS	*n* pl. -ES dullness
DULSE	*n* pl. -S an edible seaweed
DULY	*adv* rightfully
DUMA	*n* pl. -S a Russian council
DUMB	*adj* DUMBER, DUMBEST incapable of speech **DUMBLY** *adv*
DUMB	*v* -ED, -ING, -S to make silent
DUMBBELL	*n* pl. -S a weight lifted for muscular exercise
DUMBNESS	*n* pl. -ES the state of being dumb
DUMDUM	*n* pl. -S a type of bullet
DUMFOUND	*v* -ED, -ING, -S to astonish
DUMKA	*n* pl. -KY a Slavic folk ballad
DUMMKOPF	*n* pl. -S a dolt
DUMMY	*v* -MIED, -MYING, -MIES to make a representation of
DUMP	*v* -ED, -ING, -S to let fall heavily
DUMPCART	*n* pl. -S a type of cart
DUMPER	*n* pl. -S one that dumps
DUMPIER	comparative of dumpy
DUMPIEST	superlative of dumpy
DUMPILY	*adv* in a dumpy manner
DUMPING	*n* pl. -S the selling of large quantities of goods at below the market price
DUMPISH	*adj* sad
DUMPLING	*n* pl. -S a ball of dough cooked with stew or soup
DUMPY	*adj* DUMPIER, DUMPIEST short and thick
DUN	*v* DUNNED, DUNNING, DUNS to make demands upon for payment of a debt
DUN	*adj* DUNNER, DUNNEST of a dull brown color
DUNCE	*n* pl. -S a stupid person **DUNCICAL, DUNCISH** *adj*
DUNCH	*n* pl. -ES a push
DUNE	*n* pl. -S a hill of sand **DUNELIKE** *adj*
DUNELAND	*n* pl. -S an area having many dunes
DUNG	*v* -ED, -ING, -S to fertilize with manure
DUNGAREE	*n* pl. -S a coarse cotton fabric
DUNGEON	*n* pl. -S an underground prison
DUNGHILL	*n* pl. -S a heap of manure
DUNGY	*adj* DUNGIER, DUNGIEST filthy
DUNITE	*n* pl. -S an igneous rock **DUNITIC** *adj*
DUNK	*v* -ED, -ING, -S to dip into liquid
DUNKER	*n* pl. -S one that dunks
DUNLIN	*n* pl. -S a wading bird
DUNNAGE	*n* pl. -S packing material used to protect cargo
DUNNED	past tense of dun
DUNNER	comparative of dun
DUNNESS	*n* pl. -ES the state of being dun
DUNNEST	superlative of dun
DUNNING	present participle of dun

DUNNITE *n* pl. -S an explosive

DUNT *v* -ED, -ING, -S to strike with a heavy blow

DUO *n* pl. DUOS or DUI an instrumental duet

DUODENUM *n* pl. -DENA or -DENUMS the first portion of the small intestine **DUODENAL** *adj*

DUOLOG *n* pl. -S duologue

DUOLOGUE *n* pl. -S a conversation between two persons

DUOMO *n* pl. -MOS or -MI a cathedral

DUOPOLY *n* pl. -LIES the market condition existing when there are two sellers only

DUOPSONY *n* pl. -NIES the market condition existing when there are two buyers only

DUOTONE *n* pl. -S an illustration in two tones

DUP *v* DUPPED, DUPPING, DUPS to open

DUPE *v* DUPED, DUPING, DUPES to deceive **DUPABLE** *adj*

DUPER *n* pl. -S one that dupes

DUPERY *n* pl. -ERIES the act of duping

DUPING present participle of dupe

DUPLE *adj* having two parts or elements

DUPLEX *v* -ED, -ING, -ES to make duple

DUPLEXER *n* pl. -S an electronic switching device

DUPPED past tense of dup

DUPPING present participle of dup

DURA *n* pl. -S durra

DURABLE *adj* able to withstand wear or decay **DURABLY** *adv*

DURABLES *n/pl* durable goods

DURAL *adj* of the dura mater (a brain membrane)

DURAMEN *n* pl. -S the central wood of a tree

DURANCE *n* pl. -S restraint by or as if by physical force

DURATION *n* pl. -S continuance in time

DURATIVE *n* pl. -S a type of verb

DURBAR *n* pl. -S the court of a native ruler in India

DURE *v* DURED, DURING, DURES to endure

DURESS *n* pl. -ES compulsion by threat

DURIAN *n* pl. -S an East Indian tree

DURING *prep* throughout the duration of

DURION *n* pl. -S durian

DURMAST *n* pl. -S a European oak

DURN *v* -ED, -ING, -S to damn

DURNED *adj* DURNEDER, DURNEDEST or DURNDEST damned

DURO *n* pl. -ROS a Spanish silver dollar

DUROC *n* pl. -S a large red hog

DURR *n* pl. -S durra

DURRA *n* pl. -S a cereal grain

DURST a past tense of dare

DURUM *n* pl. -S a kind of wheat

DUSK *v* -ED, -ING, -S to become dark

DUSKISH *adj* dusky

DUSKY *adj* DUSKIER, DUSKIEST somewhat dark **DUSKILY** *adv*

DUST *v* -ED, -ING, -S to make free of dust (minute particles of matter)

DUSTBIN *n* pl. -S a trash can

DUSTER *n* pl. -S one that dusts

DUSTHEAP *n* pl. -S a pile of trash

DUSTIER comparative of dusty

DUSTIEST superative of dusty

DUSTILY *adv* in a dusty manner

DUSTLESS *adj* being without dust

DUSTLIKE *adj* resembling dust

DUSTMAN *n* pl. -MEN a trashman

DUSTPAN *n* pl. -S a pan for holding swept dust

DUSTRAG *n* pl. -S a rag used for dusting

DUSTUP *n* pl. -S an argument

DUSTY *adj* DUSTIER, DUSTIEST full of dust

DUTCH *adv* with each person paying for himself

DUTCHMAN *n* pl. -MEN something used to hide structural defects

DUTEOUS *adj* dutiful

DUTIABLE *adj* subject to import tax

DUTIFUL *adj* obedient

DUTY *n* pl. -TIES a moral or legal obligation

DUUMVIR *n* pl. -VIRS or -VIRI a magistrate of ancient Rome

DUVETINE   *n* pl. -S duvetyn

DUVETYN   *n* pl. -S a soft fabric

DUVETYNE   *n* pl. -S duvetyn

DWARF   *adj* DWARFER, DWARFEST extremely small

DWARF   *n* pl. DWARFS or DWARVES an extremely small person

DWARF   *v* -ED, -ING, -S to cause to appear small

DWARFISH   *adj* resembling a dwarf

DWARFISM   *n* pl. -S a condition of stunted growth

DWARVES   a pl. of dwarf

DWELL   *v* DWELT or DWELLED, DWELLING, DWELLS to reside

DWELLER   *n* pl. -S one that dwells

DWELLING   *n* pl. -S a place of residence

DWELT   a past tense of dwell

DWINDLE   *v* -DLED, -DLING, -DLES to decrease steadily

DWINE   *v* DWINED, DWINING, DWINES to pine or waste away

DYABLE   *adj* dyeable

DYAD   *n* pl. -S a pair of units

DYADIC   *n* pl. -S a sum of mathematical dyads

DYARCHY   *n* pl. -CHIES diarchy **DYARCHIC** *adj*

DYBBUK   *n* pl. -BUKS or -BUKIM a wandering soul in Jewish folklore

DYE   *v* DYED, DYEING, DYES to treat with a dye (a coloring material or matter)

DYEABLE   *adj* capable of being dyed

DYEING   *n* pl. -S something colored with a dye

DYER   *n* pl. -S one that dyes

DYESTUFF   *n* pl. -S a material yielding or used as a dye

DYEWEED   *n* pl. -S a shrub that yields a yellow dye

DYEWOOD   *n* pl. -S a wood used as a dyestuff

DYING   *n* pl. -S a passing out of existence

DYKE   *v* DYKED, DYKING, DYKES to dike

DYNAMIC   *n* pl. -S a physical force

DYNAMISM   *n* pl. -S a theory that explains the universe in terms of force or energy

DYNAMIST   *n* pl. -S an adherent of dynamism

DYNAMITE   *v* -MITED, -MITING, -MITES to blow up with a powerful explosive

DYNAMO   *n* pl. -MOS a generator

DYNAST   *n* pl. -S a ruler

DYNASTY   *n* pl. -TIES a succession of rulers from the same line of descent **DYNASTIC** *adj*

DYNATRON   *n* pl. -S a type of electron tube

DYNE   *n* pl. -S a unit of force

DYNODE   *n* pl. -S a type of electrode

DYSGENIC   *adj* causing the deterioration of hereditary qualities

DYSLEXIA   *n* pl. -S impairment of the ability to read **DYSLEXIC** *adj*

DYSPEPSY   *n* pl. -SIES indigestion

DYSPNEA   *n* pl. -S labored breathing **DYSPNEAL, DYSPNEIC** *adj*

DYSPNOEA   *n* pl. -S dyspnea **DYSPNOIC** *adj*

DYSTAXIA   *n* pl. -S a form of muscular tremor

DYSTOCIA   *n* pl. -S difficult labor and delivery in childbirth

DYSTONIA   *n* pl. -S a condition of disordered tonicity of muscle tissue

DYSTOPIA   *n* pl. -S a wretched place

DYSURIA   *n* pl. -S painful urination **DYSURIC** *adj*

DYVOUR   *n* pl. -S one who is bankrupt

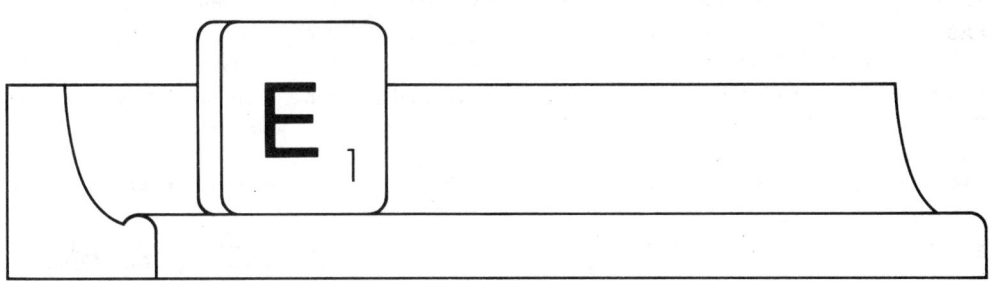

EACH	*adj* being one of two or more distinct individuals	**EARMUFF**	*n* pl. -S one of a pair of ear coverings
EAGER	*adj* -GERER, -GEREST impatiently longing **EAGERLY** *adv*	**EARN**	*v* -ED, -ING, -S to gain or deserve for one's labor or service
EAGER	*n* pl. -S eagre	**EARNER**	*n* pl. -S one that earns
EAGLE	*n* pl. -S a large bird of prey	**EARNEST**	*n* pl. -S a down payment
EAGLET	*n* pl. -S a young eagle	**EARNINGS**	*n/pl* something earned
EAGRE	*n* pl. -S a tidal flood	**EARPHONE**	*n* pl. -S a listening device worn over the ear
EANLING	*n* pl. -S yeanling	**EARPIECE**	*n* pl. -S an earphone
EAR	*n* pl. -S the organ of hearing	**EARPLUG**	*n* pl. -S a plug for the ear
EARACHE	*n* pl. -S a pain in the ear	**EARRING**	*n* pl. -S an ornament for the earlobe
EARDROP	*n* pl. -S an earring		
EARDRUM	*n* pl. -S the tympanic membrane	**EARSHOT**	*n* pl. -S the range within which sound can be heard
EARED	*adj* having ears	**EARSTONE**	*n* pl. -S an otolith
EARFLAP	*n* pl. -S a part of a cap designed to cover the ears	**EARTH**	*v* -ED, -ING, -S to cover with earth (soil)
EARFUL	*n* pl. -S a flow of information	**EARTHEN**	*adj* made of earth
EARING	*n* pl. -S a line on a ship	**EARTHIER**	comparative of earthy
EARL	*n* pl. -S a British nobleman	**EARTHIEST**	superlative of earthy
EARLAP	*n* pl. -S an earflap	**EARTHILY**	*adv* in an earthy manner
EARLDOM	*n* pl. -S the rank of an earl	**EARTHLY**	*adj* -LIER, -LIEST worldly
EARLESS	*adj* lacking ears	**EARTHMAN**	*n* pl. -MEN a person from the planet earth
EARLIER	comparative of early		
EARLIEST	superlative of early	**EARTHNUT**	*n* pl. -S a European herb
EARLOBE	*n* pl. -S a part of the ear	**EARTHPEA**	*n* pl. -S a twining plant
EARLOCK	*n* pl. -S a curl of hair by the ear	**EARTHSET**	*n* pl. -S the setting of the earth as seen from the moon
EARLSHIP	*n* pl. -S earldom		
EARLY	*adv* -LIER, -LIEST near the beginning of a period of time or a series of events	**EARTHY**	*adj* EARTHIER, EARTHIEST composed of, resembling, or suggestive of earth
EARMARK	*v* -ED, -ING, -S to designate for a specific use	**EARWAX**	*n* pl. -ES cerumen

EARWIG	*v* -WIGGED, -WIGGING, -WIGS to insinuate against in secret	**EBONIZE**	*v* -IZED, -IZING, -IZES to stain black in imitation of ebony
EARWORM	*n* pl. -S a bollworm	**EBONY**	*n* pl. -NIES a hard, heavy wood
EASE	*v* EASED, EASING, EASES to give rest of relief to	**ECARTE**	*n* pl. -S a card game
		ECAUDATE	*adj* having no tail
EASEFUL	*adj* restful	**ECBOLIC**	*n* pl. -S a type of drug
EASEL	*n* pl. -S a three-legged frame	**ECCLESIA**	*n* pl. -SIAE an assembly in ancient Greece
EASEMENT	*n* pl. -S relief		
EASIER	comparative of easy	**ECCRINE**	*adj* producing secretions externally
EASIES	pl. of easy		
EASIEST	superlative of easy	**ECDYSIS**	*n* pl. -DYSES the shedding of an outer layer of skin **ECDYSIAL** *adj*
EASILY	*adv* without difficulty		
EASINESS	*n* pl. -ES the state of being easy	**ECDYSON**	*n* pl. -S ecdysone
		ECDYSONE	*n* pl. -S an insect hormone
EASING	present participle of ease	**ECESIS**	*n* pl. -SISES the establishment of a plant or animal in a new environment
EAST	*n* pl. -S a cardinal point of the compass		
EASTER	*n* pl. -S a wind or storm from the east	**ECHARD**	*n* pl. -S the water in the soil not available to plants
EASTERLY	*n* pl. -LIES a wind from the east	**ECHE**	*v* ECHED, ECHING, ECHES to increase
EASTERN	*adj* being to, toward, or in the east	**ECHELON**	*v* -ED, -ING, -S to group in a particular formation
EASTING	*n* pl. -S a movement toward the east	**ECHIDNA**	*n* pl. -NAS or -NAE a spiny anteater
EASTWARD	*n* pl. -S a direction toward the east	**ECHINATE**	*adj* spiny
EASY	*adj* EASIER, EASIEST not difficult	**ECHING**	present participle of eche
		ECHINOID	*n* pl. -S a spiny marine animal
EASY	*n* pl. EASIES a communications code word for the letter E	**ECHINUS**	*n* pl. -NI echinoid
EAT	*v* ATE or ET, EATEN, EATING, EATS to consume food	**ECHO**	*v* -ED, -ING, -ES to produce an echo (a repetition of sound by reflection of sound waves)
EATABLE	*n* pl. -S an edible	**ECHOER**	*n* pl. -S one that echoes
EATER	*n* pl. -S one that eats	**ECHOEY**	*adj* full of echoes
EATERY	*n* pl. -ERIES a lunchroom	**ECHOIC**	*adj* resembling an echo
EATH	*adj* easy	**ECHOISM**	*n* pl. -S the formation of words in imitation of sounds
EATING	*n* pl. -S the act of consuming food		
		ECHOLESS	*adj* producing no echo
EAU	*n* pl. EAUX water	**ECLAIR**	*n* pl. -S a type of pastry
EAVE	*n* pl. -S the lower projecting edge of a roof **EAVED** *adj*	**ECLAT**	*n* pl. -S brilliance
		ECLECTIC	*n* pl. -S one who draws his beliefs from various sources
EBB	*v* -ED, -ING, -S to recede		
EBBET	*n* pl. -S a common green newt	**ECLIPSE**	*v* ECLIPSED, ECLIPSING, ECLIPSES to obscure
EBON	*n* pl. -S ebony		
EBONIES	pl. of ebony	**ECLIPSIS**	*n* pl. -SES or -SISES an ellipsis
EBONISE	*v* -ISED, -ISING, -ISES to ebonize	**ECLIPTIC**	*n* pl. -S an astronomical plane
		ECLOGITE	*n* pl. -S a type of rock
EBONITE	*n* pl. -S a hard rubber	**ECLOGUE**	*n* pl. -S a pastoral poem

ECLOSION *n* pl. -S the emergence of an insect larva from an egg

ECOLE *n* pl. -S a French school

ECOLOGY *n* pl. -GIES an environmental science **ECOLOGIC** *adj*

ECONOMIC *adj* pertaining to financial matters

ECONOMY *n* pl. -MIES thrift

ECOTONE *n* pl. -S a type of ecological zone **ECOTONAL** *adj*

ECOTYPE *n* pl. -S a subspecies adapted to specific environmental conditions **ECOTYPIC** *adj*

ECRASEUR *n* pl. -S a surgical instrument

ECRU *n* pl. -S a yellowish brown color

ECSTASY *n* pl. -SIES a state of exaltation

ECSTATIC *n* pl. -S one that is subject to ecstasies

ECTASIS *n* pl. -TASES the lengthening of a usually short syllable **ECTATIC** *adj*

ECTHYMA *n* pl. -MATA a virus disease

ECTODERM *n* pl. -S the outermost germ layer of an embryo

ECTOMERE *n* pl. -S a cell that develops into ectoderm

ECTOPIA *n* pl. -S congenital displacement of parts or organs **ECTOPIC** *adj*

ECTOSARC *n* pl. -S the outermost layer of protoplasm of certain protozoans

ECTOZOAN *n* pl. -S ectozoon

ECTOZOON *n* pl. -ZOA a parasite on the body of an animal

ECTYPE *n* pl. -S a copy **ECTYPAL** *adj*

ECU *n* pl. -S an old French coin

ECUMENIC *adj* universal

ECZEMA *n* pl. -S a skin disease

EDACIOUS *adj* voracious

EDACITY *n* pl. -TIES gluttony

EDAPHIC *adj* pertaining to the soil

EDDO *n* pl. -DOES a tropical plant

EDDY *v* -DIED, -DYING, -DIES to move against the main current

EDEMA *n* pl. -MAS or -MATA an excessive accumulation of serous fluid

EDENTATE *n* pl. -S a toothless mammal

EDGE *v* EDGED, EDGING, EDGES to provide with an edge (a bounding or dividing line)

EDGELESS *adj* lacking an edge

EDGER *n* pl. -S a tool used to trim a lawn's edge

EDGEWAYS *adv* edgewise

EDGEWISE *adv* sideways

EDGIER comparative of edgy

EDGIEST superlative of edgy

EDGILY *adv* in an edgy manner

EDGINESS *n* pl. -ES the state of being edgy

EDGING *n* pl. -S something that forms or serves as an edge

EDGY *adj* EDGIER, EDGIEST tense, nervous, or irritable

EDH *n* pl. -S an Old English letter

EDIBLE *n* pl. -S something fit to be eaten

EDICT *n* pl. -S an authoritative order having the force of law **EDICTAL** *adj*

EDIFICE *n* pl. -S a building

EDIFIER *n* pl. -S one that edifies

EDIFY *v* -FIED, -FYING, -FIES to enlighten

EDILE *n* pl. -S aedile

EDIT *v* -ED, -ING, -S to correct and prepare for publication **EDITABLE** *adj*

EDITION *n* pl. -S a particular series of printed material

EDITOR *n* pl. -S one that edits

EDITRESS *n* pl. -ES a female editor

EDUCABLE *n* pl. -S a mildly retarded person

EDUCATE *v* -CATED, -CATING, -CATES to teach

EDUCATOR *n* pl. -S one that educates

EDUCE *v* EDUCED, EDUCING, EDUCES to draw forth or bring out **EDUCIBLE** *adj*

EDUCT *n* pl. -S something educed

EDUCTION *n* pl. -S the act of educing **EDUCTIVE** *adj*

EDUCTOR *n* pl. -S one that educes

EEL *n* pl. -S a snakelike fish

EELGRASS *n* pl. -ES an aquatic plant

EELIER comparative of eely

EELIEST superlative of eely

EELLIKE *adj* resembling an eel

EELPOUT *n* pl. -S a marine fish

EELWORM	*n* pl. -S a small roundworm
EELY	*adj* EELIER, EELIEST resembling an eel
EERIE	*adj* -RIER, -RIEST weird **EERILY** *adv*
EERINESS	*n* pl. -ES the state of being eerie
EERY	*adj* -RIER, -RIEST eerie
EF	*n* pl. -S the letter F
EFF	*n* pl. -S ef
EFFABLE	*adj* capable of being uttered or expressed
EFFACE	*v* -FACED, -FACING, -FACES to rub or wipe out
EFFACER	*n* pl. -S one that effaces
EFFECT	*v* -ED, -ING, -S to bring about
EFFECTER	*n* pl. -S effector
EFFECTOR	*n* pl. -S a bodily organ that responds to a nerve impulse
EFFENDI	*n* pl. -S a Turkish title of respect
EFFERENT	*n* pl. -S an organ or part conveying nervous impulses to an effector
EFFETE	*adj* exhausted of vigor or energy **EFFETELY** *adv*
EFFICACY	*n* pl. -CIES effectiveness
EFFIGY	*n* pl. -GIES a likeness or representation
EFFLUENT	*n* pl. -S an outflow
EFFLUVIA	*n/pl* byproducts in the form of waste
EFFLUX	*n* pl. -ES an outflow
EFFORT	*n* pl. -S a deliberate exertion
EFFULGE	*v* -FULGED, -FULGING, -FULGES to shine forth
EFFUSE	*v* -FUSED, -FUSING, -FUSES to pour forth
EFFUSION	*n* pl. -S an outpouring of emotion
EFFUSIVE	*adj* pouring forth
EFT	*n* pl. -S a newt
EFTSOON	*adv* soon afterward
EFTSOONS	*adv* eftsoon
EGAD	*interj* — used as a mild oath
EGADS	*interj* egad
EGAL	*adj* equal
EGALITE	*n* pl. -S equality
EGER	*n* pl. -S eagre
EGEST	*v* -ED, -ING, -S to discharge from the body
EGESTA	*n/pl* egested matter
EGESTION	*n* pl. -S the act of egesting **EGESTIVE** *adj*
EGG	*v* -ED, -ING, -S to incite or urge
EGGAR	*n* pl. -S egger
EGGCUP	*n* pl. -S a cup from which an egg is eaten
EGGER	*n* pl. -S a kind of moth
EGGHEAD	*n* pl. -S an intellectual
EGGNOG	*n* pl. -S a beverage
EGGPLANT	*n* pl. -S a perennial herb yielding edible fruit
EGGSHELL	*n* pl. -S the hard exterior of a bird's egg
EGIS	*n* pl. EGISES aegis
EGLATERE	*n* pl. -S a wild rose
EGO	*n* pl. EGOS the conscious self
EGOISM	*n* pl. -S extreme devotion to self-interest
EGOIST	*n* pl. -S one who practices egoism **EGOISTIC** *adj*
EGOMANIA	*n* pl. -S extreme egotism
EGOTISM	*n* pl. -S self-conceit
EGOTIST	*n* pl. -S a conceited person
EGRESS	*v* -ED, -ING, -ES to go out
EGRET	*n* pl. -S a wading bird
EH	*interj* — used to express doubt or surprise
EIDE	pl. of eidos
EIDER	*n* pl. -S a large sea duck
EIDETIC	*adj* pertaining to vivid recall
EIDOLON	*n* pl. -LONS or -LA a phantom
EIDOS	*n* pl. EIDE an essence
EIGHT	*n* pl. -S a number
EIGHTEEN	*n* pl. -S a number
EIGHTH	*n* pl. -S one of eight equal parts
EIGHTHLY	*adv* in the eighth place
EIGHTVO	*n* pl. -VOS octavo
EIGHTY	*n* pl. EIGHTIES a number
EIKON	*n* pl. -S or -ES icon
EINKORN	*n* pl. -S a variety of wheat
EIRENIC	*adj* irenic
EITHER	*adj* being one or the other
EJECT	*v* -ED, -ING, -S to throw out forcibly

EJECTA *n/pl* ejected material

EJECTION *n* pl. -S the act of ejecting

EJECTIVE *n* pl. -S a sound produced with air compressed above the closed glottis

EJECTOR *n* pl. -S one that ejects

EKE *v* EKED, EKING, EKES to supplement with great effort

EKISTICS *n/pl* a science dealing with human habitats **EKISTIC** *adj*

EKTEXINE *n* pl. -S an outer layer of the exine

EL *n* pl. -S an elevated railroad or train

ELAIN *n* pl. -S olein

ELAN *n* pl. -S enthusiasm

ELAND *n* pl. -S a large antelope

ELAPHINE *adj* pertaining to a genus of deer

ELAPID *n* pl. -S a venomous snake

ELAPINE *adj* pertaining to a family of snakes

ELAPSE *v* ELAPSED, ELAPSING, ELAPSES to pass away

ELASTASE *n* pl. -S an enzyme

ELASTIC *n* pl. -S a stretchable material

ELASTIN *n* pl. -S a bodily protein

ELATE *v* ELATED, ELATING, ELATES to raise the spirits of **ELATEDLY** *adv*

ELATER *n* pl. -S a click beetle

ELATERID *n* pl. -S an elater

ELATERIN *n* pl. -S a chemical compound

ELATING present participle of elate

ELATION *n* pl. -S a feeling of great joy

ELATIVE *n* pl. -S an adjectival form in some languages

ELBOW *v* -ED, -ING, -S to jostle

ELD *n* pl. -S old age

ELDER *n* pl. -S an older person

ELDERLY *adj* rather old

ELDEST *adj* oldest

ELDRICH *adj* eldritch

ELDRITCH *adj* weird

ELECT *v* -ED, -ING, -S to select by vote for an office

ELECTION *n* pl. -S the act of electing

ELECTIVE *n* pl. -S an optional course of study

ELECTOR *n* pl. -S one that elects

ELECTRET *n* pl. -S a type of nonconductor

ELECTRIC *n* pl. -S something run by electricity

ELECTRO *v* -ED, -ING, -S to make a metallic copy of a page of type for printing

ELECTRON *n* pl. -S an atomic particle

ELECTRUM *n* pl. -S an alloy of gold and silver

ELEGANCE *n* pl. -S tasteful opulence

ELEGANCY *n* pl. -CIES elegance

ELEGANT *adj* tastefully opulent

ELEGIAC *n* pl. -S a type of verse

ELEGIES pl. of elegy

ELEGISE *v* -GISED, -GISING, -GISES to elegize

ELEGIST *n* pl. -S one that writes elegies

ELEGIT *n* pl. -S a type of judicial writ

ELEGIZE *v* -GIZED, -GIZING, -GIZES to write an elegy

ELEGY *n* pl. -GIES a mournful poem for one who is dead

ELEMENT *n* pl. -S any of a class of substances that cannot be separated into simpler substances by chemical means

ELEMI *n* pl. -S a fragrant resin

ELENCHUS *n* pl. -CHI a logical refutation **ELENCHIC, ELENCTIC** *adj*

ELEPHANT *n* pl. -S a large mammal

ELEVATE *v* -VATED, -VATING, -VATES to raise

ELEVATOR *n* pl. -S one that elevates

ELEVEN *n* pl. -S a number

ELEVENTH *n* pl. -S one of eleven equal parts

ELEVON *n* pl. -S a type of airplane control surface

ELF *n* pl. ELVES a small, often mischievous fairy

ELFIN *n* pl. -S an elf

ELFISH *adj* resembling an elf **ELFISHLY** *adv*

ELFLOCK *n* pl. -S a lock of tangled hair

ELHI *adj* pertaining to school grades 1 through 12

ELICIT *v* -ED, -ING, -S to educe

ELICITOR *n* pl. -S one that elicits

ELIDE   *v* ELIDED, ELIDING, ELIDES to omit **ELIDIBLE** *adj*

ELIGIBLE   *n* pl. -S one that is qualified to be chosen

ELIGIBLY   *adv* in a qualified manner

ELISION   *n* pl. -S the act of eliding

ELITE   *n* pl. -S a socially superior group

ELITISM   *n* pl. -S belief in rule by an elite

ELITIST   *n* pl. -S an adherent of elitism

ELIXIR   *n* pl. -S a medicinal beverage

ELK   *n* pl. -S a large deer

ELKHOUND   *n* pl. -S a hunting dog

ELL   *n* pl. -S the letter L

ELLIPSE   *n* pl. -S a type of plane curve

ELLIPSIS   *n* pl. -LIPSES an omission of a word or words in a sentence

ELLIPTIC   *adj* having the shape of an ellipse

ELM   *n* pl. -S a deciduous tree

ELMY   *adj* -MIER, -MIEST abounding in elms

ELODEA   *n* pl. -S an aquatic herb

ELOIGN   *v* -ED, -ING, -S to remove to a distant place

ELOIGNER   *n* pl. -S one that eloigns

ELOIN   *v* -ED, -ING, -S to eloign

ELOINER   *n* pl. -S one that eloins

ELONGATE   *v* -GATED, -GATING, -GATES to lengthen

ELOPE   *v* ELOPED, ELOPING, ELOPES to run off secretly to be married

ELOPER   *n* pl. -S one that elopes

ELOQUENT   *adj* fluent and convincing in speech

ELSE   *adv* in a different place, time, or way

ELUANT   *n* pl. -S a solvent

ELUATE   *n* pl. -S the material obtained by eluting

ELUDE   *v* ELUDED, ELUDING, ELUDES to evade

ELUDER   *n* pl. -S one that eludes

ELUENT   *n* pl. -S eluant

ELUSION   *n* pl. -S the act of eluding

ELUSIVE   *adj* tending to elude

ELUSORY   *adj* elusive

ELUTE   *v* ELUTED, ELUTING, ELUTES to remove by means of a solvent

ELUTION   *n* pl. -S the act of eluting

ELUVIA   a pl. of eluvium

ELUVIAL   *adj* pertaining to an eluvium

ELUVIATE   *v* -ATED, -ATING, -ATES to undergo a transfer of materials in the soil

ELUVIUM   *n* pl. -VIA or -VIUMS a soil deposit

ELVER   *n* pl. -S a young eel

ELVES   pl. of elf

ELVISH   *adj* elfish **ELVISHLY** *adv*

ELYSIAN   *adj* delightful

ELYTRON   *n* pl. -TRA a hardened forewing of certain insects **ELYTROID**, **ELYTROUS** *adj*

ELYTRUM   *n* pl. -TRA elytron

EM   *n* pl. -S the letter M

EMACIATE   *v* -ATED, -ATING, -ATES to make thin

EMANATE   *v* -NATED, -NATING, -NATES to send forth

EMANATOR   *n* pl. -S one that emanates

EMBALM   *v* -ED, -ING, -S to treat so as to protect from decay

EMBALMER   *n* pl. -S one that embalms

EMBANK   *v* -ED, -ING, -S to confine or protect with a raised structure

EMBAR   *v* -BARRED, -BARRING, -BARS to imprison

EMBARGO   *v* -ED, -ING, -ES to restrain trade by a governmental order

EMBARK   *v* -ED, -ING, -S to make a start

EMBARRED   past tense of embar

EMBARRING   present participle of embar

EMBASSY   *n* pl. -SIES the headquarters of an ambassador

EMBATTLE   *v* -TLED, -TLING, -TLES to prepare for battle

EMBAY   *v* -ED, -ING, -S to enclose in a bay

EMBED   *v* -BEDDED, -BEDDING, -BEDS to fix firmly into a surrounding mass

EMBER   *n* pl. -S a glowing fragment from a fire

EMBEZZLE   *v* -ZLED, -ZLING, -ZLES to appropriate fraudulently to one's own use

EMBITTER   *v* -ED, -ING, -S to make bitter

EMBLAZE   *v* -BLAZED, -BLAZING, -BLAZES to set on fire

EMBLAZER	*n* pl. -S one that emblazes
EMBLAZON	*v* -ED, -ING, -S to decorate with brilliant colors
EMBLEM	*v* -ED, -ING, -S to represent with an emblem (a graphical symbol)
EMBODIER	*n* pl. -S one that embodies
EMBODY	*v* -BODIED, -BODYING, -BODIES to provide with a body
EMBOLDEN	*v* -ED, -ING, -S to instill with courage
EMBOLI	pl. of embolus
EMBOLIES	pl. of emboly
EMBOLISM	*n* pl. -S the obstruction of a blood vessel by an embolus **EMBOLIC** *adj*
EMBOLUS	*n* pl. -LI an abnormal particle circulating in the blood
EMBOLY	*n* pl. -LIES a phase of embryonic growth
EMBORDER	*v* -ED, -ING, -S to provide with a border
EMBOSK	*v* -ED, -ING, -S to conceal with foliage
EMBOSOM	*v* -ED, -ING, -S to embrace
EMBOSS	*v* -ED, -ING, -ES to decorate with raised designs
EMBOSSER	*n* pl. -S one that embosses
EMBOW	*v* -ED, -ING, -S to arch
EMBOWEL	*v* -ELED, -ELING, -ELS or -ELLED, -ELLING, -ELS to disbowel
EMBOWER	*v* -ED, -ING, -S to surround with foliage
EMBRACE	*v* -BRACED, -BRACING, -BRACES to hug
EMBRACER	*n* pl. -S one that embraces
EMBROIL	*v* -ED, -ING, -S to involve in conflict
EMBROWN	*v* -ED, -ING, -S to make brown
EMBRUE	*v* -BRUED, -BRUING, -BRUES to imbrue
EMBRUTE	*v* -BRUTED, -BRUTING, -BRUTES to imbrute
EMBRYO	*n* pl. -BRYOS an organism in its early stages of development **EMBRYOID** *adj*
EMBRYON	*n* pl. -S an embryo
EMCEE	*v* -CEED, -CEEING, -CEES to serve as master of ceremonies
EME	*n* pl. -S an uncle
EMEER	*n* pl. -S emir

EMEERATE	*n* pl. -S emirate
EMEND	*v* -ED, -ING, -S to correct
EMENDATE	*v* -DATED, -DATING, -DATES to emend
EMENDER	*n* pl. -S one that emends
EMERALD	*n* pl. -S a green gem
EMERGE	*v* EMERGED, EMERGING, EMERGES to come out into view
EMERGENT	*n* pl. -S a type of aquatic plant
EMERITA	*adj* retired but retaining an honorary title — used of a woman
EMERITUS	*n* pl. -ITI a retired person who retains an honorary title
EMEROD	*n* pl. -S a tumor
EMEROID	*n* pl. -S emerod
EMERSED	*adj* standing out of water
EMERSION	*n* pl. -S the act of emerging
EMERY	*n* pl. -ERIES a granular corundum
EMESIS	*n* pl. EMESES the act of vomiting
EMETIC	*n* pl. -S a substance which induces vomiting
EMETIN	*n* pl. -S emetine
EMETINE	*n* pl. -S an alkaloid
EMEU	*n* pl. -S emu
EMEUTE	*n* pl. -S a riot
EMIGRANT	*n* pl. -S one that emigrates
EMIGRATE	*v* -GRATED, -GRATING, -GRATES to leave one country or region to settle in another
EMIGRE	*n* pl. -S an emigrant
EMINENCE	*n* pl. -S high station or rank
EMINENCY	*n* pl. -CIES eminence
EMINENT	*adj* of high station or rank
EMIR	*n* pl. -S an Arab chieftain or prince
EMIRATE	*n* pl. -S the rank of an emir
EMISSARY	*n* pl. -SARIES a person sent on a mission
EMISSION	*n* pl. -S the act of emitting **EMISSIVE** *adj*
EMIT	*v* EMITTED, EMITTING, EMITS to send forth
EMITTER	*n* pl. -S one that emits
EMMER	*n* pl. -S a type of wheat
EMMET	*n* pl. -S an ant
EMODIN	*n* pl. -S a chemical compound

EMOTE	*v* EMOTED, EMOTING, EMOTES to express emotion in an exaggerated manner	**EMPTINGS**	*n/pl* emptins
		EMPTINS	*n/pl* a liquid leavening
EMOTER	*n* pl. -S one that emotes	**EMPTY**	*adj* -TIER, -TIEST containing nothing
EMOTION	*n* pl. -S an affective state of consciousness	**EMPTY**	*v* -TIED, -TYING, -TIES to remove the contents of
EMOTIVE	*adj* pertaining to emotion	**EMPURPLE**	*v* -PLED, -PLING, -PLES to tinge with purple
EMPALE	*v* -PALED, -PALING, -PALES to impale	**EMPYEMA**	*n* pl. -EMATA or -EMAS a collection of pus in a body cavity **EMPYEMIC** *adj*
EMPALER	*n* pl. -S one that empales		
EMPANEL	*v* -ELED, -ELING, -ELS or -ELLED, -ELLING, -ELS to impanel	**EMPYREAL**	*adj* pertaining to the sky
		EMPYREAN	*n* pl. -S the highest heaven
EMPATHY	*n* pl. -THIES imaginative identification with another's thoughts and feelings **EMPATHIC** *adj*	**EMU**	*n* pl. -S a large, flightless bird
		EMULATE	*v* -LATED, -LATING, -LATES to try to equal or surpass
EMPEROR	*n* pl. -S the ruler of an empire	**EMULATOR**	*n* pl. -S one that emulates
EMPERY	*n* pl. -PERIES absolute dominion	**EMULOUS**	*adj* eager to equal or surpass another
EMPHASIS	*n* pl. -PHASES special significance imparted to something	**EMULSIFY**	*v* -FIED, -FYING, -FIES to make into an emulsion
EMPHATIC	*adj* strongly expressive	**EMULSION**	*n* pl. -S a type of liquid mixture **EMULSIVE** *adj*
EMPIRE	*n* pl. -S a major political unit		
EMPIRIC	*n* pl. -S one who relies on practical experience	**EMULSOID**	*n* pl. -S a liquid dispersed in another liquid
EMPLACE	*v* -PLACED, -PLACING, -PLACES to position	**EMYD**	*n* pl. -S a freshwater tortoise
		EMYDE	*n* pl. -S emyd
EMPLANE	*v* -PLANED, -PLANING, -PLANES to enplane	**EN**	*n* pl. -S the letter N
		ENABLE	*v* -BLED, -BLING, -BLES to make possible
EMPLOY	*v* -ED, -ING, -S to hire		
EMPLOYE	*n* pl. -S employee	**ENABLER**	*n* pl. -S one that enables
EMPLOYEE	*n* pl. -S a person who is employed	**ENACT**	*v* -ED, -ING, -S to make into a law
EMPLOYER	*n* pl. -S one that employs	**ENACTIVE**	*adj* having the power to enact
EMPOISON	*v* -ED, -ING, -S to embitter	**ENACTOR**	*n* pl. -S one that enacts
EMPORIUM	*n* pl. -RIUMS or -RIA a trading or market center	**ENACTORY**	*adj* pertaining to the enactment of law
EMPOWER	*v* -ED, -ING, -S to give legal power to	**ENAMEL**	*v* -ELED, -ELING, -ELS or -ELLED, -ELLING, -ELS to cover with a hard, glossy surface
EMPRESS	*n* pl. -ES a female ruler of an empire		
		ENAMELER	*n* pl. -S one that enamels
EMPRISE	*n* pl. -S an adventurous undertaking	**ENAMINE**	*n* pl. -S a type of amine
		ENAMOR	*v* -ED, -ING, -S to inspire with love
EMPRIZE	*n* pl. -S emprise		
EMPTIED	past tense of empty	**ENAMOUR**	*v* -ED, -ING, -S to enamor
EMPTIER	*n* pl. -S one that empties	**ENATE**	*n* pl. -S a relative on the mother's side **ENATIC** *adj*
EMPTIES	present 3d person sing. of empty		
EMPTIEST	superlative of empty	**ENATION**	*n* pl. -S an outgrowth from the surface of an organ
EMPTILY	*adv* in an empty manner		

ENCAENIA *n/pl* annual university ceremonies

ENCAGE *v* -CAGED, -CAGING, -CAGES to confine in a cage

ENCAMP *v* -ED, -ING, -S to set up a camp

ENCASE *v* -CASED, -CASING, -CASES to enclose in a case

ENCASH *v* -ED, -ING, -ES to cash

ENCEINTE *n* pl. -S an encircling fortification

ENCHAIN *v* -ED, -ING, -S to bind with chains

ENCHANT *v* -ED, -ING, -S to delight

ENCHASE *v* -CHASED, -CHASING, -CHASES to place in an ornamental setting

ENCHASER *n* pl. -S one that enchases

ENCHORIC *adj* belonging to a particular country

ENCINA *n* pl. -S an evergreen oak **ENCINAL** *adj*

ENCIPHER *v* -ED, -ING, -S to write in characters of hidden meaning

ENCIRCLE *v* -CLED, -CLING, -CLES to form a circle around

ENCLASP *v* -ED, -ING, -S to embrace

ENCLAVE *n* pl. -S a territorial unit enclosed within foreign territory

ENCLITIC *n* pl. -S a word pronounced as part of the preceding word

ENCLOSE *v* -CLOSED, -CLOSING, -CLOSES to close in on all sides

ENCLOSER *n* pl. -S one that encloses

ENCODE *v* -CODED, -CODING, -CODES to put into code

ENCODER *n* pl. -S one that encodes

ENCOMIUM *n* pl. -MIUMS or -MIA a eulogy

ENCORE *v* -CORED, -CORING, -CORES to call for the reappearance of a performer

ENCROACH *v* -ED, -ING, -ES to advance beyond the proper limits

ENCRUST *v* -ED, -ING, -S to cover with a crust

ENCRYPT *v* -ED, -ING, -S to encipher

ENCUMBER *v* -ED, -ING, -S to hinder in action or movement

ENCYCLIC *n* pl. -S a letter addressed by the pope to the bishops of the world

ENCYST *v* -ED, -ING, -S to enclose in a cyst

END *v* -ED, -ING, -S to terminate

ENDAMAGE *v* -AGED, -AGING, -AGES to damage

ENDAMEBA *n* pl. -BAS or -BAE a parasitic ameba

ENDANGER *v* -ED, -ING, -S to imperil

ENDARCH *adj* formed from the center outward

ENDARCHY *n* pl. -CHIES the condition of being endarch

ENDBRAIN *n* pl. -S a part of the brain

ENDEAR *v* -ED, -ING, -S to make dear or beloved

ENDEAVOR *v* -ED, -ING, -S to make an effort

ENDEMIAL *adj* peculiar to a country or people

ENDEMIC *n* pl. -S an endemial disease

ENDEMISM *n* pl. -S the state of being endemial

ENDER *n* pl. -S one that ends something

ENDERMIC *adj* acting by absorption through the skin

ENDEXINE *n* pl. -S an inner layer of the exine

ENDING *n* pl. -S a termination

ENDITE *v* -DITED, -DITING, -DITES to indite

ENDIVE *n* pl. -S an herb cultivated as a salad plant

ENDLEAF *n* pl. -LEAVES an endpaper

ENDLESS *adj* enduring forever

ENDLONG *adv* lengthwise

ENDMOST *adj* farthest

ENDOCARP *n* pl. -S the inner layer of a pericarp

ENDODERM *n* pl. -S the innermost germ layer of an embryo

ENDOGAMY *n* pl. -MIES marriage within a particular group

ENDOGEN *n* pl. -S a type of plant

ENDOGENY *n* pl. -NIES growth from within

ENDOPOD *n* pl. -S a branch of a crustacean limb

ENDORSE *v* -DORSED, -DORSING, -DORSES to sign the back of a negotiable document

ENDORSEE *n* pl. -S one to whom a document is transferred by endorsement

ENDORSER *n* pl. -S one that endorses

ENDORSING present participle of endorse

ENDORSOR *n* pl. -S endorser

ENDOSARC *n* pl. -S a portion of a cell

ENDOSMOS *n* pl. -ES a form of osmosis

ENDOSOME *n* pl. -S a cellular particle

ENDOSTEA *n/pl* bone membranes

ENDOW *v* -ED, -ING, -S to provide with something

ENDOWER *n* pl. -S one that endows

ENDOZOIC *adj* involving passage through an animal

ENDPAPER *n* pl. -S a sheet of paper used in bookbinding

ENDPLATE *n* pl. -S a type of nerve terminal

ENDRIN *n* pl. -S an insecticide

ENDUE *v* -DUED, -DUING, -DUES to provide with some quality or gift

ENDURE *v* -DURED, -DURING, -DURES to last

ENDURO *n* pl. -DUROS a long race

ENDWAYS *adv* endwise

ENDWISE *adv* lengthwise

ENEMA *n* pl. -MAS or -MATA a liquid injected into the rectum

ENEMY *n* pl. -MIES one that is antagonistic toward another

ENERGID *n* pl. -S a nucleus and the body of cytoplasm with which it interacts

ENERGIES pl. of energy

ENERGISE *v* -GISED, -GISING, -GISES to energize

ENERGIZE *v* -GIZED, -GIZING, -GIZES to give energy to

ENERGY *n* -GIES the capacity for vigorous activity

ENERVATE *v* -VATED, -VATING, -VATES to deprive of strength or vitality

ENFACE *v* -FACED, -FACING, -FACES to write on the front of

ENFEEBLE *v* -BLED, -BLING, -BLES to make feeble

ENFEOFF *v* -ED, -ING, -S to invest with a feudal estate

ENFETTER *v* -ED, -ING, -S to enchain

ENFEVER *v* -ED, -ING, -S to fever

ENFILADE *v* -LADED, -LADING, -LADES to direct heavy gunfire along the length of

ENFIN *adv* finally

ENFLAME *v* -FLAMED, -FLAMING, -FLAMES to inflame

ENFOLD *v* -ED, -ING, -S to envelop

ENFOLDER *n* pl. -S one that enfolds

ENFORCE *v* -FORCED, -FORCING, -FORCES to compel obedience to

ENFORCER *n* pl. -S one that enforces

ENFRAME *v* -FRAMED, -FRAMING, -FRAMES to frame

ENG *n* pl. -S a phonetic symbol

ENGAGE *v* -GAGED, -GAGING, -GAGES to employ

ENGAGER *n* pl. -S one that engages

ENGENDER *v* -ED, -ING, -S to bring into existence

ENGILD *v* -ED, -ING, -S to brighten

ENGINE *v* -GINED, -GINING, -GINES to equip with machinery

ENGINEER *v* -ED, -ING, -S to carry through or manage by contrivance

ENGINERY *n* pl. -RIES machinery

ENGINING present participle of engine

ENGINOUS *adj* ingenious

ENGIRD *v* -GIRT or -GIRDED, -GIRDING, -GIRDS to gird

ENGIRDLE *v* -DLED, -DLING, -DLES to engird

ENGLISH *v* -ED, -ING, -ES to cause a billiard ball to spin around its vertical axis

ENGLUT *v* -GLUTTED, -GLUTTING, -GLUTS to gulp down

ENGORGE *v* -GORGED, -GORGING, -GORGES to fill with blood

ENGRAFT *v* -ED, -ING, -S to graft for propagation

ENGRAIL *v* -ED, -ING, -S to ornament the edge of with curved indentations

ENGRAIN *v* -ED, -ING, -S to ingrain

ENGRAM *n* pl. -S the durable mark caused by a stimulus upon protoplasm

ENGRAMME *n* pl. -S engram

ENGRAVE *v* -GRAVED, -GRAVING, -GRAVES to form by incision

ENGRAVER *n* pl. -S one that engraves

ENGROSS *v* -ED, -ING, -ES to occupy completely

ENGULF *v* -ED, -ING, -S to surround completely

ENHALO	*v* -ED, -ING, -ES to surround with a halo
ENHANCE	*v* -HANCED, -HANCING, -HANCES to raise to a higher degree
ENHANCER	*n* pl. -S one that enhances
ENIGMA	*n* pl. -MAS or -MATA something that is hard to understand or explain
ENISLE	*v* -ISLED, -ISLING, -ISLES to isolate
ENJAMBED	*adj* marked by the continuation of a sentence from one line of a poem to the next
ENJOIN	*v* -ED, -ING, -S to command
ENJOINER	*n* pl. -S one that enjoins
ENJOY	*v* -ED, -ING, -S to receive pleasure from
ENJOYER	*n* pl. -S one that enjoys
ENKINDLE	*v* -DLED, -DLING, -DLES to set on fire
ENLACE	*v* -LACED, -LACING, -LACES to bind with laces
ENLARGE	*v* -LARGED, -LARGING, -LARGES to make or become larger
ENLARGER	*n* pl. -S a device used to enlarge photographs
ENLIST	*v* -ED, -ING, -S to engage for military service
ENLISTEE	*n* pl. -S one that is enlisted
ENLISTER	*n* pl. -S one that enlists
ENLIVEN	*v* -ED, -ING, -S to make lively
ENMESH	*v* -ED, -ING, -ES to ensnare or entangle in a net
ENMITY	*n* pl. -TIES hostility
ENNEAD	*n* pl. -S a group of nine **ENNEADIC** *adj*
ENNEAGON	*n* pl. -S a nonagon
ENNOBLE	*v* -BLED, -BLING, -BLES to make noble
ENNOBLER	*n* pl. -S one that ennobles
ENNUI	*n* pl. -S a feeling of weariness and discontent
ENNUYE	*adj* oppressed with ennui
ENNUYEE	*adj* ennuye
ENOL	*n* pl. -S a chemical compound **ENOLIC** *adj*
ENOLASE	*n* pl. -S an enzyme
ENOLOGY	*n* pl. -GIES oenology
ENORM	*adj* enormous

ENORMITY	*n* pl. -TIES a grave offense against decency
ENORMOUS	*adj* huge
ENOSIS	*n* pl. -SISES union
ENOUGH	*n* pl. -S a sufficient supply
ENOUNCE	*v* ENOUNCED, ENOUNCING, ENOUNCES to announce
ENOW	*n* pl. -S enough
ENPLANE	*v* -PLANED, -PLANING, -PLANES to board an airplane
ENQUIRE	*v* -QUIRED, -QUIRING, -QUIRES to inquire
ENQUIRY	*n* pl. -RIES inquiry
ENRAGE	*v* -RAGED, -RAGING, -RAGES to make very angry
ENRAPT	*adj* rapt
ENRAVISH	*v* -ED, -ING, -ES to delight greatly
ENRICH	*v* -ED, -ING, -ES to add desirable elements to
ENRICHER	*n* pl. -S one that enriches
ENROBE	*v* -ROBED, -ROBING, -ROBES to dress
ENROBER	*n* pl. -S one that enrobes
ENROL	*v* -ROLLED, -ROLLING, -ROLS to enroll
ENROLL	*v* -ED, -ING, -S to enter the name of in a register, record, or roll
ENROLLEE	*n* pl. -S one that is enrolled
ENROLLER	*n* pl. -S one that enrolls
ENROLLING	present participle of enrol
ENROOT	*v* -ED, -ING, -S to implant
ENS	*n* pl. ENTIA an entity
ENSAMPLE	*n* pl. -S an example
ENSCONCE	*v* -SCONCED, -SCONCING, -SCONCES to settle securely or comfortably
ENSCROLL	*v* -ED, -ING, -S to write on a scroll
ENSEMBLE	*n* pl. -S a group of complementary parts
ENSERF	*v* -ED, -ING, -S to make a serf of
ENSHEATH	*v* -ED, -ING, -S to enclose in a sheath
ENSHRINE	*v* -SHRINED, -SHRINING, -SHRINES to place in a shrine
ENSHROUD	*v* -ED, -ING, -S to conceal
ENSIFORM	*adj* sword-shaped
ENSIGN	*n* pl. -S a navy officer

ENSIGNCY *n* pl. -CIES the rank of an ensign

ENSILAGE *v* -LAGED, -LAGING, -LAGES to ensile

ENSILE *v* -SILED, -SILING, -SILES to store in a silo

ENSKY *v* -SKIED or -SKYED, -SKYING, -SKIES to raise to the skies

ENSLAVE *v* -SLAVED, -SLAVING, -SLAVES to make a slave of

ENSLAVER *n* pl. -S one that enslaves

ENSNARE *v* -SNARED, -SNARING, -SNARES to trap

ENSNARER *n* pl. -S one that ensnares

ENSNARL *v* -ED, -ING, -S to tangle

ENSORCEL *v* -ED, -ING, -S to bewitch

ENSOUL *v* -ED, -ING, -S to endow with a soul

ENSPHERE *v* -SPHERED, -SPHERING, -SPHERES to enclose in a sphere

ENSUE *v* -SUED, -SUING, -SUES to occur afterward or as a result

ENSURE *v* -SURED, -SURING, -SURES to make certain

ENSURER *n* pl. -S one that ensures

ENSWATHE *v* -SWATHED, -SWATHING, -SWATHES to swathe

ENTAIL *v* -ED, -ING, -S to restrict the inheritance of to a specified line of heirs

ENTAILER *n* pl. -S one that entails

ENTAMEBA *n* pl. -BAE or -BAS endameba

ENTANGLE *v* -TANGLED, -TANGLING, -TANGLES to tangle

ENTASIA *n* pl. -S spasmodic contraction of a muscle

ENTASIS *n* pl. -TASES a slight convexity in a column **ENTASTIC** *adj*

ENTELLUS *n* pl. -ES a hanuman

ENTENTE *n* pl. -S an agreement between nations

ENTER *v* -ED, -ING, -S to come or go into

ENTERA a pl. of enteron

ENTERAL *adj* enteric

ENTERER *n* pl. -S one that enters

ENTERIC *adj* pertaining to the enteron

ENTERON *n* pl. -TERONS or -TERA the alimentary canal

ENTHALPY *n* pl. -PIES a thermodynamic measure

ENTHETIC *adj* introduced from outside

ENTHRAL *v* -THRALLED, -THRALLING, -THRALS to enthrall

ENTHRALL *v* -ED, -ING, -S to charm

ENTHRONE *v* -THRONED, -THRONING, -THRONES to place on a throne

ENTHUSE *v* -THUSED, -THUSING, -THUSES to show enthusiasm

ENTIA pl. of ens

ENTICE *v* -TICED, -TICING, -TICES to allure

ENTICER *n* pl. -S one that entices

ENTIRE *n* pl. -S the whole of something

ENTIRELY *adv* completely

ENTIRETY *n* pl. -TIES completeness

ENTITLE *v* -TLED, -TLING, -TLES to give a title to

ENTITY *n* pl. -TIES something that has a real existence

ENTODERM *n* pl. -S endoderm

ENTOIL *v* -ED, -ING, -S to entrap

ENTOMB *v* -ED, -ING, -S to place in a tomb

ENTOPIC *adj* situated in the normal place

ENTOZOA a pl. of entozoan and pl. of entozoon

ENTOZOAL *adj* entozoic

ENTOZOAN *n* pl. -ZOANS or -ZOA an entozoic parasite

ENTOZOIC *adj* living within an animal

ENTOZOON *n* pl. -ZOA entozoan

ENTRAILS *n/pl* the internal organs

ENTRAIN *v* -ED, -ING, -S to board a train

ENTRANCE *v* -TRANCED, -TRANCING, -TRANCES to fill with delight or wonder

ENTRANT *n* pl. -S one that enters

ENTRAP *v* -TRAPPED, -TRAPPING, -TRAPS to trap

ENTREAT *v* -ED, -ING, -S to ask for earnestly

ENTREATY *n* pl. -TREATIES an earnest request

ENTREE *n* pl. -S the principal dish of a meal

ENTRENCH *v* -ED, -ING, -ES to establish firmly

ENTREPOT *n* pl. -S a warehouse

ENTRESOL	*n* pl. -S a mezzanine
ENTRIES	pl. of entry
ENTROPY	*n* pl. -PIES a thermodynamic measure
ENTRUST	*v* -ED, -ING, -S to give over for safekeeping
ENTRY	*n* pl. -TRIES a place of entrance
ENTRYWAY	*n* pl. -WAYS a passage serving as an entrance
ENTWINE	*v* -TWINED, -TWINING, -TWINES to twine around
ENTWIST	*v* -ED, -ING, -S to twist together
ENURE	*v* -URED, -URING, -URES to inure
ENURESIS	*n* pl. -SISES involuntary urination **ENURETIC** *adj*
ENVELOP	*v* -ED, -ING, -S to cover completely
ENVELOPE	*n* pl. -S a paper container
ENVENOM	*v* -ED, -ING, -S to put venom into
ENVIABLE	*adj* desirable **ENVIABLY** *adv*
ENVIED	past tense of envy
ENVIER	*n* pl. -S one that envies
ENVIES	present 3d person sing. of envy
ENVIOUS	*adj* resentful and desirous of another's possessions or qualities
ENVIRON	*v* -ED, -ING, -S to encircle
ENVISAGE	*v* -AGED, -AGING, -AGES to form a mental image of
ENVISION	*v* -ED, -ING, -S to envisage
ENVOI	*n* pl. -S the closing of a poem or prose work
ENVOY	*n* pl. -VOYS a representative
ENVY	*v* -VIED, -VYING, -VIES to be envious of
ENWHEEL	*v* -ED, -ING, -S to encircle
ENWIND	*v* -WOUND, -WINDING, -WINDS to wind around
ENWOMB	*v* -ED, -ING, -S to enclose as if in a womb
ENWRAP	*v* -WRAPPED, -WRAPPING, -WRAPS to envelop
ENZOOTIC	*n* pl. -S a type of animal disease
ENZYM	*n* pl. -S enzyme
ENZYME	*n* pl. -S a complex protein **ENZYMIC** *adj*

EOBIONT	*n* pl. -S a type of basic organism
EOHIPPUS	*n* pl. -ES an extinct horse
EOLIAN	*adj* pertaining to the wind
EOLIPILE	*n* pl. -S a type of engine
EOLITH	*n* pl. -S a prehistoric stone tool **EOLITHIC** *adj*
EOLOPILE	*n* pl. -S eolipile
EON	*n* pl. -S an indefinitely long period of time
EONIAN	*adj* everlasting
EONISM	*n* pl. -S adoption of the dress and mannerisms of the opposite sex
EOSIN	*n* pl. -S a red dye **EOSINIC** *adj*
EOSINE	*n* pl. -S eosin
EPACT	*n* pl. -S the difference between the lengths of the solar and lunar years
EPARCH	*n* pl. -S the head of an eparchy
EPARCHY	*n* pl. -CHIES a district of modern Greece
EPAULET	*n* pl. -S a shoulder ornament
EPEE	*n* pl. -S a type of sword
EPEEIST	*n* pl. -S one who fences with an epee
EPEIRIC	*adj* pertaining to vertical movement of the earth's crust
EPERGNE	*n* pl. -S an ornamental dish
EPHA	*n* pl. -S ephah
EPHAH	*n* pl. -S a Hebrew unit of dry measure
EPHEBE	*n* pl. -S ephebus **EPHEBIC** *adj*
EPHEBOS	*n* pl. -BOI ephebus
EPHEBUS	*n* pl. -BI a young man of ancient Greece
EPHEDRA	*n* pl. -S a desert shrub
EPHEDRIN	*n* pl. -S an alkaloid used to treat allergies
EPHEMERA	*n* pl. -ERAS or -ERAE something of very short life or duration
EPHOD	*n* pl. -S an ancient Hebrew vestment
EPHOR	*n* pl. -ORS or -ORI a magistrate of ancient Greece **EPHORAL** *adj*
EPHORATE	*n* pl. -S the office of ephor
EPIBLAST	*n* pl. -S the ectoderm
EPIBOLY	*n* pl. -LIES the growth of one part around another **EPIBOLIC** *adj*

EPIC   *n* pl. -S a long narrative poem **EPICAL** *adj* **EPICALLY** *adv*

EPICALYX   *n* pl. -LYXES or -LYCES a set of bracts close to and resembling a calyx

EPICARP   *n* pl. -S the outer layer of a pericarp

EPICEDIA   *n/pl* funeral songs

EPICENE   *n* pl. -S one having both male and female characteristics

EPICLIKE   *adj* resembling an epic

EPICOTYL   *n* pl. -S a part of a plant embryo

EPICURE   *n* pl. -S a gourmet

EPICYCLE   *n* pl. -S a circle that rolls on the circumference of another circle

EPIDEMIC   *n* pl. -S a rapid spread of a disease

EPIDERM   *n* pl. -S the outer layer of skin

EPIDOTE   *n* pl. -S a mineral **EPIDOTIC** *adj*

EPIDURAL   *adj* situated on the membrane that encloses the brain

EPIFAUNA   *n* pl. -FAUNAE or -FAUNAS fauna living on a hard sea floor

EPIFOCAL   *adj* pertaining to the point of origin of an earthquake

EPIGEAL   *adj* epigeous

EPIGEAN   *adj* epigeous

EPIGENE   *adj* occurring near the surface of the earth

EPIGENIC   *adj* pertaining to change in the mineral character of a rock

EPIGEOUS   *adj* growing on or close to the ground

EPIGON   *n* pl. -S epigone

EPIGONE   *n* pl. -S an inferior imitator **EPIGONIC** *adj*

EPIGONUS   *n* pl. -NI epigone

EPIGRAM   *n* pl. -S a brief, witty remark

EPIGRAPH   *n* pl. -S an engraved inscription

EPIGYNY   *n* pl. -NIES the state of having floral organs near the top of the ovary

EPILEPSY   *n* pl. -SIES a disorder of the nervous system

EPILOG   *n* pl. -S a concluding section

EPILOGUE   *v* -LOGUED, -LOGUING, -LOGUES to provide with a concluding section

EPIMER   *n* pl. -S a type of sugar compound **EPIMERIC** *adj*

EPIMERE   *n* pl. -S a part of an embryo

EPIMYSIA   *n/pl* muscle sheaths

EPINAOS   *n* pl. -NAOI a rear vestibule

EPINASTY   *n* pl. -TIES a downward bending of plant parts

EPIPHANY   *n* pl. -NIES an appearance of a deity

EPIPHYTE   *n* pl. -S a plant growing upon another plant

EPISCIA   *n* pl. -S a tropical herb

EPISCOPE   *n* pl. -S a type of projector

EPISODE   *n* pl. -S an incident in the course of a continuous experience **EPISODIC** *adj*

EPISOME   *n* pl. -S a genetic determinant **EPISOMAL** *adj*

EPISTASY   *n* pl. -SIES a suppression of genetic effect

EPISTLE   *n* pl. -S a long or formal letter

EPISTLER   *n* pl. -S one that writes epistles

EPISTYLE   *n* pl. -S a part of a classical building

EPITAPH   *n* pl. -S an inscription on a tomb

EPITASIS   *n* pl. -ASES the main part of a classical drama

EPITAXY   *n* pl. -TAXIES a type of crystalline growth

EPITHET   *n* pl. -S a term used to characterize a person or thing

EPITOME   *n* pl. -S a typical or ideal example **EPITOMIC** *adj*

EPIZOA   pl. of epizoon

EPIZOIC   *adj* living on the body of an animal

EPIZOISM   *n* pl. -S the state of being epizoic

EPIZOITE   *n* pl. -S an epizoic organism

EPIZOON   *n* pl. -ZOA an epizoic parasite

EPIZOOTY   *n* pl. -TIES a type of animal disease

EPOCH   *n* pl. -S a particular period of time **EPOCHAL** *adj*

EPODE   *n* pl. -S a type of poem

EPONYM   *n* pl. -S the person for whom something is named **EPONYMIC** *adj*

EPONYMY   *n* pl. -MIES the derivation of an eponymic name

EPOPEE   *n* pl. -S an epic poem

EPOPOEIA   *n* pl. -S epopee

EPOS   *n* pl. -ES an epic poem

EPOXIDE   *n* pl. -S an epoxy compound

EPOXY   *v* EPOXIED or EPOXYED, EPOXYING, EPOXIES to glue with epoxy (a type of resin)

EPSILON   *n* pl. -S a Greek letter

EQUABLE   *adj* not changing or varying greatly **EQUABLY** *adv*

EQUAL   *adj* having the same capability, quantity, or effect as another

EQUAL   *v* EQUALED, EQUALING, EQUALS or EQUALLED, EQUALLING, EQUALS to be equal to

EQUALISE   *v* -ISED, -ISING, -ISES to equalize

EQUALITY   *n* pl. -TIES the state of being equal

EQUALIZE   *v* -IZED, -IZING, -IZES to make equal

EQUALLED   a past tense of equal

EQUALLING   a past participle of equal

EQUALLY   *adv* in an equal manner

EQUATE   *v* EQUATED, EQUATING, EQUATES to make equal

EQUATION   *n* pl. -S the act of equating

EQUATOR   *n* pl. -S the great circle of the earth

EQUERRY   *n* pl. -RIES an officer in charge of the care of horses

EQUINE   *n* pl. -S a horse

EQUINELY   *adv* in a horselike manner

EQUINITY   *n* pl. -TIES the state of being like a horse

EQUINOX   *n* pl. -ES a point on the celestial sphere

EQUIP   *v* EQUIPPED, EQUIPPING, EQUIPS to provide with whatever is needed

EQUIPAGE   *n* pl. -S a carriage

EQUIPPER   *n* pl. -S one that equips

EQUIPPING   present participle of equip

EQUISETA   *n/pl* rushlike plants

EQUITANT   *adj* overlapping

EQUITES   *n/pl* a privileged military class of ancient Rome

EQUITY   *n* pl. -TIES fairness or impartiality

EQUIVOKE   *n* pl. -S a play on words

ER   *interj* — used to express hesitation

ERA   *n* pl. -S an epoch

ERADIATE   *v* -ATED, -ATING, -ATES to radiate

ERASE   *v* ERASED, ERASING, ERASES to rub or scrape out **ERASABLE** *adj*

ERASER   *n* pl. -S one that erases

ERASION   *n* pl. -S the act of erasing

ERASURE   *n* pl. -S erasion

ERBIUM   *n* pl. -S a metallic element

ERE   *prep* previous to; before

ERECT   *v* -ED, -ING, -S to build

ERECTER   *n* pl. -S erector

ERECTILE   *adj* capable of being raised upright

ERECTION   *n* pl. -S the act of erecting

ERECTIVE   *adj* tending to erect

ERECTLY   *adv* in an upright manner

ERECTOR   *n* pl. -S one that erects

ERELONG   *adv* soon

EREMITE   *n* pl. -S a hermit **EREMITIC** *adj*

EREMURUS   *n* pl. -URI a perennial herb

ERENOW   *adv* before this time

EREPSIN   *n* pl. -S a mixture of enzymes in the small intestine

ERETHISM   *n* pl. -S abnormal irritability **ERETHIC** *adj*

EREWHILE   *adv* some time ago

ERG   *n* pl. -S a unit of work or energy

ERGASTIC   *adj* constituting the nonliving by-products of protoplasmic activity

ERGATE   *n* pl. -S a worker ant

ERGO   *conj* therefore

ERGODIC   *adj* pertaining to the probability that any state will recur

ERGOT   *n* pl. -S a fungus **ERGOTIC** *adj*

ERGOTISM   *n* pl. -S poisoning produced by eating ergot-infected grain

ERICA   *n* pl. -S a shrub of the heath family

ERICOID   *adj* resembling heath

ERIGERON   *n* pl. -S an herb

ERINGO   *n* pl. -GOES or -GOS eryngo

ERISTIC   *n* pl. -S an expert in debate

ERLKING   *n* pl. -S an evil spirit of Germanic folklore

ERMINE   *n* pl. -S the fur of certain weasels **ERMINED** *adj*

ERN	*n* pl. -S erne	**ERVIL**	*n* pl. -S a European vetch
ERNE	*n* pl. -S a sea eagle	**ERYNGO**	*n* pl. -GOES or -GOS a medicinal herb
ERODE	*v* ERODED, ERODING, ERODES to wear away by constant friction	**ERYTHEMA**	*n* pl. -S a redness of the skin
ERODENT	*adj* erosive	**ERYTHRON**	*n* pl. -S a bodily organ consisting of the red blood cells
ERODIBLE	*adj* erosible	**ES**	*n* pl. ESES ess
ERODING	present participle of erode	**ESCALADE**	*v* -LADED, -LADING, -LADES to enter by means of ladders
EROGENIC	*adj* arousing sexual desire		
EROS	*n* pl. -ES sexual desire	**ESCALATE**	*v* -LATED, -LATING, -LATES to increase
EROSE	*adj* uneven **EROSELY** *adv*		
EROSIBLE	*adj* capable of being eroded	**ESCALLOP**	*v* -ED, -ING, -S to scallop
EROSION	*n* pl. -S the act of eroding	**ESCALOP**	*v* -ED, -ING, -S to escallop
EROSIVE	*adj* causing erosion	**ESCAPADE**	*n* pl. -S a reckless adventure
EROTIC	*n* pl. -S an amatory poem **EROTICAL** *adj*	**ESCAPE**	*v* -CAPED, -CAPING, -CAPES to get away
EROTICA	*n/pl* literature or art dealing with sexual love	**ESCAPEE**	*n* pl. -S one that has escaped
		ESCAPER	*n* pl. -S one that escapes
EROTISM	*n* pl. -S sexual excitement	**ESCAPING**	present participle of escape
ERR	*v* -ED, -ING, -S to make a mistake	**ESCAPISM**	*n* pl. -S the avoidance of reality by diversion of the mind
ERRANCY	*n* pl. -CIES an instance of erring	**ESCAPIST**	*n* pl. -S one given to escapism
ERRAND	*n* pl. -S a short trip made for a particular purpose	**ESCAR**	*n* pl. -S esker
		ESCARGOT	*n* pl. -S an edible snail
ERRANT	*n* pl. -S a wanderer	**ESCAROLE**	*n* pl. -S a variety of endive
ERRANTLY	*adv* in a wandering manner	**ESCARP**	*v* -ED, -ING, -S to cause to slope steeply
ERRANTRY	*n* pl. -RIES the state of wandering		
ERRATA	*n* pl. -S a list of printing errors	**ESCHALOT**	*n* pl. -S a shallot
ERRATIC	*n* pl. -S an eccentric person	**ESCHAR**	*n* pl. -S a hard, dry scab
ERRATUM	*n* pl. -TA a printing error	**ESCHEAT**	*v* -ED, -ING, -S to confiscate
ERRHINE	*n* pl. -S a substance that promotes nasal discharge	**ESCHEW**	*v* -ED, -ING, -S to avoid
		ESCHEWAL	*n* pl. -S the act of eschewing
ERRINGLY	*adv* in a mistaken manner	**ESCOLAR**	*n* pl. -S a food fish
ERROR	*n* pl. -S a mistake	**ESCORT**	*v* -ED, -ING, -S to accompany
ERS	*n* pl. -ES ervil	**ESCOT**	*v* -ED, -ING, -S to provide support for
ERSATZ	*n* pl. -ES a substitute		
ERST	*adv* formerly	**ESCROW**	*v* -ED, -ING, -S to place in the custody of a third party
ERUCT	*v* -ED, -ING, -S to belch	**ESCUAGE**	*n* pl. -S scutage
ERUCTATE	*v* -TATED, -TATING, -TATES to eruct	**ESCUDO**	*n* pl. -DOS a monetary unit of Portugal
ERUDITE	*adj* scholarly	**ESCULENT**	*n* pl. -S something that is edible
ERUGO	*n* pl. -GOS aerugo	**ESERINE**	*n* pl. -S a toxic alkaloid
ERUMPENT	*adj* bursting forth	**ESKAR**	*n* pl. -S esker
ERUPT	*v* -ED, -ING, -S to burst forth	**ESKER**	*n* pl. -S a narrow ridge of gravel and sand
ERUPTION	*n* pl. -S the act of erupting		
ERUPTIVE	*n* pl. -S a type of rock	**ESOPHAGI**	*n/pl* tubes connecting the mouth to the stomach

ESOTERIC   *adj* designed for a select few

ESPALIER   *v* -ED, -ING, -S to furnish with a trellis

ESPANOL   *n* pl. -ES a native of Spain

ESPARTO   *n* pl. -TOS a perennial grass

ESPECIAL   *adj* special

ESPIAL   *n* pl. -S the act of espying

ESPIED   past tense of espy

ESPIEGLE   *adj* playful

ESPIES   present 3d person sing. of espy

ESPOUSAL   *n* pl. -S a marriage ceremony

ESPOUSE   *v* -POUSED, -POUSING, -POUSES to marry

ESPOUSER   *n* pl. -S one that espouses

ESPRESSO   *n* pl. -SOS a strong coffee

ESPRIT   *n* pl. -S spirit

ESPY   *v* -PIED, -PYING, -PIES to catch sight of

ESQUIRE   *v* -QUIRED, -QUIRING, -QUIRES to escort

ESS   *n* pl. -ES the letter S

ESSAY   *v* -ED, -ING, -S to try

ESSAYER   *n* pl. -S one that essays

ESSAYIST   *n* pl. -S a writer of essays (prose compositions)

ESSENCE   *n* pl. -S a fundamental nature or quality

ESSOIN   *n* pl. -S an excuse

ESSONITE   *n* pl. -S a variety of garnet

ESTANCIA   *n* pl. -S a cattle ranch

ESTATE   *v* -TATED, -TATING, -TATES to provide with landed property

ESTEEM   *v* -ED, -ING, -S to have a high opinion of

ESTER   *n* pl. -S a type of chemical compound

ESTERASE   *n* pl. -S a type of enzyme

ESTERIFY   *v* -FIED, -FYING, -FIES to convert into an ester

ESTHESIA   *n* pl. -S the ability to receive sensation

ESTHESIS   *n* pl. -THESISES or -THESES esthesia

ESTHETE   *n* pl. -S an esthetic person

ESTHETIC   *adj* keenly appreciative of the beautiful

ESTIMATE   *v* -MATED, -MATING, -MATES to make an approximate judgment of

ESTIVAL   *adj* pertaining to summer

ESTIVATE   *v* -VATED, -VATING, -VATES to spend the summer

ESTOP   *v* -TOPPED, -TOPPING, -TOPS to impede by estoppel

ESTOPPEL   *n* pl. -S a legal restraint preventing a person from contradicting his own previous statement

ESTOVERS   *n/pl* necessities allowed by law

ESTRAGON   *n* pl. -S tarragon

ESTRAL   *adj* estrous

ESTRANGE   *v* -TRANGED, -TRANGING, -TRANGES to alienate

ESTRAY   *v* -ED, -ING, -S to stray

ESTREAT   *v* -ED, -ING, -S to copy from court records for use in prosecution

ESTRIN   *n* pl. -S estrone

ESTRIOL   *n* pl. -S an estrogen

ESTROGEN   *n* pl. -S any of a group of female hormones promoting or producing estrus

ESTRONE   *n* pl. -S an estrogen

ESTROUS   *adj* pertaining to estrus

ESTRUAL   *adj* estrous

ESTRUM   *n* pl. -S estrus

ESTRUS   *n* pl. -ES the period of heat in female mammals

ESTUARY   *n* pl. -ARIES an inlet of the sea at a river's lower end

ESURIENT   *adj* greedy

ET   a past tense of eat

ETA   *n* pl. -S a Greek letter

ETAGERE   *n* pl. -S an ornamental stand

ETAMIN   *n* pl. -S etamine

ETAMINE   *n* pl. -S a loosely woven fabric

ETAPE   *n* pl. -S a warehouse

ETATISM   *n* pl. -S state socialism
ETATIST *adj*

ETCETERA   *n* pl. -S a number of additional items

ETCH   *v* -ED, -ING, -ES to engrave with acid

ETCHER   *n* pl. -S one that etches

ETCHING   *n* pl. -S an etched design

ETERNAL   *n* pl. -S something lasting forever

ETERNE   *adj* everlasting

ETERNISE   *v* -NISED, -NISING, -NISES to eternize

ETERNITY   *n* pl. -TIES infinite time

ETERNIZE   *v* -NIZED, -NIZING, -NIZES to make everlasting

ETESIAN   *n* pl. -S an annually recurring wind

ETH   *n* pl. -S edh

ETHANE   *n* pl. -S a gaseous hydrocarbon

ETHANOL   *n* pl. -S an alcohol

ETHENE   *n* pl. -S ethylene

ETHER   *n* pl. -S a volatile liquid used as an anesthetic **ETHERIC** *adj*

ETHEREAL   *adj* airy

ETHERIFY   *v* -FIED, -FYING, -FIES to convert into ether

ETHERISH   *adj* resembling ether

ETHERIZE   *v* -IZED, -IZING, -IZES to treat with ether

ETHIC   *n* pl. -S a body of moral principles

ETHICAL   *n* pl. -S a drug sold by prescription only

ETHICIAN   *n* pl. -S an ethicist

ETHICIST   *n* pl. -S a specialist in ethics

ETHICIZE   *v* -CIZED, -CIZING, -CIZES to make ethical

ETHINYL   *n* pl. -S ethynyl

ETHION   *n* pl. -S a pesticide

ETHMOID   *n* pl. -S a bone of the nasal cavity

ETHNARCH   *n* pl. -S the ruler of a people or province

ETHNIC   *n* pl. -S a member of a particular ethnos **ETHNICAL** *adj*

ETHNOS   *n* pl. -ES a group of people who share a common and distinctive culture

ETHOLOGY   *n* pl. -GIES the study of animal behavior

ETHOS   *n* pl. -ES the fundamental character of a culture

ETHOXY   *adj* pertaining to ethoxyl

ETHOXYL   *n* pl. -S a univalent chemical radical

ETHYL   *n* pl. -S a univalent chemical radical

ETHYLATE   *v* -ATED, -ATING, -ATES to introduce the ethyl group into

ETHYLENE   *n* pl. -S a flammable gas

ETHYLIC   *adj* pertaining to ethyl

ETHYNE   *n* pl. -S a flammable gas

ETHYNYL   *n* pl. -S a univalent chemical radical

ETIOLATE   *v* -LATED, -LATING, -LATES to whiten

ETIOLOGY   *n* pl. -GIES the study of the causes of diseases

ETNA   *n* pl. -S a container for heating liquids

ETOILE   *n* pl. -S a star

ETUDE   *n* pl. -S a piece of music for the practice of a point of technique

ETUI   *n* pl. -S a case for holding small articles

ETWEE   *n* pl. -S etui

ETYMON   *n* pl. -MA or -MONS the earliest known form of a word

EUCAINE   *n* pl. -S an anesthetic

EUCALYPT   *n* pl. -S an evergreen tree

EUCHARIS   *n* pl. -RISES a flowering plant

EUCHRE   *v* -CHRED, -CHRING, -CHRES to prevent from winning three tricks in euchre (a card game)

EUCLASE   *n* pl. -S a mineral

EUCRITE   *n* pl. -S a type of meteorite **EUCRITIC** *adj*

EUDAEMON   *n* pl. -S eudemon

EUDEMON   *n* pl. -S a good spirit

EUGENICS   *n/pl* the science of hereditary improvement **EUGENIC** *adj*

EUGENIST   *n* pl. -S a student of eugenics

EUGENOL   *n* pl. -S an aromatic liquid

EUGLENA   *n* pl. -S a freshwater protozoan

EULACHAN   *n* pl. -S eulachon

EULACHON   *n* pl. -S a marine food fish

EULOGIA   *n* pl. -GIAE holy bread

EULOGIA   *n* pl. -S a blessing

EULOGISE   *v* -GISED, -GISING, -GISES to eulogize

EULOGIST   *n* pl. -S one that eulogizes

EULOGIUM   *n* pl. -GIA or -GIUMS a eulogy

EULOGIZE   *v* -GIZED, -GIZING, -GIZES to praise highly

EULOGY   *n* pl. -GIES a formal expression of high praise

EUNUCH   *n* pl. -S a castrated man

EUONYMUS   *n* pl. -ES any of a genus of shrubs or small trees

EUPATRID   *n* pl. -RIDS or -RIDAE an aristocrat of ancient Athens

EUPEPSIA   *n* pl. -S good digestion **EUPEPTIC** *adj*

EUPEPSY   *n* pl. -SIES eupepsia

EUPHENIC   *adj* dealing with biological improvement

EUPHONY   *n* pl. -NIES pleasant sound **EUPHONIC** *adj*

EUPHORIA   *n* pl. -S a feeling of well-being **EUPHORIC** *adj*

EUPHOTIC   *adj* pertaining to the upper layer of a body of water

EUPHRASY   *n* pl. -SIES an annual herb

EUPHROE   *n* pl. -S a device used to adjust a shipboard awning

EUPHUISM   *n* pl. -S an artificially elegant style of speech or writing

EUPHUIST   *n* pl. -S one given to euphuism

EUPLOID   *n* pl. -S a cell having three or more identical genomes

EUPLOIDY   *n* pl. -DIES the state of being a euploid

EUPNEA   *n* pl. -S normal breathing **EUPNEIC** *adj*

EUPNOEA   *n* pl. -S eupnea **EUPNOEIC** *adj*

EUREKA   *interj* — used to express triumph upon discovering something

EURIPUS   *n* pl. -PI a swift sea channel

EURO   *n* pl. EUROS a large kangaroo

EUROPIUM   *n* pl. -S a metallic element

EURYTHMY   *n* pl. -MIES harmony of movement or structure

EUSTACY   *n* pl. -CIES a worldwide change in sea level **EUSTATIC** *adj*

EUSTELE   *n* pl. -S a plant part

EUTAXY   *n* pl. -TAXIES good order

EUTECTIC   *n* pl. -S an alloy that has the lowest possible melting point

EUTROPHY   *n* pl. -PHIES healthful nutrition

EUXENITE   *n* pl. -S a mineral

EVACUANT   *n* pl. -S a cathartic medicine

EVACUATE   *v* -ATED, -ATING, -ATES to remove from a dangerous area

EVACUEE   *n* pl. -S one that is evacuated

EVADE   *v* EVADED, EVADING, EVADES to escape or avoid by cleverness or deceit **EVADABLE, EVADIBLE** *adj*

EVADER   *n* pl. -S one that evades

EVALUATE   *v* -ATED, -ATING, -ATES to determine the value of

EVANESCE   *v* -NESCED, -NESCING, -NESCES to fade away

EVANGEL   *n* pl. -S a preacher of the gospel

EVANISH   *v* -ED, -ING, -ES to vanish

EVASION   *n* pl. -S the act of evading

EVASIVE   *adj* tending to evade

EVE   *n* pl. -S evening

EVECTION   *n* pl. -S irregularity in the moon's motion

EVEN   *adj* EVENER, EVENEST flat and smooth

EVEN   *v* -ED, -ING, -S to make even

EVENER   *n* pl. -S one that evens

EVENFALL   *n* pl. -S twilight

EVENING   *n* pl. -S the latter part of the day and early part of the night

EVENLY   *adv* in an even manner

EVENNESS   *n* pl. -ES the state of being even

EVENSONG   *n* pl. -S an evening prayer service

EVENT   *n* pl. -S something that occurs

EVENTFUL   *adj* momentous

EVENTIDE   *n* pl. -S evening

EVENTUAL   *adj* occurring at a later time

EVER   *adv* at all times

EVERMORE   *adv* forever

EVERSION   *n* pl -S the act of everting

EVERT   *v* -ED, -ING, -S to turn outward or inside out

EVERTOR   *n* pl. -S a muscle that turns a part outward

EVERY   *adj* each without exception

EVERYDAY   *adj* ordinary

EVERYMAN   *n* pl. -MEN the typical or ordinary man

EVERYONE   *pron* every person

EVERYWAY   *adv* in every way

EVICT   *v* -ED, -ING, -S to expel by legal process

EVICTEE   *n* pl. -S one that is evicted

EVICTION	*n* pl. -S the act of evicting
EVICTOR	*n* pl. -S one that evicts
EVIDENCE	*v* -DENCED, -DENCING, -DENCES to indicate clearly
EVIDENT	*adj* clear to the vision or understanding
EVIL	*adj* EVILER, EVILEST or EVILLER, EVILLEST morally bad
EVIL	*n* pl. -S something that is evil
EVILDOER	*n* pl. -S one that does evil
EVILLER	a comparative of evil
EVILLEST	a superlative of evil
EVILLY	*adv* in an evil manner
EVILNESS	*n* pl. -ES the quality of being evil
EVINCE	*v* EVINCED, EVINCING, EVINCES to show clearly **EVINCIVE** *adj*
EVITE	*v* EVITED, EVITING, EVITES to avoid **EVITABLE** *adj*
EVOCABLE	*adj* capable of being evoked
EVOCATOR	*n* pl. -S one that evokes
EVOKE	*v* EVOKED, EVOKING, EVOKES to call forth
EVOKER	*n* pl. -S an evocator
EVOLUTE	*n* pl. -S a type of geometric curve
EVOLVE	*v* EVOLVED, EVOLVING, EVOLVES to develop
EVOLVER	*n* pl. -S one that evolves
EVONYMUS	*n* pl. -ES euonymus
EVULSION	*n* pl. -S the act of pulling out
EVZONE	*n* pl. -S a Greek soldier
EWE	*n* pl. -S a female sheep
EWER	*n* pl. -S a large pitcher
EX	*n* pl. -ES the letter X
EXACT	*adj* -ACTER, -ACTEST precise
EXACT	*v* -ED, -ING, -S to force the payment or yielding of
EXACTA	*n* pl. -S a type of horse racing bet
EXACTER	*n* pl. -S one that exacts
EXACTION	*n* pl. -S the act of exacting
EXACTLY	*adv* in an exact manner
EXACTOR	*n* pl. -S exacter
EXALT	*v* -ED, -ING, -S to raise
EXALTER	*n* pl. -S one that exalts
EXAM	*n* pl. -S an examination
EXAMEN	*n* pl. -S a critical study
EXAMINE	*v* -INED, -INING, -INES to inspect
EXAMINEE	*n* pl. -S one that is taking an examination
EXAMINER	*n* pl. -S one that examines
EXAMINING	present participle of examine
EXAMPLE	*v* -PLED, -PLING, -PLES to show by representation
EXANTHEM	*n* pl. -S a skin eruption
EXARCH	*n* pl. -S the ruler of a province in the Byzantine Empire **EXARCHAL** *adj*
EXARCHY	*n* pl. -CHIES the domain of an exarch
EXCAVATE	*v* -VATED, -VATING, -VATES to dig out
EXCEED	*v* -ED, -ING, -S to go beyond
EXCEEDER	*n* pl. -S one that exceeds
EXCEL	*v* -CELLED, -CELLING, -CELS to surpass others
EXCEPT	*v* -ED, -ING, -S to leave out
EXCERPT	*v* -ED, -ING, -S to pick out a passage from for quoting
EXCESS	*n* pl. -ES an overabundance
EXCHANGE	*v* -CHANGED, -CHANGING, -CHANGES to give and receive reciprocally
EXCIDE	*v* -CIDED, -CIDING, -CIDES to excise
EXCIPLE	*n* pl. -S a rim around the hymenium of various lichens
EXCISE	*v* -CISED, -CISING, -CISES to remove by cutting out
EXCISION	*n* pl. -S the act of excising
EXCITANT	*n* pl. -S a stimulant
EXCITE	*v* -CITED, -CITING, -CITES to arouse the emotions of
EXCITER	*n* pl. -S one that excites
EXCITON	*n* pl. -S an energy level of a crystal
EXCITOR	*n* pl. -S exciter
EXCLAIM	*v* -ED, -ING, -S to cry out suddenly
EXCLAVE	*n* pl. -S a portion of a country which is isolated in foreign territory
EXCLUDE	*v* -CLUDED, -CLUDING, -CLUDES to shut out
EXCLUDER	*n* pl. -S one that excludes
EXCRETA	*n/pl* excreted matter **EXCRETAL** *adj*

EXCRETE v -CRETED, -CRETING, -CRETES to separate and eliminate from an organic body

EXCRETER n pl. -S one that excretes

EXCUSE v -CUSED, -CUSING, -CUSES to apologize for

EXCUSER n pl. -S one that excuses

EXEC n pl. -S an executive officer

EXECRATE v -CRATED, -CRATING, -CRATES to curse

EXECUTE v -CUTED, -CUTING, -CUTES to carry out

EXECUTER n pl. -S executor

EXECUTOR n pl. -S one that executes

EXEDRA n pl. -DRAE a curved outdoor bench

EXEGESIS n pl. -GESES critical explanation or analysis **EXEGETIC** adj

EXEGETE n pl. -S one skilled in exegesis

EXEMPLAR n pl. -S one that is worthy of being copied

EXEMPLUM n pl. -PLA an example

EXEMPT v -ED, -ING, -S to free from an obligation required of others

EXEQUY n pl. -QUIES a funeral procession **EXEQUIAL** adj

EXERCISE v -CISED, -CISING, -CISES to make use of

EXERGUE n pl. -S a space on a coin **EXERGUAL** adj

EXERT v -ED, -ING, -S to put into action

EXERTION n pl. -S the act of exerting

EXERTIVE adj tending to exert

EXHALANT n pl. -S something that exhales

EXHALE v -HALED, -HALING, -HALES to expel air or vapor

EXHALENT n pl. -S exhalant

EXHAUST v -ED, -ING, -S to use up

EXHIBIT v -ED, -ING, -S to present for public viewing

EXHORT v -ED, -ING, -S to advise urgently

EXHORTER n pl. -S one that exhorts

EXHUME v -HUMED, -HUMING, -HUMES to dig out of the earth

EXHUMER n pl. -S one that exhumes

EXIGENCE n pl. -S exigency

EXIGENCY n pl. -CIES urgency

EXIGENT adj urgent

EXIGIBLE adj liable to be demanded

EXIGUITY n pl. -ITIES the state of being exiguous

EXIGUOUS adj meager

EXILE v -ILED, -ILING, -ILES to banish from one's own country

EXILIAN adj exilic

EXILIC adj pertaining to exile (banishment from one's own country)

EXIMIOUS adj excellent

EXINE n pl. -S the outer layer of certain spores

EXIST v -ED, -ING, -S to be

EXISTENT n pl. -S something that exists

EXIT v -ED, -ING, -S to go out

EXOCARP n pl. -S the epicarp

EXOCRINE n pl. -S an external secretion

EXODERM n pl. -S the ectoderm

EXODOS n pl. -DOI a concluding dramatic scene

EXODUS n pl. -ES a movement away

EXOERGIC adj releasing energy

EXOGAMY n pl. -MIES marriage outside of a particular group **EXOGAMIC** adj

EXOGEN n pl. -S a type of plant

EXORABLE adj persuadable

EXORCISE v -CISED, -CISING, -CISES to free of an evil spirit

EXORCISM n pl. -S the act of exorcising

EXORCIST n pl. -S one who practices exorcism

EXORCIZE v -CIZED, -CIZING, -CIZES to exorcise

EXORDIUM n pl. -DIUMS or -DIA a beginning **EXORDIAL** adj

EXOSMOSE n pl. -S a form of osmosis **EXOSMIC** adj

EXOSPORE n pl. -S the outer coat of a spore

EXOTERIC adj suitable for the public

EXOTIC n pl. -S something from another part of the world

EXOTICA n/pl things excitingly different or unusual

EXOTISM n pl. -S an exotic

EXOTOXIN n pl. -S an excreted toxin **EXOTOXIC** adj

EXPAND   *v* -ED, -ING, -S to increase in size or volume

EXPANDER   *n* pl. -S one that expands

EXPANSE   *n* pl. -S a wide, continuous area

EXPECT   *v* -ED, -ING, -S to anticipate

EXPEDITE   *v* -DITED, -DITING, -DITES to speed up the progress of

EXPEL   *v* -PELLED, -PELLING, -PELS to force out

EXPELLEE   *n* pl. -S a deportee

EXPELLER   *n* pl. -S one that expels

EXPELLING   present participle of expel

EXPEND   *v* -ED, -ING, -S to use up

EXPENDER   *n* pl. -S one that expends

EXPENSE   *v* -PENSED, -PENSING, -PENSES to charge with costs

EXPERT   *v* -ED, -ING, -S to serve as an authority

EXPERTLY   *adv* skillfully

EXPIABLE   *adj* capable of being expiated

EXPIATE   *v* -ATED, ATING, -ATES to atone for

EXPIATOR   *n* pl. -S one that expiates

EXPIRE   *v* -PIRED, -PIRING, -PIRES to come to an end

EXPIRER   *n* pl. -S one that expires

EXPIRY   *n* pl. -RIES a termination

EXPLAIN   *v* -ED, -ING, -S to make plain or understandable

EXPLANT   *v* -ED, -ING, -S to remove from the natural site of growth and place in a medium

EXPLICIT   *n* pl. -S a statement formerly used at the close of a book

EXPLODE   *v* -PLODED, -PLODING, -PLODES to blow up

EXPLODER   *n* pl. -S one that explodes

EXPLOIT   *v* -ED, -ING, -S to take advantage of

EXPLORE   *v* -PLORED, -PLORING, -PLORES to travel through for the purpose of discovery

EXPLORER   *n* pl. -S one that explores

EXPO   *n* pl. -POS a public exhibition

EXPONENT   *n* pl. -S one who expounds

EXPORT   *v* -ED, -ING, -S to send to other countries for commercial purposes

EXPORTER   *n* pl. -S one that exports

EXPOSAL   *n* pl. -S an exposure

EXPOSE   *v* -POSED, -POSING, -POSES to lay open to view

EXPOSER   *n* pl. -S one that exposes

EXPOSIT   *v* -ED, -ING, -S to expound

EXPOSURE   *n* pl. -S the act of exposing

EXPOUND   *v* -ED, -ING, -S to explain in detail

EXPRESS   *v* -ED, -ING, -ES to set forth in words

EXPULSE   *v* -PULSED, -PULSING, -PULSES to expel

EXPUNGE   *v* -PUNGED, PUNGING, -PUNGES to delete

EXPUNGER   *n* pl. -S one that expunges

EXSCIND   *v* -ED, -ING, -S to cut out

EXSECANT   *n* pl. -S a trigonometric function of an angle

EXSECT   *v* -ED, -ING, -S to cut out

EXSERT   *v* -ED, -ING, -S to thrust out

EXTANT   *adj* still in existence

EXTEND   *v* -ED, -ING, -S to stretch out to full length

EXTENDER   *n* pl. -S a substance added to another substance

EXTENSOR   *n* pl. -S a muscle that extends a limb

EXTENT   *n* pl. -S the range over which something extends

EXTERIOR   *n* pl. -S a part or surface that is outside

EXTERN   *n* pl. -S a nonresident of an institution

EXTERNAL   *n* pl. -S an exterior

EXTERNE   *n* pl. -S extern

EXTINCT   *v* -ED, -ING, -S to extinguish

EXTOL   *v* -TOLLED, -TOLLING, -TOLS to praise highly

EXTOLL   *v* -ED, -ING, -S to extol

EXTOLLER   *n* pl. -S one that extols

EXTOLLING   present participle of extol

EXTORT   *v* -ED, -ING, -S to obtain from a person by violence or intimidation

EXTORTER   *n* pl. -S one that extorts

EXTRA   *n* pl. -S something additional

EXTRACT   *v* -ED, -ING, -S to pull or draw out

EXTRADOS   *n* pl. -ES the outer curve of an arch

EXTREMA   pl. of extremum

EXTREME	*adj* -TREMER, -TREMEST existing in a very high degree
EXTREME	*n* pl. -S the highest degree
EXTREMUM	*n* pl. -MA a maximum or a minimum of a mathematical function
EXTRORSE	*adj* facing outward
EXTRUDE	*v* -TRUDED, -TRUDING, -TRUDES to force, thrust, or push out
EXTRUDER	*n* pl. -S one that extrudes
EXUDATE	*n* pl. -S an exuded substance
EXUDE	*v* -UDED, -UDING, -UDES to ooze forth
EXULT	*v* -ED, -ING, -S to rejoice greatly
EXULTANT	*adj* exulting
EXURB	*n* pl. -S a residential area lying beyond the suburbs of a city **EXURBAN** *adj*
EXURBIA	*n* pl. -S an exurb
EXUVIATE	*v* -ATED, -ATING, -ATES to molt
EXUVIUM	*n* pl. -VIAE or -VIA the molted covering of an animal **EXUVIAL** *adj*
EYAS	*n* pl. -ES a young hawk
EYE	*v* EYED, EYING or EYEING, EYES to watch closely **EYEABLE** *adj*
EYE	*n* pl. EYES, EYEN or EYNE the organ of sight
EYEBALL	*v* -ED, -ING, -S to eye
EYEBEAM	*n* pl. -S a glance
EYEBOLT	*n* pl. -S a type of bolt or screw
EYEBROW	*n* pl. -S the ridge over the eye
EYECUP	*n* pl. -S a cup used for applying lotions to the eyes
EYED	past tense of eye
EYEDNESS	*n* pl. -ES preference for the use of one eye over the other
EYEFUL	*n* pl. -S a complete view
EYEGLASS	*n* pl. -ES a lens used to aid vision
EYEHOLE	*n* pl. -S a small opening
EYEHOOK	*n* pl. -S a type of hook
EYELASH	*n* pl. -ES a hair growing on the edge of an eyelid
EYELESS	*adj* lacking eyes
EYELET	*v* -LETTED, -LETTING, -LETS to make a small hole in
EYELID	*n* pl. -S the lid of skin that can be closed over an eyeball
EYELIKE	*adj* resembling an eye
EYELINER	*n* pl. -S makeup for the eyes
EYEN	a pl. of eye
EYEPIECE	*n* pl. -S the lens or lens group nearest the eye in an optical instrument
EYEPOINT	*n* pl. -S the point at which an eye is placed in using an optical instrument
EYER	*n* pl. -S one that eyes
EYESHADE	*n* pl. -S a visor for shading the eyes
EYESHOT	*n* pl. -S the range of vision
EYESIGHT	*n* pl. -S the ability to see
EYESOME	*adj* pleasant to look at
EYESORE	*n* pl. -S something offensive to the sight
EYESPOT	*n* pl. -S a simple visual organ of lower animals
EYESTALK	*n* pl. -S a stalklike structure with an eye at its tip
EYESTONE	*n* pl. -S a disk used to remove foreign matter from the eye
EYETOOTH	*n* pl. -TEETH a cuspid
EYEWASH	*n* pl. -ES an eye lotion
EYEWATER	*n* pl. -S an eyewash
EYEWINK	*n* pl. -S a wink of the eye
EYING	a present participle of eye
EYNE	a pl. of eye
EYRA	*n* pl. -S a wild cat of tropical America
EYRE	*n* pl. -S a journey
EYRIE	*n* pl. -S aerie
EYRIR	*n* pl. AURAR a monetary unit of Iceland
EYRY	*n* pl. -RIES aerie

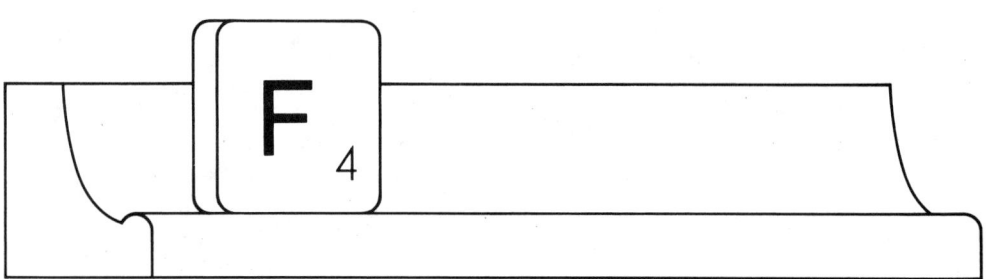

FA	*n* pl. -S the fourth tone of the diatonic musical scale	**FACIES**	*n* pl. FACIES general appearance
FABLE	*v* -BLED, -BLING, -BLES to compose or tell fictitious tales	**FACILE**	*adj* easily achieved or performed **FACILELY** *adv*
FABLER	*n* pl. -S one that fables	**FACILITY**	*n* pl. -TIES the quality of being facile
FABLIAU	*n* pl. -AUX a short metrical tale popular in medieval France	**FACING**	*n* pl. -S a lining at the edge of a garment
FABLING	present participle of fable		
FABRIC	*n* pl. -S a woven, felted, or knitted material	**FACT**	*n* pl. -S something known with certainty **FACTFUL** *adj*
FABULAR	*adj* legendary	**FACTION**	*n* pl. -S a clique within a larger group
FABULIST	*n* pl. -S a liar		
FABULOUS	*adj* almost unbelievable	**FACTIOUS**	*adj* promoting dissension
FACADE	*n* pl. -S the front of a building	**FACTOR**	*v* -ED, -ING, -S to express as a product of two or more quantities
FACE	*v* FACED, FACING, FACES to oppose or meet defiantly **FACEABLE** *adj*		
		FACTORY	*n* pl. -RIES a building or group of buildings in which goods are manufactured
FACEDOWN	*adv* with the front part down		
FACELESS	*adj* lacking personal distinction or identity	**FACTOTUM**	*n* pl. -S a person employed to do many kinds of work
FACER	*n* pl. -S one that faces	**FACTUAL**	*adj* pertaining to facts
FACET	*v* -ETED, -ETING, -ETS or -ETTED, -ETTING, -ETS to cut small plane surfaces on	**FACTURE**	*n* pl. -S the act of making something
		FACULA	*n* pl. -LAE an unusually bright spot on the sun's surface **FACULAR** *adj*
FACETE	*adj* witty **FACETELY** *adv*		
FACETIAE	*n/pl* witty sayings or writings		
FACETTED	past tense of facet	**FACULTY**	*n* pl. -TIES an inherent power or ability
FACETTING	present participle of facet		
FACEUP	*adv* with the front part up	**FAD**	*n* pl. -S a practice or interest that enjoys brief popularity
FACIA	*n* pl. -S fascia		
FACIAL	*n* pl. -S a treatment for the face	**FADABLE**	*adj* capable of fading
FACIALLY	*adv* with respect to the face	**FADDIER**	comparative of faddy
		FADDIEST	superlative of faddy
FACIEND	*n* pl. -S a number to be multiplied by another	**FADDISH**	*adj* inclined to take up fads

FADDISM	*n* pl. -S inclination to take up fads
FADDIST	*n* pl. -S a faddish person
FADDY	*adj* -DIER, -DIEST faddish
FADE	*v* FADED, FADING, FADES to lose color or brightness **FADEDLY** *adv*
FADEAWAY	*n* pl. -AWAYS a type of pitch in baseball
FADELESS	*adj* not fading
FADER	*n* pl. -S one that fades
FADGE	*v* FADGED, FADGING, FADGES to succeed
FADING	*n* pl. -S an Irish dance
FADO	*n* pl. -DOS a Portuguese folk song
FAECES	*n/pl* feces **FAECAL** *adj*
FAENA	*n* pl. -S a series of passes made by a matador in a bullfight
FAERIE	*n* pl. -S a fairy
FAERY	*n* pl. -ERIES faerie
FAG	*v* FAGGED, FAGGING, FAGS to make weary by hard work
FAGGOT	*v* -ED, -ING, -S to fagot
FAGIN	*n* pl. -S a person who instructs others in crime
FAGOT	*v* -ED, -ING, -S to bind together into a bundle
FAGOTER	*n* pl. -S one that fagots
FAGOTING	*n* pl. -S a type of embroidery
FAHLBAND	*n* pl. -S a band or stratum of rock impregnated with metallic sulfides
FAIENCE	*n* pl. -S a variety of glazed pottery
FAIL	*v* -ED, -ING, -S to be unsuccessful in an attempt
FAILING	*n* pl. -S a minor fault or weakness
FAILLE	*n* pl. -S a woven fabric
FAILURE	*n* pl. -S the act of failing
FAIN	*adj* FAINER, FAINEST glad
FAINEANT	*n* pl. -S a lazy person
FAINT	*v* -ED, -ING, -S to lose consciousness
FAINT	*adj* FAINTER, FAINTEST lacking strength or vigor
FAINTER	*n* pl. -S one that faints
FAINTISH	*adj* somewhat faint
FAINTLY	*adv* in a faint manner
FAIR	*adj* FAIRER, FAIREST free from bias, dishonesty, or injustice
FAIR	*v* -ED, -ING, -S to make smooth
FAIRIES	pl. of fairy
FAIRING	*n* pl. -S a structure on an aircraft serving to reduce drag
FAIRISH	*adj* moderately good
FAIRLEAD	*n* pl. -S a device used to hold a ship's rigging in place
FAIRLY	*adv* in a fair manner
FAIRNESS	*n* pl. -ES the quality of being fair
FAIRWAY	*n* pl. -WAYS the mowed part of a golf course between tee and green
FAIRY	*n* pl. FAIRIES an imaginary supernatural being
FAIRYISM	*n* pl. -S the quality of being like a fairy
FAITH	*v* -ED, -ING, -S to believe or trust
FAITHFUL	*n* pl. -S a loyal follower or member
FAITOUR	*n* pl. -S an impostor
FAKE	*v* FAKED, FAKING, FAKES to contrive and present as genuine
FAKEER	*n* pl. -S fakir
FAKER	*n* pl. -S one that fakes
FAKERY	*n* pl. -ERIES the practice of faking
FAKING	present participle of fake
FAKIR	*n* pl. -S a Hindu ascetic
FALBALA	*n* pl. -S a trimming for a woman's garment
FALCATE	*adj* curved and tapering to a point
FALCATED	*adj* falcate
FALCHION	*n* pl. -S a broad-bladed sword
FALCON	*n* pl. -S a bird of prey
FALCONER	*n* pl. -S one that hunts with hawks
FALCONET	*n* pl. -S a small falcon
FALCONRY	*n* pl. -RIES the sport of hunting with falcons
FALDERAL	*n* pl. -S nonsense
FALDEROL	*n* pl. -S falderal
FALL	*v* FELL, FALLEN, FALLING, FALLS to descend under the force of gravity
FALLACY	*n* pl. -CIES a false idea

FALLAL   *n* pl. -S a showy article of dress

FALLBACK   *n* pl. -S an act of retreating

FALLEN   past participle of fall

FALLER   *n* pl. -S one that falls

FALLFISH   *n* pl. -ES a freshwater fish

FALLIBLE   *adj* capable of erring **FALLIBLY** *adv*

FALLOFF   *n* pl. -S a decline in quantity or quality

FALLOUT   *n* pl. -S radioactive debris resulting from a nuclear explosion

FALLOW   *v* -ED, -ING, -S to plow and leave unseeded

FALSE   *adj* FALSER, FALSEST contrary to truth or fact **FALSELY** *adv*

FALSETTO   *n* pl. -TOS an artificially high voice

FALSIE   *n* pl. -S a pad worn within a brassiere

FALSIFY   *v* -FIED, -FYING, -FIES to represent falsely

FALSITY   *n* pl. -TIES something false

FALTBOAT   *n* pl. -S a collapsible boat resembling a kayak

FALTER   *v* -ED, -ING, -S to hesitate

FALTERER   *n* pl. -S one that falters

FAME   *v* FAMED, FAMING, FAMES to make famous

FAMELESS   *adj* not famous

FAMILIAL   *adj* pertaining to a family

FAMILIAR   *n* pl. -S a close friend or associate

FAMILY   *n* pl. -LIES a group of persons related by blood or marriage

FAMINE   *n* pl. -S a widespread scarcity of food

FAMING   present participle of fame

FAMISH   *v* -ED, -ING, -ES to suffer extreme hunger

FAMOUS   *adj* well-known **FAMOUSLY** *adv*

FAMULUS   *n* pl. -LI a servant or attendant

FAN   *v* FANNED, FANNING, FANS to cool or refresh with a fan (a device for putting air into motion)

FANATIC   *n* pl. -S a zealot

FANCIED   past tense of fancy

FANCIER   *n* pl. -S one that has a special liking for something

FANCIES   present 3d person sing. of fancy

FANCIFUL   *adj* unrealistic

FANCY   *adj* -CIER, -CIEST ornamental **FANCILY** *adv*

FANCY   *v* -CIED, -CYING, -CIES to take a liking to

FANDANGO   *n* pl. -GOS a lively Spanish dance

FANDOM   *n* pl. -S an aggregate of enthusiastic devotees

FANE   *n* pl. -S a temple

FANEGA   *n* pl. -S a Spanish unit of dry measure

FANEGADA   *n* pl. -S a Spanish unit of area

FANFARE   *n* pl. -S a short, lively musical flourish

FANFARON   *n* pl. -S a braggart

FANFOLD   *n* pl. -S a type of writing pad or tablet

FANG   *n* pl. -S a long, pointed tooth **FANGED, FANGLESS, FANGLIKE** *adj*

FANGA   *n* pl. -S fanega

FANION   *n* pl. -S a small flag

FANJET   *n* pl. -S a type of jet engine

FANLIGHT   *n* pl. -S a type of window

FANLIKE   *adj* resembling a fan

FANNED   past tase of fan

FANNER   *n* pl. -S one that fans

FANNING   present participle of fan

FANNY   *n* pl. -NIES the buttocks

FANO   *n* pl. FANOS a fanon

FANON   *n* pl. -S a cape worn by the pope

FANTAIL   *n* pl. -S a fan-shaped tail or end

FANTASIA   *n* pl. -S a free-form musical composition

FANTASIE   *n* pl. -S a fantasia

FANTASIED   past tense of fantasy

FANTASIES   present 3d person sing. of fantasy

FANTASM   *n* pl. -S phantasm

FANTAST   *n* pl. -S an impractical person

FANTASY   *v* -SIED, -SYING, -SIES to imagine

FANTOD   *n* pl. -S an emotional outburst

FANTOM   *n* pl. -S phantom

FANUM   *n* pl. -S fanon

FANWISE	*adj* spread out like an open fan	**FARM**	*v* -ED, -ING, -S to manage and cultivate as a farm (a tract of land devoted to agriculture) **FARMABLE** *adj*
FANWORT	*n* pl. -S an aquatic plant		
FAQIR	*n* pl. -S fakir		
FAQUIR	*n* pl. -S fakir	**FARMER**	*n* pl. -S one that farms
FAR	*adv* FARTHER, FARTHEST or FURTHER, FURTHEST at or to a great distance	**FARMHAND**	*n* pl. -S a farm laborer
		FARMING	*n* pl. -S the business of operating a farm
FARAD	*n* pl. -S a unit of electrical capacitance	**FARMLAND**	*n* pl. -S cultivated land
		FARMYARD	*n* pl. -S an area surrounded by farm buildings
FARADAIC	*adj* faradic		
FARADAY	*n* pl. -DAYS a unit of electricity	**FARNESOL**	*n* pl. -S an alcohol used in perfumes
FARADIC	*adj* pertaining to a type of electric current	**FARNESS**	*n* pl. -ES the state of being far off or apart
FARADISE	*v* -DISED, -DISING, -DISES to faradize	**FARO**	*n* pl. FAROS a card game
		FAROUCHE	*adj* sullenly shy
FARADISM	*n* pl. -S the use of faradic current for therapeutic purposes	**FARRAGO**	*n* pl. -GOES a confused mixture
		FARRIER	*n* pl. -S one that shoes horses
FARADIZE	*v* -DIZED, -DIZING, -DIZES to treat by faradism	**FARRIERY**	*n* pl. -ERIES the trade of a farrier
FARAWAY	*adj* distant	**FARROW**	*v* -ED, -ING, -S to give birth to a litter of pigs
FARCE	*v* FARCED, FARCING, FARCES to fill out with witty material		
		FART	*v* -ED, -ING, -S to expel gas through the anus — usually considered vulgar
FARCER	*n* pl. -S farceur		
FARCEUR	*n* pl. -S a joker		
FARCI	*adj* stuffed with finely chopped meat	**FARTHER**	a comparative of far
		FARTHEST	a superlative of far
FARCICAL	*adj* absurd	**FARTHING**	*n* pl. -S a former British coin
FARCIE	*adj* farci	**FASCES**	*n* pl. FASCES an ancient Roman symbol of power
FARCING	present participle of farce		
FARCY	*n* pl. -CIES a disease of horses	**FASCIA**	*n* pl. -CIAE or -CIAS a broad and distinct band of color **FASCIAL, FASCIATE** *adj*
FARD	*v* -ED, -ING, -S to apply cosmetics to		
FARDEL	*n* pl. -S a bundle	**FASCICLE**	*n* pl. -S a small bundle
FARE	*v* FARED, FARING, FARES to get along	**FASCINE**	*n* pl. -S a bundle of sticks used in building fortifications
FARER	*n* pl. -S a traveler	**FASCISM**	*n* pl. -S an oppressive political system
FAREWELL	*v* -ED, -ING, -S to say goodby		
FARFAL	*n* pl. FARFAL farfel	**FASCIST**	*n* pl. -S an advocate of fascism
FARFEL	*n* pl. -S noodles in the form of small pellets or granules	**FASH**	*v* -ED, -ING, -ES to annoy
		FASHION	*v* -ED, -ING, -S to give a particular shape or form to
FARINA	*n* pl. -S a fine meal made from cereal grain		
		FASHIOUS	*adj* annoying
FARING	present participle of fare	**FAST**	*adj* FASTER, FASTEST moving or able to move quickly
FARINHA	*n* pl. -S a meal made from the root of the cassava		
		FAST	*v* -ED, -ING, -S to abstain from eating
FARINOSE	*adj* resembling farina		
FARL	*n* pl. -S a thin oatmeal cake	**FASTBACK**	*n* pl. -S a type of automobile roof
FARLE	*n* pl. -S farl		

FASTBALL   *n* pl. -S a type of pitch in baseball

FASTEN   *v* -ED, -ING, -S to secure

FASTENER   *n* pl. -S one that fastens

FASTING   *n* pl. -S abstention from eating

FASTNESS   *n* pl. -ES the quality of being fast

FASTUOUS   *adj* arrogant

FAT   *adj* FATTER, FATTEST having an abundance of flesh

FAT   *v* FATTED, FATTING, FATS to make fat

FATAL   *adj* causing or capable of causing death

FATALISM   *n* pl. -S the doctrine that all events are predetermined

FATALIST   *n* pl. -S a believer in fatalism

FATALITY   *n* pl. -TIES a death resulting from an unexpected occurrence

FATALLY   *adv* in a fatal manner

FATBACK   *n* pl. -S a marine fish

FATBIRD   *n* pl. -S a wading bird

FATE   *v* FATED, FATING, FATES to destine

FATEFUL   *adj* decisively important

FATHEAD   *n* pl. -S a dolt

FATHER   *v* -ED, -ING, -S to cause to exist

FATHERLY   *adj* paternal

FATHOM   *v* -ED, -ING, -S to understand

FATIDIC   *adj* pertaining to prophecy

FATIGUE   *v* -TIGUED, -TIGUING, -TIGUES to weary

FATING   present participle of fate

FATLESS   *adj* having no fat

FATLIKE   *adj* resembling fat

FATLING   *n* pl. -S a young animal fattened for slaughter

FATLY   *adv* in the manner of one that is fat

FATNESS   *n* pl. -ES the state of being fat

FATSO   *n* pl. -SOES or -SOS a fat person

FATSTOCK   *n* pl. -S livestock that is fat and ready for market

FATTED   past tense of fat

FATTEN   *v* -ED, -ING, -S to make fat

FATTENER   *n* pl. -S one that fattens

FATTER   comparative of fat

FATTEST   superlative of fat

FATTIER   comparative of fatty

FATTIES   pl. of fatty

FATTIEST   superlative of fatty

FATTILY   *adv* in a fatty manner

FATTING   present participle of fat

FATTISH   *adj* somewhat fat

FATTY   *adj* -TIER, -TIEST greasy; oily

FATTY   *n* pl. -TIES one that is fat

FATUITY   *n* pl. -ITIES something foolish or stupid

FATUOUS   *adj* smugly stupid

FAUBOURG   *n* pl. -S a suburb

FAUCAL   *n* pl. -S a sound produced in the fauces

FAUCES   *n/pl* the passage from the mouth to the pharynx

FAUCET   *n* pl. -S a device for controlling the flow of liquid from a pipe

FAUCIAL   *adj* pertaining to the fauces

FAUGH   *interj* — used to express disgust

FAULD   *n* pl. -S a piece of armor below the breastplate

FAULT   *v* -ED, -ING, -S to criticize

FAULTY   *adj* FAULTIER, FAULTIEST imperfect **FAULTILY** *adv*

FAUN   *n* pl. -S a woodland deity of Roman mythology **FAUNLIKE** *adj*

FAUNA   *n* pl. -NAS or -NAE the animal life of a particular region **FAUNAL** *adj* **FAUNALLY** *adv*

FAUTEUIL   *n* pl. -S an armchair

FAUVE   *n* pl. -S a fauvist

FAUVISM   *n* pl. -S a movement in painting

FAUVIST   *n* pl. -S an advocate of fauvism

FAVELA   *n* pl. -S a slum area

FAVONIAN   *adj* pertaining to the west wind

FAVOR   *v* -ED, -ING, -S to regard with approval

FAVORER   *n* pl. -S one that favors

FAVORITE   *n* pl. -S a person or thing preferred above all others

FAVOUR   *v* -ED, -ING, -S to favor

FAVOURER   *n* pl. -S favorer

FAVUS   *n* pl. -ES a skin disease

FAWN   *v* -ED, -ING, -S to seek notice or favor by servile demeanor

FAWNER	*n* pl. -S one that fawns
FAWNLIKE	*adj* resembling a young deer
FAWNY	*adj* FAWNIER, FAWNIEST of a yellowish-brown color
FAX	*v* -ED, -ING, -ES to reproduce by electronic means
FAY	*v* -ED, -ING, -S to join closely
FAYALITE	*n* pl. -S a mineral
FAZE	*v* FAZED, FAZING, FAZES to disturb the composure of
FAZENDA	*n* pl. -S a Brazilian plantation
FEAL	*adj* loyal
FEALTY	*n* pl. -TIES loyalty
FEAR	*v* -ED, -ING, -S to be afraid of
FEARER	*n* pl. -S one that fears
FEARFUL	*adj* -FULLER, -FULLEST afraid
FEARLESS	*adj* unafraid
FEARSOME	*adj* frightening
FEASANCE	*n* pl. -S the performance of a condition, obligation, or duty
FEASE	*v* FEASED, FEASING, FEASES to faze
FEASIBLE	*adj* capable of being done **FEASIBLY** *adv*
FEAST	*v* -ED, -ING, -S to eat sumptuously
FEASTER	*n* pl. -S one that feasts
FEASTFUL	*adj* festive
FEAT	*n* pl. -S a notable act or achievement
FEAT	*adj* FEATER, FEATEST skillful
FEATHER	*v* -ED, -ING, -S to cover with feathers (horny structures that form the principal covering of birds)
FEATHERY	*adj* -ERIER, -ERIEST resembling feathers
FEATLY	*adj* -LIER, -LIEST graceful
FEATURE	*v* -TURED, -TURING, -TURES to give special prominence to
FEAZE	*v* FEAZED, FEAZING, FEAZES to faze
FEBRIFIC	*adj* feverish
FEBRILE	*adj* feverish
FECAL	*adj* pertaining to feces
FECES	*n/pl* bodily waste discharged through the anus
FECIAL	*n* pl. -S fetial
FECK	*n* pl. -S value
FECKLESS	*adj* worthless
FECKLY	*adv* almost
FECULA	*n* pl. -LAE fecal matter
FECULENT	*adj* foul with impurities
FECUND	*adj* fruitful
FED	*n* pl. -S a federal agent
FEDAYEE	*n* pl. -YEEN an Arab commando
FEDERACY	*n* pl. -CIES an alliance
FEDERAL	*n* pl. -S a supporter of a type of central government
FEDERATE	*v* -ATED, -ATING, -ATES to unite in an alliance
FEDORA	*n* pl. -S a type of hat
FEE	*v* FEED, FEEING, FEES to pay a fee (a fixed charge) to
FEEBLE	*adj* -BLER, -BLEST weak **FEEBLY** *adv*
FEEBLISH	*adj* somewhat feeble
FEED	*v* FED, FEEDING, FEEDS to give food to **FEEDABLE** *adj*
FEEDBACK	*n* pl. -S the return of a portion of the output to the input
FEEDBAG	*n* pl. -S a bag for feeding horses
FEEDBOX	*n* pl. -ES a box for animal feed
FEEDER	*n* pl. -S one that feeds
FEEDLOT	*n* pl. -S a plot of land on which livestock is fattened
FEEL	*v* FELT, FEELING, FEELS to perceive through the sense of touch
FEELER	*n* pl. -S a tactile organ
FEELESS	*adj* requiring no fee
FEELING	*n* pl. -S the function or power of perceiving by touch
FEET	pl. of foot **FEETLESS** *adj*
FEEZE	*v* FEEZED, FEEZING, FEEZES to faze
FEIGN	*v* -ED, -ING, -S to pretend
FEIGNER	*n* pl. -S one that feigns
FEINT	*v* -ED, -ING, -S to make a deceptive movement
FEIRIE	*adj* nimble
FEIST	*n* pl. -S a small dog of mixed breed
FEISTY	*adj* FEISTIER, FEISTIEST full of nervous energy
FELDSPAR	*n* pl. -S a mineral
FELICITY	*n* pl. -TIES happiness

FELID	*n* pl. -S a feline
FELINE	*n* pl. -S an animal of the cat family
FELINELY	*adv* in a catlike manner
FELINITY	*n* pl. -TIES the quality of being catlike
FELL	*v* -ED, -ING, -S to cause to fall
FELL	*adj* FELLER, FELLEST cruel
FELLA	*n* pl. -S a man or boy
FELLABLE	*adj* capable of being felled
FELLAH	*n* pl. -LAHS, -LAHIN, or -LAHEEN a peasant or laborer in Arab countries
FELLATIO	*n* pl. -TIOS oral stimulation of the penis
FELLER	*n* pl. -S one that fells
FELLIES	pl. of felly
FELLNESS	*n* pl. -ES extreme cruelty
FELLOE	*n* pl. -S the rim of a wheel
FELLOW	*v* -ED, -ING, -S to produce an equal to
FELLOWLY	*adj* friendly
FELLY	*n* pl. -LIES a felloe
FELON	*n* pl. -S a person who has committed a felony
FELONRY	*n* pl. -RIES the whole class of felons
FELONY	*n* pl. -NIES a grave crime
FELSITE	*n* pl. -S an igneous rock **FELSITIC** *adj*
FELSPAR	*n* pl. -S feldspar
FELSTONE	*n* pl. -S felsite
FELT	*v* -ED, -ING, -S to mat together
FELTING	*n* pl. -S felted material
FELUCCA	*n* pl. -S a swift sailing vessel
FELWORT	*n* pl. -S a flowering plant
FEMALE	*n* pl. -S an individual that bears young or produces ova
FEME	*n* pl. -S a wife
FEMINACY	*n* pl. -CIES the state of being a female
FEMINIE	*n/pl* women collectively
FEMININE	*n* pl. -S a word or form having feminine gender
FEMINISE	*v* -NISED, -NISING, -NISES to feminize
FEMINISM	*n* pl. -S a doctrine advocating rights for women equal to those of men
FEMINIST	*n* pl. -S a supporter of feminism
FEMINITY	*n* pl. -TIES the quality of being womanly
FEMINIZE	*v* -NIZED, -NIZING, -NIZES to make womanly
FEMME	*n* pl. -S a woman
FEMORAL	*adj* pertaining to the femur
FEMUR	*n* pl. -MURS or -MORA a bone of the leg
FEN	*n* pl. -S a marsh
FENAGLE	*v* -GLED, -GLING, -GLES to finagle
FENCE	*v* FENCED, FENCING, FENCES to practice the art of fencing
FENCER	*n* pl. -S one that fences
FENCIBLE	*n* pl. -S a soldier enlisted for home service only
FENCING	*n* pl. -S the art of using a sword in attack and defense
FEND	*v* -ED, -ING, -S to ward off
FENDER	*n* pl. -S a metal guard over the wheel of a motor vehicle **FENDERED** *adj*
FENESTRA	*n* pl. -TRAE a small anatomical opening
FENNEC	*n* pl. -S an African fox
FENNEL	*n* pl. -S a perennial herb
FENNY	*adj* marshy
FEOD	*n* pl. -S a fief
FEODARY	*n* pl. -RIES a vassal
FEOFF	*v* -ED, -ING, -S to grant a fief to
FEOFFEE	*n* pl. -S one to whom a fief is granted
FEOFFER	*n* pl. -S one that grants a fief to another
FEOFFOR	*n* pl. -S feoffer
FER	*prep* for
FERACITY	*n* pl. -TIES the state of being fruitful
FERAL	*adj* wild
FERBAM	*n* pl. -S a fungicide
FERE	*n* pl. -S a companion
FERETORY	*n* pl. -RIES a receptacle in which sacred relics are kept
FERIA	*n* pl. -RIAS or -RIAE a weekday of a church calendar on which no feast is celebrated **FERIAL** *adj*
FERINE	*adj* feral
FERITY	*n* pl. -TIES wildness

FERLIE	n pl. -S a strange sight
FERLY	n pl. -LIES ferlie
FERMATA	n pl. -TAS or -TE the sustaining of a musical note, chord, or rest beyond its written time value
FERMENT	v -ED, -ING, -S to undergo a type of chemical reaction
FERMI	n pl. -S a unit of length
FERMION	n pl. -S a type of atomic particle
FERMIUM	n pl. -S a radioactive element
FERN	n pl. -S a flowerless vascular plant **FERNLESS, FERNLIKE** adj
FERNERY	n pl. -ERIES a place in which ferns are grown
FERNY	adj **FERNIER, FERNIEST** abounding in ferns
FEROCITY	n pl. -TIES fierceness
FERRATE	n pl. -S a chemical salt
FERREL	v -RELED, -RELING, -RELS or -RELLED, -RELLING, -RELS ferrule
FERREOUS	adj containing iron
FERRET	v -ED, -ING, -S to search out by careful investigation
FERRETER	n pl. -S one that ferrets
FERRETY	adj suggestive of a ferret (a polecat)
FERRIAGE	n pl. -S transportation by ferry
FERRIC	adj pertaining to iron
FERRIED	past tense of ferry
FERRIES	present 3d person sing. of ferry
FERRITE	n pl. -S a magnetic substance **FERRITIC** adj
FERRITIN	n pl. -S a protein that contains iron
FERROUS	adj pertaining to iron
FERRULE	v -RULED, -RULING, -RULES to furnish with a metal ring or cap to prevent splitting
FERRUM	n pl. -S iron
FERRY	v -RIED, -RYING, -RIES to transport by ferry (a type of boat)
FERRYMAN	n pl. -MEN one who operates a ferry
FERTILE	adj capable of reproducing
FERULA	n pl. -LAE or -LAS a flat piece of wood

FERULE	v -ULED, -ULING, -ULES to ferrule
FERVENCY	n pl. -CIES fervor
FERVENT	adj marked by fervor
FERVID	adj fervent **FERVIDLY** adv
FERVOR	n pl. -S great warmth or intensity
FERVOUR	n pl. -S fervor
FESCUE	n pl. -S a perennial grass
FESS	v -ED, -ING, -ES to confess
FESSE	n pl. -S a horizontal band across the middle of a heraldic shield
FESSWISE	adv horizontally
FESTAL	adj festive **FESTALLY** adv
FESTER	v -ED, -ING, -S to generate pus
FESTIVAL	n pl. -S a day or time of celebration
FESTIVE	adj of or befitting a festival
FESTOON	v -ED, -ING, -S to hang decorative chains or strips on
FET	v FETTED, FETTING, FETS to fetch
FETA	n pl. -S a Greek cheese
FETAL	adj pertaining to a fetus
FETATION	n pl. -S the development of a fetus
FETCH	v -ED, -ING, -ES to go after and bring back
FETCHER	n pl. -S one that fetches
FETE	v FETED, FETING, FETES to honor with a celebration
FETERITA	n pl. -S a cereal grass
FETIAL	n pl. -S a priest of ancient Rome
FETIALIS	n pl. -LES fetial
FETICH	n pl. -ES fetish
FETICIDE	n pl. -S the killing of a fetus
FETID	adj having an offensive odor **FETIDLY** adv
FETING	present participle of fete
FETISH	n pl. -ES an object believed to have magical power
FETLOCK	n pl. -S a joint of a horse's leg
FETOLOGY	n pl. -GIES the branch of medicine dealing with the fetus
FETOR	n pl. -S an offensive odor
FETTED	past tense of fet
FETTER	v -ED, -ING, -S to shackle

FETTERER	*n* pl. -S one that fetters	**FIB**	*v* FIBBED, FIBBING, FIBS to tell a trivial lie
FETTING	present participle of fet	**FIBBER**	*n* pl. -S one that fibs
FETTLE	*v* -TLED, -TLING, -TLES to cover the hearth of with fettling	**FIBER**	*n* pl. -S a thread or threadlike object or structure **FIBERED** *adj*
FETTLING	*n* pl. -S loose material thrown on the hearth of a furnace to protect it	**FIBERIZE**	*v* -IZED, -IZING, -IZES to break into fibers
FETUS	*n* pl. -ES the unborn organism carried within the womb in the later stages of its development	**FIBRE**	*n* pl. -S fiber
		FIBRIL	*n* pl. -S a small fiber
FEU	*v* -ED, -ING, -S to grant land to under Scottish feudal law	**FIBRILLA**	*n* pl. -LAE a fibril
		FIBRIN	*n* pl. -S an insoluble protein
FEUAR	*n* pl. -S one granted land under Scottish feudal law	**FIBROID**	*n* pl. -S a fibroma
		FIBROIN	*n* pl. -S an insoluble protein
FEUD	*v* -ED, -ING, -S to engage in a feud (a bitter, continuous hostility)	**FIBROMA**	*n* pl. -MAS or -MATA a benign tumor composed of fibrous tissue
FEUDAL	*adj* pertaining to a political and economic system of medieval Europe **FEUDALLY** *adv*	**FIBROSIS**	*n* pl. -BROSES the development of excess fibrous tissue in a bodily organ **FIBROTIC** *adj*
FEUDARY	*n* pl. -RIES a vassal	**FIBROUS**	*adj* containing, consisting of, or resembling fibers
FEUDIST	*n* pl. -S one that feuds	**FIBULA**	*n* pl. -LAE or -LAS a bone of the leg **FIBULAR** *adj*
FEVER	*v* -ED, -ING, -S to affect with fever (abnormal elevation of the body temperature)		
		FICE	*n* pl. -S a feist
FEVERFEW	*n* pl. -S a perennial herb	**FICHE**	*n* pl. -S a sheet of microfilm
FEVERISH	*adj* having a fever	**FICHU**	*n* pl. -S a woman's scarf
FEVEROUS	*adj* feverish	**FICIN**	*n* pl. -S an enzyme
FEW	*adj* FEWER, FEWEST amounting to or consisting of a small number	**FICKLE**	*adj* -LER, -LEST not constant or loyal
		FICO	*n* pl. -COES something of little worth
FEWNESS	*n* pl. -ES the state of being few		
FEWTRILS	*n/pl* things of little value	**FICTILE**	*adj* moldable
FEY	*adj* FEYER, FEYEST crazy	**FICTION**	*n* pl. -S a literary work whose content is produced by the imagination
FEYNESS	*n* pl. -ES the state of being fey		
FEZ	*n* pl. FEZZES or FEZES a brimless cap worn by men in the Near East **FEZZED** *adj*	**FICTIVE**	*adj* imaginary
		FID	*n* pl. -S a square bar used as a support for a topmast
FIACRE	*n* pl. -S a small carriage		
FIANCE	*n* pl. -S a man engaged to be married	**FIDDLE**	*v* -DLED, -DLING, -DLES to play a violin
		FIDDLER	*n* pl. -S one that fiddles
FIANCEE	*n* pl. -S a woman engaged to be married	**FIDEISM**	*n* pl. -S reliance on faith rather than reason
FIAR	*n* pl. -S the holder of a type of absolute ownership of land under Scottish law	**FIDEIST**	*n* pl. -S a believer in fideism
		FIDELITY	*n* pl. -TIES loyalty
FIASCO	*n* pl. -COES or -CHI a wine bottle	**FIDGE**	*v* FIDGED, FIDGING, FIDGES to fidget
FIASCO	*n* pl. -COES or -COS a complete failure	**FIDGET**	*v* -ED, -ING, -S to move nervously or restlessly
FIAT	*n* pl. -S an authoritative order	**FIDGETER**	*n* pl. -S one that fidgets

FIDGETY	*adj* nervously restless
FIDGING	present participle of fidge
FIDO	*n* pl. -DOS a defective coin
FIDUCIAL	*adj* based on faith or trust
FIE	*interj* — used to express disapproval
FIEF	*n* pl. -S a feudal estate
FIEFDOM	*n* pl. -S a fief
FIELD	*v* -ED, -ING, -S to play as a fielder
FIELDER	*n* pl. -S one that catches or picks up a ball in play
FIEND	*n* pl. -S a demon
FIENDISH	*adj* extremely wicked or cruel
FIERCE	*adj* FIERCER, FIERCEST violently hostile or aggressive **FIERCELY** *adv*
FIERY	*adj* -ERIER, -ERIEST intensely hot **FIERILY** *adv*
FIESTA	*n* pl. -S a festival
FIFE	*v* FIFED, FIFING, FIFES to play a fife (a high-pitched flute)
FIFER	*n* pl. -S one that plays a fife
FIFTEEN	*n* pl. -S a number
FIFTH	*n* pl. -S one of five equal parts
FIFTHLY	*adv* in the fifth place
FIFTIETH	*n* pl. -S one of fifty equal parts
FIFTY	*n* pl. -TIES a number
FIG	*v* FIGGED, FIGGING, FIGS to adorn
FIGEATER	*n* pl. -S a large beetle
FIGHT	*v* FOUGHT, FIGHTING, FIGHTS to attempt to defeat an adversary
FIGHTER	*n* pl. -S one that fights
FIGHTING	*n* pl. -S the act of one that fights
FIGMENT	*n* pl. -S a product of mental invention
FIGULINE	*n* pl. -S a piece of pottery
FIGURAL	*adj* consisting of human or animal forms
FIGURANT	*n* pl. -S a ballet dancer who dances only in groups
FIGURATE	*adj* having a definite shape
FIGURE	*v* -URED, -URING, -URES to compute
FIGURER	*n* pl. -S one that figures
FIGURINE	*n* pl. -S a small statue
FIGURING	present participle of figure
FIGWORT	*n* pl. -S a flowering plant
FIL	*n* pl. -S a coin of Iraq and Jordan
FILA	pl. of filum
FILAGREE	*v* -GREED, -GREEING, -GREES to filigree
FILAMENT	*n* pl. -S a very thin thread or threadlike structure
FILAR	*adj* pertaining to a thread
FILAREE	*n* pl. -S a European weed
FILARIA	*n* pl. -IAE a parasitic worm **FILARIAL, FILARIAN** *adj*
FILARIID	*n* pl. -S filaria
FILATURE	*n* pl. -S the reeling of silk from cocoons
FILBERT	*n* pl. -S the edible nut of a European shrub
FILCH	*v* -ED, -ING, -ES to steal
FILCHER	*n* pl. -S one that filches
FILE	*v* FILED, FILING, FILES to remove with a file (an abrading tool)
FILEFISH	*n* pl. -ES a marine fish
FILEMOT	*adj* of a brownish yellow color
FILER	*n* pl. -S one that files
FILET	*v* -ED, -ING, -S to fillet
FILIAL	*adj* pertaining to a son or daughter **FILIALLY** *adv*
FILIATE	*v* -ATED, -ATING, -ATES to bring into close association
FILIBEG	*n* pl. -S a pleated skirt worn by Scottish Highlanders
FILICIDE	*n* pl. -S the killing of one's child
FILIFORM	*adj* shaped like a filament
FILIGREE	*v* -GREED, -GREEING, -GREES to adorn with intricate ornamental work
FILING	*n* pl. -S a particle removed by a file
FILISTER	*n* pl. -S a groove on a window frame
FILL	*v* -ED, -ING, -S to put as much as can be held into
FILLE	*n* pl. -S a girl
FILLER	*n* pl. -S one that fills
FILLET	*v* -ED, -ING, -S to cut boneless slices from
FILLIES	pl. of filly

FILLING   *n* pl. -S that which is used to fill something

FILLIP   *v* -ED, -ING, -S to strike sharply

FILLY   *n* pl. -LIES a young female horse

FILM   *v* -ED, -ING, -S to cover with a film (a thin layer or coating)

FILMCARD   *n* pl. -S a fiche

FILMDOM   *n* pl. -S the motion-picture industry

FILMGOER   *n* pl. -S one that goes to see motion pictures

FILMIC   *adj* pertaining to motion pictures

FILMIER   comparative of filmy

FILMIEST   superlative of filmy

FILMILY   *adv* in a filmy manner

FILMLAND   *n* pl. -S filmdom

FILMSET   *v* -SET, -SETTING, -SETS to photoset

FILMY   *adj* FILMIER, FILMIEST resembling or covered with film; hazy

FILOSE   *adj* resembling a thread

FILTER   *v* -ED, -ING, -S to pass through a filter (a device for removing suspended matter)

FILTERER   *n* pl. -S one that filters

FILTH   *n* pl. -S foul or dirty matter

FILTHY   *adj* FILTHIER, FILTHIEST offensively dirty **FILTHILY** *adv*

FILTRATE   *v* -TRATED, -TRATING, -TRATES to filter

FILUM   *n* pl. -LA a threadlike anatomical structure

FIMBLE   *n* pl. -S the male hemp plant

FIMBRIA   *n* pl. -BRIAE a fringe or fringe-like structure **FIMBRIAL** *adj*

FIN   *v* FINNED, FINNING, FINS to equip with fins (external paddle-like structures)

FINABLE   *adj* subject to the payment of a fine

FINAGLE   *v* -GLED, -GLING, -GLES to obtain by trickery

FINAGLER   *n* pl. -S one that finagles

FINAL   *n* pl. -S the last examination of an academic course

FINALE   *n* pl. -S a close or termination of something

FINALIS   *n* pl. -LES a type of tone in medieval music

FINALISM   *n* pl. -S the doctrine that all events are determined by ultimate purposes

FINALIST   *n* pl. -S a contestant who reaches the last part of a competition

FINALITY   *n* pl. -TIES the state of being conclusive

FINALIZE   *v* -IZED, -IZING, -IZES to put into finished form

FINALLY   *adv* at the end

FINANCE   *v* -NANCED, -NANCING, -NANCES to supply the money for

FINBACK   *n* pl. -S the rorqual

FINCH   *n* pl. -ES a small bird

FIND   *v* FOUND, FINDING, FINDS to come upon after a search

FINDER   *n* pl. -S one that finds

FINDING   *n* pl. -S something that is found

FINE   *adj* FINER, FINEST of excellent quality

FINE   *v* FINED, FINING, FINES to subject to a fine (a monetary penalty)

FINEABLE   *adj* finable

FINELY   *adv* in a fine manner

FINENESS   *n* pl. -ES the quality of being fine

FINER   comparative of fine

FINERY   *n* pl. -ERIES elaborate adornment

FINESPUN   *adj* developed with extreme care

FINESSE   *v* -NESSED, -NESSING, -NESSES to bring about by adroit maneuvering

FINEST   superlative of fine

FINFISH   *n* pl. -ES a true fish

FINFOOT   *n* pl. -S an aquatic bird

FINGER   *v* -ED, -ING, -S to touch with the fingers (the terminating members of the hand)

FINGERER   *n* pl. -S one that fingers

FINIAL   *n* pl. -S a crowning ornament **FINIALED** *adj*

FINICAL   *adj* finicky

FINICKIN   *adj* finicky

FINICKY   *adj* -ICKIER, -ICKIEST difficult to please

FINIKIN   *adj* finicky

FINIKING   *adj* finicky

FINING   *n* pl. -S the clarifying of wines

FINIS   *n* pl. -NISES the end

FINISH   *v* -ED, -ING, -ES to bring to an end

FINISHER   *n* pl. -S one that finishes

FINITE   *n* pl. -S something that is finite (having definite limits)

FINITELY   *adv* to a finite extent

FINITUDE   *n* pl. -S the state of being finite

FINK   *v* -ED, -ING, -S to inform to the police

FINLESS   *adj* having no fins

FINLIKE   *adj* resembling a fin

FINMARK   *n* pl. -S a monetary unit of Finland

FINNED   past tense of fin

FINNIER   comparative of finny

FINNIEST   superlative of finny

FINNING   present participle of fin

FINNICKY   *adj* -NICKIER, -NICKIEST finicky

FINNMARK   *n* pl. -S finmark

FINNY   *adj* -NIER, -NIEST having or characterized by fins

FINOCHIO   *n* pl. -CHIOS a perennial herb

FIORD   *n* pl. -S fjord

FIPPLE   *n* pl. -S a plug of wood at the mouth of certain wind instruments

FIQUE   *n* pl. -S a tropical plant

FIR   *n* pl. -S an evergreen tree

FIRE   *v* FIRED, FIRING, FIRES to project by discharging from a gun

FIREARM   *n* pl. -S a weapon from which a shot is discharged by gunpowder

FIREBALL   *n* pl. -S a luminous meteor

FIREBIRD   *n* pl. -S a brightly colored bird

FIREBOAT   *n* pl. -S a boat equipped with fire-fighting apparatus

FIREBOMB   *v* -ED, -ING, -S to attack with incendiary bombs

FIREBOX   *n* pl. -ES a chamber in which fuel is burned

FIREBRAT   *n* pl. -S a small, wingless insect

FIREBUG   *n* pl. -S an arsonist

FIRECLAY   *n* pl. -CLAYS a heat-resistant clay

FIRED   past tense of fire

FIREDAMP   *n* pl. -S a combustible gas

FIREDOG   *n* pl. -S an andiron

FIREFANG   *v* -ED, -ING, -S to decompose by oxidation

FIREFLY   *n* pl. -FLIES a luminous insect

FIREHALL   *n* pl. -S a fire station

FIRELESS   *adj* having no fire

FIRELOCK   *n* pl. -S a type of gun

FIREMAN   *n* pl. -MEN a man employed to extinguish fires

FIREPAN   *n* pl. -S an open pan for holding live coals

FIREPINK   *n* pl. -S a flowering plant

FIREPLUG   *n* pl. -S a hydrant

FIRER   *n* pl. -S one that fires

FIREROOM   *n* pl. -S a room containing a ship's boilers

FIRESIDE   *n* pl. -S the area immediately surrounding a fireplace

FIRETRAP   *n* pl. -S a building that is likely to catch on fire

FIREWEED   *n* pl. -S a perennial herb

FIREWOOD   *n* pl. -S wood used as fuel

FIREWORK   *n* pl. -S a device for producing a striking display of light or a loud noise

FIREWORM   *n* pl. -S a glowworm

FIRING   *n* pl. -S the process of maturing ceramic products by heat

FIRKIN   *n* pl. -S a British unit of capacity

FIRM   *adj* FIRMER, FIRMEST unyielding to pressure

FIRM   *v* -ED, -ING, -S to make firm

FIRMAN   *n* pl. -S an edict issued by a Middle Eastern sovereign

FIRMER   *n* pl. -S a woodworking tool

FIRMLY   *adv* in a firm manner

FIRMNESS   *n* pl. -ES the state of being firm

FIRN   *n* pl. -S neve

FIRRY   *adj* abounding in firs

FIRST   *n* pl. -S something that precedes all others

FIRSTLY   *adv* before all others

FIRTH   *n* pl. -S an inlet of the sea

FISC   *n* pl. -S a state or royal treasury

FISCAL   *n* pl. -S a public prosecutor

FISCALLY   *adv* with regard to financial matters

FISH   *v* -ED, -ING, -ES to catch or try to catch fish (cold-blooded aquatic vertebrates)

FISHABLE   *adj* suitable for fishing

FISHBOLT   *n* pl. -S a type of bolt

FISHBONE   *n* pl. -S a bone of a fish

FISHBOWL   *n* pl. -S a bowl in which live fish are kept

FISHER   *n* pl. -S one that fishes

FISHERY   *n* pl. -ERIES a place for catching fish

FISHEYE   *n* pl. -S a suspicious stare

FISHGIG   *n* pl. -S a pronged implement for spearing fish

FISHHOOK   *n* pl. -S a barbed hook for catching fish

FISHIER   comparative of fishy

FISHIEST   superlative of fishy

FISHILY   *adv* in a fishy manner

FISHING   *n* pl. -S the occupation or pastime of catching fish

FISHLESS   *adj* having no fish

FISHLIKE   *adj* resembling a fish

FISHLINE   *n* pl. -S a line used in fishing

FISHMEAL   *n* pl. -S ground dried fish

FISHNET   *n* pl. -S a net for catching fish

FISHPOLE   *n* pl. -S a fishing rod

FISHPOND   *n* pl. -S a pond abounding in edible fish

FISHTAIL   *v* -ED, -ING, -S to have the rear end of a moving vehicle slide from side to side

FISHWAY   *n* pl. -WAYS a device for enabling fish to pass around a dam

FISHWIFE   *n* pl. -WIVES a woman who sells fish

FISHY   *adj* FISHIER, FISHIEST of or resembling fish

FISSATE   *adj* deeply split

FISSILE   *adj* capable of being split

FISSION   *v* -ED, -ING, -S to split into parts

FISSIPED   *n* pl. -S a mammal that has separated toes

FISSURE   *v* -SURED, -SURING, -SURES to split

FIST   *v* -ED, -ING, -S to strike with the fist (the hand closed tightly)

FISTFUL   *n* pl. -S a handful

FISTIC   *adj* pertaining to pugilism

FISTNOTE   *n* pl. -S a part of a text to which attention is drawn by an index mark

FISTULA   *n* pl. -LAE or -LAS a duct formed by the imperfect closing of a wound **FISTULAR** *adj*

FIT   *adj* FITTER, FITTEST healthy

FIT   *v* FITTED, FITTING, FITS to bring to a required form and size

FITCH   *n* pl. -ES a polecat

FITCHEE   *adj* fitchy

FITCHET   *n* pl. -S a fitch

FITCHEW   *n* pl. -S a fitch

FITCHY   *adj* having the arms ending in a point — used of a heraldic cross

FITFUL   *adj* recurring irregularly **FITFULLY** *adv*

FITLY   *adv* in a fit manner

FITMENT   *n* pl. -S equipment

FITNESS   *n* pl. -ES the state of being fit

FITTABLE   *adj* capable of being fitted

FITTED   past tense of fit

FITTER   *n* pl. -S one that fits

FITTEST   superlative of fit

FITTING   *n* pl. -S a small often standardized accessory part

FIVE   *n* pl. -S a number

FIVEFOLD   *adj* five times as great

FIVEPINS   *n/pl* a bowling game

FIVER   *n* pl. -S a five-dollar bill

FIX   *v* FIXED or FIXT, FIXING, FIXES to repair **FIXABLE** *adj*

FIXATE   *v* -ATED, -ATING, -ATES to make stable or stationary

FIXATIF   *n* pl. -S fixative

FIXATION   *n* pl. -S the act of fixating

FIXATIVE   *n* pl. -S a substance for preserving paintings or drawings

FIXEDLY   *adv* firmly

FIXER   *n* pl. -S one that fixes

FIXINGS   *n/pl* accompaniments to the main dish of a meal

FIXITY   *n* pl. -TIES stability

FIXT   a past tense of fix

FIXTURE   *n* pl. -S a permanent part or appendage of a house

FIXURE   *n* pl. -S firmness

FIZ   *n* pl. FIZZES a hissing or sputtering sound

FIZGIG   *n* pl. -S fishgig

FIZZ   *v* -ED, -ING, -ES to make a hissing or sputtering sound

FIZZER   *n* pl. -S one that fizzes

FIZZES   pl. of fiz

FIZZLE   *v* -ZLED, -ZLING, -ZLES to fizz

FIZZY   *adj* FIZZIER, FIZZIEST fizzing

FJELD   *n* pl. -S a high, barren plateau

FJORD   *n* pl. -S a narrow inlet of the sea between steep cliffs

FLAB   *n* pl. -S flabby body tissue

FLABBY   *adj* -BIER, -BIEST flaccid **FLABBILY** *adv*

FLABELLA   *n/pl* fan-shaped anatomical structures

FLACCID   *adj* lacking firmness

FLACK   *n* pl. -S a press agent

FLACON   *n* pl. -S a small stoppered bottle

FLAG   *v* FLAGGED, FLAGGING, FLAGS to mark with a flag (a piece of cloth used as a symbol)

FLAGELLA   *n/pl* long, slender plant shoots

FLAGGER   *n* pl. -S one that flags

FLAGGING   *n* pl. -S a type of pavement

FLAGGY   *adj* -GIER, -GIEST drooping

FLAGLESS   *adj* having no flag

FLAGMAN   *n* pl. -MEN one who carries a flag

FLAGON   *n* pl. -S a large bulging bottle

FLAGPOLE   *n* pl. -S a pole on which a flag is displayed

FLAGRANT   *adj* extremely or deliberately conspicuous

FLAGSHIP   *n* pl. -S a ship bearing the flag of a fleet

FLAIL   *v* -ED, -ING, -S to swing freely

FLAIR   *n* pl. -S a natural aptitude

FLAK   *n* pl. FLAK antiaircraft fire

FLAKE   *v* FLAKED, FLAKING, FLAKES to peel off in flakes (flat, thin pieces)

FLAKER   *n* pl. -S one that flakes

FLAKY   *adj* FLAKIER, FLAKIEST resembling flakes **FLAKILY** *adv*

FLAM   *v* FLAMMED, FLAMMING FLAMS to deceive

FLAMBE   *v* -BEED, -BEING, -BES to douse with a liqueur and ignite

FLAMBEAU   *n* pl. -BEAUX or -BEAUS a flaming torch

FLAMBEE   *adj* flaming

FLAME   *v* FLAMED, FLAMING, FLAMES to burn brightly

FLAMEN   *n* pl. -MENS or -MINES a priest of ancient Rome

FLAMENCO   *n* pl. -COS a strongly rhythmic style of dancing

FLAMEOUT   *n* pl. -S a failure of a jet engine in flight

FLAMER   *n* pl. -S one that flames

FLAMIER   comparative of flamy

FLAMIEST   superlative of flamy

FLAMINES   a pl. of flamen

FLAMING   present participle of flame

FLAMINGO   *n* pl. -GOS or -GOES a wading bird

FLAMMED   past tense of flam

FLAMMING   present participle of flam

FLAMY   *adj* FLAMIER, FLAMIEST flaming

FLAN   *n* pl. -S or -ES a type of custard

FLANCARD   *n* pl. -S a piece of armor for the side of a horse

FLANERIE   *n* pl. -S idleness

FLANEUR   *n* pl. -S an idler

FLANGE   *v* FLANGED, FLANGING, FLANGES to provide with a protecting rim

FLANGER   *n* pl. -S one that flanges

FLANK   *v* -ED, -ING, -S to be located at the side of

FLANKER   *n* pl. -S one that flanks

FLANNEL   *v* -NELED, -NELING, -NELS or -NELLED, -NELLING, -NELS to cover with flannel (a soft fabric)

FLAP   *v* FLAPPED, FLAPPING, FLAPS to wave up and down

FLAPJACK   *n* pl. -S a pancake

FLAPLESS   *adj* having no flap (a flat appendage)

FLAPPED   past tense of flap

FLAPPER   *n* pl. -S one that flaps

FLAPPING   present participle of flap

FLAPPY   *adj* -PIER, -PIEST flapping

FLARE   v FLARED, FLARING, FLARES to burn with a bright, wavering light

FLASH   v -ED, -ING, -ES to send forth a sudden burst of light

FLASHER   n pl. -S one that flashes

FLASHGUN   n pl. -S a photographic apparatus

FLASHING   n pl. -S sheet metal used in waterproofing a roof

FLASHY   adj FLASHIER, FLASHIEST gaudy **FLASHILY** adv

FLASK   n pl. -S a narrow-necked container

FLASKET   n pl. -S a small flask

FLAT   adj FLATTER, FLATTEST having a smooth or even surface

FLAT   v FLATTED, FLATTING, FLATS to flatten

FLATBED   n pl. -S a type of truck or trailer

FLATBOAT   n pl. -S a flat-bottomed boat

FLATCAP   n pl. -S a type of hat

FLATCAR   n pl. -S a railroad car without sides or roof

FLATFISH   n pl. -ES any of an order of marine fishes

FLATFOOT   n pl. -FEET a foot condition

FLATFOOT   v -ED, -ING, -S to walk with a dragging gait

FLATHEAD   n pl. -S a marine food fish

FLATIRON   n pl. -S a device for pressing clothes

FLATLAND   n pl. -S land lacking significant variation in elevation

FLATLET   n pl. -S a type of apartment

FLATLING   adv with a flat side or edge

FLATLY   adv in a flat manner

FLATNESS   n pl. -ES the state of being flat

FLATTED   past tense of flat

FLATTEN   v -ED, -ING, -S to make or become flat

FLATTER   v -ED, -ING, -S to praise excessively

FLATTERY   n pl. -TERIES the act of flattering

FLATTEST   superlative of flat

FLATTING   present participle of flat

FLATTISH   adj somewhat flat

FLATTOP   n pl. -S an aircraft carrier

FLATUS   n pl. -ES intestinal gas

FLATWARE   n pl. -S tableware that is fairly flat

FLATWASH   n pl. -ES flatwork

FLATWAYS   adv flatwise

FLATWISE   adv with the flat side in a particular position

FLATWORK   n pl. -S laundry that can be ironed mechanically

FLATWORM   n pl. -S a flat-bodied worm

FLAUNT   v -ED, -ING, -S to exhibit in a gaudy manner

FLAUNTER   n pl. -S one that flaunts

FLAUNTY   adj FLAUNTIER, FLAUNTIEST gaudy

FLAUTIST   n pl. -S flutist

FLAVIN   n pl. -S a yellow pigment

FLAVINE   n pl. -S flavin

FLAVONE   n pl. -S a chemical compound

FLAVONOL   n pl. -S a derivative of flavone

FLAVOR   v -ED, -ING, -S to give flavor (distinctive taste) to

FLAVORER   n pl. -S one that flavors

FLAVORY   adj full of flavor

FLAVOUR   v -ED, -ING, -S to flavor

FLAVOURY   adj flavory

FLAW   v -ED, -ING, -S to produce a flaw (an imperfection) in

FLAWLESS   adj having no flaw

FLAWY   adj FLAWIER, FLAWIEST full of flaws

FLAX   n pl. -ES an annual herb

FLAXEN   adj of a pale yellow color

FLAXSEED   n pl. -S the seed of flax

FLAXY   adj FLAXIER, FLAXIEST flaxen

FLAY   v -ED, -ING, -S to strip off the skin of

FLAYER   n pl. -S one that flays

FLEA   n pl. -S a parasitic insect

FLEABAG   n pl. -S an inferior hotel

FLEABANE   n pl. -S a flowering plant

FLEABITE   n pl. -S the bite of a flea

FLEAM   n pl. -S a surgical instrument

FLEAWORT   n pl. -S a European herb

FLECHE   n pl. -S a steeple

FLECK   v -ED, -ING, -S to mark with flecks (tiny streaks or spots)

FLECKY   adj flecked

FLECTION   *n* pl. -S the act of bending

FLED   past tense of flee

FLEDGE   *v* FLEDGED, FLEDGING, FLEDGES to furnish with feathers

FLEDGY   *adj* FLEDGIER, FLEDGIEST covered with feathers

FLEE   *v* FLED, FLEEING, FLEES to run away

FLEECE   *v* FLEECED, FLEECING, FLEECES to remove the coat of wool from

FLEECER   *n* pl. -S one that fleeces

FLEECH   *v* -ED, -ING, -ES to coax

FLEECING   present participle of fleece

FLEECY   *adj* FLEECIER, FLEECIEST woolly **FLEECILY** *adv*

FLEER   *v* -ED, -ING, -S to deride

FLEET   *adj* FLEETER, FLEETEST swift **FLEETLY** *adv*

FLEET   *v* -ED, -ING, -S to move swiftly

FLEISHIG   *adj* made of meat or meat products

FLEMISH   *v* -ED, -ING, -ES to coil rope in a certain manner

FLENCH   *v* -ED, -ING, -ES to flense

FLENSE   *v* FLENSED, FLENSING, FLENSES to strip the blubber or skin from

FLENSER   *n* pl. -S one that flenses

FLESH   *v* -ED, -ING, -ES to plunge into the flesh (soft body tissue)

FLESHER   *n* pl. -S one that removes flesh from animal hides

FLESHIER   comparative of fleshy

FLESHIEST   superlative of fleshy

FLESHING   *n* pl. -S the distribution of the lean and fat on an animal

FLESHLY   *adj* -LIER, -LIEST pertaining to the body

FLESHPOT   *n* pl. -S a pot for cooking meat

FLESHY   *adj* FLESHIER, FLESHIEST having much flesh

FLETCH   *v* -ED, -ING, -ES to fledge

FLETCHER   *n* pl. -S one that makes arrows

FLEURY   *adj* having the arms terminating in three leaves — used of a heraldic cross

FLEW   *n* pl. -S a fishing net

FLEX   *v* -ED, -ING, -ES to bend

FLEXIBLE   *adj* capable of being bent **FLEXIBLY** *adv*

FLEXILE   *adj* flexible

FLEXION   *n* pl. -S flection

FLEXOR   *n* pl. -S a muscle that serves to bend a bodily part

FLEXUOSE   *adj* flexuous

FLEXUOUS   *adj* winding

FLEXURE   *n* pl. -S the act of bending **FLEXURAL** *adj*

FLEY   *v* -ED, -ING, -S to frighten

FLIC   *n* pl. -S a Parisian policeman

FLICHTER   *v* -ED, -ING, -S to flicker

FLICK   *v* -ED, -ING, -S to strike with a quick, light blow

FLICKER   *v* -ED, -ING, -S to move waveringly

FLICKERY   *adj* flickering

FLIED   a past tense of fly

FLIER   *n* pl. -S one that flies

FLIES   present 3d person sing. of fly

FLIEST   superlative of fly

FLIGHT   *v* -ED, -ING, -S to fly in a flock

FLIGHTY   *adj* FLIGHTIER, FLIGHTIEST fickle

FLIMFLAM   *v* -FLAMMED, -FLAMMING, -FLAMS to swindle

FLIMSY   *adj* -SIER, -SIEST lacking solidity or strength **FLIMSILY** *adv*

FLIMSY   *n* pl. -SIES a thin paper

FLINCH   *v* -ED, -ING, -ES to shrink back involuntarily

FLINCHER   *n* pl. -S one that flinches

FLINDER   *n* pl. -S a small fragment

FLING   *v* FLUNG, FLINGING, FLINGS to throw with force

FLINGER   *n* pl. -S one that flings

FLINT   *v* -ED, -ING, -S to provide with flint (a spark-producing rock)

FLINTY   *adj* FLINTIER, FLINTIEST resembling flint **FLINTILY** *adv*

FLIP   *v* FLIPPED, FLIPPING, FLIPS to throw with a brisk motion

FLIP   *adj* FLIPPER, FLIPPEST flippant

FLIPPANT   *adj* impudent

FLIPPED   past tense of flip

FLIPPER   *n* pl. -S a broad, flat limb adapted for swimming

FLIPPEST   superlative of flip

FLIPPING   present participle of flip

FLIRT   *v* -ED, -ING, -S to behave amorously without serious intent

FLIRTER   *n* pl. -S one that flirts

FLIRTY   *adj* FLIRTIER, FLIRTIEST given to flirting

FLIT   *v* FLITTED, FLITTING, FLITS to move lightly and swiftly

FLITCH   *v* -ED, -ING, -ES to cut into strips

FLITE   *v* FLITED, FLITING, FLITES to quarrel

FLITTED   past tense of flit

FLITTER   *v* -ED, -ING, -S to flutter

FLITTING   present participle of flit

FLIVVER   *n* pl. -S an old, battered car

FLOAT   *v* -ED, -ING, -S to rest or remain on the surface of a liquid

FLOATAGE   *n* pl. -S flotage

FLOATER   *n* pl. -S one that floats

FLOATY   *adj* FLOATIER, FLOATIEST tending to float

FLOC   *v* FLOCCED, FLOCCING, FLOCS to aggregate into floccules

FLOCCI   pl. of floccus

FLOCCOSE   *adj* having woolly tufts

FLOCCULE   *n* pl. -S a tuft-like mass

FLOCCULI   *n/pl* small, loosely aggregated masses

FLOCCUS   *n* pl. FLOCCI a floccule

FLOCK   *v* -ED, -ING, -S to gather or move in a crowd

FLOCKING   *n* pl. -S a velvety design in short fibers on cloth or paper

FLOCKY   *adj* FLOCKIER, FLOCKIEST woolly

FLOE   *n* pl. -S a large mass of floating ice

FLOG   *v* FLOGGED, FLOGGING, FLOGS to beat with a whip or rod

FLOGGER   *n* pl. -S one that flogs

FLOGGING   *n* pl. -S a whipping

FLONG   *n* pl. -S a sheet of a certain type of paper

FLOOD   *v* -ED, -ING, -S to inundate

FLOODER   *n* pl. -S one that floods

FLOODLIT   *adj* illuminated by floodlights

FLOODWAY   *n* pl. -WAYS an overflow channel

FLOOEY   *adj* awry

FLOOR   *v* -ED, -ING, -S to provide with a floor (the level base of a room)

FLOORAGE   *n* pl. -S floor space

FLOORER   *n* pl. -S one that floors

FLOORING   *n* pl. -S a floor

FLOOSY   *n* pl. -SIES floozy

FLOOZIE   *n* pl. -S floozy

FLOOZY   *n* pl. -ZIES a prostitute

FLOP   *v* FLOPPED, FLOPPING, FLOPS to fall heavily and noisily

FLOPOVER   *n* pl. -S a defect in television reception

FLOPPER   *n* pl. -S one that flops

FLOPPING   present participle of flop

FLOPPY   *adj* -PIER, -PIEST soft and flexible **FLOPPILY** *adv*

FLORA   *n* pl. -RAS or -RAE the plant life of a particular region

FLORAL   *adj* pertaining to flowers **FLORALLY** *adv*

FLORENCE   *n* pl. -S florin

FLORET   *n* pl. -S a small flower

FLORID   *adj* ruddy **FLORIDLY** *adv*

FLORIGEN   *n* pl. -S a plant hormone

FLORIN   *n* pl. -S a former gold coin of Europe

FLORIST   *n* pl. -S a grower or seller of flowers

FLORUIT   *n* pl. -S a period of flourishing

FLOSS   *n* pl. -ES a soft, light fiber

FLOSSIE   *n* pl. -S a floozy

FLOSSY   *adj* FLOSSIER, FLOSSIEST resembling floss

FLOTA   *n* pl. -S a fleet of Spanish ships

FLOTAGE   *n* pl. -S the act of floating

FLOTILLA   *n* pl. -S a fleet of ships

FLOTSAM   *n* pl. -S floating wreckage of a ship or its cargo

FLOUNCE   *v* FLOUNCED, FLOUNCING, FLOUNCES to move with exaggerated motions

FLOUNCY   *adj* FLOUNCIER, FLOUNCIEST flouncing

FLOUNDER   *v* -ED, -ING, -S to struggle clumsily

FLOUR   *v* -ED, -ING, -S to cover with flour (a finely ground meal of grain)

FLOURISH   *v* -ED, -ING, -ES to thrive

FLOURY   *adj* resembling flour

FLOUT   *v* -ED, -ING, -S to treat with contempt

FLOUTER   *n* pl. -S one that flouts

FLOW   *v* -ED, -ING, -S to move steadily and smoothly along

FLOWAGE   *n* pl. -S the act of flowing

FLOWER   *v* -ED, -ING, -S to put forth flowers (reproductive structures of seed-bearing plants)

FLOWERER   *n* pl. -S a plant that flowers at a certain time

FLOWERET   *n* pl. -S a floret

FLOWERY   *adj* -ERIER, -ERIEST abounding in flowers

FLOWN   a past participle of fly

FLU   *n* pl. -S a virus disease

FLUB   *v* FLUBBED, FLUBBING, FLUBS to bungle

FLUBDUB   *n* pl. -S pretentious nonsense

FLUE   *n* pl. -S an enclosed passageway for directing a current **FLUED** *adj*

FLUENCY   *n* pl. -CIES the quality of being fluent

FLUENT   *adj* spoken or written with effortless ease **FLUENTLY** *adv*

FLUERICS   *n/pl* fluidics **FLUERIC** *adj*

FLUFF   *v* -ED, -ING, -S to make fluffy

FLUFFY   *adj* FLUFFIER, FLUFFIEST light and soft **FLUFFILY** *adv*

FLUID   *n* pl. -S a substance that tends to flow **FLUIDAL** *adj*

FLUIDICS   *n/pl* a branch of mechanical engineering **FLUIDIC** *adj*

FLUIDISE   *v* -ISED, -ISING, -ISES to fluidize

FLUIDITY   *n* pl. -TIES the quality of being able to flow

FLUIDIZE   *v* -IZED, -IZING, -IZES to cause to flow like a fluid

FLUIDLY   *adv* with fluidity

FLUIDRAM   *n* pl. -S a unit of liquid capacity

FLUKE   *v* FLUKED, FLUKING, FLUKES to obtain by chance

FLUKEY   *adj* FLUKIER, FLUKIEST fluky

FLUKY   *adj* FLUKIER, FLUKIEST happening by or depending on chance

FLUME   *v* FLUMED, FLUMING, FLUMES to convey by means of an artificial water channel

FLUMMERY   *n* pl. -MERIES a sweet dessert

FLUMMOX   *v* -ED, -ING, -ES to confuse

FLUMP   *v* -ED, -ING, -S to fall heavily

FLUNG   past tense of fling

FLUNK   *v* -ED, -ING, -S to fail an examination or course

FLUNKER   *n* pl. -S one that flunks

FLUNKEY   *n* pl. -KEYS flunky

FLUNKY   *n* pl. -KIES a servile follower

FLUOR   *n* pl. -S fluorite **FLUORIC** *adj*

FLUORENE   *n* pl. -S a chemical compound

FLUORID   *n* pl. -S fluoride

FLUORIDE   *n* pl. -S a compound of fluorine

FLUORIN   *n* pl. -S fluorine

FLUORINE   *n* pl. -S a gaseous element

FLUORITE   *n* pl. -S a mineral

FLURRY   *v* -RIED, -RYING, -RIES to confuse

FLUSH   *adj* FLUSHER, FLUSHEST ruddy

FLUSH   *v* -ED, -ING, -ES to blush

FLUSHER   *n* pl. -S one that flushes

FLUSTER   *v* -ED, -ING, -S to put into a state of nervous confusion

FLUTE   *v* FLUTED, FLUTING, FLUTES to play on a flute (a woodwind instrument)

FLUTER   *n* pl. -S a flutist

FLUTIER   comparative of fluty

FLUTIEST   superlative of fluty

FLUTING   *n* pl. -S a series of parallel grooves

FLUTIST   *n* pl. -S one who plays the flute

FLUTTER   *v* -ED, -ING, -S to wave rapidly and irregularly

FLUTTERY   *adj* marked by fluttering

FLUTY   *adj* FLUTIER, FLUTIEST resembling a flute in sound

FLUVIAL   *adj* pertaining to a river

FLUX   *v* -ED, -ING, -ES to melt

FLUXION   *n* pl. -S the act of flowing

FLUYT   *n* pl. -S a type of ship

FLY	*v* FLEW, FLOWN, FLYING, FLIES to move through the air
FLY	*v* FLIED, FLYING, FLIES to hit a ball high into the air in baseball
FLY	*adj* FLIER, FLIEST clever
FLYABLE	*adj* suitable for flying
FLYAWAY	*n* pl. -AWAYS one that is elusive
FLYBELT	*n* pl. -S an area infested with tsetse flies
FLYBLOW	*v* -BLEW, -BLOWN, -BLOWING, -BLOWS to taint
FLYBOAT	*n* pl. -S a small, fast boat
FLYBY	*n* pl. -BYS a flight of aircraft close to a specified place
FLYER	*n* pl. -S flier
FLYING	*n* pl. -S the operation of an aircraft
FLYLEAF	*n* pl. -LEAVES a blank leaf at the beginning or end of a book
FLYMAN	*n* pl. -MEN a stage worker in a theater
FLYOVER	*n* pl. -S a flight of aircraft over a specific location
FLYPAPER	*n* pl. -S paper designed to catch or kill flies
FLYPAST	*n* pl. -S a flyby
FLYSCH	*n* pl. -ES a sandstone deposit
FLYSPECK	*v* -ED, -ING, -S to mark with minute spots
FLYTE	*v* FLYTED, FLYTING, FLYTES to flite
FLYTIER	*n* pl. -S a maker of fishing flies
FLYTING	*n* pl. -S a dispute in verse form
FLYTRAP	*n* pl. -S a trap for catching flies
FLYWAY	*n* pl. -WAYS an established air route of migratory birds
FLYWHEEL	*n* pl. -S a heavy disk used in machinery
FOAL	*v* -ED, -ING, -S to give birth to a horse
FOAM	*v* -ED, -ING, -S to form foam (a light, bubbly, gas and liquid mass)
FOAMER	*n* pl. -S one that foams
FOAMIER	comparative of foamy
FOAMIEST	superlative of foamy
FOAMILY	*adv* in a foamy manner
FOAMLESS	*adj* being without foam
FOAMLIKE	*adj* resembling foam
FOAMY	*adj* FOAMIER, FOAMIEST covered with foam
FOB	*v* FOBBED, FOBBING, FOBS to deceive
FOCAL	*adj* pertaining to a focus
FOCALISE	*v* -ISED, -ISING, -ISES to focalize
FOCALIZE	*v* -IZED, -IZING, -IZES to focus
FOCALLY	*adv* with regard to focus
FOCUS	*n* pl. -CUSES or -CI a point at which rays converge or from which they diverge
FOCUS	*v* -CUSED, -CUSING, -CUSES or -CUSSED, -CUSSING, -CUSSES to bring to a focus
FOCUSER	*n* pl. -S one that focuses
FODDER	*v* -ED, -ING, -S to feed with coarse food
FODGEL	*adj* plump
FOE	*n* pl. -S an enemy
FOEHN	*n* pl. -S a warm, dry wind
FOEMAN	*n* pl. -MEN an enemy in war
FOETAL	*adj* fetal
FOETID	*adj* fetid
FOETOR	*n* pl. -S fetor
FOETUS	*n* pl. -ES fetus
FOG	*v* FOGGED, FOGGING, FOGS, to cover with fog (condensed water vapor near the earth's surface)
FOGBOUND	*adj* surrounded by fog
FOGBOW	*n* pl. -S a nebulous arc of light sometimes seen in a fog
FOGDOG	*n* pl. -S a fogbow
FOGEY	*n* pl. -GEYS fogy
FOGFRUIT	*n* pl. -S a flowering plant
FOGGAGE	*n* pl. -S a second growth of grass
FOGGED	past tense of fog
FOGGER	*n* pl. -S one that fogs
FOGGING	present participle of fog
FOGGY	*adj* -GIER, -GIEST filled with fog **FOGGILY** *adv*
FOGHORN	*n* pl. -S a horn sounded in a fog to give warning
FOGIE	*n* pl. -S fogy
FOGLESS	*adj* having no fog
FOGY	*n* pl. -GIES an old-fashioned person **FOGYISH** *adj*
FOGYISM	*n* pl. -S old-fashioned behavior

FOH *interj* faugh

FOHN *n* pl. -S foehn

FOIBLE *n* pl. -S a minor weakness

FOIL *v* -ED, -ING, -S to prevent the success of **FOILABLE** *adj*

FOILSMAN *n* pl. -MEN a fencer

FOIN *v* -ED, -ING, -S to thrust with a pointed weapon

FOISON *n* pl. -S strength

FOIST *v* -ED, -ING, -S to force upon slyly

FOLACIN *n* pl. -S a B vitamin

FOLATE *n* pl. -S folacin

FOLD *v* -ED, -ING, -S to lay one part over another part of **FOLDABLE** *adj*

FOLDAWAY *adj* designed to fold out of the way

FOLDBOAT *n* pl. -S a faltboat

FOLDER *n* pl. -S one that folds

FOLDEROL *n* pl. -S falderal

FOLDOUT *n* pl. -S a gatefold

FOLIA a pl. of folium

FOLIAGE *n* pl. -S the growth of leaves of a plant **FOLIAGED** *adj*

FOLIAR *adj* pertaining to a leaf

FOLIATE *v* -ATED, -ATING, -ATES to hammer into thin plates

FOLIO *v* -ED, -ING, -S to number the pages of

FOLIOSE *adj* having leaves

FOLIOUS *adj* foliose

FOLIUM *n* pl. -LIA or -LIUMS a thin layer

FOLK *n* pl. -S a people or tribe

FOLKISH *adj* characteristic of the common people

FOLKLIKE *adj* folkish

FOLKLORE *n* pl. -S the lore of a people

FOLKMOOT *n* pl. -S a general assembly of the people in early England

FOLKMOT *n* pl. -S folkmoot

FOLKMOTE *n* pl. -S folkmoot

FOLKSY *adj* FOLKSIER, FOLKSIEST friendly **FOLKSILY** *adv*

FOLKTALE *n* pl. -S a tale forming part of the oral tradition of a people

FOLKWAY *n* pl. -WAYS a traditional custom of a people

FOLLICLE *n* pl. -S a small bodily cavity

FOLLIES pl. of folly

FOLLIS *n* pl. -LES a coin of ancient Rome

FOLLOW *v* -ED, -ING, -S to come or go after

FOLLOWER *n* pl. -S one that follows

FOLLY *n* pl. -LIES a foolish idea or action

FOMENT *v* -ED, -ING, -S to promote the development of

FOMENTER *n* pl. -S one that foments

FON *n* pl. -S foehn

FOND *adj* FONDER, FONDEST having an affection

FOND *v* -ED, -ING, -S to display affection

FONDANT *n* pl. -S a soft, creamy candy

FONDLE *v* -DLED, -DLING, -DLES to caress

FONDLER *n* pl. -S one that fondles

FONDLING *n* pl. -S one that is fondled

FONDLY *adv* in a fond manner

FONDNESS *n* pl. -ES affection

FONDU *n* pl. -S fondue

FONDUE *n* pl. -S a dish of melted cheese

FONT *n* pl. -S a receptacle for the water used in baptism **FONTAL** *adj*

FONTANEL *n* pl. -S a space in the fetal and infantile skull

FONTINA *n* pl. -S an Italian cheese

FOOD *n* pl. -S a substance taken into the body to maintain life and growth **FOODLESS** *adj*

FOOFARAW *n* pl. -S excessive ornamentation

FOOL *v* -ED, -ING, -S to deceive

FOOLERY *n* pl. -ERIES foolish behavior or speech

FOOLFISH *n* pl. -ES a marine fish

FOOLISH *adj* -ISHER, -ISHEST lacking good sense or judgment

FOOLSCAP *n* pl. -S a paper size

FOOT *n* pl. FEET the terminal part of the leg on which the body stands and moves

FOOT *v* -ED, -ING, -S to walk

FOOTAGE *n* pl. -S a length or quantity expressed in feet

FOOTBALL *n* pl. -S a type of ball

FOOTBATH *n* pl. -S a bath for the feet

FOOTBOY *n* pl. -BOYS a serving boy

FOOTER *n* pl. -S one that walks

FOOTFALL *n* pl. -S the sound of a footstep

FOOTGEAR *n* pl. -S footwear

FOOTHILL *n* pl. -S a low hill at the foot of higher hills

FOOTHOLD *n* pl. -S a secure support for the feet

FOOTIER comparative of footy

FOOTIEST superlative of footy

FOOTING *n* pl. -S a foothold

FOOTLE *v* -TLED, -TLING, -TLES to waste time

FOOTLER *n* pl. -S one that footles

FOOTLESS *adj* having no feet

FOOTLIKE *adj* resembling a foot

FOOTLING present participle of footle

FOOTMAN *n* pl. -MEN a male servant

FOOTMARK *n* pl. -S a mark left by the foot on a surface

FOOTNOTE *v* -NOTED, -NOTING, -NOTES to furnish with explanatory notes

FOOTPACE *n* pl. -S a walking pace

FOOTPAD *n* pl. -S one who robs a pedestrian

FOOTPATH *n* pl. -S a path for pedestrians

FOOTRACE *n* pl. -S a race run on foot

FOOTREST *n* pl. -S a support for the feet

FOOTROPE *n* pl. -S a rope used in sailing

FOOTSIE *n* pl. -S a flirting game played with the feet

FOOTSLOG *v* -SLOGGED, -SLOGGING, -SLOGS to march through mud

FOOTSORE *adj* having sore or tired feet

FOOTSTEP *n* pl. -S a step with the foot

FOOTWALL *n* pl. -S the layer of rock beneath a vein of ore

FOOTWAY *n* pl. -WAYS a footpath

FOOTWEAR *n* pl. -S wearing apparel for the feet

FOOTWORK *n* pl. -S the use of the feet

FOOTWORN *adj* footsore

FOOTY *adj* -TIER, -TIEST paltry

FOOZLE *v* -ZLED, -ZLING, -ZLES to bungle

FOOZLER *n* pl. -S one that foozles

FOP *v* FOPPED, FOPPING, FOPS to deceive

FOPPERY *n* pl. -PERIES foppish behavior

FOPPISH *adj* characteristic of a dandy

FOR *prep* directed or sent to

FORA a pl. of forum

FORAGE *v* -AGED, -AGING, -AGES to search about

FORAGER *n* pl. -S one that forages

FORAM *n* pl. -S a marine rhizopod

FORAMEN *n* pl. -MINA or -MENS a small anatomical opening

FORAY *v* -ED, -ING, -S to raid

FORAYER *n* pl. -S one that forays

FORB *n* pl. -S an herb other than grass

FORBAD a past tense of forbid

FORBADE a past tense of forbid

FORBEAR *v* -BORE, -BORNE, -BEARING, -BEARS to refrain from

FORBID *v* -BADE or -BAD, -BIDDEN, -BIDDING, -BIDS to command not to do something

FORBIDAL *n* pl. -S the act of forbidding

FORBODE *v* -BODED, -BODING, -BODES to forebode

FORBORE past tense of forbear

FORBORNE past participle of forbear

FORBY *prep* close by

FORBYE *prep* forby

FORCE *v* FORCED, FORCING, FORCES to overcome resistance by the exertion of strength **FORCEDLY** *adv*

FORCEFUL *adj* strong

FORCEPS *n* pl. -CIPES an instrument for seizing and holding objects

FORCER *n* pl. -S one that forces

FORCIBLE *adj* effected by force **FORCIBLY** *adv*

FORCING present participle of force

FORCIPES pl. of forceps

FORD *v* -ED, -ING, -S to cross by wading **FORDABLE** *adj*

FORDLESS *adj* unable to be forded

FORDO *v* -DID, -DONE, -DOING, -DOES to destroy

FORE *n* pl. -S the front part of something

FOREARM	v -ED, -ING, -S to arm in advance	**FORELOCK**	n pl. -S a lock of hair growing over the forehead
FOREBAY	n pl. -BAYS a reservoir from which water is taken to run equipment	**FOREMAN**	n pl. -MEN a man who supervises workers
FOREBEAR	n pl. -S an ancestor	**FOREMAST**	n pl. -S the forward mast of a ship
FOREBODE	v -BODED, -BODING, -BODES to indicate in advance	**FOREMILK**	n pl. -S the milk secreted immediately after childbirth
FOREBODY	n pl. -BODIES the forward part of a ship	**FOREMOST**	adj first in position
FOREBOOM	n pl. -S the boom of a ship's foremast	**FORENAME**	n pl. -S a first name
FOREBY	prep forby	**FORENOON**	n pl. -S the period of daylight before noon
FOREBYE	prep forby	**FORENSIC**	n pl. -S an argumentative exercise
FORECAST	v -ED, -ING, -S to estimate or calculate in advance	**FOREPART**	n pl. -S the front part
FOREDATE	v -DATED, -DATING, -DATES to antedate	**FOREPAST**	adj already in the past
		FOREPAW	n pl. -S the paw of a foreleg
FOREDECK	n pl. -S the forward part of a ship's deck	**FOREPEAK**	n pl. -S the forward part of a ship's hold
FOREDO	v -DID, -DONE, -DOING, -DOES to fordo	**FOREPLAY**	n pl. -PLAYS erotic stimulation preceding sexual intercourse
FOREDOOM	v -ED, -ING, -S to doom in advance	**FORERANK**	n pl. -S the first rank
FOREFACE	n pl. -S the front part of the head of a quadruped	**FORERUN**	v -RAN, -RUNNING, -RUNS to run in advance of
FOREFEEL	v -FELT, -FEELING, -FEELS to have a premonition of	**FORESAID**	adj previously said
		FORESAIL	n pl. -S the lowest sail on a foremast
FOREFEND	v -ED, -ING, -S to forfend	**FORESEE**	v -SAW, -SEEN, -SEEING, -SEES to see in advance
FOREFOOT	n pl. -FEET one of the front feet of an animal	**FORESEER**	n pl. -S one that foresees
FOREGO	v -WENT, -GONE, -GOING, -GOES to go before	**FORESHOW**	v -SHOWED, -SHOWN, -SHOWING, -SHOWS to show in advance
FOREGOER	n pl. -S one that foregoes	**FORESIDE**	n pl. -S the front side
FOREGUT	n pl. -S the front part of the embryonic alimentary canal	**FORESKIN**	n pl. -S the prepuce
FOREHAND	n pl. -S a type of tennis stroke	**FOREST**	v -ED, -ING, -S to convert into a forest (a densely wooded area)
FOREHEAD	n pl. -S the part of the face above the eyes	**FORESTAL**	adj of or pertaining to a forest
FOREHOOF	n pl. -HOOFS or -HOOVES the hoof of a forefoot	**FORESTAY**	n pl. -STAYS a wire or rope used to support a foremast
FOREIGN	adj situated outside a place or country	**FORESTER**	n pl. -S one skilled in forestry
FOREKNOW	v -KNEW, -KNOWN, -KNOWING, -KNOWS to know in advance	**FORESTRY**	n pl. -RIES the science of planting and managing forests
FORELADY	n pl. -DIES a woman who supervises workers	**FORETELL**	v -TOLD, -TELLING, -TELLS to tell of or about in advance
FORELAND	n pl. -S a projecting mass of land	**FORETIME**	n pl. -S the past
FORELEG	n pl. -S one of the front legs of an animal	**FORETOP**	n pl. -S a forelock
FORELIMB	n pl. -S a foreleg	**FOREVER**	n pl. -S an indefinite length of time

FOREWARN   *v* -ED, -ING, -S to warn in advance

FOREWENT   past tense of forego

FOREWING   *n* pl. -S an anterior wing of an insect

FOREWORD   *n* pl. -S an introductory statement

FOREWORN   *adj* forworn

FOREYARD   *n* pl. -S the lowest yard on a foremast

FORFEIT   *v* -ED, -ING, -S to lose as a penalty

FORFEND   *v* -ED, -ING, -S to protect

FORGAT   a past tense of forget

FORGAVE   past tense of forgive

FORGE   *v* FORGED, FORGING, FORGES to fashion or reproduce for fraudulent purposes

FORGER   *n* pl. -S one that forges

FORGERY   *n* pl. -ERIES the act of forging

FORGET   *v* -GOT or -GAT, -GOTTEN, -GETTING, -GETS to fail to remember

FORGING   *n* pl. -S a forgery

FORGIVE   *v* -GAVE, -GIVEN, -GIVING, -GIVES to pardon

FORGIVER   *n* pl. -S one that forgives

FORGO   *v* -WENT, -GONE, -GOING, -GOES to refrain from

FORGOER   *n* pl. -S one that forgoes

FORGOT   a past tense of forget

FORGOTTEN   past participle of forget

FORINT   *n* pl. -S a monetary unit of Hungary

FORJUDGE   *v* -JUDGED, -JUDGING, -JUDGES to deprive by judgment of a court

FORK   *v* -ED, -ING, -S to work with a fork (a pronged implement) **FORKEDLY** *adv*

FORKER   *n* pl. -S one that forks

FORKFUL   *n* pl. FORKFULS or FORKSFUL as much as a fork will hold

FORKIER   comparative of forky

FORKIEST   superlative of forky

FORKLESS   *adj* having no fork

FORKLIFT   *n* pl. -S a machine for lifting and carrying loads

FORKLIKE   *adj* resembling a fork

FORKSFUL   a pl. of forkful

FORKY   *adj* FORKIER, FORKIEST resembling a fork

FORLORN   *adj* -LORNER, -LORNEST dreary

FORM   *v* -ED, -ING, -S to produce **FORMABLE** *adj*

FORMAL   *n* pl. -S a social event that requires evening dress

FORMALIN   *n* pl. -S an aqueous solution of formaldehyde

FORMALLY   *adv* in a prescribed or customary manner

FORMANT   *n* pl. -S a characteristic component of the quality of a speech sound

FORMAT   *v* -MATTED, -MATTING, -MATS to produce in a specified style

FORMATE   *n* pl. -S a chemical salt

FORME   *n* pl. -S an assemblage of printing type secured in a metal frame

FORMEE   *adj* having the arms narrow at the center and expanding toward the ends — used of a heraldic cross

FORMER   *n* pl. -S one that forms

FORMERLY   *adv* previously

FORMFUL   *adj* exhibiting good form

FORMIC   *adj* pertaining to ants

FORMLESS   *adj* lacking structure

FORMOL   *n* pl. -S formalin

FORMULA   *n* pl. -LAS or -LAE an exact method for doing something

FORMYL   *n* pl. -S a univalent chemical radical

FORNIX   *n* pl. -NICES an arched anatomical structure **FORNICAL** *adj*

FORRADER   *adv* further ahead

FORRIT   *adv* toward the front

FORSAKE   *v* -SOOK, -SAKEN, -SAKING, -SAKES to quit or leave entirely

FORSAKER   *n* pl. -S one that forsakes

FORSOOTH   *adv* in truth

FORSPENT   *adj* worn out

FORSWEAR   *v* -SWORE, -SWORN, -SWEARING, -SWEARS to deny under oath

FORT   *n* pl. -S a fortified enclosure or structure

FORTE   *n* pl. -S a strong point

FORTH	*adv* onward in time, place, or order
FORTIES	pl. of forty
FORTIETH	*n* pl. -S one of forty equal parts
FORTIFY	*v* -FIED, -FYING, -FIES to strengthen against attack
FORTIS	*n* pl. -TES a consonant pronounced with relatively strong release of breath
FORTRESS	*v* -ED, -ING, -ES to fortify
FORTUITY	*n* pl. -ITIES an accidental occurrence
FORTUNE	*v* -TUNED, -TUNING, -TUNES to endow with wealth
FORTY	*n* pl. -TIES a number
FORUM	*n* pl. -RUMS or -RA a public meeting place
FORWARD	*adj* -WARDER, -WARDEST being at or near a point in advance
FORWARD	*v* -ED, -ING, -S to help onward
FORWENT	past tense of forgo
FORWHY	*adv* for what reason
FORWORN	*adj* worn out
FORZANDO	*n* pl. -DOS sforzato
FOSS	*n* pl. -ES fosse
FOSSA	*n* pl. -SAE an anatomical depression **FOSSATE** *adj*
FOSSE	*n* pl. -S a ditch
FOSSETTE	*n* pl. -S a small fossa
FOSSICK	*v* -ED, -ING, -S to search for gold
FOSSIL	*n* pl. -S the remains of an animal or plant preserved in the earth's crust
FOSTER	*v* -ED, -ING, -S to promote the growth of
FOSTERER	*n* pl. -S one that fosters
FOU	*adj* drunk
FOUGHT	past tense of fight
FOUGHTEN	*adj* exhausted especially from fighting
FOUL	*adj* FOULER, FOULEST offensive to the senses
FOUL	*v* -ED, -ING, -S to make foul
FOULARD	*n* pl. -S a soft fabric
FOULING	*n* pl. -S a deposit or crust
FOULLY	*adv* in a foul manner
FOULNESS	*n* pl. -ES the state of being foul
FOUND	*v* -ED, -ING, -S to establish
FOUNDER	*v* -ED, -ING, -S to become disabled
FOUNDRY	*n* pl. -RIES an establishment in which metal is cast
FOUNT	*n* pl. -S a fountain
FOUNTAIN	*v* -ED, -ING, -S to flow like a fountain (a spring of water)
FOUR	*n* pl. -S a number
FOURCHEE	*adj* having the end of each arm forked — used of a heraldic cross
FOURFOLD	*adj* four times as great
FOURGON	*n* pl. -S a wagon for carrying baggage
FOURSOME	*n* pl. -S a group of four
FOURTEEN	*n* pl. -S a number
FOURTH	*n* pl. -S one of four equal parts
FOURTHLY	*adv* in the fourth place
FOVEA	*n* pl. -VEAE a shallow anatomical depression **FOVEAL, FOVEATE, FOVEATED** *adj*
FOVEOLA	*n* pl. -LAE or -LAS a small fovea **FOVEOLAR** *adj*
FOVEOLE	*n* pl. -S a foveola
FOVEOLET	*n* pl. -S a foveola
FOWL	*v* -ED, -ING, -S to hunt birds
FOWLER	*n* pl. -S one that fowls
FOWLING	*n* pl. -S the hunting of birds
FOWLPOX	*n* pl. -ES a virus disease of poultry
FOX	*v* -ED, -ING, -ES to outwit
FOXFIRE	*n* pl. -S a glow produced by certain fungi on decaying wood
FOXFISH	*n* pl. -ES a large shark
FOXGLOVE	*n* pl. -S a flowering plant
FOXHOLE	*n* pl. -S a small pit used for cover in a battle area
FOXHOUND	*n* pl. -S a hunting dog
FOXIER	comparative of foxy
FOXIEST	superlative of foxy
FOXILY	*adv* in a foxy manner
FOXINESS	*n* pl. -ES the state of being foxy
FOXING	*n* pl. -S a piece of material used to cover the upper portion of a shoe
FOXLIKE	*adj* resembling a fox (a carnivorous mammal)
FOXSKIN	*n* pl. -S the skin of a fox
FOXTAIL	*n* pl. -S the tail of a fox

FOXY   *adj* FOXIER, FOXIEST crafty

FOY   *n* pl. FOYS a farewell feast or gift

FOYER   *n* pl. -S an entrance room or hall

FOZINESS   *n* pl. -ES the state of being fozy

FOZY   *adj* -ZIER, -ZIEST too ripe

FRACAS   *n* pl. -ES a brawl

FRACTED   *adj* broken

FRACTION   *v* -ED, -ING, -S to divide into portions

FRACTUR   *n* pl. -S fraktur

FRACTURE   *v* -TURED, -TURING, -TURES to break

FRAE   *prep* from

FRAENUM   *n* pl. -NA or -NUMS frenum

FRAG   *v* FRAGGED, FRAGGING, FRAGS to injure with a type of grenade

FRAGGING   *n* pl. -S the act of one that frags

FRAGILE   *adj* easily broken or damaged

FRAGMENT   *v* -ED, -ING, -S to break into pieces

FRAGRANT   *adj* having a pleasant odor

FRAIL   *adj* FRAILER, FRAILEST fragile **FRAILLY** *adv*

FRAIL   *n* pl. -S a basket for holding dried fruits

FRAILTY   *n* pl. -TIES a weakness of character

FRAISE   *n* pl. -S a barrier of pointed stakes

FRAKTUR   *n* pl. -S a style of type

FRAME   *v* FRAMED, FRAMING, FRAMES to construct by putting together the various parts **FRAMABLE** *adj*

FRAMER   *n* pl. -S one that frames

FRANC   *n* pl. -S a monetary unit of France

FRANCIUM   *n* pl. -S a radioactive element

FRANK   *adj* FRANKER, FRANKEST honest and unreserved in speech

FRANK   *v* -ED, -ING, -S to mark (a piece of mail) for free delivery

FRANKER   *n* pl. -S one that franks

FRANKEST   superlative of frank

FRANKLIN   *n* pl. -S a medieval English landowner

FRANKLY   *adv* in a frank manner

FRANTIC   *adj* wildly excited

FRAP   *v* FRAPPED, FRAPPING, FRAPS to bind firmly

FRAPPE   *n* pl. -S a partly frozen drink

FRAT   *n* pl. -S a college fraternity

FRATER   *n* pl. -S a comrade

FRAUD   *n* pl. -S trickery

FRAUGHT   *v* -ED, -ING, -S to load down

FRAULEIN   *n* pl. -S a German governess

FRAY   *v* -ED, -ING, -S to wear off by rubbing

FRAYING   *n* pl. -S something worn off by rubbing

FRAZZLE   *v* -ZLED, -ZLING, -ZLES to fray

FREAK   *v* -ED, -ING, -S to streak with color

FREAKIER   comparative of freaky

FREAKIEST   superlative of freaky

FREAKILY   *adv* in a freaky manner

FREAKISH   *adj* unusual

FREAKOUT   *n* pl. -S an event marked by wild excitement

FREAKY   *adj* FREAKIER, FREAKIEST freakish

FRECKLE   *v* -LED, -LING, -LES to mark with freckles (small, brownish spots)

FRECKLY   *adj* -LIER, -LIEST marked with freckles

FREE   *adj* FREER, FREEST not subject to restriction or control

FREE   *v* FREED, FREEING, FREES to make free

FREEBEE   *n* pl. -S freebie

FREEBIE   *n* pl. -S something given or received without charge

FREEBOOT   *v* -ED, -ING, -S to plunder

FREEBORN   *adj* born free

FREED   past tense of free

FREEDMAN   *n* pl. -MEN a man who has been freed from slavery

FREEDOM   *n* pl. -S the state of being free

FREEFORM   *adj* having a free flowing design or shape

FREEHAND   *adj* drawn by hand without mechanical aids

FREEHOLD   *n* pl. -S a form of tenure of real property

FREELOAD	v -ED, -ING, -S to live at the expense of others
FREELY	adv in a free manner
FREEMAN	n pl. -MEN one who is free
FREENESS	n pl. -ES freedom
FREER	n pl. -S one that frees
FREESIA	n pl. -S an African herb
FREEST	superlative of free
FREEWAY	n pl. -WAYS an express highway
FREEWILL	adj voluntary
FREEZE	v FROZE, FROZEN, FREEZING, FREEZES to become hardened into a solid body by loss of heat
FREEZER	n pl. -S an apparatus for freezing food
FREIGHT	v -ED, -ING, -S to load with goods for transportation
FREMD	adj strange
FREMITUS	n pl. -ES a palpable vibration
FRENA	a pl. of frenum
FRENCH	v -ED, -ING, -ES to cut into thin strips before cooking
FRENETIC	n pl. -S a frantic person
FRENULUM	n pl. -LA a frenum
FRENUM	n pl. -NA or -NUMS a connecting fold of membrane
FRENZILY	adv in a frantic manner
FRENZY	v -ZIED, -ZYING, -ZIES to make frantic
FREQUENT	adj -QUENTER, -QUENTEST occurring again and again
FREQUENT	v -ED, -ING, -S to be in or at often
FRERE	n pl. -S brother
FRESCO	v -ED, -ING, -ES or -S to paint on a surface of plaster
FRESCOER	n pl. -S one that frescoes
FRESH	adj FRESHER, FRESHEST new
FRESH	v -ED, -ING, -ES to freshen
FRESHEN	v -ED, -ING, -S to make or become fresh
FRESHET	n pl. -S a sudden overflow of a stream
FRESHLY	adv in a fresh manner
FRESHMAN	n pl. -MEN a first-year student
FRESNEL	n pl. -S a unit of frequency
FRET	v FRETTED, FRETTING, FRETS to worry
FRETFUL	adj inclined to fret
FRETLESS	adj having no fretwork
FRETSAW	n pl. -S a narrow-bladed saw
FRETSOME	adj fretful
FRETTED	past tense of fret
FRETTING	present participle of fret
FRETTY	adj -TIER, -TIEST fretful
FRETWORK	n pl. -S ornamental work consisting of interlacing parts
FRIABLE	adj easily crumbled
FRIAR	n pl. -S a member of a religious order **FRIARLY** adj
FRIARY	n pl. -ARIES a monastery of friars
FRIBBLE	v -BLED, -BLING, -BLES to act foolishly
FRIBBLER	n pl. -S one that fribbles
FRICANDO	n pl. -DOES a roasted loin of veal
FRICTION	n pl. -S the rubbing of one body against another
FRIDGE	n pl. -S a refrigerator
FRIED	past tense of fry
FRIEND	v -ED, -ING, -S to enter into a warm association with
FRIENDLY	adj -LIER, -LIEST inclined to approve, help, or support
FRIENDLY	n pl. -LIES one who is friendly
FRIER	n pl. -S fryer
FRIES	present 3d person sing. of fry
FRIEZE	n pl. -S a coarse woolen fabric
FRIG	v FRIGGED, FRIGGING, FRIGS to copulate — usually considered vulgar
FRIGATE	n pl. -S a sailing vessel
FRIGHT	v -ED, -ING, -S to frighten
FRIGHTEN	v -ED, -ING, -S to make afraid
FRIGID	adj very cold **FRIGIDLY** adv
FRIJOL	n pl. -ES a bean used as food
FRIJOLE	n pl. -S frijol
FRILL	v -ED, -ING, -S to provide with a frill (an ornamental ruffled edge)
FRILLER	n pl. -S one that frills
FRILLING	n pl. -S an arrangement of frills
FRILLY	adj FRILLIER, FRILLIEST having frills
FRINGE	v FRINGED, FRINGING, FRINGES to provide with a fringe (an ornamental border)

FRINGY *adj* FRINGIER, FRINGIEST resembling a fringe

FRIPPERY *n* pl. -PERIES excessive ornamentation

FRISE *n* pl. -S frieze

FRISETTE *n* pl. -S frizette

FRISEUR *n* pl. -S a hairdresser

FRISK *v* -ED, -ING, -S to move or leap about playfully

FRISKER *n* pl. -S one that frisks

FRISKET *n* pl. -S a frame used to protect paper in a printing press

FRISKY *adj* FRISKIER, FRISKIEST lively and playful **FRISKILY** *adv*

FRISSON *n* pl. -S a shudder

FRIT *v* FRITTED, FRITTING, FRITS to fuse into a vitreous substance

FRITH *n* pl. -S firth

FRITT *v* -ED, -ING, -S to frit

FRITTED past tense of frit

FRITTER *v* -ED, -ING, -S to squander little by little

FRITTING present participle of frit

FRIVOL *v* -OLED, -OLING, -OLS or -OLLED, -OLLING, -OLS to behave playfully

FRIVOLER *n* pl. -S one that frivols

FRIZ *n* pl. -ES a tight curl

FRIZ *v* -ED, -ING, -ES to frizz

FRIZER *n* pl. -S frizzer

FRIZETTE *n* pl. -S a frizzed fringe of hair

FRIZZ *n* pl. -ES friz

FRIZZ *v* -ED, -ING, -ES to form into small, tight curls

FRIZZER *n* pl. -S one that frizzes

FRIZZIER comparative of frizzy

FRIZZIEST superlative of frizzy

FRIZZILY *adv* in a frizzy manner

FRIZZLE *v* -ZLED, -ZLING, -ZLES to frizz

FRIZZLER *n* pl. -S one that frizzles

FRIZZLY *adj* -ZLIER, -ZLIEST frizzy

FRIZZY *adj* FRIZZIER, FRIZZIEST tightly curled

FRO *adv* away

FROCK *v* -ED, -ING, -S to clothe in a long, loose outer garment

FROE *n* pl. -S a cleaving tool

FROG *v* FROGGED, FROGGING, FROGS to hunt frogs (web-footed, tailless amphibians)

FROGEYE *n* pl. -S a plant disease **FROGEYED** *adj*

FROGFISH *n* pl. -ES a marine fish

FROGGED past tense of frog

FROGGING present participle of frog

FROGGY *adj* -GIER, -GIEST abounding in frogs

FROGLIKE *adj* resembling a frog

FROGMAN *n* pl. -MEN a person equipped for extended periods of underwater swimming

FROLIC *v* -ICKED, -ICKING, -ICS to play and run about merrily **FROLICKY** *adj*

FROM *prep* starting at

FROMAGE *n* pl. -S cheese

FROMENTY *n* pl. -TIES frumenty

FROND *n* pl. -S a type of leaf **FRONDED, FRONDOSE** *adj*

FRONDEUR *n* pl. -S a rebel

FRONS *n* pl. FRONTES the upper anterior portion of an insect's head

FRONT *v* -ED, -ING, -S to provide with a front (a forward part)

FRONT *adj* FRONTER articulated at the front of the oral passage

FRONTAGE *n* pl. -S the front of a building or lot

FRONTAL *n* pl. -S a bone of the skull

FRONTES pl. of frons

FRONTIER *n* pl. -S a border between two countries

FRONTLET *n* pl. -S a decorative band worn across the forehead

FRONTON *n* pl. -S a jai alai arena

FRORE *adj* frozen

FROSH *n* pl. FROSH a freshman

FROST *v* -ED, -ING, -S to cover with frost (a deposit of minute ice crystals)

FROSTBIT *adj* injured by extreme cold

FROSTED *n* pl. -S a type of milk shake

FROSTING *n* pl. -S icing

FROSTY *adj* FROSTIER, FROSTIEST covered with frost **FROSTILY** *adv*

FROTH *v* -ED, -ING, -S to foam

FROTHY   *adj* FROTHIER, FROTHIEST foamy **FROTHILY** *adv*

FROTTAGE   *n* pl. -S masturbation by rubbing against another person

FROTTEUR   *n* pl. -S one who practices frottage

FROUFROU   *n* pl. -S a rustling sound

FROUNCE   *v* FROUNCED, FROUNCING, FROUNCES to pleat

FROUZY   *adj* -ZIER, -ZIEST frowzy

FROW   *n* pl. -S froe

FROWARD   *adj* disobedient

FROWN   *v* -ED, -ING, -S to contract the brow in displeasure

FROWNER   *n* pl. -S one that frowns

FROWSTY   *adj* -TIER, -TIEST musty

FROWSY   *adj* -SIER, -SIEST frowzy

FROWZY   *adj* -ZIER, -ZIEST unkempt **FROWZILY** *adv*

FROZE   past tense of freeze

FROZEN   *adj* very cold **FROZENLY** *adv*

FRUCTIFY   *v* -FIED, -FYING, -FIES to bear fruit

FRUCTOSE   *n* pl. -S a sugar found in various fruits

FRUG   *v* FRUGGED, FRUGGING, FRUGS to perform a type of vigorous dance

FRUGAL   *adj* thrifty **FRUGALLY** *adv*

FRUIT   *v* -ED, -ING, -S to bear fruit (usually edible reproductive bodies of a seed plant)

FRUITAGE   *n* pl. -S the process of bearing fruit

FRUITER   *n* pl. -S one that grows or sells fruit

FRUITFUL   *adj* -FULLER, -FULLEST producing abundantly

FRUITIER   comparative of fruity

FRUITIEST   superlative of fruity

FRUITION   *n* pl. -S the accomplishment of something desired

FRUITLET   *n* pl. -S a small fruit

FRUITY   *adj* FRUITIER, FRUITIEST suggestive of fruit

FRUMENTY   *n* pl. -TIES a dish of wheat boiled in milk and sweetened with sugar

FRUMP   *n* pl. -S a dowdy woman **FRUMPISH** *adj*

FRUMPY   *adj* FRUMPIER, FRUMPIEST dowdy **FRUMPILY** *adv*

FRUSTA   a pl. of frustum

FRUSTULE   *n* pl. -S the shell of a diatom

FRUSTUM   *n* pl. -TA or -TUMS a part of a conical solid

FRY   *v* FRIED, FRYING, FRIES to cook over direct heat in hot fat or oil

FRYER   *n* pl. -S one that fries

FRYPAN   *n* pl. -S a pan for frying food

FUB   *v* FUBBED, FUBBING, FUBS to fob

FUBSY   *adj* FUBSIER, FUBSIEST chubby and somewhat squat

FUCHSIA   *n* pl. -S a flowering shrub

FUCHSIN   *n* pl. -S a red dye

FUCHSINE   *n* pl. -S fuchsin

FUCI   a pl. of fucus

FUCK   *v* -ED, -ING, -S to copulate — usually considered obscene

FUCOID   *n* pl. -S a brown seaweed **FUCOIDAL** *adj*

FUCOSE   *n* pl. -S a type of sugar

FUCOUS   *adj* of or pertaining to fucoids

FUCUS   *n* pl. -CI or -CUSES any of a genus of brown algae

FUD   *n* pl. -S an old-fashioned person

FUDDLE   *v* -DLED, -DLING, -DLES to confuse

FUDGE   *v* FUDGED, FUDGING, FUDGES to falsify

FUEHRER   *n* pl. -S fuhrer

FUEL   *v* -ELED, -ELING, -ELS or -ELLED, -ELLING, -ELS to provide with fuel (material used to produce energy)

FUELER   *n* pl. -S one that fuels

FUELLER   *n* pl. -S fueler

FUELLING   a present participle of fuel

FUG   *v* FUGGED, FUGGING, FUGS to make stuffy and odorous

FUGACITY   *n* pl. -TIES lack of enduring qualities

FUGAL   *adj* being in the style of a fugue **FUGALLY** *adv*

FUGATO   *n* pl. -TOS a fugal composition

FUGGED   past tense of fug

FUGGING   present participle of fug

FUGGY   *adj* -GIER, -GIEST stuffy and odorous

FUGIO   *n* pl. -GIOS a former coin of the United States

FUGITIVE   *n* pl. -S one who flees

FUGLE   *v* •GLED, -GLING, -GLES to lead

FUGLEMAN   *n* pl. -MEN a leader

FUGUE   *v* FUGUED, FUGUING, FUGUES to compose a fugue (a type of musical composition)

FUGUIST   *n* pl. -S one who composes fugues

FUHRER   *n* pl. -S a leader

FUJI   *n* pl. -S a silk fabric

FULCRUM   *n* pl. -CRUMS or -CRA a support for a lever

FULFIL   *v* -FILLED, -FILLING, -FILS to fulfill

FULFILL   *v* -ED, -ING, -S to bring about the accomplishment of

FULGENT   *adj* shining brightly

FULGID   *adj* fulgent

FULHAM   *n* pl. -S a loaded die

FULL   *adj* FULLER, FULLEST filled completely

FULL   *v* -ED, -ING, -S to shrink and thicken, as cloth

FULLAM   *n* pl. -S fulham

FULLBACK   *n* pl. -S an offensive back in football

FULLER   *v* -ED, -ING, -S to groove with a type of hammer

FULLERY   *n* pl. -ERIES a place for fulling cloth

FULLFACE   *n* pl. -S a heavy-faced type

FULLNESS   *n* pl. -ES the state of being full

FULLY   *adv* in a full manner

FULMAR   *n* pl. -S an arctic seabird

FULMINE   *v* -MINED, -MINING, -MINES to explode loudly

FULMINIC   *adj* highly explosive

FULNESS   *n* pl. -ES fullness

FULSOME   *adj* repulsive

FULVOUS   *adj* of a brownish yellow color

FUMARASE   *n* pl. -S an enzyme

FUMARATE   *n* pl. -S a chemical salt

FUMARIC   *adj* pertaining to a certain acid

FUMAROLE   *n* pl. -S a hole from which volcanic vapors issue

FUMATORY   *n* pl. -RIES a fumigation chamber

FUMBLE   *v* -BLED, -BLING, -BLES to handle clumsily

FUMBLER   *n* pl. -S one that fumbles

FUME   *v* FUMED, FUMING, FUMES to give off fumes (gaseous exhalations)

FUMELESS   *adj* having no fumes

FUMELIKE   *adj* resembling fumes

FUMER   *n* pl. -S one that fumes

FUMET   *n* pl. -S the odor of meat while cooking

FUMETTE   *n* pl. -S fumet

FUMIER   comparative of fumy

FUMIEST   superlative of fumy

FUMIGANT   *n* pl. -S a substance used in fumigating

FUMIGATE   *v* -GATED, -GATING, -GATES to subject to fumes in order to destroy pests

FUMING   present participle of fume

FUMITORY   *n* pl. -RIES a climbing plant

FUMULUS   *n* pl. -LI a thin cloud

FUMY   *adj* FUMIER, FUMIEST producing or full of fumes

FUN   *v* FUNNED, FUNNING, FUNS to act playfully

FUNCTION   *v* -ED, -ING, -S to be in action

FUNCTOR   *n* pl. -S one that functions

FUND   *v* -ED, -ING, -S to provide money for

FUNDUS   *n* pl. -DI the inner basal surface of a bodily organ **FUNDIC** *adj*

FUNERAL   *n* pl. -S a ceremony held for a dead person

FUNERARY   *adj* pertaining to a funeral

FUNEREAL   *adj* funerary

FUNEST   *adj* portending death or evil

FUNFAIR   *n* pl. -S an amusement park

FUNGAL   *n* pl. -S a fungus

FUNGI   a pl. of fungus

FUNGIBLE   *n* pl. -S something that may be exchanged for an equivalent unit of the same class

FUNGIC   *adj* fungous

FUNGO   *n* pl. -GOES a fly ball hit to a fielder for practice in baseball

FUNGOID   *n* pl. -S a growth resembling a fungus

FUNGOUS	*adj* pertaining to a fungus	**FURLESS**	*adj* having no fur
FUNGUS	*n* pl. -GI or -GUSES any of a major group of lower plants	**FURLONG**	*n* pl. -S a unit of distance
FUNICLE	*n* pl. -S a cordlike anatomical structure	**FURLOUGH**	*v* -ED, -ING, -S to grant a leave of absence to
FUNICULI	*n/pl* funicles	**FURMENTY**	*n* pl. -TIES frumenty
FUNK	*v* -ED, -ING, -S to shrink back in fear	**FURMETY**	*n* pl. -TIES frumenty
FUNKER	*n* pl. -S one that funks	**FURMITY**	*n* pl. -TIES frumenty
FUNKIA	*n* pl. -S a flowering plant	**FURNACE**	*v* -NACED, -NACING, -NACES to subject to heat
FUNKY	*adj* FUNKIER, FUNKIEST having an offensive odor	**FURNISH**	*v* -ED, -ING, -ES to equip
FUNNED	past tense of fun	**FUROR**	*n* pl. -S an uproar
FUNNEL	*v* -NELED, -NELING, -NELS or -NELLED, -NELLING, -NELS to pass through a funnel (a cone-shaped utensil)	**FURORE**	*n* pl. -S furor
		FURRED	past tense of fur
		FURRIER	*n* pl. -S one that deals in furs
FUNNING	present participle of fun	**FURRIERY**	*n* pl. -ERIES the business of a furrier
FUNNY	*adj* -NIER, -NIEST causing laughter or amusement **FUNNILY** *adv*	**FURRIEST**	superlative of furry
		FURRILY	*adv* in a furry manner
FUNNY	*n* pl. -NIES a comic strip	**FURRINER**	*n* pl. -S a foreigner
FUNNYMAN	*n* pl. -MEN a comedian	**FURRING**	*n* pl. -S a trimming or lining of fur
FUR	*v* FURRED, FURRING, FURS to cover with fur (a dressed animal pelt)	**FURROW**	*v* -ED, -ING, -S to make furrows (narrow depressions) in
FURAN	*n* pl. -S a flammable liquid	**FURROWER**	*n* pl. -S one that furrows
FURANE	*n* pl. -S furan	**FURROWY**	*adj* marked by furrows
FURANOSE	*n* pl. -S a type of sugar	**FURRY**	*adj* -RIER, -RIEST covered with fur
FURBELOW	*v* -ED, -ING, -S to decorate with ruffles	**FURTHER**	*v* -ED, -ING, -S to help forward
FURBISH	*v* -ED, -ING, -ES to polish	**FURTHEST**	a superlative of far
FURCATE	*v* -CATED, -CATING, -CATES to divide into branches	**FURTIVE**	*adj* stealthy
		FURUNCLE	*n* pl. -S a painful swelling of the skin
FURCRAEA	*n* pl. -S a tropical plant	**FURY**	*n* pl. -RIES violent anger
FURCULA	*n* pl. -LAE a forked bone **FURCULAR** *adj*	**FURZE**	*n* pl. -S a spiny shrub
FURCULUM	*n* pl. -LA a furcula	**FURZY**	*adj* FURZIER, FURZIEST abounding in furze
FURFUR	*n* pl. -ES dandruff	**FUSAIN**	*n* pl. -S a fine charcoal used in drawing
FURFURAL	*n* pl. -S a chemical compound	**FUSCOUS**	*adj* of a dusky color
FURFURAN	*n* pl. -S furan	**FUSE**	*v* FUSED, FUSING, FUSES to equip with a fuse (a detonating device)
FURIBUND	*adj* furious		
FURIES	pl. of fury		
FURIOSO	*adv* with great force — used as a musical direction	**FUSEE**	*n* pl. -S a large-headed friction match
FURIOUS	*adj* extremely angry	**FUSEL**	*n* pl. -S an oily liquid
FURL	*v* -ED, -ING, -S to roll up **FURLABLE** *adj*	**FUSELAGE**	*n* pl. -S the body of an airplane
FURLER	*n* pl. -S one that furls	**FUSELESS**	*adj* lacking a fuse

FUSIBLE   *adj* capable of being melted
FUSIBLY *adv*

FUSIFORM   *adj* tapering toward each end

FUSIL   *n* pl. -S a type of musket

FUSILE   *adj* formed by melting

FUSILEER   *n* pl. -S fusilier

FUSILIER   *n* pl. -S a soldier armed with a fusil

FUSING   present participle of fuse

FUSION   *n* pl. -S the act of melting together

FUSS   *v* -ED, -ING, -ES to be overly concerned with small details

FUSSER   *n* pl. -S one that fusses

FUSSPOT   *n* pl. -S a fusser

FUSSY   *adj* FUSSIER, FUSSIEST overly concerned with small details
FUSSILY *adv*

FUSTIAN   *n* pl. -S a cotton fabric

FUSTIC   *n* pl. -S a tropical tree

FUSTY   *adj* -TIER, -TIEST musty
FUSTILY *adv*

FUTHARC   *n* pl. -S futhark

FUTHARK   *n* pl. -S an ancient alphabet

FUTHORC   *n* pl. -S futhark

FUTHORK   *n* pl. -S futhark

FUTILE   *adj* having no useful result
FUTILELY *adv*

FUTILITY   *n* pl. -TIES the quality of being futile

FUTTOCK   *n* pl. -S a curved timber in the frame of a wooden ship

FUTURE   *n* pl. -S the time yet to come
FUTURAL *adj*

FUTURISM   *n* pl. -S an artistic and literary movement

FUTURIST   *n* pl. -S an advocate of futurism

FUTURITY   *n* pl. -TIES the future

FUZE   *v* FUZED, FUZING, FUZES to fuse

FUZEE   *n* pl. -S fusee

FUZIL   *n* pl. -S fusil

FUZING   present participle of fuze

FUZZ   *v* -ED, -ING, -ES to become fuzzy

FUZZY   *adj* FUZZIER, FUZZIEST blurry
FUZZILY *adv*

FYCE   *n* pl. -S feist

FYKE   *n* pl. -S a bag-shaped fishnet

FYLFOT   *n* pl. -S a swastika

FYTTE   *n* pl. -S a division of a poem or song

GAB	v GABBED, GABBING, GABS to chatter
GABBARD	n pl. -S a barge
GABBART	n pl. -S gabbard
GABBED	past tense of gab
GABBER	n pl. -S one that gabs
GABBING	present participle of gab
GABBLE	v -BLED, -BLING, -BLES to jabber
GABBLER	n pl. -S one that gabbles
GABBRO	n pl. -BROS a type of rock **GABBROIC, GABBROID** adj
GABBY	adj -BIER, -BIEST talkative
GABELLE	n pl. -S a tax on salt **GABELLED** adj
GABFEST	n pl. -S an informal gathering for general talk
GABIES	pl. of gaby
GABION	n pl. -S a type of basket
GABLE	v -BLED, -BLING, -BLES to form a triangular section of a wall
GABOON	n pl. -S a spittoon
GABY	n pl. -BIES a dolt
GAD	v GADDED, GADDING, GADS to roam about restlessly
GADABOUT	n pl. -S one that gads about
GADARENE	adj headlong
GADDED	past tense of gad
GADDER	n pl. -S one that gads about
GADDI	n pl. -S a hassock
GADDING	present participle of gad
GADFLY	n pl. -FLIES a biting fly
GADGET	n pl. -S a mechanical device **GADGETY** adj
GADGETRY	n pl. -RIES the devising or constructing of gadgets
GADI	n pl. -S gaddi
GADID	n pl. -S gadoid
GADOID	n pl. -S a type of fish
GADROON	n pl. -S a band of fluted or reeded molding
GADWALL	n pl. -S a wild duck
GADZOOKS	interj — used as a mild oath
GAE	v GAED, GANE, GAUN, GAES to go
GAFF	v -ED, -ING, -S to catch a fish with a sharp hook
GAFFE	n pl. -S a social blunder
GAFFER	n pl. -S an old man
GAG	v GAGGED, GAGGING, GAGS to stop up the mouth
GAGA	adj crazy
GAGE	v GAGED, GAGING, GAGES to pledge as security
GAGER	n pl. -S gauger
GAGGED	past tense of gag
GAGGER	n pl. -S one that gags
GAGGING	present participle of gag
GAGGLE	v -GLED, -GLING, -GLES to cackle
GAGING	present participle of gage
GAGMAN	n pl. -MEN one who writes jokes
GAGSTER	n pl. -S a gagman
GAHNITE	n pl. -S a mineral
GAIETY	n pl. -ETIES festive activity

GAILY	*adv* in a gay manner
GAIN	*v* -ED, -ING, -S to acquire **GAINABLE** *adj*
GAINER	*n* pl. -S one that gains
GAINFUL	*adj* profitable
GAINLESS	*adj* profitless
GAINLY	*adj* -LIER, -LIEST graceful
GAINSAY	*v* -SAID, -SAYING, -SAYS to deny
GAINST	*prep* against
GAIT	*v* -ED, -ING, -S to train a horse to move in a particular way
GAITER	*n* pl. -S a covering for the lower leg
GAL	*n* pl. -S a girl
GALA	*n* pl. -S a celebration
GALACTIC	*adj* pertaining to a galaxy
GALAGO	*n* pl. -GOS a small primate
GALAH	*n* pl. -S a cockatoo
GALANGAL	*n* pl. -S a medicinal plant
GALATEA	*n* pl. -S a strong cotton fabric
GALAVANT	*v* -ED, -ING, -S to gad about
GALAX	*n* pl. -ES an evergreen herb
GALAXY	*n* pl. -AXIES a large system of celestial bodies
GALBANUM	*n* pl. -S a gum resin
GALE	*n* pl. -S a strong wind
GALEA	*n* pl. -LEAE or -LEAS a helmet-shaped anatomical part **GALEATE, GALEATED** *adj*
GALENA	*n* pl. -S the principal ore of lead **GALENIC** *adj*
GALENITE	*n* pl. -S galena
GALERE	*n* pl. -S a group of people having a common quality
GALILEE	*n* pl. -S a type of porch
GALIOT	*n* pl. -S galliot
GALIPOT	*n* pl. -S a type of turpentine
GALIVANT	*v* -ED, -ING, -S to gad about
GALL	*v* -ED, -ING, -S to vex or irritate
GALLANT	*v* -ED, -ING, -S to court a woman
GALLATE	*n* pl. -S a chemical salt
GALLEASS	*n* pl. -ES a large war galley
GALLEIN	*n* pl. -S a green dye
GALLEON	*n* pl. -S a large sailing vessel
GALLERY	*v* -LERIED, -LERYING, -LERIES to provide with a long covered area
GALLETA	*n* pl. -S a perennial grass
GALLEY	*n* pl. -LEYS a long, low medieval ship
GALLFLY	*n* pl. -FLIES a small insect
GALLIARD	*n* pl. -S a lively dance
GALLIASS	*n* pl. -ES galleass
GALLIC	*adj* containing gallium
GALLICAN	*adj* pertaining to a French religious movement
GALLIED	past tense of gally
GALLIES	present 3d person sing. of gally
GALLIOT	*n* pl. -S a small galley
GALLIPOT	*n* pl. -S a small earthen jar
GALLIUM	*n* pl. -S a metallic element
GALLNUT	*n* pl. -S an abnormal swelling of plant tissue
GALLON	*n* pl. -S a unit of liquid measure
GALLOON	*n* pl. -S an ornamental braid
GALLOOT	*n* pl. -S galoot
GALLOP	*v* -ED, -ING, -S to ride a horse at full speed
GALLOPER	*n* pl. -S one that gallops
GALLOUS	*adj* containing gallium
GALLOWS	*n* pl. -ES a structure used for hanging a condemned person
GALLUS	*n* pl. -ES a suspender for trousers **GALLUSED** *adj*
GALLY	*v* -LIED, -LYING, -LIES to frighten
GALOOT	*n* pl. -S an awkward or uncouth person
GALOP	*n* pl. -S a lively dance
GALOPADE	*n* pl. -S a galop
GALORE	*n* pl. -S abundance
GALOSH	*n* pl. -ES an overshoe **GALOSHED** *adj*
GALOSHE	*n* pl. -S galosh
GALUMPH	*v* -ED, -ING, -S to move clumsily
GALVANIC	*adj* pertaining to a direct electric current
GALYAC	*n* pl. -S galyak
GALYAK	*n* pl. -S a fur made from lambskin
GAM	*v* GAMMED, GAMMING, GAMS to visit socially

GAMASHES *n/pl* boots worn by horseback riders

GAMB *n* pl. -S a leg

GAMBA *n* pl. -S a bass viol

GAMBADE *n* pl. -S a gambado

GAMBADO *n* pl. -DOES or -DOS a leap made by a horse

GAMBE *n* pl. -S gamb

GAMBESON *n* pl. -S a medieval coat

GAMBIA *n* pl. -S gambier

GAMBIER *n* pl. -S an extract obtained from an Asian vine

GAMBIR *n* pl. -S gambier

GAMBIT *n* pl. -S a type of chess opening

GAMBLE *v* -BLED, -BLING, -BLES to play a game of chance for money or valuables

GAMBLER *n* pl. -S one that gambles

GAMBOGE *n* pl. -S a gum resin

GAMBOL *v* -BOLED, -BOLING, -BOLS or -BOLLED, -BOLLING, -BOLS to leap about playfully

GAMBREL *n* pl. -S a part of a horse's leg

GAMBUSIA *n* pl. -S a small fish

GAME *adj* GAMER, GAMEST plucky

GAME *v* GAMED, GAMING, GAMES to gamble

GAMECOCK *n* pl. -S a rooster trained for fighting

GAMELAN *n* pl. -S a type of orchestra

GAMELIKE *adj* similar to a game (a contest governed by a set of rules)

GAMELY *adv* in a game manner

GAMENESS *n* pl. -ES the quality of being game

GAMER comparative of game

GAMESOME *adj* playful

GAMEST superlative of game

GAMESTER *n* pl. -S a gambler

GAMETE *n* pl. -S a mature reproductive cell **GAMETIC** *adj*

GAMEY *adj* GAMIER, GAMIEST gamy

GAMIC *adj* requiring fertilization

GAMIER comparative of gamy

GAMIEST superlative of gamy

GAMILY *adv* in a game manner

GAMIN *n* pl. -S an urchin

GAMINE *n* pl. -S a tomboy

GAMINESS *n* pl. -ES the quality of being gamy

GAMING *n* pl. -S the practice of gambling

GAMMA *n* pl. -S a Greek letter

GAMMADIA *n/pl* Greek ornamental designs

GAMMED past tense of gam

GAMMER *n* pl. -S an old woman

GAMMING present participle of gam

GAMMON *v* -ED, -ING, -S to mislead by deceptive talk

GAMMONER *n* pl. -S one that gammons

GAMODEME *n* pl. -S a somewhat isolated breeding community of organisms

GAMP *n* pl. -S a large umbrella

GAMUT *n* pl. -S an entire range

GAMY *adj* GAMIER, GAMIEST plucky

GAN past tense of gin

GANDER *v* -ED, -ING, -S to wander

GANE past participle of gae

GANEF *n* pl. -S a thief

GANEV *n* pl. -S ganef

GANG *v* -ED, -ING, -S to form into a gang (a group)

GANGER *n* pl. -S a foreman of a gang of laborers

GANGLAND *n* pl. -S the criminal underworld

GANGLIA a pl. of ganglion

GANGLIAL *adj* gangliar

GANGLIAR *adj* pertaining to a ganglion

GANGLIER comparative of gangly

GANGLIEST superlative of gangly

GANGLING *adj* awkwardly tall and lanky

GANGLION *n* pl. -GLIA or -GLIONS a group of nerve cells

GANGLY *adj* -GLIER, -GLIEST gangling

GANGPLOW *n* pl. -S an agricultural implement

GANGREL *n* pl. -S a vagabond

GANGRENE *v* -GRENED, -GRENING, -GRENES to suffer the loss of tissue in part of the body

GANGSTER *n* pl. -S a member of a criminal gang

GANGUE *n* pl. -S the worthless rock in which valuable minerals are found

GANGWAY *n* pl. -WAYS a passageway

GANISTER	*n* pl. -S a type of rock
GANJA	*n* pl. -S cannabis used for smoking
GANNET	*n* pl. -S a large seabird
GANOF	*n* pl. -S ganef
GANOID	*n* pl. -S a type of fish
GANTLET	*v* -ED, -ING, -S to overlap railroad tracks
GANTLINE	*n* pl. -S a rope on a ship
GANTLOPE	*n* pl. -S a former military punishment
GANTRY	*n* pl. -TRIES a structure for supporting railroad signals
GANYMEDE	*n* pl. -S a youth who serves liquors
GAOL	*v* -ED, -ING, -S to jail
GAOLER	*n* pl. -S jailer
GAP	*v* GAPPED, GAPPING, GAPS to make an opening in
GAPE	*v* GAPED, GAPING, GAPES to stare with open mouth
GAPER	*n* pl. -S one that gapes
GAPESEED	*n* pl. -S something that causes wonder
GAPEWORM	*n* pl. -S a worm that causes a disease of young birds
GAPING	present participle of gape
GAPINGLY	*adv* in a gaping manner
GAPOSIS	*n* pl. -SISES a gap in a row of buttons or snaps
GAPPED	past tense of gap
GAPPING	present participle of gap
GAPPY	*adj* -PIER, -PIEST having openings
GAPY	*adj* infested with gapeworms
GAR	*v* GARRED, GARRING, GARS to cause or compel
GARAGE	*v* -RAGED, -RAGING, -RAGES to put in a garage (a car shelter)
GARB	*v* -ED, -ING, -S to clothe
GARBAGE	*n* pl. -S food waste
GARBANZO	*n* pl. -ZOS a chickpea
GARBLE	*v* -BLED, -BLING, -BLES to distort the meaning of
GARBLER	*n* pl. -S one that garbles
GARBLESS	*adj* being without clothing
GARBOARD	*n* pl. -S a plank on a ship's bottom
GARBOIL	*n* pl. -S turmoil
GARCON	*n* pl. -S a waiter
GARDANT	*adj* turned directly toward the observer — used of a heraldic animal
GARDEN	*v* -ED, -ING, -S to cultivate a plot of ground
GARDENER	*n* pl. -S one that gardens
GARDENIA	*n* pl. -S a tropical shrub or tree
GARDYLOO	*interj* — used as a warning cry
GARFISH	*n* pl. -ES a freshwater fish
GARGANEY	*n* pl. -NEYS a small duck
GARGET	*n* pl. -S mastitis of domestic animals **GARGETY** *adj*
GARGLE	*v* -GLED, -GLING, -GLES to rinse the mouth or throat
GARGLER	*n* pl. -S one that gargles
GARGOYLE	*n* pl. -S an ornamental figure
GARISH	*adj* gaudy **GARISHLY** *adv*
GARLAND	*v* -ED, -ING, -S to deck with wreaths of flowers
GARLIC	*n* pl. -S an herb used in cooking **GARLICKY** *adj*
GARMENT	*v* -ED, -ING, -S to clothe
GARNER	*v* -ED, -ING, -S to gather and store
GARNET	*n* pl. -S a mineral
GARNISH	*v* -ED, -ING, -ES to decorate
GAROTE	*v* -ROTED, -ROTING, -ROTES to garrote
GAROTTE	*v* -ROTTED, -ROTTING, -ROTTES to garrote
GAROTTER	*n* pl. -S one that garottes
GARPIKE	*n* pl. -S a garfish
GARRED	past tense of gar
GARRET	*n* pl. -S an attic
GARRING	present participle of gar
GARRISON	*v* -ED, -ING, -S to assign to a military post
GARRON	*n* pl. -S a small, sturdy horse
GARROTE	*v* -ROTED, -ROTING, -ROTES to execute by strangling
GARROTER	*n* pl. -S one that garrotes
GARROTTE	*v* -ROTTED, -ROTTING, -ROTTES to garrote
GARTER	*v* -ED, -ING, -S to fasten with an elastic band
GARTH	*n* pl. -S a yard or garden
GARVEY	*n* pl. -VEYS a small scow

GAS   *v* GASSED, GASSING, GASES or GASSES to supply with gas (a substance capable of indefinite expansion)

GASALIER   *n* pl. -S gaselier

GASBAG   *n* pl. -S a bag for holding gas

GASCON   *n* pl. -S a boaster

GASELIER   *n* pl. -S a gaslight chandelier

GASEOUS   *adj* pertaining to gas

GASH   *v* -ED, -ING, -ES to make a long deep cut in

GASH   *adj* GASHER, GASHEST knowing

GASHOUSE   *n* pl. -S a gasworks

GASIFIED   past tense of gasify

GASIFIER   *n* pl. -S one that gasifies

GASIFORM   *adj* having the form of gas

GASIFY   *v* -IFIED, -IFYING, -IFIES to convert into gas

GASKET   *n* pl. -S packing for making something fluid-tight

GASKIN   *n* pl. -S a part of a horse's leg

GASKING   *n* pl. -S a gasket

GASLESS   *adj* having no gas

GASLIGHT   *n* pl. -S light made by burning gas

GASLIT   *adj* illuminated by gaslight

GASMAN   *n* pl. -MEN an employee of a gas company

GASOGENE   *n* pl. -S gazogene

GASOLENE   *n* pl. -S gasoline

GASOLIER   *n* pl. -S gaselier

GASOLINE   *n* pl. -S a liquid fuel

GASP   *v* -ED, -ING, -S to breathe convulsively

GASPER   *n* pl. -S a cigarette

GASSED   past tense of gas

GASSER   *n* pl. -S one that gasses

GASSES   a present 3d person sing. of gas

GASSING   *n* pl. -S a poisoning by noxious gas

GASSY   *adj* -SIER, -SIEST containing gas

GAST   *v* -ED, -ING, -S to scare

GASTIGHT   *adj* not allowing gas to escape or enter

GASTNESS   *n* pl. -ES fright

GASTRAEA   *n* pl. -S a type of metazoan

GASTRAL   *adj* pertaining to the stomach

GASTREA   *n* pl. -S gastraea

GASTRIC   *adj* pertaining to the stomach

GASTRIN   *n* pl. -S a hormone

GASTRULA   *n* pl. -LAS or -LAE a metazoan embryo

GASWORKS   *n* pl. GASWORKS a factory where gas is produced

GAT   *n* pl. -S a pistol

GATE   *v* GATED, GATING, GATES to supply with a gate (a movable barrier)

GATEFOLD   *n* pl. -S a folded insert in a book or magazine

GATELESS   *adj* lacking a gate

GATELIKE   *adj* resembling a gate

GATEMAN   *n* pl. -MEN a person in charge of a gate

GATEPOST   *n* pl. -S a post from which a gate is hung

GATEWAY   *n* pl. -WAYS a passage that may be closed by a gate

GATHER   *v* -ED, -ING, -S to bring together into one place or group

GATHERER   *n* pl. -S one that gathers

GATING   present participle of gate

GAUCHE   *adj* GAUCHER, GAUCHEST lacking social grace **GAUCHELY** *adv*

GAUCHO   *n* pl. -CHOS a cowboy of the South American pampas

GAUD   *n* pl. -S a showy ornament

GAUDERY   *n* pl. -ERIES finery

GAUDY   *adj* GAUDIER, GAUDIEST tastelessly showy **GAUDILY** *adv*

GAUDY   *n* pl. -DIES a festival

GAUFFER   *v* -ED, -ING, -S to goffer

GAUGE   *v* GAUGED, GAUGING, GAUGES to measure precisely

GAUGER   *n* pl. -S one that gauges

GAULT   *n* pl. -S a heavy, thick clay soil

GAUM   *v* -ED, -ING, -S to smear

GAUN   present participle of gae

GAUNT   *adj* GAUNTER, GAUNTEST emaciated **GAUNTLY** *adv*

GAUNTLET   *v* -ED, -ING, -S to gantlet

GAUNTRY   *n* pl. -TRIES gantry

GAUR   *n* pl. -S a wild ox

GAUSS   *n* pl. -ES a unit of magnetic induction

GAUZE   *n* pl. -S a transparent fabric

GAUZY   *adj* GAUZIER, GAUZIEST resembling gauze **GAUZILY** *adv*

GAVAGE   *n* pl. -S introduction of material into the stomach by a tube

GAVE   past tense of give

GAVEL   *v* -ELED, -ELING, -ELS or -ELLED, -ELLING, -ELS to signal for attention or order by use of a gavel (a small mallet)

GAVELOCK   *n* pl. -S a crowbar

GAVIAL   *n* pl. -S a large reptile

GAVOT   *n* pl. -S a French dance

GAVOTTE   *v* -VOTTED, -VOTTING, -VOTTES to dance a gavot

GAWK   *v* -ED, -ING, -S to stare stupidly

GAWKER   *n* pl. -S one that gawks

GAWKIER   comparative of gawky

GAWKIES   pl. of gawky

GAWKISH   *adj* gawky

GAWKY   *adj* GAWKIER, GAWKIEST awkward **GAWKILY** *adv*

GAWKY   *n* pl. GAWKIES an awkward person

GAWSIE   *adj* well-fed and healthy looking

GAWSY   *adj* gawsie

GAY   *adj* GAYER, GAYEST merry

GAY   *n* pl. GAYS a homosexual

GAYAL   *n* pl. -S a domesticated ox

GAYETY   *n* pl. -ETIES gaiety

GAYLY   *adv* in a gay manner

GAYNESS   *n* pl. -ES gaiety

GAYWINGS   *n* pl. GAYWINGS a perennial herb

GAZABO   *n* pl. -BOS or -BOES a fellow

GAZE   *v* GAZED, GAZING, GAZES to look intently

GAZEBO   *n* pl. -BOS or -BOES a roofed structure open on the sides

GAZELLE   *n* pl. -S a small antelope

GAZER   *n* pl. -S one that gazes

GAZETTE   *v* -ZETTED, -ZETTING, -ZETTES to announce in an official journal

GAZING   present participle of gaze

GAZOGENE   *n* pl. -S an apparatus for carbonating liquids

GAZPACHO   *n* pl. -CHOS a cold, spicy soup

GEAR   *v* -ED, -ING, -S to provide with gears (toothed machine parts)

GEARBOX   *n* pl. -ES an automotive transmission

GEARCASE   *n* pl. -S a casing for gears

GEARING   *n* pl. -S a system of gears

GEARLESS   *adj* being without gears

GECK   *v* -ED, -ING, -S to mock

GECKO   *n* pl. GECKOS or GECKOES a small lizard

GED   *n* pl. -S a food fish

GEE   *v* GEED, GEEING, GEES to turn to the right

GEEGAW   *n* pl. -S gewgaw

GEEK   *n* pl. -S a carnival performer

GEEPOUND   *n* pl. -S a unit of mass

GEESE   pl. of goose

GEEST   *n* pl. -S old alluvial matter

GEEZER   *n* pl. -S an eccentric man

GEISHA   *n* pl. -S a Japanese girl trained to entertain

GEL   *v* GELLED, GELLING, GELS to become like jelly **GELABLE** *adj*

GELADA   *n* pl. -S a baboon

GELANT   *n* pl. -S gellant

GELATE   *v* -ATED, -ATING, -ATES to gel

GELATIN   *n* pl. -S a glutinous substance

GELATINE   *n* pl. -S gelatin

GELATION   *n* pl. -S the process of gelling

GELD   *v* -ED, -ING, -S to castrate

GELDER   *n* pl. -S one that gelds

GELDING   *n* pl. -S a castrated animal

GELEE   *n* pl. -S a cosmetic gel

GELID   *adj* icy **GELIDLY** *adv*

GELIDITY   *n* pl. -TIES iciness

GELLANT   *n* pl. -S a substance used to produce gelling

GELLED   past tense of gel

GELLING   present participle of gel

GELSEMIA   *n/pl* medicinal plant roots

GELT   *n* pl. -S money

GEM   *v* GEMMED, GEMMING, GEMS to adorn with gems (precious stones)

GEMINAL   *adj* of or pertaining to two substituents on the same atom

GEMINATE   *v* -NATED, -NATING, -NATES to arrange in pairs

GEMLIKE	*adj* resembling a gem
GEMMA	*n* pl. -MAE an asexual reproductive structure
GEMMATE	*v* -MATED, -MATING, -MATES to produce gemmae
GEMMED	past tense of gem
GEMMIER	comparative of gemmy
GEMMIEST	superlative of gemmy
GEMMILY	*adv* in a manner suggesting a gem
GEMMING	present participle of gem
GEMMULE	*n* pl. -S a small gemma
GEMMY	*adj* -MIER, -MIEST resembling a gem
GEMOLOGY	*n* pl. -GIES the science of gems
GEMOT	*n* pl. -S a public meeting in Anglo-Saxon England
GEMOTE	*n* pl. -S gemot
GEMSBOK	*n* pl. -S a large antelope
GEMSBUCK	*n* pl. -S gemsbok
GEMSTONE	*n* pl. -S a precious stone
GENDARME	*n* pl. -S a policeman
GENDER	*v* -ED, -ING, -S to engender
GENE	*n* pl. -S a hereditary unit
GENERA	a pl. of genus
GENERAL	*n* pl. -S a military officer
GENERATE	*v* -ATED, -ATING, -ATES to bring into existence
GENERIC	*n* pl. -S a type of drug
GENEROUS	*adj* willing to give
GENESIS	*n* pl. GENESES an origin
GENET	*n* pl. -S a carnivorous mammal
GENETIC	*adj* pertaining to genetics
GENETICS	*n/pl* the science of heredity
GENETTE	*n* pl. -S genet
GENEVA	*n* pl. -S a liquor
GENIAL	*adj* having a pleasant or friendly manner **GENIALLY** *adv*
GENIC	*adj* pertaining to genes
GENIE	*n* pl. -S jinni
GENII	a pl. of genius
GENIP	*n* pl. -S a tropical tree
GENIPAP	*n* pl. -S a tropical tree
GENITAL	*adj* pertaining to reproduction
GENITALS	*n/pl* the sexual organs
GENITIVE	*n* pl. -S a grammatical case
GENITOR	*n* pl. -S a male parent
GENITURE	*n* pl. -S birth
GENIUS	*n* pl. GENIUSES or GENII an exceptional natural aptitude
GENOA	*n* pl. -S a triangular sail
GENOCIDE	*n* pl. -S the deliberate extermination of a national or racial group
GENOM	*n* pl. -S genome
GENOME	*n* pl. -S a haploid set of chromosomes **GENOMIC** *adj*
GENOTYPE	*n* pl. -S the genetic constitution of an organism
GENRE	*n* pl. -S a type or kind
GENRO	*n* pl. -ROS a group of elder statesmen in Japan
GENS	*n* pl. GENTES a type of clan
GENSENG	*n* pl. -S ginseng
GENT	*n* pl. -S a gentleman
GENTEEL	*adj* -TEELER, -TEELEST well-bred or refined
GENTES	pl. of gens
GENTIAN	*n* pl. -S a flowering plant
GENTIL	*adj* kind
GENTILE	*n* pl. -S a non-Jewish person
GENTLE	*adj* -TLER, -TLEST mild **GENTLY** *adv*
GENTLE	*v* -TLED, -TLING, -TLES to tame
GENTRICE	*n* pl. -S good breeding
GENTRY	*n* pl. -TRIES people of high social class
GENU	*n* pl. GENUA the knee
GENUINE	*adj* authentic
GENUS	*n* pl. GENERA or GENUSES a kind, sort, or class
GEODE	*n* pl. -S a type of rock
GEODESIC	*n* pl. -S a geometric line
GEODESY	*n* pl. -SIES geographical surveying
GEODETIC	*adj* pertaining to geodesy
GEODIC	*adj* of or pertaining to a geode
GEODUCK	*n* pl. -S a large, edible clam
GEOGNOSY	*n* pl. -SIES a branch of geology
GEOID	*n* pl. -S a hypothetical surface of the earth **GEOIDAL** *adj*
GEOLOGER	*n* pl. -S a specialist in geology

GEOLOGY *n* pl. -GIES the science that deals with the origin and structure of the earth **GEOLOGIC** *adj*

GEOMANCY *n* pl. -CIES a method of foretelling the future by geographical features

GEOMETER *n* pl. -S a specialist in geometry

GEOMETRY *n* pl. -TRIES a branch of mathematics

GEOPHAGY *n* pl. -GIES the practice of eating earthy substances

GEOPHONE *n* pl. -S a device that detects vibrations in the earth

GEOPHYTE *n* pl. -S a plant having underground buds

GEOPONIC *adj* pertaining to farming

GEORGIC *n* pl. -S a poem about farming

GEOTAXIS *n* pl. -TAXES the movement of an organism in response to gravity

GERAH *n* pl. -S a Hebrew unit of weight

GERANIAL *n* pl. -S citral

GERANIOL *n* pl. -S an alcohol used in perfumes

GERANIUM *n* pl. -S a flowering plant

GERARDIA *n* pl. -S an herb

GERBERA *n* pl. -S an herb

GERBIL *n* pl. -S a burrowing rodent

GERBILLE *n* pl. -S gerbil

GERENT *n* pl. -S a ruler or manager

GERENUK *n* pl. -S a long-necked antelope

GERM *n* pl. -S a microorganism that causes disease

GERMAN *n* pl. -S an elaborate dance

GERMANE *adj* relevant

GERMANIC *adj* containing germanium (a metallic element)

GERMEN *n* pl. -MENS or -MINA something that serves as an origin

GERMFREE *adj* free from germs

GERMIER comparative of germy

GERMIEST superlative of germy

GERMINA a pl. of germen

GERMINAL *adj* being in the earliest stage of development

GERMY *adj* GERMIER, GERMIEST full of germs

GERONTIC *adj* pertaining to old age

GERUND *n* pl. -S a verbal noun

GESSO *n* pl. -SOES a plaster mixture

GEST *n* pl. -S a feat

GESTALT *n* pl. -STALTS or -STALTEN a unified whole

GESTAPO *n* pl. -POS a secret-police organization

GESTATE *v* -TATED, -TATING, -TATES to carry in the uterus during pregnancy

GESTE *n* pl. -S gest

GESTIC *adj* pertaining to bodily motion

GESTICAL *adj* gestic

GESTURAL *adj* pertaining to or consisting of gestures (expressive bodily motions)

GESTURE *v* -TURED, -TURING, -TURES to express by bodily motion

GESTURER *n* pl. -S one that gestures

GET *v* GOT, GOTTEN, GETTING, GETS to obtain or acquire **GETABLE, GETTABLE** *adj*

GETAWAY *n* pl. -AWAYS an escape

GETTER *v* -ED, -ING, -S to purify with a chemically active substance

GETTING present participle of get

GETUP *n* pl. -S a costume

GEUM *n* pl. -S a perennial herb

GEWGAW *n* pl. -S a showy trinket

GEY *adv* very

GEYSER *n* pl. -S a spring that ejects jets of hot water and steam

GHARRI *n* pl. -S gharry

GHARRY *n* pl. -RIES a carriage used in India

GHAST *adj* ghastly

GHASTFUL *adj* frightful

GHASTLY *adj* -LIER, -LIEST terrifying

GHAT *n* pl. -S a passage leading down to a river

GHAUT *n* pl. -S ghat

GHAZI *n* pl. -S or -ES a Muslim war hero

GHEE *n* pl. -S a kind of liquid butter made in India

GHERAO *v* -ED, -ING, -ES to coerce by physical means

GHERKIN *n* pl. -S a small cucumber

GHETTO *v* -ED, -ING, -S or -ES to isolate in a slum

GHI *n* pl. -S ghee

GHIBLI	*n* pl. -S a hot desert wind
GHILLIE	*n* pl. -S a type of shoe
GHOST	*v* -ED, -ING, -S to haunt
GHOSTLY	*adj* -LIER, -LIEST spectral
GHOSTY	*adj* GHOSTIER, GHOSTIEST ghostly
GHOUL	*n* pl. -S a demon **GHOULISH** *adj*
GHYLL	*n* pl. -S a ravine
GIANT	*n* pl. -S a person or thing of great size
GIANTESS	*n* pl. -ES a female giant
GIANTISM	*n* pl. -S the condition of being a giant
GIAOUR	*n* pl. -S a non-Muslim
GIB	*v* GIBBED, GIBBING, GIBS to fasten with a wedge of wood or metal
GIBBER	*v* -ED, -ING, -S to jabber
GIBBET	*v* -BETED, -BETING, -BETS or -BETTED, -BETTING, -BETS to execute by hanging
GIBBING	present participle of gib
GIBBON	*n* pl. -S an arboreal ape
GIBBOSE	*adj* gibbous
GIBBOUS	*adj* irregularly rounded
GIBBSITE	*n* pl. -S a mineral
GIBE	*v* GIBED, GIBING, GIBES to jeer **GIBINGLY** *adv*
GIBER	*n* pl. -S one that gibes
GIBLET	*n* pl. -S an edible part of a fowl
GID	*n* pl. -S a disease of sheep
GIDDAP	*interj* — used as a command to a horse to go faster
GIDDY	*adj* -DIER, -DIEST dizzy **GIDDILY** *adv*
GIDDY	*v* -DIED, -DYING, -DIES to make giddy
GIE	*v* GIED, GIEN, GIEING, GIES to give
GIFT	*v* -ED, -ING, -S to present with a gift (something given without charge)
GIFTEDLY	*adv* in a talented manner
GIFTLESS	*adj* being without a gift
GIG	*v* GIGGED, GIGGING, GIGS to catch fish with a pronged spear
GIGA	*n* pl. GIGHE a gigue
GIGABIT	*n* pl. -S a unit of information
GIGANTIC	*adj* huge

GIGAS	*adj* pertaining to variations in plant development
GIGATON	*n* pl. -S a unit of weight
GIGAWATT	*n* pl. -S a unit of power
GIGGED	past tense of gig
GIGGING	present participle of gig
GIGGLE	*v* -GLED, -GLING, -GLES to laugh in a silly manner
GIGGLER	*n* pl. -S one that giggles
GIGGLY	*adj* -GLIER, -GLIEST tending to giggle
GIGHE	pl. of giga
GIGLET	*n* pl. -S a playful girl
GIGLOT	*n* pl. -S giglet
GIGOLO	*n* pl. -LOS a man supported financially by a woman
GIGOT	*n* pl. -S a leg of lamb
GIGUE	*n* pl. -S a lively dance
GILBERT	*n* pl. -S a unit of magnetomotive force
GILD	*v* GILDED or GILT, GILDING, GILDS to cover with a thin layer of gold
GILDER	*n* pl. -S one that gilds
GILDHALL	*n* pl. -S a town hall
GILDING	*n* pl. -S the application of gilt
GILL	*v* -ED, -ING, -S to catch fish with a type of net
GILLER	*n* pl. -S one that gills
GILLIE	*n* pl. -S ghillie
GILLNET	*v* -NETTED, -NETTING, -NETS to gill
GILLY	*v* -LIED, -LYING, -LIES to transport on a type of wagon
GILT	*n* pl. -S the gold with which something is gilded
GILTHEAD	*n* pl. -S a marine fish
GIMBAL	*v* -BALED, -BALING, -BALS or -BALLED, -BALLING, -BALS to support on a set of rings
GIMCRACK	*n* pl. -S a gewgaw
GIMEL	*n* pl. -S a Hebrew letter
GIMLET	*n* -ED, -ING, -S to pierce with a boring tool
GIMMAL	*n* pl. -S a pair of interlocked rings
GIMMICK	*v* -ED, -ING, -S to provide with a gimmick (a novel or tricky feature)

GIMMICKY   *adj* having or being like a gimmick

GIMP   *v* -ED, -ING, -S to limp

GIMPY   *adj* GIMPIER, GIMPIEST limping

GIN   *v* GINNED, GINNING, GINS to remove seeds from cotton

GIN   *v* GAN, GUNNEN, GINNING, GINS to begin

GINGAL   *n* pl. -S jingal

GINGALL   *n* pl. -S jingal

GINGELEY   *n* pl. -LEYS gingelly

GINGELI   *n* pl. -S gingelly

GINGELLY   *n* pl. -LIES the sesame seed or its oil

GINGELY   *n* pl. -LIES gingelly

GINGER   *v* -ED, -ING, -S to flavor with ginger (a pungent spice)

GINGERLY   *adv* in a careful manner

GINGERY   *adj* having the characteristics of ginger

GINGHAM   *n* pl. -S a cotton fabric

GINGILI   *n* pl. -LIS gingelly

GINGIVA   *n* pl. -VAE the fleshy tissue that surrounds the teeth **GINGIVAL** *adj*

GINGKO   *n* pl. -KOES ginkgo

GINK   *n* pl. -S a fellow

GINKGO   *n* pl. -GOES an ornamental tree

GINNED   past tense of gin

GINNER   *n* pl. -S one that gins cotton

GINNING   *n* pl. -S cotton as it comes from a gin

GINNY   *adj* GINNIER, GINNIEST affected with gin (a strong liquor)

GINSENG   *n* pl. -S a perennial herb

GIP   *v* GIPPED, GIPPING, GIPS to gyp

GIPON   *n* pl. -S jupon

GIPPER   *n* pl. -S one that gips

GIPPING   present participle of gip

GIPSY   *v* -SIED, -SYING, -SIES to gypsy

GIRAFFE   *n* pl. -S a long-necked mammal

GIRASOL   *n* pl. -S a variety of opal

GIRASOLE   *n* pl. -S girasol

GIRD   *v* GIRDED or GIRT, GIRDING, GIRDS to surround

GIRDER   *n* pl. -S a horizontal support

GIRDLE   *v* -DLED, -DLING, -DLES to encircle with a belt

GIRDLER   *n* pl. -S one that girdles

GIRL   *n* pl. -S a female child

GIRLHOOD   *n* pl. -S the state of being a girl

GIRLIE   *n* pl. -S a girl

GIRLISH   *adj* of, pertaining to, or having the characteristics of a girl

GIRLY   *adj* featuring scantily clothed women

GIRN   *v* -ED, -ING, -S to snarl

GIRO   *n* pl. -ROS an autogiro

GIRON   *n* pl. -S gyron

GIROSOL   *n* pl. -S girasol

GIRSH   *n* pl. -ES qursh

GIRT   *v* -ED, -ING, -S to gird

GIRTH   *v* -ED, -ING, -S to encircle

GISARME   *n* pl. -S a medieval weapon

GISMO   *n* pl. -MOS a gadget

GIST   *n* pl. -S the main point of a matter

GIT   *interj* — used as an order of dismissal

GITANO   *n* pl. -NOS a Spanish gypsy

GITTERN   *n* pl. -S a medieval guitar

GIVE   *v* GAVE, GIVEN, GIVING, GIVES to transfer freely to another's possession **GIVEABLE** *adj*

GIVEAWAY   *n* pl. -AWAYS something given away free of charge

GIVEN   *n* pl. -S something assigned as a basis for a calculation

GIVER   *n* pl. -S one that gives

GIVING   present participle of give

GIZMO   *n* pl. -MOS gismo

GIZZARD   *n* pl. -S a digestive organ

GJETOST   *n* pl. -S a hard brown cheese

GLABELLA   *n* pl. -BELLAE the smooth area between the eyebrows

GLABRATE   *adj* glabrous

GLABROUS   *adj* smooth

GLACE   *v* -CEED, -CEING, -CES to cover with icing

GLACIAL   *adj* of or pertaining to glaciers

GLACIATE   *v* -ATED, -ATING, -ATES to cover with glaciers

GLACIER   *n* pl. -S a huge mass of ice

GLACIS   *n* pl. -CISES a slope

GLAD   *adj* GLADDER, GLADDEST feeling pleasure

GLAD   *v* GLADDED, GLADDING, GLADS to gladden

GLADDEN   *v* -ED, -ING, -S to make glad

GLADDER   comparative of glad

GLADDEST   superlative of glad

GLADDING   present participle of glad

GLADE   *n* pl. -S an open space in a forest

GLADIATE   *adj* shaped like a sword

GLADIER   comparative of glady

GLADIEST   superlative of glady

GLADIOLA   *n* pl. -S a flowering plant

GLADIOLI   *n/pl* segments of the sternum

GLADLY   *adv* -LIER, -LIEST in a glad manner

GLADNESS   *n* pl. -ES the state of being glad

GLADSOME   *adj* -SOMER, -SOMEST glad

GLADY   *adj* GLADIER, GLADIEST having glades

GLAIKET   *adj* glaikit

GLAIKIT   *adj* foolish

GLAIR   *v* -ED, -ING, -S to coat with egg white

GLAIRE   *v* GLAIRED, GLAIRING, GLAIRES to glair

GLAIRY   *adj* GLAIRIER, GLAIRIEST resembling egg white

GLAIVE   *n* pl. -S a sword **GLAIVED** *adj*

GLAMOR   *n* pl. -S alluring attractiveness

GLAMOUR   *v* -ED, -ING, -S to bewitch

GLANCE   *v* GLANCED, GLANCING, GLANCES to look quickly

GLAND   *n* pl. -S a secreting organ

GLANDERS   *n/pl* a disease of horses

GLANDULE   *n* pl. -S a small gland

GLANS   *n* pl. GLANDES the tip of the penis or clitoris

GLARE   *v* GLARED, GLARING, GLARES to shine with a harshly brilliant light

GLARY   *adj* GLARIER, GLARIEST glaring

GLASS   *v* -ED, -ING, -ES to encase in glass (a transparent substance)

GLASSFUL   *n* pl. -FULS as much as a drinking glass will hold

GLASSIE   *n* pl. -S a type of playing marble

GLASSIER   comparative of glassy

GLASSIEST   superlative of glassy

GLASSILY   *adv* in a glassy manner

GLASSINE   *n* pl. -S a type of paper

GLASSMAN   *n* pl. -MEN a glazier

GLASSY   *adj* GLASSIER, GLASSIEST resembling glass

GLAUCOMA   *n* pl. -S a disease of the eye

GLAUCOUS   *adj* bluish green

GLAZE   *v* GLAZED, GLAZING, GLAZES to fit windows with glass panes

GLAZER   *n* pl. -S a glazier

GLAZIER   *n* pl. -S one that glazes

GLAZIERY   *n* pl. -ZIERIES the work of a glazier

GLAZING   *n* pl. -S glaziery

GLAZY   *adj* GLAZIER, GLAZIEST covered with a smooth, glossy coating

GLEAM   *v* -ED, -ING, -S to shine with a soft radiance

GLEAMY   *adj* GLEAMIER, GLEAMIEST gleaming

GLEAN   *v* -ED, -ING, -S to gather little by little

GLEANER   *n* pl. -S one that gleans

GLEANING   *n* pl. -S something that is gleaned

GLEBA   *n* pl. -BAE a spore-bearing mass of some fungi

GLEBE   *n* pl. -S the soil or earth

GLED   *n* pl. -S glede

GLEDE   *n* pl. -S a bird of prey

GLEE   *n* pl. -S an unaccompanied song

GLEED   *n* pl. -S a glowing coal

GLEEFUL   *adj* merry

GLEEK   *v* -ED, -ING, -S to gibe

GLEEMAN   *n* pl. -MEN a minstrel

GLEESOME   *adj* gleeful

GLEET   *v* -ED, -ING, -S to discharge mucus from the urethra

GLEETY   *adj* GLEETIER, GLEETIEST resembling mucus

GLEG   *adj* alert **GLEGLY** *adv*

GLEGNESS   *n* pl. -ES alertness

GLEN   *n* pl. -S a small valley **GLENLIKE** *adj*

GLENOID   *adj* having the shallow or slightly cupped form of a bone socket

GLEY   *n* pl. GLEYS a soil layer

GLIADIN   *n* pl. -S a simple protein

GLIADINE   *n* pl. -S gliadin

GLIAL   *adj* pertaining to the supporting tissue of the central nervous system

GLIB   *adj* GLIBBER, GLIBBEST fluent **GLIBLY** *adv*

GLIBNESS   *n* pl. -ES the quality of being glib

GLIDE   *v* GLIDED, GLIDING, GLIDES to move effortlessly

GLIDER   *n* pl. -S a type of aircraft

GLIFF   *n* pl. -S a brief moment

GLIM   *n* pl. -S a light or lamp

GLIME   *v* GLIMED, GLIMING, GLIMES to glance slyly

GLIMMER   *v* -ED, -ING, -S to shine faintly or unsteadily

GLIMPSE   *v* GLIMPSED, GLIMPSING, GLIMPSES to see for an instant

GLIMPSER   *n* pl. -S one that glimpses

GLINT   *v* -ED, -ING, -S to glitter

GLIOMA   *n* pl. -MAS or -MATA a type of tumor

GLISSADE   *v* -SADED, -SADING, -SADES to perform a gliding dance step

GLISTEN   *v* -ED, -ING, -S to shine by reflection

GLISTER   *v* -ED, -ING, -S to glisten

GLITCH   *n* pl. -ES a malfunction

GLITTER   *v* -ED, -ING, -S to sparkle

GLITTERY   *adj* glittering

GLOAM   *n* pl. -S twilight

GLOAMING   *n* pl. -S twilight

GLOAT   *v* -ED, -ING, -S to regard with great or excessive satisfaction

GLOATER   *n* pl. -S one that gloats

GLOB   *n* pl. -S a rounded mass

GLOBAL   *adj* spherical **GLOBALLY** *adv*

GLOBATE   *adj* spherical

GLOBATED   *adj* spherical

GLOBE   *v* GLOBED, GLOBING, GLOBES to form into a perfectly round body

GLOBIN   *n* pl. -S a simple protein

GLOBOID   *n* pl. -S a spheroid

GLOBOSE   *adj* spherical

GLOBOUS   *adj* spherical

GLOBULAR   *adj* spherical

GLOBULE   *n* pl. -S a small spherical mass

GLOBULIN   *n* pl. -S a simple protein

GLOCHID   *n* pl. -S a barbed hair on some plants

GLOGG   *n* pl. -S an alcoholic beverage

GLOM   *v* GLOMMED, GLOMMING, GLOMS to steal

GLOMUS   *n* pl. -MERA a type of vascular tuft

GLOOM   *v* -ED, -ING, -S to become dark

GLOOMFUL   *adj* gloomy

GLOOMING   *n* pl. -S gloaming

GLOOMY   *adj* GLOOMIER, GLOOMIEST dismally dark **GLOOMILY** *adv*

GLOP   *n* pl. -S a messy mass or mixture

GLORIA   *n* pl. -S a halo

GLORIED   past tense of glory

GLORIES   present 3d person sing. of glory

GLORIFY   *v* -FIED, -FYING, -FIES to bestow honor or praise on

GLORIOLE   *n* pl. -S a halo

GLORIOUS   *adj* magnificent

GLORY   *v* -RIED, -RYING, -RIES to rejoice proudly

GLOSS   *v* -ED, -ING, -ES to make lustrous

GLOSSA   *n* pl. -SAE or -SAS the tongue **GLOSSAL** *adj*

GLOSSARY   *n* pl. -RIES a list of terms and their definitions

GLOSSEME   *n* pl. -S the smallest linguistic unit that signals a meaning

GLOSSER   *n* pl. -S one that glosses

GLOSSIES   pl. of glossy

GLOSSINA   *n* pl. -S a tsetse fly

GLOSSY   *adj* GLOSSIER, GLOSSIEST lustrous **GLOSSILY** *adv*

GLOSSY   *n* pl. GLOSSIES a type of photograph

GLOST   *n* pl. -S pottery that has been coated with a glassy surface

GLOTTIS   *n* pl. -TISES or -TIDES the opening between the vocal cords **GLOTTAL, GLOTTIC** *adj*

GLOUT   *v* -ED, -ING, -S to scowl

GLOVE	*v* GLOVED, GLOVING, GLOVES to furnish with gloves (hand coverings)	**GLYCERIN**	*n* pl. -S a glycerol **GLYCERIC** *adj*
GLOVER	*n* pl. -S a maker or seller of gloves	**GLYCEROL**	*n* pl. -S a syrupy alcohol
		GLYCERYL	*n* pl. -S a radical derived from glycerol
GLOW	*v* -ED, -ING, -S to emit light and heat	**GLYCIN**	*n* pl. -S a compound used in photography
GLOWER	*v* -ED, -ING, -S to scowl	**GLYCINE**	*n* pl. -S an amino acid
GLOWFLY	*n* pl. -FLIES a firefly	**GLYCOGEN**	*n* pl. -S a carbohydrate
GLOWWORM	*n* pl. -S a luminous insect	**GLYCOL**	*n* pl. -S an alcohol **GLYCOLIC** *adj*
GLOXINIA	*n* pl. -S a tropical plant		
GLOZE	*v* GLOZED, GLOZING, GLOZES to explain away	**GLYCONIC**	*n* pl. -S a type of verse line
		GLYCOSYL	*n* pl. -S a radical derived from glucose
GLUCAGON	*n* pl. -S a hormone		
GLUCINUM	*n* pl. -S a metallic element **GLUCINIC** *adj*	**GLYCYL**	*n* pl. -S a radical derived from glycine
GLUCOSE	*n* pl. -S a sugar **GLUCOSIC** *adj*	**GLYPH**	*n* pl. -S an ornamental groove **GLYPHIC** *adj*
GLUE	*v* GLUED, GLUING or GLUEING, GLUES to fasten with glue (an adhesive substance)	**GLYPTIC**	*n* pl. -S the art or process of engraving on gems
GLUELIKE	*adj* resembling glue	**GNAR**	*v* GNARRED, GNARRING, GNARS to snarl
GLUER	*n* pl. -S one that glues		
GLUEY	*adj* GLUIER, GLUIEST resembling glue **GLUILY** *adv*	**GNARL**	*v* -ED, -ING, -S to twist into a state of deformity
GLUING	present participle of glue	**GNARLY**	*adj* GNARLIER, GNARLIEST gnarled
GLUM	*adj* GLUMMER, GLUMMEST being in low spirits **GLUMLY** *adv*	**GNARR**	*v* -ED, -ING, -S to gnar
GLUME	*n* pl. -S a bract on grassy plants	**GNARRED**	past tense of gnar
		GNARRING	present participle of gnar
GLUMNESS	*n* pl. -ES the state of being glum	**GNASH**	*v* -ED, -ING, -ES to grind the teeth together
GLUMPY	*adj* GLUMPIER, GLUMPIEST glum **GLUMPILY** *adv*	**GNAT**	*n* pl. -S a small winged insect
		GNATHAL	*adj* gnathic
GLUNCH	*v* -ED, -ING, -ES to frown	**GNATHIC**	*adj* of or pertaining to the jaw
GLUT	*v* GLUTTED, GLUTTING, GLUTS to feed or fill to excess	**GNATHION**	*n* pl. -S the tip of the chin
		GNATHITE	*n* pl. -S a jawlike appendage of an insect
GLUTEAL	*adj* of or pertaining to the buttock muscles	**GNATLIKE**	*adj* resembling a gnat
GLUTEI	pl. of gluteus	**GNATTY**	*adj* -TIER, -TIEST infested with gnats
GLUTELIN	*n* pl. -S a plant protein		
GLUTEN	*n* pl. -S a tough elastic plant protein substance	**GNAW**	*v* GNAWED, GNAWN, GNAWING, GNAWS to wear away by persistent biting **GNAWABLE** *adj*
GLUTEUS	*n* pl. -TEI a buttock muscle	**GNAWER**	*n* pl. -S one that gnaws
GLUTTED	past tense of glut	**GNAWING**	*n* pl. -S a persistent dull pain
GLUTTING	present participle of glut	**GNAWN**	a past participle of gnaw
GLUTTON	*n* pl. -S a person who eats to excess	**GNEISS**	*n* pl. -ES a type of rock **GNEISSIC** *adj*
GLUTTONY	*n* pl. -TONIES excessive eating	**GNOCCHI**	*n/pl* dumplings made of pasta
GLYCAN	*n* pl. -S a carbohydrate	**GNOME**	*n* pl. -S a dwarf

GNOMIC *adj* resembling or containing aphorisms

GNOMICAL *adj* gnomic

GNOMISH *adj* resembling a gnome

GNOMIST *n* pl. -S a writer of aphorisms

GNOMON *n* pl. -S a part of a sundial **GNOMONIC** *adj*

GNOSIS *n* pl. GNOSES mystical knowledge

GNOSTIC *adj* possessing knowledge

GNU *n* pl. -S a large antelope

GO *v* WENT, GONE, GOING, GOES to move along

GOA *n* pl. -S an Asian gazelle

GOAD *v* -ED, -ING, -S to drive animals with a goad (a pointed stick)

GOADLIKE *adj* resembling a goad

GOAL *v* -ED, -ING, -S to score a goal (a point-scoring play in some games)

GOALIE *n* pl. -S a player who defends against goals

GOALLESS *adj* having no goal

GOALPOST *n* pl. -S a post that marks a boundary of the scoring area in some games

GOAT *n* pl. -S a horned mammal

GOATEE *n* pl. -S a small pointed beard **GOATEED** *adj*

GOATFISH *n* pl. -ES a tropical fish

GOATHERD *n* pl. -S one who tends goats

GOATISH *adj* resembling a goat

GOATLIKE *adj* goatish

GOATSKIN *n* pl. -S the hide of a goat

GOB *v* GOBBED, GOBBING, GOBS to fill a mine pit with waste material

GOBAN *n* pl. -S gobang

GOBANG *n* pl. -S a Japanese game

GOBBED past tense of gob

GOBBET *n* pl. -S a piece of raw meat

GOBBING present participle of gob

GOBBLE *v* -BLED, -BLING, -BLES to eat hastily

GOBBLER *n* pl. -S a male turkey

GOBIES pl. of goby

GOBIOID *n* pl. -S a fish of the goby family

GOBLET *n* pl. -S a drinking vessel

GOBLIN *n* pl. -S an evil or mischievous creature

GOBO *n* pl. -BOS or -BOES a device used to shield a microphone from extraneous sounds

GOBONEE *adj* gobony

GOBONY *adj* compony

GOBY *n* pl. GOBIES a small fish

GOD *v* GODDED, GODDING, GODS to treat as a god (a supernatural being)

GODCHILD *n* pl. -CHILDREN one whom a person sponsors at baptism

GODDAM *v* -DAMMED, -DAMMING, -DAMS goddamn

GODDAMN *v* -ED, -ING, -S to damn

GODDED past tense of god

GODDESS *n* pl. -ES a female god

GODDING present participle of god

GODHEAD *n* pl. -S godhood

GODHOOD *n* pl. -S the state of being a god

GODLESS *adj* worshiping no god

GODLIER comparative of godly

GODLIEST superlative of godly

GODLIKE *adj* divine

GODLING *n* pl. -S a lesser god

GODLY *adj* -LIER, -LIEST pious **GODLILY** *adv*

GODOWN *n* pl. -S an oriental warehouse

GODROON *n* pl. -S gadroon

GODSEND *n* pl. -S an unexpected boon

GODSHIP *n* pl. -S the rank of a god

GODSON *n* pl. -S a male godchild

GODWIT *n* pl. -S a wading bird

GOER *n* pl. -S one that goes

GOETHITE *n* pl. -S an ore of iron

GOFFER *v* -ED, -ING, -S to press ridges or pleats into

GOGGLE *v* -GLED, -GLING, -GLES to stare with wide eyes

GOGGLER *n* pl. -S one that goggles

GOGGLY *adj* -GLIER, -GLIEST wide-eyed

GOGLET *n* pl. -S a long-necked jar

GOGO *n* pl. -GOS a discotheque

GOING *n* pl. -S an advance toward an objective

GOITER *n* pl. -S an enlargement of the thyroid gland **GOITROUS** *adj*

GOITRE   *n* pl. -S goiter

GOLCONDA   *n* pl. -S a source of great wealth

GOLD   *n* pl. -S a precious metallic element

GOLD   *adj* GOLDER, GOLDEST golden

GOLDARN   *n* pl. -S an expression of anger

GOLDBUG   *n* pl. -S a gold beetle

GOLDEN   *adj* -ENER, -ENEST of the color of gold **GOLDENLY** *adv*

GOLDEYE   *n* pl. -S a freshwater fish

GOLDFISH   *n* pl. -ES a freshwater fish

GOLDURN   *n* pl. -S goldarn

GOLEM   *n* pl. -S a legendary creature

GOLF   *v* -ED, -ING, -S to play golf (a type of ball game)

GOLFER   *n* pl. -S one that golfs

GOLFING   *n* pl. -S the game of golf

GOLGOTHA   *n* pl. -S a place of burial

GOLIARD   *n* pl. -S a wandering student

GOLLIWOG   *n* pl. -S a grotesque doll

GOLLY   *interj* — used as a mild oath

GOLOSH   *n* pl. -ES galosh

GOMBO   *n* pl. -BOS gumbo

GOMBROON   *n* pl. -S a kind of Persian pottery

GOMERAL   *n* pl. -S a fool

GOMEREL   *n* pl. -S gomeral

GOMERIL   *n* pl. -S gomeral

GOMUTI   *n* pl. -S a palm tree

GONAD   *n* pl. -S a sex gland **GONADAL, GONADIAL, GONADIC** *adj*

GONDOLA   *n* pl. -S a long, narrow boat

GONE   *adj* departed

GONENESS   *n* pl. -ES a state of exhaustion

GONER   *n* pl. -S one who is in a hopeless situation

GONFALON   *n* pl. -S a banner

GONFANON   *n* pl. -S gonfalon

GONG   *v* -ED, -ING, -S to make the sound of a gong (a disk-shaped percussion instrument)

GONGLIKE   *adj* resembling a gong

GONIA   pl. of gonion and of gonium

GONIDIUM   *n* pl. -IA an asexual reproductive cell **GONIDIAL, GONIDIC** *adj*

GONIF   *n* pl. -S ganef

GONION   *n* pl. -NIA a part of the lower jaw

GONIUM   *n* pl. -NIA an immature reproductive cell

GONOCYTE   *n* pl. -S a cell that produces gametes

GONOF   *n* pl. -S ganef

GONOPH   *n* pl. -S ganef

GONOPORE   *n* pl. -S a genital pore

GOO   *n* pl. GOOS a sticky or viscid substance

GOOBER   *n* pl. -S a peanut

GOOD   *adj* BETTER, BEST having positive or desirable qualities

GOOD   *n* pl. -S something that is good

GOODBY   *n* pl. -BYS goodbye

GOODBYE   *n* pl. -S a concluding remark or gesture at parting

GOODIES   pl. of goody

GOODISH   *adj* somewhat good

GOODLY   *adj* -LIER, -LIEST of pleasing appearance

GOODMAN   *n* pl. -MEN the master of a household

GOODNESS   *n* pl. -ES the state of being good

GOODWIFE   *n* pl. -WIVES the mistress of a household

GOODWILL   *n* pl. -S an attitude of friendliness

GOODY   *n* pl. GOODIES a desirable food

GOOEY   *adj* GOOIER, GOOIEST sticky or viscid

GOOF   *v* -ED, -ING, -S to blunder

GOOFBALL   *n* pl. -S a sleeping pill

GOOFY   *adj* GOOFIER, GOOFIEST silly **GOOFILY** *adv*

GOOGLY   *n* pl. -GLIES a type of bowled ball in cricket

GOOGOL   *n* pl. -S an enormous number

GOOIER   comparative of gooey

GOOIEST   superlative of gooey

GOOK   *n* pl. -S goo **GOOKY** *adj*

GOON   *n* pl. -S a hired thug

GOONEY   *n* pl. -NEYS an albatross

GOONIE   *n* pl. -S gooney

GOONY   *n* pl. -NIES gooney

GOOP   *n* pl. -S a boor

GOORAL   *n* pl. -S goral

GOOSE	*n* pl. GEESE a swimming bird
GOOSE	*v* GOOSED, GOOSING, GOOSES to poke between the buttocks
GOOSEY	*adj* GOOSIER, GOOSIEST goosy
GOOSY	*adj* GOOSIER, GOOSIEST resembling a goose
GOPHER	*n* pl. -S a burrowing rodent
GOR	*interj* — used as a mild oath
GORAL	*n* pl. -S a goat antelope
GORBELLY	*n* pl. -LIES a potbelly
GORBLIMY	*interj* blimey
GORCOCK	*n* pl. -S the male red grouse
GORE	*v* GORED, GORING, GORES to pierce with a horn or tusk
GORGE	*v* GORGED, GORGING, GORGES to stuff with food **GORGEDLY** *adv*
GORGEOUS	*adj* beautiful
GORGER	*n* pl. -S one that gorges
GORGERIN	*n* pl. -S a part of a column
GORGET	*n* pl. -S a piece of armor for the throat **GORGETED** *adj*
GORGING	present participle of gorge
GORGON	*n* pl. -S an ugly woman
GORHEN	*n* pl. -S the female red grouse
GORIER	comparative of gory
GORIEST	superlative of gory
GORILLA	*n* pl. -S a large ape
GORILY	*adv* in a gory manner
GORINESS	*n* pl. -ES the state of being gory
GORING	present participle of gore
GORMAND	*n* pl. -S gourmand
GORSE	*n* pl. -S furze
GORSY	*adj* GORSIER, GORSIEST abounding in gorse
GORY	*adj* GORIER, GORIEST bloody
GOSH	*interj* — used as an exclamation of surprise
GOSHAWK	*n* pl. -S a large hawk
GOSLING	*n* pl. -S a young goose
GOSPEL	*n* pl. -S the message concerning Christ, the kingdom of God, and salvation
GOSPELER	*n* pl. -S one that teaches the gospel
GOSPORT	*n* pl. -S a communication device in an airplane
GOSSAMER	*n* pl. -S a fine film of cobwebs
GOSSAN	*n* pl. -S a type of decomposed rock
GOSSIP	*v* -SIPED, -SIPING, -SIPS or -SIPPED, -SIPPING, -SIPS to talk idly about the affairs of others
GOSSIPER	*n* pl. -S one that gossips
GOSSIPRY	*n* pl. -RIES the practice of gossiping
GOSSIPY	*adj* inclined to gossip
GOSSOON	*n* pl. -S a boy
GOSSYPOL	*n* pl. -S a toxic pigment
GOT	past tense of get
GOTHIC	*n* pl. -S a style of printing
GOTHITE	*n* pl. -S goethite
GOTTEN	past participle of get
GOUACHE	*n* pl. -S a method of painting
GOUGE	*v* GOUGED, GOUGING, GOUGES to cut or scoop out
GOUGER	*n* pl. -S one that gouges
GOULASH	*n* pl. -ES a beef stew
GOURAMI	*n* pl. -S a food fish
GOURD	*n* pl. -S a hard-shelled fruit
GOURDE	*n* pl. -S a monetary unit of Haiti
GOURMAND	*n* pl. -S one who loves to eat
GOURMET	*n* pl. -S a connoisseur of fine food and drink
GOUT	*n* pl. -S a metabolic disease
GOUTY	*adj* GOUTIER, GOUTIEST affected with gout **GOUTILY** *adv*
GOVERN	*v* -ED, -ING, -S to rule or direct
GOVERNOR	*n* pl. -S one that governs
GOWAN	*n* pl. -S a daisy **GOWANED, GOWANY** *adj*
GOWD	*n* pl. -S gold
GOWK	*n* pl. -S a fool
GOWN	*v* -ED, -ING, -S to dress in a gown (a long, loose outer garment)
GOWNSMAN	*n* pl. -MEN a professional or academic person
GOX	*n* pl. -ES gaseous oxygen
GOY	*n* pl. GOYIM or GOYS a non-Jewish person **GOYISH** *adj*
GRAAL	*n* pl. -S grail
GRAB	*v* GRABBED, GRABBING, GRABS to grasp suddenly
GRABBER	*n* pl. -S one that grabs
GRABBIER	comparative of grabby

GRABBIEST	superlative of grabby
GRABBING	present participle of grab
GRABBLE	v -BLED, -BLING, -BLES to grope
GRABBLER	n pl. -S one that grabbles
GRABBY	adj -BIER, -BIEST tending to grab
GRABEN	n pl. -S a depression of the earth's crust
GRACE	v GRACED, GRACING, GRACES to give beauty to
GRACEFUL	adj -FULLER, -FULLEST having beauty of form or movement
GRACILE	adj gracefully slender
GRACILIS	n pl. -LES a thigh muscle
GRACING	present participle of grace
GRACIOSO	n pl. -SOS a clown in Spanish comedy
GRACIOUS	adj marked by kindness and courtesy
GRACKLE	n pl. -S a blackbird
GRAD	n pl. -S a graduate
GRADATE	v -DATED, -DATING, -DATES to change by degrees
GRADE	v GRADED, GRADING, GRADES to arrange in steps or degrees **GRADABLE** adj
GRADER	n pl. -S one that grades
GRADIENT	n pl. -S a rate of inclination
GRADIN	n pl. -S gradine
GRADINE	n pl. -S one of a series of steps
GRADING	present participle of grade
GRADUAL	n pl. -S a hymn sung in alternate parts
GRADUAND	n pl. -S one who is about to graduate
GRADUATE	v -ATED, -ATING, -ATES to receive an academic degree or diploma
GRADUS	n pl. -ES a dictionary of prosody
GRAECIZE	v -CIZED, -CIZING, -CIZES to grecize
GRAFFITO	n pl. -TI an inscription or drawing made on a rock or wall
GRAFT	v -ED, -ING, -S to unite with a growing plant by insertion
GRAFTAGE	n pl. -S the process of grafting
GRAFTER	n pl. -S one that grafts
GRAHAM	adj made of whole wheat flour
GRAIL	n pl. -S the cup used by Christ at the Last Supper
GRAIN	v -ED, -ING, -S to form into small particles
GRAINER	n pl. -S one that grains
GRAINY	adj GRAINIER, GRAINIEST granular
GRAM	pl. -S a unit of mass and weight
GRAMA	n pl. -S a pasture grass
GRAMARY	n pl. -RIES gramarye
GRAMARYE	n pl. -S occult learning; magic
GRAMERCY	n pl. -CIES an expression of gratitude
GRAMMAR	n pl. -S the study of the formal features of a language
GRAMME	n pl. -S gram
GRAMP	n pl. -S grandfather
GRAMPUS	n pl. -ES a marine mammal
GRANA	pl. of granum
GRANARY	n pl. -RIES a storehouse for grain
GRAND	adj GRANDER, GRANDEST large and impressive
GRAND	n pl. -S a type of piano
GRANDAD	n pl. -S granddad
GRANDAM	n pl. -S a grandmother
GRANDAME	n pl. -S grandam
GRANDDAD	n pl. -S a grandfather
GRANDEE	n pl. -S man of high social position
GRANDEUR	n pl. -S the state of being grand
GRANDLY	adv in a grand manner
GRANDMA	n pl. -S a grandmother
GRANDPA	n pl. -S a grandfather
GRANDSIR	n pl. -S a grandfather
GRANDSON	n pl. -S a son of one's son or daughter
GRANGE	n pl. -S a farm
GRANGER	n pl. -S a farmer
GRANITE	n pl. -S a type of rock **GRANITIC** adj
GRANNIE	n pl. -S granny
GRANNY	n pl. -NIES a grandmother
GRANT	v -ED, -ING, -S to bestow upon
GRANTEE	n pl. -S one to whom something is granted
GRANTER	n pl. -S one that grants

GRANTOR	*n* pl. -S granter
GRANULAR	*adj* composed of granules
GRANULE	*n* pl. -S a small particle
GRANUM	*n* pl. GRANA a part of a plant chloroplast
GRAPE	*n* pl. -S an edible berry
GRAPERY	*n* pl. -ERIES a vinery
GRAPH	*v* -ED, -ING, -S to represent by means of a diagram
GRAPHEME	*n* pl. -S a unit of a writing system
GRAPHIC	*n* pl. -S a product of the art of representation
GRAPHITE	*n* pl. -S a variety of carbon
GRAPIER	comparative of grapy
GRAPIEST	superlative of grapy
GRAPLIN	*n* pl. -S a grapnel
GRAPLINE	*n* pl. -S graplin
GRAPNEL	*n* pl. -S a type of anchor
GRAPPA	*n* pl. -S an Italian brandy
GRAPPLE	*v* -PLED, -PLING, -PLES to struggle or contend
GRAPPLER	*n* pl. -S one that grapples
GRAPY	*adj* GRAPIER, GRAPIEST resembling grapes
GRASP	*v* -ED, -ING, -S to seize firmly with the hand
GRASPER	*n* pl. -S one that grasps
GRASS	*v* -ED, -ING, -ES to cover with grass (herbaceous plants)
GRASSY	*adj* GRASSIER, GRASSIEST of, resembling, or pertaining to grass **GRASSILY** *adv*
GRAT	past tense of greet (to weep)
GRATE	*v* GRATED, GRATING, GRATES to reduce to shreds by rubbing
GRATEFUL	*adj* -FULLER, -FULLEST deeply thankful
GRATER	*n* pl. -S one that grates
GRATIFY	*v* -FIED, -FYING, -FIES to satisfy
GRATIN	*n* pl. -S a type of food crust
GRATING	*n* pl. -S a network of bars covering an opening
GRATIS	*adj* free of charge
GRATUITY	*n* pl. -ITIES a gift of money
GRAUPEL	*n* pl. -S precipitation consisting of granular snow pellets
GRAVAMEN	*n* pl. -MENS or -MINA the most serious part of an accusation
GRAVE	*adj* GRAVER, GRAVEST extremely serious
GRAVE	*v* GRAVED, GRAVEN, GRAVING, GRAVES to engrave
GRAVEL	*v* -ELED, -ELING, -ELS or -ELLED, -ELLING, -ELS to pave with gravel (a mixture of rock fragments)
GRAVELLY	*adj* containing gravel
GRAVELY	*adv* in a grave manner
GRAVEN	past participle of grave
GRAVER	*n* pl. -S an engraver
GRAVEST	superlative of grave
GRAVID	*adj* pregnant **GRAVIDLY** *adv*
GRAVIDA	*n* pl. -DAS or -DAE a pregnant woman
GRAVIES	pl. of gravy
GRAVING	present participle of grave
GRAVITON	*n* pl. -S a hypothetical particle
GRAVITY	*n* pl. -TIES the force of attraction toward the earth's center
GRAVURE	*n* pl. -S a printing process
GRAVY	*n* pl. -VIES a sauce of the fat and juices from cooked meat
GRAY	*adj* GRAYER, GRAYEST of a color between white and black
GRAY	*v* -ED, -ING, -S to make gray
GRAYBACK	*n* pl. -S a gray bird
GRAYFISH	*n* pl. -ES a dogfish
GRAYISH	*adj* somewhat gray
GRAYLAG	*n* pl. -S a wild goose
GRAYLING	*n* pl. -S a food fish
GRAYLY	*adv* in a gray manner
GRAYNESS	*n* pl. -ES the state of being gray
GRAYOUT	*n* pl. -S a temporary blurring of vision
GRAZE	*v* GRAZED, GRAZING, GRAZES to feed on growing grass **GRAZABLE** *adj*
GRAZER	*n* pl. -S one that grazes
GRAZIER	*n* pl. -S one that grazes cattle
GRAZING	*n* pl. -S land used for the feeding of animals
GRAZIOSO	*adj* graceful in style
GREASE	*v* GREASED, GREASING, GREASES to smear with grease (a lubricating substance)
GREASER	*n* pl. -S one that greases

GREASY	*adj* GREASIER, GREASIEST containing or resembling grease **GREASILY** *adv*
GREAT	*adj* GREATER, GREATEST large
GREAT	*n* pl. -S a distinguished or outstanding person
GREATEN	*v* -ED, -ING, -S to make greater
GREATLY	*adv* in a great manner
GREAVE	*n* pl. -S a piece of armor for the leg **GREAVED** *adj*
GREBE	*n* pl. -S a diving bird
GRECIZE	*v* -CIZED, -CIZING, -CIZES to provide with a Greek style
GREE	*v* GREED, GREEING, GREES to agree
GREED	*n* pl. -S excessive desire for gain or wealth
GREEDY	*adj* GREEDIER, GREEDIEST marked by greed **GREEDILY** *adv*
GREEGREE	*n* pl. -S grigri
GREEK	*n* pl. GREEK something unintelligible
GREEN	*adj* GREENER, GREENEST of the color of growing foliage
GREEN	*v* -ED, -ING, -S to become green
GREENBUG	*n* pl. -S a green aphid
GREENERY	*n* pl. -ERIES green vegetation
GREENFLY	*n* pl. -FLIES a green aphid
GREENIER	comparative of greeny
GREENIEST	superlative of greeny
GREENING	*n* pl. -S a variety of apple
GREENISH	*adj* somewhat green
GREENLET	*n* pl. -S a vireo
GREENLY	*adv* in a green manner
GREENTH	*n* pl. -S verdure
GREENY	*adj* GREENIER, GREENIEST somewhat green
GREET	*v* -ED, -ING, -S to address in a friendly and courteous way
GREET	*v* GRAT, GRUTTEN, GREETING, GREETS to weep
GREETER	*n* pl. -S one that greets
GREETING	*n* pl. -S a salutation
GREGO	*n* pl. -GOS a hooded coat
GREIGE	*n* pl. -S fabric in an unfinished state
GREISEN	*n* pl. -S a type of rock
GREMIAL	*n* pl. -S a lap cloth used by a bishop during a service
GREMLIN	*n* pl. -S a mischievous creature
GREMMIE	*n* pl. -S an inexperienced surfer
GREMMY	*n* pl. -MIES gremmie
GRENADE	*n* pl. -S an explosive device
GREW	past tense of grow
GREWSOME	*adj* -SOMER, -SOMEST gruesome
GREY	*adj* GREYER, GREYEST gray
GREY	*v* -ED, -ING, -S to gray
GREYHEN	*n* pl. -S the female black grouse
GREYISH	*adj* grayish
GREYLAG	*n* pl. -S graylag
GREYLY	*adv* grayly
GREYNESS	*n* pl. -ES grayness
GRIBBLE	*n* pl. -S a marine isopod
GRID	*n* pl. -S a grating
GRIDDLE	*v* -DLED, -DLING, -DLES to cook on a flat pan
GRIDE	*v* GRIDED, GRIDING, GRIDES to scrape harshly
GRIDIRON	*n* pl. -S a grate for broiling food
GRIEF	*n* pl. -S intense mental distress
GRIEVANT	*n* pl. -S one that submits a complaint for arbitration
GRIEVE	*v* GRIEVED, GRIEVING, GRIEVES to feel grief
GRIEVER	*n* pl. -S one that grieves
GRIEVOUS	*adj* causing grief
GRIFF	*n* pl. -S griffe
GRIFFE	*n* pl. -S the offspring of a black person and a mulatto
GRIFFIN	*n* pl. -S a mythological creature
GRIFFON	*n* pl. -S griffin
GRIFT	*v* -ED, -ING, -S to swindle
GRIFTER	*n* pl. -S a swindler
GRIG	*n* pl. -S a lively person
GRIGRI	*n* pl. -S a fetish or amulet
GRILL	*v* -ED, -ING, -S to broil on a gridiron
GRILLADE	*n* pl. -S a dish of grilled meat
GRILLAGE	*n* pl. -S a framework of timber
GRILLE	*n* pl. -S a grating
GRILLER	*n* pl. -S one that grills
GRILSE	*n* pl. -S a young salmon
GRIM	*adj* GRIMMER, GRIMMEST stern and unrelenting

GRIMACE	*v* -MACED, -MACING, -MACES to contort the facial features
GRIMACER	*n* pl. -S one that grimaces
GRIME	*v* GRIMED, GRIMING, GRIMES to make dirty
GRIMIER	comparative of grimy
GRIMIEST	superlative of grimy
GRIMILY	*adv* in a grimy manner
GRIMING	present participle of grime
GRIMLY	*adv* in a grim manner
GRIMMER	comparative of grim
GRIMMEST	superlative of grim
GRIMNESS	*n* pl. -ES the quality of being grim
GRIMY	*adj* GRIMIER, GRIMIEST dirty
GRIN	*v* GRINNED, GRINNING, GRINS to smile broadly
GRIND	*v* GROUND or GRINDED, GRINDING, GRINDS to wear, smooth, or sharpen by friction
GRINDER	*n* pl. -S one that grinds
GRINDERY	*n* pl. -ERIES a place where tools are ground
GRINGO	*n* pl. -GOS a foreigner in Latin America — a derogatory term
GRINNED	past tense of grin
GRINNER	*n* pl. -S one that grins
GRINNING	present participle of grin
GRIP	*v* GRIPPED or GRIPT, GRIPPING, GRIPS to grasp
GRIPE	*v* GRIPED, GRIPING, GRIPES to grasp
GRIPER	*n* pl. -S one that gripes
GRIPEY	*adj* GRIPIER, GRIPIEST gripy
GRIPIER	comparative of gripy
GRIPIEST	superlative of gripy
GRIPING	present participle of gripe
GRIPPE	*n* pl. -S a virus disease
GRIPPED	a past tense of grip
GRIPPER	*n* pl. -S one that grips
GRIPPIER	comparative of grippy
GRIPPIEST	superlative of grippy
GRIPPING	present participle of grip
GRIPPLE	*adj* greedy
GRIPPY	*adj* GRIPPIER, GRIPPIEST affected with the grippe
GRIPSACK	*n* pl. -S a valise
GRIPT	a past tense of grip
GRIPY	*adj* GRIPIER, GRIPIEST causing sharp pains in the bowels
GRISEOUS	*adj* grayish
GRISETTE	*n* pl. -S a young French working-class girl
GRISKIN	*n* pl. -S the lean part of a loin of pork
GRISLY	*adj* -LIER, -LIEST horrifying
GRISON	*n* pl. -S a carnivorous mammal
GRIST	*n* pl. -S grain for grinding
GRISTLE	*n* pl. -S the tough part of meat
GRISTLY	*adj* -TLIER, -TLIEST containing gristle
GRIT	*v* GRITTED, GRITTING, GRITS to press the teeth together
GRITH	*n* pl. -S sanctuary for a limited period of time
GRITTY	*adj* -TIER, -TIEST plucky **GRITTILY** *adv*
GRIVET	*n* pl. -S a small monkey
GRIZZLE	*v* -ZLED, -ZLING, -ZLES to complain
GRIZZLER	*n* pl. -S one that grizzles
GRIZZLY	*adj* -ZLIER, -ZLIEST grayish
GRIZZLY	*n* pl. -ZLIES a large bear
GROAN	*v* -ED, -ING, -S to utter a low, mournful sound
GROANER	*n* pl. -S one that groans
GROAT	*n* pl. -S an old English coin
GROCER	*n* pl. -S a dealer in foodstuffs and household supplies
GROCERY	*n* pl. -CERIES a grocer's store
GROG	*n* pl. -S a mixture of liquor and water
GROGGERY	*n* pl. -GERIES a barroom
GROGGY	*adj* -GIER, -GIEST dazed **GROGGILY** *adv*
GROGRAM	*n* pl. -S a coarse silk fabric
GROGSHOP	*n* pl. -S a groggery
GROIN	*v* -ED, -ING, -S to build with intersecting arches
GROMMET	*n* pl. -S a reinforcing ring of metal
GROMWELL	*n* pl. -S an herb
GROOM	*v* -ED, -ING, -S to clean and care for
GROOMER	*n* pl. -S one that grooms
GROOVE	*v* GROOVED, GROOVING, GROOVES to form a groove (a long, narrow depression)

GROOVER	*n* pl. -S one that grooves
GROOVY	*adj* GROOVIER, GROOVIEST marvelous
GROPE	*v* GROPED, GROPING, GROPES to feel about with the hands
GROPER	*n* pl. -S one that gropes
GROSBEAK	*n* pl. -S a finch
GROSCHEN	*n* pl. GROSCHEN an Austrian coin
GROSS	*adj* GROSSER, GROSSEST flagrant
GROSS	*v* -ED, -ING, -ES to earn exclusive of deductions
GROSSER	*n* pl. -S a product yielding a large volume of business
GROSSLY	*adv* in a gross manner
GROSZ	*n* pl. GROSZY a Polish coin
GROT	*n* pl. -S a grotto
GROTTO	*n* pl. -TOES or -TOS a cave
GROUCH	*v* -ED, -ING, -ES to complain
GROUCHY	*adj* GROUCHIER, GROUCHIEST ill-tempered
GROUND	*v* -ED, -ING, -S to place on a foundation
GROUNDER	*n* pl. -S a type of batted baseball
GROUP	*v* -ED, -ING, -S to arrange in a group (an assemblage of persons or things)
GROUPER	*n* pl. -S a food fish
GROUPIE	*n* pl. -S a female follower of rock groups
GROUPING	*n* pl. -S a set of objects
GROUPOID	*n* pl. -S a type of mathematical set
GROUSE	*v* GROUSED, GROUSING, GROUSES to complain
GROUSER	*n* pl. -S one that grouses
GROUT	*v* -ED, -ING, -S to fill with a thin mortar
GROUTER	*n* pl. -S one that grouts
GROUTY	*adj* GROUTIER, GROUTIEST surly
GROVE	*n* pl. -S a small forested area **GROVED** *adj*
GROVEL	*v* -ELED, -ELING, -ELS or -ELLED, -ELLING, -ELS to crawl in an abject manner
GROVELER	*n* pl. -S one that grovels

GROW	*v* GREW, GROWN, GROWING, GROWS to cultivate **GROWABLE** *adj*
GROWER	*n* pl. -S one that grows
GROWL	*v* -ED, -ING, -S to utter a deep, harsh sound
GROWLER	*n* pl. -S one that growls
GROWLY	*adj* GROWLIER, GROWLIEST deep and harsh in speech
GROWN	*adj* mature
GROWNUP	*n* pl. -S a mature person
GROWTH	*n* pl. -S development
GROYNE	*n* pl. -S a structure built to protect a shore from erosion
GRUB	*v* GRUBBED, GRUBBING, GRUBS to dig
GRUBBER	*n* pl. -S one that grubs
GRUBBY	*adj* -BIER, -BIEST dirty **GRUBBILY** *adv*
GRUBWORM	*n* pl. -S the larva of some insects
GRUDGE	*v* GRUDGED, GRUDGING, GRUDGES to be unwilling to give or admit
GRUDGER	*n* pl. -S one that grudges
GRUEL	*v* -ELED, -ELING, -ELS or -ELLED, -ELLING, -ELS to disable by hard work
GRUELER	*n* pl. -S one that gruels
GRUELING	*n* pl. -S an exhausting experience
GRUELLED	a past tense of gruel
GRUELLER	*n* pl. -S grueler
GRUELLING	*n* pl. -S grueling
GRUESOME	*adj* -SOMER, -SOMEST repugnant
GRUFF	*adj* GRUFFER, GRUFFEST low and harsh in speech
GRUFF	*v* -ED, -ING, -S to utter in a gruff voice
GRUFFIER	comparative of gruffy
GRUFFIEST	superlative of gruffy
GRUFFILY	*adv* in a gruffy manner
GRUFFISH	*adj* somewhat gruff
GRUFFLY	*adv* in a gruff manner
GRUFFY	*adj* GRUFFIER, GRUFFIEST gruff
GRUGRU	*n* pl. -S a palm tree
GRUM	*adj* GRUMMER, GRUMMEST morose

GRUMBLE   *v* -BLED, -BLING, -BLES to mutter in discontent **GRUMBLY** *adj*

GRUMBLER   *n* pl. -S one that grumbles

GRUME   *n* pl. -S a thick, viscid substance

GRUMMER   comparative of grum

GRUMMEST   superlative of grum

GRUMMET   *n* pl. -S grommet

GRUMOSE   *adj* grumous

GRUMOUS   *adj* consisting of clustered grains

GRUMP   *v* -ED, -ING, -S to complain

GRUMPHIE   *n* pl. -S a pig

GRUMPHY   *n* pl. GRUMPHIES grumphie

GRUMPISH   *adj* grumpy

GRUMPY   *adj* GRUMPIER, GRUMPIEST ill-tempered **GRUMPILY** *adv*

GRUNION   *n* pl. -S a small food fish

GRUNT   *v* -ED, -ING, -S to utter a deep, guttural sound

GRUNTER   *n* pl. -S one that grunts

GRUNTLE   *v* -TLED, -TLING, -TLES to put in a good humor

GRUSHIE   *adj* thriving

GRUTCH   *v* -ED, -ING, -ES to grudge

GRUTTEN   past participle of greet (to weep)

GRYPHON   *n* pl. -S griffin

GUACHARO   *n* pl. -ROS or -ROES a tropical bird

GUACO   *n* pl. -COS a tropical plant

GUAIAC   *n* pl. -S guaiacum

GUAIACOL   *n* pl. -S a chemical compound

GUAIACUM   *n* pl. -S a medicinal resin

GUAIOCUM   *n* pl. -S guaiacum

GUAN   *n* pl. -S a large bird

GUANACO   *n* pl. -COS a South American mammal

GUANASE   *n* pl. -S an enzyme

GUANIDIN   *n* pl. -S a chemical compound

GUANIN   *n* pl. -S guanine

GUANINE   *n* pl. -S a chemical compound

GUANO   *n* pl. -NOS the accumulated excrement of sea birds

GUAR   *n* pl. -S a drought-tolerant legume

GUARANI   *n* pl. -NIS or -NIES a monetary unit of Paraguay

GUARANTY   *v* -TIED, -TYING, -TIES to assume responsibility for the quality of

GUARD   *v* -ED, -ING, -S to protect

GUARDANT   *n* pl. -S a guardian

GUARDER   *n* pl. -S one that guards

GUARDIAN   *n* pl. -S one that guards

GUAVA   *n* pl. -S a tropical shrub

GUAYULE   *n* pl. -S a shrub that is a source of rubber

GUCK   *n* pl. -S a messy substance

GUDE   *n* pl. -S good

GUDGEON   *v* -ED, -ING, -S to dupe

GUENON   *n* pl. -S a long-tailed monkey

GUERDON   *v* -ED, -ING, -S to reward

GUERILLA   *n* pl. -S a member of a small independent band of soldiers

GUERNSEY   *n* pl. -SEYS a woolen shirt

GUESS   *v* -ED, -ING, -ES to form an opinion from little or no evidence

GUESSER   *n* pl. -S one that guesses

GUEST   *v* -ED, -ING, -S to appear as a visitor

GUFF   *n* pl. -S foolish talk

GUFFAW   *v* -ED, -ING, -S to laugh loudly

GUGGLE   *v* -GLED, -GLING, GLES to gurgle

GUGLET   *n* pl. -S goglet

GUID   *n* pl. -S good

GUIDANCE   *n* pl. -S advice

GUIDE   *v* GUIDED, GUIDING, GUIDES to show the way to **GUIDABLE** *adj*

GUIDER   *n* pl. -S one that guides

GUIDON   *n* pl. -S a small flag

GUILD   *n* pl. -S an association of people of the same trade

GUILDER   *n* pl. -S a monetary unit of the Netherlands

GUILE   *v* GUILED, GUILING, GUILES to beguile

GUILEFUL   *adj* cunning

GUILT   *n* pl. -S the fact of having committed an offense

GUILTY   *adj* GUILTIER, GUILTIEST worthy of blame for an offense **GUILTILY** *adv*

GUIMPE   *n* pl. -S a short blouse

GUINEA   *n* pl. -S a former British coin

GUIPURE	*n* pl. -S a type of lace
GUIRO	*n* pl. GUIRO a percussion instrument
GUISARD	*n* pl. -S a masker
GUISE	*v* GUISED, GUISING, GUISES to disguise
GUITAR	*n* pl. -S a stringed musical instrument
GUL	*n* pl. -S a design in oriental carpets
GULAR	*adj* of or pertaining to the throat
GULCH	*n* pl. -ES a deep, narrow ravine
GULDEN	*n* pl. -S a guilder
GULES	*n* pl. GULES the color red
GULF	*v* -ED, -ING, -S to swallow up
GULFIER	comparative of gulfy
GULFIEST	superlative of gulfy
GULFLIKE	*adj* resembling a deep chasm
GULFWEED	*n* pl. -S a brownish seaweed
GULFY	*adj* GULFIER, GULFIEST full of whirlpools
GULL	*v* -ED, -ING, -S to deceive
GULLABLE	*adj* gullible **GULLABLY** *adv*
GULLET	*n* pl. -S the throat
GULLEY	*n* pl. -LEYS a ravine
GULLIBLE	*adj* easily deceived **GULLIBLY** *adv*
GULLY	*v* -LIED, -LYING, -LIES to form ravines by the action of water
GULOSITY	*n* pl. -TIES gluttony
GULP	*v* -ED, -ING, -S to swallow rapidly
GULPER	*n* pl. -S one that gulps
GULPY	*adj* GULPIER, GULPIEST marked by gulping
GUM	*v* GUMMED, GUMMING, GUMS to smear, seal, or clog with gum (a sticky, viscid substance)
GUMBO	*n* pl. -BOS the okra plant
GUMBOIL	*n* pl. -S an abscess in the gum
GUMBOTIL	*n* pl. -S a sticky clay
GUMDROP	*n* pl. -S a chewy candy
GUMLESS	*adj* having no gum
GUMLIKE	*adj* resembling gum
GUMMA	*n* pl. -MAS or -MATA a soft tumor
GUMMED	past tense of gum
GUMMER	*n* pl. -S one that gums

GUMMIER	comparative of gummy
GUMMIEST	superlative of gummy
GUMMING	present participle of gum
GUMMITE	*n* pl. -S a mixture of various minerals
GUMMOSE	*adj* gummy
GUMMOSIS	*n* pl. -MOSES a disease of plants
GUMMOUS	*adj* gummy
GUMMY	*adj* -MIER, -MIEST resembling gum
GUMPTION	*n* pl. -S shrewdness
GUMSHOE	*v* -SHOED, -SHOEING, -SHOES to investigate stealthily
GUMTREE	*n* pl. -S a tree that yields gum
GUMWEED	*n* pl. -S a plant covered with a gummy substance
GUMWOOD	*n* pl. -S the wood of a gumtree
GUN	*v* GUNNED, GUNNING, GUNS to shoot with a gun (a portable firearm)
GUNBOAT	*n* pl. -S an armed vessel
GUNDOG	*n* pl. -S a hunting dog
GUNFIGHT	*v* -FOUGHT, -FIGHTING, -FIGHTS to fight with guns
GUNFIRE	*n* pl. -S the firing of guns
GUNFLINT	*n* pl. -S the flint in a flintlock
GUNFOUGHT	past tense of gunfight
GUNK	*n* pl. -S filthy, sticky, or greasy matter
GUNLESS	*adj* having no gun
GUNLOCK	*n* pl. -S the mechanism which ignites the charge of a gun
GUNMAN	*n* pl. -MEN one who is armed with a gun
GUNMETAL	*n* pl. -S a dark gray color
GUNNED	past tense of gun
GUNNEL	*n* pl. -S a marine fish
GUNNEN	past participle of gin
GUNNER	*n* pl. -S one that operates a gun
GUNNERY	*n* pl. -NERIES the use of guns
GUNNING	*n* pl. -S the sport of hunting with a gun
GUNNY	*n* pl. -NIES a coarse fabric
GUNPAPER	*n* pl. -S a type of explosive paper
GUNPLAY	*n* pl. -PLAYS the shooting of guns

GUNPOINT   *n* pl. -S the point or aim of a gun

GUNROOM   *n* pl. -S a room on a British warship

GUNSEL   *n* pl. -S a gunman

GUNSHIP   *n* pl. -S an armed helicopter

GUNSHOT   *n* pl. -S a projectile fired from a gun

GUNSMITH   *n* pl. -S one who makes or repairs firearms

GUNSTOCK   *n* pl. -S the rear wooden part of a rifle

GUNWALE   *n* pl. -S the upper edge of a ship's side

GUPPY   *n* pl. -PIES a small, tropical fish

GURGE   *v* GURGED, GURGING, GURGES to swirl

GURGLE   *v* -GLED, -GLING, -GLES to flow unevenly

GURGLET   *n* pl. -S goglet

GURNARD   *n* pl. -S a marine fish

GURNET   *n* pl. -S a gurnard

GURNEY   *n* pl. -NEYS a wheeled cot

GURRY   *n* pl. -RIES fish offal

GURSH   *n* pl. -ES qursh

GURU   *n* pl. -S a Hindu spiritual teacher

GURUSHIP   *n* pl. -S the office of a guru

GUSH   *v* -ED, -ING, -ES to flow forth forcefully

GUSHER   *n* pl. -S a gushing oil well

GUSHY   *adj* GUSHIER, GUSHIEST overly sentimental **GUSHILY** *adv*

GUSSET   *v* -ED, -ING, -S to furnish with a reinforcing piece of material

GUST   *v* -ED, -ING, -S to blow in gusts (sudden blasts of wind)

GUSTABLE   *n* pl. -S a savory food

GUSTIER   comparative of gusty

GUSTIEST   superlative of gusty

GUSTILY   *adv* in a gusty manner

GUSTLESS   *adj* having no gusts

GUSTO   *n* pl. -TOES vigorous enjoyment

GUSTY   *adj* GUSTIER, GUSTIEST blowing in gusts

GUT   *v* GUTTED, GUTTING, GUTS to remove the guts (intestines) of

GUTLESS   *adj* lacking courage

GUTLIKE   *adj* resembling guts

GUTSY   *adj* GUTSIER, GUTSIEST brave

GUTTA   *n* pl. -TAE a drop of liquid

GUTTATE   *adj* resembling a drop

GUTTATED   *adj* guttate

GUTTED   past tense of gut

GUTTER   *v* -ED, -ING, -S to form channels for draining off water

GUTTERY   *adj* marked by extreme vulgarity or indecency

GUTTIER   comparative of gutty

GUTTIEST   superlative of gutty

GUTTING   present participle of gut

GUTTLE   *v* -TLED, -TLING, -TLES to eat rapidly

GUTTLER   *n* pl. -S one that guttles

GUTTURAL   *n* pl. -S a throaty sound

GUTTY   *adj* -TIER, -TIEST marked by courage

GUY   *v* -ED, -ING, -S to ridicule

GUYOT   *n* pl. -S a flat-topped seamount

GUZZLE   *v* -ZLED, -ZLING, -ZLES to drink rapidly

GUZZLER   *n* pl. -S one that guzzles

GWEDUC   *n* pl. -S geoduck

GWEDUCK   *n* pl. -S geoduck

GYBE   *v* GYBED, GYBING, GYBES to shift from side to side while sailing

GYM   *n* pl. -S a room for athletic activities

GYMKHANA   *n* pl. -S an athletic meet

GYMNASIA   *n/pl* gyms

GYMNAST   *n* pl. -S one who is skilled in physical exercises

GYNAECEA   *n/pl* gynecia

GYNAECIA   *n/pl* gynecia

GYNANDRY   *n* pl. -DRIES the condition of having both male and female sexual organs

GYNARCHY   *n* pl. -CHIES government by women

GYNECIA   pl. of gynecium

GYNECIC   *adj* pertaining to women

GYNECIUM   *n* pl. -CIA the pistil of a flower

GYNECOID   *adj* resembling a woman

GYNIATRY   *n* pl. -TRIES the treatment of women's diseases

GYNOECIA   *n/pl* gynecia

GYP   *v* GYPPED, GYPPING, GYPS to swindle

GYPPER   *n* pl. -S one that gyps

GYPSEIAN   *adj* of or pertaining to gypsies

GYPSEOUS   *adj* containing gypsum

GYPSUM   *n* pl. -S a mineral

GYPSY   *v* -SIED, -SYING, -SIES to live like a gypsy (a wanderer)

GYPSYDOM   *n* pl. -S the realm of gypsies

GYPSYISH   *adj* resembling a gypsy

GYPSYISM   *n* pl. -S the mode of life of gypsies

GYRAL   *adj* gyratory **GYRALLY** *adv*

GYRATE   *v* -RATED, -RATING, -RATES to revolve or rotate

GYRATION   *n* pl. -S the act of gyrating

GYRATOR   *n* pl. -S one that gyrates

GYRATORY   *adj* moving in a circle or spiral

GYRE   *v* GYRED, GYRING, GYRES to move in a circle or spiral

GYRENE   *n* pl. -S a marine

GYRI   pl. of gyrus

GYRING   present participle of gyre

GYRO   *n* pl. -ROS a gyroscope

GYROIDAL   *adj* spiral in arrangement

GYRON   *n* pl. -S a heraldic design

GYROSE   *adj* marked with wavy lines

GYROSTAT   *n* pl. -S a type of stabilizing device

GYRUS   *n* pl. -RI a ridge in the brain

GYVE   *v* GYVED, GYVING, GYVES to shackle

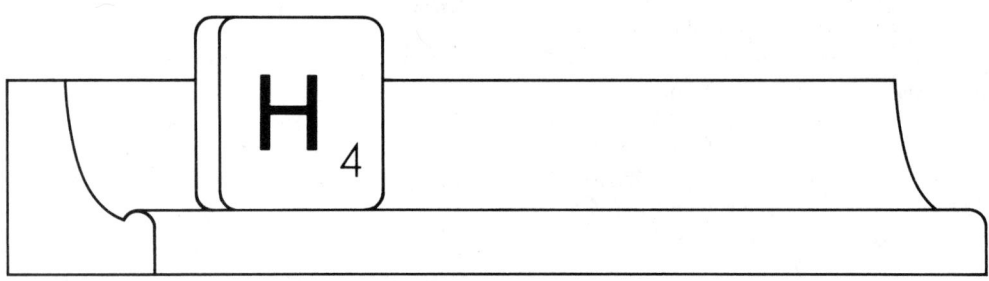

HA	*n* pl. -S a sound of surprise
HAAF	*n* pl. -S a deep-sea fishing ground
HAAR	*n* pl. -S a fog
HABANERA	*n* pl. -S a Cuban dance
HABDALAH	*n* pl. -S a Jewish ceremony
HABILE	*adj* skillful
HABIT	*v* -ED, -ING, -S to clothe or dress
HABITAN	*n* pl. -S a French settler
HABITANT	*n* pl. -S an inhabitant
HABITAT	*n* pl. -S the natural environment of an organism
HABITUAL	*adj* occurring frequently or constantly
HABITUDE	*n* pl. -S a usual course of action
HABITUE	*n* pl. -S a frequent customer
HABITUS	*n* pl. HABITUS bodily build and constitution
HABU	*n* pl. -S a poisonous snake
HACEK	*n* pl. -S a mark placed over a letter to modify it
HACHURE	*v* -CHURED, -CHURING, -CHURES to make a hatching on a map
HACIENDA	*n* pl. -S an estate
HACK	*v* -ED, -ING, -S to cut or chop roughly
HACKBUT	*n* pl. -S a type of gun
HACKEE	*n* pl. -S a chipmunk
HACKER	*n* pl. -S one that hacks
HACKIE	*n* pl. -S a taxicab driver
HACKLE	*v* -LED, -LING, -LES to hack
HACKLER	*n* pl. -S one that hackles

HACKLY	*adj* -LIER, -LIEST jagged
HACKMAN	*n* pl. -MEN a hackie
HACKNEY	*v* -NEYED, -NEYING, -NEYS to make common
HACKSAW	*n* pl. -S a type of saw
HACKWORK	*n* pl. -S artistic work done according to formula
HAD	a past tense of have
HADAL	*adj* pertaining to deep parts of the ocean
HADARIM	a pl. of heder
HADDEST	a past 2d person sing. of have
HADDOCK	*n* pl. -S a food fish
HADE	*v* HADED, HADING, HADES to incline
HADJ	*n* pl. -ES a pilgrimage to Mecca
HADJEE	*n* pl. -S hadji
HADJI	*n* pl. -S one who has made a hadj
HADRON	*n* pl. -S an elementary particle **HADRONIC** *adj*
HADST	a past 2d person sing. of have
HAE	*v* HAED, HAEN, HAEING, HAES to have
HAEM	*n* pl. -S heme
HAEMAL	*adj* hemal
HAEMATAL	*adj* hemal
HAEMATIC	*n* pl. -S hematic
HAEMATIN	*n* pl. -S hematin
HAEMIC	*adj* hemic
HAEMIN	*n* pl. -S hemin
HAEMOID	*adj* hemoid
HAEN	past participle of hae

HAERES	*n* pl. -REDES heres	**HAIRCUT**	*n* pl. -S a cutting of the hair
HAET	*n* pl. -S a small amount	**HAIRDO**	*n* pl. -DOS a style of wearing the hair
HAFFET	*n* pl. -S the cheekbone and temple	**HAIRED**	*adj* having hair
HAFFIT	*n* pl. -S haffet	**HAIRIER**	comparative of hairy
HAFIZ	*n* pl. HAFIS a Muslim who knows the Koran by heart	**HAIRIEST**	superlative of hairy
		HAIRLESS	*adj* having no hair
HAFNIUM	*n* pl. -S a metallic element	**HAIRLIKE**	*adj* resembling a hair
HAFT	*v* -ED, -ING, -S to supply with a handle	**HAIRLINE**	*n* pl. -S a very thin line
HAFTARAH	*n* pl. -RAHS, -ROTH or -ROT a biblical selection	**HAIRLOCK**	*n* pl. -S a lock of hair
		HAIRPIN	*n* pl. -S a hair fastener
HAFTER	*n* pl. -S one that hafts	**HAIRWORK**	*n* pl. -S the making of articles from hair
HAFTORAH	*n* pl. -RAHS, -ROTH or -ROT haftarah	**HAIRWORM**	*n* pl. -S a parasitic worm
HAG	*v* HAGGED, HAGGING, HAGS to hack	**HAIRY**	*adj* HAIRIER, HAIRIEST covered with hair
HAGADIC	*adj* haggadic	**HAJ**	*n* pl. -ES hadj
HAGADIST	*n* pl. -S a haggadic scholar	**HAJI**	*n* pl. -S hadji
HAGBERRY	*n* pl. -RIES a small cherry	**HAJJ**	*n* pl. -ES hadj
HAGBORN	*adj* born of a witch	**HAJJI**	*n* pl. -S hadji
HAGBUSH	*n* pl. -ES a large tree	**HAKE**	*n* pl. -S a marine fish
HAGBUT	*n* pl. -S hackbut	**HAKEEM**	*n* pl. -S hakim
HAGDON	*n* pl. -S a seabird	**HAKIM**	*n* pl. -S a Muslim physician
HAGFISH	*n* pl. -ES an eellike fish	**HALAKAH**	*n* pl. -KOTH or -KAHS the legal part of the Talmud
HAGGADIC	*adj* pertaining to the story of Exodus	**HALAKIC**	*adj* pertaining to the halakah
HAGGARD	*n* pl. -S an adult hawk	**HALAKIST**	*n* pl. -S a halakic writer
HAGGED	past tense of hag	**HALAKOTH**	a pl. of halakah
HAGGING	present participle of hag	**HALALA**	*n* pl. -S a Saudi Arabian coin
HAGGIS	*n* pl. -GISES a Scottish dish	**HALALAH**	*n* pl. -S halala
HAGGISH	*adj* resembling a hag	**HALATION**	*n* pl. -S a blurring of light in photographs
HAGGLE	*v* -GLED, -GLING, -GLES to bargain	**HALAVAH**	*n* pl. -S halvah
HAGGLER	*n* pl. -S one that haggles	**HALBERD**	*n* pl. -S an axlike weapon
HAGRIDE	*v* -RODE, -RIDDEN, -RIDING, -RIDES to harass	**HALBERT**	*n* pl. -S halberd
		HALCYON	*n* pl. -S a mythical bird
HAH	*n* pl. -S ha	**HALE**	*adj* HALER, HALEST healthy
HAIK	*n* pl. HAIKS or HAIKA an outer garment worn by Arabs	**HALE**	*v* HALED, HALING, HALES to compel to go
HAIKU	*n* pl. HAIKU a Japanese poem	**HALENESS**	*n* pl. -ES the state of being hale
HAIL	*v* -ED, -ING, -S to welcome	**HALER**	*n* pl. -LERS or -LERU a Czechoslovakian coin
HAILER	*n* pl. -S one that hails		
HAIR	*n* pl. -S a threadlike growth	**HALEST**	superlative of hale
HAIRBALL	*n* pl. -S a ball of hair	**HALING**	present participle of hale
HAIRBAND	*n* pl. -S a headband	**HALF**	*n* pl. HALVES one of two equal parts
HAIRCAP	*n* pl. -S a hat		

HALFBACK	*n* pl. -S a member of the backfield in football
HALFBEAK	*n* pl. -S a marine fish
HALFLIFE	*n* pl. -LIVES a measure of radioactive decay
HALFNESS	*n* pl. -ES the state of being half
HALFTIME	*n* pl. -S an intermission in a football game
HALFTONE	*n* pl. -S a shade between light and dark
HALFWAY	*adj* being at a point in the middle
HALIBUT	*n* pl. -S a flatfish
HALID	*n* pl. -S halide
HALIDE	*n* pl. -S a chemical compound
HALIDOM	*n* pl. -S something holy
HALIDOME	*n* pl. -S halidom
HALITE	*n* pl. -S a mineral
HALITUS	*n* pl. -ES an exhalation
HALL	*n* pl. -S a large room for assembly
HALLAH	*n* pl. -LAHS, -LOTH or -LOT challah
HALLEL	*n* pl. -S a chant of praise
HALLIARD	*n* pl. -S halyard
HALLMARK	*v* -ED, -ING, -S to mark with an official stamp
HALLO	*v* -ED, -ING, -S or -ES to shout
HALLOA	*v* -ED, -ING, -S to hallo
HALLOO	*v* -ED, -ING, -S to hallo
HALLOT	a pl. of hallah
HALLOTH	a pl. of hallah
HALLOW	*v* -ED, -ING, -S to make holy
HALLOWER	*n* pl. -S one that hallows
HALLUX	*n* pl. -LUCES the big toe
HALLWAY	*n* pl. -WAYS a hall
HALM	*n* pl. -S haulm
HALO	*v* -ED, -ING, -ES or -S to form a halo (a ring of light)
HALOGEN	*n* pl. -S a nonmetallic element
HALOID	*n* pl. -S a chemical salt
HALOLIKE	*adj* resembling a halo
HALT	*v* -ED, -ING, -S to stop
HALTER	*v* -ED, -ING, -S to put restraint upon
HALTERE	*n* pl. -S a pair of wings of an insect
HALTLESS	*adj* not hesitant

HALUTZ	*n* pl. -LUTZIM an Israeli farmer
HALVA	*n* pl. -S halvah
HALVAH	*n* pl. -S a Turkish confection
HALVE	*v* HALVED, HALVING, HALVES to divide into two equal parts
HALVERS	*n* pl. HALVERS half shares
HALVES	pl. of half
HALYARD	*n* pl. -S a line used to hoist a sail
HAM	*v* HAMMED, HAMMING, HAMS to overact
HAMAL	*n* pl. -S a porter in eastern countries
HAMARTIA	*n* pl. -S a defect of character
HAMATE	*n* pl. -S a wrist bone
HAMAUL	*n* pl. -S hamal
HAMBURG	*n* pl. -S a patty of ground beef
HAME	*n* pl. -S a part of a horse collar
HAMLET	*n* pl. -S a small town
HAMMAL	*n* pl. -S hamal
HAMMED	past tense of ham
HAMMER	*v* -ED, -ING, -S to strike repeatedly
HAMMERER	*n* pl. -S one that hammers
HAMMIER	comparative of hammy
HAMMIEST	superlative of hammy
HAMMILY	*adv* in a hammy manner
HAMMING	present participle of ham
HAMMOCK	*n* pl. -S a hanging cot
HAMMY	*adj* -MIER, -MIEST overly theatrical
HAMPER	*v* -ED, -ING, -S to hinder
HAMPERER	*n* pl. -S one that hampers
HAMSTER	*n* pl. -S a burrowing rodent
HAMULUS	*n* pl. -LI a small hook **HAMULAR, HAMULATE, HAMULOSE, HAMULOUS** *adj*
HAMZA	*n* pl. -S an Arabic diacritical mark
HAMZAH	*n* pl. -S hamza
HANAPER	*n* pl. -S a wicker receptacle
HANCE	*n* pl. -S a side of an arch
HAND	*v* -ED, -ING, -S to present with the hand (the end of the forearm)
HANDBAG	*n* pl. -S a small carrying bag
HANDBALL	*n* pl. -S a small rubber ball
HANDBILL	*n* pl. -S a circular

HANDBOOK *n* pl. -S a manual

HANDCAR *n* pl. -S a hand-operated railroad car

HANDCART *n* pl. -S a cart pushed by hand

HANDCUFF *v* -ED, -ING, -S to fetter with restraining cuffs

HANDFAST *v* -ED, -ING, -S to grip securely

HANDFUL *n* pl. HANDFULS or HANDSFUL as much as the hand can hold

HANDGRIP *n* pl. -S a grip by the hand or hands

HANDGUN *n* pl. -S a small firearm

HANDHOLD *n* pl. -S a handgrip

HANDICAP *v* -CAPPED, -CAPPING, -CAPS to hinder

HANDIER comparative of handy

HANDIEST superlative of handy

HANDILY *adv* in a handy manner

HANDLE *v* -DLED, -DLING, -DLES to touch with the hands

HANDLER *n* pl. -S one that handles

HANDLESS *adj* having no hands

HANDLIKE *adj* resembling a hand

HANDLING *n* pl. -S the manner in which something is handled

HANDLIST *n* pl. -S a reference list

HANDLOOM *n* pl. -S a manually operated loom

HANDMADE *adj* made by hand

HANDMAID *n* pl. -S a female servant

HANDOFF *n* pl. -S a play in football

HANDOUT *n* pl. -S something given out free

HANDPICK *v* -ED, -ING, -S to choose carefully

HANDRAIL *n* pl. -S a railing used for support

HANDSAW *n* pl. -S a saw used manually

HANDSEL *v* -SELED, -SELING, -SELS or -SELLED, -SELLING, -SELS to give a gift to

HANDSET *n* pl. -S a type of telephone

HANDSEWN *adj* sewn by hand

HANDSFUL a pl. of handful

HANDSOME *adj* -SOMER, -SOMEST attractive

HANDWORK *n* pl. -S manual labor

HANDWRIT *adj* written by hand

HANDY *adj* HANDIER, HANDIEST convenient for handling

HANDYMAN *n* pl. -MEN a man who does odd jobs

HANG *v* HUNG or HANGED, HANGING, HANGS to attach from above only **HANGABLE** *adj*

HANGAR *v* -ED, -ING, -S to place in an aircraft shelter

HANGBIRD *n* pl. -S a type of bird

HANGDOG *n* pl. -S a sneaky person

HANGER *n* pl. -S one that hangs

HANGFIRE *n* pl. -S a delay in detonation

HANGING *n* pl. -S an execution by strangling with a suspended noose

HANGMAN *n* pl. -MEN an executioner

HANGNAIL *n* pl. -S an agnail

HANGNEST *n* pl. -S a hangbird

HANGOUT *n* pl. -S a place often visited

HANGOVER *n* pl. -S the physical effects following a drinking binge

HANGTAG *n* pl. -S a type of tag used commercially

HANGUP *n* pl. -S an inhibition or obsession

HANK *v* -ED, -ING, -S to fasten a sail

HANKER *v* -ED, -ING, -S to long for

HANKERER *n* pl. -S one that hankers

HANKIE *n* pl. -S hanky

HANKY *n* pl. -KIES a handkerchief

HANSE *n* pl. -S a guild of merchants

HANSEL *v* -SELED, -SELING, -SELS or -SELLED, -SELLING, -SELS to handsel

HANSOM *n* pl. -S a light carriage

HANT *v* -ED, -ING, -S to haunt

HANTLE *n* pl. -S a large amount

HANUMAN *n* pl. -S an East Indian monkey

HAOLE *n* pl. -S one who is not a native Hawaiian

HAP *v* HAPPED, HAPPING, HAPS to happen

HAPAX *n* pl. -ES a word that occurs only once

HAPLESS *adj* luckless

HAPLITE *n* pl. -S aplite

HAPLOID *n* pl. -S a cell having only one set of chromosomes

HAPLOIDY   *n* pl. -DIES the state of being a haploid

HAPLONT   *n* pl. -S an organism having a particular chromosomal structure

HAPLOPIA   *n* pl. -S normal vision

HAPLOSIS   *n* pl. -LOSES the halving of the chromosome number

HAPLY   *adv* by chance

HAPPED   past tense of hap

HAPPEN   *v* -ED, -ING, -S to occur

HAPPING   present participle of hap

HAPPY   *adj* -PIER, -PIEST marked by joy **HAPPILY** *adv*

HAPTEN   *n* pl. -S a substance similar to an antigen **HAPTENIC** *adj*

HAPTENE   *n* pl. -S hapten

HAPTIC   *adj* pertaining to the sense of touch

HAPTICAL   *adj* haptic

HARANGUE   *v* -RANGUED, -RANGUING, -RANGUES to deliver a tirade to

HARASS   *v* -ED, -ING, -ES to bother persistently

HARASSER   *n* pl. -S one that harasses

HARBOR   *v* -ED, -ING, -S to shelter

HARBORER   *n* pl. -S one that harbors

HARBOUR   *v* -ED, -ING, -S to harbor

HARD   *adj* HARDER, HARDEST firm and unyielding

HARDBACK   *n* pl. -S a hardcover book

HARDBALL   *n* pl. -S baseball

HARDBOOT   *n* pl. -S a horseman

HARDCASE   *adj* tough

HARDCORE   *adj* unyielding

HARDEN   *v* -ED, -ING, -S to make hard

HARDENER   *n* pl. -S one that hardens

HARDHACK   *n* pl. -S a woody plant

HARDHAT   *n* pl. -S a conservative

HARDHEAD   *n* pl. -S a practical person

HARDIER   comparative of hardy

HARDIES   pl. of hardy

HARDIEST   superlative of hardy

HARDILY   *adv* in a hardy manner

HARDLY   *adv* scarcely

HARDNESS   *n* pl. -ES the state of being hard

HARDPAN   *n* pl. -S a layer of hard subsoil

HARDS   *n/pl* the coarse refuse of flax

HARDSET   *adj* rigid

HARDSHIP   *n* pl. -S a difficult, painful condition

HARDTACK   *n* pl. -S a hard biscuit

HARDTOP   *n* pl. -S a type of car

HARDWARE   *n* pl. -S metal goods

HARDWOOD   *n* pl. -S the hard, compact wood of various trees

HARDY   *adj* -DIER, -DIEST very sturdy

HARDY   *n* pl. -DIES a blacksmith's chisel

HARE   *v* HARED, HARING, HARES to run

HAREBELL   *n* pl. -S a perennial herb

HAREEM   *n* pl. -S harem

HARELIKE   *adj* resembling a hare (a long-eared mammal)

HARELIP   *n* pl. -S a deformity of the upper lip

HAREM   *n* pl. -S the section of a Muslim household reserved for women

HARIANA   *n* pl. -S a breed of cattle

HARICOT   *n* pl. -S the seed of various string beans

HARIJAN   *n* pl. -S an outcaste in India

HARING   present participle of hare

HARK   *v* -ED, -ING, -S to listen to

HARKEN   *v* -ED, -ING, -S to hearken

HARKENER   *n* pl. -S one that harkens

HARL   *n* pl. -S a herl

HARLOT   *n* pl. -S a prostitute

HARLOTRY   *n* pl. -RIES prostitution

HARM   *v* -ED, -ING, -S to injure

HARMER   *n* pl. -S one that harms

HARMFUL   *adj* capable of harming

HARMIN   *n* pl. -S harmine

HARMINE   *n* pl. -S an alkaloid used as a stimulant

HARMLESS   *adj* not harmful

HARMONIC   *n* pl. -S an overtone

HARMONY   *n* pl. -NIES agreement

HARNESS   *v* -ED, -ING, -ES to put tackle on a draft animal

HARP   *v* -ED, -ING, -S to play on a harp (a type of stringed musical instrument)

HARPER   *n* pl. -S a harpist

HARPIES   pl. of harpy

HARPIN	*n* pl. -S harping
HARPING	*n* pl. -S a wooden plank used in shipbuilding
HARPIST	*n* pl. -S one that plays the harp
HARPOON	*v* -ED, -ING, -S to strike with a harpoon
HARPY	*n* pl. -PIES a shrewish person
HARRIDAN	*n* pl. -S a haggard woman
HARRIED	past tense of harry
HARRIER	*n* pl. -S a hunting dog
HARRIES	present 3d person sing. of harry
HARROW	*v* -ED, -ING, -S to break up and level soil
HARROWER	*n* pl. -S one that harrows
HARRUMPH	*v* -ED, -ING, -S to make a guttural sound
HARRY	*v* -RIED, -RYING, -RIES to pillage
HARSH	*adj* HARSHER, HARSHEST severe
HARSHEN	*v* -ED, -ING, -S to make harsh
HARSHLY	*adv* in a harsh manner
HARSLET	*n* pl. -S haslet
HART	*n* pl. -S a male deer
HARTAL	*n* pl. -S a stoppage of work
HARUSPEX	*n* pl. -PICES a soothsayer of ancient Rome
HARVEST	*v* -ED, -ING, -S to gather a crop
HAS	a present 3d person sing. of have
HASH	*v* -ED, -ING, -ES to mince
HASHEESH	*n* pl. -ES hashish
HASHISH	*n* pl. -ES a mild narcotic
HASLET	*n* pl. -S the edible viscera of an animal
HASP	*v* -ED, -ING, -S to fasten with a clasp
HASSEL	*n* pl. -S an argument
HASSLE	*v* -SLED, -SLING, -SLES to argue
HASSOCK	*n* pl. -S a footstool
HAST	a present 2d person sing. of have
HASTATE	*adj* triangular
HASTE	*v* HASTED, HASTING, HASTES to hasten
HASTEFUL	*adj* hasty
HASTEN	*v* -ED, -ING, -S to hurry
HASTENER	*n* pl. -S one that hastens
HASTING	present participle of haste
HASTY	*adj* HASTIER, HASTIEST speedy **HASTILY** *adv*
HAT	*v* HATTED, HATTING, HATS to provide with a hat (a covering for the head)
HATABLE	*adj* hateable
HATBAND	*n* pl. -S a band worn on a hat
HATBOX	*n* pl. -ES a box for a hat
HATCH	*v* -ED, -ING, -ES to bring forth young from an egg
HATCHECK	*adj* pertaining to the checking of hats
HATCHEL	*v* -ELED, -ELING, -ELS or -ELLED, -ELLING, -ELS to separate flax fibers with a comb
HATCHER	*n* pl. -S one that hatches
HATCHERY	*n* pl. -ERIES a place for hatching eggs
HATCHET	*n* pl. -S a small ax
HATCHING	*n* pl. -S a series of lines used to show shading
HATCHWAY	*n* pl. -WAYS an opening in the deck of a ship
HATE	*v* HATED, HATING, HATES to despise
HATEABLE	*adj* meriting hatred
HATEFUL	*adj* detestable
HATER	*n* pl. -S one that hates
HATFUL	*n* pl. HATSFUL or HATFULS as much as a hat can hold
HATH	a present 3d person sing. of have
HATING	present participle of hate
HATLESS	*adj* lacking a hat
HATLIKE	*adj* resembling a hat
HATMAKER	*n* pl. -S one that makes hats
HATPIN	*n* pl. -S a pin for securing a hat
HATRACK	*n* pl. -S a rack for hats
HATRED	*n* pl. -S intense dislike or aversion
HATSFUL	a pl. of hatful
HATTED	past tense of hat
HATTER	*n* pl. -S a hatmaker
HATTERIA	*n* pl. -S a reptile
HATTING	present participle of hat
HAUBERK	*n* pl. -S a coat of armor
HAUGH	*n* pl. -S a low-lying meadow

HAUGHTY	*adj* -TIER, -TIEST arrogant
HAUL	*v* -ED, -ING, -S to pull with force
HAULAGE	*n* pl. -S the act of hauling
HAULER	*n* pl. -S one that hauls
HAULIER	*n* pl. -S hauler
HAULM	*n* pl. -S a plant stem
HAULMY	*adj* HAULMIER, HAULMIEST having haulms
HAULYARD	*n* pl. -S halyard
HAUNCH	*n* pl. -ES the hindquarter **HAUNCHED** *adj*
HAUNT	*v* -ED, -ING, -S to visit frequently
HAUNTER	*n* pl. -S one that haunts
HAUSEN	*n* pl. -S a Russian sturgeon
HAUSFRAU	*n* pl. -FRAUS or -FRAUEN a housewife
HAUTBOIS	*n* pl. HAUTBOIS hautboy
HAUTBOY	*n* pl. -BOYS an oboe
HAUTEUR	*n* pl. -S haughty manner or spirit
HAVDALAH	*n* pl. -S habdalah
HAVE	*v* past 2d person sing. HAD, HADDEST or HADST, present participle HAVING, present 2d person sing. HAVE or HAST, 3d person sing. HAS or HATH to be in possession of
HAVE	*n* pl. -S a wealthy person
HAVELOCK	*n* pl. -S a covering for a cap
HAVEN	*v* -ED, -ING, -S to shelter
HAVER	*v* -ED, -ING, -S to hem and haw
HAVEREL	*n* pl. -S a fool
HAVIOR	*n* pl. -S behavior
HAVIOUR	*n* pl. -S havior
HAVOC	*v* -OCKED, -OCKING, -OCS to destroy
HAVOCKER	*n* pl. -S one that havocs
HAW	*v* -ED, -ING, -S to turn left
HAWFINCH	*n* pl. -ES a Eurasian finch
HAWK	*v* -ED, -ING, -S to peddle
HAWKBILL	*n* pl. -S a sea turtle
HAWKER	*n* pl. -S one that hawks
HAWKEY	*n* pl. -EYS a hawkie
HAWKIE	*n* pl. -S a white-faced cow
HAWKING	*n* pl. -S falconry
HAWKISH	*adj* warlike
HAWKLIKE	*adj* resembling a hawk (a bird of prey)

HAWKMOTH	*n* pl. -S a large moth
HAWKNOSE	*n* pl. -S a large, curved nose
HAWKSHAW	*n* pl. -S a detective
HAWKWEED	*n* pl. -S a weedlike herb
HAWSE	*n* pl. -S a part of a ship's bow
HAWSER	*n* pl. -S a mooring rope
HAWTHORN	*n* pl. -S a thorny shrub
HAY	*v* -ED, -ING, -S to convert into hay (grass, cut and dried for fodder)
HAYCOCK	*n* pl. -S a pile of hay
HAYER	*n* pl. -S one that hays
HAYFORK	*n* pl. -S a tool for pitching hay
HAYING	*n* pl. -S the season for harvesting hay
HAYLAGE	*n* pl. -S a type of hay
HAYLOFT	*n* pl. -S a loft for hay storage
HAYMAKER	*n* pl. -S one that makes hay
HAYMOW	*n* pl. -S a hayloft
HAYRACK	*n* pl. -S a frame used in hauling hay
HAYRICK	*n* pl. -S a haystack
HAYRIDE	*n* pl. -S a wagon ride
HAYSEED	*n* pl. -S a bumpkin
HAYSTACK	*n* pl. -S a pile of hay
HAYWARD	*n* pl. -S an officer who tends cattle
HAYWIRE	*n* pl. -S wire used in baling hay
HAZAN	*n* pl. -ZANIM or -ZANS a cantor
HAZARD	*v* -ED, -ING, -S to venture
HAZE	*v* HAZED, HAZING, HAZES to subject to a humiliating initiation
HAZEL	*n* pl. -S a shrub
HAZELLY	*adj* yellowish brown
HAZELNUT	*n* pl. -S an edible nut
HAZER	*n* pl. -S one that hazes
HAZIER	comparative of hazy
HAZIEST	superlative of hazy
HAZILY	*adv* in a hazy manner
HAZINESS	*n* pl. -ES the state of being hazy
HAZING	*n* pl. -S an attempt to embarrass or ridicule
HAZY	*adj* HAZIER, HAZIEST unclear
HAZZAN	*n* pl. HAZZANIM or HAZZANS hazan
HE	*n* pl. -S a male person
HEAD	*v* -ED, -ING, -S to be chief of

HEADACHE *n* pl. -S a pain inside the head

HEADACHY *adj* -ACHIER, -ACHIEST having a headache

HEADBAND *n* pl. -S a band worn on the head

HEADER *n* pl. -S a grain harvester

HEADGATE *n* pl. -S a gate to control the flow of water

HEADGEAR *n* pl. -S a covering for the head

HEADHUNT *v* -ED, -ING, -S to seek out, decapitate, and preserve the heads of enemies

HEADIER comparative of heady

HEADIEST superlative of heady

HEADILY *adv* in a heady manner

HEADING *n* pl. -S a title

HEADLAMP *n* pl. -S a light on the front of a car

HEADLAND *n* pl. -S a cliff

HEADLESS *adj* lacking a head

HEADLINE *v* -LINED, -LINING, -LINES to provide with a title

HEADLOCK *n* pl. -S a wrestling hold

HEADLONG *adj* rash; impetuous

HEADMAN *n* pl. -MEN a foreman

HEADMOST *adj* foremost

HEADNOTE *n* pl. -S a prefixed note

HEADPIN *n* pl. -S a bowling pin

HEADRACE *n* pl. -S a water channel

HEADREST *n* pl. -S a support for the head

HEADROOM *n* pl. -S clear vertical space

HEADSAIL *n* pl. -S a type of sail

HEADSET *n* pl. -S a pair of earphones

HEADSHIP *n* pl. -S the position of a leader

HEADSMAN *n* pl. -MEN an executioner

HEADSTAY *n* pl. -STAYS a support for a ship's foremast

HEADWAY *n* pl. -WAYS forward movement

HEADWIND *n* pl. -S an oncoming wind

HEADWORD *n* pl. -S a word put at the beginning

HEADWORK *n* pl. -S mental work

HEADY *adj* HEADIER, HEADIEST intoxicating

HEAL *v* -ED, -ING, -S to make sound or whole **HEALABLE** *adj*

HEALER *n* pl. -S one that heals

HEALTH *n* pl. -S the physical condition of an organism

HEALTHY *adj* HEALTHIER, HEALTHIEST having good health

HEAP *v* -ED, -ING, -S to pile up

HEAR *v* HEARD, HEARING, HEARS to perceive by the ear **HEARABLE** *adj*

HEARER *n* pl. -S one that hears

HEARING *n* pl. -S a preliminary examination

HEARKEN *v* -ED, -ING, -S to listen to

HEARSAY *n* pl. -SAYS secondhand information

HEARSE *v* HEARSED, HEARSING, HEARSES to transport in a hearse (a vehicle for conveying corpses)

HEART *v* -ED, -ING, -S to hearten

HEARTEN *v* -ED, -ING, -S to give courage to

HEARTH *n* pl. -S the floor of a fireplace

HEARTY *adj* HEARTIER, HEARTIEST very friendly **HEARTILY** *adv*

HEARTY *n* pl. HEARTIES a comrade

HEAT *v* HEATED or HET, HEATING, HEATS to make hot **HEATABLE** *adj*

HEATEDLY *adv* in an inflamed or excited manner

HEATER *n* pl. -S an apparatus for heating

HEATH *n* pl. -S an evergreen shrub

HEATHEN *n* pl. -S an uncivilized person

HEATHER *n* pl. -S an evergreen shrub **HEATHERY** *adj*

HEATHY *adj* HEATHIER, HEATHIEST abounding in heath

HEATLESS *adj* having no warmth

HEAUME *n* pl. -S a medieval helmet

HEAVE *v* HEAVED or HOVE, HEAVING, HEAVES to lift forcefully

HEAVEN *n* pl. -S the sky

HEAVENLY *adj* -LIER, -LIEST full of beauty and peace

HEAVER *n* pl. -S one that heaves

HEAVIER comparative of heavy

HEAVIES pl. of heavy

HEAVING present participle of heave

HEAVY *adj* HEAVIER, HEAVIEST having much weight **HEAVILY** *adv*

HEAVY	*n* pl. HEAVIES a villain
HEAVYSET	*adj* solidly built; stocky
HEBDOMAD	*n* pl. -S the number seven
HEBETATE	*v* -TATED, -TATING, -TATES to make dull
HEBETIC	*adj* pertaining to puberty
HEBETUDE	*n* pl. -S mental dullness
HEBRAIZE	*v* -IZED, -IZING, -IZES to make Hebrew
HECATOMB	*n* pl. -S a great sacrifice or slaughter
HECK	*n* pl. -S hell
HECKLE	*v* -LED, -LING, -LES to harass a speaker
HECKLER	*n* pl. -S one that heckles
HECTARE	*n* pl. -S a unit of area
HECTIC	*adj* filled with turmoil **HECTICLY** *adv*
HECTICAL	*adj* hectic
HECTOR	*v* -ED, -ING, -S to bully
HEDDLE	*n* pl. -S a part of a loom
HEDER	*n* pl. HEDERS or HADARIM a Jewish school
HEDGE	*v* HEDGED, HEDGING, HEDGES to surround with a hedge
HEDGER	*n* pl. -S one that hedges
HEDGEHOG	*n* pl. -S a small mammal
HEDGEHOP	*v* -HOPPED, -HOPPING, -HOPS to fly near the ground
HEDGEPIG	*n* pl. -S a hedgehog
HEDGEROW	*n* pl. -S a row of bushes
HEDGING	present participle of hedge
HEDGY	*adj* HEDGIER, HEDGIEST abounding in hedges
HEDONIC	*adj* pertaining to pleasure
HEDONICS	*n/pl* a branch of psychology
HEDONISM	*n* pl. -S the pursuit of pleasure
HEDONIST	*n* pl. -S a follower of hedonism
HEED	*v* -ED, -ING, -S to pay attention to
HEEDER	*n* pl. -S one that heeds
HEEDFUL	*adj* paying close attention
HEEDLESS	*adj* paying little or no attention
HEEHAW	*v* -ED, -ING, -S to guffaw
HEEL	*v* -ED, -ING, -S to supply with a heel (the raised part of a shoe)
HEELBALL	*n* pl. -S a composition used for polishing

HEELER	*n* pl. -S one that puts heels on shoes
HEELING	*n* pl. -S the act of inclining laterally
HEELLESS	*adj* lacking heels
HEELPOST	*n* pl. -S a post fitted to the end of something
HEELTAP	*n* pl. -S material put on the heel of a shoe
HEEZE	*v* HEEZED, HEEZING, HEEZES to hoist
HEFT	*v* -ED, -ING, -S to lift up
HEFTER	*n* pl. -S one that hefts
HEFTY	*adj* HEFTIER, HEFTIEST heavy **HEFTILY** *adv*
HEGARI	*n* pl. -S a grain
HEGEMONY	*n* pl. -NIES great authority
HEGIRA	*n* pl. -S an exodus
HEGUMEN	*n* pl. -S the head of a monastery
HEGUMENE	*n* pl. -S the head of a nunnery
HEGUMENY	*n* pl. -NIES the office of a hegumen
HEIFER	*n* pl. -S a young cow
HEIGH	*interj* — used to attract attention
HEIGHT	*n* pl. -S the highest point
HEIGHTEN	*v* -ED, -ING, -S to raise
HEIGHTH	*n* pl. -S height
HEIL	*v* -ED, -ING, -S to salute
HEINIE	*n* pl. -S the buttocks
HEINOUS	*adj* very wicked
HEIR	*v* -ED, -ING, -S to inherit
HEIRDOM	*n* pl. -S heirship
HEIRESS	*n* pl. -ES a female inheritor
HEIRLESS	*adj* having no inheritors
HEIRLOOM	*n* pl. -S an inherited possession
HEIRSHIP	*n* pl. -S the right to inheritance
HEIST	*v* -ED, -ING, -S to steal
HEISTER	*n* pl. -S one that heists
HEJIRA	*n* pl. -S hegira
HEKTARE	*n* pl. -S hectare
HELD	past tense of hold
HELIAC	*adj* heliacal
HELIACAL	*adj* pertaining to the sun
HELIAST	*n* pl. -S an Athenian judge
HELICAL	*adj* shaped like a helix

HELICES a pl. of helix

HELICITY *n* pl. -TIES a component of a particle's spin

HELICOID *n* pl. -S a type of geometrical surface

HELICON *n* pl. -S a large bass tuba

HELICOPT *v* -ED, -ING, -S to travel by helicopter

HELIO *n* pl. -LIOS a signaling mirror

HELIPAD *n* pl. -S a heliport

HELIPORT *n* pl. -S an airport for helicopters

HELISTOP *n* pl. -S a heliport

HELIUM *n* pl. -S a gaseous element

HELIX *n* pl. -LIXES or -LICES something spiral in form

HELL *v* -ED, -ING, -S to behave raucously

HELLBENT *adj* stubbornly determined

HELLBOX *n* pl. -ES a printer's receptacle

HELLCAT *n* pl. -S a shrewish person

HELLER *n* pl. -S a hellion

HELLERI *n* pl. -ES a tropical fish

HELLERY *n* pl. -LERIES rough play

HELLFIRE *n* pl. -S the torment of hell

HELLHOLE *n* pl. -S a horrible place

HELLION *n* pl. -S a troublesome person

HELLISH *adj* horrible

HELLKITE *n* pl. -S a cruel person

HELLO *v* -ED, -ING, -ES or -S to greet

HELLUVA *adj* disagreeable

HELM *v* -ED, -ING, -S to steer a ship

HELMET *v* -ED, -ING, -S to supply with a helmet (a protective covering for the head)

HELMINTH *n* pl. -S a worm

HELMLESS *adj* lacking a helm (a steering system)

HELMSMAN *n* pl. -MEN one that steers a ship

HELOT *n* pl. -S a slave or serf

HELOTAGE *n* pl. -S helotism

HELOTISM *n* pl. -S slavery or serfdom

HELOTRY *n* pl. -RIES helotism

HELP *v* HELPED or HOLP, HOLPEN, HELPING, HELPS to give assistance to **HELPABLE** *adj*

HELPER *n* pl. -S one that helps

HELPFUL *adj* being of service or assistance

HELPING *n* pl. -S a portion of food

HELPLESS *adj* defenseless

HELPMATE *n* pl. -S a helpful companion

HELPMEET *n* pl. -S a helpmate

HELVE *v* HELVED, HELVING, HELVES to provide with a handle

HEM *v* HEMMED, HEMMING, HEMS to provide with an edge

HEMAGOG *n* pl. -S an agent that promotes blood flow

HEMAL *adj* pertaining to the blood

HEMATAL *adj* hemal

HEMATEIN *n* pl. -S a chemical compound

HEMATIC *n* pl. -S a medicine for a blood disease

HEMATIN *n* pl. -S heme

HEMATINE *n* pl. -S hematin

HEMATITE *n* pl. -S an ore of iron

HEMATOID *adj* resembling blood

HEMATOMA *n* pl. -MAS or -MATA a swelling filled with blood

HEME *n* pl. -S a component of hemoglobin

HEMIC *adj* hemal

HEMIN *n* pl. -S a chloride of heme

HEMIOLA *n* pl. -S a rhythmic alteration in music

HEMIPTER *n* pl. -S an insect

HEMLINE *n* pl. -S the bottom edge of a garment

HEMLOCK *n* pl. -S a poisonous herb

HEMMED past tense of hem

HEMMER *n* pl. -S one that hems

HEMMING present participle of hem

HEMOCOEL *n* pl. -S a body cavity

HEMOCYTE *n* pl. -S a blood cell

HEMOID *adj* hemal

HEMOLYZE *v* -LYZED, -LYZING, -LYZES to break down red blood cells

HEMOSTAT *n* pl. -S an instrument for reducing bleeding

HEMP *n* pl. -S a tall herb

HEMPEN *adj* made of hemp

HEMPIE *adj* HEMPIER, HEMPIEST hempy

HEMPIER comparative of hempy

HEMPIEST superlative of hempy

HEMPLIKE *adj* resembling hemp

HEMPSEED *n* pl. -S the seed of hemp

HEMPWEED *n* pl. -S a climbing plant

HEMPY *adj* HEMPIER, HEMPIEST mischievous

HEN *n* pl. -S a female chicken **HENLIKE** *adj*

HENBANE *n* pl. -S a poisonous herb

HENBIT *n* pl. -S a perennial herb

HENCE *adv* consequently

HENCHMAN *n* pl. -MEN an unscrupulous supporter

HENCOOP *n* pl. -S a cage for hens

HENEQUEN *n* pl. -S a fiber used to make ropes

HENEQUIN *n* pl. -S henequen

HENHOUSE *n* pl. -S a shelter for poultry

HENIQUEN *n* pl. -S henequen

HENNA *v* -ED, -ING, -S to dye with a reddish coloring

HENNERY *n* pl. -NERIES a poultry farm

HENPECK *v* -ED, -ING, -S to dominate by nagging

HENRY *n* pl. -RIES or -RYS a unit of inductance

HENT *v* -ED, -ING, -S to grasp

HEP *adj* hip

HEPARIN *n* pl. -S a biochemical

HEPATIC *n* pl. -S a drug acting on the liver

HEPATICA *n* pl. -CAS or -CAE a perennial herb

HEPATIZE *v* -TIZED, -TIZING, -TIZES to convert tissue into a firm mass

HEPATOMA *n* pl. -MAS or -MATA a tumor of the liver

HEPCAT *n* pl. -S a jazz enthusiast

HEPTAD *n* pl. -S a group of seven

HEPTAGON *n* pl. -S a seven-sided polygon

HEPTANE *n* pl. -S a hydrocarbon used as a solvent

HEPTARCH *n* pl. -S one of a group of seven rulers

HEPTOSE *n* pl. -S a chemical compound

HER *pron* the objective or possessive case of the pronoun she

HERALD *v* -ED, -ING, -S to proclaim

HERALDIC *adj* pertaining to heraldry

HERALDRY *n* pl. -RIES the art or science of armorial bearings

HERB *n* pl. -S a flowering plant with a nonwoody stem

HERBAGE *n* pl. -S nonwoody plant life

HERBAL *n* pl. -S a book about herbs and plants

HERBARIA *n/pl* collections of dried plants

HERBIER comparative of herby

HERBIEST superlative of herby

HERBLESS *adj* lacking herbs

HERBLIKE *adj* resembling an herb

HERBY *adj* HERBIER, HERBIEST abounding in herbs

HERCULES *n* pl. -LESES any man of great size and strength

HERD *v* -ED, -ING, -S to bring together in a herd (a group of animals)

HERDER *n* pl. -S one who tends a herd

HERDIC *n* pl. -S a type of carriage

HERDLIKE *adj* resembling a herd

HERDMAN *n* pl. -MEN herdsman

HERDSMAN *n* pl. -MEN a herder

HERE *n* pl. -S this place

HEREAT *adv* at this time

HEREAWAY *adv* in this vicinity

HEREBY *adv* by this means

HEREDES pl. of heres

HEREDITY *n* pl. -TIES the genetic transmission of characteristics

HEREIN *adv* in this

HEREINTO *adv* into this place

HEREOF *adv* of this

HEREON *adv* on this

HERES *n* pl. HEREDES an heir

HERESY *n* pl. -SIES a belief contrary to a church doctrine

HERETIC *n* pl. -S one that upholds heresy

HERETO *adv* to this matter

HERETRIX *n* pl. -TRIXES or -TRICES heritrix

HEREUNTO *adv* hereto

HEREUPON *adv* immediately following this

HEREWITH *adv* along with this

HERIOT *n* pl. -S a feudal tribute or payment

HERITAGE *n* pl. -S something that is inherited

HERITOR	*n* pl. -S one that inherits
HERITRIX	*n* pl. -TRIXES or -TRICES a female heritor
HERL	*n* pl. -S a feathered fishing lure
HERM	*n* pl. -S a type of statue
HERMA	*n* pl. -MAE or -MAI a herm **HERMAEAN** *adj*
HERMETIC	*adj* airtight
HERMIT	*n* pl. -S a recluse **HERMITIC** *adj*
HERMITRY	*n* pl. -RIES the state of being a hermit
HERN	*n* pl. -S a heron
HERNIA	*n* pl. -NIAS or -NIAE the protrusion of an organ through its surrounding wall **HERNIAL** *adj*
HERNIATE	*v* -ATED, -ATING, -ATES to protrude through an abnormal bodily opening
HERO	*n* pl. -ROES or -ROS one who shows great courage
HEROIC	*n* pl. -S an epic verse
HEROICAL	*adj* courageous; noble
HEROIN	*n* pl. -S an addictive narcotic
HEROINE	*n* pl. -S a brave woman
HEROISM	*n* pl. -S heroic behavior
HEROIZE	*v* -IZED, -IZING, -IZES to make heroic
HERON	*n* pl. -S a wading bird
HERONRY	*n* pl. -RIES a place where herons breed
HERPES	*n* pl. -PESES a skin infection **HERPETIC** *adj*
HERRING	*n* pl. -S a food fish
HERRY	*v* -RIED, -RYING, -RIES to harry
HERS	*pron* the possessive case of the pronoun she
HERSELF	*pron* a form of the 3d person sing. feminine pronoun
HERTZ	*n* pl. -ES a unit of frequency
HESITANT	*adj* tending to hesitate
HESITATE	*v* -TATED, -TATING, -TATES to hold back in uncertainty
HESSIAN	*n* pl. -S a coarse cloth
HESSITE	*n* pl. -S a mineral
HEST	*n* pl. -S a command
HET	a past tense of heat
HETAERA	*n* pl. -RAE or -RAS a concubine **HETAERIC** *adj*
HETAIRA	*n* pl. -RAI or -RAS hetaera
HETERO	*n* pl. -EROS a heterosexual
HETH	*n* pl. -S a Hebrew letter
HETMAN	*n* pl. -S a cossack leader
HEUCH	*n* pl. -S heugh
HEUGH	*n* pl. -S a steep cliff
HEW	*v* HEWED, HEWN, HEWING, HEWS to cut with an ax **HEWABLE** *adj*
HEWER	*n* pl. -S one that hews
HEX	*v* -ED, -ING, -ES to cast an evil spell upon
HEXAD	*n* pl. -S a group of six **HEXADIC** *adj*
HEXADE	*n* pl. -S hexad
HEXAGON	*n* pl. -S a polygon having six sides
HEXAGRAM	*n* pl. -S a six-pointed star
HEXAMINE	*n* pl. -S a chemical compound
HEXANE	*n* pl. -S a volatile liquid
HEXAPLA	*n* pl. -S an edition in which six texts are set in parallel columns **HEXAPLAR** *adj*
HEXAPOD	*n* pl. -S a six-legged insect
HEXAPODY	*n* pl. -DIES a line of verse with six feet
HEXARCHY	*n* pl. -CHIES a group of six separate states
HEXER	*n* pl. -S one that hexes
HEXEREI	*n* pl. -S witchcraft
HEXONE	*n* pl. -S a hydrocarbon solvent
HEXOSAN	*n* pl. -S a carbohydrate
HEXOSE	*n* pl. -S a simple sugar
HEXYL	*n* pl. -S a hydrocarbon radical
HEY	*interj* — used to attract attention
HEYDAY	*n* pl. -DAYS the period of one's greatest success
HEYDEY	*n* pl. -DEYS heyday
HI	*interj* — used as a greeting
HIATUS	*n* pl. -ES a gap or missing section **HIATAL** *adj*
HIBACHI	*n* pl. -S a cooking device
HIBERNAL	*adj* pertaining to winter
HIBISCUS	*n* pl. -ES a tropical plant
HIC	*interj* — used to represent a hiccup
HICCOUGH	*v* -ED, -ING, -S to hiccup

HICCUP	*v* -CUPED, -CUPING, -CUPS or -CUPPED, -CUPPING, -CUPS to make a peculiar-sounding, spasmodic inhalation
HICK	*n* pl. -S a rural person
HICKEY	*n* pl. -EYS a gadget
HICKORY	*n* pl. -RIES a hardwood tree
HID	a past tense of hide
HIDABLE	*adj* able to be hidden
HIDALGO	*n* pl. -GOS a minor Spanish nobleman
HIDDEN	*adj* concealed; obscure **HIDDENLY** *adv*
HIDE	*v* HID, HIDDEN, HIDING, HIDES to conceal
HIDE	*v* HIDED, HIDING, HIDES to flog
HIDEAWAY	*n* pl. -AWAYS a hideout
HIDELESS	*adj* lacking a skin
HIDEOUS	*adj* very ugly
HIDEOUT	*n* pl. -S a place of refuge
HIDER	*n* pl. -S one that hides
HIDING	*n* pl. -S a beating
HIDROSIS	*n* pl. -DROSES abnormal perspiration **HIDROTIC** *adj*
HIE	*v* HIED, HIEING or HYING, HIES to hurry
HIEMAL	*adj* pertaining to winter
HIERARCH	*n* pl. -S a religious leader
HIERATIC	*adj* pertaining to priests
HIGGLE	*v* -GLED, -GLING, -GLES to haggle
HIGGLER	*n* pl. -S one that higgles
HIGH	*adj* HIGHER, HIGHEST reaching far upward
HIGH	*n* pl. -S a high level
HIGHBALL	*v* -ED, -ING, -S to go at full speed
HIGHBORN	*adj* of noble birth
HIGHBOY	*n* pl. -BOYS a tall chest of drawers
HIGHBRED	*adj* highborn
HIGHBROW	*n* pl. -S a person who has superior tastes
HIGHBUSH	*adj* forming a tall bush
HIGHJACK	*v* -ED, -ING, -S to hijack
HIGHLAND	*n* pl. -S an elevated region
HIGHLY	*adv* to a high degree
HIGHNESS	*n* pl. -ES the state of being high

HIGHROAD	*n* pl. -S a highway
HIGHT	*v* -ED, -ING, -S to command
HIGHTAIL	*v* -ED, -ING, -S to retreat rapidly
HIGHTH	*n* pl. -S height
HIGHWAY	*n* pl. -WAYS a main road
HIJACK	*v* -ED, -ING, -S to seize a vehicle while in transit
HIJACKER	*n* pl. -S one that hijacks
HIJINKS	*n/pl* mischievous fun
HIKE	*v* HIKED, HIKING, HIKES to walk a long distance
HIKER	*n* pl. -S one that hikes
HILA	pl. of hilum
HILAR	*adj* pertaining to a hilum
HILARITY	*n* pl. -TIES noisy merriment
HILDING	*n* pl. -S a vile person
HILI	pl. of hilus
HILL	*v* -ED, -ING, -S to form into a hill (a rounded elevation)
HILLER	*n* pl. -S one that hills
HILLIER	comparative of hilly
HILLIEST	superlative of hilly
HILLO	*v* -ED, -ING, -S to hallo
HILLOA	*v* -ED, -ING, -S to hallo
HILLOCK	*n* pl. -S a small hill **HILLOCKY** *adj*
HILLSIDE	*n* pl. -S the side of a hill
HILLTOP	*n* pl. -S the top of a hill
HILLY	*adj* HILLIER, HILLIEST abounding in hills
HILT	*v* -ED, -ING, -S to provide with a hilt (a handle for a weapon)
HILTLESS	*adj* having no hilt
HILUM	*n* pl. HILA a small opening in a bodily organ
HILUS	*n* pl. HILI hilum
HIM	*pron* the objective case of the pronoun he
HIMATION	*n* pl. -MATIA or -MATIONS a loose outer garment
HIMSELF	*pron* a form of the 3d person sing. masculine pronoun
HIN	*n* pl. -S a Hebrew unit of liquid measure
HIND	*n* pl. -S a female red deer
HINDER	*v* -ED, -ING, -S to impede
HINDERER	*n* pl. -S one that hinders

HINDGUT	*n* pl. -S the rear part of the alimentary canal
HINDMOST	*adj* farthest to the rear
HINGE	*v* HINGED, HINGING, HINGES to attach a jointed device
HINGER	*n* pl. -S one that hinges
HINNY	*v* -NIED, -NYING, -NIES to whinny
HINT	*v* -ED, -ING, -S to suggest indirectly
HINTER	*n* pl. -S one that hints
HIP	*v* HIPPED, HIPPING, HIPS to build a type of roof
HIP	*adj* HIPPER, HIPPEST aware of the most current styles and trends
HIPBONE	*n* pl. -S a pelvic bone
HIPLESS	*adj* lacking a hip (the pelvic joint)
HIPLIKE	*adj* suggestive of a hip
HIPNESS	*n* pl. -ES the state of being hip
HIPPARCH	*n* pl. -S a cavalry commander in ancient Greece
HIPPED	past tense of hip
HIPPER	comparative of hip
HIPPEST	superlative of hip
HIPPING	present participle of hip
HIPPIE	*n* pl. -S a nonconformist
HIPPIER	comparative of hippy
HIPPIEST	superlative of hippy
HIPPISH	*adj* depressed; sad
HIPPO	*n* pl. -POS a hippopotamus
HIPPY	*adj* -PIER, -PIEST having big hips
HIPSHOT	*adj* lame; awkward
HIPSTER	*n* pl. -S one that is hip
HIRABLE	*adj* available for hire
HIRAGANA	*n* pl. -S a Japanese cursive script
HIRCINE	*adj* pertaining to a goat
HIRE	*v* HIRED, HIRING, HIRES to engage the services of for payment **HIREABLE** *adj*
HIRELING	*n* pl. -S one that works for money only
HIRER	*n* pl. -S one that hires
HIRING	present participle of hire
HIRPLE	*v* -PLED, -PLING, -PLES to limp

HIRSEL	*v* -SELED, -SELING, -SELS or -SELLED, -SELLING, -SELS to herd sheep
HIRSLE	*v* -SLED, -SLING, -SLES to slide along
HIRSUTE	*adj* hairy
HIRUDIN	*n* pl. -S an anticoagulant
HIS	*pron* the possessive form of the pronoun he
HISN	*pron* his
HISPID	*adj* covered with stiff hairs
HISS	*v* -ED, -ING, -ES to make a sibilant sound
HISSELF	*pron* himself
HISSER	*n* pl. -S one that hisses
HISSING	*n* pl. -S an object of scorn
HIST	*v* -ED, -ING, -S to hoist
HISTAMIN	*n* pl. -S an amine released in allergic reactions
HISTIDIN	*n* pl. -S an amino acid
HISTOGEN	*n* pl. -S interior plant tissue
HISTOID	*adj* pertaining to connective tissue
HISTONE	*n* pl. -S a simple protein
HISTORIC	*adj* important in history
HISTORY	*n* pl. -RIES a chronological record of past events
HIT	*v* HIT, HITTING, HITS to strike forcibly
HITCH	*v* -ED, -ING, -ES to fasten with a knot or hook
HITCHER	*n* pl. -S one that hitches
HITHER	*adv* toward this place
HITHERTO	*adv* up to now
HITLESS	*adj* being without a hit
HITTER	*n* pl. -S one that hits
HITTING	present participle of hit
HIVE	*v* HIVED, HIVING, HIVES to cause to enter a hive (a bee's nest)
HIVELESS	*adj* lacking a hive
HO	*interj* — used to express surprise
HOACTZIN	*n* pl. -S or -ES hoatzin
HOAGIE	*n* pl. -S a long sandwich
HOAGY	*n* pl. -GIES hoagie
HOAR	*n* pl. -S a white coating
HOARD	*v* -ED, -ING, -S to gather and store away

HOARDER	*n* pl. -S one that hoards	**HOELIKE**	*adj* resembling a hoe
HOARDING	*n* pl. -S something hoarded	**HOER**	*n* pl. -S one that hoes
HOARIER	comparative of hoary	**HOG**	*v* HOGGED, HOGGING, HOGS to take more than one's share
HOARIEST	superlative of hoary	**HOGAN**	*n* pl. -S a Navaho Indian dwelling
HOARILY	*adv* in a hoary manner		
HOARSE	*adj* HOARSER, HOARSEST low and rough in sound **HOARSELY** *adv*	**HOGBACK**	*n* pl. -S a sharp ridge
		HOGFISH	*n* pl. -ES a tropical fish
HOARSEN	*v* -ED, -ING, -S to make hoarse	**HOGG**	*n* pl. -S a young sheep
HOARY	*adj* HOARIER, HOARIEST white with age	**HOGGED**	past tense of hog
		HOGGER	*n* pl. -S one that hogs
HOATZIN	*n* pl. -S or -ES a tropical bird	**HOGGING**	present participle of hog
HOAX	*v* -ED, -ING, -ES to deceive	**HOGGISH**	*adj* coarsely selfish
HOAXER	*n* pl. -S one that hoaxes	**HOGLIKE**	*adj* hoggish
HOB	*v* HOBBED, HOBBING, HOBS to furnish with hobnails	**HOGMANAY**	*n* pl. -NAYS a Scottish celebration
HOBBIES	pl. of hobby	**HOGMANE**	*n* pl. -S hogmanay
HOBBLE	*v* -BLED, -BLING, -BLES to limp	**HOGMENAY**	*n* pl. -NAYS hogmanay
HOBBLER	*n* pl. -S one that hobbles	**HOGNOSE**	*n* pl. -S a nonvenomous snake
HOBBY	*n* pl. -BIES a recreational pastime	**HOGNUT**	*n* pl. -S a hickory nut
HOBBYIST	*n* pl. -S one that pursues a hobby	**HOGSHEAD**	*n* pl. -S a large cask
		HOGTIE	*v* -TIED, -TIEING or -TYING, -TIES to tie together the legs of
HOBLIKE	*adj* suggestive of an elf		
HOBNAIL	*n* pl. -S a short nail with a thick head	**HOGWASH**	*n* pl. -ES meaningless talk
		HOGWEED	*n* pl. -S a coarse plant
HOBNOB	*v* -NOBBED, -NOBBING, -NOBS to associate in a friendly way	**HOICK**	*v* -ED, -ING, -S to change directions abruptly
HOBO	*v* -ED, -ING, -S or -ES to live like a hobo (a vagrant or tramp)	**HOIDEN**	*v* -ED, -ING, -S to hoyden
		HOISE	*v* HOISED, HOISING, HOISES to hoist
HOBOISM	*n* pl. -S the state of being a hobo		
		HOIST	*v* -ED, -ING, -S to haul up by some mechanical means
HOCK	*v* -ED, -ING, -S to pawn		
HOCKER	*n* pl. -S one that hocks	**HOISTER**	*n* pl. -S one that hoists
HOCKEY	*n* pl. -EYS a game played on ice	**HOKE**	*v* HOKED, HOKING, HOKES to give false value to
HOCKSHOP	*n* pl. -S a pawnshop	**HOKEY**	*adj* false; contrived
HOCUS	*v* -CUSED, -CUSING, -CUSES or -CUSSED, -CUSSING, -CUSSES to deceive or cheat	**HOKKU**	*n* pl. HOKKU haiku
		HOKUM	*n* pl. -S nonsense
		HOKYPOKY	*n* pl. -KIES trickery
HOD	*n* pl. -S a portable trough	**HOLARD**	*n* pl. -S the total quantity of water in the soil
HODAD	*n* pl. -S a nonsurfer		
HODADDY	*n* pl. -DIES hodad	**HOLD**	*v* HELD, HOLDEN, HOLDING, HOLDS to maintain possession of **HOLDABLE** *adj*
HODDEN	*n* pl. -S a coarse cloth		
HODDIN	*n* pl. -S hodden		
HOE	*v* HOED, HOEING, HOES to use a hoe (a gardening tool)	**HOLDALL**	*n* pl. -S a carrying case
		HOLDBACK	*n* pl. -S a restraining device
HOECAKE	*n* pl. -S a cornmeal cake	**HOLDEN**	a past participle of hold
HOEDOWN	*n* pl. -S a square dance	**HOLDER**	*n* pl. -S one that holds

HOLDFAST	*n* pl. -S a fastening device
HOLDING	*n* pl. -S something held
HOLDOUT	*n* pl. -S one who delays signing a contract
HOLDOVER	*n* pl. -S something left over
HOLDUP	*n* pl. -S a delay
HOLE	*v* HOLED, HOLING, HOLES to make a hole (a cavity in a solid)
HOLELESS	*adj* lacking a hole
HOLEY	*adj* full of holes
HOLIBUT	*n* pl. -S halibut
HOLIDAY	*v* -ED, -ING, -S to take a vacation
HOLIER	comparative of holy
HOLIES	pl. of holy
HOLIEST	superlative of holy
HOLILY	*adv* in a holy manner
HOLINESS	*n* pl. -ES the state of being holy
HOLING	present participle of hole
HOLISM	*n* pl. -S a philosophical theory
HOLIST	*n* pl. -S one who adheres to the theory of holism **HOLISTIC** *adj*
HOLK	*v* -ED, -ING, -S to howk
HOLLA	*v* -ED, -ING, -S to hallo
HOLLAND	*n* pl. -S a cotton fabric
HOLLER	*v* -ED, -ING, -S to yell
HOLLO	*v* -ED, -ING, -S or -ES to hallo
HOLLOA	*v* -ED, -ING, -S to hallo
HOLLOO	*v* -ED, -ING, -S to hallo
HOLLOW	*adj* -LOWER, -LOWEST not solid **HOLLOWLY** *adv*
HOLLOW	*v* -ED, -ING, -S to make hollow
HOLLY	*n* pl. -LIES a tree
HOLM	*n* pl. -S an island in a river
HOLMIUM	*n* pl. -S a metallic element **HOLMIC** *adj*
HOLOGRAM	*n* pl. -S a three-dimensional photograph
HOLOGYNY	*n* pl. -NIES a trait transmitted solely in the female line
HOLOTYPE	*n* pl. -S an animal or plant specimen
HOLOZOIC	*adj* eating solid foods
HOLP	a past tense of help
HOLPEN	a past participle of help
HOLSTEIN	*n* pl. -S a breed of cattle
HOLSTER	*n* pl. -S a case for a pistol
HOLT	*n* pl. -S a grove
HOLY	*adj* -LIER, -LIEST having a divine nature or origin
HOLY	*n* pl. -LIES a holy place
HOLYDAY	*n* pl. -DAYS a religious holiday
HOLYTIDE	*n* pl. -S a time of religious observance
HOMAGE	*v* -AGED, -AGING, -AGES to pay tribute to
HOMAGER	*n* pl. -S a feudal vassal
HOMBRE	*n* pl. -S a fellow
HOMBURG	*n* pl. -S a felt hat
HOME	*v* HOMED, HOMING, HOMES to return to one's home (place of residence)
HOMEBODY	*n* pl. -BODIES one who likes to stay at home
HOMEBRED	*n* pl. -S a native athlete
HOMED	past tense of home
HOMELAND	*n* pl. -S one's native land
HOMELESS	*adj* lacking a home
HOMELIKE	*adj* suggestive of a home; comfortably familiar
HOMELY	*adj* -LIER, -LIEST unattractive
HOMEMADE	*adj* made at home
HOMER	*v* -ED, -ING, -S to hit a home run
HOMEROOM	*n* pl. -S the classroom where pupils report before classes begin
HOMESICK	*adj* longing for home
HOMESITE	*n* pl. -S a location for a house
HOMESPUN	*n* pl. -S a loosely woven fabric
HOMETOWN	*n* pl. -S the town of one's birth or residence
HOMEWARD	*adv* toward home
HOMEWORK	*n* pl. -S work done at home
HOMEY	*adj* HOMIER, HOMIEST homelike
HOMICIDE	*n* pl. -S the killing of one person by another
HOMIER	comparative of homy
HOMIEST	superlative of homy
HOMILIST	*n* pl. -S one that delivers a homily
HOMILY	*n* pl. -LIES a sermon
HOMINESS	*n* pl. -ES the quality of being homey
HOMING	present participle of home
HOMINIAN	*n* pl. -S a hominid

HOMINID   *n* pl. -S a manlike creature

HOMINIES   pl. of hominy

HOMININE   *adj* characteristic of man

HOMINOID   *n* pl. -S a manlike animal

HOMINY   *n* pl. -NIES hulled and dried corn

HOMMOCK   *n* pl. -S a ridge in an ice field

HOMO   *n* pl. -MOS a homosexual

HOMOGAMY   *n* pl. -MIES the bearing of sexually similar flowers

HOMOGENY   *n* pl. -NIES correspondence in form or structure

HOMOGONY   *n* pl. -NIES the condition of having flowers with uniform stamens and pistils

HOMOLOG   *n* pl. -S something that exhibits homology

HOMOLOGY   *n* pl. -GIES similarity in structure due to origin

HOMONYM   *n* pl. -S a namesake

HOMONYMY   *n* pl. -MIES the condition of having the same name

HOMY   *adj* HOMIER, HOMIEST homey

HONAN   *n* pl. -S a fine silk

HONCHO   *n* pl. -CHOS a chief

HONDA   *n* pl. -S a part of a lariat

HONE   *v* HONED, HONING, HONES to sharpen

HONER   *n* pl. -S one that hones

HONEST   *adj* -ESTER, -ESTEST truthful **HONESTLY** *adv*

HONESTY   *n* pl. -TIES the quality of being honest

HONEWORT   *n* pl. -S a perennial herb

HONEY   *v* -EYED or -IED, -EYING, -EYS to sweeten with honey (a sweet, viscid fluid)

HONEYBEE   *n* pl. -S a type of bee

HONEYBUN   *n* pl. -S a sweetheart

HONEYDEW   *n* pl. -S a sweet fluid

HONEYFUL   *adj* containing much honey

HONG   *n* pl. -S a Chinese factory

HONIED   a past tense of honey

HONING   present participle of hone

HONK   *v* -ED, -ING, -S to emit a cry like that of a goose

HONKER   *n* pl. -S one that honks

HONKEY   *n* pl. -KEYS honkie

HONKIE   *n* pl. -S a white man — a derogatory term

HONKY   *n* pl. -KIES honkie

HONOR   *v* -ED, -ING, -S to treat with respect

HONORAND   *n* pl. -S one that receives an honor

HONORARY   *n* pl. -ARIES an honor society

HONOREE   *n* pl. -S one that receives an honor

HONORER   *n* pl. -S one that honors

HONOUR   *v* -ED, -ING, -S to honor

HONOURER   *n* pl. -S honorer

HOOCH   *n* pl. -ES cheap whiskey

HOOD   *v* -ED, -ING, -S to furnish with a hood (a covering for the head)

HOODIE   *n* pl. -S a gray crow of Europe

HOODLESS   *adj* lacking a hood

HOODLIKE   *adj* resembling a hood

HOODLUM   *n* pl. -S a thug

HOODOO   *v* -ED, -ING, -S to bring bad luck to

HOODWINK   *v* -ED, -ING, -S to trick

HOOEY   *n* pl. -EYS something false or nonsensical

HOOF   *v* -ED, -ING, -S to dance

HOOF   *n* pl. HOOVES or HOOFS the hard covering on the feet of certain animals

HOOFBEAT   *n* pl. -S the sound of hooves striking the ground

HOOFER   *n* pl. -S a professional dancer

HOOFLESS   *adj* lacking hooves

HOOFLIKE   *adj* resembling a hoof

HOOK   *v* -ED, -ING, -S to catch with a hook (a bent piece of metal)

HOOKA   *n* pl. -S hookah

HOOKAH   *n* pl. -S a water pipe

HOOKED   past tense of hook

HOOKER   *n* pl. a prostitute

HOOKEY   *n* pl. -EYS hooky

HOOKIER   comparative of hooky

HOOKIES   pl. of hooky

HOOKIEST   superlative of hooky

HOOKLESS   *adj* lacking a hook

HOOKLET   *n* pl. -S a small hook

HOOKLIKE   *adj* resembling a hook

HOOKNOSE   *n* pl. -S an aquiline nose

HOOKUP	*n* pl. -S an electrical assemblage
HOOKWORM	*n* pl. -S a parasitic worm
HOOKY	*n* pl. HOOKIES truancy
HOOKY	*adj* HOOKIER, HOOKIEST full of hooks
HOOLIE	*adj* easy; slow
HOOLIGAN	*n* pl. -S a hoodlum
HOOLY	*adj* hoolie
HOOP	*v* -ED, -ING, -S to fasten with a hoop (a circular band of metal)
HOOPER	*n* pl. -S one that hoops
HOOPLA	*n* pl. -S commotion
HOOPLESS	*adj* lacking a hoop
HOOPLIKE	*adj* suggestive of a hoop
HOOPOE	*n* pl. -S a European bird
HOOPOO	*n* pl. -POOS hoopoe
HOOPSTER	*n* pl. -S a basketball player
HOORAH	*v* -ED, -ING, -S to hurrah
HOORAY	*v* -ED, -ING, -S to hurrah
HOOSEGOW	*n* pl. -S a jail
HOOSGOW	*n* pl. -S hoosegow
HOOT	*v* -ED, -ING, -S to cry like an owl
HOOTCH	*n* pl. -ES hooch
HOOTER	*n* pl. -S one that hoots
HOOVES	a pl. of hoof
HOP	*v* HOPPED, HOPPING, HOPS to move by jumping on one foot
HOPE	*v* HOPED, HOPING, HOPES to have a desire or expectation
HOPEFUL	*n* pl. -S one that seems promising
HOPELESS	*adj* despairing
HOPER	*n* pl. -S one that hopes
HOPHEAD	*n* pl. -S a drug addict
HOPING	present participle of hope
HOPLITE	*n* pl. -S a foot soldier of ancient Greece HOPLITIC *adj*
HOPPED	past tense of hop
HOPPER	*n* pl. -S one that hops
HOPPING	present participle of hop
HOPPLE	*n* -PLED, -PLING, -PLES to hobble
HOPSACK	*n* pl. -S a coarse fabric
HOPTOAD	*n* pl. -S a toad
HORA	*n* pl. -S an Israeli dance
HORAH	*n* pl. -S hora
HORAL	*adj* hourly
HORARY	*adj* hourly
HORDE	*v* HORDED, HORDING, HORDES to gather in a large group
HORDEIN	*n* pl. -S a simple protein
HORIZON	*n* pl. -S the line where the sky seems to meet the earth
HORMONE	*n* pl. -S a secretion of the endocrine organs HORMONAL, HORMONIC *adj*
HORN	*v* -ED, -ING, -S to form a horn (a hard, bonelike projection of the head)
HORNBEAM	*n* pl.-S a small tree
HORNBILL	*n* pl. -S a large-billed bird
HORNBOOK	*n* pl. -S a primer
HORNET	*n* pl. -S a stinging insect
HORNFELS	*n* pl. HORNFELS a silicate rock
HORNIER	comparative of horny
HORNIEST	superlative of horny
HORNILY	*adv* in a horny manner
HORNITO	*n* pl. -TOS a mound of volcanic matter
HORNLESS	*adj* lacking a horn
HORNLIKE	*adj* resembling a horn
HORNPIPE	*n* pl. -S a musical instrument
HORNPOUT	*n* pl. -S a catfish
HORNTAIL	*n* pl. -S a wasplike insect
HORNWORM	*n* pl. -S the larva of a hawkmoth
HORNWORT	*n* pl. -S an aquatic herb
HORNY	*adj* HORNIER, HORNIEST hornlike in hardness
HOROLOGE	*n* pl. -S a timepiece
HOROLOGY	*n* pl. -GIES the science of measuring time
HORRENT	*adj* bristling; standing erect
HORRIBLE	*n* pl. -S something that causes horror
HORRIBLY	*adv* dreadfully
HORRID	*adj* repulsive HORRIDLY *adv*
HORRIFIC	*adj* causing horror
HORRIFY	*v* -FIED, -FYING, -FIES to cause to feel horror
HORROR	*n* pl. -S a feeling of intense fear or repugnance
HORSE	*v* HORSED, HORSING, HORSES to provide with a horse (a large, hoofed mammal)

HORSECAR *n* pl. -S a streetcar drawn by a horse

HORSEFLY *n* pl. -FLIES a large fly

HORSEMAN *n* pl. -MEN one who rides a horse

HORSEY *adj* HORSIER, HORSIEST horsy

HORSIER comparative of horsy

HORSIEST superlative of horsy

HORSILY *adj* in a horsy manner

HORSING present participle of horse

HORST *n* pl. -S a portion of the earth's crust

HORSTE *n* pl. -S horst

HORSY *adj* HORSIER, HORSIEST resembling a horse

HOSANNA *v* -ED, -ING, -S to praise

HOSE *v* HOSED, HOSING, HOSES to spray with water

HOSE *n* pl. HOSEN stockings or socks

HOSEL *n* pl. -S a part of a golf club

HOSIER *n* pl. -S one that makes hose

HOSIERY *n* pl. -SIERIES hose

HOSING present participle of hose

HOSPICE *n* pl. -S a shelter

HOSPITAL *n* pl. -S a medical institution

HOSPITIA *n/pl* places of shelter

HOSPODAR *n* pl. -S a governor of a region under Turkish rule

HOST *v* -ED, -ING, -S to entertain socially

HOSTAGE *n* pl. -S a person held as security

HOSTEL *v* -ED, -ING, -S to stay at inns overnight while traveling

HOSTELER *n* pl. -S an innkeeper

HOSTELRY *n* pl. -RIES an inn

HOSTESS *v* -ED, -ING, -ES to act as a hostess (a woman who entertains socially)

HOSTILE *n* pl. -S an unfriendly person

HOSTLER *n* pl. -S a person who tends horses or mules

HOSTLY *adj* pertaining to one who hosts

HOT *adj* HOTTER, HOTTEST having a high temperature

HOT *v* HOTTED, HOTTING, HOTS to heat

HOTBED *n* pl. -S a bed of rich soil

HOTBLOOD *n* pl. -S a thoroughbred horse

HOTBOX *n* pl. -ES an overheated bearing of a railroad car

HOTCAKE *n* pl. -S a pancake

HOTCH *v* -ED, -ING, -ES to wiggle

HOTCHPOT *n* pl. -S the combining of properties in order to divide them equally among heirs

HOTDOG *v* -DOGGED, -DOGGING, -DOGS to perform in a showy manner

HOTEL *n* pl. -S a public lodging

HOTELIER *n* pl. -S a hotel manager

HOTELMAN *n* pl. -MEN a hotelier

HOTFOOT *v* -FOOTED, -FOOTING, -FOOTS to hurry

HOTHEAD *n* pl. -S a quick-tempered person

HOTHOUSE *n* pl. -S a heated greenhouse

HOTLY *adv* in a hot manner

HOTNESS *n* pl. -ES the state of being hot

HOTPRESS *v* -ED, -ING, -ES to subject to heat and pressure

HOTROD *n* pl. -S a car modified for high speeds

HOTSHOT *n* pl. -S a showily skillful person

HOTSPUR *n* pl. -S a hothead

HOTTED past tense of hot

HOTTER comparative of hot

HOTTEST superlative of hot

HOTTING present participle of hot

HOTTISH *adj* somewhat hot

HOUDAH *n* pl. -S howdah

HOUND *v* -ED, -ING, -S to pursue relentlessly

HOUNDER *n* pl. -S one that hounds

HOUR *n* pl. -S a period of sixty minutes

HOURI *n* pl. -S a beautiful maiden in Muslim belief

HOURLY *adj* occurring every hour

HOUSE *v* HOUSED, HOUSING, HOUSES to lodge in a house (a building in which people live)

HOUSEBOY *n* pl. -BOYS a male servant

HOUSEFLY *n* pl. -FLIES a common fly

HOUSEFUL *n* pl. -S as much as a house will hold

HOUSEL *v* -SELED, -SELING, -SELS or -SELLED, -SELLING, -SELS to administer the Eucharist to

HOUSEMAN *n* pl. -MEN a male servant

HOUSER *n* pl. -S one who organizes housing projects

HOUSETOP *n* pl. -S the roof of a house

HOUSING *n* pl. -S any dwelling place

HOVE a past tense of heave

HOVEL *v* -ELED, -ELING, -ELS or -ELLED, -ELLING, -ELS to live in a small, miserable dwelling

HOVER *v* -ED, -ING, -S to hang suspended in the air

HOVERER *n* pl. -S something that hovers

HOW *n* pl. -S a method of doing something

HOWBEIT *adv* nevertheless

HOWDAH *n* pl. -S a seat on an elephant or camel for riders

HOWDIE *n* pl. -S a midwife

HOWDY *n* pl. -DIES howdie

HOWE *n* pl. -S a valley

HOWEVER *adv* nevertheless

HOWF *n* pl. -S a place frequently visited

HOWFF *n* pl. -S howf

HOWITZER *n* pl. -S a short cannon

HOWK *v* -ED, -ING, -S to dig

HOWL *v* -ED, -ING, -S to cry like a dog

HOWLER *n* pl. -S one that howls

HOWLET *n* pl. -S an owl

HOY *n* pl. HOYS a heavy barge or scow

HOYDEN *v* -ED, -ING, -S to act like a tomboy

HOYLE *n* pl. -S a rule book

HUARACHE *n* pl. -S a flat-heeled sandal

HUARACHO *n* pl. -CHOS huarache

HUB *n* pl. -S the center of a wheel

HUBBUB *n* pl. -S an uproar

HUBBY *n* pl. -BIES a husband

HUBCAP *n* pl. -S a covering for the hub of a wheel

HUBRIS *n* pl. -BRISES arrogance

HUCK *n* pl. -S a durable fabric

HUCKLE *n* pl. -S the hip

HUCKSTER *v* -ED, -ING, -S to peddle

HUDDLE *v* -DLED, -DLING, -DLES to crowd together

HUDDLER *n* pl. -S one that huddles

HUE *n* pl. -S color **HUED, HUELESS** *adj*

HUFF *v* -ED, -ING, -S to breathe heavily

HUFFISH *adj* sulky

HUFFY *adj* HUFFIER, HUFFIEST easily offended **HUFFILY** *adv*

HUG *v* HUGGED, HUGGING, HUGS to clasp tightly in the arms

HUGE *adj* HUGER, HUGEST very large **HUGELY** *adj*

HUGENESS *n* pl. -ES the quality of being huge

HUGEOUS *adj* huge

HUGER comparative of huge

HUGEST superlative of huge

HUGGABLE *adj* cuddlesome

HUGGED past tense of hug

HUGGER *n* pl. -S one that hugs

HUGGING present participle of hug

HUH *interj* — used to express surprise

HUIC *interj* — used to encourage hunting hounds

HULA *n* pl. -S a Hawaiian dance

HULK *v* -ED, -ING, -S to appear impressively large

HULKY *adj* HULKIER, HULKIEST massive

HULL *v* -ED, -ING, -S to remove the shell from a seed

HULLER *n* pl. -S one that hulls

HULLO *v* -ED, -ING, -S or -ES to hallo

HULLOA *v* -ED, -ING, -S to hallo

HUM *v* HUMMED, HUMMING, HUMS to sing without opening the lips or saying words

HUMAN *n* pl. -S a person

HUMANE *adj* -MANER, -MANEST compassionate **HUMANELY** *adv*

HUMANISE *v* -ISED, -ISING, -ISES to humanize

HUMANISM *n* pl. -S the quality of being human

HUMANIST *n* pl. -S one who studies human nature

HUMANITY *n* pl. -TIES the human race

HUMANIZE *v* -IZED, -IZING, -IZES to make human

HUMANLY *adv* in a human manner

HUMANOID *n* pl. -S something having human form

HUMATE *n* pl. -S a chemical salt

HUMBLE *adj* -BLER, -BLEST modest

HUMBLE *v* -BLED, -BLING, -BLES to reduce the pride of

HUMBLER *n* pl. -S one that humbles

HUMBLEST superlative of humble

HUMBLING present participle of humble

HUMBLY *adv* in a humble manner

HUMBUG *v* -BUGGED, -BUGGING, -BUGS to deceive

HUMDRUM *n* pl. -S a dull, boring person

HUMERAL *n* pl. -S a bone of the shoulder

HUMERUS *n* pl. -MERI the large bone of the upper arm

HUMIC *adj* derived from humus

HUMID *adj* having much humidity

HUMIDIFY *v* -FIED, -FYING, -FIES to make humid

HUMIDITY *n* pl. -TIES moisture of the air

HUMIDLY *adv* in a humid manner

HUMIDOR *n* pl. -S a cigar case

HUMIFIED *adj* converted into humus

HUMILITY *n* pl. -TIES the quality of being humble

HUMMABLE *adj* capable of being hummed

HUMMED past tense of hum

HUMMER *n* pl. -S one that hums

HUMMING present participle of hum

HUMMOCK *n* pl. -S a small hill **HUMMOCKY** *adj*

HUMOR *v* -ED, -ING, -S to indulge

HUMORAL *adj* pertaining to bodily fluids

HUMORFUL *adj* humorous

HUMORIST *n* pl. -S a humorous writer or entertainer

HUMOROUS *adj* funny; witty

HUMOUR *v* -ED, -ING, -S to humor

HUMP *v* -ED, -ING, -S to arch into a hump (a rounded protuberance)

HUMPBACK *n* pl. -S a humped back

HUMPH *v* -ED, -ING, -S to utter a grunt

HUMPLESS *adj* lacking a hump

HUMPY *adj* HUMPIER, HUMPIEST full of humps

HUMUS *n* pl. -ES decomposed organic matter

HUN *n* pl. -S a barbarous, destructive person

HUNCH *v* -ED, -ING, -ES to arch forward

HUNDRED *n* pl. -S a number

HUNG a past tense of hang

HUNGER *v* -ED, -ING, -S to crave

HUNGRY *adj* -GRIER, -GRIEST wanting food **HUNGRILY** *adv*

HUNK *n* pl. -S a large piece

HUNKER *v* -ED, -ING, -S to squat

HUNKY *n* pl. -KIES an unskilled laborer

HUNNISH *adj* resembling a hun

HUNT *v* -ED, -ING, -S to pursue for food or sport **HUNTABLE** *adj* **HUNTEDLY** *adv*

HUNTER *n* pl. -S one that hunts

HUNTING *n* pl. -S an instance of searching

HUNTRESS *n* pl. -ES a female hunter

HUNTSMAN *n* pl. -MEN a hunter

HUP *interj* — used to mark a marching cadence

HURDIES *n/pl* the buttocks

HURDLE *v* -DLED, -DLING, -DLES to jump over

HURDLER *n* pl. -S one that hurdles

HURDS *n/pl* hards

HURL *v* -ED, -ING, -S to throw with great force

HURLER *n* pl. -S one that hurls

HURLEY *n* pl. -LEYS hurling

HURLING *n* pl. -S an Irish game

HURLY *n* pl. -LIES commotion

HURRAH *v* -ED, -ING, -S to cheer

HURRAY *v* -ED, -ING, -S to hurrah

HURRIER *n* pl. -S one that hurries

HURRY *v* -RIED, -RYING, -RIES to move swiftly

HURT *v* HURT, HURTING, HURTS to injure

HURTER *n* pl. -S one that hurts

HURTFUL *adj* causing injury

HURTLE *v* -TLED, -TLING, -TLES to rush violently

HURTLESS *adj* harmless

HUSBAND *v* -ED, -ING, -S to spend wisely

HUSH *v* -ED, -ING, -ES to quiet **HUSHEDLY** *adv*

HUSHABY	*v* go to sleep — used imperatively to soothe a child		**HYDATID**	*n* pl. -S a cyst caused by a tapeworm
HUSHFUL	*adj* quiet		**HYDRA**	*n* pl. -DRAS or -DRAE a freshwater polyp
HUSK	*v* -ED, -ING, -S to remove the husk (the outer covering) from		**HYDRACID**	*n* pl. -S an acid
HUSKER	*n* pl. -S one that husks		**HYDRAGOG**	*n* pl. -S a purgative causing watery discharges
HUSKIER	comparative of husky			
HUSKIES	pl. of husky		**HYDRANT**	*n* pl. -S an outlet from a water main
HUSKIEST	superlative of husky		**HYDRANTH**	*n* pl. -S the oral opening of a hydra
HUSKILY	*adv* in a husky manner			
HUSKING	*n* pl. -S a gathering of families to husk corn		**HYDRASE**	*n* pl. -S an enzyme
HUSKLIKE	*adj* resembling a husk		**HYDRATE**	*v* -DRATED, -DRATING, -DRATES to combine with water
HUSKY	*adj* -KIER, -KIEST hoarse			
HUSKY	*n* pl. -KIES an Eskimo dog		**HYDRATOR**	*n* pl. -S one that hydrates
HUSSAR	*n* pl. -S a cavalry soldier		**HYDRIA**	*n* pl. -DRIAE a water jar
HUSSY	*n* pl. -SIES a lewd woman		**HYDRIC**	*adj* pertaining to moisture
HUSTINGS	*n* pl. HUSTINGS a British court		**HYDRID**	*n* pl. -S hydride
HUSTLE	*v* -TLED, -TLING, -TLES to hurry		**HYDRIDE**	*n* pl. -S a chemical compound
HUSTLER	*n* pl. -S one that hustles		**HYDRO**	*n* pl. -DROS electricity produced by waterpower
HUSWIFE	*n* pl. -WIFES or -WIVES a sewing kit			
			HYDROGEL	*n* pl. -S a colloid
HUT	*v* HUTTED, HUTTING, HUTS to live in a hut (a simple shelter)		**HYDROGEN**	*n* pl. -S a gaseous element
			HYDROID	*n* pl. -S a polyp
HUTCH	*v* -ED, -ING, -ES to store away		**HYDROMEL**	*n* pl. -S a mixture of honey and water
HUTLIKE	*adj* resembling a hut			
HUTMENT	*n* pl. -S a group of huts		**HYDRONIC**	*adj* pertaining to heating and cooling by water
HUTTED	past tense of hut			
HUTTING	present participle of hut		**HYDROPIC**	*adj* affected with hydropsy
HUTZPA	*n* pl. -S chutzpah		**HYDROPS**	*n* pl. -ES hydropsy
HUTZPAH	*n* pl. -S chutzpah		**HYDROPSY**	*n* pl. -SIES dropsy
HUZZA	*v* -ED, -ING, -S to cheer		**HYDROSOL**	*n* pl. -S an aqueous solution of a colloid
HUZZAH	*v* -ED, -ING, -S to huzza			
HWAN	*n* pl. HWAN a monetary unit of South Korea		**HYDROUS**	*adj* containing water
			HYDROXY	*adj* containing hydroxyl
HYACINTH	*n* pl. -S a flowering plant		**HYDROXYL**	*n* pl. -S the radical or group containing oxygen and hydrogen
HYAENA	*n* pl. -S hyena **HYAENIC** *adj*			
HYALIN	*n* pl. -S hyaline		**HYENA**	*n* pl. -S a wolflike mammal **HYENIC, HYENINE, HYENOID** *adj*
HYALINE	*n* pl. -S a transparent substance			
			HYETAL	*adj* pertaining to rain
HYALITE	*n* pl. -S a colorless opal		**HYGEIST**	*n* pl. -S an expert in hygiene
HYALOGEN	*n* pl. -S a substance found in animal cells		**HYGIEIST**	*n* pl. -S hygeist
			HYGIENE	*n* pl. -S the science of health **HYGIENIC** *adj*
HYALOID	*n* pl. -S a membrane of the eye			
HYBRID	*n* pl. -S the offspring of genetically dissimilar parents		**HYING**	present participle of hie
			HYLA	*n* pl. -S a tree frog
HYBRIS	*n* pl. -BRISES hubris			

HYLOZOIC *adj* pertaining to the doctrine that life and matter are inseparable

HYMEN *n* pl. -S a vaginal membrane **HYMENAL** *adj*

HYMENEAL *n* pl. -S a wedding song or poem

HYMENIUM *n* pl. -NIA or -NIUMS a layer in certain fungi **HYMENIAL** *adj*

HYMN *v* -ED, -ING, -S to sing a hymn (a song of praise to God)

HYMNAL *n* pl. -S a book of hymns

HYMNARY *n* pl. -RIES a hymnal

HYMNBOOK *n* pl. -S a hymnal

HYMNIST *n* pl. -S one who composes hymns

HYMNLESS *adj* lacking a hymn

HYMNLIKE *adj* resembling a hymn

HYMNODY *n* pl. -DIES the singing of hymns

HYOID *n* pl. -S a bone of the tongue **HYOIDAL, HYOIDEAN** *adj*

HYOSCINE *n* pl. -S a sedative

HYP *n* pl. -S hypochondria

HYPE *n* pl. -S a deception

HYPERGOL *n* pl. -S a rocket fuel

HYPERON *n* pl. -S an atomic particle

HYPEROPE *n* pl. -S a farsighted person

HYPHA *n* pl. -PHAE a threadlike element of a fungus **HYPHAL** *adj*

HYPHEMIA *n* pl. -S deficiency of blood

HYPHEN *v* -ED, -ING, -S to connect words or syllables with a hyphen (a mark of punctuation)

HYPNIC *adj* pertaining to sleep

HYPNOID *adj* pertaining to hypnosis or sleep

HYPNOSIS *n* pl. -NOSES an artificially induced state resembling sleep

HYPNOTIC *n* pl. -S a sleep-inducing drug

HYPO *v* -ED, -ING, -S to inject with a hypodermic needle

HYPOACID *adj* having a lower than normal degree of acidity

HYPODERM *n* pl. -S a skin layer

HYPOGEAL *adj* underground

HYPOGEAN *adj* hypogeal

HYPOGENE *adj* formed underground

HYPOGEUM *n* pl. -GEA an underground chamber

HYPOGYNY *n* pl. -NIES the condition of having flowers with organs situated below the ovary

HYPONEA *n* pl. -S hyponoia

HYPONOIA *n* pl. -S dulled mental activity

HYPOPNEA *n* pl. -S abnormally shallow breathing

HYPOPYON *n* pl. -S an accumulation of pus in the eye

HYPOTHEC *n* pl. -S a type of mortgage

HYPOXIA *n* pl. -S a deficiency of oxygen in body tissue **HYPOXIC** *adj*

HYRACOID *n* pl. -S a hyrax

HYRAX *n* pl. -RAXES or -RACES a small, harelike mammal

HYSON *n* pl. -S a Chinese tea

HYSSOP *n* pl. -S a medicinal herb

HYSTERIA *n* pl. -S uncontrollable excitement or fear

HYSTERIC *n* pl. -S one who is subject to fits of hysteria

HYTE *adj* insane

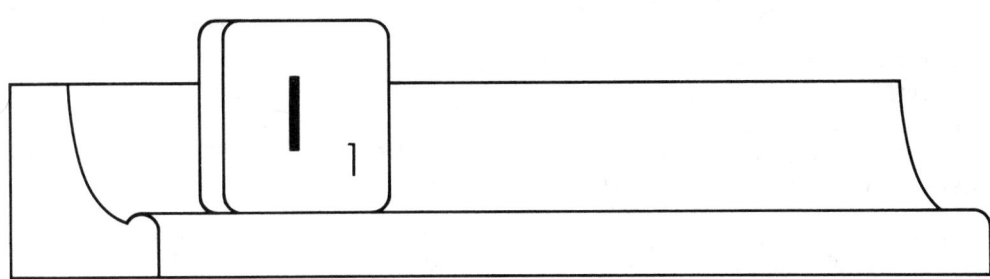

IAMB	*n* pl. -S a type of metrical foot
IAMBIC	*n* pl. -S an iamb
IAMBUS	*n* pl. -BUSES or -BI an iamb
IATRIC	*adj* pertaining to medicine
IATRICAL	*adj* iatric
IBEX	*n* pl. IBEXES or IBICES a wild goat
IBIDEM	*adv* in the same place
IBIS	*n* pl. IBISES a wading bird
ICE	*v* ICED, ICING, ICES to cover with ice (frozen water)
ICEBERG	*n* pl. -S a large floating body of ice
ICEBLINK	*n* pl. -S a glare over an ice field
ICEBOAT	*n* pl. -S a vehicle that sails on ice
ICEBOUND	*adj* surrounded by ice
ICEBOX	*n* pl. -ES a cabinet for cooling food
ICECAP	*n* pl. -S a covering of ice and snow
ICED	past tense of ice
ICEFALL	*n* pl. -S a kind of frozen waterfall
ICEHOUSE	*n* pl. -S a building for storing ice
ICEKHANA	*n* pl. -S an automotive event held on a frozen lake
ICELESS	*adj* having no ice
ICELIKE	*adj* resembling ice
ICEMAN	*n* pl. -MEN a man who supplies ice
ICH	*n* pl. ICHS a disease of certain fishes
ICHNITE	*n* pl. -S a fossil footprint

ICHOR	*n* pl. -S a watery discharge from a wound **ICHOROUS** *adj*
ICHTHYIC	*adj* pertaining to fishes
ICICLE	*n* pl. -S a hanging spike of ice **ICICLED** *adj*
ICIER	comparative of icy
ICIEST	superlative of icy
ICILY	*adv* in an icy manner
ICINESS	*n* pl. -ES the state of being icy
ICING	*n* pl. -S a sweet mixture for covering cakes
ICKER	*n* pl. -S a head of grain
ICKY	*adj* ICKIER, ICKIEST repulsive
ICON	*n* pl. -S or -ES a representation **ICONIC, ICONICAL** *adj*
ICTERIC	*n* pl. -S a remedy for icterus
ICTERUS	*n* pl. -ES a diseased condition of the liver
ICTUS	*n* pl. -ES a recurring stress or beat in a poetical form **ICTIC** *adj*
ICY	*adj* ICIER, ICIEST covered with ice
ID	*n* pl. -S a part of the psyche
IDEA	*n* pl. -S a conception existing in the mind **IDEALESS** *adj*
IDEAL	*n* pl. -S a standard of perfection
IDEALISE	*v* -ISED, -ISING, -ISES to idealize
IDEALISM	*n* pl. -S the pursuit of noble goals
IDEALIST	*n* pl. -S an adherent of idealism
IDEALITY	*n* pl. -TIES the state of being perfect; something idealized
IDEALIZE	*v* -IZED, -IZING, -IZES to regard as perfect

IDEALLY *adv* perfectly

IDEALOGY *n* pl. -GIES ideology

IDEATE *v* -ATED, -ATING, -ATES to form an idea

IDEATION *n* pl. -S the act of ideating

IDEATIVE *adj* pertaining to ideation

IDEM *adj* the same

IDENTIC *adj* identical

IDENTIFY *v* -FIED, -FYING, -FIES to establish the identity of

IDENTITY *n* pl. -TIES the essential character of a person or thing

IDEOGRAM *n* pl. -S a type of written symbol

IDEOLOGY *n* pl. -GIES a systematic body of ideas

IDES *n* pl. IDES a certain day in the ancient Roman calendar

IDIOCY *n* pl. -CIES the condition of being an idiot

IDIOLECT *n* pl. -S one's speech pattern

IDIOM *n* pl. -S an expression peculiar to a language

IDIOT *n* pl. -S a mentally deficient person **IDIOTIC** *adj*

IDIOTISM *n* pl. -S idiocy

IDLE *adj* IDLER, IDLEST inactive

IDLE *v* IDLED, IDLING, IDLES to pass time idly

IDLENESS *n* pl. -ES the state of being idle

IDLER *n* pl. -S one that idles

IDLESSE *n* pl. -S idleness

IDLEST superlative of idle

IDLING present participle of idle

IDLY *adv* in an idle manner

IDOCRASE *n* pl. -S a mineral

IDOL *n* pl. -S an object of worship

IDOLATER *n* pl. -S one that worships idols

IDOLATRY *n* pl. -TRIES the worship of idols

IDOLISE *v* -ISED, -ISING, -ISES to idolize

IDOLISER *n* pl. -S one that idolises

IDOLISM *n* pl. -S idolatry

IDOLIZE *v* -IZED, -IZING, -IZES to worship

IDOLIZER *n* pl. -S one that idolizes

IDONEITY *n* pl. -TIES the state of being idoneous

IDONEOUS *adj* suitable

IDYL *n* pl. -S a poem or prose work depicting scenes of rural simplicity

IDYLIST *n* pl. -S a writer of idyls

IDYLL *n* pl. -S idyl **IDYLLIC** *adj*

IDYLLIST *n* pl. -S idylist

IF *n* pl. -S a possibility

IFFINESS *n* pl. -ES the state of being iffy

IFFY *adj* IFFIER, IFFIEST full of uncertainty

IGLOO *n* pl. -LOOS an Eskimo dwelling

IGLU *n* pl. -S igloo

IGNATIA *n* pl. -S a medicinal seed

IGNEOUS *adj* pertaining to fire

IGNIFY *v* -FIED, -FYING, -FIES to burn

IGNITE *v* -NITED, -NITING, -NITES to set on fire

IGNITER *n* pl. -S one that ignites

IGNITION *n* pl. -S the act of igniting

IGNITOR *n* pl. -S igniter

IGNITRON *n* pl. -S a type of rectifier tube

IGNOBLE *adj* of low character **IGNOBLY** *adv*

IGNOMINY *n* pl. -NIES disgrace or dishonor

IGNORANT *adj* having no knowledge

IGNORE *v* -NORED, -NORING, -NORES to refuse to notice

IGNORER *n* pl. -S one that ignores

IGUANA *n* pl. -S a tropical lizard

IGUANIAN *n* pl. -S a lizard related to the iguana

IHRAM *n* pl. -S the garb worn by Muslim pilgrims

IKEBANA *n* pl. -S the Japanese art of flower arranging

IKON *n* pl. -S icon

ILEA pl. of ileum

ILEAC *adj* pertaining to the ileum

ILEAL *adj* ileac

ILEITIS *n* pl. ILEITIDES inflammation of the ileum

ILEUM *n* pl. ILEA a part of the small intestine

ILEUS *n* pl. -ES intestinal obstruction

ILEX *n* pl. -ES a holly

ILIA pl. of ilium

ILIAC *adj* pertaining to the ilium

ILIAD *n* pl. -S a long poem

ILIAL	*adj* iliac
ILIUM	*n* pl. ILIA a bone of the pelvis
ILK	*n* pl. -S a class or kind
ILKA	*adj* each
ILL	*n* pl. -S an evil
ILLATION	*n* pl. -S the act of inferring
ILLATIVE	*n* pl. -S a word or phrase introducing an inference
ILLEGAL	*adj* prohibited by law
ILLICIT	*adj* not permitted
ILLINIUM	*n* pl. -S a radioactive element
ILLIQUID	*adj* not readily convertible into cash
ILLITE	*n* pl. -S a group of minerals **ILLITIC** *adj*
ILLNESS	*n* pl. -ES sickness
ILLOGIC	*n* pl. -S absence of logic
ILLUME	*v* -LUMED, -LUMING, -LUMES to illuminate
ILLUMINE	*v* -MINED, -MINING, -MINES to illuminate
ILLUSION	*n* pl. -S a false perception
ILLUSIVE	*adj* illusory
ILLUSORY	*adj* based on illusion
ILLUVIUM	*n* pl. -VIA or -VIUMS a type of material accumulated in soil **ILLUVIAL** *adj*
ILLY	*adv* badly
ILMENITE	*n* pl. -S a mineral
IMAGE	*v* -AGED, -AGING, -AGES to imagine
IMAGERY	*n* pl. -ERIES mental pictures
IMAGINAL	*adj* pertaining to an imago
IMAGINE	*v* -INED, -INING, -INES to form a mental picture of
IMAGINER	*n* pl. -S one that imagines
IMAGING	present participle of image
IMAGINING	present participle of imagine
IMAGISM	*n* pl. -S a movement in poetry
IMAGIST	*n* pl. -S an adherent of imagism
IMAGO	*n* pl. -GOES an adult insect
IMAM	*n* pl. -S a Muslim priest
IMAMATE	*n* pl. -S the office of an imam
IMARET	*n* pl. -S a Turkish inn
IMAUM	*n* pl. -S imam
IMBALM	*v* -ED, -ING, -S to embalm
IMBALMER	*n* pl. -S embalmer

IMBARK	*v* -ED, -ING, -S to embark
IMBECILE	*n* pl. -S a mentally deficient person
IMBED	*v* -BEDDED, -BEDDING, -BEDS to embed
IMBIBE	*v* -BIBED, -BIBING, -BIBES to drink
IMBIBER	*n* pl. -S one that imbibes
IMBITTER	*v* -ED, -ING, -S to embitter
IMBLAZE	*v* -BLAZED, -BLAZING, -BLAZES to emblaze
IMBODY	*v* -BODIED, -BODYING, -BODIES to embody
IMBOLDEN	*v* -ED, -ING, -S to embolden
IMBOSOM	*v* -ED, -ING, -S to embosom
IMBOWER	*v* -ED, -ING, -S to embower
IMBROWN	*v* -ED, -ING, -S to embrown
IMBRUE	*v* -BRUED, -BRUING, -BRUES to stain
IMBRUTE	*v* -BRUTED, -BRUTING, -BRUTES to make brutal
IMBUE	*v* -BUED, -BUING, -BUES to make thoroughly wet
IMID	*n* pl. -S imide
IMIDE	*n* pl. -S a chemical compound **IMIDIC** *adj*
IMIDO	*adj* containing an imide
IMINE	*n* pl. -S a chemical compound
IMINO	*adj* containing an imine
IMITABLE	*adj* capable of being imitated
IMITATE	*v* -TATED, -TATING, -TATES to behave in the same way as
IMITATOR	*n* pl. -S one that imitates
IMMANE	*adj* great in size
IMMANENT	*adj* existing within
IMMATURE	*n* pl. -S an individual that is not fully grown or developed
IMMENSE	*adj* -MENSER, -MENSEST great in size
IMMERGE	*v* -MERGED, -MERGING, -MERGES to immerse
IMMERSE	*v* -MERSED, -MERSING, -MERSES to plunge into a liquid
IMMESH	*v* -ED, -ING, -ES to enmesh
IMMIES	pl. of immy
IMMINENT	*adj* ready to take place
IMMINGLE	*v* -GLED, -GLING, -GLES to blend
IMMIX	*v* -ED, -ING, -ES to mix in

IMMOBILE *adj* incapable of being moved

IMMODEST *adj* not modest

IMMOLATE *v* -LATED, -LATING, -LATES to kill as a sacrifice

IMMORAL *adj* contrary to established morality

IMMORTAL *n* pl. -S one who is not subject to death

IMMOTILE *adj* lacking mobility

IMMUNE *n* pl. -S one who is protected from a disease

IMMUNISE *n* -NISED, -NISING, -NISES to immunize

IMMUNITY *n* pl. -TIES the state of being protected from a disease

IMMUNIZE *v* -NIZED, -NIZING, -NIZES to protect from a disease

IMMURE *v* -MURED, -MURING, -MURES to imprison

IMMY *n* pl. -MIES a type of playing marble

IMP *v* -ED, -ING, -S to graft feathers onto a bird's wing

IMPACT *v* -ED, -ING, -S to pack firmly together

IMPACTER *n* pl. -S one that impacts

IMPACTOR *n* pl. -S impacter

IMPAINT *v* -ED, -ING, -S to paint or depict

IMPAIR *v* -ED, -ING, -S to make worse

IMPAIRER *n* pl. -S one that impairs

IMPALA *n* pl. -S an African antelope

IMPALE *v* -PALED, -PALING, -PALES to pierce with a pointed object

IMPALER *n* pl. -S one that impales

IMPANEL *v* -ELED, -ELING, -ELS or -ELLED, -ELLING, -ELS to enter on a list for jury duty

IMPARITY *n* pl. -TIES lack of equality

IMPARK *v* -ED, -ING, -S to confine in a park

IMPART *v* -ED, -ING, -S to make known

IMPARTER *n* pl. -S one that imparts

IMPASSE *n* pl. -S a road or passage having no exit

IMPASTE *v* -PASTED, -PASTING, -PASTES to make into a paste

IMPASTO *n* pl. -TOS a painting technique

IMPAVID *adj* brave

IMPAWN *v* -ED, -ING, -S to pawn

IMPEACH *v* -ED, -ING, -ES to charge with misconduct in office

IMPEARL *v* -ED, -ING, -S to make pearly

IMPEDE *v* -PEDED, -PEDING, -PEDES to obstruct the progress of

IMPEDER *n* pl. -S one that impedes

IMPEL *v* -PELLED, -PELLING, -PELS to force into action

IMPELLER *n* pl. -S one that impels

IMPELLOR *n* pl. -S impeller

IMPEND *v* -ED, -ING, -S to be imminent

IMPERIA a pl. of imperium

IMPERIAL *n* pl. -S an emperor or empress

IMPERIL *v* -ILED, -ILING, -ILS or -ILLED, -ILLING, -ILS to place in jeopardy

IMPERIUM *n* pl. -RIUMS or -RIA absolute power

IMPETIGO *n* pl. -GOS a skin disease

IMPETUS *n* pl. -ES an impelling force

IMPHEE *n* pl. -S an African grass

IMPI *n* pl. -S a body of warriors

IMPIETY *n* pl. -TIES lack of piety

IMPING *n* pl. -S the process of grafting

IMPINGE *v* -PINGED, -PINGING, -PINGES to collide

IMPINGER *n* pl. -S one that impinges

IMPIOUS *adj* not pious

IMPISH *adj* mischievous **IMPISHLY** *adv*

IMPLANT *v* -ED, -ING, -S to set securely

IMPLEAD *v* -ED, -ING, -S to sue in a court of law

IMPLEDGE *v* -PLEDGED, -PLEDGING, -PLEDGES to pawn

IMPLICIT *adj* implied

IMPLIED past tense of imply

IMPLIES present 3d person sing. of imply

IMPLODE *v* -PLODED, -PLODING, -PLODES to collapse inward

IMPLORE *v* -PLORED, -PLORING, -PLORES to beg for urgently

IMPLORER *n* pl. -S one that implores

IMPLY *v* -PLIED, -PLYING, -PLIES to indicate or suggest indirectly

IMPOLICY *n* pl. -CIES an unwise course of action

IMPOLITE *adj* not polite

IMPONE	*v* -PONED, -PONING, -PONES to wager
IMPOROUS	*adj* extremely dense
IMPORT	*v* -ED, -ING, -S to bring into a country from abroad
IMPORTER	*n* pl. -S one that imports
IMPOSE	*v* -POSED, -POSING, -POSES to establish as compulsory
IMPOSER	*n* pl. -S one that imposes
IMPOST	*v* -ED, -ING, -S to determine customs duties
IMPOSTER	*n* pl. -S impostor
IMPOSTOR	*n* pl. -S one that poses as another for deceptive purposes
IMPOTENT	*n* pl. -S one that is powerless
IMPOUND	*v* -ED, -ING, -S to seize and retain in legal custody
IMPOWER	*v* -ED, -ING, -S to empower
IMPREGN	*v* -ED, -ING, -S to make pregnant
IMPRESA	*n* pl. -S a type of emblem
IMPRESE	*n* pl. -S impresa
IMPRESS	*v* -ED, -ING, -ES to affect strongly
IMPREST	*n* pl. -S a loan or advance of money
IMPRIMIS	*adv* in the first place
IMPRINT	*v* -ED, -ING, -S to produce a mark by pressure
IMPRISON	*v* -ED, -ING, -S to confine
IMPROPER	*adj* not proper
IMPROVE	*v* -PROVED, -PROVING, -PROVES to make better
IMPROVER	*n* pl. -S one that improves
IMPUDENT	*adj* offensively bold or disrespectful
IMPUGN	*v* -ED, -ING, -S to make insinuations against
IMPUGNER	*n* pl. -S one that impugns
IMPULSE	*v* -PULSED, -PULSING, -PULSES to give impetus to
IMPUNITY	*n* pl. -TIES exemption from penalty
IMPURE	*adj* not pure **IMPURELY** *adv*
IMPURITY	*n* pl. -TIES something that is impure
IMPUTE	*v* -PUTED, -PUTING, -PUTES to credit to a person or a cause
IMPUTER	*n* pl. -S one that imputes
IN	*v* INNED, INNING, INS to harvest
INACTION	*n* pl. -S lack of action
INACTIVE	*adj* not active
INANE	*adj* INANER, INANEST nonsensical **INANELY** *adv*
INANE	*n* pl. -S empty space
INANITY	*n* pl. -TIES something that is inane
INAPT	*adj* not apt **INAPTLY** *adv*
INARABLE	*adj* not arable
INARCH	*v* -ED, -ING, -ES to graft with in a certain way
INARM	*v* -ED, -ING, -S to encircle with the arms
INBEING	*n* pl. -S the state of being inherent
INBOARD	*n* pl. -S a type of boat motor
INBORN	*adj* existing in one from birth
INBOUND	*adj* approaching a destination
INBOUNDS	*adj* being within certain boundaries
INBREED	*v* -BRED, -BREEDING, -BREEDS to breed closely related stock
INBUILT	*adj* forming an integral part of a structure
INBURST	*n* pl. -S the act of bursting inward
INBY	*adv* inward
INBYE	*adv* inby
INCAGE	*v* -CAGED, -CAGING, -CAGES to encage
INCASE	*v* -CASED, -CASING, -CASES to encase
INCENSE	*v* -CENSED, -CENSING, -CENSES to make angry
INCEPT	*v* -ED, -ING, -S to take in
INCEPTOR	*n* pl. -S one that incepts
INCEST	*n* pl. -S sexual intercourse between closely related persons
INCH	*v* -ED, -ING, -ES to move very slowly
INCHMEAL	*adv* little by little
INCHOATE	*adj* being in an early stage
INCHWORM	*n* pl. -S a type of worm
INCIDENT	*n* pl. -S an event
INCIPIT	*n* pl. -S the opening words of a text
INCISE	*v* -CISED, -CISING, -CISES to cut into
INCISION	*n* pl. -S the act of incising

INCISIVE	*adj* penetrating
INCISOR	*n* pl. -S a cutting tooth
INCISORY	*adj* adapted for cutting
INCISURE	*n* pl. -S a notch or cleft of a body part
INCITANT	*n* pl. -S something that incites
INCITE	*v* -CITED, -CITING, -CITES to arouse to action
INCITER	*n* pl. -S one that incites
INCIVIL	*adj* discourteous
INCLASP	*v* -ED, -ING, -S to enclasp
INCLINE	*v* -CLINED, -CLINING, -CLINES to slant
INCLINER	*n* pl. -S one that inclines
INCLIP	*v* -CLIPPED, -CLIPPING, -CLIPS to clasp
INCLOSE	*v* -CLOSED, -CLOSING, -CLOSES to enclose
INCLOSER	*n* pl. -S one that incloses
INCLUDE	*v* -CLUDED, -CLUDING, -CLUDES to have as a part
INCOG	*n* pl. -S a disguised person
INCOME	*n* pl. -S a sum of money earned regularly
INCOMER	*n* pl. -S one that comes in
INCOMING	*n* pl. -S an arrival
INCONNU	*n* pl. -S a large food fish
INCONY	*adj* pretty
INCORPSE	*v* -CORPSED, -CORPSING, -CORPSES to become combined with
INCREASE	*v* -CREASED, -CREASING, -CREASES to make or become greater
INCREATE	*adj* not created
INCROSS	*n* pl. -ES an individual produced by inbreeding
INCRUST	*v* -ED, -ING, -S to encrust
INCUBATE	*v* -BATED, -BATING, -BATES to warm eggs for hatching
INCUBUS	*n* pl. -BI or -BUSES a demon
INCUDAL	*adj* pertaining to the incus
INCUDATE	*adj* incudal
INCUDES	pl. of incus
INCULT	*adj* uncultivated
INCUMBER	*v* -ED, -ING, -S to encumber
INCUR	*v* -CURRED, -CURRING, -CURS to bring upon oneself
INCURVE	*v* -CURVED, -CURVING, -CURVES to curve inward
INCUS	*n* pl. INCUDES a bone in the middle ear
INCUSE	*v* -CUSED, -CUSING, -CUSES to mark by stamping
INDABA	*n* pl. -S a meeting of South African tribes
INDAGATE	*v* -GATED, -GATING, -GATES to investigate
INDAMIN	*n* pl. -S indamine
INDAMINE	*n* pl. -S a chemical compound
INDEBTED	*adj* beholden
INDECENT	*adj* -CENTER, -CENTEST not decent
INDEED	*adv* in truth
INDENE	*n* pl. -S a hydrocarbon
INDENT	*v* -ED, -ING, -S to cut or tear irregularly
INDENTER	*n* pl. -S one that indents
INDENTOR	*n* pl. -S indenter
INDEVOUT	*adj* not devout
INDEX	*n* pl. INDEXES or INDICES a type of reference guide at the end of a book
INDEX	*v* -ED, -ING, -ES to provide with an index
INDEXER	*n* pl. -S one that indexes
INDICAN	*n* pl. -S a chemical compound
INDICANT	*n* pl. -S something that indicates
INDICATE	*v* -CATED, -CATING, -CATES to point out
INDICES	a pl. of index
INDICIA	*n* pl. -S a distinctive mark
INDICIUM	*n* pl. -S an indicia
INDICT	*v* -ED, -ING, -S to charge with a crime
INDICTEE	*n* pl. -S one that is indicted
INDICTER	*n* pl. -S one that indicts
INDICTOR	*n* pl. -S indicter
INDIGEN	*n* pl. -S indigene
INDIGENE	*n* pl. -S a native
INDIGENT	*n* pl. -S a needy person
INDIGN	*adj* disgraceful **INDIGNLY** *adv*
INDIGO	*n* pl. -GOS or -GOES a blue dye
INDIGOID	*n* pl. -S a blue dye
INDIRECT	*adj* not direct

INDITE	*v* -DITED, -DITING, -DITES to write or compose
INDITER	*n* pl. -S one that indites
INDIUM	*n* pl. -S a metallic element
INDOCILE	*adj* not docile
INDOL	*n* pl. -S indole
INDOLE	*n* pl. -S a chemical compound
INDOLENT	*adj* lazy
INDOOR	*adj* pertaining to the interior of a building
INDOORS	*adv* in or into a house
INDORSE	*v* -DORSED, -DORSING, -DORSES to endorse
INDORSEE	*n* pl. -S endorsee
INDORSER	*n* pl. -S endorser
INDORSING	present participle of indorse
INDORSOR	*n* pl. -S endorsor
INDOW	*v* -ED, -ING, -S to endow
INDOXYL	*n* -S a chemical compound
INDRAFT	*n* pl. -S an inward flow or current
INDRAWN	*adj* drawn in
INDRI	*n* pl. -S a short-tailed lemur
INDUCE	*v* -DUCED, -DUCING, -DUCES to influence into doing something
INDUCER	*n* pl. -S one that induces
INDUCT	*v* -ED, -ING, -S to bring into military service
INDUCTEE	*n* pl. -S one that is inducted
INDUCTOR	*n* pl. -S one that inducts
INDUE	*v* -DUED, -DUING, -DUES to endue
INDULGE	*v* -DULGED, -DULGING, -DULGES to yield to the desire of
INDULGER	*n* pl. -S one that indulges
INDULIN	*n* pl. -S induline
INDULINE	*n* pl. -S a blue dye
INDULT	*n* pl. -S a privilege granted by the pope
INDURATE	*v* -RATED, -RATING, -RATES to make hard
INDUSIUM	*n* pl. -SIA an enclosing membrane **INDUSIAL** *adj*
INDUSTRY	*n* pl. -TRIES a group of productive enterprises
INDWELL	*v* -DWELT, -DWELLING, -DWELLS to live within
INEARTH	*v* -ED, -ING, -S to bury
INEDIBLE	*adj* not fit to be eaten
INEDITA	*n/pl* unpublished literary works
INEDITED	*adj* not published
INEPT	*adj* not suitable **INEPTLY** *adv*
INEQUITY	*n* pl. -TIES unfairness
INERRANT	*adj* free from error
INERT	*n* pl. -S something that lacks active properties
INERTIA	*n* pl. -TIAS or -TIAE the tendency of a body to resist acceleration **INERTIAL** *adj*
INERTLY	*adv* inactively
INEXACT	*adj* not exact
INEXPERT	*n* pl. -S a novice
INFAMOUS	*adj* having a vile reputation
INFAMY	*n* pl. -MIES the state of being infamous
INFANCY	*n* pl. -CIES the state of being an infant
INFANT	*n* pl. -S a child in the earliest stages of life
INFANTA	*n* pl. -S a daughter of a Spanish or Portuguese monarch
INFANTE	*n* pl. -S a younger son of a Spanish or Portuguese monarch
INFANTRY	*n* pl. -TRIES a branch of the army composed of foot soldiers
INFARCT	*n* pl. -S an area of dead or dying tissue
INFARE	*n* pl. -S a reception for newlyweds
INFAUNA	*n* pl. -NAS or -NAE fauna living on a soft sea floor **INFAUNAL** *adj*
INFECT	*v* -ED, -ING, -S to contaminate with disease-producing germs
INFECTER	*n* pl. -S one that infects
INFECTOR	*n* pl. -S infecter
INFECUND	*adj* barren
INFEOFF	*v* -ED, -ING, -S to enfeoff
INFER	*v* -FERRED, -FERRING, -FERS to reach or derive by reasoning
INFERIOR	*n* pl. -S one of lesser rank
INFERNAL	*adj* pertaining to hell
INFERNO	*n* pl. -NOS a place that resembles or suggests hell
INFERRED	past tense of infer
INFERRER	*n* pl. -S one that infers
INFERRING	present participle of infer

INFEST   *v* -ED, -ING, -S to overrun in large numbers

INFESTER   *n* pl. -S one that infests

INFIDEL   *n* pl. -S one who has no religious faith

INFIELD   *n* pl. -S a part of a baseball field

INFINITE   *n* pl. -S something that has no limits

INFINITY   *n* pl. -TIES the state of having no limits

INFIRM   *v* -ED, -ING, -S to weaken or destroy the validity of

INFIRMLY   *adv* in a feeble manner

INFIX   *v* -ED, -ING, -ES to implant

INFIXION   *n* pl. -S the act of infixing

INFLAME   *v* -FLAMED, -FLAMING, -FLAMES to set on fire

INFLAMER   *n* pl. -S one that inflames

INFLATE   *v* -FLATED, -FLATING, -FLATES to cause to expand by filling with gas or air

INFLATER   *n* pl. -S one that inflates

INFLATOR   *n* pl. -S inflater

INFLECT   *v* -ED, -ING, -S to bend

INFLEXED   *adj* bent inward

INFLICT   *v* -ED, -ING, -S to cause to be endured; impose

INFLIGHT   *adj* done during an air voyage

INFLOW   *n* pl. -S the act of flowing in

INFLUENT   *n* pl. -S a tributary

INFLUX   *n* pl. -ES a flowing in

INFO   *n* pl. -FOS information

INFOLD   *v* -ED, -ING, -S to fold inward

INFOLDER   *n* pl. -S one that infolds

INFORM   *v* -ED, -ING, -S to supply with information

INFORMAL   *adj* marked by the absence of formality or ceremony

INFORMER   *n* pl. -S one that informs

INFRA   *adv* below

INFRACT   *v* -ED, -ING, -S to break a legal rule

INFRARED   *n* pl. -S a part of the invisible spectrum

INFRINGE   *v* -FRINGED, -FRINGING, -FRINGES to violate an oath or a law

INFRUGAL   *adj* not frugal

INFUSE   *v* -FUSED, -FUSING, -FUSES to permeate with something

INFUSER   *n* pl. -S one that infuses

INFUSION   *n* pl. -S the act of infusing

INFUSIVE   *adj* capable of infusing

INGATE   *n* pl. -S a channel by which molten metal enters a mold

INGATHER   *v* -ED, -ING, -S to gather in

INGENUE   *n* pl. -S a naive young woman

INGEST   *v* -ED, -ING, -S to take into the body

INGESTA   *n/pl* ingested material

INGLE   *n* pl. -S a fire

INGOING   *adj* entering

INGOT   *v* -ED, -ING, -S to shape into a convenient form for storage

INGRAFT   *v* -ED, -ING, -S to engraft

INGRAIN   *v* -ED, -ING, -S to impress firmly on the mind

INGRATE   *n* pl. -S an ungrateful person

INGRESS   *n* pl. -ES the act of entering

INGROUP   *n* pl. -S a group united by common interests

INGROWN   *adj* grown into the flesh

INGROWTH   *n* pl. -S growth inward

INGUINAL   *adj* pertaining to the groin

INGULF   *v* -ED, -ING, -S to engulf

INHABIT   *v* -ED, -ING, -S to live in

INHALANT   *n* pl. -S something that is inhaled

INHALE   *v* -HALED, -HALING, -HALES to take into the lungs

INHALER   *n* pl. -S one that inhales

INHAUL   *n* pl. -S a line for bringing in a sail

INHAULER   *n* pl. -S an inhaul

INHERE   *v* -HERED, -HERING, -HERES to be inherent

INHERENT   *adj* existing in something as an essential characteristic

INHERIT   *v* -ED, -ING, -S to receive by legal succession

INHESION   *n* pl. -S the state of inhering

INHIBIT   *v* -ED, -ING, -S to restrain or hold back

INHUMAN   *adj* lacking desirable human qualities

INHUMANE   *adj* not humane

INHUME   *v* -HUMED, -HUMING, -HUMES to bury

INHUMER   *n* pl. -S one that inhumes

INIMICAL   *adj* unfriendly

INION   *n* pl. INIA a part of the skull

INIQUITY   *n* pl. -TIES a gross injustice

INITIAL   *v* -TIALED, -TIALING, -TIALS or -TIALLED, -TIALLING, -TIALS to mark with the first letters of one's name

INITIATE   *v* -ATED, -ATING, -ATES to originate

INJECT   *v* -ED, -ING, -S to force a fluid into

INJECTOR   *n* pl. -S one that injects

INJURE   *v* -JURED, -JURING, -JURES to do or cause injury to

INJURER   *n* pl. -S one that injures

INJURY   *n* pl. -RIES harm inflicted or suffered

INK   *v* -ED, -ING, -S to mark with ink (a colored fluid used for writing)

INKBERRY   *n* pl. -RIES a small shrub

INKBLOT   *n* pl. -S a blotted pattern of spilled ink

INKER   *n* pl. -S one that inks

INKHORN   *n* pl. -S a small container for ink

INKIER   comparative of inky

INKIEST   superlative of inky

INKINESS   *n* pl. -ES the state of being inky

INKLE   *n* pl. -S a tape used for trimming

INKLESS   *adj* being without ink

INKLIKE   *adj* resembling ink

INKLING   *n* pl. -S a slight suggestion

INKPOT   *n* pl. -S an inkwell

INKSTAND   *n* pl. -S an inkwell

INKWELL   *n* pl. -S a small container for ink

INKWOOD   *n* pl. -S an evergreen tree

INKY   *adj* INKIER, INKIEST resembling ink

INLACE   *v* -LACED, -LACING, -LACES to enlace

INLAID   past tense of inlay

INLAND   *n* pl. -S the interior of a region

INLANDER   *n* pl. -S one living in the interior of a region

INLAY   *v* -LAID, -LAYING, -LAYS to set into a surface

INLAYER   *n* pl. -S one that inlays

INLET   *v* -LET, -LETTING, -LETS to insert

INLIER   *n* pl. -S a type of rock formation

INLY   *adv* inwardly

INMATE   *n* pl. -S one who is confined to an institution

INMESH   *v* -ED, -ING, -ES to enmesh

INMOST   *adj* farthest within

INN   *v* -ED, -ING, -S to put up at an inn (a public lodging house)

INNARDS   *n/pl* the internal organs

INNATE   *adj* inborn **INNATELY** *adv*

INNED   past tense of in

INNER   *n* pl. -S something that is within

INNERLY   *adv* inwardly

INNERVE   *v* -NERVED, -NERVING, -NERVES to stimulate

INNING   *n* pl. -S a division of a baseball game

INNLESS   *adj* having no inns

INNOCENT   *adj* -CENTER, -CENTEST free from guilt or sin

INNOCENT   *n* pl. -S an innocent person

INNOVATE   *v* -VATED, -VATING, -VATES to introduce something new

INNUENDO   *v* -ED, -ING, -S or -ES to make a derogatory implication

INOCULUM   *n* pl. -LA or -LUMS the material used in an inoculation

INOSITE   *n* pl. -S inositol

INOSITOL   *n* pl. -S an alcohol found in plant and animal tissue

INPHASE   *adj* having matching electrical phases

INPOUR   *v* -ED, -ING, -S to pour in

INPUT   *v* -PUTTED, -PUTTING, -PUTS to enter data into a computer

INQUEST   *n* pl. -S a legal inquiry

INQUIET   *v* -ED, -ING, -S to disturb

INQUIRE   *v* -QUIRED, -QUIRING, -QUIRES to ask about

INQUIRER   *n* pl. -S one that inquires

INQUIRY   *n* pl. -RIES a question

INROAD   *n* pl. -S a hostile invasion

INRUSH   *n* pl. -ES a rushing in

INSANE   *adj* -SANER, -SANEST mentally unsound **INSANELY** *adv*

INSANITY	*n* pl. -TIES the state of being insane; something utterly foolish	**INSPAN**	*v* -SPANNED, -SPANNING, -SPANS to harness or yoke to a vehicle
INSCRIBE	*v* -SCRIBED, -SCRIBING, -SCRIBES to write or engrave as a lasting record	**INSPECT**	*v* -ED, -ING, -S to look carefully at or over
INSCROLL	*v* -ED, -ING, -S to enscroll	**INSPHERE**	*v* -SPHERED, -SPHERING, -SPHERES to ensphere
INSCULP	*v* -ED, -ING, -S to engrave	**INSPIRE**	*v* -SPIRED, -SPIRING, -SPIRES to animate the mind or emotions of
INSEAM	*n* pl. -S an inner seam		
INSECT	*n* pl. -S any of a class of small invertebrate animals	**INSPIRER**	*n* pl. -S one that inspires
INSECTAN	*adj* pertaining to insects	**INSPIRIT**	*v* -ED, -ING, -S to fill with spirit or life
INSECURE	*adj* unsafe		
INSERT	*v* -ED, -ING, -S to put in	**INSTABLE**	*adj* unstable
INSERTER	*n* pl. -S one that inserts	**INSTAL**	*v* -STALLED, -STALLING, -STALS to install
INSET	*v* -SETTED, -SETTING, -SETS to insert	**INSTALL**	*v* -ED, -ING, -S to place in position for use
INSETTER	*n* pl. -S one that inserts	**INSTANCE**	*v* -STANCED, -STANCING, -STANCES to cite as an example
INSHEATH	*v* -ED, -ING, -S to ensheath		
INSHORE	*adj* near the shore	**INSTANCY**	*n* pl. -CIES urgency
INSHRINE	*v* -SHRINED, -SHRINING, -SHRINES to enshrine	**INSTANT**	*n* pl. -S a very short time
		INSTAR	*v* -STARRED, -STARRING, -STARS to adorn with stars
INSIDE	*n* pl. -S something that lies within		
INSIDER	*n* pl. -S an accepted member of a clique	**INSTATE**	*v* -STATED, -STATING, -STATES to place in office
INSIGHT	*n* pl. -S a perception of the inner nature of things	**INSTEAD**	*adv* as a substitute or equivalent
INSIGNE	*n* pl. INSIGNIA an insignia	**INSTEP**	*n* pl. -S a part of the foot
INSIGNIA	*n* pl. -S an emblem of authority or honor	**INSTIL**	*v* -STILLED, -STILLING, -STILS to instill
INSIPID	*adj* dull and uninteresting	**INSTILL**	*v* -ED, -ING, -S to infuse slowly
INSIST	*v* -ED, -ING, -S to be resolute on some matter	**INSTINCT**	*n* pl. -S an inborn behavioral pattern
INSISTER	*n* pl. -S one that insists	**INSTROKE**	*n* pl. -S an inward stroke
INSNARE	*v* -SNARED, -SNARING, -SNARES to ensnare	**INSTRUCT**	*v* -ED, -ING, -S to supply with knowledge
INSNARER	*n* pl. -S ensnarer	**INSULANT**	*n* pl. -S an insulating material
INSOFAR	*adv* to such an extent	**INSULAR**	*n* pl. -S an islander
INSOLATE	*v* -LATED, -LATING, -LATES to expose to sunlight	**INSULATE**	*v* -LATED, -LATING, -LATES to separate with nonconducting material
INSOLE	*n* pl. -S the inner sole of a boot or shoe	**INSULIN**	*n* pl. -S a hormone
INSOLENT	*n* pl. -S an extremely rude person	**INSULT**	*v* -ED, -ING, -S to treat offensively
INSOMNIA	*n* pl. -S chronic inability to sleep	**INSULTER**	*n* pl. -S one that insults
		INSURANT	*n* pl. -S one who is insured
INSOMUCH	*adv* to such a degree	**INSURE**	*v* -SURED, -SURING, -SURES to guarantee against loss
INSOUL	*v* -ED, -ING, -S to ensoul	**INSURED**	*n* pl. -S one who is insured

INSURER *n* pl. -S one that insures

INSURING present participle of insure

INSWATHE *v* -SWATHED, -SWATHING, -SWATHES to enswathe

INSWEPT *adj* narrowed in front

INTACT *adj* not damaged in any way

INTAGLIO *n* pl. -GLIOS or -GLI an incised or sunken design

INTAKE *n* pl. -S the act of taking in

INTARSIA *n* pl. -S a decorative technique

INTEGER *n* pl. -S a whole number

INTEGRAL *n* pl. -S a total unit

INTEND *v* -ED, -ING, -S to have as a specific aim or purpose

INTENDED *n* pl. -S one's spouse to-be

INTENDER *n* pl. -S one that intends

INTENSE *adj* -TENSER, -TENSEST existing in an extreme degree

INTENT *n* pl. -S a purpose

INTENTLY *adv* in an unwavering manner

INTER *v* -TERRED, -TERRING, -TERS to bury

INTERACT *v* -ED, -ING, -S to act on each other

INTERCOM *n* pl. -S a type of communication system

INTERCUT *v* -CUT, -CUTTING, -CUTS to alternate camera shots

INTEREST *v* -ED, -ING, -S to engage the attention of

INTERIM *n* pl. -S an interval

INTERIOR *n* pl. -S the inside

INTERLAP *v* -LAPPED, -LAPPING, -LAPS to lap one over another

INTERLAY *v* -LAID, -LAYING, -LAYS to place between

INTERMIT *v* -MITTED, -MITTING, -MITS to stop temporarily

INTERMIX *v* -ED, -ING, -ES to mix together

INTERN *v* -ED, -ING, -S to confine during a war

INTERNAL *n* pl. -S an inner attribute

INTERNE *n* pl. -S a recent medical school graduate on a hospital staff

INTERNEE *n* pl. -S one who has been interned

INTERRED past tense of inter

INTERREX *n* pl. -REGES a type of sovereign

INTERRING present participle of inter

INTERSEX *n* pl. -ES a person having characteristics of both sexes

INTERTIE *n* pl. -S a type of electrical connection

INTERVAL *n* pl. -S a space of time between periods or events

INTERWAR *adj* happening between wars

INTHRAL *v* -THRALLED, -THRALLING, -THRALS to enthrall

INTHRALL *v* -ED, -ING, -S to enthrall

INTHRONE *v* -THRONED, -THRONING, -THRONES to enthrone

INTIMA *n* pl. -MAE or -MAS the innermost layer of an organ **INTIMAL** *adj*

INTIMACY *n* pl. -CIES the state of being closely associated

INTIMATE *v* -MATED, -MATING, -MATES to make known indirectly

INTIME *adj* cozy

INTINE *n* pl. -S the inner wall of a spore

INTITLE *v* -TLED, -TLING, -TLES to entitle

INTITULE *v* -ULED, -ULING, -ULES to entitle

INTO *prep* to the inside of

INTOMB *v* -ED, -ING, -S to entomb

INTONATE *v* -NATED, -NATING, -NATES to intone

INTONE *v* -TONED, -TONING, -TONES to speak in a singing voice

INTONER *n* pl. -S one that intones

INTORT *v* -ED, -ING, -S to twist inward

INTOWN *adj* located in the center of a city

INTRADOS *n* pl. -S the inner curve of an arch

INTRANT *n* pl. -S an entrant

INTREAT *v* -ED, -ING, -S to entreat

INTRENCH *v* -ED, -ING, -ES to entrench

INTREPID *adj* fearless

INTRIGUE *v* -TRIGUED, -TRIGUING, -TRIGES to arouse the curiosity of

INTRO *n* pl. -TROS an introduction

INTROFY *v* -FIED, -FYING, -FIES to increase the wetting properties of

INTROIT *n* pl. -S music sung at the beginning of a worship service

INTROMIT v -MITTED, -MITTING, -MITS to put in

INTRORSE adj facing inward

INTRUDE v -TRUDED, -TRUDING, -TRUDES to thrust or force oneself in

INTRUDER n pl. -S one that intrudes

INTRUST v -ED, -ING, -S to entrust

INTUBATE v -BATED, -BATING, -BATES to insert a tube into

INTUIT v -ED, -ING, -S to know without conscious reasoning

INTURN n pl. -S a turning inward **INTURNED** adj

INTWINE v -TWINED, -TWINING, -TWINES to entwine

INTWIST v -ED, -ING, -S to entwist

INULASE n pl. -S an enzyme

INULIN n pl. -S a chemical compound

INUNDANT adj inundating

INUNDATE v -DATED, -DATING, -DATES to overwhelm with water

INURBANE adj not urbane

INURE v -URED, -URING, -URES to accustom to accept something undesirable

INURN v -ED, -ING, -S to put in an urn

INUTILE adj useless

INVADE v -VADED, -VADING, -VADES to enter for conquest or plunder

INVADER n pl. -S one that invades

INVALID v -ED, -ING, -S to disable physically

INVAR n pl. -S a steel alloy

INVASION n pl. -S the act of invading **INVASIVE** adj

INVECTED adj edged by convex curves

INVEIGH v -ED, -ING, -S to protest angrily

INVEIGLE v -GLED, -GLING, -GLES to induce by guile or flattery

INVENT v -ED, -ING, -S to devise originally

INVENTER n pl. -S inventor

INVENTOR n pl. -S one that invents

INVERITY n pl. -TIES lack of truth

INVERSE n pl. -S something that is opposite

INVERT v -ED, -ING, -S to turn upside down

INVERTER n pl. -S one that inverts

INVERTOR n pl. -S a type of electrical device

INVEST v -ED, -ING, -S to commit something of value for future profit

INVESTOR n pl. -S one that invests

INVIABLE adj not viable **INVIABLY** adv

INVIRILE adj not virile

INVISCID adj not viscid

INVITAL adj not vital

INVITE v -VITED, -VITING, -VITES to request the presence of

INVITEE n pl. -S one that is invited

INVITER n pl. -S one that invites

INVITING present participle of invite

INVOCATE v -CATED, -CATING, -CATES to invoke

INVOICE v -VOICED, -VOICING, -VOICES to bill

INVOKE v -VOKED, -VOKING, -VOKES to appeal to for aid

INVOKER n pl. -S one that invokes

INVOLUTE v -LUTED, -LUTING, -LUTES to roll or curl up

INVOLVE v -VOLVED, -VOLVING, -VOLVES to contain or include as a part

INVOLVER n pl. -S one that involves

INWALL v -ED, -ING, -S to surround with a wall

INWARD adv toward the inside

INWARDLY adv on the inside

INWARDS adv inward

INWEAVE v -WOVE or -WEAVED, -WOVEN, -WEAVING, -WEAVES to weave together

INWIND v -WOUND, -WINDING, -WINDS to enwind

INWRAP v -WRAPPED, -WRAPPING, -WRAPS to enwrap

IODATE v -DATED, -DATING, -DATES to iodize

IODATION n pl. -S the act of iodating

IODIC adj pertaining to iodine

IODID n pl. -S iodide

IODIDE n pl. -S a compound of iodine

IODIN n pl. -S iodine

IODINATE v -ATED, -ATING, -ATES to iodize

IODINE n pl. -S a nonmetallic element

IODISM   *n* pl. -S iodine poisoning

IODIZE   *v* -DIZED, -DIZING, -DIZES to treat with iodine

IODIZER   *n* pl. -S one that iodizes

IODOFORM   *n* pl. -S an iodine compound

IODOL   *n* pl. -S an iodine compound

IODOPHOR   *n* pl. -S an iodine compound

IODOPSIN   *n* pl. -S a pigment in the retina

IODOUS   *adj* pertaining to iodine

IOLITE   *n* pl. -S a mineral

ION   *n* pl. -S an electrically charged atom

IONIC   *n* pl. -S a style of type

IONICITY   *n* pl. -TIES the state of existing as or like an ion

IONISE   *v* -ISED, -ISING, -ISES to ionize

IONIUM   *n* pl. -S an isotope of thorium

IONIZE   *v* -IZED, -IZING, -IZES to convert into ions

IONIZER   *n* pl. -S one that ionizes

IONOMER   *n* pl. -S a type of plastic

IONONE   *n* pl. -S a chemical compound

IOTA   *n* pl. -S a Greek letter

IOTACISM   *n* pl. -S excessive use of the letter iota

IPECAC   *n* pl. -S a medicinal plant

IPOMOEA   *n* pl. -S a flowering plant

IRACUND   *adj* easily angered

IRADE   *n* pl. -S a decree of a Muslim ruler

IRATE   *adj* IRATER, IRATEST angry **IRATELY** *adv*

IRE   *v* IRED, IRING, IRES to anger

IREFUL   *adj* angry **IREFULLY** *adv*

IRELESS   *adj* not angry

IRENIC   *adj* peaceful in purpose

IRENICAL   *adj* irenic

IRENICS   *n/pl* a branch of theology

IRIDES   a pl. of iris

IRIDIC   *adj* pertaining to iridium

IRIDIUM   *n* pl. -S a metallic element

IRING   present participle of ire

IRIS   *n* pl. IRISES or IRIDES a part of the eye

IRIS   *v* -ED, -ING, -ES to give the form of a rainbow to

IRITIS   *n* pl. -TISES inflammation of the iris **IRITIC** *adj*

IRK   *v* -ED, -ING, -S to annoy or weary

IRKSOME   *adj* tending to irk

IRON   *v* -ED, -ING, -S to furnish with iron (a metallic element)

IRONBARK   *n* pl. -S a timber tree

IRONCLAD   *n* pl. -S an armored warship

IRONE   *n* pl. -S an aromatic oil

IRONER   *n* pl. -S a machine for pressing clothes

IRONIC   *adj* pertaining to irony

IRONICAL   *adj* ironic

IRONIES   pl. of irony

IRONING   *n* pl. -S clothes pressed or to be pressed

IRONIST   *n* pl. -S one who uses irony

IRONLIKE   *adj* resembling iron

IRONNESS   *n* pl. -ES the state of being iron

IRONSIDE   *n* pl. -S a man of great strength

IRONWARE   *n* pl. -S articles made of iron

IRONWEED   *n* pl. -S a shrub

IRONWOOD   *n* pl. -S a hardwood tree

IRONWORK   *n* pl. -S objects made of iron

IRONY   *n* pl. -NIES the use of words to express the opposite of what is literally said

IRREAL   *adj* not real

IRRIGATE   *v* -GATED, -GATING, -GATES to supply with water by artificial means

IRRITANT   *n* pl. -S something that irritates

IRRITATE   *v* -TATED, -TATING, -TATES to excite to impatience or anger

IRRUPT   *v* -ED, -ING, -S to rush in forcibly

IS   present 3d person sing. of be

ISAGOGE   *n* pl. -S a type of introduction to a branch of study

ISAGOGIC   *n* pl. -S a branch of theology

ISARITHM   *n* pl. -S an isopleth

ISATIN   *n* pl. -S a chemical compound **ISATINIC** *adj*

ISATINE   *n* pl. -S isatin

ISBA   *n* pl. -S a Russian log hut

ISCHEMIA   *n* pl. -S a type of anemia **ISCHEMIC** *adj*

ISCHIUM *n pl.* -CHIA a pelvic bone **ISCHIAL** *adj*

ISLAND *v* -ED, -ING, -S to make into an island (a land area entirely surrounded by water)

ISLANDER *n pl.* -S one that lives on an island

ISLE *v* ISLED, ISLING, ISLES to place on an isle (a small island)

ISLELESS *adj* lacking an isle

ISLET *n pl.* -S a small island

ISLING present participle of isle

ISM *n pl.* -S a distinctive theory or doctrine

ISOBAR *n pl.* -S a type of atom **ISOBARIC** *adj*

ISOBARE *n pl.* -S isobar

ISOBATH *n pl.* -S a line on a map connecting points of equal water depth

ISOCHEIM *n pl.* -S a type of isotherm

ISOCHIME *n pl.* -S isocheim

ISOCHOR *n pl.* -S isochore

ISOCHORE *n pl.* -S a curve used to show a relationship between pressure and temperature

ISOCHRON *n pl.* -S a line on a chart connecting points representing the same time

ISOCLINE *n pl.* -S a type of rock formation

ISOCRACY *n pl.* -CIES a form of government

ISODOSE *adj* pertaining to zones that receive equal doses of radiation

ISOGAMY *n pl.* -MIES the fusion of two similar gametes

ISOGENIC *adj* genetically similar

ISOGENY *n pl.* -NIES the state of being of similar origin

ISOGLOSS *n pl.* -ES a line on a map between linguistically varied areas

ISOGON *n pl.* -S a polygon having equal angles

ISOGONAL *n pl.* -S isogone

ISOGONE *n pl.* -S a line on a map used to show characteristics of the earth's magnetic field

ISOGONIC *n pl.* -S isogone

ISOGONY *n pl.* -NIES an equivalent relative growth of parts

ISOGRAM *n pl.* -S a line on a map connecting points of equal value

ISOGRAPH *n pl.* -S a line on a map indicating areas that are linguistically similar

ISOGRIV *n pl.* -S a line drawn on a map such that all points have equal grid variation

ISOHEL *n pl.* -S a line on a map connecting points receiving equal sunshine

ISOHYET *n pl.* -S a line on a map connecting points having equal rainfall

ISOLABLE *adj* capable of being isolated

ISOLATE *n* -LATED, -LATING, -LATES to set apart from others

ISOLATOR *n pl.* -S one that isolates

ISOLEAD *n pl.* -S a line on a ballistic graph

ISOLINE *n pl.* -S an isogram

ISOLOG *n pl.* -S isologue

ISOLOGUE *n pl.* -S a type of chemical compound

ISOMER *n pl.* -S a type of chemical compound **ISOMERIC** *adj*

ISOMETRY *n pl.* -TRIES equality of measure

ISOMORPH *n pl.* -S something similar to something else in form

ISONOMY *n pl.* -MIES equality of civil rights **ISONOMIC** *adj*

ISOPHOTE *n pl.* -S a curve on a chart joining points of equal light intensity

ISOPLETH *n pl.* -S a type of isogram

ISOPOD *n pl.* -S a kind of crustacean

ISOPODAN *n pl.* -S an isopod

ISOPRENE *n pl.* -S a volatile liquid

ISOSPIN *n pl.* -S a type of quantum number

ISOSPORY *n pl.* -RIES the condition of producing sexual or asexual spores of but one kind

ISOSTASY *n pl.* -SIES the state of balance in the earth's crust

ISOTACH *n pl.* -S a line on a map connecting points of equal wind velocity

ISOTHERE *n pl.* -S a type of isotherm

ISOTHERM *n pl.* -S a line on a map connecting points of equal mean temperature

ISOTONE	*n* pl. -S a type of atom
ISOTONIC	*adj* of equal tension
ISOTOPE	*n* pl. -S a form of an element
ISOTOPIC *adj*	
ISOTOPY	*n* pl. -PIES the state of being an isotope
ISOTROPY	*n* pl. -PIES the state of being identical in all directions
ISOTYPE	*n* pl. -S a type of diagram
ISOTYPIC *adj*	
ISOZYME	*n* pl. -S a type of enzyme
ISOZYMIC *adj*	
ISSEI	*n* pl. -S a Japanese immigrant to the United States
ISSUABLE	*adj* authorized for issuing
ISSUABLY *adv*	
ISSUANCE	*n* pl. -S the act of issuing
ISSUANT	*adj* coming forth
ISSUE	*v* -SUED, -SUING, -SUES to come forth
ISSUER	*n* pl. -S one that issues
ISTHMI	a pl. of isthmus
ISTHMIAN	*n* pl. -S a native of an isthmus
ISTHMIC	*adj* pertaining to an isthmus
ISTHMOID	*adj* isthmic
ISTHMUS	*n* pl. -MUSES or -MI a strip of land connecting two larger land masses
ISTLE	*n* pl. -S a strong fiber
IT	*pron* the 3d person sing. neuter pronoun
ITALIC	*n* pl. -S a style of print

ITCH	*v* -ED, -ING, -ES to have an uneasy or tingling skin sensation
ITCHING	*n* pl. -S an uneasy or tingling skin sensation
ITCHY	*adj* ITCHIER, ITCHIEST causing an itching sensation
ITEM	*v* -ED, -ING, -S to itemize
ITEMIZE	*v* -IZED, -IZING, -IZES to set down the particulars of
ITEMIZER	*n* pl. -S one that itemizes
ITERANCE	*n* pl. -S repetition
ITERANT	*adj* repeating
ITERATE	*v* -ATED, -ATING, -ATES to repeat
ITERUM	*adv* again; once more
ITHER	*adj* other
ITS	*pron* the possessive form of the pronoun it
ITSELF	*pron* a reflexive form of the pronoun it
IVIED	*adj* covered with ivy
IVORY	*n* pl. -RIES a hard white substance found in elephant tusks
IVY	*n* pl. IVIES a climbing vine
IVYLIKE *adj*	
IWIS	*adv* certainly
IXIA	*n* pl. -S a flowering plant
IXODID	*n* pl. -S a bloodsucking insect
IXTLE	*n* pl. -S istle
IZAR	*n* pl. -S an outer garment worn by Muslim women
IZZARD	*n* pl. -S the letter Z

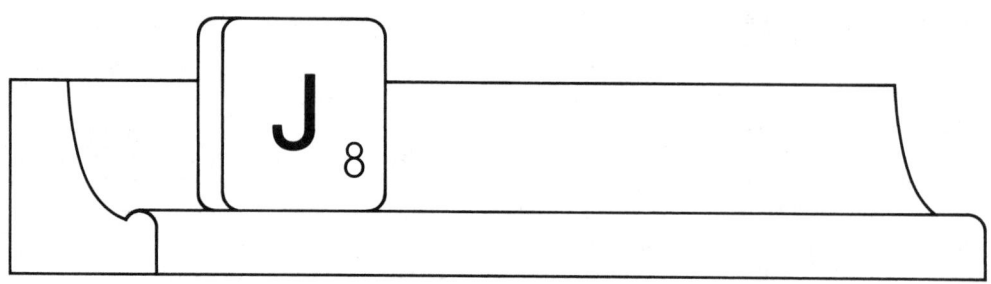

JAB	v JABBED, JABBING, JABS to poke sharply	**JACONET**	n pl. -S a cotton cloth
JABBER	v -ED, -ING, -S to talk rapidly	**JACQUARD**	n pl. -S a fabric of intricate weave
JABBERER	n pl. -S one that jabbers	**JACULATE**	v -LATED, -LATING, -LATES to throw
JABBING	present participle of jab		
JABIRU	n pl. -S a wading bird	**JADE**	v JADED, JADING, JADES to weary **JADEDLY** adv
JABOT	n pl. -S a decoration on a shirt		
JACAL	n pl. -ES or -S a hut	**JADEITE**	n pl. -S a mineral **JADITIC** adj
JACAMAR	n pl. -S a tropical bird	**JADISH**	adj worn-out **JADISHLY** adv
JACANA	n pl. -S a wading bird	**JAEGER**	n pl. -S a hunter
JACINTH	n pl. -S a variety of zircon	**JAG**	v JAGGED, JAGGING, JAGS to cut unevenly
JACINTHE	n pl. -S an orange color		
JACK	v -ED, -ING, -S to raise with a type of lever	**JAGER**	n pl. -S jaeger
		JAGG	v -ED, -ING, -S to jag
JACKAL	n pl. -S a doglike mammal	**JAGGARY**	n pl. -RIES jaggery
JACKAROO	n pl. -ROOS jackeroo	**JAGGED**	adj -GEDER, -GEDEST having a sharply uneven edge of surface **JAGGEDLY** adv
JACKASS	n pl. -ES a male donkey		
JACKBOOT	n pl. -S a heavy boot		
JACKDAW	n pl. -S a crowlike bird	**JAGGER**	n pl. -S one that jags
JACKER	n pl. -S one that jacks	**JAGGERY**	n pl. -GERIES a coarse, dark sugar
JACKEROO	n pl. -ROOS an inexperienced ranch hand		
		JAGGHERY	n pl. -GHERIES jaggery
JACKET	v -ED, -ING, -S to provide with a jacket (a short coat)	**JAGGING**	present participle of jag
		JAGGY	adj -GIER, -GIEST jagged
JACKFISH	n pl. -ES a food fish	**JAGLESS**	adj smooth and even
JACKIES	pl. of jacky	**JAGRA**	n pl. -S jaggery
JACKLEG	n pl. -S an unskilled worker	**JAGUAR**	n pl. -S a large feline animal
JACKPOT	n pl. -S a top prize or reward	**JAIL**	v -ED, -ING, -S to put in jail (a place of confinement)
JACKSTAY	n pl. -STAYS a rope on a ship		
JACKY	n pl. JACKIES a sailor	**JAILBAIT**	n pl. JAILBAIT a girl under the age of consent with whom sexual intercourse constitutes statutory rape
JACOBIN	n pl. -S a pigeon		
JACOBUS	n pl. -ES an old English coin		
		JAILBIRD	n pl. -S a prisoner

JAILER	*n* pl. -S a keeper of a jail
JAILOR	*n* pl. -S jailer
JAKE	*adj* all right; fine
JAKES	*n/pl* an outhouse
JALAP	*n* pl. -S a Mexican plant **JALAPIC** *adj*
JALAPIN	*n* pl. -S a medicinal substance contained in jalap
JALOP	*n* pl. -S jalap
JALOPPY	*n* pl. -PIES jalopy
JALOPY	*n* pl. -LOPIES a decrepit car
JALOUSIE	*n* pl. -S a type of window
JAM	*v* JAMMED, JAMMING, JAMS to force together tightly
JAMB	*v* -ED, -ING, -S to jam
JAMBE	*n* pl. -S a jambeau
JAMBEAU	*n* pl. -BEAUX a piece of armor for the leg
JAMBOREE	*n* pl. -S a noisy celebration
JAMMED	past tense of jam
JAMMER	*n* pl. -S one that jams
JAMMING	present participle of jam
JANE	*n* pl. -S a girl or woman
JANGLE	*v* -GLED, -GLING, -GLES to make a harsh, metallic sound
JANGLER	*n* pl. -S one that jangles
JANIFORM	*adj* hypocritical
JANISARY	*n* pl. -SARIES janizary
JANITOR	*n* pl. -S a maintenance man
JANIZARY	*n* pl. -ZARIES a Turkish soldier
JANTY	*adj* jaunty
JAPAN	*v* -PANNED, -PANNING, -PANS to coat with a glossy, black lacquer
JAPANIZE	*v* -NIZED, -NIZING, -NIZES to make Japanese
JAPANNER	*n* pl. -S one that japans
JAPANNING	present participle of japan
JAPE	*v* JAPED, JAPING, JAPES to mock
JAPER	*n* pl. -S one that japes
JAPERY	*n* pl. -ERIES mockery
JAPING	present participle of jape
JAPINGLY	*adv* in a japing manner
JAPONICA	*n* pl. -S an Asian shrub
JAR	*v* JARRED, JARRING, JARS to cause to shake
JARFUL	*n* pl. JARFULS or JARSFUL the quantity held by a jar (a cylindrical container)
JARGON	*v* -ED, -ING, -S to speak or write an obscure and often pretentious kind of language
JARGONEL	*n* pl. -S a variety of pear
JARGOON	*n* pl. -S a variety of zircon
JARINA	*n* pl. -S the hard seed of a palm tree
JARL	*n* pl. -S a Scandinavian nobleman
JARLDOM	*n* pl. -S the domain of a jarl
JAROSITE	*n* pl. -S a mineral
JAROVIZE	*v* -VIZED, -VIZING, -VIZES to hasten the flowering of a plant
JARRAH	*n* pl. -S an evergreen tree
JARRED	past tense of jar
JARRING	present participle of jar
JARSFUL	a pl. of jarful
JARVEY	*n* pl. -VEYS the driver of a carriage for hire
JASMINE	*n* pl. -S a climbing shrub
JASPER	*n* pl. -S a variety of quartz **JASPERY** *adj*
JASSID	*n* pl. -S any of a family of plant pests
JATO	*n* pl. -TOS a takeoff aided by jet propulsion
JAUK	*v* -ED, -ING, -S to dawdle
JAUNCE	*v* JAUNCED, JAUNCING, JAUNCES to prance
JAUNDICE	*v* -DICED, -DICING, -DICES to prejudice unfavorably
JAUNT	*v* -ED, -ING, -S to make a pleasure trip
JAUNTY	*adj* -TIER, -TIEST having a lively and self-confident manner **JAUNTILY** *adv*
JAUP	*v* -ED, -ING, -S to splash
JAVA	*n* pl. -S coffee
JAVELIN	*v* -ED, -ING, -S to pierce with a javelin (a light spear)
JAVELINA	*n* pl. -S a peccary
JAW	*v* -ED, -ING, -S to jabber
JAWAN	*n* pl. -S a soldier of India
JAWBONE	*v* -BONED, -BONING, -BONES to attempt to convince
JAWLIKE	*adj* resembling the jaw (the framework of the mouth)

JAWLINE	*n* pl. -S the outline of the lower jaw
JAY	*n* pl. JAYS a corvine bird
JAYBIRD	*n* pl. -S a jay
JAYGEE	*n* pl. -S a military officer
JAYVEE	*n* pl. -S a junior varsity player
JAYWALK	*v* -ED, -ING, -S to cross a street recklessly
JAZZ	*v* -ED, -ING, -ES to enliven
JAZZER	*n* pl. -S one that jazzes
JAZZMAN	*n* pl. -MEN a type of musician
JAZZY	*adj* JAZZIER, JAZZIEST lively **JAZZILY** *adv*
JEALOUS	*adj* resentful of another's advantages
JEALOUSY	*n* pl. -SIES a jealous feeling
JEAN	*n* pl. -S a durable cotton fabric
JEBEL	*n* pl. -S a mountain
JEE	*v* JEED, JEEING, JEES to gee
JEEP	*n* pl. -S a type of motor vehicle
JEEPERS	*interj* — used as a mild oath
JEER	*v* -ED, -ING, -S to mock
JEERER	*n* pl. -S one that jeers
JEEZ	*interj* — used as a mild oath
JEFE	*n* pl. -S a chief
JEHAD	*n* pl. -S jihad
JEHU	*n* pl. -S a fast driver
JEJUNA	pl. of jejunum
JEJUNAL	*adj* pertaining to the jejunum
JEJUNE	*adj* uninteresting; childish **JEJUNELY** *adv*
JEJUNITY	*n* pl. -TIES something that is jejune
JEJUNUM	*n* pl. -NA a part of the small intestine
JELL	*v* -ED, -ING, -S to congeal
JELLIFY	*v* -FIED, -FYING, -FIES to jelly
JELLY	*v* -LIED, -LYING, -LIES to make into a jelly (a soft, semisolid substance)
JELUTONG	*n* pl. -S a tropical tree
JEMADAR	*n* pl. -S an officer in the army of India
JEMIDAR	*n* pl. -S jemadar
JEMMY	*v* -MIED, -MYING, -MIES to jimmy
JENNET	*n* pl. -S a small horse
JENNY	*n* pl. -NIES a female donkey
JEOPARD	*v* -ED, -ING, -S to imperil
JEOPARDY	*n* pl. -DIES risk of loss or injury
JERBOA	*n* pl. -S a small rodent
JEREED	*n* pl. -S a wooden javelin
JEREMIAD	*n* pl. -S a tale of woe
JERID	*n* pl. -S jereed
JERK	*v* -ED, -ING, -S to move with a sharp, sudden motion
JERKER	*n* pl. -S one that jerks
JERKIES	pl. of jerky
JERKIN	*n* pl. -S a sleeveless jacket
JERKY	*adj* JERKIER, JERKIEST characterized by jerking movements **JERKILY** *adv*
JERKY	*n* pl. -KIES dried and smoked meat
JEROBOAM	*n* pl. -S a wine bottle
JERREED	*n* pl. -S jereed
JERRICAN	*n* pl. -S jerrycan
JERRID	*n* pl. -S jereed
JERRY	*n* pl. -RIES a German soldier
JERRYCAN	*n* pl. -S a fuel container
JERSEY	*n* pl. -SEYS a close-fitting knitted shirt **JERSEYED** *adj*
JESS	*v* -ED, -ING, -ES to fasten straps around the legs of a hawk
JESSANT	*adj* shooting forth
JESSE	*v* JESSED, JESSING, JESSES to jess
JEST	*v* -ED, -ING, -S to joke
JESTER	*n* pl. -S one that jests
JESTFUL	*adj* tending to jest
JESTING	*n* pl. -S the act of one who jests
JESUIT	*n* pl. -S a scheming person **JESUITIC** *adj*
JESUITRY	*n* pl. -RIES an unethical principle or practice
JET	*v* JETTED, JETTING, JETS to spurt forth in a stream
JETBEAD	*n* pl. -S an ornamental shrub
JETE	*n* pl. -S a ballet leap
JETLINER	*n* pl. -S a type of aircraft
JETON	*n* pl. -S jetton
JETPORT	*n* pl. -S a type of airport
JETSAM	*n* pl. -S goods cast overboard to lighten an imperiled vessel
JETSOM	*n* pl. -S jetsam
JETTED	past tense of jet

JETTIED   past tense of jetty

JETTIES   present 3d person sing. of jetty

JETTING   present participle of jet

JETTISON   *v* -ED, -ING, -S to cast overboard

JETTON   *n* pl. -S a piece used in counting

JETTY   *v* -TIED, -TYING, -TIES to jut

JEU   *n* pl. JEUX a game

JEW   *v* -ED, -ING, -S to bargain with — usually taken to be offensive

JEWEL   *v* -ELED, -ELING, -ELS or -ELLED, -ELLING, -ELS to adorn with jewels (precious stones)

JEWELER   *n* pl. -S a dealer or maker of jewelry

JEWELLER   *n* pl. -S jeweler

JEWELLING   a present participle of jewel

JEWELRY   *n* pl. -RIES an article or articles for personal adornment

JEWFISH   *n* pl. -ES a large marine fish

JEZAIL   *n* pl. -S a type of firearm

JEZEBEL   *n* pl. -S a scheming, wicked woman

JIB   *v* JIBBED, JIBBING, JIBS to refuse to proceed further

JIBB   *v* -ED, -ING, -S to shift from side to side while sailing

JIBBER   *n* pl. -S a horse that jibs

JIBBING   present participle of jib

JIBBOOM   *n* pl. -S a ship's spar

JIBE   *v* JIBED, JIBING, JIBES to gibe **JIBINGLY** *adv*

JIBER   *n* pl. -S one that jibes

JIFF   *n* pl. -S jiffy

JIFFY   *n* pl. -FIES a short time

JIG   *v* JIGGED, JIGGING, JIGS to bob

JIGABOO   *n* pl. -BOOS a black person — often taken to be offensive

JIGGER   *n* pl. -S a small whiskey glass

JIGGERED   *adj* damned

JIGGING   present participle of jig

JIGGLE   *v* -GLED, -GLING, -GLES to shake lightly

JIGGLY   *adj* -GLIER, -GLIEST unsteady

JIGSAW   *v* -SAWED, -SAWN, -SAWING, -SAWS to cut with a type of saw

JIHAD   *n* pl. -S a Muslim holy war

JILL   *n* pl. -S a unit of liquid measure

JILLION   *n* pl. -S a very large number

JILT   *v* -ED, -ING, -S to reject a lover

JILTER   *n* pl. -S one that jilts

JIMINY   *interj* — used to express surprise

JIMJAMS   *n/pl* violent delirium

JIMMINY   *interj* jiminy

JIMMY   *v* -MIED, -MYING, -MIES to pry open with a crowbar

JIMP   *adj* JIMPER, JIMPEST natty **JIMPLY** *adv*

JIMPY   *adj* jimp

JIN   *n* pl. -S jinn

JINGAL   *n* pl. -S a heavy musket

JINGALL   *n* pl. -S jingal

JINGKO   *n* pl. -KOES ginkgo

JINGLE   *v* -GLED, -GLING, -GLES to make a tinkling sound

JINGLER   *n* pl. -S one that jingles

JINGLY   *adj* -GLIER, -GLIEST jingling

JINGO   *n* pl. -GOES a zealous patriot **JINGOISH** *adj*

JINGOISM   *n* pl. -S the spirit or policy of jingoes

JINGOIST   *n* pl. -S a jingo

JINK   *v* -ED, -ING, -S to move quickly out of the way

JINKER   *n* pl. -S one that jinks

JINN   *n* pl. -S a supernatural being in Muslim mythology

JINNEE   *n* pl. JINN jinn

JINNI   *n* pl. JINN jinn

JINX   *v* -ED, -ING, -ES to bring bad luck to

JIPIJAPA   *n* pl. -S a tropical plant

JITNEY   *n* pl. -NEYS a small bus

JITTER   *v* -ED, -ING, -S to fidget

JITTERY   *adj* extremely nervous

JIUJITSU   *n* pl. -S jujitsu

JIUJUTSU   *n* pl. -S jujitsu

JIVE   *v* JIVED, JIVING, JIVES to play jazz or swing music

JNANA   *n* pl. -S knowledge acquired through meditation

JO   *n* pl. JOES a sweetheart

JOANNES   *n* pl. JOANNES johannes

JOB	*v* JOBBED, JOBBING, JOBS to work by the piece
JOBBER	*n* pl. -S a pieceworker
JOBBERY	*n* pl. -BERIES corruption in public office
JOBBING	present participle of job
JOBLESS	*adj* having no job
JOCK	*n* pl. -S an athletic supporter
JOCKEY	*v* -EYED, -EYING, -EYS to maneuver for an advantage
JOCKO	*n* pl. JOCKOS a monkey
JOCOSE	*adj* humorous **JOCOSELY** *adv*
JOCOSITY	*n* pl. -TIES the state of being jocose
JOCULAR	*adj* given to joking
JOCUND	*adj* cheerful **JOCUNDLY** *adv*
JODHPUR	*n* pl. -S a type of boot
JOE	*n* pl. -S a fellow
JOEY	*n* pl. -EYS a young kangaroo
JOG	*v* JOGGED, JOGGING, JOGS to run at a slow, steady pace
JOGGER	*n* pl. -S one that jogs
JOGGLE	*v* -GLED, -GLING, -GLES to shake slightly
JOGGLER	*n* pl. -S one that joggles
JOHANNES	*n* pl. JOHANNES a Portuguese coin
JOHN	*n* pl. -S a toilet
JOHNBOAT	*n* pl. -S a narrow square-ended boat
JOHNNY	*n* pl. -NIES a sleeveless hospital gown
JOIN	*v* -ED, -ING, -S to unite **JOINABLE** *adj*
JOINDER	*n* pl. -S a joining of parties in a lawsuit
JOINER	*n* pl. -S a carpenter
JOINERY	*n* pl. -ERIES the trade of a joiner
JOINING	*n* pl. -S a juncture
JOINT	*v* -ED, -ING, -S to fit together by means of a junction
JOINTER	*n* pl. -S one that joints
JOINTLY	*adv* together
JOINTURE	*v* -TURED, -TURING, -TURES to set aside property as an inheritance
JOIST	*v* -ED, -ING, -S to support with horizontal beams
JOJOBA	*n* pl. -S a small tree
JOKE	*v* JOKED, JOKING, JOKES to say something amusing
JOKER	*n* pl. -S one that jokes
JOKESTER	*n* pl. -S a practical joker
JOKING	present participle of joke
JOKINGLY	*adv* in a joking manner
JOLE	*n* pl. -S jowl
JOLLIED	past tense of jolly
JOLLIER	comparative of jolly
JOLLIES	present 3d person sing. of jolly
JOLLIEST	superlative of jolly
JOLLIFY	*v* -FIED, -FYING, -FIES to make jolly
JOLLITY	*n* pl. -TIES mirth
JOLLY	*adj* -LIER, -LIEST cheerful **JOLLILY** *adv*
JOLLY	*v* -LIED, -LYING, -LIES to put in a good humor for one's own purposes
JOLT	*v* -ED, -ING, -S to jar or shake roughly
JOLTER	*n* pl. -S one that jolts
JOLTY	*adj* JOLTIER, JOLTIEST marked by a jolting motion **JOLTILY** *adv*
JONGLEUR	*n* pl. -S a minstrel
JONQUIL	*n* pl. -S a perennial herb
JORAM	*n* pl. -S jorum
JORDAN	*n* pl. -S a type of container
JORUM	*n* pl. -S a large drinking bowl
JOSEPH	*n* pl. -S a woman's long cloak
JOSH	*v* -ED, -ING, -ES to tease
JOSHER	*n* pl. -S one that joshes
JOSS	*n* pl. -ES a Chinese idol
JOSTLE	*v* -TLED, -TLING, -TLES to bump or push roughly
JOSTLER	*n* pl. -S one that jostles
JOT	*v* JOTTED, JOTTING, JOTS to write down quickly
JOTA	*n* pl. -S a Spanish dance
JOTTING	*n* pl. -S a brief note
JOTTY	*adj* written down quickly
JOUK	*v* -ED, -ING, -S to dodge
JOULE	*n* pl. -S a unit of energy
JOUNCE	*v* JOUNCED, JOUNCING, JOUNCES to move roughly up and down

JOUNCY	*adj* JOUNCIER, JOUNCIEST marked by a jouncing motion	**JUDOKA**	*n* pl. -S a judoist
JOURNAL	*n* pl. -S a record of daily events	**JUG**	*v* JUGGED, JUGGING, JUGS to put into a jug (a large, deep container with a narrow mouth and a handle)
JOURNEY	*v* -ED, -ING, -S to travel		
JOUST	*v* -ED, -ING, -S to engage in personal combat	**JUGA**	a pl. of jugum
JOUSTER	*n* pl. -S one that jousts	**JUGAL**	*adj* pertaining to the cheek or cheekbone
JOVIAL	*adj* good-humored **JOVIALLY** *adv*	**JUGATE**	*adj* occurring in pairs
JOVIALTY	*n* pl. -TIES the quality or state of being jovial	**JUGFUL**	*n* pl. JUGFULS or JUGSFUL as much as a jug will hold
JOW	*v* -ED, -ING, -S to toll	**JUGGED**	past tense of jug
JOWL	*n* pl. -S the fleshy part under the lower jaw **JOWLED** *adj*	**JUGGING**	present participle of jug
		JUGGLE	*v* -GLED, -GLING, -GLES to perform feats of manual dexterity
JOWLY	*adj* JOWLIER, JOWLIEST having prominent jowls		
		JUGGLER	*n* pl. -S one that juggles
JOY	*v* -ED, -ING, -S to rejoice	**JUGGLERY**	*n* pl. -GLERIES the art of a juggler
JOYANCE	*n* pl. -S gladness		
JOYFUL	*adj* -FULLER, -FULLEST happy **JOYFULLY** *adv*	**JUGGLING**	*n* pl. -S jugglery
		JUGHEAD	*n* pl. -S a dolt
JOYLESS	*adj* being without gladness	**JUGSFUL**	a pl. of jugful
JOYOUS	*adj* joyful **JOYOUSLY** *adv*	**JUGULA**	pl. of jugulum
JOYPOP	*v* -POPPED, -POPPING, -POPS to use habit-forming drugs occasionally	**JUGULAR**	*n* pl. -S a vein of the neck
		JUGULATE	*v* -LATED, -LATING, -LATES to suppress a disease by extreme measures
JOYRIDE	*n* pl. -S a ride taken for pleasure		
		JUGULUM	*n* pl. -LA a part of a bird's neck
JOYRIDER	*n* pl. -S one that takes a joyride	**JUGUM**	*n* pl. -GA or -GUMS a pair of the opposite leaflets of a pinnate leaf
JOYSTICK	*n* pl. -S the control stick in an airplane		
JUBA	*n* pl. -S a lively dance	**JUICE**	*v* JUICED, JUICING, JUICES to extract the juice (the liquid part of a fruit or vegetable) from
JUBBAH	*n* pl. -S a loose outer garment		
JUBE	*n* pl. -S a platform in a church	**JUICER**	*n* pl. -S a juice extractor
JUBHAH	*n* pl. -S jubbah	**JUICY**	*adj* JUICIER, JUICIEST full of juice **JUICILY** *adv*
JUBILANT	*adj* exultant		
JUBILATE	*v* -LATED, -LATING, -LATES to exult	**JUJITSU**	*n* pl. -S a Japanese art of self-defense
JUBILE	*n* pl. -S jubilee	**JUJU**	*n* pl. -S an object regarded as having magical power
JUBILEE	*n* pl. -S a celebration		
JUDAS	*n* pl. -ES a peephole	**JUJUBE**	*n* pl. -S a fruit-flavored candy
JUDDER	*v* -ED, -ING, -S to vibrate	**JUJUISM**	*n* pl. -S the system of beliefs connected with jujus
JUDGE	*v* JUDGED, JUDGING, JUDGES to decide on critically		
		JUJUIST	*n* pl. -S a follower of jujuism
JUDGER	*n* pl. -S one that judges	**JUJUTSU**	*n* pl. -S jujitsu
JUDGMENT	*n* pl. -S an authoritative opinion	**JUKE**	*v* JUKED, JUKING, JUKES to fake out of position
JUDICIAL	*adj* pertaining to courts of law		
JUDO	*n* pl. -DOS a form of jujitsu	**JUKEBOX**	*n* pl. -ES a coin-operated phonograph
JUDOIST	*n* pl. -S one skilled in judo	**JULEP**	*n* pl. -S a sweet drink

JULIENNE   *n* pl. -S a clear soup

JUMBLE   *v* -BLED, -BLING, -BLES to mix in a disordered manner

JUMBLER   *n* pl. -S one that jumbles

JUMBO   *n* pl. -BOS a very large specimen of its kind

JUMBUCK   *n* pl. -S a sheep

JUMP   *v* -ED, -ING, -S to spring off the ground

JUMPER   *n* pl. -S one that jumps

JUMPOFF   *n* pl. -S a starting point

JUMPY   *adj* JUMPIER, JUMPIEST nervous **JUMPILY** *adv*

JUN   *n* pl. JUN a coin of North Korea

JUNCO   *n* pl. -COS or -COES a small finch

JUNCTION   *n* pl. -S a place where things join

JUNCTURE   *n* pl. -S the act of joining

JUNGLE   *n* pl. -S land covered with dense tropical vegetation

JUNGLY   *adj* -GLIER, -GLIEST resembling a jungle

JUNIOR   *n* pl. -S a person who is younger than another

JUNIPER   *n* pl. -S an evergreen tree

JUNK   *v* -ED, -ING, -S to discard as trash

JUNKER   *n* pl. -S something ready for junking

JUNKET   *v* -ED, -ING, -S to banquet

JUNKETER   *n* pl. -S one that junkets

JUNKIE   *n* pl. -S a drug addict

JUNKMAN   *n* pl. -MEN one who buys and sells junk

JUNKY   *adj* JUNKIER, JUNKIEST worthless

JUNKYARD   *n* pl. -S a place where junk is stored

JUNTA   *n* pl. -S a political or governmental council

JUNTO   *n* pl. -TOS a political faction

JUPE   *n* pl. -S a woman's jacket

JUPON   *n* pl. -S a tunic

JURA   pl. of jus

JURAL   *adj* pertaining to law **JURALLY** *adv*

JURANT   *n* pl. -S one that takes an oath

JURAT   *n* pl. -S a statement on an affidavit

JURATORY   *adj* pertaining to an oath

JUREL   *n* pl. -S a food fish

JURIDIC   *adj* pertaining to the law

JURIES   pl. of jury

JURIST   *n* pl. -S one versed in the law **JURISTIC** *adj*

JUROR   *n* pl. -S a member of a jury

JURY   *n* pl. -RIES a group of persons sworn to render a verdict

JURYMAN   *n* pl. -MEN a juror

JUS   *n* pl. JURA a legal right

JUSSIVE   *n* pl. -S a word used to express command

JUST   *v* -ED, -ING, -S to joust

JUST   *adj* JUSTER, JUSTEST acting in conformity with what is morally good

JUSTER   *n* pl. -S jouster

JUSTICE   *n* pl. -S a judge

JUSTIFY   *v* -FIED, -FYING, -FIES to show to be just, right, or valid

JUSTLE   *v* -TLED, -TLING, -TLES to jostle

JUSTLY   *adv* in a just manner

JUSTNESS   *n* pl. -ES the quality of being just

JUT   *v* JUTTED, JUTTING, JUTS to protrude

JUTE   *n* pl. -S a strong, coarse fiber

JUTTY   *v* -TIED, -TYING, -TIES to jut

JUVENAL   *n* pl. -S a young bird's plumage

JUVENILE   *n* pl. -S a young person

KA   *n* pl. -S the spiritual self of a human being in Egyptian religion

KAAS   *n* pl. KAAS kas

KAB   *n* pl. -S an ancient Hebrew unit of measure

KABAB   *n* pl. -S kabob

KABAKA   *n* pl. -S a Ugandan emperor

KABALA   *n* pl. -S cabala

KABAR   *n* pl. -S caber

KABAYA   *n* pl. -S a cotton jacket

KABBALA   *n* pl. -S cabala

KABBALAH   *n* pl. -S cabala

KABELJOU   *n* pl. -S a large food fish

KABIKI   *n* pl. -S a tropical tree

KABOB   *n* pl. -S cubes of meat cooked on a skewer

KABUKI   *n* pl. -S a form of Japanese theater

KACHINA   *n* pl. -S an ancestral spirit

KADDISH   *n* pl. -DISHIM a Jewish prayer

KADI   *n* pl. -S cadi

KAE   *n* pl. -S a bird resembling a crow

KAFFIR   *n* pl. -S kafir

KAFFIYEH   *n* pl. -S a large, square kerchief

KAFIR   *n* pl. -S a cereal grass

KAFTAN   *n* pl. -S caftan

KAGU   *n* pl. -S a flightless bird

KAHUNA   *n* pl. -S a medicine man

KAIAK   *n* pl. -S kayak

KAIF   *n* pl. -S kef

KAIL   *n* pl. -S kale

KAILYARD   *n* pl. -S kaleyard

KAIN   *n* pl. -S a tax paid in produce or livestock

KAINIT   *n* pl. -S kainite

KAINITE   *n* pl. -S a mineral salt

KAISER   *n* pl. -S an emperor

KAISERIN   *n* pl. -S a kaiser's wife

KAJEPUT   *n* pl. -S cajuput

KAKA   *n* pl. -S a parrot

KAKAPO   *n* pl. -POS a flightless parrot

KAKEMONO   *n* pl. -NOS a Japanese scroll

KAKI   *n* pl. -S a Japanese tree

KALAM   *n* pl. -S a type of Muslim theology

KALE   *n* pl. -S a variety of cabbage

KALENDS   *n* pl. KALENDS calends

KALEWIFE   *n* pl. -WIVES a female vegetable vendor

KALEYARD   *n* pl. -S a kitchen garden

KALIAN   *n* pl. -S a hookah

KALIF   *n* pl. -S caliph

KALIFATE   *n* pl. -S califate

KALIMBA   *n* pl. -S an African musical instrument

KALIPH   *n* pl. -S caliph

KALIUM   *n* pl. -S potassium

KALLIDIN   *n* pl. -S a hormone

KALMIA   *n* pl. -S an evergreen shrub

KALONG   *n* pl. -S a fruit-eating bat

KALPA   *n* pl. -S a period of time in Hindu religion

KALPAK   *n* pl. -S calpac

KALYPTRA	*n* pl. -S a thin veil	**KART**	*n* pl. -S a small motor vehicle
KAMAAINA	*n* pl. -S a longtime resident of Hawaii	**KARTING**	*n* pl. -S the sport of racing karts
KAMACITE	*n* pl. -S an alloy of nickel and iron	**KARYOTIN**	*n* pl. -S the nuclear material of a cell
KAMALA	*n* pl. -S an Asian tree	**KAS**	*n* pl. KAS a large cupboard
KAME	*n* pl. -S a mound of detrital material	**KASHA**	*n* pl. -S a cooked cereal
KAMI	*n* pl. KAMI a sacred power or force	**KASHER**	*v* -ED, -ING, -S to kosher
		KASHMIR	*n* pl. -S cashmere
		KASHRUT	*n* pl. -S kashruth
KAMIK	*n* pl. -S a type of boot	**KASHRUTH**	*n* pl. -S the Jewish dietary laws
KAMIKAZE	*n* pl. -S a plane to be flown in a suicide crash on a target	**KAT**	*n* pl. -S an evergreen shrub
KAMPONG	*n* pl. -S a small village	**KATAKANA**	*n* pl. -S a Japanese syllabic symbol
KAMSEEN	*n* pl. -S khamsin	**KATHODE**	*n* pl. -S cathode **KATHODAL, KATHODIC** *adj*
KAMSIN	*n* pl. -S khamsin		
KANA	*n* pl. -S the Japanese syllabic script	**KATION**	*n* pl. -S cation
		KATYDID	*n* pl. -S a grasshopper
KANE	*n* pl. -S kain	**KAURI**	*n* pl. -S a timber tree
KANGAROO	*n* pl. -ROOS an Australian mammal	**KAURY**	*n* pl. -RIES kauri
		KAVA	*n* pl. -S a tropical shrub
KANJI	*n* pl. -S a system of Japanese writing	**KAVASS**	*n* pl. -ES a Turkish policeman
		KAY	*n* pl. KAYS the letter K
KANTAR	*n* pl. -S a unit of weight	**KAYAK**	*n* pl. -S an Eskimo canoe
KANTELE	*n* pl. -S a type of harp	**KAYAKER**	*n* pl. -S one that rides in a kayak
KAOLIANG	*n* pl. -S an Asian sorghum		
KAOLIN	*n* pl. -S a fine white clay **KAOLINIC** *adj*	**KAYLES**	*n/pl* a British game
		KAYO	*v* -ED, -ING, -S or -ES to knock out
KAOLINE	*n* pl. -S kaolin		
KAON	*n* pl. -S a type of meson	**KAZOO**	*n* pl. -ZOOS a toy musical instrument
KAPA	*n* pl. -S a coarse cloth		
KAPH	*n* pl. -S a Hebrew letter	**KEA**	*n* pl. -S a parrot
KAPOK	*n* pl. -S a mass of silky fibers	**KEBAB**	*n* pl. -S kabob
KAPPA	*n* pl. -S a Greek letter	**KEBAR**	*n* pl. -S caber
KAPUT	*adj* ruined	**KEBBIE**	*n* pl. -S a rough walking stick
KAPUTT	*adj* kaput	**KEBBOCK**	*n* pl. -S kebbuck
KARAKUL	*n* pl. -S an Asian sheep	**KEBBUCK**	*n* pl. -S a whole cheese
KARAT	*n* pl. -S a unit of quality for gold	**KEBLAH**	*n* pl. -S kiblah
KARATE	*n* pl. -S a Japanese art of self-defense	**KEBOB**	*n* pl. -S kabob
		KECK	*v* -ED, -ING, -S to retch
KARMA	*n* pl. -S the force generated by a person's actions **KARMIC** *adj*	**KECKLE**	*v* -LED, -LING, -LES to wind with rope to prevent chafing
KARN	*n* pl. -S cairn	**KEDDAH**	*n* pl. -S an enclosure for elephants
KAROO	*n* pl. -ROOS karroo		
KAROSS	*n* pl. -ES an African garment	**KEDGE**	*v* KEDGED, KEDGING, KEDGES to move a vessel with the use of an anchor
KARROO	*n* pl. -ROOS a dry plateau		
KARST	*n* pl. -S a limestone region **KARSTIC** *adj*	**KEDGEREE**	*n* pl. -S a food in India

KEEF	*n* pl. -S kef
KEEK	*v* -ED, -ING, -S to peep
KEEL	*v* -ED, -ING, -S to capsize
KEELAGE	*n* pl. -S the amount paid to keep a boat in a harbor
KEELBOAT	*n* pl. -S a freight boat
KEELHALE	*v* -HALED, -HALING, -HALES to keelhaul
KEELHAUL	*v* -ED, -ING, -S to rebuke severely
KEELLESS	*adj* having no keel (the main structural part of a ship)
KEELSON	*n* pl. -S a beam in a ship
KEEN	*adj* KEENER, KEENEST enthusiastic
KEEN	*v* -ED, -ING, -S to wail loudly over the dead
KEENER	*n* pl. -S one that keens
KEENLY	*adv* in a keen manner
KEENNESS	*n* pl. -ES sharpness
KEEP	*v* KEPT, KEEPING, KEEPS to continue to possess **KEEPABLE** *adj*
KEEPER	*n* pl. -S one that keeps
KEEPING	*n* pl. -S custody
KEEPSAKE	*n* pl. -S a memento
KEESHOND	*n* pl. -HONDS or -HONDEN a small, heavy-coated dog
KEESTER	*n* pl. -S keister
KEET	*n* pl. -S a young guinea fowl
KEEVE	*n* pl. -S a tub or vat
KEF	*n* pl. -S hemp smoked to produce euphoria
KEFIR	*n* pl. -S a fermented beverage made from cow's milk
KEG	*n* pl. -S a small barrel
KEGELER	*n* pl. -S kegler
KEGLER	*n* pl. -S a bowler
KEGLING	*n* pl. -S bowling
KEIR	*n* pl. -S kier
KEISTER	*n* pl. -S the buttocks
KEITLOA	*n* pl. -S a rhinoceros
KELOID	*n* pl. -S a scar caused by excessive growth of fibrous tissue **KELOIDAL** *adj*
KELP	*v* -ED, -ING, -S to burn a type of seaweed
KELPIE	*n* pl. -S a water sprite
KELPY	*n* pl. -PIES kelpie

KELSON	*n* pl. -S keelson
KELTER	*n* pl. -S kilter
KELVIN	*n* pl. -S a unit of temperature
KEMP	*n* pl. -S a champion
KEMPT	*adj* neatly kept
KEN	*v* KENNED or KENT, KENNING, KENS to know
KENAF	*n* pl. -S an East Indian plant
KENCH	*n* pl. -ES a bin for salting fish
KENDO	*n* pl. -DOS a Japanese sport
KENNED	a past tense of ken
KENNEL	*v* -NELED, -NELING, -NELS or -NELLED, -NELLING, -NELS to keep in a shelter for dogs
KENNING	*n* pl. -S a metaphorical compound word or phrase
KENO	*n* pl. -NOS a game of chance
KENOSIS	*n* pl. -SISES the incarnation of Christ **KENOTIC** *adj*
KENOTRON	*n* pl. -S a type of diode
KENT	a past tense of ken
KEP	*v* KEPPED, KEPPEN or KIPPEN, KEPPING, KEPS to catch
KEPHALIN	*n* pl. -S cephalin
KEPI	*n* pl. -S a type of cap
KEPPED	past tense of kep
KEPPEN	a past participle of kep
KEPPING	present participle of kep
KEPT	past tense of keep
KERAMIC	*n* pl. -S ceramic
KERATIN	*n* pl. -S a fibrous protein
KERATOID	*adj* horny
KERATOMA	*n* pl. -MAS or -MATA a skin disease
KERATOSE	*adj* of or resembling horny tissue
KERB	*v* -ED, -ING, -S to provide with curbing
KERCHIEF	*n* pl. -CHIEFS or -CHIEVES a cloth worn as a head covering
KERCHOO	*interj* ahchoo
KERF	*v* -ED, -ING, -S to make an incision with a cutting tool
KERMES	*n* pl. KERMES a red dye
KERMESS	*n* pl. -ES kermis
KERMIS	*n* pl. -MISES a festival
KERN	*v* -ED, -ING, -S to be formed with a projecting typeface

KERNE   n pl. -S a medieval foot soldier

KERNEL   v -NELED, -NELING, -NELS or -NELLED, -NELLING, -NELS to envelop as a kernel (the inner part of a nut)

KERNITE   n pl. -S a mineral

KEROGEN   n pl. -S a substance found in shale

KEROSENE   n pl. -S a fuel oil

KEROSINE   n pl. -S kerosene

KERPLUNK   adv with a muffled sound

KERRIA   n pl. -S a Chinese shrub

KERRY   n pl. -RIES one of an Irish breed of cattle

KERSEY   n pl. -SEYS a woolen cloth

KERYGMA   n pl. -MATA the preaching of the gospel

KESTREL   n pl. -S a small falcon

KETCH   n pl. -ES a sailing vessel

KETCHUP   n pl. -S a spicy tomato sauce

KETENE   n pl. -S a toxic gas

KETO   adj of or pertaining to ketone

KETONE   n pl. -S a type of chemical compound **KETONIC** adj

KETOSE   n pl. -S a simple sugar

KETOSIS   n pl. -TOSES a buildup of ketones in the body **KETOTIC** adj

KETTLE   n pl. -S a vessel for boiling liquids

KEVEL   n pl. -S a belaying cleat or peg

KEVIL   n pl. -S kevel

KEX   n pl. -ES a dry, hollow stalk

KEY   v -ED, -ING, -S to provide with a key (a device used to turn the bolt in a lock)

KEYBOARD   v -ED, -ING, -S to operate a machine by means of a keyset

KEYHOLE   n pl. -S a hole for a key

KEYLESS   adj being without a key

KEYNOTE   v -NOTED, -NOTING, -NOTES to deliver the main speech at a function

KEYNOTER   n pl. -S one that keynotes

KEYPUNCH   v -ED, -ING, -ES to perforate with a machine

KEYSET   n pl. -S a system of finger levers

KEYSTER   n pl. -S keister

KEYSTONE   n pl. -S the central stone of an arch

KEYWAY   n pl. -WAYS a slot for a key

KEYWORD   n pl. -S a significant word

KHADDAR   n pl. -S a cotton cloth

KHADI   n pl. -S khaddar

KHAKI   n pl. -S a durable cloth

KHALIF   n pl. -S caliph

KHALIFA   n pl. -S caliph

KHAMSEEN   n pl. -S khamsin

KHAMSIN   n pl. -S a hot, dry wind

KHAN   n pl. -S an Asian ruler

KHANATE   n pl. -S the domain of a khan

KHAT   n pl. -S kat

KHAZEN   n pl. -ZENS or -ZENIM hazzan

KHEDA   n pl. -S keddah

KHEDAH   n pl. -S keddah

KHEDIVE   n pl. -S a Turkish viceroy **KHEDIVAL** adj

KHI   n pl. -S chi

KHIRKAH   n pl. -S a patchwork garment

KIANG   n pl. -S a wild ass

KIAUGH   n pl. -S trouble; worry

KIBBLE   v -BLED, -BLING, -BLES to grind coarsely

KIBBUTZ   n pl. -BUTZIM a collective farm in Israel

KIBE   n pl. -S a sore caused by exposure to cold

KIBITZ   v -ED, -ING, -ES to meddle

KIBITZER   n pl. -S one that kibitzes

KIBLA   n pl. -S kiblah

KIBLAH   n pl. -S the direction toward which Muslims face while praying

KIBOSH   v -ED, -ING, -ES to stop

KICK   v -ED, -ING, -S to strike out with the foot or feet

KICKBACK   n pl. -S a strong reaction

KICKER   n pl. -S one that kicks

KICKOFF   n pl. -S the kick that begins play in football

KICKSHAW   n pl. -S a trifle or trinket

KICKUP   n pl. -S a noisy argument

KID   v KIDDED, KIDDING, KIDS to tease

KIDDER   n pl. -S one that kids

KIDDIE   *n* pl. -S a small child

KIDDIES   pl. of kiddy

KIDDING   present participle of kid

KIDDISH   *adj* childish

KIDDO   *n* pl. -DOS or -DOES — used as a form of familiar address

KIDDUSH   *n* pl. -ES a Jewish prayer

KIDDY   *n* pl. -DIES kiddie

KIDLIKE   *adj* resembling a child

KIDNAP   *v* -NAPED, -NAPING, -NAPS or -NAPPED, -NAPPING, -NAPS to take a person by force and often for ransom

KIDNAPER   *n* pl. -S one that kidnaps

KIDNAPPER   *n* pl. -S kidnaper

KIDNAPPING present participle of kidnap

KIDNEY   *n* pl. -NEYS a bodily organ

KIDSKIN   *n* pl. -S a type of leather

KIEF   *n* pl. -S kef

KIELBASA   *n* pl. -BASAS or -BASY a smoked sausage

KIER   *n* pl. -S a vat for boiling and dyeing fabrics

KIESTER   *n* pl. -S keister

KIF   *n* pl. -S kef

KIKE   *n* pl. -S a Jew — usually taken to be offensive

KILIM   *n* pl. -S an oriental tapestry

KILL   *v* -ED, -ING, -S to cause to die

KILLDEE   *n* pl. -S killdeer

KILLDEER   *n* pl. -S a wading bird

KILLER   *n* pl. -S one that kills

KILLICK   *n* pl. -S a small anchor

KILLING   *n* pl. -S a sudden notable success

KILLJOY   *n* pl. -JOYS one who spoils the fun of others

KILLOCK   *n* pl. -S killick

KILN   *v* -ED, -ING, -S to bake in a type of oven

KILO   *n* pl. KILOS a kilogram or kilometer

KILOBAR   *n* pl. -S a unit of atmospheric pressure

KILOBIT   *n* pl. -S a unit of computer information

KILOGRAM   *n* pl. -S a unit of mass and weight

KILOMOLE   *n* pl. -S one thousand moles

KILORAD   *n* pl. -S a unit of nuclear radiation

KILOTON   *n* pl. -S a unit of weight

KILOVOLT   *n* pl. -S a unit of electromotive force

KILOWATT   *n* pl. -S a unit of power

KILT   *v* -ED, -ING, -S to make creases or pleats in

KILTER   *n* pl. -S good condition

KILTIE   *n* pl. -S one who wears a kilt (a type of skirt)

KILTING   *n* pl. -S an arrangement of kilt pleats

KILTY   *n* pl. KILTIES kiltie

KIMONO   *n* pl. -NOS a loose robe
KIMONOED *adj*

KIN   *n* pl. -S a group of persons of common ancestry

KINASE   *n* pl. -S an enzyme

KIND   *adj* KINDER, KINDEST having a gentle, giving nature

KIND   *n* pl. -S a class of similar or related objects or individuals

KINDLE   *v* -DLED, -DLING, -DLES to cause to burn

KINDLER   *n* pl. -S one that kindles

KINDLESS   *adj* lacking kindness

KINDLING   *n* pl. -S material that is easily ignited

KINDLY   *adj* -LIER, -LIEST kind

KINDNESS   *n* pl. -ES the quality of being kind

KINDRED   *n* pl. -S a natural grouping

KINE   *n* pl. -S a type of television tube

KINEMA   *n* pl. -S cinema

KINESICS   *n/pl* the study of body motion in relation to communication

KINESIS   *n* pl. -NESES a type of movement

KINETIC   *adj* pertaining to motion

KINETICS   *n/pl* a branch of science dealing with motion

KINETIN   *n* pl. -S a substance that increases plant growth

KINFOLK   *n/pl* relatives

KINFOLKS   *n/pl* kinfolk

KING   *v* -ED, -ING, -S to reign as king (a male monarch)

KINGBIRD   *n* pl. -S an American bird

KINGBOLT   *n* pl. -S a kingpin

KINGCUP   *n* pl. -S a marsh plant

KINGDOM   *n* pl. -S the area ruled by a king

KINGFISH   *n* pl. -ES a marine food fish

KINGHOOD   *n* pl. -S the office of a king

KINGLESS   *adj* having no king

KINGLET   *n* pl. -S a king who rules over a small area

KINGLIKE   *adj* resembling a king

KINGLY   *adj* -LIER, -LIEST of or befitting a king

KINGPIN   *n* pl. -S a central bolt connecting an axle to a vehicle

KINGPOST   *n* pl. -S a supporting structure of a roof

KINGSHIP   *n* pl. -S the power or position of a king

KINGSIDE   *n* pl. -S a part of a chessboard

KINGWOOD   *n* pl. -S a hardwood tree

KININ   *n* pl. -S a hormone

KINK   *v* -ED, -ING, -S to form a tight curl or bend in

KINKAJOU   *n* pl. -S an arboreal mammal

KINKY   *adj* KINKIER, KINKIEST tightly curled **KINKILY** *adv*

KINO   *n* pl. -NOS a gum resin

KINSFOLK   *n/pl* kinfolk

KINSHIP   *n* pl. -S relationship

KINSMAN   *n* pl. -MEN a male relative

KIOSK   *n* pl. -S an open booth

KIP   *v* KIPPED, KIPPING, KIPS to sleep

KIPPEN   a past participle of kep

KIPPER   *v* -ED, -ING, -S to cure fish by salting and smoking

KIPPING   present participle of kip

KIPSKIN   *n* pl. -S an animal hide that has not been tanned

KIRIGAMI   *n* pl. -S the Japanese art of folding paper

KIRK   *n* pl. -S a church

KIRKMAN   *n* pl. -MEN a member of a church

KIRMESS   *n* pl. -ES kermis

KIRN   *v* -ED, -ING, -S to churn

KIRSCH   *n* pl. -ES a kind of brandy

KIRTLE   *n* pl. -S a man's tunic or coat **KIRTLED** *adj*

KISHKA   *n* pl. -S kishke

KISHKE   *n* pl. -S a sausage

KISMAT   *n* pl. -S kismet

KISMET   *n* pl. -S destiny **KISMETIC** *adj*

KISS   *v* -ED, -ING, -ES to touch with the lips as a sign of affection **KISSABLE** *adj* **KISSABLY** *adv*

KISSER   *n* pl. -S one that kisses

KIST   *n* pl. -S a chest, box, or coffin

KISTFUL   *n* pl. -S as much as a kist can hold

KIT   *v* KITTED, KITTING, KITS to equip

KITCHEN   *n* pl. -S a room where food is cooked

KITE   *v* KITED, KITING, KITES to obtain money or credit fraudulently

KITER   *n* pl. -S one that kites

KITH   *n* pl. -S one's friends and neighbors

KITHARA   *n* pl. -S cithara

KITHE   *v* KITHED, KITHING, KITHES to make known

KITING   present participle of kite

KITLING   *n* pl. -S a young animal

KITSCH   *n* pl. -ES faddish art or literature **KITSCHY** *adj*

KITTED   past tense of kit

KITTEL   *n* pl. KITTEL a Jewish ceremonial robe

KITTEN   *v* -ED, -ING, -S to bear kittens (young cats)

KITTIES   pl. of kitty

KITTING   present participle of kit

KITTLE   *v* -TLED, -TLING, -TLES to tickle

KITTLE   *adj* -TLER, -TLEST ticklish

KITTY   *n* pl. -TIES a kitten or cat

KIVA   *n* pl. -S an underground ceremonial chamber

KIWI   *n* pl. -S a flightless bird

KLATCH   *n* pl. -ES a social gathering

KLATSCH   *n* pl. -ES klatch

KLAVERN   *n* pl. -S a local branch of the Ku Klux Klan

KLAXON   *n* pl. -S a low-pitched horn

KLEAGLE   *n* pl. -S an official in the Ku Klux Klan

KLEPHT   *n* pl. -S a Greek guerrilla **KLEPHTIC** *adj*

KLONG	*n* pl. -S a canal
KLOOF	*n* pl. -S a ravine
KLUDGE	*n* pl. -S a system composed of ill-fitting components
KLUTZ	*n* pl. -ES a clumsy person
KLUTZY	*adj* KLUTZIER, KLUTZIEST clumsy
KLYSTRON	*n* pl. -S a type of electron tube
KNACK	*v* -ED, -ING, -S to strike sharply
KNACKER	*n* pl. -S one that buys old livestock
KNACKERY	*n* pl. -ERIES the place of business of a knacker
KNAP	*v* KNAPPED, KNAPPING, KNAPS to strike sharply
KNAPPER	*n* pl. -S one that knaps
KNAPSACK	*n* pl. -S a bag carried on the back
KNAPWEED	*n* pl. -S a meadow plant
KNAR	*n* pl. -S a bump on a tree **KNARRED, KNARRY** *adj*
KNAVE	*n* pl. -S a dishonest person **KNAVISH** *adj*
KNAVERY	*n* pl. -ERIES trickery
KNAWEL	*n* pl. -S a Eurasian plant
KNEAD	*v* -ED, -ING, -S to work into a uniform mixture with the hands
KNEADER	*n* pl. -S one that kneads
KNEE	*v* KNEED, KNEEING, KNEES to strike with the knee (a joint of the leg)
KNEECAP	*n* pl. -S a bone at the front of the knee
KNEEHOLE	*n* pl. -S a space for the knees
KNEEL	*v* KNELT or KNEELED, KNEELING, KNEELS to rest on the knees
KNEELER	*n* pl. -S one that kneels
KNEEPAD	*n* pl. -S a covering for a knee
KNEEPAN	*n* pl. -S the kneecap
KNELL	*v* -ED, -ING, -S to sound a bell
KNELT	a past tense of kneel
KNEW	past tense of know
KNICKERS	*n/pl* loose-fitting pants gathered at the knee
KNIFE	*n* pl. KNIVES a sharp-edged instrument used for cutting
KNIFE	*v* KNIFED, KNIFING, KNIFES to cut with a knife

KNIFER	*n* pl. -S one that knifes
KNIGHT	*v* -ED, -ING, -S to make a knight (a medieval gentleman-soldier) of
KNIGHTLY	*adj* of or befitting a knight
KNISH	*n* pl. -ES dough stuffed with filling and fried
KNIT	*v* KNITTED, KNITTING, KNITS to make a fabric or garment by joining loops of yarn
KNITTER	*n* pl. -S one that knits
KNITTING	*n* pl. -S work done by a knitter
KNITWEAR	*n* pl. -S knitted clothing
KNIVES	pl. of knife
KNOB	*n* pl. -S a rounded protuberance **KNOBBED, KNOBLIKE** *adj*
KNOBBY	*adj* -BIER, -BIEST full of knobs
KNOCK	*v* -ED, -ING, -S to strike sharply
KNOCKER	*n* pl. -S one that knocks
KNOCKOFF	*n* pl. -S a copy that sells for less than the original
KNOCKOUT	*n* pl. -S a blow that induces unconsciousness
KNOLL	*v* -ED, -ING, -S to knell
KNOLLER	*n* pl. -S one that knolls
KNOLLY	*adj* hilly
KNOP	*n* pl. -S a knob **KNOPPED** *adj*
KNOSP	*n* pl. -S a knob
KNOT	*v* KNOTTED, KNOTTING, KNOTS to tie in a knot (a closed loop)
KNOTHOLE	*n* pl. -S a hole in a plank
KNOTLESS	*adj* having no knots
KNOTLIKE	*adj* resembling a knot
KNOTTER	*n* pl. -S one that knots
KNOTTY	*adj* -TIER, -TIEST full of knots **KNOTTILY** *adv*
KNOTWEED	*n* pl. -S a common weed
KNOUT	*v* -ED, -ING, -S to flog with a leather whip
KNOW	*v* KNEW, KNOWN, KNOWING, KNOWS to have a true understanding of **KNOWABLE** *adj*
KNOWER	*n* pl. -S one that knows
KNOWING	*adj* -INGER, -INGEST astute
KNOWING	*n* pl. -S knowledge
KNOWN	*n* pl. -S a mathematical quanity whose value is given

KNUCKLE *v* -LED, -LING, -LES to hit with the knuckles (the joints of the fingers)

KNUCKLER *n* pl. -S a type of baseball pitch

KNUCKLY *adj* -LIER, -LIEST having prominent knuckles

KNUR *n* pl. -S a bump on a tree

KNURL *v* -ED, -ING, -S to make grooves or ridges in

KNURLY *adj* KNURLIER, KNURLIEST gnarly

KOA *n* pl. -S a timber tree

KOALA *n* pl. -S an Australian mammal

KOAN *n* pl. -S a paradox meditated on by Buddhist monks

KOBOLD *n* pl. -S an elf

KOEL *n* pl. -S an Australian bird

KOHL *n* pl. -S a type of eye makeup

KOHLRABI *n* pl. -ES a variety of cabbage

KOINE *n* pl. -S a type of dialect

KOKANEE *n* pl. -S a food fish

KOLA *n* pl. -S cola

KOLACKY *n* pl. KOLACKY a kind of pastry

KOLHOZ *n* pl. -HOZY or -HOZES kolkhoz

KOLINSKI *n* pl. -ES kolinsky

KOLINSKY *n* pl. -SKIES an Asian mink

KOLKHOS *n* pl. -KHOSY or -KHOSES kolkhoz

KOLKHOZ *n* pl. -KHOZY or -KHOZES a collective farm in Russia

KOLKOZ *n* pl. -KOZY or -KOZES kolkhoz

KOLO *n* pl. -LOS a European folk dance

KOMATIK *n* pl. -S an Eskimo sledge

KOMONDOR *n* pl. -DORS, -DOROK, or -DOROCK a large, shaggy-coated dog

KOODOO *n* pl. -DOOS kudu

KOOK *n* pl. -S an eccentric person

KOOKIE *adj* KOOKIER, KOOKIEST kooky

KOOKY *adj* KOOKIER, KOOKIEST eccentric

KOP *n* pl. -S a hill

KOPECK *n* pl. -S a Russian coin

KOPEK *n* pl. -S kopeck

KOPH *n* pl. -S a Hebrew letter

KOPJE *n* pl. -S a small hill

KOPPA *n* pl. -S a Greek letter

KOPPIE *n* pl. -S kopje

KOR *n* pl. -S a Hebrew unit of measure

KORUNA *n* pl. KORUNAS, KORUNY, or KORUN a monetary unit of Czechoslovakia

KOS *n* pl. KOS a land measure in India

KOSHER *v* -ED, -ING, -S to make fit to be eaten according to Jewish dietary laws

KOSS *n* pl. KOSS kos

KOTO *n* pl. -TOS a musical instrument

KOTOW *v* -ED, -ING, -S to kowtow

KOTOWER *n* pl. -S one that kotows

KOUMIS *n* pl. -MISES koumiss

KOUMISS *n* pl. -ES a beverage made from camel's milk

KOUMYS *n* pl. -ES koumiss

KOUMYSS *n* pl. -ES koumiss

KOUSSO *n* pl. -SOS cusso

KOWTOW *v* -ED, -ING, -S to behave in a servile manner

KOWTOWER *n* pl. -S one that kowtows

KRAAL *v* -ED, -ING, -S to pen in a type of enclosure

KRAFT *n* pl. -S a strong paper

KRAIT *n* pl. -S a venomous snake

KRAKEN *n* pl. -S a legendary sea monster

KRATER *n* pl. -S a type of vase

KRAUT *n* pl. -S sauerkraut

KREMLIN *n* pl. -S a Russian citadel

KREUTZER *n* pl. -S an Austrian coin

KREUZER *n* pl. -S kreutzer

KRILL *n* pl. -S an aggregate of small marine crustaceans

KRIMMER *n* pl. -S a kind of fur

KRIS *n* pl. -ES a short sword

KRONA *n* pl. KRONUR a monetary unit of Iceland

KRONA *n* pl. KRONOR a monetary unit of Sweden

KRONE *n* pl. KRONER a monetary unit of Denmark

KRONE *n* pl. KRONEN a former monetary unit of Austria

KRONOR pl. of krona

KRONUR pl. of krona

KROON   *n* pl. KROONS or KROONI a former monetary unit of Estonia

KRUBI   *n* pl. -S a tropical plant

KRUBUT   *n* pl. -S krubi

KRULLER   *n* pl. -S cruller

KRYOLITE   *n* pl. -S cryolite

KRYOLITH   *n* pl. -S cryolite

KRYPTON   *n* pl. -S a gaseous element

KUCHEN   *n* pl. KUCHEN a coffee cake

KUDO   *n* pl. -DOS award; honor

KUDU   *n* pl. -S a large antelope

KUDZU   *n* pl. -S an Asian vine

KUE   *n* pl. -S the letter Q

KULAK   *n* pl. -LAKS or -LAKI a rich Russian peasant

KULTUR   *n* pl. -S culture; civilization

KUMISS   *n* pl. -ES koumiss

KUMMEL   *n* pl. -S a type of liqueur

KUMQUAT   *n* pl. -S a citrus fruit

KUMYS   *n* pl. -ES koumiss

KUNZITE   *n* pl. -S a mineral

KURBASH   *v* -ED, -ING, -ES to flog with a leather whip

KURGAN   *n* pl. -S a mound of earth over a grave

KURTA   *n* pl. -S a shirt worn in India

KURTOSIS   *n* pl. -SISES the relative degree of curvature in a statistical curve

KURU   *n* pl. -S a disease of the nervous system

KUSSO   *n* pl. -SOS cusso

KVAS   *n* pl. -ES kvass

KVASS   *n* pl. -ES a Russian beer

KVETCH   *v* -ED, -ING, -ES to complain

KWACHA   *n* pl. KWACHA a monetary unit of Zambia

KYACK   *n* pl. -S a packsack

KYANISE   *v* -ISED, -ISING, -ISES to kyanize

KYANITE   *n* pl. -S cyanite

KYANIZE   *v* -IZED, -IZING, -IZES to treat wood with a type of preservative

KYAR   *n* pl. -S coir

KYAT   *n* pl. -S a monetary unit of Burma

KYLIX   *n* pl. -LIKES a drinking vessel

KYMOGRAM   *n* pl. -S a record of fluid pressure

KYPHOSIS   *n* pl. -PHOSES abnormal curvature of the spine **KYPHOTIC** *adj*

KYRIE   *n* pl. -S a religious petition for mercy

KYTE   *n* pl. -S the stomach

KYTHE   *v* KYTHED, KYTHING, KYTHES to kithe

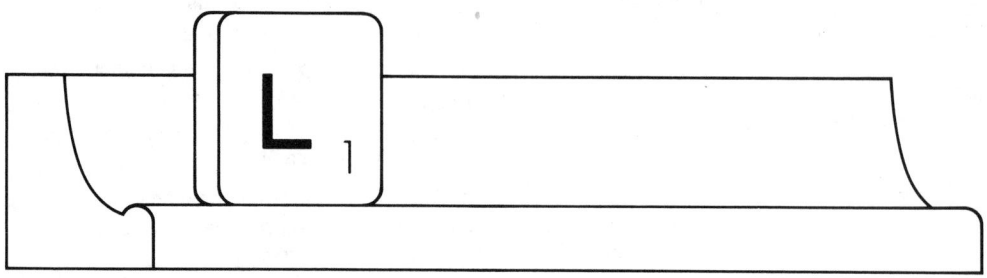

LA   *n* pl. -S the sixth tone of the diatonic musical scale

LAAGER   *v* -ED, -ING, -S to form a defensive encampment

LAB   *n* pl. -S a laboratory

LABARUM   *n* pl. -RA or -RUMS an ecclesiastical banner

LABDANUM   *n* pl. -S a fragrant resin

LABEL   *v* -BELED, -BELING, -BELS or -BELLED, -BELLING, -BELS to describe or designate

LABELER   *n* pl. -S one that labels

LABELLA   pl. of labellum

LABELLED   a past tense of label

LABELLER   *n* pl. -S labeler

LABELLING   a present participle of label

LABELLUM   *n* pl. -LA the lower petal of an orchid

LABIA   pl. of labium

LABIAL   *n* pl. -S a labially produced sound

LABIALLY   *adv* by means of the lips

LABIATE   *n* pl. -S a labiated plant

LABIATED   *adj* having corollas that are divided into two liplike parts

LABILE   *adj* likely to change

LABILITY   *n* pl. -TIES the state of being labile

LABIUM   *n* pl. -BIA a fold of the vulva

LABOR   *v* -ED, -ING, -S to work

LABORER   *n* pl. -S one that labors

LABORITE   *n* pl. -S a supporter of labor interests

LABOUR   *v* -ED, -ING, -S to labor

LABOURER   *n* pl. -S laborer

LABRA   a pl. of labrum

LABRET   *n* pl. -S an ornament worn in a perforation of the lip

LABROID   *n* pl. -S a marine fish

LABRUM   *n* pl. -BRA or -BRUMS a lip or liplike structure

LABURNUM   *n* pl. -S an ornamental tree

LAC   *n* pl. -S a resinous substance secreted by certain insects

LACE   *v* LACED, LACING, LACES to fasten by means of a lace (a cord for drawing together two edges)

LACELESS   *adj* lacking lace

LACELIKE   *adj* resembling lace

LACER   *n* pl. -S one that laces

LACERATE   *v* -ATED, -ATING, -ATES to tear roughly

LACERTID   *n* pl. -S a type of lizard

LACEWING   *n* pl. -S a winged insect

LACEWOOD   *n* pl. -S an Australian tree

LACEWORK   *n* pl. -S a delicate openwork fabric

LACEY   *adj* LACIER, LACIEST lacy

LACHES   *n* pl. LACHES undue delay in asserting a legal right

LACIER   comparative of lace

LACIEST   superlative of lace

LACILY   *adv* in a lacy manner

LACINESS   *n* pl. -ES the quality of being lacy

LACING   *n* pl. -S a contrasting marginal band of color

LACK   *v* -ED, -ING, -S to be without

LACKADAY   *interj* — used to express regret

LACKER   *v* -ED, -ING, -S to lacquer

LACKEY   *v* -ED, -ING, -S to act in a servile manner

LACONIC   *adj* using a minimum of words

LACONISM   *n* pl. -S brevity of expression

LACQUER   *v* -ED, -ING, -S to coat with a glossy substance

LACQUEY   *v* -ED, -ING, -S to lackey

LACRIMAL   *n* pl. -S a type of vase

LACROSSE   *n* pl. -S a type of ball game

LACTAM   *n* pl. -S a chemical compound

LACTARY   *adj* pertaining to milk

LACTASE   *n* pl. -S an enzyme

LACTATE   *v* -TATED, -TATING, -TATES to secrete milk

LACTEAL   *n* pl. -S a lymphatic vessel

LACTEAN   *adj* lacteous

LACTEOUS   *adj* resembling milk

LACTIC   *adj* derived from milk

LACTONE   *n* pl. -S any of a group of esters **LACTONIC** *adj*

LACTOSE   *n* pl. -S a lactic sugar

LACUNA   *n* pl. -NAE or -NAS an empty space or missing part **LACUNAL, LACUNARY, LACUNATE** *adj*

LACUNAR   *n* pl. -NARS or -NARIA a ceiling with recessed panels

LACUNE   *n* pl. -S lacuna

LACUNOSE   *adj* marked by shallow depressions

LACY   *adj* LACIER, LACIEST resembling lacework

LAD   *n* pl. -S a boy or youth

LADANUM   *n* pl. -S labdanum

LADDER   *v* -ED, -ING, -S to cause a run in a stocking

LADDIE   *n* pl. -S a lad

LADE   *v* LADED, LADEN, LADING, LADES to load with a cargo

LADEN   *v* -ED, -ING, -S to lade

LADER   *n* pl. -S one that lades

LADIES   pl. of lady

LADING   *n* pl. -S cargo; freight

LADINO   *n* pl. -NOS a fast-growing clover

LADLE   *v* -DLED, -DLING, -DLES to lift out with a ladle (a type of spoon)

LADLEFUL   *n* pl. -S as much as a ladle will hold

LADLER   *n* pl. -S one that ladles

LADRON   *n* pl. -S ladrone

LADRONE   *n* pl. -S a thief

LADY   *n* pl. -DIES a woman of refinement and gentle manners

LADYBIRD   *n* pl. -S a ladybug

LADYBUG   *n* pl. -S a small beetle

LADYFISH   *n* pl. -ES a bonefish

LADYHOOD   *n* pl. -S the state of being a lady

LADYISH   *adj* somewhat ladylike

LADYKIN   *n* pl. -S a small lady

LADYLIKE   *adj* resembling or suitable to a lady

LADYLOVE   *n* pl. -S a sweetheart

LADYPALM   *n* pl. -S a palm tree

LADYSHIP   *n* pl. -S the condition of being a lady

LAEVO   *adj* levo

LAG   *v* LAGGED, LAGGING, LAGS to stay or fall behind

LAGAN   *n* pl. -S goods thrown into the sea with a buoy attached to enable recovery

LAGEND   *n* pl. -S lagan

LAGER   *v* -ED, -ING, -S to laager

LAGGARD   *n* pl. -S one that lags

LAGGED   past tense of lag

LAGGER   *n* pl. -S a laggard

LAGGING   *n* pl. -S an insulating material

LAGNAPPE   *n* pl. -S a small gift given to a customer with his purchase

LAGOON   *n* pl. -S a shallow body of water **LAGOONAL** *adj*

LAGUNA   *n* pl. -S lagoon

LAGUNE   *n* pl. -S lagoon

LAIC   *n* pl. -S a layman **LAICAL** *adj* **LAICALLY** *adv*

LAICH   *n* pl. -S laigh

LAICISE   *v* -ICISED, -ICISING, -ICISES to laicize

LAICISM   *n* pl. -S a political system free from clerical control

LAICIZE *v* -ICIZED, -ICIZING, -ICIZES to free from clerical control

LAID a past tense of lay

LAIGH *n* pl. -S a lowland

LAIN past participle of lie

LAIR *v* -ED, -ING, -S to live in a lair (a wild animal's resting or dwelling place)

LAIRD *n* pl. -S the owner of a landed estate **LAIRDLY** *adj*

LAITANCE *n* pl. -S a milky deposit on the surface of fresh concrete

LAITH *adj* loath **LAITHLY** *adv*

LAITY *n* pl. -ITIES the nonclerical membership of a religious faith

LAKE *n* pl. -S a sizable inland body of water

LAKED *adj* subjected to the process of laking

LAKEPORT *n* pl. -S a city located on the shore of a lake

LAKER *n* pl. -S a lake fish

LAKESIDE *n* pl. -S the land along the edge of a lake

LAKH *n* pl. -S the sum of one hundred thousand

LAKING *n* pl. -S the reddening of blood plasma by the release of hemoglobin from the red corpuscles

LAKY *adj* LAKIER, LAKIEST of the color of blood

LALL *v* -ED, -ING, -S to articulate the letter *r* as *l*

LALLAN *n* pl. -S a lowland

LALLAND *n* pl. -S a lowland

LALLYGAG *v* -GAGGED, -GAGGING, -GAGS to dawdle

LAM *v* LAMMED, LAMMING, LAMS to flee hastily

LAMA *n* pl. -S a Buddhist monk

LAMASERY *n* pl. -SERIES a monastery of lamas

LAMB *v* -ED, -ING, -S to give birth to a lamb (a young sheep)

LAMBAST *v* -ED, -ING, -S to lambaste

LAMBASTE *v* -BASTED, -BASTING, -BASTES to beat severely

LAMBDA *n* pl. -S a Greek letter **LAMBDOID** *adj*

LAMBENCY *n* pl. -CIES the quality or an instance of being lambent

LAMBENT *adj* flickering lightly and gently over a surface

LAMBER *n* pl. -S a ewe that is lambing

LAMBERT *n* pl. -S a unit of brightness

LAMBIE *n* pl. -S a lambkin

LAMBKILL *n* pl. -S an evergreen shrub

LAMBKIN *n* pl. -S a small lamb

LAMBLIKE *adj* resembling a lamb

LAMBSKIN *n* pl. -S the skin of a lamb

LAME *adj* LAMER, LAMEST physically disabled

LAME *v* LAMED, LAMING, LAMES to make lame

LAMED *n* pl. -S a Hebrew letter

LAMEDH *n* pl. -S lamed

LAMELLA *n* pl. -LAE or -LAS a thin plate, scale, or membrane **LAMELLAR** *adj*

LAMELY *adv* in a lame manner

LAMENESS *n* pl. -ES the state of being lame

LAMENT *v* -ED, -ING, -S to express sorrow or regret for

LAMENTER *n* pl. -S one that laments

LAMER comparative of lame

LAMEST superlative of lame

LAMIA *n* pl. -MIAS or -MIAE a female demon

LAMINA *n* pl. -NAE or -NAS a thin plate, scale, or layer **LAMINAL, LAMINAR, LAMINARY** *adj*

LAMINATE *v* -NATED, -NATING, -NATES to compress into a thin plate

LAMING present participle of lame

LAMINOSE *adj* composed of laminae

LAMINOUS *adj* laminose

LAMISTER *n* pl. -S lamster

LAMMED past tense of lam

LAMMING present participle of lam

LAMP *v* -ED, -ING, -S to look at

LAMPAD *n* pl. -S a candlestick

LAMPAS *n* pl. -ES inflammation of the roof of a horse's mouth

LAMPERS *n* pl. -ES lampas

LAMPION *n* pl. -S a type of light-generating device

LAMPOON *v* -ED, -ING, -S to ridicule in a satirical composition

LAMPPOST   *n* pl. -S a post supporting a streetlight

LAMPREY   *n* pl. -PREYS an eellike fish

LAMPYRID   *n* pl. -S any of a family of beetles

LAMSTER   *n* pl. -S a fugitive

LANAI   *n* pl. -S a veranda

LANATE   *adj* covered with wool

LANATED   *adj* lanate

LANCE   *v* LANCED, LANCING, LANCES to pierce with a lance (a spearlike weapon)

LANCELET   *n* pl. -S a small marine organism

LANCER   *n* pl. -S a cavalryman armed with a lance

LANCET   *n* pl. -S a narrow, pointed arch **LANCETED** *adj*

LANCIERS   *n* pl. LANCIERS a French dance

LANCING   present participle of lance

LAND   *v* -ED, -ING, -S to set down upon land (solid ground)

LANDAU   *n* pl. -S a type of carriage

LANDER   *n* pl. -S one that lands

LANDFALL   *n* pl. -S a sighting or approach to land

LANDFILL   *n* pl. -S a system of waste disposal

LANDFORM   *n* pl. -S a natural feature of the earth's surface

LANDING   *n* pl. -S a place for discharging or taking on passengers or cargo

LANDLADY   *n* pl. -DIES a female landlord

LANDLER   *n* pl. -S a slow Austrian dance

LANDLESS   *adj* owning no land

LANDLORD   *n* pl. -S one who owns and rents out real estate

LANDMAN   *n* pl. -MEN one who lives and works on land

LANDMARK   *n* pl. -S an object that marks a boundary line

LANDMASS   *n* pl. -ES a large area of land

LANDMEN   pl. of landman

LANDSIDE   *n* pl. -S a part of a plow

LANDSKIP   *n* pl. -S landscape

LANDSLEIT   pl. of landsman

LANDSLID   past tense of landslide (to win an election by an overwhelming majority)

LANDSLIP   *n* pl. -S the fall of a mass of earth

LANDSMAN   *n* pl. LANDSLEIT a fellow Jew coming from one's own section of Eastern Europe

LANDSMAN   *n* pl. -MEN landman

LANDWARD   *adv* toward the land

LANE   *n* pl. -S a narrow passageway

LANELY   *adj* lonely

LANG   *adj* long

LANGLAUF   *n* pl. -S a cross-country ski run

LANGLEY   *n* pl. -LEYS a unit of illumination

LANGRAGE   *n* pl. -S a shot formerly used in naval warfare

LANGREL   *n* pl. -S langrage

LANGSHAN   *n* pl. -S any of a breed of large domestic fowl

LANGSYNE   *n* pl. -S time long past

LANGUAGE   *n* pl. -S a body of words and systems serving as a means of communication

LANGUE   *n* pl. -S a type of language

LANGUET   *n* pl. -S a tonguelike part

LANGUID   *adj* lacking in vigor or vitality

LANGUISH   *v* -ED, -ING, -ES to lose vigor or vitality

LANGUOR   *n* pl. -S the state of being languid

LANGUR   *n* pl. -S an Asian monkey

LANIARD   *n* pl. -S lanyard

LANIARY   *n* pl. -ARIES a cuspid

LANITAL   *n* pl. -S a woollike fiber

LANK   *adj* LANKER, LANKEST long and slender **LANKLY** *adv*

LANKNESS   *n* pl. -ES the state of being lank

LANKY   *adj* LANKIER, LANKIEST ungracefully tall and thin **LANKILY** *adv*

LANNER   *n* pl. -S a falcon of Europe and Asia

LANNERET   *n* pl. -S a male lanner

LANOLIN   *n* pl. -S a fatty substance obtained from wool

LANOLINE   *n* pl. -S lanolin

LANOSE   *adj* lanate

LANOSITY   *n* pl. -TIES the state of being lanose

LANTANA   *n* pl. -S a tropical shrub

LANTERN n pl. -S a protective case for a light

LANTHORN n pl. -S a lantern

LANUGO n pl. -GOS fine, soft hair

LANYARD n pl. -S a fastening rope on a ship

LAP v LAPPED, LAPPING, LAPS to fold over or around something

LAPBOARD n pl. -S a flat board used as a table or desk

LAPDOG n pl. -S a small dog

LAPEL n pl. -S an extension of the collar of a garment **LAPELLED** adj

LAPFUL n pl. -S as much as the lap can hold

LAPIDARY n pl. -DARIES one who works with precious stones

LAPIDATE v -DATED, -DATING, -DATES to hurl stones at

LAPIDES pl. of lapis

LAPIDIFY v -FIED, -FYING, -FIES to turn to stone

LAPIDIST n pl. -S a lapidary

LAPILLUS n pl. -LI a small fragment of lava

LAPIN n pl. -S a rabbit

LAPIS n pl. LAPIDES a stone

LAPIS n pl. -PISES a mineral

LAPPED past tense of lap

LAPPER v -ED, -ING, -S to lopper

LAPPET n pl. -S a decorative flap on a garment **LAPPETED** adj

LAPPING present participle of lap

LAPSE v LAPSED, LAPSING, LAPSES to fall from a previous standard **LAPSABLE, LAPSIBLE** adj

LAPSER n pl. -S one that lapses

LAPSUS n pl. LAPSUS a mistake

LAPWING n pl. -S a shore bird

LAR n pl. -ES or -S a tutelary god or spirit of an ancient Roman household

LARBOARD n pl. -S the left-hand side of a ship

LARCENER n pl. -S one that commits larceny

LARCENY n pl. -NIES the felonious taking and removal of another's personal goods

LARCH n pl. -ES a coniferous tree

LARD v -ED, -ING, -S to coat with lard (the melted fat of hogs)

LARDER n pl. -S a place where food is stored

LARDIER comparative of lardy

LARDIEST superlative of lardy

LARDLIKE adj resembling lard

LARDON n pl. -S a thin slice of bacon or pork

LARDOON n pl. -S lardon

LARDY adj LARDIER, LARDIEST resembling lard

LARES a pl. of lar

LARGE adj LARGER, LARGEST of considerable size or quantity **LARGELY** adv

LARGE n pl. -S generosity

LARGESS n pl. -ES generosity

LARGESSE n pl. -S largess

LARGISH adj somewhat large

LARGO n pl. -GOS a slow musical movement

LARIAT v -ED, -ING, -S to lasso

LARINE adj resembling a gull

LARK v -ED, -ING, -S to behave playfully

LARKER n pl. -S one that larks

LARKIER comparative of larky

LARKIEST superlative of larky

LARKSOME adj playful

LARKSPUR n pl. -S a flowering plant

LARKY adj LARKIER, LARKIEST playful

LARRIGAN n pl. -S a type of moccasin

LARRIKIN n pl. -S a rowdy

LARRUP v -ED, -ING, -S to beat or thrash

LARRUPER n pl. -S one that larrups

LARUM n pl. -S an alarm

LARVA n pl. -VAE or -VAS the immature form of various insects and animals when newly hatched **LARVAL** adj

LARYNX n pl. LARYNGES or LARYNXES an organ of the respiratory tract **LARYNGAL** adj

LASAGNA n pl. -S an Italian baked dish

LASAGNE n pl. -S lasagna

LASCAR n pl. -S an East Indian sailor

LASE v LASED, LASING, LASES to function as a laser

LASER   *n* pl. -S a device that amplifies light waves

LASH   *v* -ED, -ING, -ES to strike with a whip

LASHER   *n* pl. -S one that lashes

LASHING   *n* pl. -S a flogging

LASHINS   *n/pl* an abundance

LASHKAR   *n* pl. -S lascar

LASING   present participle of lase

LASS   *n* pl. -ES a young woman

LASSIE   *n* pl. -S a lass

LASSO   *v* -ED, -ING, -S or -ES to catch with a lasso (a long rope with a running noose)

LASSOER   *n* pl. -S one that lassos

LAST   *v* -ED, -ING, -S to continue in existence

LASTER   *n* pl. -S one that lasts

LASTING   *n* pl. -S a durable fabric

LASTLY   *adv* in conclusion

LAT   *n* pl. LATS or LATI a former monetary unit of Latvia

LATAKIA   *n* pl. -S a variety of Turkish tobacco

LATCH   *v* -ED, -ING, -ES to close with a type of fastening device

LATCHET   *n* pl. -S a thong used to fasten a shoe

LATCHKEY   *n* pl. -KEYS a key for opening a latched door

LATE   *adj* LATER, LATEST coming or occurring after the expected time

LATED   *adj* belated

LATEEN   *n* pl. -S a sailing vessel

LATEENER   *n* pl. -S a lateen

LATELY   *adv* not long ago

LATEN   *v* -ED, -ING, -S to become late

LATENCY   *n* pl. -CIES the state of being present but not manifest

LATENESS   *n* pl. -ES the state of being late

LATENT   *n* pl. -S a barely visible fingerprint that can be developed for study

LATENTLY   *adv* dormantly

LATER   comparative of late

LATERAD   *adv* toward the side

LATERAL   *v* -ED, -ING, -S to throw a sideward pass in football

LATERITE   *n* pl. -S a type of soil

LATEST   *n* pl. -S the most recent development

LATEWOOD   *n* pl. -S a part of an annual ring of wood

LATEX   *n* pl. LATICES or LATEXES a milky liquid of certain plants

LATH   *v* -ED, -ING, -S to cover with laths (thin strips of wood)

LATHE   *v* LATHED, LATHING, LATHES to cut or shape on a type of machine

LATHER   *v* -ED, -ING, -S to cover with lather (a light foam)

LATHERER   *n* pl. -S one that lathers

LATHERY   *adj* covered with lather

LATHIER   comparative of lathy

LATHIEST   superlative of lathy

LATHING   *n* pl. -S work made of or using laths

LATHWORK   *n* pl. -S lathing

LATHY   *adj* LATHIER, LATHIEST long and slender

LATI   a pl. of lat

LATICES   a pl. of latex

LATIGO   *n* pl. -GOS or -GOES a strap used to fasten a saddle

LATINITY   *n* pl. -TIES a manner of writing or speaking Latin

LATINIZE   *v* -IZED, -IZING, -IZES to translate into Latin

LATISH   *adj* somewhat late

LATITUDE   *n* pl. -S freedom from narrow restrictions

LATOSOL   *n* pl. -S a tropical soil

LATRIA   *n* pl. -S the supreme worship given to God only, in Roman Catholicism

LATRINE   *n* pl. -S a type of toilet

LATTEN   *n* pl. -S a brass-like alloy

LATTER   *adj* being the second mentioned of two

LATTERLY   *adv* lately

LATTICE   *v* -TICED, -TICING, -TICES to form a structure consisting of interlaced strips of material

LATTIN   *n* pl. -S latten

LAUAN   *n* pl. -S a Philippine timber

LAUD   *v* -ED, -ING, -S to praise

LAUDABLE *adj* worthy of praise **LAUDABLY** *adv*

LAUDANUM *n* pl. -S a type of opium preparation

LAUDATOR *n* pl. -S a lauder

LAUDER *n* pl. -S one that lauds

LAUGH *v* -ED, -ING, -S to express emotion, typically mirth, by a series of inarticulate sounds

LAUGHER *n* pl. -S one that laughs

LAUGHING *n* pl. -S laughter

LAUGHTER *n* pl. -S the act or sound of one that laughs

LAUNCE *n* pl. -S a marine fish

LAUNCH *v* -ED, -ING, -ES to set in motion

LAUNCHER *n* pl. -S a launching device

LAUNDER *v* -ED, -ING, -S to wash clothes

LAUNDRY *n* pl. -DRIES a collection of clothes to be washed

LAURA *n* pl. -RAS or -RAE a type of monastery

LAUREATE *v* -ATED, -ATING, -ATES to laurel

LAUREL *v* -RELED, -RELING, -RELS or -RELLED, -RELLING, -RELS to crown with a wreath of evergreen leaves

LAUWINE *n* pl. -S an avalanche

LAVA *n* pl. -S molten rock that issues from a volcano

LAVABO *n* pl. -BOES or -BOS a ceremonial washing in certain Christian churches

LAVAGE *n* pl. -S a washing

LAVALAVA *n* pl. -S a Polynesian garment

LAVALIER *n* pl. -S a pendant worn on a chain around the neck

LAVALIKE *adj* resembling lava

LAVATION *n* pl. -S the act of washing

LAVATORY *n* pl. -RIES a room equipped with washing and toilet facilities

LAVE *v* LAVED, LAVING, LAVES to wash

LAVEER *v* -ED, -ING, -S to sail against the wind

LAVENDER *v* -ED, -ING, -S to sprinkle with a type of perfume

LAVER *n* pl. -S a vessel used for ancient Hebrew ceremonial washings

LAVEROCK *n* pl. -S a songbird

LAVING present participle of lave

LAVISH *adj* -ISHER, -ISHEST expending or giving in great amounts **LAVISHLY** *adv*

LAVISH *v* -ED, -ING, -ES to expend or give in great amounts

LAVISHER *n* pl. -S one that lavishes

LAVROCK *n* pl. -S laverock

LAW *v* -ED, -ING, -S to take a complaint to court for settlement

LAWFUL *adj* allowed by law (the body of rules governing the affairs of a community) **LAWFULLY** *adv*

LAWGIVER *n* pl. -S one who institutes a legal system

LAWINE *n* pl. -S lauwine

LAWING *n* pl. -S a bill for food or drink in a tavern

LAWLESS *adj* having no system of laws

LAWLIKE *adj* being like the law

LAWMAKER *n* pl. -S a legislator

LAWMAN *n* pl. -MEN a law-enforcement officer

LAWN *n* pl. -S an area of grass-covered land **LAWNY** *adj*

LAWSUIT *n* pl. -S a legal action

LAWYER *n* pl. -S a member of the legal profession **LAWYERLY** *adj*

LAX *adj* LAXER, LAXEST not strict or stringent

LAXATION *n* pl. -S the act of relaxing

LAXATIVE *n* pl. -S a drug that stimulates evacuation of the bowels

LAXITY *n* pl. -ITIES the state of being lax

LAXLY *adv* in a lax manner

LAXNESS *n* pl. -ES laxity

LAY *v* LAID or LAYED, LAYING, LAYS to deposit as a wager

LAYABOUT *n* pl. -S a lazy person

LAYAWAY *n* pl. -AWAYS an item that has been reserved with a down payment

LAYER *v* -ED, -ING, -S to form a layer (a single thickness, coating, or covering)

LAYERAGE *n* pl. -S a method of plant propagation

LAYERING *n* pl. -S layerage

LAYETTE *n* pl. -S an outfit of clothing and equipment for a newborn child

LAYMAN	*n* pl. -MEN a member of the laity	**LEADLESS**	*adj* having no lead
LAYOFF	*n* pl. -S the suspension or dismissal of employees	**LEADOFF**	*n* pl. -S an opening play or move
LAYOUT	*n* pl. -S an arrangement or plan	**LEADSMAN**	*n* pl. -MEN a seaman who measures the depth of water
LAYOVER	*n* pl. -S a stopover	**LEADWORK**	*n* pl. -S something made of lead
LAYWOMAN	*n* pl. -WOMEN a female member of the laity	**LEADWORT**	*n* pl. -S a tropical plant
LAZAR	*n* pl. -S a beggar afflicted with a loathsome disease	**LEADY**	*adj* LEADIER, LEADIEST resembling lead
LAZARET	*n* pl. -S a hospital treating contagious diseases	**LEAF**	*n* pl. LEAVES a usually green, flattened organ of vascular plants
LAZE	*v* LAZED, LAZING, LAZES to pass time lazily	**LEAF**	*v* -ED, -ING, -S to turn pages rapidly
LAZIED	past tense of lazy	**LEAFAGE**	*n* pl. -S foliage
LAZIER	comparative of lazy	**LEAFIER**	comparative of leafy
LAZIES	present 3d person sing. of lazy	**LEAFIEST**	superlative of leafy
LAZIEST	superlative of lazy	**LEAFLESS**	*adj* having no leaves
LAZILY	*adv* in a lazy manner	**LEAFLET**	*n* pl. -S a small printed sheet of paper
LAZINESS	*n* pl. -ES the state of being lazy	**LEAFLIKE**	*adj* resembling a leaf
LAZING	present participle of laze	**LEAFWORM**	*n* pl. -S a moth larva that feeds on leaves
LAZULI	*n* pl. -S a mineral		
LAZULITE	*n* pl. -S a mineral	**LEAFY**	*adj* LEAFIER, LEAFIEST covered with leaves
LAZURITE	*n* pl. -S a mineral		
LAZY	*adj* LAZIER, LAZIEST disinclined to work or exertion	**LEAGUE**	*v* LEAGUED, LEAGUING, LEAGUES to come together for a common purpose
LAZY	*v* LAZIED, LAZYING, LAZIES to move or lie lazily	**LEAGUER**	*v* -ED, -ING, -S to besiege
LAZYISH	*adj* somewhat lazy	**LEAK**	*v* -ED, -ING, -S to permit the escape of something through a breach or flaw
LEA	*n* pl. -S a meadow		
LEACH	*v* -ED, -ING, -ES to subject to the filtering action of a liquid		
LEACHATE	*n* pl. -S a solution obtained by leaching	**LEAKAGE**	*n* pl. -S the act or an instance of leaking
LEACHER	*n* pl. -S one that leaches	**LEAKER**	*n* pl. -S one that leaks
LEACHY	*adj* LEACHIER, LEACHIEST porous	**LEAKLESS**	*adj* designed not to leak
		LEAKY	*adj* LEAKIER, LEAKIEST tending to leak **LEAKILY** *adv*
LEAD	*v* LED, LEADING, LEADS to show the way to by going in advance	**LEAL**	*adj* loyal **LEALLY** *adv*
		LEALTY	*n* pl. -TIES loyalty
LEAD	*v* -ED, -ING, -S to cover with lead (a heavy metallic element)	**LEAN**	*v* LEANED or LEANT, LEANING, LEANS to deviate from a vertical position
LEADEN	*adj* oppressively heavy **LEADENLY** *adv*		
LEADER	*n* pl. -S one that leads or guides	**LEAN**	*adj* LEANER, LEANEST having little fat **LEANLY** *adv*
		LEANING	*n* pl. -S a tendency
LEADIER	comparative of leady	**LEANNESS**	*n* pl. -ES the state of being lean
LEADIEST	superlative of leady	**LEANT**	a past tense of lean
LEADING	*n* pl. -S a covering or border of lead	**LEAP**	*v* LEAPED or LEAPT, LEAPING, LEAPS to spring off the ground

LEAPER *n* pl. -S one that leaps

LEAPFROG *v* -FROGGED, -FROGGING, -FROGS to jump over with the legs wide apart

LEAPT a past tense of leap

LEAR *n* pl. -S learning

LEARIER comparative of leary

LEARIEST superlative of leary

LEARN *v* LEARNED or LEARNT, LEARNING, LEARNS to gain knowledge by experience, instruction, or study

LEARNER *n* pl. -S one that learns

LEARNING *n* pl. -S acquired knowledge

LEARNT a past tense of learn

LEARY *adj* LEARIER, LEARIEST leery

LEASE *v* LEASED, LEASING, LEASES to grant temporary use of in exchange for rent **LEASABLE** *adj*

LEASER *n* pl. -S one that leases

LEASH *v* -ED, -ING, -ES to restrain an animal with a line or thong

LEASING *n* pl. -S a falsehood

LEAST *n* pl. -S something that is smallest in size or degree

LEATHER *v* -ED, -ING, -S to cover with leather (the dressed or tanned hide of an animal)

LEATHERN *adj* made of leather

LEATHERY *adj* resembling leather

LEAVE *v* LEFT, LEAVING, LEAVES to go away from

LEAVED *adj* having a leaf or leaves

LEAVEN *v* -ED, -ING, -S to produce fermentation in

LEAVER *n* pl. -S one that leaves

LEAVES pl. of leaf

LEAVING *n* pl. -S a leftover

LEAVY *adj* LEAVIER, LEAVIEST leafy

LEBEN *n* pl. -S a type of liquid food

LECH *n* pl. -ES letch

LECHAYIM *n* pl. -S lehayim

LECHER *v* -ED, -ING, -S to engage in lechery

LECHERY *n* pl. -ERIES excessive sexual indulgence

LECITHIN *n* pl. -S any of a group of fatty substances found in plant and animal tissues

LECTERN *n* pl. -S a reading desk

LECTION *n* pl. -S a portion of sacred writing read in a church service

LECTOR *n* pl. -S a low-ranking church officer

LECTURE *v* -TURED, -TURING, -TURES to expound on a specific subject

LECTURER *n* pl. -S one that lectures

LECYTHUS *n* pl. -THI lekythos

LED past tense of lead

LEDGE *n* pl. -S a narrow, shelflike projection

LEDGER *n* pl. -S an account book of final entry

LEDGY *adj* LEDGIER, LEDGIEST abounding in ledges

LEE *n* pl. -S shelter from the wind

LEEBOARD *n* pl. -S a board attached to a sailing vessel to prevent leeway

LEECH *v* -ED, -ING, -ES to cling to and feed upon or drain

LEEK *n* pl. -S an herb used in cookery

LEER *v* -ED, -ING, -S to look with a sideways glance

LEERY *adj* LEERIER, LEERIEST suspicious **LEERILY** *adv*

LEET *n* pl. -S a former English court for petty offenses

LEEWARD *n* pl. -S the direction toward which the wind is blowing

LEEWAY *n* pl. -WAYS the lateral drift of a ship

LEFT *adj* LEFTER, LEFTEST pertaining to the side of the body to the north when one faces east

LEFT *n* pl. -S the left side or hand

LEFTISM *n* pl. -S a liberal political philosophy

LEFTIST *n* pl. -S an advocate of leftism

LEFTOVER *n* pl. -S an unused or unconsumed portion

LEFTWARD *adv* toward the left

LEFTWING *adj* favoring leftism

LEFTY *n* pl. LEFTIES a left-handed person

LEG *v* LEGGED, LEGGING, LEGS to move with the legs (appendages that serve as a means of support and locomotion)

LEGACY *n* pl. -CIES something bequeathed

LEGAL	*n* pl. -S an authorized investment that may be made by investors such as savings banks	**LEGLIKE**	*adj* resembling a leg
		LEGMAN	*n* pl. -MEN a newspaperman assigned to gather information
LEGALESE	*n* pl. -S the specialized language of lawyers	**LEGROOM**	*n* pl. -S space in which to extend the legs
LEGALISE	*v* -ISED, -ISING, -ISES to legalize	**LEGUME**	*n* pl. -S a type of plant
LEGALISM	*n* pl. -S strict conformity to the law	**LEGUMIN**	*n* pl. -S a plant protein
		LEGWORK	*n* pl. -S work that involves extensive walking
LEGALIST	*n* pl. -S an adherent of legalism		
LEGALITY	*n* pl. -TIES the condition of being lawful	**LEHAYIM**	*n* pl. -S a traditional Jewish toast
LEGALIZE	*v* -IZED, -IZING, -IZES to make lawful	**LEHR**	*n* pl. -S a type of oven
		LEHUA	*n* pl. -S a tropical tree
LEGALLY	*adv* in a lawful manner	**LEI**	*n* pl. -S a wreath of flowers
LEGATE	*v* -GATED, -GATING, -GATES to bequeath	**LEISTER**	*v* -ED, -ING, -S to spear with a three-pronged fishing implement
LEGATEE	*n* pl. -S the inheritor of a legacy	**LEISURE**	*n* pl. -S freedom from the demands of work or duty **LEISURED** *adj*
LEGATINE	*adj* pertaining to an official envoy		
LEGATING	present participle of legate	**LEK**	*n* pl. -S a monetary unit of Albania
LEGATION	*n* pl. -S the sending of an official envoy	**LEKYTHOS**	*n* pl. -THOI an oil jar used in ancient Greece
LEGATO	*n* pl. -TOS a smooth and flowing musical style	**LEKYTHUS**	*n* pl. -THI lekythos
		LEMAN	*n* pl. -S a lover
LEGATOR	*n* pl. -S one that legates	**LEMMA**	*n* pl. -MAS or -MATA a type of proposition in logic
LEGEND	*n* pl. -S an unverified story from earlier times		
		LEMMING	*n* pl. -S a mouselike rodent
LEGENDRY	*n* pl. -RIES a collection of legends	**LEMNISCI**	*n/pl* bands of nerve fibers
LEGER	*n* pl. -S fishing bait made to lie on the bottom	**LEMON**	*n* pl. -S a citrus fruit **LEMONISH, LEMONY** *adj*
		LEMONADE	*n* pl. -S a beverage
LEGERITY	*n* pl. -TIES quickness of the mind or body	**LEMPIRA**	*n* pl. -S a monetary unit of Honduras
LEGES	pl. of lex	**LEMUR**	*n* pl. -S an arboreal mammal related to the monkeys
LEGGED	past tense of leg		
LEGGIER	comparative of leggy	**LEMURES**	*n/pl* the ghosts of the dead in ancient Roman religion
LEGGIEST	superlative of leggy		
LEGGIN	*n* pl. -S legging	**LEMUROID**	*n* pl. -S a lemur
LEGGING	*n* pl. -S a covering for the leg	**LEND**	*v* LENT, LENDING, LENDS to give the temporary use of
LEGGY	*adj* -GIER, -GIEST having long legs		
		LENDER	*n* pl. -S one that lends
LEGHORN	*n* pl. -S a smooth, plaited straw	**LENES**	pl. of lenis
LEGIBLE	*adj* capable of being read **LEGIBLY** *adv*	**LENGTH**	*n* pl. -S the longer or longest dimension of an object
LEGION	*n* pl. -S a large military force	**LENGTHEN**	*v* -ED, -ING, -S to make or become longer
LEGIST	*n* pl. -S one learned or skilled in the law		
		LENGTHY	*adj* LENGTHIER, LENGTHIEST very long
LEGIT	*n* pl. -S legitimate drama		
LEGLESS	*adj* having no legs	**LENIENCE**	*n* pl. -S leniency

LENIENCY *n* pl. -CIES the quality of being lenient

LENIENT *adj* gently tolerant

LENIS *n* pl. LENES a speech sound pronounced with little or no aspiration

LENITIVE *n* pl. -S a soothing medicine

LENITY *n* pl. -TIES leniency

LENO *n* pl. -NOS a style of weaving

LENS *n* pl. -ES a piece of transparent material used in changing the convergence of light rays **LENSED, LENSLESS** *adj*

LENSE *n* pl. -S lens

LENT past tense of lend

LENTANDO *adv* becoming slower — used as a musical direction

LENTEN *adj* meager

LENTIC *adj* pertaining to still water

LENTICEL *n* pl. -S a mass of cells on a plant stem

LENTIGO *n* pl. -TIGINES a freckle

LENTIL *n* pl. -S a Eurasian annual plant

LENTISK *n* pl. -S an evergreen tree

LENTO *n* pl. -TOS a slow musical movement

LENTOID *adj* lens-shaped

LEONE *n* pl. -S a monetary unit of Sierra Leone

LEONINE *adj* pertaining to a lion

LEOPARD *n* pl. -S a large, carnivorous feline mammal

LEOTARD *n* pl. -S a close-fitting garment

LEPER *n* pl. -S one affected with leprosy

LEPIDOTE *adj* covered with small scales

LEPORID *n* pl. -S a gnawing mammal

LEPORINE *adj* resembling a rabbit or hare

LEPROSE *adj* leprous

LEPROSY *n* pl. -SIES a chronic disease characterized by skin lesions and deformities

LEPROTIC *adj* leprous

LEPROUS *adj* affected with leprosy

LEPTON *n* pl. -TA a monetary unit of Greece

LEPTON *n* pl. -S an atomic particle **LEPTONIC** *adj*

LESBIAN *n* pl. -S a female homosexual

LESION *n* pl. -S an abnormal change in the structure of an organ or tissue

LESS *adj* LESSER, LEAST not as great in quantity or degree

LESSEE *n* pl. -S one to whom a lease is granted

LESSEN *v* -ED, -ING, -S to make or become less

LESSER *adj* not as large or important

LESSON *v* -ED, -ING, -S to instruct

LESSOR *n* pl. -S one that grants a lease

LEST *conj* for fear that

LET *v* LETTED, LETTING, LETS to hinder

LETCH *n* pl. -ES a strong sexual craving

LETDOWN *n* pl. -S a decrease

LETHAL *n* pl. -S a death-causing genetic defect

LETHALLY *adv* in a deadly manner

LETHARGY *n* pl. -GIES drowsiness; sluggishness

LETHE *n* pl. -S forgetfulness **LETHEAN** *adj*

LETTED past tense of let

LETTER *v* -ED, -ING, -S to mark with letters (written symbols representing speech sounds)

LETTERER *n* pl. -S one that letters

LETTING present participle of let

LETTUCE *n* pl. -S an herb cultivated as a salad plant

LETUP *n* pl. -S a lessening or relaxation

LEU *n* pl. LEI a monetary unit of Rumania

LEUCEMIA *n* pl. -S leukemia **LEUCEMIC** *adj*

LEUCIN *n* pl. -S leucine

LEUCINE *n* pl. -S an amino acid

LEUCITE *n* pl. -S a mineral **LEUCITIC** *adj*

LEUCOMA *n* pl. -S leukoma

LEUD *n* pl. -S or -ES a feudal vassal

LEUKEMIA *n* pl. -S a disease of the blood-forming organs

LEUKEMIC *n* pl. -S one affected with leukemia

LEUKOMA *n* pl. -S an opacity of the cornea

LEUKON   *n* pl. -S a bodily organ consisting of the white blood cells

LEUKOSIS   *n* pl. -KOSES leukemia **LEUKOTIC** *adj*

LEV   *n* pl. LEVA a monetary unit of Bulgaria

LEVANT   *v* -ED, -ING, -S to avoid a debt

LEVANTER   *n* pl. -S an easterly Mediterranean wind

LEVATOR   *n* pl. -ES or -S a muscle that raises an organ or part

LEVEE   *v* LEVEED, LEVEEING, LEVEES to provide with an embankment

LEVEL   *v* -ELED, -ELING, -ELS or -ELLED, -ELLING, -ELS to make even

LEVELER   *n* pl. -S one that levels

LEVELLER   *n* pl. -S leveler

LEVELLING   present participle of level

LEVELLY   *adv* in an even manner

LEVER   *v* -ED, -ING, -S to move with a lever (a rigid body used to lift weight)

LEVERAGE   *v* -AGED, -AGING, -AGES to provide with a type of economic advantage

LEVERET   *n* pl. -S a young hare

LEVIABLE   *adj* liable to be levied

LEVIED   past tense of levy

LEVIER   *n* pl. -S one that levies

LEVIES   present 3d person sing. of levy

LEVIGATE   *v* -GATED, -GATING, -GATES to reduce to a fine powder

LEVIN   *n* pl. -S lightning

LEVIRATE   *n* pl. -S the custom of marrying the widow of one's brother

LEVITATE   *v* -TATED, -TATING, -TATES to rise and float in the air

LEVITY   *n* pl. -TIES conduct characterized by a lack of seriousness

LEVO   *adj* turning toward the left

LEVOGYRE   *adj* turning toward the left

LEVULIN   *n* pl. -S a chemical compound

LEVULOSE   *n* pl. -S a very sweet sugar

LEVY   *v* LEVIED, LEVYING, LEVIES to impose or collect by legal authority

LEWD   *adj* LEWDER, LEWDEST obscene **LEWDLY** *adv*

LEWDNESS   *n* pl. -ES the state of being lewd

LEWIS   *n* pl. -ISES a hoisting device

LEWISITE   *n* pl. -S a vesicant liquid

LEWISSON   *n* pl. -S lewis

LEX   *n* pl. LEGES law

LEXICAL   *adj* pertaining to the words of a language

LEXICON   *n* pl. -CA or -CONS a dictionary

LEY   *n* pl. LEYS lea

LI   *n* pl. -S a Chinese unit of distance

LIABLE   *adj* subject or susceptible to something possible or likely

LIAISE   *v* LIAISED, LIAISING, LIAISES to establish liaison

LIAISON   *n* pl. -S a means for maintaining communication

LIANA   *n* pl. -S a tropical vine

LIANE   *n* pl. -S liana

LIANG   *n* pl. -S a Chinese unit of weight

LIANOID   *adj* pertaining to a liana

LIAR   *n* pl. -S one that speaks falsely

LIARD   *n* pl. -S a former silver coin of France

LIB   *n* pl. -S liberation

LIBATION   *n* pl. -S a ceremonial pouring of a liquid

LIBBER   *n* pl. -S one that supports a liberation movement

LIBECCIO   *n* pl. -CIOS a southwest wind

LIBEL   *v* -BELED, -BELING, -BELS or -BELLED, -BELLING, -BELS to make or publish a defamatory statement about

LIBELANT   *n* pl. -S a plaintiff in a type of lawsuit

LIBELEE   *n* pl. -S a defendant in a type of lawsuit

LIBELER   *n* pl. -S one that libels

LIBELIST   *n* pl. -S a libeler

LIBELLED   a past tense of libel

LIBELLEE   *n* pl. -S libelee

LIBELLER   *n* pl. -S libeler

LIBELLING   a present participle of libel

LIBELOUS   *adj* defamatory

LIBER   *n* pl. LIBRI or LIBERS a book of public records

LIBERAL   *n* pl. -S a person favorable to progress or reform

LIBERATE   *v* -ATED, -ATING, -ATES to set free

LIBERTY   *n* pl. -TIES the state of being free

LIBIDO   *n* pl. -DOS the energy derived from instinctual biological drives

LIBRA   *n* pl. -BRAE an ancient Roman unit of weight

LIBRA   *n* pl. -S a former gold coin of Peru

LIBRARY   *n* pl. -BRARIES a place where literary materials are kept for reading and reference

LIBRATE   *v* -BRATED, -BRATING, -BRATES to move from side to side

LIBRETTO   *n* pl. -TOS or -TI the text of an opera

LIBRI   a pl. of liber

LICE   pl. of louse

LICENCE   *v* -CENCED, -CENCING, -CENCES to license

LICENCEE   *n* pl. -S licensee

LICENCER   *n* pl. -S licenser

LICENSE   *v* -CENSED, -CENSING, -CENSES to issue or grant authoritative permission to

LICENSEE   *n* pl. -S one that is licensed

LICENSER   *n* pl. -S one that licenses

LICENSOR   *n* pl. -S licenser

LICHEE   *n* pl. -S litchi

LICHEN   *v* -ED, -ING, -S to cover with lichens (flowerless plants)

LICHENIN   *n* pl. -S a chemical compound

LICHI   *n* pl. -S litchi

LICHT   *v* -ED, -ING, -S to light

LICHTLY   *adv* lightly

LICIT   *adj* lawful **LICITLY** *adv*

LICK   *v* -ED, -ING, -S to pass the tongue over the surface of

LICKER   *n* pl. -S one that licks

LICKING   *n* pl. -S a thrashing or beating

LICKSPIT   *n* pl. -S a fawning person

LICORICE   *n* pl. -S a perennial herb

LICTOR   *n* pl. -S a magistrate's attendant in ancient Rome

LID   *v* LIDDED, LIDDING, LIDS to provide with a lid (a movable cover)

LIDAR   *n* pl. -S an electronic locating device

LIDLESS   *adj* having no lid

LIDO   *n* pl. -DOS a fashionable beach resort

LIE   *v* LIED, LYING, LIES to speak falsely

LIE   *v* LAY, LAIN, LYING, LIES to be in or get into a horizontal position

LIED   *n* pl. LIEDER a German song

LIEF   *adj* LIEFER, LIEFEST willing **LIEFLY** *adv*

LIEGE   *n* pl. -S a feudal lord

LIEGEMAN   *n* pl. -MEN a feudal vassal

LIEN   *n* pl. -S a legal right to hold or sell a debtor's property

LIENABLE   *adj* capable of being subjected to a lien

LIENAL   *adj* pertaining to the spleen

LIENTERY   *n* pl. -TERIES a form of diarrhea

LIER   *n* pl. -S one that lies or reclines

LIERNE   *n* pl. -S a connecting part in Gothic vaulting

LIEU   *n* pl. -S place; stead

LIEVE   *adv* LIEVER, LIEVEST gladly

LIFE   *n* pl. LIVES the quality that distinguishes animals and plants from inanimate matter

LIFEBOAT   *n* pl. -S a small rescue boat

LIFEFUL   *adj* full of life

LIFELESS   *adj* having no life

LIFELIKE   *adj* resembling a living thing

LIFELINE   *n* pl. -S a rope used to aid a person in distress

LIFELONG   *adj* lasting for a lifetime

LIFER   *n* pl. -S a prisoner serving a life sentence

LIFETIME   *n* pl. -S the period of living existence

LIFEWAY   *n* pl. -WAYS a way of living

LIFEWORK   *n* pl. -S the major work of one's lifetime

LIFT   *v* -ED, -ING, -S to move to a higher position **LIFTABLE** *adj*

LIFTER   *n* pl. -S one that lifts

LIFTMAN   *n* pl. -MEN an elevator operator

LIFTOFF   *n* pl. -S the vertical takeoff of a rocket

LIGAMENT   *n* pl. -S a band of firm, fibrous tissue

LIGAN   *n* pl. -S lagan

LIGAND   *n* pl. -S a type of ion or molecule

LIGASE   *n* pl. -S an enzyme

LIGATE   *v* -GATED, -GATING, -GATES to bind

LIGATION   *n* pl. -S the act of ligating **LIGATIVE** *adj*

LIGATURE   *v* -TURED, -TURING, -TURES to ligate

LIGHT   *adj* LIGHTER, LIGHTEST having little weight

LIGHT   *v* LIGHTED or LIT, LIGHTING, LIGHTS to illuminate

LIGHTEN   *v* -ED, -ING, -S to reduce the weight of

LIGHTER   *v* -ED, -ING, -S to convey in a type of barge

LIGHTFUL   *adj* brightly illuminated

LIGHTING   *n* pl. -S illumination

LIGHTISH   *adj* somewhat light

LIGHTLY   *adv* to a moderate degree

LIGNEOUS   *adj* of or resembling wood

LIGNIFY   *v* -FIED, -FYING, -FIES to convert into wood

LIGNIN   *n* pl. -S an essential part of woody tissue

LIGNITE   *n* pl. -S a type of coal **LIGNITIC** *adj*

LIGROIN   *n* pl. -S a flammable liquid

LIGROINE   *n* pl. -S ligroin

LIGULA   *n* pl. -LAE or -LAS a strap-shaped organ or part **LIGULAR, LIGULATE, LIGULOID** *adj*

LIGULE   *n* pl. -S a strap-shaped plant part

LIGURE   *n* pl. -S a precious stone

LIKABLE   *adj* pleasant

LIKE   *v* LIKED, LIKING, LIKES to find pleasant

LIKE   *adj* LIKER, LIKEST possessing the same or almost the same characteristics

LIKEABLE   *adj* likable

LIKED   past tense of like

LIKELY   *adj* -LIER, -LIEST probable

LIKEN   *v* -ED, -ING, -S to represent as similar

LIKENESS   *n* pl. -ES a pictorial representation

LIKER   *n* pl. -S one that likes

LIKEST   superlative of like

LIKEWISE   *adv* in a similar manner

LIKING   *n* pl. -S a feeling of attraction or affection

LIKUTA   *n* pl. MAKUTA a monetary unit of Zaire

LILAC   *n* pl. -S a flowering shrub

LILIED   *adj* covered with lilies

LILLIPUT   *n* pl. -S a very small person

LILT   *v* -ED, -ING, -S to sing or speak rhythmically

LILY   *n* pl. LILIES a flowering plant **LILYLIKE** *adj*

LIMA   *n* pl. -S the edible seed of a tropical American plant

LIMACINE   *adj* resembling a type of mollusk

LIMACON   *n* pl. -S a type of geometric curve

LIMAN   *n* pl. -S a lagoon

LIMB   *v* -ED, -ING, -S to cut off the arms or legs of

LIMBA   *n* pl. -S an African tree

LIMBATE   *adj* having an edge of a different color

LIMBECK   *n* pl. -S alembic

LIMBER   *adj* -BERER, -BEREST flexible **LIMBERLY** *adv*

LIMBER   *v* -ED, -ING, -S to make flexible

LIMBI   a pl. of limbus

LIMBIC   *adj* pertaining to a system of the brain

LIMBIER   comparative of limby

LIMBIEST   superlative of limby

LIMBLESS   *adj* having no arms or legs

LIMBO   *n* pl. -BOS a condition of oblivion or neglect

LIMBUS   *n* pl. -BUSES or -BI a distinctive border

LIMBY   *adj* LIMBIER, LIMBIEST having many large branches

LIME   *v* LIMED, LIMING, LIMES to treat with lime (a calcium compound)

LIMEADE   *n* pl. -S a beverage

LIMEKILN   *n* pl. -S a furnace in which shells are burned to produce lime

LIMELESS   *adj* having no lime

LIMEN   *n* pl. -MENS or -MINA a sensory threshold

LIMERICK   *n* pl. -S a humorous verse

LIMES   *n* pl. LIMITES a fortified boundary

LIMEY   *n* pl. -EYS a British sailor

LIMIER   comparative of limy

LIMIEST   superlative of limy

LIMINA   a pl. of limen

LIMINAL   *adj* pertaining to the limen

LIMINESS   *n* pl. -ES the state of being limy

LIMING   present participle of lime

LIMIT   *v* -ED, -ING, -S to restrict

LIMITARY   *adj* limiting

LIMITED   *n* pl. -S a train or bus making few stops

LIMITER   *n* pl. -S one that limits

LIMITES   pl. of limes

LIMMER   *n* pl. -S a scoundrel

LIMN   *v* -ED, -ING, -S to depict by painting or drawing

LIMNER   *n* pl. -S one that limns

LIMNETIC   *adj* pertaining to the open water of a lake or pond

LIMNIC   *adj* limnetic

LIMO   *n* pl. LIMOS a limousine

LIMONENE   *n* pl. -S a chemical compound

LIMONITE   *n* pl. -S a major ore of iron

LIMP   *v* -ED, -ING, -S to walk lamely

LIMP   *adj* LIMPER, LIMPEST lacking rigidity

LIMPER   *n* pl. -S one that limps

LIMPET   *n* pl. -S a type of mollusk

LIMPID   *adj* transparent **LIMPIDLY** *adv*

LIMPKIN   *n* pl. -S a wading bird

LIMPLY   *adv* in a limp manner

LIMPNESS   *n* pl. -ES the state of being limp

LIMPSY   *adj* lacking strength or vigor

LIMULOID   *n* pl. -S a horseshoe crab

LIMULUS   *n* pl. -LI a horseshoe crab

LIMY   *adj* LIMIER, LIMIEST resembling or containing lime

LIN   *n* pl. -S linn

LINABLE   *adj* lineable

LINAC   *n* pl. -S a device for imparting high velocities to charged particles

LINAGE   *n* pl. -S the number of lines of printed material

LINALOL   *n* pl. -S linalool

LINALOOL   *n* pl. -S a fragrant alcohol

LINCHPIN   *n* pl. -S a locking pin inserted in the end of a shaft

LINDANE   *n* pl. -S an insecticide

LINDEN   *n* pl. -S a tall forest tree

LINDY   *n* pl. -DIES a lively dance

LINE   *v* LINED, LINING, LINES to mark with lines (slender, continuous marks)

LINEABLE   *adj* lying in a straight line

LINEAGE   *n* pl. -S direct descent from an ancestor

LINEAL   *adj* being directly descended from an ancestor **LINEALLY** *adv*

LINEAR   *adj* of or resembling a straight line **LINEARLY** *adv*

LINEATE   *adj* marked with lines

LINEATED   *adj* lineate

LINEBRED   *adj* produced by interbreeding within a particular line of descent

LINECUT   *n* pl. -S a type of printing plate

LINED   past tense of line

LINELESS   *adj* having no lines

LINELIKE   *adj* resembling a line

LINEMAN   *n* pl. -MEN one who installs or repairs telephone wires

LINEN   *n* pl. -S a fabric woven from the fibers of flax **LINENY** *adj*

LINER   *n* pl. -S a commercial ship or airplane

LINESMAN   *n* pl. -MEN a football official

LINEUP   *n* pl. -S a row of persons

LINEY   *adj* LINIER, LINIEST liny

LING   *n* pl. -S a heath plant

LINGA   *n* pl. -S lingam

LINGAM   *n* pl. -S a Hindu phallic symbol

LINGCOD   *n* pl. -S a marine food fish

LINGER   *v* -ED, -ING, -S to delay leaving

LINGERER   *n* pl. -S one that lingers

LINGERIE   *n* pl. -S women's underwear

LINGIER   comparative of lingy

LINGIEST   superlative of lingy

LINGO   *n* pl. -GOES strange or incomprehensible language

LINGUA   *n* pl. -GUAE the tongue or a tonguelike part

LINGUAL   *n* pl. -S a sound articulated with the tongue

LINGUINE   *n* pl. -S linguini

LINGUINI   *n* pl. -S a type of pasta

LINGUIST   *n* pl. -S a person skilled in several languages

LINGY   *adj* LINGIER, LINGIEST covered with heaths

LINIER   comparative of liny

LINIEST   superlative of liny

LINIMENT   *n* pl. -S a medicinal liquid

LININ   *n* pl. -S a substance in the nucleus of a cell

LINING   *n* pl. -S an inner layer

LINK   *v* -ED, -ING, -S to connect **LINKABLE** *adj*

LINKAGE   *n* pl. -S the act of linking

LINKBOY   *n* pl. -BOYS a man or boy hired to carry a torch to light the way along dark streets

LINKER   *n* pl. -S one that links

LINKMAN   *n* pl. -MEN a linkboy

LINKSMAN   *n* pl. -MEN a golfer

LINKUP   *n* pl. -S something that serves as a linking device

LINKWORK   *n* pl. -S something composed of interlocking rings

LINKY   *adj* full of interlocking rings

LINN   *n* pl. -S a waterfall

LINNET   *n* pl. -S a European songbird

LINO   *n* pl. -NOS linoleum

LINOCUT   *n* pl. -S a print made from a design cut into linoleum

LINOLEUM   *n* pl. -S a durable material used as a floor covering

LINSANG   *n* pl. -S a carnivorous mammal

LINSEED   *n* pl. -S flaxseed

LINSEY   *n* pl. -SEYS a coarse fabric

LINSTOCK   *n* pl. -S a stick having one end divided to hold a match

LINT   *n* pl. -S an accumulation of bits of fiber

LINTEL   *n* pl. -S a horizontal supporting beam

LINTER   *n* pl. -S a machine for removing fibers from cotton seeds

LINTIER   comparative of linty

LINTIEST   superlative of linty

LINTLESS   *adj* free from lint

LINTOL   *n* pl. -S lintel

LINTY   *adj* LINTIER, LINTIEST covered with lint

LINUM   *n* pl. -S a plant of the flax family

LINY   *adj* LINIER, LINIEST resembling a line

LION   *n* pl. -S a large, carnivorous feline mammal

LIONESS   *n* pl. -ES a female lion

LIONFISH   *n* pl. -ES a tropical fish

LIONISE   *v* -ISED, -ISING, -ISES to lionize

LIONISER   *n* pl. -S one that lionises

LIONIZE   *v* -IZED, -IZING, -IZES to treat or regard as a celebrity

LIONIZER   *n* pl. -S one that lionizes

LIONLIKE   *adj* resembling a lion

LIP   *v* LIPPED, LIPPING, LIPS to touch with the lips (the folds of flesh around the mouth)

LIPASE   *n* pl. -S an enzyme

LIPID   *n* pl. -S any of a class of fatty substances **LIPIDIC** *adj*

LIPIDE   *n* pl. -S lipid

LIPIN   *n* pl. -S a lipid

LIPLESS   *adj* having no lips

LIPLIKE   *adj* resembling a lip

LIPOCYTE   *n* pl. -S a fat-producing cell

LIPOID   *n* pl. -S a lipid **LIPOIDAL** *adj*

LIPOMA   *n* pl. -MAS or -MATA a tumor of fatty tissue

LIPPED   past tense of lip

LIPPEN   *v* -ED, -ING, -S to trust

LIPPER   *v* -ED, -ING, -S to ripple

LIPPING   *n* pl. -S a liplike outgrowth of bone

LIPPY   *adj* -PIER, -PIEST impudent

LIPSTICK   *n* pl. -S a cosmetic used to color the lips

LIQUATE   *v* -QUATED, -QUATING, -QUATES to purify metal by heating

LIQUEFY   *v* -FIED, -FYING, -FIES to make or become liquid

LIQUEUR   *n* pl. -S a sweetened alcoholic beverage

LIQUID   *n* pl. -S a substance that flows freely

LIQUIDLY   *adv* in a free-flowing manner

LIQUIFY   *v* -FIED, -FYING, -FIES to liquefy

LIQUOR   *v* -ED, -ING, -S to intoxicate with liquor (an alcoholic beverage)

LIRA   *n* pl. LIRE or LIRAS a monetary unit of Italy

LIRA   *n* pl. LIROTH or LIROT a monetary unit of Israel

LIRIPIPE   *n* pl. -S a long scarf

LISLE   *n* pl. -S a fine, tightly twisted cotton thread

LISP   *v* -ED, -ING -S to pronounce the letters *s* and *z* imperfectly

LISPER   *n* pl. -S one that lisps

LISSOM   *adj* lissome **LISSOMLY** *adv*

LISSOME   *adj* lithe

LIST   *v* -ED, -ING, -S to write down in a particular order **LISTABLE** *adj*

LISTEL   *n* pl. -S a narrow molding

LISTEN   *v* -ED, -ING, -S to make conscious use of the sense of hearing

LISTENER   *n* pl. -S one that listens

LISTER   *n* pl. -S a type of plow

LISTING   *n* pl. -S something that is listed

LISTLESS   *adj* languid

LIT   *n* pl. -S the litas

LITANY   *n* pl. -NIES a ceremonial form of prayer

LITAS   *n* pl. LITAI or LITU a former monetary unit of Lithuania

LITCHI   *n* pl. -S the edible fruit of a Chinese tree

LITER   *n* pl. -S a unit of capacity

LITERACY   *n* pl. -CIES the ability to read and write

LITERAL   *n* pl. -S a small error in printing or writing

LITERARY   *adj* of, pertaining to, or having the characteristics of books and writings

LITERATE   *n* pl. -S one who can read and write

LITERATI   *n/pl* scholars collectively

LITHARGE   *n* pl. -S a monoxide of lead

LITHE   *adj* LITHER, LITHEST bending easily **LITHELY** *adv*

LITHEMIA   *n* pl. -S an excess of uric acid in the blood **LITHEMIC** *adj*

LITHIA   *n* pl. -S an oxide of lithium

LITHIC   *adj* pertaining to lithium

LITHIUM   *n* pl. -S a metallic element

LITHO   *n* pl. LITHOS a type of print

LITHOID   *adj* resembling stone

LITHOSOL   *n* pl. -S a type of soil

LITIGANT   *n* pl. -S one who is engaged in a lawsuit

LITIGATE   *v* -GATED, -GATING, -GATES to subject to legal proceedings

LITMUS   *n* pl. -ES a blue coloring matter

LITORAL   *adj* pertaining to a coastal region

LITOTES   *n* pl. LITOTES a figure of speech in which an assertion is made by the negation of its opposite

LITRE   *n* pl. -S liter

LITTEN   *adj* lighted

LITTER   *v* -ED, -ING, -S to scatter rubbish about

LITTERER   *n* pl. -S one that litters

LITTERY   *adj* covered with rubbish

LITTLE   *adj* -TLER, -TLEST small

LITTLE   *n* pl. -S a small amount

LITTLISH   *adj* somewhat little

LITTORAL   *n* pl. -S a coastal region

LITU   a pl. of litas

LITURGY   *n* pl. -GIES a prescribed system of public worship **LITURGIC** *adj*

LIVABLE   *adj* suitable for living in

LIVE   *v* LIVED, LIVING, LIVES to function as an animal or plant

LIVE   *adj* LIVER, LIVEST having life

LIVEABLE   *adj* livable

LIVELONG   *adj* long in passing

LIVELY   *adj* -LIER, -LIEST full of energy **LIVELILY** *adv*

LIVEN   *v* -ED, -ING, -S to make lively

LIVENER   *n* pl. -S one that livens

LIVENESS   *n* pl. -ES the state of being live

LIVER   *n* pl. -S a secreting organ

LIVERIED   *adj* wearing a livery

LIVERISH   *adj* having a liver disorder

LIVERY   *n* pl. -ERIES a uniform worn by servants

LIVES   pl. of life

LIVEST   superlative of live

LIVETRAP   *v* -TRAPPED, -TRAPPING, -TRAPS to capture in a type of animal trap

LIVID   *adj* having the skin abnormally discolored **LIVIDLY** *adv*

LIVIDITY   *n* pl. -TIES the state of being livid

LIVIER   *n* pl. -S livyer

LIVING   *n* pl. -S a means of subsistence

LIVINGLY   *adv* realistically

LIVRE   *n* pl. -S a former monetary unit of France

LIVYER   *n* pl. -S a permanent resident of Newfoundland

LIXIVIUM   *n* pl. -IA or -IUMS a solution obtained by leaching **LIXIVIAL** *adj*

LIZARD   *n* pl. -S any of a suborder of reptiles

LLAMA   *n* pl. -S a ruminant mammal

LLANO   *n* pl. -NOS an open, grassy plain

LO   *interj* — used to attract attention or to express surprise

LOACH   *n* pl. -ES a freshwater fish

LOAD   *v* -ED, -ING, -S to place in or on a means of conveyance

LOADER   *n* pl. -S one that loads

LOADING   *n* pl. -S a burden

LOADSTAR   *n* pl. -S lodestar

LOAF   *n* pl. LOAVES a shaped mass of bread

LOAF   *v* -ED, -ING, -S to pass time idly

LOAFER   *n* pl. -S one that loafs

LOAM   *v* -ED, -ING, -S to cover with loam (a type of soil)

LOAMLESS   *adj* having no loam

LOAMY   *adj* LOAMIER, LOAMIEST resembling loam

LOAN   *v* -ED, -ING, -S to lend **LOANABLE** *adj*

LOANER   *n* pl. -S one that loans

LOANING   *n* pl. -S a lane

LOANWORD   *n* pl. -S a word taken from another language

LOATH   *adj* unwilling

LOATHE   *v* LOATHED, LOATHING, LOATHES to detest greatly

LOATHER   *n* pl. -S one that loathes

LOATHFUL   *adj* repulsive

LOATHING   *n* pl. -S extreme dislike

LOATHLY   *adj* repulsive

LOAVES   pl. of loaf

LOB   *v* LOBBED, LOBBING, LOBS to throw or hit in a high arc

LOBAR   *adj* pertaining to a lobe

LOBATE   *adj* having lobes **LOBATELY** *adv*

LOBATED   *adj* lobate

LOBATION   *n* pl. -S the formation of lobes

LOBBED   past tense of lob

LOBBING   present participle of lob

LOBBY   *v* -BIED, -BYING, -BIES to attempt to influence legislators

LOBBYER   *n* pl. -S a lobbyist

LOBBYGOW   *n* pl. -S an errand boy

LOBBYISM   *n* pl. -S the practice of lobbying

LOBBYIST   *n* pl. -S one who lobbies

LOBE   *n* pl. -S a rounded, projecting anatomical part **LOBED** *adj*

LOBEFIN   *n* pl. -S a bony fish

LOBELIA   *n* pl. -S a flowering plant

LOBELINE   *n* pl. -S a poisonous alkaloid

LOBLOLLY   *n* pl. -LIES a pine tree

LOBO   *n* pl. -BOS the timber wolf

LOBOTOMY   *n* pl. -MIES a type of surgical operation

LOBSTER   *n* pl. -S an edible marine crustacean

LOBSTICK   *n* pl. -S a tree with its lower branches trimmed

LOBULE   *n* pl. -S a small lobe **LOBULAR, LOBULATE, LOBULOSE** *adj*

LOBWORM   *n* pl. -S a lugworm

LOCA   a pl. of locus

LOCAL   *n* pl. -S a train or bus making all stops

LOCALE   *n* pl. -S a locality

LOCALISE   *v* -ISED, -ISING, -ISES to localize

LOCALISM   *n* pl. -S a custom or mannerism peculiar to a locality

LOCALIST   *n* pl. -S one who is strongly concerned with the matters of a locality

LOCALITE   *n* pl. -S a resident of a locality

LOCALITY   *n* pl. -TIES an area or neighborhood

LOCALIZE   *v* -IZED, -IZING, -IZES to confine to a particular area

LOCALLY   *adv* in a particular area

LOCATE   v -CATED, -CATING, -CATES to determine the position of

LOCATER   n pl. -S one that locates

LOCATION   n pl. -S the place where something is at a given moment

LOCATIVE   n pl. -S a type of grammatical case

LOCATOR   n pl. -S locater

LOCH   n pl. -S a lake

LOCHIA   n pl. LOCHIA a vaginal discharge following childbirth **LOCHIAL** adj

LOCI   a pl. of locus

LOCK   v -ED, -ING, -S to secure by means of a mechanical fastening device **LOCKABLE** adj

LOCKAGE   n pl. -S a toll on a ship passing through a canal

LOCKBOX   n pl. -ES a box that locks

LOCKER   n pl. -S an enclosure that may be locked

LOCKET   n pl. -S a small ornamental case

LOCKJAW   n pl. -S a form of tetanus

LOCKNUT   n pl. -S a nut which keeps another from loosening

LOCKOUT   n pl. -S a closing of a business to coerce employees to agree to terms

LOCKRAM   n pl. -S a coarse, linen fabric

LOCKSTEP   n pl. -S a mode of marching in close file

LOCKUP   n pl. -S a jail

LOCO   n pl. -COS or -COES locoweed

LOCO   v -ED, -ING, -S to poison with locoweed

LOCOFOCO   n pl. -COS a type of friction match

LOCOISM   n pl. -S a disease of livestock

LOCOMOTE   v -MOTED, -MOTING, -MOTES to move about

LOCOWEED   n pl. -S a plant that causes poisoning when eaten by livestock

LOCULAR   adj having or divided into loculi

LOCULATE   adj locular

LOCULE   n pl. -S loculus **LOCULED** adj

LOCULUS   n pl. -LI a small, cell-like chamber

LOCUM   n pl. -S a temporary substitute

LOCUS   n pl. LOCI or LOCA a place

LOCUST   n pl. -S a migratory grasshopper

LOCUSTA   n pl. -TAE a spikelet **LOCUSTAL** adj

LOCUTION   n pl. -S a particular form of expression

LOCUTORY   n pl. -RIES a room in a monastery

LODE   n pl. -S a deposit of ore

LODEN   n pl. -S a thick, woolen fabric

LODESTAR   n pl. -S a star used as a point of reference

LODGE   v LODGED, LODGING, LODGES to furnish with temporary quarters

LODGER   n pl. -S one that resides in rented quarters

LODGING   n pl. -S a temporary place to live

LODGMENT   n pl. -S a lodging

LODICULE   n pl. -S a scale at the base of the ovary of a grass

LOESS   n pl. -ES a soil deposit **LOESSAL, LOESSIAL** adj

LOFT   v -ED, -ING, -S to store in a loft (an upper room)

LOFTER   n pl. -S a type of golf club

LOFTILY   adv in a lofty manner

LOFTLESS   adj having no loft

LOFTY   adj LOFTIER, LOFTIEST extending high in the air

LOG   v LOGGED, LOGGING, LOGS to cut down trees for timber

LOGAN   n pl. -S a stone balanced to permit easy movement

LOGBOOK   n pl. -S a record book of a ship or aircraft

LOGE   n pl. -S a small compartment

LOGGATS   n/pl loggets

LOGGED   past tense of log

LOGGER   n pl. -S one that logs

LOGGETS   n/pl an old English throwing game

LOGGIA   n pl. -GIAS or -GIE an open gallery

LOGGING   n pl. -S the business of cutting down trees for timber

LOGGY   adj -GIER, -GIEST logy

LOGIA   a pl. of logion

LOGIC   n pl. -S the science of reasoning

LOGICAL	*adj* pertaining to logic
LOGICIAN	*n* pl. -S one who is skilled in logic
LOGICISE	*v* -CISED, -CISING, -CISES to logicize
LOGICIZE	*v* -CIZED, -CIZING, -CIZES to reason
LOGIER	comparative of logy
LOGIEST	superlative of logy
LOGILY	*adv* in a logy manner
LOGINESS	*n* pl. -ES the state of being logy
LOGION	*n* pl. -GIA or -GIONS a saying attributed to Jesus
LOGISTIC	*n* pl. -S symbolic logic
LOGJAM	*n* pl. -S a tangled mass of logs
LOGO	*n* pl. LOGOS an identifying symbol
LOGOGRAM	*n* pl. -S a symbol used to represent an entire word
LOGOMACH	*n* pl. -S one given to arguing about words
LOGOS	*n* pl. LOGOI the rational principle that governs the universe in ancient Greek philosophy
LOGOTYPE	*n* pl. -S a piece of type bearing a syllable, word, or words
LOGOTYPY	*n* pl. -TYPIES the use of logotypes
LOGROLL	*v* -ED, -ING, -S to obtain passage of by exchanging political favors
LOGWAY	*n* pl. -WAYS a ramp used in logging
LOGWOOD	*n* pl. -S a tropical tree
LOGY	*adj* -GIER, -GIEST sluggish
LOIN	*n* pl. -S a part of the side and back between the ribs and the hipbone
LOITER	*v* -ED, -ING, -S to stand idly about
LOITERER	*n* pl. -S one that loiters
LOLL	*v* -ED, -ING, -S to lounge
LOLLER	*n* pl. -S one that lolls
LOLLIPOP	*n* pl. -S a piece of candy on the end of a stick
LOLLOP	*v* -ED, -ING, -S to loll
LOLLY	*n* pl. -LIES a lollipop
LOLLYGAG	*v* -GAGGED, -GAGGING, -GAGS to lallygag
LOLLYPOP	*n* pl. -S lollipop

LOMENT	*n* pl. -S a type of plant pod
LOMENTUM	*n* pl. -TA or -TUMS loment
LONE	*adj* having no companions
LONELY	*adj* -LIER, -LIEST sad from lack of companionship **LONELILY** *adv*
LONENESS	*n* pl. -ES the state of being lone
LONER	*n* pl. -S one that avoids others
LONESOME	*n* pl. -S self
LONG	*adj* LONGER, LONGEST extending for a considerable distance
LONG	*v* -ED, -ING, -S to desire strongly
LONGAN	*n* pl. -S the edible fruit of a Chinese tree
LONGBOAT	*n* pl. -S the largest boat carried by a sailing vessel
LONGBOW	*n* pl. -S a type of archery bow
LONGE	*v* LONGED, LONGEING, LONGES to guide a horse by means of a long rope
LONGER	*n* pl. -S one that longs
LONGERON	*n* pl. -S a longitudinal support of an airplane
LONGHAIR	*n* pl. -S an intellectual
LONGHAND	*n* pl. -S ordinary handwriting
LONGHEAD	*n* pl. -S a person having a long skull
LONGHORN	*n* pl. -S one of a breed of long-horned cattle
LONGING	*n* pl. -S a strong desire
LONGISH	*adj* somewhat long
LONGLEAF	*n* pl. -LEAVES an evergreen tree
LONGLINE	*n* pl. -S a type of fishing line
LONGLY	*adv* for a considerable distance
LONGNESS	*n* pl. -ES the state of being long
LONGSHIP	*n* pl. -S a medieval ship
LONGSOME	*adj* tediously long
LONGSPUR	*n* pl. -S a long-clawed finch
LONGTIME	*adj* of long duration
LONGUEUR	*n* pl. -S a dull and tedious section
LONGWAYS	*adv* longwise
LONGWISE	*adv* lengthwise
LOO	*v* -ED, -ING, -S to subject to a forfeit at loo (a card game)

LOOBY   *n* pl. -BIES a large, awkward person

LOOEY   *n* pl. -EYS looie

LOOF   *n* pl. -S the palm of the hand

LOOFA   *n* pl. -S loofah

LOOFAH   *n* pl. -S a tropical vine

LOOIE   *n* pl. -S a lieutenant of the armed forces

LOOK   *v* -ED, -ING, -S to use one's eyes in seeing

LOOKDOWN   *n* pl. -S a marine fish

LOOKER   *n* pl. -S one that looks

LOOKOUT   *n* pl. -S one engaged in keeping watch

LOOKUP   *n* pl. -S the process of looking something up

LOOM   *v* -ED, -ING, -S to appear in an enlarged and indistinct form

LOON   *n* pl. -S a diving waterfowl

LOONEY   *adj* -NIER, -NIEST loony

LOONY   *adj* -NIER, -NIEST crazy

LOONY   *n* pl. -NIES a loony person

LOOP   *v* -ED, -ING, -S to form loops (circular or oval openings)

LOOPER   *n* pl. -S one that loops

LOOPHOLE   *v* -HOLED, -HOLING, -HOLES to make small openings in

LOOPY   *adj* LOOPIER, LOOPIEST full of loops

LOOSE   *adj* LOOSER, LOOSEST not firm, taut, or rigid **LOOSELY** *adv*

LOOSE   *v* LOOSED, LOOSING, LOOSES to set free

LOOSEN   *v* -ED, -ING, -S to make looser

LOOSENER   *n* pl. -S one that loosens

LOOSED   past tense of loose

LOOSER   comparative of loose

LOOSEST   superlative of loose

LOOSING   present participle of loose

LOOT   *v* -ED, -ING, -S to plunder

LOOTER   *n* pl. -S one that loots

LOP   *v* LOPPED, LOPPING, LOPS to cut off branches or twigs from

LOPE   *v* LOPED, LOPING, LOPES to run with a steady, easy gait

LOPER   *n* pl. -S one that lopes

LOPPED   past tense of lop

LOPPER   *v* -ED, -ING, -S to curdle

LOPPING   present participle of lop

LOPPY   *adj* -PIER, -PIEST hanging limply

LOPSIDED   *adj* leaning to one side

LOPSTICK   *n* pl. -S lobstick

LOQUAT   *n* pl. -S a small evergreen tree

LORAL   *adj* pertaining to the space between the eye and bill of a bird

LORAN   *n* pl. -S a type of navigational system

LORD   *v* -ED, -ING, -S to invest with the power of a lord (a person having dominion over others)

LORDING   *n* pl. -S a lordling

LORDLESS   *adj* having no lord

LORDLIER   comparative of lordly

LORDLIEST   superlative of lordly

LORDLIKE   *adj* lordly

LORDLING   *n* pl. -S a young or unimportant lord

LORDLY   *adj* -LIER, -LIEST of or befitting a lord

LORDOMA   *n* pl. -S lordosis

LORDOSIS   *n* pl. -DOSES a curvature of the spinal column **LORDOTIC** *adj*

LORDSHIP   *n* pl. -S the power of a lord

LORE   *n* pl. -S traditional knowledge or belief

LOREAL   *adj* loral

LORGNON   *n* pl. -S a pair of eyeglasses with a handle

LORICA   *n* pl. -CAE a protective covering or shell

LORICATE   *n* pl. -S an animal having a lorica

LORIKEET   *n* pl. -S a small parrot

LORIMER   *n* pl. -S a maker of implements for harnesses and saddles

LORINER   *n* pl. -S lorimer

LORIS   *n* pl. -RISES an Asian lemur

LORN   *adj* abandoned

LORNNESS   *n* pl. -ES the state of being lorn

LORRY   *n* pl. -RIES a type of wagon or truck

LORY   *n* pl. -RIES a small parrot

LOSE   *v* LOST, LOSING, LOSES to come to be without and be unable to find **LOSABLE** *adj*

LOSEL   *n* pl. -S a worthless person

LOSER	*n* pl. -S one that loses
LOSING	*n* pl. -S a loss
LOSINGLY	*adv* in a manner characterized by defeat
LOSS	*n* pl. -ES the act of one that loses
LOSSY	*adj* causing dissipation of electrical energy
LOST	*adj* not to be found or recovered
LOSTNESS	*n* pl. -ES the state of being lost
LOT	*v* LOTTED, LOTTING, LOTS to distribute proportionately
LOTA	*n* pl. -S lotah
LOTAH	*n* pl. -S a small water vessel used in India
LOTH	*adj* loath
LOTHARIO	*n* pl. -IOS a seducer of women
LOTHSOME	*adj* repulsive
LOTIC	*adj* pertaining to moving water
LOTION	*n* pl. -S a liquid preparation for external application
LOTOS	*n* pl. -ES lotus
LOTTED	past tense of lot
LOTTERY	*n* pl. -TERIES a type of gambling game
LOTTING	present participle of lot
LOTTO	*n* pl. -TOS a game of chance
LOTUS	*n* pl. -ES an aquatic plant
LOUD	*adj* LOUDER, LOUDEST strongly audible
LOUDEN	*v* -ED, -ING, -S to make or become louder
LOUDISH	*adj* somewhat loud
LOUDLY	*adv* -LIER, -LIEST in a loud manner
LOUDNESS	*n* pl. -ES the quality of being loud
LOUGH	*n* pl. -S a lake
LOUIE	*n* pl. -S looie
LOUIS	*n* pl. LOUIS a former gold coin of France
LOUNGE	*v* LOUNGED, LOUNGING, LOUNGES to recline or lean in a relaxed, lazy manner
LOUNGER	*n* pl. -S one that lounges
LOUNGY	*adj* suitable for lounging
LOUP	*v* LOUPED, LOUPEN, LOUPING, LOUPS to leap
LOUPE	*n* pl. -S a small magnifying glass
LOUR	*v* -ED, -ING, -S to lower
LOURY	*adj* lowery
LOUSE	*n* pl. LICE a parasitic insect
LOUSE	*v* LOUSED, LOUSING, LOUSES to spoil or bungle
LOUSY	*adj* LOUSIER, LOUSIEST mean or contemptible **LOUSILY** *adv*
LOUT	*v* -ED, -ING, -S to bow in respect
LOUTISH	*adj* clumsy
LOUVER	*n* pl. -S a type of window **LOUVERED** *adj*
LOUVRE	*n* pl. -S louver
LOVABLE	*adj* having qualities that attract love **LOVABLY** *adv*
LOVAGE	*n* pl. -S a perennial herb
LOVE	*v* LOVED, LOVING, LOVES to feel great affection for
LOVEABLE	*adj* lovable **LOVEABLY** *adv*
LOVEBIRD	*n* pl. -S a small parrot
LOVED	past tense of love
LOVELESS	*adj* feeling no love
LOVELIER	comparative of lovely
LOVELIES	pl. of lovely
LOVELIEST	superlative of lovely
LOVELILY	*adv* in a lovely manner
LOVELOCK	*n* pl. -S a lock of hair hanging separately
LOVELORN	*adj* not loved
LOVELY	*adj* -LIER, -LIEST beautiful
LOVELY	*n* pl. -LIES a beautiful woman
LOVER	*n* pl. -S one that loves another **LOVERLY** *adj*
LOVESICK	*adj* languishing with love
LOVESOME	*adj* lovely
LOVEVINE	*n* pl. -S a twining herb
LOVING	*adj* affectionate
LOVINGLY	*adv* in a loving manner
LOW	*adj* LOWER, LOWEST having relatively little upward extension
LOW	*v* -ED, -ING, -S to utter the sound characteristic of cattle
LOWBORN	*adj* of humble birth
LOWBOY	*n* pl. -BOYS a low chest of drawers
LOWBRED	*adj* lowborn

LOWBROW	*n* pl. -S an uncultivated person
LOWDOWN	*n* pl. -S the whole truth
LOWE	*v* LOWED, LOWING, LOWES to blaze
LOWER	*v* -ED, -ING, -S to appear dark and threatening
LOWERY	*adj* dark and threatening
LOWING	*n* pl. -S the sound characteristic of cattle
LOWISH	*adj* somewhat low
LOWLAND	*n* pl. -S an area of land lying lower than the adjacent country
LOWLIFE	*n* pl. -S a despicable person
LOWLY	*adj* -LIER, -LIEST low in position or rank
LOWN	*adj* peaceful
LOWNESS	*n* pl. -ES the state of being low
LOWSE	*adj* loose
LOX	*v* -ED, -ING, -ES to supply with lox (liquid oxygen)
LOYAL	*adj* -ALER, -ALEST faithful to one's allegiance
LOYALISM	*n* pl. -S loyalty
LOYALIST	*n* pl. -S one who is loyal
LOYALLY	*adv* in a loyal manner
LOYALTY	*n* pl. -TIES the state of being loyal
LOZENGE	*n* pl. -S a small, often medicated candy
LUAU	*n* pl. -S a Hawaiian feast
LUBBER	*n* pl. -S a clumsy person **LUBBERLY** *adj*
LUBE	*n* pl. -S a lubricant
LUBRIC	*adj* slippery
LUCARNE	*n* pl. -S a type of window
LUCE	*n* pl. -S a freshwater fish
LUCENCE	*n* pl. -S lucency
LUCENCY	*n* pl. -CIES the quality of being lucent
LUCENT	*adj* giving off light **LUCENTLY** *adv*
LUCERN	*n* pl. -S lucerne
LUCERNE	*n* pl. -S alfalfa
LUCES	a pl. of lux
LUCID	*adj* easily understood **LUCIDLY** *adv*
LUCIDITY	*n* pl. -TIES the quality of being lucid
LUCIFER	*n* pl. -S a friction match

LUCK	*v* -ED, -ING, -S to succeed by chance or good fortune
LUCKIE	*n* pl. -S an old woman
LUCKLESS	*adj* unlucky
LUCKY	*adj* LUCKIER, LUCKIEST having good fortune **LUCKILY** *adv*
LUCRE	*n* pl. -S monetary gain
LUCULENT	*adj* lucid
LUES	*n* pl. LUES syphilis
LUETIC	*n* pl. -S one infected with syphilis
LUFF	*v* -ED, -ING, -S to steer a sailing vessel nearer into the wind
LUFFA	*n* pl. -S loofah
LUG	*v* LUGGED, LUGGING, LUGS to carry or pull with effort
LUGE	*n* pl. -S a small sled
LUGGAGE	*n* pl. -S articles containing a traveler's belongings
LUGGED	past tense of lug
LUGGER	*n* pl. -S a small sailing vessel
LUGGIE	*n* pl. -S a small wooden dish or pail
LUGGING	present participle of lug
LUGSAIL	*n* pl. -S a type of sail
LUGWORM	*n* pl. -S a burrowing marine worm
LUKEWARM	*adj* moderately warm
LULL	*v* -ED, -ING, -S to cause to sleep or rest
LULLABY	*v* -BIED, -BYING, -BIES to lull with a soothing song
LULU	*n* pl. -S something remarkable
LUM	*n* pl. -S a chimney
LUMBAGO	*n* pl. -GOS pain in the lower back
LUMBAR	*n* pl. -S an anatomical part situated near the loins
LUMBER	*v* -ED, -ING, -S to cut down and prepare timber for market
LUMBERER	*n* pl. -S one that lumbers
LUMEN	*n* pl. -MENS or -MINA the inner passage of a tubular organ **LUMENAL, LUMINAL** *adj*
LUMINARY	*n* pl. -NARIES a body that gives light
LUMINIST	*n* pl. -S a painter who uses the effects of light
LUMINOUS	*adj* giving off light
LUMMOX	*n* pl. -ES a clumsy person

LUMP   *v* -ED, -ING, -S to make into lumps (shapeless masses)

LUMPEN   *n* pl. -S an uprooted individual

LUMPER   *n* pl. -S a laborer employed to load and unload ships

LUMPFISH   *n* pl. -ES a marine fish

LUMPISH   *adj* stupid

LUMPY   *adj* LUMPIER, LUMPIEST full of lumps **LUMPILY** *adv*

LUNA   *n* pl. -S an alchemical designation for silver

LUNACY   *n* pl. -CIES insanity

LUNAR   *n* pl. -S an observation of the moon taken for navigational purposes

LUNARIAN   *n* pl. -S a supposed inhabitant of the moon

LUNATE   *adj* crescent-shaped **LUNATELY** *adv*

LUNATED   *adj* lunate

LUNATIC   *n* pl. -S an insane person

LUNATION   *n* pl. -S the interval between two successive new moons

LUNCH   *v* -ED, -ING, -ES to eat a noonday meal

LUNCHEON   *n* pl. -S a noonday meal

LUNCHER   *n* pl. -S one that lunches

LUNE   *n* pl. -S a crescent-shaped figure

LUNET   *n* pl. -S lunette

LUNETTE   *n* pl. -S a crescent-shaped object

LUNG   *n* pl. -S a respiratory organ

LUNGAN   *n* pl. -S longan

LUNGE   *v* LUNGED, LUNGING, LUNGES to make a forceful forward movement

LUNGEE   *n* pl. -S lungi

LUNGER   *n* pl. -S one that lunges

LUNGFISH   *n* pl. -ES a type of fish

LUNGI   *n* pl. -S a loincloth worn by men in India

LUNGING   present participle of lunge

LUNGWORM   *n* pl. -S a parasitic worm

LUNGWORT   *n* pl. -S a European herb

LUNGYI   *n* pl. -S lungi

LUNIER   comparative of luny

LUNIES   pl. of luny

LUNIEST   superlative of luny

LUNK   *n* pl. -S a lunkhead

LUNKER   *n* pl. -S a large game fish

LUNKHEAD   *n* pl. -S a stupid person

LUNT   *v* -ED, -ING, -S to emit smoke

LUNULA   *n* pl. -LAE a small crescent-shaped structure **LUNULAR, LUNULATE** *adj*

LUNULE   *n* pl. -S lunula

LUNY   *adj* -NIER, -NIEST loony

LUNY   *n* pl. -NIES a loony

LUPANAR   *n* pl. -S a brothel

LUPIN   *n* pl. -S lupine

LUPINE   *n* pl. -S a flowering plant

LUPOUS   *adj* pertaining to lupus

LUPULIN   *n* pl. -S a medicinal powder obtained from the hop plant

LUPUS   *n* pl. -ES a skin disease

LURCH   *v* -ED, -ING, -ES to sway abruptly

LURCHER   *n* pl. -S one that lurks or prowls

LURDAN   *n* pl. -S a lazy or stupid person

LURDANE   *n* pl. -S lurdan

LURE   *v* LURED, LURING, LURES to attract with something desirable

LURER   *n* pl. -S one that lures

LURID   *adj* causing shock or horror **LURIDLY** *adv*

LURING   present participle of lure

LURK   *v* -ED, -ING, -S to wait in concealment

LURKER   *n* pl. -S one that lurks

LUSCIOUS   *adj* having a very pleasing taste or smell

LUSH   *adj* LUSHER, LUSHEST abounding in vegetation **LUSHLY** *adv*

LUSH   *v* -ED, -ING, -ES to drink to excess

LUSHNESS   *n* pl. -ES the state of being lush

LUST   *v* -ED, -ING, -S to have an intense desire

LUSTER   *v* -ED, -ING -S to make or become lustrous

LUSTFUL   *adj* marked by excessive sexual desire

LUSTIER   comparative of lusty

LUSTIEST   superlative of lusty

LUSTILY   *adv* in a lusty manner

LUSTRA   a pl. of lustrum

LUSTRAL	*adj* pertaining to a lustrum
LUSTRATE	*v* -TRATED, -TRATING, -TRATES to purify ceremonially
LUSTRE	*v* -TRED, -TRING, -TRES to luster
LUSTRING	*n* pl. -S a glossy silk fabric
LUSTROUS	*adj* reflecting light evenly and efficiently
LUSTRUM	*n* pl. -TRUMS or -TRA a ceremonial purification of the population in ancient Rome
LUSTY	*adj* LUSTIER, LUSTIEST full of vigor
LUSUS	*n* pl. -ES an abnormality
LUTANIST	*n* pl. -S one who plays the lute
LUTE	*v* LUTED, LUTING, LUTES to play a lute (a stringed musical instrument)
LUTEA	pl. of luteum
LUTEAL	*adj* pertaining to the luteum
LUTECIUM	*n* pl. -S lutetium
LUTED	past tense of lute
LUTEIN	*n* pl. -S a yellow pigment
LUTENIST	*n* pl. -S lutanist
LUTEOLIN	*n* pl. -S a yellow pigment
LUTEOUS	*adj* light to moderate greenish yellow in color
LUTETIUM	*n* pl. -S a metallic element
LUTEUM	*n* pl. -TEA a hormone-secreting body
LUTHERN	*n* pl. -S a type of window
LUTING	*n* pl. -S a substance used as a sealant
LUTIST	*n* pl. -S a lutanist
LUX	*n* pl. LUXES or LUCES a unit of illumination
LUXATE	*v* -ATED, -ATING, -ATES to put out of joint
LUXATION	*n* pl. -S the act of luxating
LUXE	*n* pl. -S luxury
LUXURY	*n* pl. -RIES free indulgence in that which affords pleasure or comfort
LYARD	*adj* streaked with gray
LYART	*adj* lyard
LYASE	*n* pl. -S an enzyme
LYCEA	a pl. of lyceum
LYCEE	*n* pl. -S a French secondary school
LYCEUM	*n* pl. -CEUMS or -CEA a hall for public lectures or discussions
LYCHEE	*n* pl. -S litchi
LYCHNIS	*n* pl. -NISES a flowering plant
LYCOPENE	*n* pl. -S a red pigment
LYCOPOD	*n* pl. -S an evergreen plant
LYDDITE	*n* pl. -S an explosive
LYE	*n* pl. -S a solution used in making soap
LYING	*n* pl. -S the act of telling lies
LYINGLY	*adv* falsely
LYMPH	*n* pl. -S a body fluid containing white blood cells **LYMPHOID** *adj*
LYMPHOMA	*n* pl. -MAS or -MATA a type of tumor
LYNCEAN	*adj* of or resembling a lynx
LYNCH	*v* -ED, -ING, -ES to put to death without legal sanction
LYNCHER	*n* pl. -S one that lynches
LYNCHING	*n* pl. -S the act of one who lynches
LYNX	*n* pl. -ES a short-tailed wildcat
LYOPHILE	*adj* pertaining to a type of colloid
LYRATE	*adj* having the shape of a lyre **LYRATELY** *adv*
LYRATED	*adj* lyrate
LYRE	*n* pl. -S an ancient harp-like instrument
LYREBIRD	*n* pl. -S an Australian bird
LYRIC	*n* pl. -S a lyrical poem
LYRICAL	*adj* having the form of a song
LYRICISE	*v* -CISED, -CISING, -CISES to lyricize
LYRICISM	*n* pl. -S the quality of being lyrical
LYRICIST	*n* pl. -S one who writes the words for songs
LYRICIZE	*v* -CIZED, -CIZING, -CIZES to write lyrically
LYRIFORM	*adj* lyrate
LYRISM	*n* pl. -S lyricism
LYRIST	*n* pl. -S one who plays the lyre
LYSATE	*n* pl. -S a product of lysis
LYSE	*v* LYSED, LYSING, LYSES to cause to undergo lysis
LYSIN	*n* pl. -S a substance capable of disintegrating blood cells or bacteria

LYSINE   *n* pl. -S an amino acid

LYSING   present participle of lyse

LYSIS   *n* pl. LYSES the disintegration of cells by lysins

LYSOGEN   *n* pl. -S a type of antigen

LYSOGENY   *n* pl. -NIES the state of being like a lysogen

LYSOSOME   *n* pl. -S a saclike part of a cell

LYSOZYME   *n* pl. -S an enzyme

LYSSA   *n* pl. -S rabies

LYTIC   *adj* pertaining to lysis

LYTTA   *n* pl. -TAE or -TAS a fibrous band in the tongue of certain carnivorous mammals

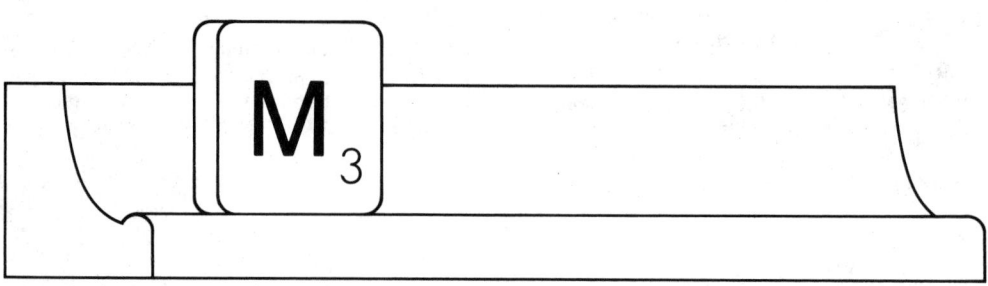

MA	*n* pl. -S mother
MAAR	*n* pl. -S a volcanic crater
MAC	*n* pl. -S a raincoat
MACABER	*adj* macabre
MACABRE	*adj* gruesome
MACACO	*n* pl. -COS a lemur
MACADAM	*n* pl. -S a type of pavement
MACAQUE	*n* pl. -S a short-tailed monkey
MACARONI	*n* pl. -NIS or -NIES a tubular pasta
MACAROON	*n* pl. -S a type of cookie
MACAW	*n* pl. -S a large parrot
MACCABAW	*n* pl. -S maccaboy
MACCABOY	*n* pl. -BOYS a type of snuff
MACCHIA	*n* pl. -CHIE a dense growth of small trees and shrubs
MACCOBOY	*n* pl. -BOYS maccaboy
MACE	*v* MACED, MACING, MACES to attack with a clublike weapon
MACER	*n* pl. -S an official who carries a ceremonial staff
MACERATE	*v* -ATED, -ATING, -ATES to soften by soaking in liquid
MACH	*n* pl. -S a number indicating the ratio of the speed of a body to the speed of sound
MACHETE	*n* pl. -S a large, heavy knife
MACHINE	*v* -CHINED, -CHINING, -CHINES to process by machine (a mechanical device)
MACHISMO	*n* pl. -MOS strong masculinity
MACHO	*n* pl. -CHOS a person who exhibits machismo
MACHREE	*n* pl. -S dear

MACHZOR	*n* pl. -ZORIM or -ZORS mahzor
MACING	present participle of mace
MACK	*n* pl. -S mac
MACKEREL	*n* pl. -S a marine food fish
MACKINAW	*n* pl. -S a woolen fabric
MACKLE	*v* -LED, -LING, -LES to blur in printing
MACLE	*n* pl. -S a spot or discoloration in a mineral **MACLED** *adj*
MACRAME	*n* pl. -S a trimming of knotted thread or cord
MACRO	*n* pl. -ROS a type of computer instruction
MACRON	*n* pl. -S a symbol placed over a vowel to show that it has a long sound
MACRURAL	*adj* pertaining to macruran
MACRURAN	*n* pl. -S any of a suborder of crustaceans
MACULA	*n* pl. -LAE or -LAS a spot **MACULAR** *adj*
MACULATE	*v* -LATED, -LATING, -LATES to mark with spots
MACULE	*v* -ULED, -ULING, -ULES to mackle
MAD	*adj* MADDER, MADDEST insane
MAD	*v* MADDED, MADDING, MADS to madden
MADAM	*n* pl. -S a woman who manages a brothel
MADAME	*n* pl. -S madam
MADAME	*n* pl. MESDAMES the French title of respect for a married woman
MADCAP	*n* pl. -S an impulsive person

MADDED	past tense of mad
MADDEN	v -ED, -ING, -S to make or become mad
MADDER	n pl. -S a perennial herb
MADDEST	superlative of mad
MADDING	present participle of mad
MADDISH	adj somewhat mad
MADE	past tense of make
MADEIRA	n pl. -S a white wine
MADHOUSE	n pl. -S an insane asylum
MADLY	adv in a mad manner
MADMAN	n pl. -MEN a man who is insane
MADNESS	n pl. -ES the state of being mad
MADONNA	n pl. -S a former Italian title of respect for a woman
MADRAS	n pl. -ES a cotton fabric
MADRE	n pl. -S mother
MADRIGAL	n pl. -S a short lyric poem
MADRONA	n pl. -S an evergreen tree
MADRONE	n pl. -S madrona
MADRONO	n pl. -NOS madrona
MADURO	n pl. -ROS a dark-colored, relatively strong cigar
MADWOMAN	n pl. -WOMEN a woman who is insane
MADWORT	n pl. -S a flowering plant
MADZOON	n pl. -S matzoon
MAE	n pl. -S more
MAENAD	n pl. -S or -ES a female participant in ancient Greek orgies **MAENADIC** adj
MAESTOSO	n pl. -SOS a stately musical passage
MAESTRO	n pl. -STROS or -STRI a master of an art
MAFFIA	n pl. -S mafia
MAFFICK	v -ED, -ING, -S to celebrate boisterously
MAFIA	n pl. -S a secret organization operating in opposition to legal authority
MAFIC	adj pertaining to minerals rich in magnesium and iron
MAFIOSO	n pl. -SI a member of the mafia
MAFTIR	n pl. -S the concluding section of a parashah
MAG	n pl. -S a magazine
MAGAZINE	n pl. -S a type of periodical publication
MAGDALEN	n pl. -S a reformed prostitute
MAGE	n pl. -S a magician
MAGENTA	n pl. -S a red dye
MAGGOT	n pl. -S the legless larva of certain insects **MAGGOTY** adj
MAGI	pl. of magus
MAGIC	v -ICKED, -ICKING, -ICS to affect by magic (sorcery)
MAGICAL	adj resembling magic
MAGICIAN	n pl. -S one skilled in magic
MAGICKED	past tense of magic
MAGICKING	present participle of magic
MAGILP	n pl. -S megilp
MAGISTER	n pl. -S a master or teacher
MAGMA	n pl. -MAS or -MATA the molten matter from which igneous rock is formed **MAGMATIC** adj
MAGNATE	n pl. -S a powerful or influential person
MAGNESIA	n pl. -S a medicinal compound **MAGNESIC** adj
MAGNET	n pl. -S a body that possesses the property of attracting iron
MAGNETIC	n pl. -S a magnet
MAGNETO	n pl. -TOS a type of electric generator
MAGNETON	n pl. -S a unit of magnetic moment
MAGNIFIC	adj magnificent
MAGNIFY	v -FIED, -FYING, -FIES to increase the perceived size of
MAGNOLIA	n pl. -S a flowering shrub or tree
MAGNUM	n pl. -S a large wine bottle
MAGOT	n pl. -S a tailless ape
MAGPIE	n pl. -S a corvine bird
MAGUEY	n pl. -GUEYS a tropical plant
MAGUS	n pl. -GI a magician
MAHARAJA	n pl. -S a king or prince in India
MAHARANI	n pl. -S the wife of a maharaja
MAHATMA	n pl. -S a Hindu sage
MAHJONG	n pl. -S a game of Chinese origin
MAHJONGG	n pl. -S mahjong
MAHOE	n pl. -S a tropical tree
MAHOGANY	n pl. -NIES a tropical tree
MAHONIA	n pl. -S a flowering shrub

MAHOUT *n* pl. -S the keeper and driver of an elephant

MAHUANG *n* pl. -S an Asian plant

MAHZOR *n* pl. -ZORIM or -ZORS a Jewish prayer book

MAID *n* pl. -S a maiden **MAIDISH** *adj*

MAIDEN *n* pl. -S a young unmarried woman **MAIDENLY** *adj*

MAIDHOOD *n* pl. -S the state of being a maiden

MAIEUTIC *adj* pertaining to a method of eliciting knowledge

MAIGRE *adj* containing neither flesh nor its juices

MAIHEM *n* pl. -S mayhem

MAIL *v* -ED,- ING, -S to send by a governmental postal system. **MAILABLE** *adj*

MAILBAG *n* pl. -S a bag for carrying mail (postal material)

MAILBOX *n* pl. -ES a box for depositing mail

MAILE *n* pl. -S a Pacific island vine

MAILER *n* pl. -S one that mails

MAILING *n* pl. -S a rented farm

MAILL *n* pl. -S a payment

MAILLESS *adj* having no armor

MAILLOT *n* pl. -S a woman's one-piece bathing suit

MAILMAN *n* pl. -MEN a man who carries and delivers mail

MAIM *v* -ED, -ING, -S to injure so as to cause lasting damage

MAIMER *n* pl. -S one that maims

MAIN *n* pl. -S the principal part

MAINLAND *n* pl. -S a principal land mass

MAINLINE *v* -LINED, -LINING, -LINES to inject a narcotic into a major vein

MAINLY *adv* for the most part

MAINMAST *n* pl. -S the principal mast of a vessel

MAINSAIL *n* pl. -S the principal sail of a vessel

MAINSTAY *n* pl. -STAYS a principal support

MAINTAIN *v* -ED, -ING, -S to keep in proper condition

MAINTOP *n* pl. -S a platform at the head of a mainmast

MAIOLICA *n* pl. -S majolica

MAIR *n* pl. -S more

MAIST *n* pl. -S most

MAIZE *n* pl. -S an American cereal grass

MAJAGUA *n* pl. -S a tropical tree

MAJESTIC *adj* having majesty

MAJESTY *n* pl. -TIES regal dignity

MAJOLICA *n* pl. -S a type of pottery

MAJOR *v* -ED, -ING, -S to pursue a specific principal course of study

MAJORITY *n* pl. -TIES the greater number or part

MAKAR *n* pl. -S a poet

MAKE *v* MADE, MAKING, MAKES to cause to exist **MAKABLE, MAKEABLE** *adj*

MAKEBATE *n* pl. -S one that encourages quarrels

MAKEFAST *n* pl. -S an object to which a boat is tied

MAKER *n* pl. -S one that makes

MAKEUP *n* pl. -S the way in which the parts or ingredients of something are put together

MAKIMONO *n* pl. -NOS a Japanese ornamental scroll

MAKING *n* pl. -S material from which something can be developed

MAKO *n* pl. -KOS a large shark

MAKUTA pl. of likuta

MALADY *n* pl. -DIES an illness

MALAISE *n* pl. -S a feeling of vague discomfort

MALAMUTE *n* pl. -S an Alaskan sled dog

MALAPERT *n* pl. -S an impudent person

MALAPROP *n* pl. -S a humorous misuse of a word

MALAR *n* pl. -S the cheekbone

MALARIA *n* pl. -S an infectious disease **MALARIAL, MALARIAN** *adj*

MALARKEY *n* pl. -KEYS nonsense

MALARKY *n* pl. -KIES malarky

MALAROMA *n* pl. -S a malodor

MALATE *n* pl. -S a chemical salt

MALE *n* pl. -S an individual that begets young by fertilizing the female

MALEATE *n* pl. -S a chemical salt

MALEDICT *v* -ED, -ING, -S to curse

MALEFIC	adj producing or causing evil
MALEMIUT	n pl. -S malamute
MALEMUTE	n pl. -S malamute
MALENESS	n pl. -ES the quality of being a male
MALFED	adj badly fed
MALGRE	prep in spite of
MALIC	adj pertaining to apples
MALICE	n pl. -S a desire to injure another
MALIGN	v -ED, -ING, -S to speak evil of
MALIGNER	n pl. -S one that maligns
MALIGNLY	adv in an evil manner
MALIHINI	n pl. -S a newcomer to Hawaii
MALINE	n pl. -S a delicate net used for veils
MALINGER	v -ED, -ING, -S to feign illness in order to avoid duty or work
MALISON	n pl. -S a curse
MALKIN	n pl. -S an untidy woman
MALL	v -ED, -ING -S to maul
MALLARD	n pl. -S a wild duck
MALLEE	n pl. -S an evergreen tree
MALLEI	pl. of malleus
MALLEOLI	n/pl bony protuberances of the ankle
MALLET	n pl. -S a type of hammer
MALLEUS	n pl. -LEI a bone of the middle ear
MALLOW	n pl. -S a flowering plant
MALM	n pl. -S a soft, friable limestone
MALMSEY	n pl. -SEYS a white wine
MALMY	adj MALMIER, MALMIEST resembling malm
MALODOR	n pl. -S an offensive odor
MALPOSED	adj being in the wrong position
MALT	v -ED, -ING, -S to treat or combine with malt (germinated grain)
MALTASE	n pl. -S an enzyme
MALTED	n pl. -S a sweet beverage
MALTHA	n pl. -S a natural tar
MALTIER	comparative of malty
MALTIEST	superlative of malty
MALTOL	n pl. -S a chemical compound
MALTOSE	n pl. -S a type of sugar
MALTREAT	v -ED, -ING, -S to treat badly
MALTSTER	n pl. -S one that makes malt
MALTY	adj MALTIER, MALTIEST resembling malt
MALVASIA	n pl. -S malmsey
MAMA	n pl. -S mother
MAMBA	n pl. -S a venomous snake
MAMBO	v -ED, -ING, -ES or -S to perform a ballroom dance
MAMELUKE	n pl. -S a slave in Muslim countries
MAMEY	n pl. -MEYS or -MEYES a tropical tree
MAMIE	n pl. -S mamey
MAMLUK	n pl. -S mameluke
MAMMA	n pl. -S mama
MAMMA	n pl. -MAE a milk-secreting organ
MAMMAL	n pl. -S any of a class of warm-blooded vertebrates
MAMMARY	adj pertaining to the mammae
MAMMATE	adj having mammae
MAMMATUS	n pl. -TI a type of cloud
MAMMEE	n pl. -S mamey
MAMMER	v -ED, -ING, -S to hesitate
MAMMET	n pl. -S maumet
MAMMEY	n pl. -MEYS mamey
MAMMIE	n pl. -S mammy
MAMMIES	pl. of mammy
MAMMILLA	n pl. -LAE a nipple
MAMMITIS	n pl. -MITIDES mastitis
MAMMOCK	v -ED, -ING, -S to shred
MAMMON	n pl. -S material wealth
MAMMOTH	n pl. -S an extinct elephant
MAMMY	n pl. -MIES mother
MAN	n pl. MEN an adult human male
MAN	v MANNED, MANNING, MANS to supply with men
MANA	n pl. -S a supernatural force in certain Pacific island religions
MANACLE	v -CLED, -CLING, -CLES to handcuff
MANAGE	v -AGED, -AGING, -AGES to control or direct
MANAGER	n pl. -S one that manages
MANAKIN	n pl. -S a tropical bird
MANANA	n pl. -S tomorrow
MANATEE	n pl. -S an aquatic mammal **MANATOID** adj

MANCHE *n* pl. -S a heraldic design

MANCHET *n* pl. -S a small loaf of fine white bread

MANCIPLE *n* pl. -S an officer authorized to purchase provisions

MANDALA *n* pl. -S a Hindu or Buddhist graphic symbol of the universe **MANDALIC** *adj*

MANDAMUS *v* -ED, -ING, -ES to command by means of writ issued by a superior court

MANDARIN *n* pl. -S a citrus fruit

MANDATE *v* -DATED, -DATING, -DATES to authorize or decree

MANDATOR *n* pl. -S one that mandates

MANDIBLE *n* pl. -S the bone of the lower jaw

MANDIOCA *n* pl. -S manioc

MANDOLA *n* pl. -S an ancient lute

MANDOLIN *n* pl. -S a stringed musical instrument

MANDRAKE *n* pl. -S a European herb

MANDREL *n* pl. -S a shaft on which a tool is mounted

MANDRIL *n* pl. -S mandrel

MANDRILL *n* pl. -S a large baboon

MANE *n* pl. -S the long hair growing on and about the neck of some animals **MANED, MANELESS** *adj*

MANEGE *n* pl. -S the art of training and riding horses

MANEUVER *v* -ED, -ING, -S to change the position of for a specific purpose

MANFUL *adj* courageous **MANFULLY** *adv*

MANGABEY *n* pl. -BEYS a long-tailed monkey

MANGABY *n* pl. -BIES mangabey

MANGANIC *adj* containing manganese (a metallic element)

MANGE *n* pl. -S a skin disease of domestic animals

MANGEL *n* pl. -S a variety of beet

MANGER *n* pl. -S a trough or box from which horses or cattle eat

MANGEY *adj* MANGIER, MANGIEST mangy

MANGIER comparative of mangy

MANGIEST superlative of mangy

MANGILY *adv* in a mangy manner

MANGLE *v* -GLED, -GLING, -GLES to cut, slash, or crush so as to disfigure

MANGLER *n* pl. -S one that mangles

MANGO *n* pl. -GOES or -GOS an edible tropical fruit

MANGOLD *n* pl. -S mangel

MANGONEL *n* pl. -S a medieval military device for hurling stones

MANGROVE *n* pl. -S a tropical tree or shrub

MANGY *adj* MANGIER, MANGIEST affected with mange

MANHOLE *n* pl. -S a hole providing entrance to an underground or enclosed structure

MANHOOD *n* pl. -S the state of being a man

MANHUNT *n* pl. -S an intensive search for a person

MANIA *n* pl. -S an excessive interest or enthusiasm

MANIAC *n* pl. -S an insane person **MANIACAL** *adj*

MANIC *n* pl. -S one that is affected with mania

MANICURE *v* -CURED, -CURING, -CURES to trim and polish the fingernails of

MANIFEST *v* -ED, -ING, -S to show clearly

MANIFOLD *v* -ED, -ING, -S to make several copies of

MANIHOT *n* pl. -S a tropical plant

MANIKIN *n* pl. -S an anatomical model of the human body

MANILA *n* pl. -S a strong paper

MANILLA *n* pl. -S manila

MANILLE *n* pl. -S the second highest trump in certain card games

MANIOC *n* pl. -S a tropical plant

MANIOCA *n* pl. -S manioc

MANIPLE *n* pl. -S a silk band worn on the left arm as a vestment

MANITO *n* pl. -TOS manitou

MANITOU *n* pl. -S an Algonquian Indian deity

MANITU *n* pl. -S manitou

MANKIND *n* pl. MANKIND the human race

MANLESS *adj* destitute of men

MANLIKE *adj* resembling a man

MANLY *adj* -LIER, -LIEST having the qualities of a man **MANLILY** *adv*

MANMADE   *adj* made by man

MANNA   *n* pl. -S divinely supplied food

MANNAN   *n* pl. -S a type of sugar

MANNED   past tense of man

MANNER   *n* pl. -S a way of acting **MANNERED** *adj*

MANNERLY   *adj* polite

MANNIKIN   *n* pl. -S manikin

MANNING   present participle of man

MANNISH   *adj* resembling or characteristic of a man

MANNITE   *n* pl. -S mannitol **MANNITIC** *adj*

MANNITOL   *n* pl. -S an alcohol

MANNOSE   *n* pl. -S a type of sugar

MANO   *n* pl. -NOS a stone used for grinding foods

MANOR   *n* pl. -S a landed estate or territorial unit **MANORIAL** *adj*

MANPACK   *adj* designed to be carried by one person

MANPOWER   *n* pl. -S the number of men available for service

MANQUE   *adj* frustrated in the fulfillment of one's aspirations

MANROPE   *n* pl. -S a rope used as a handrail

MANSARD   *n* pl. -S a type of roof

MANSE   *n* pl. -S a clergyman's house

MANSION   *n* pl. -S a large, impressive house

MANTA   *n* pl. -S a cotton fabric

MANTEAU   *n* pl. -TEAUS or -TEAUX a loose cloak

MANTEL   *n* pl. -S a shelf above a fireplace

MANTELET   *n* pl. -S a mobile screen used to protect soldiers

MANTES   a pl. of mantis

MANTIC   *adj* having powers of prophecy

MANTID   *n* pl. -S mantis

MANTILLA   *n* pl. -S a woman's scarf

MANTIS   *n* pl. -TISES or -TES a predatory insect

MANTISSA   *n* pl. -S the decimal part of a logarithm

MANTLE   *v* -TLED, -TLING, -TLES to cloak

MANTLET   *n* pl. -S mantelet

MANTLING   *n* pl. -S an ornamental cloth

MANTRA   *n* pl. -S a mystical formula of prayer or incantation in Hinduism

MANTRAP   *n* pl. -S a trap for catching men

MANTUA   *n* pl. -S a woman's gown

MANUAL   *n* pl. -S a small reference book

MANUALLY   *adv* by means of the hands

MANUARY   *adj* involving the hands

MANUBRIA   *n/pl* handle-shaped anatomical parts

MANUMIT   *v* -MITTED, -MITTING, -MITS to free from slavery

MANURE   *v* -NURED, -NURING, -NURES to fertilize with manure (animal excrement)

MANURER   *n* pl. -S one that manures

MANURIAL   *adj* of or pertaining to manure

MANURING   present participle of manure

MANUS   *n* pl. MANUS the end of the forelimb in vertebrates

MANWARD   *adv* toward man

MANWARDS   *adv* manward

MANWISE   *adv* in a manner characteristic of man

MANY   *adj* MORE, MOST consisting of or amounting to a large number

MANYFOLD   *adv* by many times

MAP   *v* MAPPED, MAPPING, MAPS to delineate on a map (a representation of a region)

MAPLE   *n* pl. -S a hardwood tree

MAPMAKER   *n* pl. -S one that makes maps

MAPPABLE   *adj* capable of being mapped

MAPPED   past tense of map

MAPPER   *n* pl. -S one that maps

MAPPING   *n* pl. -S a mathematical correspondence

MAQUETTE   *n* pl. -S a small preliminary model

MAQUI   *n* pl. -S maquis

MAQUIS   *n* pl. MAQUIS a thick underbrush

MAR   *v* MARRED, MARRING, MARS to detract from the perfection or wholeness of

MARABOU   *n* pl. -S an African stork

MARABOUT   *n* pl. -S a marabou

MARACA   *n* pl. -S a percussion instrument

MARANTA   *n* pl. -S a tropical plant

MARASCA *n* pl. -S a wild cherry

MARASMUS *n* pl. -ES a wasting away of the body **MARASMIC** *adj*

MARATHON *n* pl. -S a long-distance race

MARAUD *v* -ED, -ING, -S to rove in search of booty

MARAUDER *n* pl. -S one that marauds

MARAVEDI *n* pl. -S a former coin of Spain

MARBLE *v* -BLED, -BLING, -BLES to give a mottled appearance to

MARBLER *n* pl. -S one that marbles

MARBLING *n* pl. -S an intermixture of fat and lean in meat

MARBLY *adj* -BLIER, -BLIEST mottled

MARC *n* pl. -S the residue remaining after a fruit has been pressed

MARCEL *v* -CELLED, -CELLING, -CELS to make a deep, soft wave in the hair

MARCH *v* -ED, -ING, -ES to walk in a formal military manner

MARCHEN *n* pl. MARCHEN a folktale

MARCHER *n* pl. -S one that marches

MARCHESA *n* pl. -CHESE the wife or widow of a marchese

MARCHESE *n* p. -CHESI an Italian nobleman

MARE *n* pl. -S a mature female horse

MARE *n* pl. -RIA a dark area on the surface of the moon or Mars

MAREMMA *n* pl. -REMME a marshy coastal region

MARGARIC *adj* pearly

MARGARIN *n* pl. -S a butter substitute

MARGAY *n* pl. -GAYS a small American wildcat

MARGE *n* pl. -S a margin

MARGENT *v* -ED, -ING, -S to margin

MARGIN *v* -ED, -ING, -S to provide with a margin (a border)

MARGINAL *adj* of or pertaining to a margin

MARGRAVE *n* pl. -S the military governor of a medieval German border province

MARIA pl. of mare

MARIACHI *n* pl. -S a Mexican musical band

MARIGOLD *n* pl. -S a flowering plant

MARIMBA *n* pl. -S a percussion instrument

MARINA *n* pl. -S a docking area for small boats

MARINADE *v* -NADED, -NADING, -NADES to marinate

MARINARA *n* pl. -S a seasoned tomato sauce

MARINATE *v* -NATED, -NATING, -NATES to soak in a seasoned liquid before cooking

MARINE *n* pl. -S a soldier trained for service at sea and on land

MARINER *n* pl. -S a sailor

MARIPOSA *n* pl. -S a flowering plant

MARISH *n* pl. -ES a marsh

MARITAL *adj* pertaining to marriage

MARITIME *adj* pertaining to navigation or commerce on the sea

MARJORAM *n* pl. -S fragrant herb

MARK *v* -ED, -ING, -S to make a visible impression on

MARKDOWN *n* pl. -S a reduction in price

MARKEDLY *adv* in an evident manner

MARKER *n* pl. -S one that marks

MARKET *v* -ED, -ING, -S to offer for sale

MARKETER *n* pl. -S one that markets

MARKHOOR *n* pl. -S markhor

MARKHOR *n* pl. -S a wild goat

MARKING *n* pl. -S a pattern of marks

MARKKA *n* pl. -KAA or -KAS a monetary unit of Finland

MARKSMAN *n* pl. -MEN a person skillful at hitting a target

MARKUP *n* pl. -S an increase in price

MARL *v* -ED, -ING, -S to fertilize with marl (an earthy deposit containing lime, clay, and sand)

MARLIER comparative of marly

MARLIEST superlative of marly

MARLIN *n* pl. -S a marine game fish

MARLINE *n* pl. -S a rope used on a ship

MARLING *n* pl. -S marline

MARLITE *n* pl. -S a type of marl **MARLITIC** *adj*

MARLY *adj* MARLIER, MARLIEST abounding with marl

MARMITE *n* pl. -S a large soup kettle

MARMOSET *n* pl. -S a small monkey

MARMOT *n* pl. -S a burrowing rodent

MAROON *v* -ED, -ING, -S to abandon in an isolated place

MARPLOT	*n* pl. -S one that ruins a plan by meddling
MARQUE	*n* pl. -S reprisal
MARQUEE	*n* pl. -S a rooflike structure projecting over an entrance
MARQUESS	*n* pl. -ES marquis
MARQUIS	*n* pl. -ES a European nobleman
MARQUISE	*n* pl. -S the wife or widow of a marquis
MARRAM	*n* pl. -S a beach grass
MARRED	past tense of mar
MARRER	*n* pl. -S one that mars
MARRIAGE	*n* pl. -S the legal union of a man and woman
MARRIED	*n* pl. -S one who has entered into marriage
MARRIER	*n* pl. -S one that marries
MARRIES	present 3d person sing. of marry
MARRING	present participle of mar
MARRON	*n* pl. -S a variety of chestnut
MARROW	*v* -ED, -ING, -S to marry
MARROWY	*adj* pithy
MARRY	*v* -RIED, -RYING, -RIES to enter into marriage
MARSE	*n* pl. -S master
MARSH	*n* pl. -ES a tract of low, wet land
MARSHAL	*v* -ED, -ING, -S to put in proper order
MARSHALL	*v* -ED, -ING, -S to marshal
MARSHY	*adj* MARSHIER, MARSHIEST resembling a marsh
MARSUPIA	*n/pl* abdominal pouches of certain mammals
MART	*v* -ED, -ING, -S to market
MARTAGON	*n* pl. -S a flowering plant
MARTELLO	*n* pl. -LOS a circular fort
MARTEN	*n* pl. -S a carnivorous mammal
MARTIAL	*adj* pertaining to war
MARTIAN	*n* pl. -S a supposed inhabitant of the planet Mars
MARTIN	*n* pl. -S a small bird
MARTINET	*n* pl. -S one who demands rigid adherence to rules
MARTINI	*n* pl. -S an alcoholic beverage
MARTLET	*n* pl. -S a martin
MARTYR	*v* -ED, -ING, -S to put to death for adhering to a belief
MARTYRLY	*adj* resembling a martyr
MARTYRY	*n* pl. -TYRIES a shrine erected in honor of a martyred person
MARVEL	*v* -VELED, -VELING, -VELS or -VELLED, -VELLING, -VELS to be filled with wonder or astonishment
MARZIPAN	*n* pl. -S an almond candy
MASCARA	*n* pl. -S a cosmetic for coloring the eyelashes and eyebrows
MASCON	*n* pl. -S a concentration of dense mass beneath the moon's surface
MASCOT	*n* pl. -S a person, animal, or object believed to bring good luck
MASER	*n* pl. -S a device for amplifying electrical impulses
MASH	*v* -ED, -ING, -ES to reduce to a pulpy mass
MASHER	*n* pl. -S one that mashes
MASHIE	*n* pl. -S a golf club
MASHY	*n* pl. MASHIES mashie
MASJID	*n* pl. -S a mosque
MASK	*v* -ED, -ING, -S to cover with a mask (a covering used to disguise the face) MASKABLE *adj*
MASKEG	*n* pl. -S muskeg
MASKER	*n* pl. -S one that wears a mask
MASKING	*n* pl. -S a piece of scenery used to conceal parts of a stage from the audience
MASKLIKE	*adj* suggestive of a mask
MASON	*v* -ED, -ING, -S to build with stone or brick
MASONIC	*adj* pertaining to masonry
MASONRY	*n* pl. -RIES a structure built of stone or brick
MASQUE	*n* pl. -S a dramatic entertainment formerly popular in England
MASQUER	*n* pl. -S masker
MASS	*v* -ED, -ING, -ES to assemble in a mass (a body of coherent matter)
MASSA	*n* pl. -S master
MASSACRE	*v* -CRED, -CRING, -CRES to kill indiscriminately
MASSAGE	*v* -SAGED, -SAGING, -SAGES to manipulate parts of the body for remedial or hygienic purposes

MASSAGER *n* pl. -S one that massages

MASSE *n* pl. -S a type of shot in billiards

MASSEDLY *adv* in a massed manner

MASSETER *n* pl. -S a muscle that raises the lower jaw

MASSEUR *n* pl. -S a man who massages

MASSEUSE *n* pl. -S a woman who massages

MASSICOT *n* pl. -S a yellow pigment

MASSIER comparative of massy

MASSIEST superlative of massy

MASSIF *n* pl. -S a principal mountain mass

MASSIVE *adj* of considerable size

MASSLESS *adj* having no mass

MASSY *adj* MASSIER, MASSIEST massive

MAST *v* -ED, -ING, -S to provide with a mast (a long pole on a ship that supports the sails and rigging)

MASTABA *n* pl. -S an ancient Egyptian tomb

MASTABAH *n* pl. -S mastaba

MASTER *v* -ED, -ING, -S to become skilled in

MASTERLY *adj* very skillful

MASTERY *n* pl. -TERIES superior knowledge or skill

MASTHEAD *v* -ED, -ING, -S to raise to the top of a mast

MASTIC *n* pl. -S an aromatic resin

MASTICHE *n* pl. -S mastic

MASTIFF *n* pl. -S a large, short-haired dog

MASTITIS *n* pl. -TITIDES inflammation of the breast **MASTITIC** *adj*

MASTIX *n* pl. -ES mastic

MASTLESS *adj* having no mast

MASTLIKE *adj* resembling a mast

MASTODON *n* pl. -S an extinct elephant-like mammal

MASTOID *n* pl. -S the rear portion of the temporal bone

MASURIUM *n* pl. -S a metallic element

MAT *v* MATTED, MATTING, MATS to pack down so as to form a dense mass

MATADOR *n* pl. -S the bullfighter who kills the bull in a bullfight

MATCH *v* -ED, -ING, -ES to set in competition or opposition

MATCHBOX *n* pl. -ES a small box

MATCHER *n* pl. -S one that matches

MATE *v* MATED, MATING, MATES to join as mates (partners in a union)

MATELESS *adj* having no mate

MATELOTE *n* pl. -S a fish stew

MATER *n* pl. -TERS or -TRES mother

MATERIAL *n* pl. -S the substance of which anything is or may be composed

MATERIEL *n* pl. -S the aggregate of equipment and supplies used by an organization

MATERNAL *adj* pertaining to a mother

MATESHIP *n* pl. -S the state of being a mate

MATEY *n* pl. -EYS a friend

MATH *n* pl. -S mathematics

MATILDA *n* pl. -S a hobo's bundle

MATIN *n* pl. -S a morning song, as of birds

MATINAL *adj* pertaining to the morning

MATINEE *n* pl. -S a daytime performance

MATINESS *n* pl. -ES friendliness

MATING *n* pl. -S the period during which a seasonal-breeding animal can mate

MATLESS *adj* having no mats (small floor coverings)

MATRASS *n* pl. -ES a long-necked glass vessel

MATRES a pl. of mater

MATRIX *n* pl. -TRICES or -TRIXES something within which something else originates or develops

MATRON *n* pl. -S a married woman of established social position **MATRONAL, MATRONLY** *adj*

MATT *v* -ED, -ING, -S to matte

MATTE *v* MATTED, MATTING, MATTES to produce a dull finish on

MATTED past tense of mat, matt, and matte

MATTEDLY *adv* in a tangled manner

MATTER *v* -ED, -ING, -S to be of importance

MATTERY *adj* producing pus

MATTIN *n* pl. -S matin

MATTING *n* pl. -S a woven fabric used as a floor covering

MATTOCK *n* pl. -S a digging tool

MATTOID *n* pl. -S a mentally unbalanced person

MATTRASS *n* pl. -ES matrass

MATTRESS *n* pl. -ES a large pad filled with resilient material used on or as a bed

MATURATE *v* -RATED, -RATING, -RATES to mature

MATURE *adj* -TURER, -TUREST fully developed **MATURELY** *adv*

MATURE *v* -TURED, -TURING, -TURES to make or become mature

MATURITY *n* pl. -TIES the state of being mature

MATZA *n* pl. -S matzo

MATZAH *n* pl. -S matzo

MATZO *n* pl. -ZOS, -ZOT, or -ZOTH an unleavened bread

MATZOH *n* pl. -S matzo

MATZOON *n* pl. -S a food made from milk

MATZOT a pl. of matzo

MATZOTH a pl. of matzo

MAUDLIN *adj* excessively emotional

MAUGER *prep* maugre

MAUGRE *prep* in spite of

MAUL *v* -ED, -ING, -S to injure by beating

MAULER *n* pl. -S one that mauls

MAUMET *n* pl. -S an idol

MAUMETRY *n* pl. -RIES idolatry

MAUN *v* must — MAUN is the only form of this verb; it cannot be conjugated

MAUND *n* pl. -S an Asian unit of weight

MAUNDER *v* -ED, -ING, -S to talk incoherently

MAUNDY *n* pl. -DIES the religious ceremony of washing the feet of the poor

MAUSOLEA *n/pl* large, stately tombs

MAUT *n* pl. -S malt

MAUVE *n* pl. -S a purple color

MAVEN *n* pl. -S mavin

MAVERICK *n* pl. -S an unbranded range animal

MAVIE *n* pl. -S mavis

MAVIN *n* pl. -S an expert

MAVIS *n* pl. -VISES a songbird

MAW *v* MAWED, MAWN, MAWING, MAWS to mow

MAWKISH *adj* offensively sentimental

MAXI *n* pl. -S a long skirt or coat

MAXICOAT *n* pl. -S a long coat

MAXILLA *n* pl. -LAE or -LAS the upper jaw or jawbone

MAXIM *n* pl. -S a brief statement of a general truth or principle

MAXIMA a pl. of maximum

MAXIMAL *n* pl. -S an element of a mathematical set that is followed by no other

MAXIMIN *n* pl. -S the maximum of a set of minima

MAXIMISE *v* -MISED, -MISING, -MISES to maximize

MAXIMITE *n* pl. -S a powerful explosive

MAXIMIZE *v* -MIZED, -MIZING, -MIZES to make as great as possible

MAXIMUM *n* pl. -MUMS or -MA the greatest possible amount, quantity, or degree

MAXIXE *n* pl. -S a Brazilian dance

MAXWELL *n* pl. -S a unit of magnetic flux

MAY *v* present 2d person sing. MAY, MAYEST, or MAYST, past tense MIGHT — used as an auxiliary to express permission

MAY *v* -ED, -ING, -S to gather flowers in the spring

MAYA *n* pl. -S the power to produce illusions, in Hindu philosophy **MAYAN** *adj*

MAYAPPLE *n* pl. -S a perennial herb

MAYBE *adv* possibly

MAYBUSH *n* pl. -ES a flowering shrub

MAYDAY *n* pl. -DAYS a radio distress call

MAYEST a present 2d person sing. of may

MAYFLY *n* pl. -FLIES a winged insect

MAYHAP *adv* maybe

MAYHEM *n* pl. -S the offense of willfully maiming a person

MAYING *n* pl. -S the gathering of spring flowers

MAYOR *n* pl. -S the chief executive official of a city or borough **MAYORAL** *adj*

MAYORESS *n* pl. -ES a female mayor

MAYPOLE   *n* pl. -S a decorated pole used in a spring celebration

MAYPOP   *n* pl. -S a flowering vine

MAYST   a present 2d person sing. of may

MAYVIN   *n* pl. -S mavin

MAYWEED   *n* pl. -S a malodorous weed

MAZAEDIA   *n/pl* spore-producing organs of certain lichens

MAZARD   *n* pl. -S the head or face

MAZE   *v* MAZED, MAZING, MAZES to bewilder **MAZEDLY** *adv*

MAZELIKE   *adj* mazy

MAZER   *n* pl. -S a large drinking bowl

MAZIER   comparative of mazy

MAZIEST   superlative of mazy

MAZILY   *adv* in a mazy manner

MAZINESS   *n* pl. -ES the quality of being mazy

MAZING   present participle of maze

MAZOURKA   *n* pl. -S mazurka

MAZUMA   *n* pl. -S money

MAZURKA   *n* pl. -S a Polish dance

MAZY   *adj* MAZIER, MAZIEST full of confusing turns and passages

MAZZARD   *n* pl. -S a wild cherry

MBIRA   *n* pl. -S an African musical instrument

ME   *pron* the objective case of the pronoun I

MEAD   *n* pl. -S an alcoholic beverage

MEADOW   *n* pl. -S a tract of grassland **MEADOWY** *adj*

MEAGER   *adj* deficient in quantity or quality **MEAGERLY** *adv*

MEAGRE   *adj* meager **MEAGRELY** *adv*

MEAL   *n* pl. -S the food served and eaten in one sitting

MEALIE   *n* pl. -S an ear of corn

MEALIER   comparative of mealy

MEALIEST   superlative of mealy

MEALLESS   *adj* lacking a meal

MEALTIME   *n* pl. -S the usual time for a meal

MEALWORM   *n* pl. -S the destructive larva of certain beetles

MEALY   *adj* MEALIER, MEALIEST soft, dry, and friable

MEALYBUG   *n* pl. -S a destructive insect

MEAN   *v* MEANT, MEANING, MEANS to intend

MEAN   *adj* MEANER, MEANEST inferior in grade, quality, or character

MEANDER   *v* -ED, -ING, -S to wander

MEANER   *n* pl. -S one that means

MEANEST   superlative of mean

MEANIE   *n* pl. -S a nasty person

MEANIES   pl. of meany

MEANING   *n* pl. -S something that one intends to convey by language

MEANLY   *adv* in a mean manner

MEANNESS   *n* pl. -ES the state of being mean

MEANT   past tense of mean

MEANTIME   *n* pl. -S the intervening time

MEANY   *n* pl. MEANIES meanie

MEASLE   *n* pl. -S a tapeworm larva **MEASLED** *adj*

MEASLY   *adj* -SLIER, -SLIEST meager

MEASURE   *v* -SURED, -SURING, -SURES to ascertain the dimensions, quantity, or capacity of

MEASURER   *n* pl. -S one that measures

MEAT   *n* pl. -S animal flesh used as food

MEATAL   *adj* pertaining to a meatus

MEATBALL   *n* pl. -S a small ball of chopped meat

MEATHEAD   *n* pl. -S a dolt

MEATIER   comparative of meaty

MEATIEST   superlative of meaty

MEATILY   *adv* in a meaty manner

MEATLESS   *adj* having no meat

MEATMAN   *n* pl. -MEN a vendor of meat

MEATUS   *n* pl. -ES a natural body passage

MEATY   *adj* MEATIER, MEATIEST full of meat

MECCA   *n* pl. -S a place visited by many people

MECHANIC   *n* pl. -S a person who works with machines

MECONIUM   *n* pl. -S the first fecal excretion of a newborn child

MEDAKA   *n* pl. -S a Japanese fish

MEDAL   *v* -ALED, -ALING, -ALS or -ALLED, -ALLING, -ALS to honor with a medal (a commemorative piece of metal)

MEDALIST	*n* pl. -S a person to whom a medal has been awarded
MEDALLIC	*adj* of or pertaining to a medal
MEDALLING	a present participle of medal
MEDDLE	*v* -DLED, -DLING, -DLES to interest oneself in what is not one's concern
MEDDLER	*n* pl. -S one that meddles
MEDIA	*n* pl. -DIAE the middle layer of a blood or lymph vessel
MEDIA	*n* pl. -S a channel of communication
MEDIACY	*n* pl. -CIES the act of mediating
MEDIAD	*adv* toward the middle of a body or part
MEDIAL	*n* pl. -S a sound, syllable, or letter in the middle of a word
MEDIALLY	*adv* in a central manner
MEDIAN	*n* pl. -S a central part
MEDIANLY	*adv* medially
MEDIANT	*n* pl. -S a type of musical tone
MEDIATE	*v* -ATED, -ATING, -ATES to act between disputing parties in order to bring about a settlement
MEDIATOR	*n* pl. -S one that mediates
MEDIC	*n* pl. -S one engaged in medical work
MEDICAID	*n* pl. -S a type of governmental health program
MEDICAL	*n* pl. -S a physical examination
MEDICARE	*n* pl. -S a type of governmental health program
MEDICATE	*v* -CATED, -CATING, -CATES to treat with medicine
MEDICINE	*v* -CINED, -CINING, -CINES to administer medicine (a substance used in the treatment of disease) to
MEDICK	*n* pl. -S a flowering plant
MEDICO	*n* pl. -COS a doctor or medical student
MEDIEVAL	*n* pl. -S a person belonging to the Middle Ages
MEDII	pl. of medius
MEDIOCRE	*adj* neither good nor bad
MEDITATE	*v* -TATED, -TATING, -TATES to ponder
MEDIUM	*n* pl. -DIA or -DIUMS a surrounding environment in which something functions and thrives
MEDIUS	*n* pl. -DII the middle finger
MEDLAR	*n* pl. -S a Eurasian tree
MEDLEY	*n* pl. -LEYS a mixture
MEDULLA	*n* pl. -LAS or -LAE the central tissue in the stems of certain plants **MEDULLAR** *adj*
MEDUSA	*n* pl. -SAE or -SAS a jellyfish
MEDUSAN	*n* pl. -S medusa
MEDUSOID	*n* pl. -S medusa
MEED	*n* pl. -S a deserved reward
MEEK	*adj* MEEKER, MEEKEST lacking in spirit and courage **MEEKLY** *adv*
MEEKNESS	*n* pl. -ES the quality of being meek
MEET	*v* MET, MEETING, MEETS to come into the company or presence of
MEETER	*n* pl. -S one that meets
MEETING	*n* pl. -S an assembly for a common purpose
MEETLY	*adv* suitably
MEETNESS	*n* pl. -ES suitability
MEGABAR	*n* pl. -S a unit of pressure
MEGABIT	*n* pl. -S a unit of computer information
MEGABUCK	*n* pl. -S one million dollars
MEGADYNE	*n* pl. -S a unit of force
MEGALITH	*n* pl. -S a huge stone used in prehistoric monuments
MEGAPOD	*adj* having large feet
MEGAPODE	*n* pl. -S a large-footed bird
MEGASS	*n* pl. -ES a bagasse
MEGASSE	*n* pl. -S megass
MEGATON	*n* pl. -S a unit of explosive force
MEGAVOLT	*n* pl. -S a unit of electromotive force
MEGAWATT	*n* pl. -S a unit of power
MEGILLAH	*n* pl. -S a long, involved story
MEGILP	*n* pl. -S a substance with which pigments are mixed in painting
MEGILPH	*n* pl. -S megilp
MEGOHM	*n* pl. -S a unit of electrical resistance
MEGRIM	*n* pl. -S a migraine
MEIKLE	*adj* large
MEINIE	*n* pl. -S meiny
MEINY	*n* pl. -NIES a retinue

MEIOSIS   *n* pl. -OSES a type of cell division **MEIOTIC** *adj*

MEL   *n* pl. -S honey

MELAMINE   *n* pl. -S a chemical compound

MELANGE   *n* pl. -S a mixture

MELANIAN   *adj* pertaining to dark pigmentation

MELANIC   *n* pl. -S one who is affected with melanism

MELANIN   *n* pl. -S a dark pigment

MELANISM   *n* pl. -S abnormally dark pigmentation of the skin

MELANIST   *n* pl. -S a melanic

MELANITE   *n* pl. -S a black variety of garnet

MELANIZE   *v* -NIZED, -NIZING, -NIZES to make dark

MELANOID   *n* pl. -S a dark pigment

MELANOMA   *n* pl. -MAS or -MATA a darkly pigmented tumor

MELANOUS   *adj* having dark skin and hair

MELD   *v* -ED, -ING, -S to blend

MELDER   *n* pl. -S the amount of grain ground at one time

MELEE   *n* pl. -S a confused struggle

MELIC   *adj* pertaining to song

MELILITE   *n* pl. -S a mineral group

MELILOT   *n* pl. -S a flowering plant

MELINITE   *n* pl. -S a powerful explosive

MELISMA   *n* pl. -MAS or -MATA melodic embellishment

MELL   *v* -ED, -ING, -S to mix

MELLIFIC   *adj* producing honey

MELLOW   *adj* -LOWER, -LOWEST soft and full-flavored from ripeness **MELLOWLY** *adv*

MELLOW   *v* -ED, -ING, -S to make or become mellow

MELODEON   *n* pl. -S a musical instrument

MELODIA   *n* pl. -S a type of organ stop

MELODIC   *adj* pertaining to melody

MELODIES   pl. of melody

MELODISE   *v* -DISED, -DISING, -DISES to melodize

MELODIST   *n* pl. -S a composer of melodies

MELODIZE   *v* -DIZED, -DIZING, -DIZES to compose a melody

MELODY   *n* pl. -DIES an agreeable succession of musical sounds

MELOID   *n* pl. -S a type of beetle

MELON   *n* pl. -S any of various gourds

MELT   *v* -ED, -ING, -S to change from a solid to a liquid state by heat **MELTABLE** *adj*

MELTAGE   *n* pl. -S the process of melting

MELTER   *n* pl. -S one that melts

MELTON   *n* pl. -S a heavy woolen fabric

MEM   *n* pl. -S a Hebrew letter

MEMBER   *n* pl. -S a distinct part of a whole **MEMBERED** *adj*

MEMBRANE   *n* pl. -S a thin, pliable layer of tissue

MEMENTO   *n* pl. -TOS or -TOES something that serves as a reminder of the past

MEMO   *n* pl. MEMOS a note designating something to be remembered

MEMOIR   *n* pl. -S a biography

MEMORIAL   *n* pl. -S something that serves as a remembrance of a person or event

MEMORIZE   *v* -RIZED, -RIZING, -RIZES to commit to memory

MEMORY   *n* pl. -RIES the mental faculty of retaining and recalling past experience

MEMSAHIB   *n* pl. -S a European woman living in colonial India

MEN   pl. of man

MENACE   *v* -ACED, -ACING, -ACES to theaten

MENACER   *n* pl. -S one that menaces

MENAD   *n* pl. -S maenad

MENAGE   *n* pl. -S a household

MENARCHE   *n* pl. -S the first occurrence of menstruation

MEND   *v* -ED, -ING, -S to repair **MENDABLE** *adj*

MENDER   *n* pl. -S one that mends

MENDIGO   *n* pl. -GOS a freshwater fish

MENDING   *n* pl. -S an accumulation of articles to be mended

MENFOLK   *n/pl* the men of a family or community

MENFOLKS   *n/pl* menfolk

MENHADEN   *n* pl. -S a marine fish

MENHIR   *n* pl. -S a prehistoric monument

MENIAL   *n* pl. -S a domestic servant

MENIALLY   *adv* in a servile manner

MENINX   *n* pl. -NINGES any of the membranes enclosing the brain and spinal cord

MENISCUS   *n* pl. -CI or -CUSES a crescent-shaped body **MENISCAL** *adj*

MENO   *adv* less — used as a musical direction

MENOLOGY   *n* pl. -GIES an ecclesiastical calendar

MENORAH   *n* pl. -S a candleholder used in Jewish worship

MENSA   *n* pl. -SAS or -SAE the grinding surface of a tooth

MENSAL   *adj* pertaining to or used at the table

MENSCH   *n* pl. MENSCHES or MENSCHEN an admirable person

MENSE   *v* MENSED, MENSING, MENSES to do honor to

MENSEFUL   *adj* proper

MENSTRUA   *n/pl* solvents

MENSURAL   *adj* pertaining to measure

MENSWEAR   *n* pl. -S clothing for men

MENTA   pl. of mentum

MENTAL   *adj* pertaining to the mind **MENTALLY** *adv*

MENTHENE   *n* pl. -S a liquid hydrocarbon

MENTHOL   *n* pl. -S an alcohol

MENTION   *v* -ED, -ING, -S to refer to in a casual manner

MENTOR   *n* pl. -S a wise and trusted teacher

MENTUM   *n* pl. -TA the chin

MENU   *n* pl. -S a list of the dishes available in a restaurant

MEOW   *v* -ED, -ING, -S to make the crying sound of a cat

MEPHITIS   *n* pl. -TISES an offensive odor **MEPHITIC** *adj*

MERCAPTO   *adj* containing a particular chemical group

MERCER   *n* pl. -S a dealer in textiles

MERCERY   *n* pl. -CERIES a mercer's shop

MERCHANT   *v* -ED, -ING, -S to buy and sell goods for profit

MERCIES   pl. of mercy

MERCIFUL   *adj* full of mercy

MERCURY   *n* pl. -RIES a metallic element **MERCURIC** *adj*

MERCY   *n* pl. -CIES compassion shown to an offender or enemy

MERE   *n* pl. -S a pond or lake

MERE   *adj* MERER, MEREST being nothing more than **MERELY** *adv*

MERENGUE   *n* pl. -S a ballroom dance

MERGE   *v* MERGED, MERGING, MERGES to combine

MERGENCE   *n* pl. -S the act of merging

MERGER   *n* pl. -S the union of two or more businesses into a single enterprise

MERGING   present participle of merge

MERIDIAN   *n* pl. -S a circle around the earth passing through both poles

MERINGUE   *n* pl. -S a topping for pastries

MERINO   *n* pl. -NOS a fine wool

MERISIS   *n* pl. MERISES growth

MERISTEM   *n* pl. -S formative plant tissue

MERISTIC   *adj* made up of segments

MERIT   *v* -ED, -ING, -S to earn

MERK   *n* pl. -S a former coin of Scotland

MERL   *n* pl. -S merle

MERLE   *n* pl. -S a blackbird

MERLIN   *n* pl. -S a European falcon

MERLON   *n* pl. -S the solid part of an indented parapet

MERMAID   *n* pl. -S a legendary marine creature

MERMAN   *n* pl. -MEN a legendary marine creature

MEROPIA   *n* pl. -S partial blindness **MEROPIC** *adj*

MERRY   *adj* -RIER, -RIEST cheerful **MERRILY** *adv*

MESA   *n* pl. -S a land formation having a flat top and steep sides

MESALLY   *adv* medially

MESARCH   *adj* originating in a mesic habitat

MESCAL   *n* pl. -S a cactus

MESDAMES   pl. of madame

MESEEMS   *v* past tense MESEEMED it seems to me — MESEEMS is an impersonal verb and is used only in the 3d person sing.

MESH   *v* -ED, -ING, -ES to entangle

MESHWORK   *n* pl. -S a network

MESHY	adj MESHIER, MESHIEST netty
MESIAL	adj situated in the middle **MESIALLY** adv
MESIAN	adj mesial
MESIC	adj characterized by a medium supply of moisture
MESMERIC	adj pertaining to hypnotism
MESNALTY	n pl. -TIES a type of feudal estate
MESNE	adj being between two extremes
MESOCARP	n pl. -S the middle layer of a pericarp
MESODERM	n pl. -S the middle germ layer of an embryo
MESOGLEA	n pl. -S a gelatinous material in sponges
MESOMERE	n pl. -S an embryonic segment
MESON	n pl. -S an atomic particle **MESONIC** adj
MESOPHYL	n pl. -S the soft tissue of a leaf
MESOSOME	n pl. -S a specialized cellular part
MESOTRON	n pl. -S a meson
MESQUIT	n pl. -S mesquite
MESQUITE	n pl. -S a spiny tree or shrub
MESS	v -ED, -ING, -ES to make dirty or untidy
MESSAGE	n pl. -S an oral, written, or signaled communication
MESSAN	n pl. -S a lapdog
MESSIAH	n pl. -S an expected liberator
MESSIER	comparative of messy
MESSIEST	superlative of messy
MESSIEURS	pl. of monsieur
MESSILY	adv in a messy manner
MESSMAN	n pl. -MEN a serviceman who works in a dining facility
MESSMATE	n pl. -S a person with whom one eats regularly
MESSUAGE	n pl. -S a dwelling house with its adjacent buildings and land
MESSY	adj MESSIER, MESSIEST dirty or untidy
MESTEE	n pl. -S mustee
MESTESO	n pl. -SOS or -SOES mestizo
MESTINO	n pl. -NOS or -NOES mestizo
MESTIZA	n pl. -S a female mestizo
MESTIZO	n pl. -ZOS or -ZOES a person of mixed ancestry
MET	past tense of meet
META	adj pertaining to positions in a benzene ring separated by one carbon atom
METAGE	n pl. -S an official measurement of weight or contents
METAL	v -ALED, -ALING, -ALS or -ALLED, -ALLING, -ALS to cover with metal (any of various ductile, fusible, and lustrous substances)
METALISE	v -ISED, -ISING, -ISES to metalize
METALIST	n pl. -S one who works with metals
METALIZE	v -IZED, -IZING, -IZES to treat with metal
METALLED	past tense of metal
METALLIC	adj pertaining to or containing a metal
METALLING	a present participle of metal
METAMER	n pl. -S a type of chemical compound
METAMERE	n pl. -S a somite
METAPHOR	n pl. -S a type of figure of speech
METATE	n pl. -S a stone used for grinding grains
METAZOAN	n pl. -S any of a major division of multicellular animals **METAZOAL, METAZOIC** adj
METAZOON	n pl. -ZOA a metazoan
METE	v METED, METING, METES to distribute by measure
METEOR	n pl. -S a small celestial body that enters the earth's atmosphere **METEORIC** adj
METEPA	n pl. -S a chemical compound
METER	v -ED, -ING, -S to measure by mechanical means
METERAGE	n pl. -S the process of metering
METHADON	n pl. -S a narcotic drug
METHANE	n pl. -S a flammable gas
METHANOL	n pl. -S a toxic alcohol
METHINKS	v past tense METHOUGHT it seems to me — METHINKS is an impersonal verb and is used only in the 3d person sing.
METHOD	n pl. -S a means of procedure
METHODIC	adj systematic

METHOUGHT	past tense of methinks
METHOXY	*adj* containing a certain chemical group
METHOXYL	*adj* methoxy
METHYL	*n* pl. -S a univalent radical **METHYLIC** *adj*
METHYLAL	*n* pl. -S a flammable liquid
METIER	*n* pl. -S a vocation
METING	present participle of mete
METIS	*n* pl. METIS a person of mixed ancestry
METISSE	*n* pl. -S a female metis
METONYM	*n* pl. -S a word used in metonymy
METONYMY	*n* pl. -MIES a type of figure of speech
METOPE	*n* pl. -PES or -PAE a space between two triglyphs
METOPIC	*adj* pertaining to the forehead
METOPON	*n* pl. -S a narcotic drug
METRE	*v* -TRED, -TRING, -TRES to meter
METRIC	*n* pl. -S a standard of measurement
METRICAL	*adj* pertaining to or composed in a system of arranged and measured rhythm
METRIFY	*v* -FIED, -FYING, -FIES to compose in metrical form
METRING	present participle of metre
METRIST	*n* pl. -S one who metrifies
METRITIS	*n* pl. -TISES inflammation of the uterus
METRO	*n* pl. -ROS a subway
METTLE	*n* pl. -S quality of character **METTLED** *adj*
METUMP	*n* pl. -S a tumpline
MEUNIERE	*adj* cooked in browned butter
MEW	*v* -ED, -ING, -S to confine
MEWL	*v* -ED, -ING, -S to whimper
MEWLER	*n* pl. -S one that mewls
MEZCAL	*n* pl. -S mescal
MEZEREON	*n* pl. -S a flowering shrub
MEZEREUM	*n* pl. -S mezereon
MEZQUIT	*n* pl. -S mesquite
MEZQUITE	*n* pl. -S mesquite
MEZUZA	*n* pl. -S mezuzah
MEZUZAH	*n* pl. -ZAHS, -ZOT, or -ZOTH a Judaic scroll
MEZZO	*n* pl. -ZOS a female voice of a full, deep quality
MHO	*n* pl. MHOS a unit of electrical conductance
MI	*n* pl. -S the third tone of the diatonic musical scale
MIAOU	*v* -ED, -ING, -S to meow
MIAOW	*v* -ED, -ING, -S to meow
MIASM	*n* pl. -S miasma
MIASMA	*n* pl. -MAS or -MATA a noxious vapor **MIASMAL, MIASMIC** *adj*
MIAUL	*v* -ED, -ING, -S to meow
MIB	*n* pl. -S a type of playing marble
MICA	*n* pl. -S a mineral
MICAWBER	*n* pl. -S a person who remains hopeful despite adversity
MICE	pl. of mouse
MICELL	*n* pl. -S micelle
MICELLA	*n* pl. -LAE micelle
MICELLE	*n* pl. -S a coherent strand or structure in a fiber **MICELLAR** *adj*
MICK	*n* pl. -S an Irishman — an offensive term
MICKEY	*n* pl. -EYS a drugged drink
MICKLE	*adj* -LER, -LEST large
MICKLE	*n* pl. -S a large amount
MICRA	a pl. of micron
MICRIFY	*v* -FIED, -FYING, -FIES to make small
MICRO	*adj* very small
MICROBAR	*n* pl. -S a unit of atmospheric pressure
MICROBE	*n* pl. -S a minute life form **MICROBIC** *adj*
MICROBUS	*n* pl. -BUSES or -BUSSES a small bus
MICROHM	*n* pl. -S a unit of electrical resistance
MICROLUX	*n* pl. -LUXES or -LUCES a unit of illumination
MICROMHO	*n* pl. -S a unit of electrical conductance
MICRON	*n* pl. -CRONS or -CRA a unit of length
MICRURGY	*n* pl. -GIES the use of minute tools under high magnification
MID	*n* pl. -S the middle
MIDAIR	*n* pl. -S a region in the middle of the air

MIDBRAIN *n* pl. -S the middle region of the brain

MIDDAY *n* pl. -DAYS the middle of the day

MIDDEN *n* pl. -S a dunghill

MIDDIES pl. of middy

MIDDLE *v* -DLED, -DLING, -DLES to place in the middle (the area or point equidistant from extremes or limits)

MIDDLER *n* pl. -S a student in an intermediate grade

MIDDLING *n* pl. -S a cut of pork

MIDDY *n* pl. -DIES a loosely fitting blouse

MIDFIELD *n* pl. -S the middle portion of a playing field

MIDGE *n* pl. -S a small winged insect

MIDGET *n* pl. -S a very small person

MIDGUT *n* pl. -S the middle part of the embryonic digestive tract

MIDI *n* pl. -S a skirt or coat that extends to the middle of the calf

MIDIRON *n* pl. -S a golf club

MIDLAND *n* pl. -S the middle part of a country

MIDLEG *n* pl. -S the middle of the leg

MIDLINE *n* pl. -S a median line

MIDMONTH *n* pl. -S the middle of the month

MIDMOST *n* pl. -S a part exactly in the middle

MIDNIGHT *n* pl. -S the middle of the night

MIDNOON *n* pl. -S midday

MIDPOINT *n* pl. -S a point at the middle

MIDRANGE *n* pl. -S the middle of a range

MIDRASH *n* pl. -RASHIM an early Jewish interpretation of a biblical text

MIDRIB *n* pl. -S the central vein of a leaf

MIDRIFF *n* pl. -S the middle part of the body

MIDSHIP *adj* pertaining to the middle of a ship

MIDSHIPS *adv* toward the middle of a ship

MIDSPACE *n* pl. -S the middle of a space

MIDST *n* pl. -S the middle

MIDSTORY *n* pl. -RIES the middle of a story

MIDTERM *n* pl. -S an examination given in the middle of an academic semester

MIDTOWN *n* pl. -S the central part of a city

MIDWATCH *n* pl. -ES a watch on a ship between midnight and 4 A.M.

MIDWAY *n* pl. -WAYS an avenue at a fair or carnival for concessions and amusements

MIDWEEK *n* pl. -S the middle of the week

MIDWIFE *v* -WIFED, -WIFING, -WIFES or -WIVED, -WIVING, -WIVES to assist a woman in childbirth

MIDYEAR *n* pl. -S the middle of the year

MIEN *n* pl. -S demeanor

MIFF *v* -ED, -ING, -S to annoy

MIFFY *adj* MIFFIER, MIFFIEST easily annoyed

MIG *n* pl. -S a type of playing marble

MIGG *n* pl. -S mig

MIGGLE *n* pl. -S a mig

MIGHT *n* pl. -S strength

MIGHTY *adj* MIGHTIER, MIGHTIEST strong **MIGHTILY** *adv*

MIGNON *n* pl. -S a cut of beef

MIGNONNE *adj* daintily small

MIGRAINE *n* pl. -S a severe headache

MIGRANT *n* pl. -S one that migrates

MIGRATE *v* -GRATED, -GRATING, -GRATES to move from one region to another

MIGRATOR *n* pl. -S a migrant

MIJNHEER *n* pl. -S mynheer

MIKADO *n* pl. -DOS an emperor of Japan

MIKE *n* pl. -S a microphone

MIKRON *n* pl. -KRONS or -KRA micron

MIKVAH *n* pl. -VAHS or -VOTH a place for ritual bathing by Orthodox Jews

MIKVEH *n* pl. -S mikvah

MIL *n* pl. -S a unit of length

MILADI *n* pl. -S milady

MILADY *n* pl. -DIES an English gentlewoman

MILAGE *n* pl. -S mileage

MILCH *adj* giving milk

MILCHIG *adj* made of or derived from milk

MILD *adj* MILDER, MILDEST not harsh or rough **MILDLY** *adv*

MILDEN *v* -ED, -ING, -S to make or become mild

MILDEW	*v* -ED, -ING, -S to affect with mildew (a whitish growth produced by fungi)
MILDEWY	*adj* affected with or resembling mildew
MILDNESS	*n* pl. -ES the quality of being mild
MILE	*n* pl. -S a unit of distance
MILEAGE	*n* pl. -S total distance expressed in miles
MILEPOST	*n* pl. -S a post indicating distance in miles
MILER	*n* pl. -S one that runs a mile race
MILESIMO	*n* pl. -MOS a monetary unit of Chile
MILFOIL	*n* pl. -S a perennial herb
MILIA	pl. of milium
MILIARIA	*n* pl. -S a skin disease
MILIARY	*adj* made up of many small projections
MILIEU	*n* pl. -LIEUS or -LIEUX environment
MILITANT	*n* pl. -S a person who is aggressively engaged in a cause
MILITARY	*n* pl. -TARIES armed forces
MILITATE	*v* -TATED, -TATING, -TATES to have influence or effect
MILITIA	*n* pl. -S a citizen army
MILIUM	*n* pl. -IA a small, whitish lump in the skin
MILK	*v* -ED, -ING, -S to draw milk (a whitish, nutritious liquid) from the udder of
MILKER	*n* pl. -S one that milks
MILKFISH	*n* pl. -ES a marine food fish
MILKIER	comparative of milky
MILKIEST	superlative of milky
MILKILY	*adv* in a milky manner
MILKMAID	*n* pl. -S a woman who milks cows
MILKMAN	*n* pl. -MEN a man who sells or delivers milk
MILKSOP	*n* pl. -S an effeminate man
MILKWEED	*n* pl. -S a plant that secretes a milky juice
MILKWOOD	*n* pl. -S a tropical tree
MILKWORT	*n* pl. -S a flowering plant
MILKY	*adj* MILKIER, MILKIEST resembling or suggestive of milk

MILL	*v* -ED, -ING, -S to grind by mechanical means **MILLABLE** *adj*
MILLAGE	*n* pl. -S a type of monetary rate
MILLDAM	*n* pl. -S a dam built to form a millpond
MILLE	*n* pl. -S a thousand
MILLEPED	*n* pl. -S milliped
MILLER	*n* pl. -S one that mills
MILLET	*n* pl. -S a cereal grass
MILLIARD	*n* pl. -S a billion
MILLIARE	*n* pl. -S a unit of area
MILLIARY	*adj* marking the distance of a Roman mile
MILLIBAR	*n* pl. -S a unit of atmospheric pressure
MILLIEME	*n* pl. -S a coin of Egypt and Libya
MILLIER	*n* pl. -S a unit of weight
MILLIGAL	*n* pl. -S a unit of acceleration
MILLILUX	*n* pl. -LUXES or -LUCES a unit of illumination
MILLIME	*n* pl. -S a coin of Tunisia
MILLIMHO	*n* pl. -MHOS a unit of electrical conductance
MILLINE	*n* pl. -S a unit of advertising space
MILLINER	*n* pl. -S one who makes or sells women's hats
MILLING	*n* pl. -S a corrugated edge on a coin
MILLIOHM	*n* pl. -S a unit of electrical resistance
MILLION	*n* pl. -S a number
MILLIPED	*n* pl. -S a multi-legged arthropod
MILLIREM	*n* pl. -S a quantity of ionizing radiation
MILLPOND	*n* pl. -S a pond for supplying water to run a mill wheel (a type of waterwheel)
MILLRACE	*n* pl. -S the current of water that drives a mill wheel
MILLRUN	*n* pl. -S a millrace
MILLWORK	*n* pl. -S woodwork produced by milling
MILO	*n* pl. -LOS a cereal grass
MILORD	*n* pl. -S an English gentleman
MILPA	*n* pl. -S a field that is cleared from a jungle for farming purposes

MILREIS	*n* pl. MILREIS a former monetary unit of Portugal
MILT	*v* -ED, -ING, -S to impregnate with milt (fish sperm)
MILTER	*n* pl. -S a male fish at breeding time
MILTY	*adj* MILTIER, MILTIEST full of milt
MIM	*adj* primly demure
MIMBAR	*n* pl. -S a pulpit in a mosque
MIME	*v* MIMED, MIMING, MIMES to mimic
MIMER	*n* pl. -S one that mimes
MIMESIS	*n* pl. -SISES mimicry **MIMETIC** *adj*
MIMETITE	*n* pl. -S an ore of lead
MIMIC	*v* -ICKED, -ICKING, -ICS to imitate closely
MIMICAL	*adj* of the nature of mimicry
MIMICKER	*n* pl. -S one that mimics
MIMICKING	present participle of mimic
MIMICRY	*n* pl. -RIES an instance of mimicking
MIMING	present participle of mime
MIMOSA	*n* pl. -S a tropical plant
MINA	*n* pl. -NAS or -NAE an ancient unit of weight and value
MINABLE	*adj* capable of being mined
MINACITY	*n* pl. -TIES the state of being threatening
MINARET	*n* pl. -S a slender tower attached to a mosque
MINATORY	*adj* threatening
MINCE	*v* MINCED, MINCING, MINCES to cut into very small pieces
MINCER	*n* pl. -S one that minces
MINCY	*adj* MINCIER, MINCIEST affectedly dainty
MIND	*v* -ED, -ING, -S to heed
MINDER	*n* pl. -S one that minds
MINDFUL	*adj* heedful
MINDLESS	*adj* lacking intelligence
MINE	*v* MINED, MINING, MINES to dig into for valuable materials
MINEABLE	*adj* minable
MINER	*n* pl. -S one that mines
MINERAL	*n* pl. -S a naturally occurring inorganic substance having a characteristic set of physical properties
MINGIER	comparative of mingy
MINGIEST	superlative of mingy
MINGLE	*v* -GLED, -GLING, -GLES to mix together
MINGLER	*n* pl. -S one that mingles
MINGY	*adj* -GIER, -GIEST mean and stingy
MINI	*n* pl. -S something distinctively smaller than others of its kind
MINIBIKE	*n* pl. -S a small motorcycle
MINIBUS	*n* pl. -BUSES or -BUSSES a small bus
MINICAB	*n* pl. -S a small taxicab
MINICAR	*n* pl. -S a small automobile
MINIFY	*v* -FIED, -FYING, -FIES to make small or smaller
MINIKIN	*n* pl. -S a small or dainty creature
MINIM	*n* pl. -S a unit of liquid measure
MINIMA	a pl. of minimum
MINIMAL	*n* pl. -S an element of a mathematical set that precedes all others
MINIMAX	*n* pl. -ES the minimum of a set of maxima
MINIMISE	*v* -MISED, -MISING, -MISES to minimize
MINIMIZE	*v* -MIZED, -MIZING, -MIZES to make as small as possible
MINIMUM	*n* pl. -MUMS or -MA the least possible amount, quantity, or degree
MINING	*n* pl. -S the process or business of working mines (excavations in the earth)
MINION	*n* pl. -S a servile follower
MINISH	*v* -ED, -ING, -ES to diminish
MINISTER	*v* -ED, -ING, -S to give aid or service
MINISTRY	*n* pl. -TRIES the act of ministering
MINIUM	*n* pl. -S a red pigment
MINIVER	*n* pl. -S a white fur
MINK	*n* pl. -S a carnivorous mammal
MINNOW	*n* pl. -S a small fish
MINNY	*n* pl. -NIES minnow
MINOR	*v* -ED, -ING, -S to pursue a specific subordinate course of study
MINORCA	*n* pl. -S any of a breed of large domestic fowls

MINORITY	*n* pl. -TIES the smaller number or part
MINSTER	*n* pl. -S a large or important church
MINSTREL	*n* pl. -S a medieval musician
MINT	*v* -ED, -ING, -S to produce by stamping metal, as coins
MINTAGE	*n* pl. -S the act of minting
MINTER	*n* pl. -S one that mints
MINTY	*adj* MINTIER, MINTIEST having the flavor mint (an aromatic herb)
MINUEND	*n* pl. -S a number from which another is to be subtracted
MINUET	*n* pl. -S a slow, stately dance
MINUS	*n* pl. -ES a negative quantity
MINUTE	*v* -UTED, -UTING, -UTES to make a brief note of
MINUTE	*adj* -NUTER, -NUTEST very small **MINUTELY** *adv*
MINUTIA	*n* pl. -TIAE a small detail **MINUTIAL** *adj*
MINUTING	present participle of minute
MINX	*n* pl. -ES a pert girl **MINXISH** *adj*
MINYAN	*n* pl. -YANS or -YANIM the minimum number required to be present for the conduct of a Jewish service
MIOSIS	*n* pl. -OSES excessive contraction of the pupil of the eye
MIOTIC	*n* pl. -S an agent that causes miosis
MIQUELET	*n* pl. -S a former Spanish or French soldier
MIR	*n* pl. MIRS or MIRI a Russian peasant commune
MIRACLE	*n* pl. -S an event ascribed to supernatural or divine origin
MIRADOR	*n* pl. -S an architectural feature designed to afford an extensive view
MIRAGE	*n* pl. -S a type of optical illusion
MIRE	*v* MIRED, MIRING, MIRES to cause to stick in swampy ground
MIREX	*n* pl. -ES an insecticide
MIRI	a pl. of mir
MIRIER	comparative of miry
MIRIEST	superlative of miry
MIRINESS	*n* pl. -ES the state of being miry

MIRING	present participle of mire
MIRK	*adj* MIRKER, MIRKEST murk
MIRK	*n* pl. -S murk
MIRKY	*adj* MIRKIER, MIRKIEST murky **MIRKILY** *adv*
MIRROR	*v* -ED, -ING, -S to reflect an image of
MIRTH	*n* pl. -S spirited gaiety **MIRTHFUL** *adj*
MIRY	*adj* MIRIER, MIRIEST swampy
MIRZA	*n* pl. -S a Persian title of honor
MISACT	*v* -ED, -ING, -S to act badly
MISADAPT	*v* -ED, -ING, -S to adapt wrongly
MISADD	*v* -ED, -ING, -S to add incorrectly
MISAGENT	*n* pl. -S a bad agent
MISAIM	*v* -ED, -ING, -S to aim badly
MISALLY	*v* -LIED, -LYING, -LIES to ally badly
MISALTER	*v* -ED, -ING, -S to alter wrongly
MISAPPLY	*v* -PLIED, -PLYING, -PLIES to apply wrongly
MISASSAY	*v* -ED, -ING, -S to attempt unsuccessfully
MISATE	past tense of miseat
MISATONE	*v* -ATONED, -ATONING, -ATONES to atone wrongly
MISAVER	*v* -AVERRED, -AVERRING, -AVERS to speak erroneously
MISAWARD	*v* -ED, -ING, -S to award wrongly
MISBEGIN	*v* -GAN, -GUN, -GINNING, -GINS to begin wrongly
MISBEGOT	*adj* born out of wedlock
MISBIAS	*v* -ASED, -ASING, -ASES or -ASSED, -ASSING, -ASSES to bias wrongly
MISBILL	*v* -ED, -ING, -S to bill wrongly
MISBIND	*v* -BOUND, -BINDING, -BINDS to bind imperfectly
MISBRAND	*v* -ED, -ING, -S to brand incorrectly
MISBUILD	*v* -BUILT, -BUILDING, -BUILDS to build imperfectly
MISCALL	*v* -ED, -ING, -S to call by a wrong name
MISCARRY	*v* -RIED, -RYING, -RIES to be unsuccessful
MISCAST	*v* -CAST, -CASTING, -CASTS to cast in an unsuitable role

MISCHIEF   *n* pl. -S action that causes irritation, harm, or trouble

MISCIBLE   *adj* capable of being mixed

MISCITE   *v* -CITED, -CITING, -CITES to misquote

MISCLAIM   *v* -ED, -ING, -S to claim wrongfully

MISCLASS   *v* -ED, -ING, -ES to put in the wrong class

MISCOIN   *v* -ED, -ING, -S to coin improperly

MISCOLOR   *v* -ED, -ING, -S to color incorrectly

MISCOOK   *v* -ED, -ING, -S to cook badly

MISCOPY   *v* -COPIED, -COPYING, -COPIES to copy incorrectly

MISCOUNT   *v* -ED, -ING, -S to count incorrectly

MISCUE   *v* -CUED, -CUING, -CUES to make a faulty stroke in billiards

MISCUT   *v* -CUT, -CUTTING, -CUTS to cut incorrectly

MISDATE   *v* -DATED, -DATING, -DATES to date incorrectly

MISDEAL   *v* -DEALT, -DEALING, -DEALS to deal cards incorrectly

MISDEED   *n* pl. -S an evil act

MISDEEM   *v* -ED, -ING, -S to judge unfavorably

MISDO   *v* -DID, -DONE, -DOING, -DOES to do wrongly

MISDOER   *n* pl. -S one that misdoes

MISDOING   *n* pl. -S an instance of doing wrong

MISDONE   past participle of misdo

MISDOUBT   *v* -ED, -ING, -S to doubt

MISDRAW   *v* -DREW, -DRAWN, -DRAWING, -DRAWS to draw incorrectly

MISDRIVE   *v* -DROVE, -DRIVEN, -DRIVING, -DRIVES to drive wrongly or improperly

MISE   *n* pl. -S an agreement or settlement

MISEASE   *n* pl. -S discomfort

MISEAT   *v* -ATE, -EATING, -EATS to eat improperly

MISEDIT   *v* -ED, -ING, -S to edit incorrectly

MISENROL   *v* -ROLLED, -ROLLING, -ROLS to misenroll

MISENROLL   *v* -ED, -ING, -S to enroll improperly

MISENTER   *v* -ED, -ING, -S to enter erroneously

MISENTRY   *n* pl. -TRIES an erroneous entry

MISER   *n* pl. -S one who hoards money greedily

MISERERE   *n* pl. -S a part of a church seat

MISERLY   *adj* characteristic of a miser

MISERY   *n* pl. -ERIES a state of great suffering

MISEVENT   *n* pl. -S a mishap

MISFAITH   *n* pl. -S lack of faith; disbelief

MISFIELD   *v* -ED, -ING, -S to field badly

MISFILE   *v* -FILED, -FILING, -FILES to file in the wrong place

MISFIRE   *v* -FIRED, -FIRING, -FIRES to fail to fire

MISFIT   *v* -FITTED, -FITTING, -FITS to fit badly

MISFORM   *v* -ED, -ING, -S to misshape

MISFRAME   *v* -FRAMED, -FRAMING, -FRAMES to frame badly

MISGAUGE   *v* -GAUGED, -GAUGING, -GAUGES to gauge wrongly or inaccurately

MISGIVE   *v* -GAVE, -GIVEN, -GIVING, -GIVES to make doubtful or fearful

MISGRAFT   *v* -ED, -ING, -S to graft wrongly

MISGROW   *v* -GREW, -GROWN, -GROWING, -GROWS to grow abnormally

MISGUESS   *v* -ED, -ING, -ES to guess wrongly

MISGUIDE   *v* -GUIDED, -GUIDING, -GUIDES to guide wrongly

MISHAP   *n* pl. -S an unfortunate accident

MISHEAR   *v* -HEARD, -HEARING, -HEARS to hear incorrectly

MISHIT   *v* -HIT, -HITTING, -HITS to hit poorly

MISHMASH   *n* pl. -ES a confused mixture

MISHMOSH   *n* pl. -ES mishmash

MISINFER   *v* -FERRED, -FERRING, -FERS to infer wrongly

MISINTER   *v* -TERRED, -TERRING, -TERS to inter improperly

MISJOIN   *v* -ED, -ING, -S to join improperly

MISJUDGE   *v* -JUDGED, -JUDGING, -JUDGES to judge wrongly

MISKAL   *n* pl. -S an Oriental unit of weight

MISKEEP	*v* -KEPT, -KEEPING, -KEEPS to keep wrongly
MISKNOW	*v* -KNEW, -KNOWN, -KNOWING, -KNOWS to fail to understand or recognize
MISLABEL	*v* -BELED, -BELING, -BELS or -BELLED, -BELLING, -BELS to label incorrectly or falsely
MISLABOR	*v* -ED, -ING, -S to labor badly
MISLAIN	past participle of mislie
MISLAY	*v* -LAID, -LAYING, -LAYS to put in a forgotten place
MISLAYER	*n* pl. -S one that mislays
MISLEAD	*v* -LED, -LEADING, -LEADS to lead astray
MISLEARN	*v* -LEARNED or -LEARNT, -LEARNING, -LEARNS to learn wrongly
MISLIE	*v* -LAY, -LAIN, -LYING, -LIES to lie in a wrong position
MISLIGHT	*v* -LIGHTED or -LIT, -LIGHTING, -LIGHTS to lead astray by its light
MISLIKE	*v* -LIKED, -LIKING, -LIKES to dislike
MISLIKER	*n* pl. -S one that mislikes
MISLIT	a past tense of mislight
MISLIVE	*v* -LIVED, -LIVING, -LIVES to live a bad life
MISLODGE	*v* -LODGED, -LODGING, -LODGES to lodge in a wrong place
MISLYING	present participle of mislie
MISMARK	*v* -ED, -ING, -S to mark wrongly
MISMATCH	*v* -ED, -ING, -ES to match badly
MISMATE	*v* -MATED, -MATING, -MATES to mate unsuitably
MISMEET	*v* -MET, -MEETING, -MEETS to meet under unfortunate circumstances
MISMOVE	*v* -MOVED, -MOVING, -MOVES to move wrongly
MISNAME	*v* -NAMED, -NAMING, -NAMES to call by a wrong name
MISNOMER	*n* pl. -S a name wrongly used
MISO	*n* pl. -SOS a type of food paste
MISOGAMY	*n* pl. -MIES a hatred of marriage
MISOGYNY	*n* pl. -NIES a hatred of women
MISOLOGY	*n* pl. -GIES a hatred of debate or reasoning
MISPAGE	*v* -PAGED, -PAGING, -PAGES to page incorrectly
MISPAINT	*v* -ED, -ING, -S to paint wrongly
MISPARSE	*v* -PARSED, -PARSING, -PARSES to parse incorrectly
MISPART	*v* -ED, -ING, -S to part badly
MISPATCH	*v* -ED, -ING, -ES to patch badly
MISPEN	*v* -PENNED, -PENNING, -PENS to write incorrectly
MISPLACE	*v* -PLACED, -PLACING, -PLACES to put in a wrong place
MISPLANT	*v* -ED, -ING, -S to plant wrongly
MISPLAY	*v* -ED, -ING, -S to make a bad play in a game
MISPLEAD	*v* -PLEADED or -PLED, -PLEADING, -PLEADS to plead wrongly or falsely
MISPOINT	*v* -ED, -ING, -S to point improperly
MISPOISE	*v* -POISED, -POISING, -POISES to poise incorrectly
MISPRINT	*v* -ED, -ING, -S to print incorrectly
MISPRIZE	*v* -PRIZED, -PRIZING, -PRIZES to despise
MISQUOTE	*v* -QUOTED, -QUOTING, -QUOTES to quote incorrectly
MISRAISE	*v* -RAISED, -RAISING, -RAISES to raise wrongly
MISRATE	*v* -RATED, -RATING, -RATES to rate incorrectly
MISREAD	*v* -READ, -READING, -READS to read incorrectly
MISREFER	*v* -FERRED, -FERRING, -FERS to refer incorrectly
MISRELY	*v* -LIED, -LYING, -LIES to rely wrongly
MISRULE	*v* -RULED, -RULING, -RULES to rule unwisely or unjustly
MISS	*v* -ED, -ING, -ES to fail to make contact with
MISSAL	*n* pl. -S a prayer book
MISSAY	*v* -SAID, -SAYING, -SAYS to say incorrectly
MISSEAT	*v* -ED, -ING, -S to seat wrongly
MISSEL	*n* pl. -S a European thrush
MISSEND	*v* -SENT, -SENDING, -SENDS to send incorrectly
MISSENSE	*n* pl. -S a form of genetic mutation
MISSHAPE	*v* -SHAPED, -SHAPEN, -SHAPING, -SHAPES to shape badly
MISSHOD	*adj* improperly shod

MISSIES pl. of missy

MISSILE *n* pl. -S an object or weapon that is thrown or projected

MISSILRY *n* pl. -RIES the science of designing and operating guided missiles

MISSION *v* -ED, -ING, -S to send to perform a specific task

MISSIS *n* pl. -SISES a wife

MISSIVE *n* pl. -S a written communication

MISSORT *v* -ED, -ING, -S to sort badly or improperly

MISSOUND *v* -ED, -ING, -S to sound wrongly

MISSOUT *n* pl. -S a losing throw of dice

MISSPACE *v* -SPACED, -SPACING, -SPACES to space incorrectly

MISSPEAK *v* -SPOKE, -SPOKEN, -SPEAKING, -SPEAKS to speak incorrectly

MISSPELL *v* -SPELLED or -SPELT, -SPELLING, -SPELLS to spell incorrectly

MISSPEND *v* -SPENT, -SPENDING, -SPENDS to spend wrongly

MISSPOKE past tense of misspeak

MISSPOKEN past participle of misspeak

MISSTART *v* -ED, -ING, -S to start off badly

MISSTATE *v* -STATED, -STATING, -STATES to state wrongly

MISSTEER *v* -ED, -ING, -S to steer wrongly

MISSTEP *n* pl. -S a false step

MISSTOP *v* -STOPPED, -STOPPING, -STOPS to stop wrongly

MISSTYLE *v* -STYLED, -STYLING, -STYLES to style or call wrongly

MISSUIT *v* -ED, -ING, -S to suit badly

MISSUS *n* pl. -ES missis

MISSY *n* pl. MISSIES a young girl

MIST *v* -ED, -ING, -S to become blurry

MISTAKE *v* -TOOK or -TEUK, -TAKEN, -TAKING, -TAKES to interpret wrongly

MISTAKER *n* pl. -S one that mistakes

MISTBOW *n* pl. -S a fogbow

MISTEACH *v* -TAUGHT, -TEACHING, -TEACHES to teach wrongly or badly

MISTEND *v* -ED, -ING, -S to tend to improperly

MISTER *n* pl. -S sir

MISTERM *v* -ED, -ING, -S to call by a wrong name

MISTEUK a past tense of mistake

MISTHINK *v* -THOUGHT, -THINKING, -THINKS to think wrongly

MISTHROW *v* -THREW, -THROWN, -THROWING, -THROWS to throw errantly

MISTIER comparative of misty

MISTIEST superlative of misty

MISTILY *adv* in a misty manner

MISTIME *v* -TIMED, -TIMING, -TIMES to time wrongly

MISTITLE *v* -TLED, -TLING, -TLES to call by a wrong title

MISTOOK a past tense of mistake

MISTOUCH *v* -ED, -ING, -ES to touch improperly

MISTRACE *v* -TRACED, -TRACING, -TRACES to trace wrongly

MISTRAL *n* pl. -S a cold, dry wind

MISTREAT *v* -ED, -ING, -S to treat badly

MISTRESS *n* pl. -ES a woman in a position of authority

MISTRIAL *n* pl. -S a trial made invalid because of some error in procedure

MISTRUST *v* -ED, -ING, -S to distrust

MISTRYST *v* -ED, -ING, -S to fail to keep an appointment with

MISTUNE *v* -TUNED, -TUNING, -TUNES to tune incorrectly

MISTUTOR *v* -ED, -ING, -S to instruct or bring up badly

MISTY *adj* MISTIER, MISTIEST blurry

MISTYPE *v* -TYPED, -TYPING, -TYPES to type incorrectly

MISUNION *n* pl. -S a bad union

MISUSAGE *n* pl. -S incorrect use

MISUSE *v* -USED, -USING, -USES to use incorrectly

MISUSER *n* pl. -S one that misuses

MISVALUE *v* -UED, -UING, -UES to value incorrectly

MISWORD *v* -ED, -ING, -S to word wrongly

MISWRITE *v* -WROTE or -WRIT, -WRITTEN, -WRITING, -WRITES to write incorrectly

MISYOKE *v* -YOKED, -YOKING, -YOKES to yoke improperly

MITE *n* pl. -S a small arachnid

MITER   *v* -ED, -ING, -S to raise to the rank of a bishop

MITERER   *n pl.* -S one that miters

MITHER   *n pl.* -S mother

MITICIDE   *n pl.* -S a substance used to kill mites

MITIER   comparative of mity

MITIEST   superlative of mity

MITIGATE   *v* -GATED, -GATING, -GATES to make less severe

MITIS   *n pl.* -TISES a type of wrought iron

MITOGEN   *n pl.* -S a substance that induces mitosis

MITOSIS   *n pl.* -TOSES a type of cell division **MITOTIC** *adj*

MITRAL   *adj* pertaining to a valve of the heart

MITRE   *v* -TRED, -TRING, -TRES to miter

MITSVAH   *n pl.* -VAHS or -VOTH mitzvah

MITT   *n pl.* -S a type of baseball glove

MITTEN   *n pl.* -S a type of covering for the hand

MITTIMUS   *n pl.* -ES a warrant committing a person to prison

MITY   *adj* MITIER, MITIEST infested with mites

MITZVAH   *n pl.* -VAHS or -VOTH a commandment of Jewish law

MIX   *v* MIXED or MIXT, MIXING, MIXES to put together into one mass **MIXABLE, MIXIBLE** *adj*

MIXER   *n pl.* -S one that mixes

MIXOLOGY   *n pl.* -GIES the art of making mixed drinks

MIXT   a past tense of mix

MIXTURE   *n pl.* -S something produced by mixing

MIXUP   *n pl.* -S a state of confusion

MIZEN   *n pl.* -S mizzen

MIZZEN   *n pl.* -S a type of sail

MIZZLE   *v* -ZLED, -ZLING, -ZLES to rain in fine droplets

MIZZLY   *adj* characterized by a fine rain

MNEMONIC   *n pl.* -S a device to assist the memory

MOA   *n pl.* -S an extinct flightless bird

MOAN   *v* -ED, -ING, -S to utter a low, mournful sound

MOANFUL   *adj* moaning

MOAT   *v* -ED, -ING, -S to surround with a moat (a water-filled trench)

MOATLIKE   *adj* suggestive of a moat

MOB   *v* MOBBED, MOBBING, MOBS to crowd about

MOBBER   *n pl.* -S one that mobs

MOBBISH   *adj* characteristic of a mob (a disorderly crowd of people)

MOBCAP   *n pl.* -S a woman's cap

MOBILE   *n pl.* -S a form of sculpture

MOBILISE   *v* -LISED, -LISING, -LISES to mobilize

MOBILITY   *n pl.* -TIES the ability to move

MOBILIZE   *v* -LIZED, -LIZING, -LIZES to put into movement

MOBOCRAT   *n pl.* -S a supporter of mob rule

MOBSTER   *n pl.* -S a gangster

MOCCASIN   *n pl.* -S a type of shoe

MOCHA   *n pl.* -S a choice, pungent coffee

MOCHILA   *n pl.* -S a leather covering for a saddle

MOCK   *v* -ED, -ING, -S to ridicule **MOCKABLE** *adj*

MOCKER   *n pl.* -S one that mocks

MOCKERY   *n pl.* -ERIES the act of mocking

MOCKUP   *n pl.* -S a full-sized model

MOD   *n pl.* -S one who wears boldly stylish clothes

MODAL   *adj* pertaining to a mode **MODALLY** *adv*

MODALITY   *n pl.* -TIES the state of being modal

MODE   *n pl.* -S a method of doing or acting

MODEL   *v* -ELED, -ELING, -ELS or -ELLED, -ELLING, -ELS to plan or form after a pattern

MODELER   *n pl.* -S one that models

MODELING   *n pl.* -S the treatment of volume in sculpture

MODELLED   a past tense of model

MODELLER   *n pl.* -S modeler

MODELLING   a present participle of model

MODERATE   *v* -ATED, -ATING, -ATES to make less extreme

MODERATO   *n pl.* -TOS a musical passage played at a medium tempo

MODERN   *adj* -ERNER, -ERNEST pertaining to present or recent time **MODERNLY** *adv*

MODERN   *n* pl. -S a person of modern times or views

MODEST   *adj* -ESTER, -ESTEST having a moderate regard for oneself **MODESTLY** *adv*

MODESTY   *n* pl. -TIES the quality of being modest

MODI   pl. of modus

MODICUM   *n* pl. -CA or -CUMS a small amount

MODIFIER   *n* pl. -S one that modifies

MODIFY   *v* -FIED, -FYING, -FIES to change in form or character

MODIOLUS   *n* pl. -LI a bony shaft of the inner ear

MODISH   *adj* stylish **MODISHLY** *adv*

MODISTE   *n* pl. -S a dealer in stylish women's clothing

MODULAR   *adj* pertaining to a module

MODULATE   *v* -LATED, -LATING, -LATES to adjust to a certain proportion

MODULE   *n* pl. -S a standard of measurement

MODULO   *adv* with respect to a modulus

MODULUS   *n* pl. -LI a number that produces the same remainder when divided into each of two numbers

MODUS   *n* pl. -DI a mode

MOFETTE   *n* pl. -S a noxious emanation from a fissure in the earth

MOFFETTE   *n* pl. -S mofette

MOG   *v* MOGGED, MOGGING, MOGS to move away

MOGUL   *n* pl. -S an important person

MOHAIR   *n* pl. -S the long, silky hair of the Angora goat

MOHEL   *n* pl. -HALIM or -HELS a person who performs Jewish ritual circumcisions

MOHUR   *n* pl. -S a former gold coin of India

MOIDORE   *n* pl. -S a former gold coin of Portugal

MOIETY   *n* pl. -ETIES a half

MOIL   *v* -ED, -ING, -S to work hard

MOILER   *n* pl. -S one that moils

MOIRA   *n* pl. -RAI fate or destiny, in ancient Greek religion

MOIRE   *n* pl. -S a fabric having a wavy pattern

MOIST   *adj* MOISTER, MOISTEST slightly wet

MOISTEN   *v* -ED, -ING, -S to make or become moist

MOISTFUL   *adj* moist

MOISTLY   *adv* in a moist manner

MOISTURE   *n* pl. -S condensed or diffused liquid

MOJARRA   *n* pl. -S a marine fish

MOKE   *n* pl. -S a donkey

MOL   *n* pl. -S mole

MOLA   *n* pl. -S a marine fish

MOLAL   *adj* pertaining to a mole

MOLALITY   *n* pl. -TIES the number of moles of solute per liter of solvent

MOLAR   *n* pl. -S a grinding tooth

MOLARITY   *n* pl. -TIES the number of moles of solute per liter of solution

MOLASSES   *n* pl. -LASSESES a thick syrup

MOLD   *v* -ED, -ING, -S to work into a particular shape **MOLDABLE** *adj*

MOLDER   *v* -ED, -ING, -S to turn to dust by natural decay

MOLDIER   comparative of moldy

MOLDIEST   superlative of moldy

MOLDING   *n* pl. -S a long, narrow strip used to decorate a surface

MOLDWARP   *n* pl. -S a burrowing mammal

MOLDY   *adj* MOLDIER, MOLDIEST musty

MOLE   *n* pl. -S the quantity of a compound that has a weight equal to the compound's molecular weight

MOLECULE   *n* pl. -S the smallest physical unit of an element

MOLEHILL   *n* pl. -S a small mold of earth

MOLESKIN   *n* pl. -S a cotton fabric

MOLEST   *v* -ED, -ING, -S to disturb or annoy

MOLESTER   *n* pl. -S one that molests

MOLIES   pl. of moly

MOLINE   *adj* having arms forked and curved at the ends — used of a heraldic cross

MOLL   *n* pl. -S a gangster's girl friend

MOLLAH   *n* pl. -S mullah

MOLLIE   *n* pl. -S a tropical fish

MOLLIES pl. of molly

MOLLIFY *v* -FIED, -FYING, -FIES to soothe

MOLLUSC *n* pl. -S mollusk

MOLLUSK *n* pl. -S any of a phylum of soft-bodied invertebrates

MOLLY *n* pl. -LIES mollie

MOLOCH *n* pl. -S a spiny lizard

MOLT *v* -ED, -ING, -S to cast off an outer covering

MOLTEN *adj* made liquid by heat **MOLTENLY** *adv*

MOLTER *n* pl. -S one that molts

MOLTO *adv* very — used in musical directions

MOLY *n* pl. -LIES a wild garlic

MOLYBDIC *adj* pertaining to a certain metallic element

MOM *n* pl. -S mother

MOME *n* pl. -S a fool

MOMENT *n* pl. -S a brief period of time

MOMENTA a pl. of momentum

MOMENTLY *adv* from moment to moment

MOMENTO *n* pl. -TOS or -TOES memento

MOMENTUM *n* pl. -TA or -TUMS force of movement

MOMI a pl. of momus

MOMISM *n* pl. -S an excessive dependence on mothers

MOMMA *n* pl. -S mother

MOMMY *n* pl. -MIES mother

MOMUS *n* pl. -MUSES or -MI a carping person

MON *n* pl. MEN man

MONACHAL *adj* pertaining to monks

MONACID *n* pl. -S monoacid

MONAD *n* pl. -S a single-celled organism **MONADAL, MONADIC** *adj*

MONADES pl. of monas

MONADISM *n* pl. -S a philosophical doctrine

MONANDRY *n* pl. -DRIES the condition of having one husband at a time

MONARCH *n* pl. -S an absolute ruler

MONARCHY *n* pl. -CHIES rule by a monarch

MONARDA *n* pl. -S an aromatic herb

MONAS *n* pl. MONADES a monad

MONASTIC *n* pl. -S a monk

MONAURAL *adj* pertaining to sound transmission, recording, or reproduction involving a single transmission path

MONAXIAL *adj* having one axis

MONAZITE *n* pl. -S a mineral

MONDE *n* pl. -S the world

MONDO *n* pl. -DOS a rapid question and answer technique employed in Zen Buddhism

MONECIAN *adj* having both male and female sex organs in the same individual

MONETARY *adj* pertaining to money

MONETISE *v* -TISED, -TISING, -TISES to monetize

MONETIZE *v* -TIZED, -TIZING, -TIZES to coin into money

MONEY *n* pl. MONEYS or MONIES an official medium of exchange and measure of value

MONEYBAG *n* pl. -S a bag for holding money

MONEYED *adj* having much money

MONEYER *n* pl. -S one that coins money

MONGEESE a pl. of mongoose

MONGER *v* -ED, -ING, -S to peddle

MONGO *n* pl. -GOS mungo

MONGOE *n* pl. -S mungo

MONGOL *n* pl. -S a person affected with a form of mental deficiency

MONGOOSE *n* pl. -GOOSES or -GEESE a carnivorous mammal

MONGREL *n* pl. -S an animal or plant of mixed breed

MONGST *prep* amongst

MONICKER *n* pl. -S moniker

MONIE *adj* many

MONIED *adj* moneyed

MONIES a pl. of money

MONIKER *n* pl. -S a name

MONISH *v* -ED, -ING, -ES to warn

MONISM *n* pl. -S a philosophical theory

MONIST *n* pl. -S an adherent of monism **MONISTIC** *adj*

MONITION *n* pl. -S a warning

MONITIVE *adj* giving warning

MONITOR *v* -ED, -ING, -S to keep track of

MONITORY *n* pl. -RIES a letter of warning

MONK   *n* pl. -S a man who is a member of a secluded religious order

MONKERY   *n* pl. -ERIES the mode of life of monks

MONKEY   *v* -ED, -ING, -S to mimic

MONKFISH   *n* pl. -ES a marine fish

MONKHOOD   *n* pl. -S the state of being a monk

MONKISH   *adj* pertaining to monks

MONO   *n* pl. MONOS an infectious disease

MONOACID   *n* pl. -S a type of acid

MONOCARP   *n* pl. -S a plant that yields fruit only once before dying

MONOCLE   *n* pl. -S an eyeglass for one eye **MONOCLED** *adj*

MONOCOT   *n* pl. -S a type of seed plant

MONOCRAT   *n* pl. -S an autocrat

MONOCYTE   *n* pl. -S a type of white blood cell

MONODIST   *n* pl. -S one who writes monodies

MONODY   *n* pl. -DIES an elegy performed by one person **MONODIC** *adj*

MONOECY   *n* pl. -CIES the condition of being monecian

MONOFIL   *n* pl. -S a single filament of synthetic fiber

MONOFUEL   *n* pl. -S a type of rocket propellant

MONOGAMY   *n* pl. -MIES marriage with one person at a time

MONOGENY   *n* pl. -NIES asexual reproduction

MONOGERM   *adj* being a fruit that produces a single plant

MONOGRAM   *v* -GRAMED, -GRAMING, -GRAMS or -GRAMMED, -GRAMMING, -GRAMS to mark with a design of one's initials

MONOGYNY   *n* pl. -NIES the condition of having one wife at a time

MONOLITH   *n* pl. -S a large block of stone

MONOLOG   *n* pl. -S a lengthy speech by one person

MONOLOGY   *n* pl. -GIES the act of uttering a monolog

MONOMER   *n* pl. -S a type of chemical compound

MONOMIAL   *n* pl. -S an algebraic expression consisting of a single term

MONOPODE   *n* pl. -S a creature having one foot

MONOPODY   *n* pl. -DIES a measure consisting of a single metrical foot

MONOPOLE   *n* pl. -S a type of radio antenna

MONOPOLY   *n* pl. -LIES exclusive control of a commodity or service in a particular market

MONORAIL   *n* pl. -S a single rail serving as a track for a wheeled vehicle

MONOSOME   *n* pl. -S a type of chromosome

MONOTINT   *n* pl. -S a painting done in different shades of one color

MONOTONE   *n* pl. -S a vocal utterance in one unvaried tone

MONOTONY   *n* pl. -NIES tedious sameness

MONOTYPE   *n* pl. -S the only representative of its group

MONOXIDE   *n* pl. -S a type of oxide

MONS   *n* pl. MONTES a protuberance of the body

MONSIEUR   *n* pl. MESSIEURS a French title of courtesy for a man

MONSOON   *n* pl. -S a seasonal wind

MONSTER   *n* pl. -S a strange or terrifying creature

MONTAGE   *v* -TAGED, -TAGING, -TAGES to combine into a composite picture

MONTANE   *n* pl. -S the lower vegetation belt of a mountain

MONTE   *n* pl. -S a card game

MONTEITH   *n* pl. -S a large punch bowl

MONTERO   *n* pl. -ROS a type of cap

MONTES   pl. of mons

MONTH   *n* pl. -S a period of approximately 30 days

MONTHLY   *n* pl. -LIES a publication issued once a month

MONUMENT   *n* pl. -S a structure built as a memorial

MONURON   *n* pl. -S an herbicide

MONY   *adj* many

MOO   *v* -ED, -ING, -S to make the deep, moaning sound of a cow

MOOCH   *v* -ED, -ING, -ES to obtain without paying

MOOCHER   *n* pl. -S one that mooches

MOOD   *n* pl. -S a person's emotional state at a particular moment

MOODY   *adj* MOODIER, MOODIEST given to changing moods **MOODILY** *adv*

MOOL   *n* pl. -S soft soil

MOOLA   *n* pl. -S moolah

MOOLAH   *n* pl. -S money

MOOLEY   *n* pl. -EYS muley

MOON   *v* -ED, -ING, -S to spend time idly

MOONBEAM   *n* pl. -S a ray of light from the moon (the earth's natural satellite)

MOONBOW   *n* pl. -S a rainbow formed by light from the moon

MOONCALF   *n* pl. -CALVES a foolish person

MOONEYE   *n* pl. -S a freshwater fish

MOONFISH   *n* pl. -ES a marine fish

MOONIER   comparative of moony

MOONIEST   superlative of moony

MOONILY   *adv* in a moony manner

MOONISH   *adj* fickle

MOONLESS   *adj* lacking the light of the moon

MOONLET   *n* pl. -S a small satellite

MOONLIKE   *adj* resembling the moon

MOONLIT   *adj* lighted by the moon

MOONRISE   *n* pl. -S the rising of the moon above the horizon

MOONSAIL   *n* pl. -S a light, square sail

MOONSEED   *n* pl. -S a climbing plant

MOONSET   *n* pl. -S the setting of the moon below the horizon

MOONSHOT   *n* pl. -S the launching of a spacecraft to the moon

MOONWARD   *adv* toward the moon

MOONWORT   *n* pl. -S a flowering plant

MOONY   *adj* MOONIER, MOONIEST resembling the moon

MOOR   *v* -ED, -ING, -S to secure a vessel by means of cables

MOORAGE   *n* pl. -S the act of mooring

MOORFOWL   *n* pl. -S a game bird

MOORHEN   *n* pl. -S an aquatic bird

MOORIER   comparative of moory

MOORIEST   superlative of moory

MOORING   *n* pl. -S a place where a vessel may be moored

MOORISH   *adj* marshy

MOORLAND   *n* pl. -S a tract of marshy land

MOORWORT   *n* pl. -S a marsh plant

MOORY   *adj* MOORIER, MOORIEST marshy

MOOSE   *n* pl. MOOSE a ruminant mammal

MOOT   *v* -ED, -ING, -S to bring up for discussion

MOOTER   *n* pl. -S one that moots

MOP   *v* MOPPED, MOPPING, MOPS to wipe with a mop (an implement for cleaning floors)

MOPBOARD   *n* pl. -S a board at the base of a wall

MOPE   *v* MOPED, MOPING, MOPES to act in a dejected or gloomy manner

MOPED   *n* pl. -S a type of motorbike

MOPER   *n* pl. -S one that mopes

MOPING   present participle of mope

MOPINGLY   *adv* in a moping manner

MOPISH   *adj* given to moping **MOPISHLY** *adv*

MOPOKE   *n* pl. -S an Australian bird

MOPPED   past tense of mop

MOPPER   *n* pl. -S one that mops

MOPPET   *n* pl. -S a child

MOPPING   present participle of mop

MOQUETTE   *n* pl. -S a woolen fabric

MOR   *n* pl. -S a forest humus

MORA   *n* pl. -RAE or -RAS a unit of metrical time in prosody

MORAINE   *n* pl. -S an accumulation of debris deposited by a glacier **MORAINAL, MORAINIC** *adj*

MORAL   *adj* pertaining to principles of right and wrong **MORALLY** *adv*

MORALE   *n* pl. -S the state of the spirits of an individual or group

MORALISE   *v* -ISED, -ISING, -ISES to moralize

MORALISM   *n* pl. -S the practice of moralizing

MORALIST   *n* pl. -S a teacher of morality

MORALITY   *n* pl. -TIES conformity to the rules of right conduct

MORALIZE   *v* -IZED, -IZING, -IZES to explain in a moral sense

MORALS   *n/pl* rules of conduct with respect to right and wrong

MORASS   *n* pl. -ES a marsh **MORASSY** *adj*

MORATORY	*adj* authorizing delay of payment
MORAY	*n* pl. -RAYS a tropical eel
MORBID	*adj* gruesome **MORBIDLY** *adv*
MORBIFIC	*adj* causing disease
MORBILLI	*n/pl* a virus disease
MORCEAU	*n* pl. -CEAUX a short literary or musical composition
MORDANCY	*n* pl. -CIES a sarcastic quality
MORDANT	*v* -ED, -ING, -S to treat with a caustic substance
MORDENT	*n* pl. -S a melodic embellishment
MORE	*n* pl. -S a greater amount
MOREEN	*n* pl. -S a heavy fabric
MOREL	*n* pl. -S an edible mushroom
MORELLE	*n* pl. -S a flowering plant
MORELLO	*n* pl. -LOS a variety of sour cherry
MOREOVER	*adv* in addition
MORESQUE	*n* pl. -S an ancient decorative style
MORGEN	*n* pl. -S a Dutch unit of land area
MORGUE	*n* pl. -S a place where dead bodies are kept for identification
MORIBUND	*adj* being about to die
MORION	*n* pl. -S a type of helmet
MORN	*n* pl. -S morning
MORNING	*n* pl. -S the early part of the day
MOROCCO	*n* pl. -COS a soft leather
MORON	*n* pl. -S a mentally deficient person **MORONIC** *adj*
MORONISM	*n* pl. -S the condition of being a moron
MORONITY	*n* pl. -TIES moronism
MOROSE	*adj* sullen **MOROSELY** *adv*
MOROSITY	*n* pl. -TIES the state of being morose
MORPH	*n* pl. -S a type of phoneme
MORPHEME	*n* pl. -S a linguistic unit
MORPHIA	*n* pl. -S morphine
MORPHIC	*adj* pertaining to form
MORPHIN	*n* pl. -S morphine
MORPHINE	*n* pl. -S a narcotic alkaloid
MORPHO	*n* pl. -PHOS a tropical butterfly
MORRION	*n* pl. -S morion
MORRIS	*n* pl. -RISES an English folk dance
MORRO	*n* pl. -ROS a rounded elevation
MORROW	*n* pl. -S the next day
MORSEL	*v* -SELED, -SELING, -SELS or -SELLED, -SELLING, -SELS to divide into small pieces
MORT	*n* pl. -S a note sounded on a hunting horn to announce the killing of an animal
MORTAL	*n* pl. -S a human being
MORTALLY	*adv* fatally
MORTAR	*v* -ED, -ING, -S to secure with mortar (a type of cement)
MORTARY	*adj* containing or resembling mortar
MORTGAGE	*v* -GAGED, -GAGING, -GAGES to pledge to a creditor as security
MORTICE	*v* -TICED, -TICING, -TICES to mortise
MORTIFY	*v* -FIED, -FYING, -FIES to humiliate
MORTISE	*v* -TISED, -TISING, -TISES to join or fasten securely
MORTISER	*n* pl. -S one that mortises
MORTMAIN	*n* pl. -S perpetual ownership of land
MORTUARY	*n* pl. -ARIES a place where dead bodies are kept until burial
MORULA	*n* pl. -LAE or -LAS an embryonic mass of cells **MORULAR** *adj*
MOSAIC	*v* -ICKED, -ICKING, -ICS to form into a mosaic (a type of inlaid surface decoration)
MOSCHATE	*adj* musky
MOSEY	*v* -ED, -ING, -S to saunter
MOSHAV	*n* pl. -SHAVIM a cooperative settlement of small farms in Israel
MOSK	*n* pl. -S mosque
MOSQUE	*n* pl. -S a Muslim house of worship
MOSQUITO	*n* pl. -TOES or -TOS a winged insect
MOSS	*v* -ED, -ING, -ES to cover with moss (a growth of small, leafy-stemmed plants)
MOSSBACK	*n* pl. -S a large, old fish
MOSSER	*n* pl. -S one that gathers or works with moss
MOSSIER	comparative of mossy
MOSSIEST	superlative of mossy

MOSSLIKE *adj* resembling moss

MOSSO *adv* rapidly — used as a musical direction

MOSSY *adj* MOSSIER, MOSSIEST covered with moss

MOST *n* pl. -S the greatest amount

MOSTE past tense of mote

MOSTLY *adv* mainly

MOT *n* pl. -S a witty saying

MOTE *v* past tense MOSTE may

MOTE *n* pl. -S a small particle

MOTEL *n* pl. -S a roadside hotel

MOTET *n* pl. -S a type of choral composition

MOTEY *adj* full of motes

MOTH *n* pl. -S a winged insect

MOTHBALL *v* -ED, -ING, -S to put into storage

MOTHER *v* -ED, -ING, -S to give birth to

MOTHERLY *adj* maternal

MOTHERY *adj* slimy

MOTHY *adj* MOTHIER, MOTHIEST full of moths

MOTIF *n* pl. -S a recurring thematic element in an artistic work

MOTILE *n* pl. -S one whose mental imagery consists chiefly of inner feelings of action

MOTILITY *n* pl. -TIES the ability to move

MOTION *v* -ED, -ING, -S to signal by a bodily movement

MOTIONAL *adj* pertaining to movement

MOTIONER *n* pl. -S one that motions

MOTIVATE *v* -VATED, -VATING, -VATES to provide with an incentive

MOTIVE *v* -TIVED, -TIVING, -TIVES to motivate

MOTIVIC *adj* pertaining to a musical motif

MOTIVITY *n* pl. -TIES the ability to move

MOTLEY *adj* -LEYER, -LEYEST or -LIER, -LIEST composed of diverse elements

MOTLEY *n* pl. -LEYS a garment of various colors

MOTMOT *n* pl. -S a tropical bird

MOTOR *v* -ED, -ING, -S to travel by automobile

MOTORBUS *n* pl. -BUSES or -BUSSES a bus

MOTORCAR *n* pl. -S an automobile

MOTORIC *adj* pertaining to muscular movement

MOTORING *n* pl. -S the recreation of traveling by automobile

MOTORISE *v* -ISED, -ISING, -ISES to motorize

MOTORIST *n* pl. -S one who travels by automobile

MOTORIZE *v* -IZED, -IZING, -IZES to equip with motor vehicles

MOTORMAN *n* pl. -MEN one who operates an electric streetcar or subway train

MOTORWAY *n* pl. -WAYS a type of highway

MOTT *n* pl. -S motte

MOTTE *n* pl. -S a small growth of trees on a prairie

MOTTLE *v* -TLED, -TLING, -TLES to mark with spots or streaks of different colors

MOTTLER *n* pl. -S one that mottles

MOTTO *n* pl. -TOES or -TOS a short expression of a guiding principle

MOUCH *v* -ED, -ING, -ES to mooch

MOUCHOIR *n* pl. -S a small handkerchief

MOUE *n* pl. -S a pouting grimace

MOUFFLON *n* pl. -S mouflon

MOUFLON *n* pl. -S a wild sheep

MOUILLE *adj* pronounced with the front of the tongue against the palate

MOUJIK *n* pl. -S muzhik

MOULAGE *n* pl. -S the making of a cast or mold of a mark for use in a criminal investigation

MOULD *v* -ED, -ING, -S to mold

MOULDER *v* -ED, -ING, -S to molder

MOULDING *n* pl. -S molding

MOULDY *adj* MOULDIER, MOULDIEST moldy

MOULIN *n* pl. -S a vertical cavity in a glacier

MOULT *v* -ED, -ING, -S to molt

MOULTER *n* pl. -S molter

MOUND *v* -ED, -ING, -S to pile

MOUNT *v* -ED, -ING, -S to get up on

MOUNTAIN *n* pl. -S a large, natural elevation of the earth's surface

MOUNTER *n* pl. -S one that mounts

MOUNTING   *n* pl. -S something that provides a backing or appropriate setting for something else

MOURN   *v* -ED, -ING, -S to feel or express grief or sorrow

MOURNER   *n* pl. -S one that mourns

MOURNFUL   *adj* -FULLER, -FULLEST expressing grief or sorrow

MOURNING   *n* pl. -S an outward sign of grief

MOUSE   *n* pl. MICE a small rodent

MOUSE   *v* MOUSED, MOUSING, MOUSES to catch mice

MOUSER   *n* pl. -S an animal that catches mice

MOUSEY   *adj* MOUSIER, MOUSIEST mousy

MOUSIER   comparative of mousy

MOUSIEST   superlative of mousy

MOUSILY   *adj* in a mousy manner

MOUSING   *n* pl. -S a wrapping around the shank end of a hook

MOUSSAKA   *n* pl. -S a Middle Eastern dish of meat and eggplant

MOUSSE   *n* pl. -S a chilled dessert

MOUSY   *adj* MOUSIER, MOUSIEST resembling a mouse

MOUTH   *v* -ED, -ING, -S to put into the mouth

MOUTHER   *n* pl. -S a speaker

MOUTHFUL   *n* pl. -S as much as the mouth can hold

MOUTHY   *adj* MOUTHIER, MOUTHIEST very talkative **MOUTHILY** *adv*

MOUTON   *n* pl. -S sheepskin processed to resemble seal or beaver

MOVABLE   *n* pl. -S something that can be moved

MOVABLY   *adv* so as to be capable of being moved

MOVE   *v* MOVED, MOVING, MOVES to change from one position to another

MOVEABLE   *n* pl. -S movable

MOVEABLY   *adv* movably

MOVED   past tense of move

MOVELESS   *adj* incapable of movement

MOVEMENT   *n* pl. -S the act of moving

MOVER   *n* pl. -S one that moves

MOVIE   *n* pl. -S a motion picture

MOVIEDOM   *n* pl. -S filmdom

MOVING   present participle of move

MOVINGLY   *adv* so as to affect the emotions

MOW   *v* MOWED, MOWN, MOWING, MOWS to cut down standing herbage

MOWER   *n* pl. -S one that mows

MOXA   *n* pl. -S a Chinese plant

MOXIE   *n* pl. -S spirit or courage

MOZETTA   *n* pl. -TAS or -TE mozzetta

MOZO   *n* pl. -ZOS a manual laborer

MOZZETTA   *n* pl. -TAS or -TE a hooded cape worn by bishops

MRIDANGA   *n* pl. -S a drum of India

MU   *n* pl. -S a Greek letter

MUCH   *n* pl. -ES a great amount

MUCHNESS   *n* pl. -ES the quality of being great

MUCID   *adj* musty

MUCIDITY   *n* pl. -TIES the state of being mucid

MUCILAGE   *n* pl. -S an adhesive substance

MUCIN   *n* pl. -S a protein secreted by the mucous membranes **MUCINOID, MUCINOUS** *adj*

MUCK   *v* -ED, -ING, -S to fertilize with manure

MUCKER   *n* pl. -S a vulgar person

MUCKIER   comparative of mucky

MUCKIEST   superlative of mucky

MUCKILY   *adv* in a mucky manner

MUCKLE   *n* pl. -S a large amount

MUCKLUCK   *n* pl. -S mukluk

MUCKRAKE   *v* -RAKED, -RAKING, -RAKES to search for and expose corruption

MUCKWORM   *n* pl. -S a worm found in manure

MUCKY   *adj* MUCKIER, MUCKIEST filthy

MUCLUC   *n* pl. -S mukluk

MUCOID   *n* pl. -S a complex protein **MUCOIDAL** *adj*

MUCOR   *n* pl. -S a type of fungus

MUCOSA   *n* pl. -SAE or -SAS a mucous membrane **MUCOSAL** *adj*

MUCOSE   *adj* mucous

MUCOSITY   *n* pl. -TIES the state of being mucous

MUCOUS   *adj* secreting or containing mucus

MUCRO	*n* pl. -CRONES a sharp point at the end of certain plant and animal organs
MUCUS	*n* pl. -ES a viscid bodily fluid
MUD	*v* MUDDED, MUDDING, MUDS to cover with mud (soft, wet earth)
MUDCAP	*v* -CAPPED, -CAPPING, -CAPS to cover an explosive with mud before detonating
MUDDER	*n* pl. -S a racehorse that runs well on a muddy track
MUDDIED	past tense of muddy
MUDDIER	comparative of muddy
MUDDIES	present 3d person sing. of muddy
MUDDIEST	superlative of muddy
MUDDILY	*adj* in a muddy manner
MUDDING	present participle of mud
MUDDLE	*n* -DLED, -DLING, -DLES to mix in a disordered manner
MUDDLER	*n* pl. -S one that muddles
MUDDY	*adj* -DIER, -DIEST covered or filled with mud
MUDDY	*v* -DIED, -DYING, -DIES to make or become muddy
MUDFISH	*n* pl. -ES a fish found in mud or muddy water
MUDGUARD	*n* pl. -S a fender
MUDLARK	*n* pl. -S a street urchin
MUDPUPPY	*n* pl. -PIES a large salamander
MUDRA	*n* pl. -S a hand gesture in East Indian classical dancing
MUDROCK	*n* pl. -S pelite
MUDROOM	*n* pl. -S a room for shedding muddy clothing or footwear
MUDSILL	*n* pl. -S the lowest supporting timber of a structure
MUDSTONE	*n* pl. -S a type of rock
MUEDDIN	*n* pl. -S muezzin
MUENSTER	*n* pl. -S a mild cheese
MUEZZIN	*n* pl. -S a Muslin crier who calls the faithful to prayer
MUFF	*v* -ED, -ING, -S to bungle
MUFFIN	*n* pl. -S a small, round bread
MUFFLE	*v* -FLED, -FLING, -FLES to wrap with something to deaden sound
MUFFLER	*n* pl. -S a device for deadening sound
MUFTI	*n* pl. -S a judge who interprets Muslim religious law
MUG	*v* MUGGED, MUGGING, MUGS to assault with intent to rob
MUGG	*v* -ED, -ING, -S to make funny faces
MUGGAR	*n* pl. -S mugger
MUGGED	past tense of mug
MUGGER	*n* pl. -S a large Asian crocodile
MUGGIER	comparative of muggy
MUGGIEST	superlative of muggy
MUGGILY	*adv* in a muggy manner
MUGGING	*n* pl. -S a street assault or beating
MUGGINS	*n* pl. MUGGINS a card game
MUGGUR	*n* pl. -S mugger
MUGGY	*adj* -GIER, -GIEST warm and humid
MUGWORT	*n* pl. -S a flowering plant
MUGWUMP	*n* pl. -S a political independent
MUHLY	*n* pl. MUHLIES a perennial grass
MUJIK	*n* pl. -S muzhik
MUKLUK	*n* pl. -S a soft boot worn by Eskimos
MULATTO	*n* pl. -TOES or -TOS the offspring of one white and one black parent
MULBERRY	*n* pl. -RIES a tree bearing an edible, berrylike fruit
MULCH	*v* -ED, -ING, -ES to provide with a protective covering for the soil
MULCT	*v* -ED, -ING, -S to defraud
MULE	*v* MULED, MULING, MULES to strike from dies belonging to two different issues, as a coin
MULETA	*n* pl. -S a red cloth used by a matador
MULETEER	*n* pl. -S one who drives mules (hoofed work animals)
MULEY	*n* pl. -LEYS a hornless cow
MULING	present participle of mule
MULISH	*adj* stubborn **MULISHLY** *adv*
MULL	*v* -ED, -ING, -S to ponder
MULLA	*n* pl. -S mullah
MULLAH	*n* pl. -S a Muslim religious leader or teacher
MULLEIN	*n* pl. -S a Eurasian herb
MULLEN	*n* pl. -S mullein
MULLER	*n* pl. -S a grinding implement
MULLET	*n* pl. -S an edible fish

MULLEY	*n* pl. -LEYS muley
MULLIGAN	*n* pl. -S a stew of various meats and vegetables
MULLION	*v* -ED, -ING, -S to provide with vertical dividing strips
MULLITE	*n* pl. -S a mineral
MULLOCK	*n* pl. -S waste earth or rock from a mine **MULLOCKY** *adj*
MULTIFID	*adj* divided into many parts
MULTIJET	*adj* having more than two jets
MULTIPED	*n* pl. -S an animal having many feet
MULTIPLE	*n* pl. -S the product of a quantity by an integer
MULTIPLY	*v* -PLIED, -PLYING, -PLIES to increase in number
MULTURE	*n* pl. -S a fee paid to a miller for grinding grain
MUM	*v* MUMMED, MUMMING, MUMS to act in a disguise
MUMBLE	*v* -BLED, -BLING, -BLES to speak unclearly
MUMBLER	*n* pl. -S one that mumbles
MUMM	*v* -ED, -ING, -S to mum
MUMMED	past tense of mum and mumm
MUMMER	*n* pl. -S one that mums
MUMMERY	*n* pl. -MERIES a performance by mummers
MUMMIED	past tense of mummy
MUMMIES	present 3d person sing. of mummy
MUMMIFY	*v* -FIED, -FYING, -FIES to preserve by embalming
MUMMING	present participle of mum
MUMMY	*v* -MIED, -MYING, -MIES to mummify
MUMP	*v* -ED, -ING, -S to beg
MUMPER	*n* pl. -S one that mumps
MUN	*n* pl. -S man; fellow
MUNCH	*v* -ED, -ING, -ES to chew with a crackling sound
MUNCHER	*n* pl. -S one that munches
MUNDANE	*adj* ordinary
MUNDUNGO	*n* pl. -GOS a foul-smelling tobacco
MUNGO	*n* pl. -GOS a low-quality wool
MUNGOOSE	*n* pl. -S mongoose
MUNIMENT	*n* pl. -S a means of defense
MUNITION	*v* -ED, -ING, -S to furnish with war materiel
MUNNION	*n* pl. -S a muntin
MUNSTER	*n* pl. -S muenster
MUNTIN	*n* pl. -S a dividing strip for window panes
MUNTING	*n* pl. -S muntin
MUNTJAC	*n* pl. -S a small Asian deer
MUNTJAK	*n* pl. -S muntjac
MUON	*n* pl. -S an atomic particle **MUONIC** *adj*
MURA	*n* pl. -S a Japanese village
MURAENID	*n* pl. -S a moray
MURAL	*n* pl. -S a painting applied directly to a wall or ceiling
MURALIST	*n* pl. -S a painter of murals
MURDER	*v* -ED, -ING, -S to kill unlawfully with premediated malice
MURDEREE	*n* pl. -S one that is murdered
MURDERER	*n* pl. -S one that murders
MURE	*v* MURED, MURING, MURES to immure
MUREIN	*n* pl. -S a type of polymer
MUREX	*n* pl. -RICES or -REXES a marine mollusk
MURIATE	*n* pl. -S chloride
MURIATED	*adj* pickled
MURICATE	*adj* covered with short, sharp points
MURICES	a pl. of murex
MURID	*n* pl. -S a murine
MURINE	*n* pl. -S any of a family of small rodents
MURING	present participle of mure
MURK	*adj* MURKER, MURKEST dark **MURKLY** *adv*
MURK	*n* pl. -S darkness
MURKY	*adj* MURKIER, MURKIEST dark **MURKILY** *adv*
MURMUR	*v* -ED, -ING, -S to speak unclearly
MURMURER	*n* pl. -S one that murmurs
MURPHY	*n* pl. -PHIES a potato
MURR	*n* pl. -S murre
MURRA	*n* pl. -S a substance used to make fine vases and cups in ancient Rome
MURRAIN	*n* pl. -S a disease of cattle
MURRE	*n* pl. -S a diving bird

MURRELET	*n* pl. -S a small diving bird
MURREY	*n* pl. -REYS a dark purple color
MURRHA	*n* pl. -S murra **MURRHINE** *adj*
MURRINE	*adj* pertaining to murra
MURRY	*n* pl. -RIES a moray
MURTHER	*v* -ED, -ING, -S to murder
MUSCA	*n* pl. -CAE any of a genus of flies
MUSCADEL	*n* pl. -S muscatel
MUSCAT	*n* pl. -S a sweet, white grape
MUSCATEL	*n* pl. -S a wine made from muscat grapes
MUSCID	*n* pl. -S musca
MUSCLE	*v* -CLED, -CLING, -CLES to proceed by force
MUSCLY	*adj* composed of muscle (tissue that produces bodily movement)
MUSCULAR	*adj* pertaining to muscle
MUSE	*v* MUSED, MUSING, MUSES to ponder
MUSEFUL	*adj* pensive
MUSER	*n* pl. -S one that muses
MUSETTE	*n* pl. -S a small bagpipe
MUSEUM	*n* pl. -S a place where objects of lasting interest or value are cared for and exhibited
MUSH	*v* -ED, -ING, -ES to travel over snow with a dog sled
MUSHER	*n* pl. -S one that mushes
MUSHROOM	*v* -ED, -ING, -S to grow or spread rapidly
MUSHY	*adj* MUSHIER, MUSHIEST pulpy **MUSHILY** *adv*
MUSIC	*n* pl. -S vocal or instrumental sounds organized to produce a unified composition
MUSICAL	*n* pl. -S a play in which dialogue is interspersed with songs and dances
MUSICALE	*n* pl. -S a program of music performed at a social gathering
MUSICIAN	*n* pl. -S one who performs or composes music
MUSING	*n* pl. -S contemplation
MUSINGLY	*adv* in a pensive manner
MUSJID	*n* pl. -S a mosque
MUSK	*n* pl. -S a strongly odorous substance secreted by certain animals
MUSKEG	*n* pl. -S a marsh
MUSKET	*n* pl. -S a type of firearm
MUSKETRY	*n* pl. -RIES the technique of firing small arms
MUSKIE	*n* pl. -S a freshwater fish
MUSKIER	comparative of musky
MUSKIEST	superlative of musky
MUSKILY	*adv* in a musky manner
MUSKIT	*n* pl. -S mesquite
MUSKRAT	*n* pl. -S an aquatic rodent
MUSKY	*adj* MUSKIER, MUSKIEST resembling musk
MUSLIN	*n* pl. -S a cotton fabric
MUSPIKE	*n* pl. -S a freshwater fish
MUSQUASH	*n* pl. -ES the muskrat
MUSS	*v* -ED, -ING, -ES to mess
MUSSEL	*n* pl. -S a bivalve mollusk
MUSSY	*adj* MUSSIER, MUSSIEST messy **MUSSILY** *adv*
MUST	*v* -ED, -ING, -S to become musty
MUSTACHE	*n* pl. -S a growth of hair on the upper lip
MUSTANG	*n* pl. -S a wild horse
MUSTARD	*n* pl. -S a pungent seasoning
MUSTEE	*n* pl. -S an octoroon
MUSTER	*v* -ED, -ING, -S to summon or assemble
MUSTH	*n* pl. -S a state of frenzy occurring in male elephants
MUSTY	*adj* MUSTIER, MUSTIEST having a stale odor **MUSTILY** *adv*
MUT	*n* pl. -S mutt
MUTABLE	*adj* capable of change **MUTABLY** *adv*
MUTAGEN	*n* pl. -S a substance that causes biological mutation
MUTANT	*n* pl. -S something that undergoes mutation
MUTASE	*n* pl. -S an enzyme
MUTATE	*v* -TATED, -TATING, -TATES to undergo mutation
MUTATION	*n* pl. -S the act of changing **MUTATIVE** *adj*
MUTCH	*n* pl. -ES a close-fitting cap
MUTCHKIN	*n* pl. -S a Scottish unit of liquid measure
MUTE	*adj* MUTER, MUTEST characterized by an absence of speech **MUTELY** *adv*

MUTE   *v* MUTED, MUTING, MUTES to deaden the sound of **MUTEDLY** *adv*

MUTENESS   *n* pl. -ES the state of being mute

MUTER   comparative of mute

MUTEST   superlative of mute

MUTICOUS   *adj* lacking a point

MUTILATE   *v* -LATED, -LATING, -LATES to deprive of a limb or other essential part

MUTINE   *v* -TINED, -TINING, -TINES to mutiny

MUTINEER   *v* -ED, -ING, -S to mutiny

MUTING   present participle of mute

MUTINIED   past tense of mutiny

MUTINIES   present 3d person sing. of mutiny

MUTINING   present participle of mutine

MUTINOUS   *adj* disposed to mutiny

MUTINY   *v* -NIED, -NYING, -NIES to revolt against constituted authority

MUTISM   *n* pl. -S muteness

MUTT   *n* pl. -S a mongrel dog

MUTTER   *v* -ED, -ING, -S to speak unclearly

MUTTERER   *n* pl. -S one that mutters

MUTTON   *n* pl. -S the flesh of sheep used as food **MUTTONY** *adj*

MUTUAL   *adj* shared in common **MUTUALLY** *adv*

MUTUEL   *n* pl. -S a system of betting on races

MUTULE   *n* pl. -S an ornamental block used in classical Greek architecture **MUTULAR** *adj*

MUUMUU   *n* pl. -S a long, loose dress

MUZHIK   *n* pl. -S a Russian peasant

MUZJIK   *n* pl. -S muzhik

MUZZIER   comparative of muzzy

MUZZIEST   superlative of muzzy

MUZZILY   *adv* in a muzzy manner

MUZZLE   *v* -ZLED, -ZLING, -ZLES to put a covering over the mouth of to prevent biting or eating

MUZZLER   *n* pl. -S one that muzzles

MUZZY   *adj* -ZIER, -ZIEST confused

MY   *pron* the possessive form of the pronoun I

MYALGIA   *n* pl. -S muscular pain **MYALGIC** *adj*

MYASIS   *n* pl. MYASES myiasis

MYCELE   *n* pl. -S mycelium

MYCELIUM   *n* pl. -LIA the vegetive portion of a fungus **MYCELIAL, MYCELIAN, MYCELOID** *adj*

MYCETOMA   *n* pl. -MAS or -MATA a fungous infection

MYCOLOGY   *n* pl. -GIES the branch of botany dealing with fungi

MYCOSIS   *n* pl. -COSES a disease caused by a fungus **MYCOTIC** *adj*

MYELIN   *n* pl. -S a fatty substance that encases certain nerve fibers **MYELINIC** *adj*

MYELINE   *n* pl. -S myelin

MYELITIS   *n* pl. -LITIDES inflammation of the bone marrow

MYELOID   *adj* pertaining to bone marrow

MYELOMA   *n* pl. -MAS or -MATA a tumor of the bone marrow

MYIASIS   *n* pl. MYIASES infestation of human tissue by fly maggots

MYLONITE   *n* pl. -S a type of rock

MYNA   *n* pl. -S an Asian bird

MYNAH   *n* pl. -S myna

MYNHEER   *n* pl. -S a Dutch title of courtesy for a man

MYOBLAST   *n* pl. -S a cell capable of giving rise to muscle cells

MYOGENIC   *adj* originating in muscle tissue

MYOGRAPH   *n* pl. -S an instrument for recording muscular contractions

MYOID   *adj* resembling muscle

MYOLOGY   *n* pl. -GIES the study of muscles **MYOLOGIC** *adj*

MYOMA   *n* pl. -MAS or -MATA a tumor composed of muscle tissue

MYOPATHY   *n* pl. -THIES a disorder of muscle tissue

MYOPE   *n* pl. -S one who is affected with myopia

MYOPIA   *n* pl. -S a visual defect **MYOPIC** *adj*

MYOPY   *n* pl. -PIES myopia

MYOSCOPE   *n* pl. -S an instrument for observing muscular contractions

MYOSIN   *n* pl. -S a protein found in muscle tissue

MYOSIS   *n* pl. MYOSES miosis

MYOSOTE	*n* pl. -S myosotis
MYOSOTIS	*n* pl. -TISES a flowering plant
MYOTIC	*n* pl. -S miotic
MYOTOME	*n* pl. -S a portion of an embryonic somite
MYOTONIA	*n* pl. -S temporary muscular rigidity **MYOTONIC** *adj*
MYRIAD	*n* pl. -S a very large number
MYRIAPOD	*n* pl. -S a multi-legged arthropod
MYRICA	*n* pl. -S a medicinal tree bark
MYRIOPOD	*n* pl. -S myriapod
MYRMIDON	*n* pl. -S a loyal follower
MYRRH	*n* pl. -S an aromatic gum resin **MYRRHIC** *adj*
MYRTLE	*n* pl. -S an evergreen shrub
MYSELF	*pron* a form of the 1st person sing. pronoun
MYSOST	*n* pl. -S a mild cheese
MYSTAGOG	*n* pl. -S a teacher of religious mysteries
MYSTERY	*n* pl. -TERIES something that is not or cannot be known, understood, or explained
MYSTIC	*n* pl. -S one who professes to have had mystical experiences
MYSTICAL	*adj* spiritually significant or symbolic
MYSTICLY	*adv* in a mystical manner
MYSTIFY	*v* -FIED, -FYING, -FIES to perplex
MYSTIQUE	*n* pl. -S an aura of mystery or mystical power surrounding a particular person or thing
MYTH	*n* pl. -S a type of traditional story
MYTHIC	*adj* mythical
MYTHICAL	*adj* based on or described in a myth
MYTHOS	*n* pl. -THOI a myth
MYXEDEMA	*n* pl. -S a disease caused by decreased activity of the thyroid gland
MYXOCYTE	*n* pl. -S a large cell found in mucous tissue
MYXOID	*adj* containing mucus
MYXOMA	*n* pl. -MAS or -MATA a tumor composed of mucous tissue

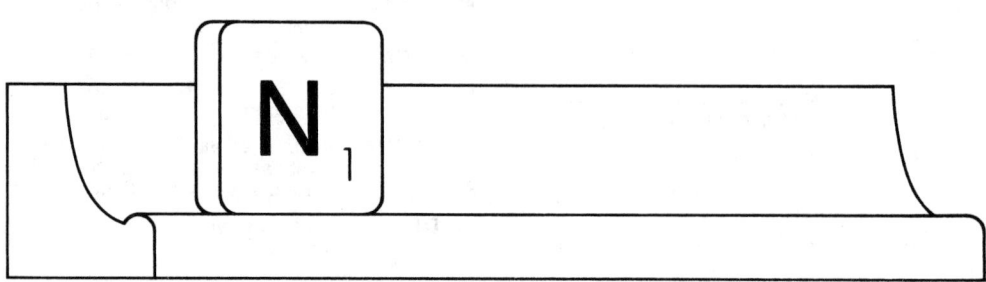

NA	*adv* no; not
NAB	*v* NABBED, NABBING, NABS to capture or arrest
NABIS	*n* pl. NABIS a group of French artists
NABOB	*n* pl. -S one who has become rich in India
NABOBERY	*n* pl. -ERIES the state of being a nabob
NABOBESS	*n* pl. -ES a female nabob
NABOBISM	*n* pl. -S great wealth and luxury
NACELLE	*n* pl. -S a shelter on an aircraft
NACRE	*n* pl. -S the pearly internal layer of certain shells **NACRED, NACREOUS** *adj*
NADIR	*n* pl. -S a point on the celestial sphere **NADIRAL** *adj*
NAE	*adv* no; not
NAETHING	*n* pl. -S nothing
NAEVUS	*n* pl. -VI nevus **NAEVOID** *adj*
NAG	*v* NAGGED, NAGGING, NAGS to find fault incessantly
NAGANA	*n* pl. -S a disease of horses in Africa
NAGGER	*n* pl. -S one that nags
NAGGING	present participle of nag
NAIAD	*n* pl. -S or -ES a water nymph
NAIF	*n* pl. -S a naive person
NAIL	*v* -ED, -ING, -S to fasten with a nail (a slender piece of metal)
NAILER	*n* pl. -S one that nails
NAILFOLD	*n* pl. -S a fold of skin around the fingernail
NAILHEAD	*n* pl. -S the top of a nail
NAILSET	*n* pl. -S a steel rod for driving a nail into something
NAINSOOK	*n* pl. -S a cotton fabric
NAIVE	*adj* NAIVER, NAIVEST lacking sophistication **NAIVELY** *adv*
NAIVE	*n* pl. -S a naive person
NAIVETE	*n* pl. -S the quality of being naive
NAIVETY	*n* pl. -TIES naivete
NAKED	*adj* -KEDER, -KEDEST being without clothing or covering **NAKEDLY** *adv*
NALED	*n* pl. -S an insecticide
NALOXONE	*n* pl. -S a chemical compound
NAME	*v* NAMED, NAMING, NAMES to give a title to **NAMABLE, NAMEABLE** *adj*
NAMELESS	*adj* lacking distinction or fame
NAMELY	*adv* that is to say
NAMER	*n* pl. -S one that names
NAMESAKE	*n* pl. -S one who is named after another
NAMING	present participle of name
NANA	*n* pl. -S a grandmother
NANCE	*n* pl. -S an effeminate male
NANDIN	*n* pl. -S an evergreen shrub
NANISM	*n* pl. -S abnormal smallness
NANKEEN	*n* pl. -S a cotton fabric
NANKIN	*n* pl. -S nankeen
NANNIE	*n* pl. -S nanny
NANNY	*n* pl. -NIES a children's nurse
NANOGRAM	*n* pl. -S a unit of mass and weight
NANOWATT	*n* pl. -S a unit of power

NAOS	*n* pl. NAOI an ancient temple		**NARRATER**	*n* pl. -S narrator
NAP	*v* NAPPED, NAPPING, NAPS to sleep briefly		**NARRATOR**	*n* pl. -S one that narrates
NAPALM	*v* -ED, -ING, -S to assault with a type of incendiary bomb		**NARROW**	*adj* -ROWER, -ROWEST of little width **NARROWLY** *adv*
NAPE	*n* pl. -S the back of the neck		**NARROW**	*v* -ED, -ING, -S to make narrow
NAPERY	*n* pl. -PERIES table linen		**NARTHEX**	*n* pl. -ES a vestibule in a church
NAPHTHA	*n* pl. -S a volatile liquid		**NARWAL**	*n* pl. -S narwhal
NAPHTHOL	*n* pl. -S a chemical compound		**NARWHAL**	*n* pl. -S an arctic aquatic mammal
NAPHTHYL	*adj* containing a certain chemical group		**NARWHALE**	*n* pl. -S narwhal
NAPHTOL	*n* pl. -S naphthol		**NARY**	*adj* not one
NAPIFORM	*adj* shaped like a turnip		**NASAL**	*n* pl. -S a sound uttered through the nose
NAPKIN	*n* pl. -S a piece of material used to wipe the hands and mouth		**NASALISE**	*v* -ISED, -ISING, -ISES to nasalize
NAPLESS	*adj* threadbare		**NASALITY**	*n* pl. -TIES the quality or an instance of being produced nasally
NAPOLEON	*n* pl. -S a type of pastry			
NAPPE	*n* pl. -S a type of rock formation		**NASALIZE**	*v* -IZED, -IZING, -IZES to produce sounds nasally
NAPPED	past tense of nap		**NASALLY**	*adv* through the nose
NAPPER	*n* pl. -S one that naps		**NASCENCE**	*n* pl. -S nascency
NAPPIE	*n* pl. -S a diaper		**NASCENCY**	*n* pl. -CIES birth; origin
NAPPING	present participle of nap		**NASCENT**	*adj* coming into existence
NAPPY	*adj* -PIER, -PIEST kinky		**NASION**	*n* pl. -S a point in the skull **NASIAL** *adj*
NARC	*n* pl. -S an undercover drug agent		**NASTIC**	*adj* pertaining to an automatic response of plants
NARCEIN	*n* pl. -S narceine			
NARCEINE	*n* pl. -S an opium derivative		**NASTY**	*adj* -TIER, -TIEST offensive to the senses **NASTILY** *adv*
NARCISM	*n* pl. -S excessive love of oneself		**NATAL**	*adj* pertaining to one's birth
NARCISSI	*n/pl* bulbous flowering plants		**NATALITY**	*n* pl. -TIES birth rate
NARCIST	*n* pl. -S one given to narcism		**NATANT**	*adj* floating or swimming **NATANTLY** *adv*
NARCO	*n* pl. -COS narc		**NATATION**	*n* pl. -S the act of swimming
NARCOSE	*adj* characterized by stupor		**NATATORY**	*adj* pertaining to swimming
NARCOSIS	*n* pl. -COSES a drug-induced stupor		**NATES**	*n/pl* the buttocks
NARCOTIC	*n* pl. -S a drug that dulls the senses		**NATHLESS**	*adv* nevertheless
			NATION	*n* pl. -S a politically organized people who share a territory, customs, and history
NARD	*n* pl. -S a fragrant ointment **NARDINE** *adj*			
NARES	pl. of naris		**NATIONAL**	*n* pl. -S a citizen of a nation
NARGHILE	*n* pl. -S a hookah		**NATIVE**	*n* pl. -S an original inhabitant of an area
NARGILE	*n* pl. -S narghile			
NARGILEH	*n* pl. -S narghile		**NATIVELY**	*adv* in an inborn manner
NARIS	*n* pl. NARES a nostril **NARIAL, NARIC, NARINE** *adj*		**NATIVISM**	*n* pl. -S a policy of favoring the interests of native inhabitants
NARK	*v* -ED, -ING, -S to spy or inform			
NARRATE	*v* -RATED, -RATING, -RATES to tell a story		**NATIVIST**	*n* pl. -S an advocate of nativism

NATIVITY *n* pl. -TIES the process of being born

NATRIUM *n* pl. -S sodium

NATRON *n* pl. -S a chemical compound

NATTER *v* -ED, -ING, -S to chatter

NATTY *adj* -TIER, -TIEST neatly dressed **NATTILY** *adv*

NATURAL *n* pl. -S a type of musical note

NATURE *n* pl. -S the essential qualities of a person or thing **NATURED** *adj*

NAUGHT *n* pl. -S a zero

NAUGHTY *adj* -TIER, -TIEST disobedient

NAUMACHY *n* pl. -CHIES a mock sea battle

NAUPLIUS *n* pl. -PLII a form of certain crustaceans **NAUPLIAL** *adj*

NAUSEA *n* pl. -S a stomach disturbance

NAUSEANT *n* pl. -S an agent that induces nausea

NAUSEATE *v* -ATED, -ATING, -ATES to affect with nausea

NAUSEOUS *adj* affected with nausea

NAUTCH *n* pl. -ES a dancing exhibition in India

NAUTICAL *adj* pertaining to ships

NAUTILUS *n* pl. -LUSES or -LI a spiral-shelled mollusk

NAVAID *n* pl. -S a navigational device

NAVAL *adj* pertaining to ships **NAVALLY** *adv*

NAVAR *n* pl. -S a system of air navigation

NAVE *n* pl. -S the main part of a church

NAVEL *n* pl. -S a depression in the abdomen

NAVETTE *n* pl. -S a gem cut in a pointed oval form

NAVICERT *n* pl. -S a document permitting a vessel passage through a naval blockade

NAVIES pl. of navy

NAVIGATE *v* -GATED, -GATING, -GATES to plan and control the course of

NAVVY *n* pl. -VIES a manual laborer

NAVY *n* pl. -VIES a nation's warships

NAWAB *n* pl. -S a nabob

NAY *n* pl. NAYS a negative vote

NAZI *n* pl. -S a type of fascist

NAZIFY *v* -FIED, -FYING, -FIES to cause to be like a nazi

NEAP *n* pl. -S a tide of lowest range

NEAR *adj* NEARER, NEAREST situated within a short distance

NEAR *v* -ED, -ING, -S to approach

NEARBY *adj* near

NEARLY *adv* -LIER, -LIEST with close approximation

NEARNESS *n* pl. -ES the state of being near

NEAT *adj* NEATER, NEATEST being in a state of cleanliness and order

NEAT *n* pl. -S a bovine

NEATEN *v* -ED, -ING, -S to make neat

NEATH *prep* beneath

NEATHERD *n* pl. -S a cowherd

NEATLY *adv* in a neat manner

NEATNESS *n* pl. -ES the state of being neat

NEB *n* pl. -S the beak of a bird

NEBBISH *n* pl. -ES a meek person

NEBULA *n* pl. -LAS or -LAE a cloud-like interstellar mass **NEBULAR** *adj*

NEBULE *adj* composed of successive short curves

NEBULISE *v* -LISED, -LISING, -LISES to nebulize

NEBULIZE *v* -LIZED, -LIZING, -LIZES to reduce to a fine spray

NEBULOSE *adj* nebulous

NEBULOUS *adj* unclear

NEBULY *adj* nebule

NECK *v* -ED, -ING, -S to kiss and caress in lovemaking

NECKBAND *n* pl. -S a band worn around the neck (the part of the body joining the head to the trunk)

NECKING *n* pl. -S a small molding near the top of a column

NECKLACE *n* pl. -S an ornament worn around the neck

NECKLESS *adj* having no neck

NECKLIKE *adj* resembling the neck

NECKLINE *n* pl. -S the line formed by the neck opening of a garment

NECKTIE *n* pl. -S a strip of fabric worn around the neck

NECKWEAR *n* pl. -S something that is worn around the neck

NECROPSY *v* -SIED, -SYING, -SIES to perform an autopsy on

NECROSE	*v* -CROSED, -CROSING, -CROSES to affect with necrosis
NECROSIS	*n* pl. -CROSES the death of living tissue **NECROTIC** *adj*
NECTAR	*n* pl. -S a delicious drink
NECTARY	*n* pl. -TARIES a plant gland
NEE	*adj* born with the name of
NEED	*v* -ED, -ING, -S to have an urgent or essential use for
NEEDER	*n* pl. -S one that needs
NEEDFUL	*n* pl. -S something that is needed
NEEDIER	comparative of needy
NEEDIEST	superlative of needy
NEEDILY	*adv* in a needy manner
NEEDLE	*v* -DLED, -DLING, -DLES to sew with a slender, pointed instrument
NEEDLER	*n* pl. -S one that needles
NEEDLESS	*adj* not necessary
NEEDLING	*n* pl. -S the act of one who needles
NEEDY	*adj* NEEDIER, NEEDIEST in a state of poverty
NEEM	*n* pl. -S an East Indian tree
NEEP	*n* pl. -S a turnip
NEGATE	*v* -GATED, -GATING, -GATES to nullify
NEGATER	*n* pl. -S one that negates
NEGATION	*n* pl. -S the act of negating
NEGATIVE	*v* -TIVED, -TIVING, -TIVES to veto
NEGATON	*n* pl. -S negatron
NEGATOR	*n* pl. -S negater
NEGATRON	*n* pl. -S an electron
NEGLECT	*v* -ED, -ING, -S to fail to pay attention to
NEGLIGE	*n* pl. -S negligee
NEGLIGEE	*n* pl. -S a woman's dressing gown
NEGRO	*n* pl. -GROES a member of the black race of mankind
NEGROID	*n* pl. -S a negro
NEGUS	*n* pl. -ES an alcoholic beverage
NEIF	*n* pl. -S nieve
NEIGH	*v* -ED, -ING, -S to utter the cry of a horse
NEIGHBOR	*v* -ED, -ING, -S to live close to
NEIST	*adj* next
NEITHER	*adj* not one or the other
NEKTON	*n* pl. -S free-swimming marine animals **NEKTONIC** *adj*
NELSON	*n* pl. -S a wrestling hold
NELUMBO	*n* pl. -BOS an aquatic herb
NEMA	*n* pl. -S a nematode
NEMATIC	*adj* pertaining to a phase of a liquid crystal
NEMATODE	*n* pl. -S a kind of worm
NEMESIS	*n* pl. NEMESES an unbeatable opponent
NENE	*n* pl. NENE a Hawaiian goose
NEOLITH	*n* pl. -S an ancient stone implement
NEOLOGY	*n* pl. -GIES a new word or phrase **NEOLOGIC** *adj*
NEOMORPH	*n* pl. -S a type of biological structure
NEOMYCIN	*n* pl. -S an antibiotic drug
NEON	*n* pl. -S a gaseous element **NEONED** *adj*
NEONATE	*n* pl. -S a newborn child **NEONATAL** *adj*
NEOPHYTE	*n* pl. -S a novice
NEOPLASM	*n* pl. -S a tumor
NEOPRENE	*n* pl. -S a synthetic rubber
NEOTENY	*n* pl. -NIES attainment of sexual maturity in the larval stage **NEOTENIC** *adj*
NEOTERIC	*n* pl. -S a modern author
NEOTYPE	*n* pl. -S a specimen of a species
NEPENTHE	*n* pl. -S a drug that induces forgetfulness
NEPHEW	*n* pl. -S a son of one's brother or sister
NEPHRIC	*adj* renal
NEPHRISM	*n* pl. -S ill health caused by a kidney disease
NEPHRITE	*n* pl. -S a mineral
NEPHRON	*n* pl. -S an excretory unit of a kidney
NEPOTISM	*n* pl. -S favoritism shown to a relative **NEPOTIC** *adj*
NEPOTIST	*n* pl. -S one who practices nepotism
NEREID	*n* pl. -S a sea nymph
NEREIS	*n* pl. -REIDES a marine worm
NERITIC	*adj* pertaining to shallow water

NEROL	*n* pl. -S a fragrant alcohol
NEROLI	*n* pl. -S a fragrant oil
NERTS	*interj* — used to express defiance or disgust
NERTZ	*interj* nerts
NERVATE	*adj* having veins
NERVE	*v* NERVED, NERVING, NERVES to give courage to
NERVIER	comparative of nervy
NERVIEST	superlative of nervy
NERVILY	*adv* in a nervy manner
NERVINE	*n* pl. -S a soothing medicine
NERVING	*n* pl. -S a type of veterinary operation
NERVOUS	*adj* easily excited
NERVULE	*n* pl. -S nervure
NERVURE	*n* pl. -S a vascular ridge on a leaf
NERVY	*adj* NERVIER, NERVIEST impudent
NESCIENT	*n* pl. -S one who is ignorant
NESS	*n* pl. -ES a headland
NEST	*v* -ED, -ING, -S to build a nest (a structure for holding bird eggs)
NESTER	*n* pl. -S one that nests
NESTLE	*v* -TLED, -TLING, -TLES to lie snugly
NESTLER	*n* pl. -S one that nestles
NESTLIKE	*adj* resembling a nest
NESTLING	*n* pl. -S a young bird
NESTOR	*n* pl. -S a wise old man
NET	*v* NETTED, NETTING, NETS to catch in a net (a type of openwork fabric)
NETHER	*adj* situated below
NETLESS	*adj* having no net
NETLIKE	*adj* resembling a net
NETOP	*n* pl. -S friend; companion
NETSUKE	*n* pl. -S a button-like fixture on Japanese clothing
NETT	*v* -ED, -ING, -S to net
NETTABLE	*adj* capable of being netted
NETTED	past tense of net, nett
NETTER	*n* pl. -S one that nets
NETTIER	comparative of netty
NETTIEST	superlative of netty
NETTING	*n* pl. -S a net

NETTLE	*v* -TLED, -TLING, -TLES to make angry
NETTLER	*n* pl. -S one that nettles
NETTLY	*adj* -TLIER, -TLIEST prickly
NETTY	*adj* -TIER, -TIEST resembling a net
NETWORK	*v* -ED, -ING, -S to cover with or as if with crossing lines
NEUM	*n* pl. -S neume
NEUME	*n* pl. -S a sign used in musical notation **NEUMATIC, NEUMIC** *adj*
NEURAL	*adj* pertaining to the nervous system **NEURALLY** *adv*
NEURAXON	*n* pl. -S a part of a neuron
NEURITIC	*n* pl. -S one affected with neuritis
NEURITIS	*n* pl. -RITIDES or -RITISES inflammation of a nerve
NEUROID	*adj* resembling a nerve
NEUROMA	*n* pl. -MAS or -MATA a type of tumor
NEURON	*n* pl. -S the basic cellular unit of the nervous system **NEURONAL, NEURONIC** *adj*
NEURONE	*n* pl. -S neuron
NEUROSIS	*n* pl. -ROSES a type of emotional disturbance **NEUROSAL** *adj*
NEUROTIC	*n* pl. -S one affected with a neurosis
NEUSTON	*n* pl. -S an aggregate of small aquatic organisms
NEUTER	*v* -ED, -ING, -S to castrate
NEUTRAL	*n* pl. -S one that is impartial
NEUTRINO	*n* pl. -NOS an atomic particle
NEUTRON	*n* pl. -S an atomic particle
NEVE	*n* pl. -S a granular snow
NEVER	*adv* at no time
NEVUS	*n* pl. -VI a birthmark **NEVOID** *adj*
NEW	*adj* NEWER, NEWEST existing only a short time
NEW	*n* pl. -S something that is new
NEWBORN	*n* pl. -S a recently born infant
NEWCOMER	*n* pl. -S one that has recently arrived
NEWEL	*n* pl. -S a staircase support
NEWFOUND	*adj* newly found
NEWISH	*adj* somewhat new

NEWLY   *adv* recently

NEWLYWED   *n* pl. -S a person recently married

NEWMOWN   *adj* recently mown

NEWNESS   *n* pl. -ES the state of being new

NEWS   *n/pl* a report of recent events

NEWSBOY   *n* pl. -BOYS a boy who delivers or sells newspapers

NEWSCAST   *n* pl. -S a news broadcast

NEWSIER   comparative of newsy

NEWSIES   pl. of newsy

NEWSIEST   superlative of newsy

NEWSLESS   *adj* having no news

NEWSMAN   *n* pl. -MEN a news reporter

NEWSPEAK   *n* pl. -S a deliberately ambiguous language

NEWSREEL   *n* pl. -S a short movie presenting current events

NEWSROOM   *n* pl. -S a room where the news is gathered

NEWSY   *adj* NEWSIER, NEWSIEST full of news

NEWSY   *n* pl. NEWSIES a newsboy

NEWT   *n* pl. -S a small salamander

NEWTON   *n* pl. -S a unit of force

NEXT   *adj* coming immediately after; adjoining

NEXTDOOR   *adj* located in the next building or room

NEXUS   *n* pl. -ES a connection or link

NGWEE   *n* pl. NGWEE a Zambian unit of currency

NIACIN   *n* pl. -S a B vitamin

NIB   *v* NIBBED, NIBBING, NIBS to provide with a penpoint

NIBBLE   *v* -BLED, -BLING, -BLES to eat with small bites

NIBBLER   *n* pl. -S one that nibbles

NIBLICK   *n* pl. -S a golf club

NIBLIKE   *adj* resembling a penpoint

NICE   *adj* NICER, NICEST pleasing to the senses **NICELY** *adv*

NICENESS   *n* pl. -ES the quality of being nice

NICETY   *n* pl. -TIES a fine point or distinction

NICHE   *v* NICHED, NICHING, NICHES to place in a receding space or hollow

NICK   *v* -ED, -ING, -S to make a shallow cut in

NICKEL   *v* -ELED, -ELING, -ELS or -ELLED, -ELLING, -ELS to plate with nickel (a metallic element)

NICKELIC   *adj* pertaining to or containing nickel

NICKER   *v* -ED, -ING, -S to neigh

NICKLE   *n* pl. -S nickel

NICKNACK   *n* pl. -S a trinket

NICKNAME   *v* -NAMED, -NAMING, -NAMES to give an alternate name to

NICOL   *n* pl. -S a type of prism

NICOTIN   *n* pl. -S nicotine

NICOTINE   *n* pl. -S a poisonous alkaloid in tobacco

NICTATE   *v* -TATED, -TATING, -TATES to wink

NIDAL   *adj* pertaining to a nidus

NIDE   *v* NIDED, NIDING, NIDES to nest

NIDERING   *n* pl. -S a coward

NIDGET   *n* pl. -S an idiot

NIDI   a pl. of nidus

NIDIFY   *v* -FIED, -FYING, -FIES to nest

NIDING   present participle of nide

NIDUS   *n* pl. NIDI or NIDUSES a nest or breeding place

NIECE   *n* pl. -S a daughter of one's brother or sister

NIELLIST   *n* pl. -S one that niellos

NIELLO   *n* pl. -LI or -LOS a black metallic substance

NIELLO   *v* -ED, -ING, -S to decorate with niello

NIEVE   *n* pl. -S the fist or hand

NIFFER   *v* -ED, -ING, -S to barter

NIFTY   *adj* -TIER, -TIEST stylish; pleasing

NIFTY   *n* pl. -TIES something that is nifty

NIGGARD   *v* -ED, -ING, -S to act stingily

NIGGER   *n* pl. -S a black person — an offensive term

NIGGLE   *v* -GLED, -GLING, -GLES to worry over petty details

NIGGLER   *n* pl. -S one that niggles

NIGGLING   *n* pl. -S petty or meticulous work

NIGH   *adj* NIGHER, NIGHEST near

NIGH	*v* -ED, -ING, -S to approach
NIGHNESS	*n* pl. -ES the state of being nigh
NIGHT	*n* pl. -S the period from sunset to sunrise
NIGHTCAP	*n* pl. -S a cap worn to bed
NIGHTIE	*n* pl. -S a nightgown
NIGHTIES	pl. of nighty
NIGHTJAR	*n* pl. -S a nocturnal bird
NIGHTLY	*adv* every night; at night
NIGHTY	*n* pl. NIGHTIES nightie
NIGRIFY	*v* -FIED, -FYING, -FIES to make black
NIGROSIN	*n* pl. -S a type of dye
NIHIL	*n* pl. -S nothing
NIHILISM	*n* pl. -S a doctrine that denies traditional values
NIHILIST	*n* pl. -S an adherent of nihilism
NIHILITY	*n* pl. -TIES the state of being nothing
NIL	*n* pl. -S nothing
NILGAI	*n* pl. -S a large antelope
NILGAU	*n* pl. -S nilgai
NILGHAI	*n* pl. -S nilgai
NILGHAU	*n* pl. -S nilgai
NILL	*v* -ED, -ING, -S to be unwilling
NIM	*v* NIMMED, NIMMING, NIMS to steal
NIMBLE	*adj* -BLER, -BLEST agile **NIMBLY** *adv*
NIMBUS	*n* pl. -BI or -BUSES a luminous cloud **NIMBUSED** *adj*
NIMIETY	*n* pl. -ETIES excess **NIMIOUS** *adj*
NIMMED	past tense of nim
NIMMING	present participle of nim
NIMROD	*n* pl. -S a hunter
NINE	*n* pl. -S a number
NINEBARK	*n* pl. -S a flowering shrub
NINEFOLD	*adj* nine times as great
NINEPIN	*n* pl. -S a wooden pin used in a bowling game
NINETEEN	*n* pl. -S a number
NINETY	*n* pl. -TIES a number
NINNY	*n* pl. -NIES a fool **NINNYISH** *adj*
NINON	*n* pl. -S a sheer fabric
NINTH	*n* pl. -S one of nine equal parts
NINTHLY	*adv* in the ninth place
NIOBIUM	*n* pl. -S a metallic element **NIOBIC, NIOBOUS** *adj*
NIP	*v* NIPPED, NIPPING, NIPS to pinch
NIPA	*n* pl. -S a palm tree
NIPPER	*n* pl. -S one that nips
NIPPIER	comparative of nippy
NIPPIEST	superlative of nippy
NIPPILY	*adv* in a nippy manner
NIPPING	present participle of nip
NIPPLE	*n* pl. -S a protuberance on the breast
NIPPY	*adj* -PIER, -PIEST sharp or biting
NIRVANA	*n* pl. -S a blessed state in Buddhism **NIRVANIC** *adj*
NISEI	*n* pl. -S one born in America of immigrant Japanese parents
NISI	*adj* not yet final
NISUS	*n* pl. NISUS an effort
NIT	*n* pl. -S the egg of a parasitic insect
NITCHIE	*n* pl. -S an American Indian — an offensive term
NITER	*n* pl. -S a chemical salt
NITID	*adj* bright
NITON	*n* pl. -S radon
NITPICK	*v* -ED, -ING, -S to fuss over petty details
NITRATE	*v* -TRATED, -TRATING, -TRATES to treat with nitric acid
NITRATOR	*n* pl. -S one that nitrates
NITRE	*n* pl. -S niter
NITRIC	*adj* containing nitrogen
NITRID	*n* pl. -S nitride
NITRIDE	*n* pl. -S a compound of nitrogen
NITRIFY	*v* -FIED, -FYING, -FIES to combine with nitrogen
NITRIL	*n* pl. -S nitrile
NITRILE	*n* pl. -S a chemical compound
NITRITE	*n* pl. -S a salt of nitrous acid
NITRO	*n* pl. -TROS a nitrated product
NITROGEN	*n* pl. -S a gaseous element
NITROLIC	*adj* pertaining to a class of acids
NITROSO	*adj* containing nitrosyl
NITROSYL	*n* pl. -S a univalent radical
NITROUS	*adj* containing nitrogen
NITTY	*adj* -TIER, -TIEST full of nits

NITWIT	*n* pl. -S a stupid person
NIVAL	*adj* pertaining to snow
NIVEOUS	*adj* resembling snow
NIX	*v* -ED, -ING, -ES to veto
NIXIE	*n* pl. -S a female water sprite
NIXY	*n* pl. NIXIES an undeliverable piece of mail
NIZAM	*n* pl. -S a former sovereign of India
NIZAMATE	*n* pl. -S the territory of a nizam
NO	*n* pl. NOS or NOES a negative reply
NOB	*n* pl. -S a wealthy person
NOBBIER	comparative of nobby
NOBBIEST	superlative of nobby
NOBBILY	*adv* in a nobby manner
NOBBLE	*v* -BLED, -BLING, -BLES to disable a racehorse
NOBBLER	*n* pl. -S one that nobbles
NOBBY	*adj* -BIER, -BIEST elegant
NOBELIUM	*n* pl. -S a radioactive element
NOBILITY	*n* pl. -TIES the social class composed of nobles
NOBLE	*adj* -BLER, -BLEST possessing qualities of excellence
NOBLE	*n* pl. -S a person of high birth, rank, or title
NOBLEMAN	*n* pl. -MEN a noble
NOBLER	comparative of noble
NOBLESSE	*n* pl. -S the nobility
NOBLEST	superlative of noble
NOBLY	*adv* in a noble manner
NOBODY	*n* pl. -BODIES an unimportant person
NOCENT	*adj* harmful
NOCK	*v* -ED, -ING, -S to notch a bow or arrow
NOCTUID	*n* pl. -S a night-flying moth **NOCTUOID** *adj*
NOCTULE	*n* pl. -S a large bat
NOCTURN	*n* pl. -S a religious service
NOCTURNE	*n* pl. -S a musical composition
NOCUOUS	*adj* harmful
NOD	*v* NODDED, NODDING, NODS to briefly lower the head forward
NODAL	*adj* of the nature of a node **NODALLY** *adv*
NODALITY	*n* pl. -TIES the state of being nodal
NODDED	past tense of nod
NODDER	*n* pl. -S one that nods
NODDIES	pl. of noddy
NODDING	present participle of nod
NODDLE	*v* -DLED, -DLING, -DLES to nod frequently
NODDY	*n* pl. -DIES a fool
NODE	*n* pl. -S a swollen enlargement
NODI	pl. of nodus
NODICAL	*adj* pertaining to an astronomical point
NODOSE	*adj* having nodes
NODOSITY	*n* pl. -TIES the state of being nodose
NODOUS	*adj* nodose
NODULE	*n* pl. -S a small node **NODULAR, NODULOSE, NODULOUS** *adj*
NODUS	*n* pl. -DI a difficulty
NOEL	*n* pl. -S a Christmas carol
NOESIS	*n* pl. -SISES the process of reason
NOETIC	*adj* pertaining to reason
NOG	*n* pl. -S a strong ale
NOGG	*n* pl. -S nog
NOGGIN	*n* pl. -S a small cup
NOGGING	*n* pl. -S a type of masonry
NOH	*n* pl. NOH the classical drama of Japan
NOHOW	*adv* in no manner
NOIL	*n* pl. -S a kind of short fiber **NOILY** *adj*
NOIR	*adj* black
NOISE	*v* NOISED, NOISING, NOISES to spread as a rumor or report
NOISOME	*adj* disgusting; harmful
NOISY	*adj* NOISIER, NOISIEST making loud sounds **NOISILY** *adv*
NOLO	*n* pl. -LOS a type of legal plea
NOM	*n* pl. -S a name
NOMA	*n* pl. -S a severe inflammation of the mouth
NOMAD	*n* pl. -S a wanderer **NOMADIC** *adj*
NOMADISM	*n* pl. -S the mode of life of a nomad
NOMARCH	*n* pl. -S the head of a nome

NOMARCHY	*n* pl. -ARCHIES a nome
NOMBLES	*n/pl* numbles
NOMBRIL	*n* pl. -S a point on a heraldic shield
NOME	*n* pl. -S a province of modern Greece
NOMEN	*n* pl. -MINA the second name of an ancient Roman
NOMINAL	*n* pl. -S a word functioning as a noun
NOMINATE	*v* -NATED, -NATING, -NATES to name as a candidate
NOMINEE	*n* pl. -S one that is nominated
NOMISM	*n* pl. -S strict adherence to moral law **NOMISTIC** *adj*
NOMOGRAM	*n* pl. -S a type of graph
NOMOLOGY	*n* pl. -GIES the science of law
NOMOS	*n* pl. NOMOI law
NONA	*n* pl. -S a virus disease
NONACID	*n* pl. -S a substance that is not an acid
NONADULT	*n* pl. -S a person who is not an adult
NONAGE	*n* pl. -S a period of immaturity
NONAGON	*n* pl. -S a nine-sided polygon
NONBANK	*adj* not involving a bank
NONBASIC	*adj* not basic
NONBEING	*n* pl. -S lack of being
NONBOOK	*n* pl. -S a book of little literary merit
NONCASH	*adj* other than cash
NONCE	*n* pl. -S the present occasion
NONCOM	*n* pl. -S a noncommissioned officer
NONDAIRY	*adj* having no milk products
NONE	*n* pl. -S one of seven canonical daily periods for prayer and devotion
NONEGO	*n* pl. -GOS all that is not part of the ego
NONELECT	*adj* not chosen
NONEMPTY	*adj* not empty
NONENTRY	*n* pl. -TRIES the fact of not entering
NONEQUAL	*n* pl. -S one that is not equal
NONESUCH	*n* pl. -ES a person or thing without an equal
NONEVENT	*n* pl. -S an expected event that does not occur

NONFARM	*adj* not pertaining to the farm
NONFAT	*adj* having no fat solids
NONFATAL	*adj* not fatal
NONFLUID	*n* pl. -S a substance that is not a fluid
NONFOCAL	*adj* not focal
NONFOOD	*adj* pertaining to something other than food
NONGAME	*adj* not hunted for food, sport, or fur
NONGREEN	*adj* not green
NONGUILT	*n* pl. -S the absence of guilt
NONHARDY	*adj* not hardy
NONHERO	*n* pl. -ROES an antihero
NONHUMAN	*adj* not human
NONIDEAL	*adj* not ideal
NONIONIC	*adj* not ionic
NONJUROR	*n* pl. -S one who refuses to take a required oath
NONLEGAL	*adj* not legal
NONLIFE	*n* pl. -LIVES the absence of life
NONLOCAL	*n* pl. -S one that is not local
NONMAN	*n* pl. -MEN a being that is not a man
NONMETAL	*n* pl. -S an element that lacks metallic properties
NONMODAL	*adj* not modal
NONMONEY	*adj* not involving money
NONMORAL	*adj* not pertaining to morals
NONNAVAL	*adj* not naval
NONOBESE	*adj* not obese
NONOWNER	*n* pl. -S one who is not the owner
NONPAGAN	*n* pl. -S one who is not a pagan
NONPAPAL	*adj* not papal
NONPAR	*adj* being a stock that has no face value
NONPARTY	*adj* not affiliated with any political party
NONPLUS	*v* -PLUSED, -PLUSING, -PLUSES or -PLUSSED, -PLUSSING, -PLUSSES to baffle
NONPOLAR	*adj* not polar
NONPROS	*v* -PROSSED, -PROSSING, -PROSSES to enter a judgment against a plaintiff who fails to prosecute
NONQUOTA	*adj* not included in or subject to a quota

NONRATED *adj* not rated

NONRIGID *adj* not rigid

NONRIVAL *n* pl. -S an unimportant rival

NONROYAL *adj* not royal

NONRURAL *adj* not rural

NONSENSE *n* pl. -S behavior or language that is meaningless or absurd

NONSKED *n* pl. -S an airline without scheduled flying times

NONSKID *adj* designed to inhibit skidding

NONSKIER *n* pl. -S one that does not ski

NONSLIP *adj* designed to prevent slipping

NONSOLAR *adj* not solar

NONSOLID *n* pl. -S a substance that is not a solid

NONSTICK *adj* allowing of easy removal of cooked food particles

NONSTOP *adj* making no stops

NONSUCH *n* pl. -ES nonesuch

NONSUGAR *n* pl. -S a substance that is not a sugar

NONSUIT *v* -ED, -ING, -S to dismiss the lawsuit of

NONTAX *n* pl. -ES a tax of little consequence

NONTIDAL *adj* not tidal

NONTITLE *adj* pertaining to an athletic contest in which a title is not at stake

NONTOXIC *adj* not toxic

NONTRUMP *adj* not having a trump

NONTRUTH *n* pl. -S something that is not true

NONUNION *n* pl. -S failure of a broken bone to heal

NONUPLE *n* pl. -S a number nine times as great as another

NONURBAN *adj* not urban

NONUSE *n* pl. -S failure to use

NONUSER *n* pl. -S one that is not a user

NONUSING *adj* not using

NONVIRAL *adj* not viral

NONVOCAL *adj* not vocal

NONVOTER *n* pl. -S one that does not vote

NONWHITE *n* pl. -S a person who is not of the white race

NONWOODY *adj* not woody

NONWOVEN *adj* made without weaving

NONZERO *adj* having a value other than zero

NOO *adv* now

NOODLE *v* -DLED, -DLING, -DLES to play idly on a musical instrument

NOOK *n* pl. -S a corner, as in a room **NOOKLIKE** *adj*

NOOKY *n* pl. NOOKIES sexual intercourse — usually considered vulgar

NOON *n* pl. -S midday

NOONDAY *n* pl. -DAYS noon

NOONING *n* pl. -S a meal eaten at noon

NOONTIDE *n* pl. -S noon

NOONTIME *n* pl. -S noon

NOOSE *v* NOOSED, NOOSING, NOOSES to secure with a type of loop

NOOSER *n* pl. -S one that nooses

NOPAL *n* pl. -S a cactus

NOPE *adv* no

NOR *conj* and not

NORIA *n* pl. -S a type of waterwheel

NORITE *n* pl. -S a granular rock **NORITIC** *adj*

NORLAND *n* pl. -S a region in the north

NORM *n* pl. -S a standard regarded as typical for a specific group

NORMAL *n* pl. -S the usual or expected state or form

NORMALCY *n* pl. -CIES conformity with the norm

NORMALLY *adv* as a rule; usually

NORMED *adj* having a norm

NORMLESS *adj* having no norm

NORTH *n* pl. -S a point of the compass

NORTHER *n* pl. -S a wind or storm from the north

NORTHERN *n* pl. -S a person living in the north

NORTHING *n* pl. -S movement toward the north

NOSE *v* NOSED, NOSING, NOSES to sniff with the nose (the organ of smell)

NOSEBAG *n* pl. -S a feedbag

NOSEBAND *n* pl. -S a part of a horse's bridle

NOSED past tense of nose

NOSEGAY *n* pl. -GAYS a bouquet

NOSELESS	*adj* having no nose
NOSELIKE	*adj* resembling a nose
NOSEY	*adj* NOSIER, NOSIEST nosy
NOSH	*v* -ED, -ING, -ES to eat snacks between meals
NOSHER	*n* pl. -S one that noshes
NOSIER	comparative of nosy, nosey
NOSIEST	superlative of nosy, nosey
NOSILY	*adv* in a nosy manner
NOSINESS	*n* pl. -ES the quality of being nosy
NOSING	*n* pl. -S a projecting edge
NOSOLOGY	*n* pl. -GIES a classification of diseases
NOSTOC	*n* pl. -S a freshwater alga
NOSTRIL	*n* pl. -S an external opening of the nose
NOSTRUM	*n* pl. -S a medicine of one's own invention
NOSY	*adj* NOSIER, NOSIEST unduly curious
NOT	*adv* in no way
NOTA	pl. of notum
NOTABLE	*n* pl. -S a person of distinction
NOTABLY	*adv* in a distinguished manner
NOTAL	*adj* pertaining to a notum
NOTARIAL	*adj* pertaining to a notary
NOTARIZE	*v* -RIZED, -RIZING, -RIZES to certify through a notary
NOTARY	*n* pl. -RIES a public officer who certifies documents
NOTATE	*v* -TATED, -TATING, -TATES to put into notation
NOTATION	*n* pl. -S a system of symbols
NOTCH	*v* -ED, -ING, -ES to make an angular cut in
NOTCHER	*n* pl. -S one that notches
NOTE	*v* NOTED, NOTING, NOTES to write down
NOTEBOOK	*n* pl. -S a book in which to write
NOTECASE	*n* pl. -S a billfold
NOTED	past tense of note
NOTEDLY	*adv* in a famous manner
NOTELESS	*adj* undistinguished
NOTER	*n* pl. -S one that notes
NOTHING	*n* pl. -S the absence of all quantity or magnitude
NOTICE	*v* -TICED, -TICING, -TICES to become aware of
NOTIFIER	*n* pl. -S one that notifies
NOTIFY	*v* -FIED, -FYING, -FIES to inform
NOTING	present participle of note
NOTION	*n* pl. -S a general idea **NOTIONAL** *adj*
NOTORNIS	*n* pl. NOTORNIS a flightless bird
NOTTURNO	*n* pl. -NI a nocturne
NOTUM	*n* pl. -TA a part of the thorax of an insect
NOUGAT	*n* pl. -S a chewy candy
NOUGHT	*n* pl. -S naught
NOUMENON	*n* pl. -MENA an object of intellectual intuition **NOUMENAL** *adj*
NOUN	*n* pl. -S a word used to denote the name of something **NOUNAL, NOUNLESS** *adj* **NOUNALLY** *adv*
NOURISH	*v* -ED, -ING, -ES to sustain with food
NOUS	*n* pl. -ES mind, reason, or intellect
NOVA	*n* pl. -VAS or -VAE a type of star **NOVALIKE** *adj*
NOVATION	*n* pl. -S the substitution of a new legal obligation for an old one
NOVEL	*n* pl. -S a fictional prose narrative
NOVELISE	*v* -ISED, -ISING, -ISES to novelize
NOVELIST	*n* pl. -S a writer of novels
NOVELIZE	*v* -IZED, -IZING, -IZES to put into the form of a novel
NOVELLA	*n* pl. -LAS or -LE a short novel
NOVELLY	*adv* in a new or unusual manner
NOVELTY	*n* pl. -TIES something new or unusual
NOVENA	*n* pl. -NAS or -NAE a religious devotion lasting nine days
NOVERCAL	*adj* pertaining to a stepmother
NOVICE	*n* pl. -S a person new to any field or activity
NOW	*n* pl. -S the present time
NOWADAYS	*adv* in these times
NOWAY	*adv* in no way
NOWAYS	*adv* noway
NOWHERE	*n* pl. -S a nonexistent place

NOWISE	*adv* not at all
NOWT	*n* pl. -S naught
NOXIOUS	*adj* harmful to health
NOYADE	*n* pl. -S an execution by drowning
NOZZLE	*n* pl. -S a projecting spout
NTH	*adj* pertaining to an indefinitely large ordinal number
NU	*n* pl. -S a Greek letter
NUANCE	*n* pl. -S a slight variation **NUANCED** *adj*
NUB	*n* pl. -S a protuberance or knob
NUBBIER	comparative of nubby
NUBBIEST	superlative of nubby
NUBBIN	*n* pl. -S an undeveloped fruit
NUBBLE	*n* pl. -S a small nub
NUBBLY	*adj* -BLIER, -BLIEST having nubbles
NUBBY	*adj* -BIER, -BIEST having nubs
NUBIA	*n* pl. -S a woman's scarf
NUBILE	*adj* suitable for marriage
NUBILITY	*n* pl. -TIES the quality of being nubile
NUBILOSE	*adj* nubilous
NUBILOUS	*adj* cloudy
NUCELLUS	*n* pl. -LI the essential part of a plant ovule **NUCELLAR** *adj*
NUCHA	*n* pl. -CHAE the nape of the neck
NUCHAL	*n* pl. -S an anatomical part lying in the region of the nape
NUCLEAL	*adj* nuclear
NUCLEAR	*adj* pertaining to a nucleus
NUCLEASE	*n* pl. -S an enzyme
NUCLEATE	*v* -ATED, -ATING, -ATES to form into a nucleus
NUCLEI	a pl. of nucleus
NUCLEIN	*n* pl. -S a protein found in nuclei
NUCLEOLE	*n* pl. -S a part of a nucleus
NUCLEOLI	*n/pl* nucleoles
NUCLEON	*n* pl. -S an atomic particle
NUCLEUS	*n* pl. -CLEI or -CLEUSES an essential part of a cell
NUCLIDE	*n* pl. -S a species of atom **NUCLIDIC** *adj*
NUDE	*adj* NUDER, NUDEST being without clothing or covering **NUDELY** *adv*
NUDE	*n* pl. -S a nude figure
NUDENESS	*n* pl. -ES nudity
NUDER	comparative of nude
NUDEST	superlative of nude
NUDGE	*v* NUDGED, NUDGING, NUDGES to push gently
NUDGER	*n* pl. -S one that nudges
NUDICAUL	*adj* having leafless stems
NUDIE	*n* pl. -S a movie featuring nude performers
NUDISM	*n* pl. -S the practice of going nude
NUDIST	*n* pl. -S an advocate of nudism
NUDITY	*n* pl. -TIES the state of being nude
NUDNICK	*n* pl. -S nudnik
NUDNIK	*n* pl. -S an annoying person
NUGATORY	*adj* having no power
NUGGET	*n* pl. -S a mass of solid matter **NUGGETY** *adj*
NUISANCE	*n* pl. -S a source of annoyance
NUKE	*n* pl. -S a nuclear weapon or power plant
NULL	*v* -ED, -ING, -S to reduce to nothing
NULLAH	*n* pl. -S a ravine
NULLIFY	*v* -FIED, -FYING, -FIES to make useless or ineffective
NULLITY	*n* pl. -TIES something of no legal force
NUMB	*adj* NUMBER, NUMBEST lacking sensation
NUMB	*v* -ED, -ING, -S to make numb
NUMBER	*v* -ED, -ING, -S to count
NUMBERER	*n* pl. -S one that numbers
NUMBFISH	*n* pl. -ES a fish capable of emitting electric shocks
NUMBLES	*n/pl* animal entrails
NUMBLY	*adv* in a numb manner
NUMBNESS	*n* pl. -ES the state of being numb
NUMEN	*n* pl. -MINA a deity
NUMERAL	*n* pl. -S a symbol that expresses a number
NUMERARY	*adj* pertaining to numbers
NUMERATE	*v* -ATED, -ATING, -ATES to count
NUMERIC	*n* pl. -S a numeral

NUMEROUS *adj* many

NUMINA pl. of numen

NUMINOUS *n* pl. -ES the presence or revelation of the numen

NUMMARY *adj* pertaining to coins

NUMMULAR *adj* shaped like a coin

NUMSKULL *n* pl. -S a dunce

NUN *n* pl. -S a woman belonging to a religious order

NUNCIO *n* pl. -CIOS an ambassador from the pope

NUNCLE *n* pl. -S an uncle

NUNLIKE *adj* resembling a nun

NUNNERY *n* pl. -NERIES a religious house for nuns

NUNNISH *adj* of, pertaining to, or characteristic of a nun

NUPTIAL *n* pl. -S a wedding

NURL *n* -ED, -ING, -S to knurl

NURSE *v* NURSED, NURSING, NURSES to care for the sick or infirm

NURSER *n* pl. -S a baby's bottle

NURSERY *n* pl. -ERIES a room for young children

NURSING *n* pl. -S the profession of one who nurses

NURSLING *n* pl. -S an infant

NURTURE *v* -TURED, -TURING, -TURES to nourish

NURTURER *n* pl. -S one that nurtures

NUT *v* NUTTED, NUTTING, NUTS to gather nuts (hard-shelled dry fruits)

NUTANT *adj* drooping

NUTATE *v* -TATED, -TATING, -TATES to exhibit nutation

NUTATION *n* pl. -S an oscillatory movement of the axis of a rotating body

NUTBROWN *adj* of a dark brown

NUTGALL *n* pl. -S a gallnut

NUTGRASS *n* pl. -ES a perennial herb

NUTHATCH *n* pl. -ES a small bird

NUTHOUSE *n* pl. -S an insane asylum

NUTLET *n* pl. -S a small nut

NUTLIKE *adj* resembling a nut

NUTMEAT *n* pl. -S the edible kernel of a nut

NUTMEG *n* pl. -S an aromatic seed used as a spice

NUTPICK *n* pl. -S a device for extracting the kernels from nuts

NUTRIA *n* pl. -S the coypu

NUTRIENT *n* pl. -S a nourishing substance

NUTSEDGE *n* pl. -S nutgrass

NUTSHELL *n* pl. -S the shell of a nut

NUTTED past tense of nut

NUTTER *n* pl. -S one that gathers nuts

NUTTING present participle of nut

NUTTY *adj* -TIER, -TIEST abounding in nuts **NUTTILY** *adv*

NUTWOOD *n* pl. -S a nut-bearing tree

NUZZLE *v* -ZLED, -ZLING, -ZLES to push with the nose

NYALA *n* pl. -S an antelope

NYLGHAI *n* pl. -S nilgai

NYLGHAU *n* pl. -S nilgai

NYLON *n* pl. -S a synthetic material

NYMPH *n* pl. -S a female spirit **NYMPHAL, NYMPHEAN** *adj*

NYMPHA *n* pl. -PHAE a fold of the vulva

NYMPHET *n* pl. -S a young nymph

NYMPHO *n* pl. -PHOS a woman obsessed by sexual desire

OAF *n* pl. OAFS or OAVES a clumsy, stupid person **OAFISH** *adj* **OAFISHLY** *adv*

OAK *n* pl. -S a hardwood tree or shrub **OAKEN, OAKLIKE** *adj*

OAKMOSS *n* pl. -ES a lichen that grows on oak trees

OAKUM *n* pl. -S loosely twisted hemp fiber

OAR *v* -ED, -ING, -S to propel with oars (long, broad-bladed poles)

OARFISH *n* pl. -ES a marine fish

OARLESS *adj* having no oars

OARLIKE *adj* resembling an oar

OARLOCK *n* pl. -S a device for holding an oar in place

OARSMAN *n* pl. -MEN a person who rows a boat

OASIS *n* pl. OASES a green area in a desert region

OAST *n* pl. -S a type of kiln

OAT *n* pl. -S a cereal grass

OATCAKE *n* pl. -S a cake made of oatmeal

OATEN *adj* pertaining to oats

OATER *n* pl. -S a cowboy movie

OATH *n* pl. -S a formal declaration or promise to fulfill a pledge

OATLIKE *adj* resembling oats

OATMEAL *n* pl. -S meal made from oats

OAVES a pl. of oaf

OBDURACY *n* pl. -CIES the quality or an instance of being obdurate

OBDURATE *adj* stubborn

OBE *n* pl. -S obeah

OBEAH *n* pl. -S a form of sorcery of African origin

OBEAHISM *n* pl. -S the use of obeah

OBEDIENT *adj* obeying or willing to obey

OBEISANT *adj* showing reverence or respect

OBELI pl. of obelus

OBELIA *n* pl. -S a marine hydroid

OBELISE *v* -LISED, -LISING, -LISES to obelize

OBELISK *n* pl. -S a four-sided shaft of stone with a pyramidal top

OBELISM *n* pl. -S the act of obelizing

OBELIZE *v* -LIZED, -LIZING, -LIZES to mark with an obelus

OBELUS *n* pl. -LI a symbol used in ancient manuscripts to indicate a doubtful passage

OBESE *adj* very fat **OBESELY** *adv*

OBESITY *n* pl. -TIES the state or condition of being obese

OBEY *v* -ED, -ING, -S to follow the commands or guidance of **OBEYABLE** *adj*

OBEYER *n* pl. -S one that obeys

OBI *n* pl. -S obeah

OBIA *n* pl. -S obeah

OBIISM *n* pl. -S obeahism

OBIT *n* pl. -S an obituary

OBITUARY *n* pl. -ARIES a published notice of a death

OBJECT *v* -ED, -ING, -S to argue in opposition

OBJECTOR *n* pl. -S one that objects

OBLAST *n* pl. -LASTS or -LASTI an administrative division of the Soviet Union

OBLATE *n* pl. -S a layman residing in a monastery

OBLATELY *adv* elliptically

OBLATION *n* pl. -S the act of making a religious offering **OBLATORY** *adj*

OBLIGATE *v* -GATED, -GATING, -GATES to oblige

OBLIGATO *n* pl. -TI or -TOS an important musical part

OBLIGE *v* OBLIGED, OBLIGING, OBLIGES to put in one's debt by a favor or service

OBLIGEE *n* pl. -S one that is obliged

OBLIGER *n* pl. -S one that obliges

OBLIGING present participle of oblige

OBLIGOR *n* pl. -S one who places himself under a legal obligation

OBLIQUE *v* OBLIQUED, OBLIQUING, OBLIQUES to slant

OBLIVION *n* pl. -S the state of being forgotten; the act of forgetting

OBLONG *n* pl. -S something that is oblong (elongated)

OBLONGLY *adv* in an oblong manner

OBLOQUY *n* pl. -QUIES abusive language

OBOE *n* pl. -S a woodwind instrument

OBOIST *n* pl. -S one who plays the oboe

OBOL *n* pl. -S a coin of ancient Greece

OBOLE *n* pl. -S a coin of medieval France

OBOLUS *n* pl. -LI an obol

OBOVATE *adj* ovate with the narrow end at the base

OBOVOID *adj* ovoid with the narrow end at the base

OBSCENE *adj* -SCENER, -SCENEST indecent

OBSCURE *adj* -SCURER, -SCUREST dark or indistinct

OBSCURE *v* -SCURED, -SCURING, -SCURES to make obscure

OBSEQUY *n* pl. -QUIES a funeral rite

OBSERVE *v* -SERVED, -SERVING, -SERVES to look attentively

OBSERVER *n* pl. -S one that observes

OBSESS *v* -ED, -ING, -ES to dominate the thoughts of

OBSESSOR *n* pl. -S something that obsesses

OBSIDIAN *n* pl. -S a volcanic glass

OBSOLETE *v* -LETED, -LETING, -LETES to make out-of-date

OBSTACLE *n* pl. -S something that obstructs

OBSTRUCT *v* -ED, -ING, -S to get in the way of

OBTAIN *v* -ED, -ING, -S to gain possession of

OBTAINER *n* pl. -S one that obtains

OBTECT *adj* covered by a hardened secretion

OBTECTED *adj* obtect

OBTEST *v* -ED, -ING, -S to beseech

OBTRUDE *v* -TRUDED, -TRUDING, -TRUDES to thrust forward

OBTRUDER *n* pl. -S one that obtrudes

OBTUND *v* -ED, -ING, -S to deaden

OBTURATE *v* -RATED, -RATING, -RATES to close or stop up

OBTUSE *adj* -TUSER, -TUSEST dull **OBTUSELY** *adv*

OBVERSE *n* pl. -S the side of a coin bearing the main design

OBVERT *v* -ED, -ING, -S to turn so as to show a different surface

OBVIATE *v* -ATED, -ATING, -ATES to prevent or eliminate by effective measures **OBVIABLE** *adj*

OBVIATOR *n* pl. -S one that obviates

OBVIOUS *adj* easily perceived or understood

OBVOLUTE *adj* rolled or tuned in

OCA *n* pl. -S a South American herb

OCARINA *n* pl. -S a wind instrument

OCCASION *v* -ED, -ING, -S to cause

OCCIDENT *n* pl. -S the west

OCCIPUT *n* pl. -PITA or -PUTS the back part of the skull

OCCLUDE *v* -CLUDED, -CLUDING, -CLUDES to close or stop up

OCCLUSAL *adj* pertaining to the biting surface of a tooth

OCCULT *v* -ED, -ING, -S to conceal

OCCULTER *n* pl -S one that occults

OCCULTLY *adv* secretly

OCCUPANT *n* pl. -S a resident

OCCUPIER *n* pl. -S one that occupies

OCCUPY   *v* -PIED, -PYING, -PIES to engage the attention or energies of

OCCUR   *v* -CURRED, -CURRING, -CURS to take place

OCEAN   *n* pl. -S the vast body of salt water that covers most of the earth's surface **OCEANIC** *adj*

OCELLAR   *adj* pertaining to an ocellus

OCELLATE   *adj* having ocelli

OCELLUS   *n* pl. -LI a minute simple eye

OCELOT   *n* pl. -S an American wildcat **OCELOID** *adj*

OCHER   *v* -ED, -ING, -S to color with ocher (a red or yellow iron ore used as a pigment)

OCHEROUS   *adj* containing or resembling ocher

OCHERY   *adj* ocherous

OCHONE   *interj* — used to express grief

OCHRE   *v* OCHRED, OCHRING, OCHRES to ocher

OCHREA   *n* pl. -REAE ocrea

OCHREOUS   *adj* ocherous

OCHRING   present participle of ochre

OCHROID   *adj* ocherous

OCHROUS   *adj* ocherous

OCHRY   *adj* ochery

OCOTILLO   *n* pl. -LOS a Mexican shrub

OCREA   *n* pl. -REAE a sheathing plant part

OCREATE   *adj* having ocreae

OCTAD   *n* pl. -S a group of eight **OCTADIC** *adj*

OCTAGON   *n* pl. -S an eight-sided polygon

OCTAL   *adj* pertaining to a number system with a base of eight

OCTANE   *n* pl. -S a liquid hydrocarbon

OCTANGLE   *n* pl. -S an octagon

OCTANT   *n* pl. -S an eighth of a circle **OCTANTAL** *adj*

OCTARCHY   *n* pl. -TARCHIES a government by eight persons

OCTAVE   *n* pl. -S a type of musical interval **OCTAVAL** *adj*

OCTAVO   *n* pl. -VOS a page size

OCTET   *n* pl. -S a group of eight

OCTETTE   *n* pl. -S octet

OCTONARY   *n* pl. -NARIES a stanza of eight lines

OCTOPI   a pl. of octopus

OCTOPOD   *n* pl. -S any of an order of eight-armed mollusks

OCTOPUS   *n* pl. -PUSES, -PI, or -PODES a nocturnal octopod

OCTOROON   *n* pl. -S a person of one-eighth black ancestry

OCTROI   *n* pl. -S a tax on certain articles brought into a city

OCTUPLE   *v* -PLED, -PLING, -PLES to multiply by eight

OCTUPLET   *n* pl. -S a group of eight related items

OCTUPLEX   *adj* being eight times as great

OCTUPLING   present participle of octuple

OCTUPLY   *adv* to eight times the degree

OCTYL   *n* pl. -S a univalent radical

OCULAR   *n* pl. -S an eyepiece

OCULARLY   *adv* by means of the eyes or sight

OCULIST   *n* pl. -S a physician who treats diseases of the eye

OD   *n* pl. -S a hypothetical force of natural power

ODALISK   *n* pl. -S a female slave in a harem

ODD   *adj* ODDER, ODDEST unusual

ODD   *n* pl. -S one that is odd

ODDBALL   *n* pl. -S an eccentric person

ODDISH   *adj* somewhat odd

ODDITY   *n* pl. -TIES one that is odd

ODDLY   *adv* in an odd manner

ODDMENT   *n* pl. -S a remnant

ODDNESS   *n* pl. -ES the state of being odd

ODE   *n* pl. -S a lyric poem

ODEON   *n* pl. -S odeum

ODEUM   *n* pl. ODEA a theater or concert hall

ODIC   *adj* pertaining to an ode

ODIOUS   *adj* deserving or causing hatred **ODIOUSLY** *adv*

ODIUM   *n* pl. -S hatred

ODOGRAPH   *n* pl. -S an odometer

ODOMETER   *n* pl. -S a device for measuring distance traveled

ODOMETRY   *n* pl. -TRIES the process of using an odometer

ODONATE   *n* pl. -S any of an order of predacious insects

ODONTOID *n* pl. -S a toothlike vertebral projection

ODOR *n* pl. -S the property of a substance that affects the sense of smell **ODORED, ODORFUL** *adj*

ODORANT *n* pl. -S an odorous substance

ODORIZE *v* -IZED, -IZING, -IZES to make odorous

ODORLESS *adj* having no odor

ODOROUS *adj* having an odor

ODOUR *n* pl. -S odor **ODOURFUL** *adj*

ODYL *n* pl. -S an od

ODYLE *n* pl. -S odyl

ODYSSEY *n* pl. -SEYS a long, wandering journey

OE *n* pl. -S a whirlwind off the Faeroe islands

OECOLOGY *n* pl. -GIES ecology

OEDEMA *n* pl. -MAS or -MATA edema

OEDIPAL *adj* pertaining to the libidinal feelings in a child toward the parent of the opposite sex

OEDIPEAN *adj* oedipal

OEILLADE *n* pl. -S an amorous look

OENOLOGY *n* pl. -GIES the study of wines

OENOMEL *n* pl. -S an ancient Greek beverage of wine and honey

OERSTED *n* pl. -S a unit of magnetic intensity

OESTRIN *n* pl. -S estrin

OESTRIOL *n* pl. -S estriol

OESTRONE *n* pl. -S estrone

OESTROUS *adj* estrous

OESTRUM *n* pl. -S estrum

OESTRUS *n* pl. -ES estrus

OEUVRE *n* pl. -S a work of art

OF *prep* coming from

OFAY *n* pl. OFAYS a white person — usually taken to be offensive

OFF *v* -ED, -ING, -S to go away

OFFAL *n* pl. -S waste material

OFFBEAT *n* pl. -S an unaccented beat in a musical measure

OFFCAST *n* pl. -S a castoff

OFFENCE *n* pl. -S offense

OFFEND *v* -ED, -ING, -S to commit an offense

OFFENDER *n* pl. -S one that offends

OFFENSE *n* pl. -S a violation of a moral or social code

OFFER *v* -ED, -ING, -S to present for acceptance or rejection

OFFERER *n* pl. -S one that offers

OFFERING *n* pl. -S a contribution

OFFEROR *n* pl. -S offerer

OFFHAND *adv* without preparation

OFFICE *n* pl. -S a position of authority

OFFICER *v* -ED, -ING, -S to furnish with officers (persons holding positions of authority)

OFFICIAL *n* pl. -S one that holds a position of authority

OFFING *n* pl. -S the near future

OFFISH *adj* aloof **OFFISHLY** *adv*

OFFLOAD *v* -ED, -ING, -S to unload

OFFPRINT *v* -ED, -ING, -S to reprint an excerpt

OFFSET *v* -SET, -SETTING, -SETS to compensate for

OFFSHOOT *n* pl. -S a lateral shoot from a main stem

OFFSHORE *adv* away from the shore

OFFSIDE *adj* being illegally in front of the ball in football

OFFSTAGE *adj* being on a part of the stage not visible to the audience

OFT *adv* OFTER, OFTEST often

OFTEN *adv* -ENER, -ENEST frequently

OFTTIMES *adv* often

OGAM *n* pl. -S ogham

OGDOAD *n* pl. -S a group of eight

OGEE *n* pl. -S an S-shaped molding

OGHAM *n* pl. -S an Old Irish alphabet **OGHAMIC** *adj*

OGHAMIST *n* pl. -S one who writes in ogham

OGIVE *n* pl. -S a pointed arch **OGIVAL** *adj*

OGLE *v* OGLED, OGLING, OGLES to stare at

OGLER *n* pl. -S one that ogles

OGRE *n* pl. -S a monster

OGREISH *adj* resembling an ogre

OGREISM *n* pl. -S the state of being ogreish

OGRESS *n* pl. -ES a female ogre

OGRISH *adj* ogreish **OGRISHLY** *adv*

OGRISM *n* pl. -S ogreism

OH *v* -ED, -ING, -S to exclaim in surprise, pain, or desire

OHIA *n* pl. -S lehua

OHM *n* pl. -S a unit of electrical resistance **OHMIC** *adj*

OHMAGE *n* pl. -S electrical resistance expressed in ohms

OHMMETER *n* pl. -S an instrument for measuring ohmage

OHO *interj* — used to express surprise or exultation

OIDIUM *n* pl. OIDIA a type of fungus

OIL *v* -ED, -ING, -S to supply with oil (a greasy liquid used for lubrication, fuel, or illumination)

OILBIRD *n* pl. -S a tropical bird

OILCAMP *n* pl. -S a living area for workers at an oil well

OILCAN *n* pl. -S a can for applying lubricating oil

OILCLOTH *n* pl. -S a waterproof fabric

OILCUP *n* pl. -S a closed cup for supplying lubricant

OILER *n* pl. -S one that oils

OILHOLE *n* pl. -S a hole through which lubricating oil is injected

OILIER comparative of oily

OILIEST superlative of oily

OILILY *adv* in an oily manner

OILINESS *n* pl. -ES the state of being oily

OILMAN *n* pl. -MEN one who owns or operates oil wells

OILPAPER *n* pl. -S a water-resistant paper

OILPROOF *adj* impervious to oil

OILSEED *n* pl. -S a seed from which oil is pressed out

OILSKIN *n* pl. -S a waterproof fabric

OILSTONE *n* pl. -S a stone for sharpening tools

OILTIGHT *adj* being so tight as to prevent the passage of oil

OILWAY *n* pl. -WAYS a channel for the passage of oil

OILY *adj* OILIER, OILIEST covered or soaked with oil

OINK *v* -ED, -ING, -S to utter the natural grunt of a hog

OINOLOGY *n* pl. -GIES oenology

OINOMEL *n* pl. -S oenomel

OINTMENT *n* pl. -S a viscous preparation applied to the skin as a medicine or cosmetic

OITICICA *n* pl. -S a South American tree

OKA *n* pl. -S a Turkish unit of weight

OKAPI *n* pl. -S an African ruminant mammal

OKAY *v* -ED, -ING, -S to approve

OKE *n* pl. -S oka

OKEH *n* pl. -S approval

OKEYDOKE *adj* perfectly all right

OKRA *n* pl. -S a tall annual herb

OLD *adj* OLDER, OLDEST or ELDER, ELDEST living or existing for a relatively long time

OLD *n* pl. -S an individual of a specified age

OLDEN *adj* pertaining to a bygone era

OLDIE *n* pl. -S a popular song of an earlier day

OLDISH *adj* somewhat old

OLDNESS *n* pl. -ES the state of being old

OLDSTER *n* pl. -S an old person

OLDSTYLE *n* pl. -S a style of printing type

OLDWIFE *n* pl. -WIVES a marine fish

OLE *n* pl. -S a shout of approval

OLEA pl. of oleum

OLEANDER *n* pl. -S a flowering shrub

OLEASTER *n* pl. -S a flowering shrub

OLEATE *n* pl. -S a chemical salt

OLEFIN *n* pl. -S an alkene **OLEFINIC** *adj*

OLEFINE *n* pl. -S olefin

OLEIC *adj* pertaining to oil

OLEIN *n* pl. -S the liquid portion of a fat

OLEINE *n* pl. -S olein

OLEO *n* pl. OLEOS margarine

OLEUM *n* pl. OLEA oil

OLEUM *n* pl. -S a corrosive liquid

OLIBANUM *n* pl. -S a fragrant resin

OLIGARCH *n* pl. -S a ruler in a government by the few

OLIGOMER *n* pl. -S a type of polymer

OLIO *n* pl. OLIOS a miscellaneous collection

OLIVARY *adj* shaped like an olive

OLIVE *n* pl. -S the small oval fruit of a Mediterranean tree

OLIVINE	*n* pl. -S a mineral **OLIVINIC** *adj*
OLLA	*n* pl. -S a wide-mouthed pot or jar
OLOGIST	*n* pl. -S an expert in a particular ology
OLOGY	*n* pl. -GIES a branch of knowledge
OLYMPIAD	*n* pl. -S a celebration of the Olympic Games
OM	*n* pl. -S a mantra used in contemplation of ultimate reality
OMASUM	*n* pl. -SA the third stomach of a ruminant
OMBER	*n* pl. -S ombre
OMBRE	*n* pl. -S a card game
OMEGA	*n* pl. -S a Greek letter
OMELET	*n* pl. -S a dish of beaten eggs cooked and folded around a filling
OMELETTE	*n* pl. -S omelet
OMEN	*v* -ED, -ING, -S to be an omen (a prophetic sign) of
OMENTUM	*n* pl. -TA or -TUMS a fold in an abdominal membrane **OMENTAL** *adj*
OMER	*n* pl. -S a Hebrew unit of dry measure
OMICRON	*n* pl. -S a Greek letter
OMIKRON	*n* pl. -S omicron
OMINOUS	*adj* portending evil
OMISSION	*n* pl. -S something left undone
OMISSIVE	*adj* marked by omission
OMIT	*v* OMITTED, OMITTING, OMITS to leave out
OMNIARCH	*n* pl. -S an almighty ruler
OMNIBUS	*n* pl. -ES a bus
OMNIFIC	*adj* unlimited in creative power
OMNIFORM	*adj* of all forms
OMNIMODE	*adj* of all modes
OMNIVORA	*n/pl* omnivores
OMNIVORE	*n* pl. -S an animal that eats all kinds of food
OMOPHAGY	*n* pl. -GIES the eating of raw flesh
OMPHALOS	*n* pl. -LI a central point
ON	*n* pl. -S the side of the wicket where a batsman stands in cricket
ONAGER	*n* pl. -GERS or -GRI a wild ass of central Asia
ONANISM	*n* pl. -S coitus deliberately interrupted to prevent insemination
ONANIST	*n* pl. -S one who practices onanism
ONCE	*n* pl. -S one single time
ONCIDIUM	*n* pl. -S a tropical orchid
ONCOLOGY	*n* pl. -GIES the science of tumors
ONCOMING	*n* pl. -S an approach
ONDOGRAM	*n* pl. -S a graph of electric wave forms
ONE	*n* pl. -S a number
ONEFOLD	*adj* constituting a single, undivided whole
ONEIRIC	*adj* pertaining to dreams
ONENESS	*n* pl. -ES unity
ONEROUS	*adj* burdensome or oppressive
ONERY	*adj* -ERIER, -ERIEST ornery
ONESELF	*pron* a person's self
ONETIME	*adj* former
ONGOING	*adj* continuing without interruption
ONION	*n* pl. -S the edible bulb of a cultivated herb
ONIUM	*adj* characterized by a complex cation
ONLOOKER	*n* pl. -S a spectator
ONLY	*adv* with nothing or no one else
ONRUSH	*n* pl. -ES a forward rush or flow
ONSET	*n* pl. -S a beginning
ONSHORE	*adv* toward the shore
ONSIDE	*adj* not offside
ONSTAGE	*adj* being on a part of the stage visible to the audience
ONTIC	*adj* having real being or existence
ONTO	*prep* to a position upon
ONTOGENY	*n* pl. -NIES the development of an individual organism
ONTOLOGY	*n* pl. -GIES the branch of philosophy that deals with being
ONUS	*n* pl. -ES a burden or responsibility
ONWARD	*adv* toward a point ahead or in front
ONWARDS	*adv* onward
ONYX	*n* pl. -ES a variety of quartz
OOCYST	*n* pl. -S a zygote

OOCYTE   *n* pl. -S an egg before maturation

OODLES   *n* pl. OODLES a large amount

OODLINS   *n* pl. OODLINS oodles

OOGAMETE   *n* pl. -S a female gamete of certain protozoa

OOGAMOUS   *adj* having structurally dissimilar gametes

OOGAMY   *n* pl. -MIES the state of being oogamous

OOGENY   *n* pl. -NIES the development of ova

OOGONIUM   *n* pl. -NIA or -NIUMS a female sexual organ in certain algae and fungi **OOGONIAL** *adj*

OOH   *v* -ED, -ING, -S to exclaim in amazement, joy, or surprise

OOLACHAN   *n* pl. -S eulachon

OOLITE   *n* pl. -S a variety of limestone **OOLITIC** *adj*

OOLITH   *n* pl. -S oolite

OOLOGIST   *n* pl. -S an expert in oology

OOLOGY   *n* pl. -GIES the study of birds' eggs **OOLOGIC** *adj*

OOLONG   *n* pl. -S a dark Chinese tea

OOMIAC   *n* pl. -S umiak

OOMIACK   *n* pl. -S umiak

OOMIAK   *n* pl. -S umiak

OOMPH   *n* pl. -S spirited vigor

OOPHYTE   *n* pl. -S a stage of development in certain plants **OOPHYTIC** *adj*

OOPS   *interj* — used to express mild apology, surprise, or dismay

OORALI   *n* pl. -S curare

OORIE   *adj* ourie

OOSPERM   *n* pl. -S a fertilized egg

OOSPHERE   *n* pl. -S an unfertilized egg within an oogonium

OOSPORE   *n* pl. -S a fertilized egg within an oogonium **OOSPORIC** *adj*

OOT   *n* pl. -S out

OOTHECA   *n* pl. -CAE an egg case of certain insects **OOTHECAL** *adj*

OOTID   *n* pl. -S one of the four sections into which a mature ovum divides

OOZE   *v* OOZED, OOZING, OOZES to flow or leak out slowly

OOZINESS   *n* pl. -ES the state of being oozy

OOZY   *adj* OOZIER, OOZIEST containing or resembling soft mud or slime **OOZILY** *adv*

OP   *n* pl. -S a style of abstract art

OPACIFY   *v* -FIED, -FYING, -FIES to make opaque

OPACITY   *n* pl. -TIES something that is opaque

OPAH   *n* pl. -S a marine fish

OPAL   *n* pl. -S a mineral

OPALESCE   *v* -ESCED, -ESCING, -ESCES to emit an iridescent shimmer of colors

OPALINE   *n* pl. -S an opaque white glass

OPAQUE   *adj* OPAQUER, OPAQUEST impervious to light **OPAQUELY** *adv*

OPAQUE   *v* OPAQUED, OPAQUING, OPAQUES to make opaque

OPE   *v* OPED, OPING, OPES to open

OPEN   *adj* OPENER, OPENEST affording unobstructed access, passage, or view

OPEN   *v* -ED, -ING, -S to cause to become open **OPENABLE** *adj*

OPENER   *n* pl. -S one that opens

OPENING   *n* pl. -S a vacant or unobstructed space

OPENLY   *adv* in an open manner

OPENNESS   *n* pl. -ES the state of being open

OPENWORK   *n* pl. -S ornamental or structural work containing numerous openings

OPERA   *n* pl. -S a form of musical drama

OPERABLE   *adj* usable **OPERABLY** *adv*

OPERAND   *n* pl. -S a quantity on which a mathematical operation is performed

OPERANT   *n* pl. -S one that operates

OPERATE   *v* -ATED, -ATING, -ATES to perform a function

OPERATIC   *n* pl. -S the technique of staging operas

OPERATOR   *n* pl. -S a symbol that represents a mathematical function

OPERCELE   *n* pl. -S opercule

OPERCULA   *n/pl* opercules

OPERCULE   *n* pl. -S an anatomical part that serves as a lid or cover

OPERETTA *n* pl. -S a light musical drama with spoken dialogue

OPERON *n* pl. -S a type of gene cluster

OPEROSE *adj* involving great labor

OPHIDIAN *n* pl. -S a snake

OPHITE *n* pl. -S an igneous rock **OPHITIC** *adj*

OPIATE *v* -ATED, -ATING, -ATES to treat with opium

OPINE *v* OPINED, OPINING, OPINES to hold or state as an opinion

OPING present participle of ope

OPINION *n* pl. -S a conclusion or judgment one holds to be true

OPIUM *n* pl. -S an addictive narcotic

OPIUMISM *n* pl. -S opium addiction

OPOSSUM *n* pl. -S an arboreal mammal

OPPIDAN *n* pl. -S a townsman

OPPILATE *v* -LATED, -LATING, -LATES to obstruct **OPPILANT** *adj*

OPPONENT *n* pl. -S one that opposes another

OPPOSE *v* -POSED, -POSING, -POSES to be in contention or conflict with

OPPOSER *n* pl. -S one that opposes

OPPOSITE *n* pl. -S one that is radically different from another in some related way

OPPRESS *v* -ED, -ING, -ES to burden by abuse of power or authority

OPPUGN *v* -ED, -ING, -S to assail with argument

OPPUGNER *n* pl. -S one that oppugns

OPSIN *n* pl. -S a type of protein

OPSONIC *adj* pertaining to opsonin

OPSONIFY *v* -FIED, -FYING, -FIES to opsonize

OPSONIN *n* pl. -S an antibody of blood serum

OPSONIZE *v* -NIZED, -NIZING, -NIZES to form opsonins in

OPT *v* -ED, -ING, -S to choose

OPTATIVE *n* pl. -S a mood of verbs that expresses a wish or desire

OPTIC *n* pl. -S an eye

OPTICAL *adj* pertaining to sight

OPTICIAN *n* pl. -S one who makes or deals in optical goods

OPTICIST *n* pl. -S one engaged in the study of light and vision

OPTIMA a pl. of optimum

OPTIMAL *adj* most desirable

OPTIME *n* pl. -S an honor student in mathematics at Cambridge University

OPTIMISE *v* -MISED, -MISING, -MISES to optimize

OPTIMISM *n* pl. -S a disposition to look on the favorable side of things

OPTIMIST *n* pl. -S one who exhibits optimism

OPTIMIZE *v* -MIZED, -MIZING, -MIZES to make as perfect, useful, or effective as possible

OPTIMUM *n* pl. -MA or -MUMS the most favorable condition for obtaining a given result

OPTION *v* -ED, -ING, -S to grant an option (a right to buy or sell something at a specified price within a specified time) on

OPTIONAL *n* pl. -S an elective course of study

OPTIONEE *n* pl. -S one who holds a legal option

OPULENCE *n* pl. -S wealth

OPULENCY *n* pl. -CIES opulence

OPULENT *adj* wealthy

OPUNTIA *n* pl. -S an American cactus

OPUS *n* pl. OPERA or OPUSES a literary or musical work

OPUSCULA *n/pl* opuscules

OPUSCULE *n* pl. -S a minor work

OQUASSA *n* pl. -S a small lake trout

OR *n* pl. -S the heraldic color gold

ORA pl. of os

ORACH *n* pl. -ES a cultivated plant

ORACHE *n* pl. -S orach

ORACLE *n* pl. -S a person through whom a deity is believed to speak **ORACULAR** *adj*

ORAL *n* pl. -S an examination requiring spoken answers

ORALITY *n* pl. -TIES the state of being produced orally

ORALLY *adv* through the mouth

ORANG *n* pl. -S a large ape

ORANGE *n* pl. -S a citrus fruit

ORANGERY *n* pl. -RIES a place where orange trees are cultivated

ORANGEY *adj* -ANGIER, -ANGIEST orangy

ORANGISH *adj* of a somewhat orange color

ORANGY *adj* -ANGIER, -ANGIEST resembling or suggestive of an orange

ORATE *v* ORATED, ORATING, ORATES to speak formally

ORATION *n* pl. -S a formal speech

ORATOR *n* pl. -S one that orates

ORATORIO *n* pl. -RIOS a type of musical composition

ORATORY *n* pl. -RIES the art of public speaking

ORATRESS *n* pl. -ES oratrix

ORATRIX *n* pl. -TRICES a female orator

ORB *v* -ED, -ING, -S to form into a circle or sphere

ORBIT *v* -ED, -ING, -S to move or revolve around

ORBITAL *n* pl. -S a subdivision of a nuclear shell

ORBITER *n* pl. -S one that orbits

ORC *n* pl. -S a marine mammal

ORCA *n* pl. -S orc

ORCEIN *n* pl. -S a reddish brown dye

ORCHARD *n* pl. -S an area for the cultivation of fruit trees

ORCHID *n* pl. -S a flowering plant

ORCHIL *n* pl. -S a purple dye

ORCHIS *n* pl. -CHISES an orchid

ORCHITIS *n* pl. -TISES inflammation of the testicle **ORCHITIC** *adj*

ORCIN *n* pl. -S orcinol

ORCINOL *n* pl. -S a chemical compound

ORDAIN *v* -ED, -ING, -S to invest with holy authority

ORDAINER *n* pl. -S one that ordains

ORDEAL *n* pl. -S a severely difficult or painful experience

ORDER *v* -ED, -ING, -S to give a command or instruction to

ORDERER *n* pl. -S one that orders

ORDERLY *n* pl. -LIES a male attendant

ORDINAL *n* pl. -S a number designating position in a series

ORDINAND *n* pl. -S a person about to be ordained

ORDINARY *adj* -NARIER, -NARIEST of a kind to be expected in the normal order of events

ORDINARY *n* pl. -NARIES something that is ordinary

ORDINATE *n* pl. -S a particular geometric coordinate

ORDINES a pl. of ordo

ORDNANCE *n* pl. -S artillery; a cannon

ORDO *n* pl. -DINES or -DOS a calendar of religious directions

ORDURE *n* pl. -S manure

ORE *n* pl. -S a mineral or rock containing a valuable metal

OREAD *n* pl. -S a mountain nymph in Greek mythology

ORECTIC *adj* pertaining to appetites or desires

ORECTIVE *adj* orectic

OREGANO *n* pl. -NOS an aromatic herb used as a seasoning

OREIDE *n* pl. -S oroide

ORFRAY *n* pl. -FRAYS orphrey

ORGAN *n* pl. -S a differentiated part of an organism performing a specific function

ORGANA a pl. of organon and organum

ORGANDIE *n* pl. -S organdy

ORGANDY *n* pl. -DIES a cotton fabric

ORGANIC *n* pl. -S a substance of animal or vegetable origin

ORGANISE *v* -NISED, -NISING, -NISES to organize

ORGANISM *n* pl. -S any form of animal or plant life

ORGANIST *n* pl. -S one who plays the organ (a keyboard musical instrument)

ORGANIZE *v* -NIZED, -NIZING, -NIZES to form into an orderly whole

ORGANON *n* pl. -GANA or -GANONS a system of rules for scientific investigation

ORGANUM *n* pl. -GANA or -GANUMS organon

ORGANZA *n* pl. -S a sheer fabric

ORGASM *n* pl. -S the climax of sexual excitement **ORGASMIC, ORGASTIC** *adj*

ORGEAT *n* pl. -S an almond-flavored syrup

ORGIAC *adj* of the nature of an orgy

ORGIC *adj* orgiac

ORGULOUS *adj* proud

ORGY   *n* pl. -GIES a party marked by unrestrained sexual indulgence

ORIBATID   *n* pl. -S any of a family of eyeless mites

ORIBI   *n* pl. -S an African antelope

ORIEL   *n* pl. -S a type of projecting window

ORIENT   *v* -ED, -ING, -S to adjust in relation to something else

ORIENTAL   *n* pl. -S an inhabitant of an eastern country

ORIFICE   *n* pl. -S a mouth or mouthlike opening

ORIGAMI   *n* pl. -S the Japanese art of paper folding

ORIGAN   *n* pl. -S marjoram

ORIGANUM   *n* pl. -S an aromatic herb

ORIGIN   *n* pl. -S a coming into being

ORIGINAL   *n* pl. -S the first form of something

ORINASAL   *n* pl. -S a sound pronounced through both the mouth and nose

ORIOLE   *n* pl. -S an American songbird

ORISON   *n* pl. -S a prayer

ORLE   *n* pl. -S a heraldic border

ORLOP   *n* pl. -S the lowest deck of a ship

ORMER   *n* pl. -S an abalone

ORMOLU   *n* pl. -S an alloy used to imitate gold

ORNAMENT   *v* -ED, -ING, -S to decorate

ORNATE   *adj* elaborately or excessively ornamented **ORNATELY** *adv*

ORNERY   *adj* -NERIER, -NERIEST stubborn and mean-spirited

ORNIS   *n* pl. ORNITHES avifauna

ORNITHIC   *adj* pertaining to birds

OROGENY   *n* pl. -NIES the process of mountain formation **OROGENIC** *adj*

OROIDE   *n* pl. -S an alloy used to imitate gold

OROLOGY   *n* pl. -GIES the study of mountains

OROMETER   *n* pl. -S a type of barometer

OROTUND   *adj* full and clear in sound

ORPHAN   *v* -ED, -ING, -S to deprive of both parents

ORPHIC   *adj* mystical

ORPHICAL   *adj* orphic

ORPHREY   *n* pl. -PHREYS an ornamental band or border

ORPIMENT   *n* pl. -S a yellow dye

ORPIN   *n* pl. -S orpine

ORPINE   *n* pl. -S a perennial herb

ORRA   *adj* occasional

ORRERY   *n* pl. -RERIES a mechanical model of the solar system

ORRICE   *n* pl. -S orris

ORRIS   *n* pl. -RISES a flowering plant

ORT   *n* pl. -S a scrap of food

ORTHICON   *n* pl. -S a type of television camera tube

ORTHO   *adj* pertaining to reproduction in a photograph of the full range of colors in nature

ORTHODOX   *n* pl. -ES one holding traditional beliefs

ORTHOEPY   *n* pl. -EPIES the study of correct pronunciation

ORTHOTIC   *adj* pertaining to the bracing of weak joints or muscles

ORTOLAN   *n* pl. -S a European bird

ORYX   *n* pl. -ES an African antelope

OS   *n* pl. ORA an orifice

OS   *n* pl. OSSA a bone

OS   *n* pl. OSAR an esker

OSCINE   *n* pl. -S any of a family of songbirds **OSCININE** *adj*

OSCITANT   *adj* yawning

OSCULA   pl. of osculum

OSCULANT   *adj* adhering closely

OSCULAR   *adj* pertaining to the mouth

OSCULATE   *v* -LATED, -LATING, -LATES to kiss

OSCULE   *n* pl. -S osculum

OSCULUM   *n* pl. -LA an opening in a sponge

OSE   *n* pl. -S an esker

OSIER   *n* pl. -S a European tree

OSMATIC   *adj* depending mainly on the sense of smell

OSMIUM   *n* pl. -S a metallic element **OSMIC, OSMIOUS** *adj*

OSMOL   *n* pl. -S a unit of osmotic pressure **OSMOLAL** *adj*

OSMOLAR   *adj* osmotic

OSMOSE *v* -MOSED, -MOSING, -MOSES to undergo osmosis

OSMOSIS *n* pl. -MOSES a form of diffusion of a fluid through a membrane

OSMOTIC *adj* pertaining to osmosis

OSMOUS *adj* containing osmium

OSMUND *n* pl. -S any of a genus of large ferns

OSMUNDA *n* pl. -S osmund

OSNABURG *n* pl. -S a cotton fabric

OSPREY *n* pl. -PREYS an American hawk

OSSA pl. of os

OSSEIN *n* pl. -S a protein substance in bone

OSSEOUS *adj* resembling bone

OSSIA *conj* or else — used as a musical direction

OSSICLE *n* pl. -S a small bone

OSSIFIC *adj* pertaining to the formation of bone

OSSIFIER *n* pl. -S one that ossifies

OSSIFY *v* -FIED, -FYING, -FIES to convert into bone

OSSUARY *n* pl. -ARIES a receptacle for the bones of the dead

OSTEAL *adj* osseous

OSTEITIS *n* pl. -ITIDES inflammation of bone **OSTEITIC** *adj*

OSTEOID *n* pl. -S uncalcified bone matrix

OSTEOMA *n* pl. -MAS or -MATA a tumor of bone tissue

OSTIA pl. of ostium

OSTIARY *n* pl. -ARIES a doorkeeper at a church

OSTINATO *n* pl. -TOS a constantly recurring musical phrase

OSTIOLE *n* pl. -S a small bodily opening **OSTIOLAR** *adj*

OSTIUM *n* pl. OSTIA an opening in a bodily organ

OSTLER *n* pl. -S hostler

OSTMARK *n* pl. -S a monetary unit of East Germany

OSTOMY *n* pl. -MIES a type of surgical operation

OSTOSIS *n* pl. -TOSES or -TOSISES the formation of bone

OSTRACOD *n* pl. -S a minute freshwater crustacean

OSTRICH *n* pl. -ES a large, flightless bird

OTALGIA *n* pl. -S pain in the ear **OTALGIC** *adj*

OTALGY *n* pl. -GIES otalgia

OTHER *n* pl. -S one that remains of two or more

OTIC *adj* pertaining to the ear

OTIOSE *adj* lazy **OTIOSELY** *adv*

OTIOSITY *n* pl. -TIES the state of being otiose

OTITIS *n* pl. OTITIDES inflammation of the ear **OTITIC** *adj*

OTOCYST *n* pl. -S an organ of balance in many invertebrates

OTOLITH *n* pl. -S a hard mass that forms in the inner ear

OTOLOGY *n* pl. -GIES the science of the ear

OTOSCOPE *n* pl. -S an instrument for examining the ear

OTOSCOPY *n* pl. -PIES the use of an otoscope

OTTAR *n* pl. -S attar

OTTAVA *n* pl. -S an octave

OTTER *n* pl. -S a carnivorous mammal

OTTO *n* pl. -TOS attar

OTTOMAN *n* pl. -S a type of sofa

OUABAIN *n* pl. -S a cardiac stimulant

OUCH *n* pl. -ES a setting for a precious stone

OUD *n* pl. -S a stringed instrument of northern Africa

OUGHT *v* -ED, -ING, -S to owe

OUISTITI *n* pl. -S a South American monkey

OUNCE *n* pl. -S a unit of weight

OUPH *n* pl. -S ouphe

OUPHE *n* pl. -S an elf

OUR *pron* a possessive form of the pronoun we

OURANG *n* pl. -S orang

OURARI *n* pl. -S curare

OUREBI *n* pl. -S oribi

OURIE *adj* shivering with cold

OURS *pron* a possessive form of the pronoun we

OURSELF *pron* myself — used in formal or regal contexts

OUSEL *n* pl. -S ouzel

OUST   *v* -ED, -ING, -S to expel or remove from a position or place

OUSTER   *n* pl. -S the act of ousting

OUT   *v* -ED, -ING, -S to be revealed

OUTACT   *v* -ED, -ING, -S to surpass in acting

OUTADD   *v* -ED, -ING, -S to surpass in adding

OUTAGE   *n* pl. -S a failure or interruption in use or functioning

OUTARGUE   *v* -GUED, -GUING, -GUES to get the better of by arguing

OUTASK   *v* -ED, -ING, -S to surpass in asking

OUTATE   past tense of outeat

OUTBACK   *n* pl. -S isolated rural country

OUTBAKE   *v* -BAKED, -BAKING, -BAKES to surpass in baking

OUTBARK   *v* -ED, -ING, -S to surpass in barking

OUTBAWL   *v* -ED, -ING, -S to surpass in bawling

OUTBEAM   *v* -ED, -ING, -S to surpass in beaming

OUTBEG   *v* -BEGGED, -BEGGING, -BEGS to surpass in begging

OUTBID   *v* -BID, -BIDDEN, -BIDDING, -BIDS to bid higher than

OUTBLAZE   *v* -BLAZED, -BLAZING, -BLAZES to surpass in brilliance of light

OUTBLEAT   *v* -ED, -ING, -S to surpass in bleating

OUTBLESS   *v* -ED, -ING, -ES to surpass in blessing

OUTBLOOM   *v* -ED, -ING, -S to surpass in blooming

OUTBLUFF   *v* -ED, -ING, -S to surpass in bluffing

OUTBLUSH   *v* -ED, -ING, -ES to surpass in blushing

OUTBOARD   *n* pl. -S a type of motor

OUTBOAST   *v* -ED, -ING, -S to surpass in boasting

OUTBOUND   *adj* outward bound

OUTBOX   *v* -ED, -ING, -ES to surpass in boxing

OUTBRAG   *v* -BRAGGED, -BRAGGING, -BRAGS to surpass in bragging

OUTBRAVE   *v* -BRAVED, -BRAVING, -BRAVES to surpass in courage

OUTBREAK   *n* pl. -S a sudden eruption

OUTBREED   *v* -BRED, -BREEDING, -BREEDS to interbreed relatively unrelated stocks

OUTBRIBE   *v* -BRIBED, -BRIBING, -BRIBES to surpass in bribing

OUTBUILD   *v* -BUILT, -BUILDING, -BUILDS to surpass in building

OUTBULLY   *v* -LIED, -LYING, -LIES to surpass in bullying

OUTBURN   *v* -BURNED or -BURNT, -BURNING, -BURNS to burn longer than

OUTBURST   *n* pl. -S a sudden and violent outpouring

OUTBY   *adv* outdoors

OUTBYE   *adv* outby

OUTCAPER   *v* -ED, -ING, -S to surpass in capering

OUTCAST   *n* pl. -S one that is cast out

OUTCASTE   *n* pl. -S a Hindu who has been expelled from his caste

OUTCATCH   *v* -CAUGHT, -CATCHING, -CATCHES to surpass in catching

OUTCAVIL   *v* -ILED, -ILING, -ILS or -ILLED, -ILLING, -ILS to surpass in caviling

OUTCHARM   *v* -ED, -ING, -S to surpass in charming

OUTCHEAT   *v* -ED, -ING, -S to surpass in cheating

OUTCHIDE   *v* -CHIDED or -CHID, -CHIDDEN, -CHIDING, -CHIDES to surpass in chiding

OUTCLASS   *v* -ED, -ING, -ES to surpass so decisively as to appear of a higher class

OUTCLIMB   *v* -CLIMBED or -CLOMB, -CLIMBING, -CLIMBS to surpass in climbing

OUTCOME   *n* pl. -S a result

OUTCOOK   *v* -ED, -ING, -S to surpass in cooking

OUTCRAWL   *v* -ED, -ING, -S to surpass in crawling

OUTCRIED   past tense of outcry

OUTCRIES   present 3d person sing. of outcry

OUTCROP   *v* -CROPPED, -CROPPING, -CROPS to protrude above the soil

OUTCROSS   *v* -ED, -ING, -ES to cross with a relatively unrelated individual

OUTCROW *v* -ED, -ING, -S to surpass in crowing

OUTCRY *v* -CRIED, -CRYING, -CRIES to cry louder than

OUTCURSE *v* -CURSED, -CURSING, -CURSES to surpass in cursing

OUTCURVE *n* pl. -S a type of pitch in baseball

OUTDANCE *v* -DANCED, -DANCING, -DANCES to surpass in dancing

OUTDARE *v* -DARED, -DARING, -DARES to surpass in daring

OUTDATE *v* -DATED, -DATING, -DATES to make out-of-date

OUTDO *v* -DID, -DONE, -DOING, -DOES to exceed in performance

OUTDODGE *v* -DODGED, -DODGING, -DODGES to surpass in dodging

OUTDOER *n* pl. -S one that outdoes

OUTDONE past participle of outdo

OUTDOOR *adj* pertaining to the open air

OUTDOORS *adv* in the open air

OUTDRANK past tense of outdrink

OUTDRAW *v* -DREW, -DRAWN, -DRAWING, -DRAWS to attract a larger audience than

OUTDREAM *v* -DREAMED or -DREAMT, -DREAMING, -DREAMS to surpass in dreaming

OUTDRESS *v* -ED, -ING, -ES to surpass in dressing

OUTDREW past tense of outdraw

OUTDRINK *v* -DRANK, -DRUNK, -DRINKING, -DRINKS to surpass in drinking

OUTDRIVE *v* -DROVE, -DRIVEN, -DRIVING, -DRIVES to drive a golf ball farther than

OUTDROP *v* -DROPPED, -DROPPING, -DROPS to surpass in dropping

OUTDRUNK past participle of outdrink

OUTEAT *v* -ATE, -EATEN, -EATING, -EATS to surpass in eating

OUTECHO *v* -ED, -ING, -ES to surpass in echoing

OUTER *n* pl. -S a part of a target

OUTFABLE *v* -BLED, -BLING, -BLES to surpass in fabling

OUTFACE *v* -FACED, -FACING, -FACES to confront unflinchingly

OUTFALL *n* pl. -S the outlet of a body of water

OUTFAST *v* -ED, -ING, -S to surpass in fasting

OUTFAWN *v* -ED, -ING, -S to surpass in fawning

OUTFEAST *v* -ED, -ING, -S to surpass in feasting

OUTFEEL *v* -FELT, -FEELING, -FEELS to surpass in feeling

OUTFIELD *n* pl. -S a part of a baseball field

OUTFIGHT *v* -FOUGHT, -FIGHTING, -FIGHTS to defeat

OUTFIND *v* -FOUND, -FINDING, -FINDS to surpass in finding

OUTFIRE *v* -FIRED, -FIRING, -FIRES to surpass in firing

OUTFIT *v* -FITTED, -FITTING, -FITS to equip

OUTFLANK *v* -ED, -ING, -S to gain a tactical advantage over

OUTFLOW *v* -ED, -ING, -S to flow out

OUTFLY *v* -FLEW, -FLOWN, -FLYING, -FLIES to surpass in speed of flight

OUTFOOL *v* -ED, -ING, -S to surpass in fooling

OUTFOOT *v* -ED, -ING, -S to surpass in speed

OUTFOUGHT past tense of outfight

OUTFOUND past tense of outfind

OUTFOX *v* -ED, -ING, -ES to outwit

OUTFROWN *v* -ED, -ING, -S to frown more than

OUTGAIN *v* -ED, -ING, -S to gain more than

OUTGAS *v* -GASSED, -GASSING, -GASSES to remove gas from

OUTGIVE *v* -GAVE, -GIVEN, -GIVING, -GIVES to give more than

OUTGLARE *v* -GLARED, -GLARING, -GLARES to surpass in glaring

OUTGLOW *v* -ED, -ING, -S to surpass in glowing

OUTGNAW *v* -GNAWED, -GNAWN, -GNAWING, -GNAWS to surpass in gnawing

OUTGO *v* -WENT, -GONE, -GOING, -GOES to go beyond

OUTGOING *n* pl. -S a departure

OUTGREW past tense of outgrow

OUTGRIN *v* -GRINNED, -GRINNING, -GRINS to surpass in grinning

OUTGROUP *n* pl. -S a group of people outside one's own group

OUTGROW *v* -GREW, -GROWN, -GROWING, -GROWS to grow too large for

OUTGUESS *v* -ED, -ING, -ES to anticipate the actions of

OUTGUIDE *v* -GUIDED, -GUIDING, -GUIDES to surpass in guiding

OUTGUN *v* -GUNNED, -GUNNING, -GUNS to surpass in firepower

OUTGUSH *n* pl. -ES a gushing out

OUTHAUL *n* pl. -S a rope for extending a sail along a spar

OUTHEAR *v* -HEARD, -HEARING, -HEARS to surpass in hearing

OUTHIT *v* -HIT, -HITTING, -HITS to get more hits than

OUTHOUSE *n* pl. -S a toilet housed in a small structure

OUTHOWL *v* -ED, -ING, -S to surpass in howling

OUTHUMOR *v* -ED, -ING, -S to surpass in humoring

OUTING *n* pl. -S a short pleasure trip

OUTJINX *v* -ED, -ING, -ES to surpass in jinxing

OUTJUMP *v* -ED, -ING, -S to surpass in jumping

OUTJUT *v* -JUTTED, -JUTTING, -JUTS to stick out

OUTKEEP *v* -KEPT, -KEEPING, -KEEPS to surpass in keeping

OUTKICK *v* -ED, -ING, -S to surpass in kicking

OUTKISS *v* -ED, -ING, -ES to surpass in kissing

OUTLAID past tense of outlay

OUTLAIN past participle of outlie

OUTLAND *n* pl. -S a foreign land

OUTLAST *v* -ED, -ING, -S to last longer than

OUTLAUGH *v* -ED, -ING, -S to surpass in laughing

OUTLAW *v* -ED, -ING, -S to prohibit

OUTLAWRY *n* pl. -RIES habitual defiance of the law

OUTLAY *n* -LAID, -LAYING, -LAYS to pay out

OUTLEAP *v* -LEAPED or -LEAPT, -LEAPING, -LEAPS to surpass in leaping

OUTLEARN *v* -LEARNED or -LEARNT, -LEARNING, -LEARNS to surpass in learning

OUTLET *n* pl. -S a passage for escape or discharge

OUTLIE *v* -LAY, -LAIN, -LYING, -LIES to lie beyond

OUTLIER *n* pl. -S an outlying area or portion

OUTLINE *v* -LINED, -LINING, -LINES to indicate the main features or different parts of

OUTLIVE *v* -LIVED, -LIVING, -LIVES to live longer than

OUTLIVER *n* pl. -S one that outlives

OUTLOOK *n* pl. -S a point of view

OUTLOVE *v* -LOVED, -LOVING, -LOVES to surpass in loving

OUTLYING present participle of outlie

OUTMAN *v* -MANNED, -MANNING, -MANS to surpass in manpower

OUTMARCH *v* -ED, -ING, -ES to surpass in marching

OUTMATCH *v* -ED, -ING, -ES to outdo

OUTMODE *v* -MODED, -MODING, -MODES to outdate

OUTMOST *adj* farthest out

OUTMOVE *v* -MOVED, -MOVING, -MOVES to move faster or farther than

OUTPACE *v* -PACED, -PACING, -PACES to surpass in speed

OUTPAINT *v* -ED, -ING, -S to surpass in painting

OUTPASS *v* -ED, -ING, -ES to excel in passing a football

OUTPITY *v* -PITIED, -PITYING, -PITIES to surpass in pitying

OUTPLAN *v* -PLANNED, -PLANNING, -PLANS to surpass in planning

OUTPLAY *v* -ED, -ING, -S to excel or defeat in a game

OUTPLOD *v* -PLODDED, -PLODDING, -PLODS to surpass in plodding

OUTPOINT *v* -ED, -ING, -S to score more points than

OUTPOLL *v* -ED, -ING, -S to get more votes than

OUTPORT *n* pl. -S a port of export or departure

OUTPOST *n* pl. -S a body of troops stationed at a distance from the main body

OUTPOUR   v -ED, -ING, -S to pour out

OUTPRAY   v -ED, -ING, -S to surpass in praying

OUTPREEN   v -ED, -ING, -S to surpass in preening

OUTPRESS   v -ED, -ING, -ES to surpass in pressing

OUTPRICE   v -PRICED, -PRICING, -PRICES to surpass in pricing

OUTPULL   v -ED, -ING, -S to attract a larger audience or following than

OUTPUSH   v -ED, -ING, -ES to surpass in pushing

OUTPUT   v -PUTTED, -PUTTING, -PUTS to produce

OUTQUOTE   v -QUOTED, -QUOTING, -QUOTES to surpass in quoting

OUTRACE   v -RACED, -RACING, -RACES to run faster or farther than

OUTRAGE   v -RAGED, -RAGING, -RAGES to arouse anger or resentment in

OUTRAISE   v -RAISED, -RAISING, -RAISES to surpass in raising

OUTRAN   past tense of outrun

OUTRANCE   n pl. -S the last extremity

OUTRANG   past tense of outring

OUTRANGE   v -RANGED, -RANGING, -RANGES to surpass in range

OUTRANK   v -ED, -ING, -S to rank higher than

OUTRAVE   v -RAVED, -RAVING, -RAVES to surpass in raving

OUTRE   adj deviating from what is usual or proper

OUTREACH   v -ED, -ING, -ES to reach beyond

OUTREAD   v -READ, -READING, -READS to surpass in reading

OUTRIDE   v -RODE, -RIDDEN, -RIDING, -RIDES to ride faster or better than

OUTRIDER   n pl. -S a mounted attendant who rides before or beside a carriage

OUTRIGHT   adj being without limit or reservation

OUTRING   v -RANG, -RUNG, -RINGING, -RINGS to ring louder than

OUTRIVAL   v -VALED, -VALING, -VALS or -VALLED, -VALLING, -VALS to outdo in a competition or rivalry

OUTROAR   v -ED, -ING, -S to roar louder than

OUTROCK   v -ED, -ING, -S to surpass in rocking

OUTRODE   past tense of outride

OUTROLL   v -ED, -ING, -S to roll out

OUTROOT   v -ED, -ING, -S to pull up by the roots

OUTRUN   v -RAN, -RUNNING, -RUNS to run faster than

OUTRUNG   past participle of outring

OUTRUSH   n pl. -ES a rushing out

OUTSAIL   v -ED, -ING, -S to sail faster than

OUTSANG   past tense of outsing

OUTSAT   past tense of outsit

OUTSAVOR   v -ED, -ING, -S to surpass in a distinctive taste or smell

OUTSAW   past tense of outsee

OUTSCOLD   v -ED, -ING, -S to surpass in scolding

OUTSCORE   v -SCORED, -SCORING, -SCORES to score more points than

OUTSCORN   v -ED, -ING, -S to surpass in scorning

OUTSEE   v -SAW, -SEEN, -SEEING, -SEES to see beyond

OUTSELL   v -SOLD, -SELLING, -SELLS to sell more than

OUTSERT   n pl. -S a folded sheet placed around a folded section of printed matter

OUTSERVE   v -SERVED, -SERVING, -SERVES to surpass in serving

OUTSET   n pl. -S a beginning

OUTSHAME   v -SHAMED, -SHAMING, -SHAMES to surpass in shaming

OUTSHINE   v -SHONE or -SHINED, -SHINING, -SHINES to shine brighter than

OUTSHOOT   v -SHOT, -SHOOTING, -SHOOTS to shoot better than

OUTSHOUT   v -ED, -ING, -S to shout louder than

OUTSIDE   n pl. -S the outer side, surface, or part

OUTSIDER   n pl. -S one that does not belong to a particular group

OUTSIGHT   n pl. -S the power of perceiving external things

OUTSIN   v -SINNED, -SINNING, -SINS to surpass in sinning

OUTSING *v* -SANG, -SUNG, -SINGING, -SINGS to surpass in singing

OUTSIT *v* -SAT, -SITTING, -SITS to remain sitting or in session longer than

OUTSIZE *n* pl. -S an unusual size
OUTSIZED *adj*

OUTSKIRT *n* pl. -S an outlying area

OUTSLEEP *v* -SLEPT, -SLEEPING, -SLEEPS to sleep later than

OUTSMART *v* -ED, -ING, -S to outwit

OUTSOAR *v* -ED, -ING, -S to soar beyond

OUTSMILE *v* -SMILED, -SMILING, -SMILES to surpass in smiling

OUTSMOKE *v* -SMOKED, -SMOKING, -SMOKES to surpass in smoking

OUTSNORE *v* -SNORED, -SNORING, -SNORES to surpass in snoring

OUTSOLD past tense of outsell

OUTSOLE *n* pl. -S the outer sole of a boot or shoe

OUTSPAN *v* -SPANNED, -SPANNING, -SPANS to unharness a draft animal

OUTSPEAK *v* -SPOKE, -SPOKEN, -SPEAKING, -SPEAKS to outdo in speaking

OUTSPELL *v* -SPELLED or -SPELT, -SPELLING, -SPELLS to surpass in spelling

OUTSPEND *v* -SPENT, -SPENDING, -SPENDS to exceed the limits of in spending

OUTSPOKE past tense of outspeak

OUTSPOKEN past participle of outspeak

OUTSTAND *v* -STOOD, -STANDING, -STANDS to endure beyond

OUTSTARE *v* -STARED, -STARING, -STARES to outface

OUTSTART *v* -ED, -ING, -S to get ahead of at the start

OUTSTATE *v* -STATED, -STATING, -STATES to surpass in stating

OUTSTAY *v* -ED, -ING, -S to surpass in staying power

OUTSTEER *v* -ED, -ING, -S to surpass in steering

OUTSTOOD past tense of outstand

OUTSTRIP *v* -STRIPPED, -STRIPPING, -STRIPS to go faster or farther than

OUTSTUDY *v* -STUDIED, -STUDYING, -STUDIES to surpass in studying

OUTSTUNT *v* -ED, -ING, -S to surpass in stunting

OUTSULK *v* -ED, -ING, -S to surpass in sulking

OUTSUNG past participle of outsing

OUTSWEAR *v* -SWORE or -SWARE, -SWORN, -SWEARING, -SWEARS to surpass in swearing

OUTSWIM *v* -SWAM, -SWUM, -SWIMMING, -SWIMS to swim faster or farther than

OUTTAKE *n* pl. -S a passage outwards

OUTTALK *v* -ED, -ING, -S to surpass in talking

OUTTASK *v* -ED, -ING, -S to surpass in tasking

OUTTELL *v* -TOLD, -TELLING, -TELLS to say openly

OUTTHANK *v* -ED, -ING, -S to surpass in thanking

OUTTHINK *v* -THOUGHT, -THINKING, -THINKS to get the better of by thinking

OUTTHROB *v* -THROBBED, -THROBBING, -THROBS to surpass in throbbing

OUTTHROW *v* -THREW, -THROWN, -THROWING, -THROWS to throw farther or more accurately than

OUTTOLD past tense of outtell

OUTTOWER *v* -ED, -ING, -S to tower above

OUTTRADE *v* -TRADED, -TRADING, -TRADES to get the better of in a trade

OUTTRICK *v* -ED, -ING, -S to get the better of by trickery

OUTTROT *v* -TROTTED, -TROTTING, -TROTS to surpass in trotting

OUTTRUMP *v* -ED, -ING, -S to outplay

OUTTURN *n* pl. -S a quantity produced

OUTVALUE *v* -UED, -UING, -UES to be worth more than

OUTVAUNT *v* -ED, -ING, -S to surpass in vaunting

OUTVOICE *v* -VOICED, -VOICING, -VOICES to surpass in loudness of voice

OUTVOTE *v* -VOTED, -VOTING, -VOTES to defeat by a majority of votes

OUTWAIT *v* -ED, -ING, -S to exceed in patience

OUTWALK *v* -ED, -ING, -S to surpass in walking

OUTWAR *v* -WARRED, -WARRING, -WARS to surpass in warring

OUTWARD *adv* toward the outside

OUTWARDS *adv* outward

OUTWARRED past tense of outwar

OUTWAR-RING present participle of outwar

OUTWASH *n* pl. -ES detritus washed from a glacier

OUTWASTE *v* -WASTED, -WASTING, -WASTES to surpass in wasting

OUTWATCH *v* -ED, -ING, -ES to watch longer than

OUTWEAR *v* -WORE, -WORN, -WEARING, -WEARS to last longer than

OUTWEARY *v* -RIED, -RYING, -RIES to surpass in wearying

OUTWEEP *v* -WEPT, -WEEPING, -WEEPS to weep more than

OUTWEIGH *v* -ED, -ING, -S to weigh more than

OUTWENT past tense of outgo

OUTWEPT past tense of outweep

OUTWHIRL *v* -ED, -ING, -S to surpass in whirling

OUTWILE *v* -WILED, -WILING, -WILES to surpass in wiling

OUTWILL *v* -ED, -ING, -S to surpass in willpower

OUTWIND *v* -ED, -ING, -S to cause to be out of breath

OUTWISH *v* -ED, -ING, -ES to surpass in wishing

OUTWIT *v* -WITTED, -WITTING, -WITS to get the better of by superior cleverness

OUTWORE past tense of outwear

OUTWORK *v* -WORKED or -WROUGHT, -WORKING, -WORKS to work faster or better than

OUTWORN past participle of outwear

OUTWRITE *v* -WROTE or -WRIT, -WRITTEN, -WRITING, -WRITES to write better than

OUT-WROUGHT a past tense of outwork

OUTYELL *v* -ED, -ING, -S to yell louder than

OUTYELP *v* -ED, -ING, -S to surpass in yelping

OUTYIELD *v* -ED, -ING, -S to surpass in yield

OUZEL *n* pl. -S a European bird

OUZO *n* pl. -ZOS a Greek liqueur

OVA pl. of ovum

OVAL *n* pl. -S an oval (egg-shaped) figure or object

OVALITY *n* pl. -TIES ovalness

OVALLY *adv* in the shape of an oval

OVALNESS *n* pl. -ES the state of being oval

OVARIAL *adj* ovarian

OVARIAN *adj* pertaining to an ovary

OVARIES pl. of ovary

OVARIOLE *n* pl. -S one of the tubes of which the ovaries of most insects are composed

OVARITIS *n* pl. -RITIDES inflammation of an ovary

OVARY *n* pl. -RIES a female reproductive gland

OVATE *adj* egg-shaped **OVATELY** *adv*

OVATION *n* pl. -S an expression or demonstration of popular acclaim

OVEN *n* pl. -S an enclosed compartment in which substances are heated **OVENLIKE** *adj*

OVENBIRD *n* pl. -S an American songbird

OVENWARE *n* pl. -S heat-resistant dishes for baking and serving food

OVER *v* -ED, -ING, -S to leap above and to the other side of

OVERABLE *adj* excessively able

OVERACT *v* -ED, -ING, -S to act with exaggeration

OVERAGE *n* pl. -S an amount in excess

OVERALL *n* pl. -S a loose outer garment

OVERAPT *adj* excessively apt

OVERARCH *v* -ED, -ING, -ES to form an arch over

OVERARM *adj* done with the arm above the shoulder

OVERATE past tense of overeat

OVERAWE *v* -AWED, -AWING, -AWES to subdue by inspiring awe

OVERBAKE *v* -BAKED, -BAKING, -BAKES to bake too long

OVERBEAR *v* -BORE, -BORNE or -BORN, -BEARING, -BEARS to bring down by superior weight or force

OVERBET *v* -BETTED, -BETTING, -BETS to bet too much

OVERBID *v* -BID, -BIDDEN, -BIDDING, -BIDS to bid higher than

OVERBIG *adj* too big

OVERBITE *n* pl. -S a faulty closure of the teeth

OVERBLOW *v* -BLEW, -BLOWN, -BLOWING, -BLOWS to give excessive importance to

OVERBOLD *adj* excessively bold or forward

OVERBOOK *v* -ED, -ING, -S to issue reservations in excess of the space available

OVERBORE past tense of overbear

OVERBORN a past participle of overbear

OVERBORNE a past participle of overbear

OVERBOUGHT past tense of overbuy

OVERBRED *adj* bred too finely or to excess

OVERBUSY *adj* too busy

OVERBUY *v* -BOUGHT, -BUYING, -BUYS to buy in quantities exceeding need or demand

OVERCALL *v* -ED, -ING, -S to overbid

OVERCAME past tense of overcome

OVERCAST *v* -CAST, -CASTING, -CASTS to become cloudy or dark

OVERCOAT *n* pl. -S a warm coat worn over indoor clothing

OVERCOLD *adj* too cold

OVERCOME *v* -CAME, -COMING, -COMES to get the better of

OVERCOOK *v* -ED, -ING, -S to cook too long

OVERCOOL *v* -ED, -ING, -S to make too cool

OVERCOY *adj* too coy

OVERCRAM *v* -CRAMMED, -CRAMMING, -CRAMS to stuff or cram to excess

OVERCROP *v* -CROPPED, -CROPPING, -CROPS to exhaust the fertility of by cultivating to excess

OVERDARE *v* -DARED, -DARING, -DARES to become too daring

OVERDEAR *adj* too dear; too costly

OVERDECK *v* -ED, -ING, -S to adorn extravagantly

OVERDO *v* -DID, -DONE, -DOING, -DOES to do to excess

OVERDOER *n* pl. -S one that overdoes

OVERDOSE *v* -DOSED, -DOSING, -DOSES to give an excessive dose to

OVERDRAW *v* -DREW, -DRAWN, -DRAWING, -DRAWS to draw checks on in excess of the balance

OVERDRY *adj* too dry

OVERDUE *adj* not paid when due

OVERDYE *v* -DYED, -DYEING, -DYES to dye with too much color

OVEREASY *adj* too easy

OVEREAT *v* -ATE, -EATEN, -EATING, -EATS to eat to excess

OVERFAR *adj* too great in distance, extent, or degree

OVERFAST *adj* too fast

OVERFAT *adj* too fat

OVERFEAR *v* -ED, -ING, -S to fear too much

OVERFEED *v* -FED, -FEEDING, -FEEDS to feed too much

OVERFILL *v* -ED, -ING, -S to fill to overflowing

OVERFISH *v* -ED, -ING, -ES to deplete the supply of fish in an area by fishing to excess

OVERFLOW *v* -FLOWED, -FLOWN, -FLOWING, -FLOWS to flow over the top of

OVERFLY *v* -FLEW, -FLOWN, -FLYING, -FLIES to fly over

OVERFOND *adj* too fond or affectionate

OVERFOUL *adj* too foul

OVERFREE *adj* too free

OVERFULL *adj* too full

OVERGILD *v* -GILDED or -GILT, -GILDING, -GILDS to gild over

OVERGIRD *v* -GIRDED or -GIRT, -GIRDING, -GIRDS to gird to excess

OVERGLAD *adj* too glad

OVERGOAD *v* -ED, -ING, -S to goad too much

OVERGROW *v* -GREW, -GROWN, -GROWING, -GROWS to grow over

OVERHAND *v* -ED, -ING, -S to sew with short, vertical stitches

OVERHANG *v* -HUNG, -HANGING, -HANGS to hang or project over

OVERHARD *adj* too hard

OVERHATE *v* -HATED, -HATING, -HATES to hate to excess

OVERHAUL *v* -ED, -ING, -S to examine carefully for needed repairs

OVERHEAD *n* pl. -S the general cost of running a business

OVERHEAP *v* -ED, -ING, -S to heap up or accumulate to excess

OVERHEAR *v* -HEARD, -HEARING, -HEARS to hear without the speaker's knowledge or intention

OVERHEAT *v* -ED, -ING, -S to heat to excess

OVERHIGH *adj* too high

OVERHOLD *v* -HELD, -HOLDING, -HOLDS to rate too highly

OVERHOLY *adj* too holy

OVERHOPE *v* -HOPED, -HOPING, -HOPES to hope exceedingly

OVERHOT *adj* too hot

OVERHUNG past tense of overhang

OVERHUNT *v* -ED, -ING, -S to deplete the supply of game in an area by hunting to excess

OVERIDLE *adj* too idle

OVERJOY *v* -ED, -ING, -S to fill with great joy

OVERJUST *adj* too just

OVERKEEN *adj* too keen

OVERKILL *v* -ED, -ING, -S to destroy with more nuclear force than required

OVERKIND *adj* too kind

OVERLADE *v* -LADED, -LADEN, -LADING, -LADES to load with too great a burden

OVERLAID past tense of overlay

OVERLAIN past participle of overlie

OVERLAND *n* pl. -S a train or stagecoach that travels over land

OVERLAP *v* -LAPPED, -LAPPING, -LAPS to extend over and cover a part of

OVERLATE *adj* too late

OVERLAX *adj* too lax

OVERLAY *v* -LAID, -LAYING, -LAYS to lay over

OVERLEAF *adv* on the other side of the page

OVERLEAP *v* -LEAPED or -LEAPT, -LEAPING, -LEAPS to leap over

OVERLET *v* -LET, -LETTING, -LETS to let to excess

OVERLEWD *adj* too lewd

OVERLIE *v* -LAY, -LAIN, -LYING, -LIES to lie over

OVERLIVE *v* -LIVED, -LIVING, -LIVES to outlive

OVERLOAD *v* -ED, -ING, -S to load to excess

OVERLONG *adj* too long

OVERLOOK *v* -ED, -ING, -S to fail to notice

OVERLORD *v* -ED, -ING, -S to rule tyrannically

OVERLOUD *adj* too loud

OVERLOVE *v* -LOVED, -LOVING, -LOVES to love to excess

OVERLY *adv* to an excessive degree

OVERLYING present participle of overlie

OVERMAN *n* pl. -MEN a foreman

OVERMAN *v* -MANNED, -MANNING, -MANS to provide with more men than are needed

OVERMANY *adj* too many

OVERMEEK *adj* excessively meek

OVERMELT *v* -ED, -ING, -S to melt too much

OVERMEN pl. of overman

OVERMILD *adj* too mild

OVERMIX *v* -ED, -ING, -ES to mix too much

OVERMUCH *n* pl. -ES an excess

OVERNEAR *adj* too near

OVERNEAT *adj* too neat

OVERNEW *adj* too new

OVERNICE *adj* excessively nice

OVERPASS *v* -PASSED or -PAST, -PASSING, -PASSES to pass over

OVERPAY *v* -PAID, -PAYING, -PAYS to pay too much

OVERPERT *adj* too pert

OVERPLAY *v* -ED, -ING, -S to exaggerate

OVERPLUS *n* pl. -ES a surplus

OVERPLY *v* -PLIED, -PLYING, -PLIES to ply to excess; overwork

OVERRAN past tense of overrun

OVERRANK *adj* too luxuriant in growth

OVERRASH *adj* too rash

OVERRATE *v* -RATED, -RATING, -RATES to rate too highly

OVERRICH *adj* too rich

OVERRIDE *v* -RODE, -RIDDEN, -RIDING, -RIDES to ride over

OVERRIFE *adj* too rife

OVERRIPE *adj* too ripe

OVERRODE past tense of override

OVERRUDE *adj* excessively rude

OVERRUFF *v* -ED, -ING, -S to trump with a higher trump card than has already been played

OVERRULE *v* -RULED, -RULING, -RULES to disallow the arguments of

OVERRUN *v* -RAN, -RUNNING, -RUNS to spread or swarm over

OVERSAD *adj* excessively sad

OVERSALE *n* pl. -S the act of overselling

OVERSALT *v* -ED, -ING, -S to salt to excess

OVERSAVE *v* -SAVED, -SAVING, -SAVES to save too much

OVERSAW past tense of oversee

OVERSEA *adv* overseas

OVERSEAS *adv* beyond or across the sea

OVERSEE *v* -SAW, -SEEN, -SEEING, -SEES to watch over and direct

OVERSEED *v* -ED, -ING, -S to seed to excess

OVERSEER *n* pl. -S one that oversees

OVERSELL *v* -SOLD, -SELLING, -SELLS to sell more of than can be delivered

OVERSET *v* -SET, -SETTING, -SETS to turn or tip over

OVERSEW *v* -SEWED, -SEWN, -SEWING, -SEWS to overhand

OVERSHOE *n* pl. -S a protective outer shoe

OVERSHOT *n* pl. -S a type of fabric weave

OVERSICK *adj* too sick

OVERSIDE *n* pl. -S the other side of a phonograph record

OVERSIZE *n* pl. -S an unusually large size

OVERSLIP *v* -SLIPPED or -SLIPT, -SLIPPING, -SLIPS to leave out

OVERSLOW *adj* too slow

OVERSOAK *v* -ED, -ING, -S to soak too much

OVERSOFT *adj* too soft

OVERSOLD past tense of oversell

OVERSOON *adv* too soon

OVERSOUL *n* pl. -S a supreme reality or mind in transcendentalism

OVERSPIN *n* pl. -S a forward spin imparted to a ball

OVERSTAY *v* -ED, -ING, -S to stay beyond the limits or duration of

OVERSTEP *v* -STEPPED, -STEPPING, -STEPS to go beyond

OVERSTIR *v* -STIRRED, -STIRRING, -STIRS to stir too much

OVERSUP *v* -SUPPED, -SUPPING, -SUPS to sup to excess

OVERSURE *adj* too sure

OVERT *adj* open to view **OVERTLY** *adv*

OVERTAKE *v* -TOOK, -TAKEN, -TAKING, -TAKES to catch up with

OVERTAME *adj* too tame

OVERTART *adj* too tart

OVERTASK *v* -ED, -ING, -S to task too severely

OVERTAX *v* -ED, -ING, -ES to tax too heavily

OVERTHIN *adj* too thin

OVERTIME *v* -TIMED, -TIMING, -TIMES to exceed the desired timing for

OVERTIRE *v* -TIRED, -TIRING, -TIRES to tire excessively

OVERTOIL *v* -ED, -ING, -S to wear out or exhaust by excessive toil

OVERTONE *n* pl. -S a higher partial tone

OVERTOOK past tense of overtake

OVERTOP *v* -TOPPED, -TOPPING, -TOPS to rise above the top of

OVERTRIM *v* -TRIMMED, -TRIMMING, -TRIMS to trim too much

OVERTURE *v* -TURED, -TURING, -TURES to propose

OVERTURN *v* -ED, -ING, -S to turn over

OVERURGE *v* -URGED, -URGING, -URGES to urge too much

OVERUSE *v* -USED, -USING, -USES to use too much

OVERVIEW *n* pl. -S a summary

OVERVOTE *v* -VOTED, -VOTING, -VOTES to defeat by a majority of votes

OVERWARM *v* -ED, -ING, -S to warm too much

OVERWARY *adj* too wary

OVERWEAK *adj* too weak

OVERWEAR *v* -WORE, -WORN, -WEARING, -WEARS to wear out

OVERWEEN *v* -ED, -ING, -S to be arrogant

OVERWET *v* -WETTED, -WETTING, -WETS to wet too much

OVERWIDE *adj* too wide

OVERWILY *adj* too wily

OVERWIND   *v* -WOUND, -WINDING, -WINDS to wind too much, as a watch

OVERWISE   *adj* too wise

OVERWORD   *n* pl. -S a word or phrase repeated at intervals in a song

OVERWORE   past tense of overwear

OVERWORK   *v* -WORKED or -WROUGHT, -WORKING, -WORKS to cause to work too hard

OVERWORN   past participle of overwear

OVER-WOUND   past tense of overwind

OVER-WROUGHT   a past tense of overwork

OVERZEAL   *n* pl. -S excess of zeal

OVIBOS   *n* pl. OVIBOS a wild ox

OVICIDE   *n* pl. -S an agent that kills eggs **OVICIDAL** *adj*

OVIDUCT   *n* pl. -S a tube through which ova travel from an ovary **OVIDUCAL** *adj*

OVIFORM   *adj* shaped like an egg

OVINE   *n* pl. -S a sheep or a closely related animal

OVIPARA   *n/pl* egg-laying animals

OVIPOSIT   *v* -ED, -ING, -S to lay eggs

OVISAC   *n* pl. -S a sac containing an ovum or ova

OVOID   *n* pl. -S an egg-shaped body **OVOIDAL** *adj*

OVOLO   *n* pl. -LI or -LOS a convex molding

OVONIC   *adj* pertaining to a branch of electronics

OVULATE   *v* -LATED, -LATING, -LATES to produce ova

OVULE   *n* pl. -S a rudimentary seed **OVULAR, OVULARY** *adj*

OVUM   *n* pl. OVA the female reproductive cell of animals

OW   *interj* — used to express sudden pain

OWE   *v* OWED, OWING, OWES to be under obligation to pay or repay

OWL   *n* pl. -S a nocturnal bird

OWLET   *n* pl. -S a young owl

OWLISH   *adj* resembling an owl **OWLISHLY** *adv*

OWLLIKE   *adj* owlish

OWN   *v* -ED, -ING, -S to have as a belonging **OWNABLE** *adj*

OWNER   *n* pl. -S one that owns

OWSE   *n* pl. OWSEN ox

OX   *n* pl. OXEN a hoofed mammal

OX   *n* pl. -ES a clumsy person

OXALATE   *v* -LATED, -LATING, -LATES to treat with an oxalate (a chemical salt)

OXALIS   *n* pl. -ALISES a flowering plant **OXALIC** *adj*

OXAZINE   *n* pl. -S a chemical compound

OXBLOOD   *n* pl. -S a deep red color

OXBOW   *n* pl. -S a U-shaped piece of wood in an ox yoke

OXCART   *n* pl. -S an ox-drawn cart

OXEN   pl. of ox

OXEYE   *n* pl. -S a flowering plant

OXFORD   *n* pl. -S a type of shoe

OXHEART   *n* pl. -S a variety of sweet cherry

OXID   *n* pl. -S oxide

OXIDABLE   *adj* capable of being oxidized

OXIDANT   *n* pl. -S an oxidizing agent

OXIDASE   *n* pl. -S an oxidizing enzyme **OXIDASIC** *adj*

OXIDATE   *v* -DATED, -DATING, -DATES to oxidize

OXIDE   *n* pl. -S a binary compound of oxygen with another element or radical **OXIDIC** *adj*

OXIDISE   *v* -DISED, -DISING, -DISES to oxidize

OXIDISER   *n* pl. -S oxidizer

OXIDIZE   *v* -DIZED, -DIZING, -DIZES to combine with oxygen

OXIDIZER   *n* pl. -S an oxidant

OXIM   *n* pl. -S oxime

OXIME   *n* pl. -S a chemical compound

OXLIP   *n* pl. -S a flowering plant

OXPECKER   *n* pl. -S an African bird

OXTAIL   *n* pl. -S the tail of an ox

OXTER   *n* pl. -S the armpit

OXTONGUE   *n* pl. -S a European herb

OXY   *adj* containing oxygen

OXYACID   *n* pl. -S an acid that contains oxygen

OXYGEN   *n* pl. -S a gaseous element **OXYGENIC** *adj*

OXYMORON *n* pl. -MORA a combination of contradictory or incongruous words

OXYPHIL *n* pl. -S oxyphile

OXYPHILE *n* pl. -S an organism that thrives in a relatively acid environment

OXYSALT *n* pl. -S of an oxyacid

OXYSOME *n* pl. -S a structural unit of cellular cristae

OXYTOCIC *n* pl. -S a drug that hastens the process of childbirth

OXYTOCIN *n* pl. -S a pituitary hormone

OXYTONE *n* pl. -S a word having heavy stress on the last syllable

OY *interj* — used to express dismay or pain

OYER *n* pl. -S a type of legal writ

OYES *n* pl. OYESSES oyez

OYEZ *n* pl. OYESSES a cry used to introduce the opening of a court of law

OYSTER *v* -ED, -ING, -S to gather oysters (edible mollusks)

OYSTERER *n* pl. -S one that gathers or sells oysters

OZONE *n* pl. -S a form of oxygen **OZONIC** *adj*

OZONIDE *n* pl. -S a compound of ozone

OZONISE *v* -ISED, -ISING, -ISES to ozonize

OZONIZE *v* -IZED, -IZING, -IZES to convert into ozone

OZONIZER *n* pl. -S a device for converting oxygen into ozone

OZONOUS *adj* pertaining to ozone

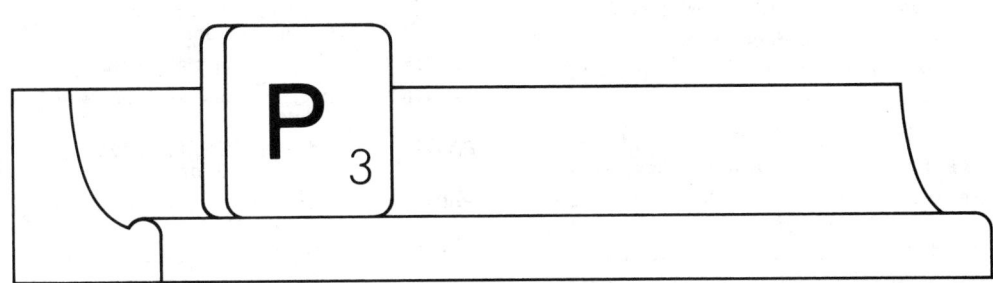

PA   n pl. -S a father

PABULUM   n pl. -S food **PABULAR** adj

PAC   n pl. -S a shoe patterned after a moccasin

PACA   n pl. -S a large rodent

PACE   v PACED, PACING, PACES to walk with a regular step

PACER   n pl. -S a horse whose gait is a pace

PACHA   n pl. -S pasha

PACHADOM   n pl. -S pashadom

PACHALIC   n pl. -S pashalik

PACHISI   n pl. -S a board game of India

PACHOULI   n pl. -S an East Indian herb

PACHUCO   n pl. -COS a flashy Mexican-American youth

PACIFIC   adj peaceful

PACIFIED   past tense of pacify

PACIFIER   n pl. -S one that pacifies

PACIFIES   present 3d person sing. of pacify

PACIFISM   n pl. -S opposition to war or violence

PACIFIST   n pl. -S an advocate of pacifism

PACIFY   v -FIED, -FYING, -FIES to make peaceful

PACING   present participle of pace

PACK   v -ED, -ING, -S to put into a receptacle for transportation or storage **PACKABLE** adj

PACKAGE   v -AGED, -AGING, -AGES to make into a package (a wrapped or boxed object)

PACKAGER   n pl. -S one that packages

PACKER   n pl. -S one that packs

PACKET   v -ED, -ING, -S to make into a small package

PACKING   n pl. -S material used to pack

PACKLY   adv intimately

PACKMAN   n pl. -MEN a peddler

PACKNESS   n pl. -ES intimacy

PACKSACK   n pl. -S a carrying bag to be worn on the back

PACKWAX   n pl. -ES paxwax

PACT   n pl. -S an agreement

PACTION   n pl. -S a pact

PAD   v PADDED, PADDING, PADS to line or stuff with soft material

PADAUK   n pl. -S a tropical tree

PADDIES   pl. of paddy

PADDING   n pl. -S material with which to pad

PADDLE   v -DLED, -DLING, -DLES to propel with a broad-bladed implement

PADDLER   n pl. -S one that paddles

PADDLING   n pl. -S the act of one who paddles

PADDOCK   v -ED, -ING, -S to confine in an enclosure for horses

PADDY   n pl. -DIES a rice field

PADISHAH   n pl. -S a sovereign

PADLE   n pl. -S a hoe

PADLOCK   v -ED, -ING, -S to secure with a type of lock

PADNAG   n pl. -S a horse that moves along at an easy pace

PADOUK   n pl. -S padauk

PADRE   *n* pl. PADRES or PADRI a Christian clergyman

PADRONE   *n* pl. -NES or -NI a master

PADSHAH   *n* pl. -S padishah

PADUASOY   *n* pl. -SOYS a strong silk fabric

PAEAN   *n* pl. -S a song of joy

PAEANISM   *n* pl. -S the chanting of a paean

PAELLA   *n* pl. -S a saffron-flavored stew

PAEON   *n* pl. -S a metrical foot of four syllables

PAGAN   *n* pl. -S an irreligious person

PAGANDOM   *n* pl. -S the realm of pagans

PAGANISE   *v* -ISED, -ISING, -ISES to paganize

PAGANISH   *adj* resembling a pagan

PAGANISM   *n* pl. -S an irreligious attitude

PAGANIST   *n* pl. -S a pagan

PAGANIZE   *v* -IZED, -IZING, -IZES to make irreligious

PAGE   *v* PAGED, PAGING, PAGES to summon by calling out the name of

PAGEANT   *n* pl. -S an elaborate public spectacle

PAGEBOY   *n* pl. -BOYS a woman's hairstyle

PAGED   past tense of page

PAGINAL   *adj* pertaining to the pages of a book

PAGINATE   *v* -NATED, -NATING, -NATES to number the pages of

PAGING   present participle of page

PAGOD   *n* pl. -S pagoda

PAGODA   *n* pl. -S a Far Eastern temple

PAGURIAN   *n* pl. -S a hermit crab

PAGURID   *n* pl. -S pagurian

PAH   *interj* — used as an exclamation of disgust

PAHLAVI   *n* pl. -S a coin of Iran

PAID   a past tense of pay

PAIK   *v* -ED, -ING, -S to beat or strike

PAIL   *n* pl. -S a watertight cylindrical container

PAILFUL   *n* pl. PAILFULS or PAILSFUL as much as a pail will hold

PAIN   *v* -ED, -ING, -S to cause pain (suffering or distress)

PAINCH   *n* pl. -ES paunch

PAINFUL   *adj* -FULLER, -FULLEST causing pain

PAINLESS   *adj* not causing pain

PAINT   *v* -ED, -ING, -S to make a representation of with paints (coloring substances)

PAINTER   *n* pl. -S one that paints

PAINTING   *n* pl. -S a picture made with paints

PAINTY   *adj* PAINTIER, PAINTIEST covered with paint

PAIR   *v* -ED, -ING, -S to arrange in sets of two

PAISA   *n* pl. PAISE or PAISAS a coin of Pakistan

PAISAN   *n* pl. -S paisano

PAISANO   *n* pl. -NOS a fellow countryman

PAISE   a pl. of paisa

PAISLEY   *n* pl. -LEYS a patterned wool fabric

PAJAMA   *n* pl. -S a garment for sleeping or lounging

PAL   *v* PALLED, PALLING, PALS to associate as friends

PALABRA   *n* pl. -S a word

PALACE   *n* pl. -S a royal residence **PALACED** *adj*

PALADIN   *n* pl. -S a knightly champion

PALAIS   *n* pl. PALAIS a palace

PALATAL   *n* pl. -S a bone of the palate

PALATE   *n* pl. -S the roof of the mouth

PALATIAL   *adj* resembling a palace

PALATINE   *n* pl. -S a high officer of an empire

PALAVER   *v* -ED, -ING, -S to chatter

PALAZZO   *n* pl. -ZI an impressive building

PALE   *adj* PALER, PALEST lacking intensity of color

PALE   *v* PALED, PALING, PALES to make or become pale

PALEA   *n* pl. -LEAE a small bract **PALEAL** *adj*

PALEFACE   *n* pl. -S a white person

PALELY   *adv* in a pale manner

PALENESS   *n* pl. -ES the quality of being pale

PALER   comparative of pale

PALEST   superlative of pale

PALESTRA   *n* pl. -TRAS or -TRAE a school for athletics in ancient Greece

PALET   *n* pl. -S a palea

PALETOT   *n* pl. -S a loose overcoat

PALETTE   *n* pl. -S a board on which an artist mixes colors

PALEWAYS   *adv* palewise

PALEWISE   *adv* vertically

PALFREY   *n* pl. -FREYS a riding horse

PALIER   comparative of paly

PALIEST   superlative of paly

PALIKAR   *n* pl. -S a Greek soldier

PALING   *n* pl. -S a picket fence

PALINODE   *n* pl. -S a formal retraction

PALISADE   *v* -SADED, -SADING, -SADES to fortify with a heavy fence

PALISH   *adj* somewhat pale

PALL   *v* -ED, -ING, -S to become insipid

PALLADIA   *n/pl* safeguards

PALLADIC   *adj* pertaining to the metallic element palladium

PALLED   past tense of pal

PALLET   *n* pl. -S a bed or mattress of straw

PALLETTE   *n* pl. -S a piece of armor protecting the armpit

PALLIA   a pl. of pallium

PALLIAL   *adj* pertaining to a part of the brain

PALLIATE   *v* -ATED, -ATING, -ATES to conceal the seriousness of

PALLID   *adj* pale **PALLIDLY** *adv*

PALLIER   comparative of pally

PALLIEST   superlative of pally

PALLING   present participle of pal

PALLIUM   *n* pl. -LIA or -LIUMS a cloak worn in ancient Rome

PALLOR   *n* pl. -S paleness

PALLY   *adj* -LIER, -LIEST marked by close friendship

PALM   *v* -ED, -ING, -S to touch with the palm (inner surface) of the hand

PALMAR   *adj* pertaining to the palm

PALMARY   *adj* worthy of praise

PALMATE   *adj* resembling an open hand

PALMATED   *adj* palmate

PALMER   *n* pl. -S a religious pilgrim

PALMETTE   *n* pl. -S a type of ornament

PALMETTO   *n* pl. -TOS or -TOES a tropical tree

PALMIER   comparative of palmy

PALMIEST   superlative of palmy

PALMIST   *n* pl. -S a fortune-teller

PALMITIN   *n* pl. -S a chemical compound

PALMLIKE   *adj* resembling a palm tree

PALMY   *adj* PALMIER, PALMIEST marked by prosperity

PALMYRA   *n* pl. -S a tropical tree

PALOMINO   *n* pl. -NOS a slender-legged horse

PALOOKA   *n* pl. -S an inferior boxer

PALP   *n* pl. -S a palpus

PALPABLE   *adj* capable of being felt **PALPABLY** *adv*

PALPAL   *adj* pertaining to a palpus

PALPATE   *v* -PATED, -PATING, -PATES to examine by touch

PALPATOR   *n* pl. -S one that palpates

PALPEBRA   *n* pl. -BRAE an eyelid

PALPUS   *n* pl. -PI a sensory organ of an arthropod

PALSY   *v* -SIED, -SYING, -SIES to paralyze

PALTER   *v* -ED, -ING, -S to talk or act insincerely

PALTERER   *n* pl. -S one that palters

PALTRY   *adj* -TRIER, -TRIEST petty **PALTRILY** *adv*

PALUDAL   *adj* pertaining to a marsh

PALUDISM   *n* pl. -S malaria

PALY   *adj* PALIER, PALIEST somewhat pale

PAM   *n* pl. -S the jack of clubs in certain card games

PAMPA   *n* pl. -S a grassland of South America

PAMPEAN   *n* pl. -S a native of the pampas

PAMPER   *v* -ED, -ING, -S to treat with extreme or excessive indulgence

PAMPERER   *n* pl. -S one that pampers

PAMPERO   *n* pl. -ROS a cold, dry wind

PAMPHLET   *n* pl. -S a printed work with a paper cover

PAN   *v* PANNED, PANNING, PANS to criticize harshly

PANACEA   *n* pl. -S a remedy for all diseases or ills **PANACEAN** *adj*

PANACHE   *n* pl. -S an ornamental tuft of feathers

PANADA	*n* pl. -S a thick sauce
PANAMA	*n* pl. -S a lightweight hat
PANATELA	*n* pl. -S a long, slender cigar
PANCAKE	*v* -CAKED, -CAKING, -CAKES to land an airplane in a certain manner
PANCHAX	*n* pl. -ES a tropical fish
PANCREAS	*n* pl. -ES a large gland
PANDA	*n* pl. -S a carnivorous mammal
PANDANUS	*n* pl. -NI or -NUSES a tropical plant
PANDECT	*n* pl. -S a complete body of laws
PANDEMIC	*n* pl. -S a widespread disease
PANDER	*v* -ED, -ING, -S to provide gratification for others' desires
PANDERER	*n* pl. -S one that panders
PANDIED	past tense of pandy
PANDIES	present 3d person sing. of pandy
PANDIT	*n* pl. -S a wise or learned man in India
PANDOOR	*n* pl. -S pandour
PANDORA	*n* pl. -S bandore
PANDORE	*n* pl. -S bandore
PANDOUR	*n* pl. -S a marauding soldier
PANDOWDY	*n* pl. -DIES an apple dessert
PANDURA	*n* pl. -S bandore
PANDY	*v* -DIED, -DYING, -DIES to punish by striking the hand
PANE	*n* pl. -S a sheet of glass for a window **PANED** *adj*
PANEL	*v* -ELED, -ELING, -ELS or -ELLED, -ELLING, -ELS to decorate with thin sheets of material
PANELING	*n* pl. -S material with which to panel
PANELIST	*n* pl. -S a member of a discussion or advisory group
PANELLED	past tense of panel
PANELLING	a present participle of panel
PANETELA	*n* pl. -S panatela
PANFISH	*n* pl. -ES any small fish that can be fried whole
PANFUL	*n* pl. -S as much as a pan will hold
PANG	*v* -ED, -ING, -S to cause to have spasms of pain
PANGA	*n* pl. -S a large knife
PANGEN	*n* pl. -S a hypothetical heredity-controlling particle of proto-plasm
PANGOLIN	*n* pl. -S a toothless mammal
PANHUMAN	*adj* pertaining to all humanity
PANIC	*v* -ICKED, -ICKING, -ICS to be overwhelmed by fear
PANICKY	*adj* -ICKIER, -ICKIEST tending to panic
PANICLE	*n* pl. -S a loosely branched flower cluster **PANICLED** *adj*
PANICUM	*n* pl. -S a grass
PANIER	*n* pl. -S pannier
PANMIXIA	*n* pl. -S random mating within a breeding population
PANNE	*n* pl. -S a lustrous velvet
PANNED	past tense of pan
PANNIER	*n* pl. -S a large basket
PANNIKIN	*n* pl. -S a small saucepan
PANNING	present participle of pan
PANOCHA	*n* pl. -S a coarse Mexican sugar
PANOCHE	*n* pl. -S panocha
PANOPLY	*n* pl. -PLIES a suit of armor
PANOPTIC	*adj* including everything visible in one view
PANORAMA	*n* pl. -S a complete view
PANPIPE	*n* pl. -S a musical instrument
PANSOPHY	*n* pl. -PHIES universal knowledge
PANSY	*n* pl. -SIES a flowering plant
PANT	*v* -ED, -ING, -S to breathe quickly and with difficulty
PANTHEON	*n* pl. -S a temple dedicated to all the gods
PANTHER	*n* pl. -S a leopard
PANTIE	*n* pl. -S a woman's or child's undergarment
PANTIES	pl. of panty
PANTILE	*n* pl. -S a roofing tile **PANTILED** *adj*
PANTOFLE	*n* pl. -S a slipper
PANTOUM	*n* pl. -S a verse form
PANTRY	*n* pl. -TRIES a closet or room for storing kitchen utensils
PANTSUIT	*n* pl. -S a type of woman's suit
PANTY	*n* pl. PANTIES pantie
PANZER	*n* pl. -S an armored combat vehicle
PAP	*n* pl. -S a soft food for infants

PAPA	*n* pl. -S a father	**PARA**	*n* pl. -S a monetary unit of Yugoslavia
PAPACY	*n* pl. -CIES the office of the pope	**PARABLE**	*n* pl. -S a simple story conveying a moral or religious lesson
PAPAIN	*n* pl. -S an enzyme		
PAPAL	*adj* pertaining to the pope **PAPALLY** *adv*	**PARABOLA**	*n* pl. -S a conic section
		PARACHOR	*n* pl. -S a mathematical constant that relates molecular volume to surface tension
PAPAW	*n* pl. -S a fleshy fruit		
PAPAYA	*n* pl. -S a melon-like fruit **PAPAYAN** *adj*	**PARADE**	*v* -RADED, -RADING, -RADES to march in a public procession
PAPER	*v* -ED, -ING, -S to cover or wrap with paper (a thin sheet material made of cellulose pulp)	**PARADER**	*n* pl. -S one that parades
		PARADIGM	*n* pl. -S a pattern or example
PAPERBOY	*n* pl. -BOYS a newsboy	**PARADING**	present participle of parade
PAPERER	*n* pl. -S one that papers	**PARADISE**	*n* pl. -S a place of extreme beauty or delight
PAPERY	*adj* resembling paper		
PAPHIAN	*n* pl. -S a prostitute	**PARADOS**	*n* pl. -ES a protective embankment
PAPILLA	*n* pl. -LAE a nipple-like projection **PAPILLAR** *adj*	**PARADOX**	*n* pl. -ES a statement seemingly contradictory or absurd yet perhaps true
PAPILLON	*n* pl. -S a small dog		
PAPIST	*n* pl. -S a Roman Catholic — usually used disparagingly **PAPISTIC** *adj*	**PARADROP**	*v* -DROPPED, -DROPPING, -DROPS to deliver by parachute
PAPISTRY	*n* pl. -TRIES the Roman Catholic religion — usually used disparagingly	**PARAFFIN**	*v* -ED, -ING, -S to coat with a waxy substance
		PARAFORM	*n* pl. -S a substance used as an antiseptic
PAPOOSE	*n* pl. -S an American Indian baby	**PARAGOGE**	*n* pl. -S the addition of a sound or sounds at the end of a word
PAPPI	*a* pl. of pappus		
PAPPIER	comparative of pappy	**PARAGON**	*v* -ED, -ING, -S to compare with
PAPPIES	pl. of pappy	**PARAKEET**	*n* pl. -S a small parrot
PAPPIEST	superlative of pappy	**PARALLAX**	*n* pl. -ES an apparent optical displacement of an object
PAPPOOSE	*n* pl. -S papoose		
PAPPUS	*n* pl. -PI a tuft of bristles on the achene of certain plants **PAPPOSE, PAPPOUS** *adj*	**PARALLEL**	*v* -LELED, -LELING, -LELS or -LELLED, -LELLING, -LELS to be similar or analogous to
PAPPY	*adj* -PIER, -PIEST resembling pap	**PARALYSE**	*v* -LYSED, -LYSING, -LYSES to paralyze
PAPPY	*n* pl. -PIES a father	**PARALYZE**	*v* -LYZED, -LYZING, -LYZES to render incapable of movement
PAPRICA	*n* pl. -S paprika		
PAPRIKA	*n* pl. -S a seasoning made from red peppers	**PARAMENT**	*n* pl. -MENTS or -MENTA an ornamental vestment
		PARAMO	*n* pl. -MOS a plateau region of South America
PAPULA	*n* pl. -LAE papule		
PAPULE	*n* pl. -S a pimple **PAPULAN, PAPULAR, PAPULOSE** *adj*	**PARAMOUR**	*n* pl. -S an illicit lover
		PARANG	*n* pl. -S a heavy knife
PAPYRUS	*n* pl. -RUSES or -RI a tall aquatic plant **PAPYRAL, PAPYRIAN, PAPYRINE** *adj*	**PARANOEA**	*n* pl. -S paranoia
		PARANOIA	*n* pl. -S a mental disorder
PAR	*v* PARRED, PARRING, PARS to shoot in a standard number of strokes in golf	**PARANOID**	*n* pl. -S one affected with paranoia
		PARAPET	*n* pl. -S a protective wall

PARAPH	*n* pl. -S a flourish at the end of a signature	**PARFAIT**	*n* pl. -S a frozen dessert
PARAQUAT	*n* pl. -S a weed killer	**PARFLESH**	*n* pl. -ES a rawhide smoked in lye to remove the hair and dried
PARAQUET	*n* pl. -S parakeet	**PARFOCAL**	*adj* having lenses with the corresponding focal points in the same plane
PARASANG	*n* pl. -S a Persian unit of distance		
PARASHAH	*n* pl. -SHOTH or -SHIOTH a passage in Jewish scripture	**PARGE**	*v* PARGED, PARGING, PARGES to parget
PARASITE	*n* pl. -S an organism that lives and feeds on or in another organism	**PARGET**	*v* -GETED, -GETING, -GETS or -GETTED, -GETTING, -GETS to cover with plaster
PARASOL	*n* pl. -S a small, light umbrella	**PARGO**	*n* pl. -GOS a food fish
PARAVANE	*n* pl. -S an underwater device used to cut cables	**PARHELIA**	*n/pl* bright circular spots appearing on a solar halo
PARBOIL	*v* -ED, -ING, -S to cook partially by boiling for a short time	**PARHELIC**	*adj* pertaining to parhelia
		PARIAH	*n* pl. -S a social outcast
PARCEL	*v* -CELED, -CELING, -CELS or -CELLED, -CELLING, -CELS to divide into parts or shares	**PARIAN**	*n* pl. -S a hard, white porcelain
		PARIES	*n* pl. PARIETES the wall of an organ
PARCENER	*n* pl. -S a joint heir	**PARIETAL**	*n* pl. -S a bone of the skull
PARCH	*v* -ED, -ING, -ES to make very dry	**PARING**	*n* pl. -S something pared off
PARD	*n* pl. -S a leopard	**PARIS**	*n* pl. -ISES a European herb
PARDAH	*n* pl. -S purdah	**PARISH**	*n* pl. -ES an ecclesiastical district
PARDEE	*interj* pardi		
PARDI	*interj* — used as a mild oath	**PARITY**	*n* pl. -TIES equality
PARDIE	*interj* pardi	**PARK**	*v* -ED, -ING, -S to leave a vehicle in a location for a time
PARDINE	*adj* pertaining to a leopard		
PARDNER	*n* pl. -S chum; friend	**PARKA**	*n* pl. -S a hooded garment
PARDON	*v* -ED, -ING, -S to release from liability for an offense	**PARKER**	*n* pl. -S one that parks
		PARKING	*n* pl. -S an area in which vehicles may be left
PARDONER	*n* pl. -S one that pardons	**PARKLAND**	*n* pl. -S a grassland region with isolated or grouped trees
PARDY	*interj* pardi		
PARE	*v* PARED, PARING, PARES to cut off the outer covering of	**PARKLIKE**	*adj* resembling an outdoor recreational area
PARECISM	*n* pl. -S the state of having the male and female sexual organs beside or near each other	**PARKWAY**	*n* pl. -WAYS a wide highway
		PARLANCE	*n* pl. -S a manner of speaking
PAREIRA	*n* pl. -S a medicinal plant root	**PARLANDO**	*adj* sung in a manner suggestive of speech
PARENT	*v* -ED, -ING, -S to exercise the functions of a parent (a father or mother)	**PARLANTE**	*adj* parlando
		PARLAY	*v* -ED, -ING, -S to bet an original wager and its winnings on a subsequent event
PARENTAL	*adj* pertaining to a parent		
PARER	*n* pl. -S one that pares		
PARESIS	*n* pl. -RESES partial loss of the ability to move	**PARLE**	*v* PARLED, PARLING, PARLES to parley
PARETIC	*n* pl. -S one affected with paresis	**PARLEY**	*v* -LEYED, -LEYING, -LEYS to discuss terms with an enemy
PAREU	*n* pl. -S a Polynesian garment	**PARLEYER**	*n* pl. -S one that parleys
PAREVE	*adj* parve	**PARLING**	present participle of parle

PARLOR *n* pl. -S a room for the entertainment of visitors

PARLOUR *n* pl. -S parlor

PARLOUS *adj* dangerous

PARODIC *adj* comically imitative

PARODIED past tense of parody

PARODIES present 3d person sing. of parody

PARODIST *n* pl. -S one who parodies

PARODOS *n* pl. -DOI an ode sung in ancient Greek drama

PARODY *v* -DIED, -DYING, -DIES to imitate a serious literary work for comic effect

PAROL *n* pl. -S an utterance

PAROLE *v* -ROLED, -ROLING, -ROLES to release from prison before completion of the imposed sentence

PAROLEE *n* pl. -S one who is paroled

PARONYM *n* pl. -S a word having the same root as another

PAROQUET *n* pl. -S parakeet

PAROTIC *adj* situated near the ear

PAROTID *n* pl. -S a salivary gland

PAROTOID *n* pl. -S a gland of certain toads and frogs

PAROUS *adj* having produced offspring

PAROXYSM *n* pl. -S a sudden fit or attack

PARQUET *v* -ED, -ING, -S to furnish with a floor of inlaid design

PARR *n* pl. -S a young salmon

PARRAL *n* pl. -S parrel

PARRED past tense of par

PARREL *n* pl. -S a sliding loop of rope or chain used on a ship

PARRIDGE *n* pl. -S porridge

PARRIED past tense of parry

PARRIES present 3d person sing. of parry

PARRING present participle of par

PARRITCH *n* pl. -ES porridge

PARROKET *n* pl. -S parakeet

PARROT *v* -ED, -ING, -S to repeat or imitate without thought or understanding

PARROTER *n* pl. -S one that parrots

PARROTY *adj* resembling a parrot (a hook-billed tropical bird)

PARRY *v* -RIED, -RYING, -RIES to ward off a blow

PARSE *v* PARSED, PARSING, PARSES to describe and analyze grammatically **PARSABLE** *adj*

PARSEC *n* pl. -S a unit of astronomical distance

PARSER *n* pl. -S one that parses

PARSING present participle of parse

PARSLEY *n* pl. -LEYS a cultivated herb

PARSNIP *n* pl. -S a European herb

PARSON *n* pl. -S a clergyman **PARSONIC** *adj*

PART *v* -ED, -ING, -S to divide or break into separate pieces

PARTAKE *v* -TOOK, -TAKEN, -TAKING, -TAKES to participate

PARTAKER *n* pl. -S one that partakes

PARTAN *n* pl. -S an edible crab

PARTERRE *n* pl. -S a section of a theater

PARTIAL *n* pl. -S a simple component of a complex tone

PARTIBLE *adj* divisible

PARTICLE *n* pl. -S a very small piece or part

PARTIED past tense of party

PARTIES present 3d person sing. of party

PARTING *n* pl. -S a division or separation

PARTISAN *n* pl. -S a firm supporter of a person, party, or cause

PARTITA *n* pl. -S a set of related instrumental pieces

PARTITE *adj* divided into parts

PARTIZAN *n* pl. -S partisan

PARTLET *n* pl. -S a woman's garment

PARTLY *adv* in some measure or degree

PARTNER *v* -ED, -ING, -S to associate with in some activity of common interest

PARTON *n* pl. -S a hypothetical atomic particle

PARTOOK past tense of partake

PARTWAY *adv* to some extent

PARTY *v* -TIED, -TYING, -TIES to attend a social gathering

PARURA *n* pl. -S parure

PARURE *n* pl. -S a set of matched jewelry

PARVE *adj* made without milk or meat

PARVENU *n pl.* -S one who has suddenly risen above his class

PARVENUE *adj* characteristic of a parvenu

PARVIS *n pl.* -VISES an enclosed area in front of a church

PARVISE *n pl.* -S parvis

PARVOLIN *n pl.* -S an oily liquid obtained from fish

PAS *n pl.* PAS a dance step

PASCHAL *n pl.* -S a candle used in certain religious ceremonies

PASE *n pl.* -S a movement of a matador's cape

PASEO *n pl.* -SEOS a leisurely stroll

PASH *v* -ED, -ING, -ES to strike violently

PASHA *n pl.* -S a former Turkish high official

PASHADOM *n pl.* -S the rank of a pasha

PASHALIC *n pl.* -S pashalik

PASHALIK *n pl.* -S the territory of a pasha

PASQUIL *n pl.* -S a satire or lampoon

PASS *v* -ED, -ING, -ES to go by

PASSABLE *adj* fairly good or acceptable **PASSABLY** *adv*

PASSADE *n pl.* -S a turn of a horse backward or forward on the same ground

PASSADO *n pl.* -DOS or -DOES a forward thrust in fencing

PASSAGE *v* -SAGED, -SAGING, -SAGES to make a voyage

PASSANT *adj* walking with the farther forepaw raised — used of a heraldic animal

PASSBAND *n pl.* -S a frequency band that permits transmission with maximum efficiency

PASSBOOK *n pl.* -S a bankbook

PASSE *adj* outmoded

PASSEE *adj* passe

PASSEL *n pl.* -S a large quantity or number

PASSER *n pl.* -S one that passes

PASSERBY *n pl.* PASSERSBY one who passes by

PASSIBLE *adj* capable of feeling or suffering

PASSIM *adv* here and there

PASSING *n pl.* -S a death

PASSION *n pl.* -S an intense emotion

PASSIVE *n pl.* -S a verb form

PASSKEY *n pl.* -KEYS a key that opens several different locks

PASSLESS *adj* incapable of being traveled over or through

PASSOVER *n pl.* -S the lamb eaten at the feast of a Jewish holiday

PASSPORT *n pl.* -S a document allowing travel from one country to another

PASSUS *n pl.* -ES a section of a story or poem

PASSWORD *n pl.* -S a secret word that must be spoken to gain admission

PAST *n pl.* -S time gone by

PASTA *n pl.* -S a food made of dough

PASTE *v* PASTED, PASTING, PASTES to fasten with a sticky mixture

PASTEL *n pl.* -S a soft, delicate hue

PASTER *n pl.* -S one that pastes

PASTERN *n pl.* -S a part of a horse's foot

PASTICCI *n/pl* pastiches

PASTICHE *n pl.* -S an artistic work made of fragments from various sources

PASTIER comparative of pasty

PASTIES pl. of pasty

PASTIEST superlative of pasty

PASTIL *n pl.* -S pastille

PASTILLE *n pl.* -S a lozenge

PASTIME *n pl.* -S a recreational activity

PASTINA *n pl.* -S a type of macaroni

PASTING present participle of paste

PASTNESS *n pl.* -ES the state of being past or gone by

PASTOR *v* -ED, -ING, -S to serve as the spiritual overseer of

PASTORAL *n pl.* -S a literary or artistic work that depicts country life

PASTRAMI *n pl.* -S a highly seasoned smoked beef

PASTROMI *n pl.* -S pastrami

PASTRY *n pl.* -TRIES a sweet baked food

PASTURAL *adj* pertaining to a pasture

PASTURE *v* -TURED, -TURING, -TURES to put in a pasture (a grazing area)

PASTURER *n pl.* -S one that pastures livestock

PASTY   adj PASTIER, PASTIEST pale and unhealthy in appearance

PASTY   n pl. PASTIES a meat pie

PAT   v PATTED, PATTING, PATS to touch lightly

PATACA   n pl. -S a monetary unit of Macao

PATAGIUM   n pl. -GIA a wing membrane of a bat

PATAMAR   n pl. -S a sailing vessel

PATCH   v -ED, -ING, -ES to mend or cover a hole or weak spot in

PATCHER   n pl. -S one that patches

PATCHY   adj PATCHIER, PATCHIEST uneven in quality **PATCHILY** adv

PATE   n pl. -S the top of the head **PATED** adj

PATELLA   n pl. -LAE or -LAS the flat movable bone at the front of the knee **PATELLAR** adj

PATEN   n pl. -S a plate

PATENCY   n pl. -CIES the state of being obvious

PATENT   v -ED, -ING, -S to obtain a patent (a government grant protecting the rights of an inventor) on

PATENTEE   n pl. -S one that holds a patent

PATENTLY   adv obviously

PATENTOR   n pl. -S one that grants a patent

PATER   n pl. -S a father

PATERNAL   adj pertaining to a father

PATH   n pl. -S a trodden way or track

PATHETIC   adj arousing pity

PATHLESS   adj having no path

PATHOGEN   n pl. -S any disease-producing organism

PATHOS   n pl. -ES a quality that arouses feelings of pity or compassion

PATHWAY   n pl. -WAYS a path

PATIENCE   n pl. -S the quality of being patient

PATIENT   adj -TIENTER, -TIENTEST able to endure disagreeable circumstances without complaint

PATIENT   n pl. -S one who is under medical treatment

PATIN   n pl. -S paten

PATINA   n pl. -NAE or -NAS a green film that forms on bronze

PATINE   v -TINED, -TINING, -TINES to cover with a patina

PATIO   n pl. -TIOS an outdoor paved area adjoining a house

PATLY   adv suitably

PATNESS   n pl. -ES suitability

PATOIS   n pl. PATOIS a dialect

PATRIOT   n pl. -S one who loves his country

PATROL   v -TROLLED, -TROLLING, -TROLS to pass through an area for the purposes of observation or security

PATRON   n pl. -S a regular customer **PATRONAL, PATRONLY** adj

PATROON   n pl. -S a landowner granted manorial rights under old Dutch law

PATSY   n pl. -SIES a person who is easily fooled

PATTAMAR   n pl. -S patamar

PATTED   past tense of pat

PATTEE   adj paty

PATTEN   n pl. -S a shoe having a thick wooden sole

PATTER   v -ED, -ING, -S to talk glibly or rapidly

PATTERER   n pl. -S one that patters

PATTERN   v -ED, -ING, -S to make according to a prescribed design

PATTIE   n pl. -S patty

PATTING   present participle of pat

PATTY   n pl. -TIES a small, flat cake of chopped food

PATTYPAN   n pl. -S a pan in which patties are baked

PATULENT   adj patulous

PATULOUS   adj spreading; open

PATY   adj formee

PAUCITY   n pl. -TIES smallness of number or quantity

PAUGHTY   adj arrogant

PAULDRON   n pl. -S a piece of armor for the shoulder

PAULIN   n pl. -S a sheet of waterproof material

PAUNCH   n pl. -ES the belly or abdomen **PAUNCHED** adj

PAUNCHY   adj PAUNCHIER, PAUNCHIEST having a protruding belly

PAUPER	*v* -ED, -ING, -S to reduce to poverty
PAUSAL	*adj* pertaining to a break or rest in speaking or writing
PAUSE	*v* PAUSED, PAUSING, PAUSES to stop temporarily
PAUSER	*n* pl. -S one that pauses
PAVAN	*n* pl. -S a slow, stately dance
PAVANE	*n* pl. -S pavan
PAVE	*v* PAVED, PAVING, PAVES to cover with material that forms a firm, level surface
PAVEMENT	*n* pl. -S a paved surface
PAVER	*n* pl. -S one that paves
PAVID	*adj* timid
PAVILION	*v* -ED, -ING, -S to cover with a large tent
PAVIN	*n* pl. -S pavan
PAVING	*n* pl. -S pavement
PAVIOR	*n* pl. -S a paver
PAVIOUR	*n* pl. -S a paver
PAVIS	*n* pl. -ISES a large medieval shield
PAVISE	*n* pl. -S pavis
PAVISER	*n* pl. -S a soldier carrying a pavis
PAVONINE	*adj* resembling a peacock
PAW	*v* -ED, -ING, -S to strike or scrape with a beating motion
PAWER	*n* pl. -S one that paws
PAWKY	*adj* PAWKIER, PAWKIEST sly **PAWKILY** *adv*
PAWL	*n* pl. -S a hinged mechanical part
PAWN	*v* -ED, -ING, -S to give as security for something borrowed **PAWNABLE** *adj*
PAWNAGE	*n* pl. -S an act of pawning
PAWNEE	*n* pl. -S one to whom something is pawned
PAWNER	*n* pl. -S one that pawns something
PAWNOR	*n* pl. -S pawner
PAWNSHOP	*n* pl. -S a place where things are pawned
PAWPAW	*n* pl. -S papaw
PAX	*n* pl. -ES a ceremonial embrace given to signify Christian love and unity
PAXWAX	*n* pl. -ES the nuchal ligament of a quadruped
PAY	*v* PAID or PAYED, PAYING, PAYS to give money or something of value in exchange for goods or services
PAYABLE	*adj* profitable **PAYABLY** *adv*
PAYCHECK	*n* pl. -S a check in payment of wages or salary
PAYDAY	*n* pl. -DAYS the day on which wages are paid
PAYEE	*n* pl. -S one to whom money is paid
PAYER	*n* pl. -S one that pays
PAYLOAD	*n* pl. -S the part of a cargo producing income
PAYMENT	*n* pl. -S something that is paid
PAYNIM	*n* pl. -S a pagan
PAYOFF	*n* pl. -S the act of distributing gains
PAYOLA	*n* pl. -S a secret payment for favors
PAYOR	*n* pl. -S payer
PAYROLL	*n* pl. -S a list of employees entitled to payment
PE	*n* pl. -S a Hebrew letter
PEA	*n* pl. -S the edible seed of an annual herb
PEACE	*v* PEACED, PEACING, PEACES to be or become silent
PEACEFUL	*adj* -FULLER, -FULLEST undisturbed; calm
PEACH	*v* -ED, -ING, -ES to inform against someone
PEACHER	*n* pl. -S one that peaches
PEACHY	*adj* PEACHIER, PEACHIEST dandy
PEACING	present participle of peace
PEACOAT	*n* pl. -S a heavy woolen jacket
PEACOCK	*v* -ED, -ING, -S to strut vainly
PEACOCKY	*adj* -COCKIER, -COCKIEST vain
PEAFOWL	*n* pl. -S a large pheasant
PEAG	*n* pl. -S wampum
PEAGE	*n* pl. -S peag
PEAHEN	*n* pl. -S a female peafowl
PEAK	*v* -ED, -ING, -S to reach a maximum
PEAKIER	comparative of peaky
PEAKIEST	superlative of peaky
PEAKISH	*adj* somewhat sickly

PEAKLESS *adj* having no peak (a pointed top)

PEAKLIKE *adj* resembling a peak

PEAKY *adj* PEAKIER, PEAKIEST sickly

PEAL *v* -ED, -ING, -S to ring out

PEALIKE *adj* resembling a pea

PEAN *n* pl. -S paean

PEANUT *n* pl. -S the nutlike seed or pod of an annual vine

PEAR *n* pl. -S a fleshy fruit

PEARL *v* -ED, -ING, -S to adorn with pearls (smooth, rounded masses formed in certain mollusks)

PEARLASH *n* pl. -ES an alkaline compound

PEARLER *n* pl. -S one that dives for pearls

PEARLITE *n* pl. -S a cast-iron alloy

PEARLY *adj* PEARLIER, PEARLIEST resembling a pearl

PEARMAIN *n* pl. -S a variety of apple

PEART *adj* PEARTER, PEARTEST lively **PEARTLY** *adv*

PEASANT *n* pl. -S a person of inferior social rank

PEASCOD *n* pl. -S peasecod

PEASE *n* pl. PEASEN or PEASES a pea

PEASECOD *n* pl. -S a pea pod

PEAT *n* pl. -S a substance composed of partially decayed vegetable matter

PEATY *adj* PEATIER, PEATIEST resembling or containing peat

PEAVEY *n* pl. -VEYS a lever used to move logs

PEAVY *n* pl. -VIES peavey

PEBBLE *v* -BLED, -BLING, -BLES to cover with pebbles (small, rounded stones)

PEBBLY *adj* -BLIER, -BLIEST resembling pebbles

PECAN *n* pl. -S a nut-bearing tree

PECCABLE *adj* liable to sin

PECCANCY *n* pl. -CIES the state of being peccant

PECCANT *adj* sinful

PECCARY *n* pl. -RIES a hoofed mammal

PECCAVI *n* pl. -S a confession of sin

PECH *v* -ED, -ING, -S to pant

PECHAN *n* pl. -S the stomach

PECK *v* -ED, -ING, -S to strike with the beak or something pointed

PECKER *n* pl. -S one that pecks

PECKY *adj* PECKIER, PECKIEST marked by decay caused by fungi

PECTASE *n* pl. -S an enzyme

PECTATE *n* pl. -S a chemical salt

PECTEN *n* pl. -TENS or -TINES a comblike anatomical part

PECTIN *n* pl. -S a carbohydrate derivative **PECTIC** *adj*

PECTIZE *v* -TIZED, -TIZING, -TIZES to change into a jelly

PECTORAL *n* pl. -S something worn on the breast

PECULATE *v* -LATED, -LATING, -LATES to embezzle

PECULIAR *n* pl. -S something belonging exclusively to a person

PECULIUM *n* pl. -LIA private property

PED *n* pl. -S a natural soil aggregate

PEDAGOG *n* pl. -S a teacher

PEDAGOGY *n* pl. -GIES the work of a teacher

PEDAL *v* -ALED, -ALING, -ALS or -ALLED, -ALLING, -ALS to operate by means of foot levers

PEDALFER *n* pl. -S a type of soil

PEDALIER *n* pl. -S the pedal keyboard of an organ

PEDALLED past tense of pedal

PEDALLING present participle of pedal

PEDANT *n* pl. -S one who flaunts his knowledge **PEDANTIC** *adj*

PEDANTRY *n* pl. -RIES ostentatious display of knowledge

PEDATE *adj* resembling a foot **PEDATELY** *adv*

PEDDLE *v* -DLED, -DLING, -DLES to travel about selling wares

PEDDLER *n* pl. -S one that peddles

PEDDLERY *n* pl. -RIES the trade of a peddler

PEDDLING present tense of peddle

PEDERAST *n* pl. -S a man who engages in sexual activities with boys

PEDES pl. of pes

PEDESTAL *v* -TALED, -TALING, -TALS or -TALLED, -TALLING, -TALS to provide with an architectural support or base

PEDICAB *n* pl. -S a passenger vehicle that is pedaled

PEDICEL *n* pl. -S a slender basal part of an organism

PEDICLE *n* pl. -S pedicel **PEDICLED** *adj*

PEDICURE *v* -CURED, -CURING, -CURES to administer a cosmetic treatment to the feet and toenails

PEDIFORM *adj* shaped like a foot

PEDIGREE *n* pl. -S a line of ancestors

PEDIMENT *n* pl. -S a triangular architectural part

PEDIPALP *n* pl. -S an appendage of an arachnid

PEDLAR *n* pl. -S peddler

PEDLARY *n* pl. -LARIES peddlery

PEDLER *n* pl. -S peddler

PEDOCAL *n* pl. -S a type of soil

PEDOLOGY *n* pl. -GIES the scientific study of the behavior and development of children

PEDRO *n* pl. -DROS a card game

PEDUNCLE *n* pl. -S a flower stalk

PEE *v* PEED, PEEING, PEES to urinate — sometimes considered vulgar

PEEBEEN *n* pl. -S an evergreen tree

PEEK *v* -ED, -ING, -S to look furtively or quickly

PEEKABOO *n* pl. -BOOS a children's game

PEEL *v* -ED, -ING, -S to strip off an outer covering of **PEELABLE** *adj*

PEELER *n* pl. -S one that peels

PEELING *n* pl. -S a piece or strip that has been peeled off

PEEN *v* -ED, -ING, -S to beat with the non-flat end of a hammerhead

PEEP *v* -ED, -ING, -S to utter a short, shrill cry

PEEPER *n* pl. -S one that peeps

PEEPHOLE *n* pl. -S a small opening through which one may look

PEEPSHOW *n* pl. -S an exhibition viewed through a small opening

PEEPUL *n* pl. -S pipal

PEER *v* -ED, -ING, -S to look narrowly or searchingly

PEERAGE *n* pl. -S the rank of a nobleman

PEERESS *n* pl. -ES a noblewoman

PEERIE *n* pl. -S peery

PEERLESS *adj* having no equal

PEERY *n* pl. PEERIES a child's toy

PEESWEEP *n* pl. -S a lapwing

PEETWEET *n* pl. -S a wading bird

PEEVE *v* PEEVED, PEEVING, PEEVES to annoy

PEEVISH *adj* irritable

PEEWEE *n* pl. -S an unusually small person or thing

PEEWIT *n* pl. -S pewit

PEG *v* PEGGED, PEGGING, PEGS to fasten with a peg (a wooden pin)

PEGBOARD *n* pl. -S a board with holes for pegs

PEGBOX *n* pl. -ES a part of a stringed instrument

PEGGED past tense of peg

PEGGING present participle of peg

PEGLESS *adj* lacking a peg

PEGLIKE *adj* resembling a peg

PEIGNOIR *n* pl. -S a woman's gown

PEIN *v* -ED, -ING, -S to peen

PEISE *v* PEISED, PEISING, PEISES to weigh

PEKAN *n* pl. -S a carnivorous mammal

PEKE *n* pl. -S a small, long-haired dog

PEKIN *n* pl. -S a silk fabric

PEKOE *n* pl. -S a black tea

PELAGE *n* pl. -S the coat or covering of a mammal **PELAGIAL** *adj*

PELAGIC *adj* oceanic

PELE *n* pl. -S a medieval fortified tower

PELERINE *n* pl. -S a woman's cape

PELF *n* pl. -S money or wealth

PELICAN *n* pl. -S a large, web-footed bird

PELISSE *n* pl. -S a long outer garment

PELITE *n* pl. -S a rock composed of fine fragments **PELITIC** *adj*

PELLAGRA *n* pl. -S a niacin-deficiency disease

PELLET *v* -ED, -ING, -S to strike with pellets (small rounded masses)

PELLETAL *adj* resembling a pellet

PELLICLE *n* pl. -S a thin skin or film

PELLMELL *n* pl. -S a jumbled mass

PELLUCID *adj* transparent

PELON	*adj* hairless
PELORIA	*n* pl. -S abnormal regularity of a flower form **PELORIAN, PELORIC** *adj*
PELORUS	*n* pl. -ES a navigational instrument
PELOTA	*n* pl. -S a court game of Spanish origin
PELT	*v* -ED, -ING, -S to strike repeatedly with blows or missiles
PELTAST	*n* pl. -S a soldier of ancient Greece
PELTATE	*adj* shaped like a shield
PELTER	*n* pl. -S one that pelts
PELTRY	*n* pl. -RIES an animal skin
PELVIC	*n* pl. -S a bone of the pelvis
PELVIS	*n* pl. -VES or -VISES a part of the skeleton
PEMBINA	*n* pl. -S a variety of cranberry
PEMICAN	*n* pl. -S pemmican
PEMMICAN	*n* pl. -S a food prepared by North American Indians
PEMOLINE	*n* pl. -S a drug used experimentally to improve memory
PEMPHIX	*n* pl. -ES a skin disease
PEN	*v* PENNED, PENNING, PENS to write with a pen (an instrument for writing with fluid ink)
PENAL	*adj* pertaining to punishment
PENALISE	*v* -ISED, -ISING, -ISES to penalize
PENALITY	*n* pl. -TIES liability to punishment
PENALIZE	*v* -IZED, -IZING, -IZES to subject to a penalty
PENALLY	*adv* in a penal manner
PENALTY	*n* pl. -TIES a punishment imposed for violation of a law, rule, or agreement
PENANCE	*v* -ANCED, -ANCING, -ANCES to impose a type of punishment upon
PENANG	*n* pl. -S a cotton fabric
PENATES	*n/pl* the Roman gods of the household
PENCE	a pl. of penny
PENCEL	*n* pl. -S a small flag
PENCHANT	*n* pl. -S a strong liking for something
PENCIL	*v* -CILED, -CILING, -CILS or -CILLED, -CILLING, -CILS to produce by using a pencil (a writing and drawing implement)
PENCILER	*n* pl. -S one that pencils
PEND	*v* -ED, -ING, -S to remain undecided or unsettled
PENDANT	*n* pl. -S a hanging ornament
PENDENCY	*n* pl. -CIES a pending state
PENDENT	*n* pl. -S pendant
PENDULUM	*n* pl. -S a type of free swinging body **PENDULAR** *adj*
PENES	a pl. of penis
PENGO	*n* pl. -GOS a former monetary unit of Hungary
PENGUIN	*n* pl. -S a flightless, aquatic bird
PENICIL	*n* pl. -S a small tuft of hairs
PENIS	*n* pl. -NES or -NISES the male organ of copulation **PENIAL, PENILE** *adj*
PENITENT	*n* pl. -S a person who repents his sins
PENKNIFE	*n* pl. -KNIVES a small pocketknife
PENLIGHT	*n* pl. -S a small flashlight
PENLITE	*n* pl. -S penlight
PENMAN	*n* pl. -MEN an author
PENNA	*n* pl. -NAE any of the feathers that determine a bird's shape
PENNAME	*n* pl. -S a name used by an author instead of his real name
PENNANT	*n* pl. -S a long, narrow flag
PENNATE	*adj* having wings or feathers
PENNATED	*adj* pennate
PENNED	past tense of pen
PENNER	*n* pl. -S one that pens
PENNI	*n* pl. -NIA or -NIS a Finnish coin
PENNIES	a pl. of penny
PENNINE	*n* pl. -S a mineral
PENNING	present participle of pen
PENNON	*n* pl. -S a pennant **PENNONED** *adj*
PENNY	*n* pl. PENNIES or PENCE a coin of the United Kingdom
PENOCHE	*n* pl. -S penuche
PENOLOGY	*n* pl. -GIES the science of the punishment of crime
PENONCEL	*n* pl. -S a small pennon
PENPOINT	*n* pl. -S the point of a pen

PENSEE *n* pl. -S a thought

PENSIL *n* pl. -S pencel

PENSILE *adj* hanging loosely

PENSION *v* -ED, -ING, -S to grant a retirement allowance to

PENSIONE *n* pl. -S a boarding house

PENSIVE *adj* engaged in deep thought

PENSTER *n* pl. -S a writer

PENSTOCK *n* pl. - S a conduit for conveying water to a waterwheel

PENT *adj* confined

PENTACLE *n* pl. -S a five-pointed star

PENTAD *n* pl. -S a group of five

PENTAGON *n* pl. -S a five-sided polygon

PENTANE *n* pl. -S a volatile liquid

PENTARCH *n* pl. -S one of five joint rulers

PENTOMIC *adj* made up of five battle groups

PENTOSAN *n* pl. -S a complex carbohydrate

PENTOSE *n* pl. -S a sugar having five carbon atoms per molecule

PENTYL *n* pl. -S amyl

PENUCHE *n* pl. -S a fudge-like candy

PENUCHI *n* pl. -S penuche

PENUCHLE *n* pl. -S pinochle

PENUCKLE *n* pl. -S pinochle

PENULT *n* pl. -S the next to last syllable in a word

PENUMBRA *n* pl. -BRAE or -BRAS a partial shadow

PENURY *n* pl. -RIES extreme poverty

PEON *n* pl. -S or -ES an unskilled laborer

PEONAGE *n* pl. -S the condition of being a peon

PEONISM *n* pl. -S peonage

PEONY *n* pl. -NIES a flowering plant

PEOPLE *v* -PLED, -PLING, -PLES to furnish with inhabitants

PEOPLER *n* pl. -S one that peoples

PEP *v* PEPPED, PEPPING, PEPS to fill with energy

PEPERONI *n* pl. -S a highly seasoned sausage

PEPLOS *n* pl. -ES a garment worn by women in ancient Greece

PEPLUM *n* pl. -LUMS or -LA a short section attached to the waistline of a garment **PEPLUMED** *adj*

PEPLUS *n* pl. -ES peplos

PEPO *n* pl. -POS a fruit having a fleshy interior and a hard rind

PEPONIDA *n* pl. -S pepo

PEPONIUM *n* pl. -S pepo

PEPPED past tense of pep

PEPPER *v* -ED, -ING, -S to season with pepper (a pungent condiment)

PEPPERER *n* pl. -S one that peppers

PEPPERY *adj* resembling pepper

PEPPING present participle of pep

PEPPY *adj* -PIER, -PIEST full of energy **PEPPILY** *adv*

PEPSIN *n* pl. -S a digestive enzyme of the stomach

PEPSINE *n* pl. -S pepsin

PEPTIC *n* pl. -S a substance that promotes digestion

PEPTID *n* pl. -S peptide

PEPTIDE *n* pl. -S a combination of amino acids **PEPTIDIC** *adj*

PEPTIZE *v* -TIZED, -TIZING, -TIZES to increase the colloidal dispersion of

PEPTIZER *n* pl. -S one that peptizes

PEPTONE *n* pl. -S a protein compound **PEPTONIC** *adj*

PER *prep* for each

PERACID *n* pl. -S a type of acid

PERCALE *n* pl. -S a cotton fabric

PERCEIVE *v* -CEIVED, -CEIVING, -CEIVES to become aware of through the senses

PERCENT *n* pl. -S one part in a hundred

PERCEPT *n* pl. -S something that is perceived

PERCH *v* -ED, -ING, -ES to sit or rest on an elevated place

PERCHER *n* pl. -S one that perches

PERCOID *n* pl. -S a spiny-finned fish

PERCUSS *v* -ED, -ING, -ES to strike with force

PERDIE *interj* pardi

PERDU *n* pl. -S a soldier sent on a dangerous mission

PERDUE *n* pl. -S perdu

PERDY *interj* pardi

PERE *n* pl. -S a father

PEREGRIN *n* pl. -S a swift falcon much used in falconry

PERFECT *adj* -FECTER, -FECTEST lacking fault or defect; of an extreme kind

PERFECT *v* -ED, -ING, -S to make perfect

PERFECTA *n pl.* -S a system of betting

PERFECTO *n pl.* -TOS a medium-sized cigar

PERFIDY *n pl.* -DIES deliberate breach of faith or trust

PERFORCE *adj* of necessity

PERFORM *v* -ED, -ING, -S to begin and carry through to completion

PERFUME *v* -FUMED, -FUMING, -FUMES to fill with a fragrant odor

PERFUMER *n pl.* -S one that perfumes

PERFUSE *v* -FUSED, -FUSING, -FUSES to spread over or through something

PERGOLA *n pl.* -S a shaded shelter or passageway

PERHAPS *n pl.* -ES something open to doubt or conjecture

PERI *n pl.* -S a supernatural being of Persian mythology

PERIANTH *n pl.* -S an outer covering of a flower

PERIAPT *n pl.* -S an amulet

PERIBLEM *n pl.* -S a region of plant tissue

PERICARP *n pl.* -S the wall of a ripened plant ovary or fruit

PERICOPE *n pl.* -PES or -PAE a selection from a book

PERIDERM *n pl.* -S an outer layer of plant tissue

PERIDIUM *n pl.* -IA the covering of the spore-bearing organ in many fungi **PERIDIAL** *adj*

PERIDOT *n pl.* -S a mineral

PERIGEE *n pl.* -S the point in the orbit of a celestial body which is nearest to the earth **PERIGEAL, PERIGEAN** *adj*

PERIGON *n pl.* -S an angle equal to 360 degrees

PERIGYNY *n pl.* -NIES the state of being situated on a cuplike organ surrounding the pistil

PERIL *v* -ILED, -ILING, -ILS or -ILLED, -ILLING, -ILS to imperil

PERILLA *n pl.* -S an Asian herb

PERILOUS *adj* dangerous

PERILUNE *n pl.* -S the point in the orbit of a celestial body which is nearest to the moon

PERINEUM *n pl.* -NEA a region of the body at the lower end of the trunk **PERINEAL** *adj*

PERIOD *n pl.* -S a portion of time

PERIODIC *adj* recurring at regular intervals

PERIODID *n pl.* -S an iodide

PERIOTIC *adj* surrounding the ear

PERIPETY *n pl.* -TIES a sudden change in a course of events

PERIPTER *n pl.* -S a structure with a row of columns around all sides

PERIQUE *n pl.* -S a dark tobacco

PERISARC *n pl.* -S a protective covering of certain hydrozoans

PERISH *v* -ED, -ING, -ES to die

PERIWIG *n pl.* -S a wig

PERJURE *v* -JURED, -JURING, -JURES to make a perjurer of

PERJURER *n pl.* -S one guilty of perjury

PERJURY *n pl.* -RIES the willful giving of false testimony under oath in a judicial proceeding

PERK *v* -ED, -ING, -S to carry oneself jauntily

PERKISH *adj* somewhat perky

PERKY *adj* PERKIER, PERKIEST jaunty **PERKILY** *adv*

PERLITE *n pl.* -S a volcanic glass **PERLITIC** *adj*

PERM *n pl.* -S a long-lasting hair setting

PERMEASE *n pl.* -S a catalyzing agent

PERMEATE *v* -ATED, -ATING, -ATES to spread through

PERMIT *v* -MITTED, -MITTING, -MITS to allow

PERMUTE *v* -MUTED, -MUTING, -MUTES to change the order of

PERONEAL *adj* pertaining to the fibula

PERORAL *adj* occurring through the mouth

PERORATE *v* -RATED, -RATING, -RATES to make a lengthy speech

PEROXID *n pl.* -S peroxide

PEROXIDE *v* -IDED, -IDING, -IDES to treat with peroxide (a bleaching agent)

PERPEND *v* -ED, -ING, -S to ponder

PERPENT *n pl.* -S a large building stone

PERPLEX *v* -ED, -ING, -ES to make mentally uncertain

PERRON *n* pl. -S an outdoor stairway

PERRY *n* pl. -RIES a beverage of pear juice often fermented

PERSALT *n* pl. -S a chemical salt

PERSE *n* pl. -S a blue color

PERSIST *v* -ED, -ING, -S to continue resolutely in some activity

PERSON *n* pl. -S a human being

PERSONA *n* pl. -NAE a character in a literary work

PERSONA *n* pl. -S the public role that a person assumes

PERSONAL *n* pl. -S a brief, private notice in a newspaper

PERSPIRE *v* -SPIRED, -SPIRING, -SPIRES to give off moisture through the pores of the skin **PERSPIRY** *adj*

PERSUADE *v* -SUADED, -SUADING, -SUADES to cause to do something by means of argument, reasoning, or entreaty

PERT *adj* PERTER, PERTEST impudent **PERTLY** *adv*

PERTAIN *v* -ED, -ING, -S to have reference or relation

PERTNESS *n* pl. -ES the quality of being pert

PERTURB *v* -ED, -ING, -S to disturb greatly

PERUKE *n* pl. -S a wig

PERUSAL *n* pl. -S the act of perusing

PERUSE *v* -RUSED, -RUSING, -RUSES to read

PERUSER *n* pl. -S one that peruses

PERVADE *v* -VADED, -VADING, -VADES to spread through every part of

PERVADER *n* pl. -S one that pervades

PERVERSE *adj* willfully deviating from desired or expected conduct

PERVERT *v* -ED, -ING, -S to turn away from the right course of action

PERVIOUS *adj* capable of being penetrated

PES *n* pl. PEDES a foot or footlike part

PESADE *n* pl. -S the position of a horse when rearing

PESETA *n* pl. -S a monetary unit of Spain

PESEWA *n* pl. -S a monetary unit of Ghana

PESKY *adj* -KIER, -KIEST annoying **PESKILY** *adv*

PESO *n* pl. -SOS a monetary unit of various Spanish-speaking countries

PESSARY *n* pl. -RIES a contraceptive device worn in the vagina

PEST *n* pl. -S an annoying person or thing

PESTER *v* -ED, -ING, -S to bother

PESTERER *n* pl. -S one that pesters

PESTHOLE *n* pl. -S a place liable to epidemic disease

PESTLE *v* -TLED, -TLING, -TLES to crush with a club-shaped hand tool

PET *v* PETTED, PETTING, PETS to caress with the hand

PETAL *n* pl. -S a leaflike part of a corolla **PETALED, PETALLED** *adj*

PETALINE *adj* resembling a petal

PETALODY *n* pl. -DIES the metamorphosis of various floral organs into petals

PETALOID *adj* resembling a petal

PETALOUS *adj* having petals

PETARD *n* pl. -S an explosive device

PETASOS *n* pl. -ES petasus

PETASUS *n* pl. -ES a broad-brimmed hat worn in ancient Greece

PETCOCK *n* pl. -S a small valve or faucet

PETECHIA *n* pl. -CHIAE a small hemorrhagic spot on a body surface

PETER *v* -ED, -ING, -S to diminish gradually

PETIOLAR *adj* pertaining to a petiole

PETIOLE *n* pl. -S the stalk of a leaf **PETIOLED** *adj*

PETIT *adj* small; minor

PETITE *n* pl. -S a clothing size for short women

PETITION *v* -ED, -ING, -S to make a formal request

PETREL *n* pl. -S a small seabird

PETRIFY *v* -FIED, -FYING, -FIES to convert into stone or a stony substance

PETROL *n* pl. -S gasoline

PETROLIC *adj* derived from petroleum

PETRONEL *n* pl. -S a portable firearm

PETROSAL	*adj* petrous
PETROUS	*adj* resembling stone in hardness
PETTED	past tense of pet
PETTEDLY	*adv* peevishly
PETTER	*n* pl. -S one that pets
PETTI	pl. of petto
PETTIER	comparative of petty
PETTIEST	superlative of petty
PETTIFOG	*v* -FOGGED, -FOGGING, -FOGS to quibble
PETTILY	*adv* in a petty manner
PETTING	present participle of pet
PETTISH	*adj* peevish
PETTLE	*v* -TLED, -TLING, -TLES to caress
PETTO	*n* pl. -TI the breast
PETTY	*adj* -TIER, -TIEST insignificant
PETULANT	*adj* peevish
PETUNIA	*n* pl. -S a tropical herb
PETUNTSE	*n* pl. -S a mineral
PETUNTZE	*n* pl. -S petuntse
PEW	*n* pl. -S a bench for seating people in church
PEWEE	*n* pl. -S a small bird
PEWIT	*n* pl. -S the lapwing
PEWTER	*n* pl. -S a tin alloy
PEWTERER	*n* pl. -S one that makes articles of pewter
PEYOTE	*n* pl. -S a cactus
PEYOTL	*n* pl. -S peyote
PEYTRAL	*n* pl. -S a piece of armor for the breast of a horse
PEYTREL	*n* pl. -S peytral
PFENNIG	*n* pl. -NIGS or -NIGE a bronze coin of Germany
PHAETON	*n* pl. -S a light carriage
PHAGE	*n* pl. -S an organism that destroys bacteria
PHALANGE	*n* pl. -S any bone of a finger or toe
PHALANX	*n* pl. -ES a formation of infantry in ancient Greece
PHALLI	a pl. of phallus
PHALLIC	*adj* pertaining to a phallus
PHALLISM	*n* pl. -S worship of the phallus as symbolic of nature's creative power
PHALLIST	*n* pl. -S one who practices phallism
PHALLUS	*n* pl. -LI or -LUSES the penis
PHANTASIED	past tense of phantasy
PHANTASIES	present 3d person sing. of phantasy
PHANTASM	*n* pl. -S a creation of the imagination
PHANTAST	*n* pl. -S fantast
PHANTASY	*v* -SIED, -SYING, -SIES to fantasy
PHANTOM	*n* pl. -S something existing in appearance only
PHARAOH	*n* pl. -S a ruler of ancient Egypt
PHARISEE	*n* pl. -S a hypocritically self-righteous person
PHARMACY	*n* pl. -CIES a drugstore
PHAROS	*n* pl. -ES a lighthouse or beacon to guide seamen
PHARYNX	*n* pl. -YNGES or -YNXES a section of the digestive tract
PHASE	*v* PHASED, PHASING, PHASES to plan or carry out by phases (distinct stages of development) **PHASEAL, PHASIC** *adj*
PHASEOUT	*n* pl. -S a gradual stopping of operations
PHASIS	*n* pl. PHASES a phase
PHASMID	*n* pl. -S a tropical insect
PHAT	*adj* susceptible of easy and rapid typesetting
PHATIC	*adj* sharing feelings rather than ideas
PHEASANT	*n* pl. -S a large, long-tailed bird
PHELLEM	*n* pl. -S a layer of plant cells
PHELONIA	*n/pl* liturgical vestments
PHENAZIN	*n* pl. -S a chemical compound
PHENETIC	*adj* pertaining to a type of classificatory system
PHENETOL	*n* pl. -S a volatile liquid
PHENIX	*n* pl. -ES phoenix
PHENOL	*n* pl. -S a caustic compound
PHENOLIC	*n* pl. -S a synthetic resin
PHENOM	*n* pl. -S a person of extraordinary ability or promise
PHENYL	*n* pl. -S a univalent chemical radical **PHENYLIC** *adj*
PHEW	*interj* — used to express relief, fatigue, or disgust
PHI	*n* pl. -S a Greek letter

PHIAL	*n* pl. -S a vial
PHILABEG	*n* pl. -S filibeg
PHILIBEG	*n* pl. -S filibeg
PHILOMEL	*n* pl. -S a songbird
PHILTER	*v* -ED, -ING, -S to put under the spell of a love potion
PHILTRE	*v* -TRED, -TRING, -TRES to philter
PHIMOSIS	*n* pl. -MOSES the abnormal constriction of the opening of the prepuce **PHIMOTIC** *adj*
PHIZ	*n* pl. -ES a face or facial expression
PHLEGM	*n* pl. -S a thick mucus secreted in the air passages
PHLEGMY	*adj* PHLEGMIER, PHLEGMIEST resembling phlegm
PHLOEM	*n* pl. -S a complex plant tissue
PHLOX	*n* pl. -ES a flowering plant
PHOBIA	*n* pl. -S an obsessive or irrational fear **PHOBIC** *adj*
PHOCINE	*adj* pertaining to seals
PHOEBE	*n* pl. -S a small bird
PHOENIX	*n* pl. -ES a mythical bird
PHON	*n* pl. -S a unit of loudness
PHONAL	*adj* pertaining to speech sounds
PHONATE	*v* -NATED, -NATING, -NATES to produce speech sounds
PHONE	*v* PHONED, PHONING, PHONES to telephone
PHONEME	*n* pl. -S a unit of speech **PHONEMIC** *adj*
PHONETIC	*adj* pertaining to speech sounds
PHONEY	*adj* -NIER, -NIEST phony
PHONEY	*n* pl. -NEYS a phony
PHONIC	*adj* pertaining to the nature of sound
PHONICS	*n/pl* the science of sound
PHONIER	comparative of phoney and phony
PHONIES	pl. of phony
PHONIEST	superlative of phoney and phony
PHONILY	*adv* in a phony manner
PHONING	present participle of phone
PHONO	*n* pl. -NOS a record player
PHONON	*n* pl. -S a quantum of vibrational energy

PHONY	*adj* -NIER, -NIEST not genuine or real
PHONY	*n* pl. -NIES one that is phony
PHOOEY	*interj* — used as an exclamation of disgust or contempt
PHORATE	*n* pl. -S an insecticide
PHOSGENE	*n* pl. -S a poisonous gas
PHOSPHID	*n* pl. -S a chemical compound
PHOSPHIN	*n* pl. -S a poisonous gas
PHOSPHOR	*n* pl. -S a substance that will emit light when exposed to radiation
PHOT	*n* pl. -S a unit of illumination
PHOTIC	*adj* pertaining to light
PHOTICS	*n/pl* the science of light
PHOTO	*v* -ED, -ING, -S to photograph
PHOTOG	*n* pl. -S one who takes photographs
PHOTOMAP	*v* -MAPPED, -MAPPING, -MAPS to map by means of aerial photography
PHOTON	*n* pl. -S a quantum of radiant energy **PHOTONIC** *adj*
PHOTOPIA	*n* pl. -S vision in bright light **PHOTOPIC** *adj*
PHOTOSET	*v* -SET, -SETTING, -SETS to prepare for printing by photographic means
PHPHT	*interj* pht
PHRASAL	*adj* pertaining to a group of two or more associated words
PHRASE	*v* PHRASED, PHRASING, PHRASES to express in words
PHRASING	*n* pl. -S manner or style of verbal expression
PHRATRY	*n* pl. -TRIES a tribal unit among primitive peoples **PHRATRAL, PHRATRIC** *adj*
PHREATIC	*adj* pertaining to underground waters
PHRENIC	*adj* pertaining to the mind
PHRENSY	*v* -SIED, -SYING, -SIES to frenzy
PHT	*interj* — used as an expression of mild anger or annoyance
PHTHALIC	*adj* pertaining to a certain acid
PHTHALIN	*n* pl. -S a chemical compound
PHTHISIC	*n* pl. -S phthisis
PHTHISIS	*n* pl. PHTHISES a disease of the lungs
PHYLA	pl. of phylon and phylum

PHYLAE	pl. of phyle
PHYLAR	*adj* pertaining to a phylum
PHYLAXIS	*n* pl. -AXISES an inhibiting of infection by the body
PHYLE	*n* pl. -LAE a political subdivision in ancient Greece **PHYLIC** *adj*
PHYLESIS	*n* pl. -LESES or -LESISES the course of evolutionary development **PHYLETIC** *adj*
PHYLLARY	*n* pl. -RIES a bract of certain plants
PHYLLITE	*n* pl. -S a foliated rock
PHYLLODE	*n* pl. -S a flattened petiole that serves as a leaf
PHYLLOID	*n* pl. -S a leaflike plant part
PHYLLOME	*n* pl. -S a leaf of a plant
PHYLON	*n* pl. -LA a genetically related group
PHYLUM	*n* pl. -LA a taxonomic division
PHYSES	pl. of physis
PHYSIC	*v* -ICKED, -ICKING, -ICS to treat with medicine
PHYSICAL	*n* pl. -S a medical examination of the body
PHYSIQUE	*n* pl. -S the form or structure of the body
PHYSIS	*n* pl. PHYSES the principle of growth or change in nature
PHYTANE	*n* pl. -S a chemical compound
PHYTIN	*n* pl. -S a chemical salt
PHYTOID	*adj* resembling a plant
PHYTON	*n* pl. -S a structural unit of a plant **PHYTONIC** *adj*
PI	*n* pl. -S a Greek letter
PI	*v* PIED, PIEING or PIING, PIES to jumble or disorder
PIA	*n* pl. -S a membrane of the brain
PIACULAR	*adj* atoning
PIAFFE	*v* PIAFFED, PIAFFING, PIAFFES to perform a piaffer
PIAFFER	*n* pl. -S a movement in horsemanship
PIAL	*adj* pertaining to a pia
PIAN	*n* pl. -S a tropical disease **PIANIC** *adj*
PIANISM	*n* pl. -S performance on the piano
PIANIST	*n* pl. -S one who plays the piano
PIANO	*n* pl. -NOS a musical instrument
PIASABA	*n* pl. -S piassava
PIASAVA	*n* pl. -S piassava
PIASSABA	*n* pl. -S piassava
PIASSAVA	*n* pl. -S a coarse, stiff fiber
PIASTER	*n* pl. -S a monetary unit of several Arab countries
PIASTRE	*n* pl. -S piaster
PIAZZA	*n* pl. -ZAS or -ZE a public square in an Italian town
PIBROCH	*n* pl. -S a musical piece played on the bagpipe
PIC	*n* pl. -S a photograph
PICA	*n* pl. -S a craving for unnatural food
PICACHO	*n* pl. -CHOS an isolated peak of a hill
PICADOR	*n* pl. -ES or -S a horseman in a bullfight
PICAL	*adj* resembling a pica
PICARA	*n* pl. -S a female picaro
PICARO	*n* pl. -ROS a vagabond
PICAROON	*v* -ED, -ING, -S to act as a pirate
PICAYUNE	*n* pl. -S a former Spanish-American coin
PICCOLO	*n* pl. -LOS a small flute
PICE	*n* pl. PICE a former coin of India and Pakistan
PICEOUS	*adj* glossy-black in color
PICK	*v* -ED, -ING, -S to select
PICKADIL	*n* pl. -S a type of collar
PICKAX	*v* -ED, -ING, -ES to use a pickax (a tool for breaking hard surfaces)
PICKAXE	*v* -AXED, -AXING, -AXES to pickax
PICKEER	*v* -ED, -ING, -S to skirmish in advance of an army
PICKER	*n* pl. -S one that picks
PICKEREL	*n* pl. -S a freshwater fish
PICKET	*v* -ED, -ING, -S to stand outside of some location, as a business, to publicize one's grievances against it
PICKETER	*n* pl. -S one who pickets
PICKIER	comparative of picky
PICKIEST	superlative of picky
PICKING	*n* pl. -S the act of one that picks

PICKLE	v -LED, -LING, -LES to preserve or flavor in a solution of brine or vinegar	**PIER**	n pl. -S a structure extending from land out over water
PICKLOCK	n pl. -S a tool for opening locks	**PIERCE**	v PIERCED, PIERCING, PIERCES to cut or pass into or through
PICKOFF	n pl. -S a play in baseball	**PIERCER**	n pl. -S one that pierces
PICKUP	n pl. -S a small truck	**PIERROT**	n pl. -S a clown
PICKWICK	n pl. -S a device for raising wicks in oil lamps	**PIETA**	n pl. -S a representation of the Virgin Mary mourning over the body of Christ
PICKY	adj PICKIER, PICKIEST fussy		
PICLORAM	n pl. -S an herbicide	**PIETIES**	pl. of piety
PICNIC	v -NICKED, -NICKING, -NICS to go on a picnic (an outdoor excursion with food)	**PIETISM**	n pl. -S piety
		PIETIST	n pl. -S a pious person
		PIETY	n pl. -TIES the quality or state of being pious
PICNICKY	adj pertaining to a picnic		
PICOGRAM	n pl. -S one trillionth of a gram	**PIFFLE**	v -FLED, -FLING, -FLES to babble
PICOLIN	n pl. -S picoline		
PICOLINE	n pl. -S a chemical compound	**PIG**	v PIGGED, PIGGING, PIGS to bear pigs (cloven-hoofed mammals)
PICOT	v -ED, -ING, -S to edge with ornamental loops		
PICOTEE	n pl. -S a variety of carnation	**PIGBOAT**	n pl. -S a submarine
PICQUET	n pl. -S piquet	**PIGEON**	n pl. -S a short-legged bird
PICRATE	n pl. -S a chemical salt	**PIGFISH**	n pl. -ES a marine fish
	PICRATED adj	**PIGGED**	past tense of pig
PICRIC	adj having a very bitter taste	**PIGGERY**	n pl. -GERIES a pigpen
PICRITE	n pl. -S an igneous rock	**PIGGIE**	n pl. -S piggy
PICTURE	v -TURED, -TURING, -TURES to make a visual representation of	**PIGGIES**	pl. of piggy
		PIGGIN	n pl. -S a small wooden pail
PICUL	n pl. -S an Asian unit of weight	**PIGGING**	present participle of pig
PIDDLE	v -DLED, -DLING, -DLES to waste time	**PIGGISH**	adj greedy or dirty
		PIGGY	n pl. -GIES a small pig
PIDDLER	n pl. -S one that piddles	**PIGLET**	n pl. -S a small pig
PIDDOCK	n pl. -S a bivalve mollusk	**PIGMENT**	v -ED, -ING, -S to add a coloring matter to
PIDGIN	n pl. -S a mixed language		
PIE	v PIED, PIEING, PIES to pi	**PIGMY**	n pl. -MIES pygmy
PIEBALD	n pl. -S a spotted animal	**PIGNUS**	n pl. -NORA property held as security for a debt
PIECE	v PIECED, PIECING, PIECES to join into a whole		
		PIGNUT	n pl. -S a hickory nut
PIECER	n pl. -S one that pieces	**PIGPEN**	n pl. -S a place where pigs are kept
PIECING	n pl. -S material to be sewn together		
		PIGSKIN	n pl. -S the skin of a pig
PIECRUST	n pl. -S the crust of a pie	**PIGSNEY**	n pl. -NEYS a darling
PIED	past tense of pie	**PIGSTICK**	v -ED, -ING, -S to hunt for wild boar
PIEDFORT	n pl. -S piefort		
PIEDMONT	n pl. -S an area lying at the foot of a mountain	**PIGSTY**	n pl. -STIES a pigpen
		PIGTAIL	n pl. -S a tight braid of hair
PIEFORT	n pl. -S an unusually thick coin	**PIGWEED**	n pl. -S a weedy plant
PIEING	a present participle of pi	**PIKA**	n pl. -S a small mammal
PIEPLANT	n pl. -S a rhubarb	**PIKAKE**	n pl. -S an East Indian vine

PIKE	*v* PIKED, PIKING, PIKES to pierce with a pike (a long spear)
PIKEMAN	*n* pl. -MEN a soldier armed with a pike
PIKER	*n* pl. -S a stingy person
PIKING	present participle of pike
PILAF	*n* pl. -S a dish made of seasoned rice and often meat
PILAFF	*n* pl. -S pilaf
PILAR	*adj* pertaining to hair
PILASTER	*n* pl. -S a rectangular column
PILAU	*n* pl. -S pilaf
PILAW	*n* pl. -S pilaf
PILCHARD	*n* pl. -S a small marine fish
PILE	*v* PILED, PILING, PILES to lay one upon the other
PILEA	pl. of pileum
PILEATE	*adj* having a pileus
PILEATED	*adj* pileate
PILED	past tense of pile
PILEI	pl. of pileus
PILEOUS	*adj* pilose
PILEUM	*n* pl. -LEA the top of a bird's head
PILEUP	*n* pl. -S a collision involving several motor vehicles
PILEUS	*n* pl. -LEI the umbrella-shaped portion of a mushroom
PILEWORT	*n* pl. -S a medicinal plant
PILFER	*v* -ED, -ING, -S to steal
PILFERER	*n* pl. -S one that pilfers
PILGRIM	*n* pl. -S a traveler or wanderer
PILI	*n* pl. -S a Philippine tree
PILIFORM	*adj* resembling a hair
PILING	*n* pl. -S a structure of building supports
PILL	*v* -ED, -ING, -S to dose with pills (small, rounded masses of medicine)
PILLAGE	*v* -LAGED, -LAGING, -LAGES to plunder
PILLAGER	*n* pl. -S one that pillages
PILLAR	*v* -ED, -ING, -S to provide with vertical building supports
PILLBOX	*n* pl. -ES a small box for pills
PILLION	*n* pl. -S a pad or cushion for an extra rider on a horse or motorcycle
PILLORY	*v* -RIED, -RYING, -RIES to expose to public ridicule or abuse
PILLOW	*v* -ED, -ING, -S to rest on a pillow (a cushion for the head)
PILLOWY	*adj* resembling a pillow
PILOSE	*adj* covered with hair
PILOSITY	*n* pl. -TIES the state of being pilose
PILOT	*v* -ED, -ING, -S to control the course of
PILOTAGE	*n* pl. -S the act of piloting
PILOTING	*n* pl. -S a branch of navigation
PILOUS	*adj* pilose
PILSENER	*n* pl. -S pilsner
PILSNER	*n* pl. -S a light beer
PILULE	*n* pl. -S a small pill **PILULAR** *adj*
PILUS	*n* pl. -LI a hair or hairlike structure
PILY	*adj* divided into a number of wedge-shaped heraldic designs
PIMA	*n* pl. -S a strong, high-grade cotton
PIMENTO	*n* pl. -TOS pimiento
PIMIENTO	*n* pl. -TOS a sweet pepper
PIMP	*v* -ED, -ING, -S to solicit clients for a prostitute
PIMPLE	*n* pl. -S an inflamed swelling of the skin **PIMPLED** *adj*
PIMPLY	*adj* -PLIER, -PLIEST covered with pimples
PIN	*v* PINNED, PINNING, PINS to fasten with a pin (a slender, pointed piece of metal)
PINA	*n* pl. -S a pineapple
PINAFORE	*n* pl. -S a child's apron
PINANG	*n* pl. -S a palm tree
PINASTER	*n* pl. -S a pine tree
PINATA	*n* pl. -S a pottery jar used in a Mexican game
PINBALL	*n* pl. -S an electric game
PINBONE	*n* pl. -S the hipbone
PINCER	*n* pl. -S one of the two pivoted parts of a grasping tool
PINCH	*v* -ED, -ING, -ES to squeeze between two edges or surfaces
PINCHBUG	*n* pl. -S a large beetle
PINCHECK	*n* pl. -S a fabric design
PINCHER	*n* pl. -S one that pinches

PINDER   *n* pl. -S an official who formerly impounded stray animals

PINDLING   *adj* puny or sickly

PINE   *v* PINED, PINING, PINES to yearn intensely

PINEAL   *adj* shaped like a pinecone

PINECONE   *n* pl. -S a cone-shaped fruit of a pine tree

PINED   past tense of pine

PINELIKE   *adj* resembling a pine (an evergreen tree)

PINENE   *n* pl. -S the main constituent of turpentine

PINERY   *n* pl. -ERIES an area where pineapples are grown

PINESAP   *n* pl. -S a fragrant herb

PINETUM   *n* pl. -TA a plantation of pine trees

PINEWOOD   *n* pl. -S the wood of a pine tree

PINEY   *adj* PINIER, PINIEST piny

PINFISH   *n* pl. -ES a small marine fish

PINFOLD   *v* -ED, -ING, -S to confine in an enclosure for stray animals

PING   *v* -ED, -ING, -S to produce a brief, high-pitched sound

PINGER   *n* pl. -S a device for producing pulses of sound

PINGO   *n* pl. -GOS a hill forced up by the effects of frost

PINGRASS   *n* pl. -ES a European weed

PINGUID   *adj* greasy

PINHEAD   *n* pl. -S the head of a pin

PINHOLE   *n* pl. -S a small hole made by a pin

PINIER   comparative of piney and piny

PINIEST   superlative of piney and piny

PINING   present participle of pine

PINION   *v* -ED, -ING, -S to remove or bind the wing feathers of to prevent flight

PINITE   *n* pl. -S a mineral

PINK   *adj* PINKER, PINKEST of a pale reddish hue

PINK   *v* -ED, -ING, -S to stab with a pointed weapon

PINKEYE   *n* pl. -S an inflammation of the eye

PINKIE   *n* pl. -S the little finger

PINKIES   pl. of pinky

PINKING   *n* pl. -S a method of cutting or decorating

PINKISH   *adj* somewhat pink

PINKLY   *adv* with a pink hue

PINKNESS   *n* pl. -ES the state of being pink

PINKO   *n* pl. PINKOS or PINKOES a person who holds somewhat radical political views

PINKROOT   *n* pl. -S a medicinal plant root

PINKY   *n* pl. PINKIES pinkie

PINNA   *n* pl. -NAE or -NAS a feather, wing, or winglike part

PINNACE   *n* pl. -S a small sailing ship

PINNACLE   *v* -CLED, -CLING, -CLES to place on a summit

PINNAE   a pl. of pinna

PINNAL   *adj* pertaining to a pinna

PINNATE   *adj* resembling a feather

PINNATED   *adj* pinnate

PINNED   past tense of pin

PINNER   *n* pl. -S one that pins

PINNING   present participle of pin

PINNIPED   *n* pl. -S a mammal with limbs modified into flippers

PINNULA   *n* pl. -LAE pinnule **PINNULAR** *adj*

PINNULE   *n* pl. -S a pinnate part or organ

PINOCHLE   *n* pl. -S a card game

PINOCLE   *n* pl. -S pinochle

PINOLE   *n* pl. -S a finely ground flour

PINON   *n* pl. -S or -ES a pine tree

PINPOINT   *v* -ED, -ING, -S to locate precisely

PINPRICK   *v* -ED, -ING, -S to puncture with a pin

PINSCHER   *n* pl. -S a large, short-haired dog

PINT   *n* pl. -S a liquid and dry measure of capacity

PINTA   *n* pl. -S a skin disease

PINTADA   *n* pl. -S pintado

PINTADO   *n* pl. -DOS or -DOES a large food fish

PINTAIL   *n* pl. -S a river duck

PINTANO   *n* pl. -NOS a tropical fish

PINTLE   *n* pl. -S a pin on which something turns

PINTO   *n* pl. -TOS or -TOES a spotted horse

PINTSIZE   *adj* small

PINUP   *n* pl. -S a picture that may be pinned up on a wall

PINWALE   *n* pl. -S a type of fabric

PINWEED   *n* pl. -S a perennial herb

PINWHEEL   *n* pl. -S a child's toy resembling a windmill

PINWORK   *n* pl. -S a type of embroidery

PINWORM   *n* pl. -S a parasitic worm

PINY   *adj* PINIER, PINIEST suggestive of or covered with pine trees

PINYON   *n* pl. -S pinon

PIOLET   *n* pl. -S an ice ax

PION   *n* pl. -S an atomic particle **PIONIC** *adj*

PIONEER   *v* -ED, -ING, -S to take part in the beginnings of

PIOSITY   *n* pl. -TIES an excessive show of piety

PIOUS   *adj* marked by religious reverence **PIOUSLY** *adv*

PIP   *v* PIPPED, PIPPING, PIPS to break through the shell of an egg

PIPAGE   *n* pl. -S a system of pipes

PIPAL   *n* pl. -S a fig tree of India

PIPE   *v* PIPED, PIPING, PIPES to convey by means of a pipe (a hollow cylinder)

PIPEAGE   *n* pl. -S pipage

PIPEFISH   *n* pl. -ES a slender fish

PIPEFUL   *n* pl. -S a quantity sufficient to fill a tobacco pipe

PIPELESS   *adj* having no pipe

PIPELIKE   *adj* resembling a pipe

PIPELINE   *v* -LINED, -LINING, -LINES to convey by a line of pipe

PIPER   *n* pl. -S one that plays on a tubular musical instrument

PIPERINE   *n* pl. -S a chemical compound

PIPESTEM   *n* pl. -S the stem of a tobacco pipe

PIPET   *v* -PETTED, -PETTING, -PETS to pipette

PIPETTE   *v* -PETTED, -PETTING, -PETTES to measure liquid with a calibrated tube

PIPIER   comparative of pipy

PIPIEST   superlative of pipy

PIPING   *n* pl. -S a system of pipes

PIPINGLY   *adv* shrilly

PIPIT   *n* pl. -S a songbird

PIPKIN   *n* pl. -S a small pot

PIPPED   past tense of pip

PIPPIN   *n* pl. -S any of several varieties of apple

PIPPING   present participle of pip

PIPY   *adj* PIPIER, PIPIEST shrill

PIQUANCY   *n* pl. -CIES the quality of being piquant

PIQUANT   *adj* having an agreeably sharp taste

PIQUE   *v* PIQUED, PIQUING, PIQUES to arouse anger or resentment in

PIQUET   *n* pl. -S a card game

PIRACY   *n* pl. -CIES robbery on the high seas

PIRAGUA   *n* pl. -S a dugout canoe

PIRANA   *n* pl. -S piranha

PIRANHA   *n* pl. -S a voracious fish

PIRARUCU   *n* pl. -S a large food fish

PIRATE   *v* -RATED, -RATING, -RATES to commit piracy

PIRATIC   *adj* pertaining to piracy

PIRAYA   *n* pl. -S piranha

PIRN   *n* pl. -S a spinning-wheel bobbin

PIROG   *n* pl. -ROGEN, -ROGHI or -ROGI a large Russian pastry

PIROGUE   *n* pl. -S piragua

PIROQUE   *n* pl. -S piragua

PIROZHOK   *n* pl. -ROZHKI, -ROSHKI or -ROJKI a small Russian pastry

PISCARY   *n* pl. -RIES a place for fishing

PISCATOR   *n* pl. -S a fisherman

PISCINA   *n* pl. -NAE or -NAS a basin used in certain church ceremonies **PISCINAL** *adj*

PISCINE   *adj* pertaining to fish

PISH   *v* -ED, -ING, -ES to express contempt

PISIFORM   *n* pl. -S a small bone of the wrist

PISMIRE   *n* pl. -S an ant

PISOLITE   *n* pl. -S a limestone

PISS   *v* -ED, -ING, -ES to urinate — sometimes considered vulgar

PISSANT   *n* pl. -S an ant

PISSOIR   *n* pl. -S a public urinal

PISTACHE *n* pl. -S a shade of green

PISTIL *n* pl. -S the seed-bearing organ of flowering plants

PISTOL *v* -TOLED, -TOLING, -TOLS or -TOLLED, -TOLLING, -TOLS to shoot with a small firearm

PISTOLE *n* pl. -S a former European gold coin

PISTON *n* pl. -S a part of an engine

PIT *v* PITTED, PITTING, PITS to mark with cavities or depressions

PITA *n* pl. -S a strong fiber

PITAPAT *v* -PATTED, -PATTING, -PATS to make a repeated tapping sound

PITCH *v* -ED, -ING, -ES to throw

PITCHER *n* pl. -S a container for holding and pouring liquids

PITCHIER comparative of pitchy

PITCHIEST superlative of pitchy

PITCHILY *adv* in a very dark manner

PITCHMAN *n* pl. -MEN a salesman of small wares

PITCHOUT *n* pl. -S a type of pitch in baseball

PITCHY *adj* PITCHIER, PITCHIEST tarry

PITEOUS *adj* pitiful

PITFALL *n* pl. -S a hidden danger or difficulty

PITH *v* -ED, -ING, -S to sever the spinal cord of

PITHEAD *n* pl. -S a mine entrance

PITHLESS *adj* lacking force

PITHY *adj* PITHIER, PITHIEST concise **PITHILY** *adv*

PITIABLE *adj* pitiful **PITIABLY** *adv*

PITIED past tense of pity

PITIER *n* pl. -S one that pities

PITIES present 3d person sing. of pity

PITIFUL *adj* -FULLER, -FULLEST arousing pity

PITILESS *adj* having no pity

PITMAN *n* pl. -MEN a mine worker

PITMAN *n* pl. -S a connecting rod

PITON *n* pl. -S a metal spike used in mountain climbing

PITSAW *n* pl. -S a large saw for cutting logs

PITTANCE *n* pl. -S a small allowance of money

PITTED past tense of pit

PITTING *n* pl. -S an arrangement of cavities or depressions

PITY *v* PITIED, PITYING, PITIES to feel pity (sorrow aroused by another's misfortune)

PIU *adv* more — used as a musical direction

PIVOT *v* -ED, -ING, -S to turn on a shaft or rod

PIVOTAL *adj* critically important

PIX *n* pl. -ES pyx

PIXIE *n* pl. -S pixy **PIXIEISH** *adj*

PIXINESS *n* pl. -ES the state of being playfully mischievous

PIXY *n* pl. PIXIES a playfully mischievous fairy or elf **PIXYISH** *adj*

PIZAZZ *n* pl. -ES the quality of being exciting or attractive

PIZZA *n* pl. -S an Italian open pie

PIZZERIA *n* pl. -S a place where pizzas are made and sold

PIZZLE *n* pl. -S the penis of an animal

PLACABLE *adj* capable of being placated **PLACABLY** *adv*

PLACARD *v* -ED, -ING, -S to publicize by means of posters

PLACATE *v* -CATED, -CATING, -CATES to soothe or mollify

PLACATER *n* pl. -S one that placates

PLACE *v* PLACED, PLACING, PLACES to set in a particular position

PLACEBO *n* pl. -BOS or -BOES a substance containing no medication that is given for its psychological effect

PLACEMAN *n* pl. -MEN a political appointee to a public office

PLACENTA *n* pl. -TAS or -TAE a vascular organ in most mammals

PLACER *n* pl. -S one that places

PLACET *n* pl. -S a vote of assent

PLACID *adj* calm or peaceful **PLACIDLY** *adv*

PLACING present participle of place

PLACK *n* pl. -S a former coin of Scotland

PLACKET *n* pl. -S a slit in a garment

PLACOID *n* pl. -S a fish having platelike scales

PLAFOND   *n* pl. -S an elaborately decorated ceiling

PLAGAL   *adj* designating a medieval musical mode

PLAGE   *n* pl. -S a bright region on the sun

PLAGIARY   *n* pl. -RIES the act of passing off another's work as one's own

PLAGUE   *v* PLAGUED, PLAGUING, PLAGUES to harass or torment

PLAGUER   *n* pl. -S one that plagues

PLAGUEY   *adj* plaguy

PLAGUING   present participle of plague

PLAGUY   *adj* troublesome **PLAGUILY** *adv*

PLAICE   *n* pl. -S a European flatfish

PLAID   *n* pl. -S a woolen scarf of a checkered pattern **PLAIDED** *adj*

PLAIN   *adj* PLAINER, PLAINEST evident **PLAINLY** *adv*

PLAIN   *v* -ED, -ING, -S to complain

PLAINT   *n* pl. -S a complaint

PLAISTER   *v* -ED, -ING, -S to plaster

PLAIT   *v* -ED, -ING, -S to braid

PLAITER   *n* pl. -S one that plaits

PLAITING   *n* pl. -S something that is plaited

PLAN   *v* PLANNED, PLANNING, PLANS to formulate a plan (a method for achieving an end)

PLANAR   *adj* flat

PLANARIA   *n* pl. -S an aquatic flatworm

PLANATE   *adj* having a flat surface

PLANCH   *n* pl. -ES a plank

PLANCHE   *n* pl. -S planch

PLANCHET   *n* pl. -S a flat piece of metal for stamping into a coin

PLANE   *v* PLANED, PLANING, PLANES to make smooth or even

PLANER   *n* pl. -S one that planes

PLANET   *n* pl. -S a celestial body

PLANFORM   *n* pl. -S the contour of an object as viewed from above

PLANGENT   *adj* resounding loudly

PLANING   present participle of plane

PLANISH   *v* -ED, -ING, -ES to toughen and smooth by hammering lightly

PLANK   *v* -ED, -ING, -S to cover with planks (long, flat pieces of lumber)

PLANKING   *n* pl. -S covering made of planks

PLANKTER   *n* pl. -S any organism that is an element of plankton

PLANKTON   *n* pl. -S the minute animal and plant life of a body of water

PLANLESS   *adj* having no plan

PLANNED   past tense of plan

PLANNER   *n* pl. -S one that plans

PLANNING   *n* pl. -S the establishment of goals or policies

PLANOSOL   *n* pl. -S a type of soil

PLANT   *v* -ED, -ING, -S to place in the ground for growing

PLANTAIN   *n* pl. -S a short-stemmed herb

PLANTAR   *adj* pertaining to the sole of the foot

PLANTER   *n* pl. -S one that plants

PLANTING   *n* pl. -S an area where plants are grown

PLANULA   *n* pl. -LAE the free-swimming larva of certain organisms **PLANULAR** *adj*

PLAQUE   *n* pl. -S an ornamental plate or disk

PLASH   *v* -ED, -ING, -ES to weave together

PLASHER   *n* pl. -S one that plashes

PLASHY   *adj* PLASHIER, PLASHIEST marshy

PLASM   *n* pl. -S plasma

PLASMA   *n* pl. -S the liquid part of blood **PLASMIC** *adj*

PLASMID   *n* pl. -S a hereditary structure of a cell

PLASMIN   *n* pl. -S an enzyme

PLASMOID   *n* pl. -S a type of high energy particle

PLASMON   *n* pl. -S a determinant of inheritance believed to exist in cells

PLASTER   *v* -ED, -ING, -S to cover with plaster (a mixture of lime, sand, and water)

PLASTERY   *adj* resembling plaster

PLASTIC   *n* pl. -S any of a group of synthetic or natural moldable materials

PLASTID   *n* pl. -S a structure in plant cells

PLASTRON   *n* pl. -S a part of the shell of a turtle **PLASTRAL** *adj*

PLASTRUM *n* pl. -S plastron

PLAT *v* PLATTED, PLATTING, PLATS to plait

PLATAN *n* pl. -S a large tree

PLATANE *n* pl. -S platan

PLATE *v* PLATED, PLATING, PLATES to coat with a thin layer of metal

PLATEAU *n* pl. -TEAUS or -TEAUX a level stretch of elevated land

PLATEAU *v* -ED, -ING, -S to reach a period or condition of stability

PLATED past tense of plate

PLATEFUL *n* pl. PLATEFULS or PLATESFUL the quantity that fills a plate (a shallow dish)

PLATELET *n* pl. -S a small, flattened body

PLATEN *n* pl. -S the roller of a typewriter

PLATER *n* pl. -S one that plates

PLATESFUL a pl. of plateful

PLATFORM *n* pl. -S a raised floor or flat surface

PLATIER comparative of platy

PLATIES a pl. of platy

PLATIEST superlative of platy

PLATINA *n* pl. -S platinum

PLATING *n* pl. -S a thin layer of metal

PLATINIC *adj* pertaining to platinum

PLATINUM *n* pl. -S a metallic element

PLATONIC *adj* purely spiritual and free from sensual desire

PLATOON *v* -ED, -ING, -S to alternate with another player at the same position

PLATTED past tense of plat

PLATTER *n* pl. -S a large, shallow dish

PLATTING present participle of plat

PLATY *adj* PLATIER, PLATIEST split into thin, flat pieces

PLATY *n* pl. PLATYS or PLATIES a small tropical fish

PLATYPUS *n* pl. -PUSES or -PI an aquatic mammal

PLAUDIT *n* pl. -S an expression of praise

PLAUSIVE *adj* expressing praise

PLAY *v* -ED, -ING, -S to engage in amusement or sport **PLAYABLE** *adj*

PLAYA *n* pl. -S the bottom of a desert basin

PLAYACT *v* -ED, -ING, -S to take part in a theatrical performance

PLAYBACK *n* pl. -S the act of replaying a newly made recording

PLAYBILL *n* pl. -S a program for a theatrical performance

PLAYBOOK *n* pl. -S a book containing one or more literary works for the stage

PLAYBOY *n* pl. -BOYS a man devoted to pleasurable activities

PLAYDAY *n* pl. -DAYS a holiday

PLAYDOWN *n* pl. -S a playoff

PLAYER *n* pl. -S one that plays

PLAYFUL *adj* frolicsome

PLAYGIRL *n* pl. -S a female playboy

PLAYGOER *n* pl. -S one who attends the theater

PLAYLAND *n* pl. -S a recreational area

PLAYLESS *adj* lacking playfulness

PLAYLET *n* pl. -S a short theatrical performance

PLAYLIKE *adj* resembling a theatrical performance

PLAYMATE *n* pl. -S a companion in play

PLAYOFF *n* pl. -S a series of games played to determine a championship

PLAYPEN *n* pl. -S an enclosure in which a young child may play

PLAYROOM *n* pl. -S a recreation room

PLAYSUIT *n* pl. -S a sports outfit for women and children

PLAYTIME *n* pl. -S a time for play or amusement

PLAYWEAR *n* pl. -S clothing worn for leisure activities

PLAZA *n* pl. -S a public square

PLEA *n* pl. -S an entreaty

PLEACH *v* -ED, -ING, -ES to weave together

PLEAD *v* PLEADED or PLED, PLEADING, PLEADS to ask for earnestly

PLEADER *n* pl. -S one that pleads

PLEADING *n* pl. -S an allegation in a legal action

PLEASANT *adj* -ANTER, -ANTEST pleasing

PLEASE *v* PLEASED, PLEASING, PLEASES to give enjoyment or satisfaction to

PLEASER   *n* pl. -S one that pleases

PLEASURE   *v* -SURED, -SURING, -SURES to please

PLEAT   *v* -ED, -ING, -S to fold in an even manner

PLEATER   *n* pl. -S one that pleats

PLEB   *n* pl. -S a commoner

PLEBE   *n* pl. -S a freshman at a military or naval academy

PLEBEIAN   *n* pl. -S a commoner

PLECTRON   *n* pl. -TRONS or -TRA plectrum

PLECTRUM   *n* pl. -TRUMS or -TRA an implement used to pluck the strings of a stringed instrument

PLED   a past tense of plead

PLEDGE   *v* PLEDGED, PLEDGING, PLEDGES to give as security for something borrowed

PLEDGEE   *n* pl. -S one to whom something is pledged

PLEDGEOR   *n* pl. -S pledger

PLEDGER   *n* pl. -S one that pledges something

PLEDGET   *n* pl. -S a pad of absorbent cotton

PLEDGING   present participle of pledge

PLEDGOR   *n* pl. -S pledger

PLEIAD   *n* pl. -S or -ES a group of seven illustrious persons

PLENA   a pl. of plenum

PLENARY   *adj* complete in every respect

PLENISH   *v* -ED, -ING, -ES to fill up

PLENISM   *n* pl. -S the doctrine that space is fully occupied by matter

PLENIST   *n* pl. -S an advocate of plenism

PLENTY   *n* pl. -TIES a sufficient or abundant amount

PLENUM   *n* pl. -NUMS or -NA space considered as fully occupied by matter

PLEONASM   *n* pl. -S the use of needless words

PLEOPOD   *n* pl. -S an appendage of crustaceans

PLESSOR   *n* pl. -S plexor

PLETHORA   *n* pl. -S an excess

PLEURA   *n* pl. -RAE or -RAS a membrane that envelops the lungs **PLEURAL** *adj*

PLEURISY   *n* pl. -SIES inflammation of the pleura

PLEURON   *n* pl. -RA a part of a thoracic segment of an insect

PLEUSTON   *n* pl. -S aquatic vegetation

PLEXOR   *n* pl. -S a small, hammer-like medical instrument

PLEXUS   *n* pl. -ES an interlacing of parts

PLIABLE   *adj* easily bent **PLIABLY** *adv*

PLIANCY   *n* pl. -CIES the quality of being pliant

PLIANT   *adj* easily bent **PLIANTLY** *adv*

PLICA   *n* pl. -CAE a fold of skin **PLICAL** *adj*

PLICATE   *adj* pleated

PLICATED   *adj* plicate

PLIE   *n* pl. -S a movement in ballet

PLIED   past tense of ply

PLIER   *n* pl. -S one that plies

PLIES   present 3d person sing. of ply

PLIGHT   *v* -ED, -ING, -S to promise or bind by a solemn pledge

PLIGHTER   *n* pl. -S one that plights

PLIMSOL   *n* pl. -S plimsoll

PLIMSOLE   *n* pl. -S plimsoll

PLIMSOLL   *n* pl. -S a rubber-soled cloth shoe

PLINK   *v* -ED, -ING, -S to shoot at random targets

PLINKER   *n* pl. -S one that plinks

PLINTH   *n* pl. -S a stone or slab upon which a column or pedestal rests

PLISKIE   *n* pl. -S a practical joke

PLISKY   *n* pl. -KIES pliskie

PLISSE   *n* pl. -S a puckered texture of cloth

PLOD   *v* PLODDED, PLODDING, PLODS to walk heavily

PLODDER   *n* pl. -S one that plods

PLOIDY   *n* pl. -DIES the extent of repetition of the basic number of chromosomes

PLONK   *v* -ED, -ING, -S to plunk

PLOP   *v* PLOPPED, PLOPPING, PLOPS to drop or fall heavily

PLOSION   *n* pl. -S a release of breath after the articulation of certain consonants

PLOSIVE   *n* pl. -S a sound produced by plosion

PLOT   *v* PLOTTED, PLOTTING, PLOTS to plan secretly

PLOTLESS   *adj* planless

PLOTTAGE   *n* pl. -S an area of land

PLOTTED   past tense of plot

PLOTTER   *n* pl. -S one that plots

PLOTTIER   comparative of plotty

PLOTTIES   pl. of plotty

PLOTTING   present participle of plot

PLOTTY   *adj* -TIER, -TIEST full of intrigue, as a novel

PLOTTY   *n* pl. -TIES a hot, spiced beverage

PLOUGH   *v* -ED, -ING, -S to plow

PLOUGHER   *n* pl. -S one that ploughs

PLOVER   *n* pl. -S a shore bird

PLOW   *v* -ED, -ING, -S to turn up land with a plow (a farm implement) **PLOWABLE** *adj*

PLOWBACK   *n* pl. -S a reinvestment of profits in a business

PLOWBOY   *n* pl. -BOYS a boy who leads a plow team

PLOWER   *n* pl. -S one that plows

PLOWHEAD   *n* pl. -S the clevis of a plow

PLOWLAND   *n* pl. -S land suitable for cultivation

PLOWMAN   *n* pl. -MEN a man who plows

PLOY   *v* -ED, -ING, -S to move from a line into column

PLUCK   *v* -ED, -ING, -S to pull out or off

PLUCKER   *n* pl. -S one that plucks

PLUCKY   *adj* PLUCKIER, PLUCKIEST brave and spirited **PLUCKILY** *adv*

PLUG   *v* PLUGGED, PLUGGING, PLUGS to seal or close with a plug (a piece of material used to fill a hole)

PLUGGER   *n* pl. -S one that plugs

PLUGLESS   *adj* having no plug

PLUGUGLY   *n* pl. -LIES a hoodlum

PLUM   *n* pl. -S a fleshy fruit

PLUMAGE   *n* pl. -S the feathers of a bird **PLUMAGED** *adj*

PLUMATE   *adj* resembling a feather

PLUMB   *v* -ED, -ING, -S to determine the depth of

PLUMBAGO   *n* pl. -GOS graphite

PLUMBER   *n* pl. -S one who installs and repairs plumbing

PLUMBERY   *n* pl. -ERIES the work of a plumber

PLUMBIC   *adj* containing lead

PLUMBING   *n* pl. -S the pipe system of a building

PLUMBISM   *n* pl. -S lead poisoning

PLUMBOUS   *adj* containing lead

PLUMBUM   *n* pl. -S lead

PLUME   *v* PLUMED, PLUMING, PLUMES to cover with feathers

PLUMELET   *n* pl. -S a small feather

PLUMIER   comparative of plumy

PLUMIEST   superlative of plumy

PLUMING   present participle of plume

PLUMIPED   *n* pl. -S a bird having feathered feet

PLUMLIKE   *adj* resembling a plum

PLUMMET   *v* -ED, -ING, -S to drop straight down

PLUMMY   *adj* -MIER, -MIEST full of plums

PLUMOSE   *adj* having feathers

PLUMP   *adj* PLUMPER, PLUMPEST well-rounded and full in form

PLUMP   *v* -ED, -ING, -S to make plump

PLUMPEN   *v* -ED, -ING, -S to plump

PLUMPER   *n* pl. -S a heavy fall

PLUMPISH   *adj* somewhat plump

PLUMPLY   *adv* in a plump way

PLUMULE   *n* pl. -S the primary bud of a plant embryo **PLUMULAR** *adj*

PLUMY   *adj* PLUMIER, PLUMIEST covered with feathers

PLUNDER   *v* -ED, -ING, -S to rob of goods by force

PLUNGE   *v* PLUNGED, PLUNGING, PLUNGES to throw or thrust suddenly or forcibly into something

PLUNGER   *n* pl. -S one that plunges

PLUNK   *v* -ED, -ING, -S to fall or drop heavily

PLUNKER   *n* pl. -S one that plunks

PLURAL   *n* pl. -S a word that expresses more than one

PLURALLY   *adv* in a manner or form that expresses more than one

PLUS   *n* pl. PLUSES or PLUSSES an additional quantity

PLUSH	*adj* PLUSHER, PLUSHEST luxurious **PLUSHLY** *adv*
PLUSH	*n* pl. -ES a fabric with a long pile
PLUSHY	*adj* PLUSHIER, PLUSHIEST luxurious **PLUSHILY** *adv*
PLUSSAGE	*n* pl. -S an amount over and above another
PLUSSES	a pl. of plus
PLUTON	*n* pl. -S a formation of igneous rock **PLUTONIC** *adj*
PLUVIAL	*n* pl. -S a prolonged period of wet climate
PLUVIOSE	*adj* pluvious
PLUVIOUS	*adj* pertaining to rain
PLY	*v* PLIED, PLYING, PLIES to supply with or offer repeatedly **PLYINGLY** *adv*
PLYER	*n* pl. -S plier
PLYWOOD	*n* pl. -S a building material
PNEUMA	*n* pl. -S the soul or spirit
POACEOUS	*adj* pertaining to plants of the grass family
POACH	*v* -ED, -ING, -ES to trespass for the purpose of taking game or fish
POACHER	*n* pl. -S one that poaches
POACHY	*adj* POACHIER, POACHIEST swampy
POCHARD	*n* pl. -S a sea duck
POCK	*v* -ED, -ING, -S to mark with pocks (pustules caused by an eruptive disease)
POCKET	*v* -ED, -ING, -S to place in a pouch sewed into a garment
POCKETER	*n* pl. -S one that pockets
POCKMARK	*v* -ED, -ING, -S to mark with scars caused by an eruptive disease
POCKY	*adj* POCKIER, POCKIEST covered with pocks **POCKILY** *adv*
POCO	*adv* a little — used as a musical direction
POCOSIN	*n* pl. -S an upland swamp
POD	*v* PODDED, PODDING, PODS to produce seed vessels
PODAGRA	*n* pl. -S gout in the foot **PODAGRAL, PODAGRIC** *adj*
PODESTA	*n* pl. -S an Italian magistrate
PODGY	*adj* PODGIER, PODGIEST pudgy **PODGILY** *adv*
PODIA	a pl. of podium
PODIATRY	*n* pl. -TRIES the study and treatment of the human foot
PODITE	*n* pl. -S a limb segment of an arthropod **PODITIC** *adj*
PODIUM	*n* pl. -DIUMS or -DIA a small platform
PODOMERE	*n* pl. -S a podite
PODSOL	*n* pl. -S podzol **PODSOLIC** *adj*
PODZOL	*n* pl. -S an infertile soil **PODZOLIC** *adj*
POECHORE	*n* pl. -S a semiarid region
POEM	*n* pl. -S a composition in verse
POESY	*n* pl. -ESIES poetry
POET	*n* pl. -S one who writes poems
POETESS	*n* pl. -ES a female poet
POETIC	*adj* pertaining to poetry
POETICAL	*adj* poetic
POETICS	*n/pl* poetic theory or practice
POETISE	*v* -ISED, -ISING, -ISES to poetize
POETISER	*n* pl. -S poetizer
POETIZE	*v* -IZED, -IZING, -IZES to write poetry
POETIZER	*n* pl. -S one that poetizes
POETLESS	*adj* lacking a poet
POETLIKE	*adj* resembling a poet
POETRY	*n* pl. -RIES literary work in metrical form
POGEY	*n* pl. -GEYS any form of government relief
POGIES	pl. of pogy
POGONIA	*n* pl. -S a small orchid
POGONIP	*n* pl. -S a dense fog of suspended ice particles
POGROM	*v* -ED, -ING, -S to massacre systematically
POGY	*n* pl. -GIES a marine fish
POH	*interj* — used to express disgust
POI	*n* pl. -S a Hawaiian food
POIGNANT	*adj* emotionally distressing
POILU	*n* pl. -S a French soldier
POIND	*v* -ED, -ING, -S to seize and sell the property of to satisfy a debt
POINT	*v* -ED, -ING, -S to indicate direction with the finger
POINTE	*n* pl. -S a ballet position
POINTER	*n* pl. -S one that points

POINTMAN *n* pl. -MEN a certain player in hockey

POINTY *adj* POINTIER, POINTIEST coming to a sharp, tapering end

POISE *v* POISED, POISING, POISES to hold in a state of equilibrium

POISER *n* pl. -S one that poises

POISON *v* -ED, -ING, -S to administer a harmful substance to

POISONER *n* pl. -S one that poisons

POITREL *n* pl. -S peytral

POKE *v* POKED, POKING, POKES to push or prod

POKER *n* pl. -S one that pokes

POKEROOT *n* pl. -S pokeweed

POKEWEED *n* pl. -S a perennial herb

POKEY *n* pl. -KEYS poky

POKIER comparative of poky

POKIES pl. of poky

POKIEST superlative of poky

POKILY *adv* in a poky manner

POKINESS *n* pl. -ES the state of being poky

POKING present participle of poke

POKY *n* pl. POKIES a jail

POKY *adj* POKIER, POKIEST slow

POL *n* pl. -S a politician

POLAR *n* pl. -S a straight line related to a point

POLARISE *v* -ISED, -ISING, -ISES to polarize

POLARITY *n* pl. -TIES the possession of two opposite qualities

POLARIZE *v* -IZED, -IZING, -IZES to give polarity to

POLARON *n* pl. -S a type of electron

POLDER *n* pl. -S a tract of low land reclaimed from a body of water

POLE *v* POLED, POLING, POLES to propel with a pole (a long, thin piece of wood or metal)

POLEAX *v* -ED, -ING, -ES to strike with an axlike weapon

POLEAXE *v* -AXED, -AXING, -AXES to poleax

POLECAT *n* pl. -S a carnivorous mammal

POLED past tense of pole

POLEIS pl. of polis

POLELESS *adj* having no pole

POLEMIC *n* pl. -S a controversial argument

POLEMIST *n* pl. -S one who engages in polemics

POLEMIZE *v* -MIZED, -MIZING, -MIZES to engage in polemics

POLENTA *n* pl. -S a thick mush of cornmeal

POLER *n* pl. -S one that poles

POLESTAR *n* pl. -S a guiding principle

POLEWARD *adv* in the direction of either extremity of the earth's axis

POLEYN *n* pl. -S a protective piece of leather for the knee

POLICE *v* -LICED, -LICING, -LICES to make clean or orderly

POLICY *n* pl. -CIES an action or a procedure considered with reference to prudence or expediency

POLING present participle of pole

POLIO *n* pl. -LIOS an infectious virus disease

POLIS *n* pl. -LEIS an ancient Greek city-state

POLISH *v* -ED, -ING, -ES to make smooth and lustrous by rubbing

POLISHER *n* pl. -S one that polishes

POLITE *adj* -LITER, -LITEST showing consideration for others **POLITELY** *adv*

POLITIC *adj* shrewd

POLITICK *v* -ED, -ING, -S to engage in politics

POLITICO *n* pl. -COS or -COES one who politicks

POLITICS *n/pl* the art or science of government

POLITY *n* pl. -TIES a form or system of government

POLKA *v* -ED, -ING, -S to perform a lively dance

POLL *v* -ED, -ING, -S to question for the purpose of surveying public opinion

POLLACK *n* pl. -S a marine food fish

POLLARD *v* -ED, -ING, -S to cut the top branches of a tree back to the trunk

POLLEE *n* pl. -S one who is polled

POLLEN	v -ED, -ING, -S to convey pollen (the fertilizing element in a seed plant) to
POLLER	n pl. -S one that polls
POLLEX	n pl. -LICES the innermost digit of the forelimb **POLLICAL** adj
POLLINIA	n/pl masses of pollen grains
POLLINIC	adj pertaining to pollen
POLLIST	n pl. -S a poller
POLLIWOG	n pl. -S a tadpole
POLLOCK	n pl. -S pollack
POLLSTER	n pl. -S a poller
POLLUTE	v -LUTED, -LUTING, -LUTES to make unclean or impure
POLLUTER	n pl. -S one that pollutes
POLLYWOG	n pl. -S polliwog
POLO	n pl. -LOS a game played on horseback
POLOIST	n pl. -S a polo player
POLONIUM	n pl. -S a radioactive element
POLTROON	n pl. -S a base coward
POLY	n pl. POLYS a type of white blood cell
POLYBRID	n pl. -S a type of hybrid plant
POLYCOT	n pl. -S a type of plant
POLYENE	n pl. -S a chemical compound **POLYENIC** adj
POLYGALA	n pl. -S a flowering plant
POLYGAMY	n pl. -MIES the condition of having more than one spouse at the same time
POLYGENE	n pl. -ES a type of gene
POLYGLOT	n pl. -S one that speaks or writes several languages
POLYGON	n pl. -S a closed plane figure bounded by straight lines
POLYGONY	n pl. -NIES an herb
POLYGYNY	n pl. -NIES the condition of having more than one wife at the same time
POLYMATH	n pl. -S a person of great and varied learning
POLYMER	n pl. -S a complex chemical compound
POLYNYA	n pl. -S an area of open water surrounded by sea ice
POLYP	n pl. -S an invertebrate
POLYPARY	n pl. -ARIES the common supporting structure of a polyp colony
POLYPI	a pl. of polypus
POLYPIDE	n pl. -S a polyp
POLYPNEA	n pl. -S rapid breathing
POLYPOD	n pl. -S a many-footed organism
POLYPODY	n pl. -DIES a fern
POLYPOID	adj resembling a polyp
POLYPORE	n pl. -S a type of fungus
POLYPOUS	adj pertaining to a polyp
POLYPUS	n pl. -PI or -PUSES a growth protruding from the mucous lining of an organ
POLYSEMY	n pl. -MIES diversity of meanings
POLYSOME	n pl. -S a cluster of protein particles
POLYTENE	adj having chromosomes of a certain type
POLYTENY	n pl. -NIES the state of being polytene
POLYTYPE	n pl. -S a crystal structure
POLYURIA	n pl. -S excessive urination **POLYURIC** adj
POLYZOAN	n pl. -S a bryozoan
POLYZOIC	adj composed of many zooids
POMACE	n pl. -S the pulpy residue of crushed fruits
POMADE	v -MADED, -MADING, -MADES to apply a perfumed hair dressing to
POMANDER	n pl. -S a mixture of aromatic substances
POMATUM	n pl. -S a perfumed hair dressing
POME	n pl. -S a fleshy fruit with a core
POMELO	n pl. -LOS a grapefruit
POMMEE	adj having arms with knoblike ends — used of a heraldic cross
POMMEL	v -MELED, -MELING, -MELS or -MELLED, -MELLING, -MELS to strike with the fists
POMOLOGY	n pl. -GIES the study of fruits
POMP	n pl. -S stately or splendid display
POMPANO	n pl. -NOS a marine food fish
POMPOM	n pl. -S an antiaircraft cannon
POMPON	n pl. -S an ornamental tuft or ball
POMPOUS	adj marked by exaggerated self-importance

PONCE   *n* pl. -S a man who solicits clients for a prostitute

PONCHO   *n* pl. -CHOS a type of cloak

POND   *n* pl. -S a body of water smaller than a lake

PONDER   *v* -ED, -ING, -S to consider something deeply and thoroughly

PONDERER   *n* pl. -S one that ponders

PONDWEED   *n* pl. -S an aquatic plant

PONE   *n* pl. -S a corn bread

PONENT   *adj* affirmative

PONGEE   *n* pl. -S a type of silk

PONGID   *n* pl. -S an anthropoid ape

PONIARD   *v* -ED, -ING, -S to stab with a dagger

PONIED   past tense of pony

PONIES   present 3d person sing. of pony

PONS   *n* pl. PONTES a band of nerve fibers in the brain

PONTIFEX   *n* pl. -FICES an ancient Roman priest

PONTIFF   *n* pl. -S a pope or bishop

PONTIFIC   *adj* pertaining to a pope or bishop

PONTIFICES   pl. of pontifex

PONTIL   *n* pl. -S a punty

PONTINE   *adj* pertaining to bridges

PONTON   *n* pl. -S pontoon

PONTOON   *n* pl. -S a flat-bottomed boat

PONY   *v* -NIED, -NYING, -NIES to prepare lessons with the aid of a literal translation

PONYTAIL   *n* pl. -S a hairstyle

POOCH   *n* pl. -ES a dog

POOD   *n* pl. -S a Russian unit of weight

POODLE   *n* pl. -S a heavy-coated dog

POOH   *v* -ED, -ING, -S to express contempt for

POOL   *v* -ED, -ING, -S to combine in a common fund

POOLHALL   *n* pl. -S a poolroom

POOLROOM   *n* pl. -S an establishment for the playing of billiards

POON   *n* pl. -S an East Indian tree

POOP   *v* -ED, -ING, -S to tire out

POOR   *adj* POORER, POOREST lacking the means of support

POORI   *n* pl. -S a light, flat wheat cake

POORISH   *adj* somewhat poor

POORLY   *adv* in a poor manner

POORNESS   *n* pl. -ES the state of being poor

POORTITH   *n* pl. -S poverty

POP   *v* POPPED, POPPING, POPS to make a sharp, explosive sound

POPCORN   *n* pl. -S a variety of corn

POPE   *n* pl. -S the head of the Roman Catholic Church **POPELESS, POPELIKE** *adj*

POPEDOM   *n* pl. -S the office of a pope

POPERY   *n* pl. -ERIES Roman Catholicism — usually used disparagingly

POPEYED   *adj* having bulging eyes

POPGUN   *n* pl. -S a toy gun

POPINJAY   *n* pl. -JAYS a vain person

POPISH   *adj* pertaining to the Roman Catholic Church — usually used disparagingly **POPISHLY** *adv*

POPLAR   *n* pl. -S a fast-growing tree

POPLIN   *n* pl. -S a durable fabric

POPLITIC   *adj* pertaining to the part of the leg behind the knee

POPOVER   *n* pl. -S a very light egg muffin

POPPA   *n* pl. -S papa

POPPED   past tense of pop

POPPER   *n* pl. -S one that pops

POPPET   *n* pl. -S a mechanical valve

POPPIED   *adj* covered with poppies

POPPIES   pl. of poppy

POPPING   present participle of pop

POPPLE   *v* -PLED, -PLING, -PLES to move in a bubbling or rippling manner

POPPY   *n* pl. -PIES a flowering plant

POPULACE   *n* pl. -S the common people

POPULAR   *adj* liked by many people

POPULATE   *v* -LATED, -LATING, -LATES to inhabit

POPULISM   *n* pl. -S populists' doctrines

POPULIST   *n* pl. -S a member of a party which represents the common people

POPULOUS   *adj* containing many inhabitants

PORCH *n* pl. -ES a covered structure at the entrance to a building

PORCINE *adj* pertaining to swine

PORE *v* PORED, PORING, PORES to gaze intently

PORGY *n* pl. -GIES a marine food fish

PORISM *n* pl. -S a type of mathematical proposition

PORK *n* pl. -S the flesh of swine used as food

PORKER *n* pl. -S a pig

PORKIER comparative of porky

PORKIES pl. of porky

PORKIEST superlative of porky

PORKPIE *n* pl. -S a man's hat

PORKWOOD *n* pl. -S a tropical tree

PORKY *adj* PORKIER, PORKIEST resembling pork

PORKY *n* pl. -KIES a porcupine

PORN *n* pl. -S pornography

PORNO *n* pl. -NOS pornography

POROSE *adj* porous

POROSITY *n* pl. -TIES the state of being porous

POROUS *adj* having minute openings **POROUSLY** *adv*

PORPHYRY *n* pl. -RIES an igneous rock

PORPOISE *n* pl. -S an aquatic mammal

PORRECT *adj* extended forward

PORRIDGE *n* pl. -S a soft food

PORT *v* -ED, -ING, -S to shift to the left side

PORTABLE *n* pl. -S something that can be carried

PORTABLY *adv* so as to be capable of being carried

PORTAGE *v* -TAGED, -TAGING, -TAGES to transport from one navigable waterway to another

PORTAL *n* pl. -S a door, gate, or entrance **PORTALED** *adj*

PORTANCE *n* pl. -S demeanor

PORTEND *v* -ED, -ING, -S to serve as an omen of

PORTENT *n* pl. -S an omen

PORTER *n* pl. -S a person employed to carry luggage

PORTHOLE *n* pl. -S a small window in a ship's side

PORTICO *n* pl. -COS or -COES a type of porch

PORTIERE *n* pl. -S a curtain for a doorway

PORTION *v* -ED, -ING, -S to divide into shares for distribution

PORTLESS *adj* having no place for ships to load or unload

PORTLY *adj* -LIER, -LIEST rather heavy or fat

PORTRAIT *n* pl. -S a likeness of a person

PORTRAY *v* -ED, -ING, -S to represent pictorially

PORTRESS *n* pl. -ES a female doorkeeper

POSADA *n* pl. -S an inn

POSE *v* POSED, POSING, POSES to assume a fixed position

POSER *n* pl. -S one that poses

POSEUR *n* pl. -S an affected or insincere person

POSH *adj* POSHER, POSHEST stylish or elegant

POSIES pl. of posy

POSING present participle of pose

POSINGLY *adv* in a posing manner

POSIT *v* -ED, -ING, -S to place

POSITION *v* -ED, -ING, -S to put in a particular location

POSITIVE *adj* -TIVER, -TIVEST certain

POSITIVE *n* pl. -S a quantity greater than zero

POSITRON *n* pl. -S an atomic particle

POSOLOGY *n* pl. -GIES a branch of medicine that deals with drug dosages

POSSE *n* pl. -S a body of men summoned to aid a peace officer

POSSESS *v* -ED, -ING, -ES to have as property

POSSET *n* pl. -S a hot, spiced drink

POSSIBLE *adj* -BLER, -BLEST capable of happening or proving true **POSSIBLY** *adv*

POSSUM *n* pl. -S opossum

POST *v* -ED, -ING, -S to affix in a public place

POSTAGE *n* pl. -S the charge for mailing an item

POSTAL *n* pl. -S a postcard

POSTALLY *adv* in a manner pertaining to the mails

POSTANAL *adj* situated behind the anus

POSTBAG *n* pl. -S a mailbag

POSTBOX *n* pl. -ES a mailbox

POSTBOY *n* pl. -BOYS a boy who carries mail

POSTCARD *n* pl. -S a card for use in the mail

POSTCAVA *n* pl. -VAE a vein in higher vertebrates

POSTDATE *v* -DATED, -DATING, -DATES to give a date later than the actual date to

POSTEEN *n* pl. -S an Afghan outer garment

POSTER *n* pl. -S a printed or written notice for posting

POSTERN *n* pl. -S a rear door or date

POSTFACE *n* pl. -S a brief note placed at the end of a publication

POSTFIX *v* -ED, -ING, -ES to affix at the end of something

POSTFORM *v* -ED, -ING, -S to shape subsequently

POSTHOLE *n* pl. -S a hole dug to secure a fence post

POSTICHE *n* pl. -S an imitation

POSTIN *n* pl. -S posteen

POSTING *n* pl. -S the act of transferring to a ledger

POSTIQUE *n* pl. -S postiche

POSTLUDE *n* pl. -S a closing musical piece

POSTMAN *n* pl. -MEN a mailman

POSTMARK *v* -ED, -ING, -S to stamp mail with an official mark

POSTORAL *adj* situated behind the mouth

POSTPAID *adv* with the postage prepaid

POSTPONE *v* -PONED, -PONING, -PONES to put off to a future time

POSTURAL *adj* pertaining to the position of the body

POSTURE *v* -TURED, -TURING, -TURES to assume a particular position

POSTURER *n* pl. -S one that postures

POSTWAR *adj* occurring or existing after a war

POSY *n* pl. -SIES a flower or bouquet

POT *v* POTTED, POTTING, POTS to put in a pot (a round, fairly deep container)

POTABLE *n* pl. -S a liquid suitable for drinking

POTAGE *n* pl. -S a thick soup

POTAMIC *adj* pertaining to rivers

POTASH *n* pl. -ES an alkaline compound

POTASSIC *adj* pertaining to potassium (a metallic element)

POTATION *n* pl. -S the act of drinking

POTATO *n* pl. -TOES the edible tuber of a cultivated plant

POTATORY *adj* pertaining to drinking

POTBELLY *n* pl. -LIES a protruding abdominal region

POTBOIL *v* -ED, -ING, -S to produce a literary or artistic work of poor quality

POTBOY *n* pl. -BOYS a boy who serves customers in a tavern

POTEEN *n* pl. -S Irish whiskey that is distilled unlawfully

POTENCE *n* pl. -S potency

POTENCY *n* pl. -CIES the quality of being potent

POTENT *adj* powerful **POTENTLY** *adv*

POTFUL *n* pl. -S as much as a pot can hold

POTHEAD *n* pl. -S one who smokes marijuana

POTHEEN *n* pl. -S poteen

POTHER *v* -ED, -ING, -S to trouble

POTHERB *n* pl. -S any herb used as a food or seasoning

POTHOLE *n* pl. -S a deep hole in a road **POTHOLED** *adj*

POTHOOK *n* pl. -S a hook for lifting or hanging pots

POTHOUSE *n* pl. -S a tavern

POTICHE *n* pl. -S a type of vase

POTION *n* pl. -S a magical or medicinal drink

POTLACH *n* pl. -ES a ceremonial feast

POTLACHE *n* pl. -S potlach

POTLATCH *v* -ED, -ING, -ES to hold a ceremonial feast for

POTLIKE *adj* resembling a pot

POTLUCK *n* pl. -S food which is incidentally available

POTMAN *n* pl. -MEN a man who serves customers in a tavern

POTPIE *n* pl. -S a deep-dish pie containing meat and vegetables

POTSHARD *n* pl. -S potsherd

POTSHERD *n* pl. -S a fragment of broken pottery

POTSHOT *v* -SHOT, -SHOTTING, -SHOTS to shoot randomly at

POTSIE *n* pl. -S potsy

POTSTONE *n* pl. -S a variety of steatite

POTSY *n* pl. -SIES a children's game

POTTAGE *n* pl. -S a thick soup

POTTED past tense of pot

POTTEEN *n* pl. -S poteen

POTTER *v* -ED, -ING, -S to putter

POTTERER *n* pl. -S one that potters

POTTERY *n* pl. -TERIES ware molded from clay and hardened by heat

POTTIER comparative of potty

POTTIES pl. of potty

POTTIEST superlative of potty

POTTING present participle of pot

POTTLE *n* pl. -S a drinking vessel

POTTO *n* pl. -TOS a lemur of tropical Africa

POTTY *adj* -TIER, -TIEST of little importance

POTTY *n* pl. -TIES a small toilet seat

POUCH *v* -ED, -ING, -ES to put in a pouch (a small, flexible receptacle)

POUCHY *adj* POUCHIER, POUCHIEST resembling a pouch

POUF *n* pl. -S a loose roll of hair **POUFED** *adj*

POUFF *n* pl. -S pouf **POUFFED** *adj*

POUFFE *n* pl. -S pouf

POULARD *n* pl. -S a spayed hen

POULARDE *n* pl. -S poulard

POULT *n* pl. -S a young domestic fowl

POULTICE *v* -TICED, -TICING, -TICES to apply a healing substance to

POULTRY *n* pl. -TRIES domestic fowls kept for eggs or meat

POUNCE *v* POUNCED, POUNCING, POUNCES to make a sudden assault or approach

POUNCER *n* pl. -S one that pounces

POUND *v* -ED, -ING, -S to strike heavily and repeatedly

POUNDAGE *n* pl. -S the act of impounding

POUNDAL *n* pl. -S a unit of force

POUNDER *n* pl. -S one that pounds

POUR *v* -ED, -ING, -S to cause to flow **POURABLE** *adj*

POURER *n* pl. -S one that pours

POUSSIE *n* pl. -S pussy

POUT *v* -ED, -ING, -S to protrude the lips in ill humor

POUTER *n* pl. -S one that pouts

POUTFUL *adj* pouty

POUTY *adj* POUTIER, POUTIEST tending to pout

POVERTY *n* pl. -TIES the state of being poor

POW *n* pl. -S an explosive sound

POWDER *v* -ED, -ING, -S to reduce to powder (matter in a finely divided state)

POWDERER *n* pl. -S one that powders

POWDERY *adj* resembling powder

POWER *v* -ED, -ING, -S to provide with means of propulsion

POWERFUL *adj* possessing great force

POWTER *n* pl. -S a domestic pigeon

POWWOW *v* -ED, -ING, -S to hold a conference

POX *v* -ED, -ING, -ES to infect with syphilis

POXVIRUS *n* pl. -ES a type of virus

POYOU *n* pl. -S an armadillo of Argentina

POZZOLAN *n* pl. -S a finely divided material used to make cement

PRAAM *n* pl. -S pram

PRACTIC *adj* practical

PRACTICE *v* -TICED, -TICING, -TICES to perform often so as to acquire skill

PRACTISE *v* -TISED, -TISING, -TISES to practice

PRAECIPE *n* pl. -S a legal writ

PRAEDIAL *adj* pertaining to land

PRAEFECT *n* pl. -S prefect

PRAELECT *v* -ED, -ING, -S to prelect

PRAETOR *n* pl. -S an ancient Roman magistrate

PRAHU *n* pl. -S prau

PRAIRIE *n* pl. -S a tract of grassland

PRAISE *v* PRAISED, PRAISING, PRAISES to express approval or admiration of

PRAISER *n* pl. -S one that praises

PRALINE *n* pl. -S a confection made of nuts cooked in sugar

PRAM *n* pl. -S a flat-bottomed boat

PRANCE *v* PRANCED, PRANCING, PRANCES to spring forward on the hind legs

PRANCER *n* pl. -S one that prances

PRANDIAL *adj* pertaining to a meal

PRANG *v* -ED, -ING, -S to cause to crash

PRANK *v* -ED, -ING, -S to adorn gaudily

PRANKISH *adj* mischievous

PRAO *n* pl. PRAOS prau

PRASE *n* pl. -S a mineral

PRAT *n* pl. -S the buttocks

PRATE *v* PRATED, PRATING, PRATES to chatter

PRATER *n* pl. -S one that prates

PRATFALL *n* pl. -S a fall on the buttocks

PRATING present participle of prate

PRATIQUE *n* pl. -S clearance given a ship by the health authority of a port

PRATTLE *v* -TLED, -TLING, -TLES to babble

PRATTLER *n* pl. -S one that prattles

PRAU *n* pl. -S a swift Malaysian sailing vessel

PRAWN *v* -ED, -ING, -S to fish for prawns (edible shellfishes)

PRAWNER *n* pl. -S one that prawns

PRAXIS *n* pl. PRAXISES or PRAXES practical use of a branch of learning

PRAY *v* -ED, -ING, -S to address prayers to

PRAYER *n* pl. -S a devout petition to a deity

PREACH *v* -ED, -ING, -ES to advocate or recommend urgently

PREACHER *n* pl. -S one that preaches

PREACHY *adj* PREACHIER, PREACHIEST tending to preach

PREACT *v* -ED, -ING, -S to act beforehand

PREADAPT *v* -ED, -ING, -S to adapt beforehand

PREADMIT *v* -MITTED, -MITTING, -MITS to admit beforehand

PREADOPT *v* -ED, -ING, -S to adopt beforehand

PREADULT *adj* preceding adulthood

PREAGED *adj* previously aged

PREALLOT *v* -LOTTED, -LOTTING, -LOTS to allot beforehand

PREAMBLE *n* pl. -S an introductory statement

PREAMP *n* pl. -S an amplifier

PREANAL *adj* situated in front of the anus

PREARM *v* -ED, -ING, -S to arm beforehand

PREAVER *v* -VERRED, -VERRING, -VERS to aver or assert beforehand

PREAXIAL *adj* situated in front of an axis

PREBASAL *adj* situated in front of a base

PREBEND *n* pl. -S a clergyman's stipend

PREBILL *v* -ED, -ING, -S to bill beforehand

PREBIND *v* -BOUND, -BINDING, -BINDS to bind in durable materials for library use

PREBLESS *v* -ED, -ING, -ES to bless beforehand

PREBOIL *v* -ED, -ING, -S to boil beforehand

PREBOUND past tense of prebind

PRECAST *v* -CAST, -CASTING, -CASTS to cast and finish before placing into position

PRECAVA *n* pl. -VAE a vein in higher vertebrates **PRECAVAL** *adj*

PRECEDE *v* -CEDED, -CEDING, -CEDES to go before

PRECENT *v* -ED, -ING, -S to lead a church choir in singing

PRECEPT *n* pl. -S a rule of conduct

PRECESS *v* -ED, -ING, -ES to rotate with a complex motion

PRECHECK *v* -ED, -ING, -S to check beforehand

PRECHILL *v* -ED, -ING, -S to chill beforehand

PRECIEUX *adj* excessively refined

PRECINCT *n* pl. -S a subdivision of a city or town

PRECIOUS *n* pl. -ES a darling

PRECIPE *n* pl. -S praecipe

PRECIS *v* -ED, -ING, -ES to make a concise summary of

PRECISE *adj* -CISER, -CISEST sharply and clearly defined or stated

PRECITED *adj* previously cited

PRECLEAN *v* -ED, -ING, -S to clean beforehand

PRECLUDE *v* -CLUDED, -CLUDING, -CLUDES to make impossible by previous action

PRECOOK *v* -ED, -ING, -S to cook beforehand

PRECOOL *v* -ED, -ING, -S to cool beforehand

PRECURE *v* -CURED, -CURING, -CURES to cure beforehand

PREDATE *v* -DATED, -DATING, -DATES to date before the actual or a specified time

PREDATOR *n* pl. -S one that plunders

PREDAWN *n* pl. -S the time just before dawn

PREDIAL *adj* praedial

PREDICT *v* -ED, -ING, -S to tell of or about in advance

PREDUSK *n* pl. -S the time just before dusk

PREE *v* PREED, PREEING, PREES to test by tasting

PREELECT *v* -ED, -ING, -S to elect or choose beforehand

PREEMIE *n* pl. -S an infant born prematurely

PREEMPT *v* -ED, -ING, -S to acquire by prior right

PREEN *v* -ED, -ING, -S to smooth or clean with the beak or tongue

PREENACT *v* -ED, -ING, -S to enact beforehand

PREENER *n* pl. -S one that preens

PREEXIST *v* -ED, -ING, -S to exist before

PREFAB *v* -FABBED, -FABBING, FABS to construct beforehand

PREFACE *v* -ACED, -ACING, -ACES to provide with an introductory statement

PREFACER *n* pl. -S one that prefaces

PREFECT *n* pl. -S an ancient Roman official

PREFER *v* -FERRED, -FERRING, -FERS to hold in higher regard or esteem

PREFIX *v* -ED, -ING, -ES to add as a prefix (a form affixed to the beginning of a root word)

PREFIXAL *adj* pertaining to or being a prefix

PREFOCUS *v* -CUSED, -CUSING, -CUSES or -CUSSED, -CUSSING, -CUSSES to focus beforehand

PREFORM *v* -ED, -ING, -S to form beforehand

PREFRANK *v* -ED, -ING, -S to frank beforehand

PREGAME *adj* preceding a game

PREGNANT *adj* carrying a developing fetus in the uterus

PREHEAT *v* -ED, -ING, -S to heat beforehand

PREHUMAN *n* pl. -S a prototype of man

PREJUDGE *v* -JUDGED, -JUDGING, -JUDGES to judge beforehand

PRELACY *n* pl. -CIES the office of a prelate

PRELATE *n* pl. -S a high-ranking clergyman **PRELATIC** *adj*

PRELECT *v* -ED, -ING, -S to lecture

PRELEGAL *adj* occurring before the commencement of studies in law

PRELIM *n* pl. -S a minor match preceding the main event

PRELIMIT *v* -ED, -ING, -S to limit beforehand

PRELUDE *v* -LUDED, -LUDING, -LUDES to play a musical introduction

PRELUDER *n* pl. -S one that preludes

PREMAN *n* pl. -MEN a hypothetical ancestor of man

PREMED *n* pl. -S a student preparing for the study of medicine

PREMEDIC *n* pl. -S a premed

PREMEN pl. of preman

PREMIE *n* pl. -S preemie

PREMIER *n* pl. -S a prime minister

PREMIERE *v* -MIERED, -MIERING, -MIERES to present publicly for the first time

PREMISE *v* -MISED, -MISING, -MISES to state in advance

PREMISS *n* pl. -ES a proposition in logic

PREMIUM *n* pl. -S an additional payment

PREMIX *v* -ED, -ING, -ES to mix before use

PREMOLAR *n* pl. -S a tooth

PREMORSE *adj* ending abruptly, as if bitten off

PREMUNE *adj* resistant to a disease

PRENAME *n* pl. -S a forename

PRENATAL adj prior to birth

PRENOMEN n pl. -MENS or -MINA the first name of an ancient Roman

PRENTICE v -TICED, -TICING, -TICES to place with an employer for instruction in a trade

PREP v PREPPED, PREPPING, PREPS to attend a preparatory school

PREPACK v -ED, -ING, -S to package before retail distribution

PREPAID past tense of prepay

PREPARE v -PARED, -PARING, -PARES to put in proper condition or readiness

PREPARER n pl. -S one that prepares

PREPAY v -PAID, -PAYING, -PAYS to pay in advance

PREPENSE adj planned in advance

PREPLACE v -PLACED, -PLACING, -PLACES to place beforehand

PREPLAN v -PLANNED, -PLANNING, -PLANS to plan in advance

PREPLANT adj occurring before planting

PREPPED past tense of prep

PREPPIE n pl. -S one who preps

PREPPING present participle of prep

PREPRINT v -ED, -ING, -S to print in advance

PREPUCE n pl. -S a fold of skin covering the penis

PREPUNCH v -ED, -ING, -ES to punch in advance

PRERENAL adj situated in front of the kidney

PRESA n pl. -SE a musical symbol

PRESAGE v -SAGED, -SAGING, -SAGES to foretell

PRESAGER n pl. -S one that presages

PRESCIND v -ED, -ING, -S to consider separately

PRESCORE v -SCORED, -SCORING, -SCORES to record the sound of before filming

PRESE pl. of presa

PRESELL v -SOLD, -SELLING, -SELLS to promote a product not yet being sold to the public

PRESENCE n pl. -S close proximity

PRESENT v -ED, -ING, -S to bring into the presence of someone

PRESERVE v -SERVED, -SERVING, -SERVES to keep free from harm or danger

PRESET v -SET, -SETTING, -SETS to set beforehand

PRESHAPE v -SHAPED, -SHAPING, -SHAPES to shape beforehand

PRESHOW v -SHOWED, -SHOWN, -SHOWING, -SHOWS to show beforehand

PRESIDE v -SIDED, -SIDING, -SIDES to occupy the position of authority

PRESIDER n pl. -S one that presides

PRESIDIA n/pl Soviet executive committees

PRESIDIO n pl. -DIOS a Spanish fort

PRESIFT v -ED, -ING, -S to sift beforehand

PRESOAK v -ED, -ING, -S to soak beforehand

PRESOLD past tense of presell

PRESS v -ED, -ING, -ES to act upon with steady force

PRESSER n pl. -S one that presses

PRESSMAN n pl. -MEN a printing press operator

PRESSOR adj causing an increase in blood pressure

PRESSRUN n pl. -S a continuous operation of a printing press

PRESSURE v -SURED, -SURING, -SURES to apply force to

PREST n pl. -S a loan

PRESTAMP v -ED, -ING, -S to stamp beforehand

PRESTER n pl. -S a priest

PRESTIGE n pl. -S distinction or reputation in the eyes of people

PRESTO n pl. -TOS a musical passage played in rapid tempo

PRESUME v -SUMED, -SUMING, -SUMES to take for granted

PRESUMER n pl. -S one that presumes

PRETASTE v -TASTED, -TASTING, -TASTES to taste beforehand

PRETAX adj existing before provision for taxes

PRETEEN n pl. -S a child under the age of thirteen

PRETENCE n pl. -S pretense

PRETEND v -ED, -ING, -S to assume or display a false appearance of

PRETENSE	*n* pl. -S the act of pretending
PRETERIT	*n* pl. -S a past tense in grammar
PRETEST	*v* -ED, -ING, -S to give a preliminary test to
PRETEXT	*v* -ED, -ING, -S to allege as an excuse
PRETOR	*n* pl. -S praetor
PRETREAT	*v* -ED, -ING, -S to treat beforehand
PRETTIED	past tense of pretty
PRETTIER	comparative of pretty
PRETTIES	present 3d person sing. of pretty
PRETTIEST	superlative of pretty
PRETTIFY	*v* -FIED, -FYING, -FIES to make pretty
PRETTY	*v* -TIED, -TYING, -TIES to make pretty
PRETTY	*adj* -TIER, -TIEST pleasing to the eye **PRETTILY** *adv*
PRETZEL	*n* pl. -S a glazed, salted cracker
PREUNION	*n* pl. -S a union beforehand
PREUNITE	*v* -UNITED, -UNITING, -UNITES to unite beforehand
PREVAIL	*v* -ED, -ING, -S to triumph
PREVENT	*v* -ED, -ING, -S to keep from happening
PREVIEW	*v* -ED, -ING, -S to view or exhibit in advance
PREVIOUS	*adj* coming or occurring before in time or order
PREVISE	*v* -VISED, -VISING, -VISES to foresee
PREVISOR	*n* pl. -S one that previses
PREVUE	*v* -VUED, -VUING, -VUES to preview
PREWAR	*adj* occurring or existing before a war
PREWARM	*v* -ED, -ING, -S to warm beforehand
PREWARN	*v* -ED, -ING, -S to warn in advance
PREWASH	*v* -ED, -ING, -ES to wash beforehand
PREWRAP	*v* -WRAPPED, -WRAPPING, -WRAPS to wrap beforehand
PREX	*n* pl. -ES prexy
PREXY	*n* pl. PREXIES a president
PREY	*v* -ED, -ING, -S to seize and devour animals for food

PREYER	*n* pl. -S one that preys
PRIAPEAN	*adj* priapic
PRIAPI	a pl. of priapus
PRIAPIC	*adj* phallic
PRIAPISM	*n* pl. -S a persistent erection of the penis
PRIAPUS	*n* pl. -PUSES or -PI a representation of the phallus
PRICE	*v* PRICED, PRICING, PRICES to set a value on
PRICER	*n* pl. -S one that prices
PRICEY	*adj* PRICIER, PRICIEST expensive
PRICIER	comparative of pricey and pricy
PRICIEST	superlative of pricey and pricy
PRICING	present participle of price
PRICK	*v* -ED, -ING, -S to puncture slightly
PRICKER	*n* pl. -S one that pricks
PRICKET	*n* pl. -S a spike for holding a candle upright
PRICKIER	comparative of pricky
PRICKIEST	superlative of pricky
PRICKLE	*v* -LED, -LING, -LES to prick
PRICKLY	*adj* -LIER, -LIEST having many sharp points
PRICKY	*adj* PRICKIER, PRICKIEST prickly
PRICY	*adj* PRICIER, PRICIEST pricey
PRIDE	*v* PRIDED, PRIDING, PRIDES to feel pride (a feeling of self-esteem)
PRIDEFUL	*adj* full of pride
PRIED	past tense of pry
PRIEDIEU	*n* pl. -DIEUS or -DIEUX a piece of furniture for kneeling on during prayer
PRIER	*n* pl. -S one that pries
PRIES	present 3d person sing. of pry
PRIEST	*v* -ED, -ING, -S to ordain as a priest (one authorized to perform religious rites)
PRIESTLY	*adj* -LIER, -LIEST characteristic of or befitting a priest
PRIG	*v* PRIGGED, PRIGGING, PRIGS to steal
PRIGGERY	*n* pl. -GERIES priggism
PRIGGISH	*adj* marked by priggism
PRIGGISM	*n* pl. -S prim adherence to convention

PRILL	*v* -ED, -ING, -S to convert into pellets
PRIM	*adj* PRIMMER, PRIMMEST formally precise or proper
PRIM	*v* PRIMMED, PRIMMING, PRIMS to give a prim expression to
PRIMA	*n* pl. -S primo
PRIMACY	*n* pl. -CIES the state of being first
PRIMAGE	*n* pl. -S an amount paid as an addition to freight charges
PRIMAL	*adj* being at the beginning or foundation
PRIMARY	*n* pl. -RIES a preliminary election
PRIMATE	*n* pl. -S any of an advanced order of mammals **PRIMATAL** *adj*
PRIME	*v* PRIMED, PRIMING, PRIMES to make ready
PRIMELY	*adv* excellently
PRIMER	*n* pl. -S a book that covers the basics of a subject
PRIMERO	*n* pl. -ROS a card game
PRIMEVAL	*adj* pertaining to the earliest ages
PRIMI	a pl. of primo
PRIMINE	*n* pl. -S the outer covering of an ovule
PRIMING	*n* pl. -S the act of one that primes
PRIMLY	*adv* in a prim manner
PRIMMED	past tense of prim
PRIMMER	comparative of prim
PRIMMEST	superlative of prim
PRIMMING	present participle of prim
PRIMNESS	*n* pl. -ES the state of being prim
PRIMO	*n* pl. -MOS or -MI the main part in a musical piece
PRIMP	*v* -ED, -ING, -S to dress or adorn carefully
PRIMROSE	*n* pl. -S a perennial herb
PRIMSIE	*adj* prim
PRIMULA	*n* pl. -S primrose
PRIMUS	*n* pl. -ES the head bishop of Scotland
PRINCE	*n* pl. -S a non-reigning male member of a royal family
PRINCELY	*adj* -LIER, -LIEST of or befitting a prince
PRINCESS	*n* pl. -ES a non-reigning female member of a royal family
PRINCIPE	*n* pl. -PI a prince
PRINCOCK	*n* pl. -S a coxcomb
PRINCOX	*n* pl. -ES princock
PRINK	*v* -ED, -ING, -S to dress or adorn in a showy manner
PRINKER	*n* pl. -S one that prinks
PRINT	*v* -ED, -ING, -S to produce by pressed type on a surface
PRINTER	*n* pl. -S one that prints
PRINTERY	*n* pl. -ERIES a place where printing is done
PRINTING	*n* pl. -S a reproduction from a printing surface
PRINTOUT	*n* pl. -S the printed output of a computer
PRIOR	*n* pl. -S an officer in a monastery
PRIORATE	*n* pl. -S the office of a prior
PRIORESS	*n* pl. -ES a nun corresponding in rank to a prior
PRIORIES	pl. of priory
PRIORITY	*n* pl. -TIES precedence established by importance
PRIORLY	*adv* previously
PRIORY	*n* pl. -RIES a religious house
PRISE	*v* PRISED, PRISING, PRISES to raise or force with a lever
PRISERE	*n* pl. -S a succession of vegetational stages
PRISM	*n* pl. -S a solid which disperses light into a spectrum
PRISMOID	*n* pl. -S a geometric solid
PRISON	*v* -ED, -ING, -S to imprison
PRISONER	*n* pl. -S one that is imprisoned
PRISS	*n* pl. -ES a prissy
PRISSY	*adj* -SIER, -SIEST excessively or affectedly proper **PRISSILY** *adv*
PRISSY	*n* pl. -SIES one who is prissy
PRISTANE	*n* pl. -S a chemical compound
PRISTINE	*adj* pertaining to the earliest time or state
PRITHEE	*interj* — used to express a wish or request
PRIVACY	*n* pl. -CIES the state of being private
PRIVATE	*adj* -VATER, -VATEST secluded from the sight, presence, or intrusion of others

PRIVATE   *n* pl. -S a soldier of lower rank

PRIVET   *n* pl. -S an ornamental shrub

PRIVIER   comparative of privy

PRIVIES   pl. of privy

PRIVITY   *n* pl. -TIES private knowledge

PRIVY   *adj* PRIVIER, PRIVIEST private **PRIVILY** *adv*

PRIVY   *n* pl. PRIVIES an outhouse

PRIZE   *v* PRIZED, PRIZING, PRIZES to value highly

PRIZER   *n* pl. -S one who vies for a reward

PRO   *n* pl. PROS an argument or vote in favor of something

PROA   *n* pl. -S prau

PROBABLE   *adj* likely to occur or prove true **PROBABLY** *adv*

PROBAND   *n* pl. -S one whose reactions or responses are studied

PROBANG   *n* pl. -S a surgical rod

PROBATE   *v* -BATED, -BATING, -BATES to establish the validity of

PROBE   *v* PROBED, PROBING, PROBES to investigate or examine thoroughly

PROBER   *n* pl. -S one that probes

PROBIT   *n* pl. -S a unit of statistical probability

PROBITY   *n* pl. -TIES complete and confirmed integrity

PROBLEM   *n* pl. -S a perplexing question or situation

PROCAINE   *n* pl. -S a compound used as a local anesthetic

PROCARP   *n* pl. -S a female sexual organ in certain algae

PROCEED   *v* -ED, -ING, -S to go forward or onward

PROCESS   *v* -ED, -ING, -ES to treat or prepare by a special method

PROCHAIN   *adj* prochein

PROCHEIN   *adj* nearest in time, relation, or degree

PROCLAIM   *v* -ED, -ING, -S to make known publicly or officially

PROCTOR   *v* -ED, -ING, -S to supervise

PROCURAL   *n* pl. -S the act of procuring

PROCURE   *v* -CURED, -CURING, -CURES to obtain by effort

PROCURER   *n* pl. -S one that procures

PROD   *v* PRODDED, PRODDING, PRODS to jab with something pointed

PRODDER   *n* pl. -S one that prods

PRODIGAL   *n* pl. -S one who spends lavishly and foolishly

PRODIGY   *n* pl. -GIES a child having exceptional talent or ability

PRODROME   *n* pl. -DROMES or -DROMATA a sign of impending disease

PRODUCE   *v* -DUCED, -DUCING, -DUCES to bring into existence

PRODUCER   *n* pl. -S one that produces

PRODUCT   *n* pl. -S something produced by labor or effort

PROEM   *n* pl. -S an introductory statement **PROEMIAL** *adj*

PROETTE   *n* pl. -S a female professional athlete

PROF   *n* pl. -S a professor

PROFANE   *v* -FANED, -FANING, -FANES to treat with irreverence or abuse

PROFANER   *n* pl. -S one that profanes

PROFESS   *v* -ED, -ING, -ES to affirm openly

PROFFER   *v* -ED, -ING, -S to present for acceptance

PROFILE   *v* -FILED, -FILING, -FILES to draw an outline of

PROFILER   *n* pl. -S one that profiles

PROFIT   *v* -ED, -ING, -S to gain an advantage or benefit

PROFITER   *n* pl. -S one that profits

PROFOUND   *adj* -FOUNDER, -FOUNDEST intellectually deep and penetrating

PROFOUND   *n* pl. -S something that is very deep

PROFUSE   *adj* pouring forth generously

PROG   *v* PROGGED, PROGGING, PROGS to prowl about for food or plunder

PROGENY   *n* pl. -NIES a descendant or offspring

PROGGER   *n* pl. -S one that progs

PROGGING   present participle of prog

PROGNOSE   *v* -NOSED, -NOSING, -NOSES to forecast the probable course of a disease

PROGRADE   *adj* pertaining to the orbital motion of a body

PROGRAM   v -GRAMED, -GRAMING, -GRAMS or -GRAMMED, -GRAMMING, -GRAMS to arrange in a plan of proceedings

PROGRESS   v -ED, -ING, -ES to move forward or onward

PROHIBIT   v -ED, -ING, -S to forbid by authority

PROJECT   v -ED, -ING, -S to extend outward

PROJET   n pl. -S a plan or outline

PROLABOR   adj favoring organized labor

PROLAMIN   n pl. -S a simple protein

PROLAN   n pl. -S a sex hormone

PROLAPSE   v -LAPSED, -LAPSING, -LAPSES to fall or slip out of place

PROLATE   adj extended lengthwise

PROLE   n pl. -S a member of the working class

PROLEG   n pl. -S an abdominal leg of certain insect larvae

PROLIFIC   adj producing abundantly

PROLINE   n pl. -S an amino acid

PROLIX   adj tediously long and wordy **PROLIXLY** adv

PROLOG   v -ED, -ING, -S to prologue

PROLOGUE   v -LOGUED, -LOGUING, -LOGUES to preface

PROLONG   v -ED, -ING, -S to lengthen in duration

PROLONGE   n pl. -S a rope used for pulling a gun carriage

PROM   n pl. -S a formal dance

PROMISE   v -ISED, -ISING, -ISES to make a declaration of assurance

PROMISEE   n pl. -S one who is promised something

PROMISER   n pl. -S promisor

PROMISING   present participle of promise

PROMISOR   n pl. -S one that promises

PROMOTE   v -MOTED, -MOTING, -MOTES to contribute to the progress of

PROMOTER   n pl. -S one that promotes

PROMPT   adj PROMPTER, PROMPTEST quick to act or respond

PROMPT   v -ED, -ING, -S to induce to action

PROMPTER   n pl. -S one that prompts

PROMPTLY   adv in a prompt manner

PROMULGE   v -MULGED, -MULGING, -MULGES to proclaim

PRONATE   v -NATED, -NATING, -NATES to turn the palm downward or backward

PRONATOR   n pl. -S or -ES a forearm or forelimb muscle

PRONE   adj lying with the front or face downward **PRONELY** adv

PRONG   v -ED, -ING, -S to pierce with a pointed projection

PRONOTUM   n pl. -NOTA a hard outer plate of an insect

PRONOUN   n pl. -S a word that may be used in place of a noun

PRONTO   adv quickly

PROOF   v -ED, -ING, -S to examine for errors

PROOFER   n pl. -S one that proofs

PROP   v PROPPED, PROPPING, PROPS to keep from falling

PROPANE   n pl. -S a flammable gas

PROPEL   v -PELLED, -PELLING, -PELS to cause to move forward or onward

PROPEND   v -ED, -ING, -S to have a tendency toward

PROPENE   n pl. -S a flammable gas

PROPENOL   n pl. -S a flammable liquid

PROPENSE   adj tending toward

PROPENYL   adj pertaining to a certain chemical group

PROPER   adj -ERER, -EREST suitable **PROPERLY** adv

PROPER   n pl. -S a portion of the Mass

PROPERTY   n pl. -TIES something owned

PROPHAGE   n pl. -S a form of virus

PROPHASE   n pl. -S the first stage in mitosis

PROPHECY   n pl. -CIES a prediction

PROPHESY   v -SIED, -SYING, -SIES to predict

PROPHET   n pl. -S one who predicts

PROPINE   v -PINED, -PINING, -PINES to offer as a gift

PROPJET   n pl. -S a type of airplane

PROPMAN   n pl. -MEN a man in charge of stage properties

PROPOLIS   n pl. -LISES a resinous substance used as a cement by bees

PROPONE	*v* -PONED, -PONING, -PONES to propose
PROPOSAL	*n* pl. -S something that is proposed
PROPOSE	*v* -POSED, -POSING, -POSES to put forward for consideration or acceptance
PROPOSER	*n* pl. -S one that proposes
PROPOUND	*v* -ED, -ING, -S to propose
PROPPED	past tense of prop
PROPPING	present participle of prop
PROPYL	*n* pl. -S a univalent radical **PROPYLIC** *adj*
PROPYLON	*n* pl. -LA an entrance to a temple
PRORATE	*v* -RATED, -RATING, -RATES to divide proportionately
PROROGUE	*v* -ROGUED, -ROGUING, -ROGUES to discontinue a session of
PROSAIC	*adj* pertaining to prose
PROSAISM	*n* pl. -S a prosaic style
PROSAIST	*n* pl. -S a writer of prose
PROSE	*v* PROSED, PROSING, PROSES to write prose (writing without metrical structure)
PROSECT	*v* -ED, -ING, -S to dissect
PROSER	*n* pl. -S a prosaist
PROSIER	comparative of prosy
PROSIEST	superlative of prosy
PROSILY	*adv* in a prosy manner
PROSING	present participle of prose
PROSIT	*interj* — used as a drinking toast
PROSO	*n* pl. -SOS millet
PROSODY	*n* pl. -DIES the study of poetical forms **PROSODIC** *adj*
PROSOMA	*n* pl. -S the front region of the body of an invertebrate **PROSOMAL** *adj*
PROSPECT	*v* -ED, -ING, -S to explore for mineral deposits
PROSPER	*v* -ED, -ING, -S to be successful or fortunate
PROST	*interj* prosit
PROSTATE	*n* pl. -S a gland in male mammals
PROSTYLE	*n* pl. -S a building having a row of columns across the front only
PROSY	*adj* PROSIER, PROSIEST prosaic

PROTAMIN	*n* pl. -S a simple protein
PROTASIS	*n* pl. -ASES the introductory part of a classical drama **PROTATIC** *adj*
PROTEA	*n* pl. -S an evergreen shrub
PROTEAN	*adj* readily taking on different shapes or forms
PROTEASE	*n* pl. -S an enzyme
PROTECT	*v* -ED, -ING, -S to keep from harm, attack, or injury
PROTEGE	*n* pl. -S one whose career is promoted by an influential person
PROTEGEE	*n* pl. -S a female protege
PROTEI	pl. of proteus
PROTEID	*n* pl. -S protein
PROTEIDE	*n* pl. -S proteid
PROTEIN	*n* pl. -S a nitrogenous organic compound
PROTEND	*v* -ED, -ING, -S to extend
PROTEOSE	*n* pl. -S a water-soluble protein
PROTEST	*v* -ED, -ING, -S to express strong objection
PROTEUS	*n* pl. -TEI any of a genus of aerobic bacteria
PROTIST	*n* pl. -S any of a group of unicellular organisms
PROTIUM	*n* pl. -S an isotope of hydrogen
PROTOCOL	*v* -COLED, -COLING, -COLS or -COLLED, -COLLING, -COLS to form a preliminary draft of an official document
PROTON	*n* pl. -S an atomic particle **PROTONIC** *adj*
PROTOPOD	*n* pl. -S a part of a crustacean appendage
PROTOXID	*n* pl. -S an oxide
PROTOZOA	*n/pl* unicellular microscopic organisms
PROTRACT	*v* -ED, -ING, -S to prolong
PROTRUDE	*v* -TRUDED, -TRUDING, -TRUDES to extend beyond the main portion
PROTYL	*n* pl. -S protyle
PROTYLE	*n* pl. -S a hypothetical substance from which all the elements are supposedly derived
PROUD	*adj* PROUDER, PROUDEST having or displaying pride **PROUDLY** *adv*
PROUDFUL	*adj* prideful

PROUNION	*adj* favoring labor unions
PROVE	*v* PROVED, PROVEN, PROVING, PROVES to establish the truth or validity of **PROVABLE** *adj* **PROVABLY** *adv*
PROVENLY	*adv* without doubt
PROVER	*n* pl. -S one that proves
PROVERB	*v* -ED, -ING, -S to make a byword of
PROVIDE	*v* -VIDED, -VIDING, -VIDES to supply
PROVIDER	*n* pl. -S one that provides
PROVINCE	*n* pl. -S an administrative division of a country
PROVING	present participle of prove
PROVIRUS	*n* pl. -ES a form of virus **PROVIRAL** *adj*
PROVISO	*n* pl. -SOS or -SOES a clause in a document introducing a condition or restriction
PROVOKE	*v* -VOKED, -VOKING, -VOKES to incite to anger or resentment
PROVOKER	*n* pl. -S one that provokes
PROVOST	*n* pl. -S a high-ranking university official
PROW	*n* pl. -S the forward part of a ship
PROW	*adj* PROWER, PROWEST brave
PROWAR	*adj* favoring war
PROWESS	*n* pl. -ES exceptional ability
PROWL	*v* -ED, -ING, -S to move about stealthily
PROWLER	*n* pl. -S one that prowls
PROXEMIC	*adj* pertaining to a branch of environmental study
PROXIES	pl. of proxy
PROXIMAL	*adj* located near the point of origin
PROXIMO	*adj* of or occurring in the following month
PROXY	*n* pl. PROXIES a person authorized to act for another
PRUDE	*n* pl. -S a prudish person
PRUDENCE	*n* pl. -S the quality of being prudent
PRUDENT	*adj* having, showing, or exercising good judgment
PRUDERY	*n* pl. -ERIES excessive regard for propriety, modesty, or morality
PRUDISH	*adj* marked by prudery
PRUINOSE	*adj* having a powdery covering
PRUNE	*v* PRUNED, PRUNING, PRUNES to cut off branches or parts from **PRUNABLE** *adj*
PRUNELLA	*n* pl. -S a strong woolen fabric
PRUNELLE	*n* pl. -S a plum-flavored liqueur
PRUNELLO	*n* pl. -LOS prunella
PRUNER	*n* pl. -S one that prunes
PRUNING	present participle of prune
PRURIENT	*adj* having lustful thoughts or desires
PRURIGO	*n* pl. -GOS a skin disease
PRURITUS	*n* pl. -ES intense itching **PRURITIC** *adj*
PRUSSIC	*adj* pertaining to a type of acid
PRUTA	*n* pl. PRUTOT prutah
PRUTAH	*n* pl. PRUTOTH a monetary unit of Israel
PRY	*v* PRIED, PRYING, PRIES to inquire impertinently into private matters **PRYINGLY** *adv*
PRYER	*n* pl. -S prier
PRYTHEE	*interj* prithee
PSALM	*v* -ED, -ING, -S to praise in psalms (sacred songs)
PSALMIC	*adj* of or pertaining to a psalm
PSALMIST	*n* pl. -S a writer of psalms
PSALMODY	*n* pl. -DIES the use of psalms in worship
PSALTER	*n* pl. -S a book of psalms
PSALTERY	*n* pl. -TERIES an ancient stringed musical instrument
PSALTRY	*n* pl. -TRIES psaltery
PSAMMITE	*n* pl. -S a fine-grained rock
PSCHENT	*n* pl. -S a crown worn by ancient Egyptian kings
PSEPHITE	*n* pl. -S a rock composed of small pebbles
PSEUDO	*adj* false or counterfeit
PSHAW	*v* -ED, -ING, -S to utter an expression of disapproval
PSI	*n* pl. -S a Greek letter
PSILOSIS	*n* pl. -LOSES a tropical disease **PSILOTIC** *adj*
PSOAS	*n* pl. PSOAI or PSOAE a muscle of the loin
PSOCID	*n* pl. -S a minute winged insect
PSORALEA	*n* pl. -S a plant of the bean family

PSST	*interj* — used to attract someone's attention
PSYCH	*v* -ED, -ING, -S to put into the proper frame of mind
PSYCHE	*n* pl. -S the mental structure of a person
PSYCHIC	*n* pl. -S one sensitive to extrasensory phenomena
PSYCHO	*n* pl. -CHOS a mentally unstable person
PSYLLA	*n* pl. -S any of various plant lice
PSYLLID	*n* pl. -S psylla
PTERIN	*n* pl. -S a chemical compound
PTEROPOD	*n* pl. -S a type of mollusk
PTERYLA	*n* pl. -LAE a feathered area on the skin of a bird
PTISAN	*n* pl. -S a tea of herbs or barley
PTOMAIN	*n* pl. -S ptomaine
PTOMAINE	*n* pl. -S a compound produced by the decomposition of protein
PTOSIS	*n* pl. PTOSES a drooping of the upper eyelid **PTOTIC** *adj*
PTYALIN	*n* pl. -S a salivary enzyme
PTYALISM	*n* pl. -S an excessive flow of saliva
PUB	*n* pl. -S a tavern
PUBERTY	*n* pl. -TIES a period of sexual maturation **PUBERAL, PUBERTAL** *adj*
PUBES	*n* pl. PUBES the lower part of the abdomen
PUBIC	*adj* pertaining to the pubes or pubis
PUBIS	*n* pl. PUBES the forward portion of either of the hipbones
PUBLIC	*n* pl. -S the community or the people as a whole
PUBLICAN	*n* pl. -S one who owns or manages a pub
PUBLICLY	*adv* by the public
PUBLISH	*v* -ED, -ING, -ES to print and issue to the public
PUCCOON	*n* pl. -S an herb that yields a red dye
PUCE	*n* pl. -S a dark red color
PUCK	*n* pl. -S a rubber disk used in ice hockey
PUCKA	*adj* pukka
PUCKER	*v* -ED, -ING, -S to gather into small wrinkles or folds
PUCKERER	*n* pl. -S one that puckers
PUCKERY	*adj* -ERIER, -ERIEST having a tendency to pucker
PUCKISH	*adj* impish
PUD	*n* pl. -S pudding
PUDDING	*n* pl. -S a thick, soft dessert
PUDDLE	*v* -DLED, -DLING, -DLES to strew with puddles (small pools of water)
PUDDLER	*n* pl. -S one who subjects iron to puddling
PUDDLING	*n* pl. -S the process of converting pig iron to wrought iron
PUDDLY	*adj* -DLIER, -DLIEST full of puddles
PUDENCY	*n* pl. -CIES modesty
PUDENDUM	*n* pl. -DA the external genital organs of a woman **PUDENDAL** *adj*
PUDGY	*adj* PUDGIER, PUDGIEST short and fat **PUDGILY** *adv*
PUDIC	*adj* pertaining to the pudendum
PUEBLO	*n* pl. -LOS a communal dwelling of certain Indian tribes
PUERILE	*adj* childish
PUFF	*v* -ED, -ING, -S to blow in short gusts
PUFFBALL	*n* pl. -S any of various globular fungi
PUFFER	*n* pl. -S one that puffs
PUFFERY	*n* pl. -ERIES excessive public praise
PUFFIN	*n* pl. -S a sea bird
PUFFY	*adj* -FIER, -FIEST swollen **PUFFILY** *adv*
PUG	*v* PUGGED, PUGGING, PUGS to fill in with clay or mortar
PUGAREE	*n* pl. -S pugree
PUGGAREE	*n* pl. -S pugree
PUGGED	past tense of pug
PUGGIER	comparative of puggy
PUGGIEST	superlative of puggy
PUGGING	present participle of pug
PUGGISH	*adj* somewhat stubby
PUGGREE	*n* pl. -S pugree
PUGGRY	*n* pl. -GRIES pugree
PUGGY	*adj* -GIER, -GIEST puggish
PUGH	*interj* — used to express disgust

PUGILISM   *n* pl. -S the art or practice of fighting with the fists

PUGILIST   *n* pl. -S one who fights with his fists

PUGMARK   *n* pl. -S a footprint

PUGREE   *n* pl. -S a cloth band wrapped around a hat

PUISNE   *n* pl. -S one of lesser rank

PUISSANT   *adj* powerful

PUKE   *v* PUKED, PUKING, PUKES to vomit

PUKKA   *adj* genuine

PUL   *n* pl. PULS or PULI a coin of Afghanistan

PULE   *v* PULED, PULING, PULES to whine

PULER   *n* pl. -S one that pules

PULI   *n* pl. -LIK or -LIS a long-haired sheepdog

PULICENE   *adj* pertaining to fleas

PULICIDE   *n* pl. -S an agent used for destroying fleas

PULIK   a pl. of puli

PULING   *n* pl. -S a plaintive cry

PULINGLY   *adv* in a whining manner

PULL   *v* -ED, -ING, -S to exert force in order to cause motion toward the force

PULLBACK   *n* pl. -S a restraint or drawback

PULLER   *n* pl. -S one that pulls

PULLET   *n* pl. -S a young hen

PULLEY   *n* pl. -LEYS a device used for lifting weight

PULLMAN   *n* pl. -S a railroad sleeping car

PULLOUT   *n* pl. -S a withdrawal

PULLOVER   *n* pl. -S a garment that is put on by being drawn over the head

PULMONIC   *adj* pertaining to the lungs

PULMOTOR   *n* pl. -S a respiratory device

PULP   *v* -ED, -ING, -S to reduce to pulp (a soft, moist mass of matter)

PULPAL   *adj* pertaining to pulp **PULPALLY** *adv*

PULPER   *n* pl. -S one that pulps

PULPIER   comparative of pulpy

PULPIEST   superlative of pulpy

PULPILY   *adv* in a pulpy manner

PULPIT   *n* pl. -S a platform in a church **PULPITAL** *adj*

PULPLESS   *adj* having no pulp

PULPOUS   *adj* pulpy

PULPWOOD   *n* pl. -S soft wood used in making paper

PULPY   *adj* PULPIER, PULPIEST resembling pulp

PULQUE   *n* pl. -S a fermented Mexican beverage

PULSANT   *adj* pulsating

PULSAR   *n* pl. -S a celestial source of radio waves

PULSATE   *v* -SATED, -SATING, -SATES to expand and contract rhythmically

PULSATOR   *n* pl. -S something that pulsates

PULSE   *v* PULSED, PULSING, PULSES to pulsate

PULSEJET   *n* pl. -S a type of engine

PULSER   *n* pl. -S a device that causes pulsations

PULSING   present participle of pulse

PULSION   *n* pl. -S propulsion

PULSOJET   *n* pl. -S pulsejet

PULVILLI   *n/pl* pads between the claws of an insect's foot

PULVINUS   *n* pl. -NI a swelling at the base of a leaf **PULVINAR** *adj*

PUMA   *n* pl. -S a cougar

PUMELO   *n* pl. -LOS pomelo

PUMICE   *v* -ICED, -ICING, -ICES to polish with a porous volcanic rock

PUMICER   *n* pl. -S one that pumices

PUMICITE   *n* pl. -S a porous volcanic rock

PUMMEL   *v* -MELED, -MELING, -MELS or -MELLED, -MELLING, -MELS to pommel

PUMP   *v* -ED, -ING, -S to cause to flow by means of a pump (a device for moving fluids)

PUMPER   *n* pl. -S one that pumps

PUMPKIN   *n* pl. -S a large, edible fruit

PUMPLESS   *adj* lacking a pump

PUMPLIKE   *adj* resembling a pump

PUN   *v* PUNNED, PUNNING, PUNS to make a pun (a play on words)

PUNA   *n* pl. -S a cold, arid plateau

PUNCH   *v* -ED, -ING, -ES to perforate with a type of tool

PUNCHEON   *n* pl. -S a vertical supporting timber

PUNCHER   *n* pl. -S one that punches

PUNCHY   *adj* PUNCHIER, PUNCHIEST dazed

PUNCTATE   *adj* covered with dots

PUNCTUAL   *adj* being on time

PUNCTURE   *v* -TURED, -TURING, -TURES to pierce with a pointed object

PUNDIT   *n* pl. -S a Hindu scholar **PUNDITIC** *adj*

PUNDITRY   *n* pl. -RIES the learning of pundits

PUNG   *n* pl. -S a box-shaped sleigh

PUNGENCY   *n* pl. -CIES the state of being pungent

PUNGENT   *adj* sharply affecting the organs of taste or smell

PUNIER   comparative of puny

PUNIEST   superlative of puny

PUNILY   *adv* in a puny manner

PUNINESS   *n* pl. -ES the state of being puny

PUNISH   *v* -ED, -ING, -ES to impose a penalty on in requital for wrongdoing

PUNISHER   *n* pl. -S one that punishes

PUNITION   *n* pl. -S the act of punishing; punishment

PUNITIVE   *adj* inflicting punishment

PUNITORY   *adj* punitive

PUNK   *n* pl. -S dry, decayed wood used as tinder

PUNK   *adj* PUNKER, PUNKEST of inferior quality

PUNKA   *n* pl. -S a ceiling fan used in India

PUNKAH   *n* pl. -S punka

PUNKEY   *n* pl. -KEYS punkie

PUNKIE   *n* pl. -S a biting gnat

PUNKIN   *n* pl. -S pumpkin

PUNKY   *adj* PUNKIER, PUNKIEST resembling punk

PUNNED   past tense of pun

PUNNER   *n* pl. -S a punster

PUNNING   present participle of pun

PUNNY   *adj* -NIER, -NIEST being or involving a pun

PUNSTER   *n* pl. -S one who is given to punning

PUNT   *v* -ED, -ING, -S to propel through water with a pole

PUNTER   *n* pl. -S one that punts

PUNTO   *n* pl. -TOS a hit or thrust in fencing

PUNTY   *n* pl. -TIES an iron rod used in glassmaking

PUNY   *adj* PUNIER, PUNIEST of inferior size, strength, or significance

PUP   *v* PUPPED, PUPPING, PUPS to give birth to puppies

PUPA   *n* pl. -PAS or -PAE an intermediate stage of a metamorphic insect **PUPAL** *adj*

PUPARIUM   *n* pl. -IA a pupal shell **PUPARIAL** *adj*

PUPATE   *v* -PATED, -PATING, -PATES to pass through the pupal stage

PUPATION   *n* pl. -S the act of pupating

PUPFISH   *n* pl. -ES a small, freshwater fish

PUPIL   *n* pl. -S a student under the close supervision of a teacher

PUPILAGE   *n* pl. -S the state of being a pupil

PUPILAR   *adj* pertaining to a part of the eye

PUPILARY   *adj* pupilar

PUPPED   past tense of pup

PUPPET   *n* pl. -S a small figure, as of a person or animal, manipulated by the hand

PUPPETRY   *n* pl. -RIES the art of making or manipulating puppets

PUPPING   present participle of pup

PUPPY   *n* pl. -PIES a young dog **PUPPYISH** *adj*

PUPPYDOM   *n* pl. -S the world of puppies

PUR   *v* PURRED, PURRING, PURS to purr

PURANA   *n* pl. -S a Hindu scripture **PURANIC** *adj*

PURBLIND   *adj* partially blind

PURCHASE   *v* -CHASED, -CHASING, -CHASES to acquire by the payment of money

PURDA   *n* pl. -S purdah

PURDAH   *n* pl. -S a curtain used in India to seclude women

PURE   *adj* PURER, PUREST free from anything different, inferior, or contaminating

PUREBRED   *n* pl. -S an animal of unmixed stock

PUREE   *v* -REED, -REEING, -REES to reduce to a thick pulp by cooking and sieving

PURELY   *adv* in a pure manner

PURENESS   *n* pl. -ES the quality of being pure

PURER   comparative of pure

PUREST   superlative of pure

PURFLE   *v* -FLED, -FLING, -FLES to decorate the border of

PURFLING   *n* pl. -S an ornamental border

PURGE   *v* PURGED, PURGING, PURGES to purify

PURGER   *n* pl. -S one that purges

PURGING   *n* pl. -S the act of purifying

PURI   *n* pl. -S poori

PURIFIER   *n* pl. -S one that purifies

PURIFY   *v* -FIED, -FYING, -FIES to free from impurities

PURIN   *n* pl. -S purine

PURINE   *n* pl. -S a chemical compound

PURISM   *n* pl. -S strict adherence to traditional correctness

PURIST   *n* pl. -S one who practices purism **PURISTIC** *adj*

PURITAN   *n* pl. -S a rigorously moral or religious person

PURITY   *n* pl. -TIES the quality of being pure

PURL   *v* -ED, -ING, -S to knit with a particular stitch

PURLIEU   *n* pl. -S an outlying or neighboring area

PURLIN   *n* pl. -S a horizontal supporting timber

PURLINE   *n* pl. -S purlin

PURLOIN   *v* -ED, -ING, -S to steal

PURPLE   *adj* -PLER, -PLEST of a color intermediate between red and blue

PURPLE   *v* -PLED, -PLING, -PLES to make purple

PURPLISH   *adj* somewhat purple

PURPLY   *adj* purplish

PURPORT   *v* -ED, -ING, -S to profess or claim

PURPOSE   *v* -POSED, -POSING, -POSES to resolve to perform or accomplish

PURPURA   *n* pl. -S a disease characterized by purple spots on the skin

PURPURE   *n* pl. -S the heraldic color purple

PURPURIC   *adj* pertaining to purpura

PURPURIN   *n* pl. -S a reddish dye

PURR   *v* -ED, -ING, -S to utter a low, vibrant sound

PURRED   past tense of pur and purr

PURRING   present participle of pur and purr

PURSE   *v* PURSED, PURSING, PURSES to pucker

PURSER   *n* pl. -S an officer in charge of a ship's accounts

PURSIER   comparative of pursy

PURSIEST   superlative of pursy

PURSILY   *adv* in a pursy manner

PURSING   present participle of purse

PURSLANE   *n* pl. -S a common garden herb

PURSUANT   *adv* in accordance

PURSUE   *v* -SUED, -SUING, -SUES to follow in order to overtake or capture

PURSUER   *n* pl. -S one that pursues

PURSUIT   *n* pl. -S the act of pursuing

PURSY   *adj* PURSIER, PURSIEST short of breath

PURULENT   *adj* secreting pus

PURVEY   *v* -ED, -ING, -S to supply

PURVEYOR   *n* pl. -S one that purveys

PURVIEW   *n* pl. -S the extent of operation, authority, or concern

PUS   *n* pl. -ES a viscous fluid formed in infected tissue

PUSH   *v* -ED, -ING, -ES to exert force in order to cause motion away from the force

PUSHBALL   *n* pl. -S a type of ball game

PUSHCART   *n* pl. -S a light cart pushed by hand

PUSHDOWN   *n* pl. -S a store of computer data

PUSHER   *n* pl. -S one that pushes

PUSHFUL   *adj* pushy

PUSHIER   comparative of pushy

PUSHIEST   superlative of pushy

PUSHILY   *adv* in a pushy manner

PUSHOVER   *n* pl. -S an easily defeated person or team

PUSHPIN   *n* pl. -S a large-headed pin

PUSHUP	*n* pl. -S a type of exercise
PUSHY	*adj* PUSHIER, PUSHIEST offensively aggressive
PUSLEY	*n* pl. -LEYS pussley
PUSLIKE	*adj* resembling pus
PUSS	*n* pl. -ES a cat
PUSSIER	comparative of pussy
PUSSIES	pl. of pussy
PUSSIEST	superlative of pussy
PUSSLEY	*n* pl. -LEYS purslane
PUSSLIKE	*adj* catlike
PUSSLY	*n* pl. -LIES pussley
PUSSY	*n* pl. PUSSIES a cat
PUSSY	*adj* -SIER, -SIEST full of pus
PUSSYCAT	*n* pl. -S a cat
PUSTULE	*n* pl. -S a small elevation of the skin containing pus **PUSTULAR, PUSTULED** *adj*
PUT	*v* PUT, PUTTING, PUTS to place in a particular position
PUTAMEN	*n* pl. -MINA the hard covering of the kernel of certain fruits
PUTATIVE	*adj* generally regarded as such
PUTLOG	*n* pl. -S a horizontal supporting timber
PUTOFF	*n* pl. -S an excuse
PUTON	*n* pl. -S a hoax or deception
PUTOUT	*n* pl. -S an act of causing an out in baseball
PUTREFY	*v* -FIED, -FYING, -FIES to make or become putrid
PUTRID	*adj* being in a decomposed, foul-smelling state **PUTRIDLY** *adv*
PUTSCH	*n* pl. -ES a suddenly executed attempt to overthrow a government
PUTT	*v* -ED, -ING, -S to hit with a light stroke in golf
PUTTEE	*n* pl. -S a strip of cloth wound around the leg
PUTTER	*v* -ED, -ING, -S to occupy oneself in a leisurely or ineffective manner
PUTTERER	*n* pl. -S one that putters
PUTTIED	past tense of putty
PUTTIER	*n* pl. -S one that putties
PUTTING	present participle of put
PUTTY	*v* -TIED, -TYING, -TIES to fill with a type of cement

PUZZLE	*v* -ZLED, -ZLING, -ZLES to cause uncertainty and indecision in
PUZZLER	*n* pl. -S something that puzzles
PYA	*n* pl. -S a copper coin of Burma
PYAEMIA	*n* pl. -S pyemia **PYAEMIC** *adj*
PYCNIDIA	*n/pl* spore-bearing organs of certain fungi
PYE	*n* pl. -S a book of ecclesiastical rules in the pre-Reformation English church
PYELITIS	*n* pl. -TISES inflammation of the pelvis or the kidney **PYELITIC** *adj*
PYEMIA	*n* pl. -S the presence of pus in the blood **PYEMIC** *adj*
PYGIDIUM	*n* pl. -IA the posterior region of certain invertebrates **PYGIDIAL** *adj*
PYGMY	*n* pl. -MIES a small person **PYGMAEAN, PYGMEAN, PYGMOID, PYGMYISH** *adj*
PYGMYISM	*n* pl. -S a stunted or dwarfish condition
PYIC	*adj* pertaining to pus
PYIN	*n* pl. -S a protein compound contained in pus
PYJAMAS	*n* pl. PYJAMAS pajamas
PYKNIC	*n* pl. -S a person having a broad, stocky build
PYLON	*n* pl. -S a tall structure marking an entrance or approach
PYLORUS	*n* pl. -RI or -RUSES the opening between the stomach and the duodenum **PYLORIC** *adj*
PYODERMA	*n* pl. -S a pus-causing skin disease
PYOGENIC	*adj* producing pus
PYOID	*adj* puslike
PYORRHEA	*n* pl. -S a discharge of pus
PYOSIS	*n* pl. -OSES the formation of pus
PYRALID	*n* pl. -S a long-legged moth
PYRAMID	*v* -ED, -ING, -S to raise or increase by adding amounts gradually
PYRAN	*n* pl. -S a chemical compound **PYRANOID** *adj*
PYRANOSE	*n* pl. -S a simple sugar
PYRE	*n* pl. -S a pile of combustible material
PYRENE	*n* pl. -S a putamen

PYRENOID   *n* pl. -S a protein body of certain lower organisms

PYRETIC   *adj* pertaining to fever

PYREXIA   *n* pl. -S fever **PYREXIAL, PYREXIC** *adj*

PYRIC   *adj* pertaining to burning

PYRIDINE   *n* pl. -S a flammable liquid **PYRIDIC** *adj*

PYRIFORM   *adj* pear-shaped

PYRITE   *n* pl. -S a metallic sulfide **PYRITIC, PYRITOUS** *adj*

PYROGEN   *n* pl. -S a substance that produces fever

PYROLA   *n* pl. -S a perennial herb

PYROLOGY   *n* pl. -GIES the scientific examination of materials by heat

PYROLYZE   *v* -LYZED, -LYZING, -LYZES to affect compounds by the application of heat

PYRONE   *n* pl. -S a chemical compound

PYRONINE   *n* pl. -S a dye

PYROPE   *n* pl. -S a variety of garnet

PYROSIS   *n* pl. -SISES heartburn

PYROSTAT   *n* pl. -S a thermostat

PYROXENE   *n* pl. -S any of a group of minerals common in igneous rocks

PYRRHIC   *n* pl. -S a type of metrical foot

PYRROL   *n* pl. -S pyrrole

PYRROLE   *n* pl. -S a chemical compound **PYRROLIC** *adj*

PYRUVATE   *n* pl. -S a chemical salt

PYTHON   *n* pl. -S a large snake **PYTHONIC** *adj*

PYURIA   *n* pl. -S the presence of pus in the urine

PYX   *n* pl. -ES a container in which the eucharistic bread is kept

PYXIDES   pl. of pyxis

PYXIDIUM   *n* pl. -IA a type of seed vessel

PYXIE   *n* pl. -S an evergreen shrub

PYXIS   *n* pl. PYXIDES a pyxidium

QAID　　　*n* pl. -S caid

QINDAR　　*n* pl. -S qintar

QINTAR　　*n* pl. -S a monetary unit of Albania

QIVIUT　　*n* pl. -S the wool of a musk-ox

QOPH　　*n* pl. -S koph

QUA　　*adv* in the capacity of

QUACK　　*v* -ED, -ING, -S to utter the characteristic cry of a duck

QUACKERY　*n* pl. -ERIES fraudulent practice

QUACKISH　*adj* fraudulent

QUACKISM　*n* pl. -S quackery

QUAD　　*v* QUADDED, QUADDING, QUADS to space out by means of quadrats

QUADRANS　*n* pl. -RANTES an ancient Roman coin

QUADRANT　*n* pl. -S a quarter section of a circle

QUADRAT　　*n* pl. -S a piece of type metal used for filling spaces

QUADRATE　*v* -RATED, -RATING, -RATES to correspond or agree

QUADRIC　　*n* pl. -S a type of geometric surface

QUADRIGA　*n* pl. -GAE a chariot drawn by four horses

QUADROON　*n* pl. -S a person of one-quarter black ancestry

QUAERE　　*n* pl. -S a question

QUAESTOR　*n* pl. -S an ancient Roman magistrate

QUAFF　　*v* -ED, -ING, -S to drink deeply

QUAFFER　　*n* pl. -S one that quaffs

QUAG　　*n* pl. -S a quagmire

QUAGGA　　*n* pl. -S an extinct zebralike mammal

QUAGGY　　*adj* -GIER, -GIEST marshy

QUAGMIRE　*n* pl. -S an area of marshy ground

QUAGMIRY　*adj* -MIRIER, -MIRIEST marshy

QUAHAUG　　*n* pl. -S quahog

QUAHOG　　*n* pl. -S an edible clam

QUAI　　*n* pl. -S quay

QUAICH　　*n* pl. -ES or -S a small drinking vessel

QUAIGH　　*n* pl. -S quaich

QUAIL　　*v* -ED, -ING, -S to cower

QUAINT　　*adj* QUAINTER, QUAINTEST pleasingly old-fashioned or unfamiliar **QUAINTLY** *adv*

QUAKE　　*v* QUAKED, QUAKING, QUAKES to shake or vibrate

QUAKER　　*n* pl. -S one that quakes

QUAKY　　*adj* QUAKIER, QUAKIEST tending to quake **QUAKILY** *adv*

QUALE　　*n* pl. -LIA a property considered apart from things having the property

QUALIFY　　*v* -FIED, -FYING, -FIES to make suitable or capable

QUALITY　　*n* pl. -TIES a characteristic or attribute

QUALM　　*n* pl. -S a feeling of doubt or misgiving

QUALMISH　*adj* having qualms

QUALMY　　*adj* QUALMIER, QUALMIEST qualmish

QUAMASH　　*n* pl. -ES camass

QUANDANG　*n* pl. -S quandong

QUANDARY *n* pl. -RIES a dilemma

QUANDONG *n* pl. -S an Australian tree

QUANT *v* -ED, -ING, -S to propel through water with a pole

QUANTA pl. of quantum

QUANTAL *adj* pertaining to a quantum

QUANTIC *n* pl. -S a type of mathematical function

QUANTIFY *v* -FIED, -FYING, -FIES to determine the quantity of

QUANTITY *n* pl. -TIES a specified or indefinite amount or number

QUANTIZE *v* -TIZED, -TIZING, -TIZES to limit the possible values of to a discrete set

QUANTONG *n* pl. -S quandong

QUANTUM *n* pl. -TA a fundamental unit of energy

QUARE *adj* queer

QUARK *n* pl. -S a hypothetical atomic particle

QUARREL *v* -RELED, -RELING, -RELS or -RELLED, -RELLING, -RELS to engage in an angry dispute

QUARRIER *n* pl. -S one that quarries

QUARRY *v* -RIED, -RYING, -RIES to dig stone from an excavation

QUART *n* pl. -S a liquid measure of capacity

QUARTAN *n* pl. -S a recurrent malarial fever

QUARTE *n* pl. -S a fencing thrust

QUARTER *v* -ED, -ING, -S to divide into four equal parts

QUARTERN *n* pl. -S one-fourth of something

QUARTET *n* pl. -S a group of four

QUARTIC *n* pl. -S a type of mathematical function

QUARTILE *n* pl. -S a portion of a frequency distribution

QUARTO *n* pl. -TOS the size of a piece of paper cut four from a sheet

QUARTZ *n* pl. -ES a mineral

QUASAR *n* pl. -S a distant celestial object emitting strong radio waves

QUASH *v* -ED, -ING, -ES to suppress completely

QUASI *adj* similar but not exactly the same

QUASS *n* pl. -ES kvass

QUASSIA *n* pl. -S a tropical tree

QUASSIN *n* pl. -S a medicinal compound obtained from the wood of a quassia

QUATE *adj* quiet

QUATORZE *n* pl. -S a set of four cards of the same denomination scoring fourteen points

QUATRAIN *n* pl. -S a stanza of four lines

QUATRE *n* pl. -S the four at cards or dice

QUAVER *v* -ED, -ING, -S to quiver

QUAVERER *n* pl. -S one that quavers

QUAVERY *adj* quivery

QUAY *n* pl. QUAYS a wharf **QUAYLIKE** *adj*

QUAYAGE *n* pl. -S a charge for the use of a quay

QUAYSIDE *n* pl. -S the area adjacent to a quay

QUEAN *n* pl. -S a harlot

QUEASY *adj* -SIER, -SIEST easily nauseated **QUEASILY** *adv*

QUEAZY *adj* -ZIER, -ZIEST queasy

QUEEN *v* -ED, -ING, -S to make a queen (a female monarch) of

QUEENLY *adj* -LIER, -LIEST of or befitting a queen

QUEER *adj* QUEERER, QUEEREST deviating from the expected or normal

QUEER *v* -ED, -ING, -S to spoil the effect or success of

QUEERISH *adj* somewhat queer

QUEERLY *adv* in a queer manner

QUELL *v* -ED, -ING, -S to suppress

QUELLER *n* pl. -S one that quells

QUENCH *v* -ED, -ING, -ES to put out or extinguish

QUENCHER *n* pl. -S one that quenches

QUENELLE *n* pl. -S a type of dumpling

QUERCINE *adj* pertaining to oaks

QUERIDA *n* pl. -S a female sweetheart

QUERIED past tense of query

QUERIER *n* pl. -S a querist

QUERIES present 3d person sing. of query

QUERIST *n* pl. -S one who queries

QUERN *n* pl. -S a hand-turned grain mill

QUERY *v* -RIED, -RYING, -RIES to question

QUEST   *v* -ED, -ING, -S to make a search

QUESTER   *n* pl. -S one that quests

QUESTION   *v* -ED, -ING, -S to put a question (an inquiry) to

QUESTOR   *n* pl. -S quaestor

QUETZAL   *n* pl. -S or -ES a tropical bird

QUEUE   *v* QUEUED, QUEUING or QUEUEING, QUEUES to line up

QUEUER   *n* pl. -S one that queues

QUEY   *n* pl. QUEYS a young cow

QUEZAL   *n* pl. -S or -ES quetzal

QUIBBLE   *v* -BLED, -BLING, -BLES to argue over trivialities

QUIBBLER   *n* pl. -S one that quibbles

QUICHE   *n* pl. -S a custard-filled pastry

QUICK   *adj* QUICKER, QUICKEST acting or capable of acting with speed

QUICK   *n* pl. -S a sensitive area of flesh

QUICKEN   *v* -ED, -ING, -S to speed up

QUICKIE   *n* pl. -S something done quickly

QUICKLY   *adv* in a quick manner

QUICKSET   *n* pl. -S a plant suitable for hedges

QUID   *n* pl. -S a portion of something to be chewed

QUIDDITY   *n* pl. -TIES the true nature of a thing

QUIDNUNC   *n* pl. -S a nosy person

QUIET   *adj* -ETER, -ETEST making little or no noise

QUIET   *v* -ED, -ING, -S to cause to be quiet

QUIETEN   *v* -ED, -ING, -S to quiet

QUIETER   *n* pl. -S one that quiets

QUIETISM   *n* pl. -S a form of religious mysticism

QUIETIST   *n* pl. -S an advocate of quietism

QUIETLY   *adv* in a quiet manner

QUIETUDE   *n* pl. -S a state of tranquillity

QUIETUS   *n* pl. -ES a final settlement

QUIFF   *n* pl. -S a forelock

QUILL   *v* -ED, -ING, -S to press small ridges in

QUILLAI   *n* pl. -S an evergreen tree

QUILLET   *n* pl. -S a trivial distinction

QUILT   *v* -ED, -ING, -S to stitch together with padding in between

QUILTER   *n* pl. -S one that quilts

QUILTING   *n* pl. -S material that is used for making quilts

QUINARY   *n* pl. -RIES a group of five

QUINATE   *adj* arranged in groups of five

QUINCE   *n* pl. -S an apple-like fruit

QUINCUNX   *n* pl. -ES an arrangement of five objects

QUINELLA   *n* pl. -S a type of bet in horse racing

QUINIC   *adj* pertaining to quinine

QUINIELA   *n* pl. -S quinella

QUININ   *n* pl. -S quinine

QUININA   *n* pl. -S quinine

QUININE   *n* pl. -S a medicinal alkaloid

QUINNAT   *n* pl. -S a food fish

QUINOA   *n* pl. -S a weedy plant

QUINOID   *n* pl. -S a chemical compound

QUINOL   *n* pl. -S a chemical compound

QUINOLIN   *n* pl. -S a chemical compound

QUINONE   *n* pl. -S a chemical compound

QUINSY   *n* pl. -SIES an inflammation of the tonsils

QUINT   *n* pl. -S a group of five

QUINTAIN   *n* pl. -S an object used as a target in a medieval sport

QUINTAL   *n* pl. -S a unit of weight

QUINTAN   *n* pl. -S a recurrent fever

QUINTAR   *n* pl. -S qintar

QUINTET   *n* pl. -S a group of five

QUINTIC   *n* pl. -S a type of mathematical function

QUINTILE   *n* pl. -S a portion of a frequency distribution

QUINTIN   *n* pl. -S a fine linen

QUIP   *v* QUIPPED, QUIPPING, QUIPS to make witty remarks

QUIPPISH   *adj* witty

QUIPPU   *n* pl. -S quipu

QUIPSTER   *n* pl. -S one that quips

QUIPU   *n* pl. -S an ancient calculating device

QUIRE   *v* QUIRED, QUIRING, QUIRES to arrange sheets of paper in sets of twenty-four

QUIRK   *v* -ED, -ING, -S to twist

QUIRKY   *adj* QUIRKIER, QUIRKIEST tricky **QUIRKILY** *adv*

QUIRT	*v* -ED, -ING, -S to strike with a riding whip
QUISLING	*n* pl. -S a traitor who aids the invaders of his country
QUIT	*v* QUITTED, QUITTING, QUITS to end one's engagement in or occupation with
QUITCH	*n* pl. -ES a perennial grass
QUITE	*adv* to the fullest extent
QUITRENT	*n* pl. -S a fixed rent due from a socage tenant
QUITTED	past tense of quit
QUITTER	*n* pl. -S one that quits
QUITTING	present participle of quit
QUITTOR	*n* pl. -S an inflammation of an animal's hoof
QUIVER	*v* -ED, -ING, -S to shake with a slight but rapid motion
QUIVERER	*n* pl. -S one that quivers
QUIVERY	*adj* marked by quivering
QUIXOTE	*n* pl. -S a quixotic person
QUIXOTIC	*adj* extremely idealistic
QUIXOTRY	*n* pl. -TRIES quixotic action or thought
QUIZ	*v* QUIZZED, QUIZZING, QUIZZES to test the knowledge of by asking questions
QUIZZER	*n* pl. -S one that quizzes

QUOD	*n* pl. -S a prison
QUOIN	*v* -ED, -ING, -S to secure with a type of wedge
QUOIT	*v* -ED, -ING, -S to play a throwing game similar to ringtoss
QUOMODO	*n* pl. -DOS a means or manner
QUONDAM	*adj* that once was
QUORUM	*n* pl. -S a particularly chosen group
QUOTA	*n* pl. -S a proportional part or share
QUOTE	*v* QUOTED, QUOTING, QUOTES to repeat the words of **QUOTABLE** *adj* **QUOTABLY** *adv*
QUOTER	*n* pl. -S one that quotes
QUOTH	*v* said — QUOTH is the only accepted form of this verb; it cannot be conjugated
QUOTHA	*interj* — used to express surprise or sarcasm
QUOTIENT	*n* pl. -S the number resulting from the division of one number by another
QUOTING	present participle of quote
QURSH	*n* pl. -ES a monetary unit of Saudi Arabia
QURUSH	*n* pl. -ES qursh

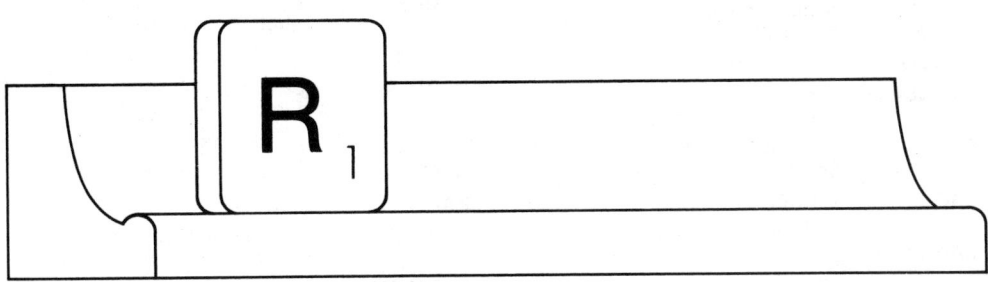

RABATO *n* pl. -TOS a wide, lace-edged collar

RABBET *v* -ED, -ING, -S to cut a groove in

RABBI *n* pl. -S or -ES a Jewish spiritual leader

RABBIN *n* pl. -S rabbi

RABBINIC *adj* pertaining to rabbis

RABBIT *v* -ED, -ING, -S to hunt rabbits (rodent-like mammals)

RABBITER *n* pl. -S one that rabbits

RABBITRY *n* pl. -RIES a place where rabbits are kept

RABBLE *v* -BLED, -BLING, -BLES to mob

RABBLER *n* pl. -S an iron bar used in puddling

RABBONI *n* pl. -S master; teacher — used as a Jewish title of respect

RABIC *adj* pertaining to rabies

RABID *adj* affected with rabies **RABIDLY** *adv*

RABIDITY *n* pl. -TIES the state of being rabid

RABIES *n* pl. RABIES an infectious virus disease **RABIETIC** *adj*

RACCOON *n* pl. -S a carnivorous mammal

RACE *v* RACED, RACING, RACES to compete in a contest of speed

RACEMATE *n* pl. -S a chemical salt

RACEME *n* pl. -S a mode of arrangement of flowers along an axis **RACEMED** *adj*

RACEMIC *adj* constituting a chemical compound that is optically inactive

RACEMISM *n* pl. -S the state of being racemic

RACEMIZE *v* -MIZED, -MIZING, -MIZES to convert into a racemic compound

RACEMOID *adj* pertaining to a raceme

RACEMOSE *adj* having the form of a raceme

RACEMOUS *adj* racemose

RACER *n* pl. -S one that races

RACEWAY *n* pl. -WAYS a channel for conducting water

RACHET *n* pl. -S ratchet

RACHIS *n* pl. -CHISES or -CHIDES the spinal column **RACHIAL** *adj*

RACHITIS *n* pl. -TIDES rickets **RACHITIC** *adj*

RACIAL *adj* pertaining to an ethnic group **RACIALLY** *adv*

RACIER comparative of racy

RACIEST superlative of racy

RACILY *adv* in a racy manner

RACINESS *n* pl. -ES the quality of being racy

RACING *n* pl. -S the sport of engaging in contests of speed

RACISM *n* pl. -S a doctrine of racial superiority

RACIST *n* pl. -S an advocate of racism

RACK *v* -ED, -ING, -S to place in a type of framework

RACKER *n* pl. -S one that racks

RACKET *v* -ED, -ING, -S to make a loud noise

RACKETY *adj* -ETIER, -ETIEST noisy

RACKLE *adj* impetuous; rash

RACKWORK *n* pl. -S a type of mechanism

RACLETTE *n* pl. -S a cheese dish

RACON *n* pl. -S a type of radar transmitter

RACOON *n* pl. -S raccoon

RACQUET *n* pl. -S a lightweight implement used in various ball games

RACY *adj* RACIER, RACIEST bordering on impropriety or indecency

RAD *v* RADDED, RADDING, RADS to fear

RADAR *n* pl. -S an electronic locating device

RADDLE *v* -DLED, -DLING, -DLES to weave together

RADIABLE *adj* capable of radiating

RADIAL *n* pl. -S a part diverging from a center

RADIALE *n* pl. -LIA a bone of the carpus

RADIALLY *adv* in a diverging manner

RADIAN *n* pl. -S a unit of angular measure

RADIANCE *n* pl. -S brightness

RADIANCY *n* pl. -CIES radiance

RADIANT *n* pl. -S a point from which rays are emitted

RADIATE *v* -ATED, -ATING, -ATES to emit rays

RADIATOR *n* pl. -S a heating device

RADICAL *n* pl. -S a group of atoms that acts as a unit in chemical compounds

RADICAND *n* pl. -S a quantity in mathematics

RADICATE *v* -CATED, -CATING, -CATES to cause to take root

RADICEL *n* pl. -S a rootlet

RADICES a pl. of radix

RADICLE *n* pl. -S a part of a plant embryo

RADII a pl. of radius

RADIO *v* -ED, -ING, -S to transmit by radio (an apparatus for wireless communication)

RADIOMAN *n* pl. -MEN a radio operator or technician

RADISH *n* pl. -ES a pungent, edible root

RADIUM *n* pl. -S a radioactive element

RADIUS *n* pl. -DII or -DIUSES a straight line from the center of a circle to the circumference

RADIX *n* pl. -DICES or -DIXES the root of a plant

RADOME *n* pl. -S a domelike device used to shelter a radar antenna

RADON *n* pl. -S a radioactive element

RADULA *n* pl. -LAE or -LAS a tonguelike organ of mollusks **RADULAR** *adj*

RAFF *n* pl. -S riffraff

RAFFIA *n* pl. -S a palm tree

RAFFISH *adj* tawdry

RAFFLE *v* -FLED, -FLING, -FLES to dispose of by a form of lottery

RAFFLER *n* pl. -S one that raffles

RAFT *v* -ED, -ING, -S to transport on a raft (a type of buoyant structure)

RAFTER *n* pl. -S a supporting beam

RAFTSMAN *n* pl. -MEN one who manages a raft

RAG *v* RAGGED, RAGGING, RAGS to scold

RAGA *n* pl. -S a Hindu musical form

RAGBAG *n* pl. -S a bag for storing scraps of cloth

RAGE *v* RAGED, RAGING, RAGES to act or speak with violent anger

RAGEE *n* pl. -S ragi

RAGGED *adj* -GEDER, -GEDEST tattered **RAGGEDLY** *adv*

RAGGEDY *adj* somewhat ragged

RAGGING present participle of rag

RAGGLE *n* pl. -S a groove cut in masonry

RAGGY *n* pl. -GIES ragi

RAGI *n* pl. -S an East Indian cereal grass

RAGING present participle of rage

RAGINGLY *adv* in a furious manner

RAGLAN *n* pl. -S a type of overcoat

RAGMAN *n* pl. -MEN one who gathers and sells scraps of cloth

RAGOUT *v* -ED, -ING, -S to make into a highly seasoned stew

RAGTAG *n* pl. -S riffraff

RAGTIME *n* pl. -S a style of American dance music

RAGWEED *n* pl. -S a weedy herb

RAGWORT *n* pl. -S a flowering plant

RAH *interj* — used to cheer on a team or player

RAIA	*n* pl. -S rayah	**RAJA**	*n* pl. -S rajah
RAID	*v* -ED, -ING, -S to make a sudden assault on	**RAJAH**	*n* pl. -S a king or prince in India
RAIDER	*n* pl. -S one that raids	**RAKE**	*v* RAKED, RAKING, RAKES to gather with a toothed implement
RAIL	*v* -ED, -ING, -S to scold in abusive or insolent language	**RAKEE**	*n* pl. -S raki
RAILBIRD	*n* pl. -S a racing enthusiast	**RAKEHELL**	*n* pl. -S a man lacking in moral restraint
RAILER	*n* pl. -S one that rails	**RAKEOFF**	*n* pl. -S a share of profits
RAILHEAD	*n* pl. -S the end of a railroad line	**RAKER**	*n* pl. -S one that rakes
RAILING	*n* pl. -S a fence-like barrier	**RAKI**	*n* pl. -S a Turkish liqueur
RAILLERY	*n* pl. -LERIES good-natured teasing	**RAKING**	present participle of rake
		RAKISH	*adj* dapper **RAKISHLY** *adv*
RAILROAD	*v* -ED, -ING, -S to transport by railroad (a type of road on which locomotives are run)	**RALE**	*n* pl. -S an abnormal respiratory sound
		RALLIED	past tense of rally
RAILWAY	*n* pl. -WAYS a railroad	**RALLIER**	*n* pl. -S one that rallies
RAIMENT	*n* pl. -S clothing	**RALLINE**	*adj* pertaining to a family of marsh birds
RAIN	*v* -ED, -ING, -S to fall like rain (drops of water condensed from atmospheric vapor)	**RALLY**	*v* -LIED, -LYING, -LIES to call together for a common purpose
RAINBAND	*n* pl. -S a dark band in the solar spectrum	**RALLYE**	*n* pl. -S a type of automobile race
RAINBIRD	*n* pl. -S a type of bird	**RALLYING**	*n* pl. -S the sport of driving in rallyes
RAINBOW	*n* pl. -S an arc of spectral colors formed in the sky	**RALLYIST**	*n* pl. -S a participant in a rallye
RAINCOAT	*n* pl. -S a waterproof coat	**RAM**	*v* RAMMED, RAMMING, RAMS to strike with great force
RAINDROP	*n* pl. -S a drop of rain	**RAMATE**	*adj* having branches
RAINFALL	*n* pl. -S a fall of rain	**RAMBLE**	*v* -BLED, -BLING, -BLES to wander
RAINIER	comparative of rainy	**RAMBLER**	*n* pl. -S one that rambles
RAINIEST	superlative of rainy	**RAMBUTAN**	*n* pl. -S the edible fruit of a Malayan tree
RAINILY	*adv* in a rainy manner	**RAMEE**	*n* pl. -S ramie
RAINLESS	*adj* having no rain	**RAMEKIN**	*n* pl. -S a cheese dish
RAINOUT	*n* pl. -S atomic fallout occurring in precipitation	**RAMENTUM**	*n* pl. -TA a scale formed on the surface of leaves
RAINWASH	*n* pl. -ES the washing away of material by rain	**RAMEQUIN**	*n* pl. -S ramekin
RAINWEAR	*n* pl. -S waterproof clothing	**RAMET**	*n* pl. -S an independent member of a clone
RAINY	*adj* RAINIER, RAINIEST marked by rain	**RAMI**	pl. of ramus
RAISE	*v* RAISED, RAISING, RAISES to move to a higher position **RAISABLE** *adj*	**RAMIE**	*n* pl. -S an Asian shrub
		RAMIFORM	*adj* shaped like a branch
RAISER	*n* pl. -S one that raises	**RAMIFY**	*v* -FIED, -FYING, -FIES to divide into branches
RAISIN	*n* pl. -S a dried grape **RAISINY** *adj*	**RAMILIE**	*n* pl. -S ramillie
RAISING	*n* pl. -S an elevation	**RAMILLIE**	*n* pl. -S a type of wig
RAISONNE	*adj* arranged systematically	**RAMJET**	*n* pl. -S a type of engine
RAJ	*n* pl. -ES dominion; sovereignty		

RAMMED	past tense of ram
RAMMER	n pl. -S one that rams
RAMMIER	comparative of rammy
RAMMIEST	superlative of rammy
RAMMING	present participle of ram
RAMMISH	adj resembling a ram (a male sheep)
RAMMY	adj -MIER, -MIEST rammish
RAMOSE	adj having many branches **RAMOSELY** adv
RAMOSITY	n pl. -TIES the state of being ramose
RAMOUS	adj ramose
RAMP	v -ED, -ING, -S to rise or stand on the hind legs
RAMPAGE	v -PAGED, -PAGING, -PAGES to move about wildly or violently
RAMPAGER	n pl. -S one that rampages
RAMPANCY	n pl. -CIES the state of being rampant
RAMPANT	adj unrestrained
RAMPART	v -ED, -ING, -S to furnish with a fortifying embankment
RAMPIKE	n pl. -S a standing dead tree
RAMPION	n pl. -S a European plant
RAMPOLE	n pl. -S rampike
RAMROD	n pl. -S a rod used in loading a firearm
RAMSHORN	n pl. -S a snail used as an aquarium scavenger
RAMSON	n pl. -S a broad-leaved garlic
RAMTIL	n pl. -S a tropical plant
RAMULOSE	adj having many small branches
RAMULOUS	adj ramulose
RAMUS	n pl. -MI a branch-like part of a structure
RAN	past tense of run and rin
RANCE	n pl. -S a variety of marble
RANCH	v -ED, -ING, -ES to work on a ranch (an establishment for raising livestock)
RANCHER	n pl. -S one that owns or works on a ranch
RANCHERO	n pl. -ROS a rancher
RANCHMAN	n pl. -MEN a rancher
RANCHO	n pl. -CHOS a ranch
RANCID	adj having an unpleasant odor or taste
RANCOR	n pl. -S bitter and vindictive enmity **RANCORED** adj
RANCOUR	n pl. -S rancor
RAND	n pl. -S a strip of leather at the heel of a shoe
RANDAN	n pl. -S a boat rowed by three persons
RANDIES	pl. of randy
RANDOM	n pl. -S a haphazard course
RANDOMLY	adv in a haphazard manner
RANDY	n pl. RANDIES a rude person
RANEE	n pl. -S rani
RANG	past tense of ring
RANGE	v RANGED, RANGING, RANGES to place in a particular order
RANGER	n pl. -S an officer supervising the care of a forest
RANGY	adj RANGIER, RANGIEST tall and slender
RANI	n pl. -S the wife of a rajah
RANID	n pl. -S any of a large family of frogs
RANK	v -ED, -ING, -S to determine the relative position of
RANK	adj RANKER, RANKEST strong and disagreeable in odor or taste
RANKER	n pl. -S an enlisted soldier
RANKISH	adj somewhat rank
RANKLE	v -KLED, -KLING, -KLES to cause irritation or resentment in
RANKLY	adv in a rank manner
RANKNESS	n pl. -ES the state of being rank
RANPIKE	n pl. -S rampike
RANSACK	v -ED, -ING, -S to search thoroughly
RANSOM	v -ED, -ING, -S to obtain the release of by paying a demanded price
RANSOMER	n pl. -S one that ransoms
RANT	v -ED, -ING, -S to speak in a loud or vehement manner
RANTER	n pl. -S one that rants
RANULA	n pl. -S a cyst formed under the tongue
RAP	v RAPPED, RAPPING, RAPS to strike sharply
RAPACITY	n pl. -TIES the quality of being ravenous

RAPE	*v* RAPED, RAPING, RAPES to force to submit to sexual intercourse
RAPER	*n* pl. -S a rapist
RAPESEED	*n* pl. -S the seed of a European herb
RAPHE	*n* pl. RAPHAE or RAPHES a seamlike ridge between two halves of an organ or part
RAPHIA	*n* pl. -S raffia
RAPHIDE	*n* pl. -S a needle-shaped crystal occurring in plant cells
RAPHIS	*n* pl. -PHIDES raphide
RAPID	*adj* -IDER, -IDEST moving or acting with great speed **RAPIDLY** *adv*
RAPID	*n* pl. -S a fast-moving part of a river
RAPIDITY	*n* pl. -TIES the state of being rapid
RAPIER	*n* pl. -S a long, slender sword **RAPIERED** *adj*
RAPINE	*n* pl. -S the taking of property by force
RAPING	present participle of rape
RAPIST	*n* pl. -S one who rapes
RAPPAREE	*n* pl. -S a plunderer
RAPPED	past tense of rap
RAPPEE	*n* pl. -S a strong snuff
RAPPEL	*v* -PELLED, -PELLING, -PELS to descend from a steep height by means of a rope
RAPPEN	*n* pl. RAPPEN a Swiss coin
RAPPER	*n* pl. -S one that raps
RAPPING	present participle of rap
RAPPINI	*n/pl* immature turnip plants
RAPPORT	*n* pl. -S a harmonious relationship
RAPT	*adj* deeply engrossed **RAPTLY** *adv*
RAPTNESS	*n* pl. -ES the state of being rapt
RAPTOR	*n* pl. -S a bird of prey
RAPTURE	*v* -TURED, -TURING, -TURES to fill with great joy
RARE	*adj* RARER, RAREST occurring infrequently
RAREBIT	*n* pl. -S a cheese dish
RAREFIER	*n* pl. -S one that rarefies
RAREFY	*v* -EFIED, -EFYING, -EFIES to make less dense
RARELY	*adv* not often
RARENESS	*n* pl. -ES the quality of being rare
RARER	comparative of rare
RARERIPE	*n* pl. -S a fruit that ripens early
RAREST	superlative of rare
RARIFY	*v* -FIED, -FYING, -FIES to rarefy
RARING	*adj* full of enthusiasm
RARITY	*n* pl. -TIES rareness
RAS	*n* pl. -ES an Ethiopian prince
RASBORA	*n* pl. -S a tropical fish
RASCAL	*n* pl. -S an unscrupulous or dishonest person
RASCALLY	*adj* characteristic of a rascal
RASE	*v* RASED, RASING, RASES to raze
RASER	*n* pl. -S one that rases
RASH	*adj* RASHER, RASHEST acting without due caution or forethought
RASH	*n* pl. -ES a skin eruption **RASHLIKE** *adj*
RASHER	*n* pl. -S a thin slice of meat
RASHLY	*adv* in a rash manner
RASHNESS	*n* pl. -ES the state of being rash
RASING	present participle of rase
RASORIAL	*adj* habitually scratching the ground for food
RASP	*v* -ED, -ING, -S to rub with something rough
RASPER	*n* pl. -S one that rasps
RASPISH	*adj* irritable
RASPY	*adj* RASPIER, RASPIEST rough
RASSLE	*v* -SLED, -SLING, -SLES to wrestle
RASTER	*n* pl. -S the area reproducing images on the picture tube of a television set
RASURE	*n* pl. -S erasure
RAT	*v* RATTED, RATTING, RATS to hunt rats (long-tailed rodents)
RATABLE	*adj* capable of being rated **RATABLY** *adv*
RATAFEE	*n* pl. -S ratafia
RATAFIA	*n* pl. -S an almond-flavored liqueur
RATAL	*n* pl. -S an amount on which rates are assessed
RATAN	*n* pl. -S rattan

RATANY	*n* pl. -NIES rhatany	**RATTED**	past tense of rat
RATAPLAN	*v* -PLANNED, -PLANNING, -PLANS to make a rapidly repeating sound	**RATTEEN**	*n* pl. -S a coarse woolen fabric
		RATTEN	*v* -ED, -ING, -S to harass
RATATAT	*n* pl. -S a quick, sharp rapping sound	**RATTENER**	*n* pl. -S one that rattens
		RATTER	*n* pl. -S an animal used for catching rats
RATCH	*n* pl. -ES a ratchet		
RATCHET	*n* pl. -S a mechanism which allows motion in one direction only	**RATTIER**	comparative of ratty
		RATTIEST	superlative of ratty
		RATTING	present participle of rat
RATE	*v* RATED, RATING, RATES to estimate the value of	**RATTISH**	*adj* ratlike
		RATTLE	*v* -TLED, -TLING, -TLES to make a quick succession of short, sharp sounds
RATEABLE	*adj* ratable **RATEABLY** *adv*		
RATEL	*n* pl. -S a carnivorous mammal		
RATER	*n* pl. -S one that rates	**RATTLER**	*n* pl. -S one that rattles
RATFINK	*n* pl. -S a contemptible person	**RATTLING**	*n* pl. -S ratline
RATFISH	*n* pl. -ES a marine fish	**RATTLY**	*adj* tending to rattle
RATH	*adj* rathe	**RATTON**	*n* pl. -S a rat
RATHE	*adj* appearing or ripening early	**RATTOON**	*v* -ED, -ING, -S to ratoon
RATHER	*adv* preferably	**RATTRAP**	*n* pl. -S a trap for catching rats
RATHOLE	*n* pl. -S a hole made by a rat	**RATTY**	*adj* -TIER, -TIEST infested with rats
RATICIDE	*n* pl. -S a substance for killing rats		
		RAUCITY	*n* pl. -TIES the state of being raucous
RATIFIER	*n* pl. -S one that ratifies		
RATIFY	*v* -FIED, -FYING, -FIES to approve and sanction formally	**RAUCOUS**	*adj* loud and unruly
		RAUNCHY	*adj* -CHIER, -CHIEST slovenly
RATINE	*n* pl. -S a heavy fabric	**RAVAGE**	*v* -AGED, -AGING, -AGES to destroy
RATING	*n* pl. -S relative estimate or evaluation		
		RAVAGER	*n* pl. -S one that ravages
RATIO	*n* pl. -TIOS a proportional relationship	**RAVE**	*v* RAVED, RAVING, RAVES to speak irrationally or incoherently
RATION	*v* -ED, -ING, -S to distribute in fixed portions		
		RAVEL	*v* -ELED, -ELING, -ELS or -ELLED, -ELLING, -ELS to separate the threads of
RATIONAL	*n* pl. -S a number that can be expressed as a quotient of integers		
		RAVELER	*n* pl. -S one that ravels
RATITE	*n* pl. -S a flightless bird	**RAVELIN**	*n* pl. -S a type of fortification
RATLIKE	*adj* resembling a rat	**RAVELING**	*n* pl. -S a loose thread
RATLIN	*n* pl. -S ratline	**RAVELLED**	a past tense of ravel
RATLINE	*n* pl. -S one of the ropes forming the steps of a rope ladder on a ship	**RAVELLER**	*n* pl. -S raveler
		RAVELLING	*n* pl. -S raveling
		RAVELLY	*adj* tangled
RATO	*n* pl. -TOS a rocket-assisted airplane takeoff	**RAVEN**	*v* -ED, -ING, -S to eat in a ravenous manner
RATOON	*v* -ED, -ING, -S to sprout from a root planted the previous year		
		RAVENER	*n* pl. -S one that ravens
RATOONER	*n* pl. -S a plant that ratoons	**RAVENING**	*n* pl. -S rapacity
RATSBANE	*n* pl. -S rat poison	**RAVENOUS**	*adj* extremely hungry
RATTAIL	*n* pl. -S a marine fish	**RAVER**	*n* pl. -S one that raves
RATTAN	*n* pl. -S a palm tree	**RAVIGOTE**	*n* pl. -S a spiced vinegar sauce

RAVIN	v -ED, -ING, -S to raven	**REACCEPT**	v -ED, -ING, -S
RAVINE	n pl. -S a narrow, steep-sided valley	**REACCUSE**	v -CUSED, -CUSING, -CUSES
		READAPT	v -ED, -ING, -S
RAVING	n pl. -S irrational, incoherent speech	**READD**	v -ED, -ING, -S
		READDICT	v -ED, -ING, -S
RAVINGLY	adv in a delirious manner	**READJUST**	v -ED, -ING, -S
RAVIOLI	n pl. -S an Italian dish	**READMIT**	v -MITTED, -MITTING, -MITS
RAVISH	v -ED, -ING, -ES to seize and carry off by force	**READOPT**	v -ED, -ING, -S
		READORN	v -ED, -ING, -S
RAVISHER	n pl. -S one that ravishes	**REAFFIRM**	v -ED, -ING, -S
RAW	adj RAWER, RAWEST uncooked	**REAFFIX**	v -ED, -ING, -ES
RAW	n pl. -S a sore or irritated spot	**REALIGN**	v -ED, -ING, -S
RAWBONED	adj having little flesh	**REALLOT**	v -LOTTED, -LOTTING, -LOTS
RAWHIDE	v -HIDED, -HIDING, -HIDES to beat with a type of whip	**REALTER**	v -ED, -ING, -S
		REANNEX	v -ED, -ING, -ES
		REANOINT	v -ED, -ING, -S
RAWISH	adj somewhat raw	**REAPPEAR**	v -ED, -ING, -S
RAWLY	adv in a raw manner	**REAPPLY**	v -PLIED, -PLYING, -PLIES
RAWNESS	n pl. -ES the state of being raw	**REARGUE**	v -GUED, -GUING, -GUES
RAX	v -ED, -ING, -ES to stretch out	**REARM**	v -ED, -ING, -S
RAY	v -ED, -ING, -S to emit rays (narrow beams of light)	**REAROUSE**	v -AROUSED, -AROUSING, -AROUSES
RAYA	n pl. -S rayah	**REARREST**	v -ED, -ING, -S
RAYAH	n pl. -S a non-Muslim inhabitant of Turkey	**REASCEND**	v -ED, -ING, -S
		REASSAIL	v -ED, -ING, -S
		REASSERT	v -ED, -ING, -S
RAYGRASS	n pl. -ES ryegrass	**REASSESS**	v -ED, -ING, -ES
RAYLESS	adj having no rays	**REASSIGN**	v -ED, -ING, -S
RAYON	n pl. -S a synthetic fiber	**REASSORT**	v -ED, -ING, -S
RAZE	v RAZED, RAZING, RAZES to tear down or demolish	**REASSUME**	v -SUMED, -SUMING, -SUMES
		REASSURE	v -SURED, -SURING, -SURES
RAZEE	v -ZEED, -ZEEING, -ZEES to make lower by removing the upper deck, as a ship	**REATTACH**	v -ED, -ING, -ES
		REATTACK	v -ED, -ING, -S
		REATTAIN	v -ED, -ING, -S
		REAVOW	v -ED, -ING, -S
RAZER	n pl. -S one that razes	**REAWAKE**	v -AWAKED or -AWOKE, -AWOKEN, -AWAKING, -AWAKES
RAZING	present participle of raze		
RAZOR	v -ED, -ING, -S to shave or cut with a sharp-edged instrument	**REAWAKEN**	v -ED, -ING, -S
		REBAIT	v -ED, -ING, -S
RAZZ	v -ED, -ING, -ES to deride	**REBID**	v -BID, -BIDDEN, -BIDDING, -BIDS
RE	n pl. -S the second tone of the diatonic musical scale	**REBILL**	v -ED, -ING, -S
		REBIND	v -BOUND, -BINDING, -BINDS
		REBLOOM	v -ED, -ING, -S
		REBOARD	v -ED, -ING, -S
		REBOIL	v -ED, -ING, -S
		REBOUND	past tense of rebind
		REBUILD	v -BUILT or -BUILDED, -BUILDING, -BUILDS

R₁ E₁

Following is a list of self-explanatory verbs containing the prefix RE- (again):

		REBURY	v -BURIED, -BURYING, -BURIES
		REBUTTON	v -ED, -ING, -S
REABSORB	v -ED, -ING, -S	**RECANE**	v -CANED, -CANING, -CANES
REACCEDE	v -CEDED, -CEDING, -CEDES	**RECARRY**	v -RIED, -RYING, -RIES
REACCENT	v -ED, -ING, -S	**RECAST**	v -CAST, -CASTING, -CASTS

RECHANGE	v -CHANGED, -CHANGING, -CHANGES
RECHARGE	v -CHARGED, -CHARGING, -CHARGES
RECHART	v -ED, -ING, -S
RECHECK	v -ED, -ING, -S
RECHOOSE	v -CHOSE, -CHOSEN, -CHOOSING, -CHOOSES
RECIRCLE	v -CLED, -CLING, -CLES
RECLAD	a past tense of reclothe
RECLASP	v -ED, -ING, -S
RECLEAN	v -ED, -ING, -S
RECLOTHE	v -CLOTHED or -CLAD, -CLOTHING, -CLOTHES
RECOAL	v -ED, -ING, -S
RECOCK	v -ED, -ING, -S
RECODIFY	v -FIED, -FYING, -FIES
RECOIN	v -ED, -ING, -S
RECOLOR	v -ED, -ING, -S
RECOMB	v -ED, -ING, -S
RECOMMIT	v -MITTED, -MITTING, -MITS
RECOOK	v -ED, -ING, -S
RECOPY	v -COPIED, -COPYING, -COPIES
RECOUPLE	v -PLED, -PLING, -PLES
RECRATE	v -CRATED, -CRATING, -CRATES
RECROSS	v -ED, -ING, -ES
RECROWN	v -ED, -ING, -S
RECUT	v -CUT, -CUTTING, -CUTS
REDATE	v -DATED, -DATING, -DATES
REDEFEAT	v -ED, -ING, -S
REDEFINE	v -FINED, -FINING, -FINES
REDEFY	v -FIED, -FYING, -FIES
REDEMAND	v -ED, -ING, -S
REDENY	v -NIED, -NYING, -NIES
REDEPLOY	v -ED, -ING, -S
REDESIGN	v -ED, -ING, -S
REDID	past tense of redo
REDIGEST	v -ED, -ING, -S
REDIP	v -DIPPED or -DIPT, -DIPPING, -DIPS
REDIVIDE	v -VIDED, -VIDING, -VIDES
REDO	v -DID, -DONE, -DOING, -DOES
REDOCK	v -ED, -ING, -S
REDRAW	v -DREW, -DRAWN, -DRAWING, -DRAWS
REDRIED	past tense of redry
REDRIES	present 3d person sing. of redry
REDRILL	v -ED, -ING, -S
REDRIVE	v -DROVE, -DRIVEN, -DRIVING, -DRIVES
REDRY	v -DRIED, -DRYING, -DRIES
REDYE	v -DYED, -DYEING, -DYES
REEARN	v -ED, -ING, -S
REECHO	v -ED, -ING, -ES
REEDIT	v -ED, -ING, -S
REEJECT	v -ED, -ING, -S
REELECT	v -ED, -ING, -S
REEMBARK	v -ED, -ING, -S
REEMBODY	v -BODIED, -BODYING, -BODIES
REEMERGE	v -EMERGED, -EMERGING, -EMERGES
REEMIT	v -EMITTED, -EMITTING, -EMITS
REEMPLOY	v -ED, -ING, -S
REENACT	v -ED, -ING, -S
REENDOW	v -ED, -ING, -S
REENGAGE	v -GAGED, -GAGING, -GAGES
REENJOY	v -ED, -ING, -S
REENLIST	v -ED, -ING, -S
REENTER	v -ED, -ING, -S
REEQUIP	v -EQUIPPED, -EQUIPPING, -EQUIPS
REERECT	v -ED, -ING, -S
REEVOKE	v -EVOKED, -EVOKING, -EVOKES
REEXPEL	v -PELLED, -PELLING, -PELS
REEXPORT	v -ED, -ING, -S
REFALL	v -FELL, -FALLEN, -FALLING, -FALLS
REFASTEN	v -ED, -ING, -S
REFEED	v -FED, -FEEDING, -FEEDS
REFELL	past tense of refall
REFIGHT	v -FOUGHT, -FIGHTING, -FIGHTS
REFIGURE	v -URED, -URING, -URES
REFILE	v -FILED, -FILING, -FILES
REFILL	v -ED, -ING, -S
REFILM	v -ED, -ING, -S
REFILTER	v -ED, -ING, -S
REFIND	v -FOUND, -FINDING, -FINDS
REFIRE	v -FIRED, -FIRING, -FIRES
REFIX	v -ED, -ING, -ES
REFLEW	past tense of refly
REFLIES	present 3d person sing. of refly
REFLOAT	v -ED, -ING, -S
REFLOOD	v -ED, -ING, -S
REFLOW	v -ED, -ING, -S
REFLOWER	v -ED, -ING, -S
REFLY	v -FLEW, -FLOWN, -FLYING, -FLIES
REFOCUS	v -CUSED, -CUSING, -CUSES or -CUSSED, -CUSSING, -CUSSES
REFOLD	v -ED, -ING, -S
REFORGE	v -FORGED, -FORGING, -FORGES
REFORMAT	v -MATTED, -MATTING, -MATS
REFOUGHT	past tense of refight
REFOUND	v -ED, -ING, -S
REFRAME	v -FRAMED, -FRAMING, -FRAMES
REFREEZE	v -FROZE, -FROZEN, -FREEZING, -FREEZES
REFRONT	v -ED, -ING, -S
REFRY	v -FRIED, -FRYING, -FRIES
REFUEL	v -ELED, -ELING, -ELS or -ELLED, -ELLING, -ELS

REGAIN	v -ED, -ING, -S
REGATHER	v -ED, -ING, -S
REGAUGE	v -GAUGED, -GAUGING, -GAUGES
REGAVE	past tense of regive
REGEAR	v -ED, -ING, -S
REGILD	v -GILDED or -GILT, -GILDING, -GILDS
REGIVE	v -GAVE, -GIVEN, -GIVING, -GIVES
REGLAZE	v -GLAZED, -GLAZING, -GLAZES
REGLOSS	v -ED, -ING, -ES
REGLOW	v -ED, -ING, -S
REGLUE	v -GLUED, -GLUING, -GLUES
REGRADE	v -GRADED, -GRADING, -GRADES
REGRAFT	v -ED, -ING, -S
REGRANT	v -ED, -ING, -S
REGREW	past tense of regrow
REGRIND	v -GROUND, -GRINDING, -GRINDS
REGROOVE	v -GROOVED, -GROOVING, -GROOVES
REGROUP	v -ED, -ING, -S
REGROW	v -GREW, -GROWN, -GROWING, -GROWS
REHAMMER	v -ED, -ING, -S
REHANDLE	v -DLED, -DLING, -DLES
REHANG	v -HUNG or -HANGED, -HANGING, -HANGS
REHARDEN	v -ED, -ING, -S
REHASH	v -ED, -ING, -ES
REHEAR	v -HEARD, -HEARING, -HEARS
REHEAT	v -ED, -ING, -S
REHEEL	v -ED, -ING, -S
REHEM	v -HEMMED, -HEMMING, -HEMS
REHINGE	v -HINGED, -HINGING, -HINGES
REHIRE	v -HIRED, -HIRING, -HIRES
REHUNG	a past tense of rehang
REIGNITE	v -NITED, -NITING, -NITES
REIMAGE	v -AGED, -AGING, -AGES
REIMPORT	v -ED, -ING, -S
REIMPOSE	v -POSED, -POSING, -POSES
REINCITE	v -CITED, -CITING, -CITES
REINCUR	v -CURRED, -CURRING, -CURS
REINDEX	v -ED, -ING, -ES
REINDUCE	v -DUCED, -DUCING, -DUCES
REINDUCT	v -ED, -ING, -S
REINFECT	v -ED, -ING, -S
REINFORM	v -ED, -ING, -S
REINFUSE	v -FUSED, -FUSING, -FUSES
REINJURE	v -JURED, -JURING, -JURES
REINSERT	v -ED, -ING, -S
REINSURE	v -SURED, -SURING, -SURES
REINTER	v -TERRED, -TERRING, -TERS
REINVENT	v -ED, -ING, -S
REINVEST	v -ED, -ING, -S
REINVITE	v -VITED, -VITING, -VITES
REINVOKE	v -VOKED, -VOKING, -VOKES
REISSUE	v -SUED, -SUING, -SUES
REJOIN	v -ED, -ING, -S
REJUDGE	v -JUDGED, -JUDGING, -JUDGES
REKEY	v -ED, -ING, -S
REKINDLE	v -DLED, -DLING, -DLES
REKNIT	v -KNITTED, -KNITTING, -KNITS
RELABEL	v -BELED, -BELING, -BELS or -BELLED, -BELLING, -BELS
RELACE	v -LACED, -LACING, -LACES
RELAUNCH	v -ED, -ING, -ES
RELAY	v -LAID, -LAYING, -LAYS
RELEARN	v -LEARNED or -LEARNT, -LEARNING, -LEARNS
RELEND	v -LENT, -LENDING, -LENDS
RELET	v -LET, -LETTING, -LETS
RELETTER	v -ED, -ING, -S
RELIGHT	v -LIGHTED or -LIT, -LIGHTING, -LIGHTS
RELINE	v -LINED, -LINING, -LINES
RELIST	v -ED, -ING, -S
RELIT	a past tense of relight
RELOAD	v -ED, -ING, -S
RELOAN	v -ED, -ING, -S
REMAIL	v -ED, -ING, -S
REMAKE	v -MADE, -MAKING, -MAKES
REMAP	v -MAPPED, -MAPPING, -MAPS
REMARRY	v -RIED, -RYING, -RIES
REMATCH	v -ED, -ING, -ES
REMEET	v -MET, -MEETING, -MEETS
REMELT	v -ED, -ING, -S
REMEND	v -ED, -ING, -S
REMERGE	v -MERGED, -MERGING, -MERGES
REMET	past tense of remeet
REMIX	v -MIXED or -MIXT, -MIXING, -MIXES
REMODIFY	v -FIED, -FYING, -FIES
REMOLD	v -ED, -ING, -S
REMOUNT	v -ED, -ING, -S
RENAME	v -NAMED, -NAMING, -NAMES
RENOTIFY	v -FIED, -FYING, -FIES
RENUMBER	v -ED, -ING, -S
REOBJECT	v -ED, -ING, -S
REOBTAIN	v -ED, -ING, -S
REOCCUPY	v -PIED, -PYING, -PIES
REOCCUR	v -CURRED, -CURRING, -CURS
REOIL	v -ED, -ING, -S
REOPEN	v -ED, -ING, -S
REOPPOSE	v -POSED, -POSING, -POSES
REORDAIN	v -ED, -ING, -S
REORDER	v -ED, -ING, -S
REORIENT	v -ED, -ING, -S
REPACIFY	v -FIED, -FYING, -FIES
REPACK	v -ED, -ING, -S
REPAINT	v -ED, -ING, -S

REPAPER	v -ED, -ING, -S	**RESHOOT**	v -SHOT, -SHOOTING, -SHOOTS
REPASS	v -ED, -ING, -ES	**RESHOW**	v -SHOWED, -SHOWN, -SHOWING, -SHOWS
REPAVE	v -PAVED, -PAVING, -PAVES	**RESIFT**	v -ED, -ING, -S
REPEOPLE	v -PLED, -PLING, -PLES	**RESILVER**	v -ED, -ING, -S
REPERK	v -ED, -ING, -S	**RESIZE**	v -SIZED, -SIZING, -SIZES
REPHRASE	v -PHRASED, -PHRASING, -PHRASES	**RESMELT**	v -ED, -ING, -S
REPIN	v -PINNED, -PINNING, -PINS	**RESMOOTH**	v -ED, -ING, -S
REPLAN	v -PLANNED, -PLANNING, -PLANS	**RESOLD**	past tense of resell
REPLANT	v -ED, -ING, -S	**RESOLDER**	v -ED, -ING, -S
REPLATE	v -PLATED, -PLATING, -PLATES	**RESOLE**	v -SOLED, -SOLING, -SOLES
REPLAY	v -ED, -ING, -S	**RESOUGHT**	past tense of reseek
REPLEDGE	v -PLEDGED, -PLEDGING, -PLEDGES	**RESOW**	v -SOWED, -SOWN, -SOWING, -SOWS
REPLUNGE	v -PLUNGED, -PLUNGING, -PLUNGES	**RESPELL**	v -SPELLED or -SPELT, -SPELLING, -SPELLS
REPOLISH	v -ED, -ING, -ES	**RESPREAD**	v -SPREAD, -SPREADING, -SPREADS
REPOUR	v -ED, -ING, -S		
REPOWER	v -ED, -ING, -S	**RESPRING**	v -SPRANG or -SPRUNG, -SPRINGING, -SPRINGS
REPRICE	v -PRICED, -PRICING, -PRICES	**RESTACK**	v -ED, -ING, -S
REPRINT	v -ED, -ING, -S	**RESTAFF**	v -ED, -ING, -S
REPROBE	v -PROBED, -PROBING, -PROBES	**RESTAGE**	v -STAGED, -STAGING, -STAGES
REPURIFY	v -FIED, -FYING, -FIES	**RESTAMP**	v -ED, -ING, -S
REPURSUE	v -SUED, -SUING, -SUES	**RESTART**	v -ED, -ING, -S
REREAD	v -READ, -READING, -READS	**RESTATE**	v -STATED, -STATING, -STATES
RERECORD	v -ED, -ING, -S	**RESTOCK**	v -ED, -ING, -S
RERISE	v -ROSE, -RISEN, -RISING, -RISES	**RESTRIKE**	v -STRUCK, -STRICKEN, -STRIKING, -STRIKES
REROLL	v -ED, -ING, -S	**RESTRING**	v -STRUNG, -STRINGING, -STRINGS
REROUTE	v -ROUTED, -ROUTING, -ROUTES	**RESTRIVE**	v -STROVE, -STRIVEN, -STRIVING, -STRIVES
RESADDLE	v -DLED, -DLING, -DLES		
RESAID	past tense of resay	**RESTRUCK**	past tense of restrike
RESAIL	v -ED, -ING, -S	**RESTRUNG**	past tense of restring
RESALUTE	v -LUTED, -LUTING, -LUTES	**RESTUDY**	v -STUDIED, -STUDYING, -STUDIES
RESAMPLE	v -PLED, -PLING, -PLES	**RESTUFF**	v -ED, -ING, -S
RESAW	v -SAWED, -SAWN, -SAWING, -SAWS	**RESTYLE**	v -STYLED, -STYLING, -STYLES
RESAY	v -SAID, -SAYING, -SAYS	**RESUBMIT**	v -MITTED, -MITTING, -MITS
RESCORE	v -SCORED, -SCORING, -SCORES	**RESUMMON**	v -ED, -ING, -S
RESCREEN	v -ED, -ING, -S	**RESUPPLY**	v -PLIED, -PLYING, -PLIES
RESEAL	v -ED, -ING, -S	**RESURVEY**	v -ED, -ING, -S
RESEAT	v -ED, -ING, -S	**RETAILOR**	v -ED, -ING, -S
RESEE	v -SAW, -SEEN, -SEEING, -SEES	**RETASTE**	v -TASTED, -TASTING, -TASTES
RESEED	v -ED, -ING, -S	**RETEACH**	v -TAUGHT, -TEACHING, -TEACHES
RESEEK	v -SOUGHT, -SEEKING, -SEEKS	**RETELL**	v -TOLD, -TELLING, -TELLS
RESEEN	past participle of resee	**RETEST**	v -ED, -ING, -S
RESEIZE	v -SEIZED, -SEIZING, -SEIZES	**RETHINK**	v -THOUGHT, -THINKING, -THINKS
RESELL	v -SOLD, -SELLING, -SELLS	**RETHREAD**	v -ED, -ING, -S
RESEND	v -SENT, -SENDING, -SENDS	**RETIE**	v -TIED, -TYING, -TIES
RESET	v -SET, -SETTING, -SETS	**RETIME**	v -TIMED, -TIMING, -TIMES
RESETTLE	v -TLED, -TLING, -TLES	**RETINT**	v -ED, -ING, -S
RESEW	v -SEWED, -SEWN, -SEWING, -SEWS	**RETITLE**	v -TLED, -TLING, -TLES
RESHAPE	v -SHAPED, -SHAPING, -SHAPES	**RETOLD**	past tense of retell
RESHIP	v -SHIPPED, -SHIPPING, -SHIPS	**RETRACK**	v -ED, -ING, -S
RESHOE	v -SHOD, -SHOEING, -SHOES	**RETRAIN**	v -ED, -ING, -S

RETRIM	v -TRIMMED, -TRIMMING, -TRIMS
RETRY	v -TRIED, -TRYING, -TRIES
RETUNE	v -TUNED, -TUNING, -TUNES
RETWIST	v -ED, -ING, -S
RETYING	present participle of retie
RETYPE	v -TYPED, -TYPING, -TYPES
REUNIFY	v -FIED, -FYING, -FIES
REUNITE	v -UNITED, -UNITING, -UNITES
REUSE	v -USED, -USING, -USES
REUTTER	v -ED, -ING, -S
REVALUE	v -UED, -UING, -UES
REVERIFY	v -FIED, -FYING, -FIES
REVEST	v -ED, -ING, -S
REVIEW	v -ED, -ING, -S
REVISIT	v -ED, -ING, -S
REVOICE	v -VOICED, -VOICING, -VOICES
REWAKE	v -WAKED or -WOKE, -WOKEN, -WAKING, -WAKES
REWAKEN	v -ED, -ING, -S
REWAN	a past tense of rewin
REWARM	v -ED, -ING, -S
REWASH	v -ED, -ING, -ES
REWAX	v -ED, -ING, -ES
REWEAVE	v -WOVE or -WEAVED, -WOVEN, -WEAVING, -WEAVES
REWEIGH	v -ED, -ING, -S
REWELD	v -ED, -ING, -S
REWIDEN	v -ED, -ING, -S
REWIN	v -WON or -WAN, -WINNING, -WINS
REWIND	v -WOUND or -WINDED, -WINDING, -WINDS
REWIRE	v -WIRED, -WIRING, -WIRES
REWOKE	a past tense of rewake
REWOKEN	past participle of rewake
REWON	a past tense of rewin
REWORK	v -WORKED or -WROUGHT, -WORKING, -WORKS
REWOUND	a past tense of rewind
REWOVE	a past tense of reweave
REWOVEN	past participle of reweave
REWRAP	v -WRAPPED, or -WRAPT, -WRAPPING, -WRAPS
REWRITE	v -WROTE, -WRITTEN, -WRITING, -WRITES
REWROUGHT	a past tense of rework
REZONE	v -ZONED, -ZONING, -ZONES
REACH	v -ED, -ING, -ES to stretch out or put forth
REACHER	n pl. -S one that reaches
REACT	v -ED, -ING, -S to respond to a stimulus

REACTANT	n pl. -S one that reacts
REACTION	n pl. -S the act of reacting
REACTIVE	adj tending to react
REACTOR	n pl. -S one that reacts
READ	v READ, READING, READS to look at so as to take in the meaning of, as something written or printed **READABLE** adj **READABLY** adv
READER	n pl. -S one that reads
READIED	past tense of ready
READIER	comparative of ready
READIES	present 3d person sing. of ready
READIEST	superlative of ready
READILY	adv in a ready manner
READING	n pl. -S material that is read
READOUT	n pl. -S a presentation of computer data
READY	adj READIER, READIEST prepared
READY	v READIED, READYING, READIES to make ready
REAGENT	n pl. -S a substance used in a chemical reaction to ascertain the nature or composition of another
REAGIN	n pl. -S a type of antibody **REAGINIC** adj
REAL	adj REALER, REALEST having actual existence
REAL	n pl. -S or -ES a former monetary unit of Spain
REAL	n pl. REIS a former monetary unit of Portugal and Brazil
REALGAR	n pl. -S a mineral
REALIA	n/pl objects used by a teacher to illustrate everyday living
REALISE	v -ISED, -ISING, -ISES to realize
REALISER	n pl. -S one that realises
REALISM	n pl. -S concern with fact or reality
REALIST	n pl. -S one who is concerned with fact or reality
REALITY	n pl. -TIES something that is real
REALIZE	v -IZED, -IZING, -IZES to understand completely
REALIZER	n pl. -S one that realizes
REALLY	adv actually
REALM	n pl. -S a kingdom

REALNESS	*n* pl. -ES the state of being real	**REBRANCH**	*v* -ED, -ING, -ES to form secondary branches
REALTY	*n* pl. -TIES property in buildings and land	**REBUFF**	*v* -ED, -ING, -S to reject or refuse curtly
REAM	*v* -ED, -ING, -S to enlarge with a reamer	**REBUKE**	*v* -BUKED, -BUKING, -BUKES to criticize sharply
REAMER	*n* pl. -S a tool used to enlarge holes	**REBUKER**	*n* pl. -S one that rebukes
REAP	*v* -ED, -ING, -S to cut for harvest **REAPABLE** *adj*	**REBURIAL**	*n* pl. -S a second burial
		REBUS	*n* pl. -ES a type of puzzle
REAPER	*n* pl. -S one that reaps	**REBUT**	*v* -BUTTED, -BUTTING, -BUTS to refute
REAPHOOK	*n* pl. -S an implement used in reaping	**REBUTTAL**	*n* pl. -S argument or proof that rebuts
REAR	*v* -ED, -ING, -S to lift upright	**REBUTTER**	*n* pl. -S one that rebuts
REARER	*n* pl. -S one that rears	**REBUTTING**	present participle of rebut
REARMICE	*n/pl* reremice	**REC**	*n* pl. -S recreation
REARMOST	*adj* coming or situated last	**RECALL**	*v* -ED, -ING, -S to call back
REARWARD	*n* pl. -S the rearmost division of an army	**RECALLER**	*n* pl. -S one that recalls
REASCENT	*n* pl. -S a new or second ascent	**RECANT**	*v* -ED, -ING, -S to make a formal retraction or disavowal of
REASON	*v* -ED, -ING, -S to derive inferences or conclusions from known or presumed facts	**RECANTER**	*n* pl. -S one that recants
		RECAP	*v* -CAPPED, -CAPPING, -CAPS to review by a brief summary
REASONER	*n* pl. -S one that reasons	**RECEDE**	*v* -CEDED, -CEDING, -CEDES to move back or away
REATA	*n* pl. -S riata		
REAVE	*v* REAVED or REFT, REAVING, REAVES to plunder	**RECEIPT**	*v* -ED, -ING, -S to mark as having been paid
REAVER	*n* pl. -S one that reaves	**RECEIVE**	*v* -CEIVED, -CEIVING, -CEIVES to come into possession of
REB	*n* pl. -S a Confederate soldier	**RECEIVER**	*n* pl. -S one that receives
REBATE	*v* -BATED, -BATING, -BATES to deduct or return from a payment or bill	**RECENCY**	*n* pl. -CIES the state of being recent
REBATER	*n* pl. -S one that rebates	**RECENT**	*adj* -CENTER, -CENTEST of or pertaining to a time not long past **RECENTLY** *adv*
REBATO	*n* pl. -TOS rabato		
REBBE	*n* pl. -S a rabbi		
REBEC	*n* pl. -S an ancient stringed instrument	**RECEPT**	*n* pl. -S a type of mental image
		RECEPTOR	*n* pl. -S a nerve ending specialized to receive stimuli
REBECK	*n* pl. -S rebec		
REBEL	*v* -BELLED, -BELLING, -BELS to oppose the established government of one's land	**RECESS**	*v* -ED, -ING, -ES to place in a receding space or hollow
		RECHEAT	*n* pl. -S a hunting call
REBELDOM	*n* pl. -S an area controlled by rebels	**RECIPE**	*n* pl. -S a set of instructions for making something
		RECISION	*n* pl. -S a cancellation
REBIRTH	*n* pl. -S a new or second birth	**RECITAL**	*n* pl. -S a detailed account
REBOANT	*adj* resounding loudly	**RECITE**	*v* -CITED, -CITING, -CITES to declaim or say from memory
REBOP	*n* pl. -S a type of music		
REBORN	*adj* born again	**RECITER**	*n* pl. -S one that recites
REBOUND	*v* -ED, -ING, -S to spring back	**RECK**	*v* -ED, -ING, -S to be concerned about
REBOZO	*n* pl. -ZOS a long scarf		

RECKLESS	*adj* foolishly heedless of danger
RECKON	*v* -ED, -ING, -S to count or compute
RECKONER	*n* pl. -S one that reckons
RECLAIM	*v* -ED, -ING, -S to make suitable for cultivation or habitation
RECLAME	*n* pl. -S publicity
RECLINE	*v* -CLINED, -CLINING, -CLINES to lean or lie back
RECLINER	*n* pl. -S one that reclines
RECLUSE	*n* pl. -S one who lives in solitude and seclusion
RECOIL	*v* -ED, -ING, -S to draw back in fear or disgust
RECOILER	*n* pl. -S one that recoils
RECON	*n* pl. -S a preliminary survey
RECONVEY	*v* -ED, -ING, -S to convey back to a previous position
RECORD	*v* -ED, -ING, -S to set down for preservation
RECORDER	*n* pl. -S one that records
RECOUNT	*v* -ED, -ING, -S to relate in detail
RECOUP	*v* -ED, -ING, -S to get back the equivalent of
RECOUPE	*adj* divided twice
RECOURSE	*n* pl. -S a turning or applying to someone or something for aid
RECOVER	*v* -ED, -ING, -S to obtain again after losing
RECOVERY	*n* pl. -ERIES an economic upturn
RECREANT	*n* pl. -S a coward
RECREATE	*v* -ATED, -ATING, -ATES to refresh mentally or physically
RECRUIT	*v* -ED, -ING, -S to engage for military service
RECTA	*a* pl. of rectum
RECTAL	*adj* pertaining to the rectum **RECTALLY** *adv*
RECTI	pl. of rectus
RECTIFY	*v* -FIED, -FYING, -FIES to correct
RECTO	*n* pl. -TOS a right-hand page of a book
RECTOR	*n* pl. -S a clergyman in charge of a parish
RECTORY	*n* pl. -RIES a rector's dwelling
RECTRIX	*n* pl. -TRICES a feather of a bird's tail
RECTUM	*n* pl. -TUMS or -TA the terminal portion of the large intestine
RECTUS	*n* pl. -TI a straight muscle
RECUR	*v* -CURRED, -CURRING, -CURS to happen again
RECURVE	*v* -CURVED, -CURVING, -CURVES to curve backward or downward
RECUSANT	*n* pl. -S one who refuses to accept established authority
RECUSE	*v* -CUSED, -CUSING, -CUSES to disqualify or challenge as judge in a particular case
RECYCLE	*v* -CLED, -CLING, -CLES to process in order to extract useful materials
RED	*adj* REDDER, REDDEST of the color of blood
RED	*v* REDDED, REDDING, REDS to redd
REDACT	*v* -ED, -ING, -S to prepare for publication
REDACTOR	*n* pl. -S one that redacts
REDAN	*n* pl. -S a type of fortification
REDARGUE	*v* -GUED, -GUING, -GUES to disprove
REDBAIT	*v* -ED, -ING, -S to denounce as Communist
REDBAY	*n* pl. -BAYS a small tree
REDBIRD	*n* pl. -S a bird with red plummage
REDBONE	*n* pl. -S a hunting dog
REDBRICK	*adj* pertaining to modern British universities
REDBUD	*n* pl. -S a small tree
REDBUG	*n* pl. -S a chigger
REDCAP	*n* pl. -S a porter
REDCOAT	*n* pl. -S a British soldier during the American Revolution
REDD	*v* -ED, -ING, -S to put in order
REDDED	past tense of red and redd
REDDEN	*v* -ED, -ING, -S to make or become red
REDDER	*n* pl. -S one that redds
REDDEST	superlative of red
REDDING	present participle of red and redd
REDDISH	*adj* somewhat red
REDDLE	*v* -DLED, -DLING, -DLES to ruddle
REDE	*v* REDED, REDING, REDES to advise
REDEAR	*n* pl. -S a common sunfish

REDEEM	v -ED, -ING, -S to buy back	**REDWARE**	n pl. -S an edible seaweed
REDEEMER	n pl. -S one that redeems	**REDWING**	n pl. -S a European thrush
REDEYE	n pl. -S a railroad danger signal	**REDWOOD**	n pl. -S a very tall evergreen tree
REDFIN	n pl. -S a freshwater fish		
REDFISH	n pl. -ES an edible rockfish	**REE**	n pl. -S the female Eurasian sandpiper
REDHEAD	n pl. -S a person with red hair	**REED**	v -ED, -ING, -S to fasten with reeds (the stalks of tall grasses)
REDHORSE	n pl. -S a freshwater fish		
REDIA	n pl. -DIAE or -DIAS the larva of certain flatworms **REDIAL** adj	**REEDBIRD**	n pl. -S the bobolink
		REEDBUCK	n pl. -S an African antelope
REDING	present participle of rede	**REEDIER**	comparative of reedy
REDIRECT	v -ED, -ING, -S to change the course or direction of	**REEDIEST**	superlative of reedy
		REEDIFY	v -FIED, -FYING, -FIES to rebuild
REDLEG	n pl. -S a bird with red legs		
REDLY	adv with red color	**REEDING**	n pl. -S a convex molding
REDNECK	n pl. -S a white, rural laborer of the southern United States	**REEDLING**	n pl. -S a marsh bird
		REEDY	adj REEDIER, REEDIEST abounding in reeds
REDNESS	n pl. -ES the state of being red		
REDO	n pl. -DOS something that is done again	**REEF**	v -ED, -ING, -S to reduce the area of a sail
REDOLENT	adj fragrant	**REEFER**	n pl. -S one that reefs
REDOUBLE	v -BLED, -BLING, -BLES to double	**REEFY**	adj REEFIER, REEFIEST abounding in ridges of rock
REDOUBT	n pl. -S an enclosed fortification		
REDOUND	v -ED, -ING, -S to have an effect or consequence	**REEK**	v -ED, -ING, -S to give off a strong, unpleasant odor
REDOUT	n pl. -S a condition in which blood is driven to the head	**REEKER**	n pl. -S one that reeks
		REEKY	adj REEKIER, REEKIEST reeking
REDOWA	n pl. -S a lively dance	**REEL**	v -ED, -ING, -S to wind on a type of rotary device **REELABLE** adj
REDOX	n pl. -ES a type of chemical reaction		
REDPOLL	n pl. -S a small finch	**REELER**	n pl. -S one that reels
REDRAFT	v -ED, -ING, -S to make a revised copy of	**REENTRY**	n pl. -TRIES a new or second entry
REDRAWER	n pl. -S one that redraws	**REEST**	v -ED, -ING, -S to balk
REDRESS	v -ED, -ING, -ES to set right	**REEVE**	v REEVED or ROVE, ROVEN, REEVING, REEVES to fasten by passing through or around something
REDROOT	n pl. -S a perennial herb		
REDSHANK	n pl. -S a shore bird		
REDSHIRT	v -ED, -ING, -S to keep a college athlete out of varsity play in order to extend his eligibility		
		REF	v REFFED, REFFING, REFS to referee
REDSKIN	n pl. -S a North American Indian	**REFACE**	v -FACED, -FACING, -FACES to repair the outer surface of
REDSTART	n pl. -S a small songbird		
REDTOP	n pl. -S a type of grass	**REFECT**	v -ED, -ING, -S to refresh with food and drink
REDUCE	v -DUCED, -DUCING, -DUCES to diminish		
		REFEL	v -FELLED, -FELLING, -FELS to reject
REDUCER	n pl. -S one that reduces		
REDUVIID	n pl. -S a bloodsucking insect	**REFER**	v -FERRED, -FERRING, -FERS to direct to a source for help or information

REFEREE	*v* -EED, -EEING, -EES to supervise the play in certain sports
REFERENT	*n* pl. -S something referred to
REFERRAL	*n* pl. -S one that is referred
REFERRED	past tense of refer
REFERRER	*n* pl. -S one that refers
REFERRING	present participle of refer
REFFED	past tense of ref
REFFING	present participle of ref
REFINE	*v* -FINED, -FINING, -FINES to free from impurities
REFINER	*n* pl. -S one that refines
REFINERY	*n* pl. -ERIES a place where crude material is refined
REFINING	present participle of refine
REFINISH	*v* -ED, -ING, -ES to give a new surface to
REFIT	*v* -FITTED, -FITTING, -FITS to prepare and equip for additional use
REFLATE	*v* -FLATED, -FLATING, -FLATES to inflate again
REFLECT	*v* -ED, -ING, -S to turn or throw back from a surface
REFLET	*n* pl. -S special brilliance of surface
REFLEX	*v* -ED, -ING, -ES to bend back
REFLEXLY	*adv* in a reflexed manner
REFLUENT	*adj* flowing back
REFLUX	*v* -ED, -ING, -ES to cause to flow back
REFOREST	*v* -ED, -ING, -S to replant with trees
REFORM	*v* -ED, -ING, -S to change to a better state
REFORMER	*n* pl. -S one that reforms
REFRACT	*v* -ED, -ING, -S to deflect in a particular manner, as a ray of light
REFRAIN	*v* -ED, -ING, -S to keep oneself back
REFRESH	*v* -ED, -ING, -ES to restore the well-being and vigor of
REFT	a past tense of reave
REFUGE	*v* -UGED, -UGING, -UGES to give or take shelter
REFUGEE	*n* pl. -S one who flees for safety
REFUGIUM	*n* pl. -GIA a stable area during a period of continental climactic change
REFUND	*v* -ED, -ING, -S to give back
REFUNDER	*n* pl. -S one that refunds
REFUSAL	*n* pl. -S the act of refusing
REFUSE	*v* -FUSED, -FUSING, -FUSES to express oneself as unwilling to accept, do, or comply with
REFUSER	*n* pl. -S one that refuses
REFUTAL	*n* pl. -S the act of refuting
REFUTE	*v* -FUTED, -FUTING, -FUTES to prove to be false or erroneous
REFUTER	*n* pl. -S one that refutes
REGAINER	*n* pl. -S one that regains
REGAL	*adj* of or befitting a king
REGALE	*v* -GALED, -GALING, -GALES to delight
REGALIA	*n/pl* the rights and privileges of a king
REGALITY	*n* pl. -TIES regal authority
REGALLY	*adv* in a regal manner
REGARD	*v* -ED, -ING, -S to look upon with a particular feeling
REGATTA	*n* pl. -S a boat race
REGELATE	*v* -LATED, -LATING, -LATES to refreeze ice by reducing the pressure
REGENCY	*n* pl. -CIES the office of a regent
REGENT	*n* pl. -S one who rules in the place of a sovereign **REGENTAL** *adj*
REGES	pl. of rex
REGICIDE	*n* pl. -S the killing of a king
REGIME	*n* pl. -S a system of government
REGIMEN	*n* pl. -S a systematic plan
REGIMENT	*v* -ED, -ING, -S to form into military units
REGINA	*n* pl. -NAE or -NAS queen **REGINAL** *adj*
REGION	*n* pl. -S an administrative area or division
REGIONAL	*n* pl. -S something that serves as a region
REGISTER	*v* -ED, -ING, -S to record officially
REGISTRY	*n* pl. -TRIES the act of registering
REGIUS	*adj* holding a professorship founded by the sovereign
REGLET	*n* pl. -S a flat, narrow molding
REGMA	*n* pl. -MATA a type of fruit

REGNA   pl. of regnum

REGNAL   *adj* pertaining to a king or his reign

REGNANCY   *n* pl. -CIES the state of being regnant

REGNANT   *adj* reigning

REGNUM   *n* pl. -NA dominion

REGOLITH   *n* pl. -S a layer of loose rock

REGORGE   *v* -GORGED, -GORGING, -GORGES to vomit

REGOSOL   *n* pl. -S a type of soil

REGRATE   *v* -GRATED, -GRATING, -GRATES to buy up in order to sell for a higher price in the same area

REGREET   *v* -ED, -ING, -S to greet in return

REGRESS   *v* -ED, -ING, -ES to go back

REGRET   *v* -GRETTED, -GRETTING, -GRETS to look back upon with sorrow or remorse

REGROWTH   *n* pl. -S a new or second growth

REGULAR   *n* pl. -S an habitual customer

REGULATE   *v* -LATED, -LATING, -LATES to control according to rule

REGULUS   *n* pl. -LI or -LUSES a mass that forms beneath the slag in a furnace **REGULINE** *adj*

REHEARSE   *v* -HEARSED, -HEARSING, -HEARSES to practice in preparation for a public appearance

REHEATER   *n* pl. -S one that reheats

REHOUSE   *v* -HOUSED, -HOUSING, -HOUSES to establish in a new housing unit

REI   *n* pl. -S an erroneous English form for a former Portuguese coin

REIF   *n* pl. -S robbery

REIFIER   *n* pl. -S one that reifies

REIFY   *v* -IFIED, -IFYING, -IFIES to regard as real or concrete

REIGN   *v* -ED, -ING, -S to exercise sovereign power

REIN   *v* -ED, -ING, -S to restrain

REINDEER   *n* pl. -S a large deer

REINLESS   *adj* unrestrained

REINSMAN   *n* pl. -MEN a skilled rider of horses

REIS   pl. of real

REISSUER   *n* pl. -S one that reissues

REITBOK   *n* pl. -S the reedbuck

REIVE   *v* REIVED, REIVING, REIVES to plunder

REIVER   *n* pl. -S one that reives

REJECT   *v* -ED, -ING, -S to refuse to accept, consider, or make use of

REJECTEE   *n* pl. -S one that is rejected

REJECTER   *n* pl. -S one that rejects

REJECTOR   *n* pl. -S rejecter

REJIGGER   *v* -ED, -ING, -S to alter

REJOICE   *v* -JOICED, -JOICING, -JOICES to feel joyful

REJOICER   *n* pl. -S one that rejoices

RELAPSE   *v* -LAPSED, -LAPSING, -LAPSES to fall or slip back into a former state

RELAPSER   *n* pl. -S one that relapses

RELATE   *v* -LATED, -LATING, -LATES to give an account of

RELATER   *n* pl. -S one that relates

RELATION   *n* pl. -S a significant association between two or more things

RELATIVE   *n* pl. -S one who is connected with another by blood or marriage

RELATOR   *n* pl. -S relater

RELAX   *v* -ED, -ING, -ES to make less tense or rigid

RELAXANT   *n* pl. -S a drug that relieves muscular tension

RELAXER   *n* pl. -S one that relaxes

RELAXIN   *n* pl. -S a female hormone

RELAY   *v* -ED, -ING, -S to send along by using fresh sets to replace tired ones

RELEASE   *v* -LEASED, -LEASING, -LEASES to set free

RELEASER   *n* pl. -S one that releases

RELEGATE   *v* -GATED, -GATING, -GATES to assign

RELENT   *v* -ED, -ING, -S to become less severe

RELEVANT   *adj* pertaining to the matter at hand

RELIABLE   *adj* suitable to be relied on **RELIABLY** *adv*

RELIANCE   *n* pl. -S confident or trustful dependence

RELIANT   *adj* showing reliance

RELIC   *n* pl. -S a surviving memorial of something past

RELICT   *n* pl. -S an organism surviving in a changed environment

RELIED   past tense of rely

RELIEF   *n* pl. -S aid in the form of money or necessities

RELIER   *n* pl. -S one that relies

RELIES   present 3d person sing. of rely

RELIEVE   *v* -LIEVED, -LIEVING, -LIEVES to lessen or free from pain or discomfort

RELIEVER   *n* pl. -S one that relieves

RELIEVO   *n* pl. -VOS the projection of figures or forms from a flat background

RELIGION   *n* pl. -S the worship of a god or the supernatural

RELIQUE   *n* pl. -S relic

RELISH   *v* -ED, -ING, -ES to enjoy

RELIVE   *v* -LIVED, -LIVING, -LIVES to experience again

RELOADER   *n* pl. -S one that reloads

RELOCATE   *v* -CATED, -CATING, -CATES to establish in a new place

RELUCENT   *adj* reflecting light

RELUCT   *v* -ED, -ING, -S to show opposition

RELUME   *v* -LUMED, -LUMING, -LUMES to light again

RELUMINE   *v* -MINED, -MINING, -MINES to relume

RELY   *v* -LIED, -LYING, -LIES to place trust or confidence

REM   *n* pl. -S a quantity of ionizing radiation

REMAIN   *v* -ED, -ING, -S to continue in the same state

REMAN   *v* -MANNED, -MANNING, -MANS to furnish with a fresh supply of men

REMAND   *v* -ED, -ING, -S to send back

REMANENT   *adj* remaining

REMANNED   past tense of reman

REMANNING   present participle of reman

REMARK   *v* -ED, -ING, -S to say or write briefly or casually

REMARKER   *n* pl. -S one that remarks

REMARQUE   *n* pl. -S a mark made in the margin of an engraved plate

REMEDIAL   *adj* intended to correct something

REMEDY   *v* -DIED, -DYING, -DIES to relieve or cure

REMEMBER   *v* -ED, -ING, -S to bring to mind again

REMEX   *n* pl. REMIGES a flight feather of a bird's wing **REMIGIAL** *adj*

REMIND   *v* -ED, -ING, -S to cause to remember

REMINDER   *n* pl. -S one that reminds

REMINT   *v* -ED, -ING, -S to melt down and make into new coin

REMISE   *v* -MISED, -MISING, -MISES to give up a claim to

REMISS   *adj* careless **REMISSLY** *adv*

REMIT   *v* -MITTED, -MITTING, -MITS to send money in payment

REMITTAL   *n* pl. -S the act of remitting

REMITTER   *n* pl. -S one that remits

REMITTING   present participle of remit

REMITTOR   *n* pl. -S remitter

REMNANT   *n* pl. -S something remaining

REMODEL   *v* -ELED, -ELING, -ELS or -ELLED, -ELLING, -ELS to make over

REMOLADE   *n* pl. -S a piquant sauce

REMORA   *n* pl. -S a type of marine fish **REMORID** *adj*

REMORSE   *n* pl. -S deep anguish caused by a sense of guilt

REMOTE   *adj* -MOTER, -MOTEST situated far away **REMOTELY** *adv*

REMOTION   *n* pl. -S the act of removing

REMOVAL   *n* pl. -S the act of removing

REMOVE   *v* -MOVED, -MOVING, -MOVES to take or move away

REMOVER   *n* pl. -S one that removes

REMUDA   *n* pl. -S a herd of horses

RENAL   *adj* pertaining to the kidneys

RENATURE   *v* -TURED, -TURING, -TURES to restore natural qualities

REND   *v* RENT or RENDED, RENDING, RENDS to tear apart forcibly

RENDER   *v* -ED, -ING, -S to cause to be or become

RENDERER   *n* pl. -S one that renders

RENDIBLE   *adj* capable of being rent

RENDZINA   *n* pl. -S a type of soil

RENEGADE *v* -GADED, -GADING, -GADES to become a traitor

RENEGADO *n* pl. -DOS or -DOES a traitor

RENEGE *v* -NEGED, -NEGING, -NEGES to fail to carry out a promise or commitment

RENEGER *n* pl. -S one that reneges

RENEW *v* -ED, -ING, -S to make new or as if new again

RENEWAL *n* pl. -S the act of renewing

RENEWER *n* pl. -S one that renews

RENIFORM *adj* kidney-shaped

RENIG *v* -NIGGED, -NIGGING, -NIGS to renege

RENIN *n* pl. -S an enzyme

RENITENT *adj* resisting physical pressure

RENNASE *n* pl. -S rennin

RENNET *n* pl. -S a lining membrane in the stomach of certain young animals

RENNIN *n* pl. -S an enzyme

RENOGRAM *n* pl. -S a photographic depiction of the course of renal excretion

RENOUNCE *v* -NOUNCED, -NOUNCING, -NOUNCES to disown

RENOVATE *v* -VATED, -VATING, -VATES to make like new

RENOWN *v* -ED, -ING, -S to make famous

RENT *v* -ED, -ING, -S to obtain temporary use of in return for compensation **RENTABLE** *adj*

RENTAL *n* pl. -S an amount paid or collected as rent

RENTE *n* pl. -S annual income under French law

RENTER *n* pl. -S one that rents

RENTIER *n* pl. -S one that receives a fixed income

RENVOI *n* pl. -S the expulsion by a government of an alien

REOFFER *v* -ED, -ING, -S to offer for public sale

REOVIRUS *n* pl. -ES a type of virus

REP *n* pl. -S a cross-ribbed fabric

REPAID past tense of repay

REPAIR *v* -ED, -ING, -S to restore to good condition

REPAIRER *n* pl. -S one that repairs

REPAND *adj* having a wavy margin **REPANDLY** *adv*

REPARTEE *n* pl. -S a quick, witty reply

REPAST *v* -ED, -ING, -S to eat or feast

REPAY *v* -PAID, -PAYING, -PAYS to pay back

REPEAL *v* -ED, -ING, -S to revoke

REPEALER *n* pl. -S one that repeals

REPEAT *v* -ED, -ING, -S to say or do again

REPEATER *n* pl. -S one that repeats

REPEL *v* -PELLED, -PELLING, -PELS to drive back

REPELLER *n* pl. -S one that repels

REPENT *v* -ED, -ING, -S to feel remorse or self-reproach for a past action

REPENTER *n* pl. -S one that repents

REPETEND *n* pl. -S a phrase or sound that is repeated

REPINE *v* -PINED, -PINING, -PINES to express discontent

REPINER *n* pl. -S one that repines

REPLACE *v* -PLACED, -PLACING, -PLACES to take the place of

REPLACER *n* pl. -S one that replaces

REPLETE *adj* abundantly supplied

REPLEVIN *v* -ED, -ING, -S to replevy

REPLEVY *v* -PLEVIED, -PLEVYING, -PLEVIES to regain possession of by legal action

REPLICA *n* pl. -S a close copy or reproduction

REPLIER *n* pl. -S one that replies

REPLY *v* -PLIED, -PLYING, -PLIES to answer

REPORT *v* -ED, -ING, -S to give an account of

REPORTER *n* pl. -S one that reports

REPOSAL *n* pl. -S the act of reposing

REPOSE *v* -POSED, -POSING, -POSES to lie at rest

REPOSER *n* pl. -S one that reposes

REPOSIT *v* -ED, -ING, -S to put away

REPOUSSE *n* pl. -S a raised design hammered in metal

REPP *n* pl. -S rep

REPPED *adj* resembling rep

REPRESS *v* -ED, -ING, -ES to keep under control

REPRIEVE   *v* -PRIEVED, -PRIEVING, -PRIEVES to postpone the punishment of

REPRISAL   *n* pl. -S an act of retaliation

REPRISE   *v* -PRISED, -PRISING, -PRISES to take back by force

REPRO   *n* pl. -PROS a trial sheet of printed material suitable for photographic reproduction

REPROACH   *v* -ED, -ING, -ES to find fault with

REPROOF   *n* pl. -S criticism for a fault

REPROVAL   *n* pl. -S reproof

REPROVE   *v* -PROVED, -PROVING, -PROVES to rebuke

REPROVER   *n* pl. -S one that reproves

REPTANT   *adj* creeping or crawling

REPTILE   *n* pl. -S any of a class of cold-blooded, air-breathing vertebrates

REPUBLIC   *n* pl. -S a constitutional form of government

REPUGN   *v* -ED, -ING, -S to oppose

REPULSE   *v* -PULSED, -PULSING, -PULSES to drive back

REPULSER   *n* pl. -S one that repulses

REPUTE   *v* -PUTED, -PUTING, -PUTES to consider to be as specified

REQUEST   *v* -ED, -ING, -S to express a desire for

REQUIEM   *n* pl. -S a musical composition for the dead

REQUIN   *n* pl. -S a voracious shark

REQUIRE   *v* -QUIRED, -QUIRING, -QUIRES to have need of

REQUIRER   *n* pl. -S one that requires

REQUITAL   *n* pl. -S something given in return, compensation, or retaliation

REQUITE   *v* -QUITED, -QUITING, -QUITES to make equivalent return for

REQUITER   *n* pl. -S one that requites

RERAN   past tense of rerun

REREDOS   *n* pl. -ES an ornamental screen behind an altar

REREMICE   *n/pl* bats (flying mammals)

REREWARD   *n* pl. -S rearward

REROLLER   *n* pl. -S one that rerolls

RERUN   *v* -RAN, -RUNNING, -RUNS to present a repetition of a recorded performance

RES   *n* pl. RES a particular thing or matter

RESALE   *n* pl. -S the act of selling again

RESCALE   *v* -SCALED, -SCALING, -SCALES to plan on a new scale

RESCIND   *v* -ED, -ING, -S to annul

RESCRIPT   *n* pl. -S something rewritten

RESCUE   *v* -CUED, -CUING, -CUES to free from danger

RESCUER   *n* pl. -S one that rescues

RESEARCH   *v* -ED, -ING, -ES to investigate thoroughly

RESEAU   *n* pl. -SEAUS or -SEAUX a filter screen for making color films

RESECT   *v* -ED, -ING, -S to excise part of an organ or structure surgically

RESEDA   *n* pl. -S a flowering plant

RESELLER   *n* pl. -S one that resells

RESEMBLE   *v* -BLED, -BLING, -BLES to be similar to

RESENT   *v* -ED, -ING, -S to feel or express annoyance or ill will at

RESERVE   *v* -SERVED, -SERVING, -SERVES to keep back for future use

RESERVER   *n* pl. -S one that reserves

RESETTER   *n* pl. -S one that resets

RESH   *n* pl. -ES a Hebrew letter

RESHAPER   *n* pl. -S one that reshapes something

RESID   *n* pl. -S a type of fuel oil

RESIDE   *v* -SIDED, -SIDING, -SIDES to dwell permanently or continuously

RESIDENT   *n* pl. -S one who resides

RESIDER   *n* pl. -S a resident

RESIDUA   a pl. of residuum

RESIDUAL   *n* pl. -S something left over

RESIDUE   *n* pl. -S something remaining after the removal of a part

RESIDUUM   *n* pl. -SIDUA or -SIDUUMS residue

RESIGN   *v* -ED, -ING, -S to give up one's office or position

RESIGNER   *n* pl. -S one that resigns

RESILE   *v* -SILED, -SILING, -SILES to spring back

RESIN   *v* -ED, -ING, -S to treat with resin (a viscous substance obtained from certain plants)

RESINATE	v -ATED, -ATING, -ATES to resin
RESINIFY	v -FIED, -FYING, -FIES to convert into resin
RESINOID	n pl. -S a resinous substance
RESINOUS	adj resembling resin
RESINY	adj resinous
RESIST	v -ED, -ING, -S to strive against
RESISTER	n pl. -S one that resists
RESISTOR	n pl. -S a device in an electric circuit
RESOJET	n pl. -S a pulsejet
RESOLUTE	adj -LUTER, -LUTEST characterized by firmness or determination
RESOLUTE	n pl. -S one who is resolute
RESOLVE	v -SOLVED, -SOLVING, -SOLVES to make a firm decision about
RESOLVER	n pl. -S one that resolves
RESONANT	n pl. -S a resounding sound
RESONATE	v -NATED, -NATING, -NATES to resound
RESORB	v -ED, -ING, -S to absorb again
RESORCIN	n pl. -S a chemical compound
RESORT	v -ED, -ING, -S to go frequently or habitually
RESORTER	n pl. -S one that resorts
RESOUND	v -ED, -ING, -S to make a loud, long, or echoing sound
RESOURCE	n pl. -S an available supply
RESPECT	v -ED, -ING, -S to have a high regard for
RESPIRE	v -SPIRED, -SPIRING, -SPIRES to breathe
RESPITE	v -SPITED, -SPITING, -SPITES to relieve temporarily
RESPOND	v -ED, -ING, -S to say or act in return
RESPONSA	n/pl written rabbinic decisions
RESPONSE	n pl. -S a reply or reaction
REST	v -ED, -ING, -S to refresh oneself by ceasing work or activity
RESTER	n pl. -S one that rests
RESTFUL	adj -FULLER, -FULLEST tranquil
RESTIVE	adj difficult to control
RESTLESS	adj unable or disinclined to remain at rest
RESTORAL	n pl. -S the act of restoring

RESTORE	v -STORED, -STORING, -STORES to bring back to a former or original condition
RESTORER	n pl. -S one that restores
RESTRAIN	v -ED, -ING, -S to hold back from action
RESTRICT	v -ED, -ING, -S to keep within certain boundaries
RESULT	v -ED, -ING, -S to occur as a consequence
RESUME	v -SUMED, -SUMING, -SUMES to take up again after interruption
RESUMER	n pl. -S one that resumes
RESUPINE	adj lying on the back
RESURGE	v -SURGED, -SURGING, -SURGES to rise again
RET	v RETTED, RETTING, RETS to soak in order to loosen the fiber from the woody tissue
RETABLE	n pl. -S a raised shelf above an altar
RETAIL	v -ED, -ING, -S to sell in small quantities
RETAILER	n pl. -S one that retails
RETAIN	v -ED, -ING, -S to keep possession of
RETAINER	n pl. -S one that retains
RETAKE	v -TOOK, -TAKEN, -TAKING, -TAKES to take back
RETAKER	n pl. -S one that retakes
RETARD	v -ED, -ING, -S to slow the progress of
RETARDER	n pl. -S one that retards
RETCH	v -ED, -ING, -ES to make an effort to vomit
RETE	n pl. -TIA an anatomical mesh or network
RETEM	n pl. -S a desert shrub
RETENE	n pl. -S a chemical compound
RETIA	pl. of rete
RETIAL	adj pertaining to a rete
RETIARII	n/pl ancient Roman gladiators
RETIARY	adj resembling a net
RETICENT	adj tending to be silent
RETICLE	n pl. -S a network of lines in the eyepiece of an optical instrument
RETICULA	n/pl netlike structures
RETICULE	n pl. -S a woman's handbag

RETIFORM	*adj* arranged like a net
RETINA	*n* pl. -NAS or -NAE a membrane of the eye
RETINAL	*n* pl. -S retinene
RETINENE	*n* pl. -S a pigment in the retina
RETINITE	*n* pl. -S a fossil resin
RETINOL	*n* pl. -S a liquid hydrocarbon
RETINUE	*n* pl. -S a group of attendants **RETINUED** *adj*
RETINULA	*n* pl. -LAE or -LAS a neural receptor of an arthropod's eye
RETIRANT	*n* pl. -S a retiree
RETIRE	*v* -TIRED, -TIRING, -TIRES to go away or withdraw
RETIREE	*n* pl. -S one who has retired from his vocation
RETIRER	*n* pl. -S one that retires
RETIRING	*adj* shy
RETOOK	past tense of retake
RETOOL	*v* -ED, -ING, -S to reequip with tools
RETORT	*v* -ED, -ING, -S to answer back
RETORTER	*n* pl. -S one that retorts
RETOUCH	*v* -ED, -ING, -ES to add new details or touches to
RETRACE	*v* -TRACED, -TRACING, -TRACES to go back over
RETRACT	*v* -ED, -ING, -S to take back
RETRAIN	*v* -ED, -ING, -S to train again
RETRAL	*adj* situated toward the back **RETRALLY** *adv*
RETREAD	*v* -ED, -ING, -S to furnish with a new tread
RETREAT	*v* -ED, -ING, -S to go back or backward
RETRENCH	*v* -ED, -ING, -ES to curtail
RETRIAL	*n* pl. -S a second trial
RETRIEVE	*v* -TRIEVED, -TRIEVING, -TRIEVES to get back
RETROACT	*v* -ED, -ING, -S to act in return
RETROFIT	*v* -FITTED, -FITTING, -FITS to furnish with new parts not originally available
RETRORSE	*adj* bent backward
RETSINA	*n* pl. -S a Greek wine
RETTED	past tense of ret
RETTING	present participle of ret
RETURN	*v* -ED, -ING, -S to come or go back

RETURNEE	*n* pl. -S one that has returned
RETURNER	*n* pl. -S one that returns
RETUSE	*adj* having a rounded apex with a shallow notch — used of leaves
REUNION	*n* pl. -S a reuniting of persons after separation
REUNITER	*n* pl. -S one that reunites
REUSABLE	*adj* capable of being used again
REV	*v* REVVED, REVVING, REVS to increase the speed of
REVAMP	*v* -ED, -ING, -S to make over
REVAMPER	*n* pl. -S one that revamps
REVANCHE	*n* pl. -S a political policy designed to regain lost territory
REVEAL	*v* -ED, -ING, -S to make known
REVEALER	*n* pl. -S one that reveals
REVEHENT	*adj* carrying back
REVEILLE	*n* pl. -S a morning bugle call
REVEL	*v* -ELED, -ELING, -ELS or -ELLED, -ELLING, -ELS to engage in revelry
REVELER	*n* pl. -S one that revels
REVELLER	*n* pl. -S reveler
REVELRY	*n* pl. -RIES noisy merrymaking
REVENANT	*n* pl. -S one that returns
REVENGE	*v* -VENGED, -VENGING, -VENGES to inflict injury in return for
REVENGER	*n* pl. -S one that revenges
REVENUE	*n* pl. -S the income of a government **REVENUAL, REVENUED** *adj*
REVENUER	*n* pl. -S a revenue officer
REVERB	*n* pl. -S an echo effect in recorded music
REVERE	*v* -VERED, -VERING, -VERES to regard with great respect
REVEREND	*n* pl. -S a clergyman
REVERENT	*adj* deeply respectful
REVERER	*n* pl. -S one that reveres
REVERIE	*n* pl. -S a daydream
REVERIES	pl. of revery
REVERING	present participle of revere
REVERS	*n* pl. REVERS a part of a garment turned back to show the inside
REVERSAL	*n* pl. -S the act of reversing

REVERSE	*v* -VERSED, -VERSING, -VERSES to turn or move in the opposite direction
REVERSER	*n* pl. -S one that reverses
REVERSO	*n* pl. -VERSOS verso
REVERT	*v* -ED, -ING, -S to return to a former state
REVERTER	*n* pl. -S one that reverts
REVERY	*n* pl. -ERIES reverie
REVET	*v* -VETTED, -VETTING, -VETS to face with masonry
REVIEWAL	*n* pl. -S the act of reviewing
REVIEWER	*n* pl. -S one that reviews
REVILE	*v* -VILED, -VILING, -VILES to denounce with abusive language
REVILER	*n* pl. -S one that reviles
REVISAL	*n* pl. -S a revision
REVISE	*v* -VISED, -VISING, -VISES to make a new or improved version of
REVISER	*n* pl. -S one that revises
REVISION	*n* pl. -S a revised version
REVISOR	*n* pl. -S reviser
REVISORY	*adj* pertaining to revision
REVIVAL	*n* pl. -S renewed attention to or interest in something
REVIVE	*v* -VIVED, -VIVING, -VIVES to bring back to life or consciousness
REVIVER	*n* pl. -S one that revives
REVIVIFY	*v* -FIED, -FYING, -FIES to give new life to
REVIVING	present participle of revive
REVOKE	*v* -VOKED, -VOKING, -VOKES to annul by taking back
REVOKER	*n* pl. -S one that revokes
REVOLT	*v* -ED, -ING, -S to rise up against authority
REVOLTER	*n* pl. -S one that revolts
REVOLUTE	*adj* rolled backward or downward
REVOLVE	*v* -VOLVED, -VOLVING, -VOLVES to turn about an axis
REVOLVER	*n* pl. -S a type of handgun
REVUE	*n* pl. -S a type of musical show
REVUIST	*n* pl. -S a writer of revues
REVULSED	*adj* affected with revulsion
REVVED	past tense of rev
REVVING	present participle of rev
REWARD	*v* -ED, -ING, -S to give recompense to for worthy behavior
REWARDER	*n* pl. -S one that rewards
REWINDER	*n* pl. -S one that rewinds
REWORD	*v* -ED, -ING, -S to state again in other words
REWRITER	*n* pl. -S one that rewrites
REX	*n* pl. REGES king
REX	*n* pl. -ES an animal with a single wavy layer of hair
REYNARD	*n* pl. -S a fox
RHABDOM	*n* pl. -S a rodlike structure in the retinula
RHABDOME	*n* pl. -S rhabdom
RHACHIS	*n* pl. -CHISES or -CHIDES rachis
RHAMNOSE	*n* pl. -S a sugar found in plants
RHAMNUS	*n* pl. -ES a thorny tree or shrub
RHAPHE	*n* pl. -PHAE or -PHES raphe
RHAPSODE	*n* pl. -S a reciter of epic poetry in ancient Greece
RHAPSODY	*n* pl. -DIES an exalted expression of feeling
RHATANY	*n* pl. -NIES a South American shrub
RHEA	*n* pl. -S a flightless bird
RHEBOK	*n* pl. -S a large antelope
RHEMATIC	*adj* pertaining to a verb
RHENIUM	*n* pl. -S a metallic element
RHEOBASE	*n* pl. -S the smallest amount of electricity required to stimulate a nerve
RHEOLOGY	*n* pl. -GIES the study of matter in the fluid state
RHEOPHIL	*adj* living in flowing water
RHEOSTAT	*n* pl. -S a resistor used to control electric current
RHESUS	*n* pl. -ES an Asian monkey
RHETOR	*n* pl. -S a teacher of rhetoric
RHETORIC	*n* pl. -S the study of effective speech and writing
RHEUM	*n* pl. -S a watery discharge from the eyes or nose **RHEUMIC** *adj*
RHEUMY	*adj* RHEUMIER, RHEUMIEST marked by rheum
RHINAL	*adj* pertaining to the nose
RHINITIS	*n* pl. RHINITIDES inflammation of the mucous membranes of the nose
RHINO	*n* pl. -NOS a rhinoceros

RHIZOBIA	*n/pl* rod-shaped bacteria	**RIBALDLY**	*adv* crudely
RHIZOID	*n* pl. -S a rootlike structure	**RIBALDRY**	*n* pl. -RIES crude language
RHIZOMA	*n* pl. -MATA rhizome	**RIBAND**	*n* pl. -S a ribbon
RHIZOME	*n* pl. -S a rootlike, underground stem **RHIZOMIC** *adj*	**RIBBAND**	*n* pl. -S a long, narrow strip used in shipbuilding
RHIZOPOD	*n* pl. -S any of a class of protozoans	**RIBBED**	past tense of rib
RHIZOPUS	*n* pl. -PI or -PUSES any of a genus of mold fungi	**RIBBER**	*n* pl. -S one that ribs
		RIBBIER	comparative of ribby
RHO	*n* pl. RHOS a Greek letter	**RIBBIEST**	superlative of ribby
RHODAMIN	*n* pl. -S a red dye	**RIBBING**	*n* pl. -S the act of one that ribs
RHODIUM	*n* pl. -S a metallic element **RHODIC** *adj*	**RIBBON**	*v* -ED, -ING, -S to decorate with ribbons (narrow strips of fine fabric)
RHODORA	*n* pl. -S a flowering shrub		
RHOMB	*n* pl. -S a rhombus	**RIBBONY**	*adj* resembling ribbon
RHOMBI	a pl. of rhombus	**RIBBY**	*adj* -BIER, -BIEST marked by prominent ribs (curved bony rods in the body)
RHOMBIC	*adj* having the shape of a rhombus		
RHOMBOID	*n* pl. -S a type of geometric figure	**RIBES**	*n* pl. RIBES a flowering shrub
		RIBGRASS	*n* pl. -ES a weedy plant
RHOMBUS	*n* pl. -BUSES or -BI a type of geometric figure	**RIBLESS**	*adj* having no ribs
RHONCHUS	*n* pl. -CHI a rattling respiratory sound **RHONCHAL** *adj*	**RIBLET**	*n* pl. -S the rib end in a breast of lamb or veal
		RIBLIKE	*adj* resembling a rib
RHUBARB	*n* pl. -S a perennial herb	**RIBOSE**	*n* pl. -S a pentose sugar
RHUMB	*n* pl. -S a point of the mariner's compass	**RIBOSOME**	*n* pl. -S a particle composed of protein and ribonucleic acid
RHUMBA	*v* -ED, -ING, -S to rumba		
RHUS	*n* pl. -ES any of a genus of shrubs and trees	**RIBWORT**	*n* pl. -S ribgrass
		RICE	*v* RICED, RICING, RICES to press through a ricer
RHYME	*v* RHYMED, RHYMING, RHYMES to compose verse with corresponding terminal sounds	**RICEBIRD**	*n* pl. -S the bobolink
		RICER	*n* pl. -S a kitchen utensil consisting of a container perforated with small holes
RHYMER	*n* pl. -S one that rhymes		
RHYOLITE	*n* pl. -S a volcanic rock		
RHYTA	pl. of rhyton	**RICERCAR**	*n* pl. -S an instrumental composition
RHYTHM	*n* pl. -S movement or procedure with uniform recurrence of strong and weak elements	**RICH**	*adj* RICHER, RICHEST having wealth
		RICHEN	*v* -ED, -ING, -S to make rich
RHYTHMIC	*n* pl. -S the science of rhythm	**RICHES**	*n/pl* wealth
RHYTON	*n* pl. -TA an ancient Greek drinking horn	**RICHLY**	*adv* in a rich manner
		RICHNESS	*n* pl. -ES the state of being rich
RIAL	*n* pl. -S a monetary unit of Iran	**RICHWEED**	*n* pl. -S a flowering plant
RIALTO	*n* pl. -TOS a marketplace	**RICIN**	*n* pl. -S a poisonous protein
RIANT	*adj* cheerful **RIANTLY** *adv*	**RICING**	present participle of rice
RIATA	*n* pl. -S a lasso	**RICINUS**	*n* pl. -ES a large-leaved plant
RIB	*v* RIBBED, RIBBING, RIBS to poke fun at	**RICK**	*v* -ED, -ING, -S to pile hay in stacks
RIBALD	*n* pl. -S one who uses crude language		

RICKETS	*n/pl* a disease resulting from vitamin D deficiency
RICKETY	*adj* -ETIER, -ETIEST likely to fall or collapse
RICKEY	*n* pl. -EYS an alcoholic beverage containing lime juice, sugar, and soda water
RICKRACK	*n* pl. -S a flat braid used as a trimming
RICKSHA	*n* pl. -S rickshaw
RICKSHAW	*n* pl. -S a small, two-wheeled passenger vehicle
RICOCHET	*v* -CHETED, -CHETING, -CHETS or -CHETTED, -CHETTING, -CHETS to rebound from a surface
RICOTTA	*n* pl. -S an Italian cheese
RICRAC	*n* pl. -S rickrack
RICTUS	*n* pl. -ES the expanse of the open mouth **RICTAL** *adj*
RID	*v* RID or RIDDED, RIDDING, RIDS to free from something objectionable
RIDABLE	*adj* capable of being ridden
RIDDANCE	*n* pl. -S deliverance
RIDDED	past tense of rid
RIDDEN	past participle of ride
RIDDER	*n* pl. -S one that rids
RIDDING	present participle of rid
RIDDLE	*v* -DLED, -DLING, -DLES to pierce with many holes
RIDDLER	*n* pl. -S one that riddles
RIDE	*v* RODE, RIDDEN, RIDING, RIDES to sit on, control, and be conveyed by an animal or machine
RIDEABLE	*adj* ridable
RIDENT	*adj* laughing
RIDER	*n* pl. -S one that rides
RIDGE	*v* RIDGED, RIDGING, RIDGES to form into ridges (long, narrow elevations)
RIDGEL	*n* pl. -S a ridgling
RIDGIER	comparative of ridgy
RIDGIEST	superlative of ridgy
RIDGIL	*n* pl. -S a ridgling
RIDGING	present participle of ridge
RIDGLING	*n* pl. -S a male animal with undescended testicles
RIDGY	*adj* RIDGIER, RIDGIEST having ridges
RIDICULE	*v* -CULED, -CULING, -CULES to make fun of
RIDING	*n* pl. -S the act of one that rides
RIDLEY	*n* pl. -LEYS a sea turtle
RIDOTTO	*n* pl. -TOS a public musical entertainment in 18th century England
RIEL	*n* pl. -S a monetary unit of Cambodia
RIEVER	*n* pl. -S reaver
RIFE	*adj* RIFER, RIFEST abundant **RIFELY** *adv*
RIFENESS	*n* pl. -ES the state of being rife
RIFF	*v* -ED, -ING, -S to riffle
RIFFLE	*v* -FLED, -FLING, -FLES to flip through hastily
RIFFLER	*n* pl. -S a filing and scraping tool
RIFFRAFF	*n* pl. -S the disreputable element of society
RIFLE	*v* -FLED, -FLING, -FLES to search through and rob
RIFLEMAN	*n* pl. -MEN a soldier armed with a rifle (a type of firearm)
RIFLER	*n* pl. -S one that rifles
RIFLERY	*n* pl. -RIES the practice of shooting at targets with a rifle
RIFLING	*n* pl. -S the system of grooves in a gun barrel
RIFT	*v* -ED, -ING, -S to form rifts (clefts)
RIFTLESS	*adj* having no rift
RIG	*v* RIGGED, RIGGING, RIGS to put in proper condition for use
RIGADOON	*n* pl. -S a lively dance
RIGATONI	*n* pl. -S a tubular pasta
RIGAUDON	*n* pl. -S rigadoon
RIGGED	past tense of rig
RIGGER	*n* pl. -S one that rigs
RIGGING	*n* pl. -S the system of lines, chains, and tackle used aboard a ship
RIGHT	*adj* RIGHTER, RIGHTEST being in accordance with what is good, proper, or just
RIGHT	*v* -ED, -ING, -S to put in proper order or condition
RIGHTER	*n* pl. -S one that rights
RIGHTFUL	*adj* just or proper
RIGHTIES	pl. of righty

RIGHTISM   *n* pl. -S a conservative political philosophy

RIGHTIST   *n* pl. -S an advocate of rightism

RIGHTLY   *adv* in a right manner

RIGHTO   *interj* — used to express cheerful consent

RIGHTY   *n* pl. RIGHTIES a right-handed person

RIGID   *adj* not flexible

RIGIDIFY   *v* -FIED, -FYING, -FIES to make rigid

RIGIDITY   *n* pl. -TIES the state of being rigid

RIGIDLY   *adv* in a rigid manner

RIGOR   *n* pl. -S strictness or severity

RIGORISM   *n* pl. -S strictness or severity in conduct or attitude

RIGORIST   *n* pl. -S one that professes rigorism

RIGOROUS   *adj* characterized by rigor

RIGOUR   *n* pl. -S rigor

RIKISHA   *n* pl. -S rickshaw

RIKSHAW   *n* pl. -S rickshaw

RILE   *v* RILED, RILING, RILES to anger

RILEY   *adj* angry

RILIEVO   *n* pl. -VI relievo

RILING   present participle of rile

RILL   *v* -ED, -ING, -S to flow like a rill (a small brook)

RILLE   *n* pl. -S a valley on the moon's surface

RILLET   *n* pl. -S a small rill

RIM   *v* RIMMED, RIMMING, RIMS to provide with a rim (an outer edge)

RIME   *v* RIMED, RIMING, RIMES to rhyme

RIMER   *n* pl. -S one that rimes

RIMESTER   *n* pl. -S a rimer

RIMFIRE   *adj* designed for the use of certain cartridges

RIMIER   comparative of rimy

RIMIEST   superlative of rimy

RIMING   present participle of rime

RIMLAND   *n* pl. -S an outlying area

RIMLESS   *adj* having no rim

RIMMED   past tense of rim

RIMMER   *n* pl. -S a reamer

RIMMING   present participle of rim

RIMOSE   *adj* marked by cracks **RIMOSELY** *adv*

RIMOSITY   *n* pl. -TIES the state of being rimose

RIMOUS   *adj* rimose

RIMPLE   *v* -PLED, -PLING, -PLES to wrinkle

RIMROCK   *n* pl. -S a type of rock formation

RIMY   *adj* RIMIER, RIMIEST frosty

RIN   *v* RAN, RINNING, RINS to run or melt

RIND   *n* pl. -S a thick and firm outer covering **RINDED** *adj*

RING   *v* -ED, -ING, -S to form a ring (a circular band) around

RING   *v* RANG, RUNG, RINGING, RINGS to give forth a clear, resonant sound

RINGBARK   *v* -ED, -ING, -S to make an encircling cut through the bark of

RINGBOLT   *n* pl. -S a type of eyebolt

RINGBONE   *n* pl. -S a bony growth on a horse's foot

RINGDOVE   *n* pl. -S a European pigeon

RINGENT   *adj* having open liplike parts

RINGER   *n* pl. -S one that rings

RINGHALS   *n* pl. -ES a venomous snake

RINGLET   *adj* a small ring

RINGLIKE   *adj* resembling a ring

RINGNECK   *n* pl. -S a bird having a ring of color around the neck

RINGSIDE   *n* pl. -S the area just outside a boxing or wrestling ring (a square enclosure)

RINGTAIL   *n* pl. -S an animal having a tail with ringlike markings

RINGTAW   *n* pl. -S a game of marbles

RINGTOSS   *n* pl. -ES a game in which the object is to toss a ring onto an upright stick

RINGWORM   *n* pl. -S a skin disease

RINK   *n* pl. -S a surface of ice for skating

RINNING   present participle of rin

RINSE   *v* RINSED, RINSING, RINSES to cleanse with clear water **RINSABLE, RINSIBLE** *adj*

RINSER   *n* pl. -S one that rinses

RINSING   *n* pl. -S the act of one that rinses

RIOT   *v* -ED, -ING, -S to take part in a violent public disturbance

RIOTER   *n* pl. -S one that riots

RIOTOUS   *adj* characterized by rioting

RIP   *v* RIPPED, RIPPING, RIPS to tear or cut apart roughly

RIPARIAN   *adj* pertaining to the bank of a river

RIPCORD   *n* pl. -S a cord pulled to release a parachute

RIPE   *adj* RIPER, RIPEST fully developed **RIPELY** *adv*

RIPE   *v* RIPED, RIPING, RIPES to cleanse

RIPEN   *v* -ED, -ING, -S to become ripe

RIPENER   *n* pl. -S one that ripens

RIPENESS   *n* pl. -ES the state of being ripe

RIPER   comparative of ripe

RIPEST   superlative of ripe

RIPIENO   *n* pl. -NI or -NOS tutti

RIPING   present participle of ripe

RIPOST   *v* -ED, -ING, -S to riposte

RIPOSTE   *v* -POSTED, -POSTING, -POSTES to make a return thrust in fencing

RIPPABLE   *adj* capable of being ripped

RIPPED   past tense of rip

RIPPER   *n* pl. -S one that rips

RIPPING   *adj* excellent

RIPPLE   *v* -PLED, -PLING, -PLES to form ripples (small waves)

RIPPLER   *n* pl. -S a toothed tool for cleaning flax fiber

RIPPLET   *n* pl. -S a small ripple

RIPPLING   present participle of ripple

RIPPLY   *adj* -PLIER, -PLIEST marked by ripples

RIPRAP   *v* -RAPPED, -RAPPING, -RAPS to strengthen with a foundation of broken stones

RIPSAW   *n* pl. -S a type of saw

RIPTIDE   *n* pl. -S a tide that opposes other tides

RISE   *v* ROSE, RISEN, RISING, RISES to move upward

RISER   *n* pl. -S one that rises

RISHI   *n* pl. -S a Hindu sage

RISIBLE   *adj* inclined to laugh **RISIBLY** *adv*

RISIBLES   *n/pl* a sense of the ridiculous

RISING   *n* pl. -S the act of one that rises

RISK   *v* -ED, -ING, -S to expose to a chance of injury or loss

RISKER   *n* pl. -S one that risks

RISKY   *adj* RISKIER, RISKIEST dangerous **RISKILY** *adv*

RISOTTO   *n* pl. -TOS a rice dish

RISQUE   *adj* bordering on impropriety or indecency

RISSOLE   *n* pl. -S a small roll filled with meat or fish

RISUS   *n* pl. -ES a grin or laugh

RITARD   *n* pl. -S a musical passage with a gradual slackening in tempo

RITE   *n* pl. -S a ceremonial act or procedure

RITTER   *n* pl. -S a knight

RITUAL   *n* pl. -S a system of rites

RITUALLY   *adv* ceremonially

RITZ   *n* pl. -ES pretentious display

RITZY   *adj* RITZIER, RITZIEST elegant **RITZILY** *adv*

RIVAGE   *n* pl. -S a coast, shore, or bank

RIVAL   *v* -VALED, -VALING, -VALS or -VALLED, -VALLING, -VALS to strive to equal or surpass

RIVALRY   *n* pl. -RIES competition

RIVE   *v* RIVED, RIVEN, RIVING, RIVES to tear apart

RIVER   *n* pl. -S a large, natural stream of water

RIVERBED   *n* pl. -S the area covered or once covered by a river

RIVERINE   *adj* pertaining to a river

RIVET   *v* -ETED, -ETING, -ETS or -ETTED, -ETTING, -ETS to fasten with a type of metal bolt

RIVETER   *n* pl. -S one that rivets

RIVIERA   *n* pl. -S a coastal resort area

RIVIERE   *n* pl. -S a necklace of precious stones

RIVING   present participle of rive

RIVULET   *n* pl. -S a small stream

RIYAL   *n* pl. -S a monetary unit of Saudi Arabia

ROACH   *v* -ED, -ING, -ES to cause to arch

ROAD   *n* pl. -S an open way for public passage

ROADBED   *n* pl. -S the foundation for a railroad track

ROADLESS   *adj* having no roads

ROADSIDE   *n* pl. -S the area along the side of a road

ROADSTER   *n* pl. -S a light, open automobile

ROADWAY   *n* pl. -WAYS a road

ROADWORK   *n* pl. -S outdoor running as a form of physical conditioning

ROAM   *v* -ED, -ING, -S to move about without purpose or plan

ROAMER   *n* pl. -S one that roams

ROAN   *n* pl. -S an animal having a coat sprinkled with white or gray

ROAR   *v* -ED, -ING, -S to utter a loud, deep sound

ROARER   *n* pl. -S one that roars

ROARING   *n* pl. -S a loud, deep sound

ROAST   *v* -ED, -ING, -S to cook with dry heat

ROASTER   *n* pl. -S one that roasts

ROB   *v* ROBBED, ROBBING, ROBS to take property from illegally

ROBALO   *n* pl. -LOS a marine food fish

ROBAND   *n* pl. -S a piece of yarn used to fasten a sail

ROBBED   past tense of rob

ROBBER   *n* pl. -S one that robs

ROBBERY   *n* pl. -BERIES the act of one who robs

ROBBIN   *n* pl. -S a roband

ROBBING   present participle of rob

ROBE   *v* ROBED, ROBING, ROBES to cover with a robe (a long, loose outer garment)

ROBIN   *n* pl. -S a songbird

ROBLE   *n* pl. -S an oak tree

ROBORANT   *n* pl. -S an invigorating drug

ROBOT   *n* pl. -S a humanlike machine that performs various functions

ROBOTICS   *n/pl* a field of interest concerned with robots

ROBOTISM   *n* pl. -S the state of being a robot

ROBOTIZE   *v* -IZED, -IZING, -IZES to make automatic

ROBOTRY   *n* pl. -RIES the science of robots

ROBUST   *adj* -BUSTER, -BUSTEST strong and healthy **ROBUSTLY** *adv*

ROC   *n* pl. -S a lengendary bird of prey

ROCHET   *n* pl. -S a linen vestment

ROCK   *v* -ED, -ING, -S to move back and forth

ROCKABY   *n* pl. -BIES a song used to lull a child to sleep

ROCKABYE   *n* pl. -S rockaby

ROCKAWAY   *n* pl. -WAYS a light carriage

ROCKER   *n* pl. -S a rocking chair

ROCKERY   *n* pl. -ERIES a rock garden

ROCKET   *v* -ED, -ING, -S to convey by means of a rocket (a device propelled by the reaction of escaping gases)

ROCKETER   *n* pl. -S one that designs or launches rockets

ROCKETRY   *n* pl. -RIES the science of rockets

ROCKFALL   *n* pl. -S a mass of fallen rocks

ROCKFISH   *n* pl. -ES a fish living around rocks

ROCKIER   comparative of rocky

ROCKIEST   superlative of rocky

ROCKLESS   *adj* having no rocks

ROCKLIKE   *adj* resembling a rock (a large mass of stone)

ROCKLING   *n* pl. -S a marine fish

ROCKOON   *n* pl. -S a small rocket

ROCKROSE   *n* pl. -S a flowering plant

ROCKWEED   *n* pl. -S a brown seaweed

ROCKWORK   *n* pl. -S a natural mass of rocks

ROCKY   *adj* ROCKIER, ROCKIEST unsteady

ROCOCO   *n* pl. -COS a style of architecture and decoration

ROD   *v* RODDED, RODDING, RODS to provide with a rod (a straight, slender piece of wood, metal, or other material)

RODE   past tense of ride

RODENT   *n* pl. -S a gnawing mammal

RODEO   *n* pl. -DEOS a public exhibition of cowboy skills

RODLESS   *adj* having no rod

RODLIKE   *adj* resembling a rod

RODMAN   *n* pl. -MEN a surveyor's assistant

RODSMAN   *n* pl. -MEN rodman

ROE   *n* pl. -S the mass of eggs within a female fish

ROEBUCK   *n* pl. -S the male of a small Eurasian deer

ROENTGEN   *n* pl. -S a unit of radiation dosage

ROGATION   *n* pl. -S the proposal of a law in ancient Rome

ROGATORY   *adj* requesting information

ROGER   *n* pl. -S the pirate flag bearing the skull and crossbones

ROGUE   *v* ROGUED, ROGUEING or ROGUING, ROGUES to defraud

ROGUERY   *n* pl. -ERIES roguish conduct

ROGUISH   *adj* dishonest

ROIL   *v* -ED, -ING, -S to make muddy

ROILY   *adj* ROILIER, ROILIEST muddy

ROISTER   *v* -ED, -ING, -S to revel

ROLAMITE   *n* pl. -S a nearly frictionless mechanical device

ROLE   *n* pl. -S a part played by an actor

ROLL   *v* -ED, -ING, -S to move along by repeatedly turning over

ROLLAWAY   *adj* mounted on rollers for easy movement

ROLLBACK   *n* pl. -S a return to a lower level of prices or wages

ROLLER   *n* pl. -S a cylindrical device that rolls or rotates

ROLLICK   *v* -ED, -ING, -S to frolic

ROLLICKY   *adj* given to rollicking

ROLLING   *n* pl. -S the act of one that rolls

ROLLMOP   *n* pl. -S a fillet of herring

ROLLOUT   *n* pl. -S a type of play in football

ROLLOVER   *n* pl. -S a motor vehicle accident in which the vehicle overturns

ROLLTOP   *adj* having a flexible, sliding cover

ROLLWAY   *n* pl. -WAYS an incline for rolling logs

ROMAINE   *n* pl. -S a variety of lettuce

ROMAN   *n* pl. -S a metrical narrative of medieval France

ROMANCE   *v* -MANCED, -MANCING, -MANCES to woo

ROMANCER   *n* pl. -S one that romances

ROMANIZE   *v* -IZED, -IZING, -IZES to write in the Roman alphabet

ROMANO   *n* pl. -NOS an Italian cheese

ROMANTIC   *n* pl. -S a fanciful person

ROMAUNT   *n* pl. -S a long, medieval narrative

ROMP   *v* -ED, -ING, -S to play boisterously

ROMPER   *n* pl. -S one that romps

ROMPISH   *adj* inclined to romp

RONDEAU   *n* pl. -DEAUX a short poem of fixed form

RONDEL   *n* pl. -S a rondeau of 14 lines

RONDELET   *n* pl. -S a rondeau of 5 or 7 lines

RONDELLE   *n* pl. -S rondel

RONDO   *n* pl. -DOS a type of musical composition

RONDURE   *n* pl. -S a circle or sphere

RONION   *n* pl. -S a mangy animal or person

RONNEL   *n* pl. -S an insecticide

RONTGEN   *n* pl. -S roentgen

RONYON   *n* pl. -S ronion

ROOD   *n* pl. -S a crucifix

ROOF   *v* -ED, -ING, -S to provide with a roof (the external upper covering of a building)

ROOFER   *n* pl. -S one that builds or repairs roofs

ROOFING   *n* pl. -S material for a roof

ROOFLESS   *adj* having no roof

ROOFLIKE   *adj* resembling a roof

ROOFLINE   *n* pl. -S the profile of a roof

ROOFTOP   *n* pl. -S a roof

ROOFTREE   *n* pl. -S a horizontal timber in a roof

ROOK   *v* -ED, -ING, -S to swindle

ROOKERY   *n* pl. -ERIES a colony of rooks (European crows)

ROOKIE   *n* pl. -S a novice

ROOKY   *adj* ROOKIER, ROOKIEST abounding in rooks

ROOM   *v* -ED, -ING, -S to occupy a room (a walled space within a building)

ROOMER   *n* pl. -S a lodger

ROOMETTE   *n* pl. -S a small room

ROOMFUL   *n* pl. -S as much as a room will hold

ROOMMATE	*n* pl. -S one with whom a room is shared
ROOMY	*adj* ROOMIER, ROOMIEST spacious **ROOMILY** *adv*
ROORBACK	*n* pl. -S a false story used for political advantage
ROOSE	*v* ROOSED, ROOSING, ROOSES to praise
ROOSER	*n* pl. -S one that rooses
ROOST	*v* -ED, -ING, -S to settle down for rest or sleep
ROOSTER	*n* pl. -S a male chicken
ROOT	*v* -ED, -ING, -S to put forth a root (an underground portion of a plant)
ROOTAGE	*n* pl. -S a system of roots
ROOTER	*n* pl. -S one that gives encouragement or support
ROOTHOLD	*n* pl. -S the embedding of a plant to soil through the growing of roots
ROOTIER	comparative of rooty
ROOTIEST	superlative of rooty
ROOTLESS	*adj* having no roots
ROOTLET	*n* pl. -S a small root
ROOTLIKE	*adj* resembling a root
ROOTY	*adj* ROOTIER, ROOTIEST full of roots
ROPE	*v* ROPED, ROPING, ROPES to bind with a rope (a thick line of twisted fibers) **ROPABLE** *adj*
ROPER	*n* pl. -S one that ropes
ROPERY	*n* pl. -ERIES a place where ropes are made
ROPEWALK	*n* pl. -S a long path where ropes are made
ROPEWAY	*n* pl. -WAYS an aerial cable used to transport freight
ROPIER	comparative of ropy
ROPIEST	superlative of ropy
ROPILY	*adv* in a ropy manner
ROPINESS	*n* pl. -ES the quality of being ropy
ROPING	present participle of rope
ROPY	*adj* ROPIER, ROPIEST resembling a rope or ropes
ROQUE	*n* pl. -S a form of croquet
ROQUET	*v* -ED, -ING, -S to cause one's own ball to hit another in croquet
RORQUAL	*n* pl. -S a large whale
ROSARIA	a pl. of rosarium
ROSARIAN	*n* pl. -S a cultivator of roses
ROSARIUM	*n* pl. -IA or -IUMS a rose garden
ROSARY	*n* pl. -RIES a series of prayers in the Roman Catholic Church
ROSCOE	*n* pl. -S a pistol
ROSE	*v* ROSED, ROSING, ROSES to make the color of a rose (a reddish flower)
ROSEATE	*adj* rose-colored
ROSEBAY	*n* pl. -BAYS an evergreen shrub
ROSEBUD	*n* pl. -S the bud of a rose
ROSEBUSH	*n* pl. -ES a shrub that bears roses
ROSED	past tense of rose
ROSEFISH	*n* pl. -ES a marine food fish
ROSELIKE	*adj* resembling a rose
ROSELLE	*n* pl. -S a tropical plant
ROSEMARY	*n* pl. -MARIES an evergreen shrub
ROSEOLA	*n* pl. -S a rose-colored skin rash **ROSEOLAR** *adj*
ROSEROOT	*n* pl. -S a perennial herb
ROSERY	*n* pl. -ERIES a place where roses are grown
ROSET	*n* pl. -S resin
ROSETTE	*n* pl. -S an ornament resembling a rose
ROSEWOOD	*n* pl. -S a tropical tree
ROSIER	comparative of rosy
ROSIEST	superlative of rosy
ROSILY	*adv* in a rosy manner
ROSIN	*v* -ED, -ING, -S to treat with rosin (a brittle resin)
ROSINESS	*n* pl. -ES the state of being rosy
ROSING	present participle of rose
ROSINOUS	*adj* resembling rosin
ROSINY	*adj* rosinous
ROSOLIO	*n* pl. -LIOS a liqueur made from raisins and brandy
ROSTELLA	*n/pl* small, beaklike structures
ROSTER	*n* pl. -S a list of names
ROSTRA	a pl. of rostrum
ROSTRAL	*adj* pertaining to a rostrum
ROSTRATE	*adj* having a rostrum
ROSTRUM	*n* pl. -TRA or -TRUMS a beaklike process or part

ROSULATE *adj* arranged in the form of a rosette

ROSY *adj* ROSIER, ROSIEST rose-colored

ROT *v* ROTTED, ROTTING, ROTS to decompose

ROTA *n* pl. -S a roster

ROTARY *n* pl. -RIES a rotating part or device

ROTATE *v* -TATED, -TATING, -TATES to turn about an axis

ROTATION *n* pl. -S the act or an instance of rotating **ROTATIVE** *adj*

ROTATOR *n* pl. -S one that rotates

ROTATOR *n* pl. -ES a muscle serving to rotate a part of the body

ROTATORY *adj* pertaining to rotation

ROTCH *n* pl. -ES rotche

ROTCHE *n* pl. -S a seabird

ROTE *n* pl. -S mechanical routine

ROTENONE *n* pl. -S an insecticide

ROTGUT *n* pl. -S inferior liquor

ROTIFER *n* pl. -S a microscopic aquatic organism

ROTIFORM *adj* shaped like a wheel

ROTL *n* pl. ROTLS or ARTAL a unit of weight in Muslim countries

ROTO *n* pl. -TOS a type of printing process

ROTOR *n* pl. -S a rotating part of a machine

ROTOTILL *v* -ED, -ING, -S to till soil with a type of farming implement

ROTTED past tense of rot

ROTTEN *adj* -TENER, -TENEST being in a state of decay **ROTTENLY** *adv*

ROTTER *n* pl. -S a scoundrel

ROTTING present participle of rot

ROTUND *adj* marked by roundness **ROTUNDLY** *adv*

ROTUNDA *n* pl. -S a round building

ROTURIER *n* pl. -S a commoner

ROUBLE *n* pl. -S ruble

ROUCHE *n* pl. -S ruche

ROUE *n* pl. -S a lecherous man

ROUEN *n* pl. -S any of a breed of domestic ducks

ROUGE *v* ROUGED, ROUGING, ROUGES to color with a red cosmetic

ROUGH *adj* ROUGHER, ROUGHEST having an uneven surface

ROUGH *v* -ED, -ING, -S to make rough

ROUGHAGE *n* pl. -S coarse, bulky food

ROUGHDRY *v* -DRIED, -DRYING, -DRIES to dry without ironing, as washed clothes

ROUGHEN *v* -ED, -ING, -S to make rough

ROUGHER *n* pl. -S one that roughs

ROUGHHEW *v* -HEWED, -HEWN, -HEWING, -HEWS to shape roughly

ROUGHISH *adj* somewhat rough

ROUGHLEG *n* pl. -S a large hawk

ROUGHLY *adv* in a rough manner

ROUGING present participle of rouge

ROULADE *n* pl. -S a musical embellishment

ROULEAU *n* pl. -LEAUX or -LEAUS a roll of coins wrapped in paper

ROULETTE *v* -LETTED, -LETTING, -LETTES to make tiny slits in

ROUND *adj* ROUNDER, ROUNDEST shaped like a sphere

ROUND *v* -ED, -ING, -S to make round

ROUNDEL *n* pl. -S a round figure or object

ROUNDER *n* pl. -S a tool for rounding

ROUNDISH *adj* somewhat round

ROUNDLET *n* pl. -S a small circle

ROUNDLY *adv* in a round manner

ROUNDUP *n* pl. -S the driving together of cattle scattered over a range

ROUP *v* -ED, -ING, -S to auction

ROUPET *adj* roupy

ROUPY *adj* ROUPIER, ROUPIEST hoarse **ROUPILY** *adv*

ROUSE *v* ROUSED, ROUSING, ROUSES to bring out of a state of sleep or inactivity

ROUSER *n* pl. -S one that rouses

ROUSSEAU *n* pl. -S fried pemmican

ROUST *v* -ED, -ING, -S to arouse and drive out

ROUSTER *n* pl. -S a wharf laborer and deckhand

ROUT *v* -ED, -ING, -S to defeat overwhelmingly

ROUTE *v* ROUTED, ROUTING, ROUTES to send on a particular course

ROUTEMAN *n* pl. -MEN one who conducts business on a customary course

ROUTER	*n* pl. -S a scooping tool	**RUBACE**	*n* pl. -S rubasse
ROUTEWAY	*n* pl. -WAYS an established course of travel	**RUBAIYAT**	*n* pl. RUBAIYAT four-lined stanzas in Persian poetry
ROUTH	*n* pl. -S an abundance	**RUBASSE**	*n* pl. -S a variety of quartz
ROUTINE	*n* pl. -S a regular course of procedure	**RUBATO**	*n* pl. -TOS a fluctuation of speed within a musical phrase
ROUTING	present participle of route	**RUBBABOO**	*n* pl. -BOOS rubaboo
ROUX	*n* pl. ROUX a mixture of butter and flour	**RUBBED**	past tense of rub
ROVE	*v* ROVED, ROVING, ROVES to roam	**RUBBER**	*n* pl. -S an elastic substance **RUBBERY** *adj*
ROVEN	a past participle of reeve	**RUBBING**	*n* pl. -S an image produced by rubbing
ROVER	*n* pl. -S one that roves	**RUBBISH**	*n* pl. -ES worthless, unwanted matter **RUBBISHY** *adj*
ROVING	*n* pl. -S a roll of textile fibers	**RUBBLE**	*v* -BLED, -BLING, -BLES to reduce to rubble (broken pieces)
ROVINGLY	*adv* in a roving manner		
ROW	*v* -ED, -ING, -S to propel by means of oars **ROWABLE** *adj*	**RUBBLY**	*adj* -BLIER, -BLIEST abounding in rubble
ROWAN	*n* pl. -S a Eurasian tree	**RUBDOWN**	*n* pl. -S a brisk rubbing of the body
ROWBOAT	*n* pl. -S a small boat designed to be rowed	**RUBE**	*n* pl. -S a rustic
ROWDY	*adj* -DIER, -DIEST disorderly in behavior **ROWDILY** *adv*	**RUBELLA**	*n* pl. -S a virus disease
		RUBEOLA	*n* pl. -S a virus disease **RUBEOLAR** *adj*
ROWDY	*n* pl. -DIES a rowdy person	**RUBICUND**	*adj* ruddy
ROWDYISH	*adj* tending to be rowdy	**RUBIDIUM**	*n* pl. -S a metallic element **RUBIDIC** *adj*
ROWDYISM	*n* pl. -S disorderly behavior		
ROWEL	*v* -ELED, -ELING, -ELS or -ELLED, -ELLING, -ELS to prick with a spiked wheel in order to urge forward	**RUBIED**	past tense of ruby
		RUBIER	comparative of ruby
		RUBIES	present 3d person sing. of ruby
ROWEN	*n* pl. -S a second growth of grass	**RUBIEST**	superlative of ruby
ROWER	*n* pl. -S one that rows	**RUBIGO**	*n* pl. -GOS red iron oxide
ROWING	*n* pl. -S the sport of racing in light, long, and narrow rowboats	**RUBIOUS**	*adj* ruby-colored
		RUBLE	*n* pl. -S a monetary unit of the Soviet Union
ROWLOCK	*n* pl. -S an oarlock		
ROWTH	*n* pl. -S routh	**RUBRIC**	*n* pl. -S a part of a manuscript or book that appears in red **RUBRICAL** *adj*
ROYAL	*n* pl. -S a size of printing paper		
ROYALISM	*n* pl. -S support of a monarch or monarchy	**RUBUS**	*n* pl. RUBUS a plant of the rose family
ROYALIST	*n* pl. -S a supporter of a monarch or monarchy	**RUBY**	*v* -BIED, -BYING, -BIES to tint with the color of a ruby (a deep-red precious stone)
ROYALLY	*adv* in a kingly manner		
ROYALTY	*n* pl. -TIES the status or power of a monarch	**RUBY**	*adj* -BIER, -BIEST of a deep-red color
ROYSTER	*v* -ED, -ING, -S to roister	**RUBYLIKE**	*adj* resembling a ruby
ROZZER	*n* pl. -S a policeman		
RUB	*v* RUBBED, RUBBING, RUBS to move along the surface of a body with pressure	**RUCHE**	*n* pl. -S a pleated strip of fine fabric
RUBABOO	*n* pl. -BOOS a type of soup	**RUCHING**	*n* pl. -S a ruche

RUCK   v -ED, -ING, -S to wrinkle or crease

RUCKSACK   n pl. -S a knapsack

RUCKUS   n pl. -ES a noisy disturbance

RUCTION   n pl. -S a ruckus

RUCTIOUS   adj quarrelsome

RUDD   n pl. -S a freshwater fish

RUDDER   n pl. -S a vertical blade used to direct the course of a vessel

RUDDIER   comparative of ruddy

RUDDIEST   superlative of ruddy

RUDDILY   adv in a ruddy manner

RUDDLE   v -DLED, -DLING, -DLES to color with a red dye

RUDDOCK   n pl. -S a European bird

RUDDY   adj -DIER, -DIEST having a healthy, reddish color

RUDE   adj RUDER, RUDEST discourteous or impolite **RUDELY** adv

RUDENESS   n pl. -ES the quality of being rude

RUDERAL   n pl. -S a plant growing in poor land

RUDESBY   n pl. -BIES a rude person

RUDEST   superlative of rude

RUDIMENT   n pl. -S a basic principle or element

RUE   v RUED, RUING, RUES to feel sorrow or remorse for

RUEFUL   adj feeling sorrow or remorse **RUEFULLY** adv

RUER   n pl. -S one that rues

RUFF   v -ED, -ING, -S to trump

RUFFE   n pl. -S a freshwater fish

RUFFIAN   n pl. -S a tough, lawless person

RUFFLE   v -FLED, -FLING, -FLES to destroy the smoothness of

RUFFLER   n pl. -S one that ruffles

RUFFLIKE   adj resembling a ruff (a pleated collar)

RUFFLING   present participle of ruffle

RUFFLY   adj not smooth

RUFOUS   adj reddish

RUG   v RUGGED, RUGGING, RUGS to tear roughly

RUGA   n pl. -GAE an anatomical fold or wrinkle **RUGAL, RUGATE** adj

RUGBY   n pl. -BIES a form of football

RUGGED   adj -GEDER, -GEDEST having an uneven surface **RUGGEDLY** adv

RUGGER   n pl. -S rugby

RUGGING   present participle of rug

RUGLIKE   adj resembling a rug (a thick fabric used as a floor covering)

RUGOSE   adj full of wrinkles **RUGOSELY** adv

RUGOSITY   n pl. -TIES the state of being rugose

RUGOUS   adj rugose

RUGULOSE   adj having small wrinkles

RUIN   v -ED, -ING, -S to destroy **RUINABLE** adj

RUINATE   v -ATED, -ATING, -ATES to ruin

RUINER   n pl. -S one that ruins

RUING   present participle of rue

RUINOUS   adj destructive

RULE   v RULED, RULING, RULES to exercise control over **RULABLE** adj

RULELESS   adj not restrained or regulated by law

RULER   n pl. -S one that rules

RULING   n pl. -S an authoritative decision

RUM   n pl. -S an alcoholic liquor

RUM   adj RUMMER, RUMMEST odd

RUMBA   v -ED, -ING, -S to perform a ballroom dance

RUMBLE   v -BLED, -BLING, -BLES to make a deep, thunderous sound

RUMBLER   n pl. -S one that rumbles

RUMBLING   n pl. -S a deep, thunderous sound

RUMBLY   adj tending to rumble

RUMEN   n pl. -MINA or -MENS a part of the stomach of a ruminant **RUMINAL** adj

RUMINANT   n pl. -S a hoofed, even-toed mammal

RUMINATE   v -NATED, -NATING, -NATES to chew again

RUMMAGE   v -MAGED, -MAGING, -MAGES to search thoroughly through

RUMMAGER   n pl. -S one that rummages

RUMMER   n pl. -S a large drinking glass

RUMMEST   superlative of rum

RUMMY   n pl. -MIES a card game

RUMMY   *adj* -MIER, -MIEST odd

RUMOR   *v* -ED, -ING, -S to spread by hearsay

RUMOUR   *v* -ED, -ING, -S to rumor

RUMP   *n* pl. -S the lower and back part of the trunk **RUMPLESS** *adj*

RUMPLE   *v* -PLED, -PLING, -PLES to wrinkle

RUMPLY   *adj* -PLIER, -PLIEST rumpled

RUMPUS   *n* pl. -ES a noisy disturbance

RUN   *v* RAN, RUNNING, RUNS to move by rapid steps

RUNABOUT   *n* pl. -S a small, open auto

RUNAGATE   *n* pl. -S a deserter

RUNAWAY   *n* pl. -AWAYS one that runs away

RUNBACK   *n* pl. -S a type of run in football

RUNDLE   *n* pl. -S a rung

RUNDLET   *n* pl. -S a small barrel

RUNDOWN   *n* pl. -S a summary

RUNE   *n* pl. -S a letter of an ancient alphabet **RUNELIKE** *adj*

RUNG   *n* pl. -S a crosspiece forming a step of a ladder **RUNGLESS** *adj*

RUNIC   *adj* pertaining to a rune

RUNKLE   *v* -KLED, -KLING, -KLES to wrinkle

RUNLESS   *adj* scoring no runs in baseball

RUNLET   *n* pl. -S a small stream

RUNNEL   *n* pl. -S a small stream

RUNNER   *n* pl. -S one that runs

RUNNING   *n* pl. -S a race

RUNNY   *adj* -NIER, -NIEST tending to drip

RUNOFF   *n* pl. -S rainfall that is not absorbed by the soil

RUNOUT   *n* pl. -S the end of a film strip

RUNOVER   *n* pl. -S matter for publication that exceeds the allotted space

RUNROUND   *n* pl. -S evasive action

RUNT   *n* pl. -S a small person or animal **RUNTISH** *adj*

RUNTY   *adj* RUNTIER, RUNTIEST small

RUNWAY   *n* pl. -WAYS a landing and takeoff strip for aircraft

RUPEE   *n* pl. -S a monetary unit of India

RUPIAH   *n* pl. -S a monetary unit of Indonesia

RUPTURE   *v* -TURED, -TURING, -TURES to burst

RURAL   *adj* pertaining to the country

RURALISE   *v* -ISED, -ISING, -ISES to ruralize

RURALISM   *n* pl. -S the state of being rural

RURALIST   *n* pl. -S one who lives in the country

RURALITE   *n* pl. -S a ruralist

RURALITY   *n* pl. -TIES the state of being rural

RURALIZE   *v* -IZED, -IZING, -IZES to make rural

RURALLY   *adv* in a rural manner

RURBAN   *adj* partially rural and urban

RUSE   *n* pl. -S a deception

RUSH   *v* -ED, -ING, -ES to move swiftly

RUSHEE   *n* pl. -S a college student seeking admission to a fraternity or sorority

RUSHER   *n* pl. -S one that rushes

RUSHIER   comparative of rushy

RUSHIEST   superlative of rushy

RUSHING   *n* pl. -S yardage gained in football by running plays

RUSHLIKE   *adj* resembling a rush (a grasslike marsh plant)

RUSHY   *adj* RUSHIER, RUSHIEST abounding in rushes

RUSINE   *adj* pertaining to a genus of deer

RUSK   *n* pl. -S a sweetened biscuit

RUSSET   *n* pl. -S a reddish or yellowish brown color **RUSSETY** *adj*

RUSSIFY   *v* -FIED, -FYING, -FIES to make Russian

RUST   *v* -ED, -ING, -S to form rust (a reddish coating that forms on iron) **RUSTABLE** *adj*

RUSTIC   *n* pl. -S one who lives in the country **RUSTICAL** *adj*

RUSTICLY   *adv* in a rural manner

RUSTIER   comparative of rusty

RUSTIEST   superlative of rusty

RUSTILY   *adv* in a rusty manner

RUSTLE   *v* -TLED, -TLING, -TLES to make a succession of slight, soft sounds

RUSTLER   *n* pl. -S one that rustles

RUSTLESS   *adj* free from rust

RUSTLING   present participle of rustle

RUSTY   *adj* RUSTIER, RUSTIEST covered with rust

RUT   *v* RUTTED, RUTTING, RUTS to make ruts (grooves) in

RUTABAGA   *n* pl. -S a plant having a thick, edible root

RUTH   *n* pl. -S compassion

RUTHENIC   *adj* pertaining to a rare, metallic element

RUTHFUL   *adj* full of compassion

RUTHLESS   *adj* having no compassion

RUTILANT   *adj* having a reddish glow

RUTILE   *n* pl. -S a mineral

RUTTED   past tense of rut

RUTTIER   comparative of rutty

RUTTIEST   superlative of rutty

RUTTILY   *adv* in a rutty manner

RUTTING   present participle of rut

RUTTISH   *adj* lustful

RUTTY   *adj* -TIER, -TIEST marked by ruts

RYA   *n* pl. -S a Scandinavian handwoven rug

RYE   *n* pl. -S a cereal grass

RYEGRASS   *n* pl. -ES a European grass

RYKE   *v* RYKED, RYKING, RYKES to reach

RYND   *n* pl. ·S an iron support

RYOT   *n* pl. -S a tenant farmer in India

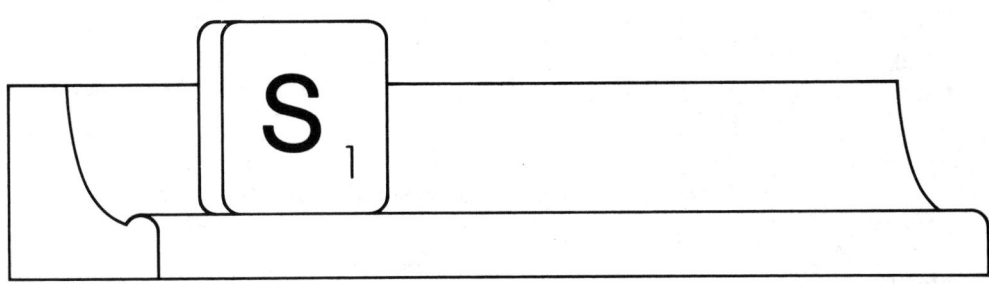

SAB	v SABBED, SABBING, SABS to sob
SABATON	n pl. -S a piece of armor for the foot
SABBAT	n pl. -S an assembly of demons and witches
SABBATH	n pl. -S sabbat
SABBATIC	adj bringing a period of rest
SABBED	past tense of sab
SABBING	present participle of sab
SABE	v SABED, SABEING, SABES to savvy
SABER	v -ED, -ING, -S to strike with a saber (a type of sword)
SABIN	n pl. -S a unit of sound absorption
SABINE	n pl. -S savin
SABIR	n pl. -S a French-based pidgin language
SABLE	n pl. -S a carnivorous mammal
SABOT	n pl. -S a wooden shoe
SABOTAGE	v -TAGED, -TAGING, -TAGES to destroy maliciously
SABOTEUR	n pl. -S one who sabotages
SABRA	n pl. -S a native Israeli
SABRE	v -BRED, -BRING, -BRES to saber
SABULOSE	adj sabulous
SABULOUS	adj sandy
SAC	n pl. -S a pouchlike structure in an animal or plant
SACATON	n pl. -S a perennial grass
SACBUT	n pl. -S sackbut

SACCADE	n pl. -S a rapid, jerky movement of the eye **SACCADIC** adj
SACCATE	adj having a sac
SACCULAR	adj resembling a sac
SACCULE	n pl. -S a small sac
SACCULUS	n pl. -LI saccule
SACHEM	n pl. -S a North American Indian chief **SACHEMIC** adj
SACHET	n pl. -S a small bag containing perfumed powder **SACHETED** adj
SACK	v -ED, -ING, -S to put into a sack (a large bag)
SACKBUT	n pl. -S a medieval trombone
SACKER	n pl. -S one that sacks
SACKFUL	n pl. SACKFULS or SACKSFUL as much as a sack will hold
SACKING	n pl. -S material for making sacks
SACKLIKE	adj resembling a sack
SACKSFUL	a pl. of sackful
SACLIKE	adj resembling a sac
SACQUE	n pl. -S a loose-fitting dress
SACRA	pl. of sacrum
SACRAL	n pl. -S a vertebra or nerve situated near the sacrum
SACRARIA	n/pl ancient Roman shrines
SACRED	adj dedicated to or set apart for the worship of a deity **SACREDLY** adv
SACRIST	n pl. -S a person in charge of a sacristy
SACRISTY	n pl. -TIES a room in which sacred vessels and vestments are kept

SACRUM	n pl. -CRA a bone of the pelvis
SAD	adj SADDER, SADDEST unhappy
SADDEN	v -ED, -ING, -S to make sad
SADDHU	n pl. -S sadhu
SADDLE	v -DLED, -DLING, -DLES to put a saddle (a leather seat for a rider) on
SADDLER	n pl. -S one that makes, repairs, or sells saddles
SADDLERY	n pl. -DLERIES the shop of a saddler
SADDLING	present participle of saddle
SADE	n pl. -S a Hebrew letter
SADHE	n pl. -S sade
SADHU	n pl. -S a Hindu holy man
SADI	n pl. -S sade
SADIRON	n pl. -S a heavy flatiron
SADISM	n pl. -S a tendency to take delight in inflicting pain
SADIST	n pl. -S one marked by sadism **SADISTIC** adj
SADLY	adv in a sad manner
SADNESS	n pl. -ES the state of being sad
SAE	adv so
SAFARI	v -ED, -ING, -S to go on a hunting expedition
SAFE	adj SAFER, SAFEST free from danger **SAFELY** adv
SAFE	n pl. -S a metal receptacle for storing valuables
SAFENESS	n pl. -ES the quality of being safe
SAFER	comparative of safe
SAFEST	superlative of safe
SAFETY	v -TIED, -TYING, -TIES to protect against failure, breakage, or accident
SAFFRON	n pl. -S a flowering plant
SAFRANIN	n pl. -S a red dye
SAFROL	n pl. -S safrole
SAFROLE	n pl. -S a poisonous liquid
SAG	v SAGGED, SAGGING, SAGS to bend or sink downward from weight or pressure
SAGA	n pl. -S a medieval Scandinavian narrative
SAGACITY	n pl. -TIES wisdom
SAGAMAN	n pl. -MEN a writer of sagas
SAGAMORE	n pl. -S an Algonquian Indian chief
SAGANASH	n pl. -ES a white man — an Algonquian Indian term
SAGBUT	n pl. -S sackbut
SAGE	adj SAGER, SAGEST wise **SAGELY** adv
SAGE	n pl. -S an aromatic herb used as seasoning
SAGENESS	n pl. -ES wisdom
SAGER	comparative of sage
SAGEST	superlative of sage
SAGGAR	v -ED, -ING, -S to bake in a saggar (a protective clay casing)
SAGGARD	n pl. -S a saggar
SAGGED	past tense of sag
SAGGER	v -ED, -ING, -S to saggar
SAGGING	present participle of sag
SAGIER	comparative of sagy
SAGIEST	superlative of sagy
SAGITTAL	adj resembling an arrow or arrowhead
SAGO	n pl. -GOS a tropical tree
SAGUARO	n pl. -ROS a tall cactus
SAGUM	n pl. -GA a cloak worn by ancient Roman soldiers
SAGY	adj SAGIER, SAGIEST flavored with sage
SAHIB	n pl. -S sir; master — used as a term of respect in colonial India
SAHIWAL	n pl. -S any of a breed of humped dairy cattle
SAHUARO	n pl. -ROS saguaro
SAICE	n pl. -S syce
SAID	n pl. -S sayyid
SAIGA	n pl. -S a small antelope
SAIL	v -ED, -ING, -S to move across the surface of water by the action of wind **SAILABLE** adj
SAILBOAT	n pl. -S a boat that sails
SAILER	n pl. -S a vessel that sails
SAILFISH	n pl. -ES a large marine fish
SAILING	n pl. -S the act of one that sails
SAILOR	n pl. -S a member of a ship's crew **SAILORLY** adj
SAIN	v -ED, -ING, -S to make the sign of the cross on
SAINFOIN	n pl. -S a perennial herb

SAINT   *v* -ED, -ING, -S to declare to be a saint (a person of exceptional holiness)

SAINTDOM   *n* pl. -S the condition of being a saint

SAINTLY   *adj* -LIER, -LIEST of or befitting a saint

SAITH   a present 3d person sing. of say

SAITHE   *n* pl. SAITHE a marine food fish

SAIYID   *n* pl. -S sayyid

SAJOU   *n* pl. -S a capuchin

SAKE   *n* pl. -S benefit, interest, or advantage

SAKER   *n* pl. -S a Eurasian falcon

SAKI   *n* pl. -S a Japanese liquor

SAL   *n* pl. -S salt

SALAAM   *v* -ED, -ING, -S to greet with a low bow

SALABLE   *adj* capable of being or fit to be sold **SALABLY** *adv*

SALACITY   *n* pl. -TIES lewdness

SALAD   *n* pl. -S a dish of green, raw vegetables

SALADANG   *n* pl. -S a wild ox

SALAMI   *n* pl. -S a seasoned sausage

SALARIAT   *n* pl. -S the class of salaried persons

SALARY   *v* -RIED, -RYING, -RIES to pay a periodic, fixed compensation to

SALE   *n* pl. -S the act or an instance of selling

SALEABLE   *adj* salable **SALEABLY** *adv*

SALEP   *n* pl. -S a starchy meal ground from the roots of certain orchids

SALEROOM   *n* pl. -S a room in which goods are displayed for sale

SALESMAN   *n* pl. -MEN a man who sells merchandise

SALIC   *adj* pertaining to a group of igneous rocks

SALICIN   *n* pl. -S a chemical compound

SALICINE   *n* pl. -S salicin

SALIENCE   *n* pl. -S a projecting feature or detail

SALIENCY   *n* pl. -CIES salience

SALIENT   *n* pl. -S the part of a fortification projecting closest to the enemy

SALIFY   *v* -FIED, -FYING, -FIES to combine with a salt

SALINA   *n* pl. -S a pond, marsh, or lake containing salt water

SALINE   *n* pl. -S a salt solution

SALINITY   *n* pl. -TIES a concentration of salt

SALINIZE   *v* -NIZED, -NIZING, -NIZES to treat with salt

SALIVA   *n* pl. -S a fluid secreted by the glands of the mouth **SALIVARY** *adj*

SALIVATE   *v* -VATED, -VATING, -VATES to secrete saliva

SALL   *v* shall — SALL is the only form of this verb; it cannot be conjugated

SALLET   *n* pl. -S a light medieval helmet

SALLIED   past tense of sally

SALLIER   *n* pl. -S one that sallies

SALLIES   present 3d person sing. of sally

SALLOW   *adj* -LOWER, -LOWEST of a sickly yellowish color **SALLOWLY** *adv*

SALLOW   *v* -ED, -ING, -S to make sallow

SALLOWY   *adj* abounding in willow trees

SALLY   *v* -LIED, -LYING, -LIES to rush out suddenly

SALMI   *n* pl. -S a dish of roasted game birds

SALMON   *n* pl. -S a food fish

SALMONID   *n* pl. -S a fish of the salmon family

SALOL   *n* pl. -S a chemical compound

SALON   *n* pl. -S a large room in which guests are received

SALOON   *n* pl. -S a tavern

SALOOP   *n* pl. -S a hot drink made from an infusion of aromatic herbs

SALP   *n* pl. -S salpa

SALPA   *n* pl. -PAE or -PAS a free-swimming tunicate

SALPIAN   *n* pl. -S salpa

SALPID   *n* pl. -S salpa

SALPINX   *n* pl. -PINGES an anatomical tube

SALSIFY   *n* pl. -FIES a European herb

SALSILLA   *n* pl. -S a tropical plant

SALT   *v* -ED, -ING, -S to treat with salt (a crystalline compound used as a seasoning and preservative)

SALT   *adj* SALTER, SALTEST salty

SALTANT	adj jumping or dancing	**SAMARA**	n pl. -S a dry, one-seeded fruit
SALTBOX	n pl. -ES a type of house	**SAMARIUM**	n pl. -S a metallic element
SALTBUSH	n pl. -ES a salt-tolerant plant	**SAMBA**	v -ED, -ING, -S to perform a Brazilian dance
SALTER	n pl. -S one that salts		
SALTERN	n pl. -S a place where salt is produced	**SAMBAR**	n pl. -S a large Asian deer
		SAMBHAR	n pl. -S sambar
SALTIE	n pl. -S a deep-sea vessel sailing the Great Lakes	**SAMBHUR**	n pl. -S sambar
		SAMBO	n pl. -BOS a Latin American of mixed black and Indian ancestry
SALTIER	n pl. -S saltire		
SALTIEST	superlative of salty	**SAMBUCA**	n pl. -S an ancient stringed instrument
SALTILY	adv in a salty manner		
SALTINE	n pl. -S a salted cracker	**SAMBUKE**	n pl. -S sambuca
SALTIRE	n pl. -S a heraldic design	**SAMBUR**	n pl. -S sambar
SALTISH	adj somewhat salty	**SAME**	adj resembling in every relevant respect
SALTLESS	adj having no salt		
SALTLIKE	adj resembling salt	**SAMECH**	n pl. -S samek
SALTNESS	n pl. -ES the state of being salty	**SAMEK**	n pl. -S a Hebrew letter
		SAMEKH	n pl. -S samek
SALTPAN	n pl. -S a large pan for making salt by evaporation	**SAMENESS**	n pl. -ES lack of change or variety
SALTWORK	n pl. -S a saltern		
SALTWORT	n pl. -S a seaside herb	**SAMIEL**	n pl. -S the simoom
SALTY	adj SALTIER, SALTIEST tasting of or containing salt	**SAMISEN**	n pl. -S a Japanese stringed instrument
		SAMITE	n pl. -S a silk fabric
SALUKI	n pl. -S a tall, slender dog	**SAMLET**	n pl. -S a young salmon
SALUTARY	adj producing a beneficial effect	**SAMOVAR**	n pl. -S a metal urn for heating water
SALUTE	v -LUTED, -LUTING, -LUTES to greet with a sign of welcome or respect	**SAMP**	n pl. -S coarsely ground corn
		SAMPAN	n pl. -S a flat-bottomed Chinese skiff
SALUTER	n pl. -S one that salutes		
SALVABLE	adj capable of being saved **SALVABLY** adv	**SAMPHIRE**	n pl. -S a European herb
		SAMPLE	v -PLED, -PLING, -PLES to test a representative portion of a whole
SALVAGE	v -VAGED, -VAGING, -VAGES to save from loss or destruction		
		SAMPLER	n pl. -S one that samples
SALVAGEE	n pl. -S one in whose favor salvage has been effected	**SAMPLING**	n pl. -S a small part selected for analysis
SALVAGER	n pl. -S one that salvages	**SAMSARA**	n pl. -S the cycle of birth, death, and rebirth in Buddhism
SALVAGING	present participle of salvage		
SALVE	v SALVED, SALVING, SALVES to soothe	**SAMSHU**	n pl. -S a Chinese liquor
		SAMURAI	n pl. -S a Japanese warrior
SALVER	n pl. -S a tray or serving platter	**SANATIVE**	adj having the power to cure or heal
SALVIA	n pl. -S a flowering plant		
SALVIFIC	adj having the power to save	**SANCTA**	a pl. of sanctum
SALVING	present participle of salve	**SANCTIFY**	v -FIED, -FYING, -FIES to make holy
SALVO	v -ED, -ING, -S or -ES to discharge firearms simultaneously		
		SANCTION	v -ED, -ING, -S to authorize
SALVOR	n pl. -S a salvager	**SANCTITY**	n pl. -TIES holiness

SANCTUM *n* pl. -TUMS or -TA a sacred place

SAND *v* -ED, -ING, -S to cover with sand (a loose, granular rock material)

SANDAL *v* -DALED, -DALING, -DALS or -DALLED, -DALLING, -DALS to provide with sandals (light, open shoes)

SANDARAC *n* pl. -S an aromatic resin

SANDBAG *v* -BAGGED, -BAGGING, -BAGS to surround with bags of sand

SANDBANK *n* pl. -S a large mass of sand

SANDBAR *n* pl. -S a ridge of sand formed in a river or sea

SANDBOX *n* pl. -ES a box containing sand for children to play in

SANDBUR *n* pl. -S an annual herb

SANDBURR *n* pl. -S sandbur

SANDER *n* pl. -S one that sands

SANDFISH *n* pl. -ES a marine fish

SANDFLY *n* pl. -FLIES a biting fly

SANDHI *n* pl. -S a process of phonetic modification

SANDHOG *n* pl. -S a worker who digs or works in sand

SANDIER comparative of sandy

SANDIEST superlative of sandy

SANDLIKE *adj* resembling sand

SANDLING *n* pl. -S a marine fish

SANDLOT *n* pl. -S a vacant lot

SANDMAN *n* pl. -MEN a mythical person who makes children sleepy by sprinkling sand in their eyes

SANDPEEP *n* pl. -S a wading bird

SANDPILE *n* pl. -S a pile of sand

SANDPIT *n* pl. -S a pit dug in sandy soil

SANDSOAP *n* pl. -S a type of soap

SANDWICH *v* -ED, -ING, -ES to place between two layers or objects

SANDWORM *n* pl. -S a sand-dwelling worm

SANDWORT *n* pl. -S a flowering plant

SANDY *adj* SANDIER, SANDIEST containing or covered with sand

SANE *adj* SANER, SANEST mentally sound **SANELY** *adv*

SANE *v* SANED, SANING, SANES to sain

SANENESS *n* pl. -ES sanity

SANER comparative of sane

SANEST superlative of sane

SANG past tense of sing

SANGA *n* pl. -S sangar

SANGAR *n* pl. -S a temporary fortification for two or three men

SANGAREE *n* pl. -S an alcoholic beverage

SANGER *n* pl. -S sangar

SANGH *n* pl. -S an association promoting unity between the different groups in Hinduism

SANGRIA *n* pl. -S an alcoholic beverage

SANGUINE *n* pl. -S a red color

SANICLE *n* pl. -S a medicinal herb

SANIES *n* pl. SANIES a fluid discharged from wounds **SANIOUS** *adj*

SANING present participle of sane

SANITARY *n* pl. -TARIES a public urinal

SANITATE *v* -TATED, -TATING, -TATES to sanitize

SANITIES pl. of sanity

SANITISE *v* -TISED, -TISING, -TISES to sanitize

SANITIZE *v* -TIZED, -TIZING, -TIZES to guard against infection or disease by cleaning or sterilizing

SANITY *n* pl. -TIES the state of being sane

SANJAK *n* pl. -S an administrative district of Turkey

SANK past tense of sink

SANNOP *n* pl. -S sannup

SANNUP *n* pl. -S a married male American Indian

SANNYASI *n* pl. -S a Hindu monk

SANS *prep* without

SANSAR *n* pl. -S sarsar

SANSEI *n* pl. -S a grandchild of Japanese immigrants to the United States

SANSERIF *n* pl. -S a typeface without serifs

SANTALIC *adj* pertaining to sandalwood

SANTIMS *n* pl. -TIMI a former coin of Latvia

SANTIR *n* pl. -S a Persian dulcimer

SANTOL *n* pl. -S a tropical tree

SANTONIN *n* pl. -S a chemical compound

SANTOUR *n* pl. -S santir

SAP	*v* SAPPED, SAPPING, SAPS to deplete or weaken gradually
SAPAJOU	*n* pl. -S a capuchin
SAPHEAD	*n* pl. -S a foolish, stupid, or gullible person
SAPHENA	*n* pl. -NAE a vein of the leg
SAPID	*adj* pleasant to the taste
SAPIDITY	*n* pl. -TIES the state of being sapid
SAPIENCE	*n* pl. -S wisdom
SAPIENCY	*n* pl. -CIES sapience
SAPIENS	*adj* pertaining to recent man
SAPIENT	*adj* wise
SAPLESS	*adj* lacking vitality
SAPLING	*n* pl. -S a young tree
SAPONIFY	*v* -FIED, -FYING, -FIES to convert into soap
SAPONIN	*n* pl. -S a soapy substance obtained from plants
SAPONINE	*n* pl. -S saponin
SAPONITE	*n* pl. -S a mineral found in veins and cavities of rocks
SAPOR	*n* pl. -S flavor **SAPOROUS** *adj*
SAPOTA	*n* pl. -S an evergreen tree
SAPOUR	*n* pl. -S sapor
SAPPED	past tense of sap
SAPPER	*n* pl. -S a military engineer
SAPPHIC	*n* pl. -S a type of verse form
SAPPHIRE	*n* pl. -S a blue gem
SAPPHISM	*n* pl. -S lesbianism
SAPPHIST	*n* pl. -S a lesbian
SAPPING	present participle of sap
SAPPY	*adj* -PIER, -PIEST silly **SAPPILY** *adv*
SAPREMIA	*n* pl. -S a form of blood poisoning **SAPREMIC** *adj*
SAPROBE	*n* pl. -S an organism that derives its nourishment from decaying organic matter **SAPROBIC** *adj*
SAPROPEL	*n* pl. -S mud consisting chiefly of decaying organic matter
SAPSAGO	*n* pl. -GOS a hard green cheese
SAPWOOD	*n* pl. -S the newly formed outer wood of a tree
SARABAND	*n* pl. -S a stately Spanish dance
SARAPE	*n* pl. -S serape
SARCASM	*n* pl. -S a sharply mocking or contemptuous remark
SARCENET	*n* pl. -S a silk fabric
SARCOID	*n* pl. -S a disease of horses
SARCOMA	*n* pl. -MAS or -MATA a type of tumor
SARCOUS	*adj* composed of flesh or muscle
SARD	*n* pl. -S a variety of quartz
SARDAR	*n* pl. -S sirdar
SARDINE	*n* pl. -S a small food fish
SARDIUS	*n* pl. -ES sard
SARDONIC	*adj* mocking
SARDONYX	*n* pl. -ES a variety of quartz
SAREE	*n* pl. -S sari
SARGASSO	*n* pl. -GASSOS a brownish seaweed
SARGE	*n* pl. -S sergeant
SARI	*n* pl. -S an outer garment worn by Hindu women
SARIN	*n* pl. -S a toxic gas
SARK	*n* pl. -S a shirt
SARMENT	*n* pl. -S a type of plant stem
SARMENTA	*n/pl* sarments
SAROD	*n* pl. -S a lute of northern India
SARODE	*n* pl. -S sarod
SARODIST	*n* pl. -S one who plays the sarod
SARONG	*n* pl. -S an outer garment worn in the Pacific islands
SARSAR	*n* pl. -S a cold, whistling wind
SARSEN	*n* pl. -S a large sandstone block
SARSENET	*n* pl. -S sarcenet
SARTOR	*n* pl. -S a tailor
SARTORII	*n/pl* flat, narrow thigh muscles
SASH	*v* -ED, -ING, -ES to furnish with a frame in which glass is set
SASHAY	*v* -ED, -ING, -S to flounce
SASHIMI	*n* pl. -S a Japanese dish of sliced raw fish
SASIN	*n* pl. -S an antelope of India
SASS	*v* -ED, -ING, -ES to talk impudently to
SASSABY	*n* pl. -BIES an African antelope
SASSIER	comparative of sassy
SASSIEST	superlative of sassy
SASSILY	*adv* in a sassy manner

SASSWOOD   *n* pl. -S an African tree

SASSY   *n* pl. -SIES sasswood

SASSY   *adj* SASSIER, SASSIEST impudent

SASTRUGA   *n* pl. -GI a ridge of snow formed by the wind in polar regions

SAT   past tense of sit

SATANG   *n* pl. -S a monetary unit of Thailand

SATANIC   *adj* extremely evil

SATANISM   *n* pl. -S worship of the powers of evil

SATANIST   *n* pl. -S one who practices satanism

SATARA   *n* pl. -S a woolen fabric

SATCHEL   *n* pl. -S a small carrying bag

SATE   *v* SATED, SATING, SATES to satiate

SATEEN   *n* pl. -S a cotton fabric

SATEM   *adj* pertaining to a group of Indo-European languages

SATI   *n* pl. -S suttee

SATIABLE   *adj* capable of being satiated SATIABLY *adv*

SATIATE   *v* -ATED, -ATING, -ATES to satisfy to or beyond capacity

SATIETY   *n* pl. -ETIES the state of being satiated

SATIN   *n* pl. -S a smooth fabric

SATINET   *n* pl. -S a thin satin

SATING   present participle of sate

SATINPOD   *n* pl. -S a flowering plant

SATINY   *adj* resembling satin

SATIRE   *n* pl. -S the use of derisive wit to attack folly or wickedness SATIRIC *adj*

SATIRISE   *v* -RISED, -RISING, -RISES to satirize

SATIRIST   *n* pl. -S one who satirizes

SATIRIZE   *v* -RIZED, -RIZING, -RIZES to subject to satire

SATISFY   *v* -FIED, -FYING, -FIES to provide fully with what is desired, expected, or needed

SATORI   *n* pl. -S the illumination of spirit sought by Zen Buddhists

SATRAP   *n* pl. -S a governor of a province in ancient Persia

SATRAPY   *n* pl. -PIES the territory of a satrap

SATURANT   *n* pl. -S a substance used to saturate

SATURATE   *v* -RATED, -RATING, -RATES to fill completely with something that permeates

SATYR   *n* pl. -S a woodland deity of Greek mythology SATYRIC *adj*

SATYRID   *n* pl. -S a brownish butterfly

SAU   *n* pl. SAU xu

SAUCE   *v* SAUCED, SAUCING, SAUCES to season with sauce (a flavorful liquid dressing)

SAUCEBOX   *n* pl. -ES a saucy person

SAUCEPAN   *n* pl. -S a cooking utensil

SAUCER   *n* pl. -S a small, shallow dish

SAUCH   *n* pl. -S saugh

SAUCING   present participle of sauce

SAUCY   *adj* SAUCIER, SAUCIEST impudent SAUCILY *adv*

SAUGER   *n* pl. -S a freshwater fish

SAUGH   *n* pl. -S a willow tree SAUGHY *adj*

SAUL   *n* pl. -S soul

SAULT   *n* pl. -S a waterfall

SAUNA   *n* pl. -S a Finnish steam bath

SAUNTER   *v* -ED, -ING, -S to walk in a leisurely manner

SAUREL   *n* pl. -S a marine fish

SAURIAN   *n* pl. -S any of a suborder of reptiles

SAUROPOD   *n* pl. -S any of a suborder of large dinosaurs

SAURY   *n* pl. -RIES a marine fish

SAUSAGE   *n* pl. -S finely chopped and seasoned meat stuffed into a casing

SAUTE   *v* -TEED or -TED, -TEING, -TES to fry in a small amount of fat

SAUTERNE   *n* pl. -S a sweet white wine

SAUTOIR   *n* pl. -S a saltire

SAUTOIRE   *n* pl. -S sautoir

SAVABLE   *adj* capable of being saved

SAVAGE   *adj* -AGER, -AGEST fierce SAVAGELY *adv*

SAVAGE   *v* -AGED, -AGING, -AGES to attack or treat brutally

SAVAGERY   *n* pl. -RIES the quality of being savage

SAVAGEST   superlative of savage

SAVAGING   present participle of savage

SAVAGISM   *n* pl. -S savagery

SAVANNA   *n* pl. -S a flat, treeless grassland

SAVANNAH   *n* pl. -S savanna

SAVANT   *n* pl. -S a man of profound learning

SAVATE   *n* pl. -S a pugilistic sport

SAVE   *v* SAVED, SAVING, SAVES to rescue from danger, injury, or loss **SAVEABLE** *adj*

SAVELOY   *n* pl. -LOYS a highly seasoned sausage

SAVER   *n* pl. -S one that saves

SAVIN   *n* pl. -S an evergreen shrub

SAVINE   *n* pl. -S savin

SAVING   *n* pl. -S the act or an instance of saving

SAVINGLY   *adv* in a thrifty manner

SAVIOR   *n* pl. -S one that saves

SAVIOUR   *n* pl. -S savior

SAVOR   *v* -ED, -ING, -S to taste or smell with pleasure

SAVORER   *n* pl. -S one that savors

SAVORIER   comparative of savory

SAVORIES   pl. of savory

SAVOROUS   *adj* savory

SAVORY   *adj* -VORIER, -VORIEST pleasant to the taste or smell **SAVORILY** *adv*

SAVORY   *n* pl. -VORIES a savory dish served before or after a meal

SAVOUR   *v* -ED, -ING, -S to savor

SAVOURER   *n* pl. -S savorer

SAVOURY   *adj* -VOURIER, -VOURIEST savory

SAVOURY   *n* pl. -VOURIES a savory

SAVOY   *n* pl. -VOYS a variety of cabbage

SAVVY   *v* -VIED, -VYING, -VIES to understand

SAW   *v* SAWED, SAWN, SAWING, SAWS to cut or divide with a saw (a type of cutting tool)

SAWBILL   *n* pl. -S a tropical bird

SAWBONES   *n* pl. -BONESES a surgeon

SAWBUCK   *n* pl. -S a sawhorse

SAWDUST   *n* pl. -S small particles of wood produced in sawing

SAWER   *n* pl. -S one that saws

SAWFISH   *n* pl. -ES a marine fish

SAWFLY   *n* pl. -FLIES a winged insect

SAWHORSE   *n* pl. -S a rack used to support a piece of wood being sawed

SAWLIKE   *adj* resembling a saw

SAWLOG   *n* pl. -S a log large enough to saw into boards

SAWMILL   *n* pl. -S a place where logs are sawed

SAWN   a past participle of saw

SAWNEY   *n* pl. -NEYS a foolish person

SAWTOOTH   *n* pl. -TEETH a cutting edge on a saw

SAWYER   *n* pl. -S one that saws wood for a living

SAX   *n* pl. -ES a saxophone

SAXATILE   *adj* living or growing among rocks

SAXHORN   *n* pl. -S a brass wind instrument

SAXONY   *n* pl. -NIES a woolen fabric

SAXTUBA   *n* pl. -S a bass saxhorn

SAY   *v* SAID, SAYING, present sing. 2d person SAY, SAYEST, or SAYST, 3d person SAYS or SAITH to utter **SAYABLE** *adj*

SAYER   *n* pl. -S one that says

SAYID   *n* pl. -S sayyid

SAYING   *n* pl. -S a maxim

SAYONARA   *n* pl. -S goodby

SAYST   a present 2d person sing. of say

SAYYID   *n* pl. -S lord; sir — used as a title of respect for a Muslim dignitary

SCAB   *v* SCABBED, SCABBING, SCABS to become covered with a scab (a crust that forms over a healing wound)

SCABBARD   *v* -ED, -ING, -S to put into a sheath, as a sword

SCABBLE   *v* -BLED, -BLING, -BLES to shape roughly

SCABBY   *adj* -BIER, -BIEST covered with scabs **SCABBILY** *adv*

SCABIES   *n* pl. SCABIES a skin disease

SCABIOSA   *n* pl. -S scabious

SCABIOUS   *n* pl. -ES a flowering plant

SCABLIKE   *adj* resembling a scab

SCABROUS   *adj* roughened with small projections

SCAD	*n* pl. -S a marine fish
SCAFFOLD	*v* -ED, -ING, -S to provide with a scaffold (a temporary platform for workmen)
SCAG	*n* pl. -S heroin
SCALABLE	*adj* capable of being scaled **SCALABLY** *adv*
SCALADE	*n* pl. -S an act of scaling the walls of a fortification
SCALADO	*n* pl. -DOS scalade
SCALAGE	*n* pl. -S a percentage deduction to compensate for shrinkage
SCALAR	*n* pl. -S a mathematical quantity possessing only magnitude
SCALARE	*n* pl. -S a tropical fish
SCALAWAG	*n* pl. -S a rascal
SCALD	*v* -ED, -ING, -S to burn with hot liquid or steam
SCALDIC	*adj* skaldic
SCALE	*v* SCALED, SCALING, SCALES to climb up or over
SCALENE	*adj* designating a triangle having no two sides equal
SCALENUS	*n* pl. -NI a muscle of the neck
SCALEPAN	*n* pl. -S a pan on a weighing scale
SCALER	*n* pl. -S one that scales
SCALIER	comparative of scaly
SCALIEST	superlative of scaly
SCALING	present participle of scale
SCALL	*n* pl. -S a scaly eruption of the skin
SCALLION	*n* pl. -S an onion-like plant
SCALLOP	*v* -ED, -ING, -S to bake in a sauce topped with bread crumbs
SCALP	*v* -ED, -ING, -S to remove an upper part from
SCALPEL	*n* pl. -S a small surgical knife
SCALPER	*n* pl. -S one that scalps
SCALY	*adj* SCALIER, SCALIEST peeling off in flakes
SCAMMONY	*n* pl. -NIES a climbing plant
SCAM	*n* pl. -S a swindle
SCAMP	*v* -ED, -ING, -S to perform in a hasty or careless manner
SCAMPER	*v* -ED, -ING, -S to run playfully about
SCAMPI	*n* pl. SCAMPI large shrimp used in Italian cooking
SCAMPISH	*adj* rascally

SCAN	*v* SCANNED, SCANNING, SCANS to examine closely
SCANDAL	*v* -DALED, -DALING, -DALS or -DALLED, -DALLING, -DALS to defame
SCANDENT	*adj* climbing, as a plant
SCANDIA	*n* pl. -S an oxide of scandium
SCANDIUM	*n* pl. -S a metallic element **SCANDIC** *adj*
SCANNED	past tense of scan
SCANNER	*n* pl. -S one that scans
SCANNING	*n* pl. -S close examination
SCANSION	*n* pl. -S the analysis of verse into metrical feet and rhythm patterns
SCANT	*adj* SCANTER, SCANTEST meager
SCANT	*v* -ED, -ING, -S to provide with a meager portion
SCANTIER	comparative of scanty
SCANTIES	*n/pl* brief panties for women
SCANTLY	*adv* in a scant manner
SCANTY	*adj* SCANTIER, SCANTIEST meager **SCANTILY** *adv*
SCAPE	*v* SCAPED, SCAPING, SCAPES to escape
SCAPHOID	*n* pl. -S a bone of the wrist
SCAPOSE	*adj* bearing a leafless stalk
SCAPULA	*n* pl. -LAE or -LAS a bone of the shoulder
SCAPULAR	*n* pl. -S a sleeveless outer garment worn by monks
SCAR	*v* SCARRED, SCARRING, SCARS to form a scar (a mark left by the healing of injured tissue)
SCARAB	*n* pl. -S a large, black beetle
SCARCE	*adj* SCARCER, SCARCEST infrequently seen or found
SCARCELY	*adv* by a narrow margin
SCARCITY	*n* pl. -TIES the quality of being scarce
SCARE	*v* SCARED, SCARING, SCARES to frighten
SCARER	*n* pl. -S one that scares
SCAREY	*adj* SCARIER, SCARIEST scary
SCARF	*n* pl. SCARFS or SCARVES a piece of cloth worn for warmth or protection
SCARF	*v* -ED, -ING, -S to cover with a scarf

SCARFPIN   *n* pl. -S a tiepin

SCARIER   comparative of scarey and scary

SCARIEST   superlative of scarey and scary

SCARIFY   *v* -FIED, -FYING, -FIES to make superficial cuts in

SCARING   present participle of scare

SCARIOSE   *adj* scarious

SCARIOUS   *adj* thin, dry, and membranous

SCARLESS   *adj* having no scars

SCARLET   *n* pl. -S a red color

SCARP   *v* -ED, -ING, -S to cut or make into a steep slope

SCARPER   *v* -ED, -ING, -S to flee

SCARPH   *v* -ED, -ING, -S to unite by means of a type of joint

SCARRED   past tense of scar

SCARRING   present participle of scar

SCARRY   *adj* -RIER, -RIEST marked with scars

SCART   *v* -ED, -ING, -S to scratch

SCARVES   a pl. of scarf

SCARY   *adj* SCARIER, SCARIEST frightening

SCAT   *v* SCATTED, SCATTING, SCATS to leave hastily

SCATBACK   *n* pl. -S a type of player in football

SCATHE   *v* SCATHED, SCATHING, SCATHES to criticize severely

SCATT   *n* pl. -S a tax

SCATTED   past tense of scat

SCATTER   *v* -ED, -ING, -S to go or send in various directions

SCATTING   present participle of scat

SCATTY   *adj* -TIER, -TIEST crazy

SCAUP   *n* pl. -S a sea duck

SCAUPER   *n* pl. -S an engraving tool

SCAUR   *n* pl. -S a protruding, isolated rock

SCAVENGE   *v* -ENGED, -ENGING, -ENGES to search through rubbish for usable items

SCENA   *n* pl. -S an elaborate composition for a single voice

SCENARIO   *n* pl. -IOS a summary of the plot of a dramatic work

SCEND   *v* -ED, -ING, -S to rise upward, as a ship on a wave

SCENE   *n* pl. -S the place where some action or event occurs

SCENERY   *n* pl. -ERIES a picturesque landscape or view

SCENIC   *adj* pertaining to scenery

SCENICAL   *adj* scenic

SCENT   *v* -ED, -ING, -S to fill with an odor

SCEPTER   *v* -ED, -ING, -S to invest with royal authority

SCEPTIC   *n* pl. -S skeptic

SCEPTRAL   *adj* pertaining to royal authority

SCEPTRE   *v* -TRED, -TRING, -TRES to scepter

SCHAPPE   *n* pl. -S a silk fabric

SCHAV   *n* pl. -S a chilled soup

SCHEDULE   *v* -ULED, -ULING, -ULES to assign to a certain date or time

SCHEMA   *n* pl. -MATA a generalized diagram or plan

SCHEME   *v* SCHEMED, SCHEMING, SCHEMES to plan or plot

SCHEMER   *n* pl. -S one that schemes

SCHERZO   *n* pl. -ZOS or -ZI a lively musical movement

SCHILLER   *n* pl. -S a brownish luster occurring on certain minerals

SCHISM   *n* pl. -S a division into opposing parties

SCHIST   *n* pl. -S a rock that readily splits into parallel layers

SCHIZO   *n* pl. SCHIZOS a schizoid

SCHIZOID   *n* pl. -S a person affected with a type of psychotic disorder

SCHIZONT   *n* pl. -S an organism that reproduces by a form of asexual reproduction

SCHLEP   *v* SCHLEPPED, SCHLEPPING, SCHLEPS to lug or drag

SCHLEPP   *v* -ED, -ING, -S to schlep

SCHLOCK   *n* pl. -S inferior merchandise

SCHMALTZ   *n* pl. -ES excessive sentimentality

SCHMALZ   *n* pl. -ES schmaltz

SCHMALZY   *adj* SCHMALZIER, SCHMALZIEST characterized by schmaltz

SCHMEER   *v* -ED, -ING, -S to bribe

SCHMELZE   *n* pl. -S a type of decorative glass

SCHMO   *n* pl. SCHMOES a stupid person

SCHMOE *n* pl. -S schmo

SCHMOOS *v* -ED, -ING, -ES to schmooze

SCHMOOSE *v* SCHMOOSED, SCHMOOSING, SCHMOOSES to schmooze

SCHMOOZE *v* SCHMOOZED, SCHMOOZING, SCHMOOZES to gossip

SCHMUCK *n* pl. -S a foolish or clumsy person

SCHNAPPS *n* pl. SCHNAPPS a strong liquor

SCHNAPS *n* pl. SCHNAPS schnapps

SCHNECKE *n* pl. -KEN a sweet roll

SCHNOOK *n* pl. -S an easily deceived person

SCHOLAR *n* pl. -S a learned person

SCHOLIUM *n* pl. -LIA or -LIUMS an explanatory marginal note

SCHOOL *v* -ED, -ING, -S to educate in an institution of learning

SCHOONER *n* pl. -S a sailing vessel

SCHORL *n* pl. -S a mineral

SCHRIK *n* pl. -S sudden fright

SCHTICK *n* pl. -S shtick

SCHUIT *n* pl. -S a Dutch sailing vessel

SCHUL *n* pl. SCHULN shul

SCHUSS *v* -ED, -ING, -ES to make a fast, straight run in skiing

SCHWA *n* pl. -S a type of vowel sound

SCIAENID *n* pl. -S a carnivorous fish

SCIATIC *n* pl. -S a nerve, vein, or artery situated near the hip

SCIATICA *n* pl. -S a painful disorder of the hip and adjoining areas

SCIENCE *n* pl. -S a department of systematized knowledge

SCILICET *adv* namely

SCILLA *n* pl. -S a flowering plant

SCIMETAR *n* pl. -S scimitar

SCIMITAR *n* pl. -S a curved Oriental sword

SCIMITER *n* pl. -S scimitar

SCINCOID *n* pl. -S one of a family of smooth, short-limbed lizards

SCIOLISM *n* pl. -S superficial knowledge

SCIOLIST *n* pl. -S one whose knowledge is superficial

SCION *n* pl. -S a child or descendant

SCIROCCO *n* pl. -COS sirocco

SCIRRHUS *n* pl. -RHI or -RHUSES a hard tumor

SCISSILE *adj* capable of being cut or split easily

SCISSION *n* pl. -S the act of cutting or splitting

SCISSOR *v* -ED, -ING, -S to cut with a two-bladed cutting implement

SCISSURE *n* pl. -S a lengthwise cut

SCIURINE *n* pl. -S a rodent of the squirrel family

SCIUROID *adj* resembling a squirrel

SCLAFF *v* -ED, -ING, -S to strike the ground with the club before hitting the ball in golf

SCLAFFER *n* pl. -S one that sclaffs

SCLERA *n* pl. -RAS or -RAE the white, fibrous outer coat of the eyeball **SCLERAL** *adj*

SCLEREID *n* pl. -S a type of plant cell

SCLERITE *n* pl. -S one of the hard plates forming the outer covering of an arthropod

SCLEROID *adj* sclerous

SCLEROMA *n* pl. -MATA a hardened patch of cellular tissue

SCLEROSE *v* -ROSED, -ROSING, -ROSES to become hard, as tissue

SCLEROUS *adj* hardened

SCOFF *v* -ED, -ING, -S to express rude doubt or derision

SCOFFER *n* pl. -S one that scoffs

SCOFFLAW *n* pl. -S an habitual law violator

SCOLD *v* -ED, -ING, -S to rebuke harshly

SCOLDER *n* pl. -S one that scolds

SCOLDING *n* pl. -S a harsh reproof

SCOLEX *n* pl. -LECES or -LICES the knoblike head of a tapeworm

SCOLIOMA *n* pl. -S abnormal curvature of the spine

SCOLLOP *v* -ED, -ING, -S to scallop

SCONCE *v* SCONCED, SCONCING, SCONCES to fine

SCONE *n* pl. -S a flat, round cake

SCOOP *v* -ED, -ING, -S to take up with a scoop (a spoonlike utensil)

SCOOPER *n* pl. -S one that scoops

SCOOPFUL *n* pl. SCOOPFULS or SCOOPSFUL as much as a scoop will hold

SCOOT *v* -ED, -ING, -S to go quickly

SCOOTER *n* pl. -S a two-wheeled vehicle

SCOP   *n* pl. -S an Old English poet

SCOPE   *n* pl. -S extent

SCOPULA   *n* pl. -LAE or -LAS a dense tuft of hairs

SCORCH   *v* -ED, -ING, -ES to burn slightly so as to alter the color or taste

SCORCHER   *n* pl. -S one that scorches

SCORE   *v* SCORED, SCORING, SCORES to make a point in a game or contest

SCOREPAD   *n* pl. -S a pad on which scored points are recorded

SCORER   *n* pl. -S one that scores

SCORIA   *n* pl. -RIAE the refuse of a smelted metal or ore

SCORIFY   *v* -FIED, -FYING, -FIES to reduce to scoria

SCORING   present participle of score

SCORN   *v* -ED, -ING, -S to treat or regard with contempt

SCORNER   *n* pl. -S one that scorns

SCORNFUL   *adj* feeling or expressing contempt

SCORPION   *n* pl. -S a stinging arachnid

SCOT   *n* pl. -S a tax

SCOTCH   *v* -ED, -ING, -ES to put a definite end to

SCOTER   *n* pl. -S a sea duck

SCOTIA   *n* pl. -S a concave molding

SCOTOMA   *n* pl. -MAS or -MATA a blind spot in the field of vision

SCOTOPIA   *n* pl. -S vision in dim light **SCOTOPIC** *adj*

SCOTTIE   *n* pl. -S a short-legged terrier

SCOUR   *v* -ED, -ING, -S to cleanse or polish by hard rubbing

SCOURER   *n* pl. -S one that scours

SCOURGE   *v* SCOURGED, SCOURGING, SCOURGES to punish severely

SCOURGER   *n* pl. -S one that scourges

SCOURING   *n* pl. -S material removed by scouring

SCOUSE   *n* pl. -S a type of meat stew

SCOUT   *v* -ED, -ING, -S to observe for the purpose of obtaining information

SCOUTER   *n* pl. -S one that scouts

SCOUTH   *n* pl. -S plenty

SCOUTHER   *v* -ED, -ING, -S to scorch

SCOUTING   *n* pl. -S the act of one that scouts

SCOW   *v* -ED, -ING, -S to transport by scow (a flat-bottomed boat)

SCOWDER   *v* -ED, -ING, -S to scouther

SCOWL   *v* -ED, -ING, -S to frown angrily

SCOWLER   *n* pl. -S one that scowls

SCRABBLE   *v* -BLED, -BLING, -BLES to claw or grope about frantically

SCRABBLY   *adj* raspy

SCRAG   *v* SCRAGGED, SCRAGGING, SCRAGS to wring the neck of

SCRAGGLY   *adj* -GLIER, -GLIEST uneven

SCRAGGY   *adj* -GIER, -GIEST scrawny

SCRAICH   *v* -ED, -ING, -S to utter a shrill cry

SCRAIGH   *v* -ED, -ING, -S to scraich

SCRAM   *v* SCRAMMED, SCRAMMING, SCRAMS to leave quickly

SCRAMBLE   *v* -BLED, -BLING, -BLES to move or climb hurriedly

SCRANNEL   *n* pl. -S a thin person

SCRAP   *v* SCRAPPED, SCRAPPING, SCRAPS to discard

SCRAPE   *v* SCRAPED, SCRAPING, SCRAPES to rub so as to remove an outer layer

SCRAPER   *n* pl. -S one that scrapes

SCRAPIE   *n* pl. -S a disease of sheep

SCRAPING   *n* pl. -S something scraped off

SCRAPPED   past tense of scrap

SCRAPPER   *n* pl. -S a fighter

SCRAPPIER   comparative of scrappy

SCRAPPIEST   superlative of scrappy

SCRAPPING   present participle of scrap

SCRAPPLE   *n* pl. -S a seasoned mixture of ground meat and cornmeal

SCRAPPY   *adj* -PIER, -PIEST marked by fighting spirit

SCRATCH   *v* -ED, -ING, -ES to make a thin, shallow cut or mark on

SCRATCHY   *adj* SCRATCHIER, SCRATCHIEST uneven in quality

SCRAWL   *v* -ED, -ING, -S to write hastily or illegibly

SCRAWLER   *n* pl. -S one that scrawls

SCRAWLY   *adj* SCRAWLIER, SCRAWLIEST written hastily or illegibly

SCRAWNY   *adj* -NIER, -NIEST extremely thin

SCREAK	*v* -ED, -ING, -S to screech
SCREAKY	*adj* screechy
SCREAM	*v* -ED, -ING, -S to utter a prolonged, piercing cry
SCREAMER	*n* pl. -S one that screams
SCREE	*n* pl. -S a mass of rocks at the foot of a slope
SCREECH	*v* -ED, -ING, -ES to utter a harsh, shrill cry
SCREECHY	*adj* SCREECHIER, SCREECHIEST screeching
SCREED	*v* -ED, -ING, -S to shred
SCREEN	*v* -ED, -ING, -S to provide with a screen (a device designed to divide, conceal, or protect)
SCREENER	*n* pl. -S one that screens
SCREW	*v* -ED, -ING, -S to attach with a screw (a type of metal fastener)
SCREWER	*n* pl. -S one that screws
SCREWY	*adj* SCREWIER, SCREWIEST crazy
SCRIBAL	*adj* pertaining to a public clerk or secretary
SCRIBBLE	*v* -BLED, -BLING, -BLES to write hastily or carelessly
SCRIBE	*v* SCRIBED, SCRIBING, SCRIBES to mark with a scriber
SCRIBER	*n* pl. -S a pointed instrument used for marking off material to be cut
SCRIEVE	*v* SCRIEVED, SCRIEVING, SCRIEVES to move along swiftly and smoothly
SCRIM	*n* pl. -S a cotton fabric
SCRIMP	*v* -ED, -ING, -S to be very or overly thrifty
SCRIMPIT	*adj* meager
SCRIMPY	*adj* SCRIMPIER, SCRIMPIEST meager
SCRIP	*n* pl. -S a small piece of paper
SCRIPT	*v* -ED, -ING, -S to prepare a written text for, as a play or motion picture
SCRIVE	*v* SCRIVED, SCRIVING, SCRIVES to engrave
SCROD	*n* pl. -S a young cod
SCROFULA	*n* pl. -S a disease of the lymph glands
SCROGGY	*adj* -GIER, -GIEST of stunted growth
SCROLL	*n* pl. -S a roll of parchment or paper with writing on it
SCROOGE	*n* pl. -S a miserly person
SCROOP	*v* -ED, -ING, -S to make a harsh, grating sound
SCROTUM	*n* -TA or -TUMS the pouch of skin that contains the testes **SCROTAL** *adj*
SCROUGE	*v* SCROUGED, SCROUGING, SCROUGES to crowd
SCROUNGE	*v* SCROUNGED, SCROUNGING, SCROUNGES to gather by foraging
SCROUNGY	*adj* SCROUNGIER, SCROUNGIEST dirty
SCRUB	*v* SCRUBBED, SCRUBBING, SCRUBS to rub hard in order to clean
SCRUBBER	*n* pl. -S one that scrubs
SCRUBBY	*adj* -BIER, -BIEST inferior in size or quality
SCRUFF	*n* pl. -S the back of the neck
SCRUFFY	*adj* -FIER, -FIEST shabby
SCRUM	*n* pl. -S a formation around the ball in rugby
SCRUNCH	*v* -ED, -ING, -ES to crush
SCRUPLE	*v* -PLED, -PLING, -PLES to hesitate because of ethical considerations
SCRUTINY	*n* pl. -NIES a close examination
SCUBA	*n* pl. -S an underwater breathing device
SCUD	*v* SCUDDED, SCUDDING, SCUDS to run or move swiftly
SCUDO	*n* pl. -DI a former Italian coin
SCUFF	*v* -ED, -ING, -S to walk without lifting the feet
SCUFFLE	*v* -FLED, -FLING, -FLES to struggle in a rough, confused manner
SCUFFLER	*n* pl. -S one that scuffles
SCULK	*v* -ED, -ING, -S to skulk
SCULKER	*n* pl. -S skulker
SCULL	*v* -ED, -ING, -S to propel with a type of oar
SCULLER	*n* pl. -S one that sculls
SCULLERY	*n* pl. -LERIES a room in which kitchen utensils are cleaned and stored
SCULLION	*n* pl. -S a kitchen servant who does menial work
SCULP	*v* -ED, -ING, -S to sculpt
SCULPIN	*n* pl. -S a freshwater fish

SCULPT   *v* -ED, -ING, -S to form an image or representation of from solid material

SCULPTOR   *n* pl. -S one that sculpts

SCUM   *v* SCUMMED, SCUMMING, SCUMS to remove the scum (impure or extraneous matter) from

SCUMBLE   *v* -BLED, -BLING, -BLES to soften the outlines or colors of by rubbing lightly

SCUMLIKE   *adj* resembling scum

SCUMMED   past tense of scum

SCUMMER   *n* pl. -S one that scums

SCUMMING   present participle of scum

SCUMMY   *adj* -MIER, -MIEST covered with scum

SCUNNER   *v* -ED, -ING, -S to feel loathing or disgust

SCUP   *n* pl. -S a marine food fish

SCUPPAUG   *n* pl. -S scup

SCUPPER   *v* -ED, -ING, -S to ambush

SCURF   *n* pl. -S scaly or shredded dry skin

SCURFY   *adj* SCURFIER, SCURFIEST covered with scurf

SCURRIED   past tense of scurry

SCURRIES   present 3d person sing. of scurry

SCURRIL   *adj* scurrile

SCURRILE   *adj* expressed in coarse and abusive language

SCURRY   *v* -RIED, -RYING, -RIES to move hurriedly

SCURVY   *adj* -VIER, -VIEST base or contemptible **SCURVILY** *adv*

SCURVY   *n* pl. -VIES a disease resulting from vitamin C deficiency

SCUT   *n* pl. -S a short tail, as of a rabbit

SCUTA   pl. of scutum

SCUTAGE   *n* pl. -S a tax exacted by a feudal lord in lieu of military service

SCUTATE   *adj* shaped like a shield

SCUTCH   *v* -ED, -ING, -ES to separate the woody fiber from by beating

SCUTCHER   *n* pl. -S one that scutches

SCUTE   *n* pl. -S a horny plate or scale

SCUTELLA   *n/pl* small, scutate organs or parts

SCUTTER   *v* -ED, -ING, -S to scurry

SCUTTLE   *v* -TLED, -TLING, -TLES to scurry

SCUTUM   *n* pl. -TA scute

SCYPHATE   *adj* shaped like a cup

SCYTHE   *v* SCYTHED, SCYTHING, SCYTHES to cut with a scythe (a single-bladed cutting implement)

SEA   *n* pl. -S the ocean

SEABAG   *n* pl. -S a bag used by a sailor

SEABEACH   *n* pl. -ES a beach lying along the sea

SEABED   *n* pl. -S a seafloor

SEABIRD   *n* pl. -S a bird frequenting the ocean or seacoast

SEABOARD   *n* pl. -S the seacoast

SEABOOT   *n* pl. -S a waterproof boot

SEABORNE   *adj* carried on or over the sea

SEACOAST   *n* pl. -S land bordering on the sea

SEACOCK   *n* pl. -S a valve in a ship's hull

SEACRAFT   *n* pl. -S skill in sea navigation

SEADOG   *n* pl. -S a fogbow

SEADROME   *n* pl. -S an airport in the sea

SEAFARER   *n* pl. -S a sailor

SEAFLOOR   *n* pl. -S the bottom of a sea

SEAFOOD   *n* pl. -S edible fish or shellfish from the sea

SEAFOWL   *n* pl. -S a seabird

SEAFRONT   *n* pl. -S an area along the edge of the sea

SEAGIRT   *adj* surrounded by the sea

SEAGOING   *adj* designed for use on the sea

SEAL   *v* -ED, -ING, -S to close or make secure against access, leakage, or passage **SEALABLE** *adj*

SEALANT   *n* pl. -S a sealing agent

SEALER   *n* pl. -S one that seals

SEALERY   *n* pl. -ERIES the occupation of hunting seals

SEALLIKE   *adj* resembling a seal (an aquatic mammal)

SEALSKIN   *n* pl. -S the skin of a seal

SEAM   *v* -ED, -ING, -S to join with a seam (a line formed by sewing two pieces of fabric together)

SEAMAN   *n* pl. -MEN a sailor **SEAMANLY** *adj*

SEAMARK *n* pl. -S a landmark serving as a navigational guide to mariners

SEAMER *n* pl. -S one that seams

SEAMIER comparative of seamy

SEAMIEST superlative of seamy

SEAMLESS *adj* having no seam

SEAMLIKE *adj* resembling a seam

SEAMOUNT *n* pl. -S an undersea mountain

SEAMSTER *n* pl. -S a person whose occupation is sewing

SEAMY *adj* SEAMIER, SEAMIEST unpleasant

SEANCE *n* pl. -S a meeting of persons seeking spiritualistic messages

SEAPIECE *n* pl. -S a seascape

SEAPLANE *n* pl. -S an airplane designed to take off from or land on the water

SEAPORT *n* pl. -S a harbor or town accessible to seagoing ships

SEAQUAKE *n* pl. -S an undersea earthquake

SEAR *adj* SEARER, SEAREST sere

SEAR *v* -ED, -ING, -S to burn the surface of

SEARCH *v* -ED, -ING, -ES to look through or over carefully in order to find something

SEARCHER *n* pl. -S one that searches

SEARER comparative of sear

SEAREST superlative of sear

SEASCAPE *n* pl. -S a picture of the sea

SEASCOUT *n* pl. -S a boy scout trained in water activities

SEASHELL *n* pl. -S the shell of a marine mollusk

SEASHORE *n* pl. -S land bordering on the sea

SEASICK *adj* affected with nausea caused by the motion of a vessel at sea

SEASIDE *n* pl. -S the seashore

SEASON *v* -ED, -ING, -S to heighten or improve the flavor of by adding savory ingredients

SEASONAL *adj* occurring at a certain time of the year

SEASONER *n* pl. -S one that seasons

SEAT *v* -ED, -ING, -S to place on a seat (something on which one sits)

SEATER *n* pl. -S one that seats

SEATING *n* pl. -S material for covering seats

SEATLESS *adj* having no seat

SEATMATE *n* pl. -S one with whom one shares a seat

SEATRAIN *n* pl. -S a ship equipped to carry railroad cars

SEATWORK *n* pl. -S work done at one's seat

SEAWALL *n* pl. -S a wall to protect a shoreline from erosion

SEAWAN *n* pl. -S wampum

SEAWANT *n* pl. -S seawan

SEAWARD *n* pl. -S the direction toward the open sea

SEAWARE *n* pl. -S seaweed used as fertilizer

SEAWATER *n* pl. -S water from the sea

SEAWAY *n* pl. -WAYS the headway made by a ship

SEAWEED *n* pl. -S a plant growing in the sea

SEBACIC *adj* derived from a certain acid

SEBASIC *adj* sebacic

SEBUM *n* pl. -S a fatty matter secreted by certain glands of the skin

SEC *n* pl. -S secant

SECANT *n* pl. -S a trigonometric function of an angle

SECANTLY *adv* in an intersecting manner

SECATEUR *n* pl. -S a pruning tool

SECCO *n* pl. -COS the art of painting on dry plaster

SECEDE *v* -CEDED, -CEDING, -CEDES to withdraw formally from an alliance or association

SECEDER *n* pl. -S one that secedes

SECERN *v* -ED, -ING, -S to discern as separate

SECLUDE *v* -CLUDED, -CLUDING, -CLUDES to remove or set apart from others

SECOND *v* -ED, -ING, -S to give support or encouragement to

SECONDE *n* pl. -S a position in fencing

SECONDER *n* pl. -S one that seconds

SECONDLY *adv* in the next place after the first

SECONDO *n* pl. -DI the lower part in a piano duet

SECPAR	*n* pl. -S a parsec
SECRECY	*n* pl. -CIES the condition of being secret
SECRET	*adj* -CRETER, -CRETEST kept from knowledge or view
SECRET	*n* pl. -S something kept from the knowledge of others
SECRETE	*v* -CRETED, -CRETING, -CRETES to generate and separate out from cells or bodily fluids
SECRETIN	*n* pl. -S a hormone
SECRETLY	*adv* in a secret manner
SECRETOR	*n* pl. -S one that secretes
SECT	*n* pl. -S a group of people united by common beliefs or interests
SECTARY	*n* pl. -RIES a member of a sect
SECTILE	*adj* capable of being cut smoothly
SECTION	*v* -ED, -ING, -S to divide into sections (distinct parts)
SECTOR	*v* -ED, -ING, -S to divide into sectors (sections)
SECTORAL	*adj* of or pertaining to a sector
SECULAR	*n* pl. -S a layman
SECUND	*adj* having the parts or organs arranged on one side only **SECUNDLY** *adv*
SECUNDUM	*adv* according to
SECURE	*adj* -CURER, -CUREST free from danger **SECURELY** *adv*
SECURE	*v* -CURED, -CURING, -CURES to make firm or tight
SECURER	*n* pl. -S one that secures
SECUREST	superlative of secure
SECURING	present participle of secure
SECURITY	*n* pl. -TIES the state of being secure
SEDAN	*n* pl. -S a type of automobile
SEDARIM	a pl. of seder
SEDATE	*adj* -DATER, -DATEST calm **SEDATELY** *adv*
SEDATE	*v* -DATED, -DATING, -DATES to administer a sedative to
SEDATION	*n* pl. -S the reduction of stress or excitement by the use of sedatives
SEDATIVE	*n* pl. -S a drug that induces a calm state
SEDER	*n* pl. -DARIM or -DERS a Jewish ceremonial dinner
SEDERUNT	*n* pl. -S a prolonged sitting
SEDGE	*n* pl. -S a marsh plant
SEDGY	*adj* SEDGIER, SEDGIEST abounding in sedge
SEDILE	*n* pl. -LIA one of the seats in a church for the use of the officiating clergy
SEDILIUM	*n* pl. -LIA sedile
SEDIMENT	*v* -ED, -ING, -S to settle to the bottom of a liquid
SEDITION	*n* pl. -S incitement of rebellion against a government
SEDUCE	*v* -DUCED, -DUCING, -DUCES to lead astray **SEDUCIVE** *adj*
SEDUCER	*n* pl. -S one that seduces
SEDULITY	*n* pl. -TIES the state of being sedulous
SEDULOUS	*adj* diligent
SEDUM	*n* pl. -S a flowering plant
SEE	*v* SAW, SEEN, SEEING, SEES to perceive with the eyes **SEEABLE** *adj*
SEECATCH	*n* pl. -CATCHIE an adult male fur seal
SEED	*v* -ED, -ING, -S to plant seeds (propagative plant structures) in
SEEDBED	*n* pl. -S land prepared for seeding
SEEDCAKE	*n* pl. -S a sweet cake containing aromatic seeds
SEEDCASE	*n* pl. -S a pericarp
SEEDER	*n* pl. -S one that seeds
SEEDIER	comparative of seedy
SEEDIEST	superlative of seedy
SEEDILY	*adv* in a seedy manner
SEEDLESS	*adj* having no seeds
SEEDLIKE	*adj* resembling a seed
SEEDLING	*n* pl. -S a young plant
SEEDMAN	*n* pl. -MEN seedsman
SEEDPOD	*n* pl. -S a type of seed vessel
SEEDSMAN	*n* pl. -MEN a dealer in seeds
SEEDTIME	*n* pl. -S the season for sowing seeds
SEEDY	*adj* SEEDIER, SEEDIEST containing seeds; inferior in condition or quality
SEEING	*n* pl. -S the act of one that sees
SEEK	*v* SOUGHT, SEEKING, SEEKS to go in search of
SEEKER	*n* pl. -S one that seeks

SEEL	*v* -ED, -ING, -S to stitch closed the eyes of, as a falcon during training
SEELY	*adj* frail
SEEM	*v* -ED, -ING, -S to give the impression of being
SEEMER	*n* pl. -S one that seems
SEEMING	*n* pl. -S outward appearance
SEEMLY	*adj* -LIER, -LIEST of pleasing appearance
SEEN	past participle of see
SEEP	*v* -ED, -ING, -S to pass slowly through small openings
SEEPAGE	*n* pl. -S the quantity of fluid that has seeped
SEEPY	*adj* SEEPIER, SEEPIEST soaked or oozing with water
SEER	*n* pl. -S a prophet
SEERESS	*n* pl. -ES a female seer
SEESAW	*v* -ED, -ING, -S to move up and down or back and forth
SEETHE	*v* SEETHED, SEETHING, SEETHES to surge or foam as if boiling
SEGETAL	*adj* growing in fields of grain
SEGGAR	*n* pl. -S a saggar
SEGMENT	*v* -ED, -ING, -S to divide into sections
SEGNO	*n* pl. -GNI or -GNOS a musical sign
SEGO	*n* pl. -GOS a perennial herb
SEGUE	*v* -GUED, -GUEING, -GUES to proceed without pause from one musical theme to another
SEI	*n* pl. -S a rorqual
SEICENTO	*n* pl. -TOS the seventeenth century
SEICHE	*n* pl. -S an oscillation of the surface of a lake or landlocked sea
SEIDEL	*n* pl. -S a large beer glass
SEIGNEUR	*n* pl. -S seignior
SEIGNIOR	*n* pl. -S a feudal lord
SEIGNORY	*n* pl. -GNORIES the power of a seignior
SEINE	*v* SEINED, SEINING, SEINES to catch fish with a large, vertically hanging net
SEINER	*n* pl. -S one that seines
SEISE	*v* SEISED, SEISING, SEISES to seize **SEISABLE** *adj*

SEISER	*n* pl. -S seizer
SEISIN	*n* pl. -S seizin
SEISING	*n* pl. -S seizing
SEISM	*n* pl. -S an earthquake **SEISMAL, SEISMIC** *adj*
SEISMISM	*n* pl. -S the natural activity involved in earthquakes
SEISOR	*n* pl. -S seizor
SEISURE	*n* pl. -S seizure
SEIZE	*v* SEIZED, SEIZING, SEIZES to take hold of suddenly and forcibly **SEIZABLE** *adj*
SEIZER	*n* pl. -S one that seizes
SEIZIN	*n* pl. -S legal possession of land
SEIZING	*n* pl. -S the act of one that seizes
SEIZOR	*n* pl. -S one that takes seizin
SEIZURE	*n* pl. -S the act of seizing
SEJANT	*adj* represented in a sitting postion — used of a heraldic animal
SEJEANT	*adj* sejant
SEL	*n* pl. -S self
SELADANG	*n* pl. -S saladang
SELAH	*n* pl. -S a word of unknown meaning often marking the end of a verse in the Psalms
SELAMLIK	*n* pl. -S the portion of a Turkish house reserved for men
SELCOUTH	*adj* unusual
SELDOM	*adj* infrequent **SELDOMLY** *adv*
SELECT	*v* -ED, -ING, -S to choose
SELECTEE	*n* pl. -S one that is selected
SELECTLY	*adv* by selection
SELECTOR	*n* pl. -S one that selects
SELENATE	*n* pl. -S a chemical salt
SELENIC	*adj* pertaining to selenium
SELENIDE	*n* pl. -S a compound of selenium
SELENITE	*n* pl. -S a variety of gypsum
SELENIUM	*n* pl. -S a nonmetallic element **SELENOUS** *adj*
SELF	*n* pl. SELVES the total, essential, or particular being of one person
SELF	*v* -ED, -ING, -S to inbreed
SELFDOM	*n* pl. -S selfhood
SELFHEAL	*n* pl. -S a perennial herb

SELFHOOD *n* pl. -S the state of being an individual person

SELFISH *adj* concerned chiefly or only with oneself

SELFLESS *adj* unselfish

SELFNESS *n* pl. -ES selfhood

SELFSAME *adj* identical

SELFWARD *adv* toward oneself

SELL *v* SOLD, SELLING, SELLS to give up to another for money or other valuable consideration **SELLABLE** *adj*

SELLE *n* pl. -S a saddle

SELLER *n* pl. -S one that sells

SELLOUT *n* pl. -S a performance for which all seats have been sold

SELSYN *n* pl. -S a type of remote-control device

SELTZER *n* pl. -S carbonated mineral water

SELVAGE *n* pl. -S the edge of a woven fabric finished to prevent raveling **SELVAGED** *adj*

SELVEDGE *n* pl. -S selvage

SELVES pl. of self

SEMANTIC *adj* pertaining to meaning

SEMATIC *adj* serving as a warning

SEME *n* pl. -S a type of ornamental pattern

SEMEME *n* pl. -S the meaning of a morpheme

SEMEN *n* pl. -MINA or -MENS a fluid produced in the male reproductive organs

SEMESTER *n* pl. -S a period constituting half of an academic year

SEMI *n* pl. -S a freight trailer

SEMIARID *adj* characterized by light rainfall

SEMIBALD *adj* partly bald

SEMICOMA *n* pl. -S a coma from which a person can be aroused

SEMIDEAF *adj* partly deaf

SEMIDOME *n* pl. -S a half dome

SEMIDRY *adj* moderately dry

SEMIFIT *adj* conforming somewhat to the lines of the body

SEMIGALA *adj* somewhat gala

SEMIHARD *adj* moderately hard

SEMIHIGH *adj* moderately high

SEMIHOBO *n* pl. -BOS or -BOES a person having some of the characteristics of a hobo

SEMILOG *adj* having one scale logarithmic and the other arithmetic

SEMIMAT *adj* having a slight luster

SEMIMATT *adj* semimat

SEMIMUTE *adj* having partially lost the faculty of speech

SEMINA a pl. of semen

SEMINAL *adj* pertaining to semen

SEMINAR *n* pl. -S an advanced study group at a college or university

SEMINARY *n* pl. -NARIES a school for the training of priests, ministers, or rabbis

SEMINUDE *adj* partly nude

SEMIOSIS *n* pl. -OSES a process in which something functions as a sign to an organism

SEMIOTIC *n* pl. -S a general theory of signs and symbolism

SEMIPRO *n* pl. -PROS one who is engaged in some field or sport for pay on a part-time basis

SEMIRAW *adj* somewhat raw

SEMIS *n* pl. -MISES a coin of ancient Rome

SEMISOFT *adj* moderately soft

SEMITIST *n* pl. -S one who favors Jewish interests

SEMITONE *n* pl. -S a type of musical tone

SEMIWILD *adj* somewhat wild

SEMOLINA *n* pl. -S a granular product of wheat used for pasta

SEMPLE *adj* of humble birth

SEMPLICE *adj* simple — used as a musical direction

SEMPRE *adv* in the same manner throughout — used as a musical direction

SEN *n* pl. SEN a monetary unit of Japan

SENARIUS *n* pl. -NARII a Greek or Latin verse consisting of six metrical feet

SENARY *adj* pertaining to the number six

SENATE *n* pl. -S an assembly having high deliberative and legislative functions

SENATOR *n* pl. -S a member of a senate

SEND   *v* SENT, SENDING, SENDS to cause to go **SENDABLE** *adj*

SENDAL   *n* pl. -S a silk fabric

SENDER   *n* pl. -S one that sends

SENDOFF   *n* pl. -S a farewell celebration

SENECA   *n* pl. -S senega

SENECIO   *n* pl. -CIOS a flowering plant

SENEGA   *n* pl. -S a medicinal plant root

SENGI   *n* pl. SENGI a monetary unit of Zaire

SENHOR   *n* pl. -S or -ES a Portuguese or Brazilian gentleman

SENHORA   *n* pl. -S a married Portuguese or Brazilian woman

SENILE   *n* pl. -S one who exhibits senility

SENILELY   *adv* in a senile manner

SENILITY   *n* pl. -TIES mental and physical infirmity due to old age

SENIOR   *n* pl. -S a person who is older than another

SENITI   *n* pl. SENITI a monetary unit of Tonga

SENNA   *n* pl. -S a medicinal plant

SENNET   *n* pl. -S a call sounded on a trumpet signaling the entrance or exit of actors

SENNIGHT   *n* pl. -S a week

SENNIT   *n* pl. -S braided straw used in making hats

SENOPIA   *n* pl. -S an improvement of near vision

SENOR   *n* pl. -S or -ES a Spanish gentleman

SENORA   *n* pl. -S a married Spanish woman

SENORITA   *n* pl. -S an unmarried Spanish girl or woman

SENSA   pl. of sensum

SENSATE   *v* -SATED, -SATING, -SATES to sense

SENSE   *v* SENSED, SENSING, SENSES to perceive by the senses (any of certain agencies through which an individual receives impressions of the external world)

SENSEFUL   *adj* sensible

SENSIBLE   *adj* -BLER, -BLEST having or showing good judgment **SENSIBLY** *adv*

SENSIBLE   *n* pl. -S something that can be sensed

SENSILLA   *n/pl* simple sense organs

SENSING   present participle of sense

SENSOR   *n* pl. -S a device that receives and responds to a stimulus

SENSORIA   *n/pl* the parts of the brain concerned with the reception and interpretation of sensory stimuli

SENSORY   *adj* pertaining to the senses or sensation

SENSUAL   *adj* pertaining to the physical senses

SENSUM   *n* pl. -SA an object of perception or sensation

SENSUOUS   *adj* pertaining to or derived from the senses

SENT   past tense of send

SENTENCE   *v* -TENCED, -TENCING, -TENCES to declare judicially the extent of punishment to be imposed

SENTI   *n* pl. SENTI a monetary unit of Tanzania

SENTIENT   *n* pl. -S a person or thing capable of sensation

SENTINEL   *v* -NELED, -NELING, -NELS or -NELLED, -NELLING, -NELS to stand guard

SENTRY   *n* pl. -TRIES one who stands guard

SEPAL   *n* pl. -S one of the individual leaves of a calyx **SEPALED, SEPALINE, SEPALLED, SEPALOID, SEPALOUS** *adj*

SEPARATE   *v* -RATED, -RATING, -RATES to set or keep apart

SEPIA   *n* pl. -S a brown pigment **SEPIC** *adj*

SEPOY   *n* pl. -POYS a native of India serving in the British army

SEPPUKU   *n* pl. -S a Japanese form of suicide

SEPSIS   *n* pl. SEPSES bacterial invasion of the body

SEPT   *n* pl. -S a clan

SEPTA   pl. of septum

SEPTAL   *adj* pertaining to a septum

SEPTARIA   *n/pl* limestone nodules

SEPTATE   *adj* having a septum

SEPTET   *n* pl. -S a group of seven

SEPTETTE   *n* pl. -S septet

SEPTIC n pl. -S an agent producing sepsis **SEPTICAL** adj

SEPTIME n pl. -S a position in fencing

SEPTUM n pl. -TA a dividing membrane or partition

SEPTUPLE v -PLED, -PLING, -PLES to make seven times as great

SEQUEL n pl. -S something that follows and serves as a continuation

SEQUELA n pl. -QUELAE an abnormal condition resulting from a preceding disease

SEQUENCE v -QUENCED, -QUENCING, -QUENCES to arrange in consecutive order

SEQUENCY n pl. -CIES the following of one thing after another

SEQUENT n pl. -S something that follows

SEQUIN n pl. -S a shiny ornamental disk **SEQUINED** adj

SEQUITUR n pl. -S the conclusion of an inference

SEQUOIA n pl. -S a large evergreen tree

SER n pl. -S a unit of weight of India

SERA a pl. of serum

SERAC n pl. -S a large mass of ice broken off of a glacier

SERAGLIO n pl. -GLIOS a harem

SERAI n pl. -S a Turkish palace

SERAIL n pl. -S a seraglio

SERAL adj pertaining to a series of ecological changes

SERAPE n pl. -S a colorful woolen shawl

SERAPH n pl. -APHS, -APHIM, or -APHIN a winged celestial being **SERAPHIC** adj

SERAPHIM n pl. -S seraph

SERDAB n pl. -S a chamber within an ancient Egyptian tomb

SERE adj SERER, SEREST withered; dry

SERE v SERED, SERING, SERES to sear

SEREIN n pl. -S a fine rain falling from an apparently clear sky

SERENADE v -NADED, -NADING, -NADES to perform an honorific evening song for

SERENATA n pl. -TAS or -TE a dramatic cantata

SERENE adj SERENER, SERENEST calm; tranquil **SERENELY** adv

SERENE n pl. -S a serene condition or expanse

SERENITY n pl. -TIES the state of being serene

SERER comparative of sere

SEREST superlative of sere

SERF n pl. -S a feudal slave

SERFAGE n pl. -S serfdom

SERFDOM n pl. -S the state of being a serf

SERFHOOD n pl. -S serfdom

SERFISH adj characteristic of a serf

SERFLIKE adj serfish

SERGE n pl. -S a twilled fabric

SERGEANT n pl. -S a noncommissioned military officer

SERGING n pl. -S a process of finishing the raw edges of a fabric

SERIAL n pl. -S a literary or dramatic work presented in successive installments

SERIALLY adv in the manner or form of a serial

SERIATE v -ATED, -ATING, -ATES to put into a series

SERIATIM adv serially

SERICIN n pl. -S a kind of protein

SERIEMA n pl. -S a Brazilian bird

SERIES n pl. SERIES an arrangement of one after another

SERIF n pl. -S a fine line used to finish off the main stroke of a letter

SERIN n pl. -S a European finch

SERINE n pl. -S an amino acid

SERING present participle of sere

SERINGA n pl. -S a Brazilian tree

SERIOUS adj thoughtful or subdued in appearance or manner

SERJEANT n pl. -S sergeant

SERMON n pl. -S a religious discourse **SERMONIC** adj

SEROLOGY n pl. -GIES the science of serums

SEROSA n pl. -SAS or -SAE a thin membrane lining certain bodily cavities **SEROSAL** adj

SEROSITY n pl. -TIES the quality or state of being serous

SEROTINE n pl. -S a European bat

SEROTYPE   *n* pl. -S a group of closely related organisms distinguished by a common set of antigens

SEROUS   *adj* of or resembling serum

SEROW   *n* pl. -S an Asian antelope

SERPENT   *n* pl. -S a snake

SERPIGO   *n* pl. -GOES or -GINES a spreading skin eruption

SERRANID   *n* pl. -S a marine fish

SERRATE   *v* -RATED, -RATING, -RATES to furnish with toothlike projections

SERRY   *v* -RIED, -RYING, -RIES to crowd together

SERUM   *n* pl. -RUMS or -RA the watery portion of whole blood **SERUMAL** *adj*

SERVABLE   *adj* capable of serving or being served

SERVAL   *n* pl. -S an African wildcat

SERVANT   *n* pl. -S one that serves others

SERVE   *v* SERVED, SERVING, SERVES to work for

SERVER   *n* pl. -S one that serves another

SERVICE   *v* -VICED, -VICING, -VICES to repair

SERVICER   *n* pl. -S one that services

SERVILE   *adj* slavishly submissive

SERVING   *n* pl. -S a portion of food

SERVITOR   *n* pl. -S a male servant

SERVO   *n* pl. -VOS an automatic device used to control another mechanism

SESAME   *n* pl. -S an East Indian plant

SESAMOID   *n* pl. -S a nodular mass of bone or cartilage

SESSILE   *adj* permanently attached

SESSION   *n* pl. -S a meeting of a legislative or judicial body for the transaction of business

SESSPOOL   *n* pl. -S cesspool

SESTERCE   *n* pl. -S a coin of ancient Rome

SESTET   *n* pl. -S a stanza of six lines

SESTINA   *n* pl. -S a type of verse form

SESTINE   *n* pl. -S sestina

SET   *v* SET, SETTING, SETS to put in a particular position

SETA   *n* pl. -TAE a coarse, stiff hair **SETAL** *adj*

SETBACK   *n* pl. -S a defeat

SETIFORM   *adj* having the form of a seta

SETLINE   *n* pl. -S a strong fishing line

SETOFF   *n* pl. -S something that offsets something else

SETON   *n* pl. -S a type of surgical thread

SETOSE   *adj* covered with setae

SETOUS   *adj* setose

SETOUT   *n* pl. -S a display

SETSCREW   *n* pl. -S a type of screw

SETTEE   *n* pl. -S a long seat with a high back

SETTER   *n* pl. -S one that sets

SETTING   *n* pl. -S the scenery used in a dramatic production

SETTLE   *v* -TLED, -TLING, -TLES to place in a desired state or order

SETTLER   *n* pl. -S one that settles

SETTLING   *n* pl. -S sediment

SETTLOR   *n* pl. -S one that makes a legal settlement

SETULOSE   *adj* covered with seta

SETULOUS   *adj* setulose

SETUP   *n* pl. -S the way something is arranged

SEVEN   *n* pl. -S a number

SEVENTH   *n* pl. -S one of seven equal parts

SEVENTY   *n* pl. -TIES a number

SEVER   *v* -ED, -ING, -S to divide or cut into parts

SEVERAL   *n* pl. -S a few persons or things

SEVERE   *adj* -VERER, -VEREST unsparing in the treatment of others **SEVERELY** *adv*

SEVERITY   *n* pl. -TIES the quality or state of being severe

SEW   *v* SEWED, SEWN, SEWING, SEWS to mend or fasten with a needle and thread

SEWAGE   *n* pl. -S the waste matter carried off by sewers

SEWAN   *n* pl. -S seawan

SEWAR   *n* pl. -S a medieval servant

SEWER   *n* pl. -S an underground conduit for carrying off liquid and solid waste

SEWERAGE   *n* pl. -S sewage

SEWING   *n* pl. -S material that has been or is to be sewed

SEWN   a past participle of sew

SEX   v -ED, -ING, -ES to determine the sex (the property by which organisms are classified according to reproductive functions) of

SEXIER   comparative of sexy

SEXIEST   superlative of sexy

SEXILY   adv in a sexy manner

SEXINESS   n pl. -ES the quality or state of being sexy

SEXISM   n pl. -S prejudice or discrimination against women

SEXIST   n pl. -S one that practices sexism

SEXLESS   adj lacking sexual characteristics

SEXOLOGY   n pl. -GIES the study of human sexual behavior

SEXPOT   n pl. -S a sexually attractive woman

SEXT   n pl. -S one of seven canonical daily periods for prayer and devotion

SEXTAIN   n pl. -S a stanza of six lines

SEXTAN   n pl. -S a recurrent malarial fever

SEXTANT   n pl. -S an instrument for measuring angular distances

SEXTARII   n/pl ancient Roman units of liquid measure

SEXTET   n pl. -S a group of six

SEXTETTE   n pl. -S sextet

SEXTILE   n pl. -S the position of two celestial bodies when they are sixty degrees apart

SEXTO   n pl. -TOS sixmo

SEXTON   n pl. -S a maintenance worker of a church

SEXTUPLE   v -PLED, -PLING, -PLES to make six times as great

SEXTUPLY   adv to six times as much or as many

SEXUAL   adj pertaining to sex **SEXUALLY** adv

SEXY   adj SEXIER, SEXIEST arousing sexual desire

SFERICS   n/pl an electronic detector of storms

SFORZATO   n pl. -TOS the playing of a tone or chord with sudden force

SFUMATO   n pl. -TOS a technique used in painting

SH   interj — used to urge silence

SHABBY   adj -BIER, -BIEST ragged **SHABBILY** adv

SHACK   n pl. -S a shanty

SHACKLE   v -LED, -LING, -LES to confine with metal fastenings placed around the wrists or ankles

SHACKLER   n pl. -S one that shackles

SHACKO   n pl. -KOS or -KOES shako

SHAD   n pl. -S a food fish

SHADBLOW   n pl. -S a shadbush

SHADBUSH   n pl. -ES a flowering tree or shrub

SHADCHAN   n pl. -CHANIM or -CHANS a Jewish marriage broker

SHADDOCK   n pl. -S a citrus fruit

SHADE   v SHADED, SHADING, SHADES to screen from light or heat

SHADER   n pl. -S one that shades

SHADFLY   n pl. -FLIES a winged insect

SHADIER   comparative of shady

SHADIEST   superlative of shady

SHADILY   adv in a shady manner

SHADING   n pl. -S protection against light or heat

SHADOOF   n pl. -S a device used in Egypt for raising water for irrigation

SHADOW   v -ED, -ING, -S to make dark or gloomy

SHADOWER   n pl. -S one that shadows

SHADOWY   adj -OWIER, -OWIEST dark

SHADRACH   n pl. -S a mass of unfused material in the hearth of a blast furnace

SHADUF   n pl. -S shadoof

SHADY   adj SHADIER, SHADIEST shaded

SHAFT   v -ED, -ING, -S to push or propel with a pole

SHAFTING   n pl. -S a system of rods for transmitting motion or power

SHAG   v SHAGGED, SHAGGING, SHAGS to make shaggy

SHAGBARK   n pl. -S a hardwood tree

SHAGGY   adj -GIER, -GIEST covered with long, coarse hair **SHAGGILY** adv

SHAGREEN   n pl. -S the rough skin of certain sharks

SHAH   n pl. -S an Iranian ruler

SHAHDOM	*n* pl. -S the territory ruled by a shah
SHAIRD	*n* pl. -S shard
SHAIRN	*n* pl. -S sharn
SHAITAN	*n* pl. -S an evil spirit
SHAKE	*v* SHOOK, SHAKEN, SHAKING, SHAKES to move to and fro with short, rapid movements **SHAKABLE** *adj*
SHAKEOUT	*n* pl. -S a minor economic recession
SHAKER	*n* pl. -S one that shakes
SHAKEUP	*n* pl. -S a total reorganization
SHAKIER	comparative of shaky
SHAKIEST	superlative of shaky
SHAKILY	*adv* in a shaky manner
SHAKING	present participle of shake
SHAKO	*n* pl. -KOS or -KOES a type of military hat
SHAKY	*adj* SHAKIER, SHAKIEST shaking
SHALE	*n* pl. -S a fissile rock
SHALED	*adj* having a shell or husk
SHALIER	comparative of shaly
SHALIEST	superlative of shaly
SHALL	*v* present sing. 2d person SHALL or SHALT, past sing. 2d person SHOULD, SHOULDST, or SHOULDEST — used as an auxiliary to express futurity, inevitability, or command
SHALLOON	*n* pl. -S a woolen fabric
SHALLOP	*n* pl. -S a small, open boat
SHALLOT	*n* pl. -S a plant resembling an onion
SHALLOW	*adj* -LOWER, -LOWEST having little depth
SHALLOW	*v* -ED, -ING, -S to make shallow
SHALOM	*interj* peace — used as a Jewish greeting and farewell
SHALT	a present 2d person sing. of shall
SHALY	*adj* SHALIER, SHALIEST resembling shale
SHAM	*v* SHAMMED, SHAMMING, SHAMS to feign
SHAMABLE	*adj* capable of being shamed
SHAMAN	*n* pl. -S a medicine man among certain North American Indians **SHAMANIC** *adj*

SHAMBLE	*v* -BLED, -BLING, -BLES to walk awkwardly
SHAME	*v* SHAMED, SHAMING, SHAMES to cause to feel a painful sense of guilt or degradation
SHAMEFUL	*adj* disgraceful
SHAMES	*n* pl. -MOSIM shammes
SHAMING	present participle of shame
SHAMMAS	*n* pl. -MASIM shammes
SHAMMASH	*n* pl. -MASHIM shammes
SHAMMED	past tense of sham
SHAMMER	*n* pl. -S one that shams
SHAMMES	*n* pl. -MOSIM a minor official of a synagogue
SHAMMIED	past tense of shammy
SHAMMIES	present 3d person sing. of shammy
SHAMMING	present participle of sham
SHAMMOS	*n* pl. -MOSIM shammes
SHAMMOSIM	pl. of shammes
SHAMMY	*v* -MIED, -MYING, -MIES to chamois
SHAMOIS	*n* pl. SHAMOIS chamois
SHAMOSIM	pl. of shames
SHAMOY	*v* -ED, -ING, -S to chamois
SHAMPOO	*v* -ED, -ING, -S to cleanse with a special preparation
SHAMROCK	*n* pl. -S a three-leaved plant
SHAMUS	*n* pl. -ES a private detective
SHANDY	*n* pl. -DIES an alcoholic drink
SHANGHAI	*v* -ED, -ING, -S to kidnap for service aboard a ship
SHANK	*v* -ED, -ING, -S to hit sharply to the right, as a golf ball
SHANTEY	*n* pl. -TEYS chantey
SHANTI	*n* pl. -S peace
SHANTIES	pl. of shanty
SHANTIH	*n* pl. -S shanti
SHANTUNG	*n* pl. -S a silk fabric
SHANTY	*n* pl. -TIES a small, crudely built dwelling
SHAPE	*v* SHAPED, SHAPEN, SHAPING, SHAPES to give shape (outward form) to **SHAPABLE** *adj*
SHAPELY	*adj* -LIER, -LIEST having a pleasing shape
SHAPER	*n* pl. -S one that shapes
SHAPEUP	*n* pl. -S a system of hiring a work crew

SHAPING present participle of shape

SHARD *n* pl. -S a fragment of broken pottery

SHARE *v* SHARED, SHARING, SHARES to have, get, or use in common with another or others **SHARABLE** *adj*

SHARER *n* pl. -S one that shares

SHARIF *n* pl. -S sherif

SHARING present participle of share

SHARK *v* -ED, -ING, -S to live by trickery

SHARKER *n* pl. -S one that sharks

SHARN *n* pl. -S cow dung **SHARNY** *adj*

SHARP *adj* SHARPER, SHARPEST suitable for or capable of cutting or piercing

SHARP *v* -ED, -ING, -S to raise in pitch, as a musical tone

SHARPEN *v* -ED, -ING, -S to make or become sharp

SHARPER *n* pl. -S a swindler

SHARPIE *n* pl. -S a very alert person

SHARPLY *adv* in a sharp manner

SHARPY *n* pl. SHARPIES sharpie

SHASHLIK *n* pl. -S kabob

SHASLIK *n* pl. -S shashlik

SHAT a past tense of shit

SHATTER *v* -ED, -ING, -S to break into pieces

SHAUGH *n* pl. -S a thicket

SHAUL *v* -ED, -ING, -S to shoal

SHAVE *v* SHAVED, SHAVEN, SHAVING, SHAVES to sever the hair close to the roots **SHAVABLE** *adj*

SHAVER *n* pl. -S one that shaves

SHAVIE *n* pl. -S a trick or prank

SHAVING *n* pl. -S something shaved off

SHAW *v* SHAWED, SHAWN, SHAWING, SHAWS to show

SHAWL *v* -ED, -ING, -S to wrap in a shawl (a piece of cloth worn as a covering)

SHAWM *n* pl. -S an early woodwind instrument

SHAWN past participle of shaw

SHAY *n* pl. SHAYS a chaise

SHE *n* pl. -S a female person

SHEA *n* pl. -S an African tree

SHEAF *v* -ED, -ING, -S to sheave

SHEAL *n* pl. -S shealing

SHEALING *n* pl. -S a shepherd's hut

SHEAR *v* SHEARED or SHORE, SHORN, SHEARING, SHEARS to cut the hair from

SHEARER *n* pl. -S one that shears

SHEATH *v* -ED, -ING, -S to sheathe

SHEATHE *v* SHEATHED, SHEATHING, SHEATHES to put into a protective case

SHEATHER *n* pl. -S one that sheathes

SHEAVE *v* SHEAVED, SHEAVING, SHEAVES to gather into a bundle

SHEBANG *n* pl. -S a situation, organization, or matter

SHEBEAN *n* pl. -S shebeen

SHEBEEN *n* pl. -S a place where liquor is sold illegally

SHED *v* SHEDDED, SHEDDING, SHEDS to house in a shed (a small, low structure)

SHEDABLE *adj* capable of being cast off

SHEDDER *n* pl. -S one that casts off something

SHEDDING present participle of shed

SHEEN *v* -ED, -ING, -S to shine

SHEENEY *n* pl. -NEYS sheenie

SHEENFUL *adj* shining

SHEENIE *n* pl. -S a Jew — an offensive term

SHEENY *adj* SHEENIER, SHEENIEST shining

SHEEP *n* pl. SHEEP a ruminant mammal

SHEEPDOG *n* pl. -S a dog trained to guard and herd sheep

SHEEPISH *adj* embarrassed

SHEEPMAN *n* pl. -MEN a person who raises sheep

SHEER *v* -ED, -ING, -S to deviate from a course

SHEER *adj* SHEERER, SHEEREST of very thin texture **SHEERLY** *adv*

SHEET *v* -ED, -ING, -S to cover with a sheet (a thin, rectangular piece of material)

SHEETER *n* pl. -S one that sheets

SHEETFED *adj* pertaining to a type of printing press

SHEETING	*n* pl. -S material in the form of sheets
SHEEVE	*n* pl. -S a grooved pulley wheel
SHEGETZ	*n* pl. SHKOTZIM a non-Jewish boy or young man
SHEIK	*n* pl. -S an Arab chief
SHEIKDOM	*n* pl. -S the area ruled by a sheik
SHEIKH	*n* pl. -S sheik
SHEITAN	*n* pl. -S shaitan
SHEKEL	*n* pl. -S an ancient unit of weight and money
SHELDUCK	*n* pl. -S a European duck
SHELF	*n* pl. SHELVES a flat rigid structure used to support articles
SHELFFUL	*n* pl. -S as much as a shelf can hold
SHELL	*v* -ED, -ING, -S to divest of a shell (a hard outer covering)
SHELLAC	*v* -LACKED, -LACKING, -LACS to cover with a thin varnish
SHELLACK	*v* -ED, -ING, -S to shellac
SHELLER	*n* pl. -S one that shells
SHELLY	*adj* SHELLIER, SHELLIEST abounding in seashells
SHELTER	*v* -ED, -ING, -S to provide cover or protection for
SHELTIE	*n* pl. -S a small, shaggy pony
SHELTY	*n* pl. -TIES sheltie
SHELVE	*v* SHELVED, SHELVING, SHELVES to place on a shelf
SHELVER	*n* pl. -S one that shelves
SHELVES	pl. of shelf
SHELVING	*n* pl. -S material for shelves
SHELVY	*adj* SHELVIER, SHELVIEST inclining gradually
SHEND	*v* SHENT, SHENDING, SHENDS to disgrace
SHEOL	*n* pl. -S hell
SHEPHERD	*v* -ED, -ING, -S to watch over carefully
SHERBERT	*n* pl. -S sherbet
SHERBET	*n* pl. -S a frozen fruit-flavored mixture
SHERD	*n* pl. -S shard
SHEREEF	*n* pl. -S sherif
SHERIF	*n* pl. -S an Arab ruler
SHERIFF	*n* pl. -S a law-enforcement officer of a county
SHERLOCK	*n* pl. -S a detective
SHEROOT	*n* pl. -S cheroot
SHERRIS	*n* pl. -RISES sherry
SHERRY	*n* pl. -RIES a type of wine
SHETLAND	*n* pl. -S a wool yarn
SHEUCH	*n* pl. -S sheugh
SHEUGH	*n* pl. -S a ditch
SHEW	*v* SHEWED, SHEWN, SHEWING, SHEWS to show
SHEWER	*n* pl. -S one that shews
SHH	*interj* sh
SHIBAH	*n* pl. -S shiva
SHICKSA	*n* pl. -S shiksa
SHIED	past tense of shy
SHIEL	*n* pl. -S shieling
SHIELD	*v* -ED, -ING, -S to provide with a protective cover or shelter
SHIELDER	*n* pl. -S one that shields
SHIELING	*n* pl. -S shealing
SHIER	*n* pl. -S a horse having a tendency to shy
SHIES	present 3d person sing. of shy
SHIEST	a superlative of shy
SHIFT	*v* -ED, -ING, -S to move from one position to another
SHIFTER	*n* pl. -S one that shifts
SHIFTY	*adj* SHIFTIER, SHIFTIEST tricky **SHIFTILY** *adv*
SHIGELLA	*n* pl. -LAE or -LAS any of a genus of aerobic bacteria
SHIKAR	*v* -KARRED, -KARRING, -KARS to hunt
SHIKAREE	*n* pl. -S a big game hunter
SHIKARI	*n* pl. -S shikaree
SHIKARRED	past tense of shikar
SHIKARRING	present participle of shikar
SHIKSA	*n* pl. -S a non-Jewish girl or young woman
SHIKSE	*n* pl. -S shiksa
SHILINGI	*n* pl. SHILINGI a monetary unit of Tanzania
SHILL	*v* -ED, -ING, -S to act as a decoy
SHILLALA	*n* pl. -S a short, thick club
SHILLING	*n* pl. -S a former monetary unit of Great Britain
SHILPIT	*adj* sickly
SHILY	*adv* in a shy manner

SHIM	*v* SHIMMED, SHIMMING, SHIMS to fill out or level by inserting a thin wedge	**SHIPPED**	past tense of ship
SHIMMER	*v* -ED, -ING, -S to glimmer	**SHIPPEN**	*n* pl. -S a cowshed
SHIMMERY	*adj* shimmering	**SHIPPER**	*n* pl. -S one that ships
SHIMMING	present participle of shim	**SHIPPING**	*n* pl. -S the business of one that ships
SHIMMY	*v* -MIED, -MYING, -MIES to vibrate or wobble	**SHIPPON**	*n* pl. -S shippen
SHIN	*v* SHINNED, SHINNING, SHINS to climb by gripping and pulling alternately with the hands and legs	**SHIPSIDE**	*n* pl. -S the area alongside a ship
		SHIPWAY	*n* pl. -WAYS a canal deep enough to serve ships
		SHIPWORM	*n* pl. -S a wormlike marine mollusk
SHINBONE	*n* pl. -S the tibia	**SHIPYARD**	*n* pl. -S a place where ships are built or repaired
SHINDIG	*n* pl. -S an elaborate dance or party	**SHIRE**	*n* pl. -S a territorial division of Great Britain
SHINDY	*n* pl. -DYS or -DIES a shindig	**SHIRK**	*v* -ED, -ING, -S to avoid work or duty
SHINE	*v* SHONE or SHINED, SHINING, SHINES to emit light		
SHINER	*n* pl. -S one that shines	**SHIRKER**	*n* pl. -S one that shirks
SHINGLE	*v* -GLED, -GLING, -GLES to cover with shingles (thin, oblong pieces of building material)	**SHIRR**	*v* -ED, -ING, -S to draw into three or more parallel rows, as cloth
SHINGLER	*n* pl. -S one that shingles	**SHIRRING**	*n* pl. -S a shirred arrangement of cloth
SHINGLY	*adj* covered with small, loose stones	**SHIRT**	*n* pl. -S a garment for the upper part of the body
SHINIER	comparative of shiny		
SHINIEST	superlative of shiny	**SHIRTING**	*n* pl. -S fabric used for making shirts
SHINILY	*adv* in a shiny manner		
SHINING	*adj* emitting or reflecting light	**SHIRTY**	*adj* SHIRTIER, SHIRTIEST angry
SHINLEAF	*n* pl. -LEAFS or -LEAVES a perennial herb	**SHIST**	*n* pl. -S schist
		SHIT	*v* SHITTED or SHAT, SHITTING, SHITS to defecate — usually considered vulgar
SHINNED	past of shin		
SHINNERY	*n* pl. -NERIES a dense growth of small trees	**SHITTAH**	*n* pl. -S a hardwood tree
SHINNEY	*n* pl. -NEYS a form of hockey	**SHITTIM**	*n* pl. -S the wood of the shittah
SHINNING	present participle of shin	**SHITTING**	present participle of shit
SHINNY	*v* -NIED, -NYING, -NIES to shin	**SHIV**	*n* pl. -S a knife
SHINY	*adj* SHINIER, SHINIEST filled with light	**SHIVA**	*n* pl. -S a period of mourning
		SHIVAH	*n* pl. -S shiva
SHIP	*v* SHIPPED, SHIPPING, SHIPS to transport by ship (a vessel suitable for navigation in deep water)	**SHIVAREE**	*v* -REED, -REEING, -REES to chivaree
		SHIVE	*n* pl. -S a thin fragment
SHIPLAP	*n* pl. -S an overlapping joint used in carpentry	**SHIVER**	*v* -ED, -ING, -S to tremble with fear or cold
SHIPLOAD	*n* pl. -S as much as a ship can carry	**SHIVERER**	*n* pl. -S one that shivers
SHIPMAN	*n* pl. -MEN a sailor	**SHIVERY**	*adj* shivering
SHIPMATE	*n* pl. -S a fellow sailor	**SHKOTZIM**	pl. of shegetz
SHIPMENT	*n* pl. -S something that is shipped	**SHLEMIEL**	*n* pl. -S an unlucky bungler
		SHLOCK	*n* pl. -S schlock

SHMO	*n* pl. SHMOES schmo
SHNAPS	*n* pl. SHNAPS schnapps
SHOAL	*adj* SHOALER, SHOALEST shallow
SHOAL	*v* -ED, -ING, -S to become shallow
SHOALY	*adj* SHOALIER, SHOALIEST full of shallow areas
SHOAT	*n* pl. -S a young hog
SHOCK	*v* -ED, -ING, -S to strike with great surprise, horror, or disgust
SHOCKER	*n* pl. -S one that shocks
SHOD	a past tense of shoe
SHODDEN	a past participle of shoe
SHODDY	*adj* -DIER, -DIEST of inferior quality **SHODDILY** *adv*
SHODDY	*n* pl. -DIES a low-quality wool
SHOE	*n* pl. SHOES or SHOON a covering for the foot
SHOE	*v* SHOD or SHOED, SHODDEN, SHOEING, SHOES to provide with shoes
SHOEBILL	*n* pl. -S a wading bird
SHOEHORN	*v* -ED, -ING, -S to force into a small space
SHOELACE	*n* pl. -S a lace for fastening a shoe
SHOEPAC	*n* pl. -S a waterproof boot
SHOEPACK	*n* pl. -S shoepac
SHOER	*n* pl. -S one that shoes horses
SHOETREE	*n* pl. -S a device shaped like a foot that is inserted into a shoe to preserve its shape
SHOFAR	*n* pl. SHOFARS or SHOFROTH a ram's-horn trumpet blown in certain Jewish rituals
SHOG	*v* SHOGGED, SHOGGING, SHOGS to move along
SHOGUN	*n* pl. -S a former military leader of Japan **SHOGUNAL** *adj*
SHOJI	*n* pl. -S a paper screen used as a partition or door in a Japanese house
SHOLOM	*interj* shalom
SHONE	a past tense of shine
SHOO	*v* -ED, -ING, -S to drive away
SHOOFLY	*n* pl. -FLIES a child's rocker
SHOOK	*n* pl. -S a set of parts for assembling a barrel or packing
SHOOL	*v* -ED, -ING, -S to shovel
SHOON	a pl. of shoe
SHOOT	*v* SHOT, SHOOTING, SHOOTS to hit, wound, or kill with a missile discharged from a weapon
SHOOTER	*n* pl. -S one that shoots
SHOOTING	*n* pl. -S the act of one that shoots
SHOP	*v* SHOPPED, SHOPPING, SHOPS to examine goods with intent to buy
SHOPBOY	*n* pl. -BOYS a salesclerk
SHOPGIRL	*n* pl. -S a salesgirl
SHOPHAR	*n* pl. -PHARS or -PHROTH shofar
SHOPLIFT	*v* -ED, -ING, -S to steal goods from a store
SHOPMAN	*n* pl. -MEN one who owns or operates a small store
SHOPPE	*n* pl. -S a small store
SHOPPED	past tense of shop
SHOPPER	*n* pl. -S one that shops
SHOPPING	*n* pl. -S the act of one that shops
SHOPTALK	*n* pl. -S conversation concerning one's business or occupation
SHOPWORN	*adj* worn out from being on display in a store
SHORAN	*n* pl. -S a type of navigational system
SHORE	*v* SHORED, SHORING, SHORES to prop with a supporting timber
SHORING	*n* pl. -S a system of supporting timbers
SHORL	*n* pl. -S schorl
SHORN	a past participle of shear
SHORT	*adj* SHORTER, SHORTEST having little length
SHORT	*v* -ED, -ING, -S to cause a type of electrical malfunction in
SHORTAGE	*n* pl. -S an insufficient supply or amount
SHORTCUT	*n* pl. -S a shorter or quicker way
SHORTEN	*v* -ED, -ING, -S to make or become shorter
SHORTIA	*n* pl. -S a perennial herb
SHORTIE	*n* pl. -S shorty
SHORTIES	pl. of shorty
SHORTISH	*adj* somewhat short
SHORTLY	*adv* in a short time

SHORTY   *n* pl. SHORTIES one that is short

SHOT   *v* SHOTTED, SHOTTING, SHOTS to load with shot (small lead or steel pellets)

SHOTE   *n* pl. -S shoat

SHOTGUN   *v* -GUNNED, -GUNNING, -GUNS to shoot with a type of gun

SHOTT   *n* pl. -S chott

SHOTTED   past tense of shot

SHOTTEN   *adj* having spawned — used of a fish

SHOTTING   present participle of shot

SHOULD   past tense of shall

SHOULDER   *v* -ED, -ING, -S to assume the burden or responsibility of

SHOULDEST   a 2d person sing. past tense of shall

SHOULDST   a 2d person sing. past tense of shall

SHOUT   *v* -ED, -ING, -S to utter loudly

SHOUTER   *n* pl. -S one that shouts

SHOVE   *v* SHOVED, SHOVING, SHOVES to push roughly

SHOVEL   *v* -ELED, -ELING, -ELS or -ELLED, -ELLING, -ELS to take up with a shovel (a digging implement)

SHOVELER   *n* pl. -S one that shovels

SHOVER   *n* pl. -S one that shoves

SHOVING   present participle of shove

SHOW   *v* SHOWED, SHOWN, SHOWING, SHOWS to cause or permit to be seen

SHOWBOAT   *n* pl. -S a boat on which theatrical performances are given

SHOWCASE   *v* -CASED, -CASING, -CASES to exhibit

SHOWDOWN   *n* pl. -S an event that forces the conclusion of an issue

SHOWER   *v* -ED, -ING, -S to fall in a brief, heavy rain

SHOWERY   *adj* showering

SHOWGIRL   *n* pl. -S a chorus girl

SHOWIER   comparative of showy

SHOWIEST   superlative of showy

SHOWILY   *adv* in a showy manner

SHOWING   *n* pl. -S an exhibition or display

SHOWMAN   *n* pl. -MEN a theatrical producer

SHOWN   past participle of show

SHOWOFF   *n* pl. -S one given to pretentious display

SHOWROOM   *n* pl. -S a room used for the display of merchandise

SHOWY   *adj* SHOWIER, SHOWIEST making a great or brilliant display

SHRANK   past tense of shrink

SHRAPNEL   *n* pl. SHRAPNEL fragments from an exploding bomb, mine, or shell

SHRED   *v* SHREDDED, SHREDDING, SHREDS to tear into small strips

SHREDDER   *n* pl. -S one that shreds

SHREW   *v* -ED, -ING, -S to curse

SHREWD   *adj* SHREWDER, SHREWDEST having keen insight **SHREWDLY** *adv*

SHREWISH   *adj* ill-tempered

SHRI   *n* pl. -S sri

SHRIEK   *v* -ED, -ING, -S to utter a shrill cry

SHRIEKER   *n* pl. -S one that shrieks

SHRIEKY   *adj* SHRIEKIER, SHRIEKIEST shrill

SHRIEVAL   *adj* pertaining to a sheriff

SHRIEVE   *v* SHRIEVED, SHRIEVING, SHRIEVES to shrive

SHRIFT   *n* pl. -S the act of shriving

SHRIKE   *n* pl. -S a predatory bird

SHRILL   *adj* SHRILLER, SHRILLEST having a high-pitched and piercing quality **SHRILLY** *adv*

SHRILL   *v* -ED, -ING, -S to utter a shrill sound

SHRIMP   *v* -ED, -ING, -S to catch shrimps (small marine decapods)

SHRIMPER   *n* pl. -S a shrimp fisher

SHRIMPY   *adj* SHRIMPIER, SHRIMPIEST abounding in shrimp

SHRINE   *v* SHRINED, SHRINING, SHRINES to place in a shrine (a receptacle for sacred relics)

SHRINK   *v* SHRANK, SHRUNK or SHRUNKEN, SHRINKING, SHRINKS to contract or draw back

SHRINKER   *n* pl. -S one that shrinks

SHRIVE   *v* SHROVE or SHRIVED, SHRIVEN, SHRIVING, SHRIVES to hear the confession of and grant absolution to

SHRIVEL   *v* -ELED, -ELING, -ELS or -ELLED, -ELLING, -ELS to contract into wrinkles

SHRIVER   *n* pl. -S one that shrives

SHRIVING   present participle of shrive

SHROFF   *v* -ED, -ING, -S to test the genuineness of, as a coin

SHROUD   *v* -ED, -ING, -S to wrap in burial clothing

SHROVE   a past tense of shrive

SHRUB   *n* pl. -S a low, woody plant

SHRUBBY   *adj* -BIER, -BIEST covered with shrubs

SHRUG   *v* SHRUGGED, SHRUGGING, SHRUGS to raise and contract the shoulders

SHRUNK   a past tense of shrink

SHRUNKEN   a past participle of shrink

SHTETEL   *n* pl. SHTETLACH a Jewish village

SHTETL   *n* pl. SHTETLACH shtetel

SHTICK   *n* pl. -S an entertainment routine

SHUCK   *v* -ED, -ING, -S to remove the husk or shell from

SHUCKER   *n* pl. -S one that shucks

SHUCKING   *n* pl. -S the act of one that shucks

SHUDDER   *v* -ED, -ING, -S to tremble

SHUDDERY   *adj* shuddering

SHUFFLE   *v* -FLED, -FLING, -FLES to walk without lifting the feet

SHUFFLER   *n* pl. -S one that shuffles

SHUL   *n* pl. SHULN or SHULS a synagogue

SHUN   *v* SHUNNED, SHUNNING, SHUNS to avoid

SHUNNER   *n* pl. -S one that shuns

SHUNPIKE   *n* pl. -S a side road taken to avoid paying tolls

SHUNT   *v* -ED, -ING, -S to turn aside

SHUNTER   *n* pl. -S one that shunts

SHUSH   *v* -ED, -ING, -ES to silence

SHUT   *v* SHUT, SHUTTING, SHUTS to close

SHUTDOWN   *n* pl. -S a temporary closing of an industrial plant

SHUTE   *v* SHUTED, SHUTING, SHUTES to chute

SHUTEYE   *n* pl. -S sleep

SHUTOFF   *n* pl. -S a device that shuts something off

SHUTOUT   *n* pl. -S a game in which one team fails to score

SHUTTER   *v* -ED, -ING, -S to provide with shutters (hinged window covers)

SHUTTING   present participle of shut

SHUTTLE   *v* -TLED, -TLING, -TLES to move or travel back and forth

SHWANPAN   *n* pl. -S swanpan

SHY   *adj* SHIER, SHIEST or SHYER, SHYEST timid

SHY   *v* SHIED, SHYING, SHIES to move suddenly back or aside, as in fear

SHYER   *n* pl. -S shier

SHYLOCK   *v* -ED, -ING, -S to lend money at high interest rates

SHYLY   *adv* in a shy manner

SHYNESS   *n* pl. -ES the state of being shy

SHYSTER   *n* pl. -S an unscrupulous lawyer or politician

SI   *n* pl. -S ti

SIAL   *n* pl. -S a type of rock formation **SIALIC** *adj*

SIALOID   *adj* resembling saliva

SIAMANG   *n* pl. -S a large, black gibbon

SIAMESE   *n* pl. -S a water pipe with a connection for two hoses

SIB   *n* pl. -S a sibling

SIBB   *n* pl. -S sib

SIBILANT   *n* pl. -S a speech sound produced by the fricative passage of breath through a narrow orifice

SIBILATE   *v* -LATED, -LATING, -LATES to hiss

SIBLING   *n* pl. -S one having the same parents as another

SIBYL   *n* pl. -S a female prophet **SIBYLIC, SIBYLLIC** *adj*

SIC   *v* SICCED, SICCING, SICS to urge to attack

SICCAN   *adj* such

SICE   *n* pl. -S syce

SICK	*adj* SICKER, SICKEST affected with disease or ill health	**SIDEWALL**	*n* pl. -S a side surface of a tire
SICK	*v* -ED, -ING, -S to sic	**SIDEWARD**	*adv* toward one side
SICKBAY	*n* pl. -BAYS a ship's hospital	**SIDEWAY**	*adv* sideways
SICKBED	*n* pl. -S a sick person's bed	**SIDEWAYS**	*adv* toward or from one side
SICKEN	*v* -ED, -ING, -S to make sick	**SIDEWISE**	*adv* sideways
SICKENER	*n* pl. -S one that sickens	**SIDING**	*n* pl. -S material used for surfacing a frame building
SICKERLY	*adv* securely	**SIDLE**	*v* -DLED, -DLING, -DLES to move sideways
SICKISH	*adj* somewhat sick		
SICKLE	*v* -LED, -LING, -LES to cut with an agricultural implement having a single blade	**SIDLER**	*n* pl. -S one that sidles
		SIEGE	*v* SIEGED, SIEGING, SIEGES to attempt to capture or gain
SICKLY	*adj* -LIER, -LIEST appearing as if sick **SICKLILY** *adv*	**SIEMENS**	*n* pl. SIEMENS a unit of electrical conductance
SICKLY	*v* -LIED, -LYING, -LIES to make sickly	**SIENITE**	*n* pl. -S syenite
		SIENNA	*n* pl. -S a brown pigment
SICKNESS	*n* pl. -ES the state of being sick	**SIEROZEM**	*n* pl. -S a type of soil
SICKROOM	*n* pl. -S a room occupied by a sick person	**SIERRA**	*n* pl. -S a mountain range **SIERRAN** *adj*
SIDDUR	*n* pl. -DURIM or -DURS a Jewish prayer book	**SIESTA**	*n* pl. -S an afternoon nap or rest
SIDE	*v* SIDED, SIDING, SIDES to agree with or support	**SIEUR**	*n* pl. -S an old French title of respect for a man
SIDEARM	*adj* thrown with a sideways sweep of the arm	**SIEVE**	*v* SIEVED, SIEVING, SIEVES to pass through a sieve (a utensil for separating the coarse parts from the fine parts of loose matter)
SIDEBAND	*n* pl. -S a band of radio frequencies		
SIDECAR	*n* pl. -S a passenger car attached to a motorcycle	**SIFFLEUR**	*n* pl. -S an animal that makes a whistling noise
SIDED	past tense of side	**SIFT**	*v* -ED, -ING, -S to sieve
SIDEHILL	*n* pl. -S a hillside	**SIFTER**	*n* pl. -S one that sifts
SIDEKICK	*n* pl. -S a close friend	**SIFTING**	*n* pl. -S the work of a sifter
SIDELINE	*v* -LINED, -LINING, -LINES to put out of action	**SIGANID**	*n* pl. -S any of a family of fishes
SIDELING	*adj* sloping	**SIGH**	*v* -ED, -ING, -S to let out a sigh (a deep, audible breath)
SIDELONG	*adj* directed to one side		
SIDEMAN	*n* pl. -MEN a member of a jazz band	**SIGHER**	*n* pl. -S one that sighs
		SIGHLESS	*adj* uttering no sigh
SIDEREAL	*adj* pertaining to the stars	**SIGHLIKE**	*adj* resembling a sigh
SIDERITE	*n* pl. -S a mineral	**SIGHT**	*v* -ED, -ING, -S to observe or notice
SIDESHOW	*n* pl. -S a small show offered in addition to a main attraction		
		SIGHTER	*n* pl. -S one that sights
SIDESLIP	*v* -SLIPPED, -SLIPPING, -SLIPS to slip to one side	**SIGHTLY**	*adj* -LIER, -LIEST pleasing to look at
SIDESPIN	*n* pl. -S a type of spin imparted to a ball	**SIGHTSEE**	*v* -SAW, -SEEN, -SEEING, -SEES to visit and view places of interest
SIDESTEP	*v* -STEPPED, -STEPPING, -STEPS to step to one side		
		SIGIL	*n* pl. -S an official seal
SIDEWALK	*n* pl. -S a paved walk for pedestrians	**SIGLOS**	*n* pl. -LOI an ancient Persian coin

SIGMA   *n* pl. -S a Greek letter **SIGMATE** *adj*

SIGMOID   *n* pl. -S an S-shaped curve in a bodily part

SIGN   *v* -ED, -ING, -S to write one's name on

SIGNAL   *v* -NALED, -NALING, -NALS or -NALLED, -NALLING, -NALS to notify by a means of communication

SIGNALER   *n* pl. -S one that signals

SIGNALLY   *adv* notably

SIGNER   *n* pl. -S one that signs

SIGNET   *v* -ED, -ING, -S to mark with an official seal

SIGNIFY   *v* -FIED, -FYING, -FIES to make known

SIGNIOR   *n* pl. -GNIORI or -GNIORS signor

SIGNIORY   *n* pl. -GNIORIES signory

SIGNOR   *n* pl. -GNORI or -GNORS an Italian title of courtesy for a man

SIGNORA   *n* pl. -GNORE or -GNORAS an Italian title of courtesy for a married woman

SIGNORE   *n* pl. -GNORI signor

SIGNORY   *n* pl. -GNORIES seignory

SIGNPOST   *v* -ED, -ING, -S to provide with signposts (posts bearing signs)

SIKE   *n* pl. -S syke

SIKER   *adj* secure

SILAGE   *n* pl. -S fodder that has been preserved in a silo

SILANE   *n* pl. -S a chemical compound

SILD   *n* pl. -S a young herring

SILENCE   *v* -LENCED, -LENCING, -LENCES to make silent

SILENCER   *n* pl. -S one that silences

SILENI   pl. of silenus

SILENT   *adj* -LENTER, -LENTEST making no sound or noise **SILENTLY** *adv*

SILENTS   *n/pl* silent movies

SILENUS   *n* pl. -NI a woodland deity of Greek mythology

SILESIA   *n* pl. -S a cotton fabric

SILEX   *n* pl. -ES silica

SILICA   *n* pl. -S a form of silicon

SILICATE   *n* pl. -S a chemical salt

SILICIC   *adj* pertaining to silicon

SILICIDE   *n* pl. -S a silicon compound

SILICIFY   *v* -FIED, -FYING, -FIES to convert into silica

SILICIUM   *n* pl. -S silicon

SILICLE   *n* pl. -S a short, flat silique

SILICON   *n* pl. -S a nonmetallic element

SILICONE   *n* pl. -S a silicon compound

SILIQUA   *n* pl. -QUAE silique

SILIQUE   *n* pl. -LIQUES a type of seed vessel

SILK   *v* -ED, -ING, -S to cover with silk (a soft, lustrous fabric)

SILKEN   *adj* made of silk

SILKIER   comparative of silky

SILKIEST   superlative of silky

SILKILY   *adv* in a silky manner

SILKLIKE   *adj* resembling silk

SILKWEED   *n* pl. -S milkweed

SILKWORM   *n* pl. -S a caterpillar that spins a cocoon of silk fibers

SILKY   *adj* SILKIER, SILKIEST resembling silk

SILL   *n* pl. -S the horizontal piece that bears the upright portion of a frame

SILLABUB   *n* pl. -S an alcoholic beverage or dessert

SILLER   *n* pl. -S silver

SILLIBUB   *n* pl. -S sillabub

SILLY   *adj* -LIER, -LIEST showing a lack of good sense **SILLILY** *adv*

SILLY   *n* pl. -LIES a silly person

SILO   *v* -ED, -ING, -S to store in a silo (a tall, cylindrical structure)

SILOXANE   *n* pl. -S a chemical compound

SILT   *v* -ED, -ING, -S to fill with silt (a sedimentary material)

SILTY   *adj* SILTIER, SILTIEST full of silt

SILURID   *n* pl. -S any of a family of catfishes

SILUROID   *n* pl. -S a silurid

SILVA   *n* pl. -VAS or -VAE sylva

SILVAN   *n* pl. -S sylvan

SILVER   *v* -ED, -ING, -S to cover with silver (a metallic element)

SILVERER   *n* pl. -S one that silvers

SILVERLY   *adv* with a silvery appearance

SILVERN   *adj* silvery

SILVERY   *adj* resembling silver

SILVICAL *adj* pertaining to silvics

SILVICS *n/pl* the study of forest trees

SIM *n* pl. -S simulation

SIMA *n* pl. -S an igneous rock

SIMAR *n* pl. -S a woman's light jacket or robe

SIMARUBA *n* pl. -S a tropical tree

SIMAZINE *n* pl. -S an herbicide

SIMIAN *n* pl. -S an ape or monkey

SIMILAR *adj* being like but not completely identical to

SIMILE *n* pl. -S a figure of speech

SIMIOID *adj* simious

SIMIOUS *adj* pertaining to simians

SIMITAR *n* pl. -S scimitar

SIMLIN *n* pl. -S cymling

SIMMER *v* -ED, -ING, -S to cook below or just at the boiling point

SIMNEL *n* pl. -S a crisp bread

SIMOLEON *n* pl. -S a dollar

SIMONIAC *n* pl. -S one who practices simony

SIMONIES pl. of simony

SIMONIST *n* pl. -S a simoniac

SIMONIZE *v* -NIZED, -NIZING, -NIZES to polish with wax

SIMONY *n* pl. -NIES the buying or selling of a church office

SIMOOM *n* pl. -S a hot, dry desert wind

SIMOON *n* pl. -S simoom

SIMP *n* pl. -S a foolish person

SIMPER *v* -ED, -ING, -S to smile in a silly manner

SIMPERER *n* pl. -S one that simpers

SIMPLE *adj* SIMPLER, SIMPLEST not complex or complicated

SIMPLE *n* pl. -S something that is simple

SIMPLEX *n* pl. -PLEXES, -PLICES, or -PLICIA a simple word

SIMPLIFY *v* -FIED, -FYING, -FIES to make simple

SIMPLISM *n* pl. -S the tendency to oversimplify an issue or problem

SIMPLY *adv* in a simple manner

SIMULANT *n* pl. -S one that simulates

SIMULAR *n* pl. -S a simulant

SIMULATE *v* -LATED, -LATING, -LATES to take on the appearance of

SIN *v* SINNED, SINNING, SINS to commit a sin (an offense against religious or moral law)

SINAPISM *n* pl. -S a pasty mixture applied to an irritated part of the body

SINCE *adv* from then until now

SINCERE *adj* -CERER, -CEREST free from hypocrisy or falseness

SINCIPUT *n* pl. -CIPUTS or -CIPITA the forehead

SINE *n* pl. -S a trigonometric function of an angle

SINECURE *n* pl. -S an office or position requiring little or no work

SINEW *v* -ED, -ING, -S to strengthen

SINEWY *adj* lean and muscular

SINFONIA *n* pl. -NIE a symphony

SINFUL *adj* marked by sin **SINFULLY** *adv*

SING *v* SANG, SUNG, SINGING, SINGS to utter with musical inflections of the voice **SINGABLE** *adj*

SINGE *v* SINGED, SINGEING, SINGES to burn slightly

SINGER *n* pl. -S one that sings

SINGLE *v* -GLED, -GLING, -GLES to select from a group

SINGLET *n* pl. -S a man's undershirt or jersey

SINGLY *adv* without the company of others

SINGSONG *n* pl. -S monotonous cadence in speaking or reading

SINGULAR *n* pl. -S a word form that denotes one person or thing

SINH *n* pl. -S a hyperbolic function of an angle

SINICIZE *v* -CIZED, -CIZING, -CIZES to modify by Chinese influence

SINISTER *adj* threatening or portending evil

SINK *v* SANK, SUNK or SUNKEN, SINKING, SINKS to move to a lower level **SINKABLE** *adj*

SINKAGE *n* pl. -S the act, process, or degree of sinking

SINKER *n* pl. -S one that sinks

SINKHOLE *n* pl. -S a natural depression in a land surface

SINLESS *adj* free from sin

SINNED past tense of sin

SINNER   *n* pl. -S one that sins

SINNING   present participle of sin

SINOLOGY   *n* pl. -GIES the study of the Chinese

SINOPIA   *n* pl. -PIAS or -PIE a red pigment

SINSYNE   *adv* since

SINTER   *v* -ED, -ING, -S to make cohesive by the combined action of heat and pressure

SINUATE   *v* -ATED, -ATING, -ATES to curve in and out

SINUOUS   *adj* characterized by curves, bends, or turns

SINUS   *n* pl. -ES a cranial cavity

SINUSOID   *n* pl. -S a mathematical curve

SIP   *v* SIPPED, SIPPING, SIPS to drink in small quantities

SIPE   *v* SIPED, SIPING, SIPES to seep

SIPHON   *v* -ED, -ING, -S to draw off through a siphon (a type of tube)

SIPHONAL   *adj* of or pertaining to a siphon

SIPHONIC   *adj* siphonal

SIPING   present participle of sipe

SIPPED   past tense of sip

SIPPER   *n* pl. -S one that sips

SIPPET   *n* pl. -S a small piece of bread soaked in gravy

SIPPING   present participle of sip

SIR   *n* pl. -S a respectful form of address used to a man

SIRDAR   *n* pl. -S a person of rank in India

SIRE   *v* SIRED, SIRING, SIRES to beget

SIREE   *n* pl. -S sirree

SIREN   *n* pl. -S a device that produces a penetrating warning sound

SIRENIAN   *n* pl. -S any of an order of aquatic mammals

SIRING   present participle of sire

SIRLOIN   *n* pl. -S a cut of beef

SIROCCO   *n* pl. -COS a hot, dry wind

SIRRA   *n* pl. -S sirrah

SIRRAH   *n* pl. -S a form of address used to inferiors

SIRREE   *n* pl. -S sir

SIRUP   *n* pl. -S syrup **SIRUPY** *adj*

SIRVENTE   *n* pl. -S a satirical medieval song or poem

SIS   *n* pl. SISES sister

SISAL   *n* pl. -S a strong fiber used for rope

SISKIN   *n* pl. -S a Eurasian finch

SISSY   *n* pl. -SIES an effeminate man or boy

SISSY   *adj* SISSIER, SISSIEST sissyish

SISSYISH   *adj* resembling a sissy

SISTER   *v* -ED, -ING, -S to treat like a sister (a female sibling)

SISTERLY   *adj* of or resembling a sister

SISTRA   a pl. of sistrum

SISTROID   *adj* included between the convex sides of two intersecting curves

SISTRUM   *n* pl. -TRUMS or -TRA an ancient Egyptian percussion instrument

SIT   *v* SAT, SITTEN, SITTING, SITS to rest on the buttocks

SITAR   *n* pl. -S a lute of India

SITARIST   *n* pl. -S one who plays the sitar

SITE   *v* SITED, SITING, SITES to place in position for operation

SITH   *adv* since

SITHENCE   *adv* since

SITHENS   *adv* since

SITI   a pl. of situs

SITING   present participle of site

SITOLOGY   *n* pl. -GIES the science of nutrition and diet

SITTEN   a past participle of sit

SITTER   *n* pl. -S one that sits

SITTING   *n* pl. -S a meeting or session

SITUATE   *v* -ATED, -ATING, -ATES to place in a certain position

SITUS   *n* pl. -TI or -TUSES a position or location

SITZMARK   *n* pl. -S a mark left in the snow by a skier who has fallen backward

SIVER   *n* pl. -S a sewer

SIX   *n* pl. -ES a number

SIXFOLD   *adj* being six times as great as

SIXMO   *n* pl. -MOS a paper size

SIXPENCE   *n* pl. -S a British coin worth six pennies

SIXPENNY *adj* worth sixpence

SIXTE *n* pl. -S a fencing parry

SIXTEEN *n* pl. -S a number

SIXTH *n* pl. -S one of six equal parts

SIXTHLY *adv* in the sixth place

SIXTIETH *n* pl. -S one of sixty equal parts

SIXTY *n* pl. -TIES a number

SIZABLE *adj* of considerable size **SIZABLY** *adv*

SIZAR *n* pl. -S a British student who receives financial assistance from his college

SIZE *v* SIZED, SIZING, SIZES to arrange according to size (physical proportions)

SIZEABLE *adj* sizable **SIZEABLY** *adv*

SIZER *n* pl. -S sizar

SIZIER comparative of sizy

SIZIEST superlative of sizy

SIZINESS *n* pl. -ES the quality or state of being sizy

SIZING *n* pl. -S a substance used as a glaze or filler for porous materials

SIZY *adj* SIZIER, SIZIEST viscid

SIZZLE *v* -ZLED, -ZLING, -ZLES to burn or fry with a hissing sound

SIZZLER *n* pl. -S a very hot day

SKAG *n* pl. -S heroin

SKALD *n* pl. -S an ancient Scandinavian poet **SKALDIC** *adj*

SKAT *n* pl. -S a card game

SKATE *v* SKATED, SKATING, SKATES to glide over ice or the ground on skates (shoes fitted with runners or wheels)

SKATER *n* pl. -S one that skates

SKATING *n* pl. -S the sport of gliding on skates

SKATOL *n* pl. -S skatole

SKATOLE *n* pl. -S a chemical compound

SKEAN *n* pl. -S a type of dagger

SKEANE *n* pl. -S a length of yarn wound in a loose coil

SKEE *v* SKEED, SKEEING, SKEES to ski

SKEEN *n* pl. -S skean

SKEET *n* pl. -S the sport of shooting at clay pigeons hurled in the air by spring traps

SKEETER *n* pl. -S a skeet shooter

SKEG *n* pl. -S a timber that connects the keel and sternpost of a ship

SKEIGH *adj* proud

SKEIN *v* -ED, -ING, -S to wind into long, loose coils

SKELETON *n* pl. -S the supporting or protective framework of a human or animal body **SKELETAL** *adj*

SKELLUM *n* pl. -S a rascal

SKELP *v* SKELPED or SKELPIT, SKELPING, SKELPS to slap

SKELTER *v* -ED, -ING, -S to scurry

SKENE *n* pl. -S skean

SKEP *n* pl. -S a beehive

SKEPSIS *n* pl. -SISES the attitude or outlook of a skeptic

SKEPTIC *n* pl. -S a person who doubts generally accepted ideas

SKERRY *n* pl. -RIES a small, rocky island

SKETCH *v* -ED, -ING, -ES to make a rough, hasty drawing of

SKETCHER *n* pl. -S one that sketches

SKETCHY *adj* SKETCHIER, SKETCHIEST lacking in completeness or clearness

SKEW *v* -ED, -ING, -S to turn aside

SKEWBACK *n* pl. -S a sloping surface against which the end of an arch rests

SKEWBALD *n* pl. -S a horse having patches of brown and white

SKEWER *v* -ED, -ING, -S to pierce with a long pin, as meat

SKEWNESS *n* pl. -ES lack of symmetry

SKI *v* -ED, -ING, -S to travel on skis (long, narrow strips of wood or metal)

SKIABLE *adj* capable of being skied over

SKIAGRAM *n* pl. -S a picture made up of shadows or outlines

SKIBOB *n* pl. -S a vehicle used for traveling over snow

SKID *v* SKIDDED, SKIDDING, SKIDS to slide sideways as a result of a loss of traction

SKIDDER *n* pl. -S one that skids

SKIDDOO *v* -ED, -ING, -S to go away

SKIDDY *adj* -DIER, -DIEST likely to cause skidding

SKIDOO	v -ED, -ING, -S to skiddoo
SKIDWAY	n pl. -WAYS a platform on which logs are piled for loading or sawing
SKIED	past tense of ski and sky
SKIER	n pl. -S one that skis
SKIES	present 3d person sing. of sky
SKIEY	adj skyey
SKIFF	n pl. -S a small, open boat
SKIFFLE	v -FLED, -FLING, -FLES to play a particular style of music
SKIING	n pl. -S the sport of traveling on skis
SKIJORER	n pl. -S a skier who is drawn over snow by a horse or vehicle
SKILFUL	adj skillful
SKILL	n pl. -S the ability to do something well **SKILLED** adj
SKILLESS	adj having no skill
SKILLET	n pl. -S a frying pan
SKILLFUL	adj having skill
SKILLING	n pl. -S a former coin of Scandinavian countries
SKIM	v SKIMMED, SKIMMING, SKIMS to remove floating matter from the surface of
SKIMMER	n pl. -S one that skims
SKIMMING	n pl. -S something that is skimmed from a liquid
SKIMO	n pl. -MOS an Eskimo
SKIMP	v -ED, -ING, -S to scrimp
SKIMPY	adj SKIMPIER, SKIMPIEST scanty **SKIMPILY** adv
SKIN	v SKINNED, SKINNING, SKINS to strip or deprive of skin (the membranous tissue covering the body of an animal)
SKINFUL	n pl. -S as much as a skin container can hold
SKINHEAD	n pl. -S one whose hair is cut very short
SKINK	v -ED, -ING, -S to pour out or serve, as liquor
SKINKER	n pl. -S one that skinks
SKINLESS	adj having no skin
SKINLIKE	adj resembling skin
SKINNED	past tense of skin
SKINNER	n pl. -S one that skins
SKINNING	present participle of skin
SKINNY	adj -NIER, -NIEST very thin
SKINT	adj having no money
SKIORING	n pl. -S a form of skiing
SKIP	v SKIPPED, SKIPPING, SKIPS to move with light springing steps
SKIPJACK	n pl. -S a marine fish
SKIPLANE	n pl. -S an airplane designed to take off from or land on snow
SKIPPED	past tense of skip
SKIPPER	v -ED, -ING, -S to act as master or captain of
SKIPPET	n pl. -S a small box for protecting an official seal
SKIPPING	present participle of skip
SKIRL	v -ED, -ING, -S to produce a shrill sound
SKIRMISH	v -ED, -ING, -ES to engage in a minor battle
SKIRR	v -ED, -ING, -S to move rapidly
SKIRRET	n pl. -S an Asian herb
SKIRT	v -ED, -ING, -S to go or pass around
SKIRTER	n pl. -S one that skirts
SKIRTING	n pl. -S a board at the base of a wall
SKIT	n pl. -S a short dramatic scene
SKITE	v SKITED, SKITING, SKITES to move away quickly
SKITTER	v -ED, -ING, -S to move lightly or rapidly along a surface
SKITTERY	adj -TERIER, -TERIEST skittish
SKITTISH	adj easily frightened
SKITTLE	n pl. -S a wooden pin used in a bowling game
SKIVE	v SKIVED, SKIVING, SKIVES to pare
SKIVER	n pl. -S one that skives
SKIVVY	n pl. -VIES a female servant
SKIWEAR	n pl. -S clothing suitable for wear while skiing
SKLENT	v -ED, -ING, -S to slant
SKOAL	v -ED, -ING, -S to drink to the health of
SKOOKUM	adj excellent
SKREEGH	v -ED, -ING, -S to screech
SKREIGH	v -ED, -ING, -S to screech
SKUA	n pl. -S a predatory seabird
SKULK	v -ED, -ING, -S to move about stealthily
SKULKER	n pl. -S one that skulks

SKULL   *n* pl. -S the framework of the head **SKULLED** *adj*

SKULLCAP   *n* pl. -S a close-fitting cap

SKUNK   *v* -ED, -ING, -S to defeat overwhelmingly

SKY   *v* SKIED or SKYED, SKYING, SKIES to hit or throw toward the sky (the upper atmosphere)

SKYBORNE   *adj* airborne

SKYCAP   *n* pl. -S a porter at an airport

SKYDIVE   *v* -DIVED or -DOVE, -DIVING, -DIVES to parachute from an airplane for sport

SKYDIVER   *n* pl. -S one that skydives

SKYEY   *adj* resembling the sky

SKYHOOK   *n* pl. -S a hook conceived as being suspended from the sky

SKYJACK   *v* -ED, -ING, -S to hijack an airplane

SKYLARK   *v* -ED, -ING, -S to frolic

SKYLIGHT   *n* pl. -S a window in a roof or ceiling

SKYLINE   *n* pl. -S the horizon

SKYMAN   *n* pl. -MEN an aviator

SKYPHOS   *n* pl. -PHOI a drinking vessel used in ancient Greece

SKYSAIL   *n* pl. -S a type of sail

SKYWARD   *adv* toward the sky

SKYWARDS   *adv* skyward

SKYWAY   *n* pl. -WAYS an elevated highway

SKYWRITE   *v* -WROTE, -WRITTEN, -WRITING, -WRITES to write in the sky by releasing a visible vapor from an airplane

SLAB   *v* SLABBED, SLABBING, SLABS to cover with slabs (broad, flat pieces of solid material)

SLABBER   *v* -ED, -ING, -S to slobber

SLABBERY   *adj* slobbery

SLABBING   present participle of slab

SLACK   *adj* SLACKER, SLACKEST not tight or taut

SLACK   *v* -ED, -ING, -S to slacken

SLACKEN   *v* -ED, -ING, -S to make less tight or taut

SLACKER   *n* pl. -S a shirker

SLACKLY   *adv* in a slack manner

SLAG   *v* SLAGGED, SLAGGING, SLAGS to convert into slag (the fused residue of a smelted ore)

SLAGGY   *adj* -GIER, -GIEST resembling slag

SLAIN   past participle of slay

SLAKE   *v* SLAKED, SLAKING, SLAKES to quench **SLAKABLE** *adj*

SLAKER   *n* pl. -S one that slakes

SLALOM   *v* -ED, -ING, -S to ski in a zigzag course

SLAM   *v* SLAMMED, SLAMMING, SLAMS to shut forcibly and noisily

SLANDER   *v* -ED, -ING, -S to defame

SLANG   *v* -ED, -ING, -S to assail with harsh or coarse language

SLANGY   *adj* SLANGIER, SLANGIEST given to vulgarity **SLANGILY** *adv*

SLANK   a past tense of slink

SLANT   *v* -ED, -ING, -S to deviate from the horizontal or vertical

SLAP   *v* SLAPPED, SLAPPING, SLAPS to strike with the open hand

SLAPDASH   *n* pl. -ES careless work

SLAPJACK   *n* pl. -S a pancake

SLAPPED   past tense of slap

SLAPPER   *n* pl. -S one that slaps

SLAPPING   present participle of slap

SLASH   *v* -ED, -ING, -ES to cut with violent sweeping strokes

SLASHER   *n* pl. -S one that slashes

SLASHING   *n* pl. -S the act of one that slashes

SLAT   *v* SLATTED, SLATTING, SLATS to provide with slats (narrow strips of wood or metal)

SLATCH   *n* pl. -ES a calm between breaking waves

SLATE   *v* SLATED, SLATING, SLATES to cover with slate (a roofing material)

SLATER   *n* pl. -S one that slates

SLATHER   *v* -ED, -ING, -S to spread thickly

SLATIER   comparative of slaty

SLATIEST   superlative of slaty

SLATING   *n* pl. -S the act of one that slates

SLATTED   past tense of slat

SLATTERN   *n* pl. -S a slovenly woman

SLATTING   present participle of slat

SLATY   *adj* SLATIER, SLATIEST resembling slate

SLAVE	v SLAVED, SLAVING, SLAVES to work like a slave (one who is owned by another)
SLAVER	v -ED, -ING, -S to drool
SLAVERER	n pl. -S one that slavers
SLAVERY	n pl. -ERIES ownership of one person by another
SLAVEY	n pl. -EYS a female servant
SLAVING	present participle of slave
SLAVISH	adj pertaining to or characteristic of a slave
SLAW	n pl. -S coleslaw
SLAY	v SLEW, SLAIN, SLAYING, SLAYS to kill violently
SLAYER	n pl. -S one that slays
SLEAVE	v SLEAVED, SLEAVING, SLEAVES to separate into filaments
SLEAZY	adj SLEAZIER, SLEAZIEST shoddy **SLEAZILY** adv
SLED	v SLEDDED, SLEDDING, SLEDS to convey on a sled (a vehicle for carrying people or loads over snow or ice)
SLEDDER	n pl. -S one that sleds
SLEDDING	n pl. -S the act of one that sleds
SLEDGE	v SLEDGED, SLEDGING, SLEDGES to convey on a type of sled
SLEEK	adj SLEEKER, SLEEKEST smooth and glossy
SLEEK	v -ED, -ING, -S to make sleek
SLEEKEN	v -ED, -ING, -S to sleek
SLEEKIER	comparative of sleeky
SLEEKIEST	superlative of sleeky
SLEEKIT	adj sleek
SLEEKLY	adv in a sleek manner
SLEEKY	adj SLEEKIER, SLEEKIEST sleek
SLEEP	v SLEPT, SLEEPING, SLEEPS to be in a natural, periodic state of rest
SLEEPER	n pl. -S one that sleeps
SLEEPING	n pl. -S the act of one that sleeps
SLEEPY	adj SLEEPIER, SLEEPIEST ready or inclined to sleep **SLEEPILY** adv
SLEET	v -ED, -ING, -S to shower sleet (frozen rain)
SLEETY	adj SLEETIER, SLEETIEST resembling sleet
SLEEVE	v SLEEVED, SLEEVING, SLEEVES to furnish with a sleeve (the part of a garment covering the arm)
SLEIGH	v -ED, -ING, -S to ride in a sled
SLEIGHER	n pl. -S one that sleighs
SLEIGHT	n pl. -S deftness
SLENDER	adj -DERER, -DEREST thin
SLEPT	past tense of sleep
SLEUTH	v -ED, -ING, -S to act as a detective
SLEW	v -ED, -ING, -S to slue
SLICE	v SLICED, SLICING, SLICES to cut into thin, flat pieces
SLICER	n pl. -S one that slices
SLICK	adj SLICKER, SLICKEST smooth and slippery
SLICK	v -ED, -ING, -S to make slick
SLICKER	n pl. -S an oilskin raincoat
SLICKLY	adv in a slick manner
SLIDE	v SLID, SLIDDEN, SLIDING, SLIDES to move smoothly along a surface **SLIDABLE** adj
SLIDER	n pl. -S one that slides
SLIDEWAY	n pl. -WAYS a route along which something slides
SLIDING	present participle of slide
SLIER	a comparative of sly
SLIEST	a superlative of sly
SLIGHT	adj SLIGHTER, SLIGHTEST small in size or amount **SLIGHTLY** adv
SLIGHT	v -ED, -ING, -S to treat with disregard
SLILY	adv in a sly manner
SLIM	adj SLIMMER, SLIMMEST slender
SLIM	v SLIMMED, SLIMMING, SLIMS to make slim
SLIME	v SLIMED, SLIMING, SLIMES to cover with slime (viscous mud)
SLIMIER	comparative of slimy
SLIMIEST	superlative of slimy
SLIMILY	adv in a slimy manner
SLIMING	present participle of slime
SLIMLY	adv in a slim manner
SLIMMED	past tense of slim

SLIMMER	comparative of slim
SLIMMEST	superlative of slim
SLIMMING	present participle of slim
SLIMNESS	n pl. -ES the state of being slim
SLIMPSY	adj -SIER, -SIEST slimsy
SLIMSY	adj -SIER, -SIEST flimsy
SLIMY	adj SLIMIER, SLIMIEST resembling slime
SLING	v SLUNG, SLINGING, SLINGS to throw with a sudden motion
SLINGER	n pl. -S one that slings
SLINK	v SLUNK or SLANK, SLINKING, SLINKS to move stealthily
SLINKY	adj SLINKIER, SLINKIEST stealthy **SLINKILY** adv
SLIP	v SLIPPED or SLIPT, SLIPPING, SLIPS to slide suddenly and accidentally
SLIPCASE	n pl. -S a protective box for a book
SLIPE	v SLIPED, SLIPING, SLIPES to peel
SLIPFORM	v -ED, -ING, -S to construct with the use of a mold in which concrete is placed to set
SLIPKNOT	n pl. -S a type of knot
SLIPLESS	adj free from errors
SLIPOUT	n pl. -S an insert in a newspaper
SLIPOVER	n pl. -S a pullover
SLIPPAGE	n pl. -S a falling off from a standard or level
SLIPPED	a past tense of slip
SLIPPER	n pl. -S a light, low shoe
SLIPPERY	adj -PERIER, -PERIEST causing or tending to cause slipping
SLIPPING	present participle of slip
SLIPPY	adj -PIER, -PIEST slippery
SLIPSHOD	adj carelessly done or made
SLIPSLOP	n pl. -S watery food
SLIPSOLE	n pl. -S a thin insole
SLIPT	a past tense of slip
SLIPUP	n pl. -S a mistake
SLIPWARE	n pl. -S a type of pottery
SLIPWAY	n pl. -WAYS an area sloping toward the water in a shipyard
SLIT	v SLITTED, SLITTING, SLITS to make a slit (a long, narrow cut) in
SLITHER	v -ED, -ING, -S to slide from side to side
SLITHERY	adj slippery
SLITLESS	adj having no slits
SLITTED	past tense of slit
SLITTER	n pl. -S one that slits
SLITTING	present participle of slit
SLIVER	v -ED, -ING, -S to cut into long, thin pieces
SLIVERER	n pl. -S one that slivers
SLIVOVIC	n pl. -S a plum brandy
SLOB	n pl. -S a slovenly or boorish person
SLOBBER	v -ED, -ING, -S to drool
SLOBBERY	adj slobbering
SLOBBISH	adj resembling a slob
SLOE	n pl. -S a plumlike fruit
SLOG	v SLOGGED, SLOGGING, SLOGS to plod
SLOGAN	n pl. -S a motto adopted by a group
SLOGGER	n pl. -S one that slogs
SLOGGING	present participle of slog
SLOID	n pl. -S sloyd
SLOJD	n pl. -S sloyd
SLOOP	n pl. -S a type of sailing vessel
SLOP	v SLOPPED, SLOPPING, SLOPS to spill or splash
SLOPE	v SLOPED, SLOPING, SLOPES to slant
SLOPER	n pl. -S one that slopes
SLOPPED	past tense of slop
SLOPPING	present participle of slop
SLOPPY	adj -PIER, -PIEST messy **SLOPPILY** adv
SLOPWORK	n pl. -S the manufacture of cheap clothing
SLOSH	v -ED, -ING, -ES to move with a splashing motion
SLOSHY	adj SLOSHIER, SLOSHIEST slushy
SLOT	v SLOTTED, SLOTTING, SLOTS to cut a long, narrow opening in
SLOTBACK	n pl. -S a type of football player
SLOTH	n pl. -S a slow-moving arboreal mammal
SLOTHFUL	adj sluggish
SLOTTED	past tense of slot

SLOTTING	present participle of slot	**SLUICE**	v SLUICED, SLUICING, SLUICES to wash with a sudden flow of water
SLOUCH	v -ED, -ING, -ES to sit, stand, or move with a drooping posture	**SLUICY**	adj falling in streams
SLOUCHER	n pl. -S one that slouches	**SLUING**	present participle of slue
SLOUCHY	adj SLOUCHIER, SLOUCHIEST slouching	**SLUM**	v SLUMMED, SLUMMING, SLUMS to visit slums (squalid urban areas)
SLOUGH	v -ED, -ING, -S to cast off	**SLUMBER**	v -ED, -ING, -S to sleep
SLOUGHY	adj SLOUGHIER, SLOUGHIEST miry	**SLUMBERY**	adj sleepy
SLOVEN	n pl. -S a slovenly person	**SLUMGUM**	n pl. -S the residue remaining after honey is extracted from a honeycomb
SLOVENLY	adj -LIER, -LIEST habitually untidy or unclean	**SLUMLORD**	n pl. -S a landlord of slum property
SLOW	adj SLOWER, SLOWEST moving with little speed	**SLUMMED**	past tense of slum
SLOW	v -ED, -ING, -S to lessen the speed of	**SLUMMER**	n pl. -S one that slums
SLOWDOWN	n pl. -S a lessening of pace	**SLUMMING**	present participle of slum
SLOWISH	adj somewhat slow	**SLUMMY**	adj -MIER, -MIEST resembling a slum
SLOWLY	adv in a slow manner	**SLUMP**	v -ED, -ING, -S to fall or sink suddenly
SLOWNESS	n pl. -ES the state of being slow	**SLUNG**	past tense of sling
SLOWPOKE	n pl. -S a slow individual	**SLUNK**	a past tense of slink
SLOWWORM	n pl. -S a European lizard having no legs	**SLUR**	v SLURRED, SLURRING, SLURS to pass over lightly or carelessly
SLOYD	n pl. -S a Swedish system of manual training	**SLURB**	n pl. -S a poorly planned suburban area **SLURBAN** adj
SLUB	v SLUBBED, SLUBBING, SLUBS to draw out and twist slightly	**SLURP**	v -ED, -ING, -S to eat or drink noisily
SLUBBER	v -ED, -ING, -S to stain or dirty	**SLURRED**	past tense of slur
SLUBBING	n pl. -S a slightly twisted roll of textile fibers	**SLURRING**	present participle of slur
SLUDGE	n pl. -S a muddy deposit	**SLURRY**	v -RIED, -RYING, -RIES to convert into a type of watery mixture
SLUDGY	adj SLUDGIER, SLUDGIEST covered with sludge	**SLUSH**	v -ED, -ING, -ES to splash with slush (partly melted snow)
SLUE	v SLUED, SLUING, SLUES to cause to move sideways	**SLUSHY**	adj SLUSHIER, SLUSHIEST resembling slush **SLUSHILY** adv
SLUFF	v -ED, -ING, -S to discard a card or cards	**SLUT**	n pl. -S a slovenly woman **SLUTTISH** adj
SLUG	v SLUGGED, SLUGGING, SLUGS to strike heavily	**SLY**	adj SLIER, SLIEST or SLYER, SLYEST crafty **SLYLY** adv
SLUGABED	n pl. -S one inclined to stay in bed out of laziness	**SLYBOOTS**	n pl. SLYBOOTS a sly person
SLUGFEST	n pl. -S a vigorous fight	**SLYNESS**	n pl. -ES the quality or state of being sly
SLUGGARD	n pl. -S an habitually lazy person	**SLYPE**	n pl. -S a narrow passage in an English cathedral
SLUGGED	past tense of slug		
SLUGGER	n pl. -S one that slugs	**SMACK**	v -ED, -ING, -S to strike sharply
SLUGGING	present participle of slug	**SMACKER**	n pl. -S one that smacks
SLUGGISH	adj displaying little movement or activity		

SMALL	adj SMALLER, SMALLEST of limited size or quantity	**SMELL**	v SMELLED or SMELT, SMELLING, SMELLS to perceive by means of the olfactory nerves
SMALL	n pl. -S a small part		
SMALLAGE	n pl. -S a wild celery	**SMELLER**	n pl. -S one that smells
SMALLISH	adj somewhat small	**SMELLY**	adj SMELLIER, SMELLIEST having an unpleasant odor
SMALLPOX	n pl. -ES a virus disease		
SMALT	n pl. -S a blue pigment	**SMELT**	v -ED, -ING, -S to melt or fuse, as ores
SMALTI	a pl. of smalto		
SMALTINE	n pl. -S smaltite	**SMELTER**	n pl. -S one that smelts
SMALTITE	n pl. -S a mineral	**SMELTERY**	n pl. -ERIES a place for smelting
SMALTO	n pl. -TOS or -TI colored glass used in mosaics		
		SMERK	v -ED, -ING, -S to smirk
SMARAGD	n pl. -S an emerald	**SMEW**	n pl. -S a Eurasian duck
SMARAGDE	n pl. -S smaragd	**SMIDGEN**	n pl. -S a very small amount
SMARM	n pl. -S trite sentimentality	**SMIDGEON**	n pl. -S smidgen
SMARMY	adj SMARMIER, SMARMIEST marked by excessive flattery	**SMIDGIN**	n pl. -S smidgen
		SMILAX	n pl. -ES a twining plant
SMART	v -ED, -ING, -S to cause a sharp, stinging pain	**SMILE**	v SMILED, SMILING, SMILES to upturn the corners of the mouth in pleasure
SMART	adj SMARTER, SMARTEST characterized by mental acuity		
		SMILER	n pl. -S one that smiles
SMARTEN	v -ED, -ING, -S to improve in appearance	**SMIRCH**	v -ED, -ING, -ES to soil
		SMIRK	v -ED, -ING, -S to smile in an affected or smug manner
SMARTIE	n pl. -S smarty		
SMARTLY	adv in a smart manner	**SMIRKER**	n pl. -S one that smirks
SMARTY	n pl. SMARTIES an obnoxiously conceited person	**SMIRKY**	adj SMIRKIER, SMIRKIEST smirking
SMASH	v -ED, -ING, -ES to shatter violently	**SMITE**	v SMOTE, SMIT or SMITTEN, SMITING, SMITES to strike heavily
SMASHER	n pl. -S one that smashes	**SMITER**	n pl. -S one that smites
SMASHUP	n pl. -S a collision of motor vehicles	**SMITH**	n pl. -S a worker in metals
		SMITHERY	n pl. -ERIES the trade of a smith
SMATTER	v -ED, -ING, -S to speak with little knowledge	**SMITHY**	n pl. SMITHIES the workshop of a smith
SMAZE	n pl. -S an atmospheric mixture of smoke and haze	**SMITING**	present participle of smite
		SMITTEN	a past participle of smite
SMEAR	v -ED, -ING, -S to spread with a sticky, greasy, or dirty substance	**SMOCK**	v -ED, -ING, -S to furnish with a smock (a loose outer garment)
		SMOCKING	n pl. -S a type of embroidery
SMEARER	n pl. -S one that smears	**SMOG**	n pl. -S an atmospheric mixture of smoke and fog **SMOGLESS** adj
SMEARY	adj SMEARIER, SMEARIEST smeared		
SMECTIC	adj pertaining to a phase of a liquid crystal	**SMOGGY**	adj -GIER, -GIEST filled with smog
SMEDDUM	n pl. -S ground malt powder	**SMOKE**	v SMOKED, SMOKING, SMOKES to emit smoke (the gaseous product of burning materials) **SMOKABLE** adj
SMEEK	v -ED, -ING, -S to smoke		
SMEGMA	n pl. -S sebum		

SMOKEPOT	*n* pl. -S a container for giving off smoke
SMOKER	*n* pl. -S one that smokes
SMOKEY	*adj* SMOKIER, SMOKIEST smoky
SMOKING	present participle of smoke
SMOKY	*adj* SMOKIER, SMOKIEST filled with smoke **SMOKILY** *adv*
SMOLDER	*v* -ED, -ING, -S to burn with no flame
SMOLT	*n* pl. -S a young salmon
SMOOCH	*v* -ED, -ING, -ES to kiss
SMOOCHY	*adj* smudgy
SMOOTH	*adj* SMOOTHER, SMOOTHEST having a surface that is free from irregularities
SMOOTH	*v* -ED, -ING, -S to make smooth
SMOOTHEN	*v* -ED, -ING, -S to smooth
SMOOTHER	*n* pl. -S one that smooths
SMOOTHIE	*n* pl. -S a person with polished manners
SMOOTHLY	*adv* in a smooth manner
SMOOTHY	*n* pl. SMOOTHIES smoothie
SMOTE	past tense of smite
SMOTHER	*v* -ED, -ING, -S to prevent from breathing
SMOTHERY	*adj* tending to smother
SMOULDER	*v* -ED, -ING, -S to smolder
SMUDGE	*v* SMUDGED, SMUDGING, SMUDGES to smear or dirty
SMUDGY	*adj* SMUDGIER, SMUDGIEST smudged **SMUDGILY** *adv*
SMUG	*adj* SMUGGER, SMUGGEST highly self-satisfied
SMUGGLE	*v* -GLED, -GLING, -GLES to import or export illicitly
SMUGGLER	*n* pl. -S one that smuggles
SMUGLY	*adv* in a smug manner
SMUGNESS	*n* pl. -ES the quality or state of being smug
SMUT	*v* SMUTTED, SMUTTING, SMUTS to soil
SMUTCH	*v* -ED, -ING, -ES to smudge
SMUTCHY	*adj* SMUTCHIER, SMUTCHIEST smudgy
SMUTTED	past tense of smut
SMUTTING	present participle of smut
SMUTTY	*adj* -TIER, -TIEST obscene **SMUTTILY** *adv*
SNACK	*v* -ED, -ING, -S to eat a light meal
SNAFFLE	*v* -FLED, -FLING, -FLES to obtain by devious means
SNAFU	*v* -ED, -ING, -S to bring into a state of confusion
SNAG	*v* SNAGGED, SNAGGING, SNAGS to catch on a snag (a jagged protuberance)
SNAGGY	*adj* -GIER, -GIEST full of snags
SNAGLIKE	*adj* resembling a snag
SNAIL	*v* -ED, -ING, -S to move slowly
SNAKE	*v* SNAKED, SNAKING, SNAKES to move like a snake (a limbless reptile)
SNAKY	*adj* SNAKIER, SNAKIEST resembling a snake **SNAKILY** *adv*
SNAP	*v* SNAPPED, SNAPPING, SNAPS to make a sharp cracking sound
SNAPBACK	*n* pl. -S a sudden rebound or recovery
SNAPLESS	*adj* lacking a snap (a type of fastening device)
SNAPPED	past tense of snap
SNAPPER	*n* pl. -S one that snaps
SNAPPIER	comparative of snappy
SNAPPIEST	superlative of snappy
SNAPPILY	*adv* in a snappy manner
SNAPPING	present participle of snap
SNAPPISH	*adj* tending to speak in an impatient or irritable manner
SNAPPY	*adj* -PIER, -PIEST snappish
SNAPSHOT	*v* -SHOTTED, -SHOTTING, -SHOTS to photograph informally and quickly
SNAPWEED	*n* pl. -S a flowering plant
SNARE	*v* SNARED, SNARING, SNARES to trap
SNARER	*n* pl. -S one that snares
SNARK	*n* pl. -S an imaginary animal
SNARL	*v* -ED, -ING, -S to growl viciously
SNARLER	*n* pl. -S one that snarls
SNARLY	*adj* SNARLIER, SNARLIEST tangled
SNASH	*n* pl. -ES abusive language
SNATCH	*v* -ED, -ING, -ES to seize suddenly
SNATCHER	*n* pl. -S one that snatches

SNATCHY *adj* SNATCHIER, SNATCHIEST occurring irregularly

SNATH *n* pl. -S the handle of a scythe

SNATHE *n* pl. -S snath

SNAW *v* -ED, -ING, -S to snow

SNAZZY *adj* -ZIER, -ZIEST very stylish

SNEAK *v* SNEAKED or SNUCK, SNEAKING, SNEAKS to move stealthily

SNEAKER *n* pl. -S one that sneaks

SNEAKY *adj* SNEAKIER, SNEAKIEST deceitful **SNEAKILY** *adv*

SNEAP *v* -ED, -ING, -S to chide

SNECK *n* pl. -S a latch

SNED *v* SNEDDED, SNEDDING, SNEDS to prune

SNEER *v* -ED, -ING, -S to curl the lip in contempt

SNEERER *n* pl. -S one that sneers

SNEERFUL *adj* given to sneering

SNEESH *n* pl. -ES snuff

SNEEZE *v* SNEEZED, SNEEZING, SNEEZES to make a sudden, involuntary expiration of breath

SNEEZER *n* pl. -S one that sneezes

SNEEZY *adj* SNEEZIER, SNEEZIEST tending to sneeze

SNELL *n* pl. -S a short line by which a fishhook is attached to a longer line

SNELL *adj* SNELLER, SNELLEST keen

SNIB *v* SNIBBED, SNIBBING, SNIBS to latch

SNICK *v* -ED, -ING, -S to nick

SNICKER *v* -ED, -ING, -S to utter a partly stifled laugh

SNICKERY *adj* tending to snicker

SNIDE *adj* SNIDER, SNIDEST maliciously derogatory **SNIDELY** *adv*

SNIFF *v* -ED, -ING, -S to inhale audibly through the nose

SNIFFER *n* pl. -S one that sniffs

SNIFFIER comparative of sniffy

SNIFFIEST superlative of sniffy

SNIFFILY *adv* in a sniffy manner

SNIFFISH *adj* haughty

SNIFFLE *v* -FLED, -FLING, -FLES to sniff repeatedly

SNIFFLER *n* pl. -S one that sniffles

SNIFFY *adj* -FIER, -FIEST sniffish

SNIFTER *n* pl. -S a pear-shaped liquor glass

SNIGGER *v* -ED, -ING, -S to snicker

SNIGGLE *v* -GLED, -GLING, -GLES to fish for eels

SNIGGLER *n* pl. -S one that sniggles

SNIP *v* SNIPPED, SNIPPING, SNIPS to cut with a short, quick stroke

SNIPE *v* SNIPED, SNIPING, SNIPES to shoot at individuals from a concealed place

SNIPER *n* pl. -S one that snipes

SNIPPED past tense of snip

SNIPPER *n* pl. -S one that snips

SNIPPET *n* pl. -S a small piece snipped off

SNIPPETY *adj* -PETIER, -PETIEST snippy

SNIPPING present participle of snip

SNIPPY *adj* -PIER, -PIEST snappish **SNIPPILY** *adv*

SNIT *n* pl. -S a state of agitation

SNITCH *v* -ED, -ING, -ES to tattle

SNITCHER *n* pl. -S one that snitches

SNIVEL *v* -ELED, -ELING, -ELS or -ELLED, -ELLING, -ELS to cry or whine with sniffling

SNIVELER *n* pl. -S one that snivels

SNOB *n* pl. -S one who tends to avoid or rebuff those regarded as inferior

SNOBBERY *n* pl. -BERIES snobbish behavior

SNOBBIER comparative of snobby

SNOBBIEST superlative of snobby

SNOBBILY *adv* in a snobby manner

SNOBBISH *adj* characteristic of a snob

SNOBBISM *n* pl. -S snobbery

SNOBBY *adj* -BIER, -BIEST snobbish

SNOOD *v* -ED, -ING, -S to secure with a snood (a net or fabric cap for the hair)

SNOOK *v* -ED, -ING, -S to sniff

SNOOKER *n* pl. -S a pocket billiards game

SNOOL *v* -ED, -ING, -S to yield meekly

SNOOP *v* -ED, -ING, -S to pry about

SNOOPER *n* pl. -S one that snoops

SNOOPY *adj* SNOOPIER, SNOOPIEST given to snooping **SNOOPILY** *adv*

SNOOT	*v* -ED, -ING, -S to treat with disdain
SNOOTY	*adj* SNOOTIER, SNOOTIEST snobbish **SNOOTILY** *adv*
SNOOZE	*v* SNOOZED, SNOOZING, SNOOZES to sleep lightly
SNOOZER	*n* pl. -S one that snoozes
SNOOZLE	*v* -ZLED, -ZLING, -ZLES to nuzzle
SNOOZY	*adj* SNOOZIER, SNOOZIEST drowsy
SNORE	*v* SNORED, SNORING, SNORES to breathe loudly while sleeping
SNORER	*n* pl. -S one that snores
SNORKEL	*v* -ED, -ING, -S to swim underwater with a type of breathing device
SNORT	*v* -ED, -ING, -S to exhale noisily through the nostrils
SNORTER	*n* pl. -S one that snorts
SNOT	*n* pl. -S nasal mucus
SNOTTY	*adj* -TIER, -TIEST arrogant **SNOTTILY** *adv*
SNOUT	*v* -ED, -ING, -S to provide with a nozzle
SNOUTISH	*adj* snouty
SNOUTY	*adj* SNOUTIER, SNOUTIEST resembling a long, projecting nose
SNOW	*v* -ED, -ING, -S to fall as snow (precipitation in the form of ice crystals)
SNOWBALL	*v* -ED, -ING, -S to increase at a rapidly accelerating rate
SNOWBANK	*n* pl. -S a mound of snow
SNOWBELL	*n* pl. -S a flowering shrub
SNOWBIRD	*n* pl. -S a small bird
SNOWBUSH	*n* pl. -ES a flowering shrub
SNOWCAP	*n* pl. -S a covering of snow
SNOWDROP	*n* pl. -S a European herb
SNOWFALL	*n* pl. -S a fall of snow
SNOWIER	comparative of snowy
SNOWIEST	superlative of snowy
SNOWILY	*adv* in a snowy manner
SNOWLAND	*n* pl. -S an area marked by a great amount of snow
SNOWLESS	*adj* having no snow
SNOWLIKE	*adj* resembling snow
SNOWMAN	*n* pl. -MEN a figure of a person that is made of snow

SNOWMELT	*n* pl. -S water produced by the melting of snow
SNOWPACK	*n* pl. -S an accumulation of packed snow
SNOWPLOW	*v* -ED, -ING, -S to execute a type of skiing maneuver
SNOWSHED	*n* pl. -S a structure built to provide protection against snow
SNOWSHOE	*v* -SHOED, -SHOEING, -SHOES to walk on snowshoes (oval frames that allow a person to walk on deep snow)
SNOWSUIT	*n* pl. -S a child's garment for winter wear
SNOWY	*adj* SNOWIER, SNOWIEST abounding in snow
SNUB	*v* SNUBBED, SNUBBING, SNUBS to treat with contempt or neglect
SNUBBER	*n* pl. -S one that snubs
SNUBBY	*adj* -BIER, -BIEST blunt
SNUBNESS	*n* pl. -ES bluntness
SNUCK	a past tense of sneak
SNUFF	*v* -ED, -ING, -S to use or inhale snuff (powdered tobacco)
SNUFFBOX	*n* pl. -ES a box for holding snuff
SNUFFER	*n* pl. -S one that snuffs
SNUFFIER	comparative of snuffy
SNUFFIEST	superlative of snuffy
SNUFFILY	*adv* in a snuffy manner
SNUFFLE	*v* -FLED, -FLING, -FLES to sniffle
SNUFFLER	*n* pl. -S one that snuffles
SNUFFLY	*adj* -FLIER, -FLIEST tending to snuffle
SNUFFY	*adj* SNUFFIER, SNUFFIEST dingy
SNUG	*adj* SNUGGER, SNUGGEST warmly comfortable
SNUG	*v* SNUGGED, SNUGGING, SNUGS to make snug
SNUGGERY	*n* pl. -GERIES a snug place
SNUGGEST	superlative of snug
SNUGGING	present participle of snug
SNUGGLE	*v* -GLED, -GLING, -GLES to lie or press closely
SNUGLY	*adv* in a snug manner
SNUGNESS	*n* pl. -ES the quality or state of being snug
SNYE	*n* pl. -S a side channel in a river or creek

SO	*n* pl. SOS sol
SOAK	*v* -ED, -ING, -S to saturate thoroughly in liquid
SOAKAGE	*n* pl. -S the act of soaking
SOAKER	*n* pl. -S one that soaks
SOAP	*v* -ED, -ING, -S to treat with soap (a cleansing agent)
SOAPBARK	*n* pl. -S a tropical tree
SOAPBOX	*n* pl. -ES a box for soap
SOAPIER	comparative of soapy
SOAPIEST	superlative of soapy
SOAPILY	*adv* in a soapy manner
SOAPLESS	*adj* having no soap
SOAPLIKE	*adj* resembling soap
SOAPSUDS	*n/pl* suds (soapy water)
SOAPWORT	*n* pl. -S a perennial herb
SOAPY	*adj* SOAPIER, SOAPIEST containing or resembling soap
SOAR	*v* -ED, -ING, -S to fly at a great height
SOARER	*n* pl. -S one that soars
SOARING	*n* pl. -S the sport of flying in a heavier-than-air craft without power
SOAVE	*n* pl. -S an Italian wine
SOB	*v* SOBBED, SOBBING, SOBS to cry with a convulsive catching of the breath
SOBBER	*n* pl. -S one that sobs
SOBEIT	*conj* provided that
SOBER	*adj* SOBERER, SOBEREST having control of one's faculties
SOBER	*v* -ED, -ING, -S to make sober
SOBERIZE	*v* -IZED, -IZING, -IZES to sober
SOBERLY	*adv* in a sober manner
SOBFUL	*adj* given to sobbing
SOBRIETY	*n* pl. -ETIES the quality or state of being sober
SOCAGE	*n* pl. -S a form of feudal land tenure
SOCAGER	*n* pl. -S a tenant by socage
SOCCAGE	*n* pl. -S socage
SOCCER	*n* pl. -S a type of ball game
SOCIABLE	*n* pl. -S a social
SOCIABLY	*adv* in a friendly manner
SOCIAL	*n* pl. -S a friendly gathering
SOCIALLY	*adv* with respect to society

SOCIETY	*n* pl. -ETIES an organized group of persons **SOCIETAL** *adj*
SOCK	*n* pl. SOCKS or SOX a knitted or woven covering for the foot
SOCK	*v* -ED, -ING, -S to strike forcefully
SOCKET	*v* -ED, -ING, -S to furnish with a socket (an opening for receiving something)
SOCKEYE	*n* pl. -S a food fish
SOCKMAN	*n* pl. -MEN socman
SOCLE	*n* pl. -S a block used as a base for a column or pedestal
SOCMAN	*n* pl. -MEN a socager
SOD	*v* SODDED, SODDING, SODS to cover with sod (turf)
SODA	*n* pl. -S a type of chemical compound **SODALESS** *adj*
SODALIST	*n* pl. -S a member of a sodality
SODALITE	*n* pl. -S a mineral
SODALITY	*n* pl. -TIES a society
SODAMIDE	*n* pl. -S a chemical compound
SODDED	past tense of sod
SODDEN	*v* -ED, -ING, -S to make soggy
SODDENLY	*adv* in a soggy manner
SODDING	present participle of sod
SODDY	*n* pl. -DIES a house built of sod
SODIUM	*n* pl. -S a metallic element **SODIC** *adj*
SODOMITE	*n* pl. -S one who practices sodomy
SODOMY	*n* pl. -OMIES unnatural copulation
SOEVER	*adv* at all
SOFA	*n* pl. -S a long, upholstered seat
SOFAR	*n* pl. -S a system for locating underwater explosions
SOFFIT	*n* pl. -S the underside of an architectural structure
SOFT	*adj* SOFTER, SOFTEST yielding readily to pressure
SOFT	*n* pl. -S a soft object or part
SOFTA	*n* pl. -S a Muslim theological student
SOFTBACK	*n* pl. -S a book bound in a flexible paper cover
SOFTBALL	*n* pl. -S a type of ball
SOFTEN	*v* -ED, -ING, -S to make soft
SOFTENER	*n* pl. -S one that softens

SOFTHEAD	n pl. -S a foolish person
SOFTIE	n pl. -S softy
SOFTIES	pl. of softy
SOFTLY	adv in a soft manner
SOFTNESS	n pl. -ES the quality or state of being soft
SOFTWARE	n pl. -S written or printed data used in computer operations
SOFTWOOD	n pl. -S the soft wood of various trees
SOFTY	n pl. SOFTIES a sentimental person
SOGGED	adj soggy
SOGGY	adj -GIER, -GIEST heavy with moisture **SOGGILY** adv
SOIGNE	adj carefully done
SOIGNEE	adj soigne
SOIL	v -ED, -ING, -S to make dirty
SOILAGE	n pl. -S green crops for feeding animals
SOILLESS	adj carried on without soil (finely divided rock mixed with organic matter)
SOILURE	n pl. -S a stain or smudge
SOIREE	n pl. -S an evening party
SOJA	n pl. -S the soybean
SOJOURN	v -ED, -ING, -S to stay temporarily
SOKE	n pl. -S a feudal right to administer justice within a certain territory
SOKEMAN	n pl. -MEN socman
SOL	n pl. -S the fifth tone of the diatonic musical scale
SOLA	a pl. of solum
SOLACE	v -LACED, -LACING, -LACES to console
SOLACER	n pl. -S one that solaces
SOLAN	n pl. -S a gannet
SOLAND	n pl. -S solan
SOLANDER	n pl. -S a protective box for library materials
SOLANIN	n pl. -S solanine
SOLANINE	n pl. -S a poisonous alkaloid
SOLANO	n pl. -NOS a strong, hot wind
SOLANUM	n pl. -S any of a genus of herbs and shrubs
SOLAR	adj pertaining to the sun
SOLARIA	a pl. of solarium

SOLARISE	v -ISED, -ISING, -ISES to solarize
SOLARISM	n pl. -S an interpretation of folk tales as concepts of the nature of the sun
SOLARIUM	n pl. -IA or -IUMS a room exposed to the sun
SOLARIZE	v -IZED, -IZING, -IZES to expose to sunlight
SOLATE	v -ATED, -ATING, -ATES to change to a fluid colloidal system
SOLATIA	pl. of solatium
SOLATION	n pl. -S the act of solating
SOLATIUM	n pl. -TIA a compensation given for damage to the feelings
SOLD	past tense of sell
SOLDAN	n pl. -S a Muslim ruler
SOLDER	v -ED, -ING, -S to join closely together
SOLDERER	n pl. -S one that solders
SOLDI	pl. of soldo
SOLDIER	v -ED, -ING, -S to perform military service
SOLDIERY	n pl. -DIERIES the military profession
SOLDO	n pl. -DI a former coin of Italy
SOLE	v SOLED, SOLING, SOLES to furnish with a sole (the bottom surface of a shoe or boot)
SOLECISE	v -CISED, -CISING, -CISES to solecize
SOLECISM	n pl. -S an ungrammatical combination of words in a sentence
SOLECIST	n pl. -S one who solecizes
SOLECIZE	v -CIZED, -CIZING, -CIZES to use solecisms
SOLED	past tense of sole
SOLELESS	adj having no sole
SOLELY	adv singly
SOLEMN	adj -EMNER, -EMNEST serious **SOLEMNLY** adv
SOLENESS	n pl. -ES the state of being the only one
SOLENOID	n pl. -S a type of electric coil
SOLERET	n pl. -S solleret
SOLFEGE	n pl. -S a type of singing exercise
SOLFEGGI	n/pl solfeges

SOLGEL   *adj* involving some changes in the state of a colloidal system

SOLI   a pl. of solo

SOLICIT   *v* -ED, -ING, -S to ask for earnestly

SOLID   *adj* -IDER, -IDEST having definite shape and volume

SOLID   *n* pl. -S a solid substance

SOLIDAGO   *n* pl. -GOS a flowering plant

SOLIDARY   *adj* united

SOLIDI   pl. of solidus

SOLIDIFY   *v* -FIED, -FYING, -FIES to make solid

SOLIDITY   *n* pl. -TIES the quality or state of being solid

SOLIDLY   *adv* in a solid manner

SOLIDUS   *n* pl. -DI a coin of ancient Rome

SOLING   present participle of sole

SOLION   *n* pl. -S an electronic detecting and amplifying device

SOLIQUID   *n* pl. -S a fluid colloidal system

SOLITARY   *n* pl. -TARIES one who lives alone

SOLITUDE   *n* pl. -S the state of being alone

SOLLERET   *n* pl. -S a sabaton

SOLO   *n* pl. -LOS or -LI a musical composition for a single voice or instrument

SOLO   *v* -ED, -ING, -S to perform alone

SOLOIST   *n* pl. -S one that performs a solo

SOLON   *n* pl. -S a wise lawgiver

SOLONETS   *n* pl. -ES solonetz

SOLONETZ   *n* pl. -ES a type of soil

SOLSTICE   *n* pl. -S the time of the year when the sun is at its greatest distance from the celestial equator

SOLUBLE   *n* pl. -S something that is soluble (capable of being dissolved)

SOLUBLY   *adv* in a soluble manner

SOLUM   *n* pl. -LA or -LUMS a soil layer

SOLUS   *adj* alone

SOLUTE   *n* pl. -S a dissolved substance

SOLUTION   *n* pl. -S a homogenous liquid mixture

SOLVABLE   *adj* capable of being solved

SOLVATE   *v* -VATED, -VATING, -VATES to convert into a type of ion

SOLVE   *v* SOLVED, SOLVING, SOLVES to find the answer or explanation for

SOLVENCY   *n* pl. -CIES the ability to pay all debts

SOLVENT   *n* pl. -S a substance capable of dissolving others

SOLVER   *n* pl. -S one that solves

SOLVING   present participle of solve

SOMA   *n* pl. -MATA or -MAS the body of an organism **SOMATIC** *adj*

SOMBER   *adj* gloomy **SOMBERLY** *adv*

SOMBRE   *adj* somber **SOMBRELY** *adv*

SOMBRERO   *n* pl. -ROS a broad-brimmed hat

SOMBROUS   *adj* somber

SOME   *adj* being an unspecified number or part

SOMEBODY   *n* pl. -BODIES an important person

SOMEDAY   *adv* at some future time

SOMEDEAL   *adv* to some degree

SOMEHOW   *adv* by some means

SOMEONE   *n* pl. -S a somebody

SOMERSET   *v* -SETED, -SETING, -SETS or -SETTED, -SETTING, -SETS to roll the body in a complete circle, head over heels

SOMETIME   *adv* at some future time

SOMEWAY   *adv* somehow

SOMEWAYS   *adv* someway

SOMEWHAT   *n* pl. -S an unspecified number or part

SOMEWHEN   *adv* sometime

SOMEWISE   *adv* somehow

SOMITE   *n* pl. -S a longitudinal segment of the body of some animals **SOMITAL, SOMITIC** *adj*

SON   *n* pl. -S a male child

SONANCE   *n* pl. -S sound

SONANT   *n* pl. -S a sound uttered with vibration of the vocal cords **SONANTAL, SONANTIC** *adj*

SONAR   *n* pl. -S an underwater locating device

SONARMAN   *n* pl. -MEN a person who operates sonar equipment

SONATA   *n* pl. -S a type of musical composition

SONATINA   *n* pl. -TINAS or -TINE a short sonata

SONDE   *n* pl. -S a device for observing atmospheric phenomena

SONDER   *n* pl. -S a class of small yachts

SONE   *n* pl. -S a unit of loudness

SONG   *n* pl. -S a musical composition written or adapted for singing

SONGBIRD   *n* pl. -S a bird that utters a musical call

SONGBOOK   *n* pl. -S a book of songs

SONGFEST   *n* pl. -S an informal gathering for group singing

SONGFUL   *adj* melodious

SONGLESS   *adj* incapable of singing

SONGLIKE   *adj* resembling a song

SONGSTER   *n* pl. -S a singer

SONIC   *adj* pertaining to sound

SONICATE   *v* -CATED, -CATING, -CATES to disrupt with sound waves

SONICS   *n/pl* the science dealing with the practical applications of sound

SONLESS   *adj* having no son

SONLIKE   *adj* resembling a son

SONLY   *adj* pertaining to a son

SONNET   *v* -NETED, -NETING, -NETS or -NETTED, -NETTING, -NETS to compose a sonnet (a type of poem)

SONNY   *n* pl. -NIES a small boy

SONORANT   *n* pl. -S a type of voiced sound

SONORITY   *n* pl. -TIES the quality or state of being sonorous

SONOROUS   *adj* characterized by a full and loud sound

SONOVOX   *n* pl. -ES a sound effects device

SONSHIP   *n* pl. -S the state of being a son

SONSIE   *adj* -SIER, -SIEST sonsy

SONSY   *adj* -SIER, -SIEST comely

SOOCHONG   *n* pl. -S souchong

SOOEY   *interj* — used in calling pigs

SOON   *adv* SOONER, SOONEST in the near future

SOONER   *n* pl. -S one who settles on government land before it is officially opened for settlement

SOOT   *v* -ED, -ING, -S to cover with soot (a black substance produced by combustion)

SOOTH   *adj* SOOTHER, SOOTHEST true

SOOTH   *n* pl. -S truth

SOOTHE   *v* SOOTHED, SOOTHING, SOOTHES to restore to a quiet or normal state

SOOTHER   *n* pl. -S one that soothes

SOOTHEST   superlative of sooth

SOOTHING   present participle of soothe

SOOTHLY   *adv* in truth

SOOTHSAY   *v* -SAID, -SAYING, -SAYS to predict

SOOTY   *adj* SOOTIER, SOOTIEST covered with soot **SOOTILY** *adv*

SOP   *v* SOPPED, SOPPING, SOPS to dip or soak in a liquid

SOPH   *n* pl. -S a sophomore

SOPHIES   pl. of sophy

SOPHISM   *n* pl. -S a plausible but fallacious argument

SOPHIST   *n* pl. -S one that uses sophisms

SOPHY   *n* pl. -PHIES a ruler of Persia

SOPITE   *v* -PITED, -PITING, -PITES to put to sleep

SOPOR   *n* pl. -S an abnormally deep sleep

SOPPED   past tense of sop

SOPPING   *adj* very wet

SOPPY   *adj* -PIER, -PIEST very wet

SOPRANO   *n* pl. -NOS or -NI the highest singing voice

SORA   *n* pl. -S a marsh bird

SORB   *v* -ED, -ING, -S to take up and hold by absorption or adsorption **SORBABLE** *adj*

SORBATE   *n* pl. -S a sorbed substance

SORBENT   *n* pl. -S a substance that sorbs

SORBET   *n* pl. -S sherbet

SORBIC   *adj* pertaining to a type of fruit

SORBITOL   *n* pl. -S a chemical compound

SORBOSE   *n* pl. -S a type of sugar

SORCERER   *n* pl. -S one who practices sorcery

SORCERY   *n* pl. -CERIES alleged use of supernatural powers

SORD   *n* pl. -S a flight of mallards

SORDID   *adj* filthy **SORDIDLY** *adv*

SORDINE   *n* pl. -S a device used to muffle the tone of a musical instrument

SORDINO   *n* pl. -NI sordine

SORE   *adj* SORER, SOREST painfully sensitive to the touch

SORE	*n* pl. -S a sore area on the body
SOREHEAD	*n* pl. -S a person who is easily angered or offended
SOREL	*n* pl. -S sorrel
SORELY	*adv* in a sore manner
SORENESS	*n* pl. -ES the quality or state of being sore
SORER	comparative of sore
SOREST	superlative of sore
SORGHO	*n* pl. -GHOS sorgo
SORGHUM	*n* pl. -S a cereal grass
SORGO	*n* pl. -GOS a variety of sorghum
SORI	pl. of sorus
SORICINE	*adj* belonging to the shrew family of mammals
SORITES	*n* pl. SORITES a type of argument used in logic **SORITIC** *adj*
SORN	*v* -ED, -ING, -S to force oneself on others for food and lodging
SORNER	*n* pl. -S one that sorns
SOROCHE	*n* pl. -S mountain sickness
SORORAL	*adj* sisterly
SORORATE	*n* pl. -S the marriage of a man usually with his deceased wife's sister
SORORITY	*n* pl. -TIES a social club for women
SOROSIS	*n* pl. -ROSES or -ROSISES a women's club or society
SORPTION	*n* pl. -S the act or process of sorbing **SORPTIVE** *adj*
SORREL	*n* pl. -S a reddish brown color
SORRIER	comparative of sorry
SORRIEST	superlative of sorry
SORRILY	*adv* in a sorry manner
SORROW	*v* -ED, -ING, -S to grieve
SORROWER	*n* pl. -S one that sorrows
SORRY	*adj* -RIER, -RIEST feeling grief or penitence
SORT	*v* -ED, -ING, -S to arrange according to kind, class, or size **SORTABLE** *adj* **SORTABLY** *adv*
SORTER	*n* pl. -S one that sorts
SORTIE	*v* -TIED, -TIEING, -TIES to attack suddenly from a defensive position
SORUS	*n* pl. -RI a cluster of plant reproductive bodies
SOT	*n* pl. -S an habitual drunkard
SOTH	*n* pl. -S sooth
SOTOL	*n* pl. -S a flowering plant
SOTTISH	*adj* resembling a sot
SOU	*n* pl. -S a former French coin
SOUARI	*n* pl. -S a tropical tree
SOUBISE	*n* pl. -S a sauce of onions and butter
SOUCAR	*n* pl. -S a Hindu banker
SOUCHONG	*n* pl. -S a Chinese tea
SOUDAN	*n* pl. -S soldan
SOUFFLE	*n* pl. -S a light, baked dish
SOUGH	*v* -ED, -ING, -S to make a moaning or sighing sound
SOUGHT	past tense of seek
SOUL	*n* pl. -S the spiritual aspect of human beings **SOULED, SOULLESS, SOULLIKE** *adj*
SOULFUL	*adj* full of emotion
SOUND	*adj* **SOUNDER, SOUNDEST** being in good health or condition
SOUND	*v* -ED, -ING, -S to make a sound (something that stimulates the auditory receptors)
SOUNDBOX	*n* pl. -ES a resonant cavity in a musical instrument
SOUNDER	*n* pl. -S one that sounds
SOUNDING	*n* pl. -S a sampling or test of opinions
SOUNDLY	*adv* in a sound manner
SOUP	*v* -ED, -ING, -S to increase the power or efficiency of
SOUPCON	*n* pl. -S a minute amount
SOUPY	*adj* **SOUPIER, SOUPIEST** foggy
SOUR	*adj* **SOURER, SOUREST** sharp or biting to the taste
SOUR	*v* -ED, -ING, -S to make or become sour
SOURBALL	*n* pl. -S a sour candy
SOURCE	*n* pl. -S a point of origin
SOURDINE	*n* pl. -S sordine
SOURISH	*adj* somewhat sour
SOURLY	*adv* in a sour manner
SOURNESS	*n* pl. -ES the quality or state of being sour
SOURPUSS	*n* pl. -ES a grouchy person
SOURSOP	*n* pl. -S a tropical tree
SOURWOOD	*n* pl. -S a flowering tree

SOUSE   v SOUSED, SOUSING, SOUSES to immerse

SOUTACHE   n pl. -S a flat, narrow braid

SOUTANE   n pl. -S a cassock

SOUTER   n pl. -S a shoemaker

SOUTH   v -ED, -ING, -S to move toward the south (a cardinal point of the compass)

SOUTHER   n pl. -S a wind or storm from the south

SOUTHERN   n pl. -S a person living in the south

SOUTHING   n pl. -S movement toward the south

SOUTHPAW   n pl. -S a left-handed person

SOUTHRON   n pl. -S a southern

SOUVENIR   n pl. -S a memento

SOVIET   n pl. -S a legislative body in a Communist country

SOVKHOZ   n pl. -KHOZES or -KHOZY a state-owned farm in the Soviet Union

SOVRAN   n pl. -S a monarch

SOVRANLY   adv supremely

SOVRANTY   n pl. -TIES a monarchy

SOW   v SOWED, SOWN, SOWING, SOWS to scatter over land for growth, as seed **SOWABLE** adj

SOWANS   n pl. SOWANS sowens

SOWAR   n pl. -S a mounted native soldier in India

SOWBELLY   n pl. -LIES pork cured in salt

SOWBREAD   n pl. -S a flowering plant

SOWCAR   n pl. -S soucar

SOWENS   n pl. SOWENS porridge made from oat husks

SOWER   n pl. -S one that sows

SOWN   past participle of sow

SOX   a pl. of sock

SOY   n pl. SOYS the soybean

SOYA   n pl. -S soy

SOYBEAN   n pl. -S the seed of a cultivated Asian herb

SOZIN   n pl. -S a type of protein

SOZINE   n pl. -S sozin

SPA   n pl. -S a mineral spring

SPACE   v SPACED, SPACING, SPACES to set some distance apart

SPACEMAN   n pl. -MEN an astronaut

SPACER   n pl. -S one that spaces

SPACIAL   adj spatial

SPACING   n pl. -S the distance between any two objects

SPACIOUS   adj vast or ample in extent

SPADE   v SPADED, SPADING, SPADES to take up with a spade (a digging implement)

SPADEFUL   n pl. -S as much as a spade can hold

SPADER   n pl. -S one that spades

SPADICES   pl. of spadix

SPADILLE   n pl. -S the highest trump in certain card games

SPADING   present participle of spade

SPADIX   n pl. -DICES a flower cluster

SPADO   n pl. -DONES a castrated man or animal

SPAE   v SPAED, SPAEING, SPAES to foretell

SPAEING   n pl. -S the act of foretelling

SPAGYRIC   n pl. -S a person skilled in alchemy

SPAHEE   n pl. -S spahi

SPAHI   n pl. -S a Turkish cavalryman

SPAIL   n pl. -S spale

SPAIT   n pl. -S spate

SPAKE   a past tense of speak

SPALE   n pl. -S a splinter or chip

SPALL   v -ED, -ING, -S to break up into fragments

SPALLER   n pl. -S one that spalls

SPALPEEN   n pl. -S a rascal

SPAN   v SPANNED, SPANNING, SPANS to extend over or across

SPANCEL   v -CELED, -CELING, -CELS or -CELLED, -CELLING, -CELS to bind or fetter with a rope

SPANDREL   n pl. -S a space between two adjoining arches

SPANDRIL   n pl. -S spandrel

SPANG   adv directly

SPANGLE   v -GLED, -GLING, -GLES to adorn with spangles (bits of sparkling metal)

SPANGLY   adj -GLIER, -GLIEST covered with spangles

SPANIEL   n pl. -S a dog with silky hair

SPANK	*v* -ED, -ING, -S to slap on the buttocks
SPANKER	*n* pl. -S one that spanks
SPANKING	*n* pl. -S the act of one that spanks
SPANLESS	*adj* having no extent
SPANNED	past tense of span
SPANNER	*n* pl. -S one that spans
SPANNING	present participle of span
SPANWORM	*n* pl. -S an inchworm
SPAR	*v* SPARRED, SPARRING, SPARS to provide with spars (stout poles used to support rigging)
SPARABLE	*n* pl. -S a type of nail
SPARE	*v* SPARED, SPARING, SPARES to refrain from punishing, harming, or destroying
SPARE	*adj* SPARER, SPAREST meager **SPARELY** *adv*
SPARER	*n* pl. -S one that spares
SPARERIB	*n* pl. -S a cut of pork
SPAREST	*adj* superlative of spare
SPARGE	*v* SPARGED, SPARGING, SPARGES to sprinkle
SPARGER	*n* pl. -S one that sparges
SPARID	*n* pl. -S any of a family of marine fishes
SPARING	present participle of spare
SPARK	*v* -ED, -ING, -S to give off sparks (small fiery particles)
SPARKER	*n* pl. -S something that sparks
SPARKIER	comparative of sparky
SPARKIEST	superlative of sparky
SPARKILY	*adv* in a lively manner
SPARKISH	*adj* jaunty
SPARKLE	*v* -KLED, -KLING, -KLES to give off or reflect flashes of light
SPARKLER	*n* pl. -S something that sparkles
SPARKY	*adj* SPARKIER, SPARKIEST lively
SPARLIKE	*adj* resembling a spar
SPARLING	*n* pl. -S a young herring
SPAROID	*n* pl. -S a sparid
SPARRED	past tense of spar
SPARRIER	comparative of sparry
SPARRIEST	superlative of sparry
SPARRING	present participle of spar
SPARROW	*n* pl. -S a small bird

SPARRY	*adj* -RIER, -RIEST resembling spar (a lustrous mineral)
SPARSE	*adj* SPARSER, SPARSEST thinly distributed **SPARSELY** *adv*
SPARSITY	*n* pl. -S the quality or state of being sparse
SPASM	*n* pl. -S an abnormal, involuntary muscular contraction
SPASTIC	*n* pl. -S one suffering from spastic paralysis (a paralysis with muscle spasms)
SPAT	*v* SPATTED, SPATTING, SPATS to strike lightly
SPATE	*n* pl. -S a freshet
SPATHE	*n* pl. -S a leaflike organ of certain plants **SPATHAL, SPATHED, SPATHOSE** *adj*
SPATHIC	*adj* sparry
SPATIAL	*adj* of or pertaining to space
SPATTED	past tense of spat
SPATTER	*v* -ED, -ING, -S to scatter in drops
SPATTING	present participle of spat
SPATULA	*n* pl. -S a mixing implement **SPATULAR** *adj*
SPAVIE	*n* pl. -S spavin **SPAVIET** *adj*
SPAVIN	*n* pl. -S a disease of horses **SPAVINED** *adj*
SPAWN	*v* -ED, -ING, -S to deposit eggs
SPAWNER	*n* pl. -S one that spawns
SPAY	*v* -ED, -ING, -S to remove the ovaries of
SPEAK	*v* SPOKE or SPAKE, SPOKEN, SPEAKING, SPEAKS to utter words
SPEAKER	*n* pl. -S one that speaks
SPEAKING	*n* pl. -S a speech or discourse
SPEAN	*v* -ED, -ING, -S to wean
SPEAR	*v* -ED, -ING, -S to pierce with a spear (a long, pointed weapon)
SPEARER	*n* pl. -S one that spears
SPEARMAN	*n* pl. -MEN a person armed with a spear
SPECIAL	*adj* -CIALER, -CIALEST of a distinct or particular kind or character
SPECIAL	*n* pl. -S a special person or thing
SPECIATE	*v* -ATED, -ATING, -ATES to undergo a type of evolutionary process

SPECIE	*n* pl. -S coined money
SPECIFIC	*n* pl. -S a remedy intended for a particular disease
SPECIFY	*v* -FIED, -FYING, -FIES to state in detail
SPECIMEN	*n* pl. -S a part or individual representative of a group or whole
SPECIOUS	*adj* having a false look of truth or authenticity
SPECK	*v* -ED, -ING, -S to mark with small spots
SPECKLE	*v* -LED, -LING, -LES to speck
SPECS	*n/pl* eyeglasses
SPECTATE	*v* -TATED, -TATING, -TATES to attend and view
SPECTER	*n* pl. -S a visible disembodied spirit
SPECTRA	a pl. of spectrum
SPECTRAL	*adj* resembling a specter
SPECTRE	*n* pl. -S specter
SPECTRUM	*n* pl. -TRA or -TRUMS an array of the components of a light wave
SPECULUM	*n* pl. -LA or -LUMS a medical instrument **SPECULAR** *adj*
SPED	a past tense of speed
SPEECH	*n* pl. -ES the faculty or act of speaking
SPEED	*v* SPED or SPEEDED, SPEEDING, SPEEDS to move swiftly
SPEEDER	*n* pl. -S one that speeds
SPEEDIER	comparative of speedy
SPEEDIEST	superlative of speedy
SPEEDILY	*adv* in a speedy manner
SPEEDING	*n* pl. -S the act of driving faster than the law allows
SPEEDUP	*n* pl. -S an acceleration of production without an increase in pay
SPEEDWAY	*n* pl. -WAYS a road designed for rapid travel
SPEEDY	*adj* SPEEDIER, SPEEDIEST swift
SPEEL	*v* -ED, -ING, -S to climb
SPEER	*v* -ED, -ING, -S to inquire
SPEERING	*n* pl. -S inquiry
SPEIL	*v* -ED, -ING, -S to speel
SPEIR	*v* -ED, -ING, -S to speer
SPEISE	*n* pl. -S speiss

SPEISS	*n* pl. -ES a metallic mixture obtained in smelting certain ores
SPELAEAN	*adj* spelean
SPELEAN	*adj* living in caves
SPELL	*v* SPELLED or SPELT, SPELLING, SPELLS to name or write the letters of in order
SPELLER	*n* pl. -S one that spells words
SPELLING	*n* pl. -S a sequence of letters composing a word
SPELT	*n* pl. -S a variety of wheat
SPELTER	*n* pl. -S zinc in the form of ingots
SPELTZ	*n* pl. -ES spelt
SPELUNK	*v* -ED, -ING, -S to explore caves
SPENCE	*n* pl. -S a pantry
SPENCER	*n* pl. -S a trysail
SPEND	*v* SPENT, SPENDING, SPENDS to pay out
SPENDER	*n* pl. -S one that spends
SPENT	past tense of spend
SPERM	*n* pl. -S a male gamete **SPERMIC** *adj*
SPERMARY	*n* pl. -RIES an organ in which sperms are formed
SPERMINE	*n* pl. -S a chemical compound
SPERMOUS	*adj* resembling or made up of sperms
SPEW	*v* -ED, -ING, -S to vomit
SPEWER	*n* pl. -S one that spews
SPHAGNUM	*n* pl. -S a grayish moss
SPHENE	*n* pl. -S a mineral
SPHENIC	*adj* shaped like a wedge
SPHENOID	*n* pl. -S a bone of the skull
SPHERAL	*adj* of, pertaining to, or having the form of a sphere
SPHERE	*v* SPHERED, SPHERING, SPHERES to form into a sphere (a type of geometric solid)
SPHERIC	*adj* spheral
SPHERICS	*n/pl* the geometry of figures on the surface of a sphere
SPHERIER	comparative of sphery
SPHERIEST	superlative of sphery
SPHERING	present participle of sphere
SPHEROID	*n* pl. -S a type of geometric solid
SPHERULE	*n* pl. -S a small sphere

SPHERY	*adj* SPHERIER, SPHERIEST resembling a sphere
SPHINGES	a pl. of sphinx
SPHINGID	*n* pl. -S the hawkmoth
SPHINX	*n* pl. SPHINXES or SPHINGES a figure of a creature of Egyptian mythology
SPHYGMUS	*n* pl. -ES the pulse **SPHYGMIC** *adj*
SPIC	*n* pl. -S a Spanish-American person — an offensive term
SPICA	*n* pl. -CAE or -CAS an ear of grain **SPICATE, SPICATED** *adj*
SPICCATO	*n* pl. -TOS a method of playing a stringed instrument
SPICE	*v* SPICED, SPICING, SPICES to season with a spice (an aromatic vegetable substance)
SPICER	*n* pl. -S one that spices
SPICERY	*n* pl. -ERIES a spicy quality
SPICEY	*adj* SPICIER, SPICIEST spicy
SPICIER	comparative of spicy
SPICIEST	superlative of spicy
SPICILY	*adv* in a spicy manner
SPICING	present participle of spice
SPICK	*n* pl. -S spic
SPICULA	*n* pl. -LAE spicule **SPICULAR** *adj*
SPICULE	*n* pl. -S a small, needlelike structure
SPICULUM	*n* pl. -LA spicule
SPICY	*adj* SPICIER, SPICIEST containing spices
SPIDER	*n* pl. -S a type of arachnid
SPIDERY	*adj* -DERIER, -DERIEST resembling a spider
SPIED	past tense of spy
SPIEGEL	*n* pl. -S a type of cast iron
SPIEL	*v* -ED, -ING, -S to talk at length
SPIELER	*n* pl. -S one that spiels
SPIER	*v* -ED, -ING, -S to speer
SPIES	present 3d person sing. of spy
SPIFFING	*adj* spiffy
SPIFFY	*adj* -FIER, -FIEST stylish **SPIFFILY** *adv*
SPIGOT	*n* pl. -S a faucet
SPIK	*n* pl. -S spic
SPIKE	*v* SPIKED, SPIKING, SPIKES to fasten with a spike (a long, thick nail)
SPIKELET	*n* pl. -S a type of flower cluster
SPIKER	*n* pl. -S one that spikes
SPIKING	present participle of spike
SPIKY	*adj* SPIKIER, SPIKIEST resembling a spike **SPIKILY** *adv*
SPILE	*v* SPILED, SPILING, SPILES to stop up with a wooden plug
SPILIKIN	*n* pl. -S a strip of wood used in a game
SPILING	*n* pl. -S a piling
SPILL	*v* SPILLED or SPILT, SPILLING, SPILLS to cause to run out of a container
SPILLAGE	*n* pl. -S something that is spilled
SPILLER	*n* pl. -S one that spills
SPILLWAY	*n* pl. -WAYS a channel for surplus water in a reservoir
SPILT	a past tense of spill
SPILTH	*n* pl. -S spillage
SPIN	*v* SPUN, SPINNING, SPINS to draw out and twist into threads
SPINACH	*n* pl. -ES a cultivated herb
SPINAGE	*n* pl. -S spinach
SPINAL	*n* pl. -S an injection of an anesthetic into the spinal cord
SPINALLY	*adv* with respect to the spine
SPINATE	*adj* bearing thorns
SPINDLE	*v* -DLED, -DLING, -DLES to impale on a slender rod
SPINDLER	*n* pl. -S one that spindles
SPINDLY	*adj* -DLIER, -DLIEST long and slender
SPINE	*n* pl. -S the vertebral column **SPINED** *adj*
SPINEL	*n* pl. -S a mineral
SPINELLE	*n* pl. -S spinel
SPINET	*n* pl. -S a small piano
SPINIER	comparative of spiny
SPINIEST	superlative of spiny
SPINIFEX	*n* pl. -ES an Australian grass
SPINLESS	*adj* having no rotation
SPINNER	*n* pl. -S one that spins
SPINNERY	*n* pl. -NERIES a spinning mill
SPINNEY	*n* pl. -NEYS a thicket

SPINNING *n* pl. -S the act of one that spins

SPINNY *n* pl. -NIES spinney

SPINOFF *n* pl. -S a new application or incidental result

SPINOR *n* pl. -S a type of mathematical vector

SPINOSE *adj* spiny

SPINOUS *adj* spiny

SPINOUT *n* pl. -S a rotational skid by an automobile

SPINSTER *n* pl. -S an unmarried woman who is past the usual age for marrying

SPINULA *n* pl. -LAE spinule

SPINULE *n* pl. -S a small thorn

SPINY *adj* SPINIER, SPINIEST bearing or covered with thorns

SPIRACLE *n* pl. -S an orifice through which breathing occurs

SPIRAEA *n* pl. -S spirea

SPIRAL *v* -RALED, -RALING, -RALS or -RALLED, -RALLING, -RALS to move like a spiral (a type of plane curve)

SPIRALLY *adv* in a spiral manner

SPIRANT *n* pl. -S a speech sound produced by the forcing of breath through a narrow passage

SPIRE *v* SPIRED, SPIRING, SPIRES to rise in a tapering manner

SPIREA *n* pl. -S a flowering shrub

SPIREM *n* pl. -S spireme

SPIREME *n* pl. -S a filament forming part of a cell nucleus during mitosis

SPIRILLA *n/pl* spirally twisted, aerobic bacteria

SPIRING present participle of spire

SPIRIT *v* -ED, -ING, -S to carry off secretly

SPIROID *adj* resembling a spiral

SPIRT *v* -ED, -ING, -S to spurt

SPIRULA *n* pl. -LAE or -LAS a spiral-shelled mollusk

SPIRY *adj* tall, slender, and tapering

SPIT *v* SPITTED, SPITTING, SPITS to impale on a spit (a pointed rod on which meat is turned)

SPITAL *n* pl. -S a hospital

SPITBALL *n* pl. -S a type of pitch in baseball

SPITE *v* SPITED, SPITING, SPITES to treat with malice

SPITEFUL *adj* -FULLER, -FULLEST malicious

SPITFIRE *n* pl. -S a quick-tempered person

SPITING present participle of spite

SPITTED past tense of spit

SPITTER *n* pl. -S a spitball

SPITTING present participle of spit

SPITTLE *n* pl. -S saliva

SPITTOON *n* pl. -S a receptacle for saliva

SPITZ *n* pl. -ES a dog having a heavy coat

SPIV *n* pl. -S a petty criminal

SPLAKE *n* pl. -S a freshwater fish

SPLASH *v* -ED, -ING, -ES to scatter a liquid about

SPLASHER *n* pl. -S one that splashes

SPLASHY *adj* SPLASHIER, SPLASHIEST showy

SPLAT *n* pl. -S a piece of wood forming the middle of a chair back

SPLATTER *v* -ED, -ING, -S to spatter

SPLAY *v* -ED, -ING, -S to spread out

SPLEEN *n* pl. -S a ductless organ of the body

SPLEENY *adj* SPLEENIER, SPLEENIEST peevish

SPLENDID *adj* -DIDER, -DIDEST magnificent

SPLENDOR *n* pl. -S magnificence

SPLENIA pl. of splenium

SPLENIAL *adj* pertaining to the splenius

SPLENIC *adj* pertaining to the spleen

SPLENIUM *n* pl. -NIA a surgical bandage

SPLENIUS *n* pl. -NII a muscle of the neck

SPLENT *n* pl. -S a splint

SPLICE *v* SPLICED, SPLICING, SPLICES to join at the ends

SPLICER *n* pl. -S one that splices

SPLINE *v* SPLINED, SPLINING, SPLINES to provide with a spline (a key that connects two rotating mechanical parts)

SPLINT *v* -ED, -ING, -S to brace with a splint (a thin piece of wood)

SPLINTER   *v* -ED, -ING, -S to split into sharp, slender pieces

SPLIT   *v* SPLIT, SPLITTING, SPLITS to separate lengthwise

SPLITTER   *n* pl. -S one that splits

SPLORE   *n* pl. -S a carousal

SPLOSH   *v* -ED, -ING, -ES to splash

SPLOTCH   *v* -ED, -ING, -ES to mark with large, irregular spots

SPLOTCHY   *adj* SPLOTCHIER, SPLOTCHIEST splotched

SPLURGE   *v* SPLURGED, SPLURGING, SPLURGES to spend money lavishly

SPLURGY   *adj* SPLURGIER, SPLURGIEST tending to splurge

SPLUTTER   *v* -ED, -ING, -S to speak rapidly and confusedly

SPODE   *n* pl. -S a fine china

SPOIL   *v* SPOILED or SPOILT, SPOILING, SPOILS to impair the value or quality of

SPOILAGE   *n* pl. -S something that is spoiled or wasted

SPOILER   *n* pl. -S one that spoils

SPOILT   a past tense of spoil

SPOKE   *v* SPOKED, SPOKING, SPOKES to provide with spokes (rods that support the rim of a wheel)

SPOKEN   past participle of speak

SPOLIATE   *v* -ATED, -ATING, -ATES to plunder

SPONDAIC   *n* pl. -S a spondee

SPONDEE   *n* pl. -S a type of metrical foot

SPONGE   *v* SPONGED, SPONGING, SPONGES to wipe with a sponge (a mass of absorbent material)

SPONGER   *n* pl. -S one that sponges

SPONGIER   comparative of spongy

SPONGIEST   superlative of spongy

SPONGILY   *adv* in a spongy manner

SPONGIN   *n* pl. -S a fibrous material

SPONGING   present participle of sponge

SPONGY   *adj* SPONGIER, SPONGIEST resembling a sponge

SPONSAL   *adj* pertaining to marriage

SPONSION   *n* pl. -S the act of sponsoring

SPONSON   *n* pl. -S a projection from the side of a ship

SPONSOR   *v* -ED, -ING, -S to make oneself responsible for

SPONTOON   *n* pl. -S a spear-like weapon

SPOOF   *v* -ED, -ING, -S to hoax

SPOOK   *v* -ED, -ING, -S to scare

SPOOKISH   *adj* spooky

SPOOKY   *adj* SPOOKIER, SPOOKIEST scary **SPOOKILY** *adv*

SPOOL   *v* -ED, -ING, -S to wind on a small cylinder

SPOON   *v* -ED, -ING, -S to take up with a spoon (a type of eating utensil)

SPOONEY   *adj* SPOONIER, SPOONIEST spoony

SPOONEY   *n* pl. -EYS a spoony

SPOONFUL   *n* pl. SPOONFULS or SPOONSFUL as much as a spoon will hold

SPOONIER   comparative of spooney

SPOONIES   pl. of spoony

SPOONIEST   superlative of spooney

SPOONING   present participle of spoon

SPOONY   *adj* SPOONIER, SPOONIEST overly sentimental **SPOONILY** *adv*

SPOONY   *n* pl. SPOONIES a spoony person

SPOOR   *v* -ED, -ING, -S to track

SPORADIC   *adj* occurring at irregular intervals

SPORAL   *adj* of, pertaining to, or resembling a spore

SPORE   *v* SPORED, SPORING, SPORES to produce spores (asexual, usually single-celled reproductive bodies)

SPOROID   *adj* resembling a spore

SPORRAN   *n* pl. -S a large purse worn by Scottish Highlanders

SPORT   *v* -ED, -ING, -S to frolic

SPORTER   *n* pl. -S one that sports

SPORTFUL   *adj* sportive

SPORTIVE   *adj* playful

SPORTY   *adj* SPORTIER, SPORTIEST showy **SPORTILY** *adv*

SPORULE   *n* pl. -S a small spore **SPORULAR** *adj*

SPOT   *v* SPOTTED, SPOTTING, SPOTS to mark with spots (small, roundish discolorations)

SPOTLESS   *adj* perfectly clean

SPOTTER	n pl. -S one that spots	**SPRINGE**	v SPRINGED, SPRINGEING, SPRINGES to catch with a type of snare
SPOTTING	present participle of spot	**SPRINGER**	n pl. -S one that springs
SPOTTY	adj -TIER, -TIEST marked with spots **SPOTTILY** adv	**SPRINGY**	adj SPRINGIER, SPRINGIEST resilient
SPOUSAL	n pl. -S marriage	**SPRINKLE**	v -KLED, -KLING, -KLES to scatter drops or particles on
SPOUSE	v SPOUSED, SPOUSING, SPOUSES to marry	**SPRINT**	v -ED, -ING, -S to run at top speed
SPOUT	v -ED, -ING, -S to eject in a rapid stream	**SPRINTER**	n pl. -S one that sprints
SPOUTER	n pl. -S one that spouts	**SPRIT**	n pl. -S a ship's spar
SPRADDLE	v -DLED, -DLING, -DLES to straddle	**SPRITE**	n pl. -S an elf or fairy
		SPROCKET	n pl. -S a toothlike projection that engages with the links of a chain
SPRAG	n pl. -S a device used to prevent a vehicle from rolling backward	**SPROUT**	v -ED, -ING, -S to begin to grow
SPRAIN	v -ED, -ING, -S to weaken by a sudden and violent twisting or wrenching	**SPRUCE**	adj SPRUCER, SPRUCEST neat and trim in appearance **SPRUCELY** adv
SPRANG	a past tense of spring	**SPRUCE**	v SPRUCED, SPRUCING, SPRUCES to make spruce
SPRAT	n pl. -S a small herring	**SPRUCY**	adj SPRUCIER, SPRUCIEST spruce
SPRATTLE	v -TLED, -TLING, -TLES to struggle	**SPRUE**	n pl. -S a tropical disease
SPRAWL	v -ED, -ING, -S to stretch out ungracefully	**SPRUG**	n pl. -S a sparrow
SPRAWLER	n pl. -S one that sprawls	**SPRUNG**	a past tense of spring
SPRAWLY	adj SPRAWLIER, SPRAWLIEST tending to sprawl	**SPRY**	adj SPRYER, SPRYEST or SPRIER, SPRIEST nimble **SPRYLY** adv
SPRAY	v -ED, -ING, -S to disperse in fine particles	**SPRYNESS**	n pl. -ES the quality or state of being spry
SPRAYER	n pl. -S one that sprays	**SPUD**	v SPUDDED, SPUDDING, SPUDS to remove with a spade-like tool
SPREAD	v SPREAD, SPREADING, SPREADS to open or expand over a larger area	**SPUDDER**	n pl. -S a tool for removing bark from trees
SPREADER	n pl. -S one that spreads	**SPUE**	v SPUED, SPUING, SPUES to spew
SPREE	n pl. -S an unrestrained indulgence in an activity	**SPUME**	v SPUMED, SPUMING, SPUMES to foam
SPRENT	adj sprinkled over	**SPUMIER**	comparative of spumy
SPRIER	a comparative of spry	**SPUMIEST**	superlative of spumy
SPRIEST	a superlative of spry	**SPUMING**	present participle of spume
SPRIG	v SPRIGGED, SPRIGGING, SPRIGS to fasten with small, thin nails	**SPUMONE**	n pl. -S an Italian ice cream
SPRIGGER	n pl. -S one that sprigs	**SPUMONI**	n pl. -S spumone
SPRIGGY	adj -GIER, -GIEST having small branches	**SPUMOUS**	adj spumy
		SPUMY	adj SPUMIER, SPUMIEST foamy
SPRIGHT	n pl. -S sprite	**SPUN**	past tense of spin
SPRING	v SPRANG or SPRUNG, SPRINGING, SPRINGS to move upward suddenly and swiftly	**SPUNK**	v -ED, -ING, -S to begin to burn
SPRINGAL	n pl. -S a young man		

SPUNKIE   *n* pl. -S a light caused by the combustion of marsh gas

SPUNKY   *adj* SPUNKIER, SPUNKIEST plucky **SPUNKILY** *adv*

SPUR   *v* SPURRED, SPURRING, SPURS to urge on with a spur (a horseman's goad)

SPURGALL   *v* -ED, -ING, -S to injure with a spur

SPURGE   *n* pl. -S a tropical plant

SPURIOUS   *adj* not genuine

SPURN   *v* -ED, -ING, -S to reject with contempt

SPURNER   *n* pl. -S one that spurns

SPURRED   past tense of spur

SPURRER   *n* pl. -S one that spurs

SPURREY   *n* pl. -REYS spurry

SPURRIER   *n* pl. -S one that makes spurs

SPURRING   present participle of spur

SPURRY   *n* pl. -RIES a European weed

SPURT   *v* -ED, -ING, -S to gush forth

SPURTLE   *n* pl. -S a stick for stirring porridge

SPUTA   pl. of sputum

SPUTNIK   *n* pl. -S a Soviet artificial earth satellite

SPUTTER   *v* -ED, -ING, -S to eject particles in short bursts

SPUTUM   *n* pl. -TA saliva

SPY   *v* SPIED, SPYING, SPIES to watch secretly

SPYGLASS   *n* pl. -ES a small telescope

SQUAB   *n* pl. -S a young pigeon

SQUABBLE   *v* -BLED, -BLING, -BLES to quarrel

SQUABBY   *adj* -BIER, -BIEST short and fat

SQUAD   *v* SQUADDED, SQUADDING, SQUADS to form into squads (small, organized groups)

SQUADRON   *v* -ED, -ING, -S to arrange in squadrons (units of military organization)

SQUALENE   *n* pl. -S a chemical compound

SQUALID   *adj* -IDER, -IDEST marked by filthiness caused by neglect or poverty

SQUALL   *v* -ED, -ING, -S to cry or scream loudly

SQUALLER   *n* pl. -S one that squalls

SQUALLY   *adj* SQUALLIER, SQUALLIEST gusty

SQUALOR   *n* pl. -S the quality or state of being squalid

SQUAMA   *n* pl. -MAE a scale **SQUAMATE, SQUAMOSE, SQUAMOUS** *adj*

SQUANDER   *v* -ED, -ING, -S to spend wastefully

SQUARE   *adj* SQUARER, SQUAREST having four equal sides and four right angles

SQUARE   *v* SQUARED, SQUARING, SQUARES to make square

SQUARELY   *adv* in a direct manner

SQUARER   *n* pl. -S one that squares

SQUAREST   superlative of square

SQUARING   present participle of square

SQUARISH   *adj* somewhat square

SQUASH   *v* -ED, -ING, -ES to press into a pulp or flat mass

SQUASHER   *n* pl. -S one that squashes

SQUASHY   *adj* SQUASHIER, SQUASHIEST soft and moist

SQUAT   *v* SQUATTED, SQUATTING, SQUATS to sit on one's heels

SQUAT   *adj* SQUATTER, SQUATTEST short and thick **SQUATLY** *adv*

SQUATTER   *v* -ED, -ING, -S to move through water

SQUATTING   present participle of squat

SQUATTY   *adj* -TIER, -TIEST squat

SQUAW   *n* pl. -S an American Indian woman

SQUAWK   *v* -ED, -ING, -S to utter a loud, harsh cry

SQUAWKER   *n* pl. -S one that squawks

SQUEAK   *v* -ED, -ING, -S to make a sharp, high-pitched sound

SQUEAKER   *n* pl. -S one that squeaks

SQUEAKY   *adj* SQUEAKIER, SQUEAKIEST tending to squeak

SQUEAL   *v* -ED, -ING, -S to utter a sharp, shrill cry

SQUEALER   *n* pl. -S one that squeals

SQUEEGEE   *v* -GEED, -GEEING, -GEES to wipe with a squeegee (an implement for removing water from a surface)

SQUEEZE   *v* SQUEEZED, SQUEEZING, SQUEEZES to press hard upon

SQUEEZER	*n* pl. -S one that squeezes
SQUEG	*v* SQUEGGED, SQUEGGING, SQUEGS to oscillate in an irregular manner
SQUELCH	*v* -ED, -ING, -ES to squash
SQUELCHY	*adj* SQUELCHIER, SQUELCHIEST squashy
SQUIB	*v* SQUIBBED, SQUIBBING, SQUIBS to lampoon
SQUID	*v* SQUIDDED, SQUIDDING, SQUIDS to fish for squid (ten-armed marine mollusks)
SQUIFFED	*adj* drunk
SQUIFFY	*adj* squiffed
SQUIGGLE	*v* -GLED, -GLING, -GLES to wriggle
SQUIGGLY	*adj* -GLIER, -GLIEST wriggly
SQUILGEE	*v* -GEED, -GEEING, -GEES to squeegee
SQUILL	*n* pl. -S a Eurasian herb
SQUILLA	*n* pl. -LAS or -LAE a burrowing crustacean
SQUINCH	*v* -ED, -ING, -ES to squint
SQUINNY	*v* -NIED, -NYING, -NIES to squint
SQUINNY	*adj* -NIER, -NIEST squinty
SQUINT	*adj* SQUINTER, SQUINTEST cross-eyed
SQUINT	*v* -ED, -ING, -S to look with the eyes partly closed
SQUINTER	*n* pl. -S one that squints
SQUINTY	*adj* SQUINTIER, SQUINTIEST marked by squinting
SQUIRE	*v* SQUIRED, SQUIRING, SQUIRES to serve as a squire (an escort)
SQUIREEN	*n* pl. -S an owner of a small estate
SQUIRISH	*adj* of, resembling, or befitting a squire
SQUIRM	*v* -ED, -ING, -S to wriggle
SQUIRMER	*n* pl. -S one that squirms
SQUIRMY	*adj* SQUIRMIER, SQUIRMIEST wriggly
SQUIRREL	*v* -RELED, -RELING, -RELS or -RELLED, -RELLING, -RELS to store up for future use
SQUIRT	*v* -ED, -ING, -S to eject in a thin, swift stream
SQUIRTER	*n* pl. -S one that squirts
SQUISH	*v* -ED, -ING, -ES to squash

SQUISHY	*adj* SQUISHIER, SQUISHIEST squashy
SQUOOSH	*v* -ED, -ING, -ES to squash
SQUUSH	*v* -ED, -ING, -ES to squash
SRADDHA	*n* pl. -S sradha
SRADHA	*n* pl. -S a Hindu ceremonial offering
SRI	*n* pl. -S mister; sir — used as a Hindu title of respect
STAB	*v* STABBED, STABBING, STABS to pierce with a pointed weapon
STABBER	*n* pl. -S one that stabs
STABILE	*n* pl. -S a stationary abstract sculpture
STABLE	*adj* -BLER, -BLEST resistant to sudden change or position or condition
STABLE	*v* -BLED, -BLING, -BLES to put in a stable (a shelter for domestic animals)
STABLER	*n* pl. -S one that keeps a stable
STABLEST	superlative of stable
STABLING	*n* pl. -S accommodation for animals in a stable
STABLISH	*v* -ED, -ING, -ES to establish
STABLY	*adv* in a stable manner
STACCATO	*n* pl. -TOS or -TI a musical passage marked by the short, clear-cut playing of tones
STACK	*v* -ED, -ING, -S to pile
STACKER	*n* pl. -S one that stacks
STACTE	*n* pl. -S a spice used by the ancient Jews in making incense
STADDLE	*n* pl. -S a platform on which hay is stacked
STADE	*n* pl. -S an ancient Greek unit of length
STADIA	*n* pl. -S a method of surveying distances
STADIUM	*n* pl. -S a structure in which athletic events are held
STAFF	*v* -ED, -ING, -S to provide with a staff (a body of assistants)
STAFFER	*n* pl. -S a member of a staff
STAG	*v* STAGGED, STAGGING, STAGS to attend a social function without a female companion
STAGE	*v* STAGED, STAGING, STAGES to produce for public view
STAGER	*n* pl. -S an experienced person
STAGEY	*adj* STAGIER, STAGIEST stagy

STAGGARD *n* pl. -S a full-grown male red deer

STAGGART *n* pl. -S staggard

STAGGED past tense of stag

STAGGER *v* -ED, -ING, -S to walk or stand unsteadily

STAGGERY *adj* unsteady

STAGGIE *n* pl. -S a colt

STAGGING present participle of stag

STAGGY *adj* -GIER, -GIEST having the appearance of a mature male

STAGIER comparative of stagey and stagy

STAGIEST superlative of stagey and stagy

STAGILY *adv* in a stagy manner

STAGING *n* pl. -S a temporary platform

STAGNANT *adj* not moving or flowing

STAGNATE *v* -NATED, -NATING, -NATES to become stagnant

STAGY *adj* STAGIER, STAGIEST having a theatrical quality

STAID *adj* STAIDER, STAIDEST sober and sedate **STAIDLY** *adv*

STAIG *n* pl. -S a colt

STAIN *v* -ED, -ING, -S to discolor or dirty

STAINER *n* pl. -S one that stains

STAIR *n* pl. -S a rest for the foot used in going from one level to another

STAIRWAY *n* pl. -WAYS a flight of stairs

STAKE *v* STAKED, STAKING, STAKES to fasten with a stake (a pointed piece of wood or metal)

STAKEOUT *n* pl. -S a surveillance of an area especially by the police

STALAG *n* pl. -S a German prisoner-of-war camp

STALE *adj* STALER, STALEST not fresh **STALELY** *adv*

STALE *v* STALED, STALING, STALES to become stale

STALK *v* -ED, -ING, -S to pursue stealthily

STALKER *n* pl. -S one that stalks

STALKY *adj* STALKIER, STALKIEST long and slender **STALKILY** *adv*

STALL *v* -ED, -ING, -S to stop the progress of

STALLION *n* pl. -S an uncastrated male horse

STALWART *n* pl. -S an unwavering partisan

STAMEN *n* pl. -S the pollen-bearing organ of flowering plants

STAMINA *n* pl. -S endurance **STAMINAL** *adj*

STAMMEL *n* pl. -S a red color

STAMMER *v* -ED, -ING, -S to speak with involuntary breaks and pauses

STAMP *v* -ED, -ING, -S to bring the foot down heavily

STAMPEDE *v* -PEDED, -PEDING, -PEDES to cause to run away in headlong panic

STAMPER *n* pl. -S one that stamps

STANCE *n* pl. -S a manner of standing

STANCH *adj* STANCHER, STANCHEST staunch

STANCH *v* -ED, -ING, -ES to stop the flow of blood from

STANCHER *n* pl. -S one that stanches

STANCHLY *adv* in a stanch manner

STAND *v* STOOD, STANDING, STANDS to assume or maintain an upright position

STANDARD *n* pl. -S an established measure of comparison

STANDBY *n* pl. -BYS one that can be relied on

STANDEE *n* pl. -S one who stands because of the lack of seats

STANDER *n* pl. -S one that stands

STANDING *n* pl. -S a position or condition in society

STANDISH *n* pl. -ES a receptacle for pens and ink

STANDOFF *n* pl. -S a tie or draw, as in a game

STANDOUT *n* pl. -S one that shows marked superiority

STANDPAT *adj* resisting or opposing change

STANDUP *adj* having an upright position

STANE *v* STANED, STANING, STANES to stone

STANG *v* -ED, -ING, -S to sting

STANHOPE *n* pl. -S a light, open carriage

STANING present participle of stane

STANK *n* pl. -S a pond

STANNARY *n* pl. -RIES a tin-mining region

STANNIC *adj* pertaining to tin

STANNITE *n* pl. -S an ore of tin

STANNOUS *adj* pertaining to tin

STANNUM *n* pl. -S tin

STANZA *n* pl. -S a division of a poem **STANZAED, STANZAIC** *adj*

STAPEDES pl. of stapes

STAPELIA *n* pl. -S an African plant

STAPES *n* pl. -PEDES a bone of the middle ear

STAPH *n* pl. -S any of various spherical bacteria

STAPLE *v* -PLED, -PLING, -PLES to fasten by means of a U-shaped metal loop

STAPLER *n* pl. -S a stapling device

STAR *v* STARRED, STARRING, STARS to shine as a star (a natural luminous body visible in the sky)

STARCH *v* -ED, -ING, -ES to treat with starch (a solid carbohydrate)

STARCHY *adj* STARCHIER, STARCHIEST containing starch

STARDOM *n* pl. -S the status of a preeminent performer

STARDUST *n* pl. -S a romantic quality

STARE *v* STARED, STARING, STARES to gaze fixedly

STARER *n* pl. -S one that stares

STARETS *n* pl. STARTSY a spiritual adviser in the Eastern Orthodox Church

STARFISH *n* pl. -ES a star-shaped marine animal

STARGAZE *v* -GAZED, -GAZING, -GAZES to gaze at the stars

STARING present participle of stare

STARK *adj* STARKER, STARKEST harsh in appearance **STARKLY** *adv*

STARLESS *adj* having no stars

STARLET *n* pl. -S a small star

STARLIKE *adj* resembling a star

STARLING *n* pl. -S a European bird

STARLIT *adj* lighted by the stars

STARNOSE *n* pl. -S a burrowing mammal

STARRED past tense of star

STARRING present participle of star

STARRY *adj* -RIER, -RIEST abounding with stars

START *v* -ED, -ING, -S to set out

STARTER *n* pl. -S one that starts

STARTLE *v* -TLED, -TLING, -TLES to frighten or surprise suddenly

STARTLER *n* pl. -S one that startles

STARTSY pl. of starets

STARVE *v* STARVED, STARVING, STARVES to die from lack of food

STARVER *n* pl. -S one that starves

STARWORT *n* pl. -S a flowering plant

STASES pl. of stasis

STASH *v* -ED, -ING, -ES to store in a secret place

STASIMON *n* pl. -MA a choral ode in ancient Greek drama

STASIS *n* pl. STASES a stoppage of the normal flow of bodily fluids

STATABLE *adj* capable of being stated

STATAL *adj* pertaining to a national government

STATANT *adj* standing with all feet on the ground — used of a heraldic animal

STATE *v* STATED, STATING, STATES to set forth in words

STATEDLY *adv* regularly

STATELY *adj* -LIER, -LIEST dignified

STATER *n* pl. -S one that states

STATIC *n* pl. -S random noise produced in a radio or television receiver **STATICAL** *adj*

STATICE *n* pl. -S a flowering plant

STATING present participle of state

STATION *v* -ED, -ING, -S to assign to a position

STATISM *n* pl. -S a theory of government

STATIST *n* pl. -S an adherent of statism

STATIVE *n* pl. -S a verb that expresses a condition

STATOR *n* pl. -S the part of a machine about which the rotor revolves

STATUARY *n* pl. -ARIES a group of statues

STATUE *n* pl. -S a three-dimensional work of art **STATUED** *adj*

STATURE *n* pl. -S the natural height of a human or animal body

STATUS *n* pl. -ES relative position

STATUTE *n* pl. -S a law enacted by the legislative branch of a government

STAUMREL *n* pl. -S a dolt

STAUNCH	*adj* STAUNCHER, STAUNCHEST firm and dependable	**STEEL**	*v* -ED, -ING, -S to cover with steel (a tough iron alloy)
STAUNCH	*v* -ED, -ING, -ES to stanch	**STEELIE**	*n* pl. -S a steel playing marble
STAVE	*v* STAVED or STOVE, STAVING, STAVES to drive or thrust away	**STEELY**	*adj* STEELIER, STEELIEST resembling steel
STAW	a past tense of steal	**STEENBOK**	*n* pl. -S an African antelope
STAY	*v* STAYED or STAID, STAYING, STAYS to continue in a place or condition	**STEEP**	*adj* STEEPER, STEEPEST inclined sharply
STAYER	*n* pl. -S one that stays	**STEEP**	*v* -ED, -ING, -S to soak in a liquid
STAYSAIL	*n* pl. -S a type of sail	**STEEPEN**	*v* -ED, -ING, -S to make steep
STEAD	*v* -ED, -ING, -S to be of advantage to	**STEEPER**	*n* pl. -S one that steeps
STEADIED	past tense of steady	**STEEPLE**	*n* pl. -S a tapering structure on a church tower **STEEPLED** *adj*
STEADIER	*n* pl. -S one that steadies	**STEEPLY**	*adv* in a steep manner
STEADIES	present 3d person sing. of steady	**STEER**	*v* -ED, -ING, -S to direct the course of
STEADING	*n* pl. -S a small farm	**STEERAGE**	*n* pl. -S the act of steering
STEADY	*adj* STEADIER, STEADIEST firm in position **STEADILY** *adv*	**STEERER**	*n* pl. -S one that steers
STEADY	*v* STEADIED, STEADYING, STEADIES to make steady	**STEEVE**	*v* STEEVED, STEEVING, STEEVES to stow in the hold of a ship
STEAK	*n* pl. -S a slice of meat	**STEEVING**	*n* pl. -S the angular elevation of a bowsprit from a ship's keel
STEAL	*v* STOLE or STAW, STOLEN, STEALING, STEALS to take without right or permission	**STEGODON**	*n* pl. -S an extinct elephant-like mammal
STEALAGE	*n* pl. -S theft	**STEIN**	*n* pl. -S a beer mug
STEALER	*n* pl. -S one that steals	**STEINBOK**	*n* pl. -S steenbok
STEALING	*n* pl. -S the act of one that steals	**STELA**	*n* pl. -LAE or -LAI an inscribed slab used as a monument **STELAR, STELENE** *adj*
STEALTH	*n* pl. -S stealthy procedure	**STELE**	*n* pl. -S the central portion of vascular tissue in a plant stem **STELIC** *adj*
STEALTHY	*adj* STEALTHIER, STEALTHIEST intended to escape observation		
STEAM	*v* -ED, -ING, -S to expose to steam (water in the form of vapor)	**STELLA**	*n* pl. -S a former coin of the United States
STEAMER	*v* -ED, -ING, -S to travel by steamship	**STELLAR**	*adj* pertaining to the stars
		STELLATE	*adj* shaped like a star
STEAMY	*adj* STEAMIER, STEAMIEST marked by steam **STEAMILY** *adv*	**STELLIFY**	*v* -FIED, -FYING, -FIES to convert into a star
STEAPSIN	*n* pl. -S an enzyme	**STEM**	*v* STEMMED, STEMMING, STEMS to remove stems (ascending axes of a plant) from
STEARATE	*n* pl. -S a chemical salt		
STEARIN	*n* pl. -S the solid portion of a fat **STEARIC** *adj*	**STEMLESS**	*adj* having no stem
STEARINE	*n* pl. -S stearin	**STEMLIKE**	*adj* resembling a stem
STEATITE	*n* pl. -S a variety of talc	**STEMMA**	*n* pl. -MAS or -MATA a scroll recording the genealogy of a family in ancient Rome
STEDFAST	*adj* staunch		
STEED	*n* pl. -S a horse	**STEMMED**	past tense of stem
STEEK	*v* -ED, -ING, -S to shut	**STEMMER**	*n* pl. -S one that removes stems

STEMMERY	*n* pl. -MERIES a place where tobacco leaves are stripped
STEMMING	present participle of stem
STEMMY	*adj* -MIER, -MIEST abounding in stems
STEMSON	*n* pl. -S a supporting timber of a ship
STEMWARE	*n* pl. -S a type of glassware
STENCH	*n* pl. -ES a foul odor
STENCHY	*adj* STENCHIER, STENCHIEST having a stench
STENCIL	*v* -CILED, -CILING, -CILS or -CILLED, -CILLING, -CILS to mark by means of a perforated sheet of material
STENGAH	*n* pl. -S a mixed drink
STENO	*n* pl. STENOS a stenographer
STENOSED	*adj* affected with stenosis
STENOSIS	*n* pl. -NOSES a narrowing of a bodily passage **STENOTIC** *adj*
STENTOR	*n* pl. -S a person having a very loud voice
STEP	*v* STEPPED, STEPPING, STEPS to move by lifting the foot and setting it down in another place
STEPDAME	*n* pl. -S a stepmother
STEPLIKE	*adj* resembling a stair
STEPPE	*n* pl. -S a vast treeless plain
STEPPED	past tense of step
STEPPER	*n* pl. -S one that steps
STEPPING	present participle of step
STEPSON	*n* pl. -S a son of one's spouse by a former marriage
STEPWISE	*adj* marked by a gradual progression
STERE	*n* pl. -S a unit of volume
STEREO	*v* -ED, -ING, -S to make a type of printing plate
STERIC	*adj* pertaining to the spatial relationships of atoms in a molecule
STERICAL	*adj* steric
STERIGMA	*n* pl. -MAS or -MATA a spore-bearing stalk of certain fungi
STERILE	*adj* incapable of producing offspring
STERLET	*n* pl. -S a small sturgeon
STERLING	*n* pl. -S British money
STERN	*adj* STERNER, STERNEST unyielding
STERN	*n* pl. -S the rear part of a ship
STERNA	a pl. of sternum
STERNAL	*adj* pertaining to the sternum
STERNITE	*n* pl. -S a somitic sclerite
STERNLY	*adv* in a stern manner
STERNSON	*n* pl. -S a reinforcing post of a ship
STERNUM	*n* pl. -NA or -NUMS a long, flat supporting bone of most vertebrates
STERNWAY	*n* pl. -WAYS the backward movement of a vessel
STEROID	*n* pl. -S a type of chemical compound
STEROL	*n* pl. -S a type of solid alcohol
STERTOR	*n* pl. -S a deep snoring sound
STET	*v* STETTED, STETTING, STETS to cancel a previously made printing correction
STETSON	*n* pl. -S a broad-brimmed hat
STEW	*v* -ED, -ING, -S to cook by boiling slowly
STEWARD	*v* -ED, -ING, -S to manage
STEWBUM	*n* pl. -S a drunken bum
STEWPAN	*n* pl. -S a pan used for stewing
STEY	*adj* steep
STHENIA	*n* pl. -S excessive energy **STHENIC** *adj*
STIBIAL	*adj* pertaining to stibium
STIBINE	*n* pl. -S a poisonous gas
STIBIUM	*n* pl. -S antimony
STIBNITE	*n* pl. -S an ore of antimony
STICH	*n* pl. -S a line of poetry **STICHIC** *adj*
STICK	*v* -ED, -ING, -S to support with slender pieces of wood
STICK	*v* STUCK, STICKING, STICKS to pierce with a pointed object
STICKER	*n* pl. -S an adhesive label
STICKFUL	*n* pl. -S an amount of set type
STICKIER	comparative of sticky
STICKIEST	superlative of sticky
STICKILY	*adv* in a sticky manner
STICKIT	*adj* unsuccessful
STICKLE	*v* -LED, -LING, -LES to argue stubbornly
STICKLER	*n* pl. -S one that stickles
STICKMAN	*n* pl. -MEN one who supervises the play at a dice table

STICKOUT	*n* pl. -S one that is conspicuous
STICKPIN	*n* pl. -S a decorative tiepin
STICKUM	*n* pl. -S a substance that causes adhesion
STICKUP	*n* pl. -S a robbery at gunpoint
STICKY	*adj* STICKIER, STICKIEST tending to adhere
STIED	a past tense of sty
STIES	present 3d person sing. of sty
STIFF	*adj* STIFFER, STIFFEST difficult to bend or stretch
STIFF	*n* pl. -S a corpse
STIFFEN	*v* -ED, -ING, -S to make stiff
STIFFISH	*adj* somewhat stiff
STIFFLY	*adv* in a stiff manner
STIFLE	*v* -FLED, -FLING, -FLES to smother
STIFLER	*n* pl. -S one that stifles
STIGMA	*n* pl. -MAS or -MATA a mark of disgrace **STIGMAL** *adj*
STILBENE	*n* pl. -S a chemical compound
STILBITE	*n* pl. -S a mineral
STILE	*n* pl. -S a series of steps for passing over a fence or wall
STILETTO	*v* -ED, -ING, -S or -ES to stab with a short dagger
STILL	*adj* STILLER, STILLEST free from sound or motion
STILL	*v* -ED, -ING, -S to make still
STILLMAN	*n* pl. -MEN one who operates a distillery
STILLY	*adj* STILLIER, STILLIEST still
STILT	*v* -ED, -ING, -S to raise on stilts (long, slender poles)
STIME	*n* pl. -S a glimpse
STIMULUS	*n* pl. -LI something that causes a response
STIMY	*v* -MIED, -MYING, -MIES to stymie
STING	*v* STUNG, STINGING, STINGS to prick painfully
STINGER	*n* pl. -S one that stings
STINGIER	comparative of stingy
STINGIEST	superlative of stingy
STINGILY	*adv* in a stingy manner
STINGO	*n* pl. -GOS a strong ale or beer
STINGRAY	*n* pl. -RAYS a flat-bodied marine fish

STINGY	*adj* -GIER, -GIEST unwilling to spend or give
STINK	*v* STANK or STUNK, STINKING, STINKS to emit a foul odor
STINKARD	*n* pl. -S a despicable person
STINKBUG	*n* pl. -S an insect that emits a foul odor
STINKER	*n* pl. -S one that stinks
STINKIER	comparative of stinky
STINKIEST	superlative of stinky
STINKO	*adj* drunk
STINKPOT	*n* pl. -S a jar containing foul-smelling combustibles formerly used in warfare
STINKY	*adj* STINKIER, STINKIEST emitting a foul odor
STINT	*v* -ED, -ING, -S to limit
STINTER	*n* pl. -S one that stints
STIPE	*n* pl. -S a slender supporting part of a plant **STIPED** *adj*
STIPEL	*n* pl. -S a small stipule
STIPEND	*n* pl. -S a fixed sum of money paid periodically
STIPES	*n* pl. STIPITES a stipe
STIPPLE	*v* -PLED, -PLING, -PLES to draw, paint, or engrave by means of dots or short touches
STIPPLER	*n* pl. -S one that stipples
STIPULE	*n* pl. -S an appendage at the base of a leaf in certain plants **STIPULAR, STIPULED** *adj*
STIR	*v* STIRRED, STIRRING, STIRS to pass an implement through in circular motions
STIRK	*n* pl. -S a young cow
STIRP	*n* pl. -S lineage
STIRPS	*n* pl. STIRPES a family or branch of a family
STIRRED	past tense of stir
STIRRER	*n* pl. -S one that stirs
STIRRING	present participle of stir
STIRRUP	*n* pl. -S a support for the foot of a horseman
STITCH	*v* -ED, -ING, -ES to join by making in-and-out movements with a threaded needle
STITCHER	*n* pl. -S one that stitches
STITHY	*v* STITHIED, STITHYING, STITHIES to forge on an anvil
STIVER	*n* pl. -S a former Dutch coin

STOA	*n* pl. STOAE, STOAI, or STOAS an ancient Greek covered walkway
STOAT	*n* pl. -S a weasel with a black-tipped tail
STOB	*v* STOBBED, STOBBING, STOBS to stab
STOCCADO	*n* pl. -DOS a thrust with a rapier
STOCCATA	*n* pl. -S stoccado
STOCK	*v* -ED, -ING, -S to keep for future sale or use
STOCKADE	*v* -ADED, -ADING, -ADES to build a type of protective fence around
STOCKCAR	*n* pl. -S a boxcar for carrying livestock
STOCKER	*n* pl. -S a young animal suitable for being fattened for market
STOCKIER	comparative of stocky
STOCKIEST	superlative of stocky
STOCKILY	*adv* in a stocky manner
STOCKING	*n* pl. -S a knitted or woven covering for the foot and leg
STOCKISH	*adj* stupid
STOCKIST	*n* pl. -S one who stocks goods
STOCKMAN	*n* pl. -MEN one who owns or raises livestock
STOCKPOT	*n* pl. -S a pot in which broth is prepared
STOCKY	*adj* STOCKIER, STOCKIEST having a short, thick body
STODGE	*v* STODGED, STODGING, STODGES to stuff full with food
STODGY	*adj* STODGIER, STODGIEST boring **STODGILY** *adv*
STOGEY	*n* pl. -GEYS stogy
STOGIE	*n* pl. -S stogy
STOGY	*n* pl. -GIES a long, slender cigar
STOIC	*n* pl. -S one who is indifferent to pleasure or pain **STOICAL** *adj*
STOICISM	*n* pl. -S indifference to pleasure or pain
STOKE	*v* STOKED, STOKING, STOKES to supply a furnace with fuel
STOKER	*n* pl. -S one that stokes
STOKESIA	*n* pl. -S a perennial herb
STOKING	present participle of stoke
STOLE	*n* pl. -S a long-wide scarf **STOLED** *adj*
STOLEN	past participle of steal
STOLID	*adj* -IDER, -IDEST showing little or no emotion **STOLIDLY** *adv*
STOLLEN	*n* pl. -S a sweet bread
STOLON	*n* pl. -S a type of plant stem **STOLONIC** *adj*
STOMA	*n* pl. -MAS or -MATA a minute opening in the epidermis of a plant organ
STOMACH	*v* -ED, -ING, -S to tolerate
STOMACHY	*adj* paunchy
STOMAL	*adj* stomatal
STOMATA	a pl. of stoma
STOMATAL	*adj* pertaining to a stoma
STOMATE	*n* pl. -S a stoma
STOMATIC	*adj* pertaining to the mouth
STOMODEA	*n/pl* embryonic oral cavities
STOMP	*v* -ED, -ING, -S to tread heavily
STOMPER	*n* pl. -S one that stomps
STONE	*v* STONED, STONING, STONES to pelt with stones (pieces of concreted earthy or mineral matter) **STONABLE** *adj*
STONEFLY	*n* pl. -FLIES a winged insect
STONER	*n* pl. -S one that stones
STONEY	*adj* STONIER, STONIEST stony
STONIER	comparative of stony
STONIEST	superlative of stony
STONILY	*adv* in a stony manner
STONING	present participle of stone
STONISH	*v* -ED, -ING, -ES to astonish
STONY	*adj* STONIER, STONIEST abounding in stones
STOOD	past tense of stand
STOOGE	*v* STOOGED, STOOGING, STOOGES to act as a comedian's straight man
STOOK	*v* -ED, -ING, -S to stack upright in a field for drying, as bundles of grain
STOOKER	*n* pl. -S one that stooks
STOOL	*v* -ED, -ING, -S to defecate
STOOLIE	*n* pl. -S an informer
STOOP	*v* -ED, -ING, -S to bend the body forward and down
STOOPER	*n* pl. -S one that stoops
STOP	*v* STOPPED or STOPT, STOPPING, STOPS to discontinue the progress or motion of

STOPCOCK *n* pl. -S a type of faucet

STOPE *v* STOPED, STOPING, STOPES to excavate in layers, as ore

STOPER *n* pl. -S one that stopes

STOPGAP *n* pl. -S a temporary substitute

STOPING present participle of stope

STOPOVER *n* pl. -S a brief stop in the course of a journey

STOPPAGE *n* pl. -S the act of stopping

STOPPED a past tense of stop

STOPPER *v* -ED, -ING, -S to plug

STOPPING present participle of stop

STOPPLE *v* -PLED, -PLING, -PLES to stopper

STOPT a past tense of stop

STORABLE *n* pl. -S something that can be stored

STORAGE *n* pl. -S a place for storing

STORAX *n* pl. -ES a fragrant resin

STORE *v* STORED, STORING, STORES to put away for future use

STOREY *n* pl. -REYS a horizontal division of a building **STOREYED** *adj*

STORIED past tense of story

STORIES present 3d person sing. of story

STORING present participle of store

STORK *n* pl. -S a wading bird

STORM *v* -ED, -ING, -S to blow violently

STORMY *adj* STORMIER, STORMIEST storming **STORMILY** *adv*

STORY *v* -RIED, -RYING, -RIES to relate as a story (an account of an event or series of events)

STOSS *adj* facing the direction from which a glacier moves

STOTINKA *n* pl. -KI a monetary unit of Bulgaria

STOUND *v* -ED, -ING, -S to ache

STOUP *n* pl. -S a basin for holy water

STOUR *n* pl. -S dust

STOURE *n* pl. -S stour

STOURIE *adj* stoury

STOURY *adj* dusty

STOUT *adj* STOUTER, STOUTEST fat

STOUT *n* pl. -S a strong, dark ale

STOUTEN *v* -ED, -ING, -S to make stout

STOUTISH *adj* somewhat stout

STOUTLY *adv* in a stout manner

STOVE *n* pl. -S a heating apparatus

STOVER *n* pl. -S coarse food for cattle

STOW *v* -ED, -ING, -S to pack **STOWABLE** *adj*

STOWAGE *n* pl. -S goods in storage

STOWAWAY *n* pl. -AWAYS one who hides aboard a conveyance to obtain free passage

STOWP *n* pl. -S stoup

STRADDLE *v* -DLED, -DLING, -DLES to sit, stand, or walk with the legs wide apart

STRAFE *v* STRAFED, STRAFING, STRAFES to attack with machine-gun fire from an airplane

STRAFER *n* pl. -S one that strafes

STRAGGLE *v* -GLED, -GLING, -GLES to stray

STRAGGLY *adj* -GLIER, -GLIEST irregularly spread out

STRAIGHT *adj* STRAIGHTER, STRAIGHTEST extending uniformly in one direction without bends or irregularities

STRAIGHT *v* -ED, -ING, -S to make straight

STRAIN *v* -ED, -ING, -S to exert to the utmost

STRAINER *n* pl. -S a utensil used to separate liquids from solids

STRAIT *n* pl. -S a narrow waterway connecting two larger bodies of water

STRAIT *adj* STRAITER, STRAITEST narrow **STRAITLY** *adv*

STRAITEN *v* -ED, -ING, -S to make strait

STRAKE *n* pl. -S a line of planking extending along a ship's hull **STRAKED** *adj*

STRAMASH *n* pl. -ES an uproar

STRAMONY *n* pl. -NIES a poisonous weed

STRAND *v* -ED, -ING, -S to leave in an unfavorable situation

STRANDER *n* pl. -S a machine that twists fibers into rope

STRANG *adj* strong

STRANGE *adj* STRANGER, STRANGEST unusual or unfamiliar

STRANGER *v* -ED, -ING, -S to estrange

STRANGLE *v* -GLED, -GLING, -GLES to choke to death

STRAP   v STRAPPED, STRAPPING, STRAPS to fasten with a strap (a narrow strip of flexible material)

STRAPPER   n pl. -S one that straps

STRASS   n pl. -ES a brilliant glass used in making imitation gems

STRATA   n pl. -S a stratum

STRATAL   adj pertaining to a stratum

STRATEGY   n pl. -GIES a plan for obtaining a specific goal

STRATH   n pl. -S a wide river valley

STRATI   pl. of stratus

STRATIFY   v -FIED, -FYING, -FIES to form or arrange in layers

STRATOUS   adj stratal

STRATUM   n pl. -TA or -TUMS a layer of material

STRATUS   n pl. -TI a type of cloud

STRAVAGE   v -VAGED, -VAGING, -VAGES to stroll

STRAVAIG   v -ED, -ING, -S to stravage

STRAW   v -ED, -ING, -S to cover with straw (stalks of threshed grain)

STRAWHAT   adj pertaining to a summer theater situated in a resort area

STRAWY   adj STRAWIER, STRAWIEST resembling straw

STRAY   v -ED, -ING, -S to wander from the proper area or course

STRAYER   n pl. -S one that strays

STREAK   v -ED, -ING, -S to cover with streaks (long, narrow marks)

STREAKER   n pl. -S one that streaks

STREAKY   adj STREAKIER, STREAKIEST covered with streaks

STREAM   v -ED, -ING, -S to flow in a steady current

STREAMER   n pl. -S a long, narrow flag

STREAMY   adj STREAMIER, STREAMIEST streaming

STREEK   v -ED, -ING, -S to stretch

STREEKER   n pl. -S one that streeks

STREET   n pl. -S a public thoroughfare

STRENGTH   n pl. -S capacity for exertion or endurance

STREP   n pl. -S any of various spherical or oval bacteria

STRESS   v -ED, -ING, -ES to place emphasis on

STRESSOR   n pl. -S a type of stimulus

STRETCH   v -ED, -ING, -ES to draw out or open to full length

STRETCHY   adj STRETCHIER, STRETCHIEST having a tendency to stretch

STRETTA   n pl. -TE or -TAS stretto

STRETTO   n pl. -TI or -TOS a concluding musical passage played at a faster tempo

STREUSEL   n pl. -S a topping for coffee cakes

STREW   v STREWED, STREWN, STREWING, STREWS to scatter about

STREWER   n pl. -S one that strews

STRIA   n pl. STRIAE a thin groove, stripe, or streak

STRIATE   v -ATED, -ATING, -ATES to mark with striae

STRICK   n pl. -S a bunch of flax fibers

STRICKEN   adj strongly affected or afflicted

STRICKLE   v -LED, -LING, -LES to shape or smooth with a strickle (an instrument for leveling off grain)

STRICT   adj STRICTER, STRICTEST kept within narrow and specific limits **STRICTLY** adv

STRIDE   v STRODE or STRID, STRIDDEN, STRIDING, STRIDES to walk with long steps

STRIDENT   adj shrill

STRIDER   n pl. -S one that strides

STRIDING   present participle of stride

STRIDOR   n pl. -S a strident sound

STRIFE   n pl. -S bitter conflict or dissension

STRIGIL   n pl. -S a scraping instrument

STRIGOSE   adj covered with short, stiff hairs

STRIKE   v STRUCK or STROOK, STRICKEN or STRUCKEN, STRIKING, STRIKES to come or cause to come into contact with

STRIKER   n pl. -S one that strikes

STRING   v STRUNG or STRINGED, STRINGING, STRINGS to provide with strings (slender cords)

STRINGER   n pl. -S one that strings

STRINGY   adj STRINGIER, STRINGIEST resembling a string or strings

STRIP   *v* STRIPPED or STRIPT, STRIPPING, STRIPS to remove the outer covering from

STRIPE   *v* STRIPED, STRIPING, STRIPES to mark with stripes (long, distinct bands)

STRIPER   *n* pl. -S a food and game fish

STRIPIER   comparative of stripy

STRIPIEST   superlative of stripy

STRIPING   *n* pl. -S the stripes marked or painted on something

STRIPPED   a past tense of strip

STRIPPER   *n* pl. -S one that strips

STRIPPING   present participle of strip

STRIPT   a past tense of strip

STRIPY   *adj* STRIPIER, STRIPIEST marked with stripes

STRIVE   *v* STROVE or STRIVED, STRIVEN, STRIVING, STRIVES to exert much effort or energy

STRIVER   *n* pl. -S one that strives

STROBE   *n* pl. -S a device that produces brief, high-intensity flashes of light

STROBIC   *adj* spinning

STROBIL   *n* pl. -S strobile

STROBILA   *n* pl. -LAE the entire body of a tapeworm

STROBILE   *n* pl. -S the conical, multiple fruit of certain trees

STROBILI   *n/pl* strobiles

STRODE   a past tense of stride

STROKE   *v* STROKED, STROKING, STROKES to rub gently

STROKER   *n* pl. -S one that strokes

STROLL   *v* -ED, -ING, -S to walk in a leisurely manner

STROLLER   *n* pl. -S one that strolls

STROMA   *n* pl. -MATA the substance that forms the framework of an organ or cell **STROMAL** *adj*

STRONG   *adj* STRONGER, STRONGEST having great strength **STRONGLY** *adv*

STRONGYL   *n* pl. -S a parasitic worm

STRONTIA   *n* pl. -S a chemical compound **STRONTIC** *adj*

STROOK   a past tense of strike

STROP   *v* STROPPED, STROPPING, STROPS to sharpen on a strip of leather

STROPHE   *n* pl. -S a part of an ancient Greek choral ode **STROPHIC** *adj*

STROUD   *n* pl. -S a coarse woolen blanket

STROVE   a past tense of strive

STROW   *v* STROWED, STROWN, STROWING, STROWS to strew

STROY   *v* -ED, -ING, -S to destroy

STROYER   *n* pl. -S one that stroys

STRUCK   a past tense of strike

STRUCKEN   a past participle of strike

STRUDEL   *n* pl. -S a type of pastry

STRUGGLE   *v* -GLED, -GLING, -GLES to make strenuous efforts against opposition

STRUM   *v* STRUMMED, STRUMMING, STRUMS to play a stringed instrument by running the fingers lightly across the strings

STRUMA   *n* pl. -MAE or -MAS scrofula

STRUMMER   *n* pl. -S one that strums

STRUMMING   present participle of strum

STRUMOSE   *adj* having a struma

STRUMOUS   *adj* having or pertaining to a struma

STRUMPET   *n* pl. -S a prostitute

STRUNG   a past tense of string

STRUNT   *v* -ED, -ING, -S to strut

STRUT   *v* STRUTTED, STRUTTING, STRUTS to walk with a pompous air

STRUTTER   *n* pl. -S one that struts

STUB   *v* STUBBED, STUBBING, STUBS to strike accidentally against a projecting object

STUBBIER   comparative of stubby

STUBBIEST   superlative of stubby

STUBBILY   *adv* in a stubby manner

STUBBING   present participle of stub

STUBBLE   *n* pl. -S a short, rough growth of beard **STUBBLED** *adj*

STUBBLY   *adj* -BLIER, -BLIEST covered with stubble

STUBBORN   *adj* unyielding

STUBBY   *adj* -BIER, -BIEST short and thick

STUCCO   *v* -ED, -ING, -ES or -S to coat with a type of plaster

STUCCOER   *n* pl. -S one that stuccoes

STUCK   past tense of stick

STUD   *v* STUDDED, STUDDING, STUDS to set thickly with small projections

STUDBOOK   *n* pl. -S a record of the pedigree of purebred animals

STUDDIE   *n* pl. -S an anvil

STUDDING   *n* pl. -S the framework of a wall

STUDENT   *n* pl. -S a person formally engaged in learning

STUDFISH   *n* pl. -ES a freshwater fish

STUDIED   past tense of study

STUDIER   *n* pl. -S one that studies

STUDIES   present 3d person sing. of study

STUDIO   *n* pl. -DIOS an artist's workroom

STUDIOUS   *adj* given to study

STUDWORK   *n* pl. -S studding

STUDY   *v* STUDIED, STUDYING, STUDIES to apply the mind to the acquisition of knowledge

STUFF   *v* -ED, -ING, -S to fill or pack tightly

STUFFER   *n* pl. -S one that stuffs

STUFFING   *n* pl. -S material with which something is stuffed

STUFFY   *adj* STUFFIER, STUFFIEST poorly ventilated **STUFFILY** *adv*

STUIVER   *n* pl. -S stiver

STULL   *n* pl. -S a supporting timber in a mine

STULTIFY   *v* -FIED, -FYING, -FIES to cause to appear absurd

STUM   *v* STUMMED, STUMMING, STUMS to increase the fermentation of by adding grape juice

STUMBLE   *v* -BLED, -BLING, -BLES to miss one's step in walking or running

STUMBLER   *n* pl. -S one that stumbles

STUMMED   past tense of stum

STUMMING   present participle of stum

STUMP   *v* -ED, -ING, -S to baffle

STUMPAGE   *n* pl. -S uncut marketable timber

STUMPER   *n* pl. -S a baffling question

STUMPY   *adj* STUMPIER, STUMPIEST short and thick

STUN   *v* STUNNED, STUNNING, STUNS to render senseless or incapable of action

STUNG   past tense of sting

STUNK   a past tense of stink

STUNNED   past tense of stun

STUNNER   *n* pl. -S one that stuns

STUNNING   *adj* strikingly beautiful or attractive

STUNSAIL   *n* pl. -S a type of sail

STUNT   *v* -ED, -ING, -S to hinder the normal growth of

STUPA   *n* pl. -S a Buddhist shrine

STUPE   *n* pl. -S a medicated cloth to be applied to a wound

STUPEFY   *v* -FIED, -FYING, -FIES to dull the senses of

STUPID   *adj* -PIDER, -PIDEST mentally slow **STUPIDLY** *adv*

STUPID   *n* pl. -S a stupid person

STUPOR   *n* pl. -S a state of reduced sensibility

STURDY   *adj* -DIER, -DIEST strong and durable **STURDILY** *adv*

STURDY   *n* pl. -DIES a disease of sheep **STURDIED** *adj*

STURGEON   *n* pl. -S an edible fish

STURT   *n* pl. -S contention

STUTTER   *v* -ED, -ING, -S to speak with spasmodic repetition

STY   *v* STIED or STYED, STYING, STIES to keep in a pigpen

STYE   *n* pl. -S an inflamed swelling of the eyelid

STYGIAN   *adj* gloomy

STYLAR   *adj* pertaining to a stylus

STYLATE   *adj* bearing a stylet

STYLE   *v* STYLED, STYLING, STYLES to name

STYLER   *n* pl. -S one that styles

STYLET   *n* pl. -S a small, stiff organ or appendage of certain animals

STYLI   a pl. of stylus

STYLING   *n* pl. -S the way in which something is styled

STYLISE   *v* -ISED, -ISING, -ISES to stylize

STYLISER   *n* pl. -S one that stylises

STYLISH   *adj* fashionable

STYLISING   present participle of stylise

STYLIST   *n* pl. -S one who is a master of a literary or rhetorical style

STYLITE   *n* pl. -S an early Christian ascetic **STYLITIC** *adj*

STYLIZE   *v* -IZED, -IZING, -IZES to make conventional

STYLIZER   *n* pl. -S one that stylizes

STYLOID   *adj* slender and pointed

STYLUS   *n* pl. -LI or -LUSES a pointed instrument for writing, marking, or engraving

STYMIE   *v* -MIED, -MIEING, -MIES to thwart

STYMY   *v* -MIED, -MYING, -MIES to stymie

STYPSIS   *n* pl. -SISES the use of a styptic

STYPTIC   *n* pl. -S a substance used to check bleeding

STYRAX   *n* pl. -ES storax

STYRENE   *n* pl. -S a liquid hydrocarbon

SUABLE   *adj* capable of being sued **SUABLY** *adv*

SUASION   *n* pl. -S persuasion **SUASIVE, SUASORY** *adj*

SUAVE   *adj* SUAVER, SUAVEST smoothly affable and polite **SUAVELY** *adv*

SUAVITY   *n* pl. -TIES the state of being suave

SUB   *v* SUBBED, SUBBING, SUBS to act as a substitute

SUBA   *n* pl. -S subah

SUBABBOT   *n* pl. -S a subordinate abbot

SUBACID   *adj* slightly sour

SUBACRID   *adj* somewhat acrid

SUBACUTE   *adj* somewhat acute

SUBADAR   *n* pl. -S subahdar

SUBADULT   *n* pl. -S an individual approaching adulthood

SUBAGENT   *n* pl. -S a subordinate agent

SUBAH   *n* pl. -S a province of India

SUBAHDAR   *n* pl. -S a governor of a subah

SUBALAR   *adj* somewhat alar

SUBAREA   *n* pl. -S a subdivision of an area

SUBARID   *adj* somewhat arid

SUBATOM   *n* pl. -S a component of an atom

SUBAXIAL   *adj* somewhat axial

SUBBASE   *n* pl. -S the lowest part of a base

SUBBASS   *n* pl. -ES a pedal stop producing the lowest tones of an organ

SUBBED   past tense of sub

SUBBING   *n* pl. -S a thin coating on the support of a photographic film

SUBBREED   *n* pl. -S a distinguishable strain within a breed

SUBCAUSE   *n* pl. -S a subordinate cause

SUBCELL   *n* pl. -S a subdivision of a cell

SUBCHIEF   *n* pl. -S a subordinate chief

SUBCLAN   *n* pl. -S a subdivision of a clan

SUBCLASS   *v* -ED, -ING, -ES to place in a subdivision of a class

SUBCLERK   *n* pl. -S a subordinate clerk

SUBCOOL   *v* -ED, -ING, -S to cool below the freezing point without solidification

SUBCUTIS   *n* pl. -CUTES or -CUTISES the deeper part of the dermis

SUBDEAN   *n* pl. -S a subordinate dean

SUBDEB   *n* pl. -S a girl the year before she becomes a debutante

SUBDEPOT   *n* pl. -S a military depot that operates under the jurisdiction of another depot

SUBDUAL   *n* pl. -S the act of subduing

SUBDUCE   *v* -DUCED, -DUCING, -DUCES to take away

SUBDUCT   *v* -ED, -ING, -S to subduce

SUBDUE   *v* -DUED, -DUING, -DUES to bring under control

SUBDUER   *n* pl. -S one that subdues

SUBECHO   *n* pl. -ECHOES an inferior echo

SUBEDIT   *v* -ED, -ING, -S to act as the assistant editor of

SUBENTRY   *n* pl. -TRIES an entry made under a more general entry

SUBEPOCH   *n* pl. -S a subdivision of an epoch

SUBER   *n* pl. -S phellem

SUBERECT   *adj* nearly erect

SUBERIC   *adj* pertaining to cork

SUBERIN   *n* pl. -S a substance found in cork cells

SUBERISE   *v* -ISED, -ISING, -ISES to suberize

SUBERIZE   *v* -IZED, -IZING, -IZES to convert into cork tissue

SUBEROSE   *adj* corky

SUBEROUS   *adj* suberose

SUBFIELD   *n* pl. -S a subset of a mathematical field that is itself a field

SUBFIX _n_ pl. -ES a distinguishing symbol or letter written below another character

SUBFLOOR _n_ pl. -S a rough floor laid as a base for a finished floor

SUBFLUID _adj_ somewhat fluid

SUBFUSC _adj_ dark in color

SUBGENUS _n_ pl. -GENERA or -GENUSES a subdivision of a genus

SUBGRADE _n_ pl. -S a surface on which a pavement is placed

SUBGROUP _n_ pl. -S a distinct group within a group

SUBGUM _adj_ prepared with mixed vegetables

SUBHEAD _n_ pl. -S the heading of a subdivision

SUBHUMAN _n_ pl. -S one that is less than human

SUBHUMID _adj_ somewhat humid

SUBIDEA _n_ pl. -S an inferior idea

SUBINDEX _n_ pl. -DEXES or -DICES a subfix

SUBITEM _n_ pl. -S an item that forms a subdivision of a larger topic

SUBITO _adv_ quickly — used as a musical direction

SUBJECT _v_ -ED, -ING, -S to cause to experience

SUBJOIN _v_ -ED, -ING, -S to add at the end

SUBLATE _v_ -LATED, -LATING, -LATES to cancel

SUBLEASE _v_ -LEASED, -LEASING, -LEASES to sublet

SUBLET _v_ -LET, -LETTING, -LETS to rent leased property to another

SUBLEVEL _n_ pl. -S a lower level

SUBLIME _adj_ -LIMER, -LIMEST of elevated or noble quality

SUBLIME _v_ -LIMED, -LIMING, -LIMES to make sublime

SUBLIMER _n_ pl. -S one that sublimes

SUBLIMEST superlative of sublime

SUBLIMING present participle of sublime

SUBMERGE _v_ -MERGED, -MERGING, -MERGES to place below the surface of a liquid

SUBMERSE _v_ -MERSED, -MERSING, -MERSES to submerge

SUBMISS _adj_ inclined to submit

SUBMIT _v_ -MITTED, -MITTING, -MITS to yield to the power of another

SUBNASAL _adj_ situated under the nose

SUBNODAL _adj_ situated under a node

SUBOPTIC _adj_ situated under the eyes

SUBORAL _adj_ situated under the mouth

SUBORDER _n_ pl. -S a category of related families within an order

SUBORN _v_ -ED, -ING, -S to induce to commit perjury

SUBORNER _n_ pl. -S one that suborns

SUBOVAL _adj_ nearly oval

SUBOVATE _adj_ nearly ovate

SUBOXIDE _n_ pl. -S an oxide containing relatively little oxygen

SUBPAR _adj_ below par

SUBPART _n_ pl. -S a subdivision of a part

SUBPENA _v_ -ED, -ING, -S to subpoena

SUBPHYLA _n/pl_ divisions within a phylum

SUBPLOT _n_ pl. -S a secondary literary plot

SUBPOENA _v_ -ED, -ING, -S to summon with a type of judicial writ

SUBPOLAR _adj_ situated just outside the polar circles

SUBPUBIC _adj_ situated under the pubis

SUBRACE _n_ pl. -S a subdivision of a race

SUBRENT _n_ pl. -S rent from a subtenant

SUBRING _n_ pl. -S a subset of a mathematical ring that is itself a ring

SUBRULE _n_ pl. -S a subordinate rule

SUBSALE _n_ pl. -S a resale of purchased goods

SUBSECT _n_ pl. -S a sect directly derived from another

SUBSERE _n_ pl. -S a type of ecological succession

SUBSERVE _v_ -SERVED, -SERVING, -SERVES to serve to promote

SUBSET _n_ pl. -S a mathematical set contained within a larger set

SUBSHAFT _n_ pl. -S a shaft that is beneath another shaft

SUBSHRUB _n_ pl. -S a low shrub

SUBSIDE _v_ -SIDED, -SIDING, -SIDES to sink to a lower or normal level

SUBSIDER _n_ pl. -S one that subsides

SUBSIDY _n_ pl. -DIES a grant or contribution of money

SUBSIST *v* -ED, -ING, -S to continue to exist

SUBSOIL *v* -ED, -ING, -S to plow so as to turn up the subsoil (the layer of earth beneath the surface soil)

SUBSOLAR *adj* situated directly beneath the sun

SUBSONIC *adj* moving at a speed less than that of sound

SUBSPACE *n* pl. -S a subset of a mathematical space

SUBSTAGE *n* pl. -S a part of a microscope for supporting accessories

SUBSUME *v* -SUMED, -SUMING, -SUMES to classify within a larger category

SUBTEEN *n* pl. -S a person approaching the teenage years

SUBTEND *v* -ED, -ING, -S to extend under or opposite to

SUBTEXT *n* pl. -S written or printed matter under a more general text

SUBTILE *adj* -TILER, -TILEST subtle

SUBTILTY *n* pl. -TIES subtlety

SUBTITLE *v* -TLED, -TLING, -TLES to give a secondary title to

SUBTLE *adj* -TLER, -TLEST so slight as to be difficult to detect **SUBTLY** *adj*

SUBTLETY *n* pl. -TIES the state of being subtle

SUBTONE *n* pl. -S a low or subdued tone

SUBTONIC *n* pl. -S a type of musical tone

SUBTOPIC *n* pl. -S a secondary topic

SUBTOTAL *v* -TALED, -TALING, -TALS or -TALLED, -TALLING, -TALS to total a portion of

SUBTRACT *v* -ED, -ING, -S to take away

SUBTRIBE *n* pl. -S a subdivision of a tribe

SUBTUNIC *n* pl. -S a tunic worn under another tunic

SUBTYPE *n* pl. -S a type that is subordinate to or included in another type

SUBULATE *adj* slender and tapering to a point

SUBUNIT *n* pl. -S a unit that is a part of a larger unit

SUBURB *n* pl. -S a residential area adjacent to a city **SUBURBED** *adj*

SUBURBAN *n* pl. -S one who lives in a suburb

SUBURBIA *n* pl. -S the suburbs of a city

SUBVENE *v* -VENED, -VENING, -VENES to arrive or occur as a support or relief

SUBVERT *v* -ED, -ING, -S to destroy completely

SUBVICAR *n* pl. -S a subordinate vicar

SUBVIRAL *adj* pertaining to a part of a virus

SUBVOCAL *adj* mentally formulated as words

SUBWAY *n* pl. -WAYS an underground railroad

SUBZONE *n* pl. -S a subdivision of a zone

SUCCAH *n* pl. -CAHS or -COTH sukkah

SUCCEED *v* -ED, -ING, -S to accomplish something desired or intended

SUCCESS *n* pl. -ES the attainment of something desired or intended

SUCCINCT *adj* -CINCTER, -CINCTEST clearly expressed in few words

SUCCINIC *adj* pertaining to amber

SUCCINYL *n* pl. -S a univalent radical

SUCCOR *v* -ED, -ING, -S to go to the aid of

SUCCORER *n* pl. -S one that succors

SUCCORY *n* pl. -RIES chicory

SUCCOTH a pl. of succah

SUCCOUR *v* -ED, -ING, -S to succor

SUCCUBA *n* pl. -BAE a succubus

SUCCUBUS *n* pl. -BI or -BUSES a female demon

SUCCUMB *v* -ED, -ING, -S to yield to superior force

SUCCUSS *v* -ED, -ING, -ES to shake violently

SUCH *adj* of that kind

SUCHLIKE *adj* of a similar kind

SUCHNESS *n* pl. -ES essential or characteristic quality

SUCK *v* -ED, -ING, -S to draw in by establishing a partial vacuum

SUCKER *v* -ED, -ING, -S to strip of lower shoots or branches

SUCKFISH *n* pl. -ES a remora

SUCKLE *v* -LED, -LING, -LES to give milk to from the breast

SUCKLER *n* pl. -S one that suckles

SUCKLESS *adj* having no juice

SUCKLING n pl. -S a young mammal that has not been weaned

SUCRASE n pl. -S an enzyme

SUCRE n pl. -S a monetary unit of Ecuador

SUCROSE n pl. -S a type of sugar

SUCTION n pl. -S the act of sucking

SUDARIUM n pl. -IA a cloth for wiping the face

SUDARY n pl. -RIES sudarium

SUDATION n pl. -S excessive sweating

SUDATORY n pl. -RIES a hot-air bath for inducing sweating

SUDD n pl. -S a floating mass of vegetation

SUDDEN adj happening quickly and without warning **SUDDENLY** adv

SUDDEN n pl. -S a sudden occurrence

SUDOR n pl. -S sweat **SUDORAL** adj

SUDS v -ED, -ING, -ES to wash in soapy water

SUDSER n pl. -S one that sudses

SUDSLESS adj having no suds

SUDSY adj SUDSIER, SUDSIEST foamy

SUE v SUED, SUING, SUES to institute legal proceedings against

SUEDE v SUEDED, SUEDING, SUEDES to finish leather with a soft, napped surface

SUER n pl. -S one that sues

SUET n pl. -S the hard, fatty tissue around the kidneys of cattle and sheep **SUETY** adj

SUFFARI n pl. -S a safari

SUFFER v -ED, -ING, -S to feel pain or distress

SUFFERER n pl. -S one that suffers

SUFFICE v -FICED, -FICING, -FICES to be adequate

SUFFICER n pl. -S one that suffices

SUFFIX v -ED, -ING, -ES to add as a suffix (a form affixed to the end of a root word)

SUFFIXAL adj pertaining to or being a suffix

SUFFLATE v -FLATED, -FLATING, -FLATES to inflate

SUFFRAGE n pl. -S the right to vote

SUFFUSE v -FUSED, -FUSING, -FUSES to spread through or over

SUGAR v -ED, -ING, -S to cover with sugar (a sweet carbohydrate)

SUGARY adj -ARIER, -ARIEST containing or resembling sugar

SUGGEST v -ED, -ING, -S to bring or put forward for consideration

SUGH v -ED, -ING, -S to sough

SUICIDAL adj self-destructive

SUICIDE v -CIDED, -CIDING, -CIDES to kill oneself intentionally

SUING present participle of sue

SUINT n pl. -S a natural grease found in the wool of sheep

SUIT v -ED, -ING, -S to be appropriate to

SUITABLE adj appropriate **SUITABLY** adv

SUITCASE n pl. -S a flat, rectangular piece of luggage

SUITE n pl. -S a series of things forming a unit

SUITING n pl. -S fabric for making suits

SUITLIKE adj resembling a suit (a set of garments)

SUITOR n pl. -S one that is courting a woman

SUKIYAKI n pl. -S a Japanese dish

SUKKAH n pl. -KAHS or -KOTH a temporary shelter in which meals are eaten during a Jewish festival

SULCATE adj having long, narrow furrows

SULCATED adj sulcate

SULCUS n pl. -CI furrow

SULDAN n pl. -S soldan

SULFA n pl. -S a bacteria-inhibiting drug

SULFATE v -FATED, -FATING, -FATES to treat with sulfuric acid

SULFID n pl. -S sulfide

SULFIDE n pl. -S a sulfur compound

SULFINYL n pl. -S a bivalent radical

SULFITE n pl. -S a chemical salt **SULFITIC** adj

SULFO adj sulfonic

SULFONAL n pl. -S a sulfone used as a sedative

SULFONE n pl. -S a sulfur compound

SULFONIC adj containing a certain univalent radical

SULFONYL n pl. -S a bivalent radical

SULFUR	*v* -ED, -ING, -S to treat with sulfur (a nonmetallic element)
SULFURET	*v* -RETED, -RETING, -RETS or -RETTED, -RETTING, -RETS to treat with sulfur
SULFURIC	*adj* pertaining to sulfur
SULFURY	*adj* resembling sulfur
SULFURYL	*n* pl. -S sulfonyl
SULK	*v* -ED, -ING, -S to be sulky
SULKER	*n* pl. -S one that sulks
SULKY	*adj* SULKIER, SULKIEST sullenly aloof or withdrawn **SULKILY** *adv*
SULKY	*n* pl. SULKIES a light horse-drawn vehicle
SULLAGE	*n* pl. -S sewage
SULLEN	*adj* -LENER, -LENEST showing a brooding ill humor or resentment **SULLENLY** *adv*
SULLY	*v* -LIED, -LYING, -LIES to soil
SULPHA	*n* pl. -S sulfa
SULPHATE	*v* -PHATED, -PHATING, -PHATES to sulfate
SULPHID	*n* pl. -S sulfide
SULPHIDE	*n* pl. -S sulfide
SULPHITE	*n* pl. -S sulfite
SULPHONE	*n* pl. -S sulfone
SULPHUR	*v* -ED, -ING, -S to sulfur
SULPHURY	*adj* sulfury
SULTAN	*n* pl. -S the ruler of a Muslim country **SULTANIC** *adj*
SULTANA	*n* pl. -S a sultan's wife
SULTRY	*adj* -TRIER, -TRIEST very hot and humid **SULTRILY** *adv*
SUM	*v* SUMMED, SUMMING, SUMS to add into one total
SUMAC	*n* pl. -S a flowering tree or shrub
SUMACH	*n* pl. -S sumac
SUMLESS	*adj* too large for calculation
SUMMA	*n* pl. -MAE or -MAS a comprehensive work covering a specific subject
SUMMABLE	*adj* capable of being summed
SUMMAND	*n* pl. -S an addend
SUMMARY	*n* pl. -RIES a condensation of the substance of a larger work
SUMMATE	*v* -MATED, -MATING, -MATES to sum
SUMMED	past tense of sum
SUMMER	*v* -ED, -ING, -S to pass the summer (the warmest season of the year)
SUMMERLY	*adj* summery
SUMMERY	*adj* -MERIER, -MERIEST characteristic of summer
SUMMING	present participle of sum
SUMMIT	*n* pl. -S the highest point **SUMMITAL** *adj*
SUMMITRY	*n* pl. -RIES the use of conferences between chiefs of state for international negotiation
SUMMON	*v* -ED, -ING, -S to order to appear
SUMMONER	*n* pl. -S one that summons
SUMMONS	*v* -ED, -ING, -ES to summon with a court order
SUMO	*n* pl. -MOS a Japanese form of wrestling
SUMP	*n* pl. -S a low area serving as a drain or receptacle for liquids
SUMPTER	*n* pl. -S a pack animal
SUMPWEED	*n* pl. -S a marsh plant
SUN	*v* SUNNED, SUNNING, SUNS to expose to the sun (the star around which the earth revolves)
SUNBACK	*adj* cut low to expose the back to sunlight
SUNBAKED	*adj* baked by the sun
SUNBATH	*n* pl. -S an exposure to sunlight
SUNBATHE	*v* -BATHED, -BATHING, -BATHES to take a sunbath
SUNBEAM	*n* pl. -S a beam of sunlight
SUNBIRD	*n* pl. -S a tropical bird
SUNBOW	*n* pl. -S an arc of spectral colors formed by the sun shining through a mist
SUNBURN	*v* -BURNED or -BURNT, -BURNING, -BURNS to burn or discolor from exposure to the sun
SUNBURST	*n* pl. -S a burst of sunlight
SUNDAE	*n* pl. -S a dish of ice cream served with a topping
SUNDER	*v* -ED, -ING, -S to break apart
SUNDERER	*n* pl. -S one that sunders
SUNDEW	*n* pl. -S a marsh plant
SUNDIAL	*n* pl. -S a type of time-telling device
SUNDOG	*n* pl. -S a small rainbow

SUNDOWN	*n* pl. -S sunset
SUNDRIES	*n/pl* miscellaneous items
SUNDROPS	*n* pl. SUNDROPS a flowering plant
SUNDRY	*adj* miscellaneous
SUNFAST	*adj* resistant to fading by the sun
SUNFISH	*n* pl. -ES a marine fish
SUNG	past participle of sing
SUNGLASS	*n* pl. -ES a lens for concentrating the sun's rays in order to produce heat
SUNGLOW	*n* pl. -S a glow in the sky caused by the sun
SUNK	a past participle of sink
SUNKEN	a past participle of sink
SUNKET	*n* pl. -S a tidbit
SUNLAMP	*n* pl. -S a lamp that radiates ultraviolet rays
SUNLAND	*n* pl. -S an area marked by a great amount of sunshine
SUNLESS	*adj* having no sunlight
SUNLIGHT	*n* pl. -S the light of the sun
SUNLIKE	*adj* resembling the sun
SUNLIT	*adj* lighted by the sun
SUNN	*n* pl. -S an East Indian shrub
SUNNA	*n* pl. -S the body of traditional Muslim law
SUNNED	past tense of sun
SUNNING	present participle of sun
SUNNY	*adj* -NIER, -NIEST filled with sunlight **SUNNILY** *adv*
SUNRISE	*n* pl. -S the ascent of the sun above the horizon in the morning
SUNROOF	*n* pl. -S an automobile roof having an openable panel
SUNROOM	*n* pl. -S a room built to admit a great amount of sunlight
SUNSCALD	*n* pl. -S an injury of woody plants caused by the sun
SUNSET	*n* pl. -S the descent of the sun below the horizon in the evening
SUNSHADE	*n* pl. -S something used as a protection from the sun
SUNSHINE	*n* pl. -S the light of the sun **SUNSHINY** *adj*
SUNSPOT	*n* pl. -S a dark spot on the surface of the sun
SUNSTONE	*n* pl. -S a variety of quartz

SUNSUIT	*n* pl. -S an outfit worn for sunbathing
SUNTAN	*n* pl. -S a brown color on the skin produced by exposure to the sun
SUNUP	*n* pl. -S sunrise
SUNWARD	*adv* toward the sun
SUNWARDS	*adv* sunward
SUNWISE	*adv* from left to right
SUP	*v* SUPPED, SUPPING, SUPS to eat supper
SUPE	*n* pl. -S an actor without a speaking part
SUPER	*v* -ED, -ING, -S to reinforce with a thin cotton mesh, as a book
SUPERADD	*n* pl. -ED, -ING, -S to add further
SUPERB	*adj* -PERBER, -PERBEST of excellent quality **SUPERBLY** *adv*
SUPEREGO	*n* pl. -EGOS a part of the psyche
SUPERFIX	*n* pl. -ES a recurrent pattern of stress in speech
SUPERIOR	*n* pl. -S one of higher rank, quality, or authority than another
SUPERJET	*n* pl. -S a type of jet airplane
SUPERLIE	*v* -LAY, -LAIN, -LYING, -LIES to lie above
SUPERMAN	*n* pl. -MEN a hypothetical superior man
SUPERNAL	*adj* pertaining to the sky
SUPERSEX	*n* pl. -ES a type of sterile organism
SUPERTAX	*n* pl. -ES an additional tax
SUPINATE	*v* -NATED, -NATING, -NATES to turn so that the palm is facing upward
SUPINE	*n* pl. -S a Latin verbal noun
SUPINELY	*adv* in an inactive manner
SUPPED	past tense of sup
SUPPER	*n* pl. -S an evening meal
SUPPING	present participle of sup
SUPPLANT	*v* -ED, -ING, -S to take the place of
SUPPLE	*adj* -PLER, -PLEST pliant **SUPPLELY** *adv*
SUPPLE	*v* -PLED, -PLING, -PLES to make supple
SUPPLIER	*n* pl. -S one that supplies
SUPPLY	*v* -PLIED, -PLYING, -PLIES to furnish with what is needed

SUPPORT	*v* -ED, -ING, -S to hold up or add strength to
SUPPOSAL	*n* pl. -S something supposed
SUPPOSE	*v* -POSED, -POSING, -POSES to assume to be true
SUPPOSER	*n* pl. -S one that supposes
SUPPRESS	*v* -ED, -ING, -ES to put an end to forcibly
SUPRA	*adv* above
SUPREME	*adj* -PREMER, -PREMEST highest in power or authority
SURA	*n* pl. -S a chapter of the Koran
SURAH	*n* pl. -S a silk fabric
SURAL	*adj* pertaining to the calf of the leg
SURBASE	*n* pl. -S a molding or border above the base of a structure **SURBASED** *adj*
SURCEASE	*v* -CEASED, -CEASING, -CEASES to cease
SURCOAT	*n* pl. -S an outer coat or cloak
SURD	*n* pl. -S a voiceless speech sound
SURE	*adj* SURER, SUREST free from doubt
SUREFIRE	*adj* sure to meet expectations
SURELY	*adv* certainly
SURENESS	*n* pl. -ES the state of being sure
SURER	comparative of sure
SUREST	superlative of sure
SURETY	*n* pl. -TIES sureness
SURF	*v* -ED, -ING, -S to ride breaking waves on a long, narrow board **SURFABLE** *adj*
SURFACE	*v* -FACED, -FACING, -FACES to apply an outer layer to
SURFACER	*n* pl. -S one that surfaces
SURFBIRD	*n* pl. -S a shore bird
SURFBOAT	*n* pl. -S a strong rowboat
SURFEIT	*v* -ED, -ING, -S to supply to excess
SURFER	*n* pl. -S one that surfs
SURFFISH	*n* pl. -ES a marine fish
SURFIER	comparative of surfy
SURFIEST	superlative of surfy
SURFING	*n* pl. -S the act or sport of riding the surf (breaking waves)
SURFLIKE	*adj* resembling breaking waves
SURFY	*adj* SURFIER, SURFIEST abounding in breaking waves
SURGE	*v* SURGED, SURGING, SURGES to move in a swelling manner
SURGEON	*n* pl. -S one who practices surgery
SURGER	*n* pl. -S one that surges
SURGERY	*n* pl. -GERIES the treatment of medical problems by operation
SURGICAL	*adj* pertaining to surgery
SURGING	present participle of surge
SURGY	*adj* surging
SURICATE	*n* pl. -S a burrowing mammal
SURLY	*adj* -LIER, -LIEST sullenly rude **SURLILY** *adv*
SURMISE	*v* -MISED, -MISING, -MISES to infer with little evidence
SURMISER	*n* pl. -S one that surmises
SURMOUNT	*v* -ED, -ING, -S to get over or across
SURNAME	*v* -NAMED, -NAMING, -NAMES to give a family name to
SURNAMER	*n* pl. -S one that surnames
SURPASS	*v* -ED, -ING, -ES to go beyond
SURPLICE	*n* pl. -S a loose-fitting vestment
SURPLUS	*n* pl. -ES an excess
SURPRINT	*v* -ED, -ING, -S to print over something already printed
SURPRISE	*v* -PRISED, -PRISING, -PRISES to come upon suddenly and unexpectedly
SURPRIZE	*v* -PRIZED, -PRIZING, -PRIZES to surprise
SURRA	*n* pl. -S a disease of domestic animals
SURREAL	*adj* having dreamlike qualities
SURREY	*n* pl. -REYS a light carriage
SURROUND	*v* -ED, -ING, -S to extend completely around
SURROYAL	*n* pl. -S the topmost prong of a stag's antler
SURTAX	*v* -ED, -ING, -ES to assess with an extra tax
SURTOUT	*n* pl. -S a close-fitting overcoat
SURVEIL	*v* -ED, -ING, -S to watch closely
SURVEY	*v* -ED, -ING, -S to determine the boundaries, area, or elevations of by measuring angles and distances
SURVEYOR	*n* pl. -S one that surveys land

SURVIVAL	*n* pl. -S a living or continuing longer than another person or thing
SURVIVE	*v* -VIVED, -VIVING, -VIVES to remain in existence
SURVIVER	*n* pl. -S survivor
SURVIVOR	*n* pl. -S one that survives
SUSLIK	*n* pl. -S a Eurasian rodent
SUSPECT	*v* -ED, -ING, -S to think guilty on slight evidence
SUSPEND	*v* -ED, -ING, -S to cause to stop for a period
SUSPENSE	*n* pl. -S a state of mental uncertainty or excitement
SUSPIRE	*v* -PIRED, -PIRING, -PIRES to sigh
SUSTAIN	*v* -ED, -ING, -S to maintain by providing with food and drink
SUSURRUS	*n* pl. -ES a soft rustling sound
SUTLER	*n* pl. -S one that peddles goods to soldiers
SUTRA	*n* pl. -S a Hindu aphorism
SUTTA	*n* pl. -S sutra
SUTTEE	*n* pl. -S a Hindu widow cremated on her husband's funeral pile to show her devotion to him
SUTURAL	*adj* pertaining to the line of junction between two bones
SUTURE	*v* -TURED, -TURING, -TURES to unite by sewing
SUZERAIN	*n* pl. -S a feudal lord
SVARAJ	*n* pl. -ES swaraj
SVEDBERG	*n* pl. -S a unit of time
SVELTE	*adj* SVELTER, SVELTEST gracefully slender **SVELTELY** *adv*
SWAB	*v* SWABBED, SWABBING, SWABS to clean with a large mop
SWABBER	*n* pl. -S one that swabs
SWABBIE	*n* pl. -S a sailor
SWABBING	present participle of swab
SWABBY	*n* pl. -BIES swabbie
SWADDLE	*v* -DLED, -DLING, -DLES to wrap in bandages
SWAG	*v* SWAGGED, SWAGGING, SWAGS to sway
SWAGE	*v* SWAGED, SWAGING, SWAGES to shape with a hammering tool
SWAGER	*n* pl. -S one that swages
SWAGGED	past tense of swag
SWAGGER	*v* -ED, -ING, -S to walk with a pompous air
SWAGGING	present participle of swag
SWAGING	present participle of swage
SWAGMAN	*n* pl. -MEN a hobo
SWAIL	*n* pl. -S swale
SWAIN	*n* pl. -S a country boy **SWAINISH** *adj*
SWALE	*n* pl. -S a tract of low, marshy ground
SWALLOW	*v* -ED, -ING, -S to take through the mouth and esophagus into the stomach
SWAM	past tense of swim
SWAMI	*n* pl. -S a Hindu religious teacher
SWAMIES	pl. of swamy
SWAMP	*v* -ED, -ING, -S to inundate
SWAMPER	*n* pl. -S one that lives in a swampy area
SWAMPISH	*adj* swampy
SWAMPY	*adj* SWAMPIER, SWAMPIEST marshy
SWAMY	*n* pl. -MIES swami
SWAN	*v* SWANNED, SWANNING, SWANS to swear
SWANG	a past tense of swing
SWANHERD	*n* pl. -S one who tends swans (large aquatic birds)
SWANK	*adj* SWANKER, SWANKEST imposingly elegant
SWANK	*v* -ED, -ING, -S to swagger
SWANKY	*adj* SWANKIER, SWANKIEST swank **SWANKILY** *adv*
SWANLIKE	*adj* resembling a swan
SWANNED	past tense of swan
SWANNERY	*n* pl. -NERIES a place where swans are raised
SWANNING	present participle of swan
SWANPAN	*n* pl. -S a Chinese abacus
SWANSKIN	*n* pl. -S the skin of a swan
SWAP	*v* SWAPPED, SWAPPING, SWAPS to trade
SWAPPER	*n* pl. -S one that swaps
SWARAJ	*n* pl. -ES self-government in British India
SWARD	*v* -ED, -ING, -S to cover with turf

SWARE   a past tense of swear

SWARF   *n* pl. -S material removed by a cutting tool

SWARM   *v* -ED, -ING, -S to move in a large group

SWARMER   *n* pl. -S one that swarms

SWART   *adj* swarthy

SWARTH   *n* pl. -S turf

SWARTHY   *adj* -THIER, -THIEST having a dark complexion

SWARTY   *adj* swarthy

SWASH   *v* -ED, -ING, -ES to swagger

SWASHER   *n* pl. -S one that swashes

SWASTICA   *n* pl. -S swastika

SWASTIKA   *n* pl. -S a geometrical figure used as a symbol or ornament

SWAT   *v* SWATTED, SWATTING, SWATS to hit sharply

SWATCH   *n* pl. -ES a sample piece of cloth

SWATH   *n* pl. -S a row of cut grass or grain

SWATHE   *v* SWATHED, SWATHING, SWATHES to wrap in bandages

SWATHER   *n* pl. -S one that swathes

SWATTED   past tense of swat

SWATTER   *n* pl. -S one that swats

SWATTING   present participle of swat

SWAY   *v* -ED, -ING, -S to move slowly back and forth **SWAYABLE** *adj*

SWAYBACK   *n* pl. -S an abnormal sagging of the back

SWAYER   *n* pl. -S one that sways

SWAYFUL   *adj* capable of influencing

SWEAR   *v* SWORE or SWARE, SWORN, SWEARING, SWEARS to utter a solemn oath

SWEARER   *n* pl. -S one that swears

SWEAT   *v* -ED, -ING, -S to perspire

SWEATBOX   *n* pl. -ES a small enclosure in which one is made to sweat

SWEATER   *n* pl. -S a knitted outer garment

SWEATY   *adj* SWEATIER, SWEATIEST covered with perspiration **SWEATILY** *adv*

SWEDE   *n* pl. -S a rutabaga

SWEENY   *n* pl. -NIES atrophy of the shoulder muscles in horses

SWEEP   *v* SWEPT, SWEEPING, SWEEPS to clear or clean with a brush or broom

SWEEPER   *n* pl. -S one that sweeps

SWEEPING   *n* pl. -S the act of one that sweeps

SWEEPY   *adj* SWEEPIER, SWEEPIEST of wide range or scope

SWEER   *adj* lazy

SWEET   *adj* SWEETER, SWEETEST pleasing to the taste

SWEET   *n* pl. -S something that is sweet

SWEETEN   *v* -ED, -ING, -S to make sweet

SWEETIE   *n* pl. -S darling

SWEETING   *n* pl. -S a sweet apple

SWEETISH   *adj* somewhat sweet

SWEETLY   *adv* in a sweet manner

SWEETSOP   *n* pl. -S a tropical tree

SWELL   *v* SWELLED, SWOLLEN, SWELLING, SWELLS to increase in size or volume

SWELL   *adj* SWELLER, SWELLEST stylish

SWELLING   *n* pl. -S something that is swollen

SWELTER   *v* -ED, -ING, -S to suffer from oppressive heat

SWELTRY   *adj* -TRIER, -TRIEST oppressively hot

SWEPT   past tense of sweep

SWERVE   *v* SWERVED, SWERVING, SWERVES to turn aside suddenly from a straight course

SWERVER   *n* pl. -S one that swerves

SWEVEN   *n* pl. -S a dream or vision

SWIFT   *adj* SWIFTER, SWIFTEST moving with a great rate of motion

SWIFT   *n* pl. -S a fast-flying bird

SWIFTER   *n* pl. -S a rope on a ship

SWIFTLY   *adv* in a swift manner

SWIG   *v* SWIGGED, SWIGGING, SWIGS to drink deeply or rapidly

SWIGGER   *n* pl. -S one that swigs

SWILL   *v* -ED, -ING, -S to swig

SWILLER   *n* pl. -S one that swills

SWIM   *v* SWAM, SWUM, SWIMMING, SWIMS to propel oneself in water by natural means

SWIMMER   *n* pl. -S one that swims

SWIMMING	*n* pl. -S the act of one that swims
SWIMMY	*adj* -MIER, -MIEST dizzy **SWIMMILY** *adv*
SWIMSUIT	*n* pl. -S a bathing suit
SWINDLE	*v* -DLED, -DLING, -DLES to take money or property from by fraudulent means
SWINDLER	*n* pl. -S one that swindles
SWINE	*n* pl. SWINE a domestic pig
SWINEPOX	*n* pl. -ES a disease of swine
SWING	*v* SWUNG or SWANG, SWINGING, SWINGS to move freely back and forth
SWINGE	*v* SWINGED, SWINGEING, SWINGES to flog
SWINGER	*n* pl. -S one that swings
SWINGLE	*v* -GLED, -GLING, -GLES to scutch
SWINGY	*adj* SWINGIER, SWINGIEST marked by swinging
SWINISH	*adj* resembling or befitting swine
SWINK	*v* -ED, -ING, -S to toil
SWINNEY	*n* pl. -NEYS sweeny
SWIPE	*v* SWIPED, SWIPING, SWIPES to strike with a sweeping blow
SWIPLE	*n* pl. -S a part of a threshing device
SWIPPLE	*n* pl. -S swiple
SWIRL	*v* -ED, -ING, -S to move with a whirling motion
SWIRLY	*adj* SWIRLIER, SWIRLIEST swirling
SWISH	*v* -ED, -ING, -ES to move with a prolonged hissing sound
SWISHER	*n* pl. -S one that swishes
SWISHY	*adj* SWISHIER, SWISHIEST swishing
SWISS	*n* pl. -ES a cotton fabric
SWITCH	*v* -ED, -ING, -ES to beat with a flexible rod
SWITCHER	*n* pl. -S one that switches
SWITH	*adv* quickly
SWITHE	*adv* swith
SWITHER	*v* -ED, -ING, -S to doubt
SWITHLY	*adv* swith
SWIVE	*v* SWIVED, SWIVING, SWIVES to copulate with
SWIVEL	*v* -ELED, -ELING, -ELS or -ELLED, -ELLING, -ELS to turn on a pivoted support
SWIVET	*n* pl. -S a state of nervous excitement
SWIVING	present participle of swive
SWIZZLE	*v* -ZLED, -ZLING, -ZLES to drink excessively
SWIZZLER	*n* pl. -S one that swizzles
SWOB	*v* SWOBBED, SWOBBING, SWOBS to swab
SWOBBER	*n* pl. -S swabber
SWOLLEN	past participle of swell
SWOON	*v* -ED, -ING, -S to faint
SWOONER	*n* pl. -S one that swoons
SWOOP	*v* -ED, -ING, -S to make a sudden descent
SWOOPER	*n* pl. -S one that swoops
SWOOSH	*v* -ED, -ING, -ES to move with a rustling sound
SWOP	*v* SWOPPED, SWOPPING, SWOPS to swap
SWORD	*n* pl. -S a weapon having a long blade for cutting or thrusting
SWORDMAN	*n* pl. -MEN one skilled in the use of a sword
SWORE	a past tense of swear
SWORN	past participle of swear
SWOT	*v* SWOTTED, SWOTTING, SWOTS to swat
SWOTTER	*n* pl. -S one that swots
SWOUN	*v* -ED, -ING, -S to swoon
SWOUND	*v* -ED, -ING, -S to swoon
SWUM	past participle of swim
SWUNG	a past tense of swing
SYBARITE	*n* pl. -S a person devoted to pleasure and luxury
SYBO	*n* pl. -BOES the cibol
SYCAMINE	*n* pl. -S the mulberry tree
SYCAMORE	*n* pl. -S a North American tree
SYCE	*n* pl. -S a male servant in India
SYCEE	*n* pl. -S fine uncoined silver formerly used in China as money
SYCOMORE	*n* pl. -S sycamore
SYCONIUM	*n* pl. -NIA a fleshy multiple fruit
SYCOSIS	*n* pl. -COSES an inflammatory disease of the hair follicles
SYENITE	*n* pl. -S an igneous rock **SYENITIC** *adj*

SYKE   *n* pl. -S a small stream

SYLLABI   a pl. of syllabus

SYLLABIC   *n* pl. -S a speech sound of high sonority

SYLLABLE   *v* -BLED, -BLING, -BLES to pronounce syllables (units of spoken language)

SYLLABUB   *n* pl. -S sillabub

SYLLABUS   *n* pl. -BI or -BUSES an outline of a course of study

SYLPH   *n* pl. -S a slender, graceful girl or woman **SYLPHIC, SYLPHISH, SYLPHY** *adj*

SYLPHID   *n* pl. -S a young sylph

SYLVA   *n* pl. -VAS or -VAE the forest trees of an area

SYLVAN   *n* pl. -S one that lives in a forest

SYLVATIC   *adj* pertaining to a forest

SYLVIN   *n* pl. -S sylvite

SYLVINE   *n* pl. -S sylvite

SYLVITE   *n* pl. -S an ore of potassium

SYMBION   *n* pl. -S symbiont

SYMBIONT   *n* pl. -S an organism living in close association with another

SYMBIOT   *n* pl. -S symbiont

SYMBIOTE   *n* pl. -S symbiont

SYMBOL   *v* -BOLED, -BOLING, -BOLS or -BOLLED, -BOLLING, -BOLS to serve as a symbol (a representation) of

SYMBOLIC   *adj* pertaining to a symbol

SYMMETRY   *n* pl. -TRIES an exact correspondence between the opposite halves of a figure

SYMPATHY   *n* pl. -THIES a feeling of compassion for another's suffering

SYMPATRY   *n* pl. -RIES the state of occupying the same area without loss of identity from interbreeding

SYMPHONY   *n* pl. -NIES an orchestral composition

SYMPODIA   *n/pl* plant stems made up of a series of superposed branches

SYMPOSIA   *n/pl* conferences for the purpose of discussion

SYMPTOM   *n* pl. -S an indication of something

SYN   *adv* syne

SYNAGOG   *n* pl. -S a building for Jewish worship

SYNAPSE   *v* -APSED, -APSING, -APSES to come together in synapsis

SYNAPSIS   *n* pl. -APSES the point at which a nervous impulse passes from one neuron to another **SYNAPTIC** *adj*

SYNC   *v* -ED, -ING, -S to cause to operate in unison

SYNCARP   *n* pl. -S a fleshy multiple fruit

SYNCARPY   *n* pl. -PIES the state of being a syncarp

SYNCH   *v* -ED, -ING, -S to sync

SYNCHRO   *n* pl. -CHROS a selsyn

SYNCLINE   *n* pl. -S a type of rock formation

SYNCOM   *n* pl. -S a type of communications satellite

SYNCOPE   *n* pl. -S the contraction of a word by omitting one or more sounds from the middle **SYNCOPAL, SYNCOPIC** *adj*

SYNCYTIA   *n/pl* masses of protoplasm resulting from cell fusion

SYNDESIS   *n* pl. -DESES or -DESISES synapsis

SYNDET   *n* pl. -S a synthetic detergent

SYNDETIC   *adj* serving to connect

SYNDIC   *n* pl. -S a business agent **SYNDICAL** *adj*

SYNDROME   *n* pl. -S a group of symptoms that characterize a particular disorder

SYNE   *adv* since

SYNECTIC   *adj* pertaining to a system of problem solving

SYNERGIA   *n* pl. -S synergy

SYNERGID   *n* pl. -S a cell found in the embryo sac of a seed plant

SYNERGY   *n* pl. -GIES combined action **SYNERGIC** *adj*

SYNESIS   *n* pl. -SISES a type of grammatical construction

SYNGAMY   *n* pl. -MIES the union of two gametes **SYNGAMIC** *adj*

SYNOD   *n* pl. -S a church council **SYNODAL, SYNODIC** *adj*

SYNONYM   *n* pl. -S a word having the same meaning as another

SYNONYME   *n* pl. -S synonym

SYNONYMY   *n* pl. -MIES equivalence of meaning

SYNOPSIS   *n* pl. -OPSES a summary **SYNOPTIC** *adj*

SYNOVIA   *n* pl. -S a lubricating fluid secreted by certain membranes **SYNOVIAL** *adj*

SYNTAX   *n* pl. -ES the way in which words are put together to form phrases and sentences

SYNTONY   *n* pl. -NIES the tuning of transmitters and receivers with each other **SYNTONIC** *adj*

SYNURA   *n* pl. -RAE any of a genus of protozoa

SYPHER   *v* -ED, -ING, -S to overlap so as to make an even surface, as beveled plank edges

SYPHILIS   *n* pl. -LISES a venereal disease

SYPHON   *v* -ED, -ING, -S to siphon

SYREN   *n* pl. -S siren

SYRINGA   *n* pl. -S an ornamental shrub

SYRINGE   *v* -RINGED, -RINGING, -RINGES to cleanse or treat with injected fluid

SYRINX   *n* pl. -INGES or -INXES the vocal organ of a bird

SYRPHIAN   *n* pl. -S syrphid

SYRPHID   *n* pl. -S a winged insect

SYRUP   *n* pl. -S a thick, sweet liquid **SYRUPY** *adj*

SYSTEM   *n* pl. -S a group of interacting elements forming a unified whole

SYSTEMIC   *n* pl. -S a type of pesticide

SYSTOLE   *n* pl. -S the normal rhythmic contraction of the heart **SYSTOLIC** *adj*

SYZYGY   *n* pl. -GIES the configuration of the earth, moon, and sun lying in a straight line **SYZYGAL, SYZYGIAL** *adj*

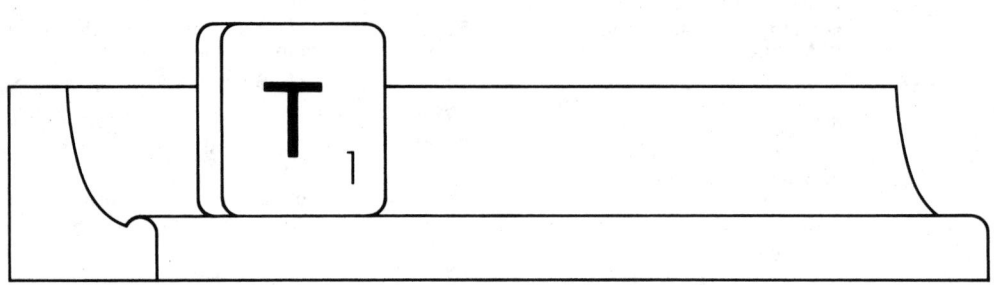

TA	*n* pl. -S an expression of gratitude	**TABLOID**	*n* pl. -S a small newspaper
TAB	*v* TABBED, TABBING, TABS to name or designate	**TABOO**	*v* -ED, -ING, -S to exclude from use, approach, or mention
TABANID	*n* pl. -S a bloodsucking insect	**TABOR**	*v* -ED, -ING, -S to beat on a small drum
TABARD	*n* pl. -S a sleeveless outer garment **TABARDED** *adj*	**TABORER**	*n* pl. -S one that tabors
TABARET	*n* pl. -S a silk fabric	**TABORET**	*n* pl. -S a small drum
TABBED	past tense of tab	**TABORIN**	*n* pl. -S taborine
TABBIED	past tense of tabby	**TABORINE**	*n* pl. -S a taboret
TABBIES	present 3d person sing. of tabby	**TABOUR**	*v* -ED, -ING, -S to tabor
TABBING	present participle of tab	**TABOURER**	*n* pl. -S taborer
TABBIS	*n* pl. -BISES a silk fabric	**TABOURET**	*n* pl. -S taboret
TABBY	*v* -BIED, -BYING, -BIES to give a wavy appearance to	**TABU**	*v* -ED, -ING, -S to taboo
TABER	*v* -ED, -ING, -S to tabor	**TABULAR**	*adj* of or pertaining to a list
TABES	*n* pl. TABES a syphilitic disease	**TABULATE**	*v* -LATED, -LATING, -LATES to arrange in a list
TABETIC	*n* pl. -S one affected with tabes	**TACE**	*n* pl. -S tasse
TABID	*adj* affected with tabes	**TACET**	*interj* be silent — used as a musical direction
TABLA	*n* pl. -S a small drum	**TACH**	*n* pl. -S a device for indicating speed of rotation
TABLE	*v* -BLED, -BLING, -BLES to place on a table (a piece of furniture having a flat upper surface)	**TACHE**	*n* pl. -S a clasp or buckle
TABLEAU	*n* pl. -LEAUX or -LEAUS a picture	**TACHINID**	*n* pl. -S a grayish fly
		TACHISM	*n* pl. -S action painting
TABLEFUL	*n* pl. TABLEFULS or TABLESFUL as much as a table can hold	**TACHIST**	*n* pl. -S an action painter
		TACHISTE	*n* pl. -S tachist
TABLET	*v* -LETED, -LETING, -LETS or -LETTED, -LETTING, -LETS to inscribe on a small, flat surface	**TACIT**	*adj* unspoken **TACITLY** *adv*
		TACITURN	*adj* habitually silent
		TACK	*v* -ED, -ING, -S to fasten with tacks (short, sharp-pointed nails)
TABLETOP	*n* pl. -S the top of a table	**TACKER**	*n* pl. -S one that tacks
TABLING	present participle of table	**TACKET**	*n* pl. -S a hobnail

TACKEY	*adj* TACKIER, TACKIEST tacky	**TAGGED**	past tense of tag
TACKIER	comparative of tacky	**TAGGER**	*n* pl. -S one that tags
TACKIEST	superlative of tacky	**TAGGING**	present participle of tag
TACKIFY	*v* -FIED, -FYING, -FIES to make tacky	**TAGLIKE**	*adj* resembling a tag
TACKILY	*adv* in a tacky manner	**TAGMEME**	*n* pl. -S the smallest unit of meaningful grammatical relation
TACKLE	*v* -LED, -LING, -LES to seize and throw to the ground	**TAGRAG**	*n* pl. -S riffraff
TACKLER	*n* pl. -S one that tackles	**TAHR**	*n* pl. -S a goatlike mammal
TACKLESS	*adj* having no tacks	**TAHSIL**	*n* pl. -S a district in India
TACKLING	*n* pl. -S equipment	**TAIGA**	*n* pl. -S a subarctic evergreen forest
TACKY	*adj* TACKIER, TACKIEST adhesive	**TAIGLACH**	*n* pl. TAIGLACH teiglach
TACNODE	*n* pl. -S a point of contact between two curves	**TAIL**	*v* -ED, -ING, -S to provide with a tail (a hindmost part)
TACO	*n* pl. -COS a tortilla folded around a filling	**TAILBACK**	*n* pl. -S a member of the backfield in some football formations
TACONITE	*n* pl. -S a low-grade iron ore	**TAILBONE**	*n* pl. -S the coccyx
TACT	*n* pl. -S skill in dealing with delicate situations	**TAILCOAT**	*n* pl. -S a man's coat
TACTFUL	*adj* having tact	**TAILER**	*n* pl. -S one that secretly follows another
TACTIC	*n* pl. -S a maneuver for gaining an objective **TACTICAL** *adj*	**TAILGATE**	*v* -GATED, -GATING, -GATES to drive dangerously close behind another vehicle
TACTILE	*adj* pertaining to the sense of touch	**TAILING**	*n* pl. -S the part of a projecting stone or brick that is inserted into a wall
TACTION	*n* pl. -S the act of touching		
TACTLESS	*adj* lacking tact	**TAILLE**	*n* pl. -S a former French tax
TACTUAL	*adj* tactile	**TAILLESS**	*adj* having no tail
TAD	*n* pl. -S a small boy	**TAILLIKE**	*adj* resembling a tail
TADPOLE	*n* pl. -S the aquatic larva of an amphibian	**TAILOR**	*v* -ED, -ING, -S to fit with clothes
TAE	*prep* to	**TAILPIPE**	*n* pl. -S an exhaust pipe
TAEL	*n* pl. -S a Chinese unit of weight	**TAILRACE**	*n* pl. -S a part of a millrace
TAENIA	*n* pl. -NIAE or -NIAS a headband worn in ancient Greece	**TAILSKID**	*n* pl. -S a support on which the tail of an airplane rests
TAFFAREL	*n* pl. -S taffrail	**TAILSPIN**	*n* pl. -S the spiral descent of a stalled airplane
TAFFEREL	*n* pl. -S taffrail		
TAFFETA	*n* pl. -S a lustrous fabric	**TAILWIND**	*n* pl. -S a wind coming from behind a moving vehicle
TAFFIA	*n* pl. -S tafia		
TAFFRAIL	*n* pl. -S a rail around the stern of a ship	**TAIN**	*n* pl. -S a thin plate
TAFFY	*n* pl. -FIES a chewy candy	**TAINT**	*v* -ED, -ING, -S to touch or affect slightly with something bad
TAFIA	*n* pl. -S an inferior rum		
TAG	*v* TAGGED, TAGGING, TAGS to provide with a tag (an identifying marker)	**TAIPAN**	*n* pl. -S a venomous snake
		TAJ	*n* pl. -ES a tall, conical cap worn in Muslim countries
TAGALONG	*n* pl. -S one that follows another		
TAGBOARD	*n* pl. -S a material for making shipping tags	**TAKAHE**	*n* pl. -S a flightless bird

TAKE | *v* TOOK, TAKEN, TAKING, TAKES to get possession of **TAKABLE, TAKEABLE** *adj*

TAKEDOWN | *n* pl. -S an article that can be taken apart easily

TAKEOFF | *n* pl. -S the act of rising in flight

TAKEOUT | *n* pl. -S the act of removing

TAKEOVER | *n* pl. -S the act of assuming control

TAKER | *n* pl. -S one that takes

TAKIN | *n* pl. -S a goatlike mammal

TAKING | *n* pl. -S a seizure

TAKINGLY | *adv* in an attractive manner

TALA | *n* pl. -S a traditional rhythmic pattern of music in India

TALAPOIN | *n* pl. -S a small African monkey

TALAR | *n* pl. -S a long cloak

TALARIA | *n/pl* winged sandals worn by various figures of classical mythology

TALC | *v* TALCKED, TALCKING, TALCS or TALCED, TALCING, TALCS to treat with talc (a soft mineral with a soapy texture) **TALCKY, TALCOSE, TALCOUS** *adj*

TALCUM | *n* pl. -S a powder made from talc

TALE | *n* pl. -S a story

TALENT | *n* pl. -S a special natural ability **TALENTED** *adj*

TALER | *n* pl. -S a former German coin

TALESMAN | *n* pl. -MEN a person summoned to fill a vacancy on a jury

TALEYSIM | a pl. of tallith

TALI | pl. of talus

TALION | *n* pl. -S a retaliation for a crime

TALIPED | *n* pl. -S a person afflicted with clubfoot

TALIPES | *n* pl. TALIPES clubfoot

TALIPOT | *n* pl. -S a tall palm tree

TALISMAN | *n* pl. -S an object believed to possess magical powers

TALK | *v* -ED, -ING, -S to communicate by speaking

TALKABLE | *adj* able to be talked about

TALKER | *n* pl. -S one that talks

TALKIE | *n* pl. -S a moving picture with synchronized sound

TALKING | *n* pl. -S conversation

TALKY | *adj* TALKIER, TALKIEST tending to talk a great deal

TALL | *adj* TALLER, TALLEST having great height

TALLAGE | *v* -LAGED, -LAGING, -LAGES to tax

TALLAISIM | a pl. of tallith

TALLBOY | *n* pl. -BOYS a highboy

TALLIED | past tense of tally

TALLIER | *n* pl. -S one that tallies

TALLIES | present 3d person sing. of tally

TALLISH | *adj* somewhat tall

TALLITH | *n* pl. TALLITHES, TALLITHIM, TALLITOTH, TALEYSIM, or TALLAISIM a Jewish prayer shawl

TALLNESS | *n* pl. -ES the state of being tall

TALLOL | *n* pl. -S a resinous liquid

TALLOW | *v* -ED, -ING, -S to smear with tallow (a mixture of animal fats)

TALLOWY | *adj* resembling tallow

TALLY | *v* -LIED, -LYING, -LIES to count

TALLYHO | *v* -ED, -ING, -S to make an encouraging shout to hunting hounds

TALLYMAN | *n* pl. -MEN a person who tallies

TALMUDIC | *adj* pertaining to the body of Jewish civil and religious law

TALON | *n* pl. -S a claw of a bird of prey **TALONED** *adj*

TALOOKA | *n* pl. -S taluk

TALUK | *n* pl. -S an estate in India

TALUKA | *n* pl. -S taluk

TALUS | *n* pl. -LI a bone of the foot

TALUS | *n* pl. -ES a slope formed by an accumulation of rock debris

TAM | *n* pl. -S a tight-fitting Scottish cap

TAMABLE | *adj* capable of being tamed

TAMAL | *n* pl. -S tamale

TAMALE | *n* pl. -S a Mexican dish

TAMANDU | *n* pl. -S tamandua

TAMANDUA | *n* pl. -S an arboreal anteater

TAMARACK | *n* pl. -S a timber tree

TAMARAO | *n* pl. -RAOS tamarau

TAMARAU | *n* pl. -S a small buffalo of the Philippines

TAMARIN | *n* pl. -S a South American monkey

TAMARIND	*n* pl. -S a tropical tree	**TANDEM**	*n* pl. -S a bicycle built for two
TAMARISK	*n* pl. -S an evergreen shrub	**TANG**	*v* -ED, -ING, -S to provide with a pungent flavor
TAMASHA	*n* pl. -S a public entertainment in India	**TANGELO**	*n* pl. -LOS a citrus fruit
TAMBAC	*n* pl. -S tombac	**TANGENCE**	*n* pl. -S tangency
TAMBALA	*n* pl. -S a monetary unit of Malawi	**TANGENCY**	*n* pl. -CIES the state of being in immediate physical contact
TAMBOUR	*v* -ED, -ING, -S to embroider on a round wooden frame	**TANGENT**	*n* pl. -S a straight line in contact with a curve at one point
TAMBOURA	*n* pl. -S tambura	**TANGIBLE**	*n* pl. -S something palpable
TAMBUR	*n* pl. -S tambura	**TANGIBLY**	*adv* palpably
TAMBURA	*n* pl. -S a stringed instrument	**TANGIER**	comparative of tangy
TAME	*adj* TAMER, TAMEST gentle or docile	**TANGIEST**	superlative of tangy
TAME	*v* TAMED, TAMING, TAMES to make tame	**TANGLE**	*v* -GLED, -GLING, -GLES to bring together in intricate confusion
TAMEABLE	*adj* tamable	**TANGLER**	*n* pl. -S one that tangles
TAMEIN	*n* pl. -S a garment worn by Burmese women	**TANGLY**	*adj* -GLIER, -GLIEST tangled
TAMELESS	*adj* not capable of being tamed	**TANGO**	*v* -ED, -ING, -S to perform a Latin-American dance
TAMELY	*adv* in a tame manner	**TANGRAM**	*n* pl. -S a Chinese puzzle
TAMENESS	*n* pl. -ES the state of being tame	**TANGY**	*adj* TANGIER, TANGIEST pungent
TAMER	*n* pl. -S one that tames	**TANIST**	*n* pl. -S the heir apparent to a Celtic chief
TAMEST	superlative of tame	**TANISTRY**	*n* pl. -RIES the system of electing a tanist
TAMING	present participle of tame	
TAMIS	*n* pl. -ISES a strainer made of cloth mesh	**TANK**	*v* -ED, -ING, -S to store in a tank (a container usually for liquids)
TAMMIE	*n* pl. -S tammy	**TANKA**	*n* pl. -S a Japanese verse form
TAMMY	*n* pl. -MIES a fabric of mixed fibers	**TANKAGE**	*n* pl. -S the capacity of a tank
TAMP	*v* -ED, -ING, -S to pack down by tapping	**TANKARD**	*n* pl. -S a tall drinking vessel
TAMPALA	*n* pl. -S an annual herb	**TANKER**	*n* pl. -S a ship designed to transport liquids
TAMPAN	*n* pl. -S a biting insect	**TANKFUL**	*n* pl. -S the amount a tank can hold
TAMPER	*v* -ED, -ING, -S to interfere in a harmful manner	**TANKSHIP**	*n* pl. -S a tanker
TAMPERER	*n* pl. -S one that tampers	**TANNABLE**	*adj* capable of being tanned
TAMPION	*n* pl. -S a plug for the muzzle of a cannon	**TANNAGE**	*n* pl. -S the process of tanning
TAMPON	*v* -ED, -ING, -S to plug with a cotton pad	**TANNATE**	*n* pl. -S a chemical salt
TAN	*v* TANNED, TANNING, TANS to convert hide into leather by soaking in chemicals	**TANNED**	past tense of tan
		TANNER	*n* pl. -S one that tans
TAN	*adj* TANNER, TANNEST brown from the sun's rays	**TANNERY**	*n* pl. -NERIES a place where hides are tanned
TANAGER	*n* pl. -S a brightly colored bird	**TANNEST**	superlative of tan
TANBARK	*n* pl. -S a tree bark used as a source of tannin	**TANNIC**	*adj* pertaining to tannin
		TANNIN	*n* pl. -S a chemical compound used in tanning

TANNING	*n* pl. -S the process of converting hides into leather
TANNISH	*adj* somewhat tan
TANREC	*n* pl. -S tenrec
TANSY	*n* pl. -SIES a perennial herb
TANTALUM	*n* pl. -S a metallic element **TANTALIC** *adj*
TANTALUS	*n* pl. -ES a case for wine bottles
TANTARA	*n* pl. -S the sound of a trumpet or horn
TANTIVY	*n* pl. -TIVIES a hunting cry
TANTO	*adv* so much — used as a musical direction
TANTRA	*n* pl. -S one of a class of Hindu religious writings **TANTRIC** *adj*
TANTRUM	*n* pl. -S a fit of rage
TANYARD	*n* pl. -S the section of a tannery containing the vats
TAO	*n* pl. -S the path of virtuous conduct according to a Chinese philosophy
TAP	*v* TAPPED, TAPPING, TAPS to strike gently
TAPA	*n* pl. -S a cloth made from tree bark
TAPADERA	*n* pl. -S a part of a saddle
TAPADERO	*n* pl. -ROS tapadera
TAPALO	*n* pl. -LOS a scarf worn in Latin-American countries
TAPE	*v* TAPED, TAPING, TAPES to fasten with tape (a long, narrow strip or band)
TAPELESS	*adj* being without tape
TAPELIKE	*adj* resembling tape
TAPELINE	*n* pl. -S a tape for measuring distances
TAPER	*v* -ED, -ING, -S to become gradually narrower toward one end
TAPERER	*n* pl. -S one that carries a candle in a religious procession
TAPESTRY	*v* -TRIED, -TRYING, -TRIES to decorate with woven wall hangings
TAPETUM	*n* pl. -TA a layer of cells in some plants **TAPETAL** *adj*
TAPEWORM	*n* pl. -S a parasitic worm
TAPHOLE	*n* pl. -S a hole in a blast furnace
TAPHOUSE	*n* pl. -S a tavern
TAPING	present participle of tape
TAPIOCA	*n* pl. -S a starchy food
TAPIR	*n* pl. -S a hoofed mammal
TAPIS	*n* pl. -PISES material used for wall hangings and floor coverings
TAPPED	past tense of tap
TAPPER	*n* pl. -S one that taps
TAPPET	*n* pl. -S a sliding rod that causes another part of a mechanism to move
TAPPING	*n* pl. -S the process or means by which something is tapped
TAPROOM	*n* pl. -S a barroom
TAPROOT	*n* pl. -S the main root of a plant
TAPSTER	*n* pl. -S one that dispenses liquor in a barroom
TAR	*v* TARRED, TARRING, TARS to cover with tar (a black viscous liquid)
TARANTAS	*n* pl. -ES a Russian carriage
TARBOOSH	*n* pl. -ES a cap worn by Muslim men
TARBUSH	*n* pl. -ES tarboosh
TARDIER	comparative of tardy
TARDIES	pl. of tardy
TARDO	*adj* slow — used as a musical direction
TARDY	*adj* TARDIER, TARDIEST late **TARDILY** *adv*
TARDY	*n* pl. -DIES an instance of being late
TARE	*v* TARED, TARING, TARES to determine the weight of a container holding goods
TARGE	*n* pl. -S a small, round shield
TARGET	*v* -ED, -ING, -S to make a goal of
TARIFF	*v* -ED, -ING, -S to tax imported or exported goods
TARING	present participle of tare
TARLATAN	*n* pl. -S a cotton fabric
TARLETAN	*n* pl. -S tarlatan
TARMAC	*n* pl. -S an asphalt road
TARN	*n* pl. -S a small mountain lake
TARNAL	*adj* damned **TARNALLY** *adv*
TARNISH	*v* -ED, -ING, -ES to dull the luster of
TARO	*n* pl. -ROS a tropical plant
TAROC	*n* pl. -S tarok
TAROK	*n* pl. -S a card game

TAROT   *n* pl. -S any of a set of playing cards used for fortune-telling

TARP   *n* pl. -S a protective canvas covering

TARPAN   *n* pl. -S an Asian wild horse

TARPAPER   *n* pl. -S a heavy paper coated with tar

TARPON   *n* pl. -S a marine game fish

TARRAGON   *n* pl. -S a perennial herb

TARRE   *v* TARRED, TARRING, TARRES to urge to action

TARRED   past tense of tar

TARRIED   past tense of tarry

TARRIER   *n* pl. -S one that tarries

TARRIES   present 3d person sing. of tarry

TARRIEST   superlative of tarry

TARRING   present participle of tar and tarre

TARRY   *v* -RIED, -RYING, -RIES to delay or be slow in acting or doing

TARRY   *adj* -RIER, -RIEST resembling tar

TARSAL   *n* pl. -S a bone of the foot

TARSI   pl. of tarsus

TARSIA   *n* pl. -S intarsia

TARSIER   *n* pl. -S a nocturnal primate

TARSUS   *n* pl. TARSI a part of the foot

TART   *adj* TARTER, TARTEST having a sharp, sour taste

TART   *v* -ED, -ING, -S to dress up

TARTAN   *n* pl. -S a patterned woolen fabric

TARTANA   *n* pl. -S a Mediterranean sailing vessel

TARTAR   *n* pl. -S a crust on the teeth **TARTARIC** *adj*

TARTISH   *adj* somewhat tart

TARTLET   *n* pl. -S a small pie

TARTLY   *adv* in a tart manner

TARTNESS   *n* pl. -ES the state of being tart

TARTRATE   *n* pl. -S a chemical salt

TARTUFE   *n* pl. -S tartuffe

TARTUFFE   *n* pl. -S a hypocrite

TARWEED   *n* pl. -S a flowering plant

TARZAN   *n* pl. -S a person of superior strength and agility

TASK   *v* -ED, -ING, -S to assign a job to

TASKWORK   *n* pl. -S hard work

TASS   *n* pl. -ES a drinking cup

TASSE   *n* pl. -S tasset

TASSEL   *v* -SELED, -SELING, -SELS or -SELLED, -SELLING, -SELS to adorn with dangling ornaments

TASSET   *n* pl. -S a piece of plate armor for the upper thigh

TASSIE   *n* pl. -S tass

TASTE   *v* TASTED, TASTING, TASTES to perceive the flavor of by taking into the mouth **TASTABLE** *adj*

TASTEFUL   *adj* tasty

TASTER   *n* pl. -S one that tastes

TASTING   present participle of taste

TASTY   *adj* TASTIER, TASTIEST pleasant to the taste **TASTILY** *adv*

TAT   *v* TATTED, TATTING, TATS to make tatting

TATAMI   *n* pl. -S straw matting used as a floor covering

TATE   *n* pl. -S a tuft of hair

TATER   *n* pl. -S a potato

TATOUAY   *n* pl. -AYS a South American armadillo

TATTED   past tense of tat

TATTER   *v* -ED, -ING, -S to become torn and worn

TATTIER   comparative of tatty

TATTIEST   superlative of tatty

TATTING   *n* pl. -S delicate handmade lace

TATTLE   *v* -TLED, -TLING, -TLES to reveal the activities of another

TATTLER   *n* pl. -S one that tattles

TATTOO   *v* -ED, -ING, -S to mark the skin with indelible pigments

TATTOOER   *n* pl. -S one that tattoos

TATTY   *adj* -TIER, -TIEST shabby

TAU   *n* pl. -S a Greek letter

TAUGHT   past tense of teach

TAUNT   *v* -ED, -ING, -S to challenge or reproach sarcastically

TAUNTER   *n* pl. -S one that taunts

TAUPE   *n* pl. -S a dark gray color

TAURINE   *n* pl. -S a chemical compound

TAUT   *adj* TAUTER, TAUTEST fully stretched, so as not to be slack

TAUT   *v* -ED, -ING, -S to tangle

TAUTAUG _n_ pl. -S tautog

TAUTEN _v_ -ED, -ING, -S to make taut

TAUTLY _adv_ in a taut manner

TAUTNESS _n_ pl. -ES the state of being taut

TAUTOG _n_ pl. -S a marine fish

TAUTOMER _n_ pl. -S a type of chemical compound

TAUTONYM _n_ pl. -S a type of taxonomic designation

TAV _n_ pl. -S a Hebrew letter

TAVERN _n_ pl. -S a place where liquor is sold to be drunk on the premises

TAVERNER _n_ pl. -S one that runs a tavern

TAW _v_ -ED, -ING, -S to convert into white leather by the application of minerals

TAWDRY _adj_ -DRIER, -DRIEST gaudy **TAWDRILY** _adv_

TAWDRY _n_ pl. -DRIES gaudy finery

TAWER _n_ pl. -S one that taws

TAWIE _adj_ docile

TAWNEY _n_ pl. -NEYS tawny

TAWNY _adj_ -NIER, -NIEST light brown **TAWNILY** _adv_

TAWNY _n_ pl. -NIES a light brown color

TAWPIE _n_ pl. -S a foolish young person

TAWSE _v_ TAWSED, TAWSING, TAWSES to flog

TAX _v_ -ED, -ING, -ES to place a tax (a charge imposed by authority for public purposes) on

TAXA a pl. of taxon

TAXABLE _adj_ subject to tax **TAXABLY** _adv_

TAXABLE _n_ pl. -S a taxable item

TAXATION _n_ pl. -S the process of taxing

TAXEME _n_ pl. -S a minimum grammatical feature of selection **TAXEMIC** _adj_

TAXER _n_ pl. -S one that taxes

TAXI _v_ TAXIED, TAXIING or TAXYING, TAXIS or TAXIES to travel in a taxicab

TAXICAB _n_ pl. -S an automobile for hire

TAXIMAN _n_ pl. -MEN the operator of a taxicab

TAXINGLY _adv_ in an onerous manner

TAXITE _n_ pl. -S a volcanic rock **TAXITIC** _adj_

TAXIWAY _n_ pl. -WAYS a paved strip at an airport

TAXLESS _adj_ free from taxation

TAXMAN _n_ pl. -MEN one who collects taxes

TAXON _n_ pl. TAXA or TAXONS a unit of scientific classification

TAXONOMY _n_ pl. -MIES the study of scientific classification

TAXPAID _adj_ paid for by taxes

TAXPAYER _n_ pl. -S one that pays taxes

TAXUS _n_ pl. TAXUS an evergreen tree or shrub

TAXWISE _adj_ pertaining to taxes

TAXYING a present participle of taxi

TAZZA _n_ pl. -ZAS or -ZE an ornamental bowl

TEA _n_ pl. -S a beverage made by infusing dried leaves in boiling water

TEABERRY _n_ pl. -RIES a North American shrub

TEABOARD _n_ pl. -S a tray for serving tea

TEABOWL _n_ pl. -S a teacup having no handle

TEABOX _n_ pl. -ES a box for tea leaves

TEACAKE _n_ pl. -S a small cake served with tea

TEACART _n_ pl. -S a wheeled table used in serving tea

TEACH _v_ TAUGHT, TEACHING, TEACHES to impart knowledge or skill to

TEACHER _n_ pl. -S one that teaches

TEACHING _n_ pl. -S a doctrine

TEACUP _n_ pl. -S a cup in which tea is served

TEAHOUSE _n_ pl. -S a public establishment serving tea

TEAK _n_ pl. -S an East Indian tree

TEAKWOOD _n_ pl. -S the wood of the teak

TEAL _n_ pl. -S a river duck

TEAM _v_ -ED, -ING, -S to form a team (a group of persons associated in a joint action)

TEAMAKER _n_ pl. -S one that makes tea

TEAMMATE _n_ pl. -S a member of the same team

TEAMSTER _n_ pl. -S a truck driver

TEAMWORK _n_ pl. -S cooperative effort to achieve a common goal

TEAPOT   *n* pl. -S a vessel used in making and serving tea

TEAPOY   *n* pl. -POYS a small table used in serving tea

TEAR   *v* -ED, -ING, -S to emit tears (drops of saline liquid secreted by a gland of the eye)

TEAR   *v* TORE, TORN, TEARING, TEARS to pull apart or into pieces **TEARABLE** *adj*

TEARDOWN   *n* pl. -S the process of disassembling

TEARDROP   *n* pl. -S a tear

TEARER   *n* pl. -S one that tears or rips

TEARFUL   *adj* full of tears

TEARGAS   *v* -GASSED, -GASSING, -GASES or -GASSES to subject to a gas that irritates the eyes

TEARIER   comparative of teary

TEARIEST   superlative of teary

TEARILY   *adv* in a teary manner

TEARLESS   *adj* being without tears

TEAROOM   *n* pl. -S a restaurant serving tea

TEARY   *adj* TEARIER, TEARIEST tearful

TEASE   *v* TEASED, TEASING, TEASES to make fun of

TEASEL   *v* -SELED, -SELING, -SELS or -SELLED, -SELLING, -SELS to raise a soft surface on fabric with a bristly flower head

TEASELER   *n* pl. -S one that teasels

TEASER   *n* pl. -S one that teases

TEASHOP   *n* pl. -S a tearoom

TEASING   present participle of tease

TEASPOON   *n* pl. -S a small spoon

TEAT   *n* pl. -S a mammary gland **TEATED** *adj*

TEATIME   *n* pl. -S the customary time for tea

TEAWARE   *n* pl. -S a tea service

TEAZEL   *v* -ZELED, -ZELING, -ZELS or -ZELLED, -ZELLING, -ZELS to teasel

TEAZLE   *v* -ZLED, -ZLING, -ZLES to teasel

TECHED   *adj* crazy

TECHNIC   *n* pl. -S technique

TECHY   *adj* TECHIER, TECHIEST tetchy **TECHILY** *adj*

TECTA   pl. of tectum

TECTAL   *adj* pertaining to a tectum

TECTONIC   *adj* pertaining to construction

TECTRIX   *n* pl. -TRICES a small feather of a bird's wing

TECTUM   *n* pl. -TA a bodily structure resembling or serving as a roof

TED   *v* TEDDED, TEDDING, TEDS to spread for drying

TEDDER   *n* pl. -S one that teds

TEDDY   *n* pl. -DIES a woman's undergarment

TEDIOUS   *adj* causing weariness

TEDIUM   *n* pl. -S the state of being tedious

TEE   *v* TEED, TEEING, TEES to place a golf ball on a small peg

TEEM   *v* -ED, -ING, -S to be full to overflowing

TEEMER   *n* pl. -S one that teems

TEEN   *n* pl. -S a teenager

TEENAGE   *adj* pertaining to teenagers

TEENAGED   *adj* teenage

TEENAGER   *n* pl. -S a person between the ages of thirteen and nineteen

TEENER   *n* pl. -S a teenager

TEENFUL   *adj* filled with grief

TEENSY   *adj* -SIER, -SIEST tiny

TEENTSY   *adj* -SIER, -SIEST tiny

TEENY   *adj* -NIER, -NIEST tiny

TEEPEE   *n* pl. -S tepee

TEETER   *v* -ED, -ING, -S to move unsteadily

TEETH   pl. of tooth

TEETHE   *v* TEETHED, TEETHING, TEETHES to cut teeth

TEETHER   *n* pl. -S an object for a baby to bite on during teething

TEETHING   *n* pl. -S the first growth of teeth

TEETOTAL   *v* -TALED, -TALING, -TALS or -TALLED, -TALLING, -TALS to abstain completely from alcoholic beverages

TEETOTUM   *n* pl. -S a spinning toy

TEFF   *n* pl. -S a cereal grass

TEG   *n* pl. -S a yearling sheep

TEGMEN   *n* pl. -MINA a covering

TEGMENTA   *n/pl* anatomical coverings

TEGMINAL   *adj* pertaining to a tegmen

TEGUA   *n* pl. -S a type of moccasin

TEGULAR *adj* resembling a tile

TEGUMEN *n pl.* -MINA tegmen

TEGUMENT *n pl.* -S a covering

TEIGLACH *n pl.* TEIGLACH a confection consisting of balls of dough boiled in honey

TEIID *n pl.* -S a tropical American lizard

TEIND *n pl.* -S a tithe

TEKTITE *n pl.* -S a glassy body believed to be of meteoritic origin **TEKTITIC** *adj*

TELA *n pl.* -LAE an anatomical tissue

TELAMON *n pl.* -ES a male figure used as a supporting column

TELE *n pl.* -S a television set

TELECAST *v* -ED, -ING, -S to broadcast by television

TELEDU *n pl.* -S a carnivorous mammal

TELEFILM *n pl.* -S a motion picture made for television

TELEGA *n pl.* -S a Russian wagon

TELEGONY *n pl.* -NIES the supposed influence of a previous sire on the offspring of later matings of the mother with other males

TELEGRAM *v* -GRAMMED, -GRAMMING, -GRAMS to send a message by telegraph

TELEMAN *n pl.* -MEN a naval officer

TELEMARK *n pl.* -S a type of turn in skiing

TELEOST *n pl.* -S a bony fish

TELEPLAY *n pl.* -PLAYS a play written for television

TELEPORT *v* -ED, -ING, -S to transport by a process that involves no physical means

TELERAN *n pl.* -S a system of air navigation

TELESIS *n pl.* TELESES planned progress

TELETHON *n pl.* -S a fund-raising television program

TELEVIEW *v* -ED, -ING, -S to observe by means of television

TELEVISE *v* -VISED, -VISING, -VISES to broadcast by television (an electronic system of transmitting images and sound)

TELEX *v* -ED, -ING, -ES to send a message by a type of telegraphic system

TELFER *v* -ED, -ING, -S to telpher

TELFORD *n pl.* -S a road made of stones

TELIA *pl.* of telium

TELIAL *adj* pertaining to a telium

TELIC *adj* directed toward a goal

TELIUM *n pl.* -LIA a sorus on the host plant of a rust fungus

TELL *v* TOLD, TELLING, TELLS to give a detailed account of **TELLABLE** *adj*

TELLER *n pl.* -S a bank employee who receives and pays out money

TELLIES *pl.* of telly

TELLTALE *n pl.* -S a tattler

TELLURIC *adj* pertaining to the earth

TELLY *n pl.* -LIES a television set

TELOME *n pl.* -S a structural unit of a vascular plant **TELOMIC** *adj*

TELOS *n pl.* TELOI an ultimate end

TELPHER *v* -ED, -ING, -S to transport by a system of aerial cable cars

TELSON *n pl.* -S the terminal segment of an arthropod **TELSONIC** *adj*

TEMBLOR *n pl.* -S or -ES an earthquake

TEMERITY *n pl.* -TIES foolish boldness

TEMPEH *n pl.* -S an Asian food

TEMPER *v* -ED, -ING, -S to moderate by adding a counterbalancing agent

TEMPERA *n pl.* -S a technique of painting

TEMPERER *n pl.* -S one that tempers

TEMPEST *v* -ED, -ING, -S to agitate violently

TEMPI *a pl.* of tempo

TEMPLAR *n pl.* -S a lawyer or student of law in London

TEMPLATE *n pl.* -S a pattern used as a guide in making something

TEMPLE *n pl.* -S a house of worship **TEMPLED** *adj*

TEMPLET *n pl.* -S template

TEMPO *n pl.* -PI or -POS the rate of speed of a musical piece

TEMPORAL *n pl.* -S a bone of the skull

TEMPT *v* -ED, -ING, -S to entice to commit an unwise or immoral act

TEMPTER *n pl.* -S one that tempts

TEMPURA *n pl.* -S a Japanese dish

TEN	*n* pl. -S a number
TENABLE	*adj* capable of being held **TENABLY** *adv*
TENACE	*n* pl. -S a combination of two high cards in some card games
TENACITY	*n* pl. -TIES perseverance or persistence
TENACULA	*n/pl* hooked surgical instruments
TENAIL	*n* pl. -S tenaille
TENAILLE	*n* pl. -S an outer defense
TENANCY	*n* pl. -CIES the temporary occupancy of something that belongs to another
TENANT	*v* -ED, -ING, -S to inhabit
TENANTRY	*n* pl. -RIES tenancy
TENCH	*n* pl. -ES a freshwater fish
TEND	*v* -ED, -ING, -S to be disposed or inclined
TENDANCE	*n* pl. -S watchful care
TENDENCE	*n* pl. -S tendance
TENDENCY	*n* pl. -CIES an inclination to act or think in a particular way
TENDER	*adj* -DERER, -DEREST soft or delicate
TENDER	*v* -ED, -ING, -S to present for acceptance
TENDERER	*n* pl. -S one that tenders
TENDERLY	*adv* in a tender manner
TENDON	*n* pl. -S a band of tough, fibrous tissue
TENDRIL	*n* pl. -S a leafless organ of climbing plants
TENEBRAE	*n/pl* a religious service
TENEMENT	*n* pl. -S an apartment house
TENESMUS	*n* pl. -ES an urgent but ineffectual effort to defecate or urinate **TENESMIC** *adj*
TENET	*n* pl. -S a principle, belief, or doctrine held to be true
TENFOLD	*n* pl. -S an amount ten times as great as a given unit
TENIA	*n* pl. -NIAE or -NIAS a tapeworm
TENIASIS	*n* pl. -SISES infestation with tapeworms
TENNER	*n* pl. -S a ten-dollar bill
TENNIS	*n* pl. -NISES an outdoor ball game
TENNIST	*n* pl. -S a tennis player
TENON	*v* -ED, -ING, -S to unite by means of a tenon (a projection on the end of a piece of wood)
TENONER	*n* pl. -S one that tenons
TENOR	*n* pl. -S a high male singing voice
TENORITE	*n* pl. -S a mineral
TENOTOMY	*n* pl. -MIES the surgical division of a tendon
TENOUR	*n* pl. -S tenor
TENPENCE	*n* pl. -S the sum of ten pennies
TENPENNY	*adj* worth tenpence
TENPIN	*n* pl. -S a bowling pin
TENREC	*n* pl. -S a mammal that feeds on insects
TENSE	*adj* TENSER, TENSEST taut **TENSELY** *adv*
TENSE	*v* TENSED, TENSING, TENSES to make tense
TENSIBLE	*adj* capable of being stretched **TENSIBLY** *adv*
TENSILE	*adj* tensible
TENSING	present participle of tense
TENSION	*v* -ED, -ING, -S to make tense
TENSITY	*n* pl. -TIES the state of being tense
TENSIVE	*adj* causing tensity
TENSOR	*n* pl. -S a muscle that stretches a body part
TENT	*v* -ED, -ING, -S to live in a tent (a type of portable shelter)
TENTACLE	*n* pl. -S an elongated, flexible appendage of some animals
TENTAGE	*n* pl. -S a supply of tents
TENTER	*v* -ED, -ING, -S to stretch on a type of frame
TENTH	*n* pl. -S one of ten equal parts
TENTHLY	*adv* in the tenth place
TENTIE	*adj* TENTIER, TENTIEST tenty
TENTIER	comparative of tenty
TENTIEST	superlative of tenty
TENTLESS	*adj* having no tent
TENTLIKE	*adj* resembling a tent
TENTY	*adj* TENTIER, TENTIEST watchful
TENUIS	*n* pl. -UES a voiceless phonetic stop
TENUITY	*n* pl. -ITIES lack of substance or strength

TENUOUS *adj* having little substance or strength

TENURE *n* pl. -S the holding of something **TENURED, TENURIAL** *adj*

TENUTO *n* pl. -TI or -TOS a musical note or chord held longer than its normal duration

TEOCALLI *n* pl. -S an Aztec temple

TEOPAN *n* pl. -S a teocalli

TEOSINTE *n* pl. -S an annual grass

TEPA *n* pl. -S a chemical compound

TEPAL *n* pl. -S a division of a perianth

TEPEE *n* pl. -S a conical tent of some North American Indians

TEPEFY *v* -FIED, -FYING, -FIES to make tepid

TEPHRA *n* pl. -S solid material ejected from a volcano

TEPHRITE *n* pl. -S a volcanic rock

TEPID *adj* moderately warm **TEPIDLY** *adv*

TEPIDITY *n* pl. -TIES the state of being tepid

TEQUILA *n* pl. -S a Mexican liquor

TERAI *n* pl. -S a sun hat with a wide brim

TERAOHM *n* pl. -S one trillion ohms

TERAPH *n* pl. -APHIM an image of a Semitic household god

TERATISM *n* pl. -S a malformed fetus **TERATOID** *adj*

TERATOMA *n* pl. -MAS or -MATA a type of tumor

TERBIA *n* pl. -S an oxide of terbium

TERBIUM *n* pl. -S a metallic element **TERBIC** *adj*

TERCE *n* pl. -S tierce

TERCEL *n* pl. -S a male falcon

TERCELET *n* pl. -S tercel

TERCET *n* pl. -S a group of three lines of verse

TEREBENE *n* pl. -S a mixture of terpenes

TEREBIC *adj* pertaining to an acid derived from oil of turpentine

TEREDO *n* pl. -DOS or -DINES a bivalve mollusk

TEREFAH *adj* tref

TERETE *adj* cylindrical and slightly tapering

TERGA pl. of tergum

TERGAL *adj* pertaining to a tergum

TERGITE *n* pl. -S a tergum

TERGUM *n* pl. -GA a back part of a segment of an arthropod

TERIYAKI *n* pl. -S a Japanese food

TERM *v* -ED, -ING, -S to give a name to

TERMER *n* pl. -S a prisoner serving a specified sentence

TERMINAL *n* pl. -S an end or extremity

TERMINUS *n* pl. -NI or -NUSES a terminal

TERMITE *n* pl. -S an insect resembling an ant **TERMITIC** *adj*

TERMLESS *adj* having no limits

TERMLY *adv* periodically

TERMOR *n* pl. -S one that holds land for a certain number of years

TERMTIME *n* pl. -S the time when a school or court is in session

TERN *n* pl. -S a seabird

TERNARY *n* pl. -RIES a group of three

TERNATE *adj* arranged in groups of three

TERNE *n* pl. -S an alloy of lead and tin

TERNION *n* pl. -S a group of three

TERPENE *n* pl. -S a chemical compound **TERPENIC** *adj*

TERPINOL *n* pl. -S a fragrant liquid

TERRA *n* pl. -RAE earth; land

TERRACE *v* -RACED, -RACING, -RACES to provide with a terrace (a raised embankment)

TERRAIN *n* pl. -S a tract of land

TERRANE *n* pl. -S a rock formation

TERRAPIN *n* pl. -S a North American tortoise

TERRARIA *n/pl* glass enclosures for plants or small animals

TERRAS *n* pl. -ES trass

TERRAZZO *n* pl. -ZOS a mosaic flooring

TERREEN *n* pl. -S terrine

TERRELLA *n* pl. -S a spherical magnet

TERRENE *n* pl. -S a land area

TERRET *n* pl. -S a metal ring on a harness

TERRIBLE *adj* very bad **TERRIBLY** *adv*

TERRIER *n* pl. -S a small, active dog

TERRIES pl. of terry

TERRIFIC	*adj* very good; fine
TERRIFY	*v* -FIED, -FYING, -FIES to fill with terror
TERRINE	*n* pl. -S an earthenware jar
TERRIT	*n* pl. -S terret
TERROR	*n* pl. -S intense fear
TERRY	*n* pl. -RIES an absorbent fabric
TERSE	*adj* TERSER, TERSEST succinct **TERSELY** *adv*
TERTIAL	*n* pl. -S a flight feather of a bird's wing
TERTIAN	*n* pl. -S a recurrent fever
TERTIARY	*n* pl. -ARIES a tertial
TESLA	*n* pl. -S a unit of magnetic induction
TESSERA	*n* pl. -SERAE a small square used in mosaic work
TEST	*v* -ED, -ING, -S to subject to an examination **TESTABLE** *adj*
TESTA	*n* pl. -TAE the hard outer coating of a seed
TESTACY	*n* pl. -CIES the state of being testate
TESTATE	*adj* having made a valid will before death
TESTATOR	*n* pl. -S one that makes a will
TESTEE	*n* pl. -S one that is tested
TESTER	*n* pl. -S one that tests
TESTES	pl. of testis
TESTICLE	*n* pl. -S a testis
TESTIER	comparative of testy
TESTIEST	superlative of testy
TESTIFY	*v* -FIED, -FYING, -FIES to make a declaration of truth under oath
TESTILY	*adv* in a testy manner
TESTING	present participle of test
TESTIS	*n* pl. TESTES a male reproductive gland
TESTON	*n* pl. -S a former French coin
TESTOON	*n* pl. -S teston
TESTUDO	*n* pl. -DINES or -DOS a portable screen used as a shield by the ancient Romans
TESTY	*adj* TESTIER, TESTIEST irritable
TETANAL	*adj* pertaining to tetanus
TETANIC	*n* pl. -S a drug capable of causing convulsions
TETANIES	pl. of tetany

TETANISE	*v* -NISED, -NISING, -NISES to tetanize
TETANIZE	*v* -NIZED, -NIZING, -NIZES to affect with convulsions
TETANUS	*n* pl. -ES an infectious disease **TETANOID** *adj*
TETANY	*n* pl. -NIES a condition marked by painful muscular spasms
TETCHED	*adj* crazy
TETCHY	*adj* TETCHIER, TETCHIEST irritable **TETCHILY** *adv*
TETH	*n* pl. -S a Hebrew letter
TETHER	*v* -ED, -ING, -S to fasten to a fixed object with a rope
TETOTUM	*n* pl. -S teetotum
TETRA	*n* pl. -S a tropical fish
TETRACID	*n* pl. -S a type of acid
TETRAD	*n* pl. -S a group of four **TETRADIC** *adj*
TETRAGON	*n* pl. -S a four-sided polygon
TETRAMER	*n* pl. -S a type of polymer
TETRAPOD	*n* pl. -S a four-footed animal
TETRARCH	*n* pl. -S one of four joint rulers
TETRODE	*n* pl. -S a type of electron tube
TETROXID	*n* pl. -S a type of oxide
TETRYL	*n* pl. -S a chemical compound
TETTER	*n* pl. -S a skin disease
TEUCH	*adj* teugh
TEUGH	*adj* tough **TEUGHLY** *adv*
TEW	*v* -ED, -ING, -S to work hard
TEXAS	*n* pl. -ES the uppermost structure on a steamboat
TEXT	*n* pl. -S the main body of a written or printed work
TEXTBOOK	*n* pl. -S a book used in the study of a subject
TEXTILE	*n* pl. -S a woven fabric
TEXTLESS	*adj* having no text
TEXTUAL	*adj* pertaining to a text
TEXTUARY	*n* pl. -ARIES a specialist in the study of the Scriptures
TEXTURE	*v* -TURED, -TURING, -TURES to make by weaving
TEXTURAL	*adj* pertaining to the surface characteristics of something
THACK	*v* -ED, -ING, -S to thatch
THAE	*adj* these; those
THAIRM	*n* pl. -S tharm

THALAMUS   *n* pl. -MI a part of the brain **THALAMIC** *adj*

THALER   *n* pl. -S taler

THALLIUM   *n* pl. -S a metallic element **THALLIC, THALLOUS** *adj*

THALLUS   *n* pl. -LI or -LUSES a plant body without true root, stem, or leaf **THALLOID** *adj*

THAN   *conj* — used to introduce the second element of a comparison

THANAGE   *n* pl. -S the land held by a thane

THANATOS   *n* pl. -ES an instinctual desire for death

THANE   *n* pl. -S a man holding land by military service in Anglo-Saxon England

THANK   *v* -ED, -ING, -S to express gratitude to

THANKER   *n* pl. -S one that thanks

THANKFUL   *adj* -FULLER, -FULLEST feeling gratitude

THARM   *n* pl. -S the belly

THAT   *pron* pl. THOSE the one indicated

THATAWAY   *adv* in that direction

THATCH   *v* -ED, -ING, -ES to cover with thatch (plant stalks or foliage)

THATCHER   *n* pl. -S one that thatches

THATCHY   *adj* resembling thatch

THAW   *v* -ED, -ING, -S to melt

THAWER   *n* pl. -S one that thaws

THAWLESS   *adj* never thawing

THE   *definite article* — used to specify or make particular

THEARCHY   *n* pl. -CHIES rule by a god

THEATER   *n* pl. -S a building for dramatic presentations **THEATRIC** *adj*

THEATRE   *n* pl. -S theater

THEBAINE   *n* pl. -S a poisonous alkaloid

THECA   *n* pl. -CAE a protective anatomical covering **THECAL, THECATE** *adj*

THEE   *pron* the objective case of the pronoun thou

THEELIN   *n* pl. -S estrone

THEELOL   *n* pl. -S estriol

THEFT   *n* pl. -S the act of stealing

THEGN   *n* pl. -S thane **THEGNLY** *adj*

THEIN   *n* pl. -S theine

THEINE   *n* pl. -S caffeine

THEIR   *pron* a possessive form of the pronoun they

THEIRS   *pron* a possessive form of the pronoun they

THEISM   *n* pl. -S belief in the existence of a god

THEIST   *n* pl. -S one who belives in the existence of a god **THEISTIC** *adj*

THELITIS   *n* pl. -TISES inflammation of the nipple

THEM   *pron* the objective case of the pronoun they

THEMATIC   *adj* pertaining to a theme

THEME   *n* pl. -S a subject discussed in speech or writing

THEN   *n* pl. -S that time

THENAGE   *n* pl. -S thanage

THENAL   *adj* pertaining to the palm of the hand

THENAR   *n* pl. -S the palm of the hand

THENCE   *adv* from that place

THEOCRAT   *n* pl. -S a person who rules as a representative of a god

THEODICY   *n* pl. -CIES a defense of God's goodness in respect to the existence of evil

THEOGONY   *n* pl. -NIES an account of the origin of the gods

THEOLOG   *n* pl. -S a student of theology

THEOLOGY   *n* pl. -GIES the study of religion

THEONOMY   *n* pl. -MIES rule by a god

THEORBO   *n* pl. -BOS an ancient lute

THEOREM   *n* pl. -S a proposition that is demonstrably true or is assumed to be so

THEORIES   pl. of theory

THEORISE   *v* -RISED, -RISING, -RISES to theorize

THEORIST   *n* pl. -S one that theorizes

THEORIZE   *v* -RIZED, -RIZING, -RIZES to form theories

THEORY   *n* pl. -RIES a group of propositions used to explain a class of phenomena

THERAPY   *n* pl. -PIES the treatment of illness or disability

THERE   *n* pl. -S that place

THEREAT   *adv* at that place or time

THEREBY   *adv* by that means

THEREFOR	*adv* for that
THEREIN	*adv* in that place
THEREMIN	*n* pl. -S a musical instrument
THEREOF	*adv* of that
THEREON	*adv* on that
THERETO	*adv* to that
THERIAC	*n* pl. -S molasses
THERIACA	*n* pl. -S theriac
THERM	*n* pl. -S a unit of quantity of heat
THERMAE	*n/pl* hot springs
THERMAL	*n* pl. -S a rising mass of warm air
THERME	*n* pl. -S therm
THERMEL	*n* pl. -S a device for temperature measurement
THERMIC	*adj* pertaining to heat
THERMION	*n* pl. -S an ion emitted by a heated body
THERMIT	*n* pl. -S thermite
THERMITE	*n* pl. -S a metallic mixture that produces intense heat when ignited
THERMOS	*n* pl. -ES a container used to keep liquids either hot or cold
THEROID	*adj* resembling a beast
THEROPOD	*n* pl. -S a carnivorous dinosaur
THESAURI	*n/pl* dictionaries of synonyms and antonyms
THESE	pl. of this
THESIS	*n* pl. THESES a proposition put forward for discussion
THESPIAN	*n* pl. -S an actor or actress
THETA	*n* pl. -S a Greek letter
THETIC	*adj* arbitrary
THETICAL	*adj* thetic
THEURGY	*n* pl. -GIES divine intervention in human affairs **THEURGIC** *adj*
THEW	*n* pl. -S a well-developed muscle **THEWY** *adj*
THEWLESS	*adj* weak
THEY	*pron* the 3d person pl. pronoun in the nominative case
THIAMIN	*n* pl. -S thiamine
THIAMINE	*n* pl. -S a B vitamin
THIAZIDE	*n* pl. -S a drug used to treat high blood pressure
THIAZIN	*n* pl. -S thiazine

THIAZINE	*n* pl. -S a chemical compound
THIAZOL	*n* pl. -S thiazole
THIAZOLE	*n* pl. -S a chemical compound
THICK	*adj* THICKER, THICKEST having relatively great extent from one surface to its opposite
THICK	*n* pl. -S the thickest part
THICKEN	*v* -ED, -ING, -S to make thick
THICKET	*n* pl. -S a dense growth of shrubs or small trees **THICKETY** *adj*
THICKISH	*adj* somewhat thick
THICKLY	*adv* in a thick manner
THICKSET	*n* pl. -S a thicket
THIEF	*n* pl. THIEVES one that steals
THIEVE	*v* THIEVED, THIEVING, THIEVES to steal
THIEVERY	*n* pl. -ERIES the act or practice of stealing
THIEVES	pl. of thief
THIEVING	present participle of thieve
THIEVISH	*adj* given to stealing
THIGH	*n* pl. -S a part of the leg **THIGHED** *adj*
THILL	*n* pl. -S a shaft of a vehicle
THIMBLE	*n* pl. -S a cap used to protect the fingertip during sewing
THIN	*adj* THINNER, THINNEST having relatively little density or thickness
THIN	*v* THINNED, THINNING, THINS to make thin
THINCLAD	*n* pl. -S a runner on a track team
THINDOWN	*n* pl. -S a lessening in the number of atomic particles and cosmic rays passing through the earth's atmosphere
THINE	*pron* a possessive form of the pronoun thou
THING	*n* pl. -S an inanimate object
THINK	*v* THOUGHT, THINKING, THINKS to formulate in the mind
THINKER	*n* pl. -S one that thinks
THINKING	*n* pl. -S an opinion or judgment
THINLY	*adv* in a thin manner
THINNED	past tense of thin
THINNER	*n* pl. -S one that thins
THINNESS	*n* pl. -ES the quality or state of being thin

THINNEST	superlative of thin
THINNING	present participle of thin
THINNISH	*adj* somewhat thin
THIO	*adj* containing sulfur
THIOL	*n* pl. -S a sulfur compound **THIOLIC** *adj*
THIONATE	*n* pl. -S a chemical salt
THIONIC	*adj* pertaining to sulfur
THIONIN	*n* pl. -S a violet dye
THIONINE	*n* pl. -S thionin
THIONYL	*n* pl. -S sulfinyl
THIOPHEN	*n* pl. -S a chemical compound
THIOTEPA	*n* pl. -S a chemical compound
THIOUREA	*n* pl. -S a chemical compound
THIR	*pron* these
THIRAM	*n* pl. -S a chemical compound
THIRD	*n* pl. -S one of three equal parts
THIRDLY	*adv* in the third place
THIRL	*v* -ED, -ING, -S to thrill
THIRLAGE	*n* pl. -S an obligation requiring feudal tenants to grind grain at a certain mill
THIRST	*v* -ED, -ING, -S to feel a desire or need to drink
THIRSTER	*n* pl. -S one that thirsts
THIRSTY	*adj* THIRSTIER, THIRSTIEST feeling a desire or need to drink
THIRTEEN	*n* pl. -S a number
THIRTY	*n* pl. -TIES a number
THIS	*pron* pl. THESE the person or thing just mentioned
THISTLE	*n* pl. -S a prickly plant **THISTLY** *adj*
THITHER	*adv* in that direction
THO	*conj* though
THOLE	*v* THOLED, THOLING, THOLES to endure
THOLEPIN	*n* pl. -S a pin that serves as an oarlock
THOLOS	*n* pl. -LOI a circular, underground tomb
THONG	*n* pl. -S a narrow strip of leather used for binding **THONGED** *adj*
THORAX	*n* pl. -RACES or -RAXES the part of the body between the neck and the abdomen **THORACAL, THORACIC** *adj*
THORIA	*n* pl. -S an oxide of thorium
THORIC	*adj* pertaining to thorium
THORITE	*n* pl. -S a thorium ore
THORIUM	*n* pl. -S a metallic element
THORN	*v* -ED, -ING, -S to prick with a thorn (a sharp, rigid projection on a plant)
THORNY	*adj* THORNIER, THORNIEST full of thorns **THORNILY** *adv*
THORO	*adj* thorough
THORON	*n* pl. -S a radioactive isotope of radon
THOROUGH	*adj* -OUGHER, -OUGHEST complete in all respects
THORP	*n* pl. -S a small village
THORPE	*n* pl. -S thorp
THOSE	pl. of that
THOU	*v* -ED, -ING, -S to address as "thou" (the 2d person sing. pronoun in the nominative case)
THOUGH	*conj* despite the fact that
THOUGHT	*n* pl. -S a product of thinking
THOUSAND	*n* pl. -S a number
THOWLESS	*adj* listless
THRALDOM	*n* pl. -S servitude
THRALL	*v* -ED, -ING, -S to enslave
THRASH	*v* -ED, -ING, -ES to beat
THRASHER	*n* pl. -S one that thrashes
THRAVE	*n* pl. -S a unit of measure for grain
THRAW	*v* -ED, -ING, -S to twist
THRAWART	*adj* stubborn
THRAWN	*adj* twisted **THRAWNLY** *adv*
THREAD	*v* -ED, -ING, -S to pass a thread (a very slender cord) through
THREADER	*n* pl. -S one that threads
THREADY	*adj* THREADIER, THREADIEST resembling a thread
THREAP	*v* -ED, -ING, -S to dispute
THREAPER	*n* pl. -S one that threaps
THREAT	*v* -ED, -ING, -S to threaten
THREATEN	*v* -ED, -ING, -S to be a source of danger to
THREE	*n* pl. -S a number
THREEP	*v* -ED, -ING, -S to threap
THRENODE	*n* pl. -S a threnody
THRENODY	*n* pl. -DIES a song of lamentation
THRESH	*v* -ED, -ING, -ES to separate the grain or seeds from a plant mechanically

THRESHER	*n* pl. -S one that threshes
THREW	past tense of throw
THRICE	*adv* three times
THRIFT	*n* pl. -S care and wisdom in the management of one's resources
THRIFTY	*adj* THRIFTIER, THRIFTIEST displaying thrift
THRILL	*v* -ED, -ING, -S to excite greatly
THRILLER	*n* pl. -S one that thrills
THRIP	*n* pl. -S a British coin
THRIVE	*v* THROVE or THRIVED, THRIVEN, THRIVING, THRIVES to grow vigorously
THRIVER	*n* pl. -S one that thrives
THRO	*prep* through
THROAT	*v* -ED, -ING, -S to utter in a hoarse voice
THROATY	*adj* THROATIER, THROATIEST hoarse
THROB	*v* THROBBED, THROBBING, THROBS to pulsate
THROBBER	*n* pl. -S one that throbs
THROE	*n* pl. -S a violent spasm of pain
THROMBIN	*n* pl. -S an enzyme
THROMBUS	*n* pl. -BI a clot occluding a blood vessel
THRONE	*v* THRONED, THRONING, THRONES to place on a throne (a royal chair)
THRONG	*v* -ED, -ING, -S to crowd into
THROSTLE	*n* pl. -S a songbird
THROTTLE	*v* -TLED, -TLING, -TLES to strangle
THROUGH	*prep* by way of
THROVE	a past tense of thrive
THROW	*v* THREW, THROWN, THROWING, THROWS to propel through the air with a movement of the arm
THROWER	*n* pl. -S one that throws
THRU	*prep* through
THRUM	*v* THRUMMED, THRUMMING, THRUMS to play a stringed instrument idly or monotonously
THRUMMER	*n* pl. -S one that thrums
THRUMMY	*adj* -MIER, -MIEST shaggy
THRUPUT	*n* pl. -S the amount of raw material processed within a given time
THRUSH	*n* pl. -ES a songbird
THRUST	*v* -ED, -ING, -S to push forcibly
THRUSTER	*n* pl. -S one that thrusts
THRUSTOR	*n* pl. -S thruster
THRUWAY	*n* pl. -WAYS an express highway
THUD	*v* THUDDED, THUDDING, THUDS to make a dull, heavy sound
THUG	*n* pl. -S a brutal ruffian or assassin
THUGGEE	*n* pl. -S thuggery in India
THUGGERY	*n* pl. -GERIES thuggish behavior
THUGGISH	*adj* characteristic of a thug
THUJA	*n* pl. -S an evergreen tree or shrub
THULIA	*n* pl. -S an oxide of thulium
THULIUM	*n* pl. -S a metallic element
THUMB	*v* -ED, -ING, -S to leaf through with the thumb (the short, thick digit of the human hand)
THUMBKIN	*n* pl. -S a screw that is turned by the thumb and fingers
THUMBNUT	*n* pl. -S a nut that is turned by the thumb and fingers
THUMP	*v* -ED, -ING, -S to strike so as to make a dull, heavy sound
THUMPER	*n* pl. -S one that thumps
THUNDER	*v* -ED, -ING, -S to produce a loud, resounding sound
THUNDERY	*adj* accompanied with thunder
THURIBLE	*n* pl. -S a censer
THURIFER	*n* pl. -S one who carries a thurible in a religious ceremony
THURL	*n* pl. -S the hip joint in cattle
THUS	*adv* in this manner
THUSLY	*adv* thus
THUYA	*n* pl. -S thuja
THWACK	*v* -ED, -ING, -S to strike with something flat
THWACKER	*n* pl. -S one that thwacks
THWART	*v* -ED, -ING, -S to prevent the accomplishment of
THWARTER	*n* pl. -S one that thwarts
THWARTLY	*adv* athwart
THY	*pron* a possessive form of the pronoun thou
THYME	*n* pl. -S an aromatic herb
THYMEY	*adj* THYMIER, THYMIEST thymy
THYMI	a pl. of thymus
THYMIC	*adj* pertaining to thyme

THYMIER	comparative of thymey and thymy
THYMIEST	superlative of thymey and thymy
THYMINE	*n* pl. -S a chemical compound
THYMOL	*n* pl. -S a chemical compound
THYMUS	*n* pl. -MI or -MUSES a glandular structure in the body
THYMY	*adj* THYMIER, THYMIEST abounding in thyme
THYREOID	*adj* pertaining to the thyroid
THYROID	*n* pl. -S an endocrine gland
THYROXIN	*n* pl. -S an amino acid
THYRSE	*n* pl. -S thyrsus
THYRSUS	*n* pl. -SI a type of flower cluster **THYRSOID** *adj*
THYSELF	*pron* yourself
TI	*n* pl. -S the seventh tone of the diatonic musical scale
TIARA	*n* pl. -S a jeweled headpiece worn by women **TIARAED** *adj*
TIBIA	*n* pl. -IAE or -IAS a bone of the leg **TIBIAL** *adj*
TIC	*n* pl. -S an involuntary muscular contraction
TICAL	*n* pl. -S a former Thai unit of weight
TICK	*v* -ED, -ING, -S to make a recurrent clicking sound
TICKER	*n* pl. -S one that ticks
TICKET	*v* -ED, -ING, -S to attach a tag to
TICKING	*n* pl. -S a strong cotton fabric
TICKLE	*v* -LED, -LING, -LES to touch lightly so as to produce a tingling sensation
TICKLER	*n* pl. -S one that tickles
TICKLISH	*adj* sensitive to tickling
TICKSEED	*n* pl. -S a flowering plant
TICKTACK	*v* -ED, -ING, -S to ticktock
TICKTOCK	*v* -ED, -ING, -S to make the ticking sound of a clock
TICTAC	*v* -TACKED, -TACKING, -TACS to ticktack
TICTOC	*v* -TOCKED, -TOCKING, -TOCS to ticktock
TIDAL	*adj* pertaining to the tides **TIDALLY** *adv*
TIDBIT	*n* pl. -S a choice bit of food
TIDDLY	*adj* slightly drunk
TIDE	*v* TIDED, TIDING, TIDES to flow like the tide (the rise and fall of the ocean's waters)
TIDELAND	*n* pl. -S land alternately covered and uncovered by the tide
TIDELESS	*adj* lacking a tide
TIDELIKE	*adj* resembling a tide
TIDEMARK	*n* pl. -S a mark showing the highest or lowest point of a tide
TIDERIP	*n* pl. -S a riptide
TIDEWAY	*n* pl. -WAYS a tidal channel
TIDIED	past tense of tidy
TIDIER	comparative of tidy
TIDIES	present 3d person sing. of tidy
TIDIEST	superlative of tidy
TIDILY	*adv* in a tidy manner
TIDINESS	*n* pl. -ES the state of being tidy
TIDING	*n* pl. -S a piece of news
TIDY	*adj* -DIER, -DIEST neat and orderly
TIDY	*v* -DIED, -DYING, -DIES to make tidy
TIDYTIPS	*n* pl. TIDYTIPS an annual herb
TIE	*v* TIED, TYING or TIEING, TIES to fasten with a cord or rope
TIEBACK	*n* pl. -S a loop for holding a curtain back to one side
TIECLASP	*n* pl. -S a clasp for securing a necktie
TIED	past tense of tie
TIEPIN	*n* pl. -S a pin for securing a necktie
TIER	*v* -ED, -ING, -S to arrange in tiers (rows placed one above another)
TIERCE	*n* pl. -S one of seven canonical daily periods for prayer and devotion
TIERCED	*adj* divided into three equal parts
TIERCEL	*n* pl. -S tercel
TIFF	*v* -ED, -ING, -S to have a petty quarrel
TIFFANY	*n* pl. -NIES a thin, mesh fabric
TIFFIN	*v* -ED, -ING, -S to lunch
TIGER	*n* pl. -S a large feline mammal
TIGEREYE	*n* pl. -S a gemstone
TIGERISH	*adj* resembling a tiger

TIGHT	*adj* TIGHTER, TIGHTEST firmly or closely fixed in place **TIGHTLY** *adv*
TIGHTEN	*v* -ED, -ING, -S to make tight
TIGHTS	*n/pl* a close-fitting garment
TIGHTWAD	*n* pl. -S a miser
TIGLON	*n* pl. -S the offspring of a male tiger and a female lion
TIGON	*n* pl. -S tiglon
TIGRESS	*n* pl. -ES a female tiger
TIGRISH	*adj* tigerish
TIKE	*n* pl. -S tyke
TIKI	*n* pl. -S a wood or stone image of a Polynesian god
TIL	*n* pl. -S the sesame plant
TILAPIA	*n* pl. -S an African fish
TILBURY	*n* pl. -BURIES a carriage having two wheels
TILDE	*n* pl. -S a mark placed over a letter to indicate its sound
TILE	*v* TILED, TILING, TILES to cover with tiles (thin slabs of baked clay)
TILEFISH	*n* pl. -ES a marine food fish
TILELIKE	*adj* resembling a tile
TILER	*n* pl. -S one that tiles
TILING	*n* pl. -S a surface of tiles
TILL	*v* -ED, -ING, -S to prepare land for crops by plowing **TILLABLE** *adj*
TILLAGE	*n* pl. -S cultivated land
TILLER	*v* -ED, -ING, -S to put forth stems from a root
TILT	*v* -ED, -ING, -S to cause to slant **TILTABLE** *adj*
TILTER	*n* pl. -S one that tilts
TILTH	*n* pl. -S tillage
TILTYARD	*n* pl. -S an area for jousting contests
TIMARAU	*n* pl. -S tamarau
TIMBAL	*n* pl. -S a large drum
TIMBALE	*n* pl. -S a pastry shell shaped like a drum
TIMBER	*v* -ED, -ING, -S to furnish with timber (wood used as a building material)
TIMBRE	*n* pl. -S the quality given to a sound by its overtones
TIMBREL	*n* pl. -S a percussion instrument

TIME	*v* TIMED, TIMING, TIMES to determine the speed or duration of
TIMECARD	*n* pl. -S a card for recording an employee's times of arrival and departure
TIMELESS	*adj* having no beginning or end
TIMELY	*adj* -LIER, -LIEST occurring at the right moment
TIMEOUS	*adj* timely
TIMEOUT	*n* pl. -S a brief suspension of activity
TIMER	*n* pl. -S one that times
TIMEWORK	*n* pl. -S work paid for by the hour or by the day
TIMEWORN	*adj* showing the effects of long use or wear
TIMID	*adj* -IDER, -IDEST lacking courage or self-confidence **TIMIDLY** *adv*
TIMIDITY	*n* pl. -TIES the quality of being timid
TIMING	*n* pl. -S the selection of the proper moment for doing something
TIMOROUS	*adj* fearful
TIMOTHY	*n* pl. -THIES a European grass
TIMPANO	*n* pl. -NI a kettledrum
TIMPANUM	*n* pl. -NA or -NUMS tympanum
TIN	*v* TINNED, TINNING, TINS to coat with tin (a metallic element)
TINAMOU	*n* pl. -S a South American game bird
TINCAL	*n* pl. -S crude borax
TINCT	*v* -ED, -ING, -S to tinge
TINCTURE	*v* -TURED, -TURING, -TURES to tinge
TINDER	*n* pl. -S readily combustible material **TINDERY** *adj*
TINE	*v* TINED, TINING, TINES to lose
TINEA	*n* pl. -S a fungous skin disease **TINEAL** *adj*
TINEID	*n* pl. -S one of a family of moths
TINFOIL	*n* pl. -S a thin metal sheeting
TINFUL	*n* pl. -S as much as a tin container can hold
TING	*v* -ED, -ING, -S to emit a high-pitched metallic sound
TINGE	*v* TINGED, TINGEING or TINGING, TINGES to apply a trace of color to

TINGLE	v -GLED, -GLING, -GLES to cause a prickly, stinging sensation
TINGLER	n pl. -S one that tingles
TINGLY	adj -GLIER, -GLIEST tingling
TINHORN	n pl. -S a showily pretentious person
TINIER	comparative of tiny
TINIEST	superlative of tiny
TINILY	adv in a tiny manner
TININESS	n pl. -ES the quality of being tiny
TINING	present participle of tine
TINKER	v -ED, -ING, -S to repair in an unskilled or experimental manner
TINKERER	n pl. -S one that tinkers
TINKLE	v -KLED, -KLING, -KLES to make slight, sharp, metallic sounds
TINKLING	n pl. -S the sound made by something that tinkles
TINKLY	adj -KLIER, -KLIEST producing a tinkling sound
TINLIKE	adj resembling tin
TINMAN	n pl. -MEN a tinsmith
TINNED	past tense of tin
TINNER	n pl. -S a tin miner
TINNIER	comparative of tinny
TINNIEST	superlative of tinny
TINNILY	adv in a tinny manner
TINNING	present participle of tin
TINNITUS	n pl. -ES a ringing sound in the ears
TINNY	adj -NIER, -NIEST of or resembling tin
TINPLATE	n pl. -S thin sheet iron coated with tin
TINSEL	v -SELED, -SELING, -SELS or -SELLED, -SELLING, -SELS to give a showy or gaudy appearance to
TINSELLY	adj cheaply gaudy
TINSMITH	n pl. -S one who works with tin
TINSTONE	n pl. -S a tin ore
TINT	v -ED, -ING, -S to color slightly or delicately
TINTER	n pl. -S one that tints
TINTING	n pl. -S the process of one that tints
TINTLESS	adj lacking color
TINTYPE	n pl. -S a kind of photograph
TINWARE	n pl. -S articles made of tinplate
TINWORK	n pl. -S something made of tin
TINY	adj TINIER, TINIEST very small
TIP	v TIPPED, TIPPING, TIPS to tilt
TIPCART	n pl. -S a type of cart
TIPCAT	n pl. -S a game resembling baseball
TIPI	n pl. -S tepee
TIPLESS	adj having no point or extremity
TIPOFF	n pl. -S a hint or warning
TIPPABLE	adj capable of being tipped
TIPPED	past tense of tip
TIPPER	n pl. -S one that tips
TIPPET	n pl. -S a covering for the shoulders
TIPPIER	comparative of tippy
TIPPIEST	superlative of tippy
TIPPING	present participle of tip
TIPPLE	v -PLED, -PLING, -PLES to drink alcoholic beverages
TIPPLER	n pl. -S one that tipples
TIPPY	adj -PIER, -PIEST unsteady
TIPSIER	comparative of tipsy
TIPSIEST	superlative of tipsy
TIPSILY	adv in a tipsy manner
TIPSTAFF	n pl. -STAFFS or -STAVES an attendant in a court of law
TIPSTER	n pl. -S one that sells information to gamblers
TIPSTOCK	n pl. -S a part of a gun
TIPSY	adj -SIER, -SIEST slightly drunk
TIPTOE	v -TOED, -TOEING, -TOES to walk on the tips of one's toes
TIPTOP	n pl. -S the highest point
TIRADE	n pl. -S a long, vehement speech
TIRE	v TIRED, TIRING, TIRES to grow tired
TIRED	adj TIREDER, TIREDEST sapped of strength **TIREDLY** adv
TIRELESS	adj seemingly incapable of tiring
TIRESOME	adj tedious
TIRING	present participle of tire
TIRL	v -ED, -ING, -S to make a vibrating sound

TIRO	*n* pl. -ROS tyro
TIRRIVEE	*n* pl. -S a tantrum
TISANE	*n* pl. -S a ptisan
TISSUAL	*adj* pertaining to tissue
TISSUE	*v* -SUED, -SUING, -SUES to weave into tissue (a fine sheer fabric)
TISSUEY	*adj* resembling tissue
TIT	*n* pl. -S a small bird
TITAN	*n* pl. -S a person of great size
TITANATE	*n* pl. -S a chemical salt
TITANESS	*n* pl. -ES a female titan
TITANIA	*n* pl. -S a mineral
TITANIC	*adj* of great size
TITANISM	*n* pl. -S revolt against social conventions
TITANITE	*n* pl. -S a mineral
TITANIUM	*n* pl. -S a metallic element
TITANOUS	*adj* pertaining to titanium
TITBIT	*n* pl. -S tidbit
TITER	*n* pl. -S the strength of a chemical solution
TITHABLE	*adj* subject to the payment of tithes
TITHE	*v* TITHED, TITHING, TITHES to pay a tithe (a small tax)
TITHER	*n* pl. -S one that tithes
TITHING	*n* pl. -S the act of levying tithes
TITHONIA	*n* pl. -S a tall herb
TITI	*n* pl. -S an evergreen shrub or tree
TITIAN	*n* pl. -S a reddish brown color
TITIVATE	*v* -VATED, -VATING, -VATES to dress smartly
TITLARK	*n* pl. -S a songbird
TITLE	*v* -TLED, -TLING, -TLES to furnish with a title (a distinctive appellation)
TITLIST	*n* pl. -S a sports champion
TITMAN	*n* pl. -MEN the smallest of a litter of pigs
TITMOUSE	*n* pl. -MICE a small bird
TITRABLE	*adj* capable of being titrated
TITRANT	*n* pl. -S the reagent used in titration
TITRATE	*v* -TRATED, -TRATING, -TRATES to determine the strength of a solution by adding a reagent until a desired reaction occurs
TITRATOR	*n* pl. -S one that titrates
TITRE	*n* pl. -S titer
TITTER	*v* -ED, -ING, -S to utter a restrained, nervous laugh
TITTERER	*n* pl. -S one that titters
TITTIE	*n* pl. -S a sister
TITTIES	pl. of titty
TITTLE	*n* pl. -S a very small mark in writing or printing
TITTUP	*v* -TUPED, -TUPING, -TUPS or -TUPPED, -TUPPING, -TUPS to move in a lively manner
TITTUPPY	*adj* shaky; unsteady
TITTY	*n* pl. -TIES a teat
TITULAR	*n* pl. -S one who holds a title
TITULARY	*n* pl. -LARIES a titular
TIVY	*adv* with great speed
TIZZY	*n* pl. -ZIES a state of nervous confusion
TMESIS	*n* pl. TMESES the separation of the parts of a compound word by an intervening word or words
TO	*prep* in the direction of
TOAD	*n* pl. -S a tailless, jumping amphibian
TOADFISH	*n* pl. -ES a marine fish
TOADFLAX	*n* pl. -ES a perennial herb
TOADIED	past tense of toady
TOADIES	present 3d person sing. of toady
TOADISH	*adj* resembling a toad
TOADLESS	*adj* having no toads
TOADLIKE	*adj* resembling a toad
TOADY	*v* TOADIED, TOADYING, TOADIES to engage in servile flattering
TOADYISH	*adj* characteristic of one that toadies
TOADYISM	*n* pl. -S toadyish behavior
TOAST	*v* -ED, -ING, -S to brown by exposure to heat
TOASTER	*n* pl. -S a device for toasting
TOASTY	*adj* TOASTIER, TOASTIEST comfortably warm
TOBACCO	*n* pl. -COS or -COES an annual herb cultivated for its leaves
TOBOGGAN	*v* -ED, -ING, -S to ride on a long, narrow sled
TOBY	*n* pl. -BIES a type of drinking mug

TOCCATA *n* pl. -TAS or -TE a musical composition usually for an organ

TOCHER *v* -ED, -ING, -S to give a dowry to

TOCOLOGY *n* pl. -GIES the branch of medicine dealing with childbirth

TOCSIN *n* pl. -S an alarm sounded on a bell

TOD *n* pl. -S a British unit of weight

TODAY *n* pl. -DAYS the present day

TODDIES pl. of toddy

TODDLE *v* -DLED, -DLING, -DLES to walk unsteadily

TODDLER *n* pl. -S one that toddles

TODDY *n* pl. -DIES an alcoholic beverage

TODY *n* pl. -DIES a West Indian bird

TOE *v* TOED, TOEING, TOES to touch with the toe (one of the terminal members of the foot)

TOECAP *n* pl. -S a covering for the tip of a shoe or boot

TOEHOLD *n* pl. -S a space that supports the toes in climbing

TOELESS *adj* having no toes

TOELIKE *adj* resembling a toe

TOENAIL *v* -ED, -ING, -S to fasten with obliquely driven nails

TOEPIECE *n* pl. -S a piece of a shoe designed to cover the toes

TOEPLATE *n* pl. -S a metal tab attached to the tip of a shoe

TOESHOE *n* pl. -S a dance slipper without a heel

TOFF *n* pl. -S a dandy

TOFFEE *n* pl. -S a chewy candy

TOFFY *n* pl. -FIES toffee

TOFT *n* pl. -S a hillock

TOFU *n* pl. -S a soft Oriental cheese made from soybean milk

TOG *v* TOGGED, TOGGING, TOGS to clothe

TOGA *n* pl. -GAS or -GAE an outer garment worn in ancient Rome **TOGAED** *adj*

TOGATE *adj* pertaining to ancient Rome

TOGATED *adj* wearing a toga

TOGETHER *adv* into a union or relationship

TOGGED past tense of tog

TOGGERY *n* pl. -GERIES clothing

TOGGING present participle of tog

TOGGLE *v* -GLED, -GLING, -GLES to fasten with a type of pin or short rod

TOGGLER *n* pl. -S one that toggles

TOGUE *n* pl. -S a freshwater fish

TOIL *v* -ED, -ING, -S to work strenuously

TOILE *n* pl. -S a sheer linen fabric

TOILER *n* pl. -S one that toils

TOILET *v* -ED, -ING, -S to dress and groom oneself

TOILETRY *n* pl. -TRIES an article used in dressing and grooming oneself

TOILETTE *n* pl. -S the act of dressing and grooming oneself

TOILFUL *adj* toilsome

TOILSOME *adj* demanding much exertion

TOILWORN *adj* worn by toil

TOIT *v* -ED, -ING, -S to saunter

TOKAY *n* pl. -KAYS a Malaysian gecko

TOKE *n* pl. -S a puff on a marijuana cigarette

TOKEN *v* -ED, -ING, -S to serve as a sign of

TOKENISM *n* pl. -S the policy of making only a superficial effort

TOKOLOGY *n* pl. -GIES tocology

TOKONOMA *n* pl. -S a small alcove in a Japanese house

TOLA *n* pl. -S a unit of weight used in India

TOLAN *n* pl. -S a chemical compound

TOLANE *n* pl. -S tolan

TOLBOOTH *n* pl. -S a prison

TOLD past tense of tell

TOLE *v* TOLED, TOLING, TOLES to allure

TOLEDO *n* pl. -DOS a finely tempered sword

TOLERANT *adj* inclined to tolerate

TOLERATE *v* -ATED, -ATING, -ATES to allow without active opposition

TOLIDIN *n* pl. -S tolidine

TOLIDINE *n* pl. -S a chemical compound

TOLING present participle of tole

TOLL	*v* -ED, -ING, -S to collect or impose a toll (a fixed charge for a service or privilege)
TOLLAGE	*n* pl. -S a toll
TOLLBAR	*n* pl. -S a tollgate
TOLLER	*n* pl. -S a collector of tolls
TOLLGATE	*n* pl. -S a gate where a toll is collected
TOLLMAN	*n* pl. -MEN a toller
TOLLWAY	*n* pl. -WAYS a road on which tolls are collected
TOLU	*n* pl. -S a fragrant resin
TOLUATE	*n* pl. -S a chemical salt
TOLUENE	*n* pl. -S a flammable liquid
TOLUIC	*adj* pertaining to any of four isomeric acids derived from toluene
TOLUID	*n* pl. -S toluide
TOLUIDE	*n* pl. -S an amide
TOLUIDIN	*n* pl. -S an amine
TOLUOL	*n* pl. -S toluene
TOLUOLE	*n* pl. -S toluol
TOLUYL	*n* pl. -S a univalent chemical radical
TOLYL	*n* pl. -S a univalent chemical radical
TOM	*n* pl. -S the male of various animals
TOMAHAWK	*v* -ED, -ING, -S to strike with a light ax
TOMALLEY	*n* pl. -LEYS the liver of a lobster
TOMAN	*n* pl. -S a coin of Iran
TOMATO	*n* pl. -TOES the fleshy, edible fruit of a perennial plant
TOMB	*v* -ED, -ING, -S to place in a tomb (a burial vault or chamber)
TOMBAC	*n* pl. -S an alloy of copper and zinc
TOMBACK	*n* pl. -S tombac
TOMBAK	*n* pl. -S tombac
TOMBAL	*adj* pertaining to a tomb
TOMBLESS	*adj* having no tomb
TOMBLIKE	*adj* resembling a tomb
TOMBOLO	*n* pl. -LOS a sandbar connecting an island to the mainland
TOMBOY	*n* pl. -BOYS a girl who prefers boyish activities
TOMCAT	*n* pl. -S a male cat

TOMCOD	*n* pl. -S a marine fish
TOME	*n* pl. -S a large book
TOMENTUM	*n* pl. -TA a network of small blood vessels
TOMFOOL	*n* pl. -S a foolish person
TOMMY	*n* pl. -MIES a loaf of bread
TOMMYROT	*n* pl. -S nonsense
TOMOGRAM	*n* pl. -S a photograph made with X rays
TOMORROW	*n* pl. -S the day following today
TOMPION	*n* pl. -S tampion
TOMTIT	*n* pl. -S a small bird
TON	*n* pl. -S a unit of weight
TONAL	*adj* pertaining to tone **TONALLY** *adv*
TONALITY	*n* pl. -TIES a system of tones
TONDO	*n* pl. -DI a circular painting
TONE	*v* TONED, TONING, TONES to give a particular tone (a sound of definite pitch and vibration) to
TONELESS	*adj* lacking in tone
TONEME	*n* pl. -S a tonal unit of speech **TONEMIC** *adj*
TONER	*n* pl. -S one that tones
TONETICS	*n/pl* the phonetic study of tone in language **TONETIC** *adj*
TONETTE	*n* pl. -S a simple flute
TONG	*v* -ED, -ING, -S to lift with a type of grasping device
TONGA	*n* pl. -S a light cart used in India
TONGER	*n* pl. -S one that tongs
TONGMAN	*n* pl. -MEN a member of a Chinese secret society
TONGUE	*v* TONGUED, TONGUING, TONGUES to touch with the tongue (an organ of the mouth)
TONGUING	*n* pl. -S the use of the tongue in articulating notes on a wind instrument
TONIC	*n* pl. -S something that invigorates or refreshes
TONICITY	*n* pl. -TIES normal, healthy bodily condition
TONIER	comparative of tony
TONIEST	superlative of tony
TONIGHT	*n* pl. -S the present night
TONING	present participle of tone
TONISH	*adj* stylish **TONISHLY** *adv*
TONLET	*n* pl. -S a skirt of plate armor

TONNAGE *n* pl. -S total weight in tons

TONNE *n* pl. -S a unit of weight

TONNEAU *n* pl. -NEAUS or -NEAUX the rear seating compartment of an automobile

TONNER *n* pl. -S an object having a specified tonnage

TONNISH *adj* tonish

TONSIL *n* pl. -S a lymphoid organ **TONSILAR** *adj*

TONSURE *v* -SURED, -SURING, -SURES to shave the head of

TONTINE *n* pl. -S a form of collective life insurance

TONUS *n* pl. -ES a normal state of tension in muscle tissue

TONY *adj* TONIER, TONIEST stylish

TOO *adv* in addition

TOOK past tense of take

TOOL *v* -ED, -ING, -S to form or finish with a tool (an implement used in manual work)

TOOLBOX *n* pl. -ES a box for tools

TOOLER *n* pl. -S one that tools

TOOLHEAD *n* pl. -S a part of a machine

TOOLING *n* pl. -S ornamentation done with tools

TOOLLESS *adj* having no tools

TOOLROOM *n* pl. -S a room where tools are stored

TOOLSHED *n* pl. -S a building where tools are stored

TOOM *adj* empty

TOON *n* pl. -S an East Indian tree

TOOT *v* -ED, -ING, -S to sound a horn or whistle in short blasts

TOOTER *n* pl. -S one that toots

TOOTH *n* pl. TEETH one of the hard structures attached in a row to each jaw

TOOTH *v* -ED, -ING, -S to furnish with toothlike projections

TOOTHY *adj* TOOTHIER, TOOTHIEST having or showing prominent teeth **TOOTHILY** *adv*

TOOTLE *v* -TLED, -TLING, -TLES to toot softly or repeatedly

TOOTLER *n* pl. -S one that tootles

TOOTS *n* pl. -ES a woman or girl — usually used as a form of address

TOOTSIE *n* pl. -S tootsy

TOOTSY *n* pl. -SIES a foot

TOP *v* TOPPED, TOPPING, TOPS to cut off the top (the highest part, point, or surface) of

TOPAZ *n* pl. -ES a mineral **TOPAZINE** *adj*

TOPCOAT *n* pl. -S a lightweight overcoat

TOPCROSS *n* pl. -ES a cross between a purebred male and inferior female stock

TOPE *v* TOPED, TOPING, TOPES to drink liquor to excess

TOPEE *n* pl. -S topi

TOPER *n* pl. -S one that topes

TOPFUL *adj* topfull

TOPFULL *adj* full to the top

TOPH *n* pl. -S tufa

TOPHE *n* pl. -S tufa

TOPHUS *n* pl. -PHI a deposit of urates in the tissue around a joint

TOPI *n* pl. -S a sun helmet

TOPIARY *n* pl. -ARIES the art of trimming shrubs into shapes

TOPIC *n* pl. -S a subject of discourse **TOPICAL** *adj*

TOPING present participle of tope

TOPKICK *n* pl. -S a first sergeant

TOPKNOT *n* pl. -S an ornament for the hair

TOPLESS *adj* having no top

TOPLOFTY *adj* -LOFTIER, -LOFTIEST haughty

TOPMAST *n* pl. -S a mast of a ship

TOPMOST *adj* highest

TOPNOTCH *adj* excellent

TOPOI pl. of topos

TOPOLOGY *n* pl. -GIES a branch of mathematics

TOPONYM *n* pl. -S the name of a place

TOPONYMY *n* pl. -MIES the study of toponyms

TOPOS *n* pl. -POI a stock rhetorical theme

TOPOTYPE *n* pl. -S a specimen selected from a locality typical of a species

TOPPED past tense of top

TOPPER *n* pl. -S one that tops

TOPPING   *n* pl. -S something that forms a top

TOPPLE   *v* -PLED, -PLING, -PLES to fall forward

TOPSAIL   *n* pl. -S a sail of a ship

TOPSIDE   *n* pl. -S the upper portion of a ship

TOPSOIL   *v* -ED, -ING, -S to remove the surface layer of soil from

TOPSTONE   *n* pl. -S the stone at the top of a structure

TOPWORK   *v* -ED, -ING, -S to graft scions of another variety of plant on the main branches of

TOQUE   *n* pl. -S a close-fitting woman's hat

TOQUET   *n* pl. -S toque

TOR   *n* pl. -S a high, craggy hill

TORA   *n* pl. -S torah

TORAH   *n* pl. -S the body of Jewish law

TORC   *n* pl. -S a metal collar or necklace

TORCH   *v* -ED, -ING, -ES to set on fire

TORCHERE   *n* pl. -S a type of electric lamp

TORCHIER   *n* pl. -S torchere

TORCHON   *n* pl. -S a coarse lace

TORE   *n* pl. -S a torus

TOREADOR   *n* pl. -S a bullfighter

TORERO   *n* pl. -ROS a bullfighter

TOREUTIC   *adj* pertaining to a type of metalwork

TORI   pl. of torus

TORIC   *adj* pertaining to a torus

TORIES   pl. of tory

TORII   *n* pl. TORII the gateway of a Japanese temple

TORMENT   *v* -ED, -ING, -S to inflict with great bodily or mental suffering

TORN   past participle of tear

TORNADO   *n* pl. -DOES or -DOS a violent windstorm **TORNADIC** *adj*

TORNILLO   *n* pl. -LOS a flowering shrub

TORO   *n* pl. -ROS a bull

TOROID   *n* pl. -S a type of geometric surface **TOROIDAL** *adj*

TOROSE   *adj* cylindrical and swollen at intervals

TOROSITY   *n* pl. -TIES the quality or state of being torose

TOROUS   *adj* torose

TORPEDO   *v* -ED, -ING, -ES or -S to damage or sink with an underwater missile

TORPID   *n* pl. -S a racing boat

TORPIDLY   *adv* in a sluggish manner

TORPOR   *n* pl. -S mental or physical inactivity

TORQUATE   *adj* having a torques

TORQUE   *v* TORQUED, TORQUING, TORQUES to cause to twist

TORQUER   *n* pl. -S one that torques

TORQUES   *n* pl. -QUESES a band of feathers, hair, or coloration around the neck

TORQUING   present participle of torque

TORR   *n* pl. TORR a unit of pressure

TORREFY   *v* -FIED, -FYING, -FIES to subject to intense heat

TORRENT   *n* pl. -S a rapid stream of water

TORRID   *adj* -RIDER, -RIDEST extremely hot **TORRIDLY** *adv*

TORRIFY   *v* -FIED, -FYING, -FIES to torrefy

TORSADE   *n* pl. -S a twisted cord

TORSE   *n* pl. -S a wreath of twisted silks

TORSI   a pl. of torso

TORSION   *n* pl. -S the act of twisting

TORSK   *n* pl. -S a marine food fish

TORSO   *n* pl. -SI or -SOS the trunk of the human body

TORT   *n* pl. -S a civil wrong

TORTE   *n* pl. TORTEN or TORTES a rich cake

TORTILE   *adj* twisted; coiled

TORTILLA   *n* pl. -S a round, flat cake of unleavened cornmeal

TORTIOUS   *adj* of the nature of a tort

TORTOISE   *n* pl. -S any of an order of reptiles having the body enclosed in a bony shell

TORTONI   *n* pl. -S a type of ice cream

TORTRIX   *n* pl. -ES a small moth

TORTUOUS   *adj* marked by repeated turns or bends

TORTURE   *v* -TURED, -TURING, -TURES to subject to severe physical pain

TORTURER   *n* pl. -S one that tortures

TORULA   *n* pl. -LAE or -LAS a type of fungus

TORUS	*n* pl. -RI a large convex molding	**TOUCHE**	*interj* — used to acknowledge a hit in fencing
TORY	*n* pl. -RIES a political conservative	**TOUCHER**	*n* pl. -S one that touches
TOSH	*n* pl. -ES nonsense	**TOUCHUP**	*n* pl. -S an act of finishing by adding minor improvements
TOSS	*v* TOSSED or TOST, TOSSING, TOSSES to throw lightly	**TOUCHY**	*adj* TOUCHIER, TOUCHIEST overly sensitive **TOUCHILY** *adv*
TOSSER	*n* pl. -S one that tosses	**TOUGH**	*adj* TOUGHER, TOUGHEST strong and resilient
TOSSPOT	*n* pl. -S a drunkard		
TOSSUP	*n* pl. -S an even choice or chance	**TOUGH**	*n* pl. -S a rowdy
TOST	a past tense of toss	**TOUGHEN**	*v* -ED, -ING, -S to make tough
TOT	*v* TOTTED, TOTTING, TOTS to total	**TOUGHIE**	*n* pl. -S a tough
		TOUGHIES	pl. of toughy
TOTABLE	*adj* capable of being toted	**TOUGHISH**	*adj* somewhat tough
TOTAL	*v* -TALED, -TALING, -TALS or -TALLED, -TALLING, -TALS to ascertain the entire amount of	**TOUGHLY**	*adv* in a tough manner
		TOUGHY	*n* pl. TOUGHIES toughie
TOTALISE	*v* -ISED, -ISING, -ISES to totalize	**TOUPEE**	*n* pl. -S a wig worn to cover a bald spot
TOTALISM	*n* pl. -S centralized control by an autocratic authority	**TOUR**	*v* -ED, -ING, -S to travel from place to place
TOTALITY	*n* pl. -TIES the quality or state of being complete	**TOURACO**	*n* pl. -COS an African bird
TOTALIZE	*v* -IZED, -IZING, -IZES to make complete	**TOURER**	*n* pl. -S a large, open automobile
TOTALLED	a past tense of total	**TOURING**	*n* pl. -S cross-country skiing for pleasure
TOTALLING	a present participle of total	**TOURISM**	*n* pl. -S the practice of touring for pleasure
TOTALLY	*adv* completely		
TOTE	*v* TOTED, TOTING, TOTES to carry by hand	**TOURIST**	*n* pl. -S one who tours for pleasure **TOURISTY** *adj*
TOTEM	*n* pl. -S a natural object serving as the emblem of a family or clan **TOTEMIC** *adj*	**TOURNEY**	*v* -ED, -ING, -S to compete in a tournament
		TOUSE	*v* TOUSED, TOUSING, TOUSES to tousle
TOTEMISM	*n* pl. -S a system of tribal division according to totems	**TOUSLE**	*v* -SLED, -SLING, -SLES to dishevel
TOTEMIST	*n* pl. -S a specialist in totemism	**TOUT**	*v* -ED, -ING, -S to solicit brazenly
TOTEMITE	*n* pl. -S a totemist		
TOTER	*n* pl. -S one that totes	**TOUTER**	*n* pl. -S one that touts
TOTHER	*pron* the other	**TOUZLE**	*v* -ZLED, -ZLING, -ZLES to tousle
TOTING	present participle of tote		
TOTTED	past tense of tot	**TOVARICH**	*n* pl. -ES comrade
TOTTER	*v* -ED, -ING, -S to walk unsteadily	**TOVARISH**	*n* pl. -ES tovarich
		TOW	*v* -ED, -ING, -S to pull by means of a rope or chain
TOTTERER	*n* pl. -S one that totters	**TOWAGE**	*n* pl. -S the price paid for towing
TOTTERY	*adj* shaky	**TOWARD**	*prep* in the direction of
TOTTING	present participle of tot	**TOWARDLY**	*adj* favorable
TOUCAN	*n* pl. -S a tropical bird	**TOWARDS**	*prep* toward
TOUCH	*v* -ED, -ING, -ES to be in or come into contact with	**TOWAWAY**	*n* pl. -AWAYS the act of towing away a vehicle

TOWBOAT	*n* pl. -S a tugboat	**TOY**	*v* -ED, -ING, -S to amuse oneself as if with a toy (a child's plaything)
TOWEL	*v* -ELED, -ELING, -ELS or -ELLED, -ELLING, -ELS to wipe with a towel (an absorbent cloth)	**TOYER**	*n* pl. -S one that toys
		TOYISH	*adj* frivolous
TOWELING	*n* pl. -S material used for towels	**TOYLESS**	*adj* having no toy
TOWER	*v* -ED, -ING, -S to rise to a great height	**TOYLIKE**	*adj* resembling a toy
		TOYO	*n* pl. -YOS a smooth straw used in making hats
TOWERY	*adj* -ERIER, -ERIEST very tall	**TOYON**	*n* pl. -S an evergreen shrub
TOWHEAD	*n* pl. -S a head of light blond hair	**TRABEATE**	*adj* constructed with horizontal beams
TOWHEE	*n* pl. -S a common finch	**TRACE**	*v* TRACED, TRACING, TRACES to follow the course of
TOWIE	*n* pl. -S a form of contract bridge for three players	**TRACER**	*n* pl. -S one that traces
TOWLINE	*n* pl. -S a line used in towing	**TRACERY**	*n* pl. -ERIES ornamental work of interlaced lines
TOWMOND	*n* pl. -S a year	**TRACING**	present participle of trace
TOWMONT	*n* pl. -S towmond	**TRACHEA**	*n* pl. -CHEAE or -CHEAS the passage for conveying air to the lungs **TRACHEAL** *adj*
TOWN	*n* pl. -S a center of population smaller than a city		
TOWNEE	*n* pl. -S a townsman	**TRACHEID**	*n* pl. -S a long, tubular plant cell
TOWNFOLK	*n/pl* the inhabitants of a town	**TRACHLE**	*v* -LED, -LING, -LES to draggle
TOWNIE	*n* pl. -S a nonstudent who lives in a college town	**TRACHOMA**	*n* pl. -S a disease of the eye
		TRACHYTE	*n* pl. -S an igneous rock
TOWNIES	pl. of towny	**TRACING**	*n* pl. -S something that is traced
TOWNISH	*adj* characteristic of a town	**TRACK**	*v* -ED, -ING, -S to follow the marks left by an animal, a person, or a vehicle
TOWNLESS	*adj* having no towns		
TOWNLET	*n* pl. -S a small town		
TOWNSHIP	*n* pl. -S an administrative division of a county	**TRACKAGE**	*n* pl. -S the track system of a railroad
TOWNSMAN	*n* pl. -MEN a resident of a town	**TRACKER**	*n* pl. -S one that tracks
TOWNWEAR	*n* pl. -S apparel that is suitable for wear in the city	**TRACKING**	*n* pl. -S the placement of students within a curriculum
TOWNY	*n* pl. TOWNIES townie	**TRACKMAN**	*n* pl. -MEN a railroad worker
TOWPATH	*n* pl. -S a path along a river that is used by animals towing boats	**TRACT**	*n* pl. -S an expanse of land
		TRACTATE	*n* pl. -S a treatise
TOWROPE	*n* pl. -S a rope used in towing	**TRACTILE**	*adj* capable of being drawn out in length
TOWY	*adj* resembling coarse hemp or flax fiber		
TOXAEMIA	*n* pl. -S toxemia **TOXAEMIC** *adj*	**TRACTION**	*n* pl. -S the act of pulling or drawing over a surface **TRACTIVE** *adj*
TOXEMIA	*n* pl. -S the condition of having toxins in the blood **TOXEMIC** *adj*		
		TRACTOR	*n* pl. -S a motor vehicle used in farming
TOXIC	*adj* pertaining to a toxin		
TOXICAL	*adj* toxic	**TRAD**	*adj* traditional
TOXICANT	*n* pl. -S a poisonous substance	**TRADE**	*v* TRADED, TRADING, TRADES to give in exchange for another commodity **TRADABLE** *adj*
TOXICITY	*n* pl. -TIES the quality of being poisonous		
TOXIN	*n* pl. -S a poisonous substance		
TOXINE	*n* pl. -S toxin		
TOXOID	*n* pl. -S a type of toxin	**TRADER**	*n* pl. -S one that trades

TRADITOR *n* pl. -ES a traitor among the early Christians

TRADUCE *v* -DUCED, -DUCING, -DUCES to defame

TRADUCER *n* pl. -S one that traduces

TRAFFIC *v* -FICKED, -FICKING, -FICS to engage in buying and selling

TRAGEDY *n* pl. -DIES a disastrous event

TRAGI pl. of tragus

TRAGIC *adj* of the nature of a tragedy

TRAGICAL *adj* tragic

TRAGOPAN *n* pl. -S an Asian pheasant

TRAGUS *n* pl. -GI a part of the external opening of the ear

TRAIK *v* -ED, -ING, -S to trudge

TRAIL *v* -ED, -ING, -S to drag along a surface

TRAILER *v* -ED, -ING, -S to transport by means of a trailer (a vehicle drawn by another)

TRAIN *v* -ED, -ING, -S to instruct systematically

TRAINEE *n* pl. -S a person receiving training

TRAINER *n* pl. -S one that trains

TRAINFUL *n* pl. -S as much as a railroad train will hold

TRAINING *n* pl. -S systematic instruction

TRAINMAN *n* pl. -MEN a railroad employee

TRAINWAY *n* pl. -WAYS a railway

TRAIPSE *v* TRAIPSED, TRAIPSING, TRAIPSES to walk about in an idle or aimless manner

TRAIT *n* pl. -S a distinguishing characteristic

TRAITOR *n* pl. -S one who betrays another

TRAJECT *v* -ED, -ING, -S to transmit

TRAM *v* TRAMMED, TRAMMING, TRAMS to convey in a tramcar

TRAMCAR *n* pl. -S a streetcar

TRAMEL *v* -ELED, -ELING, -ELS or -ELLED, -ELLING, -ELS to trammel

TRAMELL *v* -ED, -ING, -S to trammel

TRAMLESS *adj* having no tramcar

TRAMLINE *n* pl. -S a streetcar line

TRAMMED past tense of tram

TRAMMEL *v* -MELED, -MELING, -MELS or -MELLED, -MELLING, -MELS to hinder

TRAMMING present participle of tram

TRAMP *v* -ED, -ING, -S to walk with a firm, heavy step

TRAMPER *n* pl. -S one that tramps

TRAMPISH *adj* resembling a vagabond

TRAMPLE *v* -PLED, -PLING, -PLES to tread on heavily

TRAMPLER *n* pl. -S one that tramples

TRAMROAD *n* pl. -S a railway in a mine

TRAMWAY *n* pl. -WAYS a tramline

TRANCE *v* TRANCED, TRANCING, TRANCES to put into a trance (a semiconscious state)

TRANGAM *n* pl. -S a gewgaw

TRANQUIL *adj* -QUILER, -QUILEST or -QUILLER, -QUILLEST free from disturbance

TRANS *adj* characterized by the arrangement of different atoms on opposite sides of the molecule

TRANSACT *v* -ED, -ING, -S to carry out

TRANSECT *v* -ED, -ING, -S to cut across

TRANSEPT *n* pl. -S a major transverse part of the body of a church

TRANSFER *v* -FERRED, -FERRING, -FERS to convey from one source to another

TRANSFIX *v* -FIXED or -FIXT, -FIXING, -FIXES to impale

TRANSHIP *v* -SHIPPED, -SHIPPING, -SHIPS to transfer from one conveyance to another

TRANSIT *v* -ED, -ING, -S to pass across or through

TRANSMIT *v* -MITTED, -MITTING, -MITS to send from one place or person to another

TRANSOM *n* pl. -S a small window above a door or another window

TRANSUDE *v* -SUDED, -SUDING, -SUDES to pass through a membrane

TRAP *v* TRAPPED or TRAPT, TRAPPING, TRAPS to catch in a trap (a device for capturing and holding animals)

TRAPAN *v* -PANNED, -PANNING, -PANS to trepan

TRAPBALL *n* pl. -S a type of ball game

TRAPDOOR   *n* pl. -S a lifting or sliding door covering an opening

TRAPES   *v* -ED, -ING, -ES to traipse

TRAPEZE   *n* pl. -S a gymnastic apparatus

TRAPEZIA   *n/pl* four-sided polygons having no parallel sides

TRAPLIKE   *adj* resembling a trap

TRAPNEST   *v* -ED, -ING, -S to determine the productivity of hens with a type of nest

TRAPPEAN   *adj* pertaining to traprock

TRAPPED   a past tense of trap

TRAPPER   *n* pl. -S one that traps

TRAPPING   *n* pl. -S a covering for a horse

TRAPPOSE   *adj* trappean

TRAPPOUS   *adj* trappean

TRAPROCK   *n* pl. -S an igneous rock

TRAPT   a past tense of trap

TRAPUNTO   *n* pl. -TOS a decorative quilted design

TRASH   *v* -ED, -ING, -ES to free from trash (worthless or waste matter)

TRASHMAN   *n* pl. -MEN a person who removes trash

TRASHY   *adj* TRASHIER, TRASHIEST resembling trash **TRASHILY** *adv*

TRASS   *n* pl. -ES a volcanic rock

TRAUCHLE   *v* -LED, -LING, -LES to trachle

TRAUMA   *n* pl. -MAS or -MATA a severe emotional shock

TRAVAIL   *v* -ED, -ING, -S to toil

TRAVE   *n* pl. -S a frame for confining a horse

TRAVEL   *v* -ELED, -ELING, -ELS or -ELLED, -ELLING, -ELS to go from one place to another

TRAVELER   *n* pl. -S one that travels

TRAVELOG   *n* pl. -S a lecture or film on traveling

TRAVERSE   *v* -VERSED, -VERSING, -VERSES to pass across or through

TRAVESTY   *v* -TIED, -TYING, -TIES to parody

TRAVOIS   *n* pl. -ES a type of sled

TRAVOISE   *n* pl. -S travois

TRAWL   *v* -ED, -ING, -S to fish by dragging a net along the sea bottom

TRAWLER   *n* pl. -S a boat used for trawling

TRAWLEY   *n* pl. -LEYS a small truck or car for conveying material

TRAY   *n* pl. TRAYS a flat, shallow receptacle

TRAYFUL   *n* pl. -S as much as a tray will hold

TREACLE   *n* pl. -S molasses **TREACLY** *adj*

TREAD   *v* TROD, TRODE, or TREADED, TRODDEN, TREADING, TREADS to walk on, over, or along

TREADER   *n* pl. -S one that treads

TREADLE   *v* -LED, -LING, -LES to work a foot lever

TREADLER   *n* pl. -S one that treadles

TREASON   *n* pl. -S violation of allegiance toward one's country

TREASURE   *v* -URED, -URING, -URES to value highly

TREASURY   *n* pl. -URIES a place where funds are received, kept, and disbursed

TREAT   *v* -ED, -ING, -S to behave in a particular way toward

TREATER   *n* pl. -S one that treats

TREATISE   *n* pl. -S a formal and systematic written account of a subject

TREATY   *n* pl. -TIES a formal agreement between two or more nations

TREBLE   *v* -BLED, -BLING, -BLES to triple

TREBLY   *adv* triply

TRECENTO   *n* pl. -TOS the fourteenth century

TREDDLE   *v* -DLED, -DLING, -DLES to treadle

TREE   *v* TREED, TREEING, TREES to drive up a tree (a tall, woody plant)

TREELESS   *adj* having no tree

TREELIKE   *adj* resembling a tree

TREENAIL   *n* pl. -S a wooden peg used for fastening timbers

TREETOP   *n* pl. -S the top of a tree

TREF   *adj* unfit for use according to Jewish law

TREFAH   *adj* tref

TREFOIL   *n* pl. -S a plant having ternate leaves

TREHALA   *n* pl. -S a sweet, edible substance forming the pupal case of certain weevils

TREK	v TREKKED, TREKKING, TREKS to make a slow or arduous journey	**TREY**	n pl. TREYS a three in cards, dice, or dominoes
TREKKER	n pl. -S one that treks	**TRIABLE**	adj subject to judicial examination
TRELLIS	v -ED, -ING, -ES to provide with a trellis (a frame used as a support for climbing plants)	**TRIACID**	n pl. -S a type of acid
		TRIAD	n pl. -S a group of three
TREMBLE	v -BLED, -BLING, -BLES to shake involuntarily	**TRIADIC**	n pl. -S a member of a triad
		TRIADISM	n pl. -S the quality or state of being a triad
TREMBLER	n pl. -S one that trembles		
TREMBLY	adj -BLIER, -BLIEST marked by trembling	**TRIAGE**	n pl. -S a system of treating disaster victims
TREMOLO	n pl. -LOS a vibrating musical effect	**TRIAL**	n pl. -S a judicial examination
		TRIANGLE	n pl. -S a polygon having three sides
TREMOR	n pl. -S a shaking movement		
TRENAIL	n pl. -S treenail	**TRIARCHY**	n pl. -CHIES government by three persons
TRENCH	v -ED, -ING, -ES to dig a long, narrow excavation in the ground	**TRIAXIAL**	adj having three axes
TRENCHER	n pl. -S a wooden platter for serving food	**TRIAZIN**	n pl. -S triazine
		TRIAZINE	n pl. -S a chemical compound
TREND	v -ED, -ING, -S to take a particular course	**TRIAZOLE**	n pl. -S a chemical compound
		TRIBADE	n pl. -S a lesbian **TRIBADIC** adj
TRENDY	adj TRENDIER, TRENDIEST very fashionable **TRENDILY** adv	**TRIBAL**	adj pertaining to a tribe **TRIBALLY** adv
TREPAN	v -PANNED, -PANNING, -PANS to trephine	**TRIBASIC**	adj having three replaceable hydrogen atoms
TREPANG	n pl. -S a marine animal	**TRIBE**	n pl. -S a group of people sharing a common ancestry, language, and culture
TREPHINE	v -PHINED, -PHINING, -PHINES to operate on with a surgical saw		
		TRIBRACH	n pl. -S a type of metrical foot
TREPID	adj timorous	**TRIBUNAL**	n pl. -S a court of justice
TRESPASS	v -ED, -ING, -ES to enter upon the land of another unlawfully	**TRIBUNE**	n pl. -S a defender of the rights of the people
TRESS	n pl. -ES a long lock of hair **TRESSED** adj	**TRIBUTE**	n pl. -S something given to show respect, gratitude, or admiration
TRESSEL	n pl. -S trestle		
TRESSIER	comparative of tressy	**TRICE**	v TRICED, TRICING, TRICES to haul up with a rope
TRESSIEST	superlative of tressy		
TRESSOUR	n pl. -S tressure	**TRICEPS**	n pl. -ES an arm muscle
TRESSURE	n pl. -S a type of heraldic design	**TRICHINA**	n pl. -NAE or -NAS a parasitic worm
TRESSY	adj TRESSIER, TRESSIEST abounding in tresses	**TRICHITE**	n pl. -S a minute mineral body found in volcanic rocks
TRESTLE	n pl. -S a framework for supporting a bridge	**TRICHOID**	adj hairlike
		TRICHOME	n pl. -S a hairlike outgrowth
TRET	n pl. -S an allowance formerly paid to purchasers for waste incurred in transit	**TRICING**	present participle of trice
		TRICK	v -ED, -ING, -S to deceive
		TRICKER	n pl. -S one that tricks
TREVET	n pl. -S trivet	**TRICKERY**	n pl. -ERIES deception
TREWS	n/pl close-fitting tartan trousers	**TRICKIE**	adj TRICKIER, TRICKIEST tricky

TRICKIER	comparative of tricky	**TRIGGEST**	superlative of trig
TRICKIEST	superlative of tricky	**TRIGGING**	present participle of trig
TRICKILY	*adv* in a tricky manner	**TRIGLY**	*adv* in a trig manner
TRICKISH	*adj* tricky	**TRIGLYPH**	*n* pl. -S an architectural ornament
TRICKLE	*v* -LED, -LING, -LES to flow or fall in drops	**TRIGNESS**	*n* pl. -ES the quality or state of being trig
TRICKLY	*adj* -LIER, -LIEST marked by trickling	**TRIGO**	*n* pl. -GOS wheat
TRICKSY	*adj* -SIER, -SIEST mischievous	**TRIGON**	*n* pl. -S an ancient stringed instrument
TRICKY	*adj* TRICKIER, TRICKIEST characterized by deception	**TRIGONAL**	*adj* shaped like a triangle
TRICLAD	*n* pl. -S an aquatic flatworm	**TRIGRAPH**	*n* pl. -S a group of three letters representing one sound
TRICOLOR	*n* pl. -S a flag having three colors	**TRIHEDRA**	*n/pl* figures having three plane surfaces meeting at a point
TRICORN	*n* pl. -S a hat with the brim turned up on three sides	**TRIJET**	*n* pl. -S an airplane powered by three jet engines
TRICORNE	*n* pl. -S tricorn	**TRILBY**	*n* pl. -BIES a soft felt hat
TRICOT	*n* pl. -S a knitted fabric	**TRILL**	*v* -ED, -ING, -S to sing or play with a vibrating effect
TRICTRAC	*n* pl. -S a form of backgammon		
TRICYCLE	*n* pl. -S a vehicle having three wheels	**TRILLER**	*n* pl. -S one that trills
TRIDENT	*n* pl. -S a spear having three prongs	**TRILLION**	*n* pl. -S a number
		TRILLIUM	*n* pl. -S a flowering plant
TRIDUUM	*n* pl. -S a period of three days of prayer	**TRILOBAL**	*adj* trilobed
		TRILOBED	*adj* having three lobes
TRIED	past tense of try	**TRILOGY**	*n* pl. -GIES a group of three related literary works
TRIENE	*n* pl. -S a type of chemical compound		
TRIENNIA	*n/pl* periods of three years	**TRIM**	*adj* TRIMMER, TRIMMEST neat and orderly
TRIENS	*n* pl. -ENTES a coin of ancient Rome	**TRIM**	*v* TRIMMED, TRIMMING, TRIMS to make trim by cutting
TRIER	*n* pl. -S one that tries	**TRIMARAN**	*n* pl. -S a sailing vessel
TRIES	present 3d person sing. of try	**TRIMER**	*n* pl. -S a type of chemical compound
TRIETHYL	*adj* containing three ethyl groups	**TRIMETER**	*n* pl. -S a verse of three metrical feet
TRIFID	*adj* divided into three parts	**TRIMLY**	*adv* in a trim manner
TRIFLE	*v* -FLED, -FLING, -FLES to waste time	**TRIMMED**	past tense of trim
		TRIMMER	*n* pl. -S one that trims
TRIFLER	*n* pl. -S one that trifles	**TRIMMEST**	superlative of trim
TRIFLING	*n* pl. -S a waste of time	**TRIMMING**	*n* pl. -S something added as a decoration
TRIFOCAL	*n* pl. -S a type of lens		
TRIFOLD	*adj* having three parts	**TRIMNESS**	*n* pl. -ES the state of being trim
TRIFORIA	*n/pl* galleries in a church	**TRIMORPH**	*n* pl. -S a substance existing in three forms
TRIFORM	*adj* having three forms		
TRIG	*adj* TRIGGER, TRIGGEST neat	**TRIMOTOR**	*n* pl. -S an airplane powered by three engines
TRIG	*v* TRIGGED, TRIGGING, TRIGS to make trig	**TRINAL**	*adj* having three parts
TRIGGER	*v* -ED, -ING, -S to actuate	**TRINARY**	*adj* consisting of three parts

TRINDLE v -DLED, -DLING, -DLES to trundle

TRINE v TRINED, TRINING, TRINES to place in a particular astrological position

TRINITY n pl. -TIES a group of three

TRINKET v -ED, -ING, -S to deal secretly

TRINKUMS n/pl small ornaments

TRINODAL adj having three nodes

TRIO n pl. TRIOS a group of three

TRIODE n pl. -S a type of electron tube

TRIOL n pl. -S a type of chemical compound

TRIOLET n pl. -S a short poem of fixed form

TRIOSE n pl. -S a simple sugar

TRIOXID n pl. -S trioxide

TRIOXIDE n pl. -S a type of oxide

TRIP v TRIPPED, TRIPPING, TRIPS to stumble

TRIPACK n pl. -S a type of film pack

TRIPART adj divided into three parts

TRIPE n pl. -S a part of the stomach of a ruminant that is used as food

TRIPEDAL adj having three feet

TRIPHASE adj having three phases

TRIPLANE n pl. -S a type of airplane

TRIPLE v -PLED, -PLING, -PLES to make three times as great

TRIPLET n pl. -S a group of three of one kind

TRIPLEX n pl. -ES an apartment having three floors

TRIPLING present participle of triple

TRIPLITE n pl. -S a mineral

TRIPLOID n pl. -S a cell having a chromosome number that is three times the basic number

TRIPLY adv in a triple degree, manner, or number

TRIPOD n pl. -S a stand having three legs **TRIPODAL, TRIPODIC** adj

TRIPODY n pl. -DIES a verse of three metrical feet

TRIPOLI n pl. -S a soft, friable rock

TRIPOS n pl. -ES a tripod

TRIPPED past tense of trip

TRIPPER n pl. -S one that trips

TRIPPET n pl. -S a part of a mechanism designed to strike another part

TRIPPING n pl. -S the act of one that trips

TRIPTANE n pl. -S a chemical compound

TRIPTYCA n pl. -S a triptych

TRIPTYCH n pl. -S an ancient writing tablet

TRIREME n pl. -S an ancient Greek or Roman warship

TRISCELE n pl. -S triskele

TRISECT v -ED, -ING, -S to divide into three equal parts

TRISEME n pl. -S a type of metrical foot **TRISEMIC** adj

TRISKELE n pl. -S a figure consisting of three branches radiating from a center

TRISMUS n pl. -ES lockjaw **TRISMIC** adj

TRISOME n pl. -S an organism having one chromosome in addition to the usual diploid number

TRISOMIC n pl. -S a trisome

TRISOMY n pl. -MIES the condition of being a trisome

TRISTATE adj pertaining to an area made up of three adjoining states

TRISTE adj sad

TRISTEZA n pl. -S a disease of citrus trees

TRISTFUL adj sad

TRISTICH n pl. -S a stanza of three lines

TRITE adj TRITER, TRITEST used so often as to be made commonplace **TRITELY** adv

TRITHING n pl. -S an administrative division in England

TRITICUM n pl. -S a cereal grass

TRITIUM n pl. -S an isotope of hydrogen

TRITOMA n pl. -S an African herb

TRITON n pl. -S a marine mollusk

TRITONE n pl. -S a musical interval of three whole tones

TRIUMPH v -ED, -ING, -S to be victorious

TRIUMVIR n pl. -VIRS or -VIRI one of a ruling body of three in ancient Rome

TRIUNE n pl. -S a trinity

TRIUNITY n pl. -TIES a trinity

TRIVALVE n pl. -S a type of shell

TRIVET n pl. -S a small stand having three legs

TRIVIA	*n/pl* insignificant matters
TRIVIAL	*adj* insignificant
TRIVIUM	*n* pl. -IA a group of studies in medieval schools
TROAK	*v* -ED, -ING, -S to troke
TROCAR	*n* pl. -S a surgical instrument
TROCHAIC	*n* pl. -S a trochee
TROCHAL	*adj* shaped like a wheel
TROCHAR	*n* pl. -S trocar
TROCHE	*n* pl. -S a medicated lozenge
TROCHEE	*n* pl. -S a type of metrical foot
TROCHIL	*n* pl. -S an African bird
TROCHILI	*n/pl* trochils
TROCHLEA	*n* pl. -LEAE or -LEAS an anatomical structure resembling a pulley
TROCHOID	*n* pl. -S a type of geometric curve
TROCK	*v* -ED, -ING, -S to troke
TROD	a past tense of tread
TRODDEN	past participle of tread
TRODE	a past tense of tread
TROFFER	*n* pl. -S a fixture for fluorescent lighting
TROGON	*n* pl. -S a tropical bird
TROIKA	*n* pl. -S a Russian carriage
TROILITE	*n* pl. -S a mineral
TROILUS	*n* pl. -ES a large butterfly
TROIS	*n* pl. TROIS the number three
TROKE	*v* TROKED, TROKING, TROKES to exchange
TROLAND	*n* pl. -S a unit of measurement of retinal response to light
TROLL	*n* pl. -S a dwarf or giant of Teutonic folklore
TROLL	*v* -ED, -ING, -S to fish with a slowly trailing line
TROLLER	*n* pl. -S one that trolls
TROLLEY	*v* -ED, -ING, -S to convey by streetcar
TROLLIED	past tense of trolly
TROLLIES	present 3d person sing. of trolly
TROLLING	*n* pl. -S the act of one that trolls
TROLLOP	*n* pl. -S a prostitute **TROLLOPY** *adj*
TROLLY	*v* -LIED, -LYING, -LIES to trolley
TROMBONE	*n* pl. -S a brass wind instrument
TROMMEL	*n* pl. -S a screen used for sifting rock, ore, or coal
TROMP	*v* -ED, -ING, -S to tramp
TROMPE	*n* pl. -S a device used for supplying air to a furnace
TRONA	*n* pl. -S a mineral
TRONE	*n* pl. -S a weighing device
TROOP	*v* -ED, -ING, -S to move or gather in crowds
TROOPER	*n* pl. -S a cavalryman
TROOPIAL	*n* pl. -S troupial
TROOZ	*n/pl* trews
TROP	*adv* too much
TROPE	*n* pl. -S the figurative use of a word
TROPHIC	*adj* pertaining to nutrition
TROPHY	*v* -PHIED, -PHYING, -PHIES to honor with a trophy (a symbol of victory)
TROPIC	*n* pl. -S either of two circles of the celestial sphere on each side of the equator **TROPICAL** *adj*
TROPIN	*n* pl. -S tropine
TROPINE	*n* pl. -S a poisonous alkaloid
TROPISM	*n* pl. -S the involuntary response of an organism to an external stimulus
TROT	*v* TROTTED, TROTTING, TROTS to go at a gait between a walk and a run
TROTH	*v* -ED, -ING, -S to betroth
TROTLINE	*n* pl. -S a strong fishing line
TROTTED	past tense of trot
TROTTER	*n* pl. -S a horse that trots
TROTTING	present participle of trot
TROTYL	*n* pl. -S an explosive
TROUBLE	*v* -BLED, -BLING, -BLES to distress
TROUBLER	*n* pl. -S one that troubles
TROUGH	*n* pl. -S a long, narrow receptacle
TROUNCE	*v* TROUNCED, TROUNCING, TROUNCES to beat severely
TROUPE	*v* TROUPED, TROUPING, TROUPES to tour with a theatrical company
TROUPER	*n* pl. -S a member of a theatrical company
TROUPIAL	*n* pl. -S a tropical bird

TROUPING	present participle of troupe
TROUSER	*adj* pertaining to trousers
TROUSERS	*n/pl* a garment for the lower part of the body
TROUT	*n* pl. -S a freshwater fish
TROUTY	*adj* TROUTIER, TROUTIEST abounding in trout
TROUVERE	*n* pl. -S a medieval poet
TROUVEUR	*n* pl. -S trouvere
TROVE	*n* pl. -S a valuable discovery
TROVER	*n* pl. -S a type of legal action
TROW	*v* -ED, -ING, -S to suppose
TROWEL	*v* -ELED, -ELING, -ELS or -ELLED, -ELLING, -ELS to smooth with a trowel (a hand tool having a flat blade)
TROWELER	*n* pl. -S one that trowels
TROWSERS	*n/pl* trousers
TROWTH	*n* pl. -S truth
TROY	*n* pl. TROYS a system of weights
TRUANCY	*n* pl. -CIES an act of truanting
TRUANT	*v* -ED, -ING, -S to stay out of school without permission
TRUANTRY	*n* pl. -RIES truancy
TRUCE	*v* TRUCED, TRUCING, TRUCES to suspend hostilities by mutual agreement
TRUCK	*v* -ED, -ING, -S to transport by truck (an automotive vehicle designed to carry loads)
TRUCKAGE	*n* pl. -S transportation of goods by trucks
TRUCKER	*n* pl. -S a truck driver
TRUCKING	*n* pl. -S truckage
TRUCKLE	*v* -LED, -LING, -LES to yield weakly
TRUCKLER	*n* pl. -S one that truckles
TRUCKMAN	*n* pl. -MEN a trucker
TRUDGE	*v* TRUDGED, TRUDGING, TRUDGES to walk tiredly
TRUDGEN	*n* pl. -S a swimming stroke
TRUDGEON	*n* pl. -S trudgen
TRUDGER	*n* pl. -S one that trudges
TRUDGING	present participle of trudge
TRUE	*adj* TRUER, TRUEST consistent with fact or reality
TRUE	*v* TRUED, TRUING or TRUEING, TRUES to bring to conformity with a standard or requirement
TRUEBLUE	*n* pl. -S a person of unwavering loyalty
TRUEBORN	*adj* genuinely such by birth
TRUED	past tense of true
TRUELOVE	*n* pl. -S a sweetheart
TRUENESS	*n* pl. -ES the quality or state of being true
TRUER	comparative of true
TRUEST	superlative of true
TRUFFE	*n* pl. -S truffle
TRUFFLE	*n* pl. -S an edible fungus **TRUFFLED** *adj*
TRUING	a present participle of true
TRUISM	*n* pl. -S an obvious truth **TRUISTIC** *adj*
TRULL	*n* pl. -S a prostitute
TRULY	*adv* in conformity with fact or reality
TRUMEAU	*n* pl. -MEAUX a column supporting part of a doorway
TRUMP	*v* -ED, -ING, -S to outdo
TRUMPERY	*n* pl. -ERIES worthless finery
TRUMPET	*v* -ED, -ING, -S to sound on a trumpet (a brass wind instrument)
TRUNCATE	*v* -CATED, -CATING, -CATES to shorten by cutting off a part
TRUNDLE	*v* -DLED, -DLING, -DLES to propel by causing to rotate
TRUNDLER	*n* pl. -S one that trundles
TRUNK	*n* pl. -S the main stem of a tree **TRUNKED** *adj*
TRUNNEL	*n* pl. -S treenail
TRUNNION	*n* pl. -S a pin or pivot on which something can be rotated
TRUSS	*v* -ED, -ING, -ES to secure tightly
TRUSSER	*n* pl. -S one that trusses
TRUSSING	*n* pl. -S the framework of a structure
TRUST	*v* -ED, -ING, -S to place confidence in
TRUSTEE	*v* -TEED, -TEEING, -TEES to commit to the care of an administrator
TRUSTER	*n* pl. -S one that trusts
TRUSTFUL	*adj* inclined to trust
TRUSTY	*adj* TRUSTIER, TRUSTIEST worthy of trust **TRUSTILY** *adv*

TRUSTY	*n* pl. TRUSTIES one worthy of trust
TRUTH	*n* pl. -S conformity to fact or reality
TRUTHFUL	*adj* telling the truth
TRY	*v* TRIED, TRYING, TRIES to attempt
TRYINGLY	*adv* in a distressing manner
TRYMA	*n* pl. -MATA a type of nut
TRYOUT	*n* pl. -S a test of ability
TRYPSIN	*n* pl. -S an enzyme **TRYPTIC** *adj*
TRYSAIL	*n* pl. -S a type of sail
TRYST	*v* -ED, -ING, -S to agree to meet
TRYSTE	*n* pl. -S a market
TRYSTER	*n* pl. -S one that trysts
TRYWORKS	*n/pl* a type of furnace
TSADE	*n* pl. -S sade
TSADI	*n* pl. -S sade
TSAR	*n* pl. -S czar
TSARDOM	*n* pl. -S czardom
TSAREVNA	*n* pl. -S czarevna
TSARINA	*n* pl. -S czarina
TSARISM	*n* pl. -S czarism
TSARIST	*n* pl. -S czarist
TSARITZA	*n* pl. -S czaritza
TSETSE	*n* pl. -S an African fly
TSIMMES	*n* pl. TSIMMES tzimmes
TSK	*v* -ED, -ING, -S to utter an exclamation of annoyance
TSKTSK	*v* -ED, -ING, -S to tsk
TSUBA	*n* pl. TSUBA a part of a Japanese sword
TSUNAMI	*n* pl. -S a very large ocean wave **TSUNAMIC** *adj*
TSURIS	*n* pl. TSURIS a series of misfortunes
TUATARA	*n* pl. -S a large reptile
TUATERA	*n* pl. -S tuatara
TUB	*v* TUBBED, TUBBING, TUBS to wash in a tub (a round, open vessel)
TUBA	*n* pl. -BAS or -BAE a brass wind instrument
TUBAL	*adj* pertaining to a tube
TUBATE	*adj* tubular
TUBBABLE	*adj* suitable for washing in a tub
TUBBED	past tense of tub

TUBBER	*n* pl. -S one that tubs
TUBBING	present participle of tub
TUBBY	*adj* -BIER, -BIEST short and fat
TUBE	*v* TUBED, TUBING, TUBES to provide with a tube (a long, hollow cylinder)
TUBELESS	*adj* having no tube
TUBELIKE	*adj* resembling a tube
TUBER	*n* pl. -S a thick underground stem
TUBERCLE	*n* pl. -S a small, rounded swelling
TUBEROID	*adj* pertaining to a tuber
TUBEROSE	*n* pl. -S a Mexican herb
TUBEROUS	*adj* pertaining to a tuber
TUBEWORK	*n* pl. -S tubing
TUBFUL	*n* pl. -S as much as a tub will hold
TUBIFEX	*n* pl. -ES an aquatic worm
TUBIFORM	*adj* tubular
TUBING	*n* pl. -S material in the form of a tube
TUBLIKE	*adj* resembling a tub
TUBULAR	*adj* shaped like a tube
TUBULATE	*v* -LATED, -LATING, -LATES to form into a tube
TUBULE	*n* pl. -S a small tube
TUBULOSE	*adj* tubular
TUBULOUS	*adj* tubular
TUBULURE	*n* pl. -S a short tubular opening
TUCHUN	*n* pl. -S a Chinese military governor
TUCK	*v* -ED, -ING, -S to fold under
TUCKAHOE	*n* pl. -S the edible root of certain arums
TUCKER	*v* -ED, -ING, -S to weary
TUCKET	*n* pl. -S a trumpet fanfare
TUFA	*n* pl. -S a porous limestone
TUFF	*n* pl. -S a volcanic rock
TUFFET	*n* pl. -S a clump of grass
TUFT	*v* -ED, -ING, -S to form into tufts (clusters of flexible outgrowths attached at the base)
TUFTER	*n* pl. -S one that tufts
TUFTY	*adj* TUFTIER, TUFTIEST abounding in tufts **TUFTILY** *adv*
TUG	*v* TUGGED, TUGGING, TUGS to pull with force

TUGBOAT   *n* pl. -S a boat built for towing

TUGGER   *n* pl. -S one that tugs

TUGGING   present participle of tug

TUGLESS   *adj* being without a rope or chain with which to pull

TUGRIK   *n* pl. -S a Mongolian unit of currency

TUI   *n* pl. -S a bird of New Zealand

TUILLE   *n* pl. -S a tasset

TUITION   *n* pl. -S a fee for instruction

TULADI   *n* pl. -S a freshwater fish

TULE   *n* pl. -S a tall marsh plant

TULIP   *n* pl. -S a flowering plant

TULLE   *n* pl. -S a silk material

TULLIBEE   *n* pl. -S a freshwater fish

TUMBLE   *v* -BLED, -BLING, -BLES to fall or roll end over end

TUMBLER   *n* pl. -S one that tumbles

TUMBLING   *n* pl. -S the sport of gymnastics

TUMBREL   *n* pl. -S a type of cart

TUMBRIL   *n* pl. -S tumbrel

TUMEFY   *v* -FIED, -FYING, -FIES to swell

TUMID   *adj* swollen **TUMIDLY** *adv*

TUMIDITY   *n* pl. -TIES the quality or state of being tumid

TUMMY   *n* pl. -MIES the stomach

TUMOR   *n* pl. -S an abnormal swelling **TUMORAL, TUMOROUS** *adj*

TUMOUR   *n* pl. -S tumor

TUMP   *n* pl. -S tumpline

TUMPLINE   *n* pl. -S a strap for supporting a load on the back

TUMULAR   *adj* having the form of a mound

TUMULI   *a* pl. of tumulus

TUMULOSE   *adj* full of mounds

TUMULOUS   *adj* tumulose

TUMULT   *n* pl. -S a great din and commotion

TUMULUS   *n* pl. -LI or -LUSES a mound over a grave

TUN   *v* TUNNED, TUNNING, TUNS to store in a large cask

TUNA   *n* pl. -S a marine food fish

TUNABLE   *adj* capable of being tuned **TUNABLY** *adv*

TUNDISH   *n* pl. -ES a receptacle for molten metal

TUNDRA   *n* pl. -S a level, treeless expanse of arctic land

TUNE   *v* TUNED, TUNING, TUNES to put into the proper pitch

TUNEABLE   *adj* tunable **TUNEABLY** *adv*

TUNEFUL   *adj* melodious

TUNELESS   *adj* not tuneful

TUNER   *n* pl. -S one that tunes

TUNG   *n* pl. -S a Chinese tree

TUNGSTEN   *n* pl. -S a metallic element **TUNGSTIC** *adj*

TUNIC   *n* pl. -S a loose-fitting garment

TUNICA   *n* pl. -CAE an enveloping membrane or layer of body tissue

TUNICATE   *n* pl. -S a small marine animal

TUNICLE   *n* pl. -S a type of vestment

TUNING   present participle of tune

TUNNAGE   *n* pl. -S tonnage

TUNNED   past tense of tun

TUNNEL   *v* -NELED, -NELING, -NELS or -NELLED, -NELLING, -NELS to dig a tunnel (an underground passageway)

TUNNELER   *n* pl. -S one that tunnels

TUNNING   present participle of tun

TUNNY   *n* pl. -NIES a tuna

TUP   *v* TUPPED, TUPPING, TUPS to copulate with a ewe

TUPELO   *n* pl. -LOS a softwood tree

TUPIK   *n* pl. -S an Eskimo tent

TUPPED   past tense of tup

TUPPENCE   *n* pl. -S twopence

TUPPING   present participle of tup

TUPPENNY   *adj* twopenny

TUQUE   *n* pl. -S a knitted woolen cap

TURACO   *n* pl. -COS touraco

TURACOU   *n* pl. -S touraco

TURBAN   *n* pl. -S a head covering worn by Muslims **TURBANED** *adj*

TURBARY   *n* pl. -RIES a place where peat can be dug

TURBETH   *n* pl. -S turpeth

TURBID   *adj* thick or opaque with roiled sediment **TURBIDLY** *adv*

TURBINAL   *n* pl. -S a bone of the nasal passage

TURBINE   *n* pl. -S a type of engine

TURBIT	*n* pl. -S a domestic pigeon
TURBITH	*n* pl. -S turpeth
TURBO	*n* pl. -BOS a turbine
TURBOCAR	*n* pl. -S an auto powered by a gas turbine
TURBOFAN	*n* pl. -S a type of jet engine
TURBOJET	*n* pl. -S a type of jet engine
TURBOT	*n* pl. -S a European flatfish
TURD	*n* pl. -S a piece of dung
TURDINE	*adj* belonging to a large family of singing birds
TUREEN	*n* pl. -S a large, deep bowl
TURF	*n* pl. TURFS or TURVES a surface layer of earth containing a dense growth of grass and its roots
TURF	*v* -ED, -ING, -S to cover with turf
TURFIER	comparative of turfy
TURFIEST	superlative of turfy
TURFLESS	*adj* having no turf
TURFLIKE	*adj* resembling turf
TURFMAN	*n* pl. -MEN a person who is devoted to horse racing
TURFSKI	*n* pl. -S a type of ski
TURFY	*adj* TURFIER, TURFIEST covered with turf
TURGENCY	*n* pl. -CIES turgor
TURGENT	*adj* turgid
TURGID	*adj* swollen **TURGIDLY** *adv*
TURGITE	*n* pl. -S an iron ore
TURGOR	*n* pl. -S the quality or state of being turgid
TURKEY	*n* pl. -KEYS a large American bird
TURKOIS	*n* pl. -ES turquois
TURMERIC	*n* pl. -S an East Indian herb
TURMOIL	*v* -ED, -ING, -S to throw into an uproar
TURN	*v* -ED, -ING, -S to move around a central point **TURNABLE** *adj*
TURNCOAT	*n* pl. -S a traitor
TURNDOWN	*n* pl. -S a rejection
TURNER	*n* pl. -S one that turns
TURNERY	*n* pl. -ERIES the process of shaping articles on a lathe
TURNHALL	*n* pl. -S a building where gymnasts practice
TURNING	*n* pl. -S a rotation about an axis
TURNIP	*n* pl. -S an edible plant root
TURNKEY	*n* pl. -KEYS a person who has charge of a prison's keys
TURNOFF	*n* pl. -S a road that branches off from a larger one
TURNOUT	*n* pl. -S an assemblage of people
TURNOVER	*n* pl. -S an upset or overthrow
TURNPIKE	*n* pl. -S a highway on which tolls are collected
TURNSOLE	*n* pl. -S a plant that turns with the sun
TURNSPIT	*n* pl. -S one that turns a roasting spit
TURNUP	*n* pl. -S a part of a garment that is turned up
TURPETH	*n* pl. -S a medicinal plant root
TURPS	*n* pl. TURPS turpentine
TURQUOIS	*n* pl. -ES a greenish blue gem
TURRET	*n* pl. -S a small tower **TURRETED** *adj*
TURRICAL	*adj* resembling a turret
TURTLE	*v* -TLED, -TLING, -TLES to catch turtles (tortoises)
TURTLER	*n* pl. -S one that turtles
TURTLING	*n* pl. -S the act of one that turtles
TURVES	a pl. of turf
TUSCHE	*n* pl. -S a liquid used in lithography
TUSH	*v* -ED, -ING, -ES to tusk
TUSK	*v* -ED, -ING, -S to gore with a tusk (a long, pointed tooth extending outside of the mouth)
TUSKER	*n* pl. -S an animal with tusks
TUSKLESS	*adj* having no tusk
TUSKLIKE	*adj* resembling a tusk
TUSSAH	*n* pl. -S an Asian silkworm
TUSSAL	*adj* pertaining to a cough
TUSSAR	*n* pl. -S tussah
TUSSEH	*n* pl. -S tussah
TUSSER	*n* pl. -S tussah
TUSSIS	*n* pl. -SISES a cough **TUSSIVE** *adj*
TUSSLE	*v* -SLED, -SLING, -SLES to struggle
TUSSOCK	*n* pl. -S a clump of grass **TUSSOCKY** *adj*
TUSSOR	*n* pl. -S tussah

TUSSORE	*n* pl. -S tussah	**TWASOME**	*n* pl. -S twosome
TUSSUCK	*n* pl. -S tussock	**TWAT**	*n* pl. -S the vulva — usually considered vulgar
TUSSUR	*n* pl. -S tussah		
TUT	*v* TUTTED, TUTTING, TUTS to utter an exclamation of impatience	**TWATTLE**	*v* -TLED, -TLING, -TLES to twaddle
		TWEAK	*v* -ED, -ING, -S to pinch and twist sharply
TUTEE	*n* pl. -S one who is being tutored	**TWEAKY**	*adj* TWEAKIER, TWEAKIEST twitchy
TUTELAGE	*n* pl. -S the act of tutoring	**TWEED**	*n* pl. -S a coarse woolen fabric
TUTELAR	*n* pl. -S a tutelary		
TUTELARY	*n* pl. -LARIES one who has the power to protect	**TWEEDLE**	*v* -DLED, -DLING, -DLES to perform casually on a musical instrument
TUTOR	*v* -ED, -ING, -S to instruct privately	**TWEEDY**	*adj* TWEEDIER, TWEEDIEST resembling tweed
TUTORAGE	*n* pl. -S tutelage	**TWEEN**	*prep* between
TUTORESS	*n* pl. -ES a female who tutors	**TWEET**	*v* -ED, -ING, -S to chirp
TUTORIAL	*n* pl. -S a session of tutoring	**TWEETER**	*n* pl. -S a loudspeaker designed to reproduce high-pitched sounds
TUTOYER	*v* -TOYERED or -TOYED, -TOYERING, -TOYERS to address familiarly		
		TWEEZE	*v* TWEEZED, TWEEZING, TWEEZES to pluck with a tweezer
TUTTED	past tense of tut		
TUTTI	*n* pl. -S a musical passage performed by all the performers	**TWEEZER**	*n* pl. -S a pincerlike tool
		TWELFTH	*n* pl. -S the number twelve in a series
TUTTING	present participle of tut		
TUTTY	*n* pl. -TIES an impure zinc oxide	**TWELVE**	*n* pl. -S a number
TUTU	*n* pl. -S a short ballet skirt	**TWELVEMO**	*n* pl. -MOS a page size
TUX	*n* pl. -ES a tuxedo	**TWENTY**	*n* pl. -TIES a number
TUXEDO	*n* pl. -DOES or -DOS a man's semiformal dinner coat	**TWERP**	*n* pl. -S a small, impudent person
TUYER	*n* pl. -S tuyere	**TWIBIL**	*n* pl. -S a battle-ax with two cutting edges
TUYERE	*n* pl. -S a pipe through which air is forced into a blast furnace		
		TWIBILL	*n* pl. -S twibil
TWA	*n* pl. -S two	**TWICE**	*adv* two times
TWADDLE	*v* -DLED, -DLING, -DLES to talk foolishly	**TWIDDLE**	*v* -DLED, -DLING, -DLES to play idly with something
TWADDLER	*n* pl. -S one that twaddles	**TWIDDLER**	*n* pl. -S one that twiddles
TWAE	*n* pl. -S two	**TWIER**	*n* pl. -S tuyere
TWAIN	*n* pl. -S a set of two	**TWIG**	*v* TWIGGED, TWIGGING, TWIGS to observe
TWANG	*v* -ED, -ING, -S to make a sharp, vibrating sound		
		TWIGGEN	*adj* made of twigs (small branches)
TWANGIER	comparative of twangy		
TWANGIEST	superlative of twangy	**TWIGGY**	*adj* -GIER, -GIEST twiglike
TWANGLE	*v* -GLED, -GLING, -GLES to twang	**TWIGLESS**	*adj* having no twigs
		TWIGLIKE	*adj* resembling a twig
TWANGLER	*n* pl. -S one that twangles	**TWILIGHT**	*n* pl. -S the early evening light
TWANGY	*adj* TWANGIER, TWANGIEST twanging	**TWILIT**	*adj* lighted by twilight
TWANKY	*n* pl. -KIES a variety of green tea	**TWILL**	*v* -ED, -ING, -S to weave so as to produce a diagonal pattern

TWILLING	*n* pl. -S a twilled fabric
TWIN	*v* TWINNED, TWINNING, TWINS to bring together in close association
TWINBORN	*adj* born at the same birth
TWINE	*v* TWINED, TWINING, TWINES to twist together
TWINER	*n* pl. -S one that twines
TWINGE	*v* TWINGED, TWINGING, TWINGES to affect with a sharp pain
TWINIER	comparative of twiny
TWINIEST	superlative of twiny
TWINIGHT	*adj* pertaining to a baseball doubleheader that begins in the late afternoon
TWINING	present participle of twine
TWINKLE	*v* -KLED, -KLING, -KLES to shine with a flickering or sparkling light
TWINKLER	*n* pl. -S one that twinkles
TWINKLY	*adj* twinkling
TWINNED	past tense of twin
TWINNING	*n* pl. -S the bearing of two children at the same birth
TWINSHIP	*n* pl. -S close similarity or association
TWINY	*adj* TWINIER, TWINIEST resembling twine (a strong string)
TWIRL	*v* -ED, -ING, -S to rotate rapidly
TWIRLER	*n* pl. -S one that twirls
TWIRLY	*adj* TWIRLIER, TWIRLIEST curved
TWIRP	*n* pl. -S twerp
TWIST	*v* -ED, -ING, -S to combine by winding together
TWISTER	*n* pl. -S one that twists
TWISTING	*n* pl. -S a form of trickery used in selling life insurance
TWIT	*v* TWITTED, TWITTING, TWITS to ridicule
TWITCH	*v* -ED, -ING, -ES to move or pull with a sudden motion
TWITCHER	*n* pl. -S one that twitches
TWITCHY	*adj* TWITCHIER, TWITCHIEST fidgety
TWITTED	past tense of twit
TWITTER	*v* -ED, -ING, -S to utter a succession of chirping sounds
TWITTERY	*adj* nervously agitated
TWITTING	present participle of twit
TWIXT	*prep* between
TWO	*n* pl. TWOS a number
TWOFER	*n* pl. -S something sold at the rate of two for the price of one
TWOFOLD	*n* pl. -S an amount twice as great as a given unit
TWOPENCE	*n* pl. -S a British coin worth two pennies
TWOPENNY	*adj* worth twopence
TWOSOME	*n* pl. -S a group of two
TWYER	*n* pl. -S tuyere
TYCOON	*n* pl. -S a wealthy and powerful business person
TYE	*n* pl. -S a chain on a ship
TYEE	*n* pl. -S a food fish
TYING	a present participle of tie
TYKE	*n* pl. -S a small child
TYMBAL	*n* pl. -S timbal
TYMPAN	*n* pl. -S a drum
TYMPANA	a pl. of tympanum
TYMPANAL	*adj* tympanic
TYMPANI	*n/pl* kettledrums
TYMPANIC	*adj* pertaining to the tympanum
TYMPANUM	*n* pl. -NA or -NUMS the middle ear
TYMPANY	*n* pl. -NIES a swelling of the abdomen
TYNE	*v* TYNED, TYNING, TYNES to tine
TYPAL	*adj* typical
TYPE	*v* TYPED, TYPING, TYPES to write with a typewriter **TYPEABLE** *adj*
TYPEBAR	*n* pl. -S a part of a typewriter
TYPECASE	*n* pl. -S a tray for holding printing type
TYPECAST	*v* -CAST, -CASTING, -CASTS to cast in an acting role befitting one's own nature
TYPED	past tense of type
TYPEFACE	*n* pl. -S the face of printing type
TYPESET	*v* -SET, -SETTING, -SETS to set in type
TYPEY	*adj* TYPIER, TYPIEST typy
TYPHOID	*n* pl. -S an infectious disease
TYPHON	*n* pl. -S a type of signal horn
TYPHOON	*n* pl. -S a tropical hurricane **TYPHONIC** *adj*

TYPHOSE	*adj* pertaining to typhoid	**TYRANT**	*n* pl. -S an absolute ruler
TYPHUS	*n* pl. -ES an infectious disease **TYPHOUS** *adj*	**TYRE**	*v* TYRED, TYRING, TYRES to furnish with a covering for a wheel
TYPIC	*adj* typical		
TYPICAL	*adj* having the nature of a representative specimen	**TYRO**	*n* pl. -ROS a beginner **TYRONIC** *adj*
TYPIER	comparative of typey and typy	**TYROSINE**	*n* pl. -S an amino acid
TYPIEST	superlative of typey and typy	**TYTHE**	*v* TYTHED, TYTHING, TYTHES to tithe
TYPIFIER	*n* pl. -S one that typifies		
TYPIFY	*v* -FIED, -FYING, -FIES to serve as a typical example of	**TZADDIK**	*n* pl. -DIKIM zaddik
		TZAR	*n* pl. -S czar
TYPING	present participle of type	**TZARDOM**	*n* pl. -S czardom
TYPIST	*n* pl. -S one who types	**TZAREVNA**	*n* pl. -S czarevna
TYPO	*n* pl. -POS a typographical error	**TZARINA**	*n* pl. -S czarina
TYPOLOGY	*n* pl. -GIES the study of classification according to common characteristics	**TZARISM**	*n* pl. -S czarism
		TZARIST	*n* pl. -S czarist
TYPP	*n* pl. -S a unit of yarn size	**TZARITZA**	*n* pl. -S czaritza
TYPY	*adj* TYPIER, TYPIEST characterized by strict conformance to the characteristics of a group	**TZETZE**	*n* pl. -S tsetse
		TZIGANE	*n* pl. -S a gypsy
		TZIMMES	*n* pl. TZIMMES a vegetable stew
TYRAMINE	*n* pl. -S a chemical compound	**TZITZIS**	*n* pl. TZITZIS zizith
TYRANNIC	*adj* characteristic of a tyrant	**TZITZITH**	*n* pl. TZITZITH zizith
TYRANNY	*n* pl. -NIES the rule of a tyrant	**TZURIS**	*n* pl. TZURIS tsuris

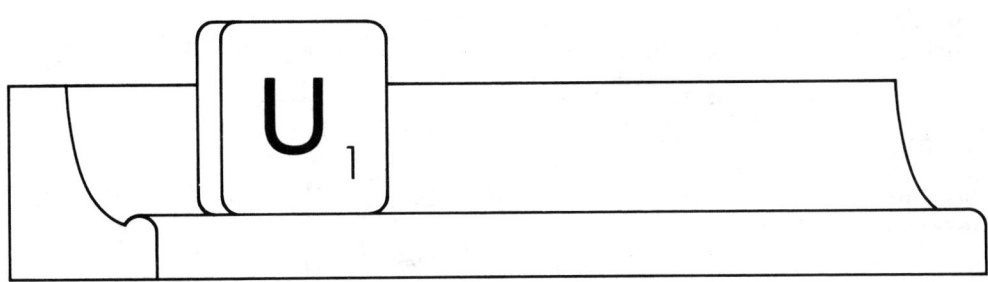

UBIETY	*n* pl. -ETIES the state of having a definite location
UBIQUE	*adv* everywhere
UBIQUITY	*n* pl. -TIES the state of being everywhere at the same time
UDDER	*n* pl. -S a mammary gland
UDO	*n* pl. UDOS a Japanese herb
UDOMETER	*n* pl. -S a rain gauge
UDOMETRY	*n* pl. -TRIES the measurement of rain
UGH	*n* pl. -S the sound of a cough or grunt
UGLIER	comparative of ugly
UGLIEST	superlative of ugly
UGLIFIER	*n* pl. -S one that uglifies
UGLIFY	*v* -FIED, -FYING, -FIES to make ugly
UGLINESS	*n* pl. -ES the state of being ugly
UGLY	*adj* -LIER, -LIEST displeasing to the sight **UGLILY** *adv*
UGSOME	*adj* disgusting
UHLAN	*n* pl. -S one of a body of Prussian cavalry
UINTAITE	*n* pl. -S a variety of asphalt
UIT	*prep* out of
UKASE	*n* pl. -S an edict
UKE	*n* pl. -S ukelele
UKELELE	*n* pl. -S ukulele
UKULELE	*n* pl. -S a small guitar-like instrument
ULAMA	*n* pl. -S ulema
ULAN	*n* pl. -S uhlan
ULCER	*v* -ED, -ING, -S to affect with an ulcer (a type of lesion)
ULCERATE	*v* -ATED, -ATING, -ATES to ulcer
ULCEROUS	*adj* being or affected with an ulcer
ULEMA	*n* pl. -S a Muslim scholar
ULEXITE	*n* pl. -S a mineral
ULLAGE	*n* pl. -S the amount that a container lacks of being full **ULLAGED** *adj*
ULNA	*n* pl. -NAE or -NAS a bone of the forearm **ULNAR** *adj*
ULSTER	*n* pl. -S a long, loose overcoat
ULTERIOR	*adj* more remote
ULTIMA	*n* pl. -S the last syllable of a word
ULTIMACY	*n* pl. -CIES an ultimate
ULTIMATA	*n/pl* final proposals
ULTIMATE	*n* pl. -S something final or fundamental
ULTIMO	*adj* of or occurring in the preceding month
ULTRA	*n* pl. -S an ultraist
ULTRAISM	*n* pl. -S advocacy of extreme measures
ULTRAIST	*n* pl. -S an advocate of extreme measures
ULTRARED	*n* pl. -S infrared
ULULANT	*adj* howling
ULULATE	*v* -LATED, -LATING, -LATES to howl
ULVA	*n* pl. -S an edible seaweed
UMBEL	*n* pl. -S a type of flower cluster **UMBELED, UMBELLAR, UMBELLED** *adj*
UMBELLET	*n* pl. -S a small umbel

UMBER   *v* -ED, -ING, -S to color with a brown pigment

UMBILICI   *n/pl* navels

UMBLES   *n/pl* the entrails of a deer

UMBO   *n* pl. -BONES or -BOS the rounded elevation at the center of a shield **UMBONAL, UMBONATE, UMBONIC** *adj*

UMBRA   *n* pl. -BRAE or -BRAS a dark area **UMBRAL** *adj*

UMBRAGE   *n* pl. -S resentment

UMBRELLA   *v* -ED, -ING, -S to provide with an umbrella (a portable cover for protection from rain or sun)

UMBRETTE   *n* pl. -S a wading bird

UMIAC   *n* pl. -S umiak

UMIACK   *n* pl. -S umiak

UMIAK   *n* pl. -S an open Eskimo boat

UMLAUT   *v* -ED, -ING, -S to modify a vowel sound by partial assimilation to a succeeding sound

UMP   *v* -ED, -ING, -S to umpire

UMPIRAGE   *n* pl. -S the function of an umpire

UMPIRE   *v* -PIRED, -PIRING, -PIRES to act as umpire (a person appointed to rule on the plays in a game)

UMPTEEN   *adj* indefinitely numerous

UMTEENTH   *adj* being the last in an indefinitely numerous series

UN   *pron* pl. -S one

| U₁ | N₁ | Following is a list of self-explanatory adjectives and adverbs containing the prefix UN- (not): |

UNABATED	*adj*
UNABLE	*adj*
UNABUSED	*adj*
UNACTED	*adj*
UNAFRAID	*adj*
UNAGED	*adj*
UNAGEING	*adj*
UNAGILE	*adj*
UNAGING	*adj*
UNAIDED	*adj*
UNAIMED	*adj*
UNAIRED	*adj*

UNALIKE	*adj*
UNALLIED	*adj*
UNAMUSED	*adj*
UNANELED	*adj*
UNAPT	*adj*
UNAPTLY	*adv*
UNARGUED	*adj*
UNARTFUL	*adj*
UNASKED	*adj*
UNATONED	*adj*
UNAVOWED	*adj*
UNAWAKED	*adj*
UNAWARE	*adj*
UNAWED	*adj*
UNBACKED	*adj*
UNBAKED	*adj*
UNBARBED	*adj*
UNBASED	*adj*
UNBEATEN	*adj*
UNBENIGN	*adj*
UNBIASED	*adj*
UNBITTED	*adj*
UNBLAMED	*adj*
UNBLEST	*adj*
UNBLOODY	*adj*
UNBONED	*adj*
UNBORN	*adj*
UNBOUGHT	*adj*
UNBOWED	*adj*
UNBRED	*adj*
UNBROKE	*adj*
UNBROKEN	*adj*
UNBURIED	*adj*
UNBURNED	*adj*
UNBURNT	*adj*
UNCALLED	*adj*
UNCANDID	*adj*
UNCARING	*adj*
UNCASHED	*adj*
UNCAUGHT	*adj*
UNCAUSED	*adj*
UNCHARY	*adj*
UNCHASTE	*adj*
UNCHEWED	*adj*
UNCHIC	*adj*
UNCHOSEN	*adj*
UNCIVIL	*adj*
UNCLEAN	*adj* -CLEANER, -CLEANEST
UNCLEAR	*adj* -CLEARER, -CLEAREST
UNCLOYED	*adj*
UNCOATED	*adj*
UNCOINED	*adj*
UNCOMBED	*adj*

UNCOMELY	adj	
UNCOMIC	adj	
UNCOMMON	adj -MONER, -MONEST	
UNCOOKED	adj	
UNCOOL	adj	
UNCOUTH	adj	
UNCURED	adj	
UNCURSED	adj	
UNCUT	adj	
UNDAMPED	adj	
UNDARING	adj	
UNDATED	adj	
UNDECKED	adj	
UNDENIED	adj	
UNDEVOUT	adj	
UNDIMMED	adj	
UNDREAMT	adj	
UNDRIED	adj	
UNDULLED	adj	
UNDYED	adj	
UNEAGER	adj	
UNEARNED	adj	
UNEATEN	adj	
UNEDIBLE	adj	
UNEDITED	adj	
UNENDED	adj	
UNENDING	adj	
UNENVIED	adj	
UNERASED	adj	
UNERRING	adj	
UNEVADED	adj	
UNEVEN	adj -EVENER, -EVENEST	
UNEVENLY	adv	
UNEXOTIC	adj	
UNEXPERT	adj	
UNFADED	adj	
UNFADING	adj	
UNFAIR	adj -FAIRER, -FAIREST	
UNFAIRLY	adv	
UNFALLEN	adj	
UNFANCY	adj	
UNFAZED	adj	
UNFEARED	adj	
UNFED	adj	
UNFELT	adj	
UNFILIAL	adj	
UNFILLED	adj	
UNFILMED	adj	
UNFIRED	adj	
UNFISHED	adj	
UNFLEXED	adj	
UNFOILED	adj	
UNFOND	adj	
UNFORCED	adj	
UNFORGED	adj	
UNFORKED	adj	
UNFORMED	adj	
UNFOUGHT	adj	
UNFOUND	adj	
UNFRAMED	adj	
UNFUNDED	adj	
UNFUNNY	adj	
UNFUSED	adj	
UNFUSSY	adj	
UNGALLED	adj	
UNGENIAL	adj	
UNGENTLE	adj	
UNGENTLY	adv	
UNGIFTED	adj	
UNGLAZED	adj	
UNGOWNED	adj	
UNGRACED	adj	
UNGRADED	adj	
UNGREEDY	adj	
UNGUIDED	adj	
UNHAILED	adj	
UNHALVED	adj	
UNHAPPY	adj -PIER, -PIEST	
UNHARMED	adj	
UNHASTY	adj	
UNHEALED	adj	
UNHEARD	adj	
UNHEATED	adj	
UNHEEDED	adj	
UNHELPED	adj	
UNHEROIC	adj	
UNHEWN	adj	
UNHIP	adj	
UNHIRED	adj	
UNHOLILY	adv	
UNHOLY	adj -LIER, -LIEST	
UNHUMAN	adj	
UNHUNG	adj	
UNHURT	adj	
UNIDEAL	adj	
UNIMBUED	adj	
UNIRONED	adj	
UNISSUED	adj	
UNJADED	adj	
UNJOINED	adj	
UNJOYFUL	adj	
UNJUDGED	adj	
UNJUST	adj	
UNJUSTLY	adv	
UNKEPT	adj	
UNKIND	adj -KINDER, -KINDEST	

UNKINDLY	adv -LIER, -LIEST		**UNPARTED**	adj
UNKINGLY	adj		**UNPAVED**	adj
UNKISSED	adj		**UNPAYING**	adj
UNKOSHER	adj		**UNPITIED**	adj
UNLAWFUL	adj		**UNPLACED**	adj
UNLEASED	adj		**UNPLAYED**	adj
UNLED	adj		**UNPLIANT**	adj
UNLETHAL	adj		**UNPLOWED**	adj
UNLETTED	adj		**UNPOETIC**	adj
UNLEVIED	adj		**UNPOISED**	adj
UNLICKED	adj		**UNPOLITE**	adj
UNLIKE	adj		**UNPOLLED**	adj
UNLIKELY	adj -LIER, -LIEST		**UNPOSED**	adj
UNLINED	adj		**UNPOSTED**	adj
UNLISTED	adj		**UNPRETTY**	adj
UNLIT	adj		**UNPRICED**	adj
UNLIVELY	adj		**UNPRIMED**	adj
UNLOBED	adj		**UNPRIZED**	adj
UNLOVED	adj		**UNPROBED**	adj
UNLOVELY	adj -LIER, -LIEST		**UNPROVED**	adj
UNLOVING	adj		**UNPROVEN**	adj
UNLUCKY	adj -LUCKIER, -LUCKIEST		**UNPRUNED**	adj
UNMANFUL	adj		**UNPURE**	adj
UNMANLY	adj		**UNPURGED**	adj
UNMAPPED	adj		**UNQUIET**	adj -ETER, -ETEST
UNMARKED	adj		**UNRAISED**	adj
UNMARRED	adj		**UNRAKED**	adj
UNMATED	adj		**UNRANKED**	adj
UNMATTED	adj		**UNRATED**	adj
UNMEANT	adj		**UNRAZED**	adj
UNMELLOW	adj		**UNREAD**	adj
UNMELTED	adj		**UNREADY**	adj -READIER, -READIEST
UNMENDED	adj		**UNREAL**	adj
UNMET	adj		**UNREALLY**	adv
UNMILLED	adj		**UNRENTED**	adj
UNMIXED	adj		**UNREPAID**	adj
UNMIXT	adj		**UNRESTED**	adj
UNMODISH	adj		**UNRHYMED**	adj
UNMOLTEN	adj		**UNRIFLED**	adj
UNMOVED	adj		**UNRIMED**	adj
UNMOVING	adj		**UNRINSED**	adj
UNMOWN	adj		**UNRISEN**	adj
UNNAMED	adj		**UNROUGH**	adj
UNNEEDED	adj		**UNRULED**	adj
UNNOISY	adj		**UNRUSHED**	adj
UNNOTED	adj		**UNSAFE**	adj
UNOILED	adj		**UNSAFELY**	adv
UNOPEN	adj		**UNSALTED**	adj
UNOPENED	adj		**UNSATED**	adj
UNORNATE	adj		**UNSAVED**	adj
UNOWNED	adj		**UNSAVORY**	adj
UNPAID	adj		**UNSAWED**	adj
UNPAIRED	adj		**UNSAWN**	adj

UNSCALED	*adj*	**UNSTUNG**	*adj*
UNSEARED	*adj*	**UNSUBTLE**	*adj*
UNSEEDED	*adj*	**UNSUITED**	*adj*
UNSEEING	*adj*	**UNSUNG**	*adj*
UNSEEMLY	*adj* -LIER, -LIEST	**UNSUNK**	*adj*
UNSEEN	*adj*	**UNSURE**	*adj*
UNSEIZED	*adj*	**UNSURELY**	*adv*
UNSENT	*adj*	**UNSWAYED**	*adj*
UNSERVED	*adj*	**UNSWEPT**	*adj*
UNSEXUAL	*adj*	**UNTAGGED**	*adj*
UNSHADED	*adj*	**UNTAKEN**	*adj*
UNSHAKEN	*adj*	**UNTAME**	*adj*
UNSHAMED	*adj*	**UNTAMED**	*adj*
UNSHAPED	*adj*	**UNTANNED**	*adj*
UNSHAPEN	*adj*	**UNTAPPED**	*adj*
UNSHARED	*adj*	**UNTASTED**	*adj*
UNSHARP	*adj*	**UNTAXED**	*adj*
UNSHAVED	*adj*	**UNTENDED**	*adj*
UNSHAVEN	*adj*	**UNTESTED**	*adj*
UNSHED	*adj*	**UNTHAWED**	*adj*
UNSHOD	*adj*	**UNTIDILY**	*adv*
UNSHORN	*adj*	**UNTIDY**	*adj* -DIER, -DIEST
UNSHRUNK	*adj*	**UNTILLED**	*adj*
UNSHUT	*adj*	**UNTILTED**	*adj*
UNSIFTED	*adj*	**UNTIMELY**	*adj* -LIER, -LIEST
UNSIGNED	*adj*	**UNTINGED**	*adj*
UNSILENT	*adj*	**UNTIRED**	*adj*
UNSINFUL	*adj*	**UNTIRING**	*adj*
UNSIZED	*adj*	**UNTITLED**	*adj*
UNSLAKED	*adj*	**UNTOLD**	*adj*
UNSMOKED	*adj*	**UNTRACED**	*adj*
UNSOAKED	*adj*	**UNTRIED**	*adj*
UNSOBER	*adj*	**UNTRUE**	*adj* -TRUER, -TRUEST
UNSOCIAL	*adj*	**UNTRULY**	*adv*
UNSOILED	*adj*	**UNTRUSTY**	*adj*
UNSOLD	*adj*	**UNTUFTED**	*adj*
UNSOLID	*adj*	**UNTURNED**	*adj*
UNSOLVED	*adj*	**UNUNITED**	*adj*
UNSORTED	*adj*	**UNURGED**	*adj*
UNSOUGHT	*adj*	**UNUSABLE**	*adj*
UNSOUND	*adj* -SOUNDER, -SOUNDEST	**UNUSED**	*adj*
UNSOURED	*adj*	**UNUSUAL**	*adj*
UNSOWED	*adj*	**UNVALUED**	*adj*
UNSOWN	*adj*	**UNVARIED**	*adj*
UNSPENT	*adj*	**UNVEINED**	*adj*
UNSPILT	*adj*	**UNVERSED**	*adj*
UNSPLIT	*adj*	**UNVEXED**	*adj*
UNSPOILT	*adj*	**UNVEXT**	*adj*
UNSPRUNG	*adj*	**UNVIABLE**	*adj*
UNSPUN	*adj*	**UNVOCAL**	*adj*
UNSTABLE	*adj* -BLER, -BLEST	**UNWALLED**	*adj*
UNSTABLY	*adv*	**UNWANTED**	*adj*
UNSTEADY	*adj* -STEADIER, -STEADIEST	**UNWARIER**	comparative of unwary

UNWARIEST	superlative of unwary	**UNBELT**	v -ED, -ING, -S to remove the belt of
UNWARILY	adv		
UNWARMED	adj	**UNBEND**	v -BENT or -BENDED, -BENDING, -BENDS to make or allow to become straight
UNWARNED	adj		
UNWARPED	adj		
UNWARY	adj -WARIER, -WARIEST	**UNBID**	adj unbidden
UNWASTED	adj	**UNBIDDEN**	adj not invited
UNWAXED	adj	**UNBIND**	v -BOUND, -BINDING, -BINDS to free from bindings
UNWEANED	adj		
UNWEARY	adj	**UNBLOCK**	v -ED, -ING, -S to free from being blocked
UNWED	adj		
UNWEDDED	adj	**UNBODIED**	adj having no body
UNWEEDED	adj	**UNBOLT**	v -ED, -ING, -S to open by withdrawing a bolt (a metal bar)
UNWELDED	adj		
UNWELL	adj	**UNBONNET**	v -ED, -ING, -S to uncover the head
UNWEPT	adj		
UNWETTED	adj	**UNBOSOM**	v -ED, -ING, -S to reveal
UNWIELDY	adj -WIELDIER, -WIELDIEST	**UNBOUND**	past tense of unbind
UNWIFELY	adj	**UNBOX**	v -ED, -ING, -ES to remove from a box
UNWILLED	adj		
UNWISE	adj -WISER, -WISEST	**UNBRACE**	v -BRACED, -BRACING, -BRACES to free from braces
UNWISELY	adv		
UNWON	adj	**UNBRAID**	v -ED, -ING, -S to separate the strands of
UNWOODED	adj		
UNWOOED	adj	**UNBREECH**	v -ED, -ING, -ES to remove the breeches of
UNWORKED	adj		
UNWORN	adj	**UNBRIDLE**	v -DLED, -DLING, -DLES to set loose
UNWORTHY	adj -THIER, -THIEST		
UNWRUNG	adj	**UNBUCKLE**	v -LED, -LING, -LES to loosen a buckle
UNZONED	adj		
		UNBUILD	v -BUILT, -BUILDING, -BUILDS to demolish
UNAI	n pl. -S unau	**UNBUNDLE**	v -DLED, -DLING, -DLES to price separately
UNANCHOR	v -ED, -ING, -S to loosen from an anchor		
		UNBURDEN	v -ED, -ING, -S to free from a burden
UNARM	v -ED, -ING, -S to disarm		
UNARY	adj consisting of a single element	**UNBUTTON**	v -ED, -ING, -S to unfasten the buttons of
		UNCAGE	v -CAGED, -CAGING, -CAGES to release from a cage
UNAU	n pl. -S a two-toed sloth		
UNAWARES	adv without warning	**UNCAKE**	v -CAKED, -CAKING, -CAKES to break up a cake (a block of compacted matter)
UNBAR	v -BARRED, -BARRING, -BARS to remove a bar from		
		UNCANNY	adj -NIER, -NIEST strange and inexplicable
UNBATED	adj unabated		
UNBE	v to cease to have being — UNBE is the only accepted form of this verb; it cannot be conjugated	**UNCAP**	v -CAPPED, -CAPPING, -CAPS to remove the cap from
		UNCASE	v -CASED, -CASING, -CASES to remove from a case
		UNCHAIN	v -ED, -ING, -S to free by removing a chain
UNBEAR	v -BEARED, -BEARING, -BEARS to free from the pressure of a rein		
		UNCHANCY	adj unlucky
UNBELIEF	n pl. -S lack of belief		

UNCHARGE	*v* -CHARGED, -CHARGING, -CHARGES to acquit	**UNCRATE**	*v* -CRATED, -CRATING, -CRATES to remove from a crate
UNCHOKE	*v* -CHOKED, -CHOKING, -CHOKES to free from obstruction	**UNCREATE**	*v* -ATED, -ATING, -ATES to deprive of existence
UNCHURCH	*v* -ED, -ING, -ES to expel from a church	**UNCROSS**	*v* -ED, -ING, -ES to change from a crossed position
UNCI	pl. of uncus	**UNCROWN**	*v* -ED, -ING, -S to deprive of a crown
UNCIA	*n* pl. -CIAE a coin of ancient Rome	**UNCTION**	*n* pl. -S the act of anointing
UNCIAL	*n* pl. -S a style of writing	**UNCTUOUS**	*adj* greasy
UNCIALLY	*adv* in the uncial style	**UNCURB**	*v* -ED, -ING, -S to remove restraints from
UNCIFORM	*n* pl. -S a bone of the wrist	**UNCURL**	*v* -ED, -ING, -S to straighten the curls of
UNCINAL	*adj* uncinate		
UNCINATE	*adj* bent at the end like a hook	**UNCUS**	*n* pl. -CI a hook-shaped anatomical part
UNCINUS	*n* pl. -NI an uncinate structure		
UNCLAD	a past tense of unclothe	**UNDE**	*adj* wavy
UNCLAMP	*v* -ED, -ING, -S to free from a clamp	**UNDEE**	*adj* unde
		UNDER	*prep* in a lower position than
UNCLASP	*v* -ED, -ING, -S to free from a clasp	**UNDERACT**	*v* -ED, -ING, -S to act subtly and with restraint
UNCLE	*n* pl. -S the brother of one's father or mother	**UNDERAGE**	*n* pl. -S a shortage
		UNDERARM	*n* pl. -S the armpit
UNCLENCH	*v* -ED, -ING, -ES to open from a clenched position	**UNDERATE**	past tense of undereat
UNCLINCH	*v* -ED, -ING, -ES to unclench	**UNDERBID**	*v* -BID, -BIDDING, -BIDS to bid lower than
UNCLOAK	*v* -ED, -ING, -S to remove a cloak from	**UNDERBUD**	*v* -BUDDED, -BUDDING, -BUDS to bud from beneath
UNCLOG	*v* -CLOGGED, -CLOGGING, -CLOGS to free from a difficulty or obstruction	**UNDERBUY**	*v* -BOUGHT, -BUYING, -BUYS to buy at a lower price than
UNCLOSE	*v* -CLOSED, -CLOSING, -CLOSES to open	**UNDERCUT**	*v* -CUT, -CUTTING, -CUTS to cut under
UNCLOTHE	*v* -CLOTHED or -CLAD, -CLOTHING, -CLOTHES to divest of clothing	**UNDERDO**	*v* -DID, -DONE, -DOING, -DOES to do insufficiently
		UNDERDOG	*n* pl. -S one who is expected to lose
UNCLOUD	*v* -ED, -ING, -S to free from clouds	**UNDEREAT**	*v* -ATE, -EATEN, -EATING, -EATS to eat an insufficient amount
UNCO	*n* pl. -COS a stranger		
UNCOCK	*v* -ED, -ING, -S to remove from a cocked position	**UNDERFED**	*adj* fed an insufficient amount
UNCOFFIN	*v* -ED, -ING, -S to remove from a coffin	**UNDERFUR**	*n* pl. -S the thick, soft fur beneath the outer coat of certain mammals
UNCOIL	*v* -ED, -ING, -S to release from a coiled position	**UNDERGO**	*v* -WENT, -GONE, -GOING, -GOES to be subjected to
UNCORK	*v* -ED, -ING, -S to draw the cork from	**UNDERGOD**	*n* pl. -S a lesser god
UNCOUPLE	*v* -PLED, -PLING, -PLES to disconnect	**UNDERJAW**	*n* pl. -S the lower jaw
		UNDERLAIN	past participle of underlie
UNCOVER	*v* -ED, -ING, -S to remove the covering from	**UNDERLAP**	*v* -LAPPED, -LAPPING, -LAPS to extend partly under

UNDERLAY	*v* -LAID, -LAYING, -LAYS to place under
UNDERLET	*v* -LET, -LETTING, -LETS to lease at less than the usual value
UNDERLIE	*v* -LAY, -LAIN, -LYING, -LIES to lie under
UNDERLIP	*n* pl. -S the lower lip
UNDERLIT	*adj* lacking adequate light
UNDERLYING	present participle of underlie
UNDERPAY	*v* -PAID, -PAYING, -PAYS to pay less than is deserved
UNDERPIN	*v* -PINNED, -PINNING, -PINS to support from below
UNDERRUN	*v* -RAN, -RUNNING, -RUNS to pass or extend under
UNDERSEA	*adv* beneath the surface of the sea
UNDERSET	*n* pl. -S a current below the surface of the ocean
UNDERTAX	*v* -ED, -ING, -ES to tax less than the usual amount
UNDERTOW	*n* pl. -S the seaward pull of receding waves breaking on a shore
UNDERWAY	*adv* in progress
UNDERWENT	past tense of undergo
UNDID	past tense of undo
UNDIES	*n/pl* underwear
UNDINE	*n* pl. -S a female water spirit
UNDO	*v* -DID, -DONE, -DOING, -DOES to bring to ruin
UNDOCK	*v* -ED, -ING, -S to move away from a dock
UNDOER	*n* pl. -S one that undoes
UNDOING	*n* pl. -S a cause of ruin
UNDONE	past participle of undo
UNDOUBLE	*v* -BLED, -BLING, -BLES to unfold
UNDRAPE	*v* -DRAPED, -DRAPING, -DRAPES to strip of drapery
UNDRAW	*v* -DREW, -DRAWN, -DRAWING, -DRAWS to draw open
UNDRESS	*v* -DRESSED or -DREST, -DRESSING, -DRESSES to remove one's clothing
UNDRUNK	*adj* not swallowed
UNDUE	*adj* exceeding what is appropriate or normal
UNDULANT	*adj* undulating

UNDULATE	*v* -LATED, -LATING, -LATES to move with a wavelike motion
UNDULY	*adv* in an undue manner
UNDY	*adj* unde
UNDYING	*adj* not subject to death
UNEARTH	*v* -ED, -ING, -S to dig up
UNEASE	*n* pl. -S mental or physical discomfort
UNEASY	*adj* -EASIER, -EASIEST marked by mental or physical discomfort **UNEASILY** *adv*
UNEQUAL	*n* pl. -S one that is not equal to another
UNFAITH	*n* pl. -S lack of faith
UNFASTEN	*v* -ED, -ING, -S to release from fastenings
UNFENCE	*v* -FENCED, -FENCING, -FENCES to remove a fence from
UNFETTER	*v* -ED, -ING, -S to free from fetters
UNFIT	*v* -FITTED, -FITTING, -FITS to make unsuitable
UNFITLY	*adv* in an unsuitable manner
UNFIX	*v* -FIXED or -FIXT, -FIXING, -FIXES to unfasten
UNFOLD	*v* -ED, -ING, -S to open something that is folded
UNFOLDER	*n* pl. -S one that unfolds
UNFORGOT	*adj* not forgotten
UNFREE	*v* -FREED, -FREEING, -FREES to deprive of freedom
UNFREEZE	*v* -FROZE, -FROZEN, -FREEZING, -FREEZES to cause to thaw
UNFROCK	*v* -ED, -ING, -S to divest of ecclesiastical authority
UNFURL	*v* -ED, -ING, -S to unroll
UNGAINLY	*adj* -LIER, -LIEST awkward
UNGIRD	*v* -GIRDED or -GIRT, -GIRDING, -GIRDS to remove a belt from
UNGLOVE	*v* -GLOVED, -GLOVING, -GLOVES to uncover by removing a glove
UNGLUE	*v* -GLUED, -GLUING, -GLUES to disjoin
UNGODLY	*adj* -LIER, -LIEST impious
UNGOT	*adj* ungotten
UNGOTTEN	*adj* not obtained
UNGUAL	*adj* pertaining to an unguis

UNGUARD   *v* -ED, -ING, -S to leave unprotected

UNGUENT   *n* pl. -S an ointment

UNGUIS   *n* pl. -GUES a nail, claw, or hoof

UNGULA   *n* pl. -LAE an unguis **UNGULAR** *adj*

UNGULATE   *n* pl. -S a hoofed mammal

UNHAIR   *v* -ED, -ING, -S to remove the hair from

UNHALLOW   *v* -ED, -ING, -S to profane

UNHAND   *v* -ED, -ING, -S to remove the hand from

UNHANDY   *adj* -HANDIER, -HANDIEST difficult to handle

UNHANG   *v* -HUNG or -HANGED, -HANGING, -HANGS to detach from a hanging support

UNHAT   *v* -HATTED, -HATTING, -HATS to remove one's hat

UNHELM   *v* -ED, -ING, -S to remove the helmet of

UNHINGE   *v* -HINGED, -HINGING, -HINGES to remove from hinges

UNHITCH   *v* -ED, -ING, -ES to free from being hitched

UNHOOD   *v* -ED, -ING, -S to remove a hood from

UNHOOK   *v* -ED, -ING, -S to remove from a hook

UNHOPED   *adj* not hoped for or expected

UNHORSE   *v* -HORSED, -HORSING, -HORSES to cause to fall from a horse

UNHOUSE   *v* -HOUSED, -HOUSING, -HOUSES to deprive of a protective shelter

UNHUSK   *v* -ED, -ING, -S to remove the husk from

UNIALGAL   *adj* pertaining to a single algal cell

UNIAXIAL   *adj* having one axis

UNICOLOR   *adj* of one color

UNICORN   *n* pl. -S a mythical horselike creature

UNICYCLE   *n* pl. -S a one-wheeled vehicle

UNIDEAED   *adj* lacking ideas

UNIFACE   *n* pl. -S a coin having a design on only one side

UNIFIC   *adj* unifying

UNIFIED   past tense of unify

UNIFIER   *n* pl. -S one that unifies

UNIFIES   present 3d person sing. of unify

UNIFILAR   *adj* having only one thread, wire, or fiber

UNIFORM   *adj* -FORMER, -FORMEST unchanging

UNIFORM   *v* -ED, -ING, -S to make uniform

UNIFY   *v* -FIED, -FYING, -FIES to make into a coherent whole

UNILOBED   *adj* having one lobe

UNION   *n* pl. -S a number of persons, parties, or political entities united for a common purpose

UNIONISE   *v* -ISED, -ISING, -ISES to unionize

UNIONISM   *n* pl. -S the principle of forming a union

UNIONIST   *n* pl. -S an advocate of unionism

UNIONIZE   *v* -IZED, -IZING, -IZES to form into a union

UNIPOD   *n* pl. -S a one-legged support

UNIPOLAR   *adj* showing only one kind of polarity

UNIQUE   *adj* UNIQUER, UNIQUEST existing as the only one of its kind; very unusual **UNIQUELY** *adv*

UNIQUE   *n* pl. -S something that is unique

UNISEX   *n* pl. -ES the condition of not being distinguishable as to sex

UNISON   *n* pl. -S complete agreement **UNISONAL** *adj*

UNIT   *n* pl. -S a specific quantity used as a standard of measurement

UNITAGE   *n* pl. -S amount in units

UNITARY   *adj* pertaining to a unit

UNITE   *v* UNITED, UNITING, UNITES to bring together so as to form a whole **UNITEDLY** *adv*

UNITER   *n* pl. -S one that unites

UNITIES   pl. of unity

UNITIVE   *adj* serving to unite

UNITIZE   *v* -IZED, -IZING, -IZES to divide into units

UNITY   *n* pl. -TIES the state of being one single entity

UNIVALVE   *n* pl. -S a mollusk having a single shell

UNIVERSE   *n* pl. -S the totality of all existing things

UNIVOCAL *n* pl. -S a word having only one meaning

UNKEMPT *adj* untidy

UNKEND *adj* unkenned

UNKENNED *adj* not known or recognized

UNKENNEL *v* -NELED, -NELING, -NELS or -NELLED, -NELLING, -NELS to release from a kennel

UNKENT *adj* unkenned

UNKNIT *v* -KNITTED, -KNITTING, -KNITS to unravel

UNKNOT *v* -KNOTTED, -KNOTTING, -KNOTS to undo a knot in

UNKNOWN *n* pl. -S one that is not known

UNLACE *v* -LACED, -LACING, -LACES to unfasten the laces of

UNLADE *v* -LADED, -LADEN, -LADING, -LADES to unload

UNLAID past tense of unlay

UNLASH *v* -ED, -ING, -ES to untie the lashing (a type of binding) of

UNLATCH *v* -ED, -ING, -ES to open by lifting the latch (a fastening device)

UNLAY *v* -LAID, -LAYING, -LAYS to untwist

UNLEAD *v* -ED, -ING, -S to remove the lead from

UNLEARN *v* -LEARNED or -LEARNT, -LEARNING, -LEARNS to put out of one's knowledge or memory

UNLEASH *v* -ED, -ING, -ES to free from a leash

UNLESS *conj* except on the condition that

UNLET *adj* not rented

UNLEVEL *v* -ELED, -ELING, -ELS or -ELLED, -ELLING, -ELS to make uneven

UNLIMBER *v* -ED, -ING, -S to prepare for action

UNLINK *v* -ED, -ING, -S to unfasten the links (connecting devices) of

UNLIVE *v* -LIVED, -LIVING, -LIVES to live so as to make amends for

UNLOAD *v* -ED, -ING, -S to remove the load or cargo from

UNLOADER *n* pl. -S one that unloads

UNLOCK *v* -ED, -ING, -S to unfasten the lock of

UNLOOSE *v* -LOOSED, -LOOSING, -LOOSES to set free

UNLOOSEN *v* -ED, -ING, -S to unloose

UNMAKE *v* -MADE, -MAKING, -MAKES to destroy

UNMAKER *n* pl. -S one that unmakes

UNMAN *v* -MANNED, -MANNING, -MANS to deprive of courage

UNMASK *v* -ED, -ING, -S to remove a mask from

UNMASKER *n* pl. -S one that unmasks

UNMEET *adj* improper **UNMEETLY** *adv*

UNMEW *v* -ED, -ING, -S to set free

UNMINGLE *v* -GLED, -GLING, -GLES to separate things that are mixed

UNMITER *v* -ED, -ING, -S to depose from the rank of bishop

UNMITRE *v* -TRED, -TRING, -TRES to unmiter

UNMOLD *v* -ED, -ING, -S to remove from a mold

UNMOOR *v* -ED, -ING, -S to release from moorings

UNMORAL *adj* amoral

UNMUFFLE *v* -FLED, -FLING, -FLES to free from something that muffles

UNMUZZLE *v* -ZLED, -ZLING, -ZLES to remove a muzzle from

UNNAIL *v* -ED, -ING, -S to remove the nails from

UNNERVE *v* -NERVED, -NERVING, -NERVES to deprive of courage

UNPACK *v* -ED, -ING, -S to remove the contents of

UNPACKER *n* pl. -S one that unpacks

UNPAGED *adj* having no page numbers

UNPEG *v* -PEGGED, -PEGGING, -PEGS to remove the pegs from

UNPEN *v* -PENNED or -PENT, -PENNING, -PENS to release from confinement

UNPEOPLE *v* -PLED, -PLING, -PLES to remove people from

UNPERSON *n* pl. -S one who is removed completely from recognition

UNPICK *v* -ED, -ING, -S to remove the stitches from

UNPILE *v* -PILED, -PILING, -PILES to take or disentangle from a pile

UNPIN *v* -PINNED, -PINNING, -PINS to remove the pins from

UNPLAIT *v* -ED, -ING, -S to undo the plaits of

UNPLUG   *v* -PLUGGED, -PLUGGING, -PLUGS to take a plug out of

UNPUCKER   *v* -ED, -ING, -S to remove the wrinkles from

UNPUZZLE   *v* -ZLED, -ZLING, -ZLES to work out the obscured meaning of

UNQUIET   *n* pl. -S a state of unrest

UNQUOTE   *v* -QUOTED, -QUOTING, -QUOTES to close a quotation

UNRAVEL   *v* -ELED, -ELING, -ELS or -ELLED, -ELLING, -ELS to separate the threads of

UNREASON   *v* -ED, -ING, -S to disrupt the sanity of

UNREEL   *v* -ED, -ING, -S to unwind from a reel

UNREELER   *n* pl. -S one that unreels

UNREEVE   *v* -REEVED or -ROVE, -ROVEN, -REEVING, -REEVES to withdraw a rope from an opening

UNRENT   *adj* not torn

UNREPAIR   *n* pl. -S lack of repair

UNREST   *n* pl. -S a disturbed or uneasy state

UNRIDDLE   *v* -DLED, -DLING, -DLES to solve

UNRIG   *v* -RIGGED, -RIGGING, -RIGS to divest of rigging

UNRIP   *v* -RIPPED, -RIPPING, -RIPS to rip open

UNRIPE   *adj* -RIPER, -RIPEST not ripe
UNRIPELY *adv*

UNROBE   *v* -ROBED, -ROBING, -ROBES to undress

UNROLL   *v* -ED, -ING, -S to open something that is rolled up

UNROOF   *v* -ED, -ING, -S to strip off the roof of

UNROOT   *v* -ED, -ING, -S to uproot

UNROUND   *v* -ED, -ING, -S to articulate without rounding the lips

UNROVE   a past tense of unreeve

UNROVEN   a past participle of unreeve

UNRULY   *adj* -LIER, -LIEST difficult to control

UNSADDLE   *v* -DLED, -DLING, -DLES to remove the saddle from

UNSAFETY   *n* pl. -TIES lack of safety

UNSAY   *v* -SAID, -SAYING, -SAYS to retract something said

UNSCREW   *v* -ED, -ING, -S to remove the screws from

UNSEAL   *v* -ED, -ING, -S to remove the seal of

UNSEAM   *v* -ED, -ING, -S to open the seams of

UNSEAT   *v* -ED, -ING, -S to remove from a seat

UNSET   *v* -SET, -SETTING, -SETS to unsettle

UNSETTLE   *v* -TLED, -TLING, -TLES to make unstable

UNSEW   *v* -SEWED, -SEWN, -SEWING, -SEWS to undo the sewing of

UNSEX   *v* -ED, -ING, -ES to deprive of sexual power

UNSHELL   *v* -ED, -ING, -S to remove the shell from

UNSHIFT   *v* -ED, -ING, -S to release the shift key on a typewriter

UNSHIP   *v* -SHIPPED, -SHIPPING, -SHIPS to unload from a ship

UNSICKER   *adj* unreliable

UNSIGHT   *v* -ED, -ING, -S to prevent from seeing

UNSLING   *v* -SLUNG, -SLINGING, -SLINGS to remove from a slung position

UNSNAP   *v* -SNAPPED, -SNAPPING, -SNAPS to undo the snaps (fastening devices) of

UNSNARL   *v* -ED, -ING, -S to untangle

UNSOLDER   *v* -ED, -ING, -S to separate

UNSONCY   *adj* unsonsie

UNSONSIE   *adj* unlucky

UNSONSY   *adj* unsonsie

UNSPEAK   *v* -SPOKE, -SPOKEN, -SPEAKING, -SPEAKS to unsay

UNSPHERE   *v* -SPHERED, -SPHERING, -SPHERES to remove from a sphere

UNSTACK   *v* -ED, -ING, -S to remove from a stack

UNSTATE   *v* -STATED, -STATING, -STATES to deprive of status

UNSTEADY   *v* -STEADIED, -STEADYING, -STEADIES to make unsteady

UNSTEEL   *v* -ED, -ING, -S to make soft

UNSTEP   *v* -STEPPED, -STEPPING, -STEPS to remove from a socket

UNSTICK   *v* -ED, -ING, -S to disjoin

UNSTOP   *v* -STOPPED, -STOPPING, -STOPS to remove a stopper from

UNSTRAP v -STRAPPED, -STRAPPING, -STRAPS to remove a strap from

UNSTRESS n pl. -ES a syllable having relatively weak stress

UNSTRING v -STRUNG, -STRINGING, -STRINGS to remove from a string

UNSWATHE v -SWATHED, -SWATHING, -SWATHES to unbind

UNSWEAR v -SWORE, -SWORN, -SWEARING, -SWEARS to retract something sworn

UNTACK v -ED, -ING, -S to remove a tack from

UNTANGLE v -GLED, -GLING, -GLES to free from tangles

UNTEACH v -TAUGHT, -TEACHING, -TEACHES to cause to unlearn something

UNTETHER v -ED, -ING, -S to free from a tether

UNTHINK v -THOUGHT, -THINKING, -THINKS to dismiss from the mind

UNTHREAD v -ED, -ING, -S to remove the thread from

UNTHRONE v -THRONED, -THRONING, -THRONES to remove from a throne

UNTIDY v -DIED, -DYING, -DIES to make untidy

UNTIE v -TIED, -TYING, -TIES to free from something that ties

UNTIL prep up to the time of

UNTO prep to

UNTOWARD adj unruly

UNTREAD v -TROD, -TRODDEN, -TREADING, -TREADS to retrace

UNTRIM v -TRIMMED, -TRIMMING, -TRIMS to strip of trimming

UNTRUSS v -ED, -ING, -ES to free from a truss

UNTRUTH n pl. -S something that is untrue

UNTUCK v -ED, -ING, -S to release from being tucked up

UNTUNE v -TUNED, -TUNING, -TUNES to put out of tune

UNTWINE v -TWINED, -TWINING, -TWINES to separate the twisted or tangled parts of

UNTWIST v -ED, -ING, -S to untwine

UNTYING present participle of untie

UNVEIL v -ED, -ING, -S to remove a covering from

UNVOICE v -VOICED, -VOICING, -VOICES to deprive of voice or vocal quality

UNWASHED n pl. -S an ignorant or underprivileged group

UNWEAVE v -WOVE, -WOVEN, -WEAVING, -WEAVES to undo something woven

UNWEIGHT v -ED, -ING, -S to reduce the weight of

UNWIND v -WOUND, -WINDING, -WINDS to reverse the winding of

UNWINDER n pl. -S one that unwinds

UNWISDOM n pl. -S lack of wisdom

UNWISH v -ED, -ING, -ES to cease to wish for

UNWIT v -WITTED, -WITTING, -WITS to make insane

UNWONTED adj unusual

UNWORTHY n pl. -THIES an unworthy person

UNWOUND past tense of unwind

UNWOVE past tense of unweave

UNWOVEN past participle of unweave

UNWRAP v -WRAPPED, -WRAPPING, -WRAPS to remove the wrapping from

UNYEANED adj unborn

UNYOKE v -YOKED, -YOKING, -YOKES to free from a yoke

UNZIP v -ZIPPED, -ZIPPING, -ZIPS to open the zipper of

UP v UPPED, UPPING, UPS to raise

UPAS n pl. -ES an Asian tree

UPBEAR v -BORE, -BORNE, -BEARING, -BEARS to raise aloft

UPBEARER n pl. -S one that upbears

UPBEAT n pl. -S an unaccented beat in a musical measure

UPBIND v -BOUND, -BINDING, -BINDS to bind completely

UPBOIL v -ED, -ING, -S to boil up

UPBORE past tense of upbear

UPBORNE past participle of upbear

UPBOUND past tense of upbind

UPBRAID v -ED, -ING, -S to reproach severely

UPBUILD v -BUILT, -BUILDING, -BUILDS to build up

UPBY	*adv* upbye
UPBYE	*adv* a little farther on
UPCAST	*v* -CAST, -CASTING, -CASTS to cast up
UPCHUCK	*v* -ED, -ING, -S to vomit
UPCLIMB	*v* -ED, -ING, -S to climb up
UPCOIL	*v* -ED, -ING, -S to coil up
UPCOMING	*adj* about to happen or appear
UPCURL	*v* -ED, -ING, -S to curl up
UPCURVE	*v* -CURVED, -CURVING, -CURVES to curve upward
UPDART	*v* -ED, -ING, -S to dart up
UPDATE	*v* -DATED, -DATING, -DATES to bring up to date
UPDATER	*n* pl. -S one that updates
UPDIVE	*v* -DIVED or -DOVE, -DIVING, -DIVES to spring upward
UPDO	*n* pl. -DOS an upswept hairdo
UPDRAFT	*n* pl. -S an upward movement of air
UPDRY	*v* -DRIED, -DRYING, -DRIES to dry completely
UPEND	*v* -ED, -ING, -S to set or stand on end
UPFIELD	*adv* into the part of the field toward which the offensive team is going
UPFLING	*v* -FLUNG, -FLINGING, -FLINGS to fling up
UPFLOW	*v* -ED, -ING, -S to flow up
UPFOLD	*v* -ED, -ING, -S to fold up
UPGATHER	*v* -ED, -ING, -S to gather up
UPGAZE	*v* -GAZED, -GAZING, -GAZES to gaze up
UPGIRD	*v* -GIRDED or -GIRT, -GIRDING, -GIRDS to gird completely
UPGOING	*adj* going up
UPGRADE	*v* -GRADED, -GRADING, -GRADES to raise to a higher grade or standard
UPGROW	*v* -GREW, -GROWN, -GROWING, -GROWS to grow up
UPGROWTH	*n* pl. -S the process of growing up
UPHEAP	*v* -ED, -ING, -S to heap up
UPHEAVAL	*n* pl. -S the act of upheaving
UPHEAVE	*v* -HEAVED or -HOVE, -HEAVING, -HEAVES to heave up
UPHEAVER	*n* pl. -S one that upheaves
UPHELD	past tense of uphold
UPHILL	*n* pl. -S an upward slope
UPHOARD	*v* -ED, -ING, -S to hoard up
UPHOLD	*v* -HELD, -HOLDING, -HOLDS to hold aloft
UPHOLDER	*n* pl. -S one that upholds
UPHOVE	a past tense of upheave
UPHROE	*n* pl. -S euphroe
UPKEEP	*n* pl. -S the cost of maintaining something in good condition
UPLAND	*n* pl. -S the higher land of a region
UPLANDER	*n* pl. -S an inhabitant of an upland
UPLEAP	*v* -LEAPED or -LEAPT, -LEAPING, -LEAPS to leap up
UPLIFT	*v* -ED, -ING, -S to lift up
UPLIFTER	*n* pl. -S one that uplifts
UPLIGHT	*v* -LIGHTED or -LIT, -LIGHTING, -LIGHTS to light to a higher degree
UPMOST	*adj* highest
UPO	*prep* upon
UPON	*prep* on
UPPED	past tense of up
UPPER	*n* pl. -S the part of a boot or shoe above the sole
UPPERCUT	*v* -CUT, -CUTTING, -CUTS to strike an upward blow
UPPILE	*v* -PILED, -PILING, -PILES to pile up
UPPING	*n* pl. -S the process of marking young swans for identification purposes
UPPISH	*adj* uppity **UPPISHLY** *adv*
UPPITY	*adj* tending to be snobbish and arrogant
UPPROP	*v* -PROPPED, -PROPPING, -PROPS to prop up
UPRAISE	*v* -RAISED, -RAISING, -RAISES to raise up
UPRAISER	*n* pl. -S one that upraises
UPREACH	*v* -ED, -ING, -ES to reach up
UPREAR	*v* -ED, -ING, -S to upraise
UPRIGHT	*v* -ED, -ING, -S to make vertical
UPRISE	*v* -ROSE, -RISEN, -RISING, -RISES to rise up
UPRISER	*n* pl. -S one that uprises
UPRISING	*n* pl. -S a revolt
UPRIVER	*n* pl. -S an area lying toward the source of a river

UPROAR *n* pl. -S a state of noisy excitement and confusion

UPROOT *v* -ED, -ING, -S to pull up by the roots

UPROOTAL *n* pl. -S the act of uprooting

UPROOTER *n* pl. -S one that uproots

UPROSE past tense of uprise

UPROUSE *v* -ROUSED, -ROUSING, -ROUSES to rouse up

UPRUSH *v* -ED, -ING, -ES to rush up

UPSEND *v* -SENT, -SENDING, -SENDS to send upward

UPSET *v* -SET, -SETTING, -SETS to overturn

UPSETTER *n* pl. -S one that upsets

UPSHIFT *v* -ED, -ING, -S to shift an automotive vehicle into a higher gear

UPSHOOT *v* -SHOT, -SHOOTING, -SHOOTS to shoot upward

UPSHOT *n* pl. -S the final result

UPSIDE *n* pl. -S the upper side

UPSILON *n* pl. -S a Greek letter

UPSOAR *v* -ED, -ING, -S to soar upward

UPSPRING *v* -SPRANG or -SPRUNG, -SPRINGING, -SPRINGS to spring up

UPSTAGE *v* -STAGED, -STAGING, -STAGES to outdo theatrically

UPSTAIR *adj* pertaining to an upper floor

UPSTAIRS *adv* up the stairs

UPSTAND *v* -STOOD, -STANDING, -STANDS to stand up on one's feet

UPSTARE *v* -STARED, -STARING, -STARES to stare upward

UPSTART *v* -ED, -ING, -S to spring up suddenly

UPSTATE *n* pl. -S the northern region of a state

UPSTATER *n* pl. -S an inhabitant of an upstate region

UPSTEP *v* -STEPPED, -STEPPING, -STEPS to step up

UPSTIR *v* -STIRRED, -STIRRING, -STIRS to stir up

UPSTOOD past tense of upstand

UPSTREAM *adv* toward the source of a stream

UPSTROKE *n* pl. -S an upward stroke

UPSURGE *v* -SURGED, -SURGING, -SURGES to surge up

UPSWEEP *v* -SWEPT, -SWEEPING, -SWEEPS to sweep upward

UPSWELL *v* -SWELLED, -SWOLLEN, -SWELLING, -SWELLS, to swell up

UPSWING *v* -SWUNG, -SWINGING, -SWINGS to swing upward

UPTAKE *n* pl. -S an upward ventilating shaft

UPTEAR *v* -TORE, -TORN, -TEARING, -TEARS to tear out by the roots

UPTHROW *v* -THREW, -THROWN, -THROWING, -THROWS to throw upward

UPTHRUST *v* -THRUST, -THRUSTING, -THRUSTS to thrust up

UPTIGHT *adj* nervous

UPTILT *v* -ED, -ING, -S to tilt upward

UPTIME *n* pl. -S the time during which machinery is functioning

UPTORE past tense of uptear

UPTORN past participle of uptear

UPTOSS *v* -ED, -ING, -ES to toss upward

UPTOWN *n* pl. -S the upper part of a city

UPTOWNER *n* pl. -S one that lives uptown

UPTREND *n* pl. -S a tendency upward or toward growth

UPTURN *v* -ED, -ING, -S to turn up or over

UPWAFT *v* -ED, -ING, -S to waft upward

UPWARD *adv* toward a higher place or position **UPWARDLY** *adv*

UPWARDS *adv* upward

UPWELL *v* -ED, -ING, -S to well up

UPWIND *n* pl. -S a wind that blows against one's course

URACIL *n* pl. -S a chemical compound

URAEI a pl. of uraeus

URAEMIA *n* pl. -S uremia **URAEMIC** *adj*

URAEUS *n* pl. URAEI or URAEUSES the figure of the sacred serpent on the headdress of ancient Egyptian rulers

URALITE *n* pl. -S a mineral **URALITIC** *adj*

URANIC *adj* pertaining to uranium

URANIDE *n* pl. -S uranium

URANISM *n* pl. -S homosexuality

URANITE *n* pl. -S a mineral **URANITIC** *adj*

URANIUM	*n* pl. -S a radioactive element
URANOUS	*adj* pertaining to uranium
URANYL	*n* pl. -S a bivalent radical **URANYLIC** *adj*
URARE	*n* pl. -S curare
URARI	*n* pl. -S curare
URASE	*n* pl. -S urease
URATE	*n* pl. -S a chemical salt **URATIC** *adj*
URBAN	*adj* pertaining to a city
URBANE	*adj* -BANER, -BANEST refined and elegant **URBANELY** *adv*
URBANISE	*v* -ISED, -ISING, -ISES to urbanize
URBANISM	*n* pl. -S the life-style of city dwellers
URBANIST	*n* pl. -S a specialist in city planning
URBANITE	*n* pl. -S one who lives in a city
URBANITY	*n* pl. -TIES the quality of being urbane
URBANIZE	*v* -IZED, -IZING, -IZES to cause to take on urban characteristics
URCHIN	*n* pl. -S a mischievous boy
URD	*n* pl. -S an annual bean grown in India
UREA	*n* pl. -S a chemical compound **UREAL** *adj*
UREASE	*n* pl. -S an enzyme
UREDIA	pl. of uredium
UREDIAL	*adj* pertaining to a uredium
UREDINIA	*n/pl* uredia
UREDIUM	*n* pl. -DIA a spore-producing organ of certain fungi
UREDO	*n* pl. -DOS a skin irritation
UREIC	*adj* pertaining to urea
UREIDE	*n* pl. -S a chemical compound
UREMIA	*n* pl. -S an abnormal condition of the blood **UREMIC** *adj*
URETER	*n* pl. -S the duct that conveys urine from the kidney to the bladder **URETERAL, URETERIC** *adj*
URETHAN	*n* pl. -S urethane
URETHANE	*n* pl. -S a chemical compound
URETHRA	*n* pl. -THRAE or -THRAS the duct through which urine is discharged from the bladder **URETHRAL** *adj*
URETIC	*adj* pertaining to urine
URGE	*v* URGED, URGING, URGES to force forward
URGENCY	*n* pl. -CIES the quality of being urgent
URGENT	*adj* requiring immediate attention **URGENTLY** *adv*
URGER	*n* pl. -S one that urges
URGING	present participle of urge
URGINGLY	*adv* in an urging manner
URIC	*adj* pertaining to urine
URIDINE	*n* pl. -S a chemical compound
URINAL	*n* pl. -S a fixture used for urinating
URINARY	*n* pl. -NARIES a urinal
URINATE	*v* -NATED, -NATING, -NATES to discharge urine
URINE	*n* pl. -S a liquid containing body wastes
URINEMIA	*n* pl. -S uremia **URINEMIC** *adj*
URINOSE	*adj* pertaining to urine
URINOUS	*adj* pertaining to urine
URN	*n* pl. -S a type of vase **URNLIKE** *adj*
UROCHORD	*n* pl. -S a rodlike structure in certain lower vertebrates
URODELE	*n* pl. -S a type of amphibian
UROLITH	*n* pl. -S a concretion in the urinary tract
UROLOGY	*n* pl. -GIES the branch of medicine dealing with the urinary tract **UROLOGIC** *adj*
UROPOD	*n* pl. -S an abdominal limb of an arthropod **UROPODAL** *adj*
UROSCOPY	*n* pl. -PIES analysis of the urine as a means of diagnosis
UROSTYLE	*n* pl. -S a part of the vertebral column of frogs and toads
URSA	*n* pl. -SAE a female bear
URSIFORM	*adj* having the form of a bear
URSINE	*adj* pertaining to a bear
URTICANT	*n* pl. -S an urticating substance
URTICATE	*v* -CATED, -CATING, -CATES to cause itching or stinging
URUS	*n* pl. -ES an extinct European ox
URUSHIOL	*n* pl. -S a toxic liquid
US	*pron* the objective case of the pronoun we
USABLE	*adj* capable of being used **USABLY** *adv*

USAGE	*n* pl. -S a firmly established and generally accepted practice or procedure	**UTERUS**	*n* pl. UTERI or UTERUSES an organ of female mammals **UTERINE** *adj*
USANCE	*n* pl. -S usage	**UTILE**	*adj* useful
USAUNCE	*n* pl. -S usance	**UTILIDOR**	*n* pl. -S an insulated system of pipes for use in arctic regions
USE	*v* USED, USING, USES to put into service	**UTILISE**	*v* -LISED, -LISING, -LISES to utilize
USEABLE	*adj* usable **USEABLY** *adv*	**UTILISER**	*n* pl. -S utilizer
USEFUL	*adj* serving a purpose **USEFULLY** *adv*	**UTILITY**	*n* pl. -TIES the quality of being useful
USELESS	*adj* serving no purpose	**UTILIZE**	*v* -LIZED, -LIZING, -LIZES to make use of
USER	*n* pl. -S one that uses	**UTILIZER**	*n* pl. -S one that utilizes
USHER	*v* -ED, -ING, -S to conduct to a place	**UTMOST**	*n* pl. -S the greatest degree or amount
USING	present participle of use	**UTOPIA**	*n* pl. -S a place of ideal perfection
USNEA	*n* pl. -S any of a genus of lichens	**UTOPIAN**	*n* pl. -S one who believes in the perfectibility of human society
USQUABAE	*n* pl. -S usquebae	**UTOPISM**	*n* pl. -S the body of ideals or principles of a utopian
USQUE	*n* pl. -S usquebae	**UTOPIST**	*n* pl. -S a utopian
USQUEBAE	*n* pl. -S whiskey	**UTRICLE**	*n* pl. -S a saclike cavity in the inner ear
USTULATE	*adj* scorched		
USUAL	*n* pl. -S something that is usual (ordinary)	**UTRICULI**	*n/pl* utricles
USUALLY	*adv* ordinarily	**UTTER**	*v* -ED, -ING, -S to give audible expression to
USUFRUCT	*n* pl. -S the legal right to use another's property so long as it is not damaged or altered	**UTTERER**	*n* pl. -S one that utters
		UTTERLY	*adv* totally
USURER	*n* pl. -S one that practices usury	**UVEA**	*n* pl. -S a layer of the eye **UVEAL** *adj*
USURIES	pl. of usury	**UVEITIS**	*n* pl. -ITISES inflammation of the uvea **UVEITIC** *adj*
USURIOUS	*adj* practicing usury		
USURP	*v* -ED, -ING, -S to seize and hold without legal authority	**UVEOUS**	*adj* pertaining to the uvea
USURPER	*n* pl. -S one that usurps	**UVULA**	*n* pl. -LAE or -LAS the pendent, fleshy portion of the soft palate
USURY	*n* pl. -RIES the lending of money at an exorbitant interest rate	**UVULAR**	*n* pl. -S a uvularly produced sound
UT	*n* pl. -S the musical tone C in the French solmization system now replaced by do	**UVULARLY**	*adv* with the use of the uvula
		UVULITIS	*n* pl. -TISES inflammation of the uvula
UTA	*n* pl. -S any of a genus of large lizards	**UXORIAL**	*adj* pertaining to a wife
UTENSIL	*n* pl. -S a useful implement	**UXORIOUS**	*adj* excessively submissive or devoted to one's wife

VACANCY   *n* pl. -CIES the quality or state of being vacant

VACANT   *adj* empty **VACANTLY** *adv*

VACATE   *v* -CATED, -CATING, -CATES to make vacant

VACATION   *v* -ED, -ING, -S to take a vacation (a period of time devoted to rest and relaxation)

VACCINA   *n* pl. -S vaccinia

VACCINE   *n* pl. -S a preparation given to produce immunity to a specific disease **VACCINAL** *adj*

VACCINIA   *n* pl. -S cowpox

VACUA   a pl. of vacuum

VACUITY   *n* pl. -ITIES an empty space

VACUOLE   *n* pl. -S a small cavity in organic tissue **VACUOLAR** *adj*

VACUOUS   *adj* empty

VACUUM   *n* pl. VACUUMS or VACUA a space entirely devoid of matter

VACUUM   *v* -ED, -ING, -S to use a device that cleans by suction

VADOSE   *adj* located above the permanent groundwater level

VAGABOND   *v* -ED, -ING, -S to live like a vagabond (a vagrant)

VAGAL   *adj* pertaining to the vagus nerve **VAGALLY** *adv*

VAGARY   *n* pl. -RIES a whim

VAGI   pl. of vagus

VAGILE   *adj* free to move about

VAGILITY   *n* pl. -TIES freedom of movement

VAGINA   *n* pl. -NAE or -NAS the passage leading from the uterus to the vulva **VAGINAL** *adj*

VAGINATE   *adj* enclosed in a sheath

VAGOTOMY   *n* pl. -MIES surgical division of the vagus nerve

VAGRANCY   *n* pl. -CIES the state of being a vagrant

VAGRANT   *n* pl. -S a wanderer with no apparent means of support

VAGROM   *adj* wandering

VAGUE   *adj* VAGUER, VAGUEST not clearly expressed or understood **VAGUELY** *adv*

VAGUS   *n* pl. -GI a cranial nerve

VAHINE   *n* pl. -S wahine

VAIL   *v* -ED, -ING, -S to lower

VAIN   *adj* VAINER, VAINEST filled with undue admiration for oneself **VAINLY** *adv*

VAINNESS   *n* pl. -ES the quality or state of being vain

VAIR   *n* pl. -S a fur used for lining and trimming medieval garments

VAKEEL   *n* pl. -S a native lawyer in India

VAKIL   *n* pl. -S vakeel

VALANCE   *v* -LANCED, -LANCING, -LANCES to furnish with a short drapery

VALE   *n* pl. -S a valley

VALENCE   *n* pl. -S the degree of combining power of an element or radical

VALENCIA   *n* pl. -S a woven fabric

VALENCY   *n* pl. -CIES valence

VALERATE   *n* pl. -S a chemical salt

VALERIAN   *n* pl. -S a perennial herb **VALERIC** *adj*

VALET	v -ED, -ING, -S to act as a personal servant to	**VALVATE**	adj having valves or parts resembling valves
VALGUS	n pl. -ES the position of a joint that is abnormally turned outward **VALGOID** adj	**VALVE**	v VALVED, VALVING, VALVES to provide with a valve (a device for controlling the flow of a liquid or gas)
VALIANCE	n pl. -S valor	**VALVELET**	n pl. -S a small valve
VALIANCY	n pl. -CIES valor	**VALVULA**	n pl. -LAE valvule
VALIANT	n pl. -S a courageous person	**VALVULAR**	adj pertaining to a valve
VALID	adj based on evidence that can be supported	**VALVULE**	n pl. -S a small valve
VALIDATE	v -DATED, -DATING, -DATES to give legal force to	**VAMBRACE**	n pl. -S a piece of armor for the forearm
VALIDITY	n pl. -TIES the quality or state of being valid	**VAMOOSE**	v -MOOSED, -MOOSING, -MOOSES to leave quickly
VALIDLY	adv in a valid manner	**VAMOSE**	v -MOSED, -MOSING, -MOSES to vamoose
VALINE	n pl. -S an amino acid	**VAMP**	v -ED, -ING, -S to repair or patch
VALISE	n pl. -S a small piece of hand luggage	**VAMPER**	n pl. -S one that vamps
VALKYR	n pl. -S valkyrie	**VAMPIRE**	n pl. -S a reanimated corpse believed to feed on sleeping persons' blood **VAMPIRIC** adj
VALKYRIE	n pl. -S a maiden in Norse mythology		
VALLATE	adj bordered by a raised edge	**VAMPISH**	adj seductive
VALLEY	n pl. -LEYS a depression of the earth's surface	**VAN**	n pl. -S a large motor vehicle
VALONIA	n pl. -S a substance obtained from dried acorn cups and used in tanning and dyeing	**VANADATE**	n pl. -S a chemical salt
		VANADIUM	n pl. -S a metallic element **VANADIC, VANADOUS** adj
VALOR	n pl. -S courage	**VANDA**	n pl. -S a tropical orchid
VALORISE	v -ISED, -ISING, -ISES to valorize	**VANDAL**	n pl. -S one who willfully destroys or defaces property **VANDALIC** adj
VALORIZE	v -IZED, -IZING, -IZES to establish and maintain the price of by governmental action	**VANDYKE**	n pl. -S a short, pointed beard **VANDYKED** adj
VALOROUS	adj courageous	**VANE**	n pl. -S a device for showing the direction of the wind **VANED** adj
VALOUR	n pl. -S valor		
VALSE	n pl. -S a concert waltz	**VANG**	n pl. -S a rope on a ship
VALUABLE	n pl. -S a possession of value	**VANGUARD**	n pl. -S the forefront of a movement
VALUABLY	adv with value		
VALUATE	v -ATED, -ATING, -ATES to appraise	**VANILLA**	n pl. -S a flavoring extract **VANILLIC** adj
VALUATOR	n pl. -S one that valuates	**VANILLIN**	n pl. -S a chemical compound used in flavoring
VALUE	v -UED, -UING, -UES to estimate the value (the quality that renders a thing useful or desirable) of	**VANISH**	v -ED, -ING, -ES to disappear
		VANISHER	n pl. -S one that vanishes
VALUER	n pl. -S one that values	**VANITY**	n pl. -TIES inflated pride in oneself **VANITIED** adj
VALUTA	n pl. -S the agreed or exchange value of a currency		
		VANMAN	n pl. -MEN a person who drives a van
VALVAL	adj resembling or pertaining to a valve		
VALVAR	adj valval	**VANQUISH**	v -ED, -ING, -ES to defeat in battle

VANTAGE   *n* pl. -S superiority over a competitor

VANWARD   *adv* toward the front

VAPID   *adj* insipid **VAPIDLY** *adv*

VAPIDITY   *n* pl. -TIES the quality or state of being vapid

VAPOR   *v* -ED, -ING, -S to emit vapor (visible floating moisture)

VAPORER   *n* pl. -S one that vapors

VAPORING   *n* pl. -S boastful talk

VAPORISE   *v* -ISED, -ISING, -ISES to vaporize

VAPORISH   *adj* resembling vapor

VAPORIZE   *v* -IZED, -IZING, -IZES to convert into vapor

VAPOROUS   *adj* vaporish

VAPORY   *adj* vaporish

VAPOUR   *v* -ED, -ING, -S to vapor

VAPOURER   *n* pl. -S vaporer

VAPOURY   *adj* vapory

VAQUERO   *n* pl. -ROS a cowboy

VARA   *n* pl. -S a Spanish unit of length

VARIA   *n/pl* a collection of various literary works

VARIABLE   *n* pl. -S something that varies

VARIABLY   *adv* in a varying manner

VARIANCE   *n* pl. -S a license to perform an act contrary to the usual rule

VARIANT   *n* pl. -S a variable

VARIATE   *v* -ATED, -ATING, -ATES to vary

VARICES   pl. of varix

VARICOSE   *adj* abnormally swollen or dilated

VARIED   past tense of vary

VARIEDLY   *adv* in a varied manner

VARIER   *n* pl. -S one that varies

VARIES   present 3d person sing. of vary

VARIETY   *n* pl. -ETIES something differing from others of the same general kind **VARIETAL** *adj*

VARIFORM   *adj* having various forms

VARIOLA   *n* pl. -S smallpox **VARIOLAR** *adj*

VARIOLE   *n* pl. -S a foveola

VARIORUM   *n* pl. -S an edition containing various versions of a text

VARIOUS   *adj* of diverse kinds

VARISTOR   *n* pl. -S a type of electrical resistor

VARIX   *n* pl. VARICES a varicose vein

VARLET   *n* pl. -S a knave

VARLETRY   *n* pl. -RIES a group of common people

VARMENT   *n* pl. -S varmint

VARMINT   *n* pl. -S an animal considered to be a pest

VARNA   *n* pl. -S any of the four main Hindu social classes

VARNISH   *v* -ED, -ING, -ES to give a glossy appearance to

VARNISHY   *adj* glossy

VARSITY   *n* pl. -TIES the principal team representing a university, college, or school in any activity

VARUS   *n* pl. -ES a malformation of a bone or joint

VARVE   *n* pl. -S a deposit of sedimentary material **VARVED** *adj*

VARY   *v* VARIED, VARYING, VARIES to become or make different

VAS   *n* pl. VASA an anatomical duct **VASAL** *adj*

VASCULAR   *adj* pertaining to ducts that convey body liquids

VASCULUM   *n* pl. -LA or -LUMS a box used to hold plant specimens

VASE   *n* pl. -S a rounded, decorative container **VASELIKE** *adj*

VASIFORM   *adj* having the form of a vase

VASSAL   *n* pl. -S a person granted the use of land by a feudal lord in return for homage and allegiance

VAST   *adj* VASTER, VASTEST of great extent or size

VAST   *n* pl. -S a vast space

VASTIER   comparative of vasty

VASTIEST   superlative of vasty

VASTITY   *n* pl. -TIES vastness

VASTLY   *adv* to a vast extent or degree

VASTNESS   *n* pl. -ES the quality or state of being vast

VASTY   *adj* VASTIER, VASTIEST vast

VAT   *v* VATTED, VATTING, VATS to put into a vat (a large container for holding liquids)

VATFUL   *n* pl. -S as much as a vat will hold

VATIC   *adj* pertaining to a prophet

VATICAL	*adj* vatic
VATICIDE	*n* pl. -S the killing of a prophet
VATTED	past tense of vat
VATTING	present participle of vat
VAU	*n* pl. -S vav
VAULT	*v* -ED, -ING, -S to provide with a vault (an arched ceiling)
VAULTER	*n* pl. -S one that leaps
VAULTING	*n* pl. -S the structure forming a vault
VAULTY	*adj* VAULTIER, VAULTIEST resembling a vault
VAUNT	*v* -ED, -ING, -S to brag
VAUNTER	*n* pl. -S one that vaunts
VAUNTFUL	*adj* boastful
VAUNTIE	*adj* boastful
VAUNTY	*adj* vauntie
VAV	*n* pl. -S a Hebrew letter
VAVASOR	*n* pl. -S a high-ranking vassal
VAVASOUR	*n* pl. -S vavasor
VAVASSOR	*n* pl. -S vavasor
VAW	*n* pl. -S vav
VAWARD	*n* pl. -S the foremost part
VAWNTIE	*adj* vaunty
VEAL	*v* -ED, -ING, -S to kill and prepare a calf for food
VEALER	*n* pl. -S a calf raised for food
VEALY	*adj* VEALIER, VEALIEST immature
VECTOR	*v* -ED, -ING, -S to guide in flight by means of radioed directions
VEDALIA	*n* pl. -S an Australian ladybug
VEDETTE	*n* pl. -S a small boat used for scouting
VEE	*n* pl. -S the letter V
VEENA	*n* pl. -S vina
VEEP	*n* pl. -S a vice-president
VEEPEE	*n* pl. -S veep
VEER	*v* -ED, -ING, -S to change direction
VEERY	*n* pl. -RIES a songbird
VEG	*n* pl. VEG a vegetable
VEGAN	*n* pl. -S one that eats only plant products
VEGANISM	*n* pl. -S the practice of eating only plant products
VEGETAL	*adj* pertaining to plants
VEGETANT	*adj* characteristic of plant life
VEGETATE	*v* -TATED, -TATING, -TATES to grow in the manner of a plant
VEGETE	*adj* healthy
VEGETIST	*n* pl. -S one that eats only plant products
VEGETIVE	*adj* growing or capable of growing
VEHEMENT	*adj* ardent
VEHICLE	*n* pl. -S a device used as a means of conveyance
VEIL	*v* -ED, -ING, -S to provide with a veil (a piece of sheer fabric worn over the face)
VEILEDLY	*adv* in a disguised manner
VEILER	*n* pl. -S one that veils
VEILING	*n* pl. -S a veil
VEILLIKE	*adj* resembling a veil
VEIN	*v* -ED, -ING, -S to fill with veins (tubular blood vessels)
VEINAL	*adj* of or pertaining to the veins
VEINER	*n* pl. -S a tool used in wood carving
VEINIER	comparative of veiny
VEINIEST	superlative of veiny
VEINING	*n* pl. -S a network of veins
VEINLESS	*adj* having no veins
VEINLET	*n* pl. -S a small vein
VEINLIKE	*adj* resembling a vein
VEINULE	*n* pl. -S venule
VEINULET	*n* pl. -S venule
VEINY	*adj* VEINIER, VEINIEST full of veins
VELA	pl. of velum
VELAMEN	*n* pl. -MINA a velum
VELAR	*n* pl. -S a kind of speech sound
VELARIUM	*n* pl. -IA an awning over an ancient Roman theater
VELARIZE	*v* -IZED, -IZING, -IZES to pronounce with the back of the tongue touching the soft palate
VELATE	*adj* having a velum
VELD	*n* pl. -S veldt
VELDT	*n* pl. -S a grassland of southern Africa
VELIGER	*n* pl. -S a larval stage of certain mollusks

VELITES	*n/pl* foot soldiers of ancient Rome
VELLEITY	*n* pl. -ITIES a very low degree of desire
VELLUM	*n* pl. -S a fine parchment
VELOCE	*adv* rapidly — used as a musical direction
VELOCITY	*n* pl. -TIES rapidity of motion
VELOUR	*n* pl. -S a fabric resembling velvet
VELOUTE	*n* pl. -S a type of sauce
VELUM	*n* pl. -LA a thin membranous covering or partition
VELURE	*v* -LURED, -LURING, -LURES to smooth with a velvet or silk pad, as a hat
VELVERET	*n* pl. -S a fabric resembling velvet
VELVET	*n* pl. -S a soft, smooth fabric **VELVETED, VELVETY** *adj*
VENA	*n* pl. -NAE a vein
VENAL	*adj* open to bribery **VENALLY** *adv*
VENALITY	*n* pl. -TIES the quality or state of being venal
VENATIC	*adj* pertaining to hunting
VENATION	*n* pl. -S an arrangement of veins
VEND	*v* -ED, -ING, -S to sell **VENDABLE** *adj*
VENDACE	*n* pl. -S a European fish
VENDEE	*n* pl. -S a buyer
VENDER	*n* pl. -S vendor
VENDETTA	*n* pl. -S a feud between two families
VENDIBLE	*n* pl. -S a salable article
VENDIBLY	*adv* salably
VENDOR	*n* pl. -S a seller
VENDUE	*n* pl. -S a public sale
VENEER	*v* -ED, -ING, -S to overlay with thin layers of material
VENEERER	*n* pl. -S one that veneers
VENENATE	*v* -NATED, -NATING, -NATES to poison
VENENOSE	*adj* poisonous
VENERATE	*v* -ATED, -ATING, -ATES to revere
VENEREAL	*adj* involving the genital organs
VENERY	*n* pl. -ERIES sexual intercourse
VENETIAN	*n* pl. -S a flexible window screen

VENGE	*v* VENGED, VENGING, VENGES to avenge
VENGEFUL	*adj* seeking to avenge
VENIAL	*adj* easily excused or forgiven **VENIALLY** *adv*
VENIN	*n* pl. -S a toxin found in snake venom
VENINE	*n* pl. -S venin
VENIRE	*n* pl. -S a type of judicial writ
VENISON	*n* pl. -S the edible flesh of a deer
VENOM	*v* -ED, -ING, -S to inject with venom (a poisonous secretion of certain animals)
VENOMER	*n* pl. -S one that venoms
VENOMOUS	*adj* poisonous
VENOSE	*adj* venous
VENOSITY	*n* pl. -TIES the quality of state of being venous
VENOUS	*adj* full of veins **VENOUSLY** *adv*
VENT	*v* -ED, -ING, -S to provide with a vent (an opening for the escape of gas or liquid)
VENTAGE	*n* pl. -S a small opening
VENTAIL	*n* pl. -S the adjustable front of a medieval helmet
VENTER	*n* pl. -S the abdomen
VENTLESS	*adj* having no vent
VENTRAL	*n* pl. -S a fin located on the underside of a fish
VENTURE	*v* -TURED, -TURING, -TURES to risk
VENTURER	*n* pl. -S one that ventures
VENTURI	*n* pl. -S a device for measuring the flow of a fluid
VENTURING	present participle of venture
VENUE	*n* pl. -S the locale of an event
VENULE	*n* pl. -S a small vein **VENULAR, VENULOSE, VENULOUS** *adj*
VERA	*adj* very
VERACITY	*n* pl. -TIES conformity to truth
VERANDA	*n* pl. -S a type of porch
VERANDAH	*n* pl. -S veranda
VERATRIA	*n* pl. -S veratrin
VERATRIN	*n* pl. -S a poisonous mixture of alkaloids
VERATRUM	*n* pl. -S a poisonous herb
VERB	*n* pl. -S a word used to express an act, occurrence, or mode of being

VERBAL *n* pl. -S a word derived from a verb

VERBALLY *adv* in a spoken manner

VERBATIM *adv* word for word

VERBENA *n* pl. -S a flowering plant

VERBIAGE *n* pl. -S an excess of words

VERBID *n* pl. -S a verbal

VERBIFY *v* -FIED, -FYING, -FIES to use as a verb

VERBILE *n* pl. -S one whose mental imagery consists of words

VERBLESS *adj* lacking a verb

VERBOSE *adj* wordy

VERBOTEN *adj* forbidden

VERDANCY *n* pl. -CIES the quality or state of being verdant

VERDANT *adj* green with vegetation

VERDERER *n* pl. -S an officer in charge of the royal forests of England

VERDEROR *n* pl. -S verderer

VERDICT *n* pl. -S the decision of a jury at the end of a legal proceeding

VERDIN *n* pl. -S a small bird

VERDITER *n* pl. -S a blue or green pigment

VERDURE *n* pl. -S green vegetation **VERDURED** *adj*

VERECUND *adj* shy

VERGE *v* VERGED, VERGING, VERGES to come near

VERGENCE *n* pl. -S a movement of one eye in relation to the other

VERGER *n* pl. -S a church official

VERGING present participle of verge

VERGLAS *n* pl. -ES a thin coating of ice on rock

VERIDIC *adj* truthful

VERIER comparative of very

VERIEST superlative of very

VERIFIER *n* pl. -S one that verifies

VERIFY *v* -FIED, -FYING, -FIES to prove to be true

VERILY *adv* in truth

VERISM *n* pl. -S realism in art or literature

VERISMO *n* pl. -MOS verism

VERIST *n* pl. -S one who practices verism **VERISTIC** *adj*

VERITAS *n* pl. -TATES truth

VERITY *n* pl. -TIES truth

VERJUICE *n* pl. -S the juice of sour or unripe fruit

VERMEIL *n* pl. -S a red color

VERMES pl. of vermis

VERMIAN *adj* pertaining to worms

VERMIN *n* pl. VERMIN small, common, harmful, or objectionable animals

VERMIS *n* pl. -MES a part of the brain

VERMOULU *adj* eaten by worms

VERMOUTH *n* pl. -S a liqueur

VERMUTH *n* pl. -S vermouth

VERNACLE *n* pl. -S vernicle

VERNAL *adj* pertaining to spring **VERNALLY** *adv*

VERNICLE *n* pl. -S veronica

VERNIER *n* pl. -S an auxiliary scale used with a main scale to obtain fine measurements

VERNIX *n* pl. -ES a fatty substance covering the skin of a fetus

VERONICA *n* pl. -S a handkerchief bearing the image of Christ's face

VERRUCA *n* pl. -CAE a wart

VERSAL *adj* entire

VERSANT *n* pl. -S the slope of a mountain or mountain chain

VERSE *v* VERSED, VERSING, VERSES to versify

VERSEMAN *n* pl. -MEN one who versifies

VERSER *n* pl. -S a verseman

VERSET *n* pl. -S a versicle

VERSICLE *n* pl. -S a short line of metrical writing

VERSIFY *v* -FIED, -FYING, -FIES to change from prose into metrical form

VERSINE *n* pl. -S a trigonometric function of an angle

VERSING present participle of verse

VERSION *n* pl. -S an account or description from a particular point of view

VERSO *n* pl. -SOS a left-hand page of a book

VERST *n* pl. -S a Russian measure of distance

VERSTE *n* pl. -S verst

VERSUS *prep* against

VERT   *n* pl. -S the heraldic color green

VERTEBRA   *n* pl. -BRAE or -BRAS any of the bones or segments forming the spinal column

VERTEX   *n* pl. -TEXES or -TICES the highest point of something

VERTICAL   *n* pl. -S something that is vertical (extending up and down)

VERTICIL   *n* pl. -S a circular arrangement, as of flowers or leaves, about a point on an axis

VERTIGO   *n* pl. -GOES, -GOS, or -GINES a disordered state in which the individual or his surroundings seem to whirl dizzily

VERTU   *n* pl. -S virtu

VERVAIN   *n* pl. -S a flowering plant

VERVE   *n* pl. -S vivacity

VERVET   *n* pl. -S an African monkey

VERY   *adj* VERIER, VERIEST absolute

VESICA   *n* pl. -CAE a bladder **VESICAL** *adj*

VESICANT   *n* pl. -S a chemical warfare agent that induces blistering

VESICATE   *v* -CATED, -CATING, -CATES to blister

VESICLE   *n* pl. -S a small bladder

VESICULA   *n* pl. -LAE a vesicle

VESPER   *n* pl. -S an evening service, prayer, or song

VESPERAL   *n* pl. -S a covering for an altar cloth

VESPIARY   *n* pl. -ARIES a nest of wasps

VESPID   *n* pl. -S a wasp

VESPINE   *adj* pertaining to wasps

VESSEL   *n* pl. -S a craft for traveling on water **VESSELED** *adj*

VEST   *v* -ED, -ING, -S to place in the control of

VESTA   *n* pl. -S a short friction match

VESTAL   *n* pl. -S a chaste woman

VESTALLY   *adv* chastely

VESTEE   *n* pl. -S a garment worn under a woman's jacket or blouse

VESTIARY   *n* pl. -ARIES a dressing room

VESTIGE   *n* pl. -S a visible sign of something that is no longer in existence

VESTIGIA   *n/pl* vestiges

VESTING   *n* pl. -S the right of an employee to share in and withdraw from a pension fund without penalty

VESTLESS   *adj* being without a vest

VESTLIKE   *adj* resembling a vest (a short, sleeveless garment)

VESTMENT   *n* pl. -S one of the ceremonial garments of the clergy

VESTRY   *n* pl. -TRIES a room in which vestments are kept **VESTRAL** *adj*

VESTURAL   *adj* pertaining to clothing

VESTURE   *v* -TURED, -TURING, -TURES to clothe

VESUVIAN   *n* pl. -S a mineral

VET   *v* VETTED, VETTING, VETS to treat animals medically

VETCH   *n* pl. -ES a climbing plant

VETERAN   *n* pl. -S a former member of the armed forces

VETIVER   *n* pl. -S an Asian grass

VETO   *v* -ED, -ING, -ES to forbid or prevent authoritatively

VETOER   *n* pl. -S one that vetoes

VETTED   past tense of vet

VETTING   present participle of vet

VEX   *v* VEXED or VEXT, VEXING, VEXES to annoy

VEXATION   *n* pl. -S a cause of trouble

VEXEDLY   *adv* in a vexed manner

VEXER   *n* pl. -S one that vexes

VEXIL   *n* pl. -S vexillum

VEXILLUM   *n* pl. -LA the web or vane of a feather **VEXILLAR** *adj*

VEXINGLY   *adv* in a vexing manner

VEXT   a past tense of vex

VIA   *prep* by way of

VIABLE   *adj* capable of living **VIABLY** *adv*

VIADUCT   *n* pl. -S a type of bridge

VIAL   *v* VIALED, VIALING, VIALS or VIALLED, VIALLING, VIALS to put in a vial (a small container for liquids)

VIAND   *n* pl. -S an article of food

VIATIC   *adj* pertaining to traveling

VIATICAL   *adj* viatic

VIATICUM   *n* pl. -CA or -CUMS an allowance for traveling expenses

VIATOR   *n* pl. -ES or -S a traveler

VIBES   *n/pl* a percussion instrument

VIBIST   *n* pl. -S one who plays the vibes

VIBRANCE   *n* pl. -S vibrancy

VIBRANCY   *n* pl. -CIES the quality or state of being vibrant

VIBRANT   *n* pl. -S a sonant

VIBRATE   *v* -BRATED, -BRATING, -BRATES to move back and forth rapidly

VIBRATO   *n* pl. -TOS a tremulous or pulsating musical effect

VIBRATOR   *n* pl. -S something that vibrates

VIBRIO   *n* pl. -RIOS any of a genus of bacteria shaped like a comma **VIBRIOID** *adj*

VIBRION   *n* pl. -S vibrio

VIBRISSA   *n* pl. -SAE one of the stiff hairs growing about the mouth of certain mammals

VIBURNUM   *n* pl. -S a flowering shrub

VICAR   *n* pl. -S a church official

VICARAGE   *n* pl. -S the office of a vicar

VICARATE   *n* pl. -S vicarage

VICARIAL   *adj* pertaining to a vicar

VICARLY   *adj* vicarial

VICE   *v* VICED, VICING, VICES to vise

VICELESS   *adj* having no immoral habits

VICENARY   *adj* pertaining to the number twenty

VICEROY   *n* pl. -ROYS one who rules as the representative of a sovereign

VICHY   *n* pl. -CHIES a type of mineral water

VICINAGE   *n* pl. -S vicinity

VICINAL   *adj* nearby

VICING   present participle of vice

VICINITY   *n* pl. -TIES the region near or about a place

VICIOUS   *adj* dangerously aggressive

VICOMTE   *n* pl. -S a French nobleman

VICTIM   *n* pl. -S one who suffers from a destructive or injurious action

VICTOR   *n* pl. -S one who defeats an adversary

VICTORIA   *n* pl. -S a light carriage

VICTORY   *n* pl. -RIES a successful outcome in a contest or struggle

VICTRESS   *n* pl. -ES a female victor

VICTUAL   *v* -UALED, -UALING, -UALS or -UALLED, -UALLING, -UALS to provide with food

VICUGNA   *n* pl. -S vicuna

VICUNA   *n* pl. -S a ruminant mammal

VIDE   *v* see — used to direct a reader to another item; VIDE is the only form of this verb; it cannot be conjugated

VIDEO   *n* pl. -EOS television

VIDETTE   *n* pl. -S vedette

VIDICON   *n* pl. -S a type of television camera tube

VIDUITY   *n* pl. -ITIES the quality or state of being a widow

VIE   *v* VIED, VYING, VIES to strive for superiority

VIER   *n* pl. -S one that vies

VIEW   *v* -ED, -ING, -S to look at **VIEWABLE** *adj*

VIEWER   *n* pl. -S one that views

VIEWIER   comparative of viewy

VIEWIEST   superlative of viewy

VIEWING   *n* pl. -S an act of seeing, watching, or looking

VIEWLESS   *adj* having no opinions

VIEWY   *adj* VIEWIER, VIEWIEST showy

VIGIL   *n* pl. -S a period of watchfulness maintained during normal sleeping hours

VIGILANT   *adj* watchful

VIGNETTE   *v* -GNETTED, -GNETTING, -GNETTES to describe briefly

VIGOR   *n* pl. -S active strength or force

VIGORISH   *n* pl. -ES a charge paid to a bookie on a bet

VIGOROSO   *adv* with emphasis and spirit — used as a musical direction

VIGOROUS   *adj* full of vigor

VIGOUR   *n* pl. -S vigor

VIKING   *n* pl. -S a Scandinavian pirate

VILAYET   *n* pl. -S an administrative division of Turkey

VILE   *adj* VILER, VILEST physically repulsive **VILELY** *adv*

VILENESS   *n* pl. -ES the state of being vile

VILIFIER   *n* pl. -S one that vilifies

VILIFY   *v* -FIED, -FYING, -FIES to defame

VILIPEND   *v* -ED, -ING, -S to vilify

VILL   *n* pl. -S a village

VILLA   *n* pl. -LAE or -LAS an agricultural estate of ancient Rome

VILLADOM   *n* pl. -S the world constituted by suburban residences and their occupants

VILLAGE   *n* pl. -S a small community in a rural area

VILLAGER   *n* pl. -S one who lives in a village

VILLAIN   *n* pl. -S a cruelly malicious person

VILLAINY   *n* pl. -LAINIES conduct characteristic of a villain

VILLATIC   *adj* rural

VILLEIN   *n* pl. -S a type of serf

VILLUS   *n* pl. -LI one of the hairlike projections found on certain membranes **VILLOSE, VILLOUS** *adj*

VIM   *n* pl. -S energy

VIMEN   *n* pl. -MINA a long, flexible branch of a plant **VIMINAL** *adj*

VIN   *n* pl. -S wine

VINA   *n* pl. -S a stringed instrument of India

VINAL   *n* pl. -S a synthetic textile fiber

VINASSE   *n* pl. -S a residue left after the distillation of liquor

VINCA   *n* pl. -S a flowering plant

VINCIBLE   *adj* capable of being conquered

VINCULUM   *n* pl. -LA or -LUMS a unifying bond

VINE   *v* VINED, VINING, VINES to grow like a vine (a climbing plant)

VINEAL   *adj* vinous

VINEGAR   *n* pl. -S a sour liquid used as a condiment or preservative **VINEGARY** *adj*

VINERY   *n* pl. -ERIES a place in which grapevines are grown

VINEYARD   *n* pl. -S an area planted with grapevines

VINIC   *adj* derived from wine

VINIER   comparative of viny

VINIEST   superlative of viny

VINIFERA   *n* pl. -S a European grape

VINING   present participle of vine

VINO   *n* pl. -NOS wine

VINOSITY   *n* pl. -TIES the character of a wine

VINOUS   *adj* pertaining to wine **VINOUSLY** *adv*

VINTAGE   *n* pl. -S a season's yield of wine from a vineyard

VINTAGER   *n* pl. -S one that harvests wine grapes

VINTNER   *n* pl. -S a wine merchant

VINY   *adj* VINIER, VINIEST covered with vines

VINYL   *n* pl. -S a type of plastic **VINYLIC** *adj*

VIOL   *n* pl. -S a stringed instrument

VIOLA   *n* pl. -S a stringed instrument

VIOLABLE   *adj* capable of being violated **VIOLABLY** *adv*

VIOLATE   *v* -LATED, -LATING, -LATES to break or disregard the terms or requirements of

VIOLATER   *n* pl. -S violator

VIOLATOR   *n* pl. -S one that violates

VIOLENCE   *n* pl. -S violent action

VIOLENT   *adj* marked by intense physical force or roughness

VIOLET   *n* pl. -S a flowering plant

VIOLIN   *n* pl. -S a stringed instrument

VIOLIST   *n* pl. -S one who plays the viol or viola

VIOLONE   *n* pl. -S a stringed instrument

VIOMYCIN   *n* pl. -S an antibiotic

VIPER   *n* pl. -S a venomous snake **VIPERINE, VIPERISH, VIPEROUS** *adj*

VIRAGO   *n* pl. -GOES or -GOS a noisy, domineering woman

VIRAL   *adj* pertaining to or caused by a virus **VIRALLY** *adv*

VIRELAI   *n* pl. -S virelay

VIRELAY   *n* pl. -LAYS a medieval French verse form

VIREMIA   *n* pl. -S the presence of a virus in the blood **VIREMIC** *adj*

VIREO   *n* pl. -EOS a small bird

VIRES   pl. of vis

VIRGA   *n* pl. -S wisps of precipitation evaporating before reaching ground

VIRGATE   *n* pl. -S an early English measure of land area

VIRGIN   *n* pl. -S a person who has never had sexual intercourse

VIRGINAL   *n* pl. -S a musical instrument

VIRGULE   *n* pl. -S a diagonal printing mark used to separate alternatives

VIRICIDE   *n* pl. -S a substance that destroys viruses

VIRID   *adj* verdant

VIRIDIAN   *n* pl. -S a bluish-green pigment

VIRIDITY   *n* pl. -TIES verdancy

VIRILE   *adj* having masculine vigor

VIRILISM   *n* pl. -S the development of male secondary sex characteristics in a female

VIRILITY   *n* pl. -TIES the quality or state of being virile

VIRION   *n* pl. -S a virus particle

VIRL   *n* pl. -S a metal ring or cap put around a shaft to prevent splitting

VIROLOGY   *n* pl. -GIES the study of viruses

VIROSIS   *n* pl. -ROSES infection with a virus

VIRTU   *n* pl. -S a love or taste for the fine arts

VIRTUAL   *adj* having the effect but not the actual form of what is specified

VIRTUE   *n* pl. -S moral excellence

VIRTUOSA   *n* pl. -SAS or -SE a female virtuoso

VIRTUOSO   *n* pl. -SOS or -SI a highly skilled artistic performer

VIRTUOUS   *adj* characterized by virtue

VIRUCIDE   *n* pl. -S viricide

VIRULENT   *adj* extremely poisonous

VIRUS   *n* pl. -ES any of a class of submicroscopic pathogens

VIS   *n* pl. VIRES force or power

VISA   *v* -ED, -ING, -S to put an official endorsement on, as a passport

VISAGE   *n* pl. -S the face or facial expression of a person **VISAGED** *adj*

VISARD   *n* pl. -S vizard

VISCACHA   *n* pl. -S a burrowing rodent

VISCERA   pl. of viscus

VISCERAL   *adj* pertaining to the internal organs

VISCID   *adj* thick and adhesive **VISCIDLY** *adv*

VISCOID   *adj* somewhat viscid

VISCOSE   *n* pl. -S a viscous solution

VISCOUNT   *n* pl. -S a British nobleman

VISCOUS   *adj* having relatively high resistance to flow

VISCUS   *n* pl. -CERA an internal organ

VISE   *v* VISED, VISING, VISES to hold in a vise (a clamping device)

VISE   *v* VISEED, VISEING, VISES to visa

VISELIKE   *adj* resembling a vice

VISIBLE   *adj* capable of being seen **VISIBLY** *adv*

VISING   present participle of vise

VISION   *v* -ED, -ING, -S to imagine

VISIONAL   *adj* imaginary

VISIT   *v* -ED, -ING, -S to go or come to see someone or something

VISITANT   *n* pl. -S a visitor

VISITER   *n* pl. -S visitor

VISITOR   *n* pl. -S one that visits

VISIVE   *adj* visible

VISOR   *v* -ED, -ING, -S to provide with a visor (a projecting brim)

VISTA   *n* pl. -S a distant view **VISTAED** *adj*

VISUAL   *adj* pertaining to the sense of sight **VISUALLY** *adv*

VITA   *n* pl. -TAE a brief, autobiographical sketch

VITAL   *adj* necessary to life

VITALISE   *v* -ISED, -ISING, -ISES to vitalize

VITALISM   *n* pl. -S a philosophical doctrine

VITALIST   *n* pl. -S an advocate of vitalism

VITALITY   *n* pl. -TIES exuberant physical strength or mental vigor

VITALIZE   *v* -IZED, -IZING, -IZES to give life to

VITALLY   *adv* in a vital manner

VITALS   *n/pl* vital organs

VITAMER   *n* pl. -S a type of chemical compound

VITAMIN   *n* pl. -S any of various organic substances essential to proper nutrition

VITAMINE   *n* pl. -S vitamin

VITELLIN   *n* pl. -S a protein found in egg yolk

VITELLUS   *n* pl. -ES the yolk of an egg

VITESSE	*n* pl. -S speed
VITIATE	*v* -ATED, -ATING, ATES to impair the value or quality of **VITIABLE** *adj*
VITIATOR	*n* pl. -S one that vitiates
VITILIGO	*n* pl. -GOS a skin disease
VITREOUS	*adj* resembling glass
VITRIC	*adj* pertaining to glass
VITRIFY	*v* -FIED, -FYING, -FIES to convert into glass
VITRINE	*n* pl. -S a glass showcase for art objects
VITRIOL	*v* -OLED, -OLING, -OLS or -OLLED, -OLLING, -OLS to treat with sulfuric acid
VITTA	*n* pl. -TAE a streak or band of color **VITTATE** *adj*
VITTLE	*v* -TLED, -TLING, -TLES to victual
VITULINE	*adj* pertaining to a calf
VIVA	*n* pl. -S a shout or cry used to express approval
VIVACE	*adj* lively — used as a musical direction
VIVACITY	*n* pl. -TIES the quality or state of being lively
VIVARIUM	*n* pl. -IA or -IUMS a place for raising and keeping live animals
VIVARY	*n* pl. -RIES vivarium
VIVE	*interj* — used as an exclamation of approval
VIVERRID	*n* pl. -S any of a family of small carnivorous mammals
VIVERS	*n/pl* food
VIVID	*adj* -IDER, -IDEST strikingly bright or intense **VIVIDLY** *adv*
VIVIFIC	*adj* vivifying
VIVIFIER	*n* pl. -S one that vivifies
VIVIFY	*v* -FIED, -FYING, -FIES to give life to
VIVIPARA	*n/pl* animals that bring forth living young
VIVISECT	*v* -ED, -ING, -S to dissect the living body of
VIXEN	*n* pl. -S a shrewish woman **VIXENISH, VIXENLY** *adj*
VIZARD	*n* pl. -S a mask **VIZARDED** *adj*
VIZCACHA	*n* pl. -S viscacha
VIZIER	*n* pl. -S a high official in some Muslim countries
VIZIR	*n* pl. -S vizier **VIZIRIAL** *adj*

VIZIRATE	*n* pl. -S the office of a vizir
VIZOR	*v* -ED, -ING, -S to visor
VIZSLA	*n* pl. -S a Hungarian breed of dog
VOCABLE	*n* pl. -S a word
VOCABLY	*adv* in a manner that may be voiced aloud
VOCAL	*n* pl. -S a sound produced with the voice
VOCALIC	*n* pl. -S a vowel sound
VOCALISE	*v* -ISED, -ISING, -ISES to vocalize
VOCALISM	*n* pl. -S the act of vocalizing
VOCALIST	*n* pl. -S a singer
VOCALITY	*n* pl. -TIES possession or exercise of vocal powers
VOCALIZE	*v* -IZED, -IZING, -IZES to produce with the voice
VOCALLY	*adv* with the voice
VOCATION	*n* pl. -S the work in which a person is regularly employed
VOCATIVE	*n* pl. -S a grammatical case used in some languages
VOCES	pl. of vox
VOCODER	*n* pl. -S an electronic device used in transmitting speech signals
VODKA	*n* pl. -S a liquor
VODUM	*n* pl. -S a primitive religion of the West Indies
VOE	*n* pl. -S a small bay, creek, or inlet
VOGIE	*adj* vain
VOGUE	*n* pl. -S the current trend or style **VOGUISH** *adj*
VOICE	*v* VOICED, VOICING, VOICES to express or utter
VOICEFUL	*adj* sonorous
VOICER	*n* pl. -S one that voices
VOICING	present participle of voice
VOID	*v* -ED, -ING, -S to make void (of no legal force or effect) **VOIDABLE** *adj*
VOIDANCE	*n* pl. -S the act or process of voiding
VOIDER	*n* pl. -S one that voids
VOIDNESS	*n* pl. -ES the quality or state of being void
VOILE	*n* pl. -S a sheer fabric
VOLANT	*adj* flying or capable of flying

VOLANTE *adj* moving with light rapidity — used as a musical direction

VOLAR *adj* pertaining to flight

VOLATILE *n* pl. -S a winged creature

VOLCANIC *n* pl. -S a rock produced by a volcano

VOLCANO *n* pl. -NOES or -NOS an opening in the earth's crust through which molten rock and gases are ejected

VOLE *v* VOLED, VOLING, VOLES to win all the tricks in a card game

VOLERY *n* pl. -ERIES a large birdcage

VOLITANT *adj* volant

VOLITION *n* pl. -S the power of choosing or determining

VOLITIVE *adj* pertaining to volition

VOLLEY *v* -ED, -ING, -S to return a tennis ball before it touches the ground

VOLLEYER *n* pl. -S one that volleys

VOLOST *n* pl. -S an administrative district in Russia

VOLPLANE *v* -PLANED, -PLANING, -PLANES to glide in an airplane

VOLT *n* pl. -S a unit of electromotive force

VOLTA *n* pl. -TE a turning

VOLTAGE *n* pl. -S electromotive force expressed in volts

VOLTAISM *n* pl. -S electricity produced by chemical action **VOLTAIC** *adj*

VOLTE *n* pl. -S a fencing movement

VOLTI *interj* — used to direct musicians to turn the page

VOLUBLE *adj* talkative **VOLUBLY** *adv*

VOLUME *v* -UMED, -UMING, -UMES to send or give out in large quantities

VOLUTE *n* pl. -S a spiral architectural ornament **VOLUTED** *adj*

VOLUTIN *n* pl. -S a granular substance that is common in microorganisms

VOLUTION *n* pl. -S a spiral

VOLVA *n* pl. -S a membranous sac that encloses certain immature mushrooms **VOLVATE** *adj*

VOLVOX *n* pl. -ES any of a genus of freshwater protozoa

VOLVULUS *n* pl. -LI or -LUSES a twisting of the intestine that causes obstruction

VOMER *n* pl. -S a bone of the skull **VOMERINE** *adj*

VOMICA *n* pl. -CAE a cavity in the body containing pus

VOMIT *v* -ED, -ING, -S to eject the contents of the stomach through the mouth

VOMITER *n* pl. -S one that vomits

VOMITIVE *n* pl. -S an emetic

VOMITO *n* pl. -TOS the black vomit of yellow fever

VOMITORY *n* pl. -RIES an emetic

VOMITOUS *adj* pertaining to vomiting

VOMITUS *n* pl. -ES vomited matter

VON *prep* of; from — used in some surnames

VOODOO *v* -ED, -ING, -S to hex

VORACITY *n* pl. -TIES the quality or state of being ravenous

VORLAGE *n* pl. -S a position in skiing

VORTEX *n* pl. -TEXES or -TICES a whirling mass of fluid **VORTICAL** *adj*

VOTABLE *adj* capable of being voted on

VOTARESS *n* pl. -ES a female votary

VOTARIST *n* pl. -S a votary

VOTARY *n* pl. -RIES a person who is bound by religious vows

VOTE *v* VOTED, VOTING, VOTES to cast a vote (a formal expression of will or opinion)

VOTEABLE *adj* votable

VOTELESS *adj* having no vote

VOTER *n* pl. -S one that votes

VOTING present participle of vote

VOTIVE *adj* performed in fullfillment of a vow **VOTIVELY** *adv*

VOTRESS *n* pl. -ES votaress

VOUCH *v* -ED, -ING, -ES to give one's personal assurance or guarantee

VOUCHEE *n* pl. -S one for whom another vouches

VOUCHER *v* -ED, -ING, -S to establish the authenticity of

VOUSSOIR *n* pl. -S a wedge-shaped building stone

VOW   *v* -ED, -ING, -S to make a vow (a solemn promise)

VOWEL   *n* pl. -S a type of speech sound

VOWELIZE   *v* -IZED, -IZING, -IZES to provide with symbols used to indicate vowels

VOWER   *n* pl. -S one that vows

VOWLESS   *adj* having made no vow

VOX   *n* pl. VOCES voice

VOYAGE   *v* -AGED, -AGING, -AGES to travel

VOYAGER   *n* pl. -S one that voyages

VOYAGEUR   *n* pl. -S a person employed by a fur company to transport goods between distant stations

VOYEUR   *n* pl. -S one who is sexually gratified by looking at sexual objects or acts

VROOM   *v* -ED, -ING, -S to run an engine at high speed

VROUW   *n* pl. -S a Dutch woman

VROW   *n* pl. -S vrouw

VUG   *n* pl. -S a small cavity in a rock or lode **VUGGY** *adj*

VUGG   *n* pl. -S vug

VUGH   *n* pl. -S vug

VULCANIC   *adj* pertaining to a volcano

VULGAR   *adj* -GARER, -GAREST crude **VULGARLY** *adv*

VULGAR   *n* pl. -S a common person

VULGATE   *n* pl. -S the common speech of a people

VULGO   *adv* commonly

VULGUS   *n* pl. -ES an exercise in Latin formerly required of pupils in some English public schools

VULPINE   *adj* pertaining to a fox

VULTURE   *n* pl. -S a bird of prey

VULVA   *n* pl. -VAE or -VAS the external genital organs of a female **VULVAL, VULVAR, VULVATE** *adj*

VULVITIS   *n* pl. -TISES inflammation of the vulva

VYING   present participle of vie

VYINGLY   *adv* in a vying manner

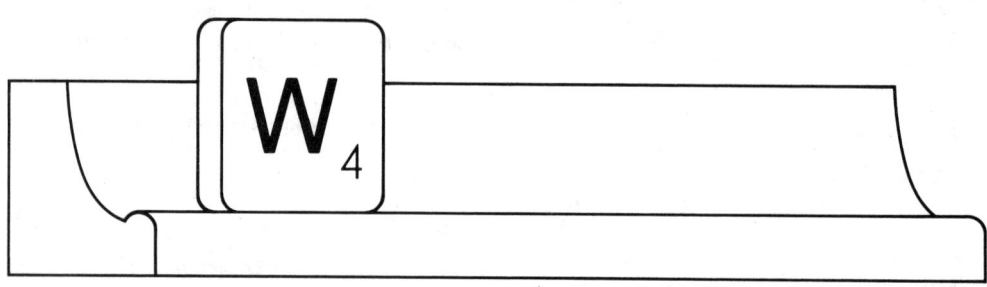

WAB	*n* pl. -S a web
WABBLE	*v* -BLED, -BLING, -BLES to wobble
WABBLER	*n* pl. -S one that wabbles
WABBLY	*adj* -BLIER, -BLIEST wobbly
WACK	*n* pl. -S a wacky person
WACKE	*n* pl. -S a type of basaltic rock
WACKY	*adj* WACKIER, WACKIEST very irrational **WACKILY** *adv*
WAD	*v* WADDED, WADDING, WADS to form into a wad (a small mass of soft material)
WADABLE	*adj* wadeable
WADDER	*n* pl. -S one that wads
WADDIE	*n* pl. -S a cowboy
WADDIED	past tense of waddy
WADDIES	present 3d person sing. of waddy
WADDING	*n* pl. -S a wad
WADDLE	*v* -DLED, -DLING, -DLES to walk with short, swaying steps
WADDLER	*n* pl. -S one that waddles
WADDLY	*adj* having or being a waddling gait
WADDY	*v* -DIED, -DYING, -DIES to strike with a thick club
WADE	*v* WADED, WADING, WADES to walk through water
WADEABLE	*adj* capable of being passed through by wading
WADER	*n* pl. -S one that wades
WADI	*n* pl. -S the bed of a usually dry watercourse
WADIES	pl. of wady
WADING	present participle of wade
WADMAAL	*n* pl. -S wadmal
WADMAL	*n* pl. -S a thick woolen fabric
WADMEL	*n* pl. -S wadmal
WADMOL	*n* pl. -S wadmal
WADMOLL	*n* pl. -S wadmal
WADSET	*v* -SETTED, -SETTING, -SETS to mortgage
WADY	*n* pl. -DIES wadi
WAE	*n* pl. -S woe
WAEFU	*adj* waeful
WAEFUL	*adj* woeful
WAENESS	*n* pl. -ES woeness
WAESUCK	*interj* waesucks
WAESUCKS	*interj* — used to express pity
WAFER	*v* -ED, -ING, -S to seal with an adhesive disk
WAFERY	*adj* resembling a wafer (a thin, crisp biscuit)
WAFF	*v* -ED, -ING, -S to wave
WAFFIE	*n* pl. -S a vagabond
WAFFLE	*v* -FLED, -FLING, -FLES to talk foolishly
WAFT	*v* -ED, -ING, -S to carry lightly over air or water
WAFTAGE	*n* pl. -S the act of wafting
WAFTER	*n* pl. -S one that wafts
WAFTURE	*n* pl. -S waftage
WAG	*v* WAGGED, WAGGING, WAGS to move briskly up and down or to and fro
WAGE	*v* WAGED, WAGING, WAGES to engage in or carry on

WAGELESS *adj* unpaid

WAGER *v* -ED, -ING, -S to risk on an uncertain outcome

WAGERER *n* pl. -S one that wagers

WAGGED past tense of wag

WAGGER *n* pl. -S one that wags

WAGGERY *n* pl. -GERIES waggish behavior

WAGGING present participle of wag

WAGGISH *adj* playfully humorous

WAGGLE *v* -GLED, -GLING, -GLES to wag

WAGGLY *adj* waggling

WAGGON *v* -ED, -ING, -S to wagon

WAGGONER *n* pl. -S wagoner

WAGING present participle of wage

WAGON *v* -ED, -ING, -S to convey by wagon (a four-wheeled, horse-drawn vehicle)

WAGONAGE *n* pl. -S conveyance by wagon

WAGONER *n* pl. -S one who drives a wagon

WAGSOME *adj* waggish

WAGTAIL *n* pl. -S a songbird

WAHCONDA *n* pl. -S wakanda

WAHINE *n* pl. -S a Hawaiian woman

WAHOO *n* pl. -HOOS a flowering shrub

WAIF *v* -ED, -ING, -S to throw away

WAIL *v* -ED, -ING, -S to utter a long, mournful cry

WAILER *n* pl. -S one that wails

WAILFUL *adj* mournful

WAILSOME *adj* wailful

WAIN *n* pl. -S a large, open wagon

WAINSCOT *v* -SCOTED, -SCOTING, -SCOTS or -SCOTTED, -SCOTTING, -SCOTS to line the walls of with wooden paneling

WAIR *v* -ED, -ING, -S to spend

WAIST *n* pl. -S the part of the body between the ribs and the hips **WAISTED** *adj*

WAISTER *n* pl. -S a seaman stationed in the middle section of a ship

WAISTING *n* pl. -S a type of dressmaking material

WAIT *v* -ED, -ING, -S to stay in expectation of

WAITER *n* pl. -S one who serves food in a restaurant

WAITING *n* pl. -S the act of one who waits

WAITRESS *n* pl. -ES a woman who serves food in a restaurant

WAIVE *v* WAIVED, WAIVING, WAIVES to give up intentionally

WAIVER *n* pl. -S the act of waiving something

WAKANDA *n* pl. -S a supernatural force in Sioux beliefs

WAKE *v* WAKED or WOKE, WOKEN, WAKING, WAKES to rouse from sleep

WAKEFUL *adj* not sleeping or able to sleep

WAKELESS *adj* unbroken — used of sleep

WAKEN *v* -ED, -ING, -S to wake

WAKENER *n* pl. -S one that wakens

WAKENING *n* pl. -S the act of one that wakens

WAKER *n* pl. -S one that wakes

WAKERIFE *adj* wakeful

WAKIKI *n* pl. -S shell money of the South Sea Islands

WAKING present participle of wake

WALE *v* WALED, WALING, WALES to mark with welts

WALER *n* pl. -S an Australian-bred saddle horse

WALIES pl. of waly

WALING present participle of wale

WALK *v* -ED, -ING, -S to advance on foot **WALKABLE** *adj*

WALKAWAY *n* pl. -AWAYS an easy victory

WALKER *n* pl. -S one that walks

WALKING *n* pl. -S the act of one that walks

WALKOUT *n* pl. -S a strike by workers

WALKOVER *n* pl. -S a walkaway

WALKUP *n* pl. -S an apartment house having no elevator

WALKWAY *n* pl. -WAYS a passage for walking

WALKYRIE *n* pl. -S valkyrie

WALL *v* -ED, -ING, -S to provide with a wall (an upright structure built to enclose an area)

WALLA *n* pl. -S wallah

WALLABY *n* pl. -BIES a small kangaroo

WALLAH *n* pl. -S a person engaged in a particular occupation or activity

WALLAROO *n* pl. -ROOS a large kangaroo

WALLET	*n* pl. -S a flat folding case
WALLEYE	*n* pl. -S an eye having a white cornea **WALLEYED** *adj*
WALLIE	*n* pl. -S a valet
WALLIES	pl. of wally
WALLOP	*v* -ED, -ING, -S to beat soundly
WALLOPER	*n* pl. -S one that wallops
WALLOW	*v* -ED, -ING, -S to roll about
WALLOWER	*n* pl. -S one that wallows
WALLY	*n* pl. -LIES waly
WALNUT	*n* pl. -S an edible nut
WALRUS	*n* pl. -ES a marine mammal
WALTZ	*v* -ED, -ING, -ES to perform a ballroom dance
WALTZER	*n* pl. -S one that waltzes
WALY	*n* pl. WALIES something visually pleasing
WAMBLE	*v* -BLED, -BLING, -BLES to move unsteadily
WAMBLY	*adj* -BLIER, -BLIEST unsteady
WAME	*n* pl. -S the belly
WAMEFOU	*n* pl. -S a bellyful
WAMEFUL	*n* pl. -S wamefou
WAMMUS	*n* pl. -ES wamus
WAMPISH	*v* -ED, -ING, -ES to throw about
WAMPUM	*n* pl. -S a form of currency formerly used by North American Indians
WAMPUS	*n* pl. -ES wamus
WAMUS	*n* pl. -ES a heavy outer jacket
WAN	*adj* WANNER, WANNEST unnaturally pale
WAN	*v* WANNED, WANNING, WANS to become wan
WAND	*n* pl. -S a slender rod
WANDER	*v* -ED, -ING, -S to move about with no destination or purpose
WANDERER	*n* pl. -S one that wanders
WANDEROO	*n* pl. -ROOS an Asian monkey
WANDLE	*adj* supple
WANE	*v* WANED, WANING, WANES to decrease in size or extent
WANEY	*adj* WANIER, WANIEST wany
WANGAN	*n* pl. -S wanigan
WANGLE	*v* -GLED, -GLING, -GLES to obtain or accomplish by contrivance
WANGLER	*n* pl. -S one that wangles
WANGUN	*n* pl. -S wanigan
WANIER	comparative of waney and wany
WANIEST	superlative of waney and wany
WANIGAN	*n* pl. -S a supply chest used in a logging camp
WANING	present participle of wane
WANION	*n* pl. -S vengeance
WANLY	*adv* in a wan manner
WANNED	past tense of wan
WANNER	comparative of wan
WANNESS	*n* pl. -ES the quality of being wan
WANNEST	superlative of wan
WANNIGAN	*n* pl. -S wanigan
WANNING	present participle of wan
WANT	*v* -ED, -ING, -S to have a desire for
WANTAGE	*n* pl. -S something that is lacking
WANTER	*n* pl. -S one that wants
WANTON	*v* -ED, -ING, -S to behave immorally
WANTONER	*n* pl. -S one that wantons
WANTONLY	*adv* immorally
WANY	*adj* WANIER, WANIEST waning in some parts
WAP	*v* WAPPED, WAPPING, WAPS to wrap
WAPITI	*n* pl. -S a large deer
WAR	*v* WARRED, WARRING, WARS to engage in war (a state of open, armed conflict)
WARBLE	*v* -BLED, -BLING, -BLES to sing with melodic embellishments
WARBLER	*n* pl. -S one that warbles
WARCRAFT	*n* pl. -S the art of war
WARD	*v* -ED, -ING, -S to turn aside
WARDEN	*n* pl. -S the chief officer of a prison
WARDENRY	*n* pl. -RIES the office of a warden
WARDER	*n* pl. -S a person who guards something
WARDRESS	*n* pl. -ES a female warden
WARDROBE	*n* pl. -S a collection of garments
WARDROOM	*n* pl. -S a recreation area on a warship

WARDSHIP	*n* pl. -S the state of being under a guardian
WARE	*v* WARED, WARING, WARES to beware of
WAREROOM	*n* pl. -S a room in which goods are displayed for sale
WARFARE	*n* pl. -S the act of engaging in war
WARFARIN	*n* pl. -S a chemical compound
WARHEAD	*n* pl. -S the front part of a missile containing the explosive
WARIER	comparative of wary
WARIEST	superlative of wary
WARILY	*adv* in a wary manner
WARINESS	*n* pl. -ES the state of being wary
WARING	present participle of ware
WARISON	*n* pl. -S a call to attack
WARK	*v* -ED, -ING, -S to endure pain
WARLESS	*adj* free from war
WARLIKE	*adj* disposed to engage in war
WARLOCK	*n* pl. -S a sorcerer
WARLORD	*n* pl. -S a military leader of a warlike nation
WARM	*adj* WARMER, WARMEST moderately hot
WARM	*v* -ED, -ING, -S to make warm
WARMAKER	*n* pl. -S one that wars
WARMER	*n* pl. -S one that warms
WARMISH	*adj* somewhat warm
WARMLY	*adv* in a warm manner
WARMNESS	*n* pl. -ES the state of being warm
WARMOUTH	*n* -S a freshwater fish
WARMTH	*n* pl. -S warmness
WARMUP	*n* pl. -S a preparatory exercise or procedure
WARN	*v* -ED, -ING, -S to make aware of impending or possible danger
WARNER	*n* pl. -S one that warns
WARNING	*n* pl. -S something that warns
WARP	*v* -ED, -ING, -S to turn or twist out of shape
WARPAGE	*n* pl. -S the act of warping
WARPATH	*n* pl. -S the route taken by attacking American Indians
WARPER	*n* pl. -S one that warps
WARPLANE	*n* pl. -S an airplane armed for combat
WARPOWER	*n* pl. -S the power to make war
WARPWISE	*adv* in a vertical direction
WARRAGAL	*n* pl. -S warrigal
WARRANT	*v* -ED, -ING, -S to give authority to
WARRANTY	*n* pl. -TIES the act of warranting
WARRED	past tense of war
WARREN	*n* pl. -S a place where rabbits live and breed
WARRENER	*n* pl. -S the keeper of a warren
WARRIGAL	*n* pl. -S a dingo
WARRING	present participle of war
WARRIOR	*n* pl. -S one engaged or experienced in warfare
WARSAW	*n* pl. -S a marine fish
WARSHIP	*n* pl. -S a ship armed for combat
WARSLE	*v* -SLED, -SLING, -SLES to wrestle
WARSLER	*n* pl. -S a wrestler
WARSTLE	*v* -TLED, -TLING, -TLES to wrestle
WARSTLER	*n* pl. -S a wrestler
WART	*n* pl. -S a protuberance on the skin **WARTED** *adj*
WARTHOG	*n* pl. -S an African wild hog
WARTIER	comparative of warty
WARTIEST	superlative of warty
WARTIME	*n* pl. -S a time of war
WARTLIKE	*adj* resembling a wart
WARTY	*adj* WARTIER, WARTIEST covered with warts
WARWORK	*n* pl. -S work done during a war
WARWORN	*adj* showing the effects of war
WARY	*adj* WARIER, WARIEST watchful
WAS	1st and 3d person sing. past indicative of be
WASH	*v* -ED, -ING, -ES to cleanse by immersing in or applying a liquid
WASHABLE	*adj* capable of being washed without damage
WASHBOWL	*n* pl. -S a bowl used for washing oneself
WASHDAY	*n* pl. -DAYS a day set aside for washing clothes
WASHER	*n* pl. -S one that washes
WASHIER	comparative of washy
WASHIEST	superlative of washy

WASHING   *n* pl. -S articles washed or to be washed

WASHOUT   *n* pl. -S an erosion of earth by the action of water

WASHRAG   *n* pl. -S a small cloth used for washing oneself

WASHROOM   *n* pl. -S a lavatory

WASHTUB   *n* pl. -S a tub used for washing clothes

WASHY   *adj* WASHIER, WASHIEST overly diluted

WASP   *n* pl. -S a stinging insect **WASPISH, WASPLIKE** *adj*

WASPY   *adj* WASPIER, WASPIEST resembling a wasp **WASPILY** *adv*

WASSAIL   *v* -ED, -ING, -S to drink to the health of

WAST   *n* pl. -S west

WASTABLE   *adj* capable of being wasted

WASTAGE   *n* pl. -S something that is wasted

WASTE   *v* WASTED, WASTING, WASTES to use thoughtlessly

WASTEFUL   *adj* tending to waste

WASTELOT   *n* pl. -S a vacant lot

WASTER   *n* pl. -S one that wastes

WASTERIE   *n* pl. -S wastry

WASTERY   *n* pl. -RIES wastry

WASTEWAY   *n* pl. -WAYS a channel for excess water

WASTING   present participle of waste

WASTREL   *n* pl. -S one that wastes

WASTRIE   *n* pl. -S wastry

WASTRY   *n* pl. -RIES reckless extravagance

WAT   *adj* WATTER, WATTEST wet

WAT   *n* pl. -S a hare

WATAP   *n* pl. -S a thread made from the roots of various trees

WATAPE   *n* pl. -S watap

WATCH   *v* -ED, -ING, -ES to observe carefully

WATCHCRY   *n* pl. -CRIES a password

WATCHDOG   *v* -DOGGED, -DOGGING, -DOGS to act as a guardian for

WATCHER   *n* pl. -S one that watches

WATCHEYE   *n* pl. -S a walleye

WATCHFUL   *adj* closely observant or alert

WATCHMAN   *n* pl. -MEN a man employed to stand guard

WATCHOUT   *n* pl. -S the act of looking out for something

WATER   *v* -ED, -ING, -S to sprinkle with water (a transparent, odorless, tasteless liquid)

WATERAGE   *n* pl. -S the conveyance of goods by water

WATERBED   *n* pl. -S a bed whose mattress is a plastic bag filled with water

WATERDOG   *n* pl. -S a large salamander

WATERER   *n* pl. -S one that waters

WATERIER   comparative of watery

WATERIEST   superlative of watery

WATERILY   *adv* in a watery manner

WATERING   *n* pl. -S the act of one that waters

WATERISH   *adj* watery

WATERLOG   *v* -LOGGED, -LOGGING, -LOGS to soak with water

WATERLOO   *n* pl. -LOOS a decisive defeat

WATERMAN   *n* pl. -MEN a boatman

WATERWAY   *n* pl. -WAYS a navigable body of water

WATERY   *adj* -TERIER, -TERIEST containing water

WATT   *n* pl. -S a unit of power

WATTAGE   *n* pl. -S an amount of power in terms of watts

WATTAPE   *n* pl. -S watap

WATTER   comparative of wat

WATTEST   superlative of wat

WATTHOUR   *n* pl. -S a unit of energy

WATTLE   *v* -TLED, -TLING, -TLES to weave into a network

WATTLESS   *adj* denoting a type of electric current

WAUCHT   *v* -ED, -ING, -S to waught

WAUGH   *adj* damp

WAUGHT   *v* -ED, -ING, -S to drink deeply

WAUK   *v* -ED, -ING, -S to wake

WAUL   *v* -ED, -ING, -S to cry like a cat

WAUR   *adj* worse

WAVE   *v* WAVED, WAVING, WAVES to move freely back and forth or up and down

WAVEBAND   *n* pl. -S a range of radio frequencies

WAVEFORM *n* pl. -S a type of mathematical graph

WAVELESS *adj* having no waves (moving ridges on the surface of a liquid)

WAVELET *n* pl. -S a small wave

WAVELIKE *adj* resembling a wave

WAVEOFF *n* pl. -S the act of denying landing permission to an approaching aircraft

WAVER *v* -ED, -ING, -S to move back and forth

WAVERER *n* pl. -S one that wavers

WAVERY *adj* wavering

WAVEY *n* pl. -VEYS the snow goose

WAVIER comparative of wavy

WAVIES present 3d person sing. of wavy

WAVIEST superlative of wavy

WAVILY *adv* in a wavy manner

WAVINESS *n* pl. -ES the state of being wavy

WAVING present participle of wave

WAVY *adj* WAVIER, WAVIEST full of waves

WAVY *n* pl. -VIES wavey

WAW *n* pl. -S vav

WAWL *v* -ED, -ING, -S to waul

WAX *v* -ED, -ING, -ES to coat with wax (a natural, heat-sensitive substance)

WAXBERRY *n* pl. -RIES a berry with a waxy coating

WAXBILL *n* pl. -S a tropical bird

WAXEN *adj* covered with wax

WAXER *n* pl. -S one that waxes

WAXIER comparative of waxy

WAXIEST superlative of waxy

WAXILY *adv* in a waxy manner

WAXINESS *n* pl. -ES the quality of being waxy

WAXING *n* pl. -S the act of one that waxes

WAXLIKE *adj* resembling wax

WAXPLANT *n* pl. -S a tropical plant

WAXWEED *n* pl. -S an annual herb

WAXWING *n* pl. -S a type of bird

WAXWORK *n* pl. -S an effigy made of wax

WAXWORM *n* pl. -S a moth that infests beehives

WAXY *adj* WAXIER, WAXIEST resembling wax

WAY *n* pl. WAYS a method of doing something

WAYBILL *n* pl. -S a list of goods relative to a shipment

WAYFARER *n* pl. -S a traveler

WAYGOING *n* pl. -S the act of leaving

WAYLAY *v* -LAID, -LAYING, -LAYS to ambush

WAYLAYER *n* pl. -S one that waylays

WAYLESS *adj* having no road or path

WAYSIDE *n* pl. -S the side of a road

WAYWARD *adj* willful

WAYWORN *adj* fatigued by travel

WE *pron* 1st person pl. pronoun in the nominative case

WEAK *adj* WEAKER, WEAKEST lacking strength

WEAKEN *v* -ED, -ING, -S to make weak

WEAKENER *n* pl. -S one that weakens

WEAKFISH *n* pl. -ES a marine fish

WEAKISH *adj* somewhat weak

WEAKLING *n* pl. -S a weak person

WEAKLY *adj* -LIER, -LIEST weak and sickly

WEAKNESS *n* pl. -ES the state of being weak

WEAL *n* pl. -S a welt

WEALD *n* pl. -S a woodland

WEALTH *n* pl. -S a great quantity of valuable material

WEALTHY *adj* WEALTHIER, WEALTHIEST having wealth

WEAN *v* -ED, -ING, -S to withhold mother's milk from and substitute other nourishment

WEANER *n* pl. -S one that weans

WEANLING *n* pl. -S a recently weaned child or animal

WEAPON *v* -ED, -ING, -S to supply with a weapon (an instrument used in combat)

WEAPONRY *n* pl. -RIES an aggregate of weapons

WEAR *v* WORE, WORN, WEARING, WEARS to have on one's person

WEARABLE *n* pl. -S a garment

WEARER *n* pl. -S one that wears something

WEARIED	past tense of weary
WEARIER	comparative of weary
WEARIES	present 3d person sing. of weary
WEARIEST	superlative of weary
WEARIFUL	*adj* tiresome
WEARISH	*adj* tasteless
WEARY	*adj* -RIER, -RIEST tired **WEARILY** *adv*
WEARY	*v* -RIED, -RYING, -RIES to make or become weary
WEASAND	*n* pl. -S the throat
WEASEL	*v* -ED, -ING, -S to act evasively
WEASON	*n* pl. -S weasand
WEATHER	*v* -ED, -ING, -S to expose to atmospheric conditions
WEAVE	*v* WOVE or WEAVED, WOVEN, WEAVING, WEAVES to form by interlacing threads
WEAVER	*n* pl. -S one that weaves
WEAZAND	*n* pl. -S weasand
WEB	*v* WEBBED, WEBBING, WEBS to provide with a web (an interlaced fabric or structure)
WEBBING	*n* pl. -S a woven strip of fiber
WEBBY	*adj* -BIER, -BIEST weblike
WEBER	*n* pl. -S a unit of magnetic flux
WEBFED	*adj* pertaining to a type of printing press
WEBFOOT	*n* pl. -FEET a foot having the toes joined by a membrane
WEBLESS	*adj* having no webs
WEBLIKE	*adj* resembling a web
WEBSTER	*n* pl. -S a weaver
WEBWORM	*n* pl. -S a web-spinning caterpillar
WECHT	*n* pl. -S weight
WED	*v* WEDDED, WEDDING, WEDS to marry
WEDDER	*n* pl. -S one that weds
WEDDING	*n* pl. -S a marriage ceremony
WEDEL	*v* -ED, -ING, -S to perform a wedeln
WEDELN	*n* pl. -S a skiing technique
WEDGE	*v* WEDGED, WEDGING, WEDGES to force apart with a wedge (a tapering piece of wood or metal)
WEDGIE	*n* pl. -S a type of woman's shoe
WEDGY	*adj* WEDGIER, WEDGIEST resembling a wedge
WEDLOCK	*n* pl. -S the state of being married
WEE	*adj* WEER, WEEST very small
WEE	*n* pl. -S a short time
WEED	*v* -ED, -ING, -S to remove weeds (undesirable plants)
WEEDER	*n* pl. -S one that weeds
WEEDIER	comparative of weedy
WEEDIEST	superlative of weedy
WEEDILY	*adv* in a weedy manner
WEEDLESS	*adj* having no weeds
WEEDLIKE	*adj* resembling a weed
WEEDY	*adj* WEEDIER, WEEDIEST resembling a weed
WEEK	*n* pl. -S a period of seven days
WEEKDAY	*n* pl. -DAYS any day of the week except Sunday
WEEKEND	*v* -ED, -ING, -S to spend the weekend (the end of the week)
WEEKLONG	*adj* continuing for a week
WEEKLY	*n* pl. -LIES a publication issued once a week
WEEL	*adj* well
WEEN	*v* -ED, -ING, -S to suppose
WEENIE	*n* pl. -S a wiener
WEENSY	*adj* -SIER, -SIEST tiny
WEENY	*adj* -NIER, -NIEST tiny
WEEP	*v* WEPT, WEEPING, WEEPS to express sorrow by shedding tears
WEEPER	*n* pl. -S one that weeps
WEEPY	*adj* WEEPIER, WEEPIEST tending to weep
WEER	comparative of wee
WEEST	superlative of wee
WEET	*v* -ED, -ING, -S to know
WEEVER	*n* pl. -S a marine fish
WEEVIL	*n* pl. -S a small beetle **WEEVILED, WEEVILLY, WEEVILY** *adj*
WEEWEE	*v* -WEED, -WEEING, -WEES to urinate
WEFT	*n* pl. -S a woven fabric or garment
WEFTWISE	*adv* in a horizontal direction
WEIGELA	*n* pl. -S a flowering shrub
WEIGELIA	*n* pl. -S weigela

WEIGH *v* -ED, -ING, -S to determine the weight of

WEIGHER *n* pl. -S one that weighs

WEIGHMAN *n* pl. -MEN one whose occupation is weighing goods

WEIGHT *v* -ED, -ING, -S to add weight (heaviness) to

WEIGHTER *n* pl. -S one that weights

WEIGHTY *adj* WEIGHTIER, WEIGHTIEST having great weight

WEINER *n* pl. -S wiener

WEIR *n* pl. -S a fence placed in a stream to catch fish

WEIRD *adj* WEIRDER, WEIRDEST mysteriously strange

WEIRD *n* pl. -S destiny

WEIRDIE *n* pl. -S a very strange person

WEIRDIES pl. of weirdy

WEIRDLY *adv* in a weird manner

WEIRDO *n* pl. WEIRDOES or WEIRDOS weirdie

WEIRDY *n* pl. WEIRDIES weirdie

WEKA *n* pl. -S a flightless bird

WELCH *v* -ED, -ING, -ES to welsh

WELCHER *n* pl. -S one that welshes

WELCOME *v* -COMED, -COMING, -COMES to greet cordially

WELCOMER *n* pl. -S one that welcomes

WELD *v* -ED, -ING, -S to join by applying heat **WELDABLE** *adj*

WELDER *n* pl. -S one that welds

WELDLESS *adj* having no welded joints

WELDMENT *n* pl. -S a unit composed of welded pieces

WELDOR *n* pl. -S welder

WELFARE *n* pl. -S general well-being

WELKIN *n* pl. -S the sky

WELL *v* -ED, -ING, -S to rise to the surface and flow forth

WELLADAY *n* pl. -DAYS wellaway

WELLAWAY *n* pl. -WAYS an expression of sorrow

WELLBORN *adj* of good birth or ancestry

WELLCURB *n* pl. -S the stone ring around a well (a hole dug in the ground to obtain water)

WELLDOER *n* pl. -S a doer of good deeds

WELLHEAD *n* pl. -S the source of a spring or stream

WELLHOLE *n* pl. -S the shaft of a well

WELLNESS *n* pl. -ES the state of being healthy

WELLSITE *n* pl. -S a mineral

WELSH *v* -ED, -ING, -ES to fail to pay a debt

WELSHER *n* pl. -S one that welshes

WELT *v* -ED, -ING, -S to mark with welts (ridges or lumps raised on the skin)

WELTER *v* -ED, -ING, -S to roll about

WELTING *n* pl. -S a cord or strip used to reinforce a seam

WEN *n* pl. -S a benign tumor of the skin

WENCH *v* -ED, -ING, -ES to consort with prostitutes

WENCHER *n* pl. -S one that wenches

WEND *v* -ED, -ING, -S to proceed along

WENDIGO *n* pl. -GOS windigo

WENNISH *adj* wenny

WENNY *adj* -NIER, -NIEST resembling a wen

WENT past tense of go

WEPT past tense of weep

WERE a pl. and 2d person sing. past indicative, and past subjunctive of be

WEREGILD *n* pl. -S wergeld

WEREWOLF *n* pl. -WOLVES a person capable of assuming the form of a wolf

WERGELD *n* pl. -S a price paid for the taking of a man's life in Anglo-Saxon law

WERGELT *n* pl. -S wergeld

WERGILD *n* pl. -S wergeld

WERT a 2d person sing. past tense of be

WERWOLF *n* pl. -WOLVES werewolf

WESKIT *n* pl. -S a vest

WESSAND *n* pl. -S weasand

WEST *n* pl. -S a cardinal point of the compass

WESTER *v* -ED, -ING, -S to move toward the west

WESTERLY *n* pl. -LIES a wind from the west

WESTERN *n* pl. -S one who lives in the west

WESTING *n* pl. -S a shifting west

WESTMOST	*adj* farthest west
WESTWARD	*n* pl. -S a direction toward the west
WET	*adj* WETTER, WETTEST covered or saturated with a liquid
WET	*v* WETTED, WETTING, WETS to make wet
WETBACK	*n* pl. -S a Mexican who enters the United States illegally
WETHER	*n* pl. -S a gelded male sheep
WETLAND	*n* pl. -S land containing much soil moisture
WETLY	*adv* in a wet manner
WETNESS	*n* pl. -ES the state of being wet
WETPROOF	*adj* waterproof
WETTABLE	*adj* capable of being wetted
WETTED	past tense of wet
WETTER	*,n* pl. -S one that wets
WETTEST	superlative of wet
WETTING	*n* pl. -S a liquid used in moistening something
WETTISH	*adj* somewhat wet
WHA	*pron* who
WHACK	*v* -ED, -ING, -S to strike sharply
WHACKER	*n* pl. -S one that whacks
WHACKY	*adj* WHACKIER, WHACKIEST wacky
WHALE	*v* WHALED, WHALING, WHALES to engage in the hunting of whales (large marine mammals)
WHALEMAN	*n* pl. -MEN a whaler
WHALER	*n* pl. -S a person engaged in whaling
WHALING	*n* pl. -S the industry of capturing and processing whales
WHAM	*v* WHAMMED, WHAMMING, WHAMS to hit with a loud impact
WHAMMY	*n* pl. -MIES a supernatural spell bringing bad luck
WHANG	*v* -ED, -ING, -S to beat with a whip
WHANGEE	*n* pl. -S an Asian grass
WHAP	*v* WHAPPED, WHAPPING, WHAPS to whop
WHAPPER	*n* pl. -S whopper
WHARF	*v* -ED, -ING, -S to moor to a wharf (a landing place for vessels)
WHARFAGE	*n* pl. -S the use of a wharf
WHARVE	*n* pl. -S a round piece of wood used in spinning thread
WHAT	*n* pl. -S the true nature of something
WHATEVER	*adj* being what or who it may be
WHATNOT	*n* pl. -S an ornamental set of shelves
WHAUP	*n* pl. -S a European bird
WHEAL	*n* pl. -S a welt
WHEAT	*n* pl. -S a cereal grass
WHEATEAR	*n* pl. -S a small bird of northern regions
WHEATEN	*adj* pertaining to wheat
WHEE	*interj* — used to express delight
WHEEDLE	*v* -DLED, -DLING, -DLES to attempt to persuade by flattery
WHEEDLER	*n* pl. -S one that wheedles
WHEEL	*v* -ED, -ING, -S to convey on wheels (circular frames designed to turn on an axis)
WHEELER	*n* pl. -S one that wheels
WHEELIE	*n* pl. -S a maneuver made on a wheeled vehicle
WHEELING	*n* pl. -S the condition of a road for vehicles
WHEELMAN	*n* pl. -MEN a helmsman
WHEEN	*n* pl. -S a fairly large amount
WHEEP	*v* -ED, -ING, -S to wheeple
WHEEPLE	*v* -PLED, -PLING, -PLES to give forth a prolonged whistle
WHEEZE	*v* WHEEZED, WHEEZING, WHEEZES to breathe with a whistling sound
WHEEZER	*n* pl. -S one that wheezes
WHEEZY	*adj* WHEEZIER, WHEEZIEST characterized by wheezing **WHEEZILY** *adv*
WHELK	*n* pl. -S a pustule
WHELKY	*adj* WHELKIER, WHELKIEST marked with whelks
WHELM	*v* -ED, -ING, -S to cover with water
WHELP	*v* -ED, -ING, -S to give birth to
WHEN	*n* pl. -S the time in which something is done or occurs
WHENAS	*conj* at which time
WHENCE	*adv* from what place
WHENEVER	*adv* at whatever time

WHERE	*n* pl. -S the place at or in which something is located or occurs
WHEREAS	*n* pl. -ES an introductory statement of a formal document
WHEREAT	*adv* at what
WHEREBY	*adv* by what
WHEREIN	*adv* in what
WHEREOF	*adv* of what
WHEREON	*adv* on what
WHERETO	*adv* to what
WHEREVER	*adv* in or to whatever place
WHERRY	*v* -RIED, -RYING, -RIES to transport in a light rowboat
WHERVE	*n* pl. -S wharve
WHET	*v* WHETTED, WHETTING, WHETS to sharpen by friction
WHETHER	*conj* if it be the case that
WHETTER	*n* pl. -S one that whets
WHETTING	present participle of whet
WHEW	*n* pl. -S a whistling sound
WHEY	*n* pl. WHEYS the watery part of milk **WHEYEY, WHEYISH** *adj*
WHEYFACE	*n* pl. -S a pale, sallow face
WHICH	*pron* what particular one or ones
WHICKER	*v* -ED, -ING, -S to whinny
WHID	*v* WHIDDED, WHIDDING, WHIDS to move rapidly and quietly
WHIDAH	*n* pl. -S whydah
WHIFF	*v* -ED, -ING, -S to blow or convey with slight gusts of air
WHIFFER	*n* pl. -S one that whiffs
WHIFFET	*n* pl. -S an insignificant person
WHIFFLE	*v* -FLED, -FLING, -FLES to move or think erratically
WHIFFLER	*n* pl. -S one that whiffles
WHILE	*v* WHILED, WHILING, WHILES to cause to pass pleasantly
WHILOM	*adv* formerly
WHILST	*conj* during the time that
WHIM	*n* pl. -S an impulsive idea
WHIMBREL	*n* pl. -S a shore bird
WHIMPER	*v* -ED, -ING, -S to cry with plaintive, broken sounds
WHIMSEY	*n* pl. -SEYS whimsy
WHIMSY	*n* pl. -SIES a whim **WHIMSIED** *adj*
WHIN	*n* pl. -S furze

WHINCHAT	*n* pl. -S a songbird
WHINE	*v* WHINED, WHINING, WHINES to utter a plaintive, high-pitched sound
WHINER	*n* pl. -S one that whines
WHINEY	*adj* WHINIER, WHINIEST whiny
WHINIER	comparative of whiny
WHINIEST	superlative of whiny
WHINING	present participle of whine
WHINNY	*v* -NIED, -NYING, -NIES to neigh in a low or gentle manner
WHINNY	*adj* -NIER, -NIEST abounding in whin
WHINY	*adj* WHINIER, WHINIEST tending to whine
WHIP	*v* WHIPPED or WHIPT, WHIPPING, WHIPS to strike with a whip (an instrument for administering corporal punishment)
WHIPCORD	*n* pl. -S a strong, twisted cord
WHIPLASH	*n* pl. -ES the lash of a whip
WHIPLIKE	*adj* resembling a whip
WHIPPED	a past tense of whip
WHIPPER	*n* pl. -S one that whips
WHIPPET	*n* pl. -S a small, swift dog
WHIPPIER	comparative of whippy
WHIPPIEST	superlative of whippy
WHIPPING	*n* pl. -S material used to whip
WHIPPY	*adj* -PIER, -PIEST pertaining to or resembling a whip
WHIPRAY	*n* pl. -RAYS a stingray
WHIPSAW	*v* -SAWED, -SAWN, -SAWING, -SAWS to cut with a narrow, tapering saw
WHIPT	a past tense of whip
WHIPTAIL	*n* pl. -S a lizard having a long, slender tail
WHIPWORM	*n* pl. -S a parasitic worm
WHIR	*v* WHIRRED, WHIRRING, WHIRS to move with a buzzing sound
WHIRL	*v* -ED, -ING, -S to revolve rapidly
WHIRLER	*n* pl. -S one that whirls
WHIRLY	*adj* WHIRLIER, WHIRLIEST marked by a whirling motion
WHIRLY	*n* pl. WHIRLIES a small tornado
WHIRR	*v* -ED, -ING, -S to whir
WHIRRED	past tense of whir
WHIRRING	present participle of whir

WHIRRY	*v* -RIED, -RYING, -RIES to hurry
WHISH	*v* -ED, -ING, -ES to move with a hissing sound
WHISHT	*v* -ED, -ING, -S to hush
WHISK	*v* -ED, -ING, -S to move quickly and easily
WHISKER	*n* pl. -S a hair on a man's face **WHISKERY** *adj*
WHISKEY	*n* pl. -KEYS a liquor
WHISKY	*n* pl. -KIES whiskey
WHISPER	*v* -ED, -ING, -S to speak softly
WHISPERY	*adj* resembling a whisper
WHIST	*v* -ED, -ING, -S to hush
WHISTLE	*v* -TLED, -TLING, -TLES to make a shrill, clear musical sound
WHISTLER	*n* pl. -S one that whistles
WHIT	*n* pl. -S a particle
WHITE	*adj* WHITER, WHITEST of the color of pure snow
WHITE	*v* WHITED, WHITING, WHITES to whiten
WHITECAP	*n* pl. -S a wave with a crest of foam
WHITEFLY	*n* pl. -FLIES a small whitish insect
WHITELY	*adv* in a white manner
WHITEN	*v* -ED, -ING, -S to make white
WHITENER	*n* pl. -S one that whitens
WHITEOUT	*n* pl. -S an arctic weather condition
WHITER	comparative of white
WHITEST	superlative of white
WHITEY	*n* pl. -EYS a white man — an offensive term
WHITHER	*adv* to what place
WHITIES	pl. of whity
WHITING	*n* pl. -S a marine food fish
WHITISH	*adj* somewhat white
WHITLOW	*n* pl. -S an inflammation of the finger or toe
WHITRACK	*n* pl. -S a weasel
WHITTER	*n* pl. -S a large draft of liquor
WHITTLE	*v* -TLED, -TLING, -TLES to cut or shave bits from
WHITTLER	*n* pl. -S one that whittles
WHITTRET	*n* pl. -S a weasel
WHITY	*n* pl. WHITIES whitey

WHIZ	*v* WHIZZED, WHIZZING, WHIZZES to move with a buzzing or hissing sound
WHIZBANG	*n* pl. -S a type of explosive shell
WHIZZ	*v* -ED, -ING, -ES to whiz
WHIZZED	past tense of whiz
WHIZZER	*n* pl. -S one that whizzes
WHIZZES	present 3d person sing. of whiz
WHIZZING	present participle of whiz
WHO	*pron* what or which person or persons
WHOA	*interj* — used to command an animal to stop
WHODUNIT	*n* pl. -S a mystery story
WHOEVER	*pron* whatever person
WHOLE	*n* pl. -S all the parts or elements entering into and making up a thing
WHOLISM	*n* pl. -S holism
WHOLLY	*adv* totally
WHOM	*pron* the objective case of who
WHOMEVER	*pron* the objective case of whoever
WHOMP	*v* -ED, -ING, -S to defeat decisively
WHOMSO	*pron* the objective case of whoso
WHOOP	*v* -ED, -ING, -S to utter loud cries
WHOOPEE	*n* pl. -S boisterous fun
WHOOPER	*n* pl. -S one that whoops
WHOOPLA	*n* pl. -S a noisy commotion
WHOOSH	*v* -ED, -ING, -ES to move with a hissing sound
WHOOSIS	*n* pl. -SISES an object or person whose name is not known
WHOP	*v* WHOPPED, WHOPPING, WHOPS to strike forcibly
WHOPPER	*n* pl. -S something unusually large
WHORE	*v* WHORED, WHORING, WHORES to consort with prostitutes
WHOREDOM	*n* pl. -S prostitution
WHORESON	*n* pl. -S a bastard
WHORING	present participle of whore
WHORISH	*adj* lewd
WHORL	*n* pl. -S a circular arrangement of similar parts **WHORLED** *adj*
WHORT	*n* pl. -S an edible berry

WHORTLE	*n* pl. -S whort
WHOSE	*pron* the possessive case of who
WHOSEVER	*pron* the possessive case of whoever
WHOSIS	*n* pl. -SISES whoosis
WHOSO	*pron* whoever
WHUMP	*v* -ED, -ING, -S to thump
WHY	*n* pl. WHYS the reason or cause of something
WHYDAH	*n* pl. -S an African bird
WICH	*n* pl. -ES wych
WICK	*n* pl. -S a bundle of loosely twisted fibers in a candle or oil lamp
WICKAPE	*n* pl. -S wicopy
WICKED	*adj* -EDER, -EDEST evil **WICKEDLY** *adv*
WICKER	*n* pl. -S a slender, pliant twig or branch
WICKET	*n* pl. -S a small door or gate
WICKING	*n* pl. -S material for wicks
WICKIUP	*n* pl. -S an American Indian hut
WICKYUP	*n* pl. -S wickiup
WICOPY	*n* pl. -PIES a flowering shrub
WIDDER	*n* pl. -S a widow
WIDDIE	*n* pl. -S widdy
WIDDLE	*v* -DLED, -DLING, -DLES to wriggle
WIDDY	*n* pl. -DIES a hangman's noose
WIDE	*adj* WIDER, WIDEST having great extent from side to side **WIDELY** *adv*
WIDE	*n* pl. -S a type of bowled ball in cricket
WIDEN	*v* -ED, -ING, -S to make wide or wider
WIDENER	*n* pl. -S one that widens
WIDENESS	*n* pl. -ES the state of being wide
WIDER	comparative of wide
WIDEST	superlative of wide
WIDGEON	*n* pl. -S a river duck
WIDGET	*n* pl. -S a gadget
WIDISH	*adj* somewhat wide
WIDOW	*v* -ED, -ING, -S to deprive of a husband
WIDOWER	*n* pl. -S a man whose wife has died and who has not remarried
WIDTH	*n* pl. -S extent from side to side

WIDTHWAY	*adv* from side to side
WIELD	*v* -ED, -ING, -S to handle or use effectively
WIELDER	*n* pl. -S one that wields
WIELDY	*adj* WIELDIER, WIELDIEST easily wielded
WIENER	*n* pl. -S a frankfurter
WIENIE	*n* pl. -S a wiener
WIFE	*n* pl. WIVES a woman married to a man
WIFE	*v* WIFED, WIFING, WIFES to wive
WIFEDOM	*n* pl. -S the status or function of a wife
WIFEHOOD	*n* pl. -S the state of being a wife
WIFELESS	*adj* having no wife
WIFELIKE	*adj* wifely
WIFELY	*adj* -LIER, -LIEST of or befitting a wife
WIFING	present participle of wife
WIG	*v* WIGGED, WIGGING, WIGS to provide with a wig (an artificial covering of hair for the head)
WIGAN	*n* pl. -S a stiff fabric
WIGEON	*n* pl. -S widgeon
WIGGED	past tense of wig
WIGGERY	*n* pl. -GERIES a wig
WIGGING	*n* pl. -S a scolding
WIGGLE	*v* -GLED, -GLING, -GLES to move with short, quick movements from side to side
WIGGLER	*n* pl. -S one that wiggles
WIGGLY	*adj* -GLIER, -GLIEST tending to wiggle
WIGHT	*n* pl. -S a living being
WIGLESS	*adj* having no wig
WIGLET	*n* pl. -S a small wig
WIGLIKE	*adj* resembling a wig
WIGMAKER	*n* pl. -S one that makes wigs
WIGWAG	*v* -WAGGED, -WAGGING, -WAGS to move back and forth
WIGWAM	*n* pl. -S an American Indian dwelling
WIKIUP	*n* pl. -S wickiup
WILCO	*interj* — used to indicate that a message received will be complied with
WILD	*adj* WILDER, WILDEST living in a natural state

WILD	*n* pl. -S an uninhabited or uncultivated area
WILDCAT	*v* -CATTED, -CATTING, -CATS to search for oil in an area of doubtful productivity
WILDER	*v* -ED, -ING, -S to bewilder
WILDFIRE	*n* pl. -S a raging, destructive fire
WILDFOWL	*n* pl. -S a wild game bird
WILDING	*n* pl. -S a wild plant or animal
WILDISH	*adj* somewhat wild
WILDLIFE	*n* pl. WILDLIFE wild animals and vegetation
WILDLING	*n* pl. -S a wilding
WILDLY	*adv* in a wild manner
WILDNESS	*n* pl. -ES the state of being wild
WILDWOOD	*n* pl. -S natural forest land
WILE	*v* WILED, WILING, WILES to entice
WILFUL	*adj* willful **WILFULLY** *adv*
WILIER	comparative of wily
WILIEST	superlative of wily
WILILY	*adv* in a wily manner
WILINESS	*n* pl. -ES the quality of being wily
WILING	present participle of wile
WILL	*v* -ED, -ING, -S to decide upon **WILLABLE** *adj*
WILL	*v* past sing. 2d person WOULD, WOULDEST, or WOULDST — used as an auxiliary followed by a simple infinitive to express futurity, inclination, likelihood, or requirement
WILLER	*n* pl. -S one that wills
WILLET	*n* pl. -S a shore bird
WILLFUL	*adj* bent on having one's own way
WILLIED	past tense of willy
WILLIES	present 3d person sing. of willy
WILLING	*adj* -INGER, -INGEST inclined or favorably disposed in mind
WILLIWAU	*n* pl. -S williwaw
WILLIWAW	*n* pl. -S a violent gust of cold wind
WILLOW	*v* -ED, -ING, -S to clean textile fibers with a certain machine
WILLOWER	*n* pl. -S one that willows
WILLOWY	*adj* -LOWIER, -LOWIEST pliant
WILLY	*v* -LIED, -LYING, -LIES to willow
WILLYARD	*adj* willful
WILLYART	*adj* willyard
WILLYWAW	*n* pl. -S williwaw
WILT	*v* -ED, -ING, -S to become limp
WILY	*adj* WILIER, WILIEST crafty
WIMBLE	*v* -BLED, -BLING, -BLES to bore with a hand tool
WIMPLE	*v* -PLED, -PLING, -PLES to pleat
WIN	*v* WON or WAN, WINNING, WINS to be victorious
WIN	*v* WINNED, WINNING, WINS to winnow
WINCE	*v* WINCED, WINCING, WINCES to flinch
WINCER	*n* pl. -S one that winces
WINCEY	*n* pl. -CEYS a type of fabric
WINCH	*v* -ED, -ING, -ES to raise with a winch (a hoisting machine)
WINCHER	*n* pl. -S one that winches
WINCING	present participle of wince
WIND	*v* WOUND or WINDED, WINDING, WINDS to pass around an object or fixed center **WINDABLE** *adj*
WINDAGE	*n* pl. -S the effect of the wind (air in natural motion) on a projectile
WINDBAG	*n* pl. -S a talkative person
WINDBURN	*v* -BURNED or -BURNT, -BURNING, -BURNS to be affected with skin irritation caused by exposure to the wind
WINDER	*n* pl. -S one that winds
WINDFALL	*n* pl. -S a sudden and unexpected gain
WINDFLAW	*n* pl. -S a gust of wind
WINDGALL	*n* pl. -S a swelling on a horse's leg
WINDIER	comparative of windy
WINDIEST	superlative of windy
WINDIGO	*n* pl. -GOS an evil demon in Algonquian mythology
WINDILY	*adv* in a windy manner
WINDING	*n* pl. -S material wound about an object
WINDLASS	*v* -ED, -ING, -ES to raise with a windlass (a hoisting machine)
WINDLE	*v* -DLED, -DLING, -DLES to wind
WINDLESS	*adj* being without wind
WINDLING	*n* pl. -S a bundle of straw

WINDMILL   *v* -ED, -ING, -S to rotate solely under the force of a passing airstream

WINDOW   *v* -ED, -ING, -S to provide with a window (an opening in a wall to admit light and air)

WINDPIPE   *n* pl. -S the trachea

WINDROW   *v* -ED, -ING, -S to arrange in long rows, as hay or grain

WINDSOCK   *n* pl. -S a device used to indicate wind direction

WINDUP   *n* pl. -S a conclusion

WINDWARD   *n* pl. -S the direction from which the wind blows

WINDWAY   *n* pl. -WAYS a passage for air

WINDY   *adj* WINDIER, WINDIEST marked by strong wind

WINE   *v* WINED, WINING, WINES to provide with wine (the fermented juice of the grape)

WINELESS   *adj* having no wine

WINERY   *n* pl. -ERIES an establishment for making wine

WINESHOP   *n* pl. -S a shop where wine is sold

WINESKIN   *n* pl. -S a goatskin bag for holding wine

WINESOP   *n* pl. -S a food sopped in wine

WINEY   *adj* WINIER, WINIEST winy

WING   *v* -ED, -ING, -S to travel by means of wings (organs of flight)

WINGBACK   *n* pl. -S a certain player in football

WINGBOW   *n* pl. -S a mark on the wing of a domestic fowl

WINGDING   *n* pl. -S a lively party

WINGEDLY   *adv* swiftly

WINGER   *n* pl. -S a certain player in soccer

WINGIER   comparative of wingy

WINGIEST   superlative of wingy

WINGLESS   *adj* having no wings

WINGLET   *n* pl. -S a small wing

WINGLIKE   *adj* resembling a wing

WINGMAN   *n* pl. -MEN a pilot behind the leader of a flying formation

WINGOVER   *n* pl. -S a flight maneuver

WINGSPAN   *n* pl. -S the distance from the tip of one of a pair of wings to that of the other

WINGY   *adj* WINGIER, WINGIEST swift

WINIER   comparative of winey and winy

WINIEST   superlative of winey and winy

WINING   present participle of wine

WINISH   *adj* winy

WINK   *v* -ED, -ING, -S to close and open one eye quickly

WINKER   *n* pl. -S one that winks

WINKLE   *v* -KLED, -KLING, -KLES to displace, extract, or evict from a position

WINNABLE   *adj* able to be won

WINNED   past tense of win (to winnow)

WINNER   *n* pl. -S one that wins

WINNING   *n* pl. -S money won in a game or competition

WINNOCK   *n* pl. -S a window

WINNOW   *v* -ED, -ING, -S to free grain from impurities

WINNOWER   *n* pl. -S one that winnows

WINO   *n* pl. WINOES or WINOS one who is habitually drunk on wine

WINSOME   *adj* -SOMER, -SOMEST charming

WINTER   *v* -ED, -ING, -S to pass the winter (the coldest season of the year)

WINTERER   *n* pl. -S one that winters

WINTERLY   *adj* wintry

WINTERY   *adj* -TERIER, -TERIEST wintry

WINTLE   *v* -TLED, -TLING, -TLES to stagger

WINTRY   *adj* -TRIER, -TRIEST characteristic of winter **WINTRILY** *adv*

WINY   *adj* WINIER, WINIEST having the taste or qualities of wine

WINZE   *n* pl. -S a steeply inclined mine shaft

WIPE   *v* WIPED, WIPING, WIPES to rub lightly in order to clean or dry

WIPEOUT   *n* pl. -S a fall from a surfboard

WIPER   *n* pl. -S one that wipes

WIPING   present participle of wipe

WIRE   *v* WIRED, WIRING, WIRES to fasten with wire (a slender rod, strand, or thread of ductile metal) **WIRABLE** *adj*

WIREDRAW   *v* -DREW, -DRAWN, -DRAWING, -DRAWS to draw into wire

WIREHAIR	*n* pl. -S a dog having a wiry coat	**WISHER**	*n* pl. -S one that wishes
WIRELESS	*v* -ED, -ING, -ES to radio	**WISHFUL**	*adj* desirous
WIRELIKE	*adj* resembling wire	**WISHLESS**	*adj* not wishful
WIREMAN	*n* pl. -MEN one who makes or works with wire	**WISING**	present participle of wise
WIRER	*n* pl. -S one that wires	**WISP**	*v* -ED, -ING, -S to twist into a wisp (a small bunch or bundle)
WIRETAP	*v* -TAPPED, -TAPPING, -TAPS to intercept messages by means of a concealed monitoring device	**WISPIER**	comparative of wispy
		WISPIEST	superlative of wispy
WIREWAY	*n* pl. -WAYS a tube for protecting electric wires	**WISPILY**	*adv* in a wispy manner
		WISPISH	*adj* wispy
WIREWORK	*n* pl. -S an article made of wire	**WISPLIKE**	*adj* wispy
WIREWORM	*n* pl. -S a wirelike worm	**WISPY**	*adj* WISPIER, WISPIEST resembling a wisp
WIRIER	comparative of wiry		
WIRIEST	superlative of wiry	**WISS**	*v* -ED, -ING, -ES to wish
WIRILY	*adv* in a wiry manner	**WIST**	*v* -ED, -ING, -S to know
WIRINESS	*n* pl. -ES the quality of being wiry	**WISTARIA**	*n* pl. -S wisteria
		WISTERIA	*n* pl. -S a flowering shrub
WIRING	*n* pl. -S a system of electric wires	**WISTFUL**	*adj* yearning
		WIT	*n* pl. -S intelligence
WIRRA	*interj* — used to express sorrow	**WIT**	*v* WIST, WITING or WITTING, present sing. 1st person WOT, 2d WOST or WOSTTETH, 3d WOT or WOTTETH, present pl. WITE or WITEN to know
WIRY	*adj* WIRIER, WIRIEST resembling wire		
WIS	*v* past tense WIST to know — WIS and WIST are the only accepted forms of this verb; it cannot be conjugated further	**WITAN**	*n/pl* the members of a national council in Anglo-Saxon England
		WITCH	*v* -ED, -ING, -ES to bewitch
WISDOM	*n* pl. -S the power of true and right discernment	**WITCHERY**	*n* pl. -ERIES sorcery
		WITCHING	*n* pl. -S sorcery
WISE	*v* WISED, WISING, WISES to become aware or informed	**WITCHY**	*adj* WITCHIER, WITCHIEST malicious
WISE	*adj* WISER, WISEST having wisdom	**WITE**	*v* WITED, WITING, WITES to blame
WISEACRE	*n* pl. -S a pretentiously wise person	**WITEN**	a present pl. of wit
WISED	past tense of wise	**WITH**	*prep* in the company of
WISELY	*adv* -LIER, -LIEST in a wise manner	**WITHAL**	*adv* in addition
		WITHDRAW	*v* -DREW, -DRAWN, -DRAWING, -DRAWS to move back or away
WISENESS	*n* pl. -ES wisdom		
WISENT	*n* pl. -S a European bison	**WITHE**	*v* WITHED, WITHING, WITHES to bind with flexible twigs
WISER	comparative of wise		
WISEST	superlative of wise	**WITHER**	*v* -ED, -ING, -S to dry up and wilt
WISH	*v* -ED, -ING, -ES to feel an impulse toward attainment or possession of something		
		WITHERER	*n* pl. -S one that withers
		WITHHOLD	*v* -HELD, -HOLDING, -HOLDS to hold back
WISHA	*interj* — used to express surprise	**WITHIER**	comparative of withy
		WITHIES	pl. of withy
WISHBONE	*n* pl. -S a forked bone in front of a bird's breastbone	**WITHIEST**	superlative of withy

WITHIN	*n* pl. -S an interior place or area	**WOBBLY**	*n* pl. -BLIES a member of the Industrial Workers of the World
WITHING	present participle of withe		
WITHOUT	*n* pl. -S an exterior place or area	**WOBEGONE**	*adj* affected with woe
		WOE	*n* pl. -S tremendous grief
WITHY	*n* pl. WITHIES a flexible twig	**WOEFUL**	*adj* -FULLER, -FULLEST full of woe **WOEFULLY** *adv*
WITHY	*adj* WITHIER, WITHIEST flexible and tough		
		WOENESS	*n* pl. -ES sadness
WITING	present participle of wit and wite	**WOESOME**	*adj* woeful
		WOFUL	*adj* woeful **WOFULLY** *adv*
WITLESS	*adj* lacking intelligence	**WOK**	*n* pl. -S a cooking utensil
WITLING	*n* pl. -S one who considers himself witty	**WOKE**	a past tense of wake
		WOKEN	a past participle of wake
WITLOOF	*n* pl. -S chicory	**WOLD**	*n* pl. -S an elevated tract of open land
WITNESS	*v* -ED, -ING, -ES to see or know by personal experience		
		WOLF	*n* pl. WOLVES a carnivorous mammal
WITNEY	*n* pl. -NEYS a heavy woolen fabric		
		WOLF	*v* -ED, -ING, -S to devour voraciously
WITTED	*adj* having intelligence		
WITTIER	comparative of witty	**WOLFER**	*n* pl. -S one who hunts wolves
WITTIEST	superlative of witty	**WOLFFISH**	*n* pl. -ES a marine fish
WITTILY	*adv* in a witty manner	**WOLFISH**	*adj* wolflike
WITTING	*n* pl. -S knowledge	**WOLFLIKE**	*adj* resembling a wolf
WITTOL	*n* pl. -S a man who tolerates his wife's infidelity	**WOLFRAM**	*n* pl. -S tungsten
		WOLVER	*n* pl. -S wolfer
WITTY	*adj* -TIER, -TIEST humorously clever	**WOLVES**	pl. of wolf
		WOMAN	*n* pl. WOMEN an adult human female
WIVE	*v* WIVED, WIVING, WIVES to marry a woman		
		WOMAN	*v* -ED, -ING, -S to play the part of a woman
WIVER	*n* pl. -S wivern		
WIVERN	*n* pl. -S a two-legged dragon	**WOMANISE**	*v* -ISED, -ISING, -ISES to womanize
WIVES	pl. of wife		
WIVING	present participle of wive	**WOMANISH**	*adj* characteristic of a woman
WIZ	*n* pl. -ES a very clever or skillful person	**WOMANIZE**	*v* -IZED, -IZING, -IZES to make effeminate
		WOMANLY	*adj* -LIER, -LIEST having the qualities of a woman
WIZARD	*n* pl. -S a sorcerer **WIZARDLY** *adj*		
WIZARDRY	*n* pl. -RIES sorcery	**WOMB**	*n* pl. -S the uterus **WOMBED** *adj*
WIZEN	*v* -ED, -ING, -S to shrivel		
WIZZEN	*n* pl. -S weasand	**WOMBAT**	*n* pl. -S a nocturnal mammal
WO	*n* pl. WOS woe	**WOMBY**	*adj* WOMBIER, WOMBIEST hollow
WOAD	*n* pl. -S a blue dye **WOADED** *adj*		
		WOMEN	pl. of woman
WOADWAX	*n* pl. -ES an ornamental shrub	**WOMERA**	*n* pl. -S a device used to propel spears
WOALD	*n* pl. -S a yellow pigment		
WOBBLE	*v* -BLED, -BLING, -BLES to move unsteadily	**WOMMERA**	*n* pl. -S womera
		WON	*v* WONNED, WONNING, WONS to dwell
WOBBLER	*n* pl. -S one that wobbles		
WOBBLY	*adj* -BLIER, -BLIEST unsteady	**WONDER**	*v* -ED, -ING, -S to have a feeling of curiosity or doubt

WONDERER *n* pl. -S one that wonders

WONDROUS *adj* marvelous

WONKY *adj* -KIER, -KIEST unsteady

WONNED past tense of won

WONNER *n* pl. -S a prodigy

WONNING present participle of won

WONT *v* -ED, -ING, -S to make accustomed to

WONTEDLY *adv* in a usual manner

WONTON *n* pl. -S a pork-filled dumpling used in Chinese cooking

WOO *v* -ED, -ING, -S to seek the affection of

WOOD *v* -ED, -ING, -S to furnish with wood (the hard, fibrous substance beneath the bark of a tree or shrub)

WOODBIN *n* pl. -S a bin for holding firewood

WOODBIND *n* pl. -S woodbine

WOODBINE *n* pl. -S a European shrub

WOODBOX *n* pl. -ES a woodbin

WOODCHAT *n* pl. -S a European shrike

WOODCOCK *n* pl. -S a game bird

WOODCUT *n* pl. -S an engraved block of wood

WOODEN *adj* -ENER, -ENEST resembling wood in stiffness **WOODENLY** *adv*

WOODHEN *n* pl. -S the weka

WOODIER comparative of woody

WOODIEST superlative of woody

WOODLAND *n* pl. -S land covered with trees

WOODLARK *n* pl. -S a songbird

WOODLESS *adj* having no wood

WOODLORE *n* pl. -S knowledge of the forest

WOODLOT *n* pl. -S an area restricted to the growing of forest trees

WOODMAN *n* pl. -MEN woodsman

WOODNOTE *n* pl. -S a song or call of a forest bird

WOODPILE *n* pl. -S a pile of wood

WOODRUFF *n* pl. -S an aromatic herb

WOODSHED *v* -SHEDDED, -SHEDDING, -SHEDS to practice on a musical instrument

WOODSIA *n* pl. -S a small fern

WOODSMAN *n* pl. -MEN one who works or lives in the forest

WOODSY *adj* WOODSIER, WOODSIEST suggestive of a forest

WOODWAX *n* pl. -ES woadwax

WOODWIND *n* pl. -S a musical wind instrument

WOODWORK *n* pl. -S work made of wood

WOODWORM *n* pl. -S a wood-boring worm

WOODY *adj* WOODIER, WOODIEST containing or resembling wood

WOOER *n* pl. -S one that woos

WOOF *v* -ED, -ING, -S to utter a gruff barking sound

WOOFER *n* pl. -S a loudspeaker designed to reproduce low-pitched sounds

WOOINGLY *adv* attractively

WOOL *n* pl. -S the dense, soft hair forming the coat of certain mammals **WOOLED** *adj*

WOOLEN *n* pl. -S a fabric made of wool

WOOLER *n* pl. -S a domestic animal raised for its wool

WOOLFELL *n* pl. -S woolskin

WOOLIE *n* pl. -S a woolly

WOOLIER comparative of wooly

WOOLIES pl. of wooly

WOOLIEST superlative of wooly

WOOLLEN *n* pl. -S woolen

WOOLLIER comparative of woolly

WOOLLIES pl. of woolly

WOOLLIEST superlative of woolly

WOOLLIKE *adj* resembling wool

WOOLLY *adj* -LIER, -LIEST consisting of or resembling wool

WOOLLY *n* pl. -LIES a garment made of wool

WOOLMAN *n* pl. -MEN a dealer in wool

WOOLPACK *n* pl. -S a bag for packing a bale of wool

WOOLSACK *n* pl. -S a sack of wool

WOOLSHED *n* pl. -S a building in which sheep are sheared

WOOLSKIN *n* pl. -S a sheepskin with the wool still on it

WOOLY *adj* WOOLIER, WOOLIEST woolly

WOOLY *n* pl. WOOLIES a woolly

WOOMERA *n* pl. -S womera

WOOPS *interj* oops

WOORALI *n* pl. -S curare

WOORARI   *n* pl. -S curare

WOOSH   *v* -ED, -ING, -ES to whoosh

WOOZY   *adj* -ZIER, -ZIEST dazed **WOOZILY** *adv*

WOP   *n* pl. -S an Italian — an offensive term

WORD   *v* -ED, -ING, -S to express in words (speech sounds that communicate meaning)

WORDAGE   *n* pl. -S the number of words used

WORDBOOK   *n* pl. -S a dictionary

WORDIER   comparative of wordy

WORDIEST   superlative of wordy

WORDILY   *adv* in a wordy manner

WORDING   *n* pl. -S the act or style of expressing in words

WORDLESS   *adj* being without words

WORDPLAY   *n* pl. -PLAYS a witty exchange of words

WORDY   *adj* WORDIER, WORDIEST using many or too many words

WORE   past tense of wear

WORK   *v* WORKED or WROUGHT, WORKING, WORKS to exert one's powers of body or mind for some purpose

WORKABLE   *adj* capable of being done

WORKADAY   *adj* everyday

WORKBAG   *n* pl. -S a bag for holding work instuments and materials

WORKBOAT   *n* pl. -S a boat used for commercial purposes

WORKBOOK   *n* pl. -S an exercise book for a student

WORKBOX   *n* pl. -ES a box for holding work instruments and materials

WORKDAY   *n* pl. -DAYS a day on which work is done

WORKER   *n* pl. -S one that works

WORKFOLK   *n/pl* manual laborers

WORKING   *n* pl. -S a mining excavation

WORKLESS   *adj* unemployed

WORKLOAD   *n* pl. -S the amount of work assigned to an employee

WORKMAN   *n* pl. -MEN a male worker

WORKOUT   *n* pl. -S a period of physical exercise

WORKROOM   *n* pl. -S a room in which work is done

WORKSHOP   *n* pl. -S a workroom

WORKUP   *n* pl. -S an intensive diagnostic study

WORKWEEK   *n* pl. -S the number of hours worked in a week

WORLD   *n* pl. -S the earth and all its inhabitants

WORLDLY   *adj* -LIER, -LIEST pertaining to the world

WORM   *v* -ED, -ING, -S to rid of worms (small, limbless invertebrates)

WORMER   *n* pl. -S one that worms

WORMHOLE   *n* pl. -S a hole made by a burrowing worm

WORMIER   comparative of wormy

WORMIEST   superlative of wormy

WORMIL   *n* pl. -S a lump in the skin of an animal's back

WORMISH   *adj* wormlike

WORMLIKE   *adj* resembling a worm

WORMROOT   *n* pl. -S pinkroot

WORMSEED   *n* pl. -S a tropical plant

WORMWOOD   *n* pl. -S a European herb

WORMY   *adj* WORMIER, WORMIEST infested with worms

WORN   *adj* affected by wear or use

WORNNESS   *n* pl. -ES the state of being worn

WORRIED   past tense of worry

WORRIER   *n* pl. -S one that worries

WORRIT   *v* -ED, -ING, -S to worry

WORRY   *v* -RIED, -RYING, -RIES to feel anxious and uneasy about something

WORSE   *n* pl. -S something that is worse (bad in a greater degree)

WORSEN   *v* -ED, -ING, -S to make or become worse

WORSER   *adj* worse

WORSET   *n* pl. -S worsted

WORSHIP   *v* -SHIPED, -SHIPING, -SHIPS or -SHIPPED, -SHIPPING, -SHIPS to honor and love as a divine being

WORST   *v* -ED, -ING, -S to defeat

WORSTED   *n* pl. -S a woolen yarn

WORT   *n* pl. -S a plant, herb, or vegetable

WORTH   *v* -ED, -ING, -S to befall

WORTHFUL   *adj* worthy

WORTHY   *adj* -THIER, -THIEST having value or merit **WORTHILY** *adv*

WORTHY   *n* pl. -THIES a worthy person

WOST   a present 2d person sing. of wit

WOSTTETH   a present 2d person sing. of wit

WOT   *v* WOTTED, WOTTING, WOTS to know

WOTTETH   a present 3d person sing. of wit

WOULD   past tense of will

WOULDEST   a 2d person sing. past tense of will

WOULDST   a 2d person sing. past tense of will

WOUND   *v* -ED, -ING, -S to inflict an injury upon

WOVE   a past tense of weave

WOVEN   past participle of weave

WOW   *v* -ED, -ING, -S to excite to enthusiastic approval

WOWSER   *n* pl. -S a puritanical person

WRACK   *v* -ED, -ING, -S to wreck

WRACKFUL   *adj* destructive

WRAITH   *n* pl. -S a ghost

WRANG   *n* pl. -S a wrong

WRANGLE   *v* -GLED, -GLING, -GLES to argue noisily

WRANGLER   *n* pl. -S one that wrangles

WRAP   *v* WRAPPED or WRAPT, WRAPPING, WRAPS to enclose in something wound or folded about

WRAPPER   *n* pl. -S one that wraps

WRAPPING   *n* pl. -S the material in which something is wrapped

WRAPT   a past tense of wrap

WRASSE   *n* pl. -S a marine fish

WRASTLE   *v* -TLED, -TLING, -TLES to wrestle

WRATH   *v* -ED, -ING, -S to make wrathful

WRATHFUL   *adj* extremely angry

WRATHY   *adj* WRATHIER, WRATHIEST wrathful **WRATHILY** *adv*

WREAK   *v* -ED, -ING, -S to inflict

WREAKER   *n* pl. -S one that wreaks

WREATH   *n* pl. -S a band of flowers **WREATHY** *adj*

WREATHE   *v* WREATHED, WREATHEN, WREATHING, WREATHES to shape into a wreathe

WRECK   *v* -ED, -ING, -S to cause the ruin of

WRECKAGE   *n* pl. -S the act of wrecking

WRECKER   *n* pl. -S one that wrecks

WRECKFUL   *adj* destructive

WRECKING   *n* pl. -S the occupation of salvaging wrecked objects

WREN   *n* pl. -S a small songbird

WRENCH   *v* -ED, -ING, -ES to twist suddenly and forcibly

WREST   *v* -ED, -ING, -S to take away by force

WRESTER   *n* pl. -S one that wrests

WRESTLE   *v* -TLED, -TLING, -TLES to engage in a type of hand-to-hand contest

WRESTLER   *n* pl. -S one that wrestles

WRETCH   *n* pl. -ES a wretched person

WRETCHED   *adj* -EDER, -EDEST extremely unhappy

WRIED   past tense of wry

WRIER   a comparative of wry

WRIES   present 3d person sing. of wry

WRIEST   a superlative of wry

WRIGGLE   *v* -GLED, -GLING, -GLES to turn or twist in a sinuous manner

WRIGGLER   *n* pl. -S one that wriggles

WRIGGLY   *adj* -GLIER, -GLIEST wriggling

WRIGHT   *n* pl. -S one who constructs or creates

WRING   *v* WRUNG or WRINGED, WRINGING, WRINGS to twist so as to compress

WRINGER   *n* pl. -S one that wrings

WRINKLE   *v* -KLED, -KLING, -KLES to make wrinkles (small ridges or furrows) in

WRINKLY   *adj* -KLIER, -KLIEST having wrinkles

WRIST   *n* pl. -S the junction between the hand and forearm

WRISTLET   *n* pl. -S a band worn around the wrist

WRISTY   *adj* WRISTIER, WRISTIEST using much wrist action

WRIT   *n* pl. -S a written legal order

WRITE	*v* WROTE, WRITTEN, WRITING, WRITES to form characters or symbols on a surface with an instrument **WRITABLE** *adj*
WRITER	*n* pl. -S one that writes
WRITHE	*v* WRITHED, WRITHING, WRITHES to squirm or twist in pain
WRITHEN	*adj* twisted
WRITHER	*n* pl. -S one that writhes
WRITHING	present participle of writhe
WRITING	*n* pl. -S a written composition
WRITTEN	past participle of write
WRONG	*adj* WRONGER, WRONGEST not according to what is right, proper, or correct
WRONG	*v* -ED, -ING, -S to treat injuriously or unjustly
WRONGER	*n* pl. -S one that wrongs
WRONGFUL	*adj* wrong
WRONGLY	*adv* in a wrong manner
WROTE	past tense of write
WROTH	*adj* very angry
WROTHFUL	*adj* wroth
WROUGHT	a past tense of work
WRUNG	a past tense of wring
WRY	*adj* WRIER, WRIEST or WRYER, WRYEST contorted **WRYLY** *adv*
WRY	*v* WRIED, WRYING, WRIES to contort
WRYNECK	*n* pl. -S a European bird
WRYNESS	*n* pl. -ES the state of being wry
WUD	*adj* insane
WURST	*n* pl. -S sausage
WURZEL	*n* pl. -S a variety of beet
WYCH	*n* pl. -ES a European elm
WYE	*n* pl. -S the letter Y
WYLE	*v* WYLED, WYLING, WYLES to beguile
WYND	*n* pl. -S a narrow street
WYNN	*n* pl. -S the rune for W
WYTE	*v* WYTED, WYTING, WYTES to wite
WYVERN	*n* pl. -S wivern

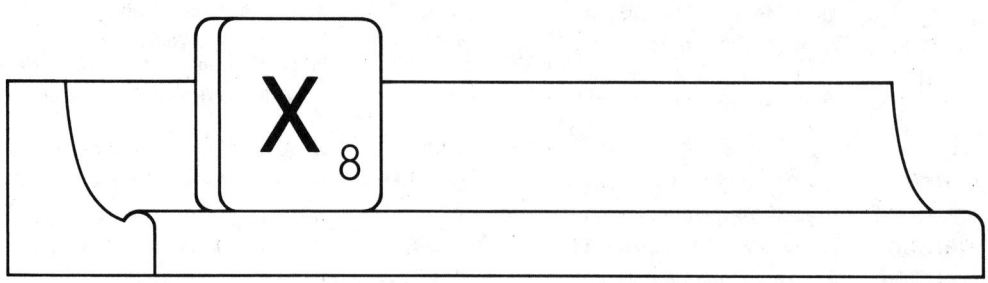

XANTHATE *n* pl. -S a chemical salt

XANTHEIN *n* pl. -S the water-soluble part of the coloring matter in yellow flowers

XANTHENE *n* pl. -S a chemical compound

XANTHIC *adj* tending to have a yellow color

XANTHIN *n* pl. -S a yellow pigment

XANTHINE *n* pl. -S a chemical compound

XANTHOMA *n* pl. -MAS or -MATA a skin disease

XANTHONE *n* pl. -S a chemical compound

XANTHOUS *adj* yellow

XEBEC *n* pl. -S a Mediterranean sailing vessel

XENIA *n* pl. -S the effect of pollen on certain plant structures **XENIAL** *adj*

XENIC *adj* pertaining to a type of culture medium

XENOGAMY *n* pl. -MIES the transfer of pollen from one plant to another

XENOGENY *n* pl. -NIES the supposed production of offspring totally different from the parent

XENOLITH *n* pl. -S a rock fragment included in another rock

XENON *n* pl. -S a gaseous element

XERARCH *adj* developing in a dry area

XERIC *adj* requiring only a small amount of moisture

XEROSERE *n* pl. -S a dry-land sere

XEROSIS *n* pl. -ROSES abnormal dryness of a body part or tissue **XEROTIC** *adj*

XERUS *n* pl. -ES an African ground squirrel

XI *n* pl. -S a Greek letter

XIPHOID *n* pl. -S a part of the sternum

XU *n* pl. XU a monetary unit of Vietnam

XYLAN *n* pl. -S a substance found in cell walls of plants

XYLEM *n* pl. -S a complex plant tissue

XYLENE *n* pl. -S a flammable hydrocarbon

XYLIDIN *n* pl. -S xylidine

XYLIDINE *n* pl. -S a chemical compound

XYLOCARP *n* pl. -S a hard, woody fruit

XYLOID *adj* resembling wood

XYLOL *n* pl. -S xylene

XYLOSE *n* pl. -S a type of sugar

XYLOTOMY *n* pl. -MIES the preparation of sections of wood for microscopic examination

XYLYL *n* pl. -S a univalent radical

XYST *n* pl. -S xystus

XYSTER *n* pl. -S a surgical instrument for scraping bones

XYSTOS *n* pl. -TOI xystus

XYSTUS *n* pl. -TI a roofed area where athletes trained in ancient Greece

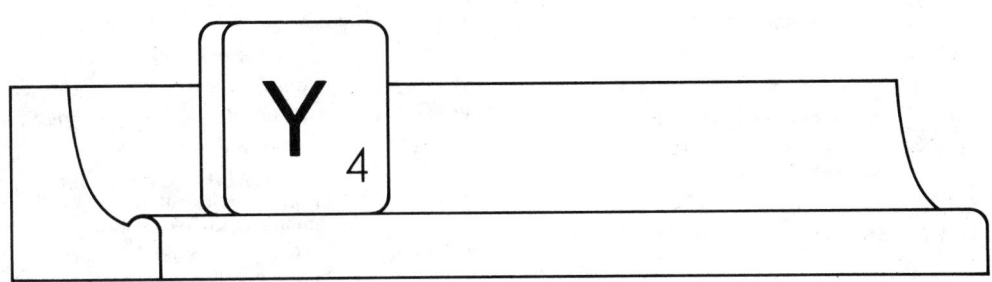

YA	*pron* you	**YANQUI**	*n* pl. -S a United States citizen
YABBER	*v* -ED, -ING, -S to jabber	**YAP**	*v* YAPPED, YAPPING, YAPS to bark shrilly
YACHT	*v* -ED, -ING, -S to sail in a yacht (a vessel used for pleasure cruising or racing)	**YAPOCK**	*n* pl. -S an aquatic mammal
		YAPOK	*n* pl. -S yapock
YACHTER	*n* pl. -S one who sails a yacht	**YAPON**	*n* pl. -S yaupon
YACHTING	*n* pl. -S the sport of sailing in yachts	**YAPPED**	past tense of yap
		YAPPER	*n* pl. -S one that yaps
YACHTMAN	*n* pl. -MEN a yachter	**YAPPING**	present participle of yap
YACK	*v* -ED, -ING, -S to yak	**YAR**	*adj* yare
YAFF	*v* -ED, -ING, -S to bark	**YARD**	*v* -ED, -ING, -S to put in a yard (a tract of ground adjacent to a building)
YAGER	*n* pl. -S jaeger		
YAGI	*n* pl. -S a type of shortwave antenna	**YARDAGE**	*n* pl. -S the use of an enclosure for livestock at a railroad station
YAH	*interj* — used as an exclamation of disgust	**YARDARM**	*n* pl. -S either end of a ship's spar
YAHOO	*n* pl. -HOOS a coarse, uncouth person	**YARDBIRD**	*n* pl. -S an army recruit
YAHOOISM	*n* pl. -S coarse, uncouth behavior	**YARDMAN**	*n* pl. -MEN a man employed to do outdoor work
YAIRD	*n* pl. -S a garden	**YARDWAND**	*n* pl. -S a measuring stick
YAK	*v* YAKKED, YAKKING, YAKS to chatter	**YARE**	*adj* YARER, YAREST nimble **YARELY** *adv*
YALD	*adj* yauld	**YARMELKE**	*n* pl. -S yarmulke
YAM	*n* pl. -S a plant having an edible root	**YARMULKE**	*n* pl. -S a skullcap worn by Jewish males
YAMEN	*n* pl. -S the residence of a Chinese public official	**YARN**	*v* -ED, -ING, -S to tell a long story
YAMMER	*v* -ED, -ING, -S to whine or complain peevishly	**YARROW**	*n* pl. -S a perennial herb
YAMMERER	*n* pl. -S one that yammers	**YASHMAC**	*n* pl. -S yashmak
YAMUN	*n* pl. -S yamen	**YASHMAK**	*n* pl. -S a veil worn by Muslim women
YANG	*n* pl. -S the masculine active principle in Chinese cosmology	**YASMAK**	*n* pl. -S yashmak
YANK	*v* -ED, -ING, -S to pull suddenly	**YATAGAN**	*n* pl. -S yataghan

YATAGHAN	*n* pl. -S a Turkish sword	**YEGG**	*n* pl. -S a burglar
YAUD	*n* pl. -S an old mare	**YEGGMAN**	*n* pl. -MEN a yegg
YAULD	*adj* vigorous	**YEH**	*adv* yeah
YAUP	*v* -ED, -ING, -S to yawp	**YELD**	*adj* not giving milk
YAUPER	*n* pl. -S one that yaups	**YELK**	*n* pl. -S yolk
YAUPON	*n* pl. -S an evergreen shrub	**YELL**	*v* -ED, -ING, -S to cry out loudly
YAW	*v* -ED, -ING, -S to deviate from an intended course	**YELLER**	*n* pl. -S one that yells
YAWL	*v* -ED, -ING, -S to yowl	**YELLOW**	*adj* -LOWER, -LOWEST of a bright color like that of ripe lemons **YELLOWLY** *adv*
YAWMETER	*n* pl. -S an instrument in an aircraft	**YELLOW**	*v* -ED, -ING, -S to make or become yellow
YAWN	*v* -ED, -ING, -S to open the mouth wide with a deep inhalation of air	**YELLOWY**	*adj* somewhat yellow
		YELP	*v* -ED, -ING, -S to utter a sharp, shrill cry
YAWNER	*n* pl. -S one that yawns	**YELPER**	*n* pl. -S one that yelps
YAWP	*v* -ED, -ING, -S to utter a loud, harsh cry	**YEN**	*v* YENNED, YENNING, YENS to yearn
YAWPER	*n* pl. -S one that yawps	**YENTA**	*n* pl. -S a gossipy woman
YAWPING	*n* pl. -S a loud, harsh cry	**YEOMAN**	*n* pl. -MEN an independent farmer **YEOMANLY** *adj*
YAY	*adv* to this extent	**YEOMANRY**	*n* pl. -RIES the collective body of yeomen
YCLEPED	*adj* yclept		
YCLEPT	*adj* called; named	**YEP**	*adv* yes
YE	*pron* you	**YERBA**	*n* pl. -S a South American beverage resembling tea
YEA	*n* pl. -S an affirmative vote	**YERK**	*v* -ED, -ING, -S to beat vigorously
YEAH	*adv* yes		
YEALING	*n* pl. -S a person of the same age	**YES**	*v* YESSED, YESSING, YESSES or YESES to give an affirmative reply to
YEAN	*v* -ED, -ING, -S to bear young		
YEANLING	*n* pl. -S the young of a sheep or goat	**YESHIVA**	*n* pl. -VAS or -VOTH an orthodox Jewish school
YEAR	*n* pl. -S a period of time consisting of 365 or 366 days	**YESHIVAH**	*n* pl. -S yeshiva
YEARBOOK	*n* pl. -S a book published each year by a graduating class	**YESSED**	past tense of yes
		YESSES	a 3d person sing. of yes
YEARLIES	pl. of yearly	**YESSING**	present participle of yes
YEARLING	*n* pl. -S an animal past its first year and not yet two years old	**YESTER**	*adj* pertaining to yesterday
YEARLONG	*adj* lasting through a year	**YESTERN**	*adj* yester
YEARLY	*n* pl. -LIES a publication appearing once a year	**YESTREEN**	*n* pl. -S the previous evening
		YET	*adv* up to now
YEARN	*v* -ED, -ING, -S to have a stong or deep desire	**YETI**	*n* pl. -S the abominable snowman
YEARNER	*n* pl. -S one that yearns	**YETT**	*n* pl. -S a gate
YEARNING	*n* pl. -S a strong or deep desire	**YEUK**	*v* -ED, -ING, -S to itch
YEAST	*v* -ED, -ING, -S to foam	**YEUKY**	*adj* itchy
YEASTY	*adj* YEASTIER, YEASTIEST foamy **YEASTILY** *adv*	**YEW**	*n* pl. -S an evergreen tree or shrub
YEELIN	*n* pl. -S yealing		

YID	*n* pl. -S a Jew — an offensive term	**YOKE**	*v* YOKED, YOKING, YOKES to fit with a yoke (a wooden frame for joining together draft animals)
YIELD	*v* -ED, -ING, -S to give up		
YIELDER	*n* pl. -S one that yields	**YOKEL**	*n* pl. -S a naive or gullible rustic
YILL	*n* pl. -S ale	**YOKELESS**	*adj* having no yoke
YIN	*n* pl. -S the feminine passive principle in Chinese cosmology	**YOKELISH**	*adj* resembling a yokel
		YOKEMATE	*n* pl. -S a companion in work
YINCE	*adv* once	**YOKING**	present participle of yoke
YIP	*v* YIPPED, YIPPING, YIPS to yelp	**YOLK**	*n* pl. -S the yellow portion of an egg **YOLKED** *adj*
YIPE	*interj* — used to express fear or surprise	**YOLKY**	*adj* YOLKIER, YOLKIEST resembling a yolk
YIPES	*interj* yipe	**YOM**	*n* pl. YOMIM day
YIPPED	past tense of yip	**YON**	*adv* yonder
YIPPEE	*interj* — used to express joy	**YOND**	*adv* yonder
YIPPIE	*n* pl. -S a politically radical hippie	**YONDER**	*adv* over there
		YONI	*n* pl. -S a symbol for the vulva in Hindu religion
YIPPING	present participle of yip		
YIRD	*n* pl. -S earth	**YONKER**	*n* pl. -S younker
YIRR	*v* -ED, -ING, -S to snarl	**YORE**	*n* pl. -S time past
YIRTH	*n* pl. -S yird	**YOU**	*pron* the 2d person sing. or pl. pronoun
YOD	*n* pl. -S a Hebrew letter		
YODEL	*v* -DELED, -DELING, -DELS or -DELLED, -DELLING, -DELS to sing with a fluctuating voice	**YOUNG**	*adj* YOUNGER, YOUNGEST being in the early period of life or growth
		YOUNG	*n* pl. -S offspring
YODELER	*n* pl. -S one that yodels	**YOUNGER**	*n* pl. -S an inferior in age
YODELLER	*n* pl. -S yodeler	**YOUNGISH**	*adj* somewhat young
YODH	*n* pl. -S yod	**YOUNKER**	*n* pl. -S a young gentleman
YODLE	*v* -DLED, -DLING, -DLES to yodel	**YOUPON**	*n* pl. -S yaupon
		YOUR	*adj* a possessive form of the pronoun you
YODLER	*n* pl. -S yodeler		
YOGA	*n* pl. -S a Hindu philosophy involving physical and mental disciplines	**YOURN**	*pron* yours
		YOURS	*pron* a possessive form of the pronoun you
YOGEE	*n* pl. -S yogi	**YOURSELF**	*pron* pl. -SELVES a form of the 2d person pronoun
YOGH	*n* pl. -S a Middle English letter		
YOGHOURT	*n* pl. -S yogurt	**YOUSE**	*pron* you
YOGHURT	*n* pl. -S yogurt	**YOUTH**	*n* pl. -S a young person
YOGI	*n* pl. -S a person who practices yoga	**YOUTHEN**	*v* -ED, -ING, -S to make youthful
		YOUTHFUL	*adj* young
YOGIC	*adj* pertaining to yoga	**YOW**	*v* -ED, -ING, -S to yowl
YOGIN	*n* pl. -S yogi	**YOWE**	*n* pl. -S a ewe
YOGINI	*n* pl. -S a female yogi	**YOWIE**	*n* pl. -S a small ewe
YOGURT	*n* pl. -S a food made from milk	**YOWL**	*v* -ED, -ING, -S to utter a loud, long, mournful cry
YOICKS	*interj* — used to encourage hunting hounds		
		YOWLER	*n* pl. -S one that yowls

YPERITE   *n* pl. -S a poisonous gas

YTTERBIA   *n* pl. -S a chemical compound **YTTERBIC** *adj*

YTTRIA   *n* pl. -S a chemical compound

YTTRIUM   *n* pl. -S a metallic element **YTTRIC** *adj*

YUAN   *n* pl. -S a monetary unit of China

YUCCA   *n* pl. -S a tropical plant

YUGA   *n* pl. -S an age of time in Hinduism

YUK   *v* YUKKED, YUKKING, YUKS to laugh loudly

YULAN   *n* pl. -S a Chinese tree

YULE   *n* pl. -S Christmas time

YULETIDE   *n* pl. -S yule

YUMMY   *adj* -MIER, -MIEST delicious

YUMMY   *n* pl. -MIES something delicious

YUP   *adv* yep

YUPON   *n* pl. -S yaupon

YURT   *n* pl. YURTA or YURTS a portable tent

YWIS   *adv* iwis

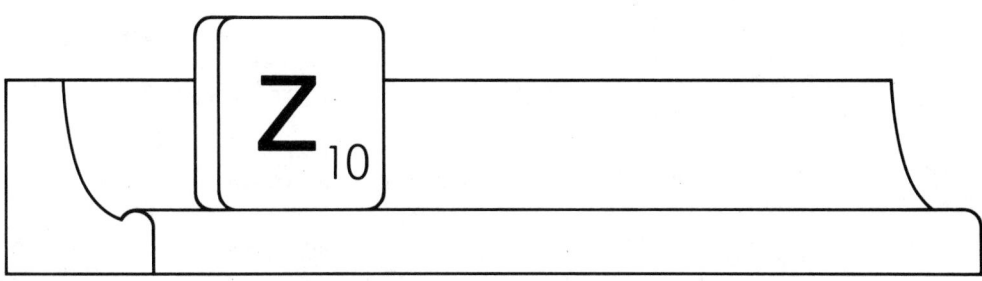

ZABAIONE	*n* pl. -S a dessert resembling custard
ZABAJONE	*n* pl. -S zabaione
ZACATON	*n* pl. -S a Mexican grass
ZADDIK	*n* pl. -DIKIM a virtuous person by Jewish religious standards
ZAFFAR	*n* pl. -S zaffer
ZAFFER	*n* pl. -S a blue ceramic coloring
ZAFFIR	*n* pl. -S zaffer
ZAFFRE	*n* pl. -S zaffer
ZAFTIG	*adj* full-bosomed
ZAG	*v* ZAGGED, ZAGGING, ZAGS to turn sharply
ZAIBATSU	*n* pl. ZAIBATSU a powerful family combine in Japan
ZAIRE	*n* pl. -S a monetary unit of Zaire
ZAMARRA	*n* pl. -S a sheepskin coat
ZAMARRO	*n* pl. -ROS zamarra
ZAMIA	*n* pl. -S a tropical plant
ZAMINDAR	*n* pl. -S a tax collector in precolonial India
ZANANA	*n* pl. -S zenana
ZANDER	*n* pl. -S a freshwater fish
ZANIER	comparative of zany
ZANIES	pl. of zany
ZANINESS	*n* pl. -ES the quality or state of being zany
ZANY	*adj* ZANIER, ZANIEST ludicrously comical **ZANILY** *adv*
ZANY	*n* pl. -NIES a zany person
ZANYISH	*adj* somewhat zany
ZANZA	*n* pl. -S an African musical instrument
ZAP	*v* ZAPPED, ZAPPING, ZAPS to kill or destroy
ZAPATEO	*n* pl. -TEOS a Spanish dance
ZAPTIAH	*n* pl. -S a Turkish policeman
ZAPTIEH	*n* pl. -S zaptiah
ZARATITE	*n* pl. -S a chemical compound
ZAREBA	*n* pl. -S an improvised stockade
ZAREEBA	*n* pl. -S zareba
ZARF	*n* pl. -S a metal holder for a coffee cup
ZARIBA	*n* pl. -S zareba
ZARZUELA	*n* pl. -S a Spanish operetta
ZASTRUGA	*n* pl. -GI sastruga
ZAX	*n* pl. -ES a tool for cutting roof slates
ZAYIN	*n* pl. -S a Hebrew letter
ZEAL	*n* pl. -S enthusiastic devotion
ZEALOT	*n* pl. -S one who is zealous
ZEALOTRY	*n* pl. -RIES excessive zeal
ZEALOUS	*adj* filled with zeal
ZEATIN	*n* pl. -S a chemical compound found in maize
ZEBEC	*n* pl. -S xebec
ZEBECK	*n* pl. -S xebec
ZEBRA	*n* pl. -S an African mammal that is related to the horse **ZEBRAIC** *adj*
ZEBRASS	*n* pl. -ES the offspring of a zebra and an ass
ZEBRINE	*adj* pertaining to a zebra
ZEBROID	*adj* zebrine
ZEBU	*n* pl. -S an Asian ox
ZECCHIN	*n* pl. -S zecchino

ZECCHINO   *n* pl. -NI or -NOS a former gold coin of Italy

ZECHIN   *n* pl. -S zecchino

ZED   *n* pl. -S the letter Z

ZEDOARY   *n* pl. -ARIES the medicinal root of a tropical plant

ZEE   *n* pl. -S the letter Z

ZEIN   *n* pl. -S a simple protein

ZELKOVA   *n* pl. -S a Japanese tree

ZEMINDAR   *n* pl. -S zamindar

ZEMSTVO   *n* pl. -VOS an elective council in czarist Russia

ZENANA   *n* pl. -S the section of a house in India reserved for women

ZENITH   *n* pl. -S the highest point **ZENITHAL** *adj*

ZEOLITE   *n* pl. -S a mineral **ZEOLITIC** *adj*

ZEPHYR   *n* pl. -S a gentle breeze

ZEPPELIN   *n* pl. -S a long, rigid airship

ZERO   *v* -ED, -ING, -ES or -S to aim at the exact center of a target

ZEST   *v* -ED, -ING, -S to fill with zest (invigorating excitement)

ZESTFUL   *adj* full of zest

ZESTY   *adj* ZESTIER, ZESTIEST marked by zest

ZETA   *n* pl. -S a Greek letter

ZEUGMA   *n* pl. -S the use of a word to modify or govern two or more words, while applying to each in a different sense

ZIBELINE   *n* pl. -S a soft fabric

ZIBET   *n* pl. -S an Asian civet

ZIBETH   *n* pl. -S zibet

ZIG   *v* ZIGGED, ZIGGING, ZIGS to turn sharply

ZIGGURAT   *n* pl. -S an ancient Babylonian temple tower

ZIGZAG   *v* -ZAGGED, -ZAGGING, -ZAGS to proceed on a course marked by sharp turns

ZIKKURAT   *n* pl. -S ziggurat

ZIKURAT   *n* pl. -S ziggurat

ZILCH   *n* pl. -ES nothing

ZILLAH   *n* pl. -S an administrative district in India

ZILLION   *n* pl. -S an indeterminately large number

ZINC   *v* ZINCED, ZINCING, ZINCS or ZINCKED, ZINCKING, ZINCS to coat with zinc (a metallic element)

ZINCATE   *n* pl. -S a chemical salt

ZINCIC   *adj* pertaining to zinc

ZINCIFY   *v* -FIED, -FYING, -FIES to coat with zinc

ZINCITE   *n* pl. -S an ore of zinc

ZINCKED   a past tense of zinc

ZINCKING   a present participle of zinc

ZINCKY   *adj* resembling zinc

ZINCOID   *adj* zincic

ZINCOUS   *adj* zincic

ZINCY   *adj* zincky

ZING   *v* -ED, -ING, -S to move with a high-pitched humming sound

ZINGANO   *n* pl. -NI zingaro

ZINGARA   *n* pl. -RE a female gypsy

ZINGARO   *n* pl. -RI a gypsy

ZINGY   *adj* ZINGIER, ZINGIEST enjoyably exciting

ZINKIFY   *v* -FIED, -FYING, -FIES to zincify

ZINKY   *adj* zincky

ZINNIA   *n* pl. -S a tropical plant

ZIP   *v* ZIPPED, ZIPPING, ZIPS to move with speed and vigor

ZIPPER   *v* -ED, -ING, -S to fasten with a zipper (a fastener consisting of two rows of interlocking teeth)

ZIPPY   *adj* -PIER, -PIEST full of energy

ZIRAM   *n* pl. -S a chemical salt

ZIRCON   *n* pl. -S a mineral

ZIRCONIA   *n* pl. -S a chemical compound

ZIRCONIC   *adj* pertaining to a certain metallic element

ZITHER   *n* pl. -S a stringed instrument

ZITHERN   *n* pl. -S zither

ZITI   *n* pl. -S a tubular pasta

ZIZITH   *n/pl* the tassels on the four corners of a Jewish prayer shawl

ZIZZLE   *v* -ZLED, -ZLING, -ZLES to sizzle

ZLOTY   *n* pl. ZLOTYS a monetary unit of Poland

ZOA   a pl. of zoon

ZOARIUM   *n* pl. -IA a colony of bryozoans **ZOARIAL** *adj*